THE SAPIRSTEIN EDITION

The ArtScroll Series®

Rabbi Nosson Scherman / Rabbi Meir Zlotowitz
General Editors

ספר ויקרא
VAYIKRA/LEVITICUS

The ArtScroll Series®

Published by

Mesorah Publications, ltd

A PROJECT OF THE

Mesorah Heritage Foundation

BOARD OF TRUSTEES

RABBI DAVID FEINSTEIN
Rosh HaYeshivah, Mesivtha Tifereth Jerusalem

ABRAHAM BIDERMAN
Chairman,
Eagle Advisers LLC

JUDAH I. SEPTIMUS*
Pres., Atlantic Land Title & Abstract, Ltd.

RABBI NOSSON SCHERMAN
General Editor, ArtScroll Series

JOEL L. FLEISHMAN*
Director, Duke University Philanthropic
Foundations Research Program

JAMES S. TISCH*
President, Loews Corp.

RABBI MEIR ZLOTOWITZ
Chairman

AUDIT COMMITTEE

SAMUEL ASTROF
CFO, United Jewish Communities

JOSEPH C. SHENKER
Vice Chairman, Sullivan & Cromwell

* The indicated Trustees also serve on the Audit Committee

INTERNATIONAL BOARD OF GOVERNORS

JAY SCHOTTENSTEIN *(Columbus, OH)*
Chairman

STEVEN ADELSBERG
HOWARD BALTER
RABBI RAPHAEL B. BUTLER
YOSEF DAVIS *(Chicago)*
REUVEN D. DESSLER *(Cleveland)*
BENJAMIN C. FISHOFF
HOWARD TZVI FRIEDMAN *(Baltimore)*
YITZCHOK GANGER
JACOB M.M. GRAFF *(Los Angeles)*
HASHI HERZKA
SHIMMIE HORN
AMIR JAFFA *(Cleveland)*
LLOYD F. KEILSON
LESTER KLAUS
MENACHEM KLEIN *(Los Angeles)*
MOTTY KLEIN
ELLY KLEINMAN
IRA A. LIPMAN
EZRA MARCOS *(Genève)*
RABBI MEYER H. MAY *(Los Angeles)*
ANDREW J. NEFF
BARRY M. RAY *(Chicago)*

ZVI RYZMAN *(Los Angeles)*
ELLIS A. SAFDEYE
A. GEORGE SAKS
JOSEPH A. SCHOTTENSTEIN
JONATHAN R. SCHOTTENSTEIN
JEFFREY A. SCHOTTENSTEIN
FRED SCHULMAN
ELLIOT SCHWARTZ
HERBERT E. SEIF *(Englewood, NJ)*
NATHAN B. SILBERMAN
SOLI SPIRA *(Jerusalem / Antwerp)*
A. JOSEPH STERN *(Edison, NJ)*
MOSHE TALANSKY
ELLIOT TANNENBAUM
SOL TEICHMAN *(Encino, CA)*
THOMAS J. TISCH
GARY TORGOW *(Detroit)*
STANLEY WASSERMAN *(New Rochelle)*
JOSEPH H. WEISS
STEVEN WEISZ
HIRSCH WOLF

The Sapirstein Edition

THE TORAH: WITH RASHI'S COMMENTARY
TRANSLATED, ANNOTATED, AND ELUCIDATED

by Rabbi Yisrael Isser Zvi Herczeg
in collaboration with
Rabbi Yaakov Petroff
and Rabbi Yoseph Kamenetsky
Contributing Editor: Rabbi Avie Gold

Designed by
Rabbi Sheah Brander

FIRST FULL SIZE EDITION
November 1994

FIRST STUDENT SIZE EDITION
Eight Impressions . . . October 1999 — July 2007
Ninth Impression . . . April 2009

Published and Distributed by
MESORAH PUBLICATIONS, Ltd.
4401 Second Avenue
Brooklyn, New York 11232

Distributed in Europe by
LEHMANNS
Unit E, Viking Business Park
Rolling Mill Road
Jarrow, Tyne & Wear NE32 3DP
England

Distributed in Israel by
SIFRIATI / A. GITLER — BOOKS
6 Hayarkon Street
Bnei Brak 51127

Distributed in Australia & New Zealand by
GOLDS WORLD OF JUDAICA
3-13 William Street
Balaclava, Melbourne 3183
Victoria Australia

Distributed in South Africa by
KOLLEL BOOKSHOP
Ivy Common 105 William Road
Norwood 2192, Johannesburg, South Africa

ARTSCROLL SERIES® / THE SAPIRSTEIN EDITION
RASHI / COMMENTARY ON THE TORAH
STUDENT SIZE EDITION
VOL. 3 — VAYIKRA / LEVITICUS

© Copyright 1994, 1999, by MESORAH PUBLICATIONS, Ltd.
4401 Second Avenue / Brooklyn, N.Y. 11232 / (718) 921-9000 / www.artscroll.com

---

ALL RIGHTS RESERVED. The texts of Onkelos and Rashi have been edited, corrected, and newly set;
the English translation and commentary — including introductory material, notes, and insights —
as well as the typographic layout and cover artwork, have been written, designed,
edited and/or revised as to content, form and style.
Additionally, new fonts have been designed for the Chumash, Onkelos and Rashi texts.
All of the above are fully protected under this international copyright.

> No part of this volume may be reproduced
> **IN ANY FORM — PHOTOCOPY, ELECTRONIC MEDIA, OR OTHERWISE**
> **— EVEN FOR PERSONAL, STUDY GROUP, OR CLASSROOM USE —**
> without WRITTEN permission from the copyright holder,
> except by a reviewer who wishes to quote brief passages in connection
> with a review written for inclusion in magazines or newspapers.

NOTICE IS HEREBY GIVEN THAT THE PUBLICATION OF THIS WORK
INVOLVED EXTENSIVE RESEARCH AND COSTS,
AND THE RIGHTS OF THE COPYRIGHT HOLDER WILL BE STRICTLY ENFORCED

ISBN 10: 1-57819-327-3
ISBN 13: 978-1-57819-327-1

Typography by Compuscribe at ArtScroll Studios, Ltd.
Custom bound by **Sefercraft, Inc.,** Brooklyn, N.Y.

✺ Table of Contents

Preface
Glossary of Transliterated Terms
Cantillation Marks / טעמי המקרא
Blessings of the Torah / ברכות התורה
Pronouncing the Names of God

The Parshiyos / הפרשיות

Vayikra / ויקרא	2
Tzav / צו	60
Shemini / שמיני	94
Tazria / תזריע	136
Metzora / מצורע	160
Acharei / אחרי	192
Kedoshim / קדושים	226
Emor / אמור	262
Behar / בהר	318
Bechukosai / בחקתי	348

The Haftaros / ההפטרות   388

The SAPIRSTEIN EDITION OF RASHI is dedicated
to the memory of our parents

Jacob and Jennie Sapirstein ע"ה

ר' יעקב בן הרב יצחק ע"ה
נפטר כ"ז סיון תשמ"ז

שיינא חיה שרה בת ר' נחמיה ע"ה
נפטרה כ' כסלו תש"ל

They came from little Grajeyvo, Poland, a Jewish shtetl that revered Torah, lived in poverty, and whose farmers brought a tenth of their crops to town to be divided among the needy.

Whether in their early years of struggle or on the peak of success, the values of their youth sustained them. Economic conditions might change, but Judaism, integrity, and charity remained the constants of their lives.

Jacob Sapirstein began as a door to door peddler of picture postcards. With his sons, Irving, Morris, ע"ה and Harry, and his daughter Bernice Davis, he became an international leader of his industry.

But he never changed.

Jacob Sapirstein lived for 102 active, fruitful years, 82 of them in the United States. In his century of life, he accomplished much — but his greatest success was his legacy, uncompromised and untarnished, of loyalty to Judaism, commitment to excellence, and concern for others.

Mr. and Mrs. Irving I. Stone

◆§ Publisher's Preface

For nine centuries, Rashi — Rabbi Shlomo ben Yitzchak of medieval France — has been universally acknowledged as the "Father of Commentators," the quintessential elucidator of the Five Books of Moses. As *Ramban* puts it, "to Rashi belongs the right of the firstborn." More than three hundred works have been published on his commentary to the Torah. In short, almost by definition, the study of *Chumash* has come to mean *Chumash/Rashi*.

The deceptive simplicity of the commentary masks profound thought and encyclopedic knowledge; Rashi's choice of citations from the voluminous literature of the Sages is in itself a commentary for those who understand the reasons he selected one or two opinions out of many. So essential is Rashi's commentary to the study of God's Torah, that it is incumbent upon each generation to strip away the barriers of language and lack of sophistication that prevent its fellow Jews from, in effect, sitting in Rashi's study hall and joining him in plumbing the depths of the Torah. Hence this new edition of *Chumash/Rashi* in the vernacular.

This volume is far more than a translation. In addition to an accurate rendering of Rashi's text in bold-face type, we add whatever words are necessary to clarify the flow of the commentary and explain Rashi's point, and to show how it is indicated in the text of the *Chumash*. The notes provide further clarification and provide further insight into Rashi's ideas, as well as questions and clarifications of other major commentators.

In sum, this treatment presents Rashi with unexcelled clarity and grace. For teachers, for parents, for students, for anyone seeking an improved understanding of the Torah and its foremost expositor, the SAPIRSTEIN EDITION OF RASHI will be a welcome book, and by enabling people to understand Rashi better, this work will prod its readers to delve more deeply into the infinite wealth of the Torah. That intensification of Torah study and knowledge will be the authors' greatest reward.

TEXT, TRANSLATION AND ELUCIDATION

The translation of the *Chumash* in this volume attempts to render the text as Rashi understood it. We attempt to follow the Hebrew as closely as possible and to avoid paraphrase, but, occasionally, English syntax or idiom forces us to deviate somewhat.

We use "HASHEM," or "the Name," as the translation of the Tetragrammaton, the sacred Hebrew Four-letter Name of God." For the Hebrew *Elohim*, which is the more general and less "personal" Name of the Deity, we use the translation "God."

Transliteration presents a problem in all works of this sort. Ashkenazi, pure Sephardi, current Israeli, and generally accepted scholarly usages frequently diverge, and such familiar names as Isaac, Jacob, and Moses conform to none of them. We have adopted a cross between the Sephardi and Ashkenazi transliterations, using Sephardi vowel and Ashkenazi pronunciations. Thus: *Akeidas Yitzchak*, rather than *Akeidat Izhak* or *Akeidas Yitzchok*. True, this blend may require some adjustment on the part of many readers, but it has proven successful. For proper names of Biblical personalities, however, we have followed the commonly accepted English usage such as Abraham, Moses, Methuselah, and so on.

In the present edition, the Hebrew text of Rashi's commentary appears twice. The first time, it is printed in the classical typeface known as *Ksav Rashi*, or Rashi Script. Commas and periods have been inserted by the editors in order to facilitate the reading. Variant readings are enclosed by brackets, and sources are noted in parentheses. In the elucidated English version, the Hebrew text is repeated phrase by phrase, in fully vowelized regular Hebrew type. All abbreviations are spelled out in full, and all numbers are given as Hebrew words rather than letter/numerals. The translation of Rashi's words is given in bold-face type, while the words interpolated to elucidate and clarify are in regular type. Variant readings are either enclosed in braces or appear in the footnotes, along with the sources from which Rashi drew his commentary.

Special emphasis has been placed on elucidating the *"dikduk"* comments in which Rashi analyzes a word or phrase from a grammatical point of view. These comments are often skimmed over in a perfunctory manner by those who are unfamiliar with Rashi's terminology or with Hebrew grammar in general. The footnotes of this edition explain both the grammatical difficulties addressed by Rashi and the principles needed to understand his solutions.

Another often neglected area is the *"lo'ez"* in which Rashi uses an Old French word or phrase to translate the Torah text. A dearth of knowledge of Old French has led many educators to dismiss these comments with, "Well, Rashi is just giving the French translation," as a result of which Rashi's intended nuance is often lost. For this edition, every foreign word used by Rashi has been thoroughly researched. To assist the reader, the Modern French and English equivalents are given, along with other English words derived from the same root. The reader thus gets an understanding of the meaning Rashi wishes to convey with his French translation.

SHMUEL BLITZ, director of the Foundation's activities in Israel, is a friend and counselor of the first order. He coordinated the production, and his suggestions and comments were most valuable throughout.

The MESORAH HERITAGE FOUNDATION, which makes possible the research and writing of this and other important works of Jewish scholarship, has become a major source of Jewish learning. For this, we are grateful to its trustees and governors, who are listed above.

A major project of the Foundation is the monumental SCHOTTENSTEIN EDITION OF THE TALMUD, which was made possible by the vision and generosity of JEROME SCHOTTENSTEIN ז״ל and his wife GERALDINE, who carries on his resolve, and of SAUL AND SONIA SCHOTTENSTEIN. Jerome Schottenstein's legacy of dedication to Jewish eternity is carried on by JAY AND JEANIE SCHOTTENSTEIN in a host of worthy causes around the world, and by SUSIE AND JON DIAMOND, ANN AND ARI DESHE, and LORI SCHOTTENSTEIN. We treasure their friendship.

We are grateful for the invaluable guidance and encouragement of the many leaders of organizational and rabbinic life. In addition to those mentioned above, some of them are: RABBI MOSHE SHERER, RABBI PINCHAS STOLPER, RABBI RAPHAEL BUTLER, RABBI BORUCH B. BORCHARDT, RABBI MOSHE GLUSTEIN, MR. DAVID H. SCHWARTZ, RABBI BURTON JAFFA, RABBI MICHAEL LEVI, RABBI YISRAEL EIDELMAN, and RABBI ELI DESSLER.

A huge investment of time and resources was required to make this edition a reality. Only thanks to the generous support of many people was it possible to undertake ambitious projects such as this and to make the finished volumes affordable to the average family and institution. We are grateful to the many who enabled us to do so, especially to MR. AND MRS. LAURENCE A. TISCH and family, MR. AND MRS. ALBERT REICHMANN, MR. AND MRS. LOUIS GLICK, MR. AND MRS. ELLIS A. SAFDEYE, MR. AND MRS. A. JOSEPH STERN, MR. AND MRS. REUVEN DESSLER, and MR. AND MRS. HOWARD ZUCKERMAN.

The entire staffs of the Mesorah Heritage Foundation and Mesorah Publications have shown an inspiring spirit of cooperation and dedication to the shared goals of both organizations. In particular we must single out those who worked on the very arduous and often complex work of typing and revising this work: MRS. CHANAH MARGALIOT, MRS. ESTHER FEIERSTEIN, MRS. MINDY BREIER, MRS. BASSIE GUTMAN, YEHUDA GORDON, DEVORAH GLATZER, UDI HERSHKOWITZ, LEAH BRACHAH LASKER, and CHAYA G. ZAIDMAN; we are grateful to them. We are grateful to SHLOMO BENZAQUEN who ably rendered the diagrams and illustrations. We are also grateful to RABBI SHMUEL GRUNFELD, MRS. MINDY STERN, MRS. JUDI DICK and MRS. FAIGY WEINBAUM, who proofread with diligence and skill. Vital and difficult administrative work was done by our comptroller LEA FREIER. This volume is a credit to all of them and their colleagues in the Foundation and in Mesorah Publications.

Finally, we and our colleagues thank the Almighty for the privilege of helping disseminate His Word to countless Jewish hearts and homes.

Rabbi Meir Zlotowitz / Rabbi Nosson Scherman

Brooklyn, New York
Kislev 5755/November 1994

Glossary of Transliterated Terms

Amora – Any of the sages of the **Gemara** (about 180-400 C.E.).
aninus – The state of being an **onein.**
arayos – The most serious class of sexual sin including incest, adultery, and relations with a **niddah.**
Avneit – A sash; one of four garments worn by **Kohanim** during the Temple service. See *Exodus* 28:4,40.
Beis HaMikdash – The Holy Temple in Jerusalem.
chalal (pl. **chalalim**) – A child born from a union specifically forbidden to **Kohanim,** and the descendants of male children born from such unions. A *chalal* does not inherit the priestly status of his father.
Cheishev – The belt of the **Eiphod.** See *Exodus* 28:8.
Choshen – The breastplate; one of eight garments worn by the **Kohen Gadol** while he officiated in the Temple. See *Exodus* 28:15-30.
Eiphod – An apronlike garment; one of eight garments worn by the **Kohen Gadol** while he officiated in the Temple. See *Exodus* 28:6-12.
Gemara – Portion of the Talmud that discusses the **Mishnah.**
kares – Literally, "excision." A punishment imposed by the Torah for the violation of certain sins, by which the sinner and his offspring die prematurely.
kehunah – The state of being a **Kohen.**
Kiyyor – Wash basin. See *Exodus* 30:17-21.
kodashim – Objects imbued with ritual sanctity.
Kohen (pl. **Kohanim**) – A priest; Aaron and his male descendants.
Kohen Gadol – The High Priest.
korban pesach – The paschal offering. See *Exodus* 12:3-28.
korban tamid – The **olah-offering** brought morning and evening in the **Mishkan** and **Beis HaMikdash.** See *Numbers* 28:1-8.
Kutoness – A robe; one of four garments worn by **Kohanim** during the Temple service. See *Exodus* 28:39,40.
Me'il – A robe; one of eight garments worn by the **Kohen Gadol** while he officiated in the Temple. See *Exodus* 28:31-35.
metzora – One afflicted with **tzara'as.**
Michnasaim – Pants; one of four garments worn by **Kohanim** during the Temple service. See *Exodus* 28:42.
Migba'as (pl. **Migba'os**) – A headdress; one of four garments worn by **Kohanim** other than the **Kohen Gadol** while they performed the Temple Service. See *Exodus* 28:40.
Mishkan – The Tabernacle. See *Exodus* Chs. 25-27.
Mishnah – The basis of the Talmud; the original teachings of the **Tannaim** (compiled about 180 C.E.).
Mitznefes – A headdress; one of eight garments worn by the **Kohen Gadol** while he officiated in the Temple. See *Exodus* 28:4,39.
Mizbe'ach – The sacrificial Altar in the **Mishkan** and **Beis HaMikdash.**
mussaf-offerings – The additional **Mizbe'ach** offerings brought on the Sabbath, Festivals and the New Moon. See *Numbers* Chs. 28-29.
nazir – One who takes a vow of abstinence which forbids him from: drinking or eating grape products; becoming impure through contact with the dead; and cutting his hair. See *Numbers* 6:1-21.
niddah – A woman impure due to menstruation. See *Leviticus* 15:19-24.
olah-offering – An animal offering, all of the meat of which is burned upon the Altar. See *Leviticus* Ch. 1.
onein – A mourner on the day on which certain relatives die.
par he'elem davar – Literally, "bull of the obscurement of an issue"; an offering brought when the public acts upon an erroneous decision of the Sanhedrin where the court permitted an act punishable by **kares.** See *Leviticus* 4:13-21.
Paroches – The partition between the Holy of Holies and the rest of the Sanctuary. See *Exodus* 26:31-33.
shifchah charufah – Literally, "a designated slavewoman." A Canaanite woman who is half free and half slave who has been designated as the wife of a Hebrew servant. See *Leviticus* 19:20-22.
Shulchan – The Table in the Sanctuary. See *Exodus* 25:23-30.
sotah – A suspected adulteress, i.e., a married woman who has secluded herself with a man other than her husband after having been warned not to. See *Numbers* 5:5-31.
tamid – See **korban tamid.**
Tanna (pl. **Tannaim**) – Any of the sages of the **Mishnah** (about 350 B.C.E. – 180 C.E.).
tereifah – Literally, "a mauled animal." An animal that has a mortal defect and therefore cannot become kosher even if it is slaughtered in accordance with halachah. See *Exodus* 22:30.
terumah – The portion of the yearly crop given to the **Kohanim.** See *Numbers* 18:12.
tzara'as – An eruption indicating spiritual impurity. It can appear on the skin of the sufferer, or on the surfaces of houses or garments. See *Leviticus* Chs. 13-14.
Tzitz – A golden forehead plate; one of eight garments worn by the **Kohen Gadol** while he officiated in the Temple. See *Exodus* 28:36-38.
zav (fem. **zavah**) – A person impure due to certain bodily discharges. See *Leviticus* 15:1-18, 25-30.

ACKNOWLEDGMENTS

This work combines the contributions of many people and was made possible by the guidance and encouragement of many others. Foremost among them are the Torah giants of the last generation, our teachers and mentors, who put their stamp on the ArtScroll Series, as they did on the new generations of Torah institutions and families in the Western Hemisphere. Their teachings remain, though they are no longer with us. There are no words to describe our gratitude to them all — indeed the gratitude that our and future generations must feel for their enormous contributions to the survival of Torah Judaism after the horrors of the Holocaust and the ravages of assimilation.

In many ways, the father of the ArtScroll Series is our revered mentor, the Telshe Rosh HaYeshivah, RABBI MORDECHAI GIFTER שליט״א. His support and suggestions were indispensable, especially in the formative years.

RABBI DAVID FEINSTEIN שליט״א has been guide and counselor, and a friend at every difficult juncture.

We have enjoyed the friendship, advice, and help of many distinguished Torah authorities, and we are grateful that they have permitted us to benefit from their wisdom. Among them are such luminaries as RABBI ZELIK EPSTEIN, RABBI SHIMON SCHWAB, RABBI AVRAHAM PAM, RABBI A. HENACH LEIBOWITZ, RABBI AHARON SHECHTER, RABBI SHMUEL KAMENETSKY, RABBI YAAKOV PERLOW, RABBI DAVID COHEN, RABBI HILLEL DAVID, and RABBI AVRAHAM AUSBAND שליט״א.

RABBI NOCHUM ZEV DESSLER, has been a confidant of the Stone family and a partner in their work on behalf of Jewish education for over half a century. We are grateful for his friendship and counsel.

The trustees of the Mesorah Heritage Foundation join the Stone-Weiss families in thanking RABBI DR. NORMAN LAMM for his warm encouragement. He has been unfailingly gracious.

RABBI YISRAEL HERCZEG, the author of this volume, has made the study and analysis of *Rashi* the major focus of a distinguished life of teaching and scholarship. We are proud to bring his outstanding work to the public. RABBI YOSEPH KAMENETSKY and RABBI YAAKOV PETROFF, his collaborators, have edited and commented with a quality commensurate with the skill of the author. These outstanding scholars from the Holy City have produced a work that is a credit to them and a service to the Jewish people.

RABBI AVIE GOLD, a mainstay of the ArtScroll Series, has made a fine work even better, with the skill and diligence ArtScroll readers have come to expect from this consummate craftsman and scholar. RABBI MOSHE ROSENBLUM, a distinguished Talmudic and Hebraic scholar, reviewed and corrected the texts of *Onkelos* and Rashi, making this one of the most accurate editions currently available.

SHEAH BRANDER is deservedly famous as the graphics genius of Jewish publishing. That he surely is, but he is more. In addition to being instrumental in designing this work, his brilliance is reflected in the commentary and translation, thanks to his perceptive comments and illuminating suggestions.

Preface / xii

THE SAPIRSTEIN EDITION

It is appropriate, that this major work be dedicated to the memory of a couple that appreciated Torah knowledge and utilized their business success to help plant the seeds of Torah life in the New World.

JACOB AND JENNIE SAPIRSTEIN were both born in Grajevo, Poland, and married in the United States, where they came as young adults to make a new life. That they did, but they never abandoned the values they absorbed from their families: respect for learning, uncompromising honesty, hard work, and dedication to Jewish continuity, despite living in a land that preached the assimilation of the melting pot.

As a new immigrant, Jacob Sapirstein worked in a little postcard store, then peddled postcards, store to store, on foot, on street cars, on horse and buggy, and in an old Ford. By dint of determination, integrity, and an unfailing zeal to anticipate the needs of customers and provide them, he and his children, IRVING I., MORRIS S. ע״ה, HARRY H., and BERNICE M. DAVIS, created the world's largest publicly held manufacturer of greeting cards and related social expression products, a company in which "J.S." remained actively involved to the very end of his long and productive life.

Throughout those years of creative struggle, Jacob and Jennie remained true to the ideals of Jewish eternity, and transmitted them to their children. Those were years when Jewish education was almost non-existent in Middle America, but the Sapirsteins imbued their children with the conviction that outstanding educators matter more than bricks and mortar. They demonstrated their love of Torah education by serving on the boards of the then fledgling Telshe Yeshiva and Hebrew Academy of Cleveland.

They came to America and planted seeds. They persevered when most others fell by the wayside. And thanks to their example, their son Irving I. Stone has become one of the world's master builders of undiluted excellence in Torah education, as exemplified by the STONE EDITION OF THE CHUMASH and now the SAPIRSTEIN EDITION OF RASHI, both of which were dedicated by him and his family, including MORRY AND JUDY WEISS. Mr. Stone's son-in-law and colleague, Morry Weiss is an example of America's strong and committed new generation of Jewish leaders.

We pray that this great undertaking will be a source of merit for the entire Stone-Weiss family, including Mr. Stone's other children HENSHA, NEIL, and MYRNA and their families, and all his grandchildren and great-grandchildren.

The SAPIRSTEIN EDITION OF RASHI is a fitting memorial to an unforgettable couple. Thanks to this work, their names will live for generations to come in the halls and hearts of all who are dedicated to the values the Sapirsteins kept vibrant.

❧ ❧ ❧

ספר ויקרא
Vayikra/Leviticus

טעמי המקרא / Cantillation Marks

פַּשְׁטָא֙ מֻנַּ֣ח זַרְקָ֘א מֻ֥נַּח סֶגּוֹל֒ מֻנַּ֣ח ׀ מֻנַּ֣ח רְבִיעִ֗י מַהְפַּ֤ךְ
פַּשְׁטָא֙ זָקֵֽף־קָטֹ֔ן זָקֵף־גָּד֕וֹל מֵרְכָ֥א טִפְחָ֖א מֻנַּ֣ח
אֶתְנַחְתָּ֑א פָּזֵ֡ר תְּלִישָׁא־קְטַנָּה֩ תְּלִישָׁא־גְדוֹלָ֜ה קַדְמָ֨א
וְאַזְלָ֨א אַזְלָא־גֵ֜רֶשׁ גֵּרְשַׁ֞יִם דַּרְגָּ֧א תְּבִ֨יר יְ֪תִיב פְּסִ֣יק ׀
סוֹף־פָּסֽוּק׃ שַׁלְשֶׁ֓לֶת קַרְנֵי־פָרָ֟ה מֵרְכָ֦א כְּפוּלָ֦ה
יֶֽרַח־בֶּן־יוֹמֽוֹ׃

BLESSINGS OF THE TORAH / ברכות התורה

The reader shows the oleh *(person called to the Torah) the place in the Torah. The* oleh *touches the Torah with a corner of his* tallis, *or the belt or mantle of the Torah, and kisses it. He then begins the blessing, bowing at* בָּרְכוּ, *"Bless," and straightening up at* ה', *"*HASHEM.*"*

Bless HASHEM, *the blessed One.* בָּרְכוּ אֶת יהוה הַמְבֹרָךְ.

Congregation, followed by oleh, *responds bowing at* בָּרוּךְ, *"Blessed," and straightening up at* ה', *"*HASHEM.*"*

Blessed is HASHEM, *the blessed One, for all eternity.* בָּרוּךְ יהוה הַמְבֹרָךְ לְעוֹלָם וָעֶד.

Oleh continues:

Blessed are You, HASHEM, *our God, King of the universe, Who selected us from all the peoples and gave us His Torah. Blessed are You,* HASHEM, *Giver of the Torah.*
(Cong. — Amen.)

בָּרוּךְ אַתָּה יהוה אֱלֹהֵינוּ מֶלֶךְ הָעוֹלָם, אֲשֶׁר בָּחַר בָּנוּ מִכָּל הָעַמִּים, וְנָתַן לָנוּ אֶת תּוֹרָתוֹ. בָּרוּךְ אַתָּה יהוה, נוֹתֵן הַתּוֹרָה.
(קהל — אָמֵן)

After his Torah portion has been read, the oleh *recites:*

Blessed are You, HASHEM, *our God, King of the universe, Who gave us the Torah of truth and implanted eternal life within us. Blessed are You,* HASHEM, *Giver of the Torah.*
(Cong. — Amen.)

בָּרוּךְ אַתָּה יהוה אֱלֹהֵינוּ מֶלֶךְ הָעוֹלָם, אֲשֶׁר נָתַן לָנוּ תּוֹרַת אֱמֶת, וְחַיֵּי עוֹלָם נָטַע בְּתוֹכֵנוּ. בָּרוּךְ אַתָּה יהוה, נוֹתֵן הַתּוֹרָה.
(קהל — אָמֵן)

Pronouncing the Names of God

The Four-Letter Name of HASHEM [י־ה־ו־ה] indicates that God is timeless and infinite, for the letters of this Name are those of the words הָיָה הֹוֶה וְיִהְיֶה, "He was, He is, and He will be." This name appears in some editions with vowel points [יְ־הֹ־וָ־ה] and in others, such as the present edition, without vowels. In either case, this Name is *never* pronounced as it is spelled.

During prayer, or when a blessing is recited, or when a Torah verse is read, the Four-Letter Name should be pronounced as if it were spelled אֲדֹנָי, *ä dō nai'*, the Name that identifies God as the Master of All. At other times, it should be pronounced הַשֵּׁם, "Hashem," literally, "the Name."

In this work, the Four-Letter Name of God is translated "HASHEM," the pronounciation traditionally used for the Name to avoid pronouncing it unnecessarily.

The following table gives the pronunciations of the Name when it appears with a prefix.

בְּי־ה־ו־ה, — *bä dō nai'*
וַי־ה־ו־ה, — *vä dō nai'*
כְּי־ה־ו־ה, — *kä dō nai'*
לַי־ה־ו־ה, — *lä dō nai'*
מֵי־ה־ו־ה, — *mä ä dō nai'*
שֶׁי־ה־ו־ה, — *she ä dō nai'*

Sometimes the Name appears with the vowelization יֱ־ה־וִ־ה. This version of the Name is pronounced as if it were spelled אֱלֹהִים, *e lō him'*, the Name that refers to God as the One Who is all-powerful. When it appears with a prefix לֱי־ה־וִ־ה, it is pronounced *lä lō him'*. We have translated this Name as HASHEM/ELOHIM to indicate that it refers to the aspects inherent in each of those Names.

פרשת ויקרא
Parashas Vayikra

1

¹ He called to Moses, and HASHEM spoke

א × וַיִּקְרָ֖א אֶל־מֹשֶׁ֑ה וַיְדַבֵּ֤ר יהוה֙

───── אונקלוס ─────
א וּקְרָא לְמֹשֶׁה וּמַלִיל יְיָ

───── רש"י ─────

(א) ויקרא אל משה. לכל דברות ולכל אמירות ולכל צוויים קדמה קריאה (ת"כ פרשתא אזריח), לשון חבה, לשון שמלאכי השרת משתמשין בו שנ׳ וקרא זה אל זה ואמר קדוש (ישעיה ו:ג), אבל נביאי אומות העולם נגלה עליהן בל׳ ערעי וטומאה שנא׳ ויקר אלהים אל בלעם (במדבר כג:ד; ב"ר נב:ה): ויקרא אל משה. הקול הולך ומגיע לאזניו וכל ישראל לא שומעין (ת"כ פרק ב:ז-ט, תנחומא ויקרא א). יכול אף להפסקות היתה קריאה ת"ל וידבר לדבור היתה קריאה ולא להפסקות. ומה היו הפסקות משמשות, ליתן ריוח למשה להתבונן בין פרשה לפרשה ובין ענין לענין, ק"ו להדיוט הלומד מן ההדיוט (ת"כ פרשתא א:ח-ט):

───── RASHI ELUCIDATED ─────

1.

1. וַיִּקְרָא אֶל מֹשֶׁה — HE CALLED TO MOSES.[2] קָרִיאָה קָדְמָה צִוּוּיִים וּלְכָל אֲמִירוֹת וּלְכָל דִּבְּרוֹת לְכָל — "Calling"[1] preceded every statement, and every saying, and every command.[2] לְשׁוֹן חִבָּה — It is language of affection, i.e., language that indicates affection; לָשׁוֹן שֶׁמַּלְאֲכֵי הַשָּׁרֵת מִשְׁתַּמְּשִׁין בּוֹ — language that the ministering angels use,[3] שֶׁנֶּאֱמַר — as it says, ״וְקָרָא זֶה אֶל זֶה וְאָמַר קָדוֹשׁ״, — "One called to the other and said, 'Holy . . . ' "[3] — אֲבָל נְבִיאֵי אֻמּוֹת הָעוֹלָם But prophets of the other nations of the world, נִגְלָה עֲלֵיהֶן בִּלְשׁוֹן עֲרָאי וְטֻמְאָה — He revealed Himself to them in language of transitoriness and impurity, שֶׁנֶּאֱמַר — as it says, ״וַיִּקָּר אֱלֹהִים אֶל בִּלְעָם״ — "God happened upon Balaam."[4,5] ☐ וַיִּקְרָא אֶל מֹשֶׁה — HE CALLED TO MOSES. הַקּוֹל הוֹלֵךְ וּמַגִּיעַ לְאָזְנָיו — The voice of God would go, and reach [Moses'] ears, וְכָל יִשְׂרָאֵל לֹא שׁוֹמְעִין[6] — and all of Israel would not hear it.[6] יָכוֹל אַף לְהַפְסָקוֹת הָיְתָה קְרִיאָה — One might be able to think that there was "calling" at breaks,[7] as well. תַּלְמוּד לוֹמַר ״וַיְדַבֵּר״, — To teach us otherwise, the verse says, "and [HASHEM] spoke," לְדִבּוּר הָיְתָה קְרִיאָה — which implies, for speaking, i.e., for instances where the Torah says explicitly that God spoke to Moses there was "calling," וְלֹא לַהַפְסָקוֹת — but not for breaks. וּמֶה הָיוּ הַפְסָקוֹת מְשַׁמְּשׁוֹת — What purpose did breaks serve? לִתֵּן רֶוַח לְמֹשֶׁה לְהִתְבּוֹנֵן — To give Moses an interval of time for contemplation בֵּין פָּרָשָׁה לְפָרָשָׁה — between one section of the Torah and another, וּבֵין עִנְיָן לְעִנְיָן — and between one topic and another. קַל וָחוֹמֶר[8] לְהֶדְיוֹט הַלּוֹמֵד מִן הֶדְיוֹט[9] — All the more so[8] that time for contemplation between subjects is necessary for an ordinary person who learns from an ordinary person.[9]

---

1. That is, calling to Moses by name (*Mizrachi; Sifsei Chachamim*).

2. *Toras Kohanim, parshasa* 1:6-7. "He called . . . and HASHEM spoke" appears redundant. Rashi explains that "He called" indicates that the "speaking" which follows was made endearingly; the call consisted of a loving pronouncement of Moses' name. Although the Torah does not say so explicitly, whenever it says that God addressed Moses using a form of the verb "to speak" (דבר) or "to say" (אמר) or "to command" (צוה) to introduce what is stated (e.g. מֹשֶׁה ה׳ וַיְדַבֵּר, "And HASHEM spoke to Moses"), God first "called"; that is, He first addressed Moses by calling his name twice. The word וַיְדַבֵּר of our verse indicates that calling preceded "speaking"; the word לֵאמֹר at the end of the verse indicates that it preceded "saying"; and the word דַּבֵּר of verse 2, which is an imperative ("Speak!"), indicates that it preceded "commanding" (*Gur Aryeh*).

3. *Isaiah* 6:3.

4. *Numbers* 23:4. The basic meaning of וַיִּקָּר, "and he happened," connotes transitoriness. It also connotes impurity as it is similar to קֶרִי, "seminal emission," which is a cause of impurity (see *Mizrachi; Sifsei Chachamim*).

5. *Bereishis Rabbah* 52:5.

6. *Toras Kohanim, perek* 2:7-9; *Tanchuma* 1. Since God called Moses by name, the verse could have said, וַיִּקְרָא מֹשֶׁה, "And He called, 'Moses.' " The phrase וַיִּקְרָא אֶל מֹשֶׁה, "And He called *to* Moses," indicates that only Moses heard his name being called (*Gur Aryeh*).

7. Breaks in the text of the Torah indicated by blank spaces. A break may be פְּתוּחָה, "open" (i.e., the blank space that indicates the break continues until the end of the line, and the text resumes on the next line, e.g., the break after 1:13), or סְתוּמָה, "closed," (i.e., after a short break of open space, the text resumes on the same line, closing in the blank space, e.g., the break after 1:9). These breaks are the rough equivalent of the end of a paragraph.

One might have thought that a break indicates the beginning of a new, distinct prophecy which would be preceded by a new "calling." Rashi explains that this is not so (*Mizrachi*).

8. A קַל וָחוֹמֶר, "*kal vachomer*," is an *a fortiori*, a logical argument which states that if a rule has been given for a particular situation where there is relatively little reason for it to apply, all the more so should it apply to a situation in which the rule has not been explicitly stated, but where there is more reason to apply it, even though the rule has not been given explicitly in the second case.

9. *Toras Kohanim, parshasa* 1:8-9.

3 / VAYIKRA/LEVITICUS — PARASHAS VAYIKRA — 1/1 — א/א

אֵלָיו מֵאֹהֶל מוֹעֵד לֵאמֹר: *to him from the Tent of Meeting, saying:*

— אונקלוס —
עִמֵּהּ מִמַּשְׁכַּן זִמְנָא לְמֵימָר:

— רש"י —

אליו. למעט את אהרן. ר' יהודה בן בתירה אומר, י"ג דברות נאמרו בתורה למשה ולאהרן וכנגדן נאמרו י"ג מיעוטין, ללמדך שלא לאהרן נאמרו אלא למשה שיאמר לאהרן (שם פרק ב:א). ואלו הן י"ג מיעוטין, לדבר אתו (במדבר ז:פט), מדבר אליו (שם), וידבר אליו (שם), וגועדתי לך (שמות כה:כב), כולן בתורת כהנים (שם ב). יכול ישמעו [ס"א שמעו] את קול הדבור [ס"א הקריאה], ת"ל קול לו קול אליו, משה שמע וכל ישראל לא שמעו (ת"כ פרק ב:ט, יומא ד:ב): **מאהל מועד.** מלמד שהי' הקול נפסק ולא הי' יוצא חוץ לאהל.

————— RASHI ELUCIDATED —————

□ **אֵלָיו — TO HIM.** — לְמַעֵט אֶת אַהֲרֹן — **This was said to exclude Aaron.** — רַבִּי יְהוּדָה בֶּן בְּתֵירָה אוֹמֵר — **The** *Tanna* **R' Yehudah ben Beseirah says:** שְׁלֹשׁ עֶשְׂרֵה דִבְּרוֹת נֶאֶמְרוּ בַּתּוֹרָה לְמֹשֶׁה וּלְאַהֲרֹן — **Thirteen statements were said in the Torah to both Moses and Aaron,**[1] — וּכְנֶגְדָן נֶאֶמְרוּ שְׁלֹשׁ עֶשְׂרֵה מִיעוּטִין — **Corresponding to them, thirteen exclusions,** i.e., phrases that imply exclusion, **were said in** other statements of which ours is one, — לְלַמֶּדְךָ שֶׁלֹּא לְאַהֲרֹן נֶאֶמְרוּ — **to teach you that they,** i.e., the thirteen statements which appear to be addressed to Aaron, as well as Moses, **were not said to Aaron,** אֶלָּא לְמֹשֶׁה — **but rather to Moses** alone, ²שֶׁיֹּאמַר לְאַהֲרֹן — with the intention **that he should say** them **to Aaron.**[2] — וְאֵלּוּ הֵן שְׁלֹשׁ עֶשְׂרֵה מִיעוּטִין — **The thirteen exclusions are the following:** ³,,לְדַבֵּר אִתּוֹ'' — **"to speak with him,"**[3] — ³,,מְדַבֵּר אֵלָיו'' — **"communicating to him,"**[3] — ,,וַיְדַבֵּר אֵלָיו'' — **"and He spoke to him,"**[3] — ⁴,,וְנוֹעַדְתִּי לְךָ'' — **"and I will arrange audience for you."**[4] — ⁵כֻּלָּן בְּתוֹרַת כֹּהֲנִים — **All of them** are listed in *Toras Kohanim.*[5] — ⁷יָכוֹל יִשְׁמְעוּ אֶת קוֹל הַדִּבּוּר — **One might be able** to think that [Israel] would hear[6] the sound of the speech.[7,8] — ⁷,,קוֹל אֵלָיו'' תַּלְמוּד לוֹמַר קוֹל לוֹ — **To show that this is not so, the Torah says** instead of, **"[the] voice** [communicating] **to him,"** using the shorter word לוֹ for "to him," **"[the] voice** [communicating] **to him,"**[9] with the longer word אֵלָיו.[10] — מֹשֶׁה שׁוֹמֵעַ — **This** implies that **Moses would hear,** ¹¹וְכָל יִשְׂרָאֵל לֹא שָׁמְעוּ — **and all of Israel would not hear.**[11]

□ **מֵאֹהֶל מוֹעֵד — FROM THE TENT OF MEETING.** — מְלַמֵּד שֶׁהָיָה הַקּוֹל נִפְסָק — **This teaches** us that the sound of **the voice would be cut off** — וְלֹא הָיָה יוֹצֵא חוּץ לָאֹהֶל — **and would not go outside the Tent.**[12]

---

1. *Malbim* (to *Shemos* 12:1) enumerates the thirteen verses; eleven of them mention both Moses and Aaron, the other two mention Aaron alone. The eleven are: *Exodus* 6:13; *Leviticus* 11:1, 13:1, 14:33, 15:1; *Numbers* 2:1, 4:1, 4:17, 14:26, 16:20, and 19:1. The two are *Leviticus* 10:8 and *Numbers* 18:8.

2. *Toras Kohanim, perek* 2:1. When the Torah states that God spoke to Moses, as it does in our verse, we can assume that no one other than Moses was addressed. It would thus seem unnecessary to introduce a limiting word such as אֵלָיו of our verse to exclude Aaron or anybody else. If the Torah does use such words, it is to teach us that in other instances in which Aaron appears, he was not addressed directly even when the Torah seems to say that he was (*Gur Aryeh*).

3. *Numbers* 7:89.

4. *Exodus* 25:22.

5. *Toras Kohanim, perek* 2:2. Rashi here lists only four of the exclusionary phrases. The remaining nine phrases listed in *Toras Kohanim* are: דִּבַּרְתִּי אִתָּךְ, "and I shall speak with you," and אֶת כָּל אֲשֶׁר אֲצַוֶּה אוֹתָךְ, "all that I shall command you" (both in *Exodus* 25:22); אֲשֶׁר אִוָּעֵד לָכֶם שָׁמָּה, לְדַבֵּר אֵלֶיךָ שָׁם, "where I will arrange audience for you to speak to you there" (*Exodus* 29:42); אֲשֶׁר אִוָּעֵד לָכֶם שָׁמָּה, "where I will arrange audience for you" (*Exodus* 30:6); אֲשֶׁר צִוָּה ה' אֶת מֹשֶׁה בְּהַר סִינַי בְּיוֹם צַוֹּתוֹ, "which Hashem commanded Moses on Mount Sinai, on the day He commanded . . ." (*Leviticus* 7:38); עַד בֹּאוֹ לְדַבֵּר אִתּוֹ, "until

he would come to speak with Him" (*Exodus* 34:35); וַיְהִי בְּיוֹם דִּבֶּר ה' אֶל מֹשֶׁה בְּאֶרֶץ מִצְרָיִם, "And it was on the day that Hashem spoke to Moses in the land of Egypt" (*Exodus* 6:28); וְאֵלֶּה תּוֹלְדֹת אַהֲרֹן וּמֹשֶׁה בְּיוֹם דִּבֶּר ה' אֶת מֹשֶׁה בְּהַר סִינָי, "These are the offspring of Aaron and Moses on the day Hashem spoke to Moses at Mount Sinai" (*Numbers* 3:1); and our verse.

6. Some editions read שָׁמְעוּ, "[Israel] heard."

7. Some editions read קוֹל הַקְּרִיאָה, "the sound of the call."

8. One might think that although the rest of Israel could not make out the individual words which God said to Moses, they could nonetheless hear the sound of His voice (*Mizrachi; Be'er Yitzchak*).

9. *Numbers* 7:89.

10. The verse could have used the shorter word, לוֹ. The longer word, אֵלָיו, connotes "to him" in a narrower sense, and can imply "to him to the exclusion of others." Since the verse chose the longer word, it indicates that no one but Moses heard the speech (*Be'er Yitzchak*; see, too, Rashi to *Yoma* 4b).

11. *Toras Kohanim, perek* 2:9; *Yoma* 4b.

12. If by the words "from the Tent of Meeting" the verse is interested only in telling us from where God's voice emanated when He communicated with Moses, it should have informed us of the location at its outset. It should have said, "He called to Moses from the Tent of Meeting, and Hashem spoke to him, saying." This would

4 / ויקרא – פרשת ויקרא   א/א – 1/1

───────────────── רש"י ─────────────────

יכול מפני שהקול נמוך, ת"ל את הקול (במדבר ז:פט), מהו הקול, הוא הקול המפרש בתהלים, קול ה' בכח קול ה' בהדר קול ה' שובר ארזים (כט:ד-ה) א"כ למה נא' מאהל מועד, מלמד שהיה הקול נפסק. כיוצא בו, וקול כנפי הכרובים נשמע עד החצר החיצונה (יחזקאל י:ה), יכול מפני שהקול נמוך, ת"ל כקול אל שדי בדברו (שם), ת"כ למה נא' עד החצר החיצונה, שכיון שמגיע שם הי' נפסק (ת"כ פרק ב:י"א): **מאהל מועד לאמר.** יכול מכל הבית, ת"ל מעל הכפורת (במדבר ז:פט). יכול מעל הכפורת כולה, ת"ל מבין שני הכרובים (שם; ת"כ שם יב): **לאמר.** צא ואמור להם דברי כבושין, בשבילכם הוא נדבר עמי.

──────────── RASHI ELUCIDATED ────────────

יָכוֹל מִפְּנֵי שֶׁהַקּוֹל נָמוּךְ — **One might be able** to think that it was not heard beyond the Tent **because** the sound of **the voice was low.** ¹״אֶת הַקּוֹל״ **תַּלְמוּד לוֹמַר** — **To teach us otherwise, the Torah says, *"the* voice."**¹ ״הַקּוֹל״, **מַהוּ** — **What is** meant by ***"the* voice"?** **הוּא הַקּוֹל הַמְפוֹרָשׁ בִּתְהִלִּים** — It is the voice which is described explicitly in *Psalms*, ״קוֹל ה' בַּכֹּחַ קוֹל ה' בֶּהָדָר קוֹל ²ה' שׁבֵר אֲרָזִים״ — **"The voice of HASHEM is powerful! The voice of HASHEM is majestic! The voice of HASHEM breaks cedars."**² ״מֵאֹהֶל מוֹעֵד״ **אִם כֵּן לָמָּה נֶאֱמַר** — **If so, why does it say, "from the Tent of Meeting"?**³ **מְלַמֵּד שֶׁהָיָה הַקּוֹל נִפְסָק** — **This teaches** us that the sound of **the voice would be cut off** when it reached the Tent walls and would not be heard outside of the Tent. **כַּיּוֹצֵא בוֹ** — **Similar to it,** i.e., the same idea is implied in the verse, ⁴״וְקוֹל כַּנְפֵי הַכְּרוּבִים נִשְׁמַע עַד הֶחָצֵר הַחִיצֹנָה״ — **"The sound of the wings of the cherubim was heard up to the outer courtyard."**⁴ **יָכוֹל מִפְּנֵי שֶׁהַקּוֹל נָמוּךְ** — **One might be able** to think that it was not heard beyond the outer courtyard **because the voice was low.** ⁴״כְּקוֹל אֵל שַׁדַּי בְּדַבְּרוֹ״ **תַּלְמוּד לוֹמַר** — **To teach us otherwise, the verse says, "like the sound of EL SHADDAI when He speaks."**⁴ **אִם כֵּן לָמָּה נֶאֱמַר** — **If so, why does it say, "up to the outer courtyard"?** ⁵**שֶׁכֵּיוָן שֶׁמַּגִּיעַ שָׁם הָיָה נִפְסָק** — **Because once it reached there it would stop.**⁵

□ **מֵאֹהֶל מוֹעֵד לֵאמֹר** — **FROM THE TENT OF MEETING, SAYING.** **יָכוֹל מִכָּל הַבַּיִת** — **One might be able** to think that the voice came **from the entire House,** i.e., the *Mishkan* (Tabernacle). **תַּלְמוּד לוֹמַר** ⁶**״מֵעַל הַכַּפֹּרֶת״** — **To teach us otherwise, the Torah says, "from above the lid"** (of the Ark).⁶ **יָכוֹל מֵעַל הַכַּפֹּרֶת כֻּלָּהּ** — **One might be able** to think that the voice came **from the entire *kapores*.** **תַּלְמוּד** **לוֹמַר** ״מִבֵּין שְׁנֵי הַכְּרוּבִים״⁶,⁷ — **To teach us otherwise, the Torah says, "from between the two cherubim."**⁶,⁷

□ **לֵאמֹר** — **SAYING.** **צֵא וֶאֱמוֹר לָהֶם דִּבְרֵי כִּבּוּשִׁין** — God said to Moses, **"Go out and say winning words to them."** **בִּשְׁבִילְכֶם הוּא נִדְבָּר עִמִּי** — Say to them, **'On your account He communicates with me.' "**⁸

---

have expressed more clearly that it was not only the speaking which took place from the Tent of Meeting, but the calling, as well. Since "from the Tent of Meeting" appears at the end of the verse, it is in order to juxtapose it with "to him," to say that the voice was heard only by Moses because he was inside the Tent of Meeting, and the sound did not travel beyond there (*Mizrachi; Sifsei Chachamim*).

Alternatively, our verse gives the impression that the voice of God came from the Tent of Meeting and was heard by Moses outside of it. But this is not so, for it says, "And when Moses would come to the Tent of Meeting to speak with Him, he would hear the voice communicating with him from above the cover which was on the Ark of the Testimony, from between the two cherubim" (*Numbers* 7:89). Rather, the voice emanated from between the cherubim, as stated in the verse quoted above, and in *Exodus* 25:22: "I shall arrange audience for you there, and I shall speak with you from atop the cover, from between the cherubim that are on the Ark of the Testimony." "From the Tent of Meeting" of our verse indicates that the sound which emerged from there could be heard throughout the Tent of Meeting, but not beyond it (*Malbim*).

1. *Numbers* 7:89. The use of the definite article "the" indicates that the Torah has a specific voice in mind.

2. *Psalms* 29:4-5.

3. If the voice was powerful, why does the verse indicate that it did not carry beyond the Tent of Meeting?

4. *Ezekiel* 10:5.

5. *Toras Kohanim, perek* 2:10-11.

6. *Numbers* 7:89.

7. *Toras Kohanim, perek* 2:12.

8. "Saying" often indicates that the individual addressed — in this case, Moses — should relate to others what he is being told. This cannot be so here, for the next verse says explicitly that he is to relate the following commandments to Israel. That is why Rashi explains that "saying" implies that Moses is to convey a message to Israel in addition to the commandments that he is instructed to tell them in the following verse (*Mesiach Ilmim; Maskil LeDavid; Amar N'kei*).

VAYIKRA/LEVITICUS — PARASHAS VAYIKRA — 1/2

דַּבֵּר אֶל־בְּנֵי יִשְׂרָאֵל וְאָמַרְתָּ אֲלֵהֶם אָדָם כִּי־יַקְרִיב מִכֶּם קָרְבָּן לַיהוָה מִן־הַבְּהֵמָה מִן־הַבָּקָר וּמִן־הַצֹּאן

² Speak to the Children of Israel and say to them: When a person from among you will bring an offering to HASHEM: from the animals — from the cattle and from the flocks

— אונקלוס —
ב מַלֵּל עִם בְּנֵי יִשְׂרָאֵל וְתֵימַר לְהוֹן אֱנָשׁ אֲרֵי יְקָרֵב מִנְּכוֹן קֻרְבָּנָא קֳדָם יְיָ מִן בְּעִירָא מִן תּוֹרֵי וּמִן עָנָא

— רש"י —

שֶׁכֵּן מָצִינוּ שֶׁכָּל ל"ח שָׁנָה שֶׁהָיוּ יִשְׂרָאֵל בַּמִּדְבָּר כִּמְנֻדִּים, מִן הַמְרַגְּלִים וָאֵילָךְ, לֹא נִתְיַחֵד הַדִּבּוּר עִם מֹשֶׁה, שֶׁנֶּאֱמַר וַיְהִי כַאֲשֶׁר תַּמּוּ כָּל אַנְשֵׁי הַמִּלְחָמָה לָמוּת וַיְדַבֵּר ה' אֵלַי לֵאמֹר (דברים ב:טז-יז) אֵלַי הָיָה הַדִּבּוּר. דָּ"אַ צֵא וֶאֱמֹר לָהֶם דְּבָרַי וַהֲשִׁיבֵנִי אִם יְקַבְּלוּם, כְּמָה שֶׁנֶּאֱמַר וַיָּשֶׁב מֹשֶׁה אֶת דִּבְרֵי הָעָם וְגוֹ' (שמות יט:ח; ת"כ שם יג): **(ב) אָדָם כִּי יַקְרִיב מִכֶּם.** כְּשֶׁיַּקְרִיב. בְּקָרְבָּנוֹת נְדָבָה דִּבֶּר הָעִנְיָן: **אָדָם.** לָמָּה נֶאֱמַר, מָה אָדָם הָרִאשׁוֹן לֹא הִקְרִיב מִן הַגָּזֵל, שֶׁהַכֹּל הָיָה שֶׁלּוֹ, אַף אַתֶּם לֹא תַקְרִיבוּ מִן הַגָּזֵל (ויק"ר ב:ז): **הַבְּהֵמָה.** יָכוֹל אַף חַיָּה בַּכְּלָל, ת"ל בָּקָר וָצֹאן (ת"כ פַּרְשְׁתָא ב:ו):

— RASHI ELUCIDATED —

שֶׁכֵּן מָצִינוּ שֶׁכָּל שְׁלֹשִׁים וּשְׁמוֹנֶה שָׁנָה שֶׁהָיוּ יִשְׂרָאֵל בַּמִּדְבָּר כִּמְנֻדִּים — **As we have found that the entire thirty-eight years that Israel were in the desert like those who are excommunicated,** מִן הַמְרַגְּלִים וָאֵילָךְ — **from** the sin of **the spies**[1] **onward,** לֹא נִתְיַחֵד הַדִּבּוּר עִם מֹשֶׁה — **the speech** of God **did not seclude itself with Moses,**[2] שֶׁנֶּאֱמַר ,,וַיְהִי כַאֲשֶׁר תַּמּוּ כָּל אַנְשֵׁי הַמִּלְחָמָה לָמוּת — **as it says, "And it came to pass, when all of the men of war ceased to die,** וַיְדַבֵּר ה' אֵלַי לֵאמֹר" — **HASHEM spoke to me, saying."**[3] אֵלַי הָיָה הַדִּבּוּר — Only then **was the speech *to me.***[4] וַהֲשִׁיבֵנִי אִם יְקַבְּלוּם, דָּבָר אַחֵר — **Alternatively,** צֵא וֶאֱמֹר לָהֶם דְּבָרַי — **Go out and tell them My words,** — **and report to Me whether or not they will accept them,**[5] כְּמָה שֶׁנֶּאֱמַר ,,וַיָּשֶׁב מֹשֶׁה אֶת דִּבְרֵי הָעָם — **as it says, "and Moses reported the words of the people, etc."**[6,7] וְגוֹמֵר"[6,7] **2.** אָדָם כִּי יַקְרִיב מִכֶּם — **WHEN A PERSON FROM AMONG YOU WILL BRING.** כְּשֶׁיַּקְרִיב — **When he will bring;**[8] בְּקָרְבְּנוֹת נְדָבָה דִּבֶּר הָעִנְיָן — **this topic discusses voluntary offerings.**[9] □ אָדָם — **A PERSON.** לָמָּה נֶאֱמַר — **Why was it said?**[10] מָה אָדָם הָרִאשׁוֹן לֹא הִקְרִיב מִן הַגָּזֵל — **Just as Adam, the first** man, **did not bring** an offering **from that which was stolen,** שֶׁהַכֹּל הָיָה שֶׁלּוֹ — **since everything was his,** אַף אַתֶּם — **you, too,** [11]לֹא תַקְרִיבוּ מִן הַגָּזֵל — **do not bring** an offering **from that which was stolen.**[11]

□ הַבְּהֵמָה — **THE ANIMALS.** יָכוֹל אַף חַיָּה בַּכְּלָל — **One might be able to think that wild animals are also included.** תַּלְמוּד לוֹמַר ,,בָּקָר וָצֹאן" — **To teach us otherwise, the Torah says, "cattle and flocks."**[12]

---

1. See *Numbers* 13:1-14:38.
2. He did not speak with him intimately and endearingly during that time (Rashi to *Deuteronomy* 2:17).
3. *Deuteronomy* 2:16-17.
4. Only after the "men of war" — those twenty and above at the time of the sin of the spies — died out, was the speech of God addressed *to me*, in an intimate fashion.
5. According to this explanation, "saying" implies not that Moses should say something to Israel, but that he is to "say" something to God, i.e., he should report to Him.
6. *Exodus* 19:8; see *Mechilta* there.
7. *Toras Kohanim, perek* 2:13.
8. The word כי can mean "because," which would render our verse, "A person from among you, because he shall bring an offering to HASHEM . . ." This could be understood to imply that the offering must be brought. Rashi explains that it is used here in the sense of "when." This can imply that the offering need not necessarily be offered, and is compatible with the subject of this section, voluntary offerings (see *Korban Aharon*; *Mishmeres HaKodesh*).

9. מכם, literally, "from you," implies that the initiative for this offering came "from you," not from an obligation imposed by the Torah (*Levush HaOrah*).
   Toras Kohanim, parshasa 2:4, draws the same conclusion, but derives it from the word כי, which is usually not used for obligations (see *Malbim*).
10. The more common term for "man" is אישׁ. Why did the Torah use אָדָם (*Mizrachi*)? Furthermore, the term אָדָם connotes a Jew, as opposed to a non-Jew (*Yevamos* 61a). Yet Rashi has previously determined that this passage discusses voluntary offerings, which in fact non-Jews may bring. Rashi therefore explains that here אָדָם refers not only to man in general, but is also a proper noun referring to the first man, Adam (*Minchas Yehudah; Sifsei Chachamim*).
11. *Vayikra Rabbah* 2:7.
12. *Toras Kohanim, parshasa* 2:6. Wild animals are sometimes included in the term בְּהֵמָה (e.g., *Deuteronomy* 14:4-5). By mentioning "cattle and flocks," which never include wild animals, immediately after בְּהֵמָה, the Torah indicates that it is to be understood in its narrow sense, to the exclusion of wild animals (*Mizrachi; Sifsei Chachamim*).

ג תַּקְרִיבוּ אֶת־קָרְבַּנְכֶם: אִם־עֹלָה
קָרְבָּנוֹ מִן־הַבָּקָר זָכָר תָּמִים
יַקְרִיבֶנּוּ אֶל־פֶּתַח אֹהֶל מוֹעֵד
יַקְרִיב אֹתוֹ לִרְצֹנוֹ לִפְנֵי יהוה:

you shall bring your offering.
³ If one's offering is an olah-offering from the cattle, he shall bring a perfect male; he shall bring it to the entrance of the Tent of Meeting, in accordance with his will, before HASHEM.

---— אונקלוס ---—

תְּקָרְבוּן יָת קֻרְבַּנְכוֹן: ג אִם עֲלָתָא קֻרְבָּנֵהּ מִן תּוֹרֵי דְּכַר שְׁלִים יְקָרְבִנֵּהּ מִן תְּרַע מַשְׁכַּן זִמְנָא יְקָרֵב יָתֵהּ לְרַעֲוָא לֵהּ קֳדָם יְיָ:

---— רש"י ---—

מן הבהמה. ולא כולה להוציא את הרובע ואת הנרבע: מן הבקר. להוציא את הנעבד: מן הצאן. להוציא את המוקצה (תמורה כת.-כט.): ומן הצאן. להוציא הנוגח שהמית (שם) [על פי עד אחד או על פי הבעלים (בכורות מא.)] כשהוא אומר למטה מן הענין ,,מן הבקר״, שאין ת״ל, להוציא את הטריפה (ת״כ פרק ג:א׳): קרבנכם. מלמד שהיא באה נדבת ציבור היא עולת קיץ המזבח הבאה מן המותרות (שבועות יב א-ב):
למטה מן הענין מן הבקר, שאין ת"ל, תמורה כת.-כט.: תקריבו. מלמד ששנים מתנדבים עולה בשותפות (ת"כ פרק ג:א'): קרבנכם. מלמד שהיא באה נדבת ציבור היא עולת קיץ המזבח הבאה מן המותרות (שבועות יב א-ב):

---— RASHI ELUCIDATED ---—

☐ מִן הַבְּהֵמָה — FROM THE ANIMALS. וְלֹא כֻלָּהּ — But not all of [the category of animals].[1] לְהוֹצִיא אֶת הָרוֹבֵעַ וְאֶת הַנִּרְבָּע — To exclude an animal that was the active or the passive partner in an act of bestiality.[2]

☐ מִן הַבָּקָר — FROM THE CATTLE. This word מִן, "from," appears in the verse לְהוֹצִיא אֶת הַנֶּעֱבָד — to exclude that which has been worshiped as an idol.

☐ מִן הַצֹּאן — FROM THE FLOCKS. This word מִן, "from," appears in the verse לְהוֹצִיא אֶת הַמֻּקְצֶה — to exclude that which has been set aside as a sacrifice for pagan worship.[3]

☐ וּמִן הַצֹּאן — AND FROM THE FLOCKS. The word וּמִן, "and from," appears in the verse לְהוֹצִיא אֶת הַנּוֹגֵחַ שֶׁהֵמִית — to exclude a goring animal that killed a person[4] {עַל פִּי עֵד אֶחָד אוֹ עַל פִּי הַבְּעָלִים — according to the testimony of a single witness or of the owner[5]}. כְּשֶׁהוּא אוֹמֵר לְמַטָּה מִן הָעִנְיָן ,,מִן הַבָּקָר״ — When it says below this topic, in the next verse, *"from the cattle,"* שֶׁאֵין תַּלְמוּד לוֹמַר — let the Torah not say it.[6] Why was it written? לְהוֹצִיא אֶת הַטְּרֵפָה — To exclude an animal which is a *tereifah*.[7,8]

☐ תַּקְרִיבוּ — YOU SHALL BRING.[9] מְלַמֵּד שֶׁשְּׁנַיִם מִתְנַדְּבִים עוֹלָה בְּשׁוּתָפוּת — This teaches us that two or more may donate an *olah*-offering in partnership.[9]

☐ קָרְבַּנְכֶם — YOUR OFFERING. מְלַמֵּד שֶׁהִיא בָּאָה נִדְבַת צִבּוּר — This teaches us that [the *olah*-offering] can come as a voluntary contribution of the entire community.[10] הִיא עוֹלַת קַיִץ הַמִּזְבֵּחַ — This is the *olah*-offering of "the dessert of the *Mizbe'ach* (Altar)"[11] הַבָּאָה מִן הַמּוֹתָרוֹת — which comes from the extra [funds].[12]

---

1. The word מִן, "from," places a limitation on the broad category of animals.
2. *Toras Kohanim, parshasa* 2:7.
3. *Temurah* 28a-29a.
4. *Temurah* 28a-29a. The "and" of "and from" implies an exclusion in addition to the one implied by "from" alone (*Mizrachi*).
5. *Bechoros* 41a. Had there been two valid witnesses to the killing, the animal would have been put to death by the *beis din*.
6. The word מִן of the following verse appears superfluous. The verse could have said, אִם עֹלָה קָרְבָּנוֹ בָּקָר זָכָר תָּמִים יַקְרִיבֶנּוּ, "If one's offering is a cattle *olah*-offering, he is to bring an unblemished male" (*Mesiach Ilmim; Ho'il Moshe*).
7. A *tereifah*, literally, "a torn animal," is one that has a physical defect which will lead to its death. Such a defect renders the animal prohibited for consumption.
8. *Toras Kohanim, parshasa* 2:7-11; *Temurah* 28a-29a.
9. *Toras Kohanim, perek* 3:1. This is implied by the shift

from the singular subject of the subordinate clause, כִּי אָדָם, "when a person from among you will bring," to the plural object of the main clause, תַּקְרִיבוּ, "you (plural) shall bring" (*Mizrachi; Sifsei Chachamim; Be'er Yitzchak*).

10. "You shall bring [lit., offer] your offering" sounds redundant. The verse could have simply said, "you shall offer," and "your offering" would have been understood. The Torah nonetheless wrote קָרְבַּנְכֶם, "your offering," with the plural suffix כֶם, "your," to teach us that there can be voluntary communal *olah*-offerings (*Be'er Yitzchak*).

11. קַיִץ are fruits which are dried in the summertime, often eaten as a dessert. "The dessert of the *Mizbe'ach*" consisted of *olah*-offerings purchased from communal funds; these were offered on the *Mizbe'ach* when no other offerings were being brought (see Rashi to *II Samuel* 16:1, *Succah* 56a, *Shevuos* 12b and *Bava Metzia* 106b).

12. *Shevuos* 12a-b. Certain sin-offerings and guilt-offerings that cannot be offered on the *Mizbe'ach* are sold when they develop a blemish. The funds are then given to

---------- רש"י ----------

(ג) זָכָר. וְלֹא נְקֵבָה כְּשֶׁהוּא אוֹמֵר זָכָר לְמַטָּה (פס' י) שְׁאֵין ת"ל, זְכַר
וְלֹא טוּמְטוּם וְאַנְדְּרוֹגִינוֹס (ת"כ פרשתא ג:ז; בכורות מא:): תָּמִים.
בְּלֹא מוּם: אֶל פֶּתַח אֹהֶל מוֹעֵד. מְטַפֵּל בַּהֲבָאָתוֹ עַד הָעֲזָרָה
(ת"כ שם יג). מַהוּ אוֹמֵר יַקְרִיב יַקְרִיב, אֲפִי' נִתְעָרְבָה עוֹלָה בְּעוֹלָה
בְּעוֹלַת שִׁמְעוֹן יַקְרִיב כָּל אַחַת לְשֵׁם מִי שֶׁהוּא. וְכֵן עוֹלָה בְּחוּלִין
יִמָּכְרוּ הַחוּלִין לְצָרְכֵי עוֹלוֹת, וַהֲרֵי הֵן כֻּלָּן עוֹלוֹת וְתִקְרַב כָּל אַחַת לְשֵׁם
מִי שֶׁהוּא. יָכוֹל אֲפִי' נִתְעָרֵב בִּפְסוּלִין אוֹ בְּשֶׁאֵינוֹ מִינוֹ, ת"ל יַקְרִיבֶנּוּ
(ת"כ שם; זבחים ע:-עא:): יַקְרִיב אֹתוֹ. מְלַמֵּד שֶׁכּוֹפִין אוֹתוֹ.

---------- RASHI ELUCIDATED ----------

3. זָכָר — MALE. וְלֹא נְקֵבָה — But not female. כְּשֶׁהוּא אוֹמֵר זָכָר לְמַטָּה — When it says "male" below,[1] שְׁאֵין תַּלְמוּד לוֹמַר — let the Torah not say it, for our verse has already stated explicitly that we are dealing with a male. [3] זָכָר וְלֹא טוּמְטוּם וְאַנְדְּרוֹגִינוֹס — Why did the Torah repeat it? To teach you that the animal must be a male, but not a *"toomtoom"*[2] or an androgyne.[3]

☐ תָּמִים — PERFECT. בְּלֹא מוּם — Without blemish.[4]

☐ אֶל פֶּתַח אֹהֶל מוֹעֵד — TO THE ENTRANCE OF THE TENT OF MEETING. מְטַפֵּל בַּהֲבָאָתוֹ עַד הָעֲזָרָה[5] — [The owner of the offering] tends to its bringing until it arrives at the Courtyard of the *Beis HaMikdash* or the *Mishkan*.[5] מַהוּ אוֹמֵר יַקְרִיב יַקְרִיב — Why does it say יַקְרִיב twice in this verse, once in the form of יַקְרִיב and once in the form of יַקְרִיבֶנּוּ? אֲפִילוּ נִתְעָרְבָה עוֹלַת רְאוּבֵן בְּעוֹלַת שִׁמְעוֹן — To teach us that even if Reuven's *olah*-offering became mixed up with Shimon's[6] *olah*-offering, and it cannot be determined which animal belongs to whom, יַקְרִיב כָּל אַחַת לְשֵׁם מִי שֶׁהוּא[7] — [the one performing the service] shall offer each one in the name of whomever it may belong to.[7] וְכֵן עוֹלָה בְּחוּלִין — Similarly, if an *olah*-offering became mixed up with an animal which was not holy, יִמָּכְרוּ הַחוּלִין לְצָרְכֵי עוֹלוֹת — that which is not holy should be sold for the need of *olah*-offerings, וַהֲרֵי הֵן כֻּלָּן עוֹלוֹת — and then they are all *olah*-offerings, וְתִקְרַב כָּל אַחַת — and each one should be offered לְשֵׁם מִי שֶׁהוּא — in the name of whomever it may belong to.[8] יָכוֹל אֲפִילוּ נִתְעָרֵב בִּפְסוּלִין — One might be able to think that the offering should be brought even if it became mixed up with those that are unfit[9] אוֹ בְּשֶׁאֵינוֹ מִינוֹ — or that which is not its kind.[10] תַּלְמוּד לוֹמַר ,,יַקְרִיבֶנּוּ" — To teach us otherwise, the verse says, "he shall bring it."[11]

☐ יַקְרִיב אֹתוֹ — HE SHALL BRING IT. מְלַמֵּד שֶׁכּוֹפִין אוֹתוֹ — This teaches us that they force him.[12]

---

the *Beis HaMikdash* for voluntary offerings. It is from these extra funds that "the dessert of the *Mizbe'ach*" is purchased (Rashi to *Yoma* 55b and *Succah* 56a; see also *Shekalim* 4:4).

1. Verse 10.

2. A טוּמְטוּם, *"toomtoom"* (cognate with טמטום, "blockage" or "closing"), is a person or animal whose genitals are blocked so that its sex cannot be determined. This differs from an אַנְדְּרוֹגִינוֹס, "androgyne" (or, "hermaphrodite"), who has both male and female characteristics.

3. *Toras Kohanim, parshasa* 3:7; *Bechoros* 41b.

4. "Male" and "perfect" are two distinct requirements. The verse does not mean to say "a perfect male" — an animal which is completely male. Were this the meaning, this verse rather than the one referred to by Rashi above would exclude animals of indeterminate and dual gender (*Gur Aryeh*).

5. *Toras Kohanim, parshasa* 3:13.

6. The hypothetical owners of the offerings are called Reuven and Shimon, the names of Jacob's two oldest sons. These names are commonly used to illustrate particular cases.

7. "He shall offer" is repeated to imply that he offer even offerings that have become mixed up with each other (*Mizrachi*). In this situation, whoever is performing the service says, "This offering is being brought for the sake of whoever is its owner" (see variant of Rashi from manuscript, *Zevachim* 71a, s.v., יקרב, and *Tosafos*, s.v., לשם מי שהוא).

8. If Reuven's *olah*-offering becomes mixed up with another animal of his which is not an offering, he does not have to consecrate the second animal and offer them both. He can have Shimon, who wishes to bring an *olah*-offering, buy whichever of the two animals has not been consecrated and designate it as his own *olah*-offering. Each animal will then be offered in the name of whomever it belongs to, as in the case of two *olah*-offerings which have become mixed up with each other (*Mizrachi*).

9. Animals unfit for offering; for example, one which has been used for idolatry (*Mizrachi*).

10. A different variety of offering; for example, an *olah*-offering became mixed up with a sin-offering (*Mizrachi*).

11. *Toras Kohanim, parshasa* 3:13; *Zevachim* 70b-71b. The verse could have said זָכָר תָּמִים יַקְרִיב, "An unblemished male he shall bring." The apparently superfluous "it" implies a limitation of the mixtures whose offering has been sanctioned by the repetition of "he shall bring" (*Nachalas Yaakov*).

12. The apparently superfluous אתו implies that *it* — the offering — must be offered in any case, even if the one who must bring it is unwilling (*Gur Aryeh*).

⁴ He shall lean his hands on the head of the olah-offering; and it will be considered pleasing on his behalf, to atone for him. **⁵** He

ד וְסָמַךְ יָדוֹ עַל רֹאשׁ הָעֹלָה וְנִרְצָה
ה לוֹ לְכַפֵּר עָלָיו: וְשָׁחַט אֶת־בֶּן

───────── אונקלוס ─────────

ד וְיִסְמוֹךְ יְדֵהּ עַל רֵישׁ עֲלָתָא וְיִתְרְעֵי לֵהּ לְכַפָּרָא עֲלוֹהִי: ה וְיִכּוֹס יָת בַּר

───────── רש"י ─────────

יָכוֹל בְּעַל כָּרְחוֹ, ת"ל לִרְצוֹנוֹ. הָא כֵּיצַד, כּוֹפִין אוֹתוֹ עַד שֶׁיֹּאמַר רוֹצֶה אֲנִי (ת"כ שם ג) (ולהביא עולת הצאן (שם ה)): **הָעֹלָה.** פְּרָט לְעוֹלַת הָעוֹף (ת"כ שם עוז; ר"ה ו.): **לִפְנֵי ה' וְסָמַךְ.** אֵין סְמִיכָה בַּבָּמָה (ת"כ שם ז): **וְנִרְצָה לוֹ.** עַל מַה הוּא מְרַצֶּה לוֹ, אִם תֹּאמַר עַל כְּרִיתוֹת וּמִיתוֹת בֵּין דִּין אוֹ מִיתָה בִּידֵי שָׁמַיִם אוֹ מַלְקוֹת הֲרֵי עָנְשָׁן אָמוּר (פרק ד:א): **(ד) עַל רֹאשׁ הָעֹלָה.** לְהָבִיא עוֹלַת חוֹבָה לַסְּמִיכָה

───────── RASHI ELUCIDATED ─────────

יָכוֹל בְּעַל כָּרְחוֹ — One might be able to think that they can force him to bring an offering **against his will.** **תַּלְמוּד לוֹמַר ,,לִרְצוֹנוֹ"** — To teach us otherwise, **the verse says, "in accordance with his will." הָא כֵּיצַד** — How can this be?[1] **²כּוֹפִין אוֹתוֹ עַד שֶׁיֹּאמַר רוֹצֶה אֲנִי** — They force him until he says, "I am willing."[2]

□ **לִפְנֵי ה' וְסָמַךְ** — BEFORE HASHEM. HE SHALL LEAN [HIS HANDS].[4] **אֵין סְמִיכָה בַּבָּמָה** — There is no leaning of hands upon an offering **at a bamah.**[3,4]

4. **עַל רֹאשׁ הָעֹלָה** — ON THE HEAD OF THE *OLAH*-OFFERING.[5] **לְהָבִיא עוֹלַת חוֹבָה לַסְּמִיכָה** — To include an obligatory *olah*-offering for, i.e., in the law of, leaning of hands,[5] {**וּלְהָבִיא עוֹלַת הַצֹּאן**[6] — and to include an *olah*-offering of the flock.[6]}

□ **הָעֹלָה** — THE *OLAH*-OFFERING.[7] **פְּרָט לְעוֹלַת הָעוֹף** — To the exclusion of the *olah*-offering of the fowl.[7]

□ **וְנִרְצָה לוֹ** — AND IT WILL BE CONSIDERED PLEASING ON HIS BEHALF. **עַל מַה הוּא מְרַצֶּה לוֹ** — For what does it "please" on his behalf? **אִם תֹּאמַר עַל כְּרִיתוֹת וּמִיתוֹת בֵּין דִּין** — If you will say that it brings forgiveness **for sins punished by excision,**[8] or sins punished by execution by the court, **אוֹ מִיתָה בִּידֵי שָׁמַיִם** — or sins punished by death at the hands of Heaven,[9] **אוֹ מַלְקוֹת** — or sins punished by lashes, **הֲרֵי עָנְשָׁן אָמוּר** — this cannot be so; **see, now, that their punishment has been stated** by the Torah. The

---

1. How can we reconcile the part of the verse that teaches us to force him to bring his offering with the part of the verse which says that he brings it of his own accord?

2. *Toras Kohanim, parshasa* 3:15; *Rosh Hashanah* 6a. They pressure him until he consents to fulfill his obligation. This is not considered to be against his will, for the true will of a Jew is to please his Creator. Man's desire to do wrong is a distortion of his true will caused by the evil inclination (*Mizrachi; Gur Aryeh*; based on *Rambam, Hilchos Gerushin*, II:20).

3. A *bamah*, literally, "platform" or "high place," is an altar other than the *Mizbe'ach* of the *Beis HaMikdash* or of the *Mishkan*. It was permitted to bring voluntary offerings on such altars until the *Beis HaMikdash* was built, except in the desert after the *Mishkan* had been erected, and during the period in which the *Mishkan* was located in Shiloh (see time line below).

4. *Toras Kohanim, perek* 4:1; *Zevachim* 119a. The words לִפְנֵי ה', "before HASHEM," appear superfluous, for the verse has already stated explicitly, "to the entrance of the Tent of Meeting." According to Rashi, they were written to juxtapose these words to "he shall lean" of the following verse to teach us that leaning of hands is required only "before HASHEM," but not for those offerings brought on the *bamos* (*Devek Tov*).

5. *Toras Kohanim, perek* 4:3.

6. *Toras Kohanim, perek* 4:5. The preceding verse has already stated explicitly that this passage deals with *olah*-offerings. Our verse could have said עַל רֹאשׁוֹ, "on its head" and it would have been clear that it meant the head of the *olah*-offering. "Of the *olah*-offering" seems superfluous. Rashi has stated above that this passage discusses voluntary *olah*-offerings. The preceding verse speaks of offerings brought from "cattle" — large species such as oxen. The apparently superfluous "of the *olah*-offering" indicates that the law of leaning of hands applies to other types of *olah*-offerings, obligatory offerings, and those which are brought from "the flock" — sheep or goats (*Mizrachi; Sifsei Chachamim*). Burnt-offerings of the flock are discussed in verses 10-13, but no mention of leaning of hands is made there.

7. *Toras Kohanim, perek* 4:7. Although "the *olah*-offering" applies the law of leaning of hands to *olah*-offerings other than those mentioned in this passage, the definite article "the" limits the extent of that application. It does not apply to *olah*-offerings of fowl (*Mizrachi; Sifsei Chachamim*).

8. According to Rashi (*Genesis* 17:14; *Leviticus* 17:9) this means premature death of the sinner and his offspring.

9. Death before the age of sixty. See *Moed Katan* 28a.

MISHKAN NOT YET ERECTED	MISHKAN IN THE DESERT 39 YEARS	MISHKAN IN GILGAL 14 YEARS	MISHKAN IN SHILOH 369 YEARS	MISHKAN IN NOB AND GIBEON 57 YEARS	BEIS HAMIKDASH IS ERECTED
BAMOS PERMITTED	BAMOS FORBIDDEN	BAMOS PERMITTED	BAMOS FORBIDDEN	BAMOS PERMITTED	BAMOS FORBIDDEN FOREVER

9 / VAYIKRA/LEVITICUS — PARASHAS VAYIKRA — 1/5 — א/ה

הַבָּקָר לִפְנֵי יהוה וְהִקְרִיבוּ בְּנֵי אַהֲרֹן הַכֹּהֲנִים אֶת־הַדָּם וְזָרְקוּ

shall slaughter the bull before HASHEM; *the sons of Aaron, the Kohanim, shall bring the blood and they shall throw*

— אונקלוס —

תּוֹרֵי קֳדָם יְיָ וִיקָרְבוּן בְּנֵי אַהֲרֹן כָּהֲנַיָּא יָת דְּמָא וְיִזְרְקוּן

— רש"י —

לג.): **לִפְנֵי ה'**: בָּעֲזָרָה: **וְהִקְרִיבוּ**: זוֹ קַבָּלָה שֶׁהִיא הָרִאשׁוֹנָה, וּמַשְׁמָעָהּ לְשׁוֹן הוֹלָכָה, לִמְדָנוּ שְׁתֵּיהֶן וְ[שֶׁ]א שְׁתֵּיהֶן בִּבְנֵי אַהֲרֹן (חֲגִיגָה י"א.; זְבָחִים ד'.): **בְּנֵי אַהֲרֹן**. יָכוֹל חֲלָלִים

הָא אֵינוֹ מַרְלֶה אֶלָּא עַל עֲשֵׂה וְעַל לֹאו שֶׁנִּתַּק לַעֲשֵׂה (שָׁם ח): **(ה) וְשָׁחַט וְהִקְרִיבוּ הַכֹּהֲנִים**. מִקַּבָּלָה וָאֵילָךְ מִצְוַת כְּהֻנָּה, לִמֵּד עַל הַשְּׁחִיטָה שֶׁכְּשֵׁרָה בְּזָר (ת"כ פָּרָשְׁתָא ד:ב; זְבָחִים

— RASHI ELUCIDATED —

option of substituting an offering has not been given. הָא אֵינוֹ מְרַצֶּה אֶלָּא עַל עֲשֵׂה — So then, [an olah-offering] "pleases" only for failure to fulfill **a positive commandment**, where no other punishment is stated, וְעַל לָאו שֶׁנִּתַּק לַעֲשֵׂה — and **a negative commandment which is commuted to a positive commandment**.[1]

5. וְשָׁחַט וְהִקְרִיבוּ הַכֹּהֲנִים — HE SHALL SLAUGHTER ... THE KOHANIM SHALL BRING. מִקַּבָּלָה וָאֵילָךְ — Fulfillment of the procedures **from** the stage of **receiving** the blood of the slaughtered animal in a vessel **onward**[2] מִצְוַת כְּהֻנָּה — **is a commandment of the kehunah**, i.e., it is a commandment which must be carried out by the Kohanim.[3] לִמֵּד עַל הַשְּׁחִיטָה שֶׁכְּשֵׁרָה בְּזָר — **This teaches** us **with regard to the slaughtering, that it is valid** if performed **by one who is not a Kohen**.[3]

☐ לִפְנֵי ה' — BEFORE HASHEM. בָּעֲזָרָה — **In the Courtyard of the Beis HaMikdash.**[4]

☐ וְהִקְרִיבוּ — [THE SONS OF AARON] SHALL BRING. זוֹ קַבָּלָה — **This refers to receiving** the blood of the slaughtered animal in a vessel, שֶׁהִיא הָרִאשׁוֹנָה — **for it is the first** procedure in the service after slaughtering. וּמַשְׁמָעָהּ לְשׁוֹן הוֹלָכָה — **By implication it is a term indicating "carrying."** לִמְדָנוּ [שֶׁ]שְׁתֵּיהֶן {בִּבְנֵי אַהֲרֹן}[5] — **We have** thus **learned {that} both of them**, i.e., receiving and carrying, are procedures of the services {and, as such, may only be performed **by the sons of Aaron**}.[5]

☐ בְּנֵי אַהֲרֹן — THE SONS OF AARON. יָכוֹל חֲלָלִים — **One might be able** to think that the service can be

---

1. *Toras Kohanim, perek* 4:8. There are positive commandments which come into effect only after the transgression of a negative commandment. For instance, it is forbidden to leave the meat of offerings uneaten beyond a given time limit. If one violates this commandment and the meat remains uneaten, a positive commandment to burn the uneaten remnants comes into effect. The negative commandment becomes commuted, as it were, to a positive commandment, and lashes do not apply to it (Rashi to *Makkos* 15a).

2. The essence of the *Mizbe'ach* service for an animal offering is its blood *avodah*. This consists of four procedures:
(a) שְׁחִיטָה, "slaughter" — The animal is slaughtered through *shechitah* the same way that a non-consecrated animal is slaughtered as food; all the rules that apply to the *shechitah* of ordinary animals (for kosher meat) apply to the slaughter of offerings as well.
(b) קַבָּלָה, "receiving" — The blood of the slaughtered offering is caught in a כְּלִי שָׁרֵת, "sacred vessel," as it spurts from the animal's neck.
(c) הוֹלָכָה, "carrying" — The vessel containing the blood is carried to the appropriate part of the Altar.
(d) זְרִיקָה, "throwing" — The blood is applied to the Altar. The procedure for applying and the number of applications vary for different offerings.
    In this and the next comment, Rashi derives the rule that the first procedure, slaughter, may be done by a non-Kohen, but the other three procedures must be done only by a Kohen.

3. *Toras Kohanim, parshasa* 4:2; *Zevachim* 32a. The subject of "he shall slaughter" is the same as that of the verbs of the preceding verses — the person bringing the offering, a non-Kohen. The Kohanim are introduced when the verse speaks of bringing the blood (*Mizrachi; Sifsei Chachamim*).

4. The term "before HASHEM" can mean in the Sanctuary of the *Beis HaMikdash* or the Mishkan. It stands to reason that here, however, it means the Courtyard area, for verse 11 states that the slaughtering takes place at the side of the *Mizbe'ach* upon which the blood of the *olah*-offering is sprinkled. This is the *Mizbe'ach* that stands in the Courtyard, for it is only the blood of certain sin-offerings that is sprinkled on the *Mizbe'ach* inside the Sanctuary (*Gur Aryeh*).

5. *Chagigah* 11a; *Zevachim* 4a. וְהִקְרִיבוּ is understood to refer to receiving the blood because the verse, no matter how it expresses itself, must be referring to the first procedure in the service after the slaughtering. By its use of a word which implies "carrying," the Torah teaches us that both receiving, the logical follow-up to slaughtering, and "carrying," which appears more directly in the verse, can be performed only by the sons of Aaron (*Mizrachi; Sifsei Chachamim*).

אֶת־הַדָּם֙ עַל־הַמִּזְבֵּ֖חַ סָבִ֑יב — *the blood on the Mizbe'ach, all around*

——— אונקלוס ———
יָת דְּמָא עַל מַדְבְּחָא סְחוֹר סְחוֹר

——— רש"י ———
ת"ל הכהנים (ת"כ שם ו): **את הדם וזרקו את הדם.** בשאינו מינו. יכול אף בפסולים או בחטאות הפנימיות או מה ת"ל דם ב' פעמים, להביא את שנתערב במינו או בחטאות החיצוניות שאלו למעלה והיא למטה, ת"ל במקום

——— RASHI ELUCIDATED ———

performed by **chalalim**.[1] הַכֹּהֲנִים,, [2] — **תַּלְמוּד לוֹמַר** — To teach us otherwise, **the Torah says, "the Kohanim."**[2]

מַה תַּלְמוּד לוֹמַר דָּם — אֶת הַדָּם וְזָרְקוּ אֶת הַדָּם — **THE BLOOD, AND THEY SHALL THROW THE BLOOD.** דָּם שְׁנֵי פְעָמִים — **Why does the Torah say blood twice?**[3] לְהָבִיא אֶת שֶׁנִּתְעָרֵב בְּמִינוֹ אוֹ בְּשֶׁאֵינוֹ מִינוֹ — **To include [blood] that has become mingled with its own kind**[4] **or with [blood] that is not its own kind.**[5] יָכוֹל אַף בִּפְסוּלִים — **One might be able** to think that it should be thrown if it became mingled **even with** the blood **of those that are disqualified**[6] אוֹ בְחַטָּאוֹת הַפְּנִימִיּוֹת — **or with the inner sin-offerings,**[7] אוֹ בְחַטָּאוֹת הַחִיצוֹנִיּוֹת — **or with the outer sin-offerings,**[8] שֶׁאֵלּוּ לְמַעְלָה וְהִיא לְמַטָּה — **even though these are above and this is below.**[9] תַּלְמוּד לוֹמַר בְּמָקוֹם

---

1. *Chalalim* are children born from unions specifically forbidden to Kohanim, and the descendants of male children born from such unions. The phrase בְּנֵי אַהֲרֹן need not exclude *chalalim,* for they, too, are descendants of Aaron.

2. *Toras Kohanim, parshasa* 4:6. A *chalal* does not inherit the priestly status of his father.

The commentaries note that "the sons of Aaron" now appears superfluous, as "the Kohanim" alone covers the entire category of those who may perform the service — Kohanim, to the exclusion of *chalalim.* They cite the conclusion of the *Toras Kohanim* (upon which Rashi is based): The term "the Kohanim" includes Kohanim who are physically blemished. They retain their priestly status, as seen from the fact that they may eat *terumah* (the portion of the yearly crop which is given to the Kohen). "The sons of Aaron" is then interpreted to exclude blemished Kohanim as follows: Just as Aaron is free of defect, so, too, only those of his sons who are free of defect may perform the *Mizbe'ach* service.

This gives rise to another question. A verse similar to ours below (21:1): אֱמֹר אֶל הַכֹּהֲנִים בְּנֵי אַהֲרֹן וְאָמַרְתָּ אֲלֵהֶם לְנֶפֶשׁ לֹא יִטַּמָּא בְּעַמָּיו, "Say to the Kohanim, the sons of Aaron, and tell them: No one may make himself impure to a [dead] person among his people." There *Toras Kohanim* uses "the sons of Aaron" to *include* blemished Kohanim in the prohibition against making themselves impure. How can the same phrase be used to exclude blemished Kohanim in one context, and include them in another?

The answer lies in the order of the words. בְּנֵי אַהֲרֹן, "the sons of Aaron," is a broader term than הַכֹּהֲנִים, "the Kohanim," for it includes *chalalim.* In our verse הַכֹּהֲנִים follows בְּנֵי אַהֲרֹן and thus limits it. Once we see that the verse is interested in narrowing the scope of those who may perform the service, we interpret the now apparently superfluous בְּנֵי אַהֲרֹן in a limitative sense, as well. In the verse in Chapter 21, however, בְּנֵי אַהֲרֹן follows הַכֹּהֲנִים and thus expands it to include blemished Kohanim. That verse could not have used בְּנֵי אַהֲרֹן alone, however, because that would have implied that even *chalalim* fall under the

prohibition against making themselves impure (see *Mizrachi*; *Tzeidah LaDerech*; *Malbim*).

Rashi on our verse most likely does not mention that "the sons of Aaron" excludes blemished Kohanim because they are excluded by the verse, "Speak to Aaron saying: Any man of your offspring throughout their generations in whom there will be a blemish shall not come near to offer the food of his God" (21:17). *Toras Kohanim,* on the other hand, might not be content to use that verse alone because it could be referring only to the more significant steps of the sacrificial procedure, such as throwing the blood on the *Mizbe'ach* and putting the flesh of the offering onto the fire. It uses "the sons of Aaron" of our verse to exclude blemished Kohanim even from such lesser steps as receiving the blood and taking it to the *Mizbe'ach* (*Nachalas Yaakov*).

3. The verse could have said, "The sons of Aaron, the Kohanim, shall bring the blood and throw *it* on the *Mizbe'ach.*" Why does it say "the blood" again? (*Mizrachi*).

4. For example, when blood of one person's *olah-*offering mingles with the blood of another person's *olah-*offering, the law of throwing blood on the *Mizbe'ach* also applies (*Mizrachi*; *Sifsei Chachamim*).

5. For example, blood of an *olah-*offering that mingled with blood of any offering other than an *olah-*offering (*Mizrachi*; *Sifsei Chachamim*).

6. Animals that are unfit for offering; for example, one which has been used for idolatrous purposes.

7. These are sin-offerings whose blood is sprinkled on the *Paroches* — the partition between the Holy of Holies and the Sanctuary — and on the Golden *Mizbe'ach* inside the Sanctuary, whereas the blood of the *olah-*offerings is sprinkled on the *Mizbe'ach* outside the Sanctuary.

8. These are sin-offerings whose blood is placed on the *Mizbe'ach* outside the Sanctuary.

9. The blood of the outer sin-offerings is placed upon the upper part of the *Mizbe'ach,* whereas the blood of the *olah-*offerings and all other offerings is sprinkled below the halfway mark (*Mizrachi*; *Sifsei Chachamim*).

1 אֲשֶׁר־פֶּתַח אֹהֶל מוֹעֵד: וְהִפְשִׁיט — *which is at the entrance of the Tent of Meeting.* ⁶ *He shall skin the olah-*

אונקלוס

דִּי בִתְרַע מַשְׁכַּן זִמְנָא: וְיַשְׁלַח

רש"י

אֹתוֹ דָמוֹ (וזבחים פּה.: ת"כ שם ז״ח): וְזָרְקוּ. עוֹמֵד לְמַטָּה בְּזְרִיקָה. אִי וְרַקִין יָכוֹל בִּזְרִיקָה אַחַת. הָא כֵּיצַד,
וְזוֹרֵק מִן הַכְּלִי לְכוֹתֶל הַמִּזְבֵּחַ לְמַטָּה מִחוּט הַסִּיקְרָא כְּנֶגֶד נוֹתֵן שְׁתֵּי מַתָּנוֹת שֶׁהֵן ד׳ (שם טו): אֲשֶׁר פֶּתַח אֹהֶל מוֹעֵד.
הַזָּוִיּוֹת, לְכָךְ נֶאֱ' סָבִיב שֶׁיְּהֵא הַדָּם נִיתָּן בְד' רוּחוֹת הַמִּזְבֵּחַ. אוֹ וְלֹא בִּזְמַן שֶׁהוּא מְפוֹרָק (שם יד): (ו) וְהִפְשִׁיט וְגוֹ'. מַה ת"ל
יָכוֹל יַקִּיפֶנּוּ כְּחוּט [שם ת"ח בחוטם], ת"ל וְזָרְקוּ, וְאִי אֶפְשָׁר לְהַקִּיף הָעוֹלָה, לְרַבּוֹת אֶת כָּל הָעוֹלוֹת לְהֶפְשֵׁט וְנִתּוּחַ (שם פרק ה:ד):

RASHI ELUCIDATED
---

[1] אַחֵר — To teach us otherwise, **the Torah says elsewhere,**[1] ²״דָּמוֹ,, — **"its blood."**[2]

□ וְזָרְקוּ — **AND THEY SHALL THROW.** — עוֹמֵד לְמַטָּה — **He stands below**[3] וְזוֹרֵק מִן הַכְּלִי לְכוֹתֶל הַמִּזְבֵּחַ — **and throws** the blood **from the vessel to the wall of the** *Mizbe'ach* — לְמַטָּה מִחוּט הַסִּקְרָא — **below the band of red paint** which went around the middle of the *Mizbe'ach* — כְּנֶגֶד הַזָּוִיּוֹת — **toward the** diagonally opposite **corners** of the *Mizbe'ach*. ״לְכָךְ נֶאֱמַר סָבִיב,, — **This is why it says, "all around,"** to teach us שֶׁיְּהֵא הַדָּם נָתוּן בְּאַרְבַּע רוּחוֹת הַמִּזְבֵּחַ — **that the blood should be put on the four sides of the** ***Mizbe'ach***.[4] ⁵אוֹ יָכוֹל יַקִּיפֶנּוּ כְּחוּט — **Or one would be able** to conclude that "all around" means that **he should encircle it like a thread,**[5] i.e., he should make a thread of blood around the entire perimeter of the *Mizbe'ach*. תַּלְמוּד לוֹמַר ״וְזָרְקוּ,, — To teach us otherwise, **the Torah says, "and they shall throw,"** וְאִי אֶפְשָׁר לְהַקִּיף בִּזְרִיקָה — **and it is impossible to encircle** an object **by throwing.** אִי ״וְזָרְקוּ,, — If it says, **"and they shall throw,"** יָכוֹל בִּזְרִיקָה אַחַת — **one might be able** to think that the act may be done **with one throw.** תַּלְמוּד לוֹמַר ״סָבִיב,, — To teach us otherwise, **the Torah says, "all around."** הָא כֵּיצַד — **How can this be?**[6] נוֹתֵן שְׁתֵּי מַתָּנוֹת שֶׁהֵן אַרְבַּע — **He puts two applications** of blood **which are four** on the *Mizbe'ach*.[7]

□ אֲשֶׁר פֶּתַח אֹהֶל מוֹעֵד — **WHICH IS AT THE ENTRANCE OF THE TENT OF MEETING.** — וְלֹא בִּזְמַן שֶׁהוּא מְפֹרָק — **But not at the time when it has been dismantled.**[8]

6. וְהִפְשִׁיט וְגוֹמֵר — **HE SHALL SKIN, ETC.** — מַה תַּלְמוּד לוֹמַר ״הָעוֹלָה,, — **Why does the Torah say, "the** *olah*-**offering"?**[9] ¹⁰לְרַבּוֹת אֶת כָּל הָעוֹלוֹת לְהַפְשֵׁט וְנִתּוּחַ — **To include all** *olah*- **offerings in** the law of **skinning and cutting into pieces.**[10]

---

1. Verse 11.

2. *Toras Kohanim, parshasa* 4:7-8; *Zevachim* 81b. "Its" implies exclusion. Rashi has stated above that our verse repeats the word הַדָּם, "the blood," to include the blood of *olah*-offerings that has become mingled with certain other blood. The "its" of דָמוֹ, "its blood," now excludes blood of an *olah*-offering that became mingled with the blood of disqualified animals or with sacrificial blood that must be thrown on a part of the *Mizbe'ach* other than where the blood of the *olah*-offering must be thrown (*Mizruchi, Sifsei Chachamim*).

3. He stands on the ground and does not ascend the *Mizbe'ach* as he does with the blood of the sin-offering (*Mizrachi; Sifsei Chachamim*).

4. The blood is thrown onto the northeastern and southwestern corners of the *Mizbe'ach*, so that there should be some blood on each of the four sides of the *Mizbe'ach*.

5. Some editions read בְּחוּט, "with a thread." The basic meaning, however, is unchanged.

6. How can "they shall throw" and "all around" be reconciled?

7. *Toras Kohanim, parshasa* 4:9. He applies the blood to two corners of the *Mizbe'ach* which are diagonal from each other. The blood is thus applied to all four sides of the *Mizbe'ach*; hence, "two which are four." [The Talmud (*Zevachim* 53b-54a) explains why "all around" would not be fulfilled by four separate applications at the four corners.]

8. *Toras Kohanim, parshasa* 4:14. When the Torah refers to the *Mizbe'ach*, it means the one outside the entrance of the Tent of Meeting unless it specifies otherwise (*Mizrachi*). If the Torah here gives the position of the *Mizbe'ach*, which is apparently unnecessary information, it is to teach us that the *olah*-offering may be sacrificed on the *Mizbe'ach* only when the *Mishkan* is assembled.

9. Since this section has been talking about the *olah*-offering, why state it here explicitly? The Torah could have stated, וְהִפְשִׁיט אֹתָה, "he shall skin it," and it would have been clear that it refers to the *olah*-offering (*Mizrachi; Sifsei Chachamim*).

10. *Toras Kohanim, perek* 5:4. The verse says "the *olah*-offering" to teach us that all *olah*-offerings are skinned and cut into pieces, not only those brought voluntarily from cattle, which is the subject of our verse (*Mizrachi; Sifsei Chachamim*).

offering and cut it into its pieces. **⁷ The sons of Aaron the Kohen shall put fire on the Mizbe'ach, and arrange wood on the fire. ⁸ The sons of Aaron, the Kohanim, shall arrange the pieces, the head and the fats,**

אֶת־הָעֹלָה וְנִתַּח אֹתָהּ לִנְתָחֶיהָ: ז וְנָתְנוּ בְּנֵי אַהֲרֹן הַכֹּהֵן אֵשׁ עַל־הַמִּזְבֵּחַ וְעָרְכוּ עֵצִים עַל־הָאֵשׁ: ח וְעָרְכוּ בְּנֵי אַהֲרֹן הַכֹּהֲנִים אֵת הַנְּתָחִים אֶת־הָרֹאשׁ וְאֶת־הַפָּדֶר

──────── אונקלוס ────────

יָת עֲלָתָא וִיפַלַּג יָתַהּ לְאֵבְרָהָא: ז וְיִתְּנוּן בְּנֵי אַהֲרֹן כָּהֲנָא אֶשָּׁתָא עַל מַדְבְּחָא וִיסַדְּרוּן אָעַיָּא עַל אֶשָּׁתָא: ח וִיסַדְּרוּן בְּנֵי אַהֲרֹן כָּהֲנַיָּא יָת אֶבְרַיָּא יָת רֵישָׁא וְיָת תַּרְבָּא

──────── רש"י ────────

אתה לנתחיה. ולא נתחיה לנתחים (שם ז; חולין י"א.): (ז) **ונתנו אש.** אע"פ שהאש יורדת מן השמים מצוה להביא מן ההדיוט (ת"כ שם י'): **בני אהרן הכהן.** כשהוא בכיהונו הא אם עבד בבגדי כהן הדיוט עבודתו פסולה (שם ט): (ח) **בני אהרן הכהנים.** כשהם בכיהונם הא כהן הדיוט ששמש במלה של ח בגדים עבודתו פסולה (שם): **את הנתחים את הראש.** לפי שאין הראש בכלל הפשט שכבר הותז בשחיטה לפיכך הוצרך למנותו לעצמו (שם פרק ו:ג; חולין כז.): **ואת הפדר.** למה נאמר ללמדך שמעלהו עם הראש

──────── RASHI ELUCIDATED ────────

□ אֹתָהּ לִנְתָחֶיהָ – **IT INTO ITS PIECES.** ² וְלֹא נְתָחֶיהָ לִנְתָחִים – But he may **not cut its pieces**[1] **into pieces.**[2]

7. אֵשׁ . . . וְנָתְנוּ – [THE SONS OF AARON THE KOHEN] SHALL PUT FIRE. אַף עַל פִּי שֶׁהָאֵשׁ יוֹרֶדֶת מִן הַשָּׁמַיִם – **Even though the fire would descend from the heaven** and ignite the wood on the *Mizbe'ach*,[3] מִצְוָה לְהָבִיא מִן הַהֶדְיוֹט – there is a commandment to bring fire from that which is ordinary, i.e., kindled by man.[4]

□ בְּנֵי אַהֲרֹן הַכֹּהֵן – THE SONS OF AARON THE KOHEN. כְּשֶׁהוּא בְּכִיהוּנוֹ – When he is in his state of *kehunah*. הָא אִם עָבַד בְּבִגְדֵי כֹּהֵן הֶדְיוֹט – But if he were to serve in the garments of an ordinary Kohen, עֲבוֹדָתוֹ פְּסוּלָה[5] – his service is invalid.[5]

8. בְּנֵי אַהֲרֹן הַכֹּהֲנִים – THE SONS OF AARON, THE KOHANIM. כְּשֶׁהֵם בְּכִיהוּנָם – When they are in their state of *kehunah*. הָא כֹּהֵן הֶדְיוֹט שֶׁשִּׁמֵּשׁ בִּשְׁמוֹנָה בְגָדִים – But if an ordinary Kohen were to serve in, i.e., while wearing, the **eight garments** of the Kohen Gadol, עֲבוֹדָתוֹ פְּסוּלָה[6] – his service is disqualified.[6]

□ אֶת הַנְּתָחִים אֶת הָרֹאשׁ – THE PIECES, THE HEAD. לְפִי שֶׁאֵין הָרֹאשׁ בִּכְלָל הֶפְשֵׁט – Since the head is not included in skinning, שֶׁכְּבָר הוּתַּז בִּשְׁחִיטָה – for it has already been cut off through slaughtering, לְפִיכָךְ הֻצְרַךְ לִמְנוֹתוֹ לְעַצְמוֹ[7] – for this reason [the Torah] had to list it individually.[7]

□ וְאֶת הַפָּדֶר – AND THE FATS. לָמָּה נֶאֱמַר – Why is it stated?[8] לְלַמֶּדְךָ שֶׁמַּעֲלֵהוּ עִם הָרֹאשׁ – To teach

1. "Into *its* pieces" rather than simply "into pieces" indicates that the *olah*-offering must be cut into the ten pieces set forth in the Mishnah (*Tamid* 4:2-3) that conform to the different sections of the animal's body. They are "*its* pieces," i.e., the natural pieces of the animal; as *Targum Onkelos* translates it לְאֵבְרָהָא, "into its limbs" (*Nefesh HaGer*).

2. *Toras Kohanim, perek* 5:7, *Chullin* 11a. The apparently superfluous אֹתָהּ teaches us that "its pieces," i.e., those ten pieces set forth in the Mishnah (*Tamid* 4:2-3), are not to be cut up into smaller pieces (*Be'er Yitzchak*).

3. Heavenly fire descended upon the copper *Mizbe'ach* of the *Mishkan* in the days of Moses. It moved to the stone *Mizbe'ach* of the first *Beis HaMikdash* built by Solomon and remained there until the reign of Manasseh (*Mizrachi*; *Sifsei Chachamim*).

4. *Toras Kohanim, perek* 5:10.

5. *Toras Kohanim, perek* 5:9. It is obvious that Aaron is a Kohen. The verse states this to teach us that the service of a Kohen Gadol, of which Aaron is the exemplar, is valid only when he is wearing all of the garments which reflect the status of his office (*Mizrachi*; *Sifsei Chachamim*).

6. *Toras Kohanim, perek* 5:9. It is obvious that the sons of Aaron are Kohanim. The verse states this to teach us that the service of an ordinary Kohen is valid only when he is wearing those garments which reflect his status as an ordinary Kohen (*Gur Aryeh*; *Sifsei Chachamim*).

7. *Toras Kohanim, perek* 6:3; *Chullin* 27a. Verse 6 says, "He shall skin the *olah*-offering and cut it into its pieces." On this basis, one could say that the pieces referred to here are only those included in the commandment of skinning. The head, which is not skinned, would thus not be arranged on the *Mizbe'ach*. For this reason, the Torah had to include the head specifically among the pieces (*Chullin* 27a and Rashi there).

8. The reason given above for the specific mention of the head does not apply to the fats, for they are among the body parts which are skinned (Rashi, *Chullin* 27b).

on the wood that is on the fire, which is on the Mizbe'ach. ⁹ He shall wash its innards and its feet with water; and the Kohen shall cause it all to go up in smoke on the Mizbe'ach — an olah-offering, a fire-offering, a pleasing fragrance to Hashem. ¹⁰ And if his offering is from the flock,	עַל־הָעֵצִים֙ אֲשֶׁ֣ר עַל־הָאֵ֔שׁ אֲשֶׁ֖ר עַל־הַמִּזְבֵּֽחַ: ⁹ וְקִרְבּ֥וֹ וּכְרָעָ֖יו יִרְחַ֣ץ בַּמָּ֑יִם וְהִקְטִ֨יר הַכֹּהֵ֤ן אֶת־הַכֹּל֙ הַמִּזְבֵּ֔חָה עֹלָ֛ה אִשֵּׁ֥ה רֵֽיחַ־נִיח֖וֹחַ לַֽיהוָֽה: ¹⁰ וְאִם־מִן־הַצֹּ֥אן קָרְבָּנ֛וֹ

― אונקלוס ―

עַל אָעַיָּא דִּי עַל אֶשָּׁתָא דִּי עַל מַדְבְּחָא: ט וְגַוֵּהּ וּכְרָעוֹהִי יְחַלֵּל בְּמַיָּא וְיַסֵּק כַּהֲנָא יָת כֹּלָּא לְמַדְבְּחָא עֲלָתָא קֻרְבַּן דְּמִתְקַבַּל בְּרַעֲוָא קֳדָם יְיָ: י וְאִם מִן עָנָא קֻרְבָּנֵהּ

― רש"י ―

ומכסה בו את בית השחיטה וזהו דרך כבוד של מעלה (ת"כ שם ב; חולין כז:): **אשר על המזבח.** שלא יהיו הגזירין יוצאין חוץ למערכה (שם ה): (ט) **עולה.** לשם עולה יקטירנו (שם ו): **אשה.** | כשישחטנו יהא שחטנו לשם האש וכל אשה ל' אש פויי"ר בלע"ז: **ניחוח.** נחת רוח לפני שאמרתי ונעשה רצוני (שם טו): (י) **ואם מן הצאן.** וי"ו מוסיף על ענין ראשון. ולמה הפסק, ליתן ריוח למשה

― RASHI ELUCIDATED ―

□ וּמְכַסֶּה בּוֹ אֶת בֵּית הַשְּׁחִיטָה — **and you that he brings it up** to the top of the *Mizbe'ach* **with the head, covers the place of the slaughtering,** i.e., the opening in the throat caused by the act of slaughtering, **with it.** וְזֶהוּ דֶּרֶךְ כָּבוֹד שֶׁל מַעְלָה — **This is respectful conduct towards** He Who is **Above.**¹

□ אֲשֶׁר עַל הַמִּזְבֵּחַ — **WHICH IS ON THE *MIZBE'ACH*.** שֶׁלֹּא יְהוּ הַגְּזִירִין יוֹצְאִין — **That the logs should not protrude** חוּץ לַמַּעֲרָכָה — **outside the arrangement** of wood on the top of the *Mizbe'ach*.²

9. עֹלָה — AN *OLAH*-OFFERING. {לְשֵׁם עוֹלָה יַקְטִירֶנּוּ} — {He should set it smoking} with intent for an *olah*-offering.³

□ אִשֶּׁה — A FIRE-OFFERING. כְּשֶׁיִּשְׁחָטֶנּוּ — When he slaughters it, יְהֵא שׁוֹחֲטוֹ לְשֵׁם הָאֵשׁ — he should slaughter it with intent for the fire.⁴ וְכָל אִשֶּׁה — Any example of the word אִשֶּׁה in Scripture לְשׁוֹן אֵשׁ — is related to fire. פויי"ר בְּלַעַ"ז — *Foier* in Old French.⁵

□ נִיחוֹחַ — PLEASING. נַחַת רוּחַ לְפָנַי — It is a source of **contentment before Me,** שֶׁאָמַרְתִּי וְנַעֲשָׂה רְצוֹנִי — **as I said** that the offering should be brought **and My will was done.**⁶

10. וְאִם מִן הַצֹּאן — AND IF [HIS OFFERING IS] FROM THE FLOCK. וָי"ו מוֹסִיף עַל עִנְיָן רִאשׁוֹן — The prefix ו **adds to the preceding topic.**⁷ וְלָמָּה הֻפְסַק — **Why was it interrupted?**⁸ לִתֵּן רֶוַח לְמֹשֶׁה

---

1. *Toras Kohanim*, *perek* 6:2; *Chullin* 27b.

2. *Toras Kohanim*, *perek* 6:5. It has already been stated explicitly in the preceding verse that the fire is on the *Mizbe'ach*. It is repeated here to teach us that the logs must be in the area on top of the *Mizbe'ach* designated for the arrangement of wood. They must not protrude into the walkway for the Kohanim which went around the top of the *Mizbe'ach* (*Mizrachi; Sifsei Chachamim*; see Rashi to *Exodus* 27:5 for a description of the walkway).

3. *Zevachim* 46b. This entire passage has been discussing an *olah*-offering. The Torah repeats this point here to teach us that when the Kohen sets fire to the pieces of the *olah*-offering, he should do so thinking that it is an *olah*-offering, not any other offering (*Mizrachi; Sifsei Chachamim*).

4. It has already been stated explicitly that the offering is burnt by fire. The Torah repeats this point to teach us that the one slaughtering the offering should have in mind at the time of the slaughtering that it will be consumed by the fire, not merely roasted by it (see Rashi to *Zevachim* 46b, *Ramban*).

5. "Hearth" or "fireplace"; in Modern French, *foyer*. The English word "foyer" originally referred to a hearth, and was later expanded to mean "a room with a hearth."

6. *Toras Kohanim*, *perek* 6:9.

7. *Toras Kohanim*, *parshasa* 5:1; *Zevachim* 48a. The ו connects this section of the Torah which deals with *olah*-offerings of the flock with the preceding one which deals with *olah*-offerings of cattle. Because they are joined, laws stated in one section apply to the other. The law that the offering must be slaughtered at the northern side of the *Mizbe'ach* which is stated in the context of the *olah*-offering of the flock applies to *olah*-offerings of cattle. The laws of placing of the hands, skinning, and cutting into pieces which are stated in the context of the *olah*-offering of cattle apply to *olah*-offerings of the flock (*Mizrachi; Sifsei Chachamim*).

8. Why is there a break in the text of the Torah between the two sections if they are meant to be connected (*Mizrachi; Sifsei Chachamim*)?

מִן־הַכְּשָׂבִים אוֹ מִן־הָעִזִּים לְעֹלָה זָכָר תָּמִים יַקְרִיבֶנּוּ: וְשָׁחַט אֹתוֹ עַל יֶרֶךְ הַמִּזְבֵּחַ צָפֹנָה לִפְנֵי יְהוָה וְזָרְקוּ בְּנֵי אַהֲרֹן הַכֹּהֲנִים אֶת־דָּמוֹ עַל־הַמִּזְבֵּחַ סָבִיב: וְנִתַּח אֹתוֹ לִנְתָחָיו וְאֶת־רֹאשׁוֹ וְאֶת־פִּדְרוֹ וְעָרַךְ הַכֹּהֵן אֹתָם עַל־הָעֵצִים אֲשֶׁר עַל־הָאֵשׁ אֲשֶׁר עַל־הַמִּזְבֵּחַ: וְהַקֶּרֶב וְהַכְּרָעַיִם יִרְחַץ בַּמָּיִם וְהִקְרִיב הַכֹּהֵן אֶת־הַכֹּל וְהִקְטִיר הַמִּזְבֵּחָה עֹלָה הוּא אִשֵּׁה רֵיחַ נִיחֹחַ לַיהוָה:

יא

יב

יג

יד **שני** וְאִם מִן־הָעוֹף עֹלָה קָרְבָּנוֹ לַיהוָה

from the sheep or from the goats, for an olah-offering: he shall offer an unblemished male. ¹¹ *He shall slaughter it at the side of the Mizbe'ach, on the north, before* HASHEM; *and the sons of Aaron, the Kohanim, shall throw its blood on the Mizbe'ach, all around.* ¹² *He shall cut it into its pieces, its head, and its fats. The Kohen shall arrange them on the wood that is on the fire that is on the Mizbe'ach.* ¹³ *He shall wash the innards and the feet in water; the Kohen shall bring it all and cause it to go up in smoke on the Mizbe'ach — it is an olah-offering, a fire-offering, a pleasing fragrance to* HASHEM.

¹⁴ *If one's offering to* HASHEM *is an olah-*

─────── אונקלוס ───────

מִן אִמְּרַיָּא אוֹ מִן בְּנֵי עִזַּיָּא לַעֲלָתָא דְּכַר שְׁלִים יְקָרְבִנֵּהּ: יא וְיִכּוֹס יָתֵהּ עַל צִדָּא (נ״א שְׁדָא) דְּמַדְבְּחָא צִפּוּנָא קֳדָם יְיָ וְיִזְרְקוּן בְּנֵי אַהֲרֹן כָּהֲנַיָּא יָת דְּמֵהּ עַל מַדְבְּחָא סְחוֹר סְחוֹר: יב וִיפַלַּג יָתֵהּ לְאֶבְרוֹהִי וְיָת רֵישֵׁהּ וְיָת תַּרְבֵּהּ וִיסַדַּר כָּהֲנָא יָתְהוֹן עַל אָעַיָּא דִּי עַל אֶשָּׁתָא דִּי עַל מַדְבְּחָא: יג וְגַוָּא וּכְרָעַיָּא יְחַלֵּל בְּמַיָּא וִיקָרֵב כָּהֲנָא יָת כֹּלָּא וְיַסֵּק לְמַדְבְּחָא עֲלָתָא הוּא קֻרְבַּן דְּמִתְקַבֵּל בְּרַעֲוָא קֳדָם יְיָ: יד וְאִם מִן עוֹפָא עֲלָתָא קֻרְבָּנֵהּ קֳדָם יְיָ.

─────── רש"י ───────

לְהִתְבּוֹנֵן בֵּין פָּרָשָׁה לְפָרָשָׁה (ת"כ פרשתא ה:א). **מִן הַצֹּאן מִן הַכְּבָשִׂים אוֹ מִן הָעִזִּים.** הֲרֵי אֵלוּ שְׁלֹשָׁה מִעוּטִין, הֲרֵי אָלוּ ג' מִעוּטִין, פְּרָט לְזָקֵן וּלְחוֹלֶה וְלִמְזֻהָם (שם ב; בכורות מא.). **עַל יֶרֶךְ הַמִּזְבֵּחַ.** לַד הַמִּזְבֵּחַ: **צָפֹנָה לִפְנֵי ה'.** וְאֵין צָפוֹן בְּבָמָה (ת"כ פרק ה:ח; זבחים קיט:). **(יד) מִן הָעוֹף.** וְלֹא כָל הָעוֹף, לְפִי שֶׁנֶּאֱמַר תָּמִים זָכָר בַּבָּקָר, בַּכְּבָשִׂים וּבָעִזִּים תְּמוּת וְזַכְרוּת בִּבְהֵמָה

─────── RASHI ELUCIDATED ───────

— לְהִתְבּוֹנֵן בֵּין פָּרָשָׁה לְפָרָשָׁה¹ — **To give Moses an interval for contemplation between one section** of the Torah **and another.**¹

□ מִן הַצֹּאן מִן הַכְּבָשִׂים אוֹ מִן הָעִזִּים — **FROM THE FLOCK, FROM THE SHEEP OR FROM THE GOATS.** — הֲרֵי אֵלוּ שְׁלֹשָׁה מִעוּטִין — **We have here three limitative terms,** i.e., the three instances of מִן, פְּרָט לְזָקֵן וּלְחוֹלֶה — **excluding an old one, and a sick one, and a filthy one.**² וְלִמְזֻהָם

11. עַל יֶרֶךְ הַמִּזְבֵּחַ — This means עַל צַד הַמִּזְבֵּחַ — **on the side of the** *Mizbe'ach*.³

□ צָפֹנָה לִפְנֵי ה' — **ON THE NORTH, BEFORE HASHEM.** — וְאֵין צָפוֹן בְּבָמָה — **But there is no** requirement to slaughter on the **northern** side of the *Mizbe'ach* when bringing an offering **at a** *bamah*.⁴

14. מִן הָעוֹף — **FROM THE FOWL.** — וְלֹא כָל הָעוֹף — **But not all the fowl.** — לְפִי שֶׁנֶּאֱמַר ,,תָּמִים זָכָר בַּבָּקָר, בַּכְּבָשִׂים וּבָעִזִּים — **Because it says** that the *olah-*offering must be **"unblemished, male, from the cattle, from the sheep, or from the goats,"**⁵ — תְּמוּת וְזַכְרוּת בִּבְהֵמָה — **the requirements of perfection**

---

1. *Toras Kohanim, parshasa* 5:1. Rashi has already stated above (v. 1, see note 7 on p. 2) that the breaks were intended to allow Moses to pause for contemplation. He repeats his point here because it is this verse which is the source for this idea. Were it not for this verse, we could have explained the breaks as indications of a change in subject matter, much as we use paragraphs in English. It is the break of our verse, which appears before a verse expressly intended to be linked to the one that precedes it, that allows us to conclude that the breaks were intended to provide a pause for Moses (*Be'er BaSadeh*).

2. *Toras Kohanim, parshasa* 5:2; *Bechoros* 41a. "A filthy one" means one which is sweaty and foul smelling (Rashi to *Temurah* 28b).

3. The literal meaning of יֶרֶךְ is "thigh." It is used in the sense of "side" because the thigh is at a person's side (Rashi to *Exodus* 40:22).

4. *Toras Kohanim, perek* 4:1; *Zevachim* 119b. The requirement to slaughter on the north applies only "before HASHEM," which often means in the *Beis HaMikdash* or the *Mishkan,* but not at a *bamah.* For the definition of *bamah,* see note 3 on p. 8.

5. Below 22:19.

offering from the fowl, he shall bring his offering from the turtledoves or from the young doves. **15** *The Kohen shall bring it to the Mizbe'ach, and he shall perform Melikah and*

וְהִקְרִיב מִן־הַתֹּרִים אוֹ מִן־בְּנֵי הַיּוֹנָה אֶת־קָרְבָּנוֹ: טו וְהִקְרִיבוֹ הַכֹּהֵן אֶל־הַמִּזְבֵּחַ וּמָלַק אֶת־רֹאשׁוֹ

— אונקלוס —

וִיקָרֵב מִן שַׁפְנִינַיָּא אוֹ מִן בְּנֵי יוֹנָתָא יָת קָרְבָּנֵהּ: טו וִיקָרְבִנֵּהּ כַּהֲנָא לְמַדְבְּחָא וְיִמְלוֹק יָת רֵישֵׁהּ

— רש"י —

וְאֵין תַּמּוּת וְזַכְרוּת בְּעוֹפוֹת. יָכוֹל אַף מְחֻסַּר אֵבֶר, תַּלְמוּד לוֹמַר **מִן הָעוֹף** (ת"כ פרשתא ו:ג; קידושין כד:): **תּוֹרִים**. גְּדוֹלִים וְלֹא קְטַנִּים (שם פרק ח:ב; חולין כב א-ב): **בְּנֵי יוֹנָה**. קְטַנִּים וְלֹא גְדוֹלִים (ת"כ שם ד; חולין שם): **מִן הַתּוֹרִים אוֹ מִן בְּנֵי הַיּוֹנָה**. פְּרָט לִתְחִלַּת הַצִּהוּב שֶׁבָּזֶה וּשֶׁבָּזֶה שֶׁהוּא פָסוּל (ת"כ שם ה; חולין כב.), שֶׁגָּדוֹל הוּא אֵצֶל בְּנֵי יוֹנָה וְקָטָן אֵצֶל תּוֹרִים: **(טו) וְהִקְרִיבוֹ**. אֲפִלּוּ פְּרִידָה אַחַת יָבִיא (ת"כ פרשתא ז:א; זבחים סה.): **הַכֹּהֵן וּמָלַק**. אֵין מְלִיקָה בִּכְלִי אֶלָּא בְּעַצְמוֹ שֶׁל כֹּהֵן, קוֹצֵץ בְּצִפָּרְנוֹ מִמּוּל הָעוֹרֶף וְחוֹתֵךְ מַפְרַקְתּוֹ עַד שֶׁמַּגִּיעַ לְסִימָנִין וְקוֹצְצָן (שם ב-ה; זבחים סד:-סה; חולין כא.):

— RASHI ELUCIDATED —

and maleness apply **to livestock** בְּעוֹפוֹת וְזַכְרוּת תַּמּוּת וְאֵין — but the requirements of **perfection and maleness do not** apply **to fowl.**[1] אֵבֶר מְחֻסַּר אַף יָכוֹל — **One might be able** to think that **even** a fowl which is **lacking a limb** might be acceptable for an *olah-* offering. [2]מִן הָעוֹף,, לוֹמַר תַּלְמוּד — To teach us otherwise, the verse says, "from the fowl."[2]

□ תֹּרִים — TURTLEDOVES. קְטַנִּים וְלֹא גְדוֹלִים[3] — Mature ones, not young ones.[3]

□ בְּנֵי יוֹנָה — YOUNG DOVES. גְדוֹלִים וְלֹא קְטַנִּים[4] — Young ones, not mature ones.[4]

□ מִן הַתֹּרִים אוֹ מִן בְּנֵי הַיּוֹנָה — FROM THE TURTLEDOVES OR FROM THE YOUNG DOVES. הַצִּיהוּב לִתְחִלַּת פְּרָט — **To the exclusion of the beginning of the yellowing** in both **this** species **and that,** פָסוּל שֶׁהוּא — **which is invalid** for offering[5] יוֹנָה בְּנֵי אֵצֶל הוּא שֶׁגָּדוֹל — **because** [such a bird] **is mature with regard to doves,** תּוֹרִים אֵצֶל וְקָטָן — **and immature with regard to turtledoves.**

15. וְהִקְרִיבוֹ — [THE KOHEN] SHALL BRING IT. יָבִיא אַחַת פְּרִידָה אֲפִלּוּ[6] — **He may bring even a single fledgling.**[6]

□ הַכֹּהֵן וּמָלַק — THE KOHEN [SHALL BRING IT,] AND HE SHALL PERFORM *MELIKAH*. בִּכְלִי מְלִיקָה אֵין — **Slaughtering by the method of *melikah* is not** performed **with an implement,** כֹּהֵן שֶׁל בְּעַצְמוֹ אֶלָּא — rather, **by the very self of the Kohen,**[7] הָעוֹרֶף מִמּוּל בְּצִפָּרְנוֹ קוֹצֵץ — **He cuts with his fingernail at the** bird's **nape,**[8] מַפְרַקְתּוֹ וְחוֹתֵךְ — **and severs its backbone** לַסִּימָנִין שֶׁמַּגִּיעַ עַד — **until he reaches the signs,** i.e., the gullet (esophagus) and the windpipe (trachea), וְקוֹצְצָן[9] — **and cuts them.**[9]

---

1. Verse 3 states that an *olah-*offering brought from cattle must be male and unblemished. In 22:19, the Torah repeats the requirement that *olah-*offerings from the cattle, the flock and the goats be blemish-free, without mentioning fowl. This indicates that fowl need not be blemish-free (*Gur Aryeh*; Rashi, *Kiddushin* 24b).

2. *Toras Kohanim, parshasa* 6:3; *Kiddushin* 24b. Although blemishes which disqualify livestock are acceptable in fowl, "from" excludes a bird which lacks a limb or organ.

3. *Toras Kohanim, perek* 8:3; *Chullin* 22a-b. See next note.

4. *Toras Kohanim, perek* 8:4; *Chullin* 22a-b. The term בְּנֵי יוֹנָה, literally, "the children of doves," implies young birds. Since the turtledoves are not referred to as בְּנֵי תוֹרִים, but rather as simply תוֹרִים, no limitation regarding age is implied. However, the juxtaposition of בְּנֵי יוֹנָה with תוֹרִים teaches us that just as בְּנֵי יוֹנָה is a limited category, so, too, תוֹרִים of our verse is a limited category. The absence of בְּנֵי with regard to תוֹרִים indicates that the category is that of mature birds (*Mizrachi*; *Sifsei Chachamim* based on *Chullin* 22b).

5. *Toras Kohanim, perek* 8:5; *Chullin* 22b. The neck feathers of both the turtledove and the dove take on a yellowish shine when they reach maturity. The exclusionary term "from" invalidates a bird of either species from being used as an offering at the beginning of the yellowing process.

6. *Toras Kohanim, parshasa* 7:1; *Zevachim* 65a. Since the preceding verse spoke of "turtledoves" and "doves" in the plural, one might think that a minimum of two birds must be brought for an *olah-*offering of fowl. The singular "it" here indicates that this is not so (*Mizrachi*).

7. The verse could have used "he" and it would have been clear that a Kohen must do the *melikah*, for *melikah* is done at the top of the *Mizbe'ach*, an area restricted to Kohanim. The verse uses "the Kohen" to teach us that *melikah* is done directly by the Kohen, not with an instrument (*Mizrachi*).

8. For a precise description of מִמּוּל הָעֹרֶף, literally, "opposite the back of the head," see Rashi to 5:8 below and note 4 there.

9. *Toras Kohanim, parshasa* 7:2-5; *Zevachim* 64b-65a; *Chullin* 21a.

וְהִקְטִיר הַמִּזְבֵּחָה וְנִמְצָה דָמוֹ עַל קִיר הַמִּזְבֵּחַ: וְהֵסִיר אֶת־ טז מֻרְאָתוֹ בְּנֹצָתָהּ וְהִשְׁלִיךְ אֹתָהּ

cause it to go up in smoke on the *Mizbe'ach*, and its blood shall be squeezed out against the wall of the *Mizbe'ach*. [16] He shall remove its crop with its innards, and he shall throw it

──────── אונקלוס ────────

וְיַסֵּק לְמַדְבְּחָא וְיִתְמְצֵי דְּמֵהּ עַל כֹּתֶל מַדְבְּחָא: טז וְיַעֲדֵי יָת זְפָקָהּ בְּאֻכְלֵהּ וְיִרְמֵי יָתַהּ

──────── רש״י ────────

(טז) מֻרְאָתוֹ. מְקוֹם הָרְאִי [סַ״א הָרְעִי] וְזֶה הַזֶּפֶק וְתִרְגֵּם אוּנְקְלוֹס זַפְקֵהּ: **בְּנֹצָתָהּ.** עִם בְּנֵי מֵעֶיהָ. וְנוֹצָה לְ׳ דָּבָר הַמָּאוּס כְּמוֹ כִּי נָצוּ גַּם נָעוּ (איכה ד:טו), וְזֶהוּ שֶׁתִּ״א בְּאוּכְלֵהּ, וְזֶהוּ מִדְרָשׁוֹ שֶׁל אַבָּא יוֹסֵי בֶּן חָנָן שֶׁאָמַר נוֹטֵל אֶת הַקֻּרְקְבָן עִמָּהּ. וְרַבּוֹתֵינוּ זִכְרוֹנָם לִבְרָכָה אָמְרוּ

מִסוֹרָס הוּא, וּמָלַק וְהִקְטִיר וְקֹדֶם הַקְּטָרָה וְנִמְצָה דָמוֹ כְּבָר: (טז) **מֻרְאָתוֹ.** מְקוֹם הָרְאִי [סַ״א הָרְעִי] וְזֶה הַזֶּפֶק: **בְּנֹצָתָהּ.** עִם בְּנֵי מֵעֶיהָ. וְנוֹצָה לְ׳ דָּבָר הַמָּאוּס כְּמוֹ כִּי נָצוּ גַּם נָעוּ, וְזֶהוּ שֶׁתִּ״א בְּאוּכְלֵהּ, וְזֶהוּ מִדְרָשׁוֹ שֶׁל אַבָּא יוֹסֵי בֶּן חָנָן שֶׁאָמַר נוֹטֵל אֶת הַקֻּרְקְבָן עִמָּהּ. וְרַבּוֹתֵינוּ ז״ל אָמְרוּ

──────── RASHI ELUCIDATED ────────

□ וְנִמְצָה דָמוֹ — **AND ITS BLOOD SHALL BE SQUEEZED OUT.** [1] וְנִמְצָה is related to מִיץ in, לָשׁוֹן מִיץ אַפַּיִם, "extract of anger," [1] [2] כִּי אָפֵס הַמֵּץ — and the הַמֵּץ in, "for the juice has been depleted." [2] כּוֹבֵשׁ בֵּית הַשְׁחִיטָה — [The *Kohen*] presses the place of the slaughtering (the opening caused by the act of *melikah*) עַל קִיר הַמִּזְבֵּחַ — **against the wall of the *Mizbe'ach*,** [3] וְהַדָּם מִתְמַצֶּה וְיוֹרֵד — **and the blood is squeezed out, and runs down** the side of the wall. [3]

□ וְהִקְטִיר . . . וְנִמְצָה — **AND HE SHALL PERFORM** *MELIKAH* . . . **AND HE SHALL CAUSE IT TO GO UP IN SMOKE . . . AND [ITS BLOOD] SHALL BE SQUEEZED OUT.** אֶפְשָׁר לוֹמַר כֵּן — **Is it possible to say this?** — אֶלָּא מַה הַקְטָרָה — מֵאַחַר שֶׁהוּא מַקְטִיר הוּא מוֹצֵא — **After he puts it to smoke, does he squeeze it?** [4] **But, just as** with regard to **putting it to smoke** הָרֹאשׁ בְּעַצְמוֹ וְהַגּוּף בְּעַצְמוֹ — **the head is by itself and the body is by itself,** i.e., the head is completely detached from the body, [5] אַף מְלִיקָה כֵּן — **so, too, is it with** *melikah*. [6] וּפְשׁוּטוֹ שֶׁל מִקְרָא מְסֹרָס הוּא — **The simple understanding of the verse is that it is inverted.** וּמָלַק וְהִקְטִיר — The verse is saying that **he shall perform** *melikah* **and he shall put it to smoke,** וְקוֹדֶם הַקְטָרָה — **and before putting** it **to smoke,** וְנִמְצָה דָמוֹ כְּבָר — **its blood will have already been squeezed out.**

16. מֻרְאָתוֹ — It is מְקוֹם הָרְאִי — **the place of the waste.** [7] זֶה הַזֶּפֶק — **This is the crop.** [7]

□ בְּנֹצָתָהּ — **WITH ITS INNARDS.** This word is translated as if it read עִם בְּנֵי מֵעֶיהָ — **with its innards.** נָצָה — The word נוֹצָה **means something repulsive,** [8] כְּמוֹ נָצוּ — **like** נָצוּ **in:** כִּי נָצוּ גַם נָעוּ, "**They have become repulsive, and even slip.**" [8] וְזֶהוּ שֶׁתִּרְגֵם אוּנְקְלוֹס — **This is why** *Onkelos* **rendered** it, בְּאֻכְלֵהּ, — **literally, "with its digested food."** וְזֶהוּ מִדְרָשׁוֹ שֶׁל אַבָּא יוֹסֵי בֶּן חָנָן — **This is the interpretation of** the *Amora* **Abba Yose ben Chanan** [9] שֶׁאָמַר נוֹטֵל אֶת הַקֻּרְקְבָן עִמָּהּ — **who says that he takes the gizzard with [the crop].** [9] וְרַבּוֹתֵינוּ זִכְרוֹנָם לִבְרָכָה אָמְרוּ — **But our Rabbis, of**

---

1. *Proverbs* 30:33.
2. *Isaiah* 16:4.
3. *Toras Kohanim, parshasa* 7:8; *Zevachim* 65a.
4. Although our verse speaks only of burning the head, he could not squeeze the blood out of the body afterwards, for animal offerings are never burned on the *Mizbe'ach* prior to the sprinkling of their blood (*Be'er Yitzchak* based on *Zevachim* 43a).
5. For our verse speaks of burning the head and verse 17 speaks of burning the body (*Toras Kohanim* quoted by Rashi to *Chullin* 21b).
6. *Toras Kohanim, parshasa* 7:6; *Zevachim* 65a. The verse juxtaposes *melikah* with putting to smoke to teach us that just as the head has been detached from the body by the time the offering is burned, so, too, must the head be detached from the body at the time of *melikah* (Rashi to *Chullin* 21b). However, they are considered detached when the windpipe and gullet are severed. The

flesh and skin of the bird may be cut with a knife afterward (*Mizrachi*; *Sifsei Chachamim*).

7. *Toras Kohanim, parshasa* 7:9; *Zevachim* 65a. Rashi first notes that מֻרְאָתוֹ is related to רְאִי (in some editions this is spelled רְעִי, although the two words are identical in meaning, Rashi apparently sees מֻרְאָתוֹ as cognate with רְאִי), and then goes on to define it as זֶפֶק (*Mizrachi*; *Sefer Zikaron*). The crop (or, craw) is a sac in a bird's gullet in which food is stored and partially digested before it passes into the stomach.

8. *Lamentations* 4:15. Rashi (to *Lamentations*) explains that they slip in their blood.

9. *Toras Kohanim, parshasa* 7:9; *Zevachim* 65a.

17 / VAYIKRA/LEVITICUS — PARASHAS VAYIKRA

אֵ֣צֶל הַמִּזְבֵּ֗חַ קֵ֖דְמָה אֶל־מְק֣וֹם *next to the Mizbe'ach, on the east, to the place of the ashes.* ¹⁷ *He shall tear it apart — with its feathers — he need not*
הַדָּ֑שֶׁן: יז וְשִׁסַּ֨ע אֹת֤וֹ בִכְנָפָיו֙ לֹ֣א

—————— אונקלוס ——————

לִסְטַר מַדְבְּחָא קִדּוּמָא לַאֲתַר דְּמוֹשְׁדִין קִטְמָא: יז וִיפָרֵק יָתֵהּ בְּגַדְפוֹהִי לָא

—————— רש"י ——————

ע:ג:): **אל מקום הדשן**. מָקוֹם שֶׁנּוֹתְנִין שָׁם תְּרוּמַת הַדֶּשֶׁן בְּכָל בֹּקֶר וְדִשּׁוּן מִזְבַּח הַפְּנִימִי וְהַמְּנוֹרָה, וְכֻלָּם נִבְלָעִים שָׁם בִּמְקוֹמָן (שם; יומא כא:): **(יז) ושסע**. אֵין שִׁסּוּעַ אֶלָּא בַיָּד, וְכֵן הוּא אוֹמֵר בְּשִׁמְשׁוֹן וַיְשַׁסְּעֵהוּ כְּשַׁסַּע הַגְּדִי וְגוֹ' (שׁוֹפְטִים יד:ו): **בכנפיו**. עִם כְּנָפָיו אֵינוֹ צָרִיךְ לִמְרוֹט כַּנְפֵי נוֹצָתוֹ (שַׁבָּת קח.):

קוֹדֵר סָבִיב הַזֶּפֶק בְּסַכִּין כְּעֵין אֲרוּבָּה וְנוֹטְלוֹ עִם הַנּוֹצָה שֶׁעַל הָעוֹר (זְבָחִים שָׁם). בְּעוֹלַת בְּהֵמָה שֶׁאֵינָהּ אוֹכֶלֶת אֶלָּא בְּאֵבוּס בְּעָלֶיהָ נֶאֱמַר וְהַקֶּרֶב וְהַכְּרָעַיִם יִרְחַץ בַּמָּיִם וְהִקְטִיר (לְעֵיל פָּסוּק ט). וּבְעוֹף שֶׁנִּזּוֹן מִן הַגָּזֵל נֶאֱמַר וְהִשְׁלִיךְ אֶת הַמֻּרְאָה, שֶׁאָכַל מִן הַגָּזֵל (וַיִּקְרָא רַבָּה ג:ד): **אצל המזבח קדמה**. בְּמִזְרָחוֹ שֶׁל כֶּבֶשׁ (ת"כ פֶּרֶק

—————— RASHI ELUCIDATED ——————

blessed memory, said: קוֹדֵר סָבִיב הַזֶּפֶק בְּסַכִּין כְּעֵין אֲרוּבָּה — He cuts a window-like hole in the body of the bird **around the crop with a knife,** ¹ וְנוֹטְלוֹ עִם הַנּוֹצָה שֶׁעַל הָעוֹר — **and removes it with the feathers that are on the skin.**¹

בְּעוֹלַת בְּהֵמָה — **Regarding the** *olah***-offering of an animal,** שֶׁאֵינָהּ אוֹכֶלֶת אֶלָּא בְּאֵבוּס בְּעָלֶיהָ — which **eats only from the feeding trough of its owner,** נֶאֱמַר ,,וְהַקֶּרֶב וְהַכְּרָעַיִם יִרְחַץ בַּמָּיִם . . . וְהִקְטִיר,, ² — **it says, "He shall wash its innards and its feet with water . . . and cause it to go up in smoke."**² וּבְעוֹף — But with regard to fowl, שֶׁנִּזּוֹן מִן הַגָּזֵל — which generally **takes its sustenance from that which is stolen,** נֶאֱמַר ,,וְהִשְׁלִיךְ,, אֶת הַמֻּרְאָה — **it says, "he shall throw** away" **the innards,** שֶׁאָכַל מִן הַגָּזֵל — **for it ate from that which is stolen.**³

□ אֵצֶל הַמִּזְבֵּחַ קֵדְמָה — **NEXT TO THE** *MIZBE'ACH,* **ON THE EAST.** בְּמִזְרָחוֹ שֶׁל כֶּבֶשׁ⁴ — **To the east of the ramp.**⁴

□ אֶל מְקוֹם הַדָּשֶׁן — **TO THE PLACE OF THE ASHES.** מָקוֹם שֶׁנּוֹתְנִין שָׁם תְּרוּמַת הַדֶּשֶׁן בְּכָל בֹּקֶר — **The place where they put the raising of the ashes every morning,**⁵ וְדִשּׁוּן מִזְבַּח הַפְּנִימִי⁶ — **and the ashes removed from the interior** *Mizbe'ach,*⁶ וְהַמְּנוֹרָה — **and the Menorah.**⁷ וְכֻלָּם נִבְלָעִים שָׁם בִּמְקוֹמָן — **They are all** miraculously **swallowed up there in their place.**⁷

17. וְשִׁסַּע — **HE SHALL TEAR [IT] APART.** אֵין שִׁסּוּעַ אֶלָּא בַיָּד — **"Tearing apart"** is done **only by hand.** וְכֵן הוּא אוֹמֵר בְּשִׁמְשׁוֹן — **And so it says of Samson:** ,,וַיְשַׁסְּעֵהוּ כְּשַׁסַּע הַגְּדִי וְגוֹמֵר,,⁸,⁹ — **"And he tore it apart as a kid is torn apart, etc."**⁸,⁹

□ בִכְנָפָיו — **This means** עִם כְּנָפָיו — **along with its feathers.**¹⁰ ¹¹אֵינוֹ צָרִיךְ לִמְרוֹט כַּנְפֵי נוֹצָתוֹ — **He does not have to pluck the feathers of its plumage.**¹¹

---

1. *Zevachim* 65a. According to the Rabbis, נוֹצָה means "feathers" (specifically, the soft, fluffy inner feathers [Rashi to *Shabbos* 108a, s.v., בכנפיו]). In their opinion the verse says that the Kohen makes an incision in the body opposite the position of the crop, cuts down to the depth of the crop, and removes it along with the flesh and feathers that lie above it. According to Abba Yose ben Chanan, the Kohen removes only the crop and the gizzard. He makes a straight line incision through which he removes the crop, but he does not remove any flesh or feathers. According to *Levush HaOrah*, Rashi understands that the Rabbis disagree with Abba Yose regarding removal of the gizzard along with the crop. According to *Mizrachi*, Rashi understands that the Rabbis agree with Abba Yose that the gizzard was removed, too.

2. Above v. 13.

3. *Vayikra Rabbah* 3:4.

4. *Toras Kohanim, perek* 9:3. If the verse had meant that the Kohen should throw the crop to the east of the *Mizbe'ach*, it would have said, קֵדְמָה לַמִּזְבֵּחַ, "east of the *Mizbe'ach*." The phrase "next to the *Mizbe'ach*, on the east" is interpreted as "east of that which is next to the *Mizbe'ach*," i.e., the ramp (*Gur Aryeh*).

5. The ashes removed from the outer *Mizbe'ach*. The Torah uses the term "raising" with reference to the removal of those ashes (6:3 below).

6. The ashes of the incense burned each day on the interior *Mizbe'ach*.

7. *Toras Kohanim, perek* 9:3; *Yoma* 21b. This explains why the verse says, "to the *place* of the ashes," rather than, "to the ashes" (*Minchas Yehudah; Sifsei Chachamim*).

8. *Judges* 14:6. The verse goes on, "and there was nothing in his hand" (*Be'er Yitzchak*).

9. *Zevachim* 65b.

10. Not "at its feathers," i.e., along its back, as *Ramban* explains it. The word כָּנָף is often translated "wing." Here, Rashi's explanation of why the כְּנָפַיִם are not removed (see Rashi's next comment) cannot refer to the wings. Moreover, some editions include the French word פלומ"ש, "plumes." And in his commentary to *Shabbos* 108a and *Chullin* 56b, Rashi explains כְּנָפַיִם as the large, stiff feathers, as opposed to the soft, fluffy ones.

11. *Shabbos* 108a.

divide it; the Kohen shall cause it to go up in smoke on the Mizbe'ach, on the wood that is on the fire — it is an olah-offering, a fire-offering, a pleasing fragrance to HASHEM.

2 ¹ **W**hen a soul will bring a meal-offering to HASHEM, his offering shall be of fine flour; he shall pour oil on it and place

יַבְדִּיל וְהִקְטִיר אֹתוֹ הַכֹּהֵן הַמִּזְבֵּחָה עַל־הָעֵצִים אֲשֶׁר עַל־הָאֵשׁ עֹלָה הוּא אִשֵּׁה רֵיחַ נִיחֹחַ לַיהוה: ב א וְנֶפֶשׁ כִּי־תַקְרִיב קָרְבַּן מִנְחָה לַיהוה סֹלֶת יִהְיֶה קָרְבָּנוֹ וְיָצַק עָלֶיהָ שֶׁמֶן וְנָתַן

—————— אונקלוס ——————

יַפְרֵשׁ וְיַסֵּק כַּהֲנָא יָתֵהּ לְמַדְבְּחָא עַל אָעַיָּא דִּי עַל אֶשָּׁתָא עֲלָתָא הוּא קֻרְבַּן דְּמִתְקַבַּל בְּרַעֲוָא קֳדָם יְיָ: א וֶאֱנָשׁ אֲרֵי יְקָרֵב קֻרְבַּן מִנְחָתָא קֳדָם יְיָ סֻלְתָּא יְהֵי קֻרְבָּנֵהּ וִירִיק עֲלַהּ מִשְׁחָא וְיִתֵּן

—————— רש"י ——————

בכנפיו. נוצה ממש, והלא אין לך הדיוט שמריח ריח [רע] של כנפים נשרפים ואין נפשו קצה עליו, ולמה אמר הכתוב והקטיר, כדי שיהא המזבח שבע ומהודר בקרבנו של עני (ויק"ר ג:ה): **לא יבדיל.** אינו מפרקו לגמרי לב' חתיכות אלא קורעו מגבו. נא' באוף ריח ניחוח ונאמר בבהמה ריח ניחוח (לעיל פס' ט) לומר לך אחד המרבה ואחד הממעיט ובלבד שיכוין את לבו לשמים (ת"כ פרק ט:ח: מנחות קי.): **(א) ונפש כי תקריב.** לא נאמר נפש בכל קרבנות נדבה אלא במנחה מי דרכו להתנדב מנחה, עני. אמר הקב"ה מעלה אני עליו כאלו הקריב נפשו (מנחות קד:): **סלת יהיה קרבנו.** האומר הרי עלי מנחה סתם מביא מנחת סלת

—————— RASHI ELUCIDATED ——————

☐ **בִּכְנָפָיו** — ALONG WITH ITS FEATHERS. This refers to **נוֹצָה מַמָּשׁ** — actual plumage.¹ **וַהֲלֹא אֵין לְךָ הֶדְיוֹט** — But is it not true that there is no ordinary person **שֶׁמֵּרִיחַ רֵיחַ {רַע} שֶׁל כְּנָפַיִם נִשְׂרָפִים** — who smells the {harsh} smell of burning feathers **וְאֵין נַפְשׁוֹ קָצָה עָלָיו** — without becoming nauseated by it? **וְלָמָּה אָמַר הַכָּתוּב ,,וְהִקְטִיר,,** — Why did Scripture say that "he shall cause it to go up in smoke"? **כְּדֵי שֶׁיְּהֵא הַמִּזְבֵּחַ שָׂבֵעַ** — In order that the *Mizbe'ach* should be full **וּמְהֻדָּר** — and beautified **בְּקָרְבָּנוֹ שֶׁל עָנִי** — with the offering of a poor man.²

☐ **לֹא יַבְדִּיל** — HE NEED NOT DIVIDE. **אֵינוֹ מְפָרְקוֹ לְגַמְרֵי** — He does not take it apart completely, **לִשְׁתֵּי חֲתִיכוֹת** — into two pieces, **אֶלָּא קוֹרְעוֹ מִגַּבּוֹ** — but he tears it along its back and leaves it intact at its front. **נֶאֱמַר בְּעוֹף ,,רֵיחַ נִיחוֹחַ,,** — It says "a pleasing fragrance" about *olah-* offerings of fowl, **וְנֶאֱמַר** **,,רֵיחַ נִיחוֹחַ,,** **בִּבְהֵמָה** — and it says "a pleasing fragrance"³ about *olah-* offerings of livestock, **לוֹמַר לְךָ** — to tell you that **אֶחָד הַמַּרְבֶּה וְאֶחָד הַמַּמְעִיט** — one who gives much, i.e., an expensive offering, is the same as one who gives less, i.e., a modest offering, **וּבִלְבַד שֶׁיְּכַוֵּן אֶת לִבּוֹ לַשָּׁמַיִם** — as long as his heart is directed toward Heaven.⁴

2.

1. וְנֶפֶשׁ כִּי תַקְרִיב — WHEN A SOUL WILL BRING. **לֹא נֶאֱמַר נֶפֶשׁ בְּכָל קָרְבְּנוֹת נְדָבָה** — "Soul" was not used with reference to any voluntary offerings **אֶלָּא בַּמִּנְחָה** — except for the meal-offering. The reason for this is as follows: **מִי דַרְכּוֹ לְהִתְנַדֵּב מִנְחָה** — Whose practice is it to dedicate a meal-offering? **עָנִי** — A poor person.⁵ **אָמַר הַקָּדוֹשׁ בָּרוּךְ הוּא** — The Holy One, Blessed is He, said: Although the poor man's offering is modest, **מַעֲלֶה אֲנִי עָלָיו** — I consider it on his behalf **כְּאִלּוּ הִקְרִיב נַפְשׁוֹ** — as if he offered his soul.⁶

☐ **סֹלֶת יִהְיֶה קָרְבָּנוֹ** — HIS OFFERING SHALL BE OF FINE FLOUR. **הָאוֹמֵר הֲרֵי עָלַי מִנְחָה** — One who says, "I take upon myself to bring **a meal-offering," סְתָם** — without specifying what sort of meal-offering he wishes to bring, **מֵבִיא מִנְחַת סֹלֶת** — brings a meal-offering of unbaked **fine flour,**

---

1. In line with his preceding comment, Rashi points out that the verse speaks of the feathers in a concrete sense; they are burned on the *Mizbe'ach*. This is in contrast to the explanation of the *Ramban*, who maintains that the feathers are mentioned as an indication of the location of the dividing. According to him, the verse does not treat the feathers as an object involved in the sacrificial procedure.

2. *Vayikra Rabbah* 3:5. Fowl are usually the offering of the poor. Such offerings would look scant if put on the *Mizbe'ach* stripped of feathers (*Mizrachi*).

3. Above vv. 9, 13.

4. *Toras Kohanim, perek* 9:7; *Menachos* 110a.

5. Because he owns no livestock (*Rashi* to *Menachos* 104b).

6. *Menachos* 104b.

19 / VAYIKRA/LEVITICUS — PARASHAS VAYIKRA — ב/ב – 2/2

בּ עָלֶיהָ לְבֹנָה׃ וֶהֱבִיאָהּ אֶל־בְּנֵי *He shall bring it to* ² *.frankincense on it*

— אונקלוס —

עֲלַהּ לְבֻנְתָּא׃ ² וְיַיְתִנַּהּ לְוַת בְּנֵי

— רש"י —

שֶׁהִיא הָרִאשׁוֹנָה שֶׁבַּמְּנָחוֹת וְנִקְמֶצֶת כְּשֶׁהִיא סֹלֶת כְּמוֹ שֶׁמְּפוֹרָשׁ פְּתוּתָהּ מְעַשְּׂרוֹן שֶׁגָּל' וְעִשָּׂרוֹן סֹלֶת לַמִּנְחָה (הלן יד:כא) עֶשָּׂרוֹן
בָּעִנְיָן (שם). לְפִי שֶׁנֶּאֶמְרוּ כָּאן ה' מִינֵי מְנָחוֹת וְכוּלָּן בָּאוֹת אֲפוּיוֹת לְכָל מִנְחָה (ת"כ פרק י:א‑ד): **וְיָצַק עָלֶיהָ שֶׁמֶן.** עַל כֻּלָּהּ:
קֹדֶם קְמִיצָה חוּץ מִזּוֹ לְכָךְ קְרוּיָה מִנְחַת סֹלֶת: **סֹלֶת.** אֵין סֹלֶת **וְנָתַן עָלֶיהָ לְבֹנָה.** עַל מִקְצָתָהּ. מַנִּיחַ קוֹמֶץ לְבוֹנָה עָלֶיהָ
אֶלָּא מִן הַחִטִּין שֶׁנֶּאֱמַר סֹלֶת חִטִּים (שמות כט:ב) וְאֵין מִנְחָה לְצַד אֶחָד. וּמַה רָאִיתָ לוֹמַר כֵּן, שֶׁאֵין רִבּוּי אַחַר רִבּוּי בַּתּוֹרָה

— RASHI ELUCIDATED —

וְנִקְמֶצֶת כְּשֶׁהִיא סֹלֶת — It is **שֶׁהִיא הָרִאשׁוֹנָה שֶׁבַּמְּנָחוֹת** — which is the first of the meal-offerings.[1] scooped from it while it is still in a state of being fine flour,[2] **כְּמוֹ שֶׁמְּפוֹרָשׁ בָּעִנְיָן** — as stated explicitly[3] further on in this passage.[4] **לְפִי שֶׁנֶּאֶמְרוּ כָּאן חֲמִשָּׁה מִינֵי מְנָחוֹת** — Since five varieties of meal-offerings are mentioned here,[5] **וְכֻלָּן בָּאוֹת אֲפוּיוֹת קֹדֶם קְמִיצָה** — and all of them come baked before the scooping procedure — except for this one, **חוּץ מִזּוֹ** — **לְכָךְ קְרוּיָה מִנְחַת סֹלֶת** — therefore it is called "a meal-offering of fine flour."[6]

□ **סֹלֶת** — FINE FLOUR. **אֵין "סֹלֶת״ אֶלָּא מִן הַחִטִּין** — Whenever סֹלֶת, "fine flour," is mentioned in Scripture, it means only flour that is of wheat, **שֶׁנֶּאֱמַר "סֹלֶת חִטִּים״** — as it says, "fine flour of wheat."[7] **וְאֵין מִנְחָה פְּחוּתָה מֵעִשָּׂרוֹן** — A meal-offering cannot be less than a tenth-*ephah*[8] of fine flour, **שֶׁנֶּאֱמַר "וְעִשָּׂרוֹן סֹלֶת לַמִּנְחָה״** — as it says, "and a tenth-*ephah* of fine flour ... for a meal-offering,"[9] which means, **עִשָּׂרוֹן לְכָל מִנְחָה** — a tenth-*ephah* for every meal-offering.[10]

□ **וְיָצַק עָלֶיהָ שֶׁמֶן** — HE SHALL POUR OIL ON IT. **עַל כֻּלָּהּ** — On all of it.

□ **וְנָתַן עָלֶיהָ לְבֹנָה** — AND PLACE FRANKINCENSE ON IT.[11] **עַל מִקְצָתָהּ** — On part of it. **מַנִּיחַ קוֹמֶץ לְבוֹנָה עָלֶיהָ** — He places threefingersful of frankincense on part of it **לְצַד אֶחָד** — on one side. **וּמַה רָאִיתָ** — What did you see to say thus?[12] **שֶׁאֵין רִבּוּי אַחַר רִבּוּי בַּתּוֹרָה** — Because there is no **לוֹמַר כֵּן** —

---

1. Rashi's use of the word הָרִאשׁוֹנָה, "the first," does not refer to the fact that this is the first of the meal-offerings mentioned in the Torah. Rather, it means that this is the meal-offering that most quickly (i.e. first) becomes a valid offering, since it does not require baking before it is brought (*Gur Aryeh* based on *Menachos* 104b-105a).

2. *Menachos* 104b.
   The Kohen cups the three middle fingers of his right hand over his palm and scoops up as much of the flour-and-oil mixture as his hand will hold. His three fingers must be filled to capacity, but none of the mixture may poke out from between or outside his fingers. The act of scooping is known as *kemitzah* and the amount scooped is called a *kometz*. Because there is no English equivalent for the measure of a *kometz*, we have coined the word "three-fingersful" for the translation; in the notes, however, we use "*kometz*." (See Rashi to v. 2 below, s.v., וְקָמַץ מִשָּׁם, "he shall scoop from there.")
   A *kometz* of each meal-offering is burned on the *Mizbe'ach*, while the rest is eaten by the Kohanim, as stated in the coming verses.

3. Verse 2.
4. *Menachos* 104b.
5. The five varieties are: (a) מִנְחַת סֹלֶת, "the meal-offering of fine flour" (vv. 1-3); (b,c) מִנְחַת מַאֲפֵה תַנּוּר, "the meal-offering baked in an oven," which can consist of either חַלּוֹת מַצּוֹת, "unleavened loaves," or רְקִיקֵי מַצּוֹת, "unleavened wafers" (v. 4); (d) מִנְחַת עַל הַמַּחֲבַת, "the meal-offering on the pan" (vv. 5-6); (e) מִנְחַת מַרְחֶשֶׁת, "the meal-offering in a deep pan" (v. 7).

6. All of the meal-offerings discussed here are of fine flour. It is this particular one which is referred to by the name "meal-offering of fine flour" because it is the only one whose *kometz* is placed on the *Mizbe'ach* while it is still flour (*Mizrachi; Sifsei Chachamim*).

7. *Exodus* 29:2.
8. An *ephah* is a volume measure equal to the volume of 432 *beitzim* (average-size chicken eggs). Opinions regarding the modern-day equivalent of the basic *beitzah* range from 2 to 3.5 fluid ounces. Thus, the volume of a tenth-*ephah* is approximately $2^{2}/_{3}$-$4^{2}/_{3}$ quarts.
9. Below 14:21.
10. *Toras Kohanim, perek* 10:1-4. The context of the verse shows clearly that the tenth-*ephah* of fine flour is brought as a meal-offering. The Torah nonetheless states לְמִנְחָה, "as a meal-offering," to teach us that the offering has the volume of a tenth-*ephah* because of the very fact that it is a meal-offering. Thus, we can derive from here that all meal-offerings must be a minimum of a tenth-*ephah* (*Be'er Yitzchak*).
11. The English word "frankincense" is derived from the two Old French words *franc*, "pure," and *encens*, "incense." It is in this sense that we use it here, and not as the definitive name of a particular spice. Moreover, "frankincense" is not the translation of לְבוֹנָה, but of the phrase לְבוֹנָה זַכָּה (see 24:7 below). To distinguish between the two, we translate "pure frankincense" for לְבוֹנָה זַכָּה, and "frankincense" when לְבוֹנָה appears without the adjective זַכָּה.
12. Why did you interpret the first עָלֶיהָ of the verse as "on all of it," and the second as "on part of it"?

אַהֲרֹן֙ הַכֹּהֲנִ֔ים וְקָמַ֨ץ מִשָּׁ֜ם מְלֹ֣א קֻמְצ֗וֹ מִסָּלְתָּהּ֙ וּמִשַּׁמְנָ֔הּ עַ֖ל כָּל־

the sons of Aaron, the Kohanim, and he shall scoop from there his full threefingersful, of its fine flour and of its oil, as well

──────────── אונקלוס ────────────

אַהֲרֹן כָּהֲנַיָּא וְיִקְמוֹץ מִתַּמָּן מְלֵי קֻמְצֵהּ מִסֻּלְתַּהּ וּמִמִּשְׁחַהּ עַל כָּל

──────────── רש"י ────────────

אֶלָּא לְמַעֵט (ת"כ פרק יז:ז). ד"א שמן על כולה מפני שהוא נבלל עמה ונקמץ עמה כמ"ש מסלתה ומשמנה (פסוק ב), ולבונה על מקצתה שאינה נבללת עמה ולא נקמצת עמה שנאמר על כל לבונתה, שלאחר שקמץ מלקט את הלבונה כולה מעליה ומקטירה (שם ח): **וְיָצַק וְנָתַן**

וְהֵבִיאָה. מלמד שיציקה ובלילה כשרים בזר (שם י; מנחות יח:): **(ב) הַכֹּהֲנִים וְקָמַץ.** מקמיצה ואילך מצות כהונה (מנחות פט:ל): **וְקָמַץ מִשָּׁם.** ממקום שרגלי הזר עומדות. ללמדך שהקמיצה כשרה בכל מקום בעזרה אף בי"א אמה של מקום דריסת רגלי ישראל

──────────── RASHI ELUCIDATED ────────────

inclusion after an inclusion in the Torah [4] אֶלָּא לְמַעֵט — except to exclude.[1] דָּבָר אַחֵר — Alternatively, שֶׁמֶן עַל כֻּלָּהּ — oil is poured on all of it מִפְּנֵי שֶׁהוּא נִבְלָל עִמָּהּ — because it is mixed with [the flour] וְנִקְמָץ עִמָּהּ — and is scooped with it and burnt on the *Mizbe'ach*, כְּמוֹ שֶׁנֶּאֱמַר — as it says, "He shall scoop from there his threefingersful [2] מִסָּלְתָּהּ וּמִשַּׁמְנָהּ — of its fine flour and of its oil." וּלְבוֹנָה עַל מִקְצָתָהּ — Frankincense is placed on part of it, שֶׁאֵינָהּ נִבְלֶלֶת עִמָּהּ — because it is not mixed with [the flour] וְלֹא נִקְמֶצֶת עִמָּהּ — nor scooped with it, שֶׁנֶּאֱמַר — as it says, [2] עַל כָּל לְבֹנָתָהּ — "as well as all its frankincense." The verse implies שֶׁלְּאַחַר שֶׁקָּמַץ — that after he has scooped the threefingersful מְלַקֵּט אֶת הַלְּבוֹנָה כֻּלָּהּ מֵעָלֶיהָ — he gathers all of the frankincense from upon it [3] וּמַקְטִירָהּ — and sets it smoking on the *Mizbe'ach*.[3]

☐ וְיָצַק וְנָתַן וְהֵבִיאָה — HE SHALL POUR...HE SHALL PLACE...HE SHALL BRING. מְלַמֵּד — This teaches us שֶׁיְּצִיקָה וּבְלִילָה כְּשֵׁרִים בְּזָר — that pouring the oil on the flour and mixing the oil and the flour are valid if performed by a non-Kohen.[4]

2. הַכֹּהֲנִים וְקָמַץ — THE KOHANIM, HE SHALL SCOOP. מִקְּמִיצָה וְאֵילָךְ — From the procedure of scooping and onward [5] מִצְוַת כְּהֻנָּה — is a commandment of the *kehunah* and can be performed only by Kohanim.[5]

☐ וְקָמַץ מִשָּׁם — HE SHALL SCOOP FROM THERE. מִמָּקוֹם שֶׁרַגְלֵי הַזָּר עוֹמְדוֹת — From the place where the feet of a non-Kohen may stand. לְלַמֶּדְךָ שֶׁהַקְּמִיצָה כְּשֵׁרָה בְּכָל מָקוֹם בָּעֲזָרָה — This serves to teach you that the scooping is valid anywhere in the Courtyard of the *Beis HaMikdash*, אַף בְּאַחַת עֶשְׂרֵה — even in the eleven *amos* where the feet of Yisrael, i.e., those who are neither Kohanim nor Levites, may tread.[6]

---

1. *Toras Kohanim, perek* 10:7. When the Torah makes two statements, each of which would be considered an inclusive statement if it stood alone, the second statement is then interpreted as exclusionary rather than inclusive. The term עָלֶיהָ, "on it," is an inclusive statement which is understood in its broadest sense, "on all of it," unless there is reason to understand it otherwise. Thus, the first עָלֶיהָ is an inclusive statement. The second עָלֶיהָ is an inclusive statement which follows an inclusive statement, and is therefore interpreted as excluding, or limiting. In our verse, the first עָלֶיהָ is interpreted in the broad sense — oil is poured over all of the flour. But the second is interpreted to limit the spreading of the frankincense — it is put over only part of the meal-offering (*Mizrachi; Sifsei Chachamim*).

2. Below v. 2.

3. *Toras Kohanim, perek* 10:8. The oil is poured on all of the flour because it will be mixed with the flour and a handful of that mixture will be burned upon the *Mizbe'ach*. The frankincense is put in one spot because all of it will be gathered up to be burned upon the *Mizbe'ach*. The less it is spread out, the easier it will be to gather it together.

4. *Toras Kohanim, perek* 10:10; *Menachos* 18b. Our passage does not introduce the Kohen until the performance of the scooping (v. 2), implying that all prior steps in the procedure, such as pouring and mixing, may be performed by a non-Kohen. Rashi makes specific mention of mixing because it is not stated explicitly in the verse. It is implied by "he shall pour." If pouring, a later step in the sacrificial procedure (see Rashi to v. 5 below and note 4 there), can be performed by a non-Kohen, all the more so can the mixing which precedes it be done by a non-Kohen (*Mizrachi*).

5. *Menachos* 9a. Verse 8 below speaks of bringing the offering to the *Mizbe'ach*. This precedes the scooping of the *kometz* and nevertheless must be performed only by a Kohen. Rashi here refers only to stages which precede scooping that have been mentioned in the Torah up to this point, not those that first appear later (*Ramban; Mizrachi*).

6. *Menachos* 8b (see Rashi there, s.v., רגלי הזר עומדות); *Zevachim* 63a. "From there" implies that the Kohen

21 / VAYIKRA/LEVITICUS — PARASHAS VAYIKRA

לְבֹנָתָהּ וְהִקְטִיר הַכֹּהֵן אֶת־
אַזְכָּרָתָהּ הַמִּזְבֵּחָה אִשֵּׁה רֵיחַ
ג נִיחֹחַ לַיהוה: וְהַנּוֹתֶ֫רֶת מִן־

as all its frankincense; and the Kohen shall cause its memorial portion to go up in smoke upon the Mizbe'ach — a fire-offering, a satisfying aroma to HASHEM. *[3] The remnant of*

― אונקלוס ―

לְבֻנְתַהּ וְיַסֵּק כַּהֲנָא יָת אִדְכַּרְתַּהּ לְמַדְבְּחָא קֻרְבַּן דְּמִתְקַבַּל בְּרַעֲוָא קֳדָם יְיָ: גוּדְאִשְׁתְּאַר מִן

― רש"י ―

(מנחות ח:; זבחים סג.): **מלא קמצו.** יכול מבורץ מבוצבץ
ויוצא לכל צד, ת"ל במקום אחר והרים ממנו בקמצו (להלן ו:ח)
לא יהא כשר אלא מה שבתוך הקומץ. אי בקמצו יכול חסר, ת"ל
מלא. הא כיצד, חופה ג' אצבעותיו על פס ידו (ת"כ פרשתא
ט:ו; מנחות יא.) וזהו קומץ במשמע לשון העברית: **על כל**

לבונתה: לבד כל הלבונה יהא הקומץ מלא: **לבונתה
והקטיר.** אף הלבונה בהקטרה (שם י): **מלא קמצו מסלתה
ומשמנה.** הא אם קמץ ועלה בידו גרגיר מלח או קורט
לבונה פסולה (ת"כ שם; מנחות ו.): **אזכרתה.** הקומץ
העולה לגבוה הוא זכרון המנחה שבו נזכר בעליה לטובה

― RASHI ELUCIDATED ―

☐ **מְלֹא קֻמְצוֹ — HIS FULL THREEFINGERSFUL.** יָכוֹל מְבוֹרָץ — **One might be able to** think that the threefingersful should be **brimming,** מְצַבְצֵב — **overflowing,** וְיוֹצֵא לְכָל צַד — **and** with flour **coming out** of his grasp **in every direction.** תַּלְמוּד לוֹמַר בְּמָקוֹם אַחֵר — **To teach us otherwise, the Torah says elsewhere,** ,,וְהֵרִים מִמֶּנּוּ בְּקֻמְצוֹ,,[1] — **"and he shall separate from it in his threefingersful,"**[1] implying לֹא יְהֵא כָשֵׁר אֶלָּא מַה שֶּׁבְּתוֹךְ הַקּוֹמֶץ — **only that which is within the threefingersful is fit** to be offered on the *Mizbe'ach.* ,,אִי ,,בְּקֻמְצוֹ — **If** we were to draw our conclusion on the basis of **"his threefingersful"** alone, יָכוֹל חָסֵר — **one might be able** to think that the scoop could be **less** than a full threefingersful.[2] תַּלְמוּד לוֹמַר ,,מְלֹא,, — **To teach us otherwise, the Torah says, "full."** הָא כֵּיצַד — **How is this** scooping done? After he puts his hand into the flour, חוֹפֶה שָׁלֹשׁ אֶצְבְּעוֹתָיו עַל פַּס יָדוֹ[2] — **he covers,** i.e., bends, **his three** middle **fingers, but not his** little finger, **on,** i.e., toward, **his palm,** and removes the flour held between his palm and his fingers from the rest of the meal-offering.[3] וְזֶהוּ קוֹמֶץ בְּמַשְׁמַע לָשׁוֹן הָעִבְרִית — **This is the meaning of** קוֹמֶץ **in the Hebrew language.**

☐ **עַל כָּל לְבֹנָתָהּ — AS WELL AS ALL ITS FRANKINCENSE.** This means, לְבַד כָּל הַלְּבוֹנָה — **aside from all the frankincense** יְהֵא הַקּוֹמֶץ מָלֵא — **the** *kometz* **should be full,** i.e., the threefingersful may not include any of the frankincense.

☐ **לְבֹנָתָהּ וְהִקְטִיר — ITS FRANKINCENSE; AND [THE KOHEN] SHALL CAUSE TO GO UP IN SMOKE.** אַף הַלְּבוֹנָה בְּהַקְטָרָה[4] — **The frankincense is also** included **in the burning.**[4]

☐ **מְלֹא קֻמְצוֹ מִסָּלְתָּהּ וּמִשַּׁמְנָהּ — HIS FULL THREEFINGERSFUL OF ITS FINE FLOUR AND OF ITS OIL.** הָא אִם קָמַץ — **But if he scooped** וְעָלָה בְיָדוֹ — **and there came up in his hand** גַּרְגִּיר מֶלַח אוֹ קוֹרֶט לְבוֹנָה — **a grain of salt**[5] **or a particle of frankincense,** פְּסוּלָה[6] — **[the scooping] is invalid.**[6]

☐ **אַזְכָּרָתָהּ — ITS MEMORIAL PORTION.** הַקּוֹמֶץ הָעוֹלֶה לַגָּבוֹהַּ — **The threefingersful which ascends to** He Who is **on high** הוּא זִכְרוֹן הַמִּנְחָה — **is the memorial of the meal-offering,** שֶׁבּוֹ נִזְכָּר בְּעָלֶיהָ לְטוֹבָה

קוֹמֶץ — KOMETZ

מבורץ
BRIMMING-OVER
(INVALID)

חסר — DEFICIENT
(INVALID)

מלא — FULL (VALID)

---

does the scooping at the spot where the non-Kohen who brings the offering gives it to him. Hence, the scooping may be done in the part of the Courtyard in which non-Kohanim may stand. The Courtyard was 187 *amos* long. Non-Kohanim were allowed to stand only in the first eleven *amos* from the entrance (*Mizrachi*; *Be'er Yitzchak*).

1. Below 6:8. "In his threefingersful" implies that none of it should overflow.

2. The term קֹמֶץ could be understood as referring to that which is held by his three fingers, even though it does not fill all of the available space.

3. *Toras Kohanim, parshasa* 9:6; *Menachos* 11a.

4. *Toras Kohanim, parshasa* 9:10. The Torah juxtaposes "frankincense" and "the Kohen shall cause to go up in smoke" to teach you that the frankincense is also burned (*Mizrachi*). Alternatively, since the Torah does not state explicitly what is to be done with the frankincense, it stands to reason that it is included in the burning (*Mesiach Ilmim*).

5. See v. 13 below.

6. *Toras Kohanim, parshasa* 9:10; *Menachos* 6a. Because then his hand is not full of oil and flour (*Mizrachi*; *Sifsei Chachamim*).

הַמִּנְחָה לְאַהֲרֹן וּלְבָנָיו קֹדֶשׁ קָדָשִׁים מֵאִשֵּׁי יהוה: ד וְכִי תַקְרִב קָרְבַּן מִנְחָה מַאֲפֵה תַנּוּר סֹלֶת

the meal-offering is for Aaron and his sons; most holy, from the fire-offerings of HASHEM. **4** *When you offer a meal-offering that is baked in an oven, it shall be of fine flour:*

---- אונקלוס ----

מִנְחָתָא לְאַהֲרֹן וְלִבְנוֹהִי קֹדֶשׁ קוּדְשִׁין מִקֻּרְבָּנַיָּא דַיָי: ד וַאֲרֵי תְקָרֵב קֻרְבַּן מִנְחָתָא מַאֲפֵה תַנּוּרָא סֻלְתָּא

---- רש"י ----

(ג) **לאהרן ולבניו.** כהן גדול נוטל חלק בראש שלא במחלוקת וההדיוט במחלוקת (שם פרק יא:א; יומא יד.): **קדש קדשים.** היא להם: **מאשי ה'.** אין להם חלק בה אלא לאחר מתנות האישים (שם ה): (ד) **וכי תקריב וגו'.** שאמר הרי עלי מנחת מאפה תנור, ולימד הכתוב שיביא או חלות או רקיקין, החלות בלולות והרקיקין משוחין (שם פרשתא י״ד-ה; מנחות עה:). ונחלקו רבותינו במשיחתן, י״א מושחן וחוזר ומושחן עד שיכלה כל השמן שבלוג, שכל המנחות טעונות לוג שמן, וי״א מושחן כמין כ"י

---- RASHI ELUCIDATED ----

[1] **וּלְנַחַת רוּחַ** – *for by means of it its owner is remembered for goodness and for contentment,* i.e., the owner is remembered for having done something good, and for having brought contentment to God.[1]

3. לְאַהֲרֹן וּלְבָנָיו – FOR AARON AND HIS SONS. – כֹּהֵן גָּדוֹל נוֹטֵל חֵלֶק בָּרֹאשׁ – The Kohen Gadol takes a portion of the meal-offering **first,** שֶׁלֹּא בְמַחֲלוֹקֶת – *without apportionment,* וְהַהֶדְיוֹט בְּמַחֲלוֹקֶת – **and the ordinary Kohen** takes his portion **through apportionment.**[2]

□ קֹדֶשׁ קָדָשִׁים – IT IS MOST HOLY הִיא לָהֶם – **for them.**

□ מֵאִשֵּׁי ה' – FROM THE FIRE-OFFERINGS OF HASHEM. – אֵין לָהֶם חֵלֶק בָּהּ – **They have no share in it** אֶלָּא לְאַחַר מַתְּנוֹת הָאִשִּׁים – **until after the offerings of the parts which are placed onto the pyres** of the *Mizbe'ach*.[3]

4. וְכִי תַקְרִיב וְגוֹמֵר – WHEN YOU OFFER, ETC. – שֶׁאָמַר הֲרֵי עָלַי מִנְחַת מַאֲפֵה תַנּוּר – The verse speaks of a case in which he says, "I take upon myself to bring **a meal-offering that is baked in an oven."** וְלִמֵּד הַכָּתוּב – The verse teaches you שֶׁיָּבִיא אוֹ חַלּוֹת – **that he should bring either loaves** אוֹ רְקִיקִין – **or wafers.**[4] הַחַלּוֹת בְּלוּלוֹת – The loaves are mixed with oil, [5] וְהָרְקִיקִין מְשׁוּחִין – **and the wafers are smeared.**[5] וְנֶחְלְקוּ רַבּוֹתֵינוּ בִּמְשִׁיחָתָן – Our Rabbis argue with respect to their smearing. יֵשׁ אוֹמְרִים – מוֹשְׁחָן – **There are those who say** that **he smears them** וְחוֹזֵר וּמוֹשְׁחָן – **and smears them again,** i.e., continues to smear them, עַד שֶׁכָּלָה כָּל הַשֶּׁמֶן שֶׁבַּלּוֹג – **until all of the oil in the** *log* **is finished,** שֶׁכָּל הַמְּנָחוֹת טְעוּנוֹת לוֹג שֶׁמֶן – **for all the meal-offerings require a** *log* **of oil.**[6] וְיֵשׁ אוֹמְרִים – **And there are those who say** that מוֹשְׁחָן כְּמִין כִי – **he smears them** once **in the shape of** the Greek letter **chi**[7]

---

1. *Toras Kohanim, parshasa* 9:12.

2. *Toras Kohanim, perek* 11:1; *Yoma* 14a. All the Kohanim on duty in the *Beis HaMikdash* on any given day share equally in the portions of the offerings the Torah assigns to the Kohanim. The Kohen Gadol is not included in this apportionment. He may take whatever and as much as he wishes as his share (*Mizrachi; Sefer Zikaron*). Our verse could have said, "the remnant of the meal offering is for the Kohanim." It says instead, "for Aaron and his sons," to teach us that Aaron and the Kohanim Gedolim who follow him each takes his portion separately, before "his sons," that is, before the ordinary Kohanim (*Minchas Yehudah; Sifsei Chachamim*).

3. *Toras Kohanim, perek* 11:5. It does not seem appropriate to refer to the remnant as being "from the fire-offerings of HASHEM," because the remnant is not offered upon the fire. The מ prefix of מֵאִשֵּׁי is therefore interpreted as, "from the time of"; the remnant of the meal-offering is for Aaron and his sons, from the time of the burning of the fire-offerings of HASHEM (*Mesiach Ilmim*).

4. *Menachos* 63b. The ו of וּרְקִיקֵי is understood as "or," not "and" (*Mizrachi; Sifsei Chachamim*).

5. *Toras Kohanim, parshasa* 10:4-5; *Menachos* 74b.

6. The *log* is a volume measure equal to six *beitzim* (average-size chicken eggs). Opinions regarding the modern-day equivalents of the basic *beitzah* range from 2 to 3.5 fluid ounces. Thus, the volume of a *log* is approximately 12 to 21 fluid ounces.

7. Sometimes called כִי (or כי) and often called כִּי יְוָנִית or כַּף יְוָנִית in the Talmud and commentaries, the identity of this letter is a much disputed point in the writings of the *Rishonim* and *Acharonim*. All agree, however, that it is a Greek letter as the term יְוָנִית implies.
— According to the *Rambam* (Hil. Klei HaMikdash 1:9), it is the twenty-second letter of the Greek alphabet, pronounced *chi* (כִי) and written X.
— The Talmudic dictionary *Aruch* (compiled in 1101 by R' Nosson of Rome) maintains that it is the eleventh letter in the Greek alphabet, called *lambda* and written Λ like an inverted V. This opinion is cited by *Tosafos* to *Menachos* 75a. *Yad Avraham* (*Menachos* 6:3) suggests that *lambda* may be called כִי or כ"ף

23 / VAYIKRA/LEVITICUS — PARASHAS VAYIKRA — ב/ד – ה 2/4

חַלּוֹת מַצֹּת בְּלוּלֹת בַּשֶּׁמֶן וּרְקִיקֵי *unleavened loaves mixed with oil, or un-*
ה מַצּוֹת מְשֻׁחִים בַּשָּׁמֶן: וְאִם־ *leavened wafers smeared with oil.*

───────── אונקלוס ─────────

גְרִיצָן פַּטִּירָן דְּפִילָן בִּמְשַׁח וְאֶסְפּוֹגִין פַּטִּירִין דִּמְשִׁיחִין בִּמְשָׁח: הוְאִם

───────── רש"י ─────────

[ס"א כ"ף יונית] ושאר השמן נאכל בפני עצמן לכהנים (מנחות   למנורה שנאמר בו זך (שמות כז:כ) וטנינו במנחות (עו.) כל
עה.). מה ת"ל בשמן בשני פעמים, להכשיר שמן שני   המנחות האפויות לפני קמיצתן וקמצותיה ע"י פתיתה כולן באות
ושלישי היוצא מן הזיתים (ת"כ שם ו) ואין צריך שמן ראשון אלא   עשר עשר חלות והאמור בה רקיקין באה עשר רקיקין:

───────── RASHI ELUCIDATED ─────────

וּשְׁאָר הַשֶּׁמֶן — and the rest of the oil נֶאֱכָל בִּפְנֵי עַצְמוֹ **— is consumed by itself,** without being used for the offering, לַכֹּהֲנִים¹ **— by the Kohanim.**¹ מַה תַּלְמוּד לוֹמַר בַּשֶּׁמֶן שְׁנֵי פְעָמִים **— Why does the Torah say בַּשֶּׁמֶן, "in oil," twice?** לְהַכְשִׁיר שֶׁמֶן שֵׁנִי וּשְׁלִישִׁי **— To permit the second and third oil,** i.e., the oil of the second and third extracting procedure, הַיּוֹצֵא מִן הַזֵּיתִים **— which comes out of the olives.**² וְאֵין צָרִיךְ שֶׁמֶן רִאשׁוֹן **— First oil,** i.e., oil of the first pressing, **is not necessary** אֶלָּא לַמְּנוֹרָה **— except for the Menorah,** שֶׁנֶּאֱמַר בּוֹ **— about which it says,** ³זָךְ, **— "pure."**³ ⁴וְטָנִינוּ בִּמְנָחוֹת **— We have learned in** *Menachos*:⁴ כָּל הַמְּנָחוֹת הָאֲפוּיוֹת לִפְנֵי קְמִיצָתָן **— Those meal-offerings which are baked before their threefingersful is taken,** i.e., all the meal-offerings in this chapter with the exception of the first, the "meal-offering of fine flour," וְנִקְמָצוֹת עַל יְדֵי פְּתִיתָה **— and whose threefingersful is taken by crumbling,** as baking has already made them hard, כֻּלָּן בָּאוֹת עֶשֶׂר עֶשֶׂר חַלּוֹת **— all come,** i.e., consist, **of ten loaves,** וְהָאָמוּר בָּהּ רְקִיקִין **— And [the meal-offering] about which "wafers" is said,** i.e., which is called "wafers," בָּאָה עֲשָׂרָה רְקִיקִין **— comes,** i.e., consists, **of ten wafers.**

because like the Hebrew כ it is the eleventh letter in its alphabet.

— *Tosefos Yom Tov* (*Menachos* 6:3 and *Keilim* 20:7) contends that כ"י יונית refers to the lower-case form of the twentieth letter of the Greek alphabet, called *upsilon* and written U. *Yad Avraham* (*Menachos* 6:3) suggests that *upsilon* may be called כ"י or כ"ף because it is the twentieth letter and the *gematria* of the Hebrew letter כ is twenty.

However, Rashi's opinion is difficult to ascertain because of apparently conflicting statements in his commentary: (a) In his commentary to Exodus 29:2, he describes the כ"י as our letter ג; in the first printed edition this is enhanced by a picture of the letter U – Ո (see *Yosef Hallel*), but no letter in the Greek alphabet has this shape, except perhaps an inverted lower-case *upsilon*; (b) in his commentary to Exodus 29:7, Rashi describes the anointing of the Kohen Gadol as "in the form of the letter כ"י; he puts oil on the Kohen Gadol's head and among his eyelashes, and connects these with his finger," a description that seems to fit the picture of the inverted *upsilon* mentioned above; (c) in his commentary to *Menachos* 74a, Rashi describes the כ"י as "a Greek letter, something like a ט, as when the index finger is separated from the thumb"; here, too, there is no Greek letter that looks quite like a ט; however, the spreading of the thumb and index finger apart does yield a U of sorts; (d) in his commentary to *Horayos* 12a, Rashi describes the anointing of a Kohen Gadol, "He begins to anoint with his finger among the eyelashes and draws the oil over the head until he reaches the back of the neck, like a כ"י יוֹנִי, like a ח" — until here, all the various descriptions given by Rashi were of rounded letters, but here he shows a square

letter which seems to be the sixteenth letter in the Greek alphabet, called *pi* and written Π; (e) most puzzling, however, is the letter pictured in Rashi's commentary to *Kereisos* 5b, which is clearly the letter X; Rashi continues there, "He pours oil on his head, then between his eyelids, and connects them across the forehead"; in this last comment Rashi seems to agree with *Rambam*'s view and differ with his own comment in *Horayos* regarding the size of the oil mark; (f) finally, *Tosafos* to *Menachos* 75a write, "Rashi draws a sort of ט, and in his commentary to the *Chumash* he describes a ג, and some describe a sort of נ or a sort of ב."

1. *Menachos* 75a.

2. *Toras Kohanim, parshasa* 10:6. See the following note.

3. *Exodus* 27:20. The Mishnah (*Menachos* 86a) explains that the olive tree is harvested three times a year. The first harvest is for the earliest ripening olives at the top of the tree. The second is for the olives on the middle branches which ripen later. Finally, a third harvest is for the fruit of the lowest branches that never receive the full sunlight and so do not ripen until after they have been harvested and left to stand packed tightly together in a vessel. Oil is extracted from the olives of each harvest through three consecutive methods: First, they are crushed in a mortar; then, they are pressed with a beam; finally, they are ground with millstones. The Mishnah goes on to say that only the oil extracted from each of the three harvests by crushing the olives in a mortar is fit for use in the Menorah, but the oil extracted by the other two methods is valid for the meal-offerings.

4. *Menachos* 76a.

מִנְחָה עַל־הַמַּחֲבַת קָרְבָּנֶךָ סֹלֶת בְּלוּלָה בַשֶּׁמֶן מַצָּה תִהְיֶה: פָּתוֹת אֹתָהּ פִּתִּים וְיָצַקְתָּ עָלֶיהָ שָׁמֶן מִנְחָה הִוא: שלישי וְאִם־

5 If your offering is a meal-offering on the pan, it shall be of fine flour mixed with oil, it shall be unleavened. **6** You shall crumble it into bits and pour oil upon it — it is a meal-offering.

— אונקלוס —

מִנְחָתָא עַל מַסְרֵתָא קָרְבָּנָךְ סֻלְתָּא דְּפִילָא בִמְשַׁח פַּטִּיר תְּהֵי: ו בְּצַע יָתַהּ בְּצוֹעִין וּתְרִיק עֲלַהּ מִשְׁחָא מִנְחָתָא הִיא: זוְאִם

— רש"י —

(ה) **ואם מנחה על המחבת.** שֶׁאָמַר הֲרֵי עָלַי מִנְחַת מַחֲבַת. לְעִטּוּיָן (ת"כ שם א־ב; מנחות עד:): **סלת בלולה בשמן.** וּכְלִי הוּא שֶׁהָיָה בַּמִּקְדָּשׁ שֶׁאוֹפִין בּוֹ מִנְחָה [זוֹ] עַל הָאוּר בַּשֶּׁמֶן, מְלַמֵּד שֶׁבּוֹלְלָן בְּעוֹדָן סֹלֶת (ת"כ שם): (ו) **פתות** וְהַכְּלִי אֵינוֹ עָמֹק אֶלָּא צָף, וּמַעֲשֵׂי הַמִּנְחָה שֶׁבְּתוֹכוֹ קָשִׁין (ת"כ **אותה פתים.** לְרַבּוֹת כָּל הַמְּנָחוֹת הַנֶּאֱפוֹת קֹדֶם קְמִיצָה פֶּרֶק יב:ז), מִנָּחוֹת סג.), שֶׁמְּתוֹךְ שֶׁהִיא צָפָה הָאוּר שׂוֹרֵף אֶת הַשֶּׁמֶן, לִפְתִיתָה (ת"כ שם ה): **ויצקת עליה שמן.** מִנְחָה הִיא. לְרַבּוֹת וְכֻלָּן טְעוּנוֹת ג' מַתְּנוֹת שֶׁמֶן, יְצִיקָה וּבְלִילָה וּמַתַּן שֶׁמֶן בַּכְּלִי קֹדֶם כָּל הַמְּנָחוֹת לִיצִיקָה (שם ו), יָכוֹל אַף מִנְחָה מַאֲפֵה תַנּוּר כֵּן,

— RASHI ELUCIDATED —

5. שֶׁאָמַר הֲרֵי עָלַי מִנְחָת הַמַּחֲבַת — וְאִם מִנְחָה עַל הַמַּחֲבַת IF [YOUR OFFERING IS] A MEAL-OFFERING ON THE PAN. מַחֲבַת — The verse speaks of a case **in which he says, "I take upon myself** to bring **a meal-offering of a pan."** וּכְלִי הוּא שֶׁהָיָה בַּמִּקְדָּשׁ — [The pan] is **a vessel that was in the *Beis HaMikdash*** שֶׁאוֹפִין בּוֹ {זוֹ} מִנְחָה — **in which they baked {this} meal-offering** עַל הָאוּר — **on the fire** בַּשֶּׁמֶן — **in oil.** וּמַעֲשֵׂי הַמִּנְחָה שֶׁבְּתוֹכוֹ קָשִׁין — וְהַכְּלִי אֵינוֹ עָמֹק The **vessel is not deep,** אֶלָּא צָף — **but shallow.**[1] שֶׁמִּתּוֹךְ שֶׁהִיא צָפָה — for due to its **being shallow, meal-offerings made in it are crisp,**[2] הָאוּר שׂוֹרֵף — **the fire burns up the oil** and does not allow it to soften the texture of the meal-offering. וְכֻלָּן טְעוּנוֹת שָׁלֹשׁ מַתְּנוֹת שֶׁמֶן — **All of them**[3] **require three applications of oil,** namely, יְצִיקָה — **pouring,** וּבְלִילָה — **and mixing,** וּמַתַּן שֶׁמֶן בִּכְלִי קֹדֶם לַעֲשִׂיָּתָן[4] — **and putting oil in a vessel before they are made,** i.e., before the flour is placed in the vessel.[4] סֹלֶת בְּלוּלָה בַשֶּׁמֶן — FINE FLOUR MIXED WITH OIL. מְלַמֵּד שֶׁבּוֹלְלָן בְּעוֹדָן סֹלֶת — This teaches us **that he mixes them while it is still fine flour.**[5]

6. פָּתוֹת אוֹתָהּ פִּתִּים — YOU SHALL CRUMBLE IT INTO BITS. לְרַבּוֹת כָּל הַמְּנָחוֹת — **To include all meal-offerings** הַנֶּאֱפוֹת קֹדֶם קְמִיצָה — **which are baked before scooping** is performed[6] לִפְתִיתָה[7] — **in** the law of **crumbling.**[7]

וְיָצַקְתָּ עָלֶיהָ שֶׁמֶן מִנְחָה הִיא — AND POUR OIL UPON IT — IT IS A MEAL-OFFERING. לְרַבּוֹת כָּל הַמְּנָחוֹת — **To include all meal-offerings** in the law of **pouring.**[8] לִיצִיקָה[8] — יָכוֹל אַף מִנְחָה מַאֲפֵה תַנּוּר כֵּן — **One might be able** to think that **a meal-offering baked in an oven** should **also** have oil poured over it after

---

1. The oil does not collect in quantity at the bottom as it would in a deep pan. Rashi defines צָף as "shallow" in his comments to *Menachos* 63a.

2. *Toras Kohanim, perek* 12:7; *Menachos* 63a.

3. The meal-offerings brought in a shallow pan and a deep pan (*Mizrachi; Nachalas Yaakov*), and the meal-offering of unbaked fine flour (*Be'er Yitzchak*), see *Mishneh LaMelech, Hil. Maasei HaKorbonos* 13:5, s.v., ‏(ודע שכבר החליט).

4. *Toras Kohanim, perek* 12:1-2; *Menachos* 74b. Our verse mentions the oil that is mixed with the flour. Verse 6 mentions a pouring which is done after the mixing. Verse 7 refers to putting oil in the vessel before the flour is placed into it. Although verses 5 and 6 speak of a meal-offering brought in a shallow pan, and verse 7 speaks of a meal-offering brought in a deep pan, *Toras Kohanim* uses a *gezeirah shavah* (see p. 155, note 10) based on the appearance of the word קָרְבָּנְךָ in both contexts to apply the laws of one type of offering to the other (*Mizrachi; Sifsei Chachamim*).

5. *Toras Kohanim, perek* 12:1-2; *Menachos* 74b. Rashi reflects the opinion of the Sages cited anonymously in *Toras Kohanim.* R' Yehudah HaNasi holds that the mixing is done after it is baked (*Mesiach Ilmim*).

6. By this description, Rashi (based on *Menachos* 75a) excludes שְׁתֵּי הַלֶּחֶם, "the Two Breads" meal-offering brought on Shavuos, and לֶחֶם הַפָּנִים, "the Bread of Surfaces" that was on the *Shulchan* (Table) in the *Beis HaMikdash* from week to week. A *kometz* was not scooped from these offerings (*Mizrachi; Sifsei Chachamim*).

7. *Toras Kohanim, perek* 12:5. See next note.

8. *Toras Kohanim, perek* 12:6. The apparently superfluous "it is a meal-offering" is used to apply both laws of this verse, crumbling and pouring, to other meal-offerings (*Gur Aryeh*).

25 / VAYIKRA/LEVITICUS — PARASHAS VAYIKRA — 2/7-10 — ב/ז-י

⁷ *If your offering is a meal-offering in a deep pan, it shall be made of fine flour with oil.* ⁸ *You shall present to* HASHEM *the meal-offering that will be prepared from these; he shall bring it to the Kohen and he shall bring it close to the Mizbe'ach.*

⁹ *The Kohen shall separate from the meal-offering its memorial portion and cause it to go up in smoke on the Mizbe'ach — a fire-offering, a satisfying aroma to* HASHEM. ¹⁰ *The remnant of the meal-offering is for Aaron and his sons — most holy, from the fire-offerings of* HASHEM.

ח מִנְחַת מַרְחֶשֶׁת קָרְבָּנֶךָ סֹלֶת בַּשֶּׁמֶן תֵּעָשֶׂה: וְהֵבֵאתָ אֶת־הַמִּנְחָה אֲשֶׁר יֵעָשֶׂה מֵאֵלֶּה לַיהוָה וְהִקְרִיבָהּ אֶל־הַכֹּהֵן וְהִגִּישָׁהּ ט אֶל־הַמִּזְבֵּחַ: וְהֵרִים הַכֹּהֵן מִן־הַמִּנְחָה אֶת־אַזְכָּרָתָהּ וְהִקְטִיר הַמִּזְבֵּחָה אִשֵּׁה רֵיחַ נִיחֹחַ לַיהוָה: י וְהַנּוֹתֶרֶת מִן־הַמִּנְחָה לְאַהֲרֹן וּלְבָנָיו קֹדֶשׁ קָדָשִׁים מֵאִשֵּׁי יְהוָה:

— אונקלוס —

מִנְחַת רְדִתָּא קָרְבָּנָךְ סֻלְתָּא בִּמְשַׁח תִּתְעֲבֵד: חוְתַיְתֵי יָת מִנְחָתָא דִּי תִתְעֲבֵד מֵאִלֵּין קֳדָם יְיָ וִיקָרְבִנַּהּ לְוָת כָּהֲנָא וִיקָרְבִנַּהּ לְמַדְבְּחָא: טוְיַפְרֵשׁ כַּהֲנָא מִן מִנְחָתָא יָת אִדְכַּרְתַּהּ וְיַסֵּק לְמַדְבְּחָא קֻרְבַּן דְּמִתְקַבַּל בְּרַעֲוָא קֳדָם יְיָ: יוּדְאִשְׁתָּאַר מִן מִנְחָתָא לְאַהֲרֹן וְלִבְנוֹהִי קֹדֶשׁ קוּדְשִׁין מִקֻּרְבָּנַיָּא דַּייָ:

— רש"י —

(ז) **מרחשת.** כְּלִי הוּא שֶׁהָיָה בַּמִּקְדָּשׁ עָמוֹק, וּמִתּוֹךְ שֶׁהִיא עֲמֻקָּה שַׁמְנָהּ צָבוּר וְאֵין הָאוּר שׂוֹרְפוֹ, לְפִיכָךְ מַעֲשֵׂי מִנְחָה הָעֲשׂוּיִין לְתוֹכָהּ רוֹחֲשִׁין (ת"כ פרק יב:ז; מנחות סג.). כָּל דָּבָר רַךְ ע"י מַשְׁקֶה נִרְאֶה כְּרוֹחֵשׁ וּמִתְנַעְנֵעַ. מֵאֶחָד מִן הַמִּינִים הַלָּלוּ. **והקריבה.** בְּעָלֶיהָ אֶל הַכֹּהֵן. **והגישה** הַכֹּהֵן **אל המזבח.** מַגִּיעָה [ס"א מגישה] לְקֶרֶן דְּרוֹמִית מַעֲרָבִית שֶׁל מִזְבֵּחַ (סוטה יד:): (ט) **את אזכרתה.** הִיא הַקּוֹמֶץ (ת"כ פרשתא ט:יב):

— RASHI ELUCIDATED —

it has been mixed. עֲלֶיהָ תַּלְמוּד לוֹמַר — To teach us otherwise, **the verse says, "upon** *it***,"** to exclude the meal-offering baked in an oven. אוֹצִיא אֶת הַחַלּוֹת — **I could** still **exclude** only **the loaves** baked in an oven וְלֹא אוֹצִיא אֶת הָרְקִיקִין — **but I would not exclude the wafers** baked in an oven. תַּלְמוּד לוֹמַר ״הוּא״ — To exclude the wafers, as well, **the verse says, "it,"** a second limiting word which excludes wafers baked in an oven.

7. מַרְחֶשֶׁת — A DEEP PAN. כְּלִי הוּא — **It is a vessel** שֶׁהָיָה בַּמִּקְדָּשׁ — **that was in the** *Beis HaMikdash;* עָמוֹק — it was **deep** וּמִתּוֹךְ שֶׁהִיא עֲמֻקָּה — **and, because it was deep,** שַׁמְנָהּ צָבוּר — **its oil gathered** to a considerable depth וְאֵין הָאוּר שׂוֹרְפוֹ — **and the fire did not burn it up** as it did to the oil in the shallow pan. לְפִיכָךְ — **Therefore,** מַעֲשֵׂי מִנְחָה הָעֲשׂוּיִין לְתוֹכָהּ רוֹחֲשִׁין[1] — **meal-offerings made in it "creep."**[1] כָּל דָּבָר רַךְ עַל יְדֵי מַשְׁקֶה — For **anything which is soft because of liquid** absorbed in it נִרְאֶה כְּרוֹחֵשׁ וּמִתְנַעְנֵעַ — **appears as if it is creeping and moving.**[2]

8. אֲשֶׁר יֵעָשֶׂה מֵאֵלֶּה — THAT WILL BE PREPARED FROM THESE. מֵאֶחָד מִן הַמִּינִים הַלָּלוּ — **From one of** these varieties.[3]

□ וְהִקְרִיבָהּ — HE SHALL BRING IT. That is, בְּעָלֶיהָ אֶל הַכֹּהֵן — **the owner** shall bring it **to the Kohen.**

□ וְהִגִּישָׁהּ — AND HE SHALL BRING IT CLOSE. That is, הַכֹּהֵן — **the Kohen** shall bring it.[4]

□ אֶל הַמִּזְבֵּחַ — TO THE *MIZBE'ACH.* מַגִּיעָה לְקֶרֶן דְּרוֹמִית מַעֲרָבִית שֶׁל מִזְבֵּחַ[5] — **He touches it to the** southwestern corner of the *Mizbe'ach.*[5]

9. אֶת אַזְכָּרָתָהּ — ITS MEMORIAL PORTION. הִיא הַקּוֹמֶץ[6] — **This is the threefingersful.**[6]

---

1. *Toras Kohanim, perek* 12:7; *Menachos* 63a.

2. The oil in such a cake gives it a resilient quality which causes it to move in a manner similar to creeping when pressed with a finger (see Rashi, *Menachos* 63a).

3. That is, from any of the varieties of meal-offering mentioned in this passage, to the exclusion of the Two Breads of Shavuos and the Bread of Surfaces which do not have to be brought to the southwestern corner of the *Mizbe'ach* (*Mizrachi; Sifsei Chachamim*).

4. The subjects of וְהִקְרִיבָהּ, "he shall bring it," and וְהִגִּישָׁהּ, "and he shall bring it close," are not the same. The first refers to the owner, the second to the Kohen (*Mizrachi; Sifsei Chachamim*).

5. *Sotah* 14b. Some editions of Rashi read מַגִּישָׁהּ instead of מַגִּיעָהּ, but the meaning is unchanged.

6. *Toras Kohanim, parshasa* 9:12. See Rashi to v. 2 above, s.v., אַזְכָּרָתָהּ.

¹¹ Any meal-offering that you offer to Hashem shall not be prepared leavened, for you shall not cause to go up in smoke from any leavening or any honey as a fire-offering to Hashem. ¹² You shall offer them as a first-fruit offering to Hashem, but they may not go up upon the Mizbe'ach for a satisfying aroma. ¹³ You shall salt your every meal-offering with salt; you may not discontinue the salt of your God's covenant from upon your meal-offering — on all your offerings shall you offer salt.

יא כָּל־הַמִּנְחָ֗ה אֲשֶׁ֤ר תַּקְרִ֙יבוּ֙ לַיהוָ֔ה לֹ֥א תֵעָשֶׂ֖ה חָמֵ֑ץ כִּ֤י כָל־שְׂאֹר֙ וְכָל־דְּבַ֔שׁ לֹא־תַקְטִ֧ירוּ מִמֶּ֛נּוּ אִשֶּׁ֖ה לַיהוָה׃ יב קָרְבַּ֥ן רֵאשִׁ֛ית תַּקְרִ֥יבוּ אֹתָ֖ם לַיהוָ֑ה וְאֶל־הַמִּזְבֵּ֥חַ לֹא־יַעֲל֖וּ לְרֵ֥יחַ נִיחֹֽחַ׃ יג וְכָל־קָרְבַּ֣ן מִנְחָתְךָ֮ בַּמֶּ֣לַח תִּמְלָח֒ וְלֹ֣א תַשְׁבִּ֗ית מֶ֚לַח בְּרִ֣ית אֱלֹהֶ֔יךָ מֵעַ֖ל מִנְחָתֶ֑ךָ עַ֥ל כָּל־קָרְבָּנְךָ֖ תַּקְרִ֥יב מֶֽלַח׃ יד וְאִם־

───── אונקלוס ─────

יא כָּל מִנְחָתָא דִּי תְקָרְבוּן קֳדָם יְיָ לָא תִתְעֲבֵד חֲמִיעַ אֲרֵי כָל חֲמִיר וְכָל דְּבַשׁ לָא תַסְּקוּן מִנֵּהּ קֻרְבָּנָא קֳדָם יְיָ: יב קֻרְבַּן קַדְמָי תְּקָרְבוּן יָתְהוֹן קֳדָם יְיָ וּלְמַדְבְּחָא לָא תַסְּקוּן לְאִתְקַבָּלָא בְרַעֲוָא: יג וְכָל קֻרְבַּן מִנְחָתָךְ בְּמִלְחָא תִמְלַח וְלָא תְבַטֵּל מְלַח קְיָם אֱלָהָךְ מֵעַל מִנְחָתָךְ עַל כָּל קֻרְבָּנָךְ תְּקָרֵב מִלְחָא: יד וְאִם

───── רש״י ─────

(יא) וְכָל דְּבָשׁ. כָּל מְתִיקַת פְּרִי קְרוּיָה דְּבַשׁ: (יב) קָרְבַּן רֵאשִׁית תַּקְרִיבוּ אוֹתָם. מַה יֵשׁ לְךָ לְהָבִיא מִן הַשְּׂאוֹר וּמִן הַדְּבַשׁ, קָרְבַּן רֵאשִׁית. שְׁתֵּי הַלֶּחֶם שֶׁל עֲצֶרֶת הַבָּאִים מִן הֶחָמֵץ, שֶׁנֶּאֱמַר חָמֵץ תֵּאָפֶינָה, וּבִכּוּרִים מִן הַדְּבַשׁ, כְּמוֹ בִּכּוּרֵי תְאֵנִים וּתְמָרִים: (יג) מֶלַח בְּרִית. שֶׁהַבְּרִית כְּרוּתָה לַמֶּלַח מִשֵּׁשֶׁת יְמֵי בְרֵאשִׁית, שֶׁהֻבְטְחוּ הַמַּיִם הַתַּחְתּוֹנִים לִקָּרֵב בַּמִּזְבֵּחַ בְּמֶלַח, וְנִסּוּךְ הַמַּיִם בֶּחָג: עַל כָּל קָרְבָּנְךָ. עַל עוֹלַת בְּהֵמָה וָעוֹף וְאֵמוּרֵי כָּל הַקֳּדָשִׁים כֻּלָּן (ת״כ פרק יד:ג; מנחות כ.):

───── RASHI ELUCIDATED ─────

11. וְכָל דְּבַשׁ — **OR ANY HONEY.** כָּל מְתִיקַת פְּרִי קְרוּיָה דְּבַשׁ — **Anything sweet which comes from fruit is referred to as honey.**[1]

12. קָרְבַּן רֵאשִׁית תַּקְרִיבוּ אֹתָם — **YOU SHALL OFFER THEM AS A FIRST-FRUIT OFFERING.** מַה יֵּשׁ לְךָ לְהָבִיא ״קָרְבַּן רֵאשִׁית״ מִן הַשְּׂאוֹר וּמִן הַדְּבַשׁ — **What can you bring from the leavening and from the honey?** — "The first-fruit offering," which includes שְׁתֵּי הַלֶּחֶם שֶׁל עֲצֶרֶת — **the Two Breads of Shavuos** הַבָּאִים מִן הַשְּׂאוֹר — **which come from the leavening,** שֶׁנֶּאֱמַר חָמֵץ תֵּאָפֶינָה — **as it says, "they shall be baked leavened,"**[2] וּבִכּוּרִים מִן הַדְּבַשׁ — **and the first fruits** which can be brought **from the honey,** כְּמוֹ בִּכּוּרֵי תְאֵנִים וּתְמָרִים — **such as the first fruits of figs and dates** from which honey can be made.[3]

13. מֶלַח בְּרִית — **THE SALT OF [YOUR GOD'S] COVENANT.** שֶׁהַבְּרִית כְּרוּתָה לַמֶּלַח — **For a covenant has been made with salt** מִשֵּׁשֶׁת יְמֵי בְרֵאשִׁית — **since the six days of Creation,** שֶׁהֻבְטְחוּ הַמַּיִם הַתַּחְתּוֹנִים — **for the lower,** i.e., earthly, **waters were promised** לִקָּרֵב בַּמִּזְבֵּחַ — **to be offered on the** *Mizbe'ach* בְּמֶלַח — **in the form of salt**[4] וְנִסּוּךְ הַמַּיִם בֶּחָג — **and at the pouring of the water** on the *Mizbe'ach* on Succos.[5]

עַל כָּל קָרְבָּנְךָ — **ON ALL YOUR OFFERINGS.** עַל עוֹלַת בְּהֵמָה וָעוֹף — **On** *olah*-**offerings of livestock and fowl** וְאֵמוּרֵי כָּל הַקֳּדָשִׁים כֻּלָּן — **and the parts burned upon the** *Mizbe'ach* **of all that is consecrated.**[6]

---

1. The next verse says that the offering of first fruits can come from this honey. It cannot therefore refer exclusively to bee's honey (*Mizrachi; Sifsei Chachamim*). Rashi to *Exodus* 13:5 (based on *Kesubos* 111b) explains the phrase "a land flowing with milk and honey" in a similar manner: "Milk flows from the goats and honey flows from the dates and from the figs."
 Nevertheless, the prohibition of this verse does include bee's honey (*Be'er BaSadeh*).

2. Below 23:17. The Two Breads is a first-fruit offering in that it permits flour from the new crop to be brought as offerings.

3. *Menachos* 58a.

4. Dead Sea salt was used if it was available (see *Menachos* 21a), for it represented the covenant with the waters of the earth.

5. *Ramban* cites this passage from Rashi and adds וּמִדְרַשׁ חֲכָמִים הוּא, "It is a Midrash of the Sages." A similar teaching appears in *Midrash Aseres HaDibros*, Chap. 1, and is cited by *Rabbeinu Bachya*.

6. *Toras Kohanim, perek* 14:3; *Menachos* 20a.

27 / VAYIKRA/LEVITICUS — PARASHAS VAYIKRA — ב/יד

תַּקְרִיב מִנְחַת בִּכּוּרִים לַיהוָה
אָבִיב קָלוּי בָּאֵשׁ גֶּרֶשׂ כַּרְמֶל
תַּקְרִיב אֶת מִנְחַת בִּכּוּרֶיךָ:

14 *When you will bring a meal-offering of first fruits to* Hashem: *from ripe ears, parched over fire, ground from plump kernels, shall you offer the meal-offering of your first grain.*

— אונקלוס —

תְּקָרֵב מִנְחַת בִּכּוּרִין קֳדָם יְיָ אָבִיב קְלֵי בְּנוּר פֵּרוּכָן רַכִּיכָן תְּקָרֵב יָת מִנְחַת בִּכּוּרָךְ:

— רש״י —

(יד) וְאִם תַּקְרִיב. הֲרֵי אִם מְשַׁמֵּשׁ בְּלָ׳, כִּי שֶׁהֲרֵי אֵין זֶה רְשׁוּת, שֶׁהֲרֵי בְּמִנְחַת הָעוֹמֶר הַכָּתוּב מְדַבֵּר שֶׁהִיא חוֹבָה, וְכֵן וְאִם יִהְיֶה הַיּוֹבֵל וְגוֹ׳ (במדבר לו:ד); ת״כ פרשתא יג:ב): **מִנְחַת בִּכּוּרִים.** בְּמִנְחַת הָעוֹמֶר הַכָּתוּב מְדַבֵּר, שֶׁהִיא בָאָה אָבִיב בִּשְׁעַת בִּשּׁוּל הַתְּבוּאָה וּמִן הַשְּׂעוֹרִים הִיא בָאָה, נֶאֱמַר כָּאן אָבִיב וְנֶאֱמַר לְהַלָּן ,,כִּי הַשְּׂעֹרָה אָבִיב״: **קָלוּי בָּאֵשׁ.** שֶׁמְּיַבְּשִׁין

אוֹתָהּ עַל הָאוּר בְּאַבּוּב שֶׁל קְלָאִים (מנחות סו:) שֶׁאִלּוּלֵי כֵן אֵינָהּ נִטְחֶנֶת בָּרֵחַיִם לְפִי שֶׁהִיא לַחָה: **גֶּרֶשׂ כַּרְמֶל.** גְּרוּסָה בְּעוֹדָהּ לַחָה: **גֶּרֶשׂ.** לְ׳ שְׁבִירָה וּטְחִינָה (גסה), גּוֹרְסָהּ בְּרֵחַיִם שֶׁל גְּרוּסוֹת כְּמוֹ וַיַּגְרֵס בֶּחָצָץ (איכה ג:טז) וְכֵן גָּרְסָה נַפְשִׁי (תהלים קיט:כ): **כַּרְמֶל.** בְּעוֹד הַכַּר מָלֵא (מנחות שם) שֶׁהַתְּבוּאָה לַחָה וּמְלֵאָה בְּקַשִּׁין שֶׁלָּה וְעַל כֵּן נִקְרָאִים הַמְּלִילוֹת כַּרְמֶל,

— RASHI ELUCIDATED —

14. וְאִם תַּקְרִיב — WHEN YOU WILL BRING. הֲרֵי ,,אִם״ מְשַׁמֵּשׁ בִּלְשׁוֹן ,,כִּי״ — Here the word אִם is used in the sense of כִּי, "when,"[1] שֶׁהֲרֵי אֵין זֶה רְשׁוּת — for this offering is not optional שֶׁהֲרֵי בְּמִנְחַת הָעוֹמֶר — שֶׁהִיא חוֹבָה — which is an obligation, הַכָּתוּב מְדַבֵּר — as the verse speaks of the meal-offering of the *omer*[2] וְכֵן ,,וְאִם יִהְיֶה הַיּוֹבֵל וְגוֹמֵר״ — Similarly the word אִם as used in "when the Children of Israel will have the *yovel*, etc."[3] means "when."[4]

□ מִנְחַת בִּכּוּרִים — A MEAL-OFFERING OF FIRST FRUITS. בְּמִנְחַת הָעוֹמֶר הַכָּתוּב מְדַבֵּר — The verse speaks of the meal-offering of the *omer* שֶׁהִיא בָאָה אָבִיב — which comes, i.e., is brought, from nearly ripe ears בִּשְׁעַת בִּשּׁוּל הַתְּבוּאָה — at the time of the ripening of the crop.[5] וּמִן הַשְּׂעוֹרִים הִיא בָאָה — It comes from barley.[6] The source for this is the following: נֶאֱמַר כָּאן אָבִיב — The word אָבִיב is said here,[7,8] וְנֶאֱמַר לְהַלָּן ,,כִּי הַשְּׂעֹרָה אָבִיב״ — and the word אָבִיב is said elsewhere, in the verse, "for the barley had nearly ripened."[7] Just as that verse speaks of barley, so, too, does this one.[8]

□ קָלוּי בָּאֵשׁ — PARCHED OVER FIRE. שֶׁמְּיַבְּשִׁין אוֹתָהּ עַל הָאוּר — For they dry it over fire בְּאַבּוּב שֶׁל קְלָאִים[9] — in a grain-roasters' cylinder,[9] שֶׁאִלּוּלֵי כֵן — because otherwise, אֵינָהּ נִטְחֶנֶת בָּרֵחַיִם — it cannot be ground in a mill, לְפִי שֶׁהִיא לַחָה — because it is too moist.

□ גֶּרֶשׂ כַּרְמֶל — GROUND FROM PLUMP KERNELS. This means, גְּרוּסָה בְּעוֹדָהּ לַחָה — it is ground while it is still moist.[10]

□ גֶּרֶשׂ — GROUND. לְשׁוֹן שְׁבִירָה וּטְחִינָה — The word גֶּרֶשׂ expresses breaking and grinding. גּוֹרְסָהּ[11] — He crushes it[11] בְּרֵחַיִם שֶׁל גְּרוּסוֹת — in a grist-grinders' mill. כְּמוֹ ,,וַיַּגְרֵס בֶּחָצָץ״[12] — The term גֶּרֶשׂ is akin to וַיַּגְרֵס in, "He broke [my teeth] with gravel."[12] וְכֵן ,,גָּרְסָה נַפְשִׁי״[13] — And similarly גָּרְסָה in, "My soul is shattered."[13]

□ כַּרְמֶל — PLUMP KERNELS. בְּעוֹד הַכַּר מָלֵא[14] — While the pillow is full,[14] שֶׁהַתְּבוּאָה לַחָה — because the crop is moist וּמְלֵאָה בְּקַשִּׁין שֶׁלָּה — and full in its spikes. וְעַל כֵּן נִקְרָאִים הַמְּלִילוֹת כַּרְמֶל — This

---

1. אִם usually means "if."
2. See below 23:9-13; see also Rashi's next comment.
3. *Numbers* 36:4.
4. *Toras Kohanim, parshasa* 13:2.
5. Barley is the earliest of the grains of Eretz Yisrael to ripen. It is fully ripe when other grains are beginning to ripen. See Rashi to *Nedarim* 62b.
6. As opposed to other meal-offerings which are of wheat flour.
7. *Exodus* 9:31.
8. *Toras Kohanim, parshasa* 13:4.
9. *Menachos* 66b.
10. Although the barley was parched over fire, it still retained some of its moisture (*Leket Bahir*).
11. Some editions of Rashi read וּטְחִינָה גַסָּה, "and coarse grinding." Some omit both גַסָּה and גּוֹרְסָהּ.
12. *Lamentations* 3:16.
13. *Psalms* 119:20. The letters ס and שׂ are virtually the same letter and may be interchanged. Some other examples are: שְׂטִים (*Hosea* 5:2) and סֵטִים (*Psalms* 101:3), "wayward"; מַּבְעֵשׂ (*Psalms* 6:8) and מְבַעֵשׂ (*Job* 17:7), "because of anger"; שׂוֹכְרִים (*II Chronicles* 24:12) and וְסֹכְרִים (*Ezra* 4:5), "they hired." It is also noteworthy that many of the *piyutim* (liturgical poems) composed with an alphabetic acrostic use a שׂ where a ס is expected.
14. *Menachos* 66b. When the stalks are full of ripe kernels, and resemble a full pillow (*Sefer Zikaron*).

15 You shall put oil on it and place frankincense on it — a meal-offering. **16** The Kohen shall cause its memorial portion to go up in smoke — from its flour and its oil, as well as its frankincense — a fire-offering to HASHEM.

3

1 If his offering is a sacrifice of a peace-offering, if he offers it from the cattle — whether male or female — unblemished shall he offer it before HASHEM. **2** He shall lean his hands upon the head of his offering and slaughter it at the entrance of the Tent of Meeting; the sons of Aaron, the Kohanim, shall throw the blood upon the Mizbe'ach, all around. **3** From the sacrifice of the peace-offering he shall offer as a fire-offering to HASHEM: the fat that covers the innards, and all the fat that is upon the innards; **4** and the two

טו וְנָתַתָּ עָלֶיהָ שֶׁמֶן וְשַׂמְתָּ עָלֶיהָ לְבֹנָה מִנְחָה הִוא: וְהִקְטִיר הַכֹּהֵן אֶת־אַזְכָּרָתָהּ מִגִּרְשָׂהּ וּמִשַּׁמְנָהּ עַל כָּל־לְבֹנָתָהּ אִשֶּׁה לַיהוָה:

ג א רביעי וְאִם־זֶבַח שְׁלָמִים קָרְבָּנוֹ אִם מִן־הַבָּקָר הוּא מַקְרִיב אִם־זָכָר אִם־נְקֵבָה תָּמִים יַקְרִיבֶנּוּ לִפְנֵי יְהוָה: וְסָמַךְ יָדוֹ עַל־רֹאשׁ קָרְבָּנוֹ וּשְׁחָטוֹ פֶּתַח אֹהֶל מוֹעֵד וְזָרְקוּ בְּנֵי אַהֲרֹן הַכֹּהֲנִים אֶת־הַדָּם עַל־הַמִּזְבֵּחַ סָבִיב: וְהִקְרִיב מִזֶּבַח הַשְּׁלָמִים אִשֶּׁה לַיהוָה אֶת־הַחֵלֶב הַמְכַסֶּה אֶת־הַקֶּרֶב וְאֵת כָּל־הַחֵלֶב אֲשֶׁר עַל־הַקֶּרֶב: וְאֵת שְׁתֵּי

אונקלוס — טו וְתִתֵּן עֲלַהּ מִשְׁחָא וּתְשַׁוֵּי עֲלַהּ לְבוֹנְתָּא מִנְחָתָא הִיא: טז וְיַסֵּק כַּהֲנָא יָת אִדְכַּרְתַּהּ מִפֵּירוּכַהּ וּמִמִּשְׁחַהּ עַל כָּל לְבוֹנְתַּהּ קֻרְבָּנָא קֳדָם יְיָ: א וְאִם נִכְסַת קוּדְשַׁיָּא קֻרְבָּנֵהּ אִם מִן תּוֹרֵי הוּא מְקָרֵב אִם דְּכַר אִם נֻקְבָּא שְׁלִים יְקָרְבִנֵּהּ קֳדָם יְיָ: ב וְיִסְמוֹךְ יְדֵהּ עַל רֵישׁ קֻרְבָּנֵהּ וְיִכְסִנֵּהּ בִּתְרַע מַשְׁכַּן זִמְנָא וְיִזְרְקוּן בְּנֵי אַהֲרֹן כַּהֲנַיָּא יָת דְּמָא עַל מַדְבְּחָא סְחוֹר סְחוֹר: ג וִיקָרֵב מִנִּכְסַת קוּדְשַׁיָּא קֻרְבָּנָא קֳדָם יְיָ יָת תַּרְבָּא דְּחָפֵי יָת גַּוָּא וְיָת כָּל תַּרְבָּא דִּי עַל גַּוָּא: ד וְיָת תַּרְתֵּין

רש"י — וכן בצלקלונו (מלכים ב ד:מב): **(א) שלמים.** שמטילים שלום ולבעלים (שם ב): **(ג) ואת כל החלב וגו'.** להביא חלב שעל הקבה, דברי רבי ישמעאל. רבי עקיבא אומר, להביא חלב שעל הדקין בעולם (ת"כ פרק טז:א). ד"א שלמים שיש בהם שלום למזבח ולכהנים

RASHI ELUCIDATED

is why the kernels are called בַּרְמֶל."[1] — וְכֵן, Similarly, וְכַרְמֶל בְּצִקְלוֹנוֹ[2] — in, "and plump kernels in their husks."[2]

3.

1. שְׁלָמִים — PEACE-OFFERING[S]. — שֶׁמְּטִילִים שָׁלוֹם בָּעוֹלָם[3] — They are called "peace-offerings" **because they bring peace into the world.**[3] {דָּבָר אַחֵר — **Alternatively:**} שְׁלָמִים — They are called **"peace-offerings"** שֶׁיֵּשׁ בָּהֶם שָׁלוֹם — **because there is peace in them** — לַמִּזְבֵּחַ — **for the** *Mizbe'ach*, וְלַכֹּהֲנִים — **and for the** Kohanim, וְלַבְּעָלִים[4] — **and for the owner,** i.e., the one bringing the offering.[4]

3. וְאֵת כָּל הַחֵלֶב וְגוֹמֵר — AND ALL THE FAT, ETC. — לְהָבִיא חֵלֶב שֶׁעַל הַקֵּבָה — This is stated **to include the fat that is on the stomach.** דִּבְרֵי רַבִּי יִשְׁמָעֵאל — **This is the opinion** of the *Tanna* **R' Yishmael.** רַבִּי עֲקִיבָא אוֹמֵר — The *Tanna* **R' Akiva says** that this is stated לְהָבִיא חֵלֶב שֶׁעַל הַדַּקִּין — **to include the fat that is on the small intestines.**[5]

---

1. כַּרְמֶל is a contraction of בַּר, "pillow," and מָלֵא, "full" (*Mizrachi; Sifsei Chachamim*; based on *Shabbos* 105a).
2. *II Kings* 4:42.
3. *Toras Kohanim, perek* 16:1.
4. *Toras Kohanim, perek* 16:2. The offering "brings peace" in that all involved receive a portion in it — there are parts which are burned on the *Mizbe'ach*, the breast and part of the rear right leg go to the Kohanim, and the rest of the flesh goes to those who are bringing the offering (*Be'er Yitzchak*). Rashi's alternative explanation also explains why שְׁלָמִים is a plural word — it brings many types of peace.

Some early editions omit the words דָּבָר אַחֵר, "alternatively." *Gur Aryeh* apparently had that reading before him, for he explains that the plural form of the word שְׁלָמִים indicates two types of peace: (a) peace in the world; (b) peace for the *Mizbe'ach*, the Kohanim, and the owner.

5. *Toras Kohanim, parshasa* 14:6. "All the fat" mentioned here must be similar to "the fat on the innards" (קֶרֶב) mentioned before it in the verse. R' Yishmael is of the opinion that all fats referred to are similar because they all are covered by a membrane that can be peeled away. This applies to the fat on the

kidneys with the fat that is upon them, that is upon the flanks, and he shall remove the diaphragm with the liver, with the kidneys. ⁵ *The sons of Aaron shall cause it to go up in smoke on the Mizbe'ach,*

הַכְּלָיֹת וְאֶת־הַחֵלֶב אֲשֶׁר עֲלֵהֶן אֲשֶׁר עַל־הַכְּסָלִים וְאֶת־הַיֹּתֶרֶת עַל־הַכָּבֵד עַל־הַכְּלָיוֹת יְסִירֶנָּה: ה וְהִקְטִירוּ אֹתוֹ בְנֵי־אַהֲרֹן הַמִּזְבֵּחָה

— אונקלוס —

כָּלְיָן וְיָת תַּרְבָּא דִי עֲלֵיהֶן עַל גִּסְסַיָּא וְיָת חִצְרָא דְעַל כַּבְדָּא עַל כָּלְיָתָא יַעְדִּנַּהּ: ה וְיַסְּקוּן יָתֵהּ בְּנֵי אַהֲרֹן לְמַדְבְּחָא

— רש"י —

(שם פרשתא יד:ו): (ד) **הכסלים**. פלנק"ש בלע"ז שהחלב שעל הכליות כשהבהמה חיה הוא בגובה הכסלים והם מלמטה, וזהו החלב שתחת המתנים שקורין בלע"ז לונביל"ש, לובן הנראה למעלה בגובה הכסלים ובתחתיתו הבשר חופהו: **היותרת**. הוא דופן המסך שקורין איברי"ש, ובל' ארמי חצרא דכבדא: **על הכבד**. שיטול מן הכבד עמה מעט (ת"כ שם ח), ובמקום אחר הוא אומר ואת היותרת מן הכבד (להלן ט:י): **על הכבד ועל הכליות**. לבד מן הכבד ולבד מן הכליות יסירנה לזו:

— RASHI ELUCIDATED —

4. שֶׁהַחֵלֶב שֶׁעַל הַכְּלָיוֹת — **For the fat that is on the kidneys,** הַכְּסָלִים — THE FLANKS. {פלנק"ש בלע"ז — *flancs* in Old French.} כְּשֶׁהַבְּהֵמָה חַיָּה — **when the animal is alive** and standing up הוּא בְּגוֹבַהּ הַכְּסָלִים — **is at the upper part of the flanks,** וְהֵם מִלְּמַטָּה — **and they,** the kidneys, **are below** in a lower position than the fat.[1] וְזֶהוּ הַחֵלֶב שֶׁתַּחַת הַמָּתְנַיִם — **This is the fat which is under the loins** שֶׁקּוֹרִין בלע"ז לונביל"ש — **which they call** *lonbels* **in Old French.**[2] לוֹבֶן הַנִּרְאֶה לְמַעְלָה — **It is the whiteness visible at the top,** i.e., the whiteness whose upper part is visible, בְּגוֹבַהּ הַכְּסָלִים — **at the upper part of the flanks,** וּבְתַחְתִּיתוֹ הַבָּשָׂר חוֹפֵהוּ — **and the flesh covers it [this fat] at its lower part.**

□ הַיֹּתֶרֶת — THE DIAPHRAGM. הוּא דֹפֶן הַמָּסָךְ — **It is the wall which acts as a partition**[3] שֶׁקּוֹרִין איברי"ש — **which they call** *ebres* in Old French, וּבִלְשׁוֹן אֲרַמִּי — **and in the Aramaic language,** חִצְרָא דְכַבְדָּא — "**the courtyard of the liver.**"[4]

□ עַל הַכָּבֵד — WITH THE LIVER. שֶׁיִּטּוֹל מִן הַכָּבֵד עִמָּהּ מְעַט — **That he should take a bit of the liver along with it.**[5] We see that not all of the liver is burned because וּבְמָקוֹם אַחֵר הוּא אוֹמֵר — **elsewhere it says,** וְאֶת הַיֹּתֶרֶת מִן הַכָּבֵד — "**the diaphragm, [and] from the liver.**"[6]

□ עַל הַכָּבֵד עַל הַכְּלָיוֹת — WITH THE LIVER, WITH THE KIDNEYS. This means, לְבַד מִן הַכָּבֵד וּלְבַד מִן הַכְּלָיוֹת יְסִירֶנָּה לָזוֹ — **aside from the liver, and aside from the kidneys, he** also **should remove [the diaphragm].**[7]

---

stomach (קֵבָה), as well as to the fat on the small intestines. R' Akiva holds that the fat referred to here must be similar to "the fat on the innards" in an additional aspect. It must lie as an unbroken covering, like a garment spread out over the flesh. This additional qualification excludes the fat on the stomach, for that fat is composed of several pieces and thus does not lie as an unbroken covering. Therefore, "all the fat" applies only to the fat on the small intestines (see *Chullin* 49a-b and Rashi there; *Mizrachi*; *Sifsei Chachamim*).

1. Rashi explains in what sense this fat is "on" the flanks. When the animal is alive and standing, the fat is situated toward the top of the flanks. עַל, "on," is being used in the sense of "above," and not in the sense of "which is part of" (*Devek Tov*).

2. This old French word, also spelled *"lombles"* or *"lonbels,"* was used for both "loins" and "kidneys." The Modern French derivative *"lombes"* means "loins." The Modern English "lumbar" refers to the loins and the vertebrae that are adjacent to the loins.

3. It is the membrane that separates the digestive organs from the respiratory organs (*Mizrachi*; *Sifsei Chachamim*). The digestive organ adjacent to the diaphragm is the liver; therefore the Torah always mentions the כָּבֵד, "liver," when it mentions the יֹתֶרֶת, "diaphragm."

4. The Hebrew form of this Aramaic term, חֲצַר כָּבֵד, appears in *Chullin* 38b. Rashi there (and in Exodus 29:13) also gives the Old French translation *"ebres."* The Aramaic translation of *Targum Onkelos* reads חִצְרָא דְעַל כַּבְדָּא to account for the word עַל of the Hebrew verse. When the phrase omits the word עַל (e.g. 9:19 below), *Onkelos* translates חֲצַר כַּבְדָּא.

5. *Toras Kohanim, parshasa* 14:8. עַל here is understood as "along with," or "as well as," not as "on" (*Mizrachi*; *Sifsei Chachamim*). See Rashi to *Exodus* 35:22 for another example of this usage. עַל הַכָּבֵד of our verse cannot be understood as "on the liver," giving the location of the diaphragm, for the diaphragm is not situated *on* the liver, but rather, next to it (*Sefer Zikaron*).

6. Below 9:10. Rashi cites the verse below which uses מִן to show that only part of the liver is burned — one offers *from* the liver, not all of the liver (*Sefer Zikaron*).

7. Rashi gives a similar interpretation of עַל in 2:2 above (s.v., עַל כָּל לְבֹנָתָהּ) and in *Exodus* 29:13.

עַל־הָעֹלָה אֲשֶׁר עַל־הָעֵצִים אֲשֶׁר עַל־הָאֵשׁ אִשֵּׁה רֵיחַ נִיחֹחַ לַיהוָה׃ וְאִם־מִן־הַצֹּאן קָרְבָּנוֹ לְזֶבַח שְׁלָמִים לַיהוָה זָכָר אוֹ נְקֵבָה תָּמִים יַקְרִיבֶנּוּ׃ אִם־כֶּשֶׂב הוּא־מַקְרִיב אֶת־קָרְבָּנוֹ וְהִקְרִיב אֹתוֹ לִפְנֵי יְהוָה׃ וְסָמַךְ אֶת־יָדוֹ עַל־רֹאשׁ קָרְבָּנוֹ וְשָׁחַט אֹתוֹ לִפְנֵי אֹהֶל מוֹעֵד וְזָרְקוּ בְּנֵי אַהֲרֹן אֶת־דָּמוֹ עַל־הַמִּזְבֵּחַ סָבִיב׃ וְהִקְרִיב מִזֶּבַח הַשְּׁלָמִים אִשֶּׁה לַיהוָה חֶלְבּוֹ הָאַלְיָה תְמִימָה

with the olah-offering that is on the wood that is on the fire — a fire-offering, a satisfying aroma to Hashem. **⁶** If his offering to Hashem is a sacrifice of a peace-offering from the flock — male or female — unblemished shall he offer it. **⁷** If he offers a sheep as his offering, he shall bring it before Hashem. **⁸** He shall lean his hands upon the head of his offering and slaughter it before the Tent of Meeting; and the sons of Aaron shall throw its blood upon the Mizbe'ach, all around. **⁹** From the sacrifice of the peace-offering he shall offer as a fire-offering to Hashem its choicest part — the entire tail

──── אונקלוס ────

עַל עֲלָתָא דִּי עַל אָעַיָּא דִּי עַל אֶשָּׁתָא קָרְבַּן דְּמִתְקַבֵּל בְּרַעֲוָא קֳדָם יְיָ: ו וְאִם מִן עָנָא קָרְבָּנֵהּ לְנִכְסַת קוּדְשַׁיָּא קֳדָם יְיָ דְּכַר אוֹ נוּקְבָא שְׁלִים יְקָרְבִנֵּיהּ: ז אִם אִמַּר הוּא מְקָרֵב יָת קָרְבָּנֵהּ וִיקָרֵב יָתֵהּ קֳדָם יְיָ: ח וְיִסְמֹךְ יָת יְדֵהּ עַל רֵישׁ קָרְבָּנֵהּ וְיִכּוֹס יָתֵהּ קֳדָם מַשְׁכַּן זִמְנָא וְיִזְרְקוּן בְּנֵי אַהֲרֹן יָת דְּמֵהּ עַל מַדְבְּחָא סְחוֹר סְחוֹר: ט וִיקָרֵב מִנִּכְסַת קוּדְשַׁיָּא קָרְבָּנָא קֳדָם יְיָ תַּרְבֵּהּ אַלִּיתָא שְׁלֶמְתָּא

──── רש"י ────

(ה) **על העולה.** מלבד העולה. למדנו שתקדוס עולת תמיד לכל קרבן על המערכה: (ז) **אם כשב.** לפי שיש באימורי הכשב מה שאין באימורי העז שהכשב אליתו קריבה, לכך

נחלקו לשתי פרשיות: (ח) **וזרקו.** שתי מתנות שהן ד׳, ועל ידי הכלי הוא זורק ואינו נותן באצבע אלא בחטאת (וזבחיס נג.): (ט) **חלבו.** המובחר שבו ומהו זה האליה תמימה

──── RASHI ELUCIDATED ────

5. עַל הָעֹלָה — WITH THE OLAH-OFFERING. This means מִלְּבַד הָעוֹלָה — aside from the *olah-* offering. לָמַדְנוּ — We have learned from here שֶׁתִּקְדּוֹם עוֹלַת תָּמִיד — that the regular *olah-* offering should precede לְכָל קָרְבָּן — any other offering עַל הַמַּעֲרָכָה — on the arrangement of wood on the *Mizbe'ach*.[1]

7. אִם כֶּשֶׂב — IF [HE OFFERS] A SHEEP. לְפִי שֶׁיֵּשׁ בְּאִימוּרֵי הַכֶּשֶׂב — Because there is an item among the parts specified of a sheep for burning on the *Mizbe'ach* מַה שֶׁאֵין בְּאִימוּרֵי הָעֵז — which is not among the specified parts of a goat, שֶׁהַכֶּשֶׂב אַלְיָתוֹ קְרֵבָה — for in the case of the sheep its tail is offered, לְכָךְ נֶחְלְקוּ לִשְׁתֵּי פָרָשִׁיּוֹת — therefore [the peace-offerings of the sheep and the goat] were divided into two separate passages.[2]

8. וְזָרְקוּ — AND [THE SONS OF AARON] SHALL THROW. שְׁתֵּי מַתָּנוֹת שֶׁהֵן אַרְבַּע — Two applications which are four.[3] וְעַל יְדֵי הַכְּלִי הוּא זוֹרֵק — He throws the blood by means of a vessel, וְאֵינוֹ נוֹתֵן בְּאֶצְבַּע — and he does not apply it with a finger אֶלָּא בְחַטָּאת[4] — except in the case of a sin-offering.[4]

9. חֶלְבּוֹ — ITS CHOICEST PART. This means הַמּוּבְחָר שֶׁבּוֹ — the choicest part that is in it. וּמַהוּ — And what is it? זֶה — This is הָאַלְיָה תְמִימָה — the entire tail.[5]

---

1. The *olah-* offering of the expression עַל הָעֹלָה, which Rashi interprets as "aside from the *olah-* offering," is the *tamid*, the regular *olah-* offering brought each morning. Since the peace-offering that is the subject of our verse is to be offered "aside from the *tamid*," the *tamid* must already have been offered, otherwise the term "aside from" makes no sense (*Gur Aryeh*; see, too, *Numbers* 28:10 and Rashi and *Sifsei Chachamim* there).

2. This is in contrast to the *olah-* offering (above 1:10-13) in which offerings of sheep and goats were discussed in the same passage (*Mizrachi; Sifsei Chachamim*).

3. See Rashi to 1:5 above, s.v., וְזָרְקוּ.

4. *Zevachim* 53a; see below 4:25,30.

5. In his comments on *Genesis* 45:18, Rashi notes that (although חֵלֶב is usually translated "fat") the basic meaning of חֵלֶב is "the choicest," "the best." There, the context rules out "fat." Here, too, חֶלְבּוֹ cannot be "its fat." For without a ו in front of it הָאַלְיָה rather than (וְהָאַלְיָה), הָאַלְיָה stands in apposition to חֶלְבּוֹ, i.e., הָאַלְיָה is one and the same as חֶלְבּוֹ, and not something else. Since the tail is not composed wholly of fat, חֶלְבּוֹ in our verse cannot mean "its fat" (*Be'er Yitzchak*).

31 / VAYIKRA/LEVITICUS — PARASHAS VAYIKRA — 3/10-15

— he shall remove it above the kidneys; and the fat that covers the innards and all the fat that is upon the innards; **10** *and the two kidneys and the fat that is upon them, that is upon the flanks; and he shall remove the diaphragm with the liver, with the kidneys.* **11** *The Kohen shall cause it to go up in smoke on the Mizbe'ach; it is the food of the fire, for* Hashem.

12 *If his offering is a goat, he shall bring it before* Hashem. **13** *He shall lean his hands upon its head and slaughter it before the Tent of Meeting; and the sons of Aaron shall throw its blood upon the Mizbe'ach, all around.* **14** *He shall bring his offering from it as a fire-offering to* Hashem: *the fat that covers the innards and all the fat that is upon the innards;* **15** *and the two kidneys and the fat that is upon them, that is upon the flanks;*

לְעֻמַּ֤ת הֶֽעָצֶה֙ יְסִירֶ֔נָּה וְאֶת־הַחֵ֗לֶב הַֽמְכַסֶּה֙ אֶת־הַקֶּ֔רֶב וְאֵ֥ת כָּל־הַחֵ֖לֶב אֲשֶׁ֥ר עַל־הַקֶּֽרֶב: י וְאֵת֙ שְׁתֵּ֣י הַכְּלָיֹ֔ת וְאֶת־הַחֵ֨לֶב֙ אֲשֶׁ֣ר עֲלֵהֶ֔ן אֲשֶׁ֖ר עַל־הַכְּסָלִ֑ים וְאֶת־הַיֹּתֶ֙רֶת֙ עַל־הַכָּבֵ֔ד עַל־הַכְּלָיֹ֖ת יְסִירֶֽנָּה: יא וְהִקְטִיר֥וֹ הַכֹּהֵ֖ן הַמִּזְבֵּ֑חָה לֶ֥חֶם אִשֶּׁ֖ה לַֽיהֹוָֽה: יב וְאִם־עֵ֖ז קָרְבָּנ֑וֹ וְהִקְרִיב֖וֹ לִפְנֵ֥י יְהֹוָֽה: יג וְסָמַ֤ךְ אֶת־יָדוֹ֙ עַל־רֹאשׁ֔וֹ וְשָׁחַ֣ט אֹת֔וֹ לִפְנֵ֖י אֹ֣הֶל מוֹעֵ֑ד וְ֠זָרְק֠וּ בְּנֵ֨י אַהֲרֹ֧ן אֶת־דָּמ֛וֹ עַל־הַמִּזְבֵּ֖חַ סָבִֽיב: יד וְהִקְרִ֤יב מִמֶּ֙נּוּ֙ קָרְבָּנ֔וֹ אִשֶּׁ֖ה לַֽיהֹוָ֑ה אֶת־הַחֵ֙לֶב֙ הַֽמְכַסֶּ֣ה אֶת־הַקֶּ֔רֶב וְאֵת֙ כָּל־הַחֵ֔לֶב אֲשֶׁ֖ר עַל־הַקֶּֽרֶב: טו וְאֵת֙ שְׁתֵּ֣י הַכְּלָיֹ֔ת וְאֶת־הַחֵ֙לֶב֙ אֲשֶׁ֣ר עֲלֵהֶ֔ן אֲשֶׁ֖ר עַל־הַכְּסָלִ֑ים

— אונקלוס —

לָקֳבֵל שְׁזַרְתָּא יְעַדִּנַּהּ וְיָת תַּרְבָּא דְּחָפֵי יָת גַּוָּא וְיָת כָּל תַּרְבָּא דִּי עַל גַּוָּא: י וְיָת תַּרְתֵּין כָּלְיָן וְיָת תַּרְבָּא דִּי עֲלֵיהֶן דִּי עַל גִּסְסַיָּא וְיָת חִצְרָא דְּעַל כַּבְדָּא עַל כָּלְיָתָא יְעַדִּנַּהּ: יא וְיַסֵּיקִנֵּהּ כַּהֲנָא לְמַדְבְּחָא לְחֵם קֻרְבָּנָא קֳדָם יְיָ: יב וְאִם מִן בְּנֵי עִזַּיָּא קֻרְבָּנֵהּ וִיקָרְבִנֵּהּ קֳדָם יְיָ: יג וְיִסְמוֹךְ יָת יְדֵהּ עַל רֵישֵׁהּ וְיִכּוֹס יָתֵהּ קֳדָם מַשְׁכַּן זִמְנָא וְיִזְרְקוּן בְּנֵי אַהֲרֹן יָת דְּמֵהּ עַל מַדְבְּחָא סְחוֹר סְחוֹר: יד וִיקָרֵב מִנֵּהּ קֻרְבָּנֵהּ קֻרְבָּן קֳדָם יְיָ יָת תַּרְבָּא דְּחָפֵי יָת גַּוָּא וְיָת כָּל תַּרְבָּא דִּי עַל גַּוָּא: טו וְיָת תַּרְתֵּין כָּלְיָן וְיָת תַּרְבָּא דִּי עֲלֵיהֶן דִּי עַל גִּסְסַיָּא

— רש"י —

לעמת העצה. למעלה מן הכליות היועצות (חולין יא.): עבד (יא) **לחם אשה לה׳.** לחמו של אש לשם גבוה (קהלת ייט):

לחם. לשון מאכל וכן נשחיתה עץ בלחמו (ירמיה יא:יט). לחם רב (דניאל ה:א). לשחוק עושים לחם (קהלת ייט):

— RASHI ELUCIDATED —

☐ לְעֻמַּת הֶעָצֶה — ABOVE THE KIDNEYS. This means לְמַעְלָה מִן הַכְּלָיוֹת הַיוֹעֲצוֹת[1] — above the kidneys which give advice.[1]

11. לֶחֶם אִשֶּׁה לַה׳ — IT IS THE FOOD OF THE FIRE, FOR HASHEM. לַחְמוֹ שֶׁל אֵשׁ — Food of the fire לְשֵׁם גָּבוֹהַּ — in the name of He Who is on high.[2]

☐ לֶחֶם — FOOD. The word לֶחֶם is לְשׁוֹן מַאֲכָל — an expression for food in general.[3] וְכֵן ,,נַשְׁחִיתָה עֵץ בְּלַחְמוֹ'' — Similarly, בְּלַחְמוֹ in, "let us put poison in his food";[4] ,,עֲבַד לְחֶם רַב'' — and the word לֶחֶם in, "made a great meal";[5] ,,לִשְׂחוֹק עֹשִׂים לָחֶם'' — and the word לָחֶם in, "for revelry they make a meal."[6]

---

1. *Chullin* 11a. Rashi explains why עֵצָה means "kidney." The kidneys are the part of the body associated with the power of judgment and advice, עֵצָה. "From where do we know that the kidneys give advice? As it says, 'I bless Hashem for He has advised me; even at nights my kidneys admonish me' (*Psalms* 16:7)" — Rashi to *Berachos* 61a.

2. לֶחֶם by its vowelization could be either a construct or absolute form. Rashi explains that it is a construct. The verse should not be understood as "food, a fiery offering unto Hashem," for God does not need food (*Mizrachi*; *Sifsei Chachamim*).

[God says,] "I did not tell you to bring a sacrifice because I need to eat; rather [because] it is a source of contentment before Me that I have spoken and My will has been done" (*Rashi* to *Psalms* 50:13).

3. It cannot be understood in the usual sense of "bread" in our verse.

4. *Jeremiah* 11:19.

5. *Daniel* 5:1.

6. *Ecclesiastes* 10:19.

and he shall remove the diaphragm with the liver, with the kidneys. *16* The Kohen shall cause them to go up in smoke on the Mizbe'ach — the food of the fire for a satisfying aroma, all the choice parts for HASHEM. *17* An eternal decree for your generations in all your dwelling places; you may not consume any fat or any blood.

4

1 HASHEM spoke to Moses, saying: *2* Speak to the Children of Israel, saying: When a person will sin unintentionally from among all the commandments of HASHEM that may not be done, and

וְאֶת־הַיֹּתֶרֶת עַל־הַכָּבֵד עַל־הַכְּלָיֹת יְסִירֶנָּה: וְהִקְטִירָם הַכֹּהֵן הַמִּזְבֵּחָה לֶחֶם אִשֶּׁה לְרֵיחַ נִיחֹחַ כָּל־חֵלֶב לַיהוָה: חֻקַּת עוֹלָם לְדֹרֹתֵיכֶם בְּכֹל מוֹשְׁבֹתֵיכֶם כָּל־חֵלֶב וְכָל־דָּם לֹא תֹאכֵלוּ:

ד *א* וַיְדַבֵּר יְהוָה אֶל־מֹשֶׁה לֵּאמֹר: *ב* דַּבֵּר אֶל־בְּנֵי יִשְׂרָאֵל לֵאמֹר נֶפֶשׁ כִּי־תֶחֱטָא בִשְׁגָגָה מִכֹּל מִצְוֹת יְהוָה אֲשֶׁר לֹא תֵעָשֶׂינָה

---------- אונקלוס ----------

וְיָת חַצְרָא דִּי עַל כַּבְדָּא עַל כֻּלְיָתָא יַעְדִּנַּהּ: *טו* וְיַסֵּיקִנּוּן כַּהֲנָא לְמַדְבְּחָא לְחֵם קֻרְבָּנָא לְאִתְקַבָּלָא בְרַעֲוָא כָּל תַּרְבָּא קֳדָם יְיָ: *יז* קְיָם עָלַם לְדָרֵיכוֹן בְּכֹל מוֹתְבָנֵיכוֹן כָּל תַּרְבָּא וְכָל דְּמָא לָא תֵיכְלוּן: *א* וּמַלִּיל יְיָ עִם מֹשֶׁה לְמֵימָר: *ב* מַלֵּל עִם בְּנֵי יִשְׂרָאֵל לְמֵימָר אֱנַשׁ אֲרֵי יֵחוֹב בְּשָׁלוּ מִכֹּל פִּקּוּדַיָּא דַּיָי דִּי לָא כָשְׁרִין לְאִתְעֲבָדָא

---------- רש"י ----------

(יז) חֻקַּת עוֹלָם. יָפֶה מְפֹרָשׁ בְּת"כ (פֶּרֶק כ:) כֹּל חוּבָּה פָרָשָׁתָא אֹ:ח; יְבָמוֹת ט: כְּרִיתוֹת כב:) אֵין חַטָּאת הַפָּסוּק הַזֶּה: **(ב) מִכֹּל מִצְוֹת ה'.** פֵּי' רַבּוֹתֵינוּ (ת"כ בָּאָה אֶלָּא עַל דָּבָר שֶׁזְּדוֹנוֹ לָאו וְכָרֵת וְשִׁגְגָתוֹ חַטָּאת}:

========== RASHI ELUCIDATED ==========

17. חֻקַּת עוֹלָם — AN ETERNAL DECREE. — יָפֶה מְפֹרָשׁ בְּתוֹרַת כֹּהֲנִים[1] כָּל הַפָּסוּק הַזֶּה — This entire verse is explained well in *Toras Kohanim*.[1]

4.

2. מִכֹּל מִצְוֹת ה' — FROM AMONG ALL THE COMMANDMENTS OF HASHEM. — [2]פֵּרְשׁוּ רַבּוֹתֵינוּ — Our Rabbis have explained[2] that עַל דָּבָר שֶׁזְּדוֹנוֹ לָאו — אֵין חַטָּאת בָּאָה אֶלָּא — a sin-offering is not brought except for something whose intentional violation is prohibited by **a negative commandment, and** וְכָרֵת — **is punished by** *kares*,[3] {וְשִׁגְגָתוֹ חַטָּאת} — **and its unintentional violation** must be atoned for by **a sin-offering}.**[4]

---

1. *Toras Kohanim* (*Chovah, parshasa* 1:7) says: "An eternal decree" — even during the era of the *Beis HaMikdash*. We might have thought otherwise: During the years in the desert, when it was forbidden to eat meat except for peace-offerings (see *Deuteronomy* 12:20 with Rashi), all blood and fat would have been used as part of the service; consequently it would have seemed logical that only in the desert would it be forbidden to eat them. In Eretz Yisrael, however, where it was permitted to slaughter animals for personal use, there would seem to be no reason to prohibit blood and fats. Thus our verse states that the prohibition applies even then.

"For your generations" — even in subsequent generations. We might have thought otherwise: During the era of the *Beis HaMikdash*, when blood and fat are offered on the *Mizbe'ach*, it would have seemed logical that it would be forbidden to eat them. But after the *Beis HaMikdash* was destroyed, it would seem that they should be permitted. Thus our verse states that the prohibition is eternal.

"In all your dwelling places" — within the Land and outside the Land of Israel. We might have thought otherwise: Only in the Land of Israel, where blood and fat are offered, would the prohibition apply. Thus our verse states that it applies everywhere (*Gur Aryeh*).

2. *Toras Kohanim, Chovah, parshasa* 1:7; *Yevamos* 9a; *Kerisos* 22b.

3. Literally, "excision." According to Rashi (*Genesis* 17:14; *Leviticus* 17:9) this means premature death of the sinner and his offspring.

4. *Numbers* 15:29 speaks of the sin-offering of one who unintentionally commits idolatry, and uses the phrase, "There shall be one law for you, for one who acts unintentionally." *Toras Kohanim* explains that the sin-offering of idolatry serves as a model for all sin-offerings. Just as intentional commission of idolatry is punished by *kares* (if there were no witnesses or warning to the act; if there were witnesses and the sinner was warned, the punishment is death by stoning), so, too, a sin-offering is brought only for sins whose intentional violation is punished by *kares*. The negative phrase in our verse, "that may not be done," tells us that the commandment must be a negative one (*Mizrachi; Sifsei Chachamim*).

he will commit from one of them. ³ *If the anointed Kohen will sin, to the guilt of the people; for his sin that he committed he shall offer a bull, a*

וְעָשָׂה מֵאַחַת מֵהֵנָּה: אִם הַכֹּהֵן הַמָּשִׁיחַ יֶחֱטָא לְאַשְׁמַת הָעָם וְהִקְרִיב עַל חַטָּאתוֹ אֲשֶׁר חָטָא פַּר

— אונקלוס —

וְיַעְבֵּד מִן חַד מִנְּהוֹן: ג אִם כַּהֲנָא רַבָּא יֵחוֹב לְחוֹבַת עַמָּא וִיקָרֵב עַל חוֹבָתֵהּ דִּי חָב תּוֹר

— רש"י —

מֵאַחַת מֵהֵנָּה. מִמִּקְצָת אַחַת מֵהֶן כְּגוֹן הַכּוֹתֵב בְּשַׁבָּת שֵׁם מִשִּׁמְעוֹן נֹחַ מִנָּחוֹר דָּן מִדָּנִיֵּאל (שם פרק לד; שבת קג.): (ג) אִם הַכֹּהֵן הַמָּשִׁיחַ יֶחֱטָא לְאַשְׁמַת הָעָם. מִדְרָשׁוֹ אֵינוֹ חַיָּב אֶלָּא בְּהֶעְלֵם דָּבָר עִם שִׁגְגַת מַעֲשֶׂה (שם פרק ב:א) כְּמוֹ שֶׁנֶּאֱמַר לְאַשְׁמַת הָעָם [ס"א כְּמוֹ לְאַשְׁמַת הָעָם שֶׁנֶּאֱמַר] וְנֶעְלַם דָּבָר מֵעֵינֵי הַקָּהָל וְעָשׂוּ (פסוקים יג). וּפְשׁוּטוֹ לְפִי אַגָּדָה, כְּשֶׁהַכֹּהֵן הַגָּדוֹל חוֹטֵא אַשְׁמַת הָעָם הוּא זֶה, שֶׁהֵן תְּלוּיִין בּוֹ לְכַפֵּר עֲלֵיהֶם וּלְהִתְפַּלֵּל בַּעֲדָם וְנַעֲשָׂה מְקֻלְקָל (ויקרא רבה ה:ו): פַּר. יָכוֹל זָקֵן, ת"ל בֶּן.

— RASHI ELUCIDATED —

□ מֵאַחַת מֵהֵנָּה — FROM ONE OF THEM. מִמִּקְצָת אַחַת מֵהֵן — From part of one of them;¹ בְּגוֹן הַכּוֹתֵב בְּשַׁבָּת — for instance, one who writes on Shabbos שֵׁם מִשִּׁמְעוֹן — the name Shem out of Shimon or נֹחַ מִנָּחוֹר — Noach out of Nachor or דָּן מִדָּנִיֵּאל — Dan out of Daniel.²

3. אִם הַכֹּהֵן הַמָּשִׁיחַ יֶחֱטָא לְאַשְׁמַת הָעָם — IF THE ANOINTED KOHEN WILL SIN TO THE GUILT OF THE PEOPLE. מִדְרָשׁוֹ — Its midrashic interpretation is: אֵינוֹ חַיָּב אֶלָּא — He is only obligated to bring a sin-offering בְּהֶעְלֵם דָּבָר — if there is obscuring of the issue ³עִם שִׁגְגַת מַעֲשֶׂה — with lack of intention to sin in the act.³ כְּמוֹ שֶׁנֶּאֱמַר — As it says, ⁴״לְאַשְׁמַת הָעָם״ — "to the guilt of the people,"⁴ and with regard to the sin-offering brought by the entire people it says, ⁵״וְנֶעְלַם דָּבָר מֵעֵינֵי הַקָּהָל וְעָשׂוּ״ — "and a matter became obscured from the eyes of the congregation, and they commit . . ."⁵

וּפְשׁוּטוֹ לְפִי אַגָּדָה — [The verse's] simple interpretation, according to aggadah,⁶ is: כְּשֶׁהַכֹּהֵן הַגָּדוֹל חוֹטֵא — When the Kohen Gadol sins, אַשְׁמַת הָעָם הוּא זֶה — it is the guilt of the people,⁷ שֶׁהֵן תְּלוּיִין — for they are dependent upon him לְכַפֵּר עֲלֵיהֶם — to atone for them, וּלְהִתְפַּלֵּל בַּעֲדָם — and to pray on their behalf, ⁸וְנַעֲשָׂה מְקֻלְקָל — and he has become befouled by sin.⁸

□ פַּר — A BULL. יָכוֹל זָקֵן — One might be able to think that this means an old one. תַּלְמוּד לוֹמַר ״בֶּן״ —

---

1. This is implied by the Torah's use of מֵאַחַת, "from one of," rather than אַחַת, "one of" (*Mizrachi; Sifsei Chachamim*).

2. *Toras Kohanim, Chovah, perek* 1:4; *Shabbos* 103a. The minimum amount for which one must bring a sin-offering if he unintentionally transgressed the prohibition against writing on the Shabbos is two letters (*Shabbos* 73a). According to R' Yehudah (103a), these two letters must form a word (*Meiri*). Even if he intended to write a long word, but stopped before he finished it, if the letters he wrote constitute a word at least two letters long, he must bring a sin-offering. Moreover, R' Yehudah maintains that the regular and final forms of the letters מנצפך may be interchanged. Thus, even one who wrote שם or דן is considered as having written an entire word.

3. *Toras Kohanim, Chovah, perek* 2:1. The sin-offering of the Kohen Gadol is brought only if two conditions are met: (a) There is an obscuring of the issue, i.e., he makes an error in interpreting the law; and (b) he sins unintentionally on the basis of that error. Rashi explains that these requirements are derived from verse 13 which discusses the communal sin-offering brought when the masses sin unintentionally due to an erroneous decision by the Sanhedrin. Nevertheless, there is a basic difference between the two offerings: The communal offering is brought when the masses, not necessarily including the members of the Sanhedrin, sinned due to the Sanhedrin's decision. The Kohen Gadol's offering is brought only if his actions were based on his own decision. In the case of the sin-offering of a common individual, unintentional sin is sufficient cause even if there is no legal error; for instance, if one knows the laws regarding which fats are permitted and which are forbidden, but sins through wrongly identifying the fat rather than misinterpreting the law, he must still bring a sin-offering.

4. Some editions of Rashi read כְּמוֹ לְאַשְׁמַת הָעָם, "similar to the (case of) communal guilt," שֶׁנֶּאֱמַר, "as it says."

5. Below v. 13. The verse regarding the sin-offering of the entire people mentions the two conditions of error in interpreting the law: obscuring of the issue and lack of intention to sin in the act. "To the guilt of the people" implies that the Kohen Gadol brings a sin-offering when his act parallels that which requires a communal sin-offering from the people.

6. This interpretation fits the grammar and syntax better than the halachic interpretation, and explains an aggadic message of the verse rather than its legal implication.

7. The sinfulness of the Kohen Gadol leads to the people's guilt, for he does not represent them effectively before God (see *Lifshuto shel Rashi*).

8. *Vayikra Rabbah* 5:6.

young male of cattle, unblemished, to HASHEM as a sin-offering. ⁴ He shall bring the bull to the entrance of the Tent of Meeting before HASHEM; he shall lean his hands upon the head of the bull, and he shall slaughter the bull before HASHEM. ⁵ The anointed Kohen shall take from the blood of the bull and bring it to the Tent of Meeting. ⁶ The Kohen shall dip his forefinger into the blood; he shall sprinkle some of the blood seven times before HASHEM toward the Curtain of the Holy. ⁷ The Kohen shall put some of the blood on the horns of the Mizbe'ach where incense is caused to go up in smoke before HASHEM,

בֶּן־בָּקָר תָּמִים לַיהוָה לְחַטָּאת: ⁴ וְהֵבִיא אֶת־הַפָּר אֶל־פֶּתַח אֹהֶל מוֹעֵד לִפְנֵי יְהוָה וְסָמַךְ אֶת־יָדוֹ עַל־רֹאשׁ הַפָּר וְשָׁחַט אֶת־הַפָּר לִפְנֵי יְהוָה: ⁵ וְלָקַח הַכֹּהֵן הַמָּשִׁיחַ מִדַּם הַפָּר וְהֵבִיא אֹתוֹ אֶל־אֹהֶל מוֹעֵד: ⁶ וְטָבַל הַכֹּהֵן אֶת־אֶצְבָּעוֹ בַּדָּם וְהִזָּה מִן־הַדָּם שֶׁבַע פְּעָמִים לִפְנֵי יְהוָה אֶת־פְּנֵי פָּרֹכֶת הַקֹּדֶשׁ: ⁷ וְנָתַן הַכֹּהֵן מִן־הַדָּם עַל־קַרְנוֹת מִזְבַּח קְטֹרֶת הַסַּמִּים לִפְנֵי יְהוָה

---------- אונקלוס ----------

בַּר תּוֹרֵי שְׁלִים קֳדָם יְיָ לְחַטָּאתָא: ⁴ וְיָיְתֵי יָת תּוֹרָא לִתְרַע מַשְׁכַּן זִמְנָא לָקֳדָם יְיָ וְיִסְמוֹךְ יָת יְדֵהּ עַל רֵישׁ תּוֹרָא וְיִכּוֹס יָת תּוֹרָא קֳדָם יְיָ: ⁵ וְיִסַּב כַּהֲנָא רַבָּא מִדְמָא דְתוֹרָא וְיָיְתֵי יָתֵהּ לְמַשְׁכַּן זִמְנָא: ⁶ וְיִטְבּוֹל כַּהֲנָא יָת אֶצְבְּעֵהּ בִּדְמָא וְיַדֵּי מִן דְּמָא שְׁבַע זִמְנִין קֳדָם יְיָ קֳדָם פָּרֻכְתָּא דְקוּדְשָׁא: ⁷ וְיִתֵּן כַּהֲנָא מִן דְּמָא עַל קַרְנַת מַדְבְּחָא דִקְטֹרֶת בּוּסְמִין קֳדָם יְיָ

---------- רש"י ----------

אוֹ בֶּן יָכוֹל קָטָן, ת"ל פַּר. הָא כֵיצַד, זֶה פַּר בֶּן ג' (ת"כ שָׁם פֶּרֶק ג:ג): (ה) אֶל אֹהֶל מוֹעֵד. לַמִּשְׁכָּן, וּבְבֵית עוֹלָמִים לַהֵיכָל: (ו) אֶת פְּנֵי פָּרֹכֶת הַקֹּדֶשׁ. כְּנֶגֶד מְקוֹם קְדֻשָּׁתָהּ מְכֻוָּן כְּנֶגֶד בֵּין הַבַּדִּים (ת"כ שָׁם פָּרָשְׁתָא ג:י). וְלֹא הָיוּ נוֹגְעִים דָּמִים בַּפָּרֹכֶת וְאִם נָגְעוּ נָגְעוּ

---------- RASHI ELUCIDATED ----------

— To teach us otherwise, **the Torah says, "a young male."** איֶ בֶּן — **If** the verse had written only **"a young male,"** יָכוֹל קָטָן — **one would have been able** to say that this means **a small [calf].** תַּלְמוּד לוֹמַר "פַּר" — To teach us otherwise, **the Torah says, "a bull."** הָא כֵיצַד — **How is this,** i.e., how is "a bull," which implies an older animal, to be reconciled with "young"? זֶה פַּר בֶּן שָׁלֹשׁ — **This is a three-year-old bull.**[1]

5. אֶל אֹהֶל מוֹעֵד — **TO THE TENT OF MEETING.** לַמִּשְׁכָּן — **To the** *Mishkan*. וּבְבֵית עוֹלָמִים לַהֵיכָל — **In the Eternal House,** the *Beis HaMikdash,* the Kohen Gadol brings the blood of his sin-offering **to the Sanctuary.**[2]

6. אֶת פְּנֵי פָּרֹכֶת הַקֹּדֶשׁ — **TOWARD THE CURTAIN OF THE HOLY.** כְּנֶגֶד מְקוֹם קְדֻשָּׁתָהּ — **Toward the point of its** most intense **holiness.**[3] מְכֻוָּן כְּנֶגֶד בֵּין הַבַּדִּים — **Exactly opposite** the point **between the poles** of the *Aron*.[3] וְלֹא הָיוּ נוֹגְעִים דָּמִים בַּפָּרֹכֶת — **The blood did not touch the *Paroches*** curtain.[4] וְאִם נָגְעוּ נָגְעוּ — **But if it touched, it touched.**[5]

---

1. *Toras Kohanim, Chovah, perek* 3:1. See also *Parah* 1:2 with *Tos. Yom Tov.*

2. He brings the sin-offering to the actual structure of the Temple. He cannot bring it only to the Courtyard. Although the Tent of Meeting has been mentioned earlier, Rashi did not state that the same laws applied in the *Beis HaMikdash* because the laws there referred to the Courtyard of the *Mishkan*, and the Courtyard of the *Beis HaMikdash* is essentially identical to it. The two structures, however, differed significantly. Thus Rashi had to state explicitly that this law which the Torah refers to in terms of the *Mishkan* also applies to the Sanctuary of the *Beis HaMikdash* (*Mizrachi*).

3. *Toras Kohanim, Chovah, parshasa* 3:10. This is derived from the apparently superfluous "of the Holy" (*Mizrachi; Sifsei Chachamim*).

The *Aron* (Ark) was located in the *Kodesh HaKodashim,* behind the *Paroches* curtain (*Exodus* 26:33). The two carrying poles at the sides of the *Aron* were the same length as the *Kodesh HaKodashim* and thus pressed against the *Paroches* so that two protrusions were visible on the other side (*Yoma* 54a; see Rashi to *Shabbos* 88b, s.v., בין שדי ילין). The Kohen aimed his throw between these two protrusions.

4. The Kohen Gadol threw the blood in the direction of that area on the *Paroches,* but he did not throw hard enough that the blood should actually fall on it.

5. *Yoma* 57a. If the blood did touch the *Paroches,* the offering was not disqualified.

35 / VAYIKRA/LEVITICUS — PARASHAS VAYIKRA — 4/8-10 — ד/ח-י

which is in the Tent of Meeting; and all the blood of the bull he shall pour onto the base of the Olah-offering Mizbe'ach, which is at the entrance of the Tent of Meeting. ⁸ *And he shall remove from it all the fat of the bull of the sin-offering; the fat that covers the innards and all the fat that is upon the innards;* ⁹ *and the two kidneys and the fat that is upon them, which is upon the flanks; and he shall remove the diaphragm with the liver, with the kidneys — * ¹⁰ *just as it would be removed from the sacrifice of the peace-offering bull;*

אֲשֶׁ֣ר בְּאֹֽהֶל־מוֹעֵ֑ד וְאֵ֣ת ׀ כָּל־דַּ֣ם הַפָּ֗ר יִשְׁפֹּךְ֙ אֶל־יְסוֹד֙ מִזְבַּ֣ח הָֽעֹלָ֔ה
ח אֲשֶׁר־פֶּ֖תַח אֹֽהֶל מוֹעֵֽד: וְאֶת־כָּל־
חֵ֛לֶב פַּ֥ר הַֽחַטָּ֖את יָרִ֣ים מִמֶּ֑נּוּ אֶת־
הַחֵ֙לֶב֙ הַֽמְכַסֶּ֣ה עַל־הַקֶּ֔רֶב וְאֵת֙ כָּל־
ט הַחֵ֔לֶב אֲשֶׁ֖ר עַל־הַקֶּֽרֶב: וְאֵת֙ שְׁתֵּ֣י
הַכְּלָיֹ֗ת וְאֶת־הַחֵ֙לֶב֙ אֲשֶׁ֣ר עֲלֵיהֶ֔ן
אֲשֶׁ֖ר עַל־הַכְּסָלִ֑ים וְאֶת־הַיֹּתֶ֙רֶת֙
עַל־הַכָּבֵ֔ד עַל־הַכְּלָי֖וֹת יְסִירֶֽנָּה:
י כַּאֲשֶׁ֣ר יוּרַ֔ם מִשּׁ֖וֹר זֶ֣בַח הַשְּׁלָמִ֑ים

— אונקלוס —

דִּי בְמַשְׁכַּן זִמְנָא וְיָת כָּל דְּמָא דְתוֹרָא יֵשׁוֹד לִיסוֹדָא דְּמַדְבְּחָא דַעֲלָתָא דִּי בִתְרַע מַשְׁכַּן זִמְנָא: ח וְיָת כָּל תַּרְבָּא
דְּתוֹרָא דְחַטָּאתָא יַפְרֵשׁ מִנֵּיהּ יָת תַּרְבָּא דְחָפֵי עַל גַּוָּא וְיָת כָּל תַּרְבָּא דִּי עַל גַּוָּא: ט וְיָת תַּרְתֵּין כָּלְיָן וְיָת תַּרְבָּא
דִּי עֲלֵיהֶן דִּי עַל גִּסְסַיָּא וְיָת חַצְרָא דְעַל כַּבְדָּא עַל כָּלְיָתָא יֶעְדִּנַהּ: י כְּמָא דִי מִתְפָּרַשׁ מִתּוֹר נִכְסַת קוּדְשַׁיָּא

— רש"י —

(יוּמָא נג.): (ז) וְאֵת כָּל דָּם. שְׁיָרֵי הַדָּם (זבחים כה.): (ח) וְאֵת | שְׁעִירֵי ע"ז לִכְלָיוֹת וְלַחֲלָבִים וְלַיוֹתֶרֶת (שם): יָרִים
כָּל חֵלֶב פַּר. חֶלְבּוּ הָיָה ל"ל מַה ת"ל פַּר לְרַבּוֹת פַּר שֶׁל יוֹה"כ | מִמֶּנּוּ. מִן הַמְחוּבָּר (שם) שֶׁלֹּא יִנַתְּחֶנּוּ קוֹדֶם הֲסָרַת חֶלְבּוֹ: (י)
לִכְלָיוֹת וְלַחֲלָבִים וְיוֹתֶרֶת (ת"כ שם פרק ד:א): הַחַטָּאת. לְהָבִיא | כַּאֲשֶׁר יוּרָם. כְּאוֹתָן אֵימוּרִין הַמְפוֹרָשִׁין בְּשׁוֹר זֶבַח הַשְּׁלָמִים.

— RASHI ELUCIDATED —

7. וְאֵת כָּל דַּם וְגוֹמֵר — AND ALL THE BLOOD, ETC. ¹ שְׁיָרֵי הַדָּם — The remainder of the blood.¹

8. וְאֶת כָּל חֵלֶב פַּר — AND ALL THE FAT OF THE BULL. חֶלְבּוֹ הָיָה לוֹ לוֹמַר — [The verse] should have said, "all *its* fat."² פַּר, מַה תַּלְמוּד לוֹמַר — Why does the Torah say "of the bull"? לְרַבּוֹת פַּר שֶׁל יוֹם הַכִּפּוּרִים — To include the bull of, i.e., offered on, Yom Kippur לִכְלָיוֹת — in the laws pertaining to the kidneys, וְלַחֲלָבִים — and to the fats, ³וְיוֹתֶרֶת — and the diaphragm.³

□ הַחַטָּאת — OF THE SIN-OFFERING. לְהָבִיא שְׂעִירֵי עֲבוֹדָה זָרָה — To include the goats of idolatry⁴ לִכְלָיוֹת — in the laws pertaining to the kidneys, וְלַחֲלָבִים — and to the fats, ⁵וּלְיוֹתֶרֶת — and to the diaphragm.⁵

□ יָרִים מִמֶּנּוּ — HE SHALL REMOVE FROM IT. ⁶מִן הַמְחוּבָּר — From that which is connected,⁶ i.e., whole, שֶׁלֹּא יְנַתְּחֶנּוּ — that he should not cut it into pieces קוֹדֶם הֲסָרַת חֶלְבּוֹ — before the removal of its fat.⁷

10. כַּאֲשֶׁר יוּרָם — JUST AS IT WOULD BE REMOVED. כְּאוֹתָן אֵימוּרִין — Like those specified parts הַמְפוֹרָשִׁין בְּשׁוֹר זֶבַח הַשְּׁלָמִים — which are mentioned explicitly with regard to the peace-offering.

---

1. *Zevachim* 25a. "All the blood" must mean "all the *remaining* blood," for some of it has already been sprinkled (see *Sefer Zikaron* to v. 25 below).

2. Since the previous phrase mentions עַל גַּוָּא, "all the blood of the bull," our verse could have used the pronominal suffix וֹ, "its."

3. *Toras Kohanim, Chovah, perek* 4:1. The apparently superfluous "bull" implies that another bull offering has the same parts placed on the *Mizbe'ach* as the sin-offering of the Kohen Gadol. This is the bull offered on Yom Kippur (see Ch. 16). The kidneys and diaphragm are not mentioned there (*Mizrachi*).

4. This refers to the sin-offering brought for the unintentional commission of idolatry by the majority of the community due to a misinterpretation of the law by the Sanhedrin (see *Numbers* 15:22-26). Although a single goat is offered, the Sages use "goats" in the plural because in the case of mass commission of idolatry due to an incorrect ruling by the court, each tribe brings a goat of its own (*Minchas Yehudah; Sifsei Chachamim*).

5. *Toras Kohanim, Chovah, perek* 4:1. The Torah does not state that parts of the goats are sacrificed upon the *Mizbe'ach*. The apparently superfluous "the sin-offering" here teaches us that the parts placed on the *Mizbe'ach* from the sin-offering of the goat are the same as the parts placed on the *Mizbe'ach* from the bull sin-offering of the Kohen Gadol (*Mizrachi*).

6. *Toras Kohanim, Chovah, perek* 4:1.

7. The word מִמֶּנּוּ, "from it," appears superfluous (*Sefer Zikaron*). It implies that the fat must be removed while it is still whole (*Mizrachi; Sifsei Chachamim*).

וְהִקְטִירָם֙ הַכֹּהֵ֔ן עַ֥ל מִזְבַּ֖ח הָעֹלָֽה:
יא וְאֶת־ע֤וֹר הַפָּר֙ וְאֶת־כָּל־בְּשָׂר֔וֹ

and the Kohen shall cause them to go up in smoke on the Olah-offering Mizbe'ach. ¹¹ *But the hide of the bull and all its flesh*

———————— אונקלוס ————————

וְיַסְּקִנּוּן כַּהֲנָא עַל מַדְבְּחָא דַעֲלָתָא: יא וְיָת מְשַׁךְ תּוֹרָא וְיָת כָּל בִּסְרֵהּ

———————— רש"י ————————

וכי מה פי' בזבח השלמים שלא פי' כאן, אלא להקישו לשלמים,   שלוס לעולם (שם ב). ובשחיטת קדשים מצריכו ללמוד הימנו שאין
מה שלמים לשמן אף זה לשמו, ומה שלמים שלוס לעולם אף זה   למדין למד מן הלמד בקדשים, בפרק איזהו מקומן (זבחים מט:):

———————— RASHI ELUCIDATED ————————

וְכִי מַה פֵּרֵשׁ בְּזֶבַח הַשְּׁלָמִים — **But what did [the Torah] state explicitly with regard to the peace-offering** שֶׁלֹּא פֵּרֵשׁ כָּאן — **that it did not state explicitly here?**[1] אֶלָּא לְהַקִּישׁוּ לִשְׁלָמִים — Rather, this phrase was said **to compare [the sin-offering of the Kohen Gadol] to the peace-offering.** מַה שְּׁלָמִים לִשְׁמָן — **Just as the** procedures of the **peace-offering must be performed for its sake,** i.e., with intent that they are being performed for the sake of a peace-offering,[2] אַף זֶה לִשְׁמוֹ — **so, too,** this offering's procedure must be performed **for its sake.** וּמַה שְּׁלָמִים שָׁלוֹם לָעוֹלָם — **And just as the peace-offering is** a source of **peace for the world,**[3] אַף זֶה שָׁלוֹם לָעוֹלָם — **this, too, is** a source of **peace for the world.**[4] וּבִשְׁחִיטַת קָדָשִׁים — **And in** *Shechitas Kodashim*[5] מַצְרִיכוֹ — **[the Talmud] requires [the comparison]** between the parts of the Kohen Gadol's sin-offering and the parts of the peace-offering לִלְמוֹד הֵימֶנּוּ — **to learn from it** שֶׁאֵין לְמֵדִין — **that we do not derive** לָמֵד מִן הַלָּמֵד — **a derivative from a derivative** בְּקָדָשִׁים — **with regard to** *kodashim* (matters concerning offerings and the property of the *Beis HaMikdash*), בְּפֶרֶק אֵיזֶהוּ מְקוֹמָן — **in Chapter** *Eizehu Mekoman*.[6]

1. Why did the Torah have to refer back to the peace-offering? All of the parts mentioned regarding the peace-offering are mentioned here as well.

2. The Talmud in *Zevachim* 4a derives the law that the procedures of the peace-offering must be performed for its sake.

3. See Rashi to 3:1 above.

4. *Toras Kohanim, Chovah, perek* 4:2.

5. A term used by some of the *Rishonim* for Tractate *Zevachim*.

6. *Zevachim* 49b. A law of the Torah that is stated explicitly for commandment A can be applied to commandment B (where it is not stated) through the principles by which the Sages expound the Torah. The law is then considered as if it were explicitly stated for commandment B. Thus, the law can be applied to commandment C (where it is also not stated), if it can be derived from commandment B through the principles by which the Torah is expounded. In this case, a derivative – commandment B, which was derived from commandment A – generates another derivative – commandment C.

The principle that one derivative can generate another does not apply to matters concerning *kodashim*. Thus, if a law of *kodashim* is stated in the context of commandment A, in order for it to apply to other commandments, it must be linked directly to each of the other commandments; it cannot be linked to one which in turn serves as a link to a third.

From our verse the Talmud learns the exclusion of *kodashim* from this principle. The Torah does not state that parts of the goats of idolatry (see note 5 to verse 8 above) are burned on the *Mizbe'ach*. This is derived, according to one opinion, from the *par he'elem davar* (see vv. 13-21 below). The parts of the *par he'elem davar* which are burned on the *Mizbe'ach* are themselves derived from the sin-offering of the Kohen Gadol. This appears to be a case of a derivative, the goats of idolatry, being derived from another derivative, the *par he'elem davar*, which is derived from the sin-offering of the Kohen Gadol. But the Torah states the apparently superfluous "just as it would be removed from the peace-offering bull" in the context of the sin-offering of the Kohen Gadol. The Talmud says that if this phrase is unnecessary in the context in which it appears, the Torah intends that it be applied in a different context, the *par he'elem davar*. The Torah does this so that the *par he'elem davar* should no longer be considered a derivative; the application of "just as it would be removed from the peace-offering bull" constitutes an explicit statement of which parts of the *par he'elem davar* are to be offered on the *Mizbe'ach*. Thus we see that although the *par he'elem davar* could have been derived from the sin-offering of the Kohen Gadol, the Torah wrote an extra statement to give it the status of a commandment whose law has been stated explicitly, so that the law of the goats of idolatry can be derived from it. This shows us that with regard to *kodashim*, only a written statement can serve as a source for a derived law.

עַל־רֹאשׁ֖וֹ וְעַל־כְּרָעָ֑יו וְקִרְבּ֖וֹ
יב וּפִרְשׁ֑וֹ: וְהוֹצִ֣יא אֶת־כָּל־הַ֠פָּר אֶל־
מִח֨וּץ לַֽמַּחֲנֶ֜ה אֶל־מָק֤וֹם טָהוֹר֙ אֶל־
שֶׁ֣פֶךְ הַדֶּ֔שֶׁן וְשָׂרַ֥ף אֹת֛וֹ עַל־עֵצִ֖ים
בָּאֵ֑שׁ עַל־שֶׁ֥פֶךְ הַדֶּ֖שֶׁן יִשָּׂרֵֽף:

with its head and with its feet, and its innards and its waste — ¹² the entire bull shall he remove to the outside of the camp, to a pure place, to where the ashes are poured, and he shall burn it on wood in fire; on the place where the ashes are poured shall it be burned.

—————— אונקלוס ——————

עַל רֵישֵׁהּ וְעַל כְּרָעוֹהִי וְגַוֵּהּ וְאֻכְלֵהּ: יב וְיַפֵּק יָת כָּל תּוֹרָא מִבָּרָא לְמַשְׁרִיתָא לַאֲתַר דְּכֵי לַאֲתַר בֵּית מֵישַׁר קִטְמָא וְיוֹקִיד יָתֵהּ עַל אָעַיָּא בְּנוּרָא עַל אֲתַר בֵּית מֵישַׁד קִטְמָא יִתּוֹקָד:

—————— רש"י ——————

עַל הַכָּבֵד עַל הַכְּלָיוֹת עַל רֹאשׁוֹ וְעַל כְּרָעָיו. כֻּלָּן לְשׁוֹן תּוֹסֶפֶת הֵן כְּמוֹ מִלְּבַד: **(יב) אֶל מָקוֹם טָהוֹר.** לְפִי שֶׁיֵּשׁ מִחוּץ לָעִיר מָקוֹם מוּכָן לְטֻמְאָה לְהַשְׁלִיךְ אֲבָנִים מְנֻגָּעוֹת (סנהדרין ע"א) וּלְבֵית הַקְּבָרוֹת, הֻצְרַךְ לוֹמַר מִחוּץ לַמַּחֲנֶה זֶה שֶׁהוּא חוּץ לָעִיר שֶׁיְּהֵא הַמָּקוֹם טָהוֹר: **לַמַּחֲנֶה.** חוּץ לְשָׁלֹשׁ מַחֲנוֹת (ת"כ פרק ה:ג), וּבְבֵית עוֹלָמִים חוּץ לָעִיר, כְּמוֹ שֶׁפֵּרְשׁוּהוּ רַבּוֹתֵינוּ בְּמַסֶּכֶת יוֹמָא (סח.) וּבְסַנְהֶדְרִין (מב:): **אֶל שֶׁפֶךְ הַדֶּשֶׁן.** מָקוֹם שֶׁשּׁוֹפְכִין בּוֹ הַדֶּשֶׁן הַמְסֻלָּק מִן הַמִּזְבֵּחַ, כְּמָ"שׁ וְהוֹצִיא אֶת הַדֶּשֶׁן אֶל מִחוּץ לַמַּחֲנֶה (להלן ו:ד; ת"כ שם ה): **עַל שֶׁפֶךְ הַדֶּשֶׁן יִשָּׂרֵף.** שֶׁאֵין

—————— RASHI ELUCIDATED ——————

☐ עַל הַכָּבֵד עַל הַכְּלָיוֹת ... עַל רֹאשׁוֹ וְעַל כְּרָעָיו — WITH THE LIVER, WITH THE KIDNEYS ... WITH ITS HEAD, AND WITH ITS FEET. — כֻּלָּן לְשׁוֹן תּוֹסֶפֶת הֵן — All of [these instances of עַל] express addition, כְּמוֹ מִלְּבַד — like "besides."[1]

12. אֶל מָקוֹם טָהוֹר — TO A PURE PLACE. — לְפִי שֶׁיֵּשׁ מִחוּץ לָעִיר — Since there is outside the city מָקוֹם מוּכָן לְטֻמְאָה — a place prepared for impurity, i.e., for things that are impure, לְהַשְׁלִיךְ אֲבָנִים מְנֻגָּעוֹת — to throw away there plague-stricken stones[2] וּלְבֵית הַקְּבָרוֹת — and for a cemetery, הֻצְרַךְ לוֹמַר — [the verse] needed to say, מִחוּץ לַמַּחֲנֶה זֶה — with reference to this "outside of the camp" שֶׁהוּא חוּץ לָעִיר — which is also outside the city, שֶׁיְּהֵא הַמָּקוֹם טָהוֹר — that the place should be pure.

☐ מִחוּץ לַמַּחֲנֶה — OUTSIDE OF THE CAMP. — [3]חוּץ לְשָׁלֹשׁ מַחֲנוֹת — Outside three camps,[3] with respect to the Mishkan. וּבְבֵית עוֹלָמִים — And in the time of the Eternal House, the Beis HaMikdash, חוּץ לָעִיר — outside of the city,[4] כְּמוֹ שֶׁפֵּרְשׁוּהוּ רַבּוֹתֵינוּ — as our Rabbis explained it בְּמַסֶּכֶת יוֹמָא[5] וּבְסַנְהֶדְרִין — in Tractates Yoma[5] and Sanhedrin.[6]

☐ אֶל שֶׁפֶךְ הַדֶּשֶׁן — TO WHERE THE ASHES ARE POURED. This means מָקוֹם שֶׁשּׁוֹפְכִין בּוֹ הַדֶּשֶׁן — the place[7] where they pour the ashes הַמְסֻלָּק מִן הַמִּזְבֵּחַ — that are removed from the Mizbe'ach, כְּמָ"שׁ שֶׁנֶּאֱמַר — in the same manner in which it says, ,,וְהוֹצִיא אֶת הַדֶּשֶׁן אֶל מִחוּץ לַמַּחֲנֶה'' — "He shall remove the ashes to the outside of the camp."[8,9]

☐ עַל שֶׁפֶךְ הַדֶּשֶׁן יִשָּׂרֵף — ON THE PLACE WHERE THE ASHES ARE POURED SHALL IT BE BURNED. שֶׁאֵין

---

1. Some of the words in the rubric of this comment are from verse 9. The most common meaning of על is "on." However, it means "besides" in the instances cited. *Rashi* renders על in a similar sense in 2:2,4,5 above and in *Exodus* 29:13 and *Deuteronomy* 23:14.

2. *Sanhedrin* 71a; see 14:40 below.

3. *Toras Kohanim, Chovah, perek* 5:3.

4. The "camp" in the desert consisted of three camps: (a) The *Mishkan* and its courtyard was the camp of the *Shechinah*; (b) the camp of the Levites; and (c) the camp of the Israelites. In the days of the *Beis HaMikdash*, the city of Jerusalem comprised the three camps: (a) The camp of the *Shechinah* is the Temple area proper, including the Courtyard of the *Beis HaMikdash*; (b) the camp of the Levites is the area of the Temple Mount, including the *Ezras Nashim* (Women's Courtyard); and (c) the camp of the Israelites is the rest of the city up to the city walls (*Mizrachi; Sifsei Chachamim*; see also Rashi to Numbers 5:2).

5. *Yoma* 68a.

6.. *Sanhedrin* 42b. In addition to "outside of the camp" of this verse, the same phrase appears, seemingly superfluously, in verses 4:21 and 6:4 below. From the presence of three phrases, the Sages learn that the burning of those parts of the bull which are not burned on the *Mizbe'ach* was to take place outside of the three camps. While the Israelites were in the desert, this meant outside the entire camp. In the days of the *Beis HaMikdash*, it meant outside the city walls.

7. The term אֶל שֶׁפֶךְ הַדֶּשֶׁן means literally, "to the pouring of the ashes." It could have been understood as saying that the bull must be burned on the ashes which have been poured. Rashi explains that although it is preferable that there actually be ashes present, the verse here requires only that the bull is to be burned at the *location* of the pouring of the ashes (*Mizrachi*).

8. Below 6:4.

9. *Toras Kohanim, Chovah, perek* 5:5.

ויקרא – פרשת ויקרא / 38

יג וְאִ֚ם כָּל־עֲדַ֣ת יִשְׂרָאֵל֙ יִשְׁגּ֔וּ וְנֶעְלַ֣ם דָּבָ֔ר מֵעֵינֵ֖י הַקָּהָ֑ל וְ֠עָשׂ֠וּ אַחַ֨ת מִכָּל־מִצְוֺ֧ת יְהֹוָ֛ה אֲשֶׁ֥ר לֹא־תֵעָשֶׂ֖ינָה וְאָשֵֽׁמוּ׃ יד וְנֽוֹדְעָה֙ הַֽחַטָּ֔את אֲשֶׁ֥ר חָטְא֖וּ עָלֶ֑יהָ וְהִקְרִ֨יבוּ הַקָּהָ֜ל פַּ֤ר בֶּן־בָּקָר֙ לְחַטָּ֔את וְהֵבִ֣יאוּ אֹת֔וֹ לִפְנֵ֖י אֹ֥הֶל מוֹעֵֽד׃ טו וְ֠סָמְכ֠וּ זִקְנֵ֨י הָעֵדָ֧ה אֶת־יְדֵיהֶ֛ם עַל־רֹ֥אשׁ הַפָּ֖ר לִפְנֵ֣י יְהֹוָ֑ה וְשָׁחַ֥ט אֶת־הַפָּ֖ר לִפְנֵ֥י יְהֹוָֽה׃ טז וְהֵבִ֛יא הַכֹּהֵ֥ן הַמָּשִׁ֖יחַ מִדַּ֣ם הַפָּ֑ר אֶל־אֹ֖הֶל מוֹעֵֽד׃ יז וְטָבַ֧ל הַכֹּהֵ֛ן אֶצְבָּע֖וֹ מִן־הַדָּ֑ם וְהִזָּ֞ה שֶׁ֤בַע פְּעָמִים֙ לִפְנֵ֣י יְהֹוָ֔ה אֶת

13 *If the entire assembly of Israel shall err, and a matter became obscured from the eyes of the congregation; and they commit one from among all the commandments of* HASHEM *that may not be done, and they become guilty;* **14** *when the sin regarding which they committed becomes known, the congregation shall offer a bull, a young male of cattle, as a sin-offering, and they shall bring it before the Tent of Meeting.* **15** *The elders of the assembly shall lean their hands upon the head of the bull before* HASHEM, *and someone shall slaughter the bull before* HASHEM. **16** *The anointed Kohen shall bring part of the bull's blood to the Tent of Meeting.* **17** *The Kohen shall dip his finger from the blood; and he shall sprinkle seven times before* HASHEM,

──────── אונקלוס ────────

יג וְאִם כָּל כְּנִשְׁתָּא דְיִשְׂרָאֵל יִשְׁתַּלּוּן וִיהֵי מְכַסָּא פִתְגָמָא מֵעֵינֵי קְהָלָא וְיַעְבְּדוּן חַד מִכֹּל פִּקוּדַיָּא דַּייָ דִּי לָא כָשְׁרִין לְאִתְעֲבָדָא וִיחוּבוּן: יד וְתִתְיְדַע חוֹבְתָא דִּי חָבוּ עֲלַהּ וִיקָרְבוּן קְהָלָא תּוֹר בַּר תּוֹרֵי לְחַטָּאתָא וְיַעֲלוּן יָתֵהּ לָקֳדָם מַשְׁכַּן זִמְנָא: טו וְיִסְמְכוּן סָבֵי כְנִשְׁתָּא יָת יְדֵיהוֹן עַל רֵישׁ תּוֹרָא קֳדָם יְיָ וְיִכּוֹס יָת תּוֹרָא קֳדָם יְיָ: טז וְיָעֵל כַּהֲנָא רַבָּא מִן דְּמָא דְתוֹרָא לְמַשְׁכַּן זִמְנָא: יז וְיִטְבּוֹל כַּהֲנָא (בְּ)אֶצְבְּעֵהּ מִן דְּמָא וְיַדֵּי שְׁבַע זִמְנִין לָקֳדָם יְיָ יָת

──────── רש"י ────────

ת"ל, אֶלָּא לִלְמַד בְּאַחַת מִכֹּל כְּרִיתוֹת שֶׁבַּתּוֹרָה שֶׁהוּא מוּתָּר (הוריות ת.): (יג) עֲדַת יִשְׂרָאֵל. אֵלוּ סַנְהֶדְרִין (שָׁם פָּרָשָׁתָא ד:ב): וְנֶעְלַם דָּבָר. טָעוּ לְהוֹרוֹת בְּאַחַת מִכֹּל כְּרִיתוֹת שֶׁבַּתּוֹרָה (הוריות ח.): הַקָּהָל וְעָשׂוּ. שֶׁעָשׂוּ צִבּוּר עַל פִּיהֶם (ת"כ שָׁם י; הוריות ג.):

──────── RASHI ELUCIDATED ────────

תַּלְמוּד לוֹמַר – **Let the Torah not have said** this, for the verse has already said where the bull is to be burned. אֶלָּא – **But,** it is repeated¹ לְלַמֵּד שֶׁאֲפִילוּ אֵין שָׁם דֶּשֶׁן – **to teach** us **that** the burning may be done **even if there are no ashes there.**¹

13. עֲדַת יִשְׂרָאֵל – ASSEMBLY OF ISRAEL. אֵלוּ סַנְהֶדְרִין² – **These are the Sanhedrin.²**

□ וְנֶעְלַם דָּבָר – AND A MATTER BECAME OBSCURED. טָעוּ – **They erred** לְהוֹרוֹת – **by ruling** בְּאַחַת – on one, מִכֹּל כְּרִיתוֹת שֶׁבַּתּוֹרָה – **on one of all,** i.e., on any one of, **the** *kereisos*³ **that are in the Torah** about which they said שֶׁהוּא מֻתָּר⁴ – **that it is permitted** when in fact it is forbidden.⁴

□ הַקָּהָל וְעָשׂוּ – THE CONGREGATION; AND THEY COMMIT. This means שֶׁעָשׂוּ צִבּוּר עַל פִּיהֶם – **that the public acted on the word of [the Sanhedrin].**⁵

---

1. *Pesachim* 75b. The repetition of the commandment to burn the bull at the place where the ashes are poured implies the need to burn the bull in all circumstances (*Gur Aryeh*).

2. *Toras Kohanim, Chovah, parshasa* 4:2. The word "assembly" is used in reference to the courts of twenty-three judges (Lesser Sanhedrin) in *Numbers* 35:24,25. "Assembly *of Israel*" implies not just any Sanhedrin, but the one court which is unique among the courts of Israel the Great Sanhedrin of seventy-one judges that sat on the Temple Mount (*Mizrachi; Sifsei Chachamim*).

3. Acts punishable by *kares*. See note 8 on page 8.

4. *Horayos* 8a.

5. *Toras Kohanim, Chovah, parshasa* 4:10; *Horayos* 3a. The beginning of the verse used the term עֲדַת יִשְׂרָאֵל, "assembly of Israel," to refer to the Sanhedrin. But here, the verse uses a different term, עֵינֵי הַקָּהָל, "the eyes of the congregation." Moreover, the verse could have been more brief: וְאִם כָּל עֲדַת יִשְׂרָאֵל יִשְׁגּוּ וְנֶעְלַם דָּבָר מֵעֵינֵיהֶם, "If the entire assembly of Israel shall err, and a matter became obscured from *their* eyes." The verse uses עֵינֵי הַקָּהָל in order to juxtapose הַקָּהָל and וְעָשׂוּ, "and they commit." This teaches us that the subject of "and they commit" is not עֲדַת יִשְׂרָאֵל, the Sanhedrin, who were the subject of the beginning of the verse, but refers to the congregation of Israel. If the Sanhedrin alone acts upon their erroneous decision, they bring the same sin-offering as any other individual (see *Maskil LeDavid*).

39 / VAYIKRA/LEVITICUS — PARASHAS VAYIKRA — 4/18-19

toward the Curtain. ¹⁸ *He shall put some of the blood upon the horns of the Mizbe'ach that is before HASHEM, which is in the Tent of Meeting; and all the remaining blood he shall pour onto the base of the Olah-offering Mizbe'ach, which is at the entrance of the Tent of Meeting.* ¹⁹ *He shall separate all its fats from it and cause it to go up in smoke*

יח וּמִן־הַדָּם יִתֵּן ׀ עַל־קַרְנֹת הַמִּזְבֵּחַ אֲשֶׁר לִפְנֵי יהוה אֲשֶׁר בְּאֹהֶל מוֹעֵד וְאֵת כָּל־הַדָּם יִשְׁפֹּךְ אֶל־יְסוֹד מִזְבַּח הָעֹלָה אֲשֶׁר־פֶּתַח אֹהֶל מוֹעֵד: יט וְאֵת כָּל־חֶלְבּוֹ יָרִים מִמֶּנּוּ וְהִקְטִיר

—————— אונקלוס ——————

יח וּמִן דְּמָא יִתֵּן עַל קַרְנַת מַדְבְּחָא דִּי קֳדָם יְיָ דִי בְמַשְׁכַּן זִמְנָא וְיָת כָּל דְּמָא יֵשׁוֹד לִיסוֹדָא דְמַדְבְּחָא דַעֲלָתָא דִי בִתְרַע מַשְׁכַּן זִמְנָא: יט וְיָת כָּל תַּרְבֵּהּ יַפְרֵשׁ מִנֵּהּ וְיַסֵּק

—————— רש"י ——————

(יז) את פני הפרכת. ולמעלה הוא אומר את פני פרכת הקדש (לעיל פסוק ו) משל למלך שסרחה עליו מדינה, אם מיעוטה סרחו פמליא שלו מתקיימת ואם כולם סרחו אין פמליא שלו מתקיימת (זבחים מא:). אף כאן כשחטא כהן משיח עדיין [שם] קדושת המקום על המקדש, משחטאו כולם ח"ו נסתלקה הקדושה: (יח) יסוד מזבח העולה.

אשר פתח אהל מועד. זה יסוד מערבי שהוא כנגד הפתח (ת"כ פרשתא ג:יג; זבחים נא.): (יט) ואת כל חלבו ירים. אע"פ שלא פירש כאן יותרת ושתי כליות למדין הם ממוצא לפר כאשר עשה וגו'. ומפני מה לא נתפרשו בו, תנא דבי רבי ישמעאל, משל למלך שזעם על אוהבו ומיעט בסרחונו מפני חיבתו (זבחים מא:):

—————— RASHI ELUCIDATED ——————

17. אֶת פְּנֵי הַפָּרֹכֶת — TOWARD THE CURTAIN. וּלְמַעְלָה הוּא אוֹמֵר — But above it says, "הַקֹּדֶשׁ" — "toward the Curtain of the Holy."[1] מָשָׁל לְמֶלֶךְ שֶׁסָּרְחָה עָלָיו מְדִינָה — This can be compared to a king against whom the country has rebelled. אִם מִעוּטָהּ סָרְחוּ — If its minority, i.e., if the minority of its population, has rebelled, פַּמַּלְיָא שֶׁלּוֹ מִתְקַיֶּימֶת — his administration still exists. וְאִם כֻּלָּם סָרְחוּ — But if all of it has rebelled, [2]אֵין פַּמַּלְיָא שֶׁלּוֹ מִתְקַיֶּימֶת — his administration no longer exists. אַף כָּאן — Here, too, כְּשֶׁחָטָא כֹּהֵן מָשִׁיחַ — when the Anointed Kohen[3] sinned, עֲדַיִין {שָׁם} קְדֻשַּׁת הַמָּקוֹם עַל הַמִּקְדָּשׁ — {the status of} the holiness of the location still remains upon the *Beis HaMikdash*, and therefore the verse uses "the Curtain of the Holy." מִשֶּׁחָטְאוּ כֻלָּם — Once all of [Israel] has sinned, חַס וְשָׁלוֹם — Heaven forbid, נִסְתַּלְּקָה הַקְּדֻשָּׁה — the holiness has departed.

18. יְסוֹד מִזְבַּח הָעוֹלָה אֲשֶׁר פֶּתַח אֹהֶל מוֹעֵד — [HE SHALL POUR ONTO] THE BASE OF THE *OLAH*-OFFERING MIZBE'ACH, WHICH IS AT THE ENTRANCE OF THE TENT OF MEETING. זֶה יְסוֹד מַעֲרָבִי — This is the western base of the *Mizbe'ach*, the side of the base שֶׁהוּא כְּנֶגֶד הַפֶּתַח[4] — that is opposite the entrance.[4]

19. וְאֵת כָּל חֶלְבּוֹ יָרִים — HE SHALL SEPARATE ALL ITS FATS. אַף עַל פִּי שֶׁלֹּא פֵּרֵשׁ כָּאן — Although [the Torah] did not state here explicitly that in addition to the fats יוֹתֶרֶת וּשְׁתֵּי כְלָיוֹת — the diaphragm and the two kidneys are placed on the *Mizbe'ach*, לְמֵדִין הֵם — they are derived מִ..וְעָשָׂה לַפָּר כַּאֲשֶׁר עָשָׂה וְגוֹמֵר" — from the next verse, "He shall do to the bull as he had done, etc." וּמִפְּנֵי מָה לֹא נִתְפָּרְשׁוּ בּוֹ — And why were [the diaphragm and the kidneys] not stated explicitly with regard to [the *par he'elem davar*]? תָּנָא דְּבֵי רַבִּי יִשְׁמָעֵאל — It has been taught by the students of the House of Study of the *Tanna* R' Yishmael: מָשָׁל לְמֶלֶךְ שֶׁזָּעַם עַל אוֹהֲבוֹ — This can be compared to a king who became incensed at his loving friend. וּמִעֵט בְּסִרְחוֹנוֹ — [The king] was brief in his discussion of [the friend's] dishonor, מִפְּנֵי חִבָּתוֹ[5] — because of [the friend's] love [for him].[5]

---

1. Above v. 6.
2. *Zevachim* 41b.
3. The subject of verse 6.
4. *Toras Kohanim, Chovah, parshasa* 3:13; *Zevachim* 51a. The Torah has already stated (*Exodus* 40:6,39) that the *Mizbe'ach* is situated opposite the entrance to the Tent of Meeting. The apparently superfluous "which is at the entrance of the Tent of Meeting," then, modifies the base, not the *Mizbe'ach* as a whole (*Mizrachi; Sifsei Chachamim*).
5. *Zevachim* 41b. Alternatively: "because of [the king's] love [for him]."

ויקרא – פרשת ויקרא

כ הַמִּזְבֵּחַ: וְעָשָׂה לַפָּר כַּאֲשֶׁר עָשָׂה לְפַר הַחַטָּאת כֵּן יַעֲשֶׂה־לּוֹ וְכִפֶּר עֲלֵהֶם הַכֹּהֵן וְנִסְלַח לָהֶם: כא וְהוֹצִיא אֶת־הַפָּר אֶל־מִחוּץ לַמַּחֲנֶה וְשָׂרַף אֹתוֹ כַּאֲשֶׁר שָׂרַף אֵת הַפָּר הָרִאשׁוֹן חַטַּאת הַקָּהָל הוּא:

on the Mizbe'ach. [20] He shall do to the bull as he had done to the sin-offering bull, so shall he do to it; thus shall the Kohen provide them atonement and it shall be forgiven them. [21] He shall remove the bull to the outside of the camp and burn it, as he had burned the first bull; it is a sin-offering of the congregation.

אונקלוס

כ וְיַעֲבֵד לְתוֹרָא כְּמָא דִי עֲבַד לְתוֹרָא דְחַטָּאתָא כֵּן יַעֲבֵּד לֵהּ וִיכַפַּר עֲלֵיהוֹן כַּהֲנָא וְיִשְׁתְּבֵק לְהוֹן: כא וְיַפֵּק יָת תּוֹרָא לְמִבָּרָא לְמַשְׁרִיתָא וְיוֹקִיד יָתֵהּ כְּמָא דִי אוֹקִיד יָת תּוֹרָא קַדְמָאָה חַטָּאת קְהָלָא הוּא:

רש"י

(כ) **ועשה לפר** זה כאשר עשה לפר החטאת. כמו שמפורש בפר כהן משיח, להביא יותרת ושתי כליות שפירש שם (לעיל פסוק ט) מה שלא פירש כאן (זבחים מא.). ולכפול במצות העבודות

ללמד שאם חסר אחת מכל המתנות פסול (ת"כ שם פרק ו:ה; זבחים לט.). לפי שמצינו בניתנין על המזבח החיצון שנתנה מתנה אחת כיפר, הוצרך לומר כאן שמתנה אחת מהן מעכבת:

RASHI ELUCIDATED

20. וְעָשָׂה לַפָּר – **HE SHALL DO TO THE BULL**, i.e., he shall do to זֶה – **this** bull,[1] כַּאֲשֶׁר עָשָׂה לְפַר הַחַטָּאת – **as he had done to the sin-offering bull**, כְּמוֹ שֶׁמְּפוֹרָשׁ בְּפַר כֹּהֵן מָשִׁיחַ – **as stated explicitly regarding the bull of the Anointed Kohen.**[2] לְהָבִיא יוֹתֶרֶת וּשְׁתֵּי כְלָיוֹת – This is said **to include** the placing of the **diaphragm** and the **two kidneys** on the *Mizbe'ach*,[3] שֶׁפֵּרַשׁ שָׁם – **for [the Torah] stated explicitly there**[3] מַה שֶּׁלֹּא פֵּרַשׁ כָּאן – **that which it did not state explicitly here.**[4] וּלְכְפֹּל בְּמִצְוֹת הָעֲבוֹדוֹת – **And** this verse is meant **to repeat the commandment of the sacrificial procedures** לְלַמֵּד – **to teach us**[5] שֶׁאִם חִסֵּר אַחַת מִכָּל הַמַּתָּנוֹת פָּסוּל – **that if he left out** even **one of the applications** of blood to the *Mizbe'ach* or the *Paroches* [**the offering**] **is invalid.**[5] לְפִי שֶׁמָּצִינוּ בְּנִתָּנִין עַל הַמִּזְבֵּחַ הַחִיצוֹן – **Because we find with regard to those** offerings **the blood of which is put on the outer *Mizbe'ach*** שֶׁנִּתְּנָן מַתָּנָה אַחַת כִּפֵּר – **that if he put** only **one application** of blood onto the *Mizbe'ach* **it atones**, and the offering is valid,[6] הֻצְרַךְ לוֹמַר כָּאן – **it was necessary to say here** שֶׁמַּתָּנָה אַחַת מֵהֶן – **that** failure to perform even **one application** of the four on the inner *Mizbe'ach* or the seven on the *Paroches* מְעַכֶּבֶת – **prevents** the offering from being accepted.

---
1. The word זֶה, "this," does not appear in the verse. Rashi interpolates it because the structure וְעָשָׂה לַפָּר כַּאֲשֶׁר עָשָׂה לְ... ["he shall do to the bull as he had done to..."] in the Hebrew language suggests that the bull is about to be compared to some other species of animal. But this is not the case in our verse. Rashi stresses that the contrast is between *this* bull and another bull (*Mizrachi; Sifsei Chachamim*).

2. The verse compares "the bull" of the *he'elem davar* to "the bull of the sin-offering," implying that it is something other than a sin-offering, when in fact the bull of the *he'elem davar* is itself a sin-offering. Rashi resolves this by explaining that the verse means to compare the bull of *he'elem davar* to that sin-offering bull whose laws have been stated explicitly (*Mizrachi; Sifsei Chachamim*).

3. Above v. 9.

4. *Zevachim* 41b.

5. *Toras Kohanim, Chovah, perek* 6:5; *Zevachim* 39a. The apparently superfluous "so shall he do to it" is a

repetition of the directions involving the application of the blood of the offering to the *Mizbe'ach* and the *Paroches*, for those directions are also given in the context of the sin-offering of the Kohen Gadol. They are repeated to disqualify the offering if all the directions are not followed. For the rule is that failure to perform any commandment in the offering procedure which was stated only once does not disqualify the offering. Failure to perform a commandment which was *repeated* renders the offering invalid (*Maskil LeDavid*).

6. The *olah*-offering, the peace-offering, and the guilt-offering all require two applications of blood at two corners of the outer *Mizbe'ach* diagonally opposite each other so that the blood is applied to all four sides of the *Mizbe'ach*. Sin-offerings whose blood is applied to the outer *Mizbe'ach* require four applications at the four corners. In the case of these offerings, as long as one application was made, the offering is valid, because the requirement to make multiple applications was not stated and repeated.

4 / 22-24

²² When a ruler sins, and commits one from among all the commandments of HASHEM that may not be done — unintentionally — and becomes guilty: ²³ If the sin that he committed became known to him, he shall bring his offering, a male goat, unblemished. ²⁴ He shall lean his hands on the head of the goat and he shall slaughter it in the place he would slaughter the olah-offering before HASHEM; it is a sin-offering.

כב אֲשֶׁ֥ר נָשִׂ֖יא יֶחֱטָ֑א וְעָשָׂ֡ה אַחַ֣ת מִכָּל־מִצְוֺת֩ יהו֨ה אֱלֹהָ֜יו אֲשֶׁ֧ר לֹא־תֵעָשֶׂ֛ינָה בִּשְׁגָגָ֖ה וְאָשֵֽׁם: כג אֽוֹ־הוֹדַ֤ע אֵלָיו֙ חַטָּאת֔וֹ אֲשֶׁ֥ר חָטָ֖א בָּ֑הּ וְהֵבִ֧יא אֶת־קָרְבָּנ֛וֹ שְׂעִ֥יר עִזִּ֖ים זָכָ֥ר תָּמִֽים: כד וְסָמַ֤ךְ יָדוֹ֙ עַל־רֹ֣אשׁ הַשָּׂעִ֔יר וְשָׁחַ֣ט אֹת֔וֹ בִּמְק֛וֹם אֲשֶׁר־יִשְׁחַ֥ט אֶת־הָעֹלָ֖ה לִפְנֵ֣י יהו֑ה חַטָּ֖את הֽוּא׃

──────────── אונקלוס ────────────

כב דִּי רַבָּא יֵחוֹב וְיַעֲבֵּד חַד מִכָּל פִּקּוּדַיָּא דַּיְיָ אֱלָהֵהּ דִּי לָא כָשְׁרִין לְאִתְעֲבָדָא בְּשָׁלוּ וְיֵחוֹב: כג אוֹ אִתְיְדַע לֵהּ חוֹבָתֵהּ דִּי חָב בַּהּ וְיַיְתִי יָת קֻרְבָּנֵהּ צְפִיר בַּר עִזִּין דְּכַר שְׁלִים: כד וְיִסְמוֹךְ יְדֵהּ עַל רֵישׁ צְפִירָא וְיִכּוֹס יָתֵהּ בְּאַתְרָא דִּי יִכּוֹס יָת עֲלָתָא קֳדָם יְיָ חַטָּאתָא הוּא:

──────────── רש"י ────────────

(כב) אשר נשיא יחטא. לשון אשרי, אשרי הדור שהנשיא שלו נותן לב להביא כפרה על שגגתו, ק"ו שמתחרט על זדונותיו (ת"כ פרשתא ה:א; הוריות י:): (כג) או הודע. כמו אם הודע הדבר. הרבה או יש משמשין בלשון אם ואם במקום או, וכן אם נודע כי שור נגח הוא (שמות כא:לו): הודע אליו. כשחטא היה סבור שהוא היתר ולאחר מכאן נודע לו שאיסור היה: (כד) במקום אשר ישחט את העולה. בצפון שהוא מפורש בעולה (לעיל א:יא; ת"כ שם פרשתא ו:י; ת"כ שם): חטאת הוא. לשמו כשר, שלא לשמו פסול (ת"כ שם פרק ח:ו; זבחים י:):

──────────── RASHI ELUCIDATED ────────────

22. אֲשֶׁר נָשִׂיא יֶחֱטָא — WHEN A RULER SINS. לְשׁוֹן אַשְׁרֵי — The word אֲשֶׁר here is **related to** אַשְׁרֵי [fortunate], as if to say, אַשְׁרֵי הַדּוֹר — **fortunate is the generation** שֶׁהַנָּשִׂיא שֶׁלוֹ נוֹתֵן לֵב לְהָבִיא כַּפָּרָה — **whose ruler sets his heart to bring an atonement for his unintentional sin.** עַל שִׁגְגָתוֹ — All the more so ,שֶׁמִּתְחָרֵט עַל זְדוֹנוֹתָיו — **that he has regrets over his intentional sins.**[1]

23. אוֹ הוֹדַע — IF . . . BECAME KNOWN. This has the same meaning כְּמוֹ אִם הוֹדַע הַדָּבָר — as "**if [the sin that he has committed] became known.**"[2] הַרְבֵּה אוֹ יֵשׁ מְשַׁמְּשִׁין בִּלְשׁוֹן אִם — There are **many instances of** אוֹ **which serve to express** אִם,[3] וְאִם בִּמְקוֹם אוֹ — **and** there are **many instances of** אִם **in place of** אוֹ.[4] וְכֵן ,אוֹ נוֹדַע כִּי שׁוֹר נַגָּח הוּא — Similarly, אוֹ in, "**if it was known that it was a** habitually **goring ox,**"[5] means "**if.**"

□ הוֹדַע אֵלָיו — BECAME KNOWN TO HIM. כְּשֶׁחָטָא — When he sinned הָיָה סָבוּר שֶׁהוּא הֶתֵּר — he was **under the impression that [what he did] is permitted,** וּלְאַחַר מִכַּאן נוֹדַע לוֹ — **and afterwards it became known to him** שֶׁאִסּוּר הָיָה — **that it was something forbidden.**

24. בִּמְקוֹם אֲשֶׁר יִשְׁחַט אֶת הָעֹלָה — IN THE PLACE HE WOULD SLAUGHTER THE OLAH-OFFERING. בַּצָּפוֹן — At the north side of the *Mizbe'ach*, שֶׁהוּא מְפֹרָשׁ — which is stated explicitly בְּעוֹלָה — with regard to the *olah*-offering.[6,7]

□ חַטָּאת הוּא — IT IS A SIN-OFFERING. לִשְׁמוֹ כָּשֵׁר — For its sake, it is valid. שֶׁלֹּא לִשְׁמוֹ פָּסוּל — Not for its sake, it is not valid.[8]

──────────────────────────

1. *Toras Kohanim, Chovah, parshasa* 5:1; *Horayos* 10b. Verse 3 of this chapter began, "If the anointed Kohen will sin." Our verse uses אֲשֶׁר, "when," rather than אִם, "if," in order to suggest the word אַשְׁרֵי, "fortunate" (*Mizrachi; Sifsei Chachamim*).

2. The most common meaning of אוֹ is "or." Rashi explains that here it is used in the sense of אִם, "if."

3. See Rashi to 26:41 below, *Numbers* 5:30 and 15:6.

4. See Rashi and *Metzudas Tzion* to *Job* 39:13.

5. *Exodus* 21:36. Rashi there appears to explain אִם of our verse differently from the way he does here. See *Mizrachi, Gur Aryeh,* and *Divrei David* there for a discussion of the apparent contradiction.

6. Above 1:11.

7. *Toras Kohanim, Chovah, parshasa* 6:10.

8. *Toras Kohanim, Chovah, perek* 8:6. *Zevachim* 10b. The verse makes this statement to imply that throughout the entire sacrificial procedure the one who is officiating must intend that he is bringing the offering for its sake, i.e., with the intention that it is a sin-offering. If during part of the service he thought that it was some other type of offering, the offering becomes invalid (*Devek Tov; Minchas Yehudah; Sifsei Chachamim*).

²⁵ The Kohen shall take from the blood of the sin-offering with his forefinger and place it upon the horns of the Olah-offering Mizbe'ach; and he shall pour its blood upon the base of the Olah-offering Mizbe'ach. ²⁶ And he shall cause all its fats to go up in smoke on the Mizbe'ach, like the fats of the sacrifice of the peace-offering; thus shall the Kohen provide him atonement for his sin, and it shall be forgiven him.

²⁷ If an individual person from among the people of the land shall sin unintentionally, by committing one of the commandments of Hashem that may not be done, and he becomes guilty: ²⁸ If the sin that he committed becomes known to him, he shall bring as his offering a she-goat, unblemished, for the sin that he committed. ²⁹ He shall lean his hands upon the head of the sin-offering; and he shall slaughter the sin-offering in the place of the olah-offering. ³⁰ The Kohen shall take from its blood with his forefinger and place it on the horns of the Olah-offering Mizbe'ach; and he shall pour all of its [remaining] blood upon the base of the Mizbe'ach. ³¹ He shall remove all of its fat, as the fat had been removed from upon the sacrifice of the peace-offering,

כה וְלָקַח הַכֹּהֵן מִדַּם הַחַטָּאת בְּאֶצְבָּעוֹ וְנָתַן עַל־קַרְנֹת מִזְבַּח הָעֹלָה וְאֶת־דָּמוֹ יִשְׁפֹּךְ אֶל־יְסוֹד מִזְבַּח הָעֹלָה: כו וְאֶת־כָּל־חֶלְבּוֹ יַקְטִיר הַמִּזְבֵּחָה כְּחֵלֶב זֶבַח הַשְּׁלָמִים וְכִפֶּר עָלָיו הַכֹּהֵן מֵחַטָּאתוֹ וְנִסְלַח לוֹ:

ששי כז וְאִם־נֶפֶשׁ אַחַת תֶּחֱטָא בִשְׁגָגָה מֵעַם הָאָרֶץ בַּעֲשֹׂתָהּ אַחַת מִמִּצְוֹת יְהוָה אֲשֶׁר לֹא־תֵעָשֶׂינָה וְאָשֵׁם: כח אוֹ הוֹדַע אֵלָיו חַטָּאתוֹ אֲשֶׁר חָטָא וְהֵבִיא קָרְבָּנוֹ שְׂעִירַת עִזִּים תְּמִימָה נְקֵבָה עַל־חַטָּאתוֹ אֲשֶׁר חָטָא: כט וְסָמַךְ אֶת־יָדוֹ עַל רֹאשׁ הַחַטָּאת וְשָׁחַט אֶת־הַחַטָּאת בִּמְקוֹם הָעֹלָה: ל וְלָקַח הַכֹּהֵן מִדָּמָהּ בְּאֶצְבָּעוֹ וְנָתַן עַל־קַרְנֹת מִזְבַּח הָעֹלָה וְאֶת־כָּל־דָּמָהּ יִשְׁפֹּךְ אֶל־יְסוֹד הַמִּזְבֵּחַ: לא וְאֶת־כָּל־חֶלְבָּהּ יָסִיר כַּאֲשֶׁר הוּסַר חֵלֶב מֵעַל זֶבַח הַשְּׁלָמִים

─────────── אונקלוס ───────────

כה וְיִסַּב כַּהֲנָא מִדְּמָא דְחַטָּאתָא בְּאֶצְבְּעֵהּ וְיִתֵּן עַל קַרְנַת מַדְבְּחָא דַעֲלָתָא וְיָת דְּמֵהּ יֵשׁוֹד לִיסוֹדָא דְמַדְבְּחָא דַעֲלָתָא: כו וְיָת כָּל תַּרְבֵּהּ יַסֵּק לְמַדְבְּחָא כִּתְרַב נִכְסַת קוּדְשַׁיָּא וִיכַפַּר עֲלוֹהִי כַהֲנָא מֵחוֹבָתֵהּ וְיִשְׁתְּבֵק לֵהּ: כז וְאִם אֱנָשׁ חַד יֵחוֹב בְּשָׁלוּ מֵעַמָּא דְאַרְעָא בְּמֶעְבְּדֵהּ חַד מִפִּקּוּדַיָּא דַיְיָ דִּי לָא כָשְׁרִין לְאִתְעֲבָדָא וִיחוֹב: כח אוֹ יִתְיְדַע לֵהּ חוֹבָתֵהּ דִּי חָב וְיַיְתֵי קָרְבָּנֵהּ צְפִירַת בַּר עִזֵּי שְׁלֶמְתָּא נֻקְבְּתָא עַל חוֹבָתֵהּ דִּי חָב: כט וְיִסְמוֹךְ יָת יְדֵהּ עַל רֵישׁ חַטָּאתָא וְיִכּוֹס יָת חַטָּאתָא בַּאֲתַר דַּעֲלָתָא: ל וְיִסַּב כַּהֲנָא מִדְּמַהּ בְּאֶצְבְּעֵהּ וְיִתֵּן עַל קַרְנַת מַדְבְּחָא דַעֲלָתָא וְיָת כָּל דְּמַהּ יֵשׁוֹד לִיסוֹדָא דְמַדְבְּחָא: לא וְיָת כָּל תַּרְבַּהּ יֶעְדֵּי כְּמָא דִי אִתַּעֲדָא תְרַב מֵעַל נִכְסַת קוּדְשַׁיָּא

─────────── רש"י ───────────

פרק ח:ו; זבחים י:ו: (כה) וְאֶת דָּמוֹ. שִׁיָּרֵי הַדָּם: (כו) כְּחֵלֶב זֶבַח (לעיל ג:יד-טו) ת"כ שם פרק ט:ד): (לא) בַּאֲשֶׁר הוּסַר חֵלֶב הַשְּׁלָמִים. כְּאוֹתָן אֵימוּרִין הַמְפֹרָשִׁים בְּעֵז הָאָמוּר אֵצֶל שְׁלָמִים. כְּאִמּוּרֵי עֵז הָאֲמוּרִים בִּשְׁלָמִים (לעיל שם;

─────────── RASHI ELUCIDATED ───────────

25. וְאֶת דָּמוֹ — AND ... ITS BLOOD. שִׁיָּרֵי הַדָּם — The remainder of the blood.[1]

26. כְּחֵלֶב זֶבַח הַשְּׁלָמִים — LIKE THE FATS OF THE SACRIFICE OF THE PEACE-OFFERING. כְּאוֹתָן אֲמוּרִין — Like those specified parts — הַמְפֹרָשִׁים — which are mentioned explicitly [3,4] בְּעֵז הָאָמוּר אֵצֶל שְׁלָמִים — with regard to the goat[2] mentioned in the section that discusses the peace-offering.[3,4]

31. כַּאֲשֶׁר הוּסַר חֵלֶב מֵעַל זֶבַח הַשְּׁלָמִים — AS THE FAT HAD BEEN REMOVED FROM UPON THE SACRIFICE OF THE PEACE OFFERING. כָּאֲמוּרֵי עֵז — Like the specified parts of the goat[2] הָאֲמוּרִים בִּשְׁלָמִים [3,5] — which are mentioned with regard to the peace-offering.[3,5]

---

1. See note 1 to v. 7 above.
2. Unlike the sheep, the goat's tail is not offered on the Mizbe'ach.
3. Above 3:14-15.
4. Toras Kohanim, Chovah, perek 9:4.
5. Toras Kohanim, perek 10:7.

and the Kohen shall cause it to go up in smoke on the Mizbe'ach as a satisfying aroma to HASHEM; and the Kohen shall provide him atonement, and it shall be forgiven him.

³² If he shall bring a sheep as his offering for a sin-offering, he shall bring a female, unblemished. ³³ He shall lean his hands upon the head of the sin-offering; he shall slaughter it for a sin-offering in the place where he would slaughter the olah-offering. ³⁴ The Kohen shall take from the blood of the sin-offering with his forefinger and place it upon the horns of the Olah-offering Mizbe'ach; and he shall pour all its [remaining] blood upon the base of the Mizbe'ach. ³⁵ And he shall remove all its fat as the fat of the sheep would be removed from the sacrifice of the peace-offering, and the Kohen shall cause them to go up in smoke on the Mizbe'ach, on the fires of HASHEM; and the Kohen shall provide him atonement for the sin that he committed, and it shall be forgiven him.

וְהִקְטִיר הַכֹּהֵן הַמִּזְבֵּחָה לְרֵיחַ נִיחֹחַ לַיהוה וְכִפֶּר עָלָיו הַכֹּהֵן וְנִסְלַח לוֹ:
לב וְאִם־כֶּבֶשׂ יָבִיא קָרְבָּנוֹ לְחַטָּאת לג נְקֵבָה תְמִימָה יְבִיאֶנָּה: וְסָמַךְ אֶת־יָדוֹ עַל רֹאשׁ הַחַטָּאת וְשָׁחַט אֹתָהּ לְחַטָּאת בִּמְקוֹם אֲשֶׁר לד יִשְׁחַט אֶת־הָעֹלָה: וְלָקַח הַכֹּהֵן מִדַּם הַחַטָּאת בְּאֶצְבָּעוֹ וְנָתַן עַל־קַרְנֹת מִזְבַּח הָעֹלָה וְאֶת־כָּל־דָּמָהּ יִשְׁפֹּךְ אֶל־יְסוֹד הַמִּזְבֵּחַ: לה וְאֶת־כָּל־חֶלְבָּהּ יָסִיר כַּאֲשֶׁר יוּסַר חֵלֶב־הַכֶּשֶׂב מִזֶּבַח הַשְּׁלָמִים וְהִקְטִיר הַכֹּהֵן אֹתָם הַמִּזְבֵּחָה עַל אִשֵּׁי יהוה וְכִפֶּר עָלָיו הַכֹּהֵן עַל־חַטָּאתוֹ אֲשֶׁר־חָטָא וְנִסְלַח לוֹ:

──── אונקלוס ────

וְיַסֵּק כַּהֲנָא לְמַדְבְּחָא לְאִתְקַבָּלָא בְּרַעֲוָא קֳדָם יְיָ וִיכַפֵּר עֲלוֹהִי כַהֲנָא וְיִשְׁתְּבֵק לֵהּ: לב וְאִם אִמַּר יַיְתֵי קָרְבָּנֵהּ לְחַטָּאתָא נֻקְבְּתָא שְׁלֶמְתָּא יַיְתִנַּהּ: לג וְיִסְמוֹךְ יָת יְדֵהּ עַל רֵישָׁא דְחַטָּאתָא וְיִכּוֹס יָתַהּ לְחַטָּאתָא בְּאַתְרָא דִּי יִכּוֹס יָת עֲלָתָא: לד וְיִסַּב כַּהֲנָא מִדְּמָא דְחַטָּאתָא בְּאֶצְבְּעֵהּ וְיִתֵּן עַל קַרְנַת מַדְבְּחָא דַעֲלָתָא וְיָת כָּל דְּמַהּ יֵשׁוּד לִיסוֹדָא דְמַדְבְּחָא: לה וְיָת כָּל תַּרְבַּהּ יֶעְדֵּי כְּמָא דִי מִתְעֲדֵי תְרַב אִמְּרָא מִנִּכְסַת קוּדְשַׁיָּא וְיַסֵּק כַּהֲנָא יָתְהוֹן לְמַדְבְּחָא עַל קֻרְבָּנַיָּא דַיְיָ וִיכַפֵּר עֲלוֹהִי כַהֲנָא עַל חוֹבְתֵהּ דִּי חָב וְיִשְׁתְּבֵק לֵהּ:

──── רש"י ────

ת"כ שם פרק י"ז: (לג) ושחט אותה לחטאת. אף חטאת שחיטתה כשהיא באה כבשה טעונה אליה עם האמורין (ת"כ שם פרק יה:ד): (לה) על אשי ה'. על שפתא שחיקפה לשם חטאת (זבחים ז:): כאשר יוסר חלב הכשב. שנתרבו אימוריו באליה. מדורות האש העשויות לשם, פוא"יליש בלע"ז:

──── RASHI ELUCIDATED ────

33. וְשָׁחַט אֹתָהּ לְחַטָּאת — **HE SHALL SLAUGHTER IT FOR A SIN-OFFERING.** — שֶׁתְּהֵא שְׁחִיטָתָהּ — That its **slaughtering should be** ¹לְשֵׁם חַטָּאת — **for the sake of,** i.e., with intent that it be, **a sin-offering.**[1]

35. כַּאֲשֶׁר יוּסַר חֵלֶב הַכֶּשֶׂב — **AS THE FAT OF THE SHEEP WOULD BE REMOVED.** — שֶׁנִּתְרַבּוּ אֵמוּרָיו — For its **specified parts** as a peace-offering **were increased** over those of the goat בָּאַלְיָה — **by the fat tail.** אַף חַטָּאת — With regard to **the sin-offering, too,** כְּשֶׁהִיא בָּאָה כִשְׂבָּה — **when it is brought as a ewe,** ²טְעוּנָה אֵלֶיהָ עִם הָאֵמוּרִין — **it requires the fat tail among the specified parts.**[2]

עַל אִשֵּׁי ה' — This means עַל מְדוּרוֹת הָאֵשׁ — **on the pyres of fire,** i.e., on the several piles of wood that blazed on the Mizbe'ach, הָעֲשׂוּיוֹת לַשֵּׁם — **which are made for the sake of HASHEM.**[3] פוא"יליש — **Foeiles** in Old French.[4]

---

1. *Zevachim* 7b.
2. *Toras Kohanim, Chovah, perek* 11:4.
3. Rashi differs with *Targum Onkelos* who understands עַל אִשֵּׁי ה' as "with the offerings of HASHEM" (*Shaarei Aharon; Lifshuto shel Rashi*).

Furthermore, Rashi explains why the plural "fires" is used, and what is meant by "of HASHEM" (*Sefer Zikaron*).

4. In Modern French, *feu*, a blazing pile of wood such as in a bonfire or pyre.

5

¹ If a person will sin and will hear the sound of an oath, and he is a witness — either he saw or he knew — if he does not testify, he shall bear his inquity; **²** or if a person will have touched any impure object — whether the impure carcass of a beast, the impure carcass of an animal, or the impure carcass of a creeping animal — and it was concealed from him, and he is impure and he had become guilty; **³** or

ה א וְנֶפֶשׁ כִּי־תֶחֱטָא וְשָׁמְעָה קוֹל אָלָה וְהוּא עֵד אוֹ רָאָה אוֹ יָדָע אִם־לוֹא יַגִּיד וְנָשָׂא עֲוֹנוֹ: ב אוֹ נֶפֶשׁ אֲשֶׁר תִּגַּע בְּכָל־דָּבָר טָמֵא אוֹ בְנִבְלַת חַיָּה טְמֵאָה אוֹ בְּנִבְלַת בְּהֵמָה טְמֵאָה אוֹ בְּנִבְלַת שֶׁרֶץ טָמֵא וְנֶעְלַם מִמֶּנּוּ וְהוּא טָמֵא וְאָשֵׁם: ג אוֹ

אונקלוס

א וֶאֱנָשׁ אֲרֵי יֵחוֹב וְיִשְׁמַע קָל מוֹמֵי וְהוּא סָהִיד אוֹ חֲזָא אוֹ יְדַע אִם לָא חַוִּי וִיקַבֵּל חוֹבֵהּ: ב אוֹ אֱנָשׁ דִּי יִקְרַב בְּכָל מִדַּעַם מְסָאָב אוֹ בִנְבֵלַת חֵיתָא מְסָאֲבָא אוֹ בִנְבֵלַת בְּעִירָא מְסָאֲבָא אוֹ בִנְבֵלַת רִחֲשָׁא מְסָאָב וִיהֵי מְכַסָּא מִנֵּהּ וְהוּא מְסָאָב וְיֵחוֹב: ג אוֹ

רש"י

(א) ושמעה קול אלה. בדבר שהוא עד בו, שהשביעוהו שבועה שאם יודע לו עדות יעיד לו (ת"כ שם פרשתא ח ופרק יא): **(ב) או נפש אשר תגע וגו'.** ולאחר הטומאה הזו יאכל קדשים או יכנס למקדש שהוא דבר שזדונו כרת. במסכת שבועות (ו:) נדרש כן. **ונעלם ממנו.** הטומאה (ת"כ שם פרק יב:ז; שבועות יד): **ואשם.** באכילת קדש או בביאת מקדש:

RASHI ELUCIDATED

5.

1. וְשָׁמְעָה קוֹל אָלָה — AND WILL HEAR THE SOUND OF AN OATH — בְּדָבָר שֶׁהוּא עֵד בּוֹ — regarding a matter to which he is a witness. "Hear the sound of an oath" means שֶׁהִשְׁבִּיעוּהוּ שְׁבוּעָה — that they administered an oath to him ¹שֶׁאִם יוֹדֵעַ לוֹ עֵדוּת — that if he knows testimony¹ in favor of [a litigant] ²שֶׁיָּעִיד לוֹ — that he should testify on behalf of [that litigant].²

2. אוֹ נֶפֶשׁ אֲשֶׁר תִּגַּע וְגוֹמֵר — OR IF A PERSON WILL HAVE TOUCHED, ETC. — וּלְאַחַר הַטֻּמְאָה הַזּוֹ — And after this impurity יֹאכַל קָדָשִׁים — he will eat *kodashim* אוֹ יִכָּנֵס לַמִּקְדָּשׁ — or enter the *Beis HaMikdash* שֶׁהוּא דָּבָר שֶׁזְּדוֹנוֹ כָּרֵת — which is a matter whose intentional violation is punished by *kares*.³ בְּמַסֶּכֶת שְׁבוּעוֹת⁴ — In Tractate *Shevuos*⁴ נִדְרַשׁ כֵּן — [this passage] is explained thus.

□ וְנֶעְלַם מִמֶּנּוּ — AND IT WAS CONCEALED FROM HIM. That is, הַטֻּמְאָה — the impurity was concealed from him.⁵

□ וְאָשֵׁם — AND HE HAD BECOME GUILTY בַּאֲכִילַת קֹדֶשׁ — through eating that which is sacred אוֹ בְּבִיאַת מִקְדָּשׁ — or through entering the *Beis HaMikdash*.

---

1. Some editions read בְּעֵדוּת, "some testimony."

2. *Toras Kohanim*, *Chovah*, *parshasa* 8 and *perek* 11. Parties to a monetary dispute have the right to demand that those who can testify in their favor do so. If one of the litigants exercises this right, and the person asked to testify denies that he has knowledge of the case, the litigant can ask the alleged witness to swear to that effect. If the witness accepts the oath administered to him by saying *amen* (or, according to some opinions, even by remaining silent), and subsequently admits to having lied, he is subject to the offering discussed in this passage.

3. The verse makes no mention of eating *kodashim* or entering the *Beis HaMikdash* after becoming impure. However, since the verse concludes, "and had become guilty," this implies that a sin had been committed. Becoming impure in itself is not a sin. Eating *kodashim* or entering the *Beis HaMikdash* in a state of impurity is a sin punished by *kares* (*Mizrachi; Sifsei Chachamim*). *Kares* is defined on page 8, note 8.

4. *Shevuos* 6b-7b.

5. *Toras Kohanim, Chovah, perek* 12:7. *Shevuos* 14b. A guilt-offering must be brought only if one ate *kodashim* or entered the *Beis HaMikdash* having forgotten that he was impure. If he remembered that he was impure but forgot that what he ate was *kodashim* or that the place he entered was the *Beis HaMikdash*, he does not have to bring a guilt-offering (*Mizrachi; Sifsei Chachamim*). According to this interpretation, Rashi here follows the view of the *Tanna* R' Akiva. According to the *Tanna* R' Yishmael, the repetition of וְנֶעְלַם מִמֶּנּוּ, "and it was concealed from him," in the next verse indicates that there are two types of forgetfulness for which one is obligated to bring this offering: (a) He forgot that he was impure; (b) he forgot the sanctity of what he ate or where he was. The halachah follows R' Yishmael (*Rambam, Shegagos* 11:1). See *Nachalas Yaakov* (who questions this interpretation of Rashi because it does not coincide with the halachah) for another interpretation.

5/4 — ה/ד

if he will touch a human impurity through any manner of his impurity which makes him impure through it but it was concealed from him — and he knew — and he became guilty; [4] *or if a person will swear, expressing by lips to do harm or to do good,*

כִּי יִגַּע בְּטֻמְאַת אָדָם לְכֹל טֻמְאָתוֹ
אֲשֶׁר יִטְמָא בָּהּ וְנֶעְלַם מִמֶּנּוּ וְהוּא
יָדַע וְאָשֵׁם: אוֹ נֶפֶשׁ כִּי תִשָּׁבַע
לְבַטֵּא בִשְׂפָתַיִם לְהָרַע ׀ אוֹ לְהֵיטִיב

───────── אונקלוס ─────────

אֲרֵי יִקְרַב בְּסוֹאֲבַת אֱנָשָׁא לְכֹל סוֹבְתֵהּ דְּאִסְתָּאַב בַּהּ וִיהֵי מְכַסָּא מִנֵּהּ
וְהוּא יָדַע וְחָב: ד אוֹ אֱנָשׁ אֲרֵי יְקַיֵּם לְפָרָשָׁא בְּסִפְוָן לְאַבְאָשָׁא אוֹ לְאוֹטָבָא

───────── רש"י ─────────

(ג) **בְּטֻמְאַת אָדָם.** זוֹ טוּמְאַת מֵת (ת״כ שם פרק יב:ח): **לְכֹל טֻמְאָתוֹ.** לְרַבּוֹת טוּמְאַת מַגַּע זָבִין וְזָבוֹת (שם): **אֲשֶׁר יִטְמָא.** לְרַבּוֹת הַנּוֹגֵעַ בְּבוֹעֵל נִדָּה (שם): **בָּהּ.** לְרַבּוֹת בּוֹלֵעַ נִבְלַת עוֹף טָהוֹר (שם): **וְנֶעְלַם.** וְלֹא [שם ״והוא״] יָדַע, שֶׁכָּח הַטּוּמְאָה: **וְאָשֵׁם.** בַּאֲכִילַת קֹדֶשׁ אוֹ בְּבִיאַת מִקְדָּשׁ (ת״כ שם פרק יב:ח): (ד) **בִשְׂפָתָיִם.** וְלֹא בַלֵּב (שם פרשתא ט:ב; שבועות כו:): **לְהָרַע.** לְעַצְמוֹ (שם ג׳ד): **אוֹ לְהֵיטִיב.** לְעַצְמוֹ, כְּגוֹן אוֹכַל וְלֹא אוֹכַל אִישָׁן וְלֹא אִישָׁן (שבועות יט:, כה.):

───────── RASHI ELUCIDATED ─────────

3. בְּטֻמְאַת אָדָם — HUMAN IMPURITY. [1] זוֹ טֻמְאַת מֵת — **This is impurity of** one who has touched **a dead person.**[1]

☐ לְכֹל טֻמְאָתוֹ — THROUGH ANY MANNER OF HIS IMPURITY. [2] לְרַבּוֹת טֻמְאַת מַגַּע זָבִין וְזָבוֹת — This serves **to include impurity through touching** *zavin* and *zavos*.[2]

☐ אֲשֶׁר יִטְמָא — WHICH MAKES [HIM] IMPURE. [3] לְרַבּוֹת הַנּוֹגֵעַ בְּבוֹעֵל נִדָּה — This serves **to include one who touches one who had relations with a** *niddah*.[3]

☐ בָּהּ — THROUGH IT. [4] לְרַבּוֹת בּוֹלֵעַ נִבְלַת עוֹף טָהוֹר — This serves **to include one who swallows** meat from **a carcass of a pure bird,** i.e., a bird of a kosher species, **that has not been ritually slaughtered.**[4]

☐ וְנֶעְלַם — BUT IT WAS CONCEALED. [5] וְלֹא יָדַע — **And he did not know,** שֶׁשָּׁכַח הַטֻּמְאָה — **for he had forgotten** about **the impurity.**[6]

☐ וְאָשֵׁם — AND HE BECAME GUILTY — בַּאֲכִילַת קֹדֶשׁ — **by eating that which is sacred** אוֹ בְּבִיאַת מִקְדָּשׁ — **or by entering the** *Beis HaMikdash.*

4. בִשְׂפָתָיִם — BY LIPS [7] וְלֹא בַלֵּב — **but not** merely **in the heart.**[7]

☐ לְהָרַע — TO DO HARM [8] לְעַצְמוֹ — **to himself.**[8]

☐ אוֹ לְהֵיטִיב — OR TO DO GOOD — לְעַצְמוֹ — **to himself,** כְּגוֹן — **for example,** if he swears, אֹכַל — **"I will eat,"** וְלֹא אֹכַל — or, **"I will not eat,"** אִישָׁן — **"I will sleep,"** וְלֹא אִישָׁן — or, **"I will not sleep."**[9]

---

1. *Toras Kohanim, Chovah, perek* 12:8. See *Numbers* 19:13.

2. *Toras Kohanim, Chovah, perek* 12:8. *Zavin* and *zavos* are, respectively, men and women who have a discharge that causes impurity. See 15:2 and 15:25 below.

3. *Toras Kohanim, Chovah, perek* 12:8. A *niddah* is a woman in a state of impurity due to menstruation. See below 15:19-24.

4. *Toras Kohanim, Chovah, perek* 12:8; *Shevuos* 7b. See 22:8 below and Rashi there.

5. Some editions read וְהוּא יָדַע; see next note.

6. He must bring a guilt-offering only if he once knew of his impurity, and then forgot about it. If he was never aware of the impurity before eating the *kodashim* or entering the *Beis HaMikdash*, he does not bring an offering (*Gur Aryeh*).

Nachalas Yaakov (cited by *Sifsei Chachamim*) and *Sefer Zikaron* have the words וְהוּא יָדַע, "and he knew" of the verse instead of וְלֹא יָדַע of our text. According to this version, Rashi is explaining what it is that "he knew"; he was once aware that he was impure, but then he forgot.

7. *Toras Kohanim, Chovah, parshasa* 9:2; *Shevuos* 26b. A commitment not expressed verbally does not have the status of an oath (*Mizrachi; Sifsei Chachamim*).

8. *Toras Kohanim, Chovah, parshasa* 9:3-4.

9. *Shevuos* 19b, 25a. One does not bring a guilt-offering if he does not fulfill an oath to do harm to others, nor is such an oath binding (see *Afikei Yam*, vol. I, 36:4). He *does* bring a guilt-offering for failing to fulfill an oath to do harm to himself. When Rashi says, "to do good to himself," he is merely maintaining uniform language for stylistic reasons. He does not mean to exclude failure to fulfill an oath to do good to another from the guilt-offering (*Mizrachi; Sifsei Chachamim*).

Our text is that found in most common editions of Rashi, and is also the text of the first printed edition.

anything that a person will express in an oath, but it was concealed from him, and he knew — and he became guilty regarding one of these matters. ⁵ When one shall become guilty regarding one of these matters, he shall confess what he had sinned. ⁶ He shall bring as his guilt-offering to HASHEM, for his sin that he committed, a female from the flock — a sheep or a goat — for a sin-offering; and the Kohen shall provide him atonement from his sin.

⁷ But if his means are insufficient for a sheep or goat, then he shall bring as his guilt-offering for that which he sinned: two turtledoves or two young doves to HASHEM, one for a sin-offering and one for an olah-offering. ⁸ He shall bring them to the Kohen, and he shall offer first the one that is for a sin-offering; he shall perform melikah at its nape,

לְכֹל אֲשֶׁר יְבַטֵּא הָאָדָם בִּשְׁבֻעָה וְנֶעְלַם מִמֶּנּוּ וְהוּא־יָדַע וְאָשֵׁם לְאַחַת מֵאֵלֶּה: ⁵ וְהָיָה כִי־יֶאְשַׁם לְאַחַת מֵאֵלֶּה וְהִתְוַדָּה אֲשֶׁר חָטָא עָלֶיהָ: ⁶ וְהֵבִיא אֶת־אֲשָׁמוֹ לַיהוה עַל חַטָּאתוֹ אֲשֶׁר חָטָא נְקֵבָה מִן־הַצֹּאן כִּשְׂבָּה אוֹ־שְׂעִירַת עִזִּים לְחַטָּאת וְכִפֶּר עָלָיו הַכֹּהֵן מֵחַטָּאתוֹ: ⁷ וְאִם־לֹא תַגִּיעַ יָדוֹ דֵּי שֶׂה וְהֵבִיא אֶת־אֲשָׁמוֹ אֲשֶׁר חָטָא שְׁתֵּי תֹרִים אוֹ־שְׁנֵי בְנֵי־יוֹנָה לַיהוה אֶחָד לְחַטָּאת וְאֶחָד לְעֹלָה: ⁸ וְהֵבִיא אֹתָם אֶל־הַכֹּהֵן וְהִקְרִיב אֶת־אֲשֶׁר לַחַטָּאת רִאשׁוֹנָה וּמָלַק אֶת־רֹאשׁוֹ מִמּוּל עָרְפּוֹ

— אונקלוס —

לְכֹל דִּי יְפָרֵשׁ אֲנָשָׁא בְּקִיּוּם וִיהֵי מְכַסָּא מִנֵּהּ וְהוּא יְדַע וְחָב לַחֲדָא מֵאִלֵּין: וִיהֵי אֲרֵי יְחוֹב לַחֲדָא מֵאִלֵּין וְיוֹדֵי דִּי חָב עֲלַהּ: וְיַיְתִי יָת חוֹבָתֵהּ קֳדָם יְיָ עַל חוֹבָתֵהּ דִּי חָב נְקוּבְתָּא מִן עָנָא אִמַּרְתָּא אוֹ צְפִירַת עִזִּין לְחַטָּאתָא וִיכַפַּר עֲלוֹהִי כַהֲנָא מֵחוֹבָתֵהּ: וְאִם לָא תַמְטֵי יְדֵהּ מִסַּת שֵׂיתָא וְיַיְתִי יָת חוֹבָתֵהּ דִּי חָב תַּרְתֵּין שַׁפְנִינִין אוֹ תְרֵין בְּנֵי יוֹנָה קֳדָם יְיָ חַד לְחַטָּאתָא וְחַד לַעֲלָתָא: ח וְיַיְתִי יָתְהוֹן לְוָת כַּהֲנָא וִיקָרֵב יָת דִּי לְחַטָּאתָא קַדְמֵיתָא וְיִמְלוֹק יָת רֵישֵׁהּ מִלָּקֳבֵל קְדָלֵהּ

— רש"י —

לכל אשר יבטא. לְרַבּוֹת לְשֶׁעָבַר (ת"כ שם ח; שבועות כו.): **ונעלם ממנו.** וְעָבַר עַל שְׁבוּעָתוֹ. כָּל אֵלֶּה בְקָרְבַּן עוֹלֶה וְיוֹרֵד כִּמְפֹרָשׁ כָּאן, אֲבָל שְׁבוּעָה יֵשׁ בָּהּ כְּפִירַת מָמוֹן אֵינָהּ בְּקָרְבָּן זֶה אֶלָּא בְּאָשָׁם (להלן פסוקים כ-כו): (ח) **והקריב את אשר לחטאת ראשונה.** חַטָּאת קוֹדֶמֶת לְעוֹלָה. לְמָה הַדָּבָר דּוֹמֶה, לִפְרַקְלִיט שֶׁנִּכְנַס לְרַצּוֹת

— RASHI ELUCIDATED —

□ לְכֹל אֲשֶׁר יְבַטֵּא — ANYTHING THAT [A PERSON] WILL EXPRESS. ¹לְרַבּוֹת לְשֶׁעָבַר — To include that which is in the past.¹

□ וְנֶעְלַם מִמֶּנּוּ — BUT IT WAS CONCEALED FROM HIM וְעָבַר עַל שְׁבוּעָתוֹ — and he transgressed his oath.²

□ כָּל אֵלֶּה — All of these oaths are included בְּקָרְבַּן עוֹלֶה וְיוֹרֵד — in the obligation to bring an ascending and descending offering,³ כִּמְפֹרָשׁ כָּאן — as stated explicitly here.⁴ אֲבָל שְׁבוּעָה שֶׁיֵּשׁ בָּהּ כְּפִירַת מָמוֹן — But an oath which has in it, i.e., which involves, **denial of money**, i.e., a financial claim, אֵינָהּ בְּקָרְבָּן זֶה — is not included in the obligation to bring this offering, אֶלָּא בְּאָשָׁם — but rather, in the obligation to bring a guilt-offering.⁵

8. וְהִקְרִיב אֶת אֲשֶׁר לַחַטָּאת רִאשׁוֹנָה — AND HE SHALL OFFER FIRST THE ONE THAT IS FOR A SIN-OFFERING. חַטָּאת קוֹדֶמֶת לְעֹלָה — The sin-offering precedes the olah-offering. לְמָה הַדָּבָר דּוֹמֶה — What is the matter comparable to? לִפְרַקְלִיט — To an advocate שֶׁנִּכְנַס לְרַצּוֹת — who enters before the king to

---

1. *Toras Kohanim, Chovah, parshasa* 9:8; *Shevuos* 26a. "To do harm or to do good" refers to an oath that involves an undertaking to do something in the future. "Anything that a person will express" includes an oath about the past.

2. The verse says only that the vow "was concealed from him," i.e., it slipped his mind. But this in itself is not a sin, and would not require an offering. Therefore, Rashi concludes that וְעָבַר, "and he transgressed," is implicit in the verse (*Mizrachi; Sifsei Chachamim*).

3. This offering is described in the verses that follow. It is called "ascending and descending" because its contents and thus its monetary value ascend or descend in accordance with the resources of the one who brings it.

4. See verses 5-13 below and Rashi to verse 13.

5. See verses 20-26 below.

47 / VAYIKRA/LEVITICUS — PARASHAS VAYIKRA — ה/ט־י – 5/9-10

but not separate [it]. ⁹ He shall sprinkle from the blood of the sin-offering upon the wall of the Mizbe'ach, and the remainder of the blood he shall squeeze out toward the base of the Mizbe'ach; it is a sin-offering. ¹⁰ And he shall make the second one an olah-offering as prescribed; and the Kohen shall provide

ט וְלֹא יַבְדִּיל: וְהִזָּה מִדַּם הַחַטָּאת עַל־קִיר הַמִּזְבֵּחַ וְהַנִּשְׁאָר בַּדָּם יִמָּצֵה אֶל־יְסוֹד הַמִּזְבֵּחַ חַטָּאת הוּא: י וְאֶת־הַשֵּׁנִי יַעֲשֶׂה עֹלָה כַּמִּשְׁפָּט וְכִפֶּר עָלָיו הַכֹּהֵן

— אונקלוס —

וְלָא יַפְרֵשׁ: ט וְיַדֵּי מִדְּמָא דְחַטָּאתָא עַל כֹּתֶל מַדְבְּחָא וּדְאִשְׁתָּאַר בְּדָמָא יִתְמְצֵי לִיסוֹדָא דְמַדְבְּחָא חַטָּאתָא הוּא: י וְיָת תִּנְיָנָא יַעֲבֵד עֲלָתָא כִּדְחָזֵי וִיכַפֵּר עֲלוֹהִי כַהֲנָא

— רש"י —

רִיצָה פְרַקְלִיט נִכְנָס דּוֹרוֹן אַחֲרָיו (זבחים ז:): אֵינוֹ **וְלֹא יַבְדִּיל.** אֵינוֹ מוֹלֵק אֶלָּא סִימָן אֶחָד (חולין כא.): **עוֹרֶף.** הוּא גּוֹבַהּ הָרֹאשׁ הַמְשֻׁפָּע לְצַד הַצַּוָּאר. מוּל עֹרֶף. מוּל הָרוֹאֶה אֶת הָעֹרֶף (שם יט:) וְהוּא אוֹרֶךְ כָּל אֲחוֹרֵי הַצַּוָּאר: **(ט) וְהִזָּה מִדַּם הַחַטָּאת.** בְּעוֹלָה לֹא הַטְעִין אֶלָּא מִצּוּי וּבְחַטָּאת הַזָּאָה וּמִצּוּי אוֹחֵז בָּעוֹף (לְעֵיל א:טו) וּבְחַטְאַת הָעוֹף מַלּוּי, אוֹחֵז בָּעוֹף וּמַתִּיז וְהַדָּם נִתָּז וְהוֹלֵךְ לַמִּזְבֵּחַ (זבחים סד:): **חַטָּאת הוּא.** לִשְׁמָהּ כְּשֵׁרָה שֶׁלֹּא לִשְׁמָהּ פְּסוּלָה (ת"כ פרק יח:ט): **(י) כַּמִּשְׁפָּט.** כְּדָת הָאָמוּר בְּעוֹלַת הָעוֹף שֶׁל נִדְבָה בְּרֹאשׁ הַפָּרָשָׁה:

— RASHI ELUCIDATED —

placate the king on behalf of someone he is representing. רָצָה פְרַקְלִיט – Once the advocate has placated the king, נִכְנָס דּוֹרוֹן אַחֲרָיו – a gift to the king follows him.¹

□ וְלֹא יַבְדִּיל – BUT NOT SEPARATE [IT]. אֵינוֹ מוֹלֵק אֶלָּא סִימָן אֶחָד – He performs *melikah* on only one sign.²

□ עֹרֶף – The meaning of the word עֹרֶף in the phrase מִמּוּל עָרְפּוֹ – הוּא גּוֹבַהּ הָרֹאשׁ – is "the high part of the head" הַמְשֻׁפָּע לְצַד הַצַּוָּאר – which slopes toward the neck. מוּל עֹרֶף – The meaning of the phrase מִמּוּל עֹרֶף, here translated, **"at its nape,"** is ³מוּל הָרוֹאֶה אֶת הָעֹרֶף – that which faces the back of the head,³ וְהוּא אוֹרֶךְ כָּל אֲחוֹרֵי הַצַּוָּאר – which is the length of the entire back of the neck.⁴

9. וְהִזָּה מִדַּם הַחַטָּאת – HE SHALL SPRINKLE FROM THE BLOOD OF THE SIN-OFFERING. בְּעוֹלָה לֹא הַטְעִין אֶלָּא מִצּוּי⁵ – With regard to the *olah*-offering, [the Torah] required only squeezing out,⁵ וּבְחַטָּאת – but with regard to the sin-offering, הַזָּאָה וּמִצּוּי – the Torah required both **sprinkling and squeezing out.** אוֹחֵז בָּעוֹף – He holds the bird⁶ וּמַתִּיז – and sprinkles, וְהַדָּם נִתָּז וְהוֹלֵךְ לַמִּזְבֵּחַ – and the blood gets sprinkled toward the *Mizbe'ach*.⁷

□ חַטָּאת הוּא – IT IS A SIN-OFFERING. לִשְׁמָהּ כְּשֵׁרָה – If it was offered **for its sake**, i.e., with intent that it is being performed for the sake of a sin-offering, **it is valid.** But if it was offered ⁸שֶׁלֹּא לִשְׁמָהּ פְּסוּלָה – not for its sake, it is invalid.⁸

10. כַּמִּשְׁפָּט – AS PRESCRIBED. כְּדָת הָאָמוּר בְּעוֹלַת הָעוֹף שֶׁל נְדָבָה – In conformance with the law stated regarding a voluntary *olah*-offering of fowl, בְּרֹאשׁ הַפָּרָשָׁה – at the beginning of the portion.⁹

---

1. *Zevachim* 7b. The sin-offering placates God, so to speak, on behalf of the sinner. The *olah*-offering is his gift to God.

2. *Chullin* 21a. The esophagus and the trachea are called "signs." The *melikah* (see Rashi to 1:15 above, s.v., הַכֹּהֵן וּמָלַק) performed on an *olah*-offering must sever both signs. Our verse teaches that when the Kohen performs *melikah* on the sin-offering, he may not sever more than one sign.

3. *Chullin* 19b; see Rashi there.

4. The עֹרֶף is part of the back of the head, not the back of the neck, as can be seen from the verse, כִּי פָנוּ אֵלַי עֹרֶף וְלֹא פָנִים, "For they turned the back of their head to me, not their face" (*Jeremiah* 2:27). "That which faces the back of the head" refers to the back of the neck. It faces the lower part of the back of the head (i.e., the bottom of the occipital bone) because the back of the head slopes downward and inward and is not a vertical extension of the neck (see *Sefer Zikaron*).

5. See 1:15 above and Rashi there.

6. Some editions read אוֹחֵז בָּעֹרֶף, "he holds the back of the head." But it is highly unlikely that this is what Rashi wrote. *Yosef Hallel* notes that the text of the first printed edition of Rashi, אוֹחֵז בָּעוֹף, "he holds the bird," is probably the authentic version, since Rashi to *Zevachim* 64b uses אוֹחֵז בָּעוֹף in describing the process of sprinkling.

7. *Zevachim* 64b.

8. *Toras Kohanim, Chovah, perek* 18:9. See note 8 to 4:24 above.

9. See 1:14-17 above.

him atonement from his sin that he committed, and it shall be forgiven him. *⁷* ¹¹ *But if his means are insufficient for two turtledoves or for two young doves, then he shall bring, as his guilt-offering for that which he sinned, a tenth of an ephah of fine flour for a sin-offering; he shall not place oil on it nor shall he put frankincense on it, for it is a sin-offering.* ¹² *He shall bring it to the Kohen, and the Kohen shall scoop his threefingersful as its memorial portion and cause it to go up in smoke on the Mizbe'ach, on the fires of* H<small>ASHEM</small>; *it is a sin-offering.* ¹³ *The Kohen shall provide him atonement over his sin that he committed from one of these, and it will be forgiven*

מֵחַטָּאתֹ֛ו אֲשֶׁר־חָטָ֖א וְנִסְלַ֥ח
לֹֽו: *שביעי* וְאִם־לֹא֩ תַשִּׂ֨יג יא
יָד֜וֹ לִשְׁתֵּ֣י תֹרִ֗ים אוֹ֙ לִשְׁנֵ֣י בְנֵי־יוֹנָ֔ה
וְהֵבִ֨יא אֶת־קׇרְבָּנ֜וֹ אֲשֶׁ֣ר חָטָ֗א
עֲשִׂירִ֧ת הָאֵפָ֛ה סֹ֖לֶת לְחַטָּ֑את לֹא־
יָשִׂ֨ים עָלֶ֜יהָ שֶׁ֗מֶן וְלֹא־יִתֵּ֤ן עָלֶ֨יהָ֙
לְבֹנָ֔ה כִּ֥י חַטָּ֖את הִֽוא: וֶהֱבִיאָהּ֮ אֶל־ יב
הַכֹּהֵן֒ וְקָמַ֣ץ הַכֹּהֵ֣ן ׀ מִ֠מֶּ֠נָּה מְל֨וֹא
קֻמְצ֜וֹ אֶת־אַזְכָּרָתָהּ֙ וְהִקְטִ֣יר
הַמִּזְבֵּ֔חָה עַ֖ל אִשֵּׁ֣י יְהוָ֑ה חַטָּ֖את
הִֽוא: וְכִפֶּר֩ עָלָ֨יו הַכֹּהֵ֜ן עַל־חַטָּאת֧וֹ יג
אֲשֶׁר־חָטָ֛א מֵאַחַ֥ת מֵאֵ֖לֶּה וְנִסְלַ֣ח

───── אונקלוס ─────

מחוֹבְתֵהּ דִּי חָב וְיִשְׁתְּבֵיק לֵהּ: יא וְאִם לָא תַדְבֵּיק יְדֵהּ לְתַרְתֵּין שַׁפְנִינִין אוֹ לִתְרֵין בְּנֵי יוֹנָה וְיַיְתֵי יָת קֻרְבָּנֵהּ דִּי חָב חַד מִן עַסְרָא בִּתְלָת סְאִין סֻלְתָּא לְחַטָּאתָא לָא יְשַׁוֵּי עֲלַהּ מִשְׁחָא וְלָא יִתֵּן עֲלַהּ לְבוֹנְתָּא אֲרֵי חַטָּאתָא הִיא: יב וְיַיְתִנַהּ לְוָת כַּהֲנָא וְיִקְמוֹץ כַּהֲנָא מִנַּהּ מְלֵי קֻמְצֵהּ יָת אַדְכַּרְתַּהּ וְיַסֵּק לְמַדְבְּחָא עַל קֻרְבָּנַיָּא דַּיְיָ חַטָּאתָא הִיא: יג וִיכַפַּר עֲלוֹהִי כַּהֲנָא עַל חוֹבְתֵהּ דִּי חָב מֵחֲדָא מֵאִלֵּין וְיִשְׁתְּבֵיק

───── רש"י ─────

(יא) **כִּי חַטָּאת הִוא.** וְאֵין דִּין שֶׁיְּהֵא קׇרְבָּנוֹ [נ"א קׇרְבָּנָהּ] מְהֻדָּר (לְטָעֵיל פָּסוּק ו וּפָסוּק י), וְכָאן בְּדַלֵּי דַלּוּת נ"ח) עַל חַטָּאתוֹ, דִּקְדְּקוּ (מנחות ו.): **(יב) חַטָּאת הִוא.** נִקְמְצָה וְנִקְטְרָה לִשְׁמָהּ כְּשֵׁרָה, שֶׁלֹּא רַבּוֹתֵינוּ (כְּרִיתוֹת כז:) מִכָּאן שֶׁאִם חָטָא כְּשֶׁהוּא עָשִׁיר וְהִפְרִישׁ לִשְׁמָהּ פְּסוּלָה (ת"כ פֶּרֶק יט:ט; מנחות ד.): **(יג) עַל חַטָּאתוֹ אֲשֶׁר** מָעוֹת לְכִשְׂבָּה אוֹ שְׂעִירָה וְהֶעֱנִי, יָבִיא מִמִּקְצָתָן שְׁתֵּי **חָטָא.** כָּאן שִׁנָּה הַכָּתוּב, שֶׁהֲרֵי בַּעֲשִׁירוּת וּבְדַלּוּת נֶאֱמַר מֵחַטָּאתוֹ תּוֹרִים, הֶעֱנִי יוֹתֵר מִמִּקְלָטָן שְׁתֵּי תוֹרִים. הִפְרִישׁ מָעוֹת לִשְׁתֵּי תוֹרִים וְהֶעֱנִי, יָבִיא מִמִּקְלָטָן עֲשִׂירִית הָאֵיפָה

───── RASHI ELUCIDATED ─────

11. כִּי חַטָּאת הִוא — FOR IT IS A SIN-OFFERING, וְאֵין בַּדִּין — and it is not proper ² מְהֻדָּר — that [a sinner's] offering¹ be splendid.²

12. חַטָּאת הִוא — IT IS A SIN-OFFERING. נִקְמְצָה וְנִקְטְרָה לִשְׁמָהּ — If it was scooped and burned for its sake, i.e., with intent that it is being performed for the sake of a sin-offering, כְּשֵׁרָה — it is valid. שֶׁלֹּא לִשְׁמָהּ³ — Not for its sake, פְּסוּלָה — it is invalid.³

13. עַל חַטָּאתוֹ אֲשֶׁר חָטָא — OVER HIS SIN THAT HE COMMITTED. כָּאן שִׁנָּה הַכָּתוּב — Here Scripture used different wording, שֶׁהֲרֵי בַּעֲשִׁירוּת וּבְדַלּוּת — for with regard to the offerings brought out of wealth and poverty, נֶאֱמַר ,,מֵחַטָּאתוֹ״⁴ — it says, *"from his sin,"*⁴ וְכָאן בְּדַלֵּי דַלּוּת — and here, with regard to extreme poverty, נֶאֱמַר ,,עַל חַטָּאתוֹ״ — it says, *"over his sin."* ⁵ דְּקְדְּקוּ רַבּוֹתֵינוּ מִכָּאן — Our Rabbis⁵ inferred from here שֶׁאִם חָטָא כְּשֶׁהוּא עָשִׁיר — that if he sinned when he was rich וְהִפְרִישׁ מָעוֹת — and he set aside money לְכִשְׂבָּה אוֹ שְׂעִירָה — for a female sheep or goat, the offering brought by a rich man, וְהֶעֱנִי — and then he became poor, יָבִיא מִמִּקְצָתָן — he should bring from part of [the money set aside] שְׁתֵּי תוֹרִים — two turtledoves, the offering of the poor man, and he may keep the rest of the money; הִפְרִישׁ מָעוֹת לִשְׁתֵּי תוֹרִים — if he set aside money for two turtledoves, the offering of a poor man, וְהֶעֱנִי — and then he became yet poorer, יָבִיא מִמִּקְצָתָן — he should bring from part of [the money set aside] עֲשִׂירִית הָאֵיפָה — a tenth of an *ephah* of flour for a meal-offering,

---

1. The literal meaning of קׇרְבָּנוֹ is "its offering," using the masculine pronominal suffix וֹ. The antecedent must then be a masculine noun, in this case the חוֹטֵא, "sinner."
   Some editions of Rashi read קׇרְבָּנָהּ, using the feminine suffix הּ. The antecedent must then be a feminine noun, in this case the חַטָּאת, "sin." קׇרְבָּנָה then means

2. *Menachos* 6a.

3. *Toras Kohanim, Chovah, perek* 19:9; *Menachos* 4a. See note 8 to 4:24 above.

4. Above verses 6 and 10.

5. *Kereisos* 27b.

יד לוֹ וְהָיְתָה לַכֹּהֵן כַּמִּנְחָה: וַיְדַבֵּר

him; and it shall be to the Kohen, like the meal-offering.

—— אונקלוס ——

לֵהּ וּתְהֵי לְכָהֲנָא כְּמִנְחָתָא: יד וּמַלִּיל

—— רש"י ——

וְלָכָךְ נֶאֱמַר מֵחַטָּאתוֹ. הִפְרִישׁ מָעוֹת לַעֲשִׂירִית הָאֵיפָה וְהֶעֱשִׁיר, יוֹסִיף עֲלֵיהֶן וְיָבִיא קָרְבַּן עָשִׁיר, לְכָךְ נֶאֱמַר כָּאן עַל חַטָּאתוֹ: **מֵאַחַת מֵאֵלֶּה.** מֵאַחַת מִשָּׁלֹשׁ כַּפָּרוֹת הָאֲמוּרוֹת בָּעִנְיָן אוֹ בַּעֲשִׁירוּת שְׁבָהֶן יְהוּ בְּכִשְׂבָּה אוֹ שְׂעִירָה וְהַקַּלִּין שֶׁבַּקַּלִּין יִהְיוּ בְּעוֹף וְהַקַּלִּין שֶׁבַּקַּלִּין יִהְיוּ בַּעֲשִׂירִית הָאֵיפָה, תַּלְמוּד לוֹמַר ,,מֵאַחַת מֵאֵלֶּה'' לְהַשְׁווֹת קַלִּין לַחֲמוּרִין לְכִשְׂבָּה וּשְׂעִירָה וְאֶת הַחֲמוּרִין לְקַלִּין אִם הַשִּׂיגָה יָדוֹ אוֹ שְׂעִירַת הָאֵיפָה בְּדַלֵּי דַלּוּת (ת"כ שם פרק יז:יו): **וְהָיְתָה לַכֹּהֵן בַּמִּנְחָה:** לִלַמֵּד עַל מִנְחַת חוֹטֵא

—— RASHI ELUCIDATED ——

the offering of the extremely poor. {מֵחַטָּאתוֹ, נֶאֱמַר לְכָךְ – **Therefore it says, "from his sin."**}[1] הִפְרִישׁ מָעוֹת לַעֲשִׂירִית הָאֵיפָה – **If he set aside money for a tenth of an** *ephah* because he sinned when he was very poor וְהֶעֱשִׁיר – **and** then **he became rich,** יוֹסִיף עֲלֵיהֶן – **he should add on to [the money]** וְיָבִיא קָרְבַּן עָשִׁיר – **and bring the offering of a rich man.** לְכָךְ נֶאֱמַר כָּאן ,,עַל חַטָּאתוֹ'' – This is why it says here, **"over his sin."**[2]

□ מֵאַחַת מֵאֵלֶּה – **FROM ONE OF THESE.** מֵאַחַת מִשָּׁלֹשׁ כַּפָּרוֹת – **From one of the three methods of atonement,** הָאֲמוּרוֹת בָּעִנְיָן – **which are stated in this topic:** אוֹ בַּעֲשִׁירוּת – **either through** the offering brought out of **wealth,** אוֹ בְּדַלּוּת – **or through** the offering brought out of **poverty,** אוֹ בְּדַלֵּי דַלּוּת – **or through** the offering brought out of **extreme poverty.**[3] וּמַה תַּלְמוּד לוֹמַר – **Why does the Torah say this?** Is it not obvious that only one offering must be brought? שֶׁיָּכוֹל – **Because one might be able** to think, יִהְיוּ בְּכִשְׂבָּה אוֹ שְׂעִירָה – **the most severe** sins **among them should be** atoned for **through a sheep or a goat,** וְהַקַּלִּין – **and those of lesser consequence** יִהְיוּ בְּעוֹף – **should be** atoned for **through a fowl,** וְהַקַּלִּין שֶׁבַּקַּלִּין – **and those of least consequence** יִהְיוּ בַּעֲשִׂירִית הָאֵיפָה – **should be** atoned for **through a tenth of an** *ephah* of flour for a meal-offering. תַּלְמוּד לוֹמַר ,,מֵאַחַת מֵאֵלֶּה'' – **To teach us otherwise, the verse says, "from one of these,"** לְהַשְׁווֹת קַלִּין לַחֲמוּרִין – **to equate those of lesser consequence to the most severe** obligation to offer **a sheep or a goat** אִם הַשִּׂיגָה יָדוֹ – **if he can afford it,** וְאֶת הַחֲמוּרִין לְקַלִּין – **and** to equate **the most severe to those of lesser consequence** לַעֲשִׂירִית הָאֵיפָה – for the obligation to offer **a tenth of an** *ephah* of flour for a meal-offering[4] בְּדַלֵּי דַלּוּת – **in extreme poverty.**[4]

□ וְהָיְתָה לַכֹּהֵן כַּמִּנְחָה – **AND IT SHALL BE TO THE KOHEN, LIKE THE MEAL-OFFERING.** לְלַמֵּד עַל מִנְחַת חוֹטֵא

---

1. The word מֵחַטָּאתוֹ here means, "from his sin," but it can also mean, "from his sin-offering." "From" connotes reduction; thus, the Rabbis inferred that the sin-offerings of the rich man and the poor man, where the word מֵחַטָּאתוֹ appears, can be reduced (Rashi to *Kereisos* 27b).

2. עַל חַטָּאתוֹ here means, "over his sin," but it can also mean, "over his sin-offering." "Over" connotes increase; thus the Rabbis inferred that the sin-offering of the extremely poor man can be increased (Rashi to *Kereisos* 27b; the Mishnah in *Kereisos* applies this law to a poor man who became rich, as well).

3. In verse 4 above, אַחַת מֵאֵלֶּה, "one of these," referred to the *sins* for which the offering of ascending and descending value is brought. Here it refers to the types of the offering (*Sefer Zikaron*).

4. *Toras Kohanim, Chovah, perek* 19:10. One could have thought that the scale of offerings depended on the severity of the sin rather than the means of the sinner. Eating *kodashim* or entering the *Beis HaMikdash* in a state of impurity, which is punished by *kares* (premature death), would be atoned for by offering a sheep or a goat. Swearing falsely to a demand for testimony is less serious because it is not punished by *kares*. It is, however, dealt with more strictly than taking a *shevuas bitui* (a verbally expressed oath which does not deal with testimony) falsely in that one must bring an offering whether one takes the false oath intentionally or unintentionally. It would be atoned for by offering fowl. Violation of a *shevuas bitui* is dealt with least strictly, because it is not punished by *kares*, nor is it an offering required for intentional violation. It would be atoned for by a meal-offering. To prevent this interpretation, the Torah says, "from one of these," i.e., one of the above, implying that all three of the offerings are possibilities for any of the sins mentioned, and that the criterion that determines which one applies is the fiscal status of the sinner.

Although verse 7 uses וְאִם לֹא תַגִּיעַ יָדוֹ, and verse 11 uses וְאִם לֹא תַשִּׂיג יָדוֹ, both of which mean "if his means are insufficient," and which seem to clearly indicate that the criterion the scale is based on is what the sinner can afford, we could nonetheless have thought that the scale of the offerings depends on the severity of the sin. For the literal meanings of the above phrases are "but if his hand will not reach" and "but if his hand will not attain," respectively. They

ה/יד-טו

טו וַיְדַבֵּ֥ר יְהוָ֖ה אֶל־מֹשֶׁ֥ה לֵּאמֹֽר׃ נֶ֚פֶשׁ כִּֽי־תִמְעֹ֣ל מַ֔עַל וְחָֽטְאָה֙ בִּשְׁגָגָ֔ה מִקָּדְשֵׁ֖י יְהוָ֑ה וְהֵבִיא֩ אֶת־אֲשָׁמ֨וֹ

¹⁴ HASHEM spoke to Moses, saying: ¹⁵ If a person will commit a misuse, and sins unintentionally against HASHEM'S holies, he shall bring his guilt-offering

— אונקלוס —

יְיָ עִם מֹשֶׁה לְמֵימַר: **טו** אֱנָשׁ אֲרֵי יְשַׁקַּר שְׁקַר וְיֵחוֹב בְּשָׁלוּ מִקּוּדְשַׁיָּא דַייָ וְיַיְתִי יָת אֲשָׁמֵהּ

— רש"י —

שֶׁיִּהְיוּ שְׁיָרֶיהָ נֶאֱכָלִין (ת"כ פרק יט:יא; מנחות עג:), וְהִיא לְכֹהֵן, וְאִם חוֹטֵא זֶה כֹּהֵן הוּא תְּהֵא כִּשְׁאָר מִנְחַת נִדְבַת כֹּהֵן, שֶׁהִיא בְּכָלִיל תְּהִי' לֹא תֵאָכֵל (להלן ו:טז): **(טו) כִּי תִמְעֹל מָעַל.** אֵין מְעִילָה בְּכָל מָקוֹם אֶלָּא שִׁנּוּי, וְכֵן הוּא אוֹמֵר וַיִּמְעֲלוּ בֵּאלֹהֵי אֲבוֹתֵיהֶם וַיִּזְנוּ אַחֲרֵי אֱלֹהֵי עַמֵּי הָאָרֶץ (דה"א ה:כה), וְכֵן ה"א בַּסּוֹטָה וּמָעֲלָה בוֹ מָעַל (במדבר ה:יב; ת"כ פרשתא יא:א:ב): **וְחָטְאָה בִּשְׁגָגָה מִקָּדְשֵׁי ה'.** שֶׁנֶּהֱנָה מִן הַהֶקְדֵּשׁ. וְהֵיכָן הֻזְהַר, נֶאֱמַר כָּאן חֵטְא וְנֶאֱמַר לְהַלָּן חֵטְא בִּתְרוּמָה (להלן כב:ט), מָה לְהַלָּן הִזְהִיר אַף כָּאן הִזְהִיר. אִי מַה לְּהַלָּן

RASHI ELUCIDATED

שֶׁיְּהֵיוּ שְׁיָרֶיהָ נֶאֱכָלִין — that its remnants, i.e., that which remains of it after its threefingersful has been burned on the *Mizbe'ach*, should be eaten by the Kohanim. זֶהוּ לְפִי פְשׁוּטוֹ — This is its interpretation according to its simple meaning.[1] וְרַבּוֹתֵינוּ דָרְשׁוּ — And our Rabbis interpreted[1] ‏,,וְהָיְתָה לַכֹּהֵן'' — "and it shall be to the Kohen" as follows: וְאִם חוֹטֵא זֶה כֹּהֵן הוּא — If this sinner who brings the meal-offering is a Kohen, תְּהֵא כִּשְׁאָר מִנְחַת נִדְבַת כֹּהֵן — it shall be like any other voluntary meal-offering of a Kohen, שֶׁהִיא — which is spoken of in the verse, "Every meal-offering of a Kohen is to be entirely burned; it may not be eaten."[2] ‏,,בְּכָלִיל תִּהְיֶה לֹא תֵאָכֵל''

15. כִּי תִמְעֹל מַעַל — IF [A PERSON] WILL COMMIT A MISUSE. אֵין מְעִילָה בְּכָל מָקוֹם אֶלָּא שִׁנּוּי — The term מְעִילָה, wherever it appears in Scripture, can mean only change, i.e., changing the state of an entity to something other than what it ought to be. וְכֵן הוּא אוֹמֵר — Similarly it says, ‏,,וַיִּמְעֲלוּ בֵּאלֹהֵי אֲבוֹתֵיהֶם וַיִּזְנוּ אַחֲרֵי אֱלֹהֵי עַמֵּי הָאָרֶץ''[4] — "And they alienated themselves[3] from the God of their fathers, and they strayed after the gods of the peoples of the land."[4] וְכֵן הוּא אוֹמֵר בְּסוֹטָה — Similarly it says regarding a *sotah*,[5] ‏,,וּמָעֲלָה בוֹ מָעַל''[6,7] — "and she committed a trespass against him."[6,7]

□ וְחָטְאָה בִּשְׁגָגָה מִקָּדְשֵׁי ה' — AND SINS UNINTENTIONALLY AGAINST HASHEM'S HOLIES. שֶׁנֶּהֱנָה מִן הַהֶקְדֵּשׁ — That he derived personal benefit from that which is holy, i.e., that which has been consecrated as an offering or as property of the *Beis HaMikdash*. וְהֵיכָן הֻזְהַר — Where was he warned?[8] נֶאֱמַר כָּאן חֵטְא — It says חֵטְא, "sin," here, in the word וְחָטְאָה, וְנֶאֱמַר לְהַלָּן חֵטְא בִּתְרוּמָה — and it says חֵטְא further on, with regard to *terumah*,[9] in the verse, ‏,,וְלֹא יִשְׂאוּ עָלָיו חֵטְא''[10] — "and they shall not bear sin over it."[10] מַה לְּהַלָּן הִזְהִיר — Just as further on [the Torah] gave a warning, i.e., stated a prohibition, אַף כָּאן הִזְהִיר — here, too, it gave a warning.[11] אִי מַה לְּהַלָּן — If one would argue, just

---

could have been interpreted as referring to severity — "but if his hand will not attain the degree of severity required for the above offering" (*Mizrachi*; *Sifsei Chachamim*).

1. *Toras Kohanim*, *Chovah*, perek 19:11; *Menachos* 73b.
2. Below 6:16. According to the simple meaning, "it will be to the Kohen" means "it will *belong* to the Kohen." According to the interpretation of the Rabbis, the verse says, "If the meal-offering will be one of a Kohen, it will be like the voluntary meal-offering of a Kohen, in that it must be burned entirely" (*Be'er Yitzchak*).
3. Here, too, וַיִּמְעֲלוּ, "and they alienated themselves," indicates a change; Israel changed, and was no longer loyal to God. See Rashi to *Me'ilah* 18a.
4. *I Chronicles* 5:25.
5. A woman suspected of adultery. See *Numbers* 5:11-31.
6. *Numbers* 5:12. There, too, the root מעל indicates a change; the wife is no longer faithful to her husband. In our verse it denotes misuse — making profane use of that which is sacred.
7. *Toras Kohanim*, *Chovah*, perek 11:1.
8. If the verse calls this a sin, the Torah must have written a prohibition against it. Where is this prohibition? (*Mizrachi*).
9. The portion of the yearly crops which is set aside for the Kohanim. See *Numbers* 18:12.
10. Below 22:9.
11. 22:10 is a prohibition against the misappropriation of *terumah* by a non-Kohen. The fact that the root חטא appears both in our verse which deals with misuse of *hekdesh* (that which is holy), and in the context of *terumah*, teaches us that just as there is a prohibition with regard to *terumah*, so, too, there is a prohibition with regard to misuse of *hekdesh*.

to Hashem, *an unblemished ram from the flock, with a value of silver shekels, according to the sacred shekel, for a guilt-offering.* ¹⁶ *For what he has deprived the Sanctuary he shall make restitution, and add a fifth*

לַיהוָה אַיִל תָּמִים מִן־הַצֹּאן בְּעֶרְכְּךָ כֶּסֶף־שְׁקָלִים בְּשֶׁקֶל־הַקֹּדֶשׁ לְאָשָׁם: טז וְאֵת אֲשֶׁר חָטָא מִן־הַקֹּדֶשׁ יְשַׁלֵּם וְאֶת־חֲמִישִׁתוֹ

— אונקלוס —

קֳדָם יְיָ דְּכַר שְׁלִים מִן עָנָא בְּפֻרְסָנֵהּ כְּסַף סִלְעִין בְּסִלְעֵי קוּדְשָׁא לַאֲשָׁמָא: טז וְיָת דִּי חָב מִן קוּדְשָׁא יְשַׁלֵּם וְיָת חֻמְשָׁא

— רש"י —

לֹא הִזְהִיר אֶלָּא עַל הָאוֹכֵל אַף כָּאן לֹא הִזְהִיר אֶלָּא עַל הָאוֹכֵל, ת"ל תִּמְעוֹל מַעַל רִבָּה (ת"כ שם ה; מְעִילָה יח:): מִקָּדְשֵׁי ה'. הַמְיֻחָדִים לָשֵׁם, יָצְאוּ קָדָשִׁים קַלִּים (שם פרק כ:א): אַיִל. לְשׁוֹן קָשֶׁה, כְּמוֹ וְאֵת אֵילֵי הָאָרֶץ לָקָח (יחזקאל יז:יג), אַף כָּאן קָשֶׁה בֶּן שְׁתֵּי שָׁנִים (ת"כ שם): (ו) בְּעֶרְכְּךָ כֶּסֶף שְׁקָלִים. שֶׁיְּהֵא שָׁוֶה שְׁתֵּי סְלָעִים (שם; כְּרִיתוּת י:): (טז) וְאֵת אֲשֶׁר חָטָא מִן הַקֹּדֶשׁ יְשַׁלֵּם. קֶרֶן וְחוֹמֶשׁ לַהֶקְדֵּשׁ

— RASHI ELUCIDATED —

as further on אַף כָּאן, **[the Torah] gave a warning only to one who eats,** לֹא הִזְהִיר אֶלָּא עַל הָאוֹכֵל – **here, too,** לֹא הִזְהִיר אֶלָּא עַל הָאוֹכֵל – **it gave a warning only to one who eats.**[1] תַּלְמוּד לוֹמַר – **To** teach us otherwise, **the verse says,** ,,תִּמְעוֹל מַעַל'' – **"will misuse,"** using a double form of the root מַעַל. ²רִבָּה – Thus, **it has included** acts other than eating within the prohibition.[2]

□ מִקָּדְשֵׁי ה' – **AGAINST HASHEM'S HOLIES.** הַמְיֻחָדִים לַשֵּׁם – **Those which are designated** solely for Hashem. ³יָצְאוּ קָדָשִׁים קַלִּים – *Kodashim* **of the lesser degree have** thus **left** the category of consecrated objects to which the obligation to bring a guilt-offering applies.[3]

□ אַיִל – **RAM.** לְשׁוֹן קָשֶׁה – This **connotes "tough,"** ⁴,,וְאֵת אֵילֵי הָאָרֶץ לָקָח'' – **like the word** אֵילֵי in, **"and he took the tough ones of the land."**[4] אַף כָּאן קָשֶׁה – **Here, too,** the verse means **a tough one;** ⁵בֶּן שְׁתֵּי שָׁנִים – **one which is two years old.**[5]

□ בְּעֶרְכְּךָ כֶּסֶף שְׁקָלִים – **WITH A VALUE OF SILVER SHEKELS.** ⁶שֶׁיְּהֵא שָׁוֶה שְׁתֵּי סְלָעִים – **That it should be worth** at least **two shekels.**[6]

16. וְאֵת אֲשֶׁר חָטָא מִן הַקֹּדֶשׁ יְשַׁלֵּם – **FOR WHAT HE HAS DEPRIVED THE SANCTUARY HE SHALL MAKE RESTITUTION.** ⁸קֶרֶן וְחוֹמֶשׁ לַהֶקְדֵּשׁ – **The principal and a fifth**[7] **to** *hekdesh* (the *Beis HaMikdash*).[8]

1. Once we derive the laws regarding the misuse of *hekdesh* from *terumah*, we should relate the two laws even more closely and say, just as sins concerning *terumah* involve eating, so, too, the misuse of *hekdesh* in this verse would involve only personal benefit from consuming them (*Gur Aryeh*).

2. *Toras Kohanim, Chovah, perek* 11:5; *Meilah* 18b. The verse could have expressed "will misuse" through the word תִּמְעוֹל alone. The additional מַעַל broadens the category of misuse to include benefit which does not involve consumption (see *Korban Aharon*).

3. *Toras Kohanim, Chovah, perek* 20:1. Offerings of the lesser degree of sanctity are not designated "solely for Hashem" because those bringing the offering partake of them. Similarly, once the blood of sin-offerings and guilt-offerings, which are *kodashim* of the higher degree of sanctity, has been sprinkled, they are no longer designated "solely for Hashem," for they may be eaten by the Kohanim. However, those parts of offerings of the lesser degree which are burned on the *Mizbe'ach* and not eaten are considered "Hashem's holies" and fall within the prohibition of our verse (*Mizrachi; Sifsei Chachamim*).

4. *Ezekiel* 17:13.

5. *Toras Kohanim, Chovah, perek* 20:6.

6. *Toras Kohanim, Chovah, perek* 20:6; *Kereisos* 10b.

The word בְּעֶרְכְּךָ could be interpreted as in estimation," i.e., that the estimated value of the ram must be two *shekels*. Rashi, by saying "that it should be worth," explains that the verse means actual value, not estimated value (*Mizrachi; Sifsei Chachamim*). Furthermore, Rashi points out that the plural *"shekels"* implies a worth of at least two *shekels* (*Mizrachi*). [סֶלַע, as used by Rashi here, is the same coin as שֶׁקֶל.]

7. When the Torah or the Talmud speaks of raising or enlarging a number by a particular percentage, the percentage is given with reference to the final amount, not the original. Thus, when the Torah states, "for what he has deprived the Sanctuary he shall make restitution of and add a fifth to it," the fine is reckoned in the following manner: The misappropriation is divided into four parts (e.g., a one-hundred-dollar misappropriation is considered as four twenty-five-dollar parts); then one more part is added (making, in our example, one hundred twenty-five dollars). The addition is then one-fifth of the final amount. [In Modern English terminology, this would be called "an increase of one-fourth" of the original amount.]

8. *Toras Kohanim, Chovah, perek* 20:7. The word וְנָתַן אוֹתוֹ לַכֹּהֵן, "and he shall give *it* to the Kohen," could have been understood as referring to the money being returned, and would have implied that the money becomes the property of the Kohen. Rather, *it* refers to

to it, and he shall give it to the *Kohen*; then the *Kohen* shall provide him atonement with the ram of the guilt-offering and it shall be forgiven him.

¹⁷ If a person will sin and will commit one of all the commandments of HASHEM that may not be done, but was unaware and became guilty, and bears his iniquity; ¹⁸ he shall bring an unblemished ram from

יוֹסֵף עָלָיו וְנָתַן אֹתוֹ לַכֹּהֵן וְהַכֹּהֵן יְכַפֵּר עָלָיו בְּאֵיל הָאָשָׁם וְנִסְלַח לוֹ:
יז וְאִם־נֶפֶשׁ כִּי תֶחֱטָא וְעָשְׂתָה אַחַת מִכָּל־מִצְוֹת יהוה אֲשֶׁר לֹא תֵעָשֶׂינָה וְלֹא־יָדַע וְאָשֵׁם וְנָשָׂא עֲוֹנוֹ: יח וְהֵבִיא אַיִל תָּמִים מִן־

— אונקלוס —

יוֹסֵף עֲלוֹהִי וְיִתֵּן יָתֵהּ לְכַהֲנָא וִיכַפֵּר עֲלוֹהִי כַהֲנָא בְּדִכְרָא דַאֲשָׁמָא וְיִשְׁתְּבִיק לֵהּ: יז וְאִם אֱנַשׁ אֲרֵי יֵחוֹב וְיַעֲבֵד חֲדָא מִכָּל פִּקּוּדַיָּא דַּיָּי דִי לָא כָשְׁרִין לְאִתְעֲבָדָא וְלָא יְדַע וְחָב וִיקַבֵּל חוֹבֵהּ: יח וְיַיְתֵי דְּכַר שְׁלִים מִן

— רש"י —

(ת"כ שם ז:) **וְלֹא יָדַע וְאָשֵׁם וְנָשָׂא עֲוֹנוֹ.** הָעִנְיָן הַזֶּה מְדַבֵּר בְּמִי שֶׁבָּא סָפֵק כָּרֵת לְיָדוֹ וְלֹא יָדַע אִם עָבַר עָלָיו אִם לָאו, כְּגוֹן חֵלֶב וְשֻׁמָּן לְפָנָיו וּכְסָבוּר שֶׁשְּׁתֵּיהֶן הֶתֵּר וְאָכַל אֶת הָאַחַת. אָמְרוּ לוֹ אַחַת שֶׁל חֵלֶב הָיְתָה, וְלֹא יָדַע אִם זוֹ שֶׁל חֵלֶב אָכַל, הֲרֵי זֶה מֵבִיא אָשָׁם תָּלוּי (ת"כ שם פרשתא יב:ג; כריתות יב:), וּמֵגִין עָלָיו כָּל זְמַן שֶׁלֹּא נוֹדַע לוֹ שֶׁוַּדַּאי חָטָא, וְאִם נוֹדַע לוֹ לְאַחַר זְמַן יָבִיא חַטָּאת (ת"כ שם פרק כח:א):

כריתות שם): **וְלֹא יָדַע וְאָשֵׁם וְנָשָׂא עֲוֹנוֹ.** ר"ו הַגְּלִילִי אוֹמֵר הֲרֵי הַכָּתוּב עָנַשׁ אֶת מִי שֶׁלֹּא יָדַע, עַל אַחַת כַּמָּה וְכַמָּה שֶׁיַּעֲנִישׁ אֶת מִי שֶׁיֵּדַע (ת"כ שם פרשתא יב:ז). רַבִּי יוֹסֵי אוֹמֵר אִם נַפְשְׁךָ לֵידַע מַתַּן שְׂכָרָן שֶׁל צַדִּיקִים צֵא וּלְמַד מֵאָדָם הָרִאשׁוֹן, שֶׁלֹּא נִצְטַוָּה אֶלָּא עַל מִצְוַת לֹא תַעֲשֶׂה וְעָבַר עָלֶיהָ, רְאֵה כַּמָּה מִיתוֹת נִקְנְסוּ עָלָיו וּלְדוֹרוֹתָיו. וְכִי אֵיזוֹ מִדָּה מְרֻבָּה, שֶׁל טוֹבָה אוֹ שֶׁל פֻּרְעָנוּת, הֱוֵי אוֹמֵר מִדָּה טוֹבָה:

— RASHI ELUCIDATED —

17. וְלֹא יָדַע וְאָשֵׁם... וְהֵבִיא — BUT WAS UNAWARE AND BECAME GUILTY...HE SHALL BRING. הָעִנְיָן הַזֶּה מְדַבֵּר — This topic speaks בְּמִי שֶׁבָּא סָפֵק כָּרֵת לְיָדוֹ — of one to whose hand a doubt of *kares* had come,¹ וְלֹא יָדַע אִם עָבַר עָלָיו אִם לָאו — and he did not know whether he had transgressed [the sin punishable by *kares*] or had not. כְּגוֹן חֵלֶב וְשֻׁמָּן לְפָנָיו — For instance, forbidden fat and permitted fat were in front of him, וּכְסָבוּר שֶׁשְּׁתֵּיהֶן הֶתֵּר — and he was under the impression that both of them were permitted, וְאָכַל אֶת הָאַחַת — and he ate one of them. אָמְרוּ לוֹ — They said to him, אַחַת שֶׁל חֵלֶב — "One of them was a piece of forbidden fat." וְלֹא יָדַע — And he did not know אִם זוֹ שֶׁל חֵלֶב הָיְתָה — if he ate the one of forbidden fat. אָכַל — Now then, this individual brings אָשָׁם תָּלוּי — an *asham talui*,² וּמֵגִין עָלָיו — and it protects him כָּל זְמַן שֶׁלֹּא נוֹדַע לוֹ — all the while that it has not become known to him שֶׁוַּדַּאי חָטָא — that he definitely had sinned. וְאִם נוֹדַע לוֹ לְאַחַר זְמַן — But if, after some time, it became known to him that he had sinned, ³יָבִיא חַטָּאת — he should bring a sin-offering.³

רַבִּי יוֹסֵי — וְלֹא יָדַע וְאָשֵׁם וְנָשָׂא עֲוֹנוֹ — BUT IS UNAWARE AND BECAME GUILTY, AND BEARS HIS INIQUITY. הַגְּלִילִי אוֹמֵר — The *Tanna* R' Yose HaGelili says: הֲרֵי הַכָּתוּב עָנַשׁ — See that Scripture has punished אֶת מִי שֶׁלֹּא יָדַע — one who is unaware that he committed a sin. עַל אַחַת כַּמָּה וְכַמָּה — How much more so שֶׁיַּעֲנִישׁ — that it will punish ⁴אֶת מִי שֶׁיֵּדַע — he who is aware.⁴ רַבִּי יוֹסֵי אוֹמֵר — The *Tanna* R' Yose says: אִם נַפְשְׁךָ לֵידַע מַתַּן שְׂכָרָן שֶׁל צַדִּיקִים — If you wish to know the reward of the righteous, צֵא וּלְמַד מֵאָדָם הָרִאשׁוֹן — go out and learn it from Adam, the first man, שֶׁלֹּא נִצְטַוָּה אֶלָּא עַל מִצְוַת לֹא תַעֲשֶׂה — who was commanded only with respect to one negative commandment,⁵ וְעָבַר עָלֶיהָ — and transgressed it. רְאֵה כַּמָּה מִיתוֹת — See how many deaths נִקְנְסוּ — have been given as punishment עָלָיו וּלְדוֹרוֹתָיו — to him and to his posterity. וְכִי אֵיזוֹ מִדָּה מְרֻבָּה — Now, which measure of God is the greater, שֶׁל טוֹבָה — of good, i.e., of giving reward, אוֹ שֶׁל פֻּרְעָנוּת — or of punishment? הֱוֵי אוֹמֵר — You should say in answer, מִדָּה טוֹבָה — the good

the ram of the guilt-offering. The money is the property of *hekdesh* (*Be'er Yitzchak*, based on *Rashbam*).

1. One who had been in a situation where he may have committed a sin whose intentional transgression is punished by *kares* (see p. 8, note 8).
2. *Toras Kohanim, Chovah, parshasa* 12:3; *Kereisos* 17b. An אָשָׁם תָּלוּי, literally, "suspended guilt-offering,"

is a guilt-offering brought in a situation of doubt or suspense.

3. *Toras Kohanim, Chovah, perek* 21:1; *Kereisos* 17b.
4. *Toras Kohanim, Chovah, perek* 12:7.
5. "And from the tree of knowledge of good and evil, you shall not eat of it" (*Genesis* 2:17).

― רש"י ―

אם מדת פורענות המעוטה ראה כמה מיתות נקנסו לו ולדורותיו, להחמיר עליו ולעשות דינו כיוצא באלו לענין זוגע זממה
מדה טובה המרובה, היושב לו מן הפיגולין והנותרות והמתענה [ס"א והצומה]. אם כך ענש הכתוב לנטפל לעוברי עבירה כעוברי
ביוה"כ עאכ"ו שיזכה לו ולדורותיו ולדורות דורותיו עד סוף עבירה, על אחת כמה וכמה שישלם שכר טוב לנטפל לעושי
כל הדורות (שם י). רבי עקיבא אומר הרי הוא אומר ע"פ מצוה כעושי מצוה (שם יא). רבי אלעזר בן עזריה אומר כי
שנים עדים או שלשה וגו' (דברים יז:ו), אם מתקיימת תקצור קצירך בשדך ושכחת עומר בשדה (דברים כד:יט),
העדות בשנים למה פרט לך הכתוב שלשה, אלא להביא שלישי הרי הוא אומר למען יברכך וגו' (שם) קבע הכתוב ברכה

―――――― RASHI ELUCIDATED ――――――

measure. פוּרְעָנוּת מִדַּת אָם – **If** with regard to **the measure of punishment,** הַמְּעוּטָה – **the lesser** of the two measures, רָאֵה כַּמָּה מִיתוֹת נִקְנְסוּ לוֹ וּלְדוֹרוֹתָיו – **see how many deaths have been given as punishment to him and to his posterity,** מִדָּה טוֹבָה הַמְרֻבָּה – **with regard to the measure of good, the greater** of the two, הַיּוֹשֵׁב לוֹ מִן הַפִּגּוּלִין – **one who refrains from** eating offerings that are *pigul*,[1] וְהַנּוֹתָרוֹת – **and** offerings that are *nosar*,[2] וְהַמִּתְעַנֶּה בְּיוֹם הַכִּפּוּרִים – **and one who fasts on Yom Kippur,** עַל אַחַת כַּמָּה וְכַמָּה שֶׁיִּזְכֶּה – **how much more so that he will gain reward** לוֹ וּלְדוֹרוֹתָיו – **for himself and for his posterity** וּלְדוֹרוֹת דּוֹרוֹתָיו – **and for the posterity of his posterity,** עַד סוֹף כָּל הַדּוֹרוֹת – **to the end of all generations.**[3] רַבִּי עֲקִיבָא אוֹמֵר – The *Tanna* **R' Akiva says:** הֲרֵי הוּא אוֹמֵר – **See that it says,** "עַל פִּי שְׁנַיִם עֵדִים אוֹ שְׁלֹשָׁה וְגוֹמֵר" – **"by the word of two witnesses or three, etc."**[4] אִם מִתְקַיֶּמֶת הָעֵדוּת בִּשְׁנַיִם – **If the testimony is upheld through two** witnesses, לָמָּה פָּרַט לְךָ הַכָּתוּב שְׁלֹשָׁה – **why did the verse specify three for you?** אֶלָּא לְהָבִיא שְׁלִישִׁי – **But** it specifies three **to include the third** witness insofar as לְהַחֲמִיר עָלָיו – **to deal stringently with him** וְלַעֲשׂוֹת דִּינוֹ כַּיּוֹצֵא בָּאֵלּוּ – **and make the judgment meted out to him identical to** that given [the other two] [5] לְעִנְיַן עוֹנֶשׁ זְמָמָה – **with regard to the matter of punishment for falsification.**[5] אִם כָּךְ עָנַשׁ הַכָּתוּב – **If Scripture meted out such punishment** לְעוֹבְרֵי עֲבֵרָה – **to the one who affiliates with transgressors,** כְּעוֹבְרֵי עֲבֵרָה – **like transgressors** themselves, עַל אַחַת כַּמָּה וְכַמָּה – **how much more is it so** שֶׁיְּשַׁלֵּם שָׂכָר טוֹב – **that it shall pay a good reward** לַנִּטְפָּל לְעוֹשֵׂי מִצְוָה – **to one who affiliates with those who perform a commandment** כְּעוֹשֵׂי מִצְוָה – **like those who perform the commandment** themselves.[6] רַבִּי אֶלְעָזָר בֶּן עֲזַרְיָה אוֹמֵר – The *Tanna* **R' Elazar ben Azariah says:** The verse says, "כִּי תִקְצֹר קְצִירְךָ בְּשָׂדֶךָ" – **"if you will reap your reaping in your field,** וְשָׁכַחְתָּ עֹמֶר בַּשָּׂדֶה"[7] – **and you will forget a sheaf in the field..."**[7] הֲרֵי הוּא אוֹמֵר – **See that it says** at the end of that verse, "לְמַעַן יְבָרֶכְךָ וְגוֹמֵר" – **"so that HASHEM, your God, will bless you, etc."** קָבַע הַכָּתוּב בְּרָכָה – **Scripture has assigned a**

---

1. An offering during whose slaughter the slaughterer had in mind that it should be eaten beyond the restrictions of time and place set for it by the Torah. See below 7:18 and 19:7.

2. Meat of an offering left uneaten beyond the time the Torah set for it to be eaten. It is forbidden to eat *nosar* or derive any benefit from it (see *Pesachim* 24a).

3. *Toras Kohanim, Chovah, parshasa* 12:10.

4. *Deuteronomy* 17:6. The text of our Rashi quotes this verse, which reads in full, "By the word of two witnesses or three witnesses shall the condemned person die; he shall not die by the word of one witness," in conformance with one of the variants of the Mishnah in *Makkos* 5b, which is a source for this part of the Rashi. The Gaon of Vilna in his notes there, however, says that the text should read עַל פִּי שְׁנֵי עֵדִים אוֹ עַל פִּי שְׁלֹשָׁה עֵדִים יָקוּם דָּבָר, "By the word of two witnesses or three witnesses will the matter be upheld" (*Deuteronomy* 19:15). This is supported by the fact that R' Akiva as quoted by Rashi here, as well as the Mishnah in *Makkos*, both go on to speak of "upholding" testimony.

5. Our text of Rashi which reads עוֹנֶשׁ זְמָמָה, "punishment for falsification," follows the first printed edition.

Yosef Hallel considers this version most accurate. The common texts read עוֹנֶשׁ וַהֲזָמָה, "punishment and refutation."

Zomemim are witnesses whom other witnesses refute by saying that they could not have seen the event to which they testify because they were together with the second set of witnesses in another location at the time that they claim to have seen the event. The testimony of the second group of witnesses is accepted, and the first group, the *zomemim*, is presumed false. The punishment for *zomemim* is that they receive the punishment they had planned (זָמְמוּ) to have the court inflict upon the victim of their plot. One might have thought that when a group of two witnesses is joined by a third witness, and all three are found to be *zomemim*, that the third witness not be punished, because his testimony did not make the testimony of the first two any more effective. The verse therefore specifies "two witnesses or three witnesses" to make the punishment of the third witness identical to that of the first two.

6. *Toras Kohanim, Chovah, parshasa* 12:11.

7. *Deuteronomy* 24:19. That verse continues, "do not go back to retrieve it; it shall be for the stranger, for the

הַצֹּאן בְּעֶרְכְּךָ לְאָשָׁם אֶל־הַכֹּהֵן וְכִפֶּר עָלָיו הַכֹּהֵן עַל שִׁגְגָתוֹ אֲשֶׁר־שָׁגָג וְהוּא לֹא־יָדַע וְנִסְלַח לוֹ: יט אָשָׁם הוּא אָשֹׁם אָשַׁם לַיהוָה:

the flock, of the value for a guilt-offering — to the Kohen; and the Kohen shall provide him atonement for the inadvertence that he committed unwittingly and he was unaware and it shall be forgiven him. ¹⁹ *It is a guilt-offering; he has committed an act of guilt before* HASHEM.

---- אונקלוס ----

עָנָא בְּפָרְסָנֵהּ לַאֲשָׁמָא לְוָת כַּהֲנָא וִיכַפַּר עֲלוֹהִי כַהֲנָא עַל שָׁלוּתֵהּ דְּאִשְׁתְּלִי וְהוּא לָא יְדַע וְיִשְׁתְּבֵק לֵהּ: יט אֲשָׁמָא הוּא עַל חוֹבְתֵהּ דְּהוּא חָב אֲשָׁמָא קֳדָם יְיָ:

---- רש"י ----

לְמִי שֶׁבָּאתָה עַל יָדוֹ מִצְוָה. (ת"כ פרק כה:ב): (יט) אָשָׁם הוּא אָשֹׁם אָשַׁם. הָרִאשׁוֹן כֻּלּוֹ קָמוּץ שֶׁהוּא שֵׁם דָּבָר, וְהָאַחֲרוֹן חֶצְיוֹ קָמֵץ וְחֶצְיוֹ פַּתָּח שֶׁהוּא לְ׳ פָּעַל.

לְאַחַר זְמַן, לֹא נִתְכַּפֵּר לוֹ בְּאָשָׁם זֶה עַד שֶׁיָּבִיא חַטָּאת. הָא לְמָה זֶה דּוֹמֶה, לְעֶגְלָה עֲרוּפָה שֶׁנִּתְעָרְפָה וְאַחַ"כ נִמְצָא הַהוֹרֵג, הֲרֵי זֶה יֵהָרֵג (ת"כ שם יג:): (יח) בְּעֶרְכְּךָ לְאָשָׁם. בָּעֵרֶךְ הָאָמוּר לְמַעְלָה (פסוק טו; ת"כ שם יד:): אֲשֶׁר שָׁגַג וְהוּא לֹא יָדַע. הָא אִם יָדַע

---- RASHI ELUCIDATED ----

לְמִי שֶׁבָּאתָה עַל יָדוֹ מִצְוָה — **to one through whom** a fulfillment of **a commandment has come about**, בְּלֹא יָדַע — **inadvertently.** אֱמוֹר מֵעַתָּה הָיְתָה סֶלַע צְרוּרָה בִּכְנָפָיו — **Say now,** on this basis, **that if there was a coin bound up in his hem,** וְנָפְלָה הֵימֶנּוּ — **and it fell from him,** וּמְצָאָהּ הֶעָנִי — **and a poor man found it,** וְנִתְפַּרְנֵס בָּהּ — **and derived sustenance from it,** הֲרֵי הַקָּדוֹשׁ בָּרוּךְ הוּא קוֹבֵעַ לוֹ בְּרָכָה — **see, then, the Holy One, Blessed is He, assigns him a blessing.**[1]

18. בְּעֶרְכְּךָ לְאָשָׁם — OF THE VALUE FOR A GUILT-OFFERING. בָּעֵרֶךְ הָאָמוּר לְמַעְלָה — **Of the value stated above.**[2,3]

□ אֲשֶׁר שָׁגַג וְהוּא לֹא יָדַע — THAT HE COMMITTED UNWITTINGLY AND HE WAS UNAWARE. הָא אִם יָדַע לְאַחַר זְמַן — **But if he became aware after some time,** לֹא נִתְכַּפֵּר לוֹ בְּאָשָׁם זֶה — **[the sin] is not atoned for him through this guilt-offering,** עַד שֶׁיָּבִיא חַטָּאת — **until he brings a sin-offering.** הָא לְמָה זֶה דּוֹמֶה — **What is this similar to?** לְעֶגְלָה עֲרוּפָה — **To an** *eglah arufah*[4] שֶׁנִּתְעָרְפָה — **which had its neck broken,** וְאַחַר כָּךְ נִמְצָא הַהוֹרֵג — **and afterwards the killer was found.** [5] הֲרֵי זֶה יֵהָרֵג — **Now, then, this [killer] should be killed.**[5]

19. אָשָׁם הוּא אָשֹׁם אָשַׁם — IT IS A GUILT-OFFERING. HE HAS COMMITTED AN ACT OF GUILT. הָרִאשׁוֹן — **The first** אשם **in this verse** כֻּלּוֹ קָמוּץ — **is vowelized entirely with the** *kamatz*, שֶׁהוּא שֵׁם דָּבָר — **because it is a noun.** וְהָאַחֲרוֹן — **With respect to the last one,** חֶצְיוֹ קָמֵץ — **half of it,** i.e., its first syllable, **is vowelized with a** *kamatz*, וְחֶצְיוֹ פַּתָּח — **and half of it,** i.e., its final syllable, **is vowelized with a** *patach*, שֶׁהוּא לְשׁוֹן פָּעַל — **because it is a third-person singular verb in the past tense.**[6]

---

orphan, and for the widow, so that HASHEM, your God, will bless you in all the work of your hands."

1. *Toras Kohanim, Chovah, parshasa* 12:13.

2. Verse 15. See Rashi there (s.v., בְּעֶרְכְּךָ כֶּסֶף שְׁקָלִים) that this means two *shekels*. The verse could have been read, "He shall bring an unblemished ram from the flock according to your estimation, for a guilt-offering." Rashi's comment points out that this interpretation is incorrect for three reasons: (a) It understands בְּעֶרְכְּךָ in its sense of "estimation" rather than "value" (see note 6 on p. 51 above); (b) it incorrectly understands the *chaf*-suffix of בְּעֶרְכְּךָ as "your" (see Rashi to 27:3 below); and (c) it views לְאָשָׁם as connected to "he shall bring" of the beginning of the verse, when in fact it is connected to בְּעֶרְכְּךָ.

3. *Toras Kohanim, Chovah, parshasa* 12:14.

4. Literally, "calf whose neck is broken," a means of atonement for a murder whose perpetrator is unknown. See *Deuteronomy* 21:1-9.

5. *Toras Kohanim, Chovah, perek* 21:2. Just as the *eglah arufah* serves as a temporary atonement until the killing of the killer, which is an absolute atonement, so, too, the *asham talui* is a temporary atonement until the sin-offering is brought for absolute atonement.

6. The root אשם appears three times in the verse. Rashi explains the first and third appearances. The first word, אָשָׁם, is a noun, similar in construction to דָּבָר, "a matter" (e.g., above 4:13), and נָהָר, "a river" (e.g., *Numbers* 24:6). The third word, אָשַׁם, is a verb, in the simple *kal*, past tense, third person, masculine, singular, similar to שָׁמַר, "he watched" (e.g., *Genesis* 37:11), and לָמַד, "he learned" (e.g., *Isaiah* 26:10). The middle word אָשֹׁם is a *makor* or infinitive, a verb form that grammatically has neither tense nor person, which here serves to strengthen the verb (אָשַׁם) to which it is juxtaposed. The word אָשֹׁם is similar to the infinitive שָׁמוֹעַ in the phrase שָׁמוֹעַ תִּשְׁמְעוּ, "hearken well" (*Exodus* 19:5; *Leshon Chaim*).

55 / VAYIKRA/LEVITICUS — PARASHAS VAYIKRA 5/20-21 — כ/כ־כא

²⁰ HASHEM *spoke to Moses, saying:* ²¹ *If a person will sin and commit a trespass against* HASHEM *and be deceitful toward his fellow regarding a pledge or*

כ וַיְדַבֵּר יהוה אֶל־מֹשֶׁה לֵּאמֹר׃
כא נֶפֶשׁ כִּי תֶחֱטָא וּמָעֲלָה מַעַל
בַּיהוה וְכִחֵשׁ בַּעֲמִיתוֹ בְּפִקָּדוֹן אוֹ־

─────── אונקלוס ───────

כ וּמַלִּיל יְיָ עִם מֹשֶׁה לְמֵימָר: כא אֱנָשׁ אֲרֵי יֵחוֹב וִישַׁקַּר שְׁקַר קֳדָם יְיָ וִיכַדֵּב בְּחַבְרֵהּ בְּפִקְדוֹנָא אוֹ

─────── רש"י ───────

וא"ת מקרא שלא לנטרך הוא, כבר דרוש הוא בת"כ (שם ג:ז). אשם אשם, להביא אשם שפחה חרופה שיהא איל בן [שתי שנים שוה] שני סלעים. יכול שאני מרבה אשם נזיר ואשם מצורע, תלמוד לומר הוא. (שם ז): (כא) נפש כי תחטא. אמר רבי

עקיבא מה ת"ל ומעלה מעל בה', לפי שכל המלוה והלוה והנושא והנותן אינו עושה אלא בעדים ובשטר, לפיכך בזמן שהוא מכחש מכחש בעדים ובשטר. אבל המפקיד אצל חבירו [ואינו] רוצה שתדע בו נשמה אלא שלישי שביניהם,

─────── RASHI ELUCIDATED ───────

כְּבָר דְּרוּשׁ הוּא — it is an unnecessary verse,[1] וְאִם תֹּאמַר *If you will say,* מִקְרָא שֶׁלֹּא לְצוֹרֶךְ הוּא — ״אָשָׁם אָשָׁם״ — "he has committed an act of guilt" בְּתוֹרַת כֹּהֲנִים — it has already been expounded in *Toras Kohanim*[2] as follows: לְהָבִיא אֲשַׁם שִׁפְחָה חֲרוּפָה — to include the guilt-offering of a *shifchah charufah*[3] שֶׁיְּהֵא אַיִל — that it should be a ram בֶּן שְׁנֵי סְלָעִים — worth two *shekels*.[4] יָכוֹל — One might be able to think שֶׁאֲנִי מַרְבֶּה אֲשַׁם נָזִיר — that I would also include the guilt-offering of the *nazir*[5] וַאֲשַׁם מְצוֹרָע — and the guilt-offering of one who suffered from *tzara'as*[6] in the law of having a value of two *shekels*. תַּלְמוּד לוֹמַר — To teach us otherwise, **the Torah says,** ״הוּא״ — "it."[7]

21. נֶפֶשׁ כִּי תֶחֱטָא — IF A PERSON WILL SIN. אָמַר רַבִּי עֲקִיבָא — The *Tanna* R' Akiva said: מַה תַּלְמוּד לוֹמַר — Why does the Torah say, ״וּמָעֲלָה מַעַל בַּה׳״ — "and commit a trespass against HASHEM"?[8] לְפִי — Because whoever lends וְהַלֹוֶה — or borrows וְהַנּוֹשֵׂא וְהַנּוֹתֵן — or buys and sells אֵינוֹ עוֹשֶׂה אֶלָּא בְּעֵדִים וּבִשְׁטָר — does his business only by witnesses and a contract. לְפִיכָךְ בִּזְמַן שֶׁהוּא מְכַחֵשׁ — Therefore, at a time when he lies, מְכַחֵשׁ בְּעֵדִים וּבִשְׁטָר — he lies against the witnesses and against the contract. אֲבָל הַמַּפְקִיד אֵצֶל חֲבֵרוֹ — But one who gives his possessions for safekeeping to his friend אֵינוֹ רוֹצֶה[9] שֶׁתֵּדַע בּוֹ נְשָׁמָה — does not want a soul to know about it אֶלָּא הַשְּׁלִישִׁי שֶׁבֵּינֵיהֶם

---

1. If you will argue that this verse is unnecessary because the preceding verses have already identified the offering under discussion as a guilt-offering which is brought for certain actions which cause guilt.

2. *Toras Kohanim, Chovah, perek* 21:3-6. *Toras Kohanim* has various expositions and interpretations of this verse. Rashi cites only one of them. In some editions of Rashi the remainder of this comment is set off as a paragraph on its own, with the rubric אָשָׁם אָשָׁם.

3. Literally, "a designated slavewoman." A Canaanite woman who is half free and half slave who has been designated as the wife of a Hebrew servant. If a Jew other than her husband has relations with her, he must bring a guilt-offering. See 19:20-21 below.

4. Some editions read, שֶׁיְּהֵא אַיִל בֶּן שְׁתֵּי שָׁנִים, "that it should be a two-year-old ram," שָׁוֶה שְׁנֵי סְלָעִים, "worth two *shekalim*."

5. The "Nazirite." One who takes a certain vow of abstinence. See *Numbers* 6:12.

6. *Tzara'as* is a disease of the skin that renders the sufferer impure. See 14:12 below.

7. *Toras Kohanim, Chovah, perek* 21:7. "It" implies "to the exclusion of others." It is used here to exclude the guilt-offering of the *nazir* and the guilt-offering of one who suffered *tzara'as*. They need not have a value of at least two *shekels*. The verse is interpreted as including the guilt-offering of *shifchah charufah* and excluding the guilt-offerings of the *nazir* and one who suffered *tzara'as* because the guilt-offering of *shifchah charufah* is more like the *asham talui* of our passage; both are rams. However, the guilt-offerings of the *nazir* and one who suffered *tzara'as* are male lambs (*Mizrachi*).

The Mishnah describes the ages of a male sheep: Until the day before its first birthday, it qualifies as a כֶּבֶשׂ, "lamb"; from the 31st day after its first birthday until the day before its second birthday it qualifies as an אַיִל, "ram"; for the first thirty days of its second year, it is disqualified as too old for a lamb and two young for a ram (*Puruh* 1:3). Once a male sheep reaches its second birthday, it is no longer fit to be an offering (*Rambam, Maaseh HaKorbanos* 1:11; *Tiferes Yisrael*).

8. Why does the verse say "against HASHEM" when immediately afterwards it describes the sin as being "toward his fellow"? Furthermore, why does the verse use "against HASHEM" with reference to this sin which seems to be essentially between man and his fellow man, when it does not use it with reference to misusing *hekdesh* (see v. 15 above) which seems to be more directly a sin against God? (*Divrei David*).

9. Some editions read וְאֵינוֹ רוֹצֶה, "*and* he does not want."

about a putting of a hand or about robbery; or deprived his fellow; ²² or he found a lost item and denied it — and he swore falsely about any of all the things, which man does do, to sin by them — ²³ so it shall be that he will sin and become guilty,

בְּתְשׂוּמֶת יָד אוֹ בְגָזֵל אוֹ עָשַׁק אֶת־עֲמִיתוֹ: כב אוֹ־מָצָא אֲבֵדָה וְכִחֶשׁ בָּהּ וְנִשְׁבַּע עַל־שָׁקֶר עַל־אַחַת מִכֹּל אֲשֶׁר־יַעֲשֶׂה הָאָדָם לַחֲטֹא בָהֵנָּה: כג וְהָיָה כִּי־יֶחֱטָא וְאָשֵׁם

— אונקלוס —

בְּשֻׁתָּפוּת יְדָא אוֹ בִגְזֵלָא אוֹ עֲשַׁק יָת חַבְרֵיהּ: כב אוֹ אַשְׁכַּח אֲבֶדְתָּא וִיכַדֵּב בַּהּ וְיִשְׁתְּבַע עַל שִׁקְרָא עַל חֲדָא מִכֹּל דִּי יַעְבֵּד אֱנָשָׁא לְמֵיחַב בְּהֵן: כג וִיהֵי אֲרֵי יֵחוֹב וְיֵחוֹב

— רש״י —

בָּהּ. שֶׁכִּפֵּר עַל אַחַת מִכֹּל אֵלֶּה, אֲשֶׁר יַעֲשֶׂה הָאָדָם לַחֲטוֹא וְלִהִשָּׁבַע עַל שֶׁקֶר לִכְפִירַת מָמוֹן: (כב) כִּי יֶחֱטָא וְאָשֵׁם. כְּשֶׁיַּכִּיר בְּעַצְמוֹ לָשׁוּב בִּתְשׁוּבָה לָדַעַת וּלְהוֹדוֹת (ס״א וּבְדַעְתּוֹ לְהִתְוַדּוֹת) כִּי חָטָא וְאָשֵׁם: לְפִיכָךְ כְּשֶׁהוּא מְכַחֵשׁ מְכַחֵשׁ בַּשְּׁלִישִׁי שֶׁבֵּינֵיהֶם (שם פרק כב:ד): בִּתְשׂוּמֶת יָד. שָׂם בְּיָדוֹ מָמוֹן לְהִתְעַסֵּק אוֹ בְּמִלְוֶה: אוֹ בְגָזֵל. גָּזַל מִיָּדוֹ כְּלוּם: אוֹ עָשָׁק. הוּא שְׂכַר שָׂכִיר (שם ו):

━━━━━━━━━━━━━━━━ RASHI ELUCIDATED ━━━━━━━━━━━━━━━━

— except for the third party Who is between them, i.e., God, Who is the witness to the deposit. מְכַחֵשׁ — lies, Therefore, — לְפִיכָךְ כְּשֶׁהוּא מְכַחֵשׁ — when he to whom the possessions were entrusted lies, בַּשְּׁלִישִׁי שֶׁבֵּינֵיהֶם¹ — he denies the third party Who is between them, i.e., by contradicting that to which God is witness, in effect, denies the existence of God.¹

□ בִּתְשׂוּמֶת יָד — ABOUT A PUTTING OF A HAND. שָׂם בְּיָדוֹ מָמוֹן — That he put money in his hand לְהִתְעַסֵּק — to do business with אוֹ בְּמִלְוֶה — or as a loan.

□ אוֹ בְגָזֵל — OR ABOUT ROBBERY. שֶׁגָּזַל מִיָּדוֹ כְּלוּם — That he robbed something from his hand.

□ אוֹ עָשָׁק — OR DEPRIVED. ² הוּא שְׂכַר שָׂכִיר — It is the wage of a hired worker.²

22. וְכִחֶשׁ בָּהּ — AND DENIED IT.³ This means שֶׁכִּפֵּר — that he denied falsely⁴ — עַל אַחַת מִכֹּל אֵלֶּה — about any of all these, אֲשֶׁר יַעֲשֶׂה הָאָדָם לַחֲטֹא — which man does do, to sin וּלְהִשָּׁבַע עַל שֶׁקֶר — and to swear to a falsehood לִכְפִירַת מָמוֹן — for the denial of a claim of money.⁵

23. כִּי יֶחֱטָא וְאָשֵׁם — THAT HE WILL SIN AND BECOME GUILTY. כְּשֶׁיַּכִּיר בְּעַצְמוֹ — When he will develop the self-awareness לָשׁוּב בִּתְשׁוּבָה — to repent, ⁶לָדַעַת וּלְהוֹדוֹת — to know and to confess,⁶ כִּי חָטָא — that he has sinned וְאָשֵׁם — and has become guilty.⁷

---

1. *Toras Kohanim, Chovah, perek* 22:4, see *Ra'avad* there.

2. *Toras Kohanim, Chovah, perek* 22:6. Although the verb עשק can be used for any type of thievery or illicit gain, in this verse, "it is the wage of a hired worker" which it is used for, as it is in 19:13 below. Other types of illicit gain are included in the category of אוֹ בְגָזֵל, "or about robbery," which appears in the verse.

3. Rashi's comment to this verse appears as one paragraph in most printed editions, a reading confirmed by *Nachalas Yaakov.* Some editions divide it into two or three very short paragraphs (see *Yosef Hallel*).

4. In the previous verse כִּחֵשׁ means "he made a false statement." Here it means, "he denied the truth."

5. The verse could have been understood, "Or he found a lost item and lied about it, and he swore falsely; about any of all the things that a person can do and sin thereby." According to this understanding, the verse is saying that a guilt-offering must be brought "about any of all the things that a person can do and sin thereby" i.e., over any sin. If this is so, however, why does the Torah list specific sins? This points to another understanding of the verse. Rashi explains that there is an implicit "these" in the verse — "Or he found a lost item and lied about it, and he swore falsely; about any of all of *these* things," i.e., about any of the false oaths mentioned previously (*Gur Aryeh*). אֲשֶׁר יַעֲשֶׂה הָאָדָם לַחֲטֹא בָהֵנָּה, "the things which a man does do, to sin by them," is the term used by the Torah to express these sins because it explains why the Torah required the guilt-offering in these specific cases. They are acts "which man does do, to sin by them"; that is, man is prone to commit these sins which involve false denial of a debt (*Mizrachi; Sifsei Chachamim*).

6. Some editions read וְלָדַעַת וּלְהִתְוַדּוֹת, "and to know and to confess"; others read וּבְדַעְתּוֹ לְהִתְוַדּוֹת, "and it is in his mind to confess."

7. The verse says, "So it shall be, that he will sin and become guilty, he will return the robbed item." Not everyone who sins and becomes guilty returns what he robbed. Thus, it is implicit that the sinner repented of his sin — "So it shall be, when he will recognize that he has sinned and has become guilty" (*Mizrachi*).

he will return the robbed item that he robbed, or the proceeds of his fraud, or the pledge that was left with him, or the lost item that he found, ²⁴ or anything about which he had sworn falsely — he shall repay by its head and its fifths; he shall give it to the one to whom it belongs on the day he admits his guilt. ²⁵ And he shall bring his guilt-offering to Hashem — an unblemished ram from the flock, of the value for a guilt-offering — to the Kohen. ²⁶ The Kohen shall provide him atonement before Hashem, and it shall be forgiven him for any of all the things he might do to incur guilt.

וְהֵשִׁיב אֶת־הַגְּזֵלָה אֲשֶׁר גָּזָל אוֹ אֶת־הָעֹשֶׁק אֲשֶׁר עָשָׁק אוֹ אֶת־הַפִּקָּדוֹן אֲשֶׁר הָפְקַד אִתּוֹ אוֹ אֶת־הָאֲבֵדָה אֲשֶׁר מָצָא: מפטיר אוֹ מִכֹּל כד אֲשֶׁר־יִשָּׁבַע עָלָיו לַשֶּׁקֶר וְשִׁלַּם אֹתוֹ בְּרֹאשׁוֹ וַחֲמִשִׁתָיו יֹסֵף עָלָיו לַאֲשֶׁר הוּא לוֹ יִתְּנֶנּוּ בְּיוֹם אַשְׁמָתוֹ: וְאֶת־אֲשָׁמוֹ יָבִיא לַיהוָה אַיִל תָּמִים כה מִן־הַצֹּאן בְּעֶרְכְּךָ לְאָשָׁם אֶל־הַכֹּהֵן: וְכִפֶּר עָלָיו הַכֹּהֵן לִפְנֵי יהוה כו וְנִסְלַח לוֹ עַל־אַחַת מִכֹּל אֲשֶׁר־יַעֲשֶׂה לְאַשְׁמָה בָהּ: פ פ פ

THE HAFTARAH FOR VAYIKRA APPEARS ON PAGE 389.
When Parashas Zachor coincides with Vayikra, the regular Maftir and Haftarah are replaced with the readings of Parashas Zachor — see page 407.
When Rosh Chodesh Nissan coincides with Vayikra, Vayikra is divided into six aliyos; the Rosh Chodesh reading, (page 405, is the seventh aliyah; and the Parashas HaChodesh readings follow — see page 412.

─── אונקלוס ───

וְיָתֵב יָת גְזֵלָה דִּי גְזַל אוֹ יָת עֻשְׁקָא דִּי עֲשַׁק אוֹ יָת פִּקְדוֹנָא דִּי אִתְפְּקַד עִמֵּהּ אוֹ יָת אֲבֵדְתָּא דִי אַשְׁכָּח: כד אוֹ מִכֹּל דְּאִשְׁתְּבַע עֲלוֹהִי לְשִׁקְרָא וִישַׁלֵּם יָתֵהּ בְּרֵישֵׁהּ וְחֻמְשֵׁהּ יוֹסֵף עֲלוֹהִי לְדִי הוּא דִילֵהּ יִתְּנִנֵּהּ בְּיוֹמָא דְחוֹבָתֵהּ: כה וְיָת אֲשָׁמֵהּ יַיְתֵי קֳדָם יְיָ דְּכַר שְׁלִים מִן עָנָא בְּפֻרְסָנֵהּ לַאֲשָׁמָא לְוָת כַּהֲנָא: כו וִיכַפֵּר עֲלוֹהִי כַהֲנָא קֳדָם יְיָ וְיִשְׁתְּבֵק לֵהּ עַל חֲדָא מִכֹּל דִּי יַעְבֵּד לְמֵיחַב בַּהּ:

─── רש"י ───

(כד) בראשו. הוא הַקֶּרֶן רֹאשׁ הַמָּמוֹן (ב״ק ק״י.): וחמשיתיו. שִׁיתַּמְטַע הַקֶּרֶן שֶׁנִּשְׁבַּע עָלָיו פָּחוֹת מִשְׁוֵה פְּרוּטָה ת"כ שָׁם רִבְּתָה תּוֹרָה חֲמִישִׁיּוֹת הַרְבֵּה לְקֶרֶן אַחַת, שֶׁאִם כָּפַר בַּחוֹמֶשׁ וְנִשְׁבַּע פַּרְשָׁתָא יג:יב; בבא קמא קג, קח״:: לאשר הוא לו. לְמִי וְהוֹדָה חוֹזֵר וּמֵבִיא חוֹמֶשׁ עַל אוֹתוֹ חוֹמֶשׁ, וְכֵן מוֹסִיף וְהוֹלֵךְ עַד שֶׁהַמָּמוֹן שֶׁלּוֹ (ת"כ שָׁם; ב״ק קג:):

─── RASHI ELUCIDATED ───

24. בְּרֹאשׁוֹ — BY ITS HEAD. הוּא הַקֶּרֶן — This is the principal, רֹאשׁ הַמָּמוֹן — the head of the money.[1]

וַחֲמִשִׁתָיו — AND ITS FIFTHS. רִבְּתָה הַתּוֹרָה — The Torah included חֲמִישִׁיּוֹת הַרְבֵּה — many fifths לְקֶרֶן אַחַת — for one principal.[2] שֶׁאִם כָּפַר בַּחוֹמֶשׁ — For if he denied the fifth, i.e., if the fifth was claimed from him and he falsely denied owing it, וְנִשְׁבַּע — and swore falsely, וְהוֹדָה — and subsequently **confessed,** חוֹזֵר וּמֵבִיא חוֹמֶשׁ עַל אוֹתוֹ חוֹמֶשׁ — he brings another fifth for that fifth.[3] וְכֵן מוֹסִיף וְהוֹלֵךְ — And so he keeps adding fifth upon fifth, עַד שֶׁיִּתְמַעֵט הַקֶּרֶן שֶׁנִּשְׁבַּע עָלָיו פָּחוֹת מִשְׁוֵה פְּרוּטָה — until the principal about which he swears becomes less than the value of a *perutah*.[4]

לַאֲשֶׁר הוּא לוֹ — TO THE ONE TO WHOM IT BELONGS. לְמִי שֶׁהַמָּמוֹן שֶׁלּוֹ — To the one to whom the money, i.e., the principal, **belongs.**[5]

---

1. Bava Kamma 110a. "The head of the money" means the source of any profit that stems from it (*Mizrachi; Sifsei Chachamim*). Similarly, the English word "capital" is derived from the Latin word *caput*, "head."

2. By using the plural "fifths," the Torah implies that it is possible to pay many fifths which stem from the same original principal.

3. The first fifth now becomes the principal on which he swears. If he swears falsely, and then he confesses, he pays an additional fifth of that fifth.

4. *Toras Kohanim, Chovah, parshasa* 13:12; *Bava Kamma* 103a-b, 108a.

5. *Toras Kohanim, Chovah, parshasa* 13:12; *Bava Kamma* 103a. "It" of יִתְּנֶנּוּ, "he shall give it," refers to the fifth. "It" of לַאֲשֶׁר הוּא לוֹ, "to the one to whom *it* belongs" might also have been understood as referring to the fifth. But then the verse would be instructing us to give the fifth to the one to whom the fifth belongs without telling us who that is. Rashi therefore explains that "to the one to whom it belongs" refers to the principal (*Gur Aryeh*).

פרשת צו

Parashas Tzav

6

¹ **H**ASHEM spoke to Moses, saying: ² Command Aaron and his sons, saying: This is the law of the olah-offering: It is the olah-offering [that stays] on the flame, on the Mizbe'ach, all night until the morning, and the fire of the Mizbe'ach shall be kept aflame

וַיְדַבֵּ֥ר יְהוָ֖ה אֶל־מֹשֶׁ֥ה לֵּאמֹֽר: צַ֤ו אֶֽת־אַהֲרֹן֙ וְאֶת־בָּנָ֣יו לֵאמֹ֔ר זֹ֥את תּוֹרַ֖ת הָעֹלָ֑ה הִ֣וא הָעֹלָ֡ה עַל֩ מוֹקְדָ֨ה עַל־הַמִּזְבֵּ֤חַ כָּל־הַלַּ֨יְלָה֙ עַד־הַבֹּ֔קֶר וְאֵ֥שׁ הַמִּזְבֵּ֖חַ תּ֥וּקַד

אונקלוס

א וּמַלִּיל יְיָ עִם מֹשֶׁה לְמֵימָר: ב פַּקֵּד יָת אַהֲרֹן וְיָת בְּנוֹהִי לְמֵימַר דָּא אוֹרַיְתָא דַעֲלָתָא הִיא עֲלָתָא דְּמִתּוֹקְדָא עַל מַדְבְּחָא כָּל לֵילְיָא עַד צַפְרָא וְאֶשָּׁתָא דְמַדְבְּחָא תְּהֵא יָקְדָא

רש"י

(ב) צו את אהרן. אין צו אלא לשון זרוז, מיד ולדורות. אמר רבי שמעון ביותר צריך הכתוב לזרז במקום שיש בו חסרון כיס (ת"כ לו פרשתא א:א; קדושין כט.). **זאת תורת העולה וגו'.** הרי הענין הזה בא ללמד על הקטר חלבים ואיברים שיהא כשר כל הלילה (מגילה כא.). וללמד על הפסולין איזה אם עלה ירד ואיזה אם עלה לא ירד, שכל תורה לרבות הוא בא לומר תורה אחת לכל העולים ואפי' פסולין שאם עלו לא ירדו (ת"כ שם פרשתא א:ב). **הוא העולה.** למעט את הרובע ואת הנרבע וכיוצא בהן שלא היה פסולן בקדש שנפסלו קודם שבאו לעזרה (שם ח; זבחים כז:; נדה מ:):

RASHI ELUCIDATED

6.

2. צַו אֶת אַהֲרֹן — COMMAND AARON. אֵין צַו אֶלָּא לְשׁוֹן זֵרוּז — "Command" can only be meant to express urging on, מִיָּד וּלְדוֹרוֹת — for the immediate moment, and for future generations.¹ אָמַר רַבִּי שִׁמְעוֹן — The *Tanna* R' Shimon said: בְּיוֹתֵר צָרִיךְ הַכָּתוּב לְזָרֵז — Scripture must especially urge בְּמָקוֹם שֶׁיֵּשׁ — בּוֹ חֶסְרוֹן כִּיס — in a situation where there is loss of money.²

□ זֹאת תּוֹרַת הָעֹלָה וְגוֹמֵר — THIS IS THE LAW OF THE *OLAH*-OFFERING, ETC. הֲרֵי הָעִנְיָן הַזֶּה — See then, this topic בָּא לְלַמֵּד — comes to teach עַל הֶקְטֵר חֲלָבִים וְאֵבָרִים — about the burning of fats and body parts שֶׁיְּהֵא כָּשֵׁר — that it should be valid³ כָּל הַלַּיְלָה — throughout the entire night,³ וּלְלַמֵּד עַל הַפְּסוּלִין — and to teach us about offerings that have become disqualified, אֵיזֶה אִם עָלָה יֵרֵד — which of them, if it ascended upon the *Mizbe'ach* should come down, וְאֵיזֶה אִם עָלָה לֹא יֵרֵד — and which, if it ascended, should not come down. שֶׁכָּל ,,תּוֹרָה'' לְרַבּוֹת הוּא בָּא — For every instance in Scripture of the word תּוֹרָה, "law," comes to include, לוֹמַר — as if to say, תּוֹרָה אַחַת — there should be one law לְכָל הָעוֹלִים — for all offerings that ascend onto the *Mizbe'ach*, וַאֲפִילוּ פְּסוּלִין — even those that are disqualified, שֶׁאִם עָלוּ — that if they ascended, although they should not have, ⁴לֹא יֵרְדוּ — they should not descend.⁴

□ הִוא הָעֹלָה — IT IS THE *OLAH*-OFFERING. לְמַעֵט אֶת הָרוֹבֵעַ וְאֶת הַנִּרְבָּע — To exclude an animal that was the active or the passive party to an act of bestiality, וְכַיּוֹצֵא בָהֶן — and the like, שֶׁלֹּא הָיָה פְּסוּלָן בַּקֹּדֶשׁ — whose disqualification did not come about in the Sanctuary, שֶׁנִּפְסְלוּ — for they became disqualified ⁵קוֹדֶם שֶׁבָּאוּ לָעֲזָרָה — before they came to the Courtyard of the *Beis HaMikdash*.⁵

---

1. *Kiddushin* 29a. Wherever the Torah uses צַו rather than דַּבֵּר or אֱמוֹר, it indicates three points: (a) urging on; (b) that the matter commanded must be done immediately; and that (c) it must also be performed by future generations (see *Korban Aharon*).

2. *Toras Kohanim* 1:1; *Kiddushin* 29a. The Kohanim suffer financial loss because they are not paid for the sacrificial service. In order to perform it, they must give up their regular means of earning a livelihood. Even the hides that they receive from the *olah*-offerings are insufficient to make up for this loss of income (*Gur Aryeh*). The Torah makes this point in the context of the *olah*-offering rather than other offerings because the loss of income in this case is especially great. With other animal offerings, the Kohanim receive both meat and hides. With the *olah*-offering, they receive only hides (see *Divrei David*).

3. *Megillah* 21a.

4. *Toras Kohanim* 1:7.

5. *Toras Kohanim* 1:8; *Zevachim* 27b, 84a; *Niddah* 40b. "This is the law of the *olah*-offering" is an inclusionary phrase. It implies that even parts of disqualified offerings which should not have been put on the *Mizbe'ach* should remain there and be consumed by the fire. "It is the *olah*-offering" limits that inclusion to offerings that became disqualified once they entered the grounds of the *Beis HaMikdash*; for example, an offering whose blood was spilled before it was sprinkled. However, if parts of an animal that had become disqualified before it entered the grounds of the *Beis HaMikdash* were placed on the *Mizbe'ach*, they should be taken off.

on it. ³ **The Kohen shall don his fitted linen Tunic, and he shall don linen Michnasaim on his flesh; he shall raise the ashes which the fire will consume of the olah-offering on the Mizbe'ach, and place it next to the Mizbe'ach.** ⁴ **He shall remove his garments**

ג וְלָבַשׁ הַכֹּהֵן מִדּוֹ בַד וּמִכְנְסֵי־בַד יִלְבַּשׁ עַל־בְּשָׂרוֹ וְהֵרִים אֶת־הַדֶּשֶׁן אֲשֶׁר תֹּאכַל הָאֵשׁ אֶת־הָעֹלָה עַל־הַמִּזְבֵּחַ וְשָׂמוֹ אֵצֶל הַמִּזְבֵּחַ: ד וּפָשַׁט אֶת־בְּגָדָיו

─────── אונקלוס ───────

בה: ג וְיִלְבַּשׁ כָּהֲנָא לְבוּשִׁין דְּבוּץ וּמִכְנְסִין דְּבוּץ יִלְבַּשׁ עַל בִּסְרֵהּ וְיַפְרֵשׁ יָת קִטְמָא דִּי תֵיכוּל אֶשָּׁתָא יָת עֲלָתָא עַל מַדְבְּחָא וִישַׁוִּנֵּה בִּסְטַר מַדְבְּחָא: ד וְיַשְׁלַח יָת לְבוּשׁוֹהִי

─── רש"י ───

(ג) מדו בד. הִיא הַכְּתֹנֶת וּמַה תַּ"ל מִדּוֹ, שֶׁתְּהֵא כְּמִדָּתוֹ (ת"כ פרק ב:א; זבחים לה.): **עַל בְּשָׂרוֹ.** שֶׁלֹּא יְהֵא דָּבָר חוֹצֵץ בֵּינְתַיִם (ת"כ שם ג; זבחים יט.; ערכין ג:): **וְהֵרִים אֶת הַדֶּשֶׁן.** הָיָה חוֹתֶה מְלֹא הַמַּחְתָּה מִן הַמְאֻכָּלוֹת הַפְּנִימִיּוֹת וְנוֹתְנָן בְּמִזְרָחוֹ שֶׁל כֶּבֶשׁ (ת"כ שם ד; תמיד כח.): **הַדֶּשֶׁן אֲשֶׁר תֹּאכַל הָאֵשׁ אֶת הָעוֹלָה.** וַעֲשָׂאַתּוּ דֶשֶׁן מֵאוֹתוֹ דֶשֶׁן יָרִים תְּרוּמָה וְשָׂמוֹ אֵצֶל הַמִּזְבֵּחַ. **[עַל הַמִּזְבֵּחַ.** מָצָא אֵבָרִים שֶׁלֹּא נִתְאַכְּלוּ מַחֲזִירָן עַל הַמִּזְבֵּחַ לְאַחַר שֶׁחָתָה גֶּחָלִים אֵילָךְ וָאֵילָךְ וְנָטַל מִן הַפְּנִימִיּוֹת שֶׁנֶּאֱמַר אֶת הָעֹלָה עַל הַמִּזְבֵּחַ (ת"כ שם ה; יומא מה:)]: **(ד) וּפָשַׁט אֶת בְּגָדָיו.** אֵין זוֹ חוֹבָה אֶלָּא דֶּרֶךְ אֶרֶץ, שֶׁלֹּא יְלַכְלֵךְ בְּהוֹצָאַת הַדֶּשֶׁן בְּגָדִים שֶׁהוּא מְשַׁמֵּשׁ בָּהֶן תָּמִיד. בְּגָדִים שֶׁבִּשֵּׁל בָּהֶן קְדֵרָה לְרַבּוֹ

─── RASHI ELUCIDATED ───

3. מִדּוֹ בַד — HIS FITTED LINEN TUNIC. הִיא הַכְּתֹנֶת — It is the *Kutones*.[1] וּמַה תַּלְמוּד לוֹמַר מִדּוֹ — Why does the Torah say, i.e., call it, מִדּוֹ? שֶׁתְּהֵא כְּמִדָּתוֹ — So that it should be like [the Kohen's] measurement, i.e., to teach us that it should fit the Kohen.[2]

□ עַל בְּשָׂרוֹ — ON HIS FLESH. שֶׁלֹּא יְהֵא דָּבָר חוֹצֵץ בֵּינְתַיִם[3] — That there should be nothing acting as a barrier between [the garment and the Kohen's flesh].[3]

□ וְהֵרִים אֶת הַדֶּשֶׁן — HE SHALL RAISE THE ASHES. הָיָה חוֹתֶה — He would shovel מְלֹא הַמַּחְתָּה — a shovelful מִן הַמְאֻכָּלוֹת הַפְּנִימִיּוֹת — from the interior, consumed ashes,[4] וְנוֹתְנָן — and put them בְּמִזְרָחוֹ שֶׁל כֶּבֶשׁ[5] — at the east of the ramp which led to the top of the *Mizbe'ach*.[5]

□ הַדֶּשֶׁן אֲשֶׁר תֹּאכַל הָאֵשׁ אֶת הָעֹלָה — THE ASHES; WHICH THE FIRE WILL CONSUME OF THE *OLAH*-OFFERING. וַעֲשָׂאַתּוּ דֶשֶׁן — and will have made of it ashes.[6] מֵאוֹתוֹ דֶּשֶׁן — From those ashes יָרִים תְּרוּמָה — he shall raise an offering וְשָׂמוֹ אֵצֶל הַמִּזְבֵּחַ — and place it next to the *Mizbe'ach*.

□ עַל הַמִּזְבֵּחַ — ON THE *MIZBE'ACH*. מָצָא אֵבָרִים — If he found body parts שֶׁעֲדַיִן לֹא נִתְאַכְּלוּ — which were not yet consumed, מַחֲזִירָן עַל הַמִּזְבֵּחַ — he puts them back on the *Mizbe'ach* לְאַחַר שֶׁחָתָה — after he raked the embers גֶּחָלִים אֵילָךְ וָאֵילָךְ — to this side and that וְנָטַל מִן הַפְּנִימִיּוֹת — and took from the interior [ashes], שֶׁנֶּאֱמַר — as it says: אֶת הָעֹלָה עַל הַמִּזְבֵּחַ,,[7] — "the *olah*-offering on the *Mizbe'ach*."[7]}

4. וּפָשַׁט אֶת בְּגָדָיו — HE SHALL REMOVE HIS GARMENTS. אֵין זוֹ חוֹבָה — This is not an obligation, אֶלָּא דֶּרֶךְ אֶרֶץ — but rather, proper conduct, שֶׁלֹּא יְלַכְלֵךְ — so that he should not dirty, בְּהוֹצָאַת הַדֶּשֶׁן — through taking out the ashes, בְּגָדִים שֶׁהוּא מְשַׁמֵּשׁ בָּהֶן תָּמִיד — garments which he serves in constantly. בְּגָדִים שֶׁבִּשֵּׁל בָּהֶן קְדֵרָה לְרַבּוֹ — Garments in which he was dressed when **he cooked a pot**

---

1. See *Exodus* 28:40.
2. *Toras Kohanim, perek* 2:1; *Zevachim* 35a.
3. *Toras Kohanim, perek* 2:3; *Zevachim* 19a; *Arachin* 3b.
4. The ashes at the innermost part of the *Mizbe'ach* fire would be the most completely consumed by the fire. They would not contain bits of flesh or fat that were not completely burnt.
5. *Toras Kohanim, perek* 2:4; *Tamid* 28b. The word וְהֵרִים connotes separation of a part from the whole. Thus, the removal of ashes discussed here is not a thorough cleaning of the *Mizbe'ach*. Rather, it is a removal of a small amount of the ashes which serves as the opening ritual of the new day's service (*Minchas Yehudah; Sifsei Chachamim*).
6. Taken literally, the verse reads, "He shall raise the ashes which the fire will consume the *olah*-offering." Rashi explains that the verse means the ashes which have resulted from the consuming of the *olah*-offering (see *Mizrachi*).
7. *Toras Kohanim, perek* 2:5; *Yoma* 45b. The apparently superfluous "on the *Mizbe'ach*" implies that all the while that the offering is still considered an *olah*-offering, i.e., all the while that it has not yet been completely consumed, it must be kept on the *Mizbe'ach*, even if it had been taken off the top of the *Mizbe'ach* (*Be'er Yitzchak; Lifshuto shel Rashi*).

וְלָבַשׁ בְּגָדִים אֲחֵרִים וְהוֹצִיא אֶת־
הַדֶּשֶׁן אֶל־מִחוּץ לַמַּחֲנֶה אֶל־מָקוֹם
ה טָהוֹר: וְהָאֵשׁ עַל־הַמִּזְבֵּחַ תּוּקַד־בּוֹ
לֹא תִכְבֶּה וּבִעֵר עָלֶיהָ הַכֹּהֵן עֵצִים
בַּבֹּקֶר בַּבֹּקֶר וְעָרַךְ עָלֶיהָ הָעֹלָה

and he shall wear other garments, and he shall remove the ashes to the outside of the camp, to a pure place. ⁵ *The fire on the Mizbe'ach shall remain aflame on it, it shall not be extinguished; and the Kohen shall kindle wood upon it every morning; he shall arrange the olah-offering on it*

―――――― אונקלוס ――――――

וְיִלְבַּשׁ לְבוּשִׁין אָחֳרָנִין וְיַפֵּק יָת קִטְמָא לְמִבָּרָא לְמַשְׁרִיתָא לַאֲתַר דְּכֵי: ה וְאֶשָׁתָא עַל
מַדְבְּחָא תְּהֵי יָקְדָא בֵּהּ לָא תִטְפֵי וִיבַעַר עֲלַהּ כַּהֲנָא אָעַיָּא בִּצְפַר בִּצְפַר וִיסַדַּר עֲלַהּ עֲלָתָא

―――――――― רש״י ――――――――

אַל יִמְזוֹג בָּהֶן כּוֹס לְרַבּוֹ, לְכָךְ וְלָבֵשׁ בְּגָדִים אֲחֵרִים, פְּחוּתִין מֵהֶן
(יומא כ״ו פרק כג:): וְהוֹצִיא אֶת הַדֶּשֶׁן. הַצָּבוּר בַּתַּפּוּחַ
כְּשֶׁהוּא הַרְבֵּה וְאֵין מָקוֹם לַמַּעֲרָכָה מוֹצִיאוֹ מִשָּׁם וְאֵין זֶה חוֹבָה
בְּכָל יוֹם (תמיד כח:), אֲבָל הַתְּרוּמָה חוֹבָה בְּכָל יוֹם: (ה) וְהָאֵשׁ
עַל הַמִּזְבֵּחַ תּוּקַד בּוֹ. רִבָּה כָּאן יְקִידוֹת הַרְבֵּה, עַל מוֹקְדָה

(לְטוֹל פָּסוּק ב), וְאֵשׁ הַמִּזְבֵּחַ תּוּקַד בּוֹ (שָׁם), וְהָאֵשׁ עַל הַמִּזְבֵּחַ תּוּקַד
בּוֹ, אֵשׁ תָּמִיד תּוּקַד עַל הַמִּזְבֵּחַ (לְהַלָּן פָּסוּק ו) כּוּלָן נִדְרְשׁוּ בְּמַסֶּ׳
יוֹמָא (מה.) שֶׁנֶּחְלְקוּ רַבּוֹתֵינוּ בְּמִנְיַן הַמַּעֲרָכוֹת שֶׁהָיוּ שָׁם (ת״כ שָׁם
יא; יומא מג:): וְעָרַךְ עָלֶיהָ הָעֹלָה. עוֹלַת תָּמִיד הִיא תַּקְדִּים
וּמִנַּיִן שֶׁלֹּא יְהֵא דָּבָר קוֹדֶם עַל הַמַּעֲרָכָה לִתְמִיד שֶׁל שַׁחַר,

―――――― RASHI ELUCIDATED ――――――

of food **for his master,** אַל יִמְזוֹג בָּהֶן כּוֹס לְרַבּוֹ — **he should not pour,** while dressed **in them, a cup** of wine **for his master.**[1] לְכָךְ — **Therefore:** ״וְלָבַשׁ בְּגָדִים אֲחֵרִים״ — **"He shall wear other garments,"** פְּחוּתִין מֵהֶן — **inferior to them.**[2]

□ וְהוֹצִיא אֶת הַדֶּשֶׁן — **AND HE SHALL REMOVE THE ASHES** הַצָּבוּר בַּתַּפּוּחַ — which have collected in the *tapuach*.[3] כְּשֶׁהוּא הַרְבֵּה — **When they are in quantity,** וְאֵין מָקוֹם לַמַּעֲרָכָה — **and there is no room** for the arrangement of wood on the *Mizbe'ach,* מוֹצִיאוֹ מִשָּׁם — **he removes them from there.** וְאֵין זֶה חוֹבָה בְּכָל יוֹם — **This is not a duty on every day.**[4] אֲבָל הַתְּרוּמָה — **But the raising** of the ashes חוֹבָה בְּכָל יוֹם — **is a duty on every day.**[5]

5. וְהָאֵשׁ עַל הַמִּזְבֵּחַ תּוּקַד בּוֹ — **THE FIRE ON THE *MIZBE'ACH* SHALL BE KEPT BURNING ON IT.** רִבָּה כָּאן יְקִידוֹת הַרְבֵּה — [The Torah] **speaks here of several burnings,** namely: ״עַל מוֹקְדָה״[6] — **"on the flame";**[6] ״וְאֵשׁ הַמִּזְבֵּחַ תּוּקַד בּוֹ״ — **"and the fire of the *Mizbe'ach* shall be kept aflame on it";**[6] ״וְהָאֵשׁ עַל הַמִּזְבֵּחַ תּוּקַד בּוֹ״ — **"the fire on the *Mizbe'ach* shall be kept aflame on it";** and, ״אֵשׁ תָּמִיד תּוּקַד עַל הַמִּזְבֵּחַ״[7] — **"a permanent fire shall remain aflame on the *Mizbe'ach.*"**[7] שֶׁנֶּחְלְקוּ רַבּוֹתֵינוּ — כּוּלָן נִדְרְשׁוּ בְּמַסֶּכֶת יוֹמָא[8] — **All of them have been expounded in Tractate *Yoma*,**[8] as our Rabbis have disagreed[9] בְּמִנְיַן הַמַּעֲרָכוֹת שֶׁהָיוּ שָׁם — **about the number of fires that were there.**[9]

□ וְעָרַךְ עָלֶיהָ הָעֹלָה — **HE SHALL ARRANGE THE *OLAH*-OFFERING ON IT.** עוֹלַת תָּמִיד הִיא תַּקְדִּים — **The** continual *olah*-offering of the morning **shall come first,** of all the offerings of the day. וּמִנַּיִן — **And from where do we know** שֶׁלֹּא יְהֵא דָּבָר קוֹדֶם עַל הַמַּעֲרָכָה לִתְמִיד שֶׁל שַׁחַר — **that nothing should**

---

1. *Yoma* 23b. A servant should not wear the same clothes for the performance of a duty in which he gets dirty and for the performance of a duty which must be done in a dignified manner.

2. *Toras Kohanim, perek* 2:6; *Yoma* 23b.

3. The word תַּפּוּחַ literally means "apple." It is the pile of ashes at the center of the *Mizbe'ach*. The Kohanim would rake away ashes from the sides to the center so that the ashes formed a mound. That mound is referred to as the "apple" because of its round shape (*Sefer Zikaron*).

4. *Tamid* 28b.

5. The removal of the ashes of this verse is different from the "raising" of the ashes of the preceding verse. Those ashes were put next to the *Mizbe'ach*. They were not taken outside of the camp, but were swallowed up where they were placed (see Rashi to 1:16). The ashes of this verse which were taken outside the camp were those that were removed when the *Mizbe'ach* was periodically cleaned (*Gur Aryeh*).

6. Above v. 2.

7. Below v. 6.

8. *Yoma* 45a.

9. *Toras Kohanim, perek* 2:11 and *Yoma* 43b cite three opinions concerning the number of fires that burned on top of the *Mizbe'ach* each day: two, three or four. Each *Tanna's* opinion is based on the manner in which he interprets the many words with the root יקד in this passage (*Yoma* 45a).

6/6-7

וְהִקְטִיר עָלֶיהָ חֶלְבֵי הַשְּׁלָמִים: ו אֵשׁ תָּמִיד תּוּקַד עַל־הַמִּזְבֵּחַ לֹא תִכְבֶּה: ז וְזֹאת תּוֹרַת הַמִּנְחָה

and shall cause the fats of the peace-offerings to go up in smoke up it. [6] *A fire, continually, shall remain aflame on the Mizbe'ach; you shall not extinguish it.* [7] *This is the law of the meal-offering:*

―――――― אונקלוס ――――――

וְיַסֵּק עֲלַהּ תַּרְבֵּי נִכְסַת קוּדְשַׁיָּא: ו אֶשָּׁתָא תְדִירָא תְּהֵי יָקְדָא עַל מַדְבְּחָא לָא תִטְפֵי: ז וְדָא אוֹרַיְתָא דְמִנְחָתָא

―――――― רש"י ――――――

ת"ל הָעוֹלָה עוֹלָה רִאשׁוֹנָה: (פסחים נח:): **חֶלְבֵי הַשְּׁלָמִים.** אִם יָבִיאוּ שָׁם שְׁלָמִים. וְרַבּוֹתֵינוּ לָמְדוּ מִכָּאן, עָלֶיהָ, עַל עוֹלַת הַבֹּקֶר, הַשְׁלֵם כָּל הַקָּרְבָּנוֹת כֻּלָּם. מִכָּאן שֶׁלֹּא יְהֵא דָבָר מְאֻחָר לְתָמִיד שֶׁל בֵּין הָעַרְבַּיִם (שם:): **(ו) אֵשׁ תָּמִיד.** אֵשׁ שֶׁנֶּאֱמַר בָּהּ תָּמִיד, הִיא שֶׁמַּדְלִיקִין בָּהּ אֶת הַנֵּרוֹת, שֶׁנֶּאֱמַר בָּהּ לְהַעֲלֹת נֵר תָּמִיד (שמות כז:כ). אַף הִיא מֵעַל מִזְבֵּחַ הַחִיצוֹן תּוּקַד (יומא מה:): **לֹא תִכְבֶּה.** הַמְכַבֶּה אֵשׁ עַל הַמִּזְבֵּחַ עוֹבֵר בִּשְׁנֵי לָאוִין: **(ז) וְזֹאת תּוֹרַת הַמִּנְחָה.** תּוֹרָה אַחַת לְכֻלָּן לְהַטְעִינָן שֶׁמֶן וּלְבוֹנָה הָאֲמוּרִין

―――――― RASHI ELUCIDATED ――――――

precede the morning continual *olah*-offering on the fire of the *Mizbe'ach*? תַּלְמוּד לוֹמַר – **The verse states,** ״הָעֹלָה״, – **"the *olah*-offering,"** with the prefix הָ which implies that it is עוֹלָה רִאשׁוֹנָה¹ – **the first *olah*-offering.**}¹

□ חֶלְבֵי הַשְּׁלָמִים – **THE FATS OF THE PEACE-OFFERINGS.** אִם יָבִיאוּ שָׁם שְׁלָמִים – **If they will bring peace-offerings there.**² וְרַבּוֹתֵינוּ לָמְדוּ מִכָּאן – **Our Rabbis learned from here:** ״עָלֶיהָ״, – **"On it"** means, עַל עוֹלַת הַבֹּקֶר – **on the** continual *olah*-**offering of the morning,**³ הַשְׁלֵם כָּל הַקָּרְבָּנוֹת כֻּלָּם – **you must complete all of the offerings.** מִכָּאן – **From here they learned** שֶׁלֹּא יְהֵא דָבָר – **that there should not be anything** offered מְאֻחָר לְתָמִיד שֶׁל בֵּין הָעַרְבַּיִם – **later than the continual *olah*-offering of the afternoon.**⁴

6. אֵשׁ תָּמִיד – **A FIRE, CONTINUALLY.** ״תָּמִיד״, – אֵשׁ שֶׁנֶּאֱמַר בָּהּ – **A fire about which "continually" has been stated.**⁵ הִיא שֶׁמַּדְלִיקִין בָּהּ אֶת הַנֵּרוֹת – **It is the one with which they light the lamps** of the Menorah, שֶׁנֶּאֱמַר בָּהּ – **about which it says,** ⁶״לְהַעֲלֹת נֵר תָּמִיד״ – **"to light a lamp continually."**⁶ אַף הִיא⁷ – **It, too,**⁷ מֵעַל הַמִּזְבֵּחַ הַחִיצוֹן תּוּקַד – **shall be set alight from** the fire which is **on the *Mizbe'ach*.**⁷

□ לֹא תִכְבֶּה – **YOU SHALL NOT EXTINGUISH [IT].** הַמְכַבֶּה אֵשׁ עַל הַמִּזְבֵּחַ – **He who extinguishes fire on the *Mizbe'ach*** עוֹבֵר בִּשְׁנֵי לָאוִין – **transgresses two negative commandments.**⁸

7. וְזֹאת תּוֹרַת הַמִּנְחָה – **THIS IS THE LAW OF THE MEAL-OFFERING.** תּוֹרָה אַחַת לְכֻלָּן – **They all have one law** לְהַטְעִינָן שֶׁמֶן וּלְבוֹנָה – **to require them** to have oil and frankincense הָאֲמוּרִין

---

1. *Pesachim* 58b. "The *olah*-offering" implies that the verse is talking about a specific *olah*-offering — the first *olah*-offering mentioned in the series of offerings discussed in *Numbers*, Chapter 28 (Rashi to *Kesubos* 106b).

2. The statement, "he shall arrange the *olah*-offering on it," is an absolute obligation, as the continual *olah*-offering must be brought every day. But the phrase "and shall cause the fats of the peace-offering to go up in smoke on it," is not meant to imply that there is a daily obligation to bring a peace-offering. Peace-offerings are voluntary. The verse means that *if* peace-offerings are brought that day, they are to be offered on the *Mizbe'ach* (*Minchas Yehudah; Sifsei Chachamim*).

3. According to Rashi's first explanation, "on it" means on the fire of the *Mizbe'ach*. According to the explanation of the Rabbis, "it" refers to the continual *olah*-offering.

4. *Pesachim* 58b. The verse could have said, חֶלְבֵי שְׁלָמִים, "the fats of peace-offerings." The definite article prefix ה, "the," of הַשְּׁלָמִים, "*the* peace-offerings," poses a difficulty. For though "*the olah*-offering" which precedes it refers to a specific offering (see note 1 above), no particular peace-offering is referred to here. The Rabbis therefore conclude that the definite article was used so that the word could be interpreted as the imperative הַשְׁלֵם, "Complete!" According to this interpretation, "on it" refers to the morning *olah*-offering. The verse thus says that all offerings must be, in a sense, a "completion" of the *olah*-offering of the morning; that is, of the two daily continual *olah*-offerings, all offerings must follow that of the morning, but may not follow that of the evening (*Divrei David; Sifsei Chachamim*).

5. *Yoma* 45b. The verse says that the fire is not to be extinguished. It is obvious, then, that the fire burns continually. תָּמִיד is nonetheless stated explicitly to link the fire of our verse to the fire of the light of the Menorah, for that light is also called תָּמִיד (*Maskil LeDavid*).

6. *Exodus* 27:20.

7. *Yoma* 45b.

8. "You shall not extinguish" appears both here and in the preceding verse (*Mizrachi; Sifsei Chachamim*).

ויקרא – פרשת צו

הַקְרֵב אֹתָהּ בְּנֵי־אַהֲרֹן לִפְנֵי
יהוה אֶל־פְּנֵי הַמִּזְבֵּחַ: וְהֵרִים
מִמֶּנּוּ בְקֻמְצוֹ מִסֹּלֶת הַמִּנְחָה

The sons of Aaron shall bring it before Hashem, *to the front of the Mizbe'ach.* ⁸ *And he shall separate from it in his threefingersful from the fine flour of the meal-offering*

— אונקלוס —

דִּיקָרְבוּן יָתַהּ בְּנֵי אַהֲרֹן קֳדָם יְיָ לָקֳדָם מַדְבְּחָא: ⁸ וְיַפְרֵשׁ מִנַּהּ בְּקֻמְצֵיהּ מִסֻּלְתָּא דְמִנְחָתָא

— רש"י —

בְּעִנְיָן (ת"כ פרשתא ב:א). שִׁיכּוֹל אֵין לִי טְעוּנוֹת שֶׁמֶן וּלְבוֹנָה אֶלָּא מִנְחַת יִשְׂרָאֵל שֶׁהִיא נִקְמֶצֶת, מִנְחַת כֹּהֲנִים שֶׁהִיא כָּלִיל מִנַּיִן, ת"ל תּוֹרָה (שם ב): **הַקְרֵב אֹתָהּ.** הִיא הַגָּשָׁה בְּקֶרֶן דְּרוֹמִית מַעֲרָבִית (שם ד): **לִפְנֵי ה'.** הוּא מַעֲרָב שֶׁהוּא לְנֶגֶד אֹהֶל מוֹעֵד:

אֶל פְּנֵי הַמִּזְבֵּחַ. הוּא הַדָּרוֹם שֶׁהוּא פָנָיו שֶׁל מִזְבֵּחַ שֶׁהַכֶּבֶשׁ נָתוּן לְאוֹתוֹ הָרוּחַ (ת"כ שם; מנחות שס, סוטה יד:): (ח) **[וְהֵרִים] מִמֶּנּוּ.** מֵהַמְחוּבָּר, שֶׁיְּהֵא עֶשָּׂרוֹן שָׁלֵם בְּבַת אַחַת בִּשְׁעַת קְמִיצָה: **בְּקֻמְצוֹ.** שֶׁלֹּא יַעֲשֶׂה מִדָּה לַקּוֹמֶץ (ת"כ שם ה:ב; יומא מז.):

— RASHI ELUCIDATED —

בְּעִנְיָן[1] – **which are mentioned in this passage**.[1] It is necessary to say this, שֶׁיָּכוֹל – **for one would have been able** to think, אֵין לִי טְעוּנוֹת שֶׁמֶן וּלְבוֹנָה – **I have none,** i.e., I know of no meal-offerings, **which require oil and frankincense** אֶלָּא מִנְחַת יִשְׂרָאֵל – **except for the meal-offering of an Israelite,** i.e., one who is not a Kohen, שֶׁהִיא נִקְמֶצֶת – **which has a threefingersful taken from it** to be burned on the *Mizbe'ach;* מִנְחַת כֹּהֲנִים – **A meal-offering of a Kohen,** שֶׁהִיא כָּלִיל – **which is burned entirely,** מִנַּיִן – **from where do I know** that it, too, requires oil and frankincense? To tell us this, תַּלְמוּד לוֹמַר – **the verse says,** ״תּוֹרַת״,[2] – **"law."**[2]

□ הַקְרֵב אֹתָהּ – **SHALL BRING IT.** הִיא הַגָּשָׁה – **This is bringing it near** to the *Mizbe'ach,*[3] בְּקֶרֶן דְּרוֹמִית מַעֲרָבִית[4] – **at the southwestern corner,**[4] as follows:

□ לִפְנֵי ה' – **BEFORE** HASHEM, הוּא מַעֲרָב – **it is the west** side of the *Mizbe'ach,* שֶׁהוּא לְצַד אֹהֶל מוֹעֵד – **which faces the Tent of Meeting;**

□ אֶל פְּנֵי הַמִּזְבֵּחַ – **TO THE FRONT OF THE** *MIZBE'ACH,* הוּא הַדָּרוֹם – **it is the south,** שֶׁהוּא פָנָיו שֶׁל מִזְבֵּחַ – **which is the front of the** *Mizbe'ach***,** שֶׁהַכֶּבֶשׁ נָתוּן לְאוֹתוֹ הָרוּחַ – **for the ramp** which leads to the top of the *Mizbe'ach* **is put at that side.**[5]

8. {וְהֵרִים מִמֶּנּוּ} – **HE SHALL SEPARATE FROM IT.** מֵהַמְחוּבָּר – **From that which is connected,** i.e., from the entire meal-offering, with all its flour collected together, שֶׁיְּהֵא עֶשָּׂרוֹן שָׁלֵם – **that there should be a complete tenth** of an *ephah,* בְּבַת אַחַת – **at once,** i.e., in a single unit, בִּשְׁעַת קְמִיצָה – **at the time of the taking of the threefingersful.**[6]}

□ בְּקֻמְצוֹ – **IN HIS THREEFINGERSFUL.** שֶׁלֹּא יַעֲשֶׂה מִדָּה לַקּוֹמֶץ – **That he should not make a measure,** i.e., measuring cup, **for the threefingersful.**[7]

---

1. *Toras Kohanim, parshasa* 2:1.
2. *Toras Kohanim, parshasa* 2:2. In verses 2:2-3 above, the commandment to put oil and frankincense on the meal-offering is stated immediately before the commandment to offer a *kometz* (threefingersful) on the *Mizbe'ach*. One might have thought that the oil and frankincense are a preparation for removing the *kometz*. The meal-offering of a Kohen, however, does not have a *kometz* taken from it, and would be excluded from the requirement of oil and frankincense. The term תּוֹרָה, "law," connotes inclusion (see Rashi to verse 2 above), and includes the meal-offering of a Kohen in the requirement of oil and frankincense (*Mizrachi*).

   Rashi's opening statement, "They *all* have one law," is not to be taken strictly. The Torah says that the meal-offerings of a sinner (above 5:11) and a *sotah* (a woman suspected of adultery – see *Numbers* 5:15) should not have oil and frankincense (*Leket Bahir*).

3. The term הַקְרֵב does not mean "offer" as it often does, for הַקְרֵב refers to the entire meal-offering, whereas only a threefingersful of it is offered (*Mizrachi*; *Sifsei Chachamim*). For a similar use of קרב, see 2:8 above and Rashi there.

4. *Toras Kohanim, parshasa* 2:4; *Menachos* 19b.
5. *Toras Kohanim, parshasa* 2:4; *Menachos* 19b; *Sotah* 14b. "Before HASHEM" implies the west side of the *Mizbe'ach;* "the front of the *Mizbe'ach*" implies its south side. Thus, the meal-offering is brought close to the southwestern corner.

6. *Toras Kohanim, parshasa* 2:5. The pronoun "it" of the term מִמֶּנּוּ, "from it," cannot refer to the fine flour and the oil, for they are mentioned explicitly. Similarly, it cannot refer to the meal-offering, for the word מִנְחָה is feminine and the verse would have used the feminine form מִמֶּנָּה. Therefore, we must understand the "it" as referring to an implicit masculine antecedent, namely, כְּלִי, "vessel" – the single vessel that holds the entire meal-offering (*Malbim*).

7. *Yoma* 47a. The verse could have said, וְהֵרִים מִמֶּנּוּ קֻמְצוֹ, "He shall separate from it *its* threefingersful." וְהֵרִים

65 / VAYIKRA/LEVITICUS — PARASHAS TZAV — 6/9-10

and from its oil, and all of the frankincense that is on the meal-offering; and he shall cause them to go up in smoke on the Mizbe'ach for a satisfying aroma — its memorial portion unto HASHEM. ⁹ *Aaron and his sons shall eat what is left of it; it shall be eaten unleavened in a holy place, in the Courtyard of the Tent of Meeting shall they eat it.* ¹⁰ *It may not be baked leavened, I have presented it as their share*

וּמִשַּׁמְנָהּ וְאֵת כָּל־הַלְּבֹנָה אֲשֶׁר עַל־הַמִּנְחָה וְהִקְטִיר הַמִּזְבֵּחַ רֵיחַ נִיחֹחַ אַזְכָּרָתָהּ לַיהוָה: ט וְהַנּוֹתֶרֶת מִמֶּנָּה יֹאכְלוּ אַהֲרֹן וּבָנָיו מַצּוֹת תֵּאָכֵל בְּמָקוֹם קָדֹשׁ בַּחֲצַר אֹהֶל־מוֹעֵד יֹאכְלוּהָ: י לֹא תֵאָפֶה חָמֵץ חֶלְקָם נָתַתִּי אֹתָהּ

— אונקלוס —

וּמִשְׁמַהּ וְיָת כָּל לְבוֹנְתָא דִּי עַל מִנְחָתָא וְיַסֵּק לְמַדְבְּחָא לְאִתְקַבָּלָא בְּרַעֲוָא אַדְכַּרְתָּהּ קֳדָם יְיָ: ט וּדְאִשְׁתְּאַר מִנַּהּ יֵכְלוּן אַהֲרֹן וּבְנוֹהִי פַּטִּיר תִּתְאֲכֵל בַּאֲתַר קַדִּישׁ בְּדָרַת מַשְׁכַּן זִמְנָא יֵכְלֻנַּהּ: י לָא תִתְאֲפֵי חֲמִיעַ חֲלָקְהוֹן יְהָבִית יָתַהּ

— רש"י —

מסלת המנחה ומשמנה. מכאן שקומץ ממקום שנתרבה שמנה (סוטה יד:): **המנחה.** שלא תהא מעורבת באחרת (ת"כ שם): **ואת כל הלבונה אשר על המנחה והקטיר.** שמלקט את לבונתה לאחר קמיצה ומקטירה (ת"כ שם; סוטה שם). ולפי שלא פירש כן אלא באחת מן המנחות בויקרא (ולטיל ב:ב) הוזקק לשנות פרשה זו לכלול כל המנחות כמשפטן: (ט) **במקום קדוש.** ואיזהו, בחצר אהל מועד: (י) **לא תאפה חמץ חלקם.** אף השירים אסורים בחמץ (מנחות נה.):

— RASHI ELUCIDATED —

□ מִסֹּלֶת הַמִּנְחָה וּמִשַּׁמְנָהּ — FROM THE FINE FLOUR OF THE MEAL-OFFERING AND FROM ITS OIL. — מִכָּאן From here there is a source for the law שֶׁקּוֹמֵץ — that he takes the threefingersful מִמָּקוֹם שֶׁנִּתְרַבָּה שַׁמְנָהּ¹ — from where it is most oily.¹

□ הַמִּנְחָה — THE MEAL-OFFERING. שֶׁלֹּא תְהֵא מְעֹרֶבֶת בְּאַחֶרֶת — That it should not be mixed with another.²

□ וְאֵת כָּל הַלְּבֹנָה אֲשֶׁר עַל הַמִּנְחָה וְהִקְטִיר — AND ALL OF THE FRANKINCENSE THAT IS ON THE MEAL-OFFERING; AND HE SHALL CAUSE [THEM] TO GO UP IN SMOKE, that is, שֶׁמְּלַקֵּט אֶת לְבוֹנָתָהּ — that he should gather up its frankincense לְאַחַר קְמִיצָה — after the taking of the threefingersful, וּמַקְטִירוֹ³ — and cause it to go up in smoke.³ וּלְפִי שֶׁלֹּא פֵּרֵשׁ כֵּן — Since this was not stated explicitly אֶלָּא בְּאַחַת מִן הַמְּנָחוֹת — except in the case of one of the meal-offerings בְּוַיִּקְרָא,⁴ — in *Parashas Vayikra*,⁴ הֻזְקַק לִשְׁנוֹת פָּרָשָׁה זוֹ — [the Torah] had to repeat this *parashah*, in order לִכְלוֹל כָּל הַמְּנָחוֹת — to include all of the meal-offerings in the law of gathering and burning the frankincense, כְּמִשְׁפָּטָן — in accordance with their law.

9. בְּמָקוֹם קָדֹשׁ — IN A HOLY PLACE. וְאֵיזֶהוּ — And which holy place is it? ",,בַּחֲצַר אֹהֶל מוֹעֵד" — "In the Courtyard of the Tent of Meeting."⁵

10. לֹא תֵאָפֶה חָמֵץ חֶלְקָם — IT MAY NOT BE BAKED LEAVENED. [I HAVE PRESENTED IT AS] THEIR SHARE. אַף הַשִּׁירַיִם — The remainders that are left over after the *kometz* has been taken, too, ⁶אֲסוּרִים בְּחָמֵץ — are forbidden if leavened.⁶

מִמֶּנּוּ בְּקֻמְצוֹ, "He shall separate from it *in his* threefingersful," implies that it must be separated directly into the hands of the Kohen, and not by means of a vessel which holds threefingersful (*HaKesav VeHaKabbalah*).

1. *Sotah* 14b. The entire meal-offering is mixed with oil. If the Torah nonetheless states, "and from its oil," it is to teach us that the *kometz* must be taken from the oiliest part (*Mizrachi*; *Sifsei Chachamim*).

2. *Toras Kohanim, parshasa* 2:5. Had the verse said, "from *its* fine flour and from its oil," it would have been clear that it would be referring to the meal-offering mentioned at the beginning of the verse. If the verse nonetheless states "of the meal-offering" explicitly, it is to stress the definite article "the" — the threefingersful must be taken from a single, clearly defined, meal-offering, not from a mixture (*Be'er Yitzchak*).

3. *Toras Kohanim, parshasa* 2:5; *Sotah* 14b.

4. Above 2:2. See Rashi there and to 2:1.

5. The verse could have been read, "In a holy place in the Courtyard of the Tent of Meeting," without "holy place" being set off from "Courtyard." The verse would have implied that some places in the Courtyard are holy, while others are not. This is not true, however, for the entire Courtyard is holy. The verse is read, "In a holy place, in the Courtyard of the Tent of Meeting" — "Courtyard of the Tent of Meeting" *is* the "holy place" (*Gur Aryeh*).

6. *Menachos* 55a. The Torah has already prohibited that which is leavened to be offered on the *Mizbe'ach*

from My fire-offerings; it is most holy, like the sin-offering and like the guilt-offering. **11** Every male of the children of Aaron shall eat it, an eternal portion for your generations, from the fire-offerings of HASHEM; whatever touches them shall become holy.

מֵאִשָּׁי קָדְשֵׁי קָדָשִׁים הוּא כַּחַטָּאת וְכָאָשָׁם: יא כָּל־זָכָר בִּבְנֵי אַהֲרֹן יֹאכֲלֶנָּה חָק־עוֹלָם לְדֹרֹתֵיכֶם מֵאִשֵּׁי יהוה כֹּל אֲשֶׁר־יִגַּע בָּהֶם יִקְדָּשׁ:

— אונקלוס —

מִקֻּרְבָּנַי קֹדֶשׁ קוּדְשִׁין הִיא כְּחַטָּאתָא וְכַאֲשָׁמָא: יא כָּל דְּכוּרָא בִּבְנֵי אַהֲרֹן יֵכְלִנַּהּ קְיָם עָלַם לְדָרֵיכוֹן מִקֻּרְבָּנַיָּא דַּיָי כֹּל דְּיִקְרַב בְּהוֹן יִתְקַדָּשׁ:

— רש"י —

בחטאת וכאשם. מנחת חוטא הרי היא כחטאת, לפיכך קמצה שלא לשמה פסולה. מנחת נדבה הרי היא כאשם, לפיכך קמצה שלא לשמה כשרה (ת"כ פרק ג:ד; זבחים יח.; מנחות ב:): **(יא) כל זכר.** אפי' בעל מום. למה נאמר, אם לאכילה הרי כבר אמור לחם אלהיו

מקדשי הקדשים וגו' (להלן כא:כב). אלא לרבות בעלי מומין למחלוקת (ת"כ שם ה; זבחים קב.): **כל אשר יגע וגו'.** קדשים קלים או חולין שיגעו בה ויבלעו ממנה: **יקדש.** להיות כמוה שאם פסולה יפסלו ואם כשרה יאכלו כחומר המנחה (ת"כ פרק ג:ז; זבחים לז:):

— RASHI ELUCIDATED —

☐ **כַּחַטָּאת הִיא הֲרֵי חוֹטֵא מִנְחַת** — LIKE THE SIN-OFFERING AND LIKE THE GUILT-OFFERING. **וְכָאָשָׁם** — The meal-offering of a sinner[1] is thus like the sin-offering; **לְפִיכָךְ** — therefore, **שֶׁלֹּא קַמְצָה** **לִשְׁמָהּ** — if he scooped the threefingersful from it not for its sake, i.e., without conscious intent that it is being done for the sake of the meal-offering of a sinner, **פְּסוּלָה** — it is invalid. **מִנְחַת נְדָבָה הֲרֵי הִיא כָּאָשָׁם** — A voluntary meal-offering is thus like the guilt-offering; **לְפִיכָךְ** — therefore, **שֶׁלֹּא קַמְצָה** **לִשְׁמָהּ** — if he scooped the threefingersful from it not for its sake, [2] **כְּשֵׁרָה** — it is valid.[2]

11. כָּל זָכָר — EVERY MALE. **אֲפִלּוּ בַּעַל מוּם** — Even one who has a blemish which disqualifies him from participating in the offering service. **לָמָה נֶאֱמַר** — Why is this stated? **אִם לַאֲכִילָה** — If for eating, i.e., if it is stated to teach us that a blemished Kohen may eat of the meal-offering, **הֲרֵי כְּבָר אָמוּר** — it has already been stated,[3] **״לֶחֶם אֱלֹהָיו מִקָּדְשֵׁי הַקֳּדָשִׁים וְגוֹמֵר״** — "the bread of his God, from the holy of holies, etc."[3] **אֶלָּא** — Rather, the verse is meant **לְרַבּוֹת בַּעֲלֵי מוּמִין** — to include those who are blemished [4] **לְמַחֲלוֹקֶת** — for apportioning.[4]

☐ **כֹּל אֲשֶׁר יִגַּע וְגוֹמֵר** — WHATEVER TOUCHES, ETC. **קָדָשִׁים קַלִּים** — Holies of the lesser degree of sanctity **שֶׁיִּגְּעוּ בָהּ** — which will come into contact with it **וְיִבְלְעוּ מִמֶּנָּה** — or that which is not holy **וְיִבְלְעוּ מִמֶּנָּה** — and absorb of it,[5]

☐ **יִקְדָּשׁ** — SHALL BECOME HOLY **לִהְיוֹת כָּמוֹהָ** — to become like it: **שֶׁאִם פְּסוּלָה** — So that if it is invalid, **יִפָּסְלוּ** — they will become invalid; **וְאִם כְּשֵׁרָה** — and if it is valid, **יֵאָכְלוּ** — they shall be eaten **כְּחוֹמֶר הַמִּנְחָה** [6] — with the stringencies of the meal-offering.[6]

(above 2:11). חֶלְקָם, "their share," is juxtaposed here with a repetition of that commandment to teach that the prohibition also applies to the remainder of the flour, which is eaten by the Kohanim (*Minchas Yehudah; Sifsei Chachamim*).

1. See 5:11-13 above.
2. *Toras Kohanim, perek* 3:4; *Zevachim* 11a; *Menachos* 2b. The Torah compares the meal-offering to these two offerings whose laws differ from each other to teach us that some meal-offerings share the law of the sin-offering, while others share the law of the guilt-offering (*Be'er Mayim Chaim*).
3. Below 21:22. That verse reads in full, "The bread of his God, from the holy of holies and from the holies, he shall eat."
4. *Toras Kohanim, perek* 3:5; *Zevachim* 102a. Not only may a blemished Kohen eat of the offerings, but he also receives a share with the other members of his family when it is their turn to serve in the *Beis HaMikdash*.

5. The verse could have said כָּל אֲשֶׁר תִּגַּע, "whatever it will touch," with the feminine verb תִּגַּע indicating that the feminine מִנְחָה, "meal-offering," is the subject of the verse. Instead, the verse is written with the objects being touched by the meal-offering as the subject of the sentence. The Torah does this to allow the use of בָּהֶם, "in them," to imply that the sanctity of the meal-offering transfers to the objects it touches (only the meal-offering is absorbed "in them." (See *Korban Aharon*. See also *Malbim* and *Mishmeres HaKodesh* for alternative approaches to understanding this Rashi.)

6. *Toras Kohanim, perek* 3:6; *Zevachim* 97b. If something absorbs some of the meal-offering, it takes on the character of the meal-offering. If the meal-offering had become disqualified, that portion of another offering which absorbs of it also becomes disqualified. If the meal-offering was valid, the same restrictions of time

VAYIKRA/LEVITICUS — PARASHAS TZAV — 6/12-14

¹² Hashem spoke to Moses, saying: ¹³ This is the offering of Aaron and his sons, which each shall offer to Hashem on the day he is inaugurated: a tenth of an ephah of fine flour as a meal-offering; continually, half of it in the morning and half of it in the afternoon. ¹⁴ It should be made on a pan with oil, scalded shall you bring it; repeated bakings, a meal-offering of crumbs,

יב וַיְדַבֵּר יהוה אֶל־מֹשֶׁה לֵּאמֹר: יג זֶה קָרְבַּן אַהֲרֹן וּבָנָיו אֲשֶׁר־יַקְרִיבוּ לַיהוה בְּיוֹם הִמָּשַׁח אֹתוֹ עֲשִׂירִת הָאֵפָה סֹלֶת מִנְחָה תָּמִיד מַחֲצִיתָהּ בַּבֹּקֶר וּמַחֲצִיתָהּ בָּעָרֶב: יד עַל־מַחֲבַת בַּשֶּׁמֶן תֵּעָשֶׂה מֻרְבֶּכֶת תְּבִיאֶנָּה תֻּפִינֵי מִנְחַת פִּתִּים

— אונקלוס —

יב וּמַלִּיל יְיָ עִם מֹשֶׁה לְמֵימָר: יג דֵּין קֻרְבַּן אַהֲרֹן וּבְנוֹהִי דִי יְקָרְבוּן קֳדָם יְיָ בְּיוֹמָא דִירַבּוּן יָתֵהּ חַד מִן עַסְרָא בִּתְלַת סְאִין סֻלְתָּא מִנְחָתָא תְּדִירָא פַּלְגּוּתַהּ בְּצַפְרָא וּפַלְגוּתַהּ בְּרַמְשָׁא: יד עַל מַסְרֵיתָא בִּמְשַׁח תִּתְעֲבֵד רְבִיכָא תַיְתִינַהּ תֻּפִינֵי מִנְחַת צּוּצִין

— רש״י —

(יג) זֶה קָרְבַּן אַהֲרֹן וּבָנָיו. אַף הַהֶדְיוֹטוֹת מַקְרִיבִין עֲשִׂירִית הָאֵיפָה בְּיוֹם שֶׁהֵן מִתְחַנְּכִין לַעֲבוֹדָה אֲבָל כֹּהֵן גָּדוֹל בְּכָל יוֹם שֶׁנֶּאֱמַר מִנְחָה תָּמִיד וְגוֹ', וְהַכֹּהֵן הַמָּשִׁיחַ תַּחְתָּיו מִבָּנָיו וְגוֹ' חָק עוֹלָם: (יד) מֻרְבֶּכֶת. חֲלוּטָה בְּרוֹתְחִין כָּל צָרְכָּהּ: תֻּפִינֵי. אֲפוּיָה אֲפִיּוֹת הַרְבֵּה, שֶׁאַחַר חֲלִיטָתָהּ אוֹפָהּ בַּתַּנּוּר וְחוֹזֵר וּמְטַגְּנָהּ בַּמַּחֲבַת: מִנְחַת פִּתִּים. מְלַמֵּד שֶׁטְּעוּנָה פְּתִיתָה {וְלֹא פְּתִיתָה מַמָּשׁ בְּלִיעִין וּפֵרוּרִין לְפִי שֶׁאֵינָהּ נִקְמֶצֶת אֶלָּא כּוֹפְלָהּ לִשְׁנַיִם וְחוֹזֵר וְכוֹפְלָהּ לְאַרְבָּעָה וְאֵינוֹ מַבְדִּיל, וְכֵן מַקְטִיר לְאִשִּׁים}:

— RASHI ELUCIDATED —

13. זֶה קָרְבַּן אַהֲרֹן וּבָנָיו — THIS IS THE OFFERING OF AARON AND HIS SONS. — אַף הַהֶדְיוֹטוֹת — The common Kohanim, too, מַקְרִיבִין עֲשִׂירִית הָאֵיפָה — offer a tenth of an *ephah* of flour as a meal-offering בְּיוֹם שֶׁהֵן מִתְחַנְּכִין לַעֲבוֹדָה — on the day that they are initiated to the Temple service.[1] אֲבָל כֹּהֵן גָּדוֹל בְּכָל יוֹם — But the Kohen Gadol brings such an offering every day, שֶׁנֶּאֱמַר — as it says: מִנְחָה תָּמִיד — "a meal-offering, continually, etc." וְגוֹמֵר — וְהַכֹּהֵן הַמָּשִׁיחַ תַּחְתָּיו מִבָּנָיו וְגוֹמֵר חָק עוֹלָם — "The Kohen from among his sons who is anointed in his place, etc., an eternal decree."[2]

14. מֻרְבֶּכֶת — This means חֲלוּטָה בְּרוֹתְחִין — scalded with boiling water [3] כָּל צָרְכָּהּ — all that it needs.[3]

תֻּפִינֵי — REPEATED BAKINGS. — אֲפוּיָה אֲפִיּוֹת הַרְבֵּה — It was baked many bakings, שֶׁאַחַר חֲלִיטָתָהּ — for after its scalding אוֹפָהּ בַּתַּנּוּר — he bakes it in the oven [4] וְחוֹזֵר וּמְטַגְּנָהּ בַּמַּחֲבַת — and then fries it in the pan.[4]

מִנְחַת פִּתִּים — A MEAL-OFFERING OF CRUMBS. — מְלַמֵּד שֶׁטְּעוּנָה פְּתִיתָה — This teaches us that it requires crumbling. וְלֹא פְּתִיתָה מַמָּשׁ — But not actual crumbling בְּצִיעִין וּפֵרוּרִין — into pieces and crumbs, לְפִי שֶׁאֵינָהּ נִקְמֶצֶת — since it is not subject to scooping. אֶלָּא כּוֹפְלָהּ לִשְׁנַיִם — Rather, he folds it in two, וְחוֹזֵר וְכוֹפְלָהּ לְאַרְבָּעָה — then he folds it again into four, שְׁתִי וָעֵרֶב — vertically and horizontally, וְאֵינוֹ מַבְדִּיל — but he does not separate it into pieces. [5] וְכֵן מַקְטִיר לְאִשִּׁים — And so he makes it go up in smoke on the *Mizbe'ach* fires.}[5]

---

nnd place which apply to the meal-offering apply to that which absorbed of it.

1. "His sons" refers to all Kohanim, not only to those sons of Aaron who succeed him in the office of Kohen Gadol (*Gur Aryeh*).

2. *Toras Kohanim, parshasa* 3:1-3; *Menachos* 51b. Our verse begins by referring to a meal-offering brought on the day of a Kohen's inauguration. But it goes on to refer to "a continual meal-offering," which implies a meal-offering brought regularly. Rashi explains that the verse speaks of two different meal-offerings. The "continual meal-offering" is that brought by the Kohen Gadol each day. Rashi cites verse 15 in support of this, for it explicitly refers to the meal-offering of the Kohen Gadol as an "eternal decree," i.e., an offering that is brought continually. But the meal-offering brought on the day of inauguration is brought not only by the Kohen Gadol, but by "Aaron *and his sons,*" i.e., all Kohanim (see *Mesiach Ilmim; Nachalas Yaakov; Be'er Yitzchak*).

3. *Toras Kohanim, perek* 4:6. The meal-offering of the Kohanim was scalded in water, as stated by Rashi to *Menachos* 53a. *Shitah Mekubetzes* to *Menachos* 78a notes that the comment of Rashi there, which seems to indicate that it was scalded in oil, is based on a printer's error (*Shaarei Aharon*).

4. *Menachos* 50b.

5. *Toras Kohanim, perek* 4:6; *Menachos* 75b.

you shall offer it as a satisfying aroma to HASHEM. **15** *The Kohen from among his sons who is anointed in his place shall perform it; it is an eternal decree for HASHEM; it shall be caused to go up in smoke in its entirety.* **16** *Every meal-offering of a Kohen is to be an entirety; it shall not be eaten.*

17 HASHEM *spoke to Moses, saying:* **18** *Speak to Aaron and his sons, saying: This is the law of the sin-offering; in the place where the olah-offering is slaughtered shall the sin-offering be slaughtered, before* HASHEM *— it is most holy.* **19** *The Kohen who makes it into a sin-offering may eat it; it shall be eaten in a holy place:*

יַחֲ־נִיחֹחַ לַיהוָה: וְהַכֹּהֵן
הַמָּשִׁיחַ תַּחְתָּיו מִבָּנָיו יַעֲשֶׂה אֹתָהּ
חָק־עוֹלָם לַיהוָה כָּלִיל תָּקְטָר: וְכָל־מִנְחַת כֹּהֵן כָּלִיל תִּהְיֶה לֹא תֵאָכֵל:
וַיְדַבֵּר יהוה אֶל־מֹשֶׁה לֵּאמֹר: דַּבֵּר
אֶל־אַהֲרֹן וְאֶל־בָּנָיו לֵאמֹר זֹאת תּוֹרַת הַחַטָּאת בִּמְקוֹם אֲשֶׁר
תִּשָּׁחֵט הָעֹלָה תִּשָּׁחֵט הַחַטָּאת לִפְנֵי יהוה קֹדֶשׁ קָדָשִׁים הִוא: הַכֹּהֵן
הַמְחַטֵּא אֹתָהּ יֹאכֲלֶנָּה בְּמָקוֹם קָדֹשׁ

---- אונקלוס ----

תִּתְקְרֵב לְאִתְקַבָּלָא בְרַעֲוָא קֳדָם יְיָ: טוּ וְכַהֲנָא דְיִתְרַבָּא תְּחוֹתוֹהִי מִבְּנוֹהִי יַעְבֵּד יָתַהּ קְיָם עֲלָם
קֳדָם יְיָ גְּמִיר תִּתַּסָּק: טזוְכָל מִנְחָתָא דְכַהֲנָא גְּמִיר תְּהֵי לָא תִתְאֲכֵל: יזוּמַלִּיל יְיָ עִם מֹשֶׁה לְמֵימַר: יח מַלֵּל עִם אַהֲרֹן וְעִם בְּנוֹהִי לְמֵימַר דָּא אוֹרַיְתָא דְחַטָּאתָא בְּאַתְרָא דִי תִתְנְכֵס עֲלָתָא תִתְנְכֵס
חַטָּאתָא קֳדָם יְיָ קֹדֶשׁ קוּדְשִׁין הִיא: יט כַּהֲנָא דִמְכַפֵּר יָתַהּ (נ"א בִּדְמַהּ) יֵכְלִנַּהּ בַּאֲתַר קַדִּישׁ

---- רש"י ----

(טו) הַמָּשִׁיחַ תַּחְתָּיו מִבָּנָיו. הַמָּשִׁיחַ מִבָּנָיו תַּחְתָּיו: **כָּלִיל
תָּקְטָר.** אֵין נִקְמֶצֶת לִהְיוֹת שְׁיָרֶיהָ נֶאֱכָלִין אֶלָּא כֻּלָּהּ כָּלִיל
וְכֵן: **(טז) כָּל מִנְחַת כֹּהֵן.** שֶׁל נְדָבָה: **כָּלִיל תִּהְיֶה.** כָּלִיל,
כֻּלָּהּ שָׁוָה לַגָּבוֹהַּ: **(יט) הַמְחַטֵּא אֹתָהּ.** הָעוֹבֵד עֲבוֹדוֹתֶיהָ
שֶׁהִיא נַעֲשֵׂית חַטָּאת עַל יָדוֹ: **הַמְחַטֵּא אֹתָהּ יֹאכֲלֶנָּה.** הָרָאוּי
לַעֲבוֹדָה, יָצָא טָמֵא בִּשְׁעַת זְרִיקַת דָּמִים שֶׁאֵינוֹ חוֹלֵק בַּבָּשָׂר.

---- RASHI ELUCIDATED ----

15. הַמָּשִׁיחַ תַּחְתָּיו מִבָּנָיו — This means הַמָּשִׁיחַ — the anointed one מִבָּנָיו — from among his sons תַּחְתָּיו — who is **in his stead**.[1]

□ כָּלִיל תָּקְטָר — IT SHALL BE CAUSED TO GO UP IN SMOKE IN ITS ENTIRETY. אֵין נִקְמֶצֶת — It is not scooped לִהְיוֹת שְׁיָרֶיהָ נֶאֱכָלִין — for its remainder to be eaten, as is the meal-offering of a non-Kohen. אֶלָּא — Rather, כֻּלָּהּ כָּלִיל — it is burned in its entirety. וְכֵן — And likewise,

16. כָּל מִנְחַת כֹּהֵן — EVERY MEAL-OFFERING OF A KOHEN שֶׁל נְדָבָה — that is voluntary.[2]

□ כָּלִיל תִּהְיֶה — IS TO BE AN ENTIRETY. {כָּלִיל — The word כָּלִיל implies,} כֻּלָּהּ — all of it שָׁוָה לַגָּבוֹהַּ — is equally offered to the One Who is on high.[3]

19. הַמְחַטֵּא אֹתָהּ — WHO MAKES IT INTO A SIN-OFFERING. This means הָעוֹבֵד עֲבוֹדוֹתֶיהָ — who performs its services, שֶׁהִיא נַעֲשֵׂית חַטָּאת עַל יָדוֹ — so that it becomes a sin-offering through his agency.[4]

□ הַמְחַטֵּא אֹתָהּ יֹאכֲלֶנָּה — WHO MAKES IT INTO A SIN-OFFERING MAY EAT IT. This means הָרָאוּי לַעֲבוֹדָה — one who is fit for the service. יָצָא טָמֵא — This excludes one who was impure בִּשְׁעַת זְרִיקַת דָּמִים — at the time of the sprinkling of the blood, שֶׁאֵינוֹ חוֹלֵק בַּבָּשָׂר — that he does not take a share in

---

1. The *Gemara* (*Menachos* 51b) states that if a Kohen Gadol dies and his successor has not yet been appointed, his son brings the daily meal-offering of the Kohen Gadol. This law is derived there from our verse, which the Talmud reads: וְהַכֹּהֵן הַמָּשִׁיחַ, "And the Kohen who is anointed, תַּחְתָּיו, in his place, מִבָּנָיו יַעֲשֶׂה אֹתָהּ, one of his sons shall perform it." Rashi explains that this is not the simple meaning of the verse. On its simplest level, the verse is not speaking of a situation in which the Kohen Gadol has died. It is stating the general rule: The Kohen from among Aaron's sons who is anointed in his stead shall perform the service of the daily meal-offering.

2. "Every meal-offering of a Kohen is to be an entirety" does not refer only to obligatory offerings such as the one of the previous verse, but even to voluntary offerings (*Mizrachi*).

3. The verse uses כָּלִיל which has the sense of כָּל, "all" or "entirety," but it does not state explicitly what is to be done with the whole of the offering. Rashi explains that all of it is to be offered to God (*Minchas Yehudah; Sifsei Chachamim*).

4. Elsewhere, similar verbs mean to sprinkle (e.g., below 14:52). The word הַמְחַטֵּא could have been understood in this sense here, for the blood of the

in the Courtyard of the Tent of Meeting. ²⁰ *Whatever touches its flesh shall become holy; and if there will have been sprinkled from its blood on the garment, that*

תֹּאכֵ֖ל בַּחֲצַ֥ר אֹֽהֶל־מוֹעֵֽד: כֹּ֛ל אֲשֶׁר־יִגַּ֥ע בִּבְשָׂרָ֖הּ יִקְדָּ֑שׁ וַאֲשֶׁ֨ר יִזֶּ֤ה מִדָּמָהּ֙ עַל־הַבֶּ֔גֶד אֲשֶׁר֙

──────── אונקלוס ────────

תִּתְאֲכֵל בְּדָרַת מַשְׁכַּן זִמְנָא: כֹּל דִּי יִקְרַב בְּבִסְרַהּ יִתְקַדָּשׁ וְדִי יַדִּי מִדְּמַהּ עַל לְבוּשׁ דִּי

──────── רש"י ────────

וְאִי אֶפְשָׁר לוֹמַר שְׁאָר שְׁחוּטִין שֶׁאָסַר כָּאן בַּכֹּהֲנִים חוּץ מִן הַזּוֹרֵק דָּמָהּ, שֶׁהֲרֵי נֶאֱמַר לְמַטָּה כָּל זָכָר בַּכֹּהֲנִים יֹאכַל אוֹתָהּ (להלן פסוק כב, זבחים צח:־צט.): (כ) כֹּל אֲשֶׁר יִגַּע בִּבְשָׂרָהּ. כָּל דָּבָר אֹכֶל אֲשֶׁר יִגַּע וְיִבְלַע מִמֶּנָּה: יִקְדָּשׁ. לִהְיוֹת כָּמוֹהָ

אִם פְּסוּלָה תִּפָּסֵל וְאִם הִיא כְּשֵׁרָה תֵּאָכֵל כַּחוֹמֶר שֶׁבָּהּ (ת"כ פרשתא ד:ו; זבחים צז:): וַאֲשֶׁר יִזֶּה מִדָּמָהּ עַל הַבֶּגֶד. וְאִם הֻזָּה מִדָּמָהּ עַל הַבֶּגֶד אוֹתוֹ מְקוֹם דָּם שֶׁבַּבֶּגֶד אֲשֶׁר יִזֶּה עָלֶיהָ תְּכַבֵּס בְּתוֹךְ הָעֲזָרָה (ת"כ פרק ו:ז; זבחים צג:):

──────── RASHI ELUCIDATED ────────

שְׁאוּסֵר שְׁאָר כֹּהֲנִים בַּאֲכִילָתָהּ חוּץ — It is impossible to say וְאִי אֶפְשָׁר לוֹמַר מִן הַזּוֹרֵק דָּמָהּ — that [the verse] forbids the rest of the Kohanim from eating it, other than the one who sprinkles its blood, שֶׁהֲרֵי נֶאֱמַר לְמַטָּה — for it says below, "כָּל זָכָר בַּכֹּהֲנִים יֹאכַל אֹתָהּ",[1,2] "every male among the Kohanim may eat it."[1,2]

20. כֹּל אֲשֶׁר יִגַּע בִּבְשָׂרָהּ — WHATEVER TOUCHES ITS FLESH. כָּל דְּבַר אֹכֶל — Any foodstuff אֲשֶׁר יִגַּע וְיִבְלַע מִמֶּנָּה — which will touch and absorb of it,[3]

□ יִקְדָּשׁ — SHALL BECOME HOLY לִהְיוֹת כָּמוֹהָ — to become like it: אִם פְּסוּלָה — If [the sin-offering] is invalid, תִּפָּסֵל — [that which absorbs of it] becomes invalid; וְאִם הִיא כְּשֵׁרָה — and if [the sin-offering] is valid, תֵּאָכֵל כַּחוֹמֶר שֶׁבָּהּ — it shall be eaten with the stringency of [the sin-offering].[4]

□ וְאִם הֻזָּה מִדָּמָהּ — if[5] there will have been sprinkled[6] from its blood[7] וַאֲשֶׁר יִזֶּה מִדָּמָהּ עַל הַבֶּגֶד — This means "עַל הַבֶּגֶד" — "on the garment," אוֹתוֹ מְקוֹם הַדָּם — that place of blood שֶׁבַּבֶּגֶד — on the garment, אֲשֶׁר יִזֶּה עָלֶיהָ — that on which it will be sprinkled, i.e., the garment, "תְּכַבֵּס" — "you shall launder" בְּתוֹךְ הָעֲזָרָה — inside the Courtyard of the *Beis HaMikdash*.[8]

sin-offering is sprinkled. Rashi explains that הַמְחַטֵּא of our verse is a participle derived from the noun חַטָּאת, not from the verb חטא.

1. Below v. 22.
2. *Zevachim* 98b-99a.
3. The verse could have said, כָּל אֲשֶׁר יִגַּע בָּהּ, "whatever touches it." The verse uses instead, כָּל אֲשֶׁר יִגַּע בִּבְשָׂרָהּ, "whatever touches its flesh," to imply contact which is more than superficial (*Nachalas Yaakov; Sifsei Chachamim*).
4. *Toras Kohanim, parshasa* 4:6; *Zevachim* 97b. See note 6 to v. 11 above.
5. Rashi points out that וַאֲשֶׁר here means "if," not "and that which" or "whatever," as it does further on in the verse. "And that which" would seem to say that the garment ought to be splashed with the blood of the sin-offering. The verse certainly does not mean this (*Gur Aryeh; Sifsei Chachamim*).
6. *Leshon Chaim* explains a few grammatical points, necessary for an understanding of Rashi's comments to the two appearances of יִזֶּה in our verse:
(a) Verbal roots that begin with the letter נ are classified as פ״נ verbs, i.e., the first root letter (called the פֵּ׳ הַפֹּעַל) is a נ. In the simple *kal* conjugation, the נ is dropped and a *dagesh* is placed in the second root letter (ע׳ הַפֹּעַל). Thus, for example, the *kal*, future, third person masculine singular of נפל, "to fall," is יִפֹּל,

"he will fall" (11:32 below).
Verbal roots that end with the letter ה are classified as ל״ה verbs, i.e., the last root letter (ל׳ הַפֹּעַל) is a ה. In the *kal*, future tense, the middle root letter is vowelized with a *segol*. Thus, for example, the *kal*, future, third person masculine singular of קנה, "to buy," is יִקְנֶה, "he will buy" (22:11 below).
The root נזה, "to sprinkle," falls into the classifications of both פ״נ and ל״ה. Thus, in the *kal*, future tense, the נ is dropped and the ז takes a *dagesh* and a *segol*; the third person masculine singular is then יִזֶּה, which appears twice in our verse.
(b) In the *kal*, the verb נזה is intransitive, passive in meaning although active in form. Thus, יִזֶּה does not mean "he will sprinkle," but "he (or, as in our verse, "it") will be sprinkled".
(c) In the *hifil* conjugation, future tense, פ״נ ל״ה verbs take the same vowels as in the *kal*, except that the first root letter takes a *patach* instead of a *chirik*.
(d) In the *hifil*, the verb נזה is transitive and active. Thus, יַזֶּה (16:14 below) means, "he will sprinkle."
7. The verse cannot mean "he who will sprinkle from its blood," for two reasons: (a) If such were the meaning the word would be vowelized with a *patach* [see part (d) of previous note]; and (b) the object of the verb תְּכַבֵּס, "you shall launder," can only be a cloth but not a person (*Sefer Zikaron*).
8. *Toras Kohanim, perek* 6:7; *Zevachim* 93b.

הָ תְּכֻבַּס בְּמָקוֹם קָדֹשׁ: חֶרֶשׂ אֲשֶׁר תְּבֻשַּׁל־בּוֹ יִשָּׁבֵר וְאִם־בִּכְלִי נְחֹשֶׁת בֻּשָּׁלָה וּמֹרַק וְשֻׁטַּף בַּמָּיִם: כָּל־זָכָר בַּכֹּהֲנִים יֹאכַל אֹתָהּ קֹדֶשׁ קָדָשִׁים הִוא:

on which it will be sprinkled, you shall launder in a holy place. ²¹ *An earthenware vessel in which it was cooked must be broken; but if it was cooked in a copper vessel, it should be scoured and rinsed in water.* ²² *Every male among the Kohanim may eat it; it is most holy.*

───────── אונקלוס ─────────

יְדֵי עֲלַהּ תְּחַוַּר בַּאֲתַר קַדִּישׁ: כאוּמָן דַּחֲסַף דִּי תִתְבַּשַּׁל בֵּהּ יִתְּבַר וְאִם בְּמָנָא דִּנְחָשָׁא תִּתְבַּשַּׁל וְיִתְמְרֵק וְיִשְׁתַּטַּף בְּמַיָּא: כבכָּל דְּכוּרָא בְּכַהֲנַיָּא יֵכוֹל יָתַהּ קֹדֶשׁ קוּדְשִׁין הִיא:

───────── רש"י ─────────

אשר יזה. יהא כמו נזה ולא יטה לארץ מנלס (איוב טו:כט) יהא נטוי: (כא) **ישבר.** לפי שהבליעה שנבלעת בו נעשה נותר, והוא הדין לכל הקדשים (ע"ז עו.): **ומרק.** לשון תמרוקי הנשים (אסתר ב:יב) אשקורי"ר בלעז: **ומרק ושטף.** לפלוט

את בליעתו אבל כלי חרם למדך הכתוב כאן שאינו יוצא מידי דפיו לעולם (פסחים ל:): (כב) **כל זכר בכהנים יאכל אותה.** הא למדת שהמחטאת אותה האמור למעלה לא להוציא שאר הכהנים אלא להוציא את שאינו ראוי לחטוי:

───────── RASHI ELUCIDATED ─────────

□ **אֲשֶׁר יִזֶּה — THAT [ON WHICH] IT WILL BE SPRINKLED.** The word יִזֶּה means יְהֵא נִזֶּה — will be sprinkled, like יְזֶּה in, "בְּמוֹ וְלֹא יִטֶּה לָאָרֶץ מִנְלָם — *their fulfillment will not be stooped to the ground,*"[1] which means, יְהֵא נָטוּי — will be stooped.[2]

21. יִשָּׁבֵר — MUST BE BROKEN. לְפִי שֶׁהַבְּלִיעָה — Because the absorption שֶׁנִּבְלַעַת בּוֹ — that is absorbed in it, i.e., the absorbed meat juices, נַעֲשֶׂה נוֹתָר — becomes *nosar*.[3] וְהוּא הַדִּין לְכָל הַקֳּדָשִׁים[4] — The same law as applies to absorbing the juices of a sin-offering holds true for all holies, i.e., offerings.[4]

□ **וּמֹרַק — IT SHOULD BE SCOURED.** לְשׁוֹן תַּמְרוּקֵי הַנָּשִׁים[5] — This is related to תַּמְרוּקֵי in, "cosmetics of women,"[5] אשקורי"ר בלע"ז — *Escurer* in Old French.[6]

□ **וּמֹרַק וְשֻׁטַּף — IT SHOULD BE SCOURED AND RINSED** לִפְלוֹט אֶת בְּלִיעָתוֹ — to expel its absorption. אֲבָל בִּכְלִי חֶרֶס — But with regard to an earthenware vessel, לִמֶּדְךָ הַכָּתוּב כָּאן — the verse teaches you here שֶׁאֵינוֹ יוֹצֵא מִידֵי דָפְיוֹ לְעוֹלָם[7] — that [the vessel] does not ever leave the grasp of its defect,[7] i.e., does not rid itself of its defect, and so must be broken.

22. כָּל זָכָר בַּכֹּהֲנִים יֹאכַל אֹתָהּ — EVERY MALE AMONG THE KOHANIM MAY EAT IT. הָא לָמַדְתָּ — Now then, you have learned שֶׁ״הַמְחַטֵּא אוֹתָהּ״ — that "the one who makes it into a sin-offering" הָאָמוּר לְמַעְלָה[8] — that is mentioned above[8] לֹא לְהוֹצִיא שְׁאָר הַכֹּהֲנִים — is not meant to exclude the other Kohanim אֶלָּא לְהוֹצִיא אֶת שֶׁאֵינוֹ רָאוּי לְחִטּוּי — but to exclude one who is unfit to perform the

---

1. *Job* 15:29. The root of יִטֶּה is נטה which, like נזה, is a פ"נ ל"ה verb.

2. (See note 6 on page 69.) In his preceding comment, which included his remarks on the first אֲשֶׁר יִזֶּה of our verse, Rashi stressed that יִזֶּה has a passive meaning. Here he again points out the passive sense, but also stresses the future aspect of the verb by saying יְהֵא נִזֶּה. Rashi in his preceding comment used a passive form in the past (הֻזָּה). He did not then need to point out the future quality; this is implied by the "if" (אִם) which is Rashi's understanding of אֲשֶׁר. Here, in the second אֲשֶׁר יִזֶּה of our verse, אֲשֶׁר does not mean "if," but "which." That is why Rashi feels he must note the future sense with יְהֵא.

Since נזה in the *kal* appears only twice in the Torah (both times in our verse as יִזֶּה), as distinct from נזה in the *hifil*, Rashi wished to note its nature — active in form, passive in meaning. He supports his point by showing that this is not unique. נטה — in the *kal*, future tense, third person masculine singular — יִטֶּה — is also intransitive, passive in

meaning although active in form.

3. *Nosar* is the meat of an offering that has been left uneaten beyond the time the Torah set for it to be eaten. It is forbidden to eat *nosar* or derive any benefit from it (see *Pesachim* 24a). The juices absorbed by an earthenware vessel will perforce become *nosar* because they will not be eaten within the allotted time. Since they cannot be scoured from earthenware, the vessel must be broken.

4. *Avodah Zarah* 76a.

5. *Esther* 2:12. Both words connote "cleaning" (*Leket Bahir; Lifshuto shel Rashi*).

6. This is the source of the English word "scour." In Modern French *"récurer"* means "to scour" and *"curer"* means "to clean out." Rashi apparently understands תַּמְרוּקֵי הַנָּשִׁים as a kind of cleanser used by women to beautify their skin.

7. *Pesachim* 30b.

8. Verse 19. See Rashi there.

VAYIKRA/LEVITICUS — PARASHAS TZAV

23 And any sin-offering from which some blood has been brought to the Tent of Meeting, to effect atonement within the Holy, shall not be eaten; it shall be burned in fire.

7 **1** This is the law of the guilt-offering; it is most holy. **2** In the place where they shall slaughter the olah-offering shall they slaughter the guilt-offering; and he shall throw its blood upon the Mizbe'ach, all around.

כג וְכָל־חַטָּאת אֲשֶׁר יוּבָא מִדָּמָהּ אֶל־אֹהֶל מוֹעֵד לְכַפֵּר בַּקֹּדֶשׁ לֹא תֵאָכֵל בָּאֵשׁ תִּשָּׂרֵף׃

ז א וְזֹאת תּוֹרַת הָאָשָׁם קֹדֶשׁ קָדָשִׁים הוּא׃ ב בִּמְקוֹם אֲשֶׁר יִשְׁחֲטוּ אֶת־הָעֹלָה יִשְׁחֲטוּ אֶת־הָאָשָׁם וְאֶת־דָּמוֹ יִזְרֹק עַל־הַמִּזְבֵּחַ סָבִיב׃

— אונקלוס —

כג וְכָל חַטָּאתָא דִּי מִתָּעַל מִדְּמַהּ לְמַשְׁכַּן זִמְנָא לְכַפָּרָא בְּקוּדְשָׁא לָא תִתְאֲכֵל בְּנוּרָא תִתּוֹקַד׃ א וְדָא אוֹרַיְתָא דַּאֲשָׁמָא קֹדֶשׁ קוּדְשִׁין הוּא׃ ב בְּאַתְרָא דִּי יִכְּסוּן יָת עֲלָתָא יִכְּסוּן יָת אֲשָׁמָא וְיָת דְּמֵהּ יִזְרוֹק עַל מַדְבְּחָא סְחוֹר סְחוֹר׃

— רש"י —

(כג) וכל חטאת וגו׳. שֶׁאִם הִכְנִיס מִדַּם חַטָּאת הַחִיצוֹנָה לִפְנִים פְּסוּלָה. וכל. לְרַבּוֹת שְׁאָר קָדָשִׁים: (ת"כ פרק כ"ב; זבחים פ"ב.): (א) קדש קדשים הוא. הוּא קָרֵב וְאֵין תְּמוּרָתוֹ קְרֵבָה (ת"כ פרשתא ה:ב; תמורה י"ז:): (ב) וישחטו. רִבָּה לָנוּ שְׁחִיטוֹת הַרְבֵּה, לְפִי שֶׁמָּצִינוּ אָשָׁם בָּא בְּצִבּוּר נֶאֱמַר יִשְׁחֲטוּ: ותלאו עולה. תְּלָאוֹ בְּעוֹלָה לְהָבִיא עוֹלַת צִבּוּר לִצְפוֹן:

— RASHI ELUCIDATED —

sin-offering service.[1]

23. וְכָל חַטָּאת וְגוֹמֵר — AND ANY SIN-OFFERING, ETC. — שֶׁאִם הִכְנִיס מִדַּם הַחַטָּאת הַחִיצוֹנָה לִפְנִים — That if he brought some of the blood of an exterior sin-offering to the inside of the *Mishkan* or the *Beis HaMikdash*, פְּסוּלָה — it is invalid.[2,3] {וְכָל — AND ANY.[3] לְרַבּוֹת שְׁאָר קָדָשִׁים — To include other holies, i.e., offerings.[3]}

7.

1. קֹדֶשׁ קָדָשִׁים הוּא — IT IS MOST HOLY. הוּא קָרֵב — It is offered, וְאֵין תְּמוּרָתוֹ קְרֵבָה — but its substitute is not offered.[4]

2. {יִשְׁחֲטוּ} — THEY SHALL SLAUGHTER. רִבָּה לָנוּ שְׁחִיטוֹת הַרְבֵּה — [The verse] has included many slaughterings.[5] לְפִי שֶׁמָּצִינוּ אָשָׁם בָּא בְּצִבּוּר — Since we have found a guilt-offering brought by the public, נֶאֱמַר "יִשְׁחֲטוּ" — it says, "they shall slaughter," in the רַבִּים — plural.[6] וּתְלָאוֹ בְּעוֹלָה — [The Torah] made it dependent on the *olah*-offering, i.e., the Torah stated the location of the slaughtering of the guilt-offering in terms of that of the *olah*-offering, לְהָבִיא עוֹלַת צִבּוּר לַצָּפוֹן — to include an *olah*-offering of the public for slaughtering in **the north**.[7]

---

1. He is unfit, because he is impure; but a Kohen who has a blemish may eat from the sin-offering, as Rashi has noted in his comments to verse 11 above, s.v., כָּל זָכָר.
2. The blood of the sin-offering of a common person is sprinkled on the outer *Mizbe'ach* (see 4:30 above). If it was brought into the Sanctuary, the offering is invalid.
3. *Toras Kohanim*, perek 8:1; *Zevachim* 82a.
4. *Toras Kohanim*, parshasa 5:2; *Temurah* 17b. It is forbidden to substitute another animal for an animal which has been designated as an offering. If one does, however, say, "This animal should be brought as an offering instead of this one," the original animal remains sanctified and the substitute also has the sanctity of an offering (see below, 27:9-10). In the case of certain offerings — the *olah*-offering and the peace-offering — the substitute is offered on the *Mizbe'ach*, as well as the original. "*It is most holy*" implies that this is not so with regard to the guilt-offering. The substitute may not be slaughtered or used for work because of its sanctity, but it is not offered on the *Mizbe'ach*. It is allowed to graze until it develops a blemish. Then it is sold. Its sanctity transfers to the money paid for it, and that money is used to purchase voluntary offerings (*Mizrachi*; *Sifsei Chachamim*).
5. The parallel phrase in *Toras Kohanim* (*parshasa* 5:3) reads, ..., רִבָּה כָּאן שׁוֹחֲטִים הַרְבֵּה, "[The verse] here has included many slaughterers: even proselytes, even women, even slaves."
6. Rashi's comment seems to in contradict the Talmud (*Temurah* 14a) which states that there are no guilt-offerings brought by the public. Moreover, this comment is not found in most early editions of *Rashi*. Thus, most commentators are of the opinion that this was not written by Rashi, and crept into the text by error. See, however, *Yosef Hallel*, who offers two possible resolutions to the contradiction.
7. Although the Torah has stated that the *olah*-offering of an individual should be slaughtered on the northern side of the *Mizbe'ach* (1:11), it has not specified where an *olah*-offering of the public should be slaughtered. The Torah states the location of the slaughtering of the guilt-offering in terms of the

³ And he shall offer all of its fat; the fat tail and the fat that covers the innards; ⁴ and the two kidneys and the fat that covers them, which is on the flanks; and he shall remove the diaphragm as well as the liver, as well as the kidneys. ⁵ The Kohen shall cause them to go up in smoke on the Mizbe'ach, a fire-offering to HASHEM; it is a guilt-offering.

כָּל־חֶלְבּוֹ יַקְרִיב מִמֶּנּוּ אֵת הָאַלְיָה וְאֶת־הַחֵלֶב הַמְכַסֶּה אֶת־הַקֶּרֶב: ⁴ וְאֵת שְׁתֵּי הַכְּלָיֹת וְאֶת־הַחֵלֶב אֲשֶׁר עֲלֵיהֶן אֲשֶׁר עַל־הַכְּסָלִים וְאֶת־הַיֹּתֶרֶת עַל־הַכָּבֵד עַל־הַכְּלָיֹת יְסִירֶנָּה: ⁵ וְהִקְטִיר אֹתָם הַכֹּהֵן הַמִּזְבֵּחָה אִשֶּׁה לַיהוָה אָשָׁם הוּא:

אונקלוס

ג וְיַת כָּל תַּרְבֵּהּ יְקָרֵב מִנֵּהּ יָת אַלִּיתָא וְיָת תַּרְבָּא דְחָפֵי יָת גַּוָּא: ד וְיָת תַּרְתֵּין כָּלְיָן וְיָת תַּרְבָּא דִי עֲלֵיהֶן דִּי עַל גִּסְסַיָּא וְיָת חֲצָרָא דְעַל כַּבְדָּא עַל כָּלְיָתָא יֶעְדִּנַּהּ: ה וְיַסֵּק יָתְהוֹן כַּהֲנָא לְמַדְבְּחָא קֻרְבָּנָא קֳדָם יְיָ אֲשָׁמָא הוּא:

רש"י

(ג) וְאֵת כָּל חֶלְבּוֹ וְגוֹ׳. עַד כָּאן לֹא נִתְפָּרְשׁוּ אֵימוּרִין בְּאָשָׁם לְכָךְ הוּצְרַךְ לְפָרְשָׂם כָּאן אֲבָל חַטָּאת כְּבָר נִתְפָּרְשׁוּ בָּהּ בְּפָרָשַׁת וַיִּקְרָא (לְעֵיל בְּפֶרֶק ד): אֶת הָאַלְיָה. לְפִי שֶׁאָשָׁם אֵינוֹ בָא אֶלָּא אַיִל אוֹ כֶּבֶשׂ, וְאַיִל וְכֶבֶשׂ נִתְרַבּוּ בְּאַלְיָה (לְעֵיל ג:ט):

(ה) אָשָׁם הוּא. עַד שֶׁיִּנָּתֵק שְׁמוֹ מִמֶּנּוּ. לִמֵּד עַל אָשָׁם שֶׁמֵּתוּ בְּעָלָיו אוֹ שֶׁנִּתְכַּפְּרוּ בְּעָלָיו, אע"פ שֶׁעוֹמֵד לִהְיוֹת דָּמָיו עוֹלָה לְקִיץ הַמִּזְבֵּחַ, אִם שְׁחָטוֹ סְתָם אֵינוֹ כָּשֵׁר לְעוֹלָה קוֹדֶם שֶׁנִּתַּק שְׁמוֹ לִרְעִיָּה. וְאֵינוֹ בָא לְלַמֵּד עַל הָאָשָׁם שֶׁיְּהֵא פָסוּל שֶׁלֹּא לִשְׁמוֹ:

RASHI ELUCIDATED
---

3. וְאֵת כָּל חֶלְבּוֹ וְגוֹמֵר — AND [HE SHALL OFFER] ALL OF ITS FAT. עַד כָּאן — Up to this point, לֹא נִתְפָּרְשׁוּ אֵימוּרִין בְּאָשָׁם — the specified parts which are to be burned on the *Mizbe'ach* had not been stated explicitly regarding the guilt-offering. לְכָךְ הֻצְרַךְ לְפָרְשָׁם כָּאן — Therefore, [the Torah] needed to state them explicitly here. אֲבָל חַטָּאת — But with regard to the sin-offering, כְּבָר נִתְפָּרְשׁוּ בָהּ — [the specified parts] were already stated explicitly about it בְּפָרָשַׁת וַיִּקְרָא — in *Parashas Vayikra*.[1]

אֶת הָאַלְיָה — THE FAT TAIL. לְפִי שֶׁאָשָׁם אֵינוֹ בָא אֶלָּא אַיִל אוֹ כֶבֶשׂ — Because the guilt-offering can only be a ram or a sheep,[2] וְאַיִל וְכֶבֶשׂ נִתְרַבּוּ בָּאַלְיָה — and a ram and a sheep have been increased by the fat tail,[3] i.e., have the fat tail among their specified parts, in addition to the same specified parts as other animal offerings.

5. אָשָׁם הוּא — IT IS A GUILT-OFFERING עַד שֶׁיִּנָּתֵק שְׁמוֹ מִמֶּנּוּ — until its name will be disconnected from it. לִמֵּד עַל אָשָׁם שֶׁמֵּתוּ בְעָלָיו — This teaches us about a guilt-offering whose owner has died,[4] אוֹ שֶׁנִּתְכַּפְּרוּ בְעָלָיו — or whose owner has attained atonement through the offering of another animal,[5] אַף עַל פִּי שֶׁעוֹמֵד — even though it stands לִהְיוֹת דָּמָיו עוֹלָה לְקִיץ הַמִּזְבֵּחַ — to have its money, i.e., the money gained through its sale, used for an *olah*-offering for the "dessert of the *Mizbe'ach*,"[6] אִם שְׁחָטוֹ סְתָם — if he slaughtered it with no specific intent, אֵינוֹ כָּשֵׁר לְעוֹלָה — it is not valid as an *olah*-offering קוֹדֶם שֶׁנִּתַּק לִרְעִיָּה — before it has been disconnected from its status as a guilt-offering by being designated for grazing.[7] וְאֵינוֹ בָא — [The phrase אָשָׁם הוּא] does not come לְלַמֵּד עַל הָאָשָׁם — to teach about the guilt-offering שֶׁיְּהֵא פָסוּל שֶׁלֹּא לִשְׁמוֹ — that it is invalid if it was slaughtered

---

olah-offering to imply that there is yet another *olah*-offering slaughtered on the north, the *olah*-offering of the public.

1. Above Ch. 4.
2. The difference between אַיִל, "ram," and כֶּבֶשׂ, "sheep," is discussed in note 7 on page 55.
3. Above 3:9.
4. It is a tradition received by Moses at Sinai (*halachah leMoshe miSinai*) that if the owner of the guilt-offering dies before his offering is brought, it is not offered. Instead, it is set out to pasture where it remains until it develops a blemish that disqualifies it from being brought as an offering. The animal is then sold and the proceeds are used to purchase *olah*-offerings as described below (see *Temurah* 18a).

The assertion of *Sifsei Chachamim*, based on *Minchas Yehudah*, that this is so because the owner has attained atonement through his death is questionable, for the law holds true even when the owner sins by his death, i.e., in a case of suicide.

5. This occurs when an animal designated as a guilt-offering has been lost, and another animal was offered in its place before the original animal is found (*Mizrachi*; *Sifsei Chachamim*). The law mentioned in the previous note regarding what is done with the ownerless guilt-offering applies here as well.

6. See Rashi to 1:2 above and note 11 on page 6.

7. *Temurah* 18a. The apparently superfluous "it is a guilt-offering" teaches us that even though it will never be offered as a guilt-offering, it remains in that state, and can-

⁶ *Every male among the Kohanim may eat it; it shall be eaten in a holy place, it is most holy.* ⁷ *Like the sin-offering is the guilt-offering, they have the same law; it shall belong to the Kohen who performs its atonement service.* ⁸ *And the Kohen who offers a person's olah-offering*

וּ כָּל־זָכָר בַּכֹּהֲנִים יֹאכְלֶנּוּ בְּמָקוֹם
קָדוֹשׁ יֵאָכֵל קֹדֶשׁ קָדָשִׁים הוּא:
ז כַּחַטָּאת כָּאָשָׁם תּוֹרָה אַחַת לָהֶם
הַכֹּהֵן אֲשֶׁר יְכַפֶּר־בּוֹ לוֹ יִהְיֶה:
ח וְהַכֹּהֵן הַמַּקְרִיב אֶת־עֹלַת אִישׁ

אונקלוס

ו וְכָל דְּכוּרָא בְּכַהֲנַיָּא יֵכְלִנַּהּ בַּאֲתַר קַדִּישׁ יִתְאֲכֵל קֹדֶשׁ קוּדְשִׁין הוּא: ז כְּחַטָּאתָא כַּאֲשָׁמָא אוֹרַיְתָא חֲדָא לְהוֹן כַּהֲנָא דִי יְכַפֵּר בֵּהּ דִּילֵהּ יְהֵא: ח וְכַהֲנָא דִמְקָרֵב יָת עֲלַת גְּבַר

רש"י

(ו) **קדש קדשים הוא.** בְּתוֹרַת כֹּהֲנִים הוּא נִדְרָשׁ: (ז) **תורה אחת להם.** לַדָּבָר זֶה: **הכהן אשר יכפר בו.** הָרָאוּי לְכַפָּרָה חוֹלֵק בּוֹ, פְּרָט לִטְבוּל יוֹם וּמְחֻסַּר כִּפּוּרִים וְאוֹנֵן (ת"כ פרק ט:א):

כְּמוֹ שֶׁדָּרְשׁוּ הוּא הַכָּתוּב בְּחַטָּאת (לְעֵיל ד:כד), לְפִי שֶׁאָשָׁם לֹא נֶאֱמַר בּוֹ ״אָשָׁם הוּא״ אֶלָּא לְאַחַר הַקְטָרַת אֵימוּרִין וְהוּא עַצְמוֹ שֶׁלֹּא הוּקְטְרוּ אֵימוּרָיו, כָּשֵׁר (זבחים י'):

--- RASHI ELUCIDATED ---

not for its sake, but with the intent that it is slaughtered for the sake of a different kind of offering, **בַּחַטָּאת הַכָּתוּב** ״הוּא״ שֶׁדָּרְשׁוּ כְּמוֹ – as they interpreted "it is" which is written about the sin-offering,¹ אֵימוּרִין הַקְטָרַת לְאַחַר אֶלָּא בּוֹ נֶאֱמַר לֹא שֶׁאָשָׁם לְפִי – because the guilt-offering does not have "it is a guilt-offering" said about it until after the burning of the specified parts, עַצְמוֹ וְהוּא – but [the guilt-offering] itself אֵימוּרָיו הוּקְטְרוּ שֶׁלֹּא – whose specified parts were not burnt on the *Mizbe'ach* ²כָּשֵׁר – is valid.²

6. קָדָשִׁים קֹדֶשׁ הוּא – IT IS MOST HOLY. נִדְרָשׁ הוּא כֹּהֲנִים בְּתוֹרַת – This is expounded in *Toras Kohanim*.³

7. לָהֶם אַחַת תּוֹרָה – THEY HAVE THE SAME LAW. זֶה בְּדָבָר – in this matter:⁴

□ בּוֹ יְכַפֶּר אֲשֶׁר הַכֹּהֵן – THE KOHEN WHO PERFORMS ITS ATONEMENT SERVICE. בּוֹ חוֹלֵק לְכַפָּרָה הָרָאוּי – One who is fit for the performance of the atonement service takes a share in it יוֹם לִטְבוּל פְּרָט – to the exclusion of one who immersed that day,⁵ כִּפּוּרִים וּמְחֻסַּר – and one who is lacking atonement,⁶ ⁸וְאוֹנֵן – and a mourner on the day of the death of a relative.⁷,⁸

---

not be offered as an *olah*-offering, until it has been formally taken out of its state of being a guilt-offering by being handed over for grazing. At this point, although it should be left to graze until it develops a blemish, if it is slaughtered as an *olah*-offering, it is a valid offering.

1. See 4:24 above and Rashi there.

2. *Zevachim* 10b. Although the similar "it is a sin-offering" (4:24) was interpreted as teaching us that the slaughter of the sin-offering must be done for its sake, a parallel interpretation cannot be made here. For "it is a guilt-offering" appears here in the context of placing the specified parts on the *Mizbe'ach,* whereas "it is a sin-offering" appears in the context of slaughtering. Nor can the context here be interpreted as saying that the specified parts must be for the sake of the guilt-offering, for as Rashi points out, the offering is accepted even if the specified parts were not burned on the *Mizbe'ach* at all (*Mizrachi; Sifsei Chachamim*).

3. *Toras Kohanim, parshasa* 5:10. The phrase "it is most holy" appears superfluous. The interpretation in *Toras Kohanim* is as follows: "Most holy" tells us to apply this law — which restricts all but male Kohanim from eating the offering — to peace-offerings brought on behalf of the public. "It is" tells us that the law does not apply to thanksgiving-offerings (see below, vv. 11-15) and the

ram brought by a *nazir* at the end of his term of *nezirus* (see *Numbers* 6:17).

4. The matter which follows in the verse and is the subject of Rashi's next comment, but their laws differ in other respects.

5. The purification process for certain types of impurity requires immersion of the purificant in a mikveh, and waiting until sundown. Once the purificant immerses himself in the mikveh, he becomes a טְבוּל יוֹם, literally, one who "immersed that day." Although he no longer transmits impurity to non-sacred objects, he still transmits impurity to offerings and *terumah*. If he is a Kohen, he may not serve in the Temple or partake of offerings or *terumah* until sundown.

6. Some types of impurity require offerings to complete the purification process. In these cases, although the purificant has immersed himself, and sundown has passed, he may not serve in the Temple or partake of offerings until he has brought his own offering for his atonement. One in this state is called מְחֻסַּר כִּפּוּרִים, "lacking atonement."

7. Such a mourner is disqualified from serving in the Temple and from partaking of offerings. See note 2 on page 106.

8. *Toras Kohanim, perek* 9:1.

עוֹר הָעֹלָה אֲשֶׁר הִקְרִיב לַכֹּהֵן לוֹ
יִהְיֶה: וְכָל־מִנְחָה אֲשֶׁר תֵּאָפֶה
בַתַּנּוּר וְכָל־נַעֲשָׂה בַמַּרְחֶשֶׁת
וְעַל־מַחֲבַת לַכֹּהֵן הַמַּקְרִיב אֹתָהּ
לוֹ תִהְיֶה: וְכָל־מִנְחָה בְלוּלָה־
בַשֶּׁמֶן וַחֲרֵבָה לְכָל־בְּנֵי אַהֲרֹן
תִּהְיֶה אִישׁ כְּאָחִיו:
וְזֹאת תּוֹרַת זֶבַח הַשְּׁלָמִים
אֲשֶׁר יַקְרִיב לַיהוָה: אִם עַל־תּוֹדָה

— the hide of the *olah-offering* that he offered, to that *Kohen*, his shall it be.

⁹ Any meal-offering that is baked in the oven and any that is made in a deep pan or upon a shallow pan — it shall belong to the *Kohen* who offers it; it shall be his. ¹⁰ And any meal-offering that is mixed with oil or that is dry, it shall belong to all of Aaron's sons, every man alike.

¹¹ This is the law of the sacrifice of the peace-offering that one will offer to HASHEM: ¹² If he shall offer it for a thanksgiving-

―――― אונקלוס ――――

מְשַׁךְ עֲלָתָא דִּי יְקָרֵב לְכַהֲנָא דִּילֵהּ יְהֵא: ט וְכָל מִנְחָתָא דִּי תִתְאֲפֵי בְתַנּוּרָא וְכָל דְּתִתְעֲבֵד בְּרַדְתָּא וְעַל מַסְרֵיתָא לְכַהֲנָא דִּמְקָרֵב יָתַהּ דִּילֵהּ תְּהֵא: י וְכָל מִנְחָתָא דְפִילָא בִמְשַׁח וּדְלָא פִילָא לְכָל בְּנֵי אַהֲרֹן תְּהֵי גְבַר כַּאֲחוּהִי: יא וְדָא אוֹרַיְתָא דְנִכְסַת קוּדְשַׁיָּא דִּי יְקָרֵב קֳדָם יְיָ: יב אִם עַל תּוֹדְתָא

―――― רש"י ――――

(ח) **עור העולה אשר הקריב לכהן לו יהיה.** פרט לטבול יום ומחוסר כפורים ואונן שאינן חולקים בעורות (ת"כ שם ה; זבחים קג:ב): (ט) **לכהן המקריב אתה וגו'.** יכול לו לבדו, ת"ל לכל בני אהרן תהיה. יכול לכולן, ת"ל המקריב. הא כיצד, לבית אב של אותו יום שמקריבין אותה (ת"כ פרק י:ב): (י) **בלולה בשמן.** זו מנחת נדבה. **וחרבה.** זו מנחת חוטא ומנחת קנאות שאין בהן שמן:

―――― RASHI ELUCIDATED ――――

8. עוֹר הָעֹלָה אֲשֶׁר הִקְרִיב לַכֹּהֵן לוֹ יִהְיֶה — **THE HIDE OF THE *OLAH*-OFFERING THAT HE OFFERED, TO THAT KOHEN, HIS SHALL IT BE,** פְּרָט לִטְבוּל יוֹם — **to the exclusion of one who immersed that day,**[1] וּמְחֻסַּר כִּפּוּרִים — **and one who is lacking atonement,**[2] וְאוֹנֵן — **and a mourner on the day of the death of a relative,**[3] שֶׁאֵין חוֹלְקִים בָּעוֹרוֹת — **that they do not take a share in the hides.**[4]

9. לַכֹּהֵן הַמַּקְרִיב אֹתָהּ וְגוֹמֵר — **TO THE KOHEN WHO OFFERS IT, ETC.** — יָכוֹל לוֹ לְבַדּוֹ — **One might be able to** think that it goes **to him alone.** תַּלְמוּד לוֹמַר — **To teach us otherwise, the verse says,** לְכָל בְּנֵי אַהֲרֹן תִּהְיֶה — **"It shall belong to all of Aaron's sons."** יָכוֹל לְכֻלָּן — **One might be able to think on the basis of that verse alone that the meal-offerings go to all of them.** תַּלְמוּד לוֹמַר — **To teach us** otherwise, **the verse says,** לַכֹּהֵן הַמַּקְרִיב — **"to the Kohen who offers [it]."** הָא כֵּיצַד — **How is this?**[5] The meal-offering belongs לְבֵית אָב — **to the** officiating **extended family** of Kohanim[6] שֶׁל אוֹתוֹ יוֹם שֶׁמַּקְרִיבִין אוֹתָהּ — **of that day on which they offer [the meal-offering].**[7]

10. בְּלוּלָה בַשֶּׁמֶן — **MIXED WITH OIL.** זוֹ מִנְחַת נְדָבָה — **This is a voluntary meal-offering.**

וַחֲרֵבָה — **OR [THAT IS] DRY.** זוֹ מִנְחַת חוֹטֵא — **This is the meal-offering of a sinner**[8] — וּמִנְחַת קְנָאוֹת — **and the meal-offering of jealousy**[9] שֶׁאֵין בָּהֶן שֶׁמֶן — **which do not have oil in them.**

1. See above, p. 73, note 5.
2. See above, p. 73, note 6.
3. See above, p. 73, note 7.
4. *Toras Kohanim, perek* 9:5; *Zevachim* 103b.
5. How can we reconcile the verse that implies that it belongs only to the Kohen who brings the offering with the verse that implies that it belongs to all of the Kohanim?
6. The term בֵּית אָב, literally, "father's house," means "an extended family." See Rashi to *Exodus* 12:3 and our comments there. The *Kohanim* were divided into twenty-four groups called מִשְׁמָרוֹת, "watches." These were each divided into six family groupings called בָּתֵי אָבוֹת, "extended families." Each watch officiated in the *Beis HaMikdash* for one week, twice (or three times) a year. Each extended family officiated for one weekday, with the particular function of each individual in the regular communal offerings being assigned by lots. On Shabbos, the entire watch was eligible for the lottery. During the festivals, all Kohanim, regardless of the watch to which they belonged, were eligible for the lottery.

7. *Toras Kohanim, perek* 10:2.
8. See 5:11-13 above.
9. The meal-offering brought by a *sotah*, a woman suspected of adultery. See *Numbers* 5:15.

and from its oil, and all of the frankincense that is on the meal-offering; and he shall cause them to go up in smoke on the Mizbe'ach for a satisfying aroma — its memorial portion unto HASHEM. *⁹ Aaron and his sons shall eat what is left of it; it shall be eaten unleavened in a holy place, in the Courtyard of the Tent of Meeting shall they eat it. ¹⁰ It may not be baked leavened, I have presented it as their share*

וּמִשַּׁמְנָהּ וְאֵת כָּל־הַלְּבֹנָה אֲשֶׁר עַל־הַמִּנְחָה וְהִקְטִיר הַמִּזְבֵּחַ רֵיחַ נִיחֹחַ אַזְכָּרָתָהּ לַיהוָה: ט וְהַנּוֹתֶרֶת מִמֶּנָּה יֹאכְלוּ אַהֲרֹן וּבָנָיו מַצּוֹת תֵּאָכֵל בְּמָקוֹם קָדֹשׁ בַּחֲצַר אֹהֶל־מוֹעֵד יֹאכְלוּהָ: י לֹא תֵאָפֶה חָמֵץ חֶלְקָם נָתַתִּי אֹתָהּ

---------- אונקלוס ----------

וּמִמִּשְׁחַהּ וְיָת כָּל לִבְנָתָא דִּי עַל מִנְחָתָא וְיַסֵּק לְמַדְבְּחָא לְאִתְקַבָּלָא בְרַעֲוָא אִדְכַּרְתַּהּ קֳדָם יְיָ: ט וּדְאִשְׁתָּאַר מִנַּהּ יֵכְלוּן אַהֲרֹן וּבְנוֹהִי פַטִּיר תִּתְאֲכֵל בַּאֲתַר קַדִּישׁ בְּדָרַת מַשְׁכַּן זִמְנָא יֵכְלֻנַּהּ: י לָא תִתְאֲפֵי חֲמִיעַ חֳלָקְהוֹן יְהָבִית יָתַהּ

---------- רש"י ----------

מִסֹּלֶת הַמִּנְחָה וּמִשַּׁמְנָהּ. מִכָּאן שֶׁקּוֹמֵץ מִמְּקוֹם שֶׁנִּתְרַבָּה שַׁמְנָהּ (סוטה יד:): **הַמִּנְחָה.** שֶׁלֹּא תְּהֵא מְעֹרֶבֶת בְּאַחֶרֶת (ת"כ שם): **וְאֵת כָּל הַלְּבוֹנָה אֲשֶׁר עַל הַמִּנְחָה וְהִקְטִיר.** שֶׁמְּלַקֵּט אֶת לְבוֹנָתָהּ לְאַחַר קְמִיצָה וּמַקְטִירוֹ (ת"כ שם; סוטה שם). וּלְפִי שֶׁלֹּא פֵּרֵשׁ כֵּן אֶלָּא בְּאַחַת מִן הַמְּנָחוֹת בַּוַּיִּקְרָא (וְלִטֹּל שַׁמְנָהּ), הֻצְרַךְ לִשְׁנוֹת פָּרָשָׁה זוֹ לִכְלוֹל כָּל הַמְּנָחוֹת כְּמִשְׁפָּטָן: (ט) **בְּמָקוֹם קָדוֹשׁ.** וְאֵיזֶהוּ, בַּחֲצַר אֹהֶל מוֹעֵד: (י) **לֹא תֵאָפֶה חָמֵץ חֶלְקָם.** אַף הַשְּׁיָרִים אֲסוּרִים בְּחָמֵץ (מנחות נה.):

---------- RASHI ELUCIDATED ----------

□ מִסֹּלֶת הַמִּנְחָה וּמִשַּׁמְנָהּ – FROM THE FINE FLOUR OF THE MEAL-OFFERING AND FROM ITS OIL. מִכָּאן – From here there is a source for the law שֶׁקּוֹמֵץ – that he takes the threefingersful מִמָּקוֹם שֶׁנִּתְרַבָּה שַׁמְנָהּ – from where it is most oily.¹

□ הַמִּנְחָה – THE MEAL-OFFERING. שֶׁלֹּא תְהֵא מְעֹרֶבֶת בְּאַחֶרֶת – That it should not be mixed with another.²

□ וְאֵת כָּל הַלְּבֹנָה אֲשֶׁר עַל הַמִּנְחָה וְהִקְטִיר – AND ALL OF THE FRANKINCENSE THAT IS ON THE MEAL-OFFERING; AND HE SHALL CAUSE [THEM] TO GO UP IN SMOKE, that is, שֶׁמְּלַקֵּט אֶת לְבוֹנָתָהּ – that he should gather up its frankincense לְאַחַר קְמִיצָה – after the taking of the threefingersful, ³וּמַקְטִירוֹ – and cause it to go up in smoke.³ אֶלָּא – Since this was not stated explicitly וּלְפִי שֶׁלֹּא פֵּרֵשׁ כֵּן בְּאַחַת מִן הַמְּנָחוֹת – except in the case of one of the meal-offerings ⁴בַּוַּיִּקְרָא – in *Parashas Vayikra*,⁴ הֻצְרַךְ לִשְׁנוֹת פָּרָשָׁה זוֹ – [the Torah] had to repeat this *parashah*, in order לִכְלוֹל כָּל הַמְּנָחוֹת – to include all of the meal-offerings in the law of gathering and burning the frankincense, כְּמִשְׁפָּטָן – in accordance with their law.

9. בְּמָקוֹם קָדֹשׁ – IN A HOLY PLACE. וְאֵיזֶהוּ – And which holy place is it? ",בַּחֲצַר אֹהֶל מוֹעֵד,, – "In the Courtyard of the Tent of Meeting."⁵

10. לֹא תֵאָפֶה חָמֵץ חֶלְקָם – IT MAY NOT BE BAKED LEAVENED. [I HAVE PRESENTED IT AS] THEIR SHARE. אַף הַשְּׁיָרִים – The remainders that are left over after the *kometz* has been taken, too, ⁶אֲסוּרִים בְּחָמֵץ – are forbidden if leavened.⁶

מִמֶּנּוּ בְּקֻמְצוֹ, "He shall separate from it *in his* threefingersful," implies that it must be separated directly into the hands of the Kohen, and not by means of a vessel which holds threefingersful (*HaKesav VeHaKabbalah*).

1. *Sotah* 14b. The entire meal-offering is mixed with oil. If the Torah nonetheless states, "and from its oil," it is to teach us that the *kometz* must be taken from the oiliest part (*Mizrachi; Sifsei Chachamim*).

2. *Toras Kohanim, parshasa* 2:5. Had the verse said, "from *its* fine flour and from its oil," it would have been clear that it would be referring to the meal-offering mentioned at the beginning of the verse. If the verse nonetheless states "of the meal-offering" explicitly, it is to stress the definite article "the" — the threefingersful must be taken from a single, clearly defined, meal-offering, not from a mixture (*Be'er Yitzchak*).

3. *Toras Kohanim, parshasa* 2:5; *Sotah* 14b.

4. Above 2:2. See Rashi there and to 2:1.

5. The verse could have been read, "In a holy place in the Courtyard of the Tent of Meeting," without "holy place" being set off from "Courtyard." The verse would then have implied that some places in the Courtyard are holy, while others are not. This is not true, however, for the entire Courtyard is holy. The verse is read, "In a holy place, in the Courtyard of the Tent of Meeting" — "Courtyard of the Tent of Meeting" *is* the "holy place" (*Gur Aryeh*).

6. *Menachos* 55a. The Torah has already prohibited that which is leavened to be offered on the *Mizbe'ach*

מֵאִשֵּׁי קָדֶשׁ קָדָשִׁים הוּא כַּחַטָּאת
וְכָאָשָׁם: יא כָּל־זָכָר בִּבְנֵי אַהֲרֹן
יֹאכֲלֶנָּה חָק־עוֹלָם לְדֹרֹתֵיכֶם
מֵאִשֵּׁי יהוה כֹּל אֲשֶׁר־יִגַּע בָּהֶם
יִקְדָּשׁ:

from My fire-offerings; it is most holy, like the sin-offering and like the guilt-offering. ¹¹ Every male of the children of Aaron shall eat it, an eternal portion for your generations, from the fire-offerings of HASHEM; whatever touches them shall become holy.

──────────── אונקלוס ────────────

מִקֻּרְבָּנַי קֹדֶשׁ קוּדְשִׁין הִיא כְּחַטָּאתָא וְכַאֲשָׁמָא: יא כָּל דְּכוּרָא בִּבְנֵי אַהֲרֹן יֵכְלִנַּהּ קְיָם עָלַם לְדָרֵיכוֹן מִקֻּרְבָּנַיָּא דַּיָי כֹּל דְּיִקְרַב בְּהוֹן יִתְקַדָּשׁ:

──────────── רש"י ────────────

בחטאת וכאשם. מנחת חוטא הרי היא כחטאת, לפיכך קמצה שלא לשמה פסולה. מנחת נדבה הרי היא כאשם, לפיכך קמצה שלא לשמה כשרה (ת"כ פרק ג:ד; זבחים יא.; מנחות ב:): **(יא) כל זכר.** אפי׳ בעל מום. למה נאמר, אם לאכילה הרי כבר אמור לחם אלהיו

מִקְדְּשֵׁי הַקֳּדָשִׁים וגו׳ (להלן כא:כב). אלא לרבות בעלי מומין למחלוקת (ת"כ שם ה; זבחים קב.): **בל אשר יגע וגו׳.** קדשים קלים או חולין שנגעו בה ויבלעו ממנה: **יקדש.** להיות כמוהו שאם פסולה יפסלו ואם כשרה יאכלו כחומר המנחה (ת"כ פרק ג:ו; זבחים צז:):

──────────── RASHI ELUCIDATED ────────────

□ כַּחַטָּאת וְכָאָשָׁם — LIKE THE SIN-OFFERING AND LIKE THE GUILT-OFFERING. מִנְחַת חוֹטֵא הֲרֵי הִיא כַּחַטָּאת — The meal-offering of a sinner¹ is thus like the sin-offering; לְפִיכָךְ — therefore, קָמְצָה שֶׁלֹּא לִשְׁמָהּ — if he scooped the threefingersful from it not for its sake, i.e., without conscious intent that it is being done for the sake of the meal-offering of a sinner, פְּסוּלָה — it is invalid. מִנְחַת נְדָבָה הֲרֵי הִיא כָּאָשָׁם — A voluntary meal-offering is thus like the guilt-offering; לְפִיכָךְ — therefore, קָמְצָה שֶׁלֹּא לִשְׁמָהּ — if he scooped the threefingersful from it not for its sake, ²כְּשֵׁרָה — it is valid.²

11. כָּל זָכָר — EVERY MALE. אֲפִילוּ בַּעַל מוּם — Even one who has a blemish which disqualifies him from participating in the offering service. לָמָּה נֶאֱמַר — Why is this stated? אִם לַאֲכִילָה — If for eating, i.e., if it is stated to teach us that a blemished Kohen may eat of the meal-offering, הֲרֵי כְּבָר אָמוּר — it has already been stated, ³לֶחֶם אֱלֹהָיו מִקָּדְשֵׁי הַקֳּדָשִׁים וְגוֹמֵר — "the bread of his God, from the holy of holies, etc."³ אֶלָּא — Rather, the verse is meant לְרַבּוֹת בַּעֲלֵי מוּמִין — to include those who are blemished ⁴לְמַחֲלוֹקֶת — for apportioning.⁴

□ כָּל אֲשֶׁר יִגַּע וְגוֹמֵר — WHATEVER TOUCHES, ETC. קָדָשִׁים קַלִּים — Holies of the lesser degree of sanctity אוֹ חֻלִּין — or that which is not holy שֶׁנָּגְעוּ בָהּ — which will come into contact with it וְיִבְלְעוּ מִמֶּנָּה — and absorb of it,⁵

□ יִקְדָּשׁ — SHALL BECOME HOLY לִהְיוֹת כָּמוֹהָ — to become like it: שֶׁאִם פְּסוּלָה — So that if it is invalid, יִפָּסְלוּ — they will become invalid; וְאִם כְּשֵׁרָה — and if it is valid, יֵאָכְלוּ — they shall be eaten ⁶כְּחוֹמֶר הַמִּנְחָה — with the stringencies of the meal-offering.⁶

(above 2:11). חֶלְקָם, "their share," is juxtaposed here with a repetition of that commandment to teach that the prohibition also applies to the remainder of the flour, which is eaten by the Kohanim (Minchas Yehudah; Sifsei Chachamim).

1. See 5:11-13 above.

2. Toras Kohanim, perek 3:4; Zevachim 11a; Menachos 2b. The Torah compares the meal-offering to these two offerings whose laws differ from each other to teach us that some meal-offerings share the law of the sin-offering, while others share the law of the guilt-offering (Be'er Mayim Chaim).

3. Below 21:22. That verse reads in full, "The bread of his God, from the holy of holies and from the holies, he shall eat."

4. Toras Kohanim, perek 3:5; Zevachim 102a. Not only may a blemished Kohen eat of the offerings, but he also receives a share with the other members of his family when it is their turn to serve in the Beis HaMikdash.

5. The verse could have said כָּל אֲשֶׁר תִּגַּע, "whatever it will touch," with the feminine verb תִּגַּע indicating that the feminine מִנְחָה, "meal-offering," is the subject of the verse. Instead, the verse is written with the objects being touched by the meal-offering as the subject of the sentence. The Torah does this to allow the use of בָּהֶם, "in them," to imply that the sanctity of the meal-offering transfers to the objects it touches only if some of the meal-offering is absorbed "in them." (See Korban Aharon. See also Malbim and Mishmeres HaKodesh for alternative approaches to understanding this Rashi.)

6. Toras Kohanim, perek 3:6; Zevachim 97b. If something absorbs some of the meal-offering, it takes on the character of the meal-offering. If the meal-offering had become disqualified, that portion of another offering which absorbs of it also becomes disqualified. If the meal-offering was valid, the same restrictions of time

67 / VAYIKRA/LEVITICUS — PARASHAS TZAV

12 HASHEM spoke to Moses, saying: **13** This is the offering of Aaron and his sons, which each shall offer to HASHEM on the day he is inaugurated: a tenth of an ephah of fine flour as a meal-offering; continually, half of it in the morning and half of it in the afternoon. **14** It should be made on a pan with oil, scalded shall you bring it; repeated bakings, a meal-offering of crumbs,

יב וַיְדַבֵּר יהוה אֶל־מֹשֶׁה לֵּאמֹר:
יג זֶה קָרְבַּן אַהֲרֹן וּבָנָיו אֲשֶׁר־יַקְרִיבוּ לַיהוה בְּיוֹם הִמָּשַׁח אֹתוֹ עֲשִׂירִת הָאֵפָה סֹלֶת מִנְחָה תָּמִיד מַחֲצִיתָהּ בַּבֹּקֶר וּמַחֲצִיתָהּ בָּעָרֶב:
יד עַל־מַחֲבַת בַּשֶּׁמֶן תֵּעָשֶׂה מֻרְבֶּכֶת תְּבִיאֶנָּה תֻּפִינֵי מִנְחַת פִּתִּים

— אונקלוס —

יב וּמַלִּיל יְיָ עִם מֹשֶׁה לְמֵימָר: יג דֵּין קָרְבַּן אַהֲרֹן וּבְנוֹהִי דִּי יְקָרְבוּן קֳדָם יְיָ בְּיוֹמָא דִירַבּוֹן יָתֵהּ חַד מִן עַסְרָא בִּתְלַת סְאִין סֻלְתָּא מִנְחָתָא תְּדִירָא פַּלְגוּתַהּ בְּצַפְרָא וּפַלְגוּתַהּ בְּרַמְשָׁא: יד עַל מַסְרֵיתָא בִּמְשַׁח תִּתְעֲבֵד רְבִיכָא תַיְתִנַהּ תּוּפִינֵי מִנְחַת בְּצוּעִין

— רש"י —

(יג) זֶה קָרְבַּן אַהֲרֹן וּבָנָיו. אַף הֶהֶדְיוֹטוֹת מַקְרִיבִין עֲשִׂירִית הָאֵיפָה בְּיוֹם שֶׁהֵן מִתְחַנְּכִין לַעֲבוֹדָה אֲבָל כֹּהֵן גָּדוֹל בְּכָל יוֹם שֶׁנֶּאֱמַר מִנְחָה תָּמִיד וְגוֹ', וְהַכֹּהֵן הַמָּשִׁיחַ תַּחְתָּיו מִבָּנָיו וְגוֹ' חָק עוֹלָם (ת"כ פרשתא ג:א־ג; מנחות נא:): **(יד) מֻרְבֶּכֶת.** חֲלוּטָה בְּרוֹתְחִין כָּל צָרְכָּהּ (ת"כ פרק ד:ו): **תֻּפִינֵי.** אֲפוּיָה אֲפִיּוֹת הַרְבֵּה, שֶׁאַחַר חֲלִיטָתָהּ אוֹפָה בַּתַּנּוּר וּמַחֲזִירָהּ בַּמַּחֲבַת (מנחות נ:): **מִנְחַת פִּתִּים.** מְלַמֵּד שֶׁטְּעוּנָה פְתִיתָה. וְלֹא פְתִיתָה מַמָּשׁ אֶלָּא כּוֹפְלָהּ לִשְׁנַיִם וְחוֹזֵר וְכוֹפְלָהּ לְאַרְבָּעָה וְאֵינוֹ מַבְדִּיל, וְכֵן מַקְטִיר לָאִשִּׁים [ת"כ שם; מנחות עה:]:

— RASHI ELUCIDATED —

13. זֶה קָרְבַּן אַהֲרֹן וּבָנָיו — **THIS IS THE OFFERING OF AARON AND HIS SONS.** אַף הֶהֶדְיוֹטוֹת — **The common Kohanim, too,** מַקְרִיבִין עֲשִׂירִית הָאֵיפָה — **offer a tenth of an** *ephah* **of** flour as a meal-offering בְּיוֹם שֶׁהֵן מִתְחַנְּכִין לַעֲבוֹדָה — **on the day that they are initiated to the** Temple service.[1] אֲבָל כֹּהֵן גָּדוֹל בְּכָל יוֹם — **But the Kohen Gadol brings such an offering every day,** שֶׁנֶּאֱמַר — **as it says:** ,,מִנְחָה תָּמִיד,, — **"a meal-offering, continually, etc."** [2] ,,וְהַכֹּהֵן הַמָּשִׁיחַ תַּחְתָּיו מִבָּנָיו וְגוֹמֵר חָק עוֹלָם,, — **"The Kohen from among his sons who is anointed in his place, etc., an eternal decree."**[2]

14. מֻרְבֶּכֶת — **This means** חֲלוּטָה בְּרוֹתְחִין — **scalded with boiling water** [3] כָּל צָרְכָּהּ — **all that it needs.**[3]

□ תֻּפִינֵי — **REPEATED BAKINGS.** אֲפוּיָה אֲפִיּוֹת הַרְבֵּה — **It was baked many bakings,** שֶׁאַחַר חֲלִיטָתָהּ — **for after its scalding** אוֹפָה בַּתַּנּוּר — **he bakes it in the oven** [4] וְחוֹזֵר וּמַטְגְּנָהּ בַּמַּחֲבַת — **and then fries it in the pan.**[4]

□ מִנְחַת פִּתִּים — **A MEAL-OFFERING OF CRUMBS.** מְלַמֵּד שֶׁטְּעוּנָה פְתִיתָה — **This teaches us that it requires crumbling.** {וְלֹא פְתִיתָה מַמָּשׁ — **But not actual crumbling** בְּצִיעִין וּפֵרוּרִין — **into pieces and crumbs,** לְפִי שֶׁאֵינָהּ נִקְמֶצֶת — **since it is not subject to scooping.** אֶלָּא כּוֹפְלָהּ לִשְׁנַיִם — **Rather, he folds it in two,** וְחוֹזֵר וְכוֹפְלָהּ לְאַרְבָּעָה — **then he folds it again into four,** שְׁתִי וָעֵרֶב — **vertically and horizontally,** וְאֵינוֹ מַבְדִּיל — **but he does not separate** it into pieces.[5] וְכֵן מַקְטִיר לָאִשִּׁים — **And so he makes** it go up in smoke on the *Mizbe'ach* fires.}[5]

---

and place which apply to the meal-offering apply to that which absorbed of it.

1. "His sons" refers to all Kohanim, not only to those sons of Aaron who succeed him in the office of Kohen Gadol (*Gur Aryeh*).

2. *Toras Kohanim*, *parshasa* 3:1-3; *Menachos* 51b. Our verse begins by referring to a meal-offering brought on the day of a Kohen's inauguration. But it goes on to refer to "a continual meal-offering," which implies a meal-offering brought regularly. Rashi explains that the verse speaks of two different meal-offerings. The "continual meal-offering" is that brought by the Kohen Gadol each day. Rashi cites verse 15 in support of this, for it explicitly refers to the meal-offering of the Kohen Gadol as an "eternal decree," i.e., an offering that is brought continually. But the meal-offering brought on the day of inauguration is brought not only by the Kohen Gadol, but by "Aaron *and his sons,*" i.e., all Kohanim (see *Mesiach Ilmim; Nachalas Yaakov; Be'er Yitzchak*).

3. *Toras Kohanim*, *perek* 4:6. The meal-offering of the Kohanim was scalded in water, as stated by Rashi to *Menachos* 53a. *Shitah Mekubetzes* to *Menachos* 78a notes that the comment of Rashi there, which seems to indicate that it was scalded in oil, is based on a printer's error (*Shaarei Aharon*).

4. *Menachos* 50b.

5. *Toras Kohanim*, *perek* 4:6; *Menachos* 75b.

you shall offer it as a satisfying aroma to HASHEM. **15** *The Kohen from among his sons who is anointed in his place shall perform it; it is an eternal decree for* HASHEM; *it shall be caused to go up in smoke in its entirety.* **16** *Every meal-offering of a Kohen is to be an entirety; it shall not be eaten.*

17 HASHEM *spoke to Moses, saying:* **18** *Speak to Aaron and his sons, saying: This is the law of the sin-offering; in the place where the olah-offering is slaughtered shall the sin-offering be slaughtered, before* HASHEM *— it is most holy.* **19** *The Kohen who makes it into a sin-offering may eat it; it shall be eaten in a holy place:*

טו תַּקְרִיב רֵיחַ־נִיחֹחַ לַיהוָה: וְהַכֹּהֵן הַמָּשִׁיחַ תַּחְתָּיו מִבָּנָיו יַעֲשֶׂה אֹתָהּ חָק־עוֹלָם לַיהוָה כָּלִיל תָּקְטָר: טז וְכָל־מִנְחַת כֹּהֵן כָּלִיל תִּהְיֶה לֹא תֵאָכֵל:

יז וַיְדַבֵּר יְהוָה אֶל־מֹשֶׁה לֵּאמֹר: יח דַּבֵּר אֶל־אַהֲרֹן וְאֶל־בָּנָיו לֵאמֹר זֹאת תּוֹרַת הַחַטָּאת בִּמְקוֹם אֲשֶׁר תִּשָּׁחֵט הָעֹלָה תִּשָּׁחֵט הַחַטָּאת לִפְנֵי יְהוָה קֹדֶשׁ קָדָשִׁים הִוא: יט הַכֹּהֵן הַמְחַטֵּא אֹתָהּ יֹאכְלֶנָּה בְּמָקוֹם קָדֹשׁ

——— אונקלוס ———

תְּקָרֵב לְאִתְקַבָּלָא בְּרַעֲוָא קֳדָם יְיָ: טו וְכַהֲנָא דְיִתְרַבָּא תְּחוֹתוֹהִי מִבְּנוֹהִי יַעְבֵּד יָתַהּ קְיָם עָלָם קֳדָם יְיָ גְּמִיר גְּמִיר תִּתַּסָּק: טז וְכָל מִנְחָתָא דְכַהֲנָא גְּמִיר תְּהֵי לָא תִתְאֲכֵל: יז וּמַלִּיל יְיָ עִם מֹשֶׁה לְמֵימָר: יח מַלֵּל עִם אַהֲרֹן וְעִם בְּנוֹהִי לְמֵימַר דָּא אוֹרַיְתָא דְחַטָּאתָא בְּאַתְרָא דִּי תִתְנְכֵס עֲלָתָא תִּתְנְכֵס חַטָּאתָא קֳדָם יְיָ קֹדֶשׁ קוּדְשִׁין הִיא: יט כַּהֲנָא דִמְכַפַּר יָתַהּ (נ"א בְּדַמַּהּ) יֵכְלִנַּהּ בַּאֲתַר קַדִּישׁ

——— רש"י ———

(טו) הַמָּשִׁיחַ תַּחְתָּיו מִבָּנָיו. הַמָּשִׁיחַ מִבָּנָיו תַּחְתָּיו: כָּלִיל תִּהְיֶה. כֻּלָּהּ שָׁוֶה לַגָּבוֹהַּ: (יט) הַמְחַטֵּא אֹתָהּ. הָעוֹבֵד עֲבוֹדָתֶיהָ, שֶׁהִיא נַעֲשֵׂית חַטָּאת עַל יָדוֹ: הַמְחַטֵּא אֹתָהּ יֹאכְלֶנָּה. הָרָאוּי תָּקְטָר. אֵין נִקְמֶצֶת לִהְיוֹת שְׁיָרֶיהָ נֶאֱכָלִין אֶלָּא כֻלָּהּ כָּלִיל, וְכֵן: (טז) כָּל מִנְחַת כֹּהֵן. שֶׁל נְדָבָה: כָּלִיל תִּהְיֶה. שֶׁל נְדָבָה כָּלִיל, לַעֲבוֹדָה, יָצָא טָמֵא בִּשְׁעַת זְרִיקַת דָּמִים שֶׁאֵינוֹ חוֹלֵק בַּבָּשָׂר.

——— RASHI ELUCIDATED ———

15. הַמָּשִׁיחַ תַּחְתָּיו מִבָּנָיו — הַמָּשִׁיחַ — This means **the anointed one** מִבָּנָיו — **from among his sons** תַּחְתָּיו — **who is in his stead.**[1]

□ כָּלִיל תָּקְטָר — IT SHALL BE CAUSED TO GO UP IN SMOKE IN ITS ENTIRETY. אֵין נִקְמֶצֶת — It is not scooped לִהְיוֹת שְׁיָרֶיהָ נֶאֱכָלִין — **for its remainder to be eaten,** as is the meal-offering of a non-Kohen. אֶלָּא — Rather, כֻּלָּהּ כָּלִיל — **it is burned in its entirety.** וְכֵן — **And likewise,**

16. כָּל מִנְחַת כֹּהֵן — EVERY MEAL-OFFERING OF A KOHEN שֶׁל נְדָבָה — **that is voluntary.**[2]

□ כָּלִיל תִּהְיֶה — IS TO BE AN ENTIRETY. {כָּלִיל — The word כָּלִיל implies,} כֻּלָּהּ — **all of it** שָׁוֶה לַגָּבוֹהַּ — **is equally** offered **to** the One Who **is on high.**[3]

19. הַמְחַטֵּא אֹתָהּ — WHO MAKES IT INTO A SIN-OFFERING. This means הָעוֹבֵד עֲבוֹדָתֶיהָ — **who performs its services,** שֶׁהִיא נַעֲשֵׂית חַטָּאת עַל יָדוֹ — **so that it becomes a sin-offering through his agency.**[4]

□ הַמְחַטֵּא אֹתָהּ יֹאכְלֶנָּה — WHO MAKES IT INTO A SIN-OFFERING MAY EAT IT. This means הָרָאוּי לַעֲבוֹדָה — **one who is fit for the service.** יָצָא טָמֵא — This excludes one who was impure בִּשְׁעַת זְרִיקַת דָּמִים — **at the time of the sprinkling of the blood,** שֶׁאֵינוֹ חוֹלֵק בַּבָּשָׂר — **that he does not take a share in**

---

1. The *Gemara* (*Menachos* 51b) states that if a Kohen Gadol dies and his successor has not yet been appointed, his son brings the daily meal-offering of the Kohen Gadol. This law is derived there from our verse, which the Talmud reads: וְהַכֹּהֵן הַמָּשִׁיחַ, "And the Kohen who is anointed, תַּחְתָּיו, in his place, מִבָּנָיו יַעֲשֶׂה אֹתָהּ, one of his sons shall perform it." Rashi explains that this is not the simple meaning of the verse. On its simplest level, the verse is not speaking of a situation in which the Kohen Gadol has died. It is stating the general rule: The Kohen from among Aaron's sons who is anointed in his stead shall perform the service of the daily meal-offering.

2. "Every meal-offering of a Kohen is to be an entirety" does not refer only to obligatory offerings such as the one of the previous verse, but even to voluntary offerings (*Mizrachi*).

3. The verse uses כָּלִיל which has the sense of כָּל, "all" or "entirety," but it does not state explicitly what is to be done with the whole of the offering. Rashi explains that all of it is to be offered to God (*Minchas Yehudah; Sifsei Chachamim*).

4. Elsewhere, similar verbs mean to sprinkle (e.g., below 14:52). The word הַמְחַטֵּא could have been understood in this sense here, for the blood of the

in the Courtyard of the Tent of Meeting. ²⁰ *Whatever touches its flesh shall become holy; and if there will have been sprinkled from its blood on the garment, that*

תֵּאָכֵל בַּחֲצַר אֹהֶל מוֹעֵד: כֹּל אֲשֶׁר־יִגַּע בִּבְשָׂרָהּ יִקְדָּשׁ וַאֲשֶׁר יִזֶּה מִדָּמָהּ עַל־הַבֶּגֶד אֲשֶׁר

─────────── אונקלוס ───────────

תִּתְאֲכֵל בְּדָרַת מַשְׁכַּן זִמְנָא: ככֹּל דִּי יִקְרַב בְּבִסְרַהּ יִתְקַדָּשׁ וְדִי יַדִּי מִדְּמַהּ עַל לְבוּשׁ דִּי

─────────── רש"י ───────────

(כב) **כל אשר יגע בבשרה.** כָּל דָּבָר אוֹכֶל אֲשֶׁר יִגַּע וְיִבְלַע מִמֶּנָּה. **יקדש.** לִהְיוֹת כָּמוֹהָ

ואשר יזה מדמה על הבגד. וְאִם הֻזָּה מִדָּמָהּ עַל הַבֶּגֶד אוֹתוֹ מְקוֹם הַדָּם שֶׁבַּבֶּגֶד אֲשֶׁר יָזָה עָלָיו תְּכַבֵּס בְּתוֹךְ הָעֲזָרָה (ת"כ פרק ו:ז; זבחים לג:):

וְאִי אֶפְשַׁר לוֹמַר שְׁאָר כֹּהֲנִים שֶׁהֲרֵי נֶאֱמַר לְמַטָּה כָּל זָכָר בַּכֹּהֲנִים יֹאכַל אֹתָהּ (להלן פסוק כב; זבחים לח:-לט.): **אם פסולה תפסל** וְאִם הִיא כְשֵׁרָה תֵּאָכֵל כַחוֹמֶר שֶׁבָּהּ (ת"כ פרשתא ד:ו; זבחים זז:):

─────────── RASHI ELUCIDATED ───────────

שְׁאוֹסֵר שְׁאָר כֹּהֲנִים בַּאֲכִילָתָהּ חוּץ – **It is impossible to say** וְאִי אֶפְשַׁר לוֹמַר – *the flesh* of the offering. מִן הַזּוֹרֵק דָּמָהּ – that [the verse] forbids the rest of the Kohanim from eating it, other than the one who sprinkles its blood, שֶׁהֲרֵי נֶאֱמַר לְמַטָּה – for it says below,[1,2] – "כָּל זָכָר בַּכֹּהֲנִים יֹאכַל אֹתָהּ" "every male among the Kohanim may eat it."[1,2]

20. כֹּל אֲשֶׁר יִגַּע בִּבְשָׂרָהּ – WHATEVER TOUCHES ITS FLESH. כָּל דְּבַר אוֹכֶל – Any foodstuff אֲשֶׁר יִגַּע וְיִבְלַע מִמֶּנָּה – which will touch and absorb of it,[3]

□ יִקְדָּשׁ – SHALL BECOME HOLY לִהְיוֹת כָּמוֹהָ – to become like it: אִם פְּסוּלָה – If [the sin-offering] is invalid, תִּפָּסֵל – [that which absorbs of it] becomes invalid; וְאִם הִיא כְשֵׁרָה – and if [the sin-offering] is valid, תֵּאָכֵל כַחוֹמֶר שֶׁבָּהּ – it shall be eaten with the stringency of [the sin-offering].[4]

□ וַאֲשֶׁר יִזֶּה מִדָּמָהּ עַל הַבֶּגֶד – This means וְאִם הֻזָּה מִדָּמָהּ – if[5] there will have been sprinkled[6] from its blood[7] "עַל הַבֶּגֶד" – "on the garment," אוֹתוֹ מְקוֹם הַדָּם – that place of blood שֶׁבַּבֶּגֶד – on the garment, אֲשֶׁר יָזָה עָלָיו – that on which it will be sprinkled, i.e., the garment, "תְּכַבֵּס" – "you shall launder" בְּתוֹךְ הָעֲזָרָה – inside the Courtyard of the *Beis HaMikdash*.[8]

─────────────────────

sin-offering is sprinkled. Rashi explains that הַמְחַטֵּא of our verse is a participle derived from the noun חַטָּאת, not from the verb חטא.

1. Below v. 22.
2. *Zevachim* 98b-99a.
3. The verse could have said, כָּל אֲשֶׁר יִגַּע בָּהּ, "whatever touches it." The verse uses instead, כָּל אֲשֶׁר יִגַּע בִּבְשָׂרָהּ, "whatever touches its flesh," to imply contact which is more than superficial (*Nachalas Yaakov*; *Sifsei Chachamim*).
4. *Toras Kohanim, parshasa* 4:6; *Zevachim* 97b. See note 6 to v. 11 above.
5. Rashi points out that וַאֲשֶׁר here means "if," not "and that which" or "whatever," as it does further on in the verse. "And that which" would seem to say that the garment ought to be splashed with the blood of the sin-offering. The verse certainly does not mean this (*Gur Aryeh*; *Sifsei Chachamim*).
6. *Leshon Chaim* explains a few grammatical points, necessary for an understanding of Rashi's comments to the two appearances of יזה in our verse:
(a) Verbal roots that begin with the letter נ are classified as פ"נ verbs, i.e., the first root letter (called the פ' הַפֹּעַל) is a נ. In the simple *kal* conjugation, the נ is dropped in the future tense and a *dagesh* is placed in the second root letter (ע' הַפֹּעַל). Thus, for example, the *kal*, future, third person masculine singular of נפל, "to fall," is יִפֹּל,

"he will fall" (11:32 below).
Verbal roots that end with the letter ה are classified as ל"ה verbs, i.e., the last root letter (ל' הַפֹּעַל) is a ה. In the *kal*, future tense, the middle root letter is vowelized with a *segol*. Thus, for example, the *kal*, future, third person masculine singular of קנה, "to buy," is יִקְנֶה, "he will buy" (22:11 below).
The root נזה, "to sprinkle," falls into the classifications of both פ"נ and ל"ה. Thus, in the *kal*, future tense, the נ is dropped and the ו takes a *dagesh* and a *segol*; the third person masculine singular is then יִזֶּה, which appears twice in our verse.
(b) In the *kal*, the verb נזה is intransitive, passive in meaning although active in form. Thus, יִזֶּה does not mean "he will sprinkle," but "he (or, as in our verse, "it") will be sprinkled."
(c) In the *hifil* conjugation, future tense, פ"נ ל"ה verbs take the same vowels as in the *kal*, except that the first root letter takes a *patach* instead of a *chirik*.
(d) In the *hifil*, the verb נזה is transitive and active. Thus, יַזֶּה (16:14 below) means, "he will sprinkle."
7. The verse cannot mean "he who will sprinkle from its blood," for two reasons: (a) If such were the meaning the word would be vowelized with a *patach* [see part (d) of previous note]; and (b) the object of the verb תְּכַבֵּס, "you shall launder," can only be a cloth but not a person (*Sefer Zikaron*).
8. *Toras Kohanim, perek* 6:7; *Zevachim* 93b.

יִזֶּ֣ה עָלֶ֔יהָ תְּכַבֵּ֖ס בְּמָק֣וֹם קָדֹֽשׁ׃
כא וּכְלִי־חֶ֛רֶשׂ אֲשֶׁ֥ר תְּבֻשַּׁל־בּ֖וֹ יִשָּׁבֵ֑ר וְאִם־בִּכְלִ֤י נְחֹ֙שֶׁת֙ בֻּשָּׁ֔לָה וּמֹרַ֥ק
כב וְשֻׁטַּ֖ף בַּמָּֽיִם׃ כָּל־זָכָ֥ר בַּכֹּהֲנִ֖ים יֹאכַ֣ל אֹתָ֑הּ קֹ֥דֶשׁ קָֽדָשִׁ֖ים הִֽוא׃

on which it will be sprinkled, you shall launder in a holy place. [21] *An earthenware vessel in which it was cooked must be broken; but if it was cooked in a copper vessel, it should be scoured and rinsed in water.* [22] *Every male among the Kohanim may eat it; it is most holy.*

— אונקלוס —

יַדִּי עֲלַהּ תְּחַוַּר בַּאֲתַר קַדִּישׁ: כא וּמָן דַּחֲסַף דִּי תִתְבַּשַּׁל בֵּהּ יִתְּבָר וְאִם בְּמָנָא דִּנְחָשָׁא תִּתְבַּשַּׁל וְיִתְמְרֵק וְיִשְׁתַּטַּף בְּמַיָּא: כב כָּל דְּכוּרָא בְּכַהֲנַיָּא יֵכוּל יָתַהּ קֹדֶשׁ קוּדְשִׁין הִיא:

— רש"י —

אֲשֶׁר יִזֶּה. יְהֵא נִזֶּה כְּמוֹ וְלֹא יִטֶּה לָאָרֶץ מִנְלָם (איוב טו:כט) יְהֵא נָטוּי: **(כא) יִשָּׁבֵר.** לְפִי שֶׁהַבְּלִיעָה שֶׁנִּבְלַעַת בּוֹ נַעֲשֶׂה נוֹתָר, וְהוּא הַדִּין לְכָל הַקָּדָשִׁים (ע"ז עו.): **וּמֹרַק.** לְשׁוֹן תַּמְרוּקֵי הַנָּשִׁים (אסתר ב:יב) אשקור"ר בלע"ז: **וּמֹרַק וְשֻׁטַּף.** לִפְלוֹט אֶת בְּלִיעָתוֹ אֲבָל כְּלִי חֶרֶס לִמֶּדְךָ הַכָּתוּב כָּאן שֶׁאֵינוֹ יוֹצֵא מִידֵי דָפְיוֹ לְעוֹלָם (פסחים ל:): **(כב) כָּל זָכָר בַּכֹּהֲנִים יֹאכַל אֹתָהּ.** הָא לָמַדְתָּ שֶׁהַמְחַטֵּא אוֹתָהּ הָאָמוּר לְמַעְלָה (פסוק יט) לֹא לְהוֹצִיא שְׁאָר הַכֹּהֲנִים אֶלָּא לְהוֹצִיא אֶת שֶׁאֵינוֹ רָאוּי לְחִטּוּי:

RASHI ELUCIDATED

☐ **אֲשֶׁר יִזֶּה** — THAT [ON WHICH] IT WILL BE SPRINKLED. The word יִזֶּה means יְהֵא נִזֶּה — will be sprinkled, like יִטֶּה in, "בְּמוֹ ,,וְלֹא יִטֶּה לָאָרֶץ מִנְלָם — their fulfillment will not be stooped to the ground,"[1] which means, יְהֵא נָטוּי — will be stooped.[2]

21. יִשָּׁבֵר — MUST BE BROKEN. לְפִי שֶׁהַבְּלִיעָה — Because the absorption שֶׁנִּבְלַעַת בּוֹ — that is absorbed in it, i.e., the absorbed meat juices, נַעֲשֶׂה נוֹתָר — becomes *nosar*.[3] וְהוּא הַדִּין לְכָל הַקֳּדָשִׁים — The same law as applies to absorbing the juices of a sin-offering holds true for all holies, i.e., offerings.[4]

☐ **וּמֹרַק** — IT SHOULD BE SCOURED. לְשׁוֹן ,,תַּמְרוּקֵי הַנָּשִׁים[5] — This is related to תַּמְרוּקֵי in, "cosmetics of women."[5] — אשקורי"ר בְּלַעַ"ז — *Escurer* in Old French.[6]

☐ **וּמֹרַק וְשֻׁטַּף** — IT SHOULD BE SCOURED AND RINSED לִפְלוֹט אֶת בְּלִיעָתוֹ — to expel its absorption. אֲבָל בִּכְלִי חֶרֶס — But with regard to an earthenware vessel, לִמֶּדְךָ הַכָּתוּב כָּאן — the verse teaches you here שֶׁאֵינוֹ יוֹצֵא מִידֵי דָפְיוֹ לְעוֹלָם — that [the vessel] does not ever leave the grasp of its defect,[7] i.e., does not rid itself of its defect, and so must be broken.

22. כָּל זָכָר בַּכֹּהֲנִים יֹאכַל אֹתָהּ — EVERY MALE AMONG THE KOHANIM MAY EAT IT. הָא לָמַדְתָּ — Now then, you have learned שֶׁ,,הַמְחַטֵּא אוֹתָהּ'' — that "the one who makes it into a sin-offering" הָאָמוּר לְמַעְלָה[8] — that is mentioned above[8] לֹא לְהוֹצִיא שְׁאָר הַכֹּהֲנִים — is not meant to exclude the other Kohanim אֶלָּא לְהוֹצִיא אֶת שֶׁאֵינוֹ רָאוּי לְחִטּוּי — but to exclude one who is unfit to perform the

---

1. *Job* 15:29. The root of יִטֶּה is נטה which, like נזה, is a פ"י ל"ה verb.

2. (See note 6 on page 69.) In his preceding comment, which included his remarks on the first אֲשֶׁר יִזֶּה of our verse, Rashi stressed that יִזֶּה has a passive meaning. Here he again points out the passive sense, but also stresses the future aspect of the verb by saying יְהֵא נִזֶּה. Rashi in his preceding comment used a passive form in the past (הֻזָּה). He did not then need to point out the future quality; it is implied by the "if" (אִם) which is Rashi's understanding of אֲשֶׁר. Here, in the second אֲשֶׁר יִזֶּה of our verse, אֲשֶׁר does not mean "if," but "which." That is why Rashi feels he must note the future sense with יְהֵא.
Since נזה in the *kal* appears only twice in the Torah (both times in our verse as יִזֶּה), as distinct from נזה in the *hifil*, Rashi wished to note its nature — active in form, passive in meaning. He supports his point by showing that this is not unique. נטה — in the *kal*, future tense, third person masculine singular — יִטֶּה — is also intransitive, passive in

meaning although active in form.

3. *Nosar* is the meat of an offering that has been left uneaten beyond the time the Torah set for it to be eaten. It is forbidden to eat *nosar* or derive any benefit from it (see *Pesachim* 24a). The juices absorbed by an earthenware vessel will perforce become *nosar* because they will not be eaten within the allotted time. Since they cannot be scoured from earthenware, the vessel must be broken.

4. *Avodah Zarah* 76a.

5. *Esther* 2:12. Both words connote "cleaning" (*Leket Bahir; Lifshuto shel Rashi*).

6. This is the source of the English word "scour." In Modern French "*récurer*" means "to scour" and "*curer*" means "to clean out." Rashi apparently understands תַּמְרוּקֵי הַנָּשִׁים as a kind of cleanser used by women to beautify their skin.

7. *Pesachim* 30b.

8. Verse 19. See Rashi there.

²³ **And any sin-offering from which some blood has been brought to the Tent of Meeting, to effect atonement within the Holy, shall not be eaten; it shall be burned in fire.**

7 ¹ **This is the law of the guilt-offering; it is most holy.** ² **In the place where they shall slaughter the olah-offering shall they slaughter the guilt-offering; and he shall throw its blood upon the Mizbe'ach, all around.**

כג וְכָל־חַטָּאת אֲשֶׁר יוּבָא מִדָּמָהּ אֶל־אֹהֶל מוֹעֵד לְכַפֵּר בַּקֹּדֶשׁ לֹא תֵאָכֵל בָּאֵשׁ תִּשָּׂרֵף:

ז א וְזֹאת תּוֹרַת הָאָשָׁם קֹדֶשׁ קָדָשִׁים הוּא: ב בִּמְקוֹם אֲשֶׁר יִשְׁחֲטוּ אֶת־הָעֹלָה יִשְׁחֲטוּ אֶת־הָאָשָׁם וְאֶת־דָּמוֹ יִזְרֹק עַל־הַמִּזְבֵּחַ סָבִיב:

———————— אונקלוס ————————

כג וְכָל חַטָּאתָא דִּי מִתָּעַל מִדְּמַהּ לְמַשְׁכַּן זִמְנָא לְכַפָּרָא בְקוּדְשָׁא לָא תִתְאֲכֵל בְּנוּרָא תִּתּוֹקָד: א וְדָא אוֹרַיְתָא דַאֲשָׁמָא קֹדֶשׁ קוּדְשִׁין הוּא: ב בְּאַתְרָא דִּי יִכְּסוּן יָת עֲלָתָא יִכְּסוּן יָת אֲשָׁמָא וְיָת דְּמֵהּ יִזְרוֹק עַל מַדְבְּחָא סְחוֹר סְחוֹר:

———————— רש״י ————————

(כג) וכל חטאת וגו׳. אִם הִכְנִיס מִדַּם חַטַּאת הַחִיצוֹנָה לִפְנִים פְּסוּלָה **וכל.** לְרַבּוֹת שְׁאָר קָדָשִׁים (ת״כ פרק ח:א; זבחים פב.): **(א) קדש קדשים הוא.** הוּא קָרֵב וְאֵין תְּמוּרָתוֹ קְרֵבָה (ת״כ פרשתא ה:ב; תמורה יז:): **(ב) וישחטו.** רִבָּה לָנוּ שְׁחִיטוֹת הַרְבֵּה, לְפִי שֶׁמָּצִינוּ אָשָׁם בְּלָבוּר נֶאֱמַר יִשְׁחֲטוּ רַבִּים. וּתְלָאוֹ בְּעוֹלָה לְהָבִיא עוֹלַת צִבּוּר לִצְפוֹן:

———————— RASHI ELUCIDATED ————————

sin-offering service.¹

23. וְכָל חַטָּאת וְגוֹמֵר — AND ANY SIN-OFFERING, ETC. — שֶׁאִם הִכְנִיס מִדַּם חַטָּאת הַחִיצוֹנָה לִפְנִים — That if he brought some of the blood of an exterior sin-offering to the inside of the *Mishkan* or the *Beis HaMikdash*, פְּסוּלָה — it is invalid.[2,3] {וְכָל — AND ANY.³ לְרַבּוֹת שְׁאָר קָדָשִׁים — To include other holies, i.e., offerings.³}

7.

1. קֹדֶשׁ קָדָשִׁים הוּא — IT IS MOST HOLY. הוּא קָרֵב — It is offered, וְאֵין תְּמוּרָתוֹ קְרֵבָה — but its substitute is not offered.⁴

2. {יִשְׁחֲטוּ — THEY SHALL SLAUGHTER. רִבָּה לָנוּ שְׁחִיטוֹת הַרְבֵּה — [The verse] has included many slaughterings.⁵ לְפִי שֶׁמָּצִינוּ אָשָׁם בְּצִבּוּר — Since we have found a guilt-offering brought by the public, נֶאֱמַר ״יִשְׁחֲטוּ״ — it says, "they shall slaughter," in the רַבִּים — plural.⁶ וּתְלָאוֹ בְּעוֹלָה — [The Torah] made it dependent on the *olah*-offering, i.e., the Torah stated the location of slaughtering of the guilt-offering in terms of that of the *olah*-offering, לְהָבִיא עוֹלַת צִבּוּר לַצָּפוֹן — to include an *olah*-offering of the public for slaughtering in the north.⁷}

---

1. He is unfit, because he is impure; but a Kohen who has a blemish may eat from the sin-offering, as Rashi has noted in his comments to verse 11 above, s.v., כָּל זָכָר.

2. The blood of the sin-offering of a common person is sprinkled on the outer *Mizbe'ach* (see 4:30 above). If it was brought into the Sanctuary, the offering is invalid.

3. *Toras Kohanim*, perek 8:1; *Zevachim* 82a.

4. *Toras Kohanim*, parshasa 5:2; *Temurah* 17b. It is forbidden to substitute another animal for an animal which has been designated as an offering. If one does, however, say, "This animal should be brought as an offering instead of this one," the original animal remains sanctified and the substitute also has the sanctity of an offering (see below, 27:9-10). In the case of certain offerings – the *olah*-offering and the peace-offering – the substitute is offered on the *Mizbe'ach*, as well as the original. *"It is most holy"* implies that this is not so with regard to the guilt-offering. The substitute may not be slaughtered or used for work because of its sanctity, but it is not offered on the *Mizbe'ach*. It is allowed to graze until it develops a blemish. Then it is sold. Its sanctity transfers to the money paid for it, and that money is used to purchase voluntary offerings (*Mizrachi; Sifsei Chachamim*).

5. The parallel phrase in *Toras Kohanim* (parshasa 5:3) reads, . . . רִבָּה כָּאן שׁוֹחֲטִים הַרְבֵּה, "[The verse] here has included many slaughterers: even proselytes, even women, even slaves."

6. Rashi's comment seems to in contradict the Talmud (*Temurah* 14a) which states that there are no guilt-offerings brought by the public. Moreover, this comment is not found in most early editions of *Rashi*. Thus, most commentators are of the opinion that this was not written by Rashi, and crept into the text by error. See, however, *Yosef Hallel*, who offers two possible resolutions to the contradiction.

7. Although the Torah has stated that the *olah*-offering of an individual should be slaughtered on the northern side of the *Mizbe'ach* (1:11), it has not specified where an *olah*-offering of the public should be slaughtered. The Torah states the location of the slaughtering of the guilt-offering in terms of the

³ *And he shall offer all of its fat; the fat tail and the fat that covers the innards;* ⁴ *and the two kidneys and the fat that covers them, which is on the flanks; and he shall remove the diaphragm as well as the liver, as well as the kidneys.* ⁵ *The Kohen shall cause them to go up in smoke on the Mizbe'ach, a fire-offering to* HASHEM*; it is a guilt-offering.*

ג וְאֵת כָּל־חֶלְבּוֹ יַקְרִיב מִמֶּנּוּ אֵת הָאַלְיָה וְאֶת־הַחֵלֶב הַמְכַסֶּה אֶת־הַקֶּרֶב: ד וְאֵת שְׁתֵּי הַכְּלָיֹת וְאֶת־הַחֵלֶב אֲשֶׁר עֲלֵיהֶן אֲשֶׁר עַל־הַכְּסָלִים וְאֶת־הַיֹּתֶרֶת עַל־הַכָּבֵד עַל־הַכְּלָיֹת יְסִירֶנָּה: ה וְהִקְטִיר אֹתָם הַכֹּהֵן הַמִּזְבֵּחָה אִשֶּׁה לַיהוה אָשָׁם הוּא:

—————————— אונקלוס ——————————

ג וְיָת כָּל תַּרְבֵּהּ יְקָרֵב מִנֵּהּ יָת אַלְיְתָא וְיָת תַּרְבָּא דְּחָפֵי יָת גַּוָּא: ד וְיָת תַּרְתֵּין כָּלְיָן וְיָת תַּרְבָּא דִּי עֲלֵיהֶן דִּי עַל גִּסְסַיָּא וְיָת חִצְרָא דְעַל כַּבְדָּא עַל כָּלְיָתָא יַעְדִּנַּהּ: ה וְיַסֵּק יָתְהוֹן כַּהֲנָא לְמַדְבְּחָא קֻרְבָּנָא קֳדָם יְיָ אֲשָׁמָא הוּא:

—————————— רש"י ——————————

(ג) וְאֵת כָּל חֶלְבּוֹ וְגוֹ׳. עַד כָּאן לֹא נִתְפָּרְשׁוּ אֵימוּרִין בְּאָשָׁם, לְכָךְ הוּצְרַךְ לְפָרְשָׁם כָּאן, אֲבָל חַטָּאת כְּבָר נִתְפָּרְשָׁה בָּהּ בְּפָרָשַׁת וַיִּקְרָא (לְעֵיל בְּפֶרֶק ד): אֶת הָאַלְיָה. לְפִי שֶׁאָשָׁם אֵינוֹ בָא אֶלָּא אַיִל אוֹ כֶבֶשׂ, וְאַיִל וְכֶבֶשׂ נִתְרַבּוּ בָאַלְיָה (לְעֵיל ג:ט): (ה) אָשָׁם הוּא. עַד שֶׁיִּנָּתֵק שְׁמוֹ מִמֶּנּוּ. לִמֵּד עַל אָשָׁם שֶׁמֵּתוּ בְּעָלָיו אוֹ שֶׁנִּתְכַּפְּרוּ בְעָלָיו, אעַ"פ שֶׁעוֹמֵד לִהְיוֹת דָּמָיו עוֹלָה לְקַיִץ הַמִּזְבֵּחַ, אִם שְׁחָטוֹ סְתָם אֵינוֹ כָּשֵׁר לְעוֹלָה קֹדֶם שֶׁנִּתַּק לִרְעִיָּה. וְאֵינוֹ בָא לְלַמֵּד עַל הָאָשָׁם שֶׁיְּהֵא פָּסוּל שֶׁלֹּא לִשְׁמוֹ:

—————————— RASHI ELUCIDATED ——————————

3. וְאֵת כָּל חֶלְבּוֹ וְגוֹמֵר — AND [HE SHALL OFFER] ALL OF ITS FAT. עַד כָּאן — Up to this point, לֹא נִתְפָּרְשׁוּ אֵימוּרִין בְּאָשָׁם — the specified parts which are to be burned on the *Mizbe'ach* had not been stated explicitly regarding the guilt-offering. לְכָךְ הוּצְרַךְ לְפָרְשָׁם כָּאן — Therefore, [the Torah] needed to state them explicitly here. אֲבָל חַטָּאת — But with regard to the sin-offering, כְּבָר נִתְפָּרְשׁוּ בָהּ — [the specified parts] were already stated explicitly about it בְּפָרָשַׁת וַיִּקְרָא — in *Parashas Vayikra*.[1]

אֶת הָאַלְיָה — THE FAT TAIL. לְפִי שֶׁאָשָׁם אֵינוֹ בָא אֶלָּא אַיִל אוֹ כֶבֶשׂ — Because the guilt-offering can only be a ram or a sheep,[2] וְאַיִל וְכֶבֶשׂ נִתְרַבּוּ בָאַלְיָה — and a ram and a sheep have been increased by the fat tail,[3] i.e., have the fat tail among their specified parts, in addition to the same specified parts as other animal offerings.

5. אָשָׁם הוּא — IT IS A GUILT-OFFERING עַד שֶׁיִּנָּתֵק שְׁמוֹ מִמֶּנּוּ — until its name will be disconnected from it. לִמֵּד עַל אָשָׁם שֶׁמֵּתוּ בְעָלָיו — This teaches us about a guilt-offering whose owner has died,[4] אוֹ שֶׁנִּתְכַּפְּרוּ בְעָלָיו — or whose owner has attained atonement through the offering of another animal,[5] אַף עַל פִּי שֶׁעוֹמֵד — even though it stands לִהְיוֹת דָּמָיו עוֹלָה לְקַיִץ הַמִּזְבֵּחַ — to have its money, i.e., the money gained through its sale, used for an *olah*-offering for the "dessert of the *Mizbe'ach*,"[6] אִם שְׁחָטוֹ סְתָם — if he slaughtered it with no specific intent, אֵינוֹ כָּשֵׁר לְעוֹלָה — it is not valid as an *olah*-offering קֹדֶם שֶׁנִּתַּק לִרְעִיָּה — before it has been disconnected from its status as a guilt-offering by being designated for grazing.[7] וְאֵינוֹ בָא — [The phrase] אָשָׁם הוּא [does not come] לְלַמֵּד עַל הָאָשָׁם — to teach about the guilt-offering שֶׁיְּהֵא פָּסוּל שֶׁלֹּא לִשְׁמוֹ — that it is invalid if it was slaughtered

olah-offering to imply that there is yet another *olah*-offering slaughtered on the north, the *olah*-offering of the public.

1. Above Ch. 4.
2. The difference between אַיִל, "ram," and כֶּבֶשׂ, "sheep," is discussed in note 7 on page 55.
3. Above 3:9.
4. It is a tradition received by Moses at Sinai (*halachah leMoshe miSinai*) that if the owner of the guilt-offering dies before his offering is brought, it is not offered. Instead, it is set out to pasture where it remains until it develops a blemish that disqualifies it from being brought as an offering. The animal is then sold and the proceeds are used to purchase *olah*-offerings as described below (see *Temurah* 18a).

The assertion of *Sifsei Chachamim*, based on *Minchas Yehudah*, that this is so because the owner has attained atonement through his death is questionable, for the law holds true even when the owner sins by his death, i.e., in a case of suicide.

5. This occurs when an animal designated as a guilt-offering has been lost, and another animal was offered in its place before the original animal is found (*Mizrachi; Sifsei Chachamim*). The law mentioned in the previous note regarding what is done with the ownerless guilt-offering applies here as well.

6. See Rashi to 1:2 above and note 11 on page 6.

7. *Temurah* 18a. The apparently superfluous "it is a guilt-offering" teaches us that even though it will never be offered as a guilt-offering, it remains in that state, and can-

73 / VAYIKRA/LEVITICUS — PARASHAS TZAV — 7/6-8

⁶ *Every male among the Kohanim may eat it; it shall be eaten in a holy place, it is most holy.* ⁷ *Like the sin-offering is the guilt-offering, they have the same law; it shall belong to the Kohen who performs its atonement service.* ⁸ *And the Kohen who offers a person's olah-offering*

ו כָּל־זָכָר בַּכֹּהֲנִים יֹאכְלֶנּוּ בְּמָקוֹם
קָדוֹשׁ יֵאָכֵל קֹדֶשׁ קָדָשִׁים הוּא:
ז כַּחַטָּאת כָּאָשָׁם תּוֹרָה אַחַת לָהֶם
הַכֹּהֵן אֲשֶׁר יְכַפֶּר־בּוֹ לוֹ יִהְיֶה:
ח וְהַכֹּהֵן הַמַּקְרִיב אֶת־עֹלַת אִישׁ

──────── אונקלוס ────────

ו כָּל דְּכוּרָא בְכָהֲנַיָּא יֵכְלִנַּהּ בַּאֲתַר קַדִּישׁ יִתְאֲכֵל קֹדֶשׁ קוּדְשִׁין הוּא: ז כְּחַטָּאתָא כַּאֲשָׁמָא אוֹרַיְתָא חֲדָא לְהוֹן כַּהֲנָא דִּי יְכַפֵּר בֵּהּ דִּילֵהּ יְהֵא: ח וְכָהֲנָא דִמְקָרֵב יָת עֲלַת גְּבַר

──────── רש"י ────────

הוּא. בְּתוֹרַת כֹּהֲנִים הוּא נִדְרָשׁ: **(ז) תּוֹרָה אַחַת לָהֶם.** לְעִנְיָן זֶה: **הַכֹּהֵן אֲשֶׁר יְכַפֶּר בּוֹ.** הָרָאוּי לְכַפָּרָה חוֹלֵק בּוֹ, פְּרָט לִטְבוּל יוֹם וּמְחֻסַּר כִּפּוּרִים וְאוֹנֵן (ת"כ פרק ט:א): כְּמוֹ שֶׁדָּרְשׁוּ הוּא הַכָּתוּב בַּחַטָּאת (לעיל ד:כד), לְפִי שֶׁאָשָׁם לֹא נֶאֱמַר בּוֹ אָשָׁם הוּא אֶלָּא לְאַחַר הַקְטָרַת אֵמוּרִין וְהוּא עַצְמוֹ שֶׁלֹּא הוּקְטְרוּ אֵמוּרָיו, כָּשֵׁר (זבחים ט׳): **(ו) קֹדֶשׁ קָדָשִׁים**

──────── RASHI ELUCIDATED ────────

not for its sake, but with the intent that it is slaughtered for the sake of a different kind of offering, כְּמוֹ שֶׁדָּרְשׁוּ "הוּא" הַכָּתוּב בַּחַטָּאת – as they interpreted "it is" which is written about the sin-offering,[1] לְפִי שֶׁאָשָׁם לֹא נֶאֱמַר בּוֹ "אָשָׁם הוּא" אֶלָּא לְאַחַר הַקְטָרַת אֵמוּרִין – because the guilt-offering does not have "it is a guilt-offering" said about it until after the burning of the specified parts, וְהוּא עַצְמוֹ – but [the guilt-offering] itself שֶׁלֹּא הֻקְטְרוּ אֵמוּרָיו – whose specified parts were not burnt on the *Mizbe'ach* ²כָּשֵׁר – is valid.[2]

6. קֹדֶשׁ קָדָשִׁים הוּא – IT IS MOST HOLY. בְּתוֹרַת כֹּהֲנִים הוּא נִדְרָשׁ – This is expounded in *Toras Kohanim*.[3]

7. תּוֹרָה אַחַת לָהֶם – THEY HAVE THE SAME LAW בְּדָבָר זֶה – in this matter:[4]

□ הַכֹּהֵן אֲשֶׁר יְכַפֶּר בּוֹ – THE KOHEN WHO PERFORMS ITS ATONEMENT SERVICE. הָרָאוּי לְכַפָּרָה חוֹלֵק בּוֹ – One who is fit for the performance of the atonement service takes a share in it פְּרָט לִטְבוּל יוֹם – to the exclusion of one who immersed that day,[5] וּמְחֻסַּר כִּפּוּרִים – and one who is lacking atonement,[6] ⁸וְאוֹנֵן – and a mourner on the day of the death of a relative.[7,8]

not be offered as an *olah*-offering, until it has been formally taken out of its state of being a guilt-offering by being handed over for grazing. At this point, although it should be left to graze until it develops a blemish, if it is slaughtered as an *olah*-offering, it is a valid offering.

1. See 4:24 above and Rashi there.

2. *Zevachim* 10b. Although the similar "it is a sin-offering" (4:24) was interpreted as teaching us that the slaughter of the sin-offering must be done for its sake, a parallel interpretation cannot be made here. For "it is a guilt-offering" appears here in the context of placing the specified parts on the *Mizbe'ach*, whereas "it is a sin-offering" appears in the context of slaughtering. Nor can the context here be interpreted as saying that the specified parts must be offered for the sake of the guilt-offering, for as Rashi points out, the offering is accepted even if the specified parts were not burned on the *Mizbe'ach* at all (*Mizrachi; Sifsei Chachamim*).

3. *Toras Kohanim, parshasa* 5:10. The phrase "it is most holy" appears superfluous. The interpretation in *Toras Kohanim* is as follows: "Most holy" tells us to apply this law — which restricts all but male Kohanim from eating the offering — to peace-offerings brought on behalf of the public. "It is" tells us that the law does not apply to thanksgiving-offerings (see below, vv. 11-15) and the

ram brought by a *nazir* at the end of his term of *nezirus* (see *Numbers* 6:17).

4. The matter which follows in the verse and is the subject of Rashi's next comment, but their laws differ in other respects.

5. The purification process for certain types of impurity requires immersion of the purificant in a mikveh, and waiting until sundown. Once the purificant immerses himself in the mikveh, he becomes a טְבוּל יוֹם, literally, one who "immersed that day." Although he no longer transmits impurity to non-sacred objects, he still transmits impurity to offerings and *terumah*. If he is a Kohen, he may not serve in the Temple or partake of offerings or *terumah* until sundown.

6. Some types of impurity require offerings to complete the purification process. In these cases, although the purificant has immersed himself, and sundown has passed, he may not serve in the Temple or partake of offerings until he has brought his own offering for his atonement. One in this state is called מְחֻסַּר כִּפּוּרִים, "lacking atonement."

7. Such a mourner is disqualified from serving in the Temple and from partaking of offerings. See note 2 on page 106.

8. *Toras Kohanim, perek* 9:1.

— the hide of the olah-offering that he offered, to that Kohen, his shall it be. ⁹ Any meal-offering that is baked in the oven and any that is made in a deep pan or upon a shallow pan — it shall belong to the Kohen who offers it; it shall be his. ¹⁰ And any meal-offering that is mixed with oil or that is dry, it shall belong to all of Aaron's sons, every man alike.

¹¹ This is the law of the sacrifice of the peace-offering that one will offer to HASHEM: ¹² If he shall offer it for a thanksgiving-

עוֹר הָעֹלָה אֲשֶׁר הִקְרִיב לַכֹּהֵן לוֹ
יִהְיֶה: ט וְכָל־מִנְחָה אֲשֶׁר תֵּאָפֶה
בַתַּנּוּר וְכָל־נַעֲשָׂה בַמַּרְחֶשֶׁת
וְעַל־מַחֲבַת לַכֹּהֵן הַמַּקְרִיב אֹתָהּ
לוֹ תִהְיֶה: י וְכָל־מִנְחָה בְלוּלָה־
בַשֶּׁמֶן וַחֲרֵבָה לְכָל־בְּנֵי אַהֲרֹן
תִּהְיֶה אִישׁ כְּאָחִיו:

יא שלישי וְזֹאת תּוֹרַת זֶבַח הַשְּׁלָמִים
יב אֲשֶׁר יַקְרִיב לַיהוָה: אִם עַל־תּוֹדָה

— אונקלוס —

מְשַׁךְ עֲלָתָא דִּי יְקָרֵב לְכַהֲנָא דִּילֵהּ יְהֵא: ט וְכָל מִנְחָתָא דִּי תִתְאֲפֵי בְתַנּוּרָא וְכָל דְּתִתְעֲבֵד בִּרְדֻתָּא וְעַל מַסְרֵיתָא לְכַהֲנָא דִמְקָרֵב יָתַהּ דִּילֵהּ תְּהֵא: י וְכָל מִנְחָתָא דְפִילָא בִמְשַׁח וּדְלָא פִילָא לְכָל בְּנֵי אַהֲרֹן תְּהֵי גְּבַר כְּאֲחוּהִי: יא וְדָא אוֹרַיְתָא דְּנִכְסַת קוּדְשַׁיָּא דִּי יְקָרֵב קֳדָם יְיָ: יב אִם עַל תּוֹדְתָא

— רש"י —

(ח) עוֹר הָעוֹלָה אֲשֶׁר הִקְרִיב לַכֹּהֵן לוֹ יִהְיֶה. פְּרָט לִטְבוּל יוֹם וּמְחֻסַּר כִּפּוּרִים וְאוֹנֵן שֶׁאֵינָן חוֹלְקִין בָּעוֹרוֹת (ת"כ שם ה; זבחים קג:): (ט) לַכֹּהֵן הַמַּקְרִיב אֹתָהּ וְגוֹ'. יָכוֹל לוֹ לְבַדּוֹ, ת"ל לְכָל בְּנֵי אַהֲרֹן תִּהְיֶה. יָכוֹל לְכֻלָּן, ת"ל לַכֹּהֵן הַמַּקְרִיב. הָא כֵּיצַד, לְבֵית אָב שֶׁל אוֹתוֹ יוֹם שֶׁמַּקְרִיבִין אוֹתָהּ (ת"כ פרק י:ב): (י) בְּלוּלָה בַשֶּׁמֶן. זוֹ מִנְחַת נְדָבָה: וַחֲרֵבָה. זוֹ מִנְחַת חוֹטֵא וּמִנְחַת קְנָאוֹת שֶׁאֵין בָּהֶן שֶׁמֶן:

— RASHI ELUCIDATED —

8. עוֹר הָעֹלָה אֲשֶׁר הִקְרִיב לַכֹּהֵן לוֹ יִהְיֶה — THE HIDE OF THE *OLAH*-OFFERING THAT HE OFFERED, TO THAT KOHEN, HIS SHALL IT BE, פְּרָט לִטְבוּל יוֹם — to the exclusion of one who immersed that day,[1] וּמְחֻסַּר כִּפּוּרִים — and one who is lacking atonement,[2] וְאוֹנֵן — and a mourner on the day of the death of a relative,[3] שֶׁאֵינָן חוֹלְקִים בָּעוֹרוֹת — that they do not take a share in the hides.[4]

9. לַכֹּהֵן הַמַּקְרִיב אֹתָהּ וְגוֹמֵר — TO THE KOHEN WHO OFFERS IT, ETC. יָכוֹל לוֹ לְבַדּוֹ — One might be able to think that it goes **to him alone.** תַּלְמוּד לוֹמַר — To teach us otherwise, **the verse says,** ,,לְכָל בְּנֵי אַהֲרֹן תִּהְיֶה'' — "It shall belong to all of Aaron's sons." יָכוֹל לְכֻלָּן — One might be able to think on the basis of that verse alone that the meal-offerings go **to all of them.** תַּלְמוּד לוֹמַר — To teach us otherwise, **the verse says,** ,,לַכֹּהֵן הַמַּקְרִיב'' — **"to the Kohen who offers** [it]." הָא כֵּיצַד — How is this?[5] The meal-offering belongs לְבֵית אָב — **to the** officiating **extended family** of Kohanim[6] שֶׁל אוֹתוֹ יוֹם שֶׁמַּקְרִיבִין אוֹתָהּ — **of that day on which they offer** [the meal-offering].[7]

10. בְּלוּלָה בַשֶּׁמֶן — MIXED WITH OIL. זוֹ מִנְחַת נְדָבָה — **This is a voluntary meal-offering.** וַחֲרֵבָה — OR [THAT IS] DRY. זוֹ מִנְחַת חוֹטֵא — **This is the meal-offering of a sinner**[8] וּמִנְחַת קְנָאוֹת — **and the meal-offering of jealousy**[9] שֶׁאֵין בָּהֶן שֶׁמֶן — **which do not have oil in them.**

1. See above, p. 73, note 5.
2. See above, p. 73, note 6.
3. See above, p. 73, note 7.
4. *Toras Kohanim, perek* 9:5; *Zevachim* 103b.
5. How can we reconcile the verse that implies that it belongs only to the Kohen who brings the offering with the verse that implies that it belongs to all of the Kohanim?
6. The term בֵּית אָב, literally, "father's house," means "an extended family." See Rashi to *Exodus* 12:3 and our comments there. The *Kohanim* were divided into twenty-four groups called מִשְׁמָרוֹת, "watches." These were each divided into six family groupings called בָּתֵּי

אָבוֹת, "extended families." Each watch officiated in the *Beis HaMikdash* for one week, twice (or three times) a year. Each extended family officiated for one weekday, with the particular function of each individual in the regular communal offerings being assigned by lots. On Shabbos, the entire watch was eligible for the lottery. During the festivals, all Kohanim, regardless of the watch to which they belonged, were eligible for the lottery.

7. *Toras Kohanim, perek* 10:2.
8. See 5:11-13 above.
9. The meal-offering brought by a *sotah*, a woman suspected of adultery. See *Numbers* 5:15.

7/12

offering, with the sacrifice of the thanksgiving-offering shall he offer unleavened loaves mixed with oil, unleavened wafers smeared with oil, and loaves of scalded

יַקְרִיבֶ֣נּוּ וְהִקְרִ֣יב ׀ עַל־זֶ֣בַח הַתּוֹדָ֗ה
חַלּ֤וֹת מַצּוֹת֙ בְּלוּלֹ֣ת בַּשֶּׁ֔מֶן וּרְקִיקֵ֥י
מַצּ֖וֹת מְשֻׁחִ֣ים בַּשָּׁ֑מֶן וְסֹ֣לֶת מֻרְבֶּ֔כֶת

— אונקלוס —

יְקָרְבִנֵּהּ וִיקָרֵב עַל נִכְסַת תּוֹדְתָא גְּרִיצָן פַּטִּירָן דְּפִילָן בִּמְשַׁח וְאֶסְפּוֹגִין פַּטִּירִין דִּמְשִׁיחִין בִּמְשַׁח וְסֻלְתָּא רְבִיכָא

— רש״י —

(יב) אם על תודה יקריבנו. אם על דבר הודאה על נס שנעשה לו, כגון יורדי הים והולכי מדבריות וחבושי בית האסורים וחולה שנתרפא שהן צריכין להודות, שכתוב בהן יודו לה' חסדו ונפלאותיו לבני אדם (תהלים קז:ח, טו, כא, לא), וִיזְבְּחוּ זִבְחֵי תּוֹדָה (שם פס' כב). אם על אחת מאלה נדר שלמים הללו, שלמי תודה הן וטעונות לחם האמור בענין ואין נאכלין אלא ליום ולילה כמו שמפורש כאן (להלן פס' טו): **והקריב על זבח התודה.** ארבעה מיני לחם. חלות ורקיקין ורבוכה שלשה מיני מצה, וכתיב על חלת לחם חמץ וגו' (פסוק יג). וכל מין ומין עשר חלות כך מפורש במנחות (עז.) ושיעורן חמץ שאין ירושלמיות שהן שש מדבריות, עשרים עשרון (שם טו:ו): **מרבכת.** לחם חלוט ברותחין כל צרכו:

— RASHI ELUCIDATED —

12. אִם עַל תּוֹדָה יַקְרִיבֶנּוּ – **IF HE SHALL OFFER IT FOR A THANKSGIVING-OFFERING.** אִם עַל דָּבָר הוֹדָאָה – If over a matter of thanksgiving, עַל נֵס שֶׁנַּעֲשָׂה לוֹ – over a miracle, i.e., deliverance from a perilous situation, that was done for him, כְּגוֹן – for example, יוֹרְדֵי הַיָּם – seafarers, וְהוֹלְכֵי מִדְבָּרִיּוֹת – and those who travel deserts, וַחֲבוּשֵׁי בֵּית הָאֲסוּרִים – and those who were confined in prison and were released, וְחוֹלֶה שֶׁנִּתְרַפֵּא – and a sick person who was healed, שֶׁהֵן צְרִיכִין לְהוֹדוֹת – for they must give thanks, שֶׁכָּתוּב בָּהֶן – for it is written of them: "יוֹדוּ לַה' חַסְדּוֹ וְנִפְלְאוֹתָיו לִבְנֵי אָדָם" – "They should give thanks to HASHEM for His kindness, and for His wonders to mankind,"[1] וְיִזְבְּחוּ זִבְחֵי "תּוֹדָה" – "and they should slaughter thanksgiving-offerings."[2] אִם עַל אַחַת מֵאֵלֶּה נָדַר שְׁלָמִים הַלָּלוּ – If over one of these causes for thanksgiving he pledged to bring these peace-offerings, שַׁלְמֵי תּוֹדָה הֵן – they are peace-offerings of thanksgiving, וּטְעוּנוֹת לֶחֶם – and require the bread הָאָמוּר בָּעִנְיָן – stated in this topic, וְאֵין נֶאֱכָלִין אֶלָּא לְיוֹם וָלַיְלָה – and they may be eaten only for a day and a night,[3] כְּמוֹ שֶׁמְּפוֹרָשׁ כָּאן – as stated explicitly here.[4]

□ וְהִקְרִיב עַל זֶבַח הַתּוֹדָה – **WITH THE SACRIFICE OF THE THANKSGIVING-OFFERING SHALL HE OFFER** אַרְבָּעָה מִינֵי לֶחֶם – four varieties of bread: חַלּוֹת – loaves, וּרְקִיקִין – and wafers, וּרְבוּכָה – and that which is scalded, these are שְׁלֹשָׁה מִינֵי מַצָּה – three varieties of unleavened bread; וּכְתִיב – and it is written, "עַל חַלֹּת לֶחֶם חָמֵץ וְגוֹמֵר" – "with loaves of leavened bread, etc.,"[5] in addition to the three unleavened varieties. וְכָל מִין וָמִין עֶשֶׂר חַלּוֹת – Each variety consists of ten loaves. כָּךְ מְפוֹרָשׁ בִּמְנָחוֹת – Thus is it stated explicitly in *Menachos*.[6] וְשִׁעוּרָן – Their amount, i.e., their total volume, is חָמֵשׁ סְאִין יְרוּשַׁלְמִיּוֹת – five *se'in* of Jerusalem, שֶׁהֵן שֵׁשׁ מִדְבָּרִיּוֹת – which are six *se'in* of these used when the Israelites were in the desert, which equal עֶשְׂרִים עִשָּׂרוֹן – twenty *issaron* (tenth-*ephahs*).[7]

□ מֻרְבֶּכֶת – **SCALDED.** לֶחֶם חָלוּט בְּרוֹתְחִין – Bread scalded in boiling water כָּל צָרְכּוֹ – all that it needs (as much as is necessary).[8]

---

1. *Psalms* 107:8,15,21,31. Rashi in his comments on that psalm (based on *Berachos* 54b) shows how each verse refers to one of the four categories he mentions here.
2. *Psalms* 107:22.
3. Unlike other peace-offerings which may be eaten within two days and their intervening night.
4. Below v. 16.
5. Below v. 13.
6. *Menachos* 77a-b.
7. *Menachos* 76b. The *se'ah* (pl. *se'in*) measure in use at the time the Torah was given at Sinai is called the סְאָה מִדְבָּרִית, "desert *se'ah*." Some centuries later, the Sages enlarged the *se'ah* measure by twenty percent, so that each original *se'ah* was now only ⁵/₆ of its new counterpart. This new measure came to be known as the סְאָה יְרוּשַׁלְמִית, "Jerusalem *se'ah*," and was the standard of measure used in early Mishnaic times. Hence, five Jerusalem *se'ahs* are actually six desert *se'ahs*.
  The authority of the Sages to increase Biblical measures is derived by the Talmud (*Menachos* 77a) from a verse in *Ezekiel* (45:11). This is also the source for increasing the measure by one sixth (R' *Ovadiah Bertinoro* to *Menachos* 7:1). [In the late Mishnaic period, the *se'ah* was again enlarged by twenty percent in what came to be known as the סְאָה צִפּוֹרִית, "Sepphoris *se'ah*."]
8. Rashi defined the term מֻרְבֶּכֶת, "scalded," above in 6:14. But there the verse used it to describe the meal-offering — "scalded shall you bring it." Here, the verse uses it in conjunction with fine flour — "scalded fine flour." We might have thus thought that the flour is to be scalded before it is baked. Rashi therefore states that it is "*bread* scalded in boiling water," i.e., it is not the flour alone that is scalded; it is the mixture of oil and flour which composes the bread

fine flour mixed with oil. ¹³ With loaves of leavened bread shall he bring his offering, with the sacrifice of his thanksgiving peace-offering. ¹⁴ From it he shall offer one from each offering, a portion to Hashem; it shall belong to the Kohen who throws the blood of the peace-offering. ¹⁵ And the flesh of the sacrifice of his thanksgiving peace-

יג חַלֹּת בְּלוּלֹת בַּשָּׁמֶן: עַל־חַלֹּת
לֶחֶם חָמֵץ יַקְרִיב קָרְבָּנוֹ עַל־
זֶבַח תּוֹדַת שְׁלָמָיו: יד וְהִקְרִיב מִמֶּנּוּ
אֶחָד מִכָּל־קָרְבָּן תְּרוּמָה לַיהוָה
לַכֹּהֵן הַזֹּרֵק אֶת־דַּם הַשְּׁלָמִים לוֹ
יִהְיֶה: טו וּבְשַׂר זֶבַח תּוֹדַת שְׁלָמָיו

─── אונקלוס ───

גְּרִיצָן דְּפִילָן בִּמְשַׁח: יג עַל גְּרִיצָן דִּלְחֵם חֲמִיעַ יְקָרֵב קָרְבָּנֵהּ עַל נִכְסַת תּוֹדַת (נִכְסָת) קוּדְשׁוֹהִי: יד וִיקָרֵב מִנֵּהּ חַד מִכָּל קָרְבָּנָא אַפְרָשׁוּתָא קֳדָם יְיָ לְכָהֲנָא דִּיזְרוֹק יָת דַּם נִכְסַת קוּדְשַׁיָּא דִּילֵהּ יְהֵא: טו וּבְסַר נִכְסַת תּוֹדַת (נִכְסָת) קוּדְשׁוֹהִי

─── רש"י ───

(יג) יקריב קרבנו על זבח. מַגִּיד שֶׁאֵין הַלֶּחֶם קָדוֹשׁ קְדוּשַׁת הַגּוּף לִיפָּסֵל בְּיוֹצֵא וּטְבוּל יוֹם וּמְלִאכֶת לַחוּלִין בִּפְדִיוֹן עַד שֶׁיִּשָּׁחֵט הַזֶּבַח (ת"כ פרק יא:ו; מנחות עח:): (יד) אחד מכל קרבן. לֶחֶם אֶחָד מִכָּל מִין וּמִין יִטּוֹל תְּרוּמָה לַכֹּהֵן הָעוֹבֵד עֲבוֹדָתָהּ, וְהַשְּׁאָר

לִבְעָלִים. וּבְשָׂרָהּ לַבְּעָלִים חוּץ מֵחָזֶה וְשׁוֹק שֶׁבָּהּ, מַגִּיד שֶׁאֵין הַלֶּחֶם קָדוֹשׁ קְדוּשַׁת הַגּוּף כְּמוֹ שֶׁמְּפוֹרָשׁ תְּנוּפַת חָזֶה וְשׁוֹק בַּשְּׁלָמִים (פסוקים כט-לד) וְהַתּוֹדָה קְרוּיָה שְׁלָמִים: (טו) ובשר זבח תודת שלמיו. יֵשׁ כָּאן רִבּוּיִין הַרְבֵּה, לְרַבּוֹת חַטָּאת וְאָשָׁם וְאַיִל נָזִיר וַחֲגִיגַת אַרְבָּעָה עָשָׂר שֶׁיִּהְיוּ נֶאֱכָלִין לְיוֹם

─── RASHI ELUCIDATED ───

13. מַגִּיד — **This tells** us יַקְרִיב קָרְבָּנוֹ עַל זֶבַח — **SHALL HE BRING HIS OFFERING; WITH THE SACRIFICE.** לִפָּסֵל בְּיוֹצֵא — **that the bread is not holy with inherent holiness**¹ שֶׁאֵין הַלֶּחֶם קָדוֹשׁ קְדוּשַׁת הַגּוּף — **insofar as becoming invalid by leaving** the Courtyard of the *Beis HaMikdash*, וּטְבוּל יוֹם — **or** by coming in contact with **one who immersed that day**,² וּמְלִאכֶת לַחוּלִין בִּפְדִיוֹן — **and** from being prohibited **from leaving** the state of holiness **for** that of **the non-holy through redemption**,³ עַד שֶׁיִּשָּׁחֵט הַזֶּבַח — **until the sacrifice will be slaughtered.**⁴

14. אֶחָד מִכָּל קָרְבָּן — **ONE FROM EACH OFFERING.** לֶחֶם אֶחָד מִכָּל מִין וָמִין — **One bread from each variety** יִטּוֹל תְּרוּמָה — **he should remove as a portion** לַכֹּהֵן הָעוֹבֵד עֲבוֹדָתוֹ — **for the Kohen who performs his service,** וְהַשְּׁאָר — **and the rest** of the bread נֶאֱכָל לַבְּעָלִים — **is eaten by the owner.** וּבְשָׂרָהּ לַבְּעָלִים — Its meat goes **to the owner** חוּץ מֵחָזֶה וְשׁוֹק שֶׁבָּהּ — **except for its breast and thigh,** כְּמוֹ שֶׁמְפוֹרָשׁ — **just as the waving of the breast and thigh are stated explicitly below with regard to the peace-offering,**⁵ לְמַטָּה תְּנוּפַת חָזֶה וָשׁוֹק בַּשְּׁלָמִים — **just as the waving of the breast and thigh are stated explicitly below with regard to the peace-offering,**⁵ וְהַתּוֹדָה קְרוּיָה שְׁלָמִים — **and the thanksgiving-offering is called a peace-offering.**⁶

15. וּבְשַׂר זֶבַח תּוֹדַת שְׁלָמָיו — **AND THE FLESH OF THE SACRIFICE OF HIS THANKSGIVING PEACE-OFFERING.** יֵשׁ כָּאן רִבּוּיִין הַרְבֵּה — **There are many inclusions here,** לְרַבּוֹת חַטָּאת — **to include the sin-offering,** וְאָשָׁם — **and the guilt-offering,** וְאֵיל נָזִיר — **and the ram of the** *nazir*,⁷ וַחֲגִיגַת אַרְבָּעָה עָשָׂר — **and** the festival-offering of the fourteenth of Nissan,⁸ שֶׁיִּהְיוּ נֶאֱכָלִין — **that they should be eaten** לְיוֹם

that is scalded before it is baked (see *Maskil LeDavid*).

1. קְדוּשַׁת הַגּוּף [*kedushas haguf*], "inherent holiness," literally, "holiness of the body," is a holiness which renders the object fit to be a *Mizbe'ach* offering, as opposed to קְדוּשַׁת דָּמִים [*kedushas damim*], "holiness of value," by which an object becomes the property of the *Beis HaMikdash*, even if it is not fit for an offering.

2. See note 5 on page 73.

3. That which has *kedushas haguf* (see note 1 above) cannot be redeemed. That which merely has *kedushas damim* can.

4. *Toras Kohanim, perek* 11:10; *Menachos* 78b. The preceding verse has already stated that the bread is offered with the thanksgiving-offering. "With the sacrifice of his thanksgiving peace-offering" is repeated here to juxtapose יַקְרִיב קָרְבָּנוֹ, "shall he bring his offering," with עַל זֶבַח. Those words in isolation mean, "He shall bring his offering with the sacrifice"; that is, his bread attains

the status of an offering with the slaughter of the thanksgiving-offering, but not before then (*Mizrachi; Sifsei Chachamim*).

5. Verses 29-34 below.

6. Verse 34 states explicitly that the breast and the thigh of the peace-offering go to the Kohen. Our verse teaches us that the same law applies to the thanksgiving-offering, since it calls the thanksgiving-offering a peace-offering.

7. See *Numbers* 6:14.

8. See *Deuteronomy* 16:2 and Rashi there. On the fourteenth of Nissan, with the *korban pesach*, an additional offering was brought, known as the *chagigah*, "festival offering," of the festival. In contradistinction to the regular *chagigah* that *must* be brought during the course of each of the three pilgrimage festivals (Pesach, Shavuos, and Succos), the *chagigah* offered on the eve of Pesach is not absolutely obligatory. The basis of the

offering must be eaten on the day of its offering; he may not leave any of it until morning. ¹⁶ *But if the sacrifice of his offering is for a vow or a donation, it must be eaten on the day he offered his sacrifice; and on the next day, what is left over from it may be eaten.* ¹⁷ *What is left over from the flesh of the sac-*

בְּיוֹם קָרְבָּנוֹ יֵאָכֵל לֹא־יַנִּיחַ מִמֶּנּוּ
טז עַד־בֹּקֶר: וְאִם־נֶדֶר ׀ אוֹ נְדָבָה
זֶבַח קָרְבָּנוֹ בְּיוֹם הַקְרִיבוֹ אֶת־
זִבְחוֹ יֵאָכֵל וּמִמָּחֳרָת וְהַנּוֹתָר
יז מִמֶּנּוּ יֵאָכֵל: וְהַנּוֹתָר מִבְּשַׂר הַזֶּבַח

―――――― אונקלוס ――――――

בְּיוֹם קֻרְבָּנֵהּ יִתְאֲכֵל לָא יַצְנַע מִנֵּהּ עַד צַפְרָא: טזוְאִם נְדַר אוֹ נִדְבְתָא נִכְסַת קֻרְבָּנֵהּ בְּיוֹמָא דִּי יְקָרֵב נִכְסְתֵהּ יִתְאֲכֵל וּמִיּוֹמָא דְּבַתְרוֹהִי וּדְאִשְׁתְּאַר מִנֵּהּ יִתְאֲכֵל: יז וּדְאִשְׁתְּאַר מִבְּסַר נִכְסַת

―――――― רש"י ――――――

וְלַיְלָה (ת"כ פרק יב:ח; זבחים לו.). **בְּיוֹם קָרְבְּנוֹ יֵאָכֵל.** וּכְזְמַן בְּשָׂרוֹ זְמַן לַחְמוֹ: **לֹא יַנִּיחַ מִמֶּנּוּ עַד בֹּקֶר.** אֲבָל אוֹכֵל הוּא כָּל הַלַּיְלָה. אִם כֵּן לָמָּה אָמְרוּ עַד חֲצוֹת, כְּדֵי לְהַרְחִיק הָאָדָם מִן הָעֲבֵרָה (ת"כ שם ה; ברכות ב.): **(טז) וְאִם** **נֶדֶר אוֹ נְדָבָה.** שֶׁלֹּא הֱבִיאָהּ עַל הוֹדָאָה שֶׁל נֵס אֵינָהּ טְעוּנָה לֶחֶם וְנֶאֱכֶלֶת לִשְׁנֵי יָמִים כְּמוֹ שֶׁמְּפוֹרָשׁ בָּעִנְיָן: **וּמִמָּחֳרָת וְהַנּוֹתָר מִמֶּנּוּ בָּרִאשׁוֹן יֵאָכֵל.** וְהַנּוֹתָר מִמֶּנּוּ יֵאָכֵל וי"ו זוֹ יְתֵרָה הִיא וְיֵשׁ כָּמוֹהָ הַרְבֵּה בַּמִּקְרָא כְּגוֹן וְאֵלֶּה בְּנֵי צִבְעוֹן וְאַיָּה

―――――― RASHI ELUCIDATED ――――――

□ וְלַיְלָה — **for a day and a night,** the day of the sacrifice and the night which follows.¹

□ בְּיוֹם קָרְבָּנוֹ יֵאָכֵל — MUST BE EATEN ON THE DAY OF ITS OFFERING. וּכְזְמַן בְּשָׂרוֹ — And like the time of eating its meat זְמַן לַחְמוֹ — is the time of eating its bread.²

□ לֹא יַנִּיחַ מִמֶּנּוּ עַד בֹּקֶר — HE MAY NOT LEAVE ANY OF IT UNTIL MORNING. אֲבָל אוֹכֵל הוּא — But he may eat כָּל הַלַּיְלָה — the entire night. אִם כֵּן — If so, לָמָּה אָמְרוּ ,,עַד חֲצוֹת״ — why did they say, "until midnight"?³ כְּדֵי לְהַרְחִיק אָדָם מִן הָעֲבֵרָה — In order to distance man from sin.⁴

16. וְאִם נֶדֶר אוֹ נְדָבָה — [BUT] IF [THE SACRIFICE OF HIS OFFERING] IS FOR A VOW OR A DONATION, שֶׁלֹּא הֱבִיאָהּ עַל הוֹדָאָה שֶׁל נֵס — that he did not bring it over thanksgiving for a miracle,⁵ אֵינָהּ טְעוּנָה לֶחֶם — it does not require bread, וְנֶאֱכֶלֶת לִשְׁנֵי יָמִים — and it may be eaten for two days, כְּמוֹ שֶׁמְּפוֹרָשׁ בָּעִנְיָן — as stated explicitly in the topic.

□ וּמִמָּחֳרָת וְהַנּוֹתָר מִמֶּנּוּ — AND ON THE NEXT DAY, WHAT IS LEFT OVER FROM IT בָּרִאשׁוֹן — on the first day, יֵאָכֵל — may be eaten. {וְהַנּוֹתָר מִמֶּנּוּ יֵאָכֵל — "What is left over from it may be eaten,"} prefix of וְהַנּוֹתָר is superfluous,⁶ וָי"ו זוֹ יְתֵרָה הִיא — this וְ וְיֵשׁ כָּמוֹהָ הַרְבֵּה בַּמִּקְרָא — and there are many like it in Scripture, כְּגוֹן — for example the וְ of וְאַיָּה in, ,,וְאֵלֶּה בְּנֵי צִבְעוֹן וְאַיָּה

practice to bring this *chagigah* is the Torah's commandment that the *korban pesach* be eaten "when [one is] sated"; thus one eats of the *chagigah* to satisfy his hunger before partaking of the *korban pesach*. But, unlike the *korban pesach*, the Torah does not *require* that the meat of *chagigah* be eaten only at the Seder.

1. *Toras Kohanim, perek* 12:1; *Zevachim* 36a. The verse could have said, וְתוֹדָתוֹ, "and his thanksgiving-offering," instead of וּבְשַׂר זֶבַח תּוֹדַת שְׁלָמָיו, "and the flesh of the sacrifice of his thanksgiving peace offering." The lengthier wording is used to tell us that other offerings are also to be consumed within the day of their slaughter and the following night (*Mizrachi*).

2. The verse could have said, בְּיוֹמוֹ, "on its day." The lengthier בְּיוֹם קָרְבָּנוֹ, "on the day of its offering," alludes to the bread, which has been referred to in the preceding verse as an offering (*Mizrachi; Sifsei Chachamim*).

3. If the Torah permitted the offering to be eaten throughout the night, why did the Sages (*Berachos* 2a) say that it had to be eaten before midnight?

4. *Toras Kohanim, perek* 12:5; *Berachos* 2a. By insisting that the offering be eaten before midnight, the Sages ensured that there would not be a violation of the prohibition against leaving any of it over until morning.

5. A thanksgiving-offering is always a vow or a donation; that is, it is not an obligatory offering. "But if the sacrifice of his offering is for a vow or a donation" is not intended to imply that the thanksgiving-offering is not a vow or a donation. The verse means, "If the offering of his sacrifice is brought only as a vow or a donation, without a specific feeling of obligation to give thanks for deliverance or for a miracle" (*Mizrachi*).

6. If the וְ of וְהַנּוֹתָר were understood in its usual sense of "and," the verse would say, "It must be eaten on the day he offered his offering and on the next day, *and* what is left over may be eaten." This would imply that there is an obligation to eat the offering on the day it is offered and on the next day, but if there is meat left over after that time, it may still be eaten. This cannot be so, however, for the meat of a peace-offering may not be eaten on the third day after it was offered (see v. 17). Thus, the וְ of וְהַנּוֹתָר is interpreted as having no simple meaning. The verse reads, "It must be eaten on the day he offered his offering; and on the next day, what is left over from the first day may be eaten" (*Mizrachi*).

ויקרא – פרשת צו

יח בַּיּוֹם֙ הַשְּׁלִישִׁ֔י בָּאֵ֖שׁ יִשָּׂרֵֽף: וְאִ֣ם הֵאָכֹ֣ל יֵאָכֵ֡ל מִבְּשַׂר־זֶ֩בַח֩ שְׁלָמָ֨יו בַּיּ֤וֹם הַשְּׁלִישִׁי֙ לֹ֣א יֵרָצֶ֔ה הַמַּקְרִ֣יב אֹת֔וֹ לֹ֥א יֵחָשֵׁ֛ב ל֖וֹ פִּגּ֣וּל יִהְיֶ֑ה וְהַנֶּ֛פֶשׁ הָאֹכֶ֥לֶת מִמֶּ֖נּוּ עֲוֺנָ֥הּ תִּשָּֽׂא: יט וְהַבָּשָׂ֞ר אֲשֶׁר־יִגַּ֤ע בְּכָל־טָמֵא֙ לֹ֣א יֵֽאָכֵ֔ל בָּאֵ֖שׁ יִשָּׂרֵ֑ף וְהַ֨בָּשָׂ֔ר כָּל־טָה֖וֹר יֹאכַ֥ל בָּשָֽׂר:

rifice shall be burned in the fire on the third day. [18] And if some of the flesh of the sacrifice of his peace-offering will be eaten on the third day, it does not appease, the one who offers it may not intend this — it remains rejected; and the soul that eats of it shall bear its sin.

[19] But the flesh that touches anything impure may not be eaten, it shall be burned in fire; but of the flesh [that is not impure], any pure person may eat the flesh.

— אונקלוס —

בְּיוֹמָא תְלִיתָאָה בְּנוּרָא יִתּוֹקָד: יח וְאִם אִתְאֲכָלָא יִתְאֲכֵל מִבְּסַר נִכְסַת קוּדְשׁוֹהִי בְּיוֹמָא תְלִיתָאָה לָא יְהֵא לְרַעֲוָא דִמְקָרֵב יָתֵהּ לָא יִתְחַשֵּׁב לֵהּ מְרָחָק יְהֵא וֶאֱנָשָׁא דְיֵיכוּל מִנֵּהּ חוֹבֵהּ יְקַבֵּל: יט וּבְסַר קוּדְשָׁא דִי יִקְרַב בְּכָל מְסָאָב לָא יִתְאֲכֵל בְּנוּרָא יִתּוֹקָד וּבְסַר קוּדְשָׁא כָּל דִּדְכֵי לְקוּדְשֵׁי יֵיכוּל בְּסַר קוּדְשָׁא:

— רש"י —

וְטַעְנָא (בראשית לו:כד) תֵּת וָקֶדֶשׁ וְלִבָא מֵרְמָס (דניאל ח:יג): (יח) וְאִם הֵאָכֹל יֵאָכֵל וְגוֹ'. בְּמַחֲשָׁבָה שֶׁחִשֵּׁב בִּשְׁעַת הַכְּשֵׁרוֹ מְדַבֵּר. יָכוֹל אִם אָכַל מִמֶּנּוּ בַּשְּׁלִישִׁי יִפָּסֵל לְמַפְרֵעַ, ת"ל הַמַּקְרִיב אֹתוֹ לֹא יֵחָשֵׁב, בִּשְׁעַת הַקְרָבָה הוּא נִפְסָל וְאֵינוֹ נִפְסָל בַּשְּׁלִישִׁי (ת"כ פרשתא ח:א; זבחים כט.), וְכֵן פֵּרוּשׁוֹ, בִּשְׁעַת הַקְרָבָתוֹ לֹא תַּעֲלֶה זֹאת בְּמַחֲשָׁבָה וְאִם חִשֵּׁב פִּגּוּל יִהְיֶה: וְהַנֶּפֶשׁ הָאֹכֶלֶת מִמֶּנּוּ. אֲפִלּוּ בְּתוֹךְ הַזְּמַן עֲוֺנָהּ תִּשָּׂא: (יט) וְהַבָּשָׂר. שֶׁל קֹדֶשׁ שְׁלָמִים אֲשֶׁר יִגַּע בְּכָל טָמֵא לֹא יֵאָכֵל. לְרַבּוֹת אֵבֶר שֶׁיָּצָא

— RASHI ELUCIDATED —

וַעֲנָה – "and these are the sons of Zibeon: Aiah and Anah";[1] and the ו of וְקֹדֶשׁ in, תֵּת וְקֹדֶשׁ וְצָבָא ,,מִרְמָס"[2] – "allows that which is holy, and the host to be trampled."[2]

18. וְאִם הֵאָכֹל יֵאָכֵל וְגוֹמֵר – AND IF... WILL BE EATEN, ETC. בְּמַחֲשָׁבָה בַּשְּׁחִיטָה לְאָכְלוֹ בַּשְּׁלִישִׁי הַכָּתוּב מְדַבֵּר – The verse speaks of one who thinks at the time of slaughter of eating it on the third day. יָכוֹל – One might be able to think אִם אָכַל מִמֶּנּוּ בַּשְּׁלִישִׁי – that if one ate of it on the third day יִפָּסֵל לְמַפְרֵעַ – it should become invalid retroactively, as the literal meaning of the verse implies. תַּלְמוּד לוֹמַר – To teach us otherwise, the verse says, ,,הַמַּקְרִיב אֹתוֹ לֹא יֵחָשֵׁב" – "the one who offers it may not intend," implying, בִּשְׁעַת הַקְרָבָה הוּא נִפְסָל – at the time of offering it becomes invalid, וְאֵינוּ נִפְסָל בַּשְּׁלִישִׁי[3] – and it does not become invalid on the third day.[3] וְכֵן פֵּרוּשׁוּ – And this is the interpretation of [the phrase]: בִּשְׁעַת הַקְרָבָתוֹ – At the time of its being offered, לֹא תַעֲלֶה זֹאת בְּמַחֲשָׁבָה – this should not go up in thought, i.e., he should not have such a thought, וְאִם חִשֵּׁב – and if he did think that the offering should be eaten on the third day, פִּגּוּל יִהְיֶה – it shall be piggul (rejected).[4]

□ וְהַנֶּפֶשׁ הָאֹכֶלֶת מִמֶּנּוּ – AND THE SOUL THAT EATS OF IT, אֲפִלּוּ בְּתוֹךְ הַזְּמַן – even within the normally permitted time, עֲוֺנָהּ תִּשָּׂא – shall bear its sin.

19. וְהַבָּשָׂר – BUT THE FLESH שֶׁל קֹדֶשׁ – of the holy שְׁלָמִים – of a peace-offering, אֲשֶׁר יִגַּע בְּכָל טָמֵא – that touches any impure thing, לֹא יֵאָכֵל – may not be eaten.[5]

□ וְהַבָּשָׂר – BUT OF THE FLESH [THAT IS NOT IMPURE]. לְרַבּוֹת – This is meant to include אֵבֶר שֶׁיָּצָא

1. Genesis 36:24. Although the ו in וְאַיָה can be interpreted as part of the name [as we find in נָפְסִי, "Vophsi" (Numbers 13:14), וַשְׁתִּי, "Vashti" (Esther 1:9), וַיְזָתָא, "Vaizatha" (Esther 9:9), and וָשְׁנִי, "Vashni" (I Chronicles 6:13 according to some commentaries)], Rashi rejects that interpretation because the parallel verse (I Chronicles 1:40) omits the ו.

2. Daniel 8:13. Other verses in which this phenomenon occurs are: וַאֲנִי (II Samuel 15:34; once according to Rashi there, twice according to Radak there and Ramban to Genesis 36:24); וְרָכֵב (Psalms 76:7; see Rashi there); וְעָפָר (I Chronicles 5:24; see Radak there); and וְאַיָה (I Chronicles 6:13, according to some com-

mentaries there).

3. Toras Kohanim, parshasa 8:1; Zevachim 29a.

4. The phrase הַמַּקְרִיב אֹתוֹ לֹא יֵחָשֵׁב לוֹ could have been understood, "It shall not be considered on behalf of the one who offers it." Rashi explains that it should be understood, "The one who offers it may not intend this" (Mizrachi).

5. The verse as it stands could have been understood as referring to any flesh (Gur Aryeh). Alternatively, our verse refers only to "the flesh of the holy of a peace-offering," as opposed to piggul, that which is not acceptable, the subject of the preceding verse, which

20 A person who eats flesh from the sacrifice of the peace-offering that is Hashem's while his impurity is upon him, that soul will be cut off from its people.

כ וְהַנֶּפֶשׁ אֲשֶׁר־תֹּאכַל בָּשָׂר מִזֶּבַח הַשְּׁלָמִים אֲשֶׁר לַיהוה וְטֻמְאָתוֹ עָלָיו וְנִכְרְתָה הַנֶּפֶשׁ הַהִוא מֵעַמֶּיהָ:

—— אונקלוס ——

כ וֶאֱנָשׁ דִּי יֵיכוֹל בִּסְרָא מִנִּכְסַת קוּדְשַׁיָּא דִּי קֳדָם יְיָ וְסוֹבְתֵהּ עֲלוֹהִי וְיִשְׁתֵּיצֵי אֲנָשָׁא הַהוּא מֵעַמֵּהּ:

—— רש"י ——

מִקְצָתוֹ שֶׁהִסְפְּנִימִי מוּתָר (ת"כ פרשתא ט:ו): **בָּל טָהוֹר יֹאכַל בָּשָׂר**. מַה ת"ל לְפִי שֶׁנֶּאֱמַר ,,וְדַם זְבָחֶיךָ יִשָּׁפֵךְ וְגוֹ' וְהַבָּשָׂר תֹּאכֵל" (דברים יב:כז) יָכוֹל לֹא יֹאכְלוּ שְׁלָמִים אֶלָּא הַבְּעָלִים לְכָךְ נֶאֱמַר טָהוֹר יֹאכַל בָּשָׂר (ת"כ שם ז): [**וְהַבָּשָׂר כָּל טָהוֹר יֹאכַל בָּשָׂר**. כְּלוֹמַר כָּל מַה שֶּׁאָסַרְתִּי לְךָ בְּחַטָּאת וְאָשָׁם שֶׁאִם יָצְאוּ חוּץ לִקְלָעִים אָסוּרִין כְּמוֹ שֶׁכָּתוּב בַּחֲצַר אֹהֶל מוֹעֵד יֹאכְלוּהָ (לעיל ו:ט) בְּבָשָׂר זֶה אֲנִי אוֹמֵר לָךְ כָּל טָהוֹר יֹאכַל בָּשָׂר אֲפִלּוּ בְּכָל הָעִיר: **וְטֻמְאָתוֹ עָלָיו**. בְּטוּמְאַת הַגּוּף הַכָּתוּב מְדַבֵּר (ת"כ פרק יד ג־ו; זבחים מג:) אֲבָל טָהוֹר שֶׁאָכַל אֶת הַטָּמֵא אֵינוֹ עֲנוּשׁ כָּרֵת אֶלָּא אַזְהָרָה וְהַבָּשָׂר אֲשֶׁר יִגַּע בְּכָל טָמֵא וְגוֹ' (פסוק יט) וְאַזְהָרַת טָמָא

—— RASHI ELUCIDATED ——

מִקְצָתוֹ — **a limb part of which has gone outside** of the holy area where it was required to be eaten, שֶׁהַפְּנִימִי מֻתָּר — **that the inner part is still permitted.**[1]

□ כָּל טָהוֹר יֹאכַל בָּשָׂר — ANY PURE PERSON MAY EAT THE FLESH. מַה תַּלְמוּד לוֹמַר — **Why does the Torah say this?** לְפִי שֶׁנֶּאֱמַר — **Because it says,** ,,וְדַם זְבָחֶיךָ יִשָּׁפֵךְ וְגוֹמֵר וְהַבָּשָׂר תֹּאכֵל" — **"The blood of your offerings shall be poured** on the Mizbe'ach, etc., and the flesh you shall eat."[2] יָכוֹל — **One might be able** to think that לֹא יֹאכְלוּ שְׁלָמִים אֶלָּא הַבְּעָלִים — **only the owner may eat the peace-offering.**[3] לְכָךְ נֶאֱמַר — **Therefore, it says,** ,,כָּל טָהוֹר יֹאכַל בָּשָׂר"[4] — **"any pure person may eat the flesh."**[4]

□ {וְהַבָּשָׂר כָּל טָהוֹר יֹאכַל בָּשָׂר — BUT THE FLESH ... ANY PURE PERSON MAY EAT THE FLESH. כְּלוֹמַר — **As if to say:** כָּל מַה שֶּׁאָסַרְתִּי לְךָ — **All that I forbade you** בְּחַטָּאת וְאָשָׁם — **regarding a sin-offering and a guilt-offering,** namely, שֶׁאִם יָצְאוּ חוּץ לִקְלָעִים — **that if they went out beyond the Curtains** of the Courtyard of the Tent of Meeting אֲסוּרִין — **they are forbidden,** כְּמוֹ שֶׁכָּתוּב — **as it is written,** ,,בַּחֲצַר אֹהֶל מוֹעֵד יֹאכְלוּהָ"[5] — **"in the Courtyard of the Tent of Meeting they shall eat it,"**[5] בְּבָשָׂר זֶה — **regarding this flesh** of the peace-offering אֲנִי אוֹמֵר לָךְ — **I say to you,** ,,כָּל טָהוֹר יֹאכַל בָּשָׂר" — **"any pure person may eat the flesh,"** אֲפִלּוּ בְּכָל הָעִיר — **even in the entire city,** i.e., even in the entire walled city of Jerusalem, when there was a Beis HaMikdash, not only in the Courtyard.}

20. וְטֻמְאָתוֹ עָלָיו — WHILE HIS IMPURITY IS UPON HIM. בְּטֻמְאַת הַגּוּף הַכָּתוּב מְדַבֵּר — **The verse speaks of impurity of the body,** of the one who is eating, and not of the object eaten.[6] אֲבָל טָהוֹר שֶׁאָכַל אֶת הַטָּמֵא — **But a pure person who ate that which is impure,** i.e., an offering that became impure, אֵינוֹ עָנוּשׁ — is not punished כָּרֵת — by kares,[7] אֶלָּא אַזְהָרָה — **but it is a negative commandment,**[8] וְהַבָּשָׂר — ,,וְהַבָּשָׂר אֲשֶׁר יִגַּע בְּכָל טָמֵא וְגוֹמֵר"[9] — **"but the flesh that touches anything impure etc."**[9] וְאַזְהָרַת טָמֵא

may not be eaten irrespective of whether it comes into contact with that which is not pure (Mizrachi).

1. Toras Kohanim, parshasa 9:6. The second וְהַבָּשָׂר of the verse appears redundant. It teaches us that if part of a limb of an offering extends beyond the area in which it must be eaten, only the part that lies outside the prescribed area is forbidden. The rest of the piece may be eaten (Mizrachi; see also Pesachim 85b).

2. Deuteronomy 12:27.

3. Since "your offerings" of Deuteronomy 12:27 implies the owner, one may have thought that "you may eat the flesh" of that verse also applies only to the owner (Mizrachi).

4. Toras Kohanim, parshasa 9:7.

5. Above 6:9. Note, however, that that verse speaks of a meal-offering, not a sin-offering. This apparent oversight leads many commentaries to reject this passage as a later addition not written by Rashi. Their view is further supported by the absence of any comments on it by Mizrachi, Gur Aryeh and other major commentaries. It is possible, however, that the original comment adduced the phrase מוֹעֵד אֹהֶל מִפֶּתַח from 6:19 which discusses where the sin-offering may be eaten. The addition of the word יֹאכְלוּהָ would then be the error of a copyist who thought Rashi was citing 6:9.

6. Toras Kohanim, perek 14:3-6; Zevachim 43b. See note 1 on page 76.

7. See note 8 to page 8.

8. That is, it is punished by flogging, the usual punishment for transgressing a negative commandment of the Torah if no other punishment is specified.

9. Above v. 19. That verse continues, "may not be eaten."

21 *If a person touches any impurity — whether human impurity or an impure animal [carcass] or any impure detestable [carcass] — and he eats from the flesh of*

כא וְנֶ֗פֶשׁ כִּֽי־תִגַּ֣ע בְּכָל־טָמֵא֒ בְּטֻמְאַ֣ת אָדָ֗ם א֚וֹ ׀ בִּבְהֵמָ֣ה טְמֵאָ֔ה א֖וֹ בְּכָל־שֶׁ֣קֶץ טָמֵ֑א וְאָכַ֛ל מִבְּשַׂר־

— אונקלוס —

כא וֶאֱנָשׁ אֲרֵי יִקְרַב בְּכָל מְסָאָב בְּסוֹאֲבַת אֱנָשָׁא אוֹ בִּבְעִירָא מְסָאֲבָא אוֹ בְּכָל שִׁקְצָא מְסָאָב וְיֵיכוֹל מִבְּסַר

— רש"י —

שֶׁאָכַל אֶת הַטָּהוֹר — The negative commandment against one who is impure eating [an offering] that is pure אֵינָהּ מְפֹרֶשֶׁת בַּתּוֹרָה — is not stated explicitly in the Torah,[1] אֶלָּא חֲכָמִים לְמָדוּהָ — but the Sages derived it בִּגְזֵרָה שָׁוָה — through a *gezeirah shavah*.[2] שָׁלֹשׁ כְּרִיתוֹת אֲמוּרוֹת בְּאוֹכְלֵי קָדָשִׁים בְּטֻמְאַת הַגּוּף — Three *kereisos* are said with regard to those who eat that which is holy while in a state of impurity of the body.[3] וּדְרָשׁוּם רַבּוֹתֵינוּ זִכְרוֹנָם לִבְרָכָה — Our Rabbis, of blessed memory, expounded them in *Shevuos*:[4] אַחַת לִכְלָל — one for a generality,[5] וְאַחַת לִפְרָט — and one for a specific,[6] וְאַחַת לְלַמֵּד עַל קָרְבָּן עוֹלֶה וְיוֹרֵד — and one[7] to teach about the ascending and descending offering,[8] שֶׁלֹּא נֶאֱמַר אֶלָּא עַל טֻמְאַת מִקְדָּשׁ וְקָדָשָׁיו — that it was said, i.e., that the Torah said that it must be brought, only for causing **impurity of the *Beis HaMikdash* and its holies**.[9]

---

1. Although our verse states that one who is impure is punished for eating an offering, no negative commandment is given.

2. A method of deriving information in which that which is stated explicitly with regard to one context is applied to another context, as well, by virtue of an identical word or phrase appearing in the two contexts. This only applies when such association of two contexts is a matter of received tradition. It is not a procedure rooted in logical criteria that can be used at one's own initiative.

In our case, טֻמְאָתוֹ appears both here and in the context of one who enters the grounds of the *Beis HaMikdash* while impure (*Numbers* 19:13). Just as there is a negative commandment given for one who enters the grounds of the *Beis HaMikdash* while impure (*Numbers* 5:3), so, too, is there a negative commandment here. This also explains why וְטֻמְאָתוֹ עָלָיו refers to the individual ("while *his* impurity is upon *him*") and not to the offering ("while *its* impurity is upon *it*"). For just as טֻמְאָתוֹ in *Numbers* 19:13 refers to the individual, so, too, does it refer to the individual here (*Mizrachi; Sifsei Chachamim*).

3. The Torah states three times that one who eats of offerings while he is impure is punished by *kares* — in our verse, in the verse which follows, and in 22:3 below.

4. *Shevuos* 7a.

5. This refers to 22:3, which speaks in general terms of eating "the holies" without specifying what "the holies" are.

6. This refers to our verse, which makes specific mention of the peace-offering, thus limiting the punishment of *kares* — for eating that which is holy while in a state of impurity — to the peace-offering.

The eighth of the Thirteen Principles by which the Torah is expounded is: כָּל דָּבָר שֶׁהָיָה בִּכְלָל, Anything that was included in a general statement, וְיָצָא מִן הַכְּלָל לְלַמֵּד, but then left the generality to teach something, לֹא לְלַמֵּד עַל עַצְמוֹ יָצָא, did not leave to teach only about itself, אֶלָּא לְלַמֵּד עַל הַכְּלָל כֻּלּוֹ יָצָא, rather it left to teach about the entire generality. In our case, 22:3 below states a generality: Anyone who eats of "the holies" while he is in a state of impurity is liable to *kares*; that verse does not specify whether "the holies" refers to what is consecrated as *kedushas haguf* or *kedushas damim* (see note 1 on page 76). However, our verse specifies that peace-offerings may not be eaten by anyone in a state of impurity on pain of *kares*. If so, peace-offerings, which had been included in the generality "the holies," have left the generality to teach that they — and, by inference, other holies of *kedushas haguf* — render an impure person who eats them liable to *kares*. By the rule stated above, this lesson must be applied to the entire generality. Thus, the phrase "the holies" of 22:3 includes only offerings which are consecrated with *kedushas haguf* (Rashi to *Shevuos* 7a).

7. This refers to verse 21. See note 9 below.

8. An offering, the value of which ascends or descends, depending on the financial state of the one who brings it (see above 5:1-13 and Rashi's comments there).

9. Verse 21, which speaks of *kares*, is used to define in which situation one must bring an ascending and descending offering. Verse 5:3 speaks of an offering brought for a sin involving impurity, but does not specify the specific sin. Verse 21 is used to define that sin as one in which a person in a state of impurity enters the grounds of the *Beis HaMikdash* or eats the flesh of an offering (Rashi to *Shevuos* 7a).

a sacrifice of the peace-offering that is HASHEM's, then that soul will be cut off from its people.

²² HASHEM spoke to Moses, saying: ²³ Speak to the Children of Israel, saying: Any fat of oxen, sheep, or goats — you shall not eat. ²⁴ The fat of an animal that died and the fat of an animal that had been torn to death may be put to any use; but you shall not eat it. ²⁵ For anyone who eats the fat of animal species from which one may bring a fire-offering to HASHEM — the soul that eats will be cut off from its people. ²⁶ You shall not consume any blood, in any of your dwelling places, whether from fowl or from animals.

זֶבַח הַשְּׁלָמִים אֲשֶׁר לַיהוָה וְנִכְרְתָה הַנֶּפֶשׁ הַהִוא מֵעַמֶּיהָ:
כב־כג וַיְדַבֵּר יהוה אֶל־מֹשֶׁה לֵּאמֹר: דַּבֵּר אֶל־בְּנֵי יִשְׂרָאֵל לֵאמֹר כָּל־חֵלֶב
כד שׁוֹר וְכֶשֶׂב וָעֵז לֹא תֹאכֵלוּ: וְחֵלֶב נְבֵלָה וְחֵלֶב טְרֵפָה יֵעָשֶׂה לְכָל־
כה מְלָאכָה וְאָכֹל לֹא תֹאכְלֻהוּ: כִּי כָּל־אֹכֵל חֵלֶב מִן־הַבְּהֵמָה אֲשֶׁר יַקְרִיב מִמֶּנָּה אִשֶּׁה לַיהוָה וְנִכְרְתָה הַנֶּפֶשׁ
כו הָאֹכֶלֶת מֵעַמֶּיהָ: וְכָל־דָּם לֹא תֹאכְלוּ בְּכֹל מוֹשְׁבֹתֵיכֶם לָעוֹף וְלַבְּהֵמָה:

—————— אונקלוס ——————

נִכְסַת קוּדְשַׁיָּא דִּי קֳדָם יְיָ וְיִשְׁתֵּיצֵי אֲנָשָׁא הַהוּא מֵעַמֵּהּ: כב וּמַלִּיל יְיָ עִם מֹשֶׁה לְמֵימַר: כג מַלֵּל עִם בְּנֵי יִשְׂרָאֵל לְמֵימַר כָּל תְּרַב תּוֹר וְאִמַּר וְעִזָּא לָא תֵיכְלוּן: כד וּתְרַב נְבִילָא וּתְרַב תְּבִירָא יִתְעֲבֵד לְכָל עִבִידְתָּא וּמֵיכַל לָא תֵיכְלֻנֵּהּ: כה אֲרֵי כָּל דְּיֵיכוּל תַּרְבָּא מִן בְּעִירָא דִּי יְקָרֵב מִנַּהּ קֻרְבָּנָא קֳדָם יְיָ וְיִשְׁתֵּיצֵי אֲנָשָׁא דְּיֵיכוּל מֵעַמֵּהּ: כו וְכָל דְּמָא לָא תֵיכְלוּן בְּכֹל מוֹתְבָנֵיכוֹן לְעוֹפָא וְלִבְעִירָא:

—————— רש"י ——————

(כד) יעשה לכל מלאכה. בא ולימד על החלב שאינו מטמא טומאת נבלות (פסחים כג.): ואכל לא תאכלהו. אמרה תורה יבוא איסור נבילה וטריפה ויחול על איסור חלב שאם אכלו יתחייב אף על לאו של נבילה (חולין לז.; זבחים ע., קג.): ולא תאמר אין איסור חל על איסור: (כו) לעוף ולבהמה. פרט לדם דגים וחגבים (ת"כ פר' ויק'; כריתות כ:): בכל מושבותיכם. לפי שהיא חובת הגוף

—————— RASHI ELUCIDATED ——————

24. יֵעָשֶׂה לְכָל מְלָאכָה — MAY BE PUT TO ANY USE. בָּא וְלִמֵּד עַל הַחֵלֶב — [This verse] comes and teaches us about forbidden fat [1] שֶׁאֵינוֹ מְטַמֵּא טֻמְאַת נְבֵלוֹת — that it does not transmit the impurity of unslaughtered carcasses.[1]

וְאָכֹל לֹא תֹאכְלֻהוּ — BUT YOU SHALL NOT EAT IT. אָמְרָה תוֹרָה — The Torah said: יָבֹא אִסּוּר נְבֵלָה וּטְרֵפָה — Let the prohibition against eating an unslaughtered carcass and a mauled animal come וְיָחוּל עַל אִסּוּר חֵלֶב — and take effect in addition to the prohibition of forbidden fat, שֶׁאִם אֲכָלוֹ — that if he ate [the fat of an unslaughtered carcass or a mauled animal] יִתְחַיֵּב — he will be culpable אַף עַל לָאו שֶׁל נְבֵלָה — also for transgressing the negative commandment of the unslaughtered carcass.[2] וְלֹא תֹאמַר — And do not say, אֵין אִסּוּר חָל עַל אִסּוּר — a prohibition cannot take effect in addition to a pre-existing prohibition.[3]

26. לָעוֹף וְלַבְּהֵמָה — WHETHER FROM FOWL OR FROM ANIMALS. פְּרָט לְדַם דָּגִים — To the exclusion of the blood of fish [4] וַחֲגָבִים — and kosher grasshoppers.[4]

בְּכֹל מוֹשְׁבֹתֵיכֶם — IN ANY OF YOUR DWELLING PLACES. לְפִי שֶׁהִיא חוֹבַת הַגּוּף — Because it is a duty of

---

1. *Pesachim* 23a. The Torah never prohibited the use of forbidden fat. It only forbade it to be eaten. If the verse nonetheless makes a point of saying that it may be put to any use, it intends to permit a type of use one may have thought was forbidden. If the forbidden fat was part of the carcass of an animal which was not slaughtered properly, one might have thought that the fat could not be used in a manner which brought it into contact with holy objects, for it would transmit the impurity of the carcass to the object. This verse teaches us that the fat may be put to *any* use — it does not bear the impurity of carcasses and may come into contact with holy objects (*Mizrachi; Sifsei Chacha-*

mim; based on Rashi to *Pesachim* 23a).

2. *Chullin* 37a; *Zevachim* 70a and 103a.

3. In general, a prohibition does not take effect where there is a pre-existing prohibition. There is a prohibition against eating forbidden fat even from a properly slaughtered animal. Our verse speaks specifically of an animal that died without slaughter and a mauled animal to teach us that the prohibitions of eating the carcass of an animal that died and of a mauled animal take effect on the forbidden fat of the animal, even though there was a pre-existing prohibition on it (*Mizrachi; Sifsei Chachamim*).

4. *Toras Kohanim, parshasa* 10:11; *Kereisos* 20b.

ויקרא – פרשת צו

²⁷ Any person who consumes any blood — that soul will be cut off from its people. ²⁸ Hashem spoke to Moses, saying: ²⁹ Speak to the Children of Israel, saying: When one brings his sacrifice peace-offering to Hashem, he shall deliver his offering to Hashem from the sacrifice of his peace-offering. ³⁰ His hands shall bring the fire-offerings of Hashem: the fat

כז כָּל־נֶפֶשׁ אֲשֶׁר־תֹּאכַל כָּל־דָּם וְנִכְרְתָה הַנֶּפֶשׁ הַהִוא מֵעַמֶּיהָ: כח-כט וַיְדַבֵּר יהוה אֶל־מֹשֶׁה לֵּאמֹר: דַּבֵּר אֶל־בְּנֵי יִשְׂרָאֵל לֵאמֹר הַמַּקְרִיב אֶת־זֶבַח שְׁלָמָיו לַיהוה יָבִיא אֶת־קָרְבָּנוֹ לַיהוה מִזֶּבַח שְׁלָמָיו: ל יָדָיו תְּבִיאֶינָה אֵת אִשֵּׁי יהוה אֶת־הַחֵלֶב

─── אונקלוס ───

כז כָּל אֱנָשׁ דִי יֵיכוּל כָּל דְמָא וְיִשְׁתֵּיצֵי אֲנָשָׁא הַהוּא מֵעַמֵּהּ: כח וּמַלִיל יְיָ עִם מֹשֶׁה לְמֵימָר: כט מַלֵל עִם בְּנֵי יִשְׂרָאֵל לְמֵימָר דִמְקָרֵב יָת נִכְסַת קוּדְשַׁיָּא קֳדָם יְיָ יַיְתִי יָת קָרְבָּנֵהּ לָקֳדָם יְיָ מִנִּכְסַת קוּדְשׁוֹהִי: ל יְדוֹהִי יַיְתְיָן יָת קָרְבָּנַיָּא דַיְיָ יָת תַּרְבָּא

─── רש"י ───

וְאֵינָהּ חוֹבַת קַרְקַע נוֹהֶגֶת בְּכָל מוֹשָׁבוֹת וּבְמַסֶּכֶת קִדּוּשִׁין בְּפֶּ"א (דף לז:) מְפָרֵשׁ לָמָּה הוּצְרַךְ לוֹמַר: (ל) **יָדָיו תְּבִיאֶינָה וְגוֹ'.** שֶׁתְּהֵא יַד הַבְּעָלִים מִלְמַעְלָה וְהַחֵלֶב וְהֶחָזֶה נְתוּנִין בָּהּ וְיַד כֹּהֵן מִלְמַטָּן וּמְנִיפָן: **אֵת אִשֵּׁי ה'.** וּמָה הֵן הָאִשִּׁים, אֶת הַחֵלֶב עַל הֶחָזֶה. (מנחות סא.): **יְבִיאֶנּוּ.** כְּשֶׁמְּבִיאָן מִבֵּית הַמַּטְבָּחַיִם נוֹתֵן הַחֵלֶב עַל הֶחָזֶה וּכְשֶׁנּוֹתְנוֹ לְיַד [הַכֹּהֵן] הַמֵּנִיף נִמְצָא הֶחָזֶה לְמַעְלָה וְהַחֵלֶב לְמַטָּה, וְזֶהוּ הָאָמוּר

─── RASHI ELUCIDATED ───

וְאֵינָהּ חוֹבַת — the body, i.e., an obligation which falls upon the individual irrespective of his location, נוֹהֶגֶת בְּכָל — and it is not a duty of the land, i.e., an obligation bound up with the Land of Israel, קַרְקַע – מוֹשָׁבוֹת — it applies in all dwelling places. וּבְמַסֶּכֶת קִדּוּשִׁין – In Tractate *Kiddushin*, בְּפֶּרֶק רִאשׁוֹן – in the first chapter,[1] מְפָרֵשׁ לָמָּה הוּצְרַךְ לוֹמַר – it explains why this had to be stated.[2]

30. יָדָיו תְּבִיאֶינָה וְגוֹ' – HIS HANDS SHALL BRING, ETC. שֶׁתְּהֵא יַד הַבְּעָלִים מִלְמַעְלָה — That the hand of the owner should be on top, וְהַחֵלֶב וְהֶחָזֶה נְתוּנִין בָּהּ – and the fat and breasts put in it, וְיַד כֹּהֵן מִלְמַטָּה – and the hand of the Kohen below, ³וּמְנִיפָן – and he waves them.[3]

□ אֵת אִשֵּׁי ה' – THE FIRE-OFFERINGS OF HASHEM. וּמָה הֵן הָאִשִּׁים – And what are the fire-offerings? אֶת הַחֵלֶב עַל הֶחָזֶה – "The fat that he brings atop the breast."[4]

□ יְבִיאֶנּוּ – SHALL HE BRING IT. כְּשֶׁמְּבִיאָן מִבֵּית הַמַּטְבָּחַיִם – When he brings them from the butcher's quarter in the Courtyard of the *Beis HaMikdash*, נוֹתֵן חֵלֶב עַל הֶחָזֶה – he puts fat atop the breast, וּכְשֶׁנּוֹתְנוֹ לְיַד {הַכֹּהֵן} הַמֵּנִיף – and when he puts it in the hand of {the Kohen} who waves it, נִמְצָא הֶחָזֶה לְמַעְלָה – it is found that the breast is on top וְהַחֵלֶב לְמַטָּה – and the fat below.[5] וְזֶהוּ הָאָמוּר

---

1. *Kiddushin* 37b.

2. The Talmud there explains that the prohibitions against eating forbidden fat and blood are obligations that fall upon the individual irrespective of location. If so, why did the Torah need to say "in any of your dwelling places"? Because I might have thought that since these prohibitions are stated in the context of the laws of offerings [both here and in 3:17 above], they apply only during periods when offerings are brought, i.e., while the *Beis HaMikdash* is standing. "In any of your dwelling places" teaches us that they always apply.

3. *Menachos* 61b. Although our verse makes no mention of a Kohen, the Talmud derives this on the basis of the appearance of "hand" both here and in the context of waving the offering of first-fruits. Just as the Kohen participates in the waving of the first-fruits (see *Deuteronomy* 26:4 and Rashi there), so, too, does he participate in the waving of the peace-offering (*Mizrachi*; *Sifsei Chachamim*).

4. "The fat atop the breast" is in apposition to "the fire-offerings of Hashem." It is not a separate category (*Be'er Yitzchak*).

Rashi does not mean that the fat and the breast are the "fire-offerings" of this verse. That would be patently wrong, as Rashi himself states in his last comment on this verse. Rather "the fire-offerings" refers to the fats that are brought from the butcher's quarters atop the breast that will be given to the Kohen. According to *Yosef Hallel*, this comment ends with the words אֶת הַחֵלֶב, "the fat," and the phrase עַל הֶחָזֶה, "atop the breast," is part of the heading of Rashi's next comment.

5. The Kohen who brings it from the butcher's quarters turns it upside down into the hands of the owner who will perform the waving (*Mizrachi*). Many editions omit the word הַכֹּהֵן, "the Kohen," from the preceding phrase, because the breast and fat are placed into the owner's hands; the Kohen then places his hands under the owner's and they wave the fat and breast.

83 / VAYIKRA/LEVITICUS — PARASHAS TZAV — ז/לא – 7/31

atop the breast shall he bring it; the breast, in order to wave it as a wave-service before HASHEM. [31] The Kohen shall cause the fat to go up in smoke on the Mizbe'ach; and the breast shall be for Aaron and his sons.

עַל הֶחָזֶה יְבִיאֶנּוּ אֵת הֶחָזֶה לְהָנִיף
אֹתוֹ תְּנוּפָה לִפְנֵי יהוה: וְהִקְטִיר לא
הַכֹּהֵן אֶת־הַחֵלֶב הַמִּזְבֵּחָה
וְהָיָה הֶחָזֶה לְאַהֲרֹן וּלְבָנָיו:

— אונקלוס —

עַל חֶדְיָא יַיְתִנֵּהּ יָת חֶדְיָא לַאֲרָמָא יָתֵהּ אֲרָמוּתָא קֳדָם יְיָ:
לא וְיַסֵּק כַּהֲנָא יָת תַּרְבָּא לְמַדְבְּחָא וִיהֵי חֶדְיָא לְאַהֲרֹן וְלִבְנוֹהִי:

— רש"י —

בְּמָקוֹם אַחֵר שׁוֹק הַתְּרוּמָה וְחֲזֵה הַתְּנוּפָה עַל אִשֵּׁי הַחֲלָבִים יְבִיאוּ לְהָנִיף וגו' (להלן י:טו) וּלְאַחַר הַתְּנוּפָה נוֹתְנוֹ לַכֹּהֵן הַמַּקְטִיר וְנִמְצָא הֶחָזֶה לְמַטָּה, וְזֶהוּ שֶׁנֶּאֱמַר וַיָּשִׂימוּ אֶת הַחֲלָבִים עַל הֶחָזוֹת וַיַּקְטֵר הַחֲלָבִים הַמִּזְבֵּחָה (להלן ט:כ) לִמְּדָנוּ שֶׁשְּׁלֹשָׁה כֹהֲנִים זְקוּקִין לָהּ. כָּךְ מְפֹרָשׁ בִּמְנָחוֹת (סב.): אֵת הַחֵלֶב עַל הֶחָזֶה יְבִיאֶנּוּ. לְמָה מֵבִיא, לְהָנִיף אוֹתוֹ הוּא מְבִיאוֹ, וְלֹא שֶׁיְּהֵא הוּא מִן הָאִשִּׁים. שֶׁנֶּאֱמַר אֶת אִשֵּׁי ה' אֶת הַחֵלֶב עַל הֶחָזֶה, יָכוֹל אַף הֶחָזֶה לָאִשִּׁים, לְכָךְ נֶאֱמַר אֶת הֶחָזֶה לְהָנִיף וגו': (לא): וְהִקְטִיר הַכֹּהֵן אֶת הַחֵלֶב. וְאַחַ"כ וְהָיָה הֶחָזֶה לְאַהֲרֹן, לִמְּדָנוּ שֶׁאֵין הַבָּשָׂר נֶאֱכָל בְּעוֹד שֶׁהָאֵמוּרִין לְמַטָּה מִן הַמִּזְבֵּחַ (ת"כ פרק טז:ד; פסחים נט:):

— RASHI ELUCIDATED —

שׁוֹק הַתְּרוּמָה וְחֲזֵה הַתְּנוּפָה עַל אִשֵּׁי — בְּמָקוֹם אַחֵר — This is the meaning of that which is said elsewhere, הַחֲלָבִים יָבִיאוּ לְהָנִיף וְגוֹמֵר[1] — "They are to bring the thigh of the raising-up and the breast of the waving upon the fire-offering fats to wave, etc."[1] וּלְאַחַר הַתְּנוּפָה — And after the waving, נוֹתְנוֹ — לַכֹּהֵן הַמַּקְטִיר — he gives it to the Kohen who causes it to go up in smoke, וְנִמְצָא הֶחָזֶה לְמַטָּה — and the breast is found to be below.[2] וְזֶהוּ שֶׁנֶּאֱמַר — This is referred to in that which it says, וַיָּשִׂימוּ אֶת הַחֲלָבִים עַל הֶחָזוֹת וַיַּקְטֵר הַחֲלָבִים הַמִּזְבֵּחָה[3] — "They placed the fats upon the breasts, and caused the fats to go up in smoke on the Mizbe'ach."[3] לִמְּדָנוּ — This has taught us שֶׁשְּׁלֹשָׁה כֹּהֲנִים זְקוּקִין לָהּ — that it requires three Kohanim. כָּךְ מְפֹרָשׁ בִּמְנָחוֹת[4] — Thus has it been stated explicitly in Menachos.[4]

□ וְאֵת הֶחָזֶה עַל הַחֵלֶב יְבִיאֶנּוּ — THE FAT ATOP THE BREAST SHALL HE BRING, מָה מֵבִיא — and why does he bring the breast? לְהָנִיף אוֹתוֹ הוּא מְבִיאוֹ — To wave it he brings it, וְלֹא — not that it should be among the fire-offerings. לְפִי שֶׁנֶּאֱמַר — Because שֶׁהֲרֵי הוּא מֵהָאִשִּׁים — it says, אֶת אִשֵּׁי ה' אֶת הַחֵלֶב עַל הֶחָזֶה — "the fire-offerings of HASHEM, the fat atop the breast," יָכוֹל שֶׁיְּהֵא אַף הֶחָזֶה לָאִשִּׁים — one might be able to think that the breast, too, is for the fire-offerings. לְכָךְ נֶאֱמַר — Therefore it says, אֶת הֶחָזֶה לְהָנִיף וְגוֹמֵר — "the breast in order to wave, etc."[5]

31. וְהִקְטִיר הַכֹּהֵן אֶת הַחֵלֶב — THE KOHEN SHALL CAUSE THE FAT TO GO UP IN SMOKE. וְאַחַר כָּךְ — And afterwards, וְהָיָה הֶחָזֶה לְאַהֲרֹן — "and the breast shall be for Aaron." לִמְּדָנוּ — This has taught us שֶׁאֵין הַבָּשָׂר נֶאֱכָל — that the flesh of the breast may not be eaten בְּעוֹד שֶׁהָאֵמוּרִים לְמַטָּה מִן הַמִּזְבֵּחַ[6] — while the specified parts are still below the Mizbe'ach, i.e., before the parts which must be burned have been put on the Mizbe'ach.[6]

---

1. Below 10:15.

2. The one who performed waving turns it over into the hands of the Kohen who will place it on the Mizbe'ach (Mizrachi).

3. Below 9:20.

4. Menachos 62a. Our verse states that the fat is on top of the breast; 10:15 states that the breast is on top of the fat; while 9:20 says that the fat is on top of the breast. Rashi explains that the three verses refer to three different procedures of the offering service, each performed by a different Kohen: One brings the fats and the breast from the butcher's quarters; the second places his hands under the owner's hands and performs the waving; and the third places the fat on the Mizbe'ach (Mizrachi).

5. The verse has already said, "The fat atop the breast shall he bring." Why does it repeat "the breast"? To make it clear that the breast is not among "the fire-offerings of HASHEM." "The breast" is connected with that which follows, "in order to wave as a wave-service." Although the following verse states explicitly that the breast is given to the Kohanim, which indicates that they are not part of the fire-offering, if it were not for "the breast in order to wave..." of our verse, we would have concluded that part of the breast is burned as a fire-offering and part is given to the Kohanim (Gur Aryeh; Sifsei Chachamim).

6. Toras Kohanim, perek 16:4; Pesachim 59b.

ויקרא – פרשת צו

לב וְאֵת֙ שׁ֣וֹק הַיָּמִ֔ין תִּתְּנ֥וּ תְרוּמָ֖ה לַכֹּהֵ֑ן מִזִּבְחֵ֖י שַׁלְמֵיכֶֽם: לג הַמַּקְרִ֞יב אֶת־דַּ֧ם הַשְּׁלָמִ֛ים וְאֶת־הַחֵ֖לֶב מִבְּנֵ֣י אַהֲרֹ֑ן ל֣וֹ תִהְיֶ֥ה שׁ֥וֹק הַיָּמִ֖ין לְמָנָֽה: לד כִּי֩ אֶת־חֲזֵ֨ה הַתְּנוּפָ֜ה וְאֵ֣ת ׀ שׁ֣וֹק הַתְּרוּמָ֗ה לָקַ֨חְתִּי֙ מֵאֵ֣ת בְּנֵֽי־יִשְׂרָאֵ֔ל מִזִּבְחֵ֖י שַׁלְמֵיהֶ֑ם וָאֶתֵּ֣ן אֹ֠תָם לְאַהֲרֹ֨ן הַכֹּהֵ֤ן וּלְבָנָיו֙ לְחָק־עוֹלָ֔ם מֵאֵ֖ת בְּנֵ֥י יִשְׂרָאֵֽל:

³² You shall give the right leg as a raised-up gift to the Kohen, from the sacrifice of your peace-offering. ³³ Anyone from among the sons of Aaron who offers the blood of the peace-offering and the fat — the right leg shall be his as a portion. ³⁴ For the breast of the waving and the leg of the raising have I taken from the Children of Israel, from the sacrifice of their peace-offering, and I have given them to Aaron the Kohen and his sons as an eternal stipend from the Children of Israel.

— אונקלוס —

לב וְיָת שׁוֹקָא דְיַמִּינָא תִּתְּנוּן אַפְרָשׁוּתָא לְכַהֲנָא מִנִּכְסַת קוּדְשֵׁיכוֹן: לג דִּמְקָרֵב יָת דַּם קוּדְשַׁיָּא וְיָת תַּרְבָּא מִבְּנֵי אַהֲרֹן לֵהּ תְּהֵי שׁוֹקָא דְיַמִּינָא לָחֳלָק: לד אֲרֵי יָת חֶדְיָא דַּאֲרָמוּתָא וְיָת שׁוֹקָא דְאַפְרָשׁוּתָא נְסֵבִית מִן בְּנֵי יִשְׂרָאֵל מִנִּכְסַת קוּדְשֵׁיהוֹן וִיהָבִית יָתְהוֹן לְאַהֲרֹן כַּהֲנָא וְלִבְנוֹהִי לִקְיָם עֲלָם מִן בְּנֵי יִשְׂרָאֵל:

— רש״י —

(לב) שׁוֹק. מִן הַפֶּרֶק שֶׁל אַרְכּוּבָה הַנִּמְכֶּרֶת עִם הָרֹאשׁ עַד הַפֶּרֶק הָאֶמְצָעִי שֶׁהוּא סוֹבֵךְ שֶׁל רֶגֶל [חולין קל"ד] [חולין ק"ד ירך]: **(לג) הַמַּקְרִיב אֶת דַּם הַשְּׁלָמִים וְגוֹ'.** מִי שֶׁהוּא רָאוּי לְזָרְקוֹ וּלְהַקְטִיר חֲלָבָיו. יָצָא טָמֵא בִּשְׁעַת זְרִיקַת דָּמִים [אוֹ בִשְׁעַת הֶקְטֵר חֲלָבִים] שֶׁאֵינוֹ חוֹלֵק בַּבָּשָׂר (ת״כ פרק טז:ז-ח; זבחים צח.; מנחות סא.; סוכה לז.): **(לד) הַתְּנוּפָה.** מוֹלִיךְ וּמֵבִיא: **הַתְּרוּמָה.** מַעֲלֶה וּמוֹרִיד:

— RASHI ELUCIDATED —

32. שׁוֹק — LEG. הַנִּמְכֶּרֶת עִם הָרֹאשׁ — which is sold along with the head,[2] מִן הַפֶּרֶק שֶׁל אַרְכֻּבָּה — From the joint of the *arkubah*[1] עַד הַפֶּרֶק הָאֶמְצָעִי — to the middle joint,[3] שֶׁהוּא סוֹבֵךְ שֶׁל רָגֶל — which is the pivot of the leg.[3]

33. הַמַּקְרִיב אֶת דַּם הַשְּׁלָמִים וְגוֹמֵר — WHO OFFERS THE BLOOD OF THE PEACE-OFFERING. מִי שֶׁהוּא רָאוּי — One who is fit for its sprinkling, i.e., the sprinkling of its blood, וּלְהַקְטִיר חֲלָבָיו — and to cause its fats to go up in smoke. יָצָא טָמֵא בִּשְׁעַת זְרִיקַת דָּמִים — To the exclusion of one who was impure at the time of the sprinkling of blood, {אוֹ בִּשְׁעַת הֶקְטֵר חֲלָבִים — or at the time of causing fats to go up in smoke,}[4] שֶׁאֵינוֹ חוֹלֵק בַּבָּשָׂר — that he does not take a share in the meat.[4]

34. הַתְּנוּפָה . . . הַתְּרוּמָה — THE WAVING ... THE RAISING. מוֹלִיךְ וּמֵבִיא — He moves it forward and brings it back,[5] מַעֲלֶה וּמוֹרִיד — raises it up and brings it down.[5]

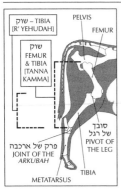

שׁוֹק – TIBIA [R' YEHUDAH]
PELVIS
FEMUR
שׁוֹק FEMUR & TIBIA [TANNA KAMMA]
סוֹבֶךְ שֶׁל רֶגֶל PIVOT OF THE LEG
פֶּרֶק שֶׁל אַרְכֻּבָּה JOINT OF THE ARKUBAH
TIBIA
METATARSUS

1. The leg of an ox, from the ankle to the top of the hip, comprises three long bones. The term *arkubah* means "section of the leg." Rashi uses it here with reference to the lowest of the three sections, the section that used to be sold with the head (see next note). The שׁוֹק is the section from the upper joint of the *arkubah* to the fleshy part of the leg, which is where the second bone connects with the third.

2. In the days of the compilation of the Talmud, it was common to purchase this joint of the animal along with the head (*Yam shel Shlomo; Chullin*, Chapter 4, Section 11).

3. *Chullin* 135b. The "pivot of the leg" (some editions of Rashi read סוֹבֶךְ שֶׁל יָרֵךְ, "pivot of the thigh") is the joint between the middle and upper bone of the leg (Rashi to *Chullin* 134b). In describing the שׁוֹק, "leg," of our verse as the middle long bone, Rashi cites the opinion of the *Tanna* R' Yehudah (in the Mishnah there). The *Tanna Kamma* holds that the שׁוֹק includes the two upper bones. *Rambam* (*Hil. Bikkurim* 9:18) states the halachah according to the view of the *Tanna Kamma*. (See *Yosef Hallel* who attempts to reconcile Rashi with the *Tanna Kamma*'s view.)

4. *Toras Kohanim, perek* 16:7-8; *Zevachim* 98b. This verse is interpreted as referring to those fit to perform the service rather than those who actually perform the service (*Mizrachi*). Other verses interpreted in this way are 6:19, 6:22, 7:7 and 7:9 above.

5. *Menachos* 61a; *Succah* 37b. Rashi (to *Exodus* 29:24, based on the Talmud) describes the procedures of "waving" and "raising": For "waving," he moves the parts back and forth for Him to Whom the four winds of the world (north, south, east, west) belong. Waving holds back and annuls punishments and harmful winds. For "raising," he lifts and lowers the parts for Him to Whom the heavens and earth belong. Raising holds back harmful dew.

7/35-8/2

35 This is the anointment [portion] of Aaron and the anointment [portion] gift of his sons from the fire-offerings of HASHEM, on the day He brought them near to minister to HASHEM; **36** that HASHEM commanded to be given them on the day He anointed them from among the Children of Israel; it is an eternal decree for their generations. **37** This is the law of the olah-offering, the meal-offering, the sin-offering, and the guilt-offering; and the inauguration-offerings, and the sacrifice of the peace-offering; **38** which HASHEM commanded Moses on Mount Sinai, on the day He commanded the Children of Israel to bring their offerings to HASHEM, in the Wilderness of Sinai.

8 **1** HASHEM spoke to Moses, saying: **2** Take Aaron and his sons with him, and the garments and the oil of anointment, and

לה זֹאת מִשְׁחַת אַהֲרֹן וּמִשְׁחַת בָּנָיו
מֵאִשֵּׁי יְהוָה בְּיוֹם הִקְרִיב אֹתָם
לו לְכַהֵן לַיהוָה: אֲשֶׁר צִוָּה יְהוָה
לָתֵת לָהֶם בְּיוֹם מָשְׁחוֹ אֹתָם מֵאֵת
בְּנֵי יִשְׂרָאֵל חֻקַּת עוֹלָם לְדֹרֹתָם:
לז זֹאת הַתּוֹרָה לָעֹלָה לַמִּנְחָה
וְלַחַטָּאת וְלָאָשָׁם וְלַמִּלּוּאִים
לח וּלְזֶבַח הַשְּׁלָמִים: אֲשֶׁר צִוָּה יְהוָה
אֶת־מֹשֶׁה בְּהַר סִינָי בְּיוֹם צַוֹּתוֹ
אֶת־בְּנֵי יִשְׂרָאֵל לְהַקְרִיב אֶת־
קָרְבְּנֵיהֶם לַיהוָה בְּמִדְבַּר סִינָי:

ח א רביעי וַיְדַבֵּר יְהוָה אֶל־מֹשֶׁה לֵּאמֹר:
ב קַח אֶת־אַהֲרֹן וְאֶת־בָּנָיו אִתּוֹ וְאֵת
הַבְּגָדִים וְאֵת שֶׁמֶן הַמִּשְׁחָה וְאֵת |

— אונקלוס —

לה דָּא רְבוּת אַהֲרֹן וּרְבוּת בְּנוֹהִי מִקֻּרְבָּנַיָּא דַייָ בְּיוֹמָא דְּקָרֵיב יָתְהוֹן לְשַׁמָּשָׁא קֳדָם יְיָ: לו דִּי פַקֵּיד יְיָ לְמִתַּן לְהוֹן בְּיוֹמָא דְרַבִּי יָתְהוֹן מִן בְּנֵי יִשְׂרָאֵל קְיָם עָלָם לְדָרֵיהוֹן: לז דָּא אוֹרָיְתָא לַעֲלָתָא לְמִנְחָתָא וּלְחַטָּאתָא וְלַאֲשָׁמָא וּלְקֻרְבָּנַיָּא וּלְנִכְסַת קוּדְשַׁיָּא: לח דִּי פַקֵּיד יְיָ יָת מֹשֶׁה בְּטוּרָא דְסִינָי בְּיוֹמָא דְּפַקֵּיד יָת בְּנֵי יִשְׂרָאֵל לְקָרָבָא יָת קֻרְבָּנֵיהוֹן קֳדָם יְיָ בְּמַדְבְּרָא דְסִינָי: א וּמַלִּיל יְיָ עִם מֹשֶׁה לְמֵימָר: ב קָרֵב יָת אַהֲרֹן וְיָת בְּנוֹהִי עִמֵּהּ וְיָת לְבוּשַׁיָּא וְיָת מִשְׁחָא דִרְבוּתָא וְיָת

— רש"י —

(לז) ולמלואים. ליום חינוך הכהונה: **(ב) קח את אהרן.** פרשה זו נאמרה שבעת ימים קודם הקמת המשכן שאין מוקדם ומאוחר בתורה (פסחים ו:): **קח את אהרן.** קחנו בדברים ומשכהו (ת"כ מלואים ב):

— RASHI ELUCIDATED —

37. וְלַמִּלּוּאִים — AND THE INAUGURATION-OFFERINGS. לְיוֹם חִנּוּךְ הַכְּהֻנָּה — This means the offerings for the day of the inauguration of the *kehunah*.[1]

8.

2. קַח אֶת אַהֲרֹן — TAKE AARON. פָּרָשָׁה זוּ נֶאֶמְרָה — This section of the Torah was said שִׁבְעַת יָמִים — seven days before the erection of the *Mishkan*,[2] שֶׁאֵין מֻקְדָּם וּמְאֻחָר בַּתּוֹרָה — for קוֹדֶם הֲקָמַת הַמִּשְׁכָּן there is no earlier and later in the Torah, i.e., the events of the Torah are not presented in chronological sequence.[2]

□ קַח אֶת אַהֲרֹן — TAKE AARON. קָחֶנּוּ בִּדְבָרִים — Take him with words, וּמָשְׁכֵהוּ — and persuade him.[3]

---

1. The literal meaning of the word is, "for the fillings." Rashi to *Exodus* 28:41 explains how "filling" connotes "inauguration" (*Mizrachi*; *Sifsei Chachamim*).

2. *Pesachim* 6b. The Torah has already related that the erection of the *Mishkan* took place on the first of Nissan of the second year of the Israelites' sojourn in the desert (*Exodus* 40:17). Although the events related here took place before that time, it is common for the Torah to relate events out of chronological order (*Mizrachi*; *Sifsei Chachamim*). The reference to Aaron and his sons being in the *Mishkan* during the procedure of their inauguration mentioned in verse 33 of our chapter does not contradict this. Moses would erect and dismantle the *Mishkan* each day of the seven days of inauguration, as mentioned by Rashi in his comments to 9:23. On the first of Nissan the *Mishkan* was first erected, to be dismantled only when camp was broken.

3. *Toras Kohanim, Miluim* 2. The term לְקִיחָה normally denotes taking in a concrete physical way. If applied to people in this sense, it would imply taking them and moving them bodily. When the Torah uses the term לְקִיחָה with reference to people, it does not intend this meaning, but rather, taking by means of persuasion (*Gur Aryeh*). Rashi explains the word similarly in his comments to *Genesis* 2:15, 16:3, *Exodus* 14:6, *Numbers* 8:6, 16:1, 20:25, 27:18, 27:22, *Deuteronomy* 1:15. See also Rashi to *Genesis* 43:15 and *Joshua* 3:12, where he explains that taking as applied to people is not to be understood in the physical sense, but does not specifically mention persuasion.

the bull of the sin-offering, and the two rams, and the basket of matzos. ³ Gather the entire assembly to the entrance of the Tent of Meeting. ⁴ Moses did as HASHEM commanded him; and the assembly was gathered to the entrance of the Tent of Meeting. ⁵ Moses said to the assembly: "This is the thing that HASHEM commanded to be done." ⁶ Moses brought Aaron and his sons forward and he immersed them in water. ⁷ He placed the Kutoness upon him and girdled him with the Avneit; he dressed him in the Me'il and placed the Ephod on him; he girdled him with the Cheshev of the Ephod and adorned him with it. ⁸ He placed the Choshen upon him; and in the Choshen he placed the Urim

פַּר הַחַטָּאת וְאֵת שְׁנֵי הָאֵילִים וְאֵת
ג סַל הַמַּצּוֹת וְאֵת כָּל־הָעֵדָה הַקְהֵל
ד אֶל־פֶּתַח אֹהֶל מוֹעֵד: וַיַּעַשׂ מֹשֶׁה
כַּאֲשֶׁר צִוָּה יְהוָה אֹתוֹ וַתִּקָּהֵל
הָעֵדָה אֶל־פֶּתַח אֹהֶל מוֹעֵד:
ה וַיֹּאמֶר מֹשֶׁה אֶל־הָעֵדָה זֶה הַדָּבָר
ו אֲשֶׁר־צִוָּה יְהוָה לַעֲשׂוֹת: וַיַּקְרֵב
מֹשֶׁה אֶת־אַהֲרֹן וְאֶת־בָּנָיו וַיִּרְחַץ
ז אֹתָם בַּמָּיִם: וַיִּתֵּן עָלָיו אֶת־הַכֻּתֹּנֶת
וַיַּחְגֹּר אֹתוֹ בָּאַבְנֵט וַיַּלְבֵּשׁ אֹתוֹ
אֶת־הַמְּעִיל וַיִּתֵּן עָלָיו אֶת־הָאֵפֹד
וַיַּחְגֹּר אֹתוֹ בְּחֵשֶׁב הָאֵפֹד וַיֶּאְפֹּד
ח לוֹ בּוֹ: וַיָּשֶׂם עָלָיו אֶת־הַחֹשֶׁן
וַיִּתֵּן אֶל־הַחֹשֶׁן אֶת־הָאוּרִים

─── אונקלוס ───

תּוֹרָא דְחַטָּאתָא וְיָת תְּרֵין דִּכְרִין וְיָת סַלָּא דְפַטִּירַיָּא: ג וְיָת כָּל כְּנִשְׁתָּא אַכְנֵשׁ לִתְרַע מַשְׁכַּן זִמְנָא: ד וַעֲבַד מֹשֶׁה כְּמָא דִי פַּקִּיד יְיָ יָתֵהּ וְאִתְכְּנֵישַׁת כְּנִשְׁתָּא לִתְרַע מַשְׁכַּן זִמְנָא: ה וַאֲמַר מֹשֶׁה לִכְנִשְׁתָּא דֵּין פִּתְגָמָא דִי פַקִּיד יְיָ לְמֶעְבַּד: ו וְקָרֵיב מֹשֶׁה יָת אַהֲרֹן וְיָת בְּנוֹהִי וְאַסְחִי יָתְהוֹן בְּמַיָּא: ז וִיהַב עֲלוֹהִי יָת כִּתּוּנָא וְזָרֵז יָתֵהּ בְּהֶמְיָנָא וְאַלְבֵּשׁ יָתֵהּ מְעִילָא וִיהַב עֲלוֹהִי יָת אֵפוֹדָא וְזָרֵז יָתֵהּ בְּהֶמְיָן אֵפוֹדָא וְאַתְקִין לֵהּ בֵּהּ: ח וְשַׁוִּי עֲלוֹהִי חוּשְׁנָא וִיהַב לְחוּשְׁנָא יָת אוּרַיָּא

─── רש"י ───

ואת פר החטאת וגו'. אֵלּוּ הָאֲמוּרִים בְּעִנְיַן צַוָּאַת הַמִּלּוּאִים בּוֹאַתָּה תְּצַוֶּה (שמות כט) וְעַכְשָׁיו בַּיּוֹם רִאשׁוֹן לַמִּלּוּאִים חָזַר וְזֵרְזוֹ בִּשְׁעַת מַעֲשֶׂה: **(ג) הקהל אל פתח אהל מועד.** זֶה אֶחָד מִן הַמְּקוֹמוֹת שֶׁהֶחֱזִיק מוּעָט אֶת הַמְּרֻבֶּה (ויק"ר י'): **(ה) זה הדבר.** דְּבָרִים שֶׁתִּרְאוּ שֶׁאֲנִי עוֹשֶׂה לִפְנֵיכֶם צִוַּנִי הַקָּבָּ"ה לַעֲשׂוֹת, וְאַל תֹּאמְרוּ לִכְבוֹדִי וְלִכְבוֹד אָחִי אֲנִי עוֹשֶׂה. כָּל הָעִנְיָן הַזֶּה פֵּרַשְׁתִּי בִּוְאַתָּה תְּצַוֶּה (שמות כט): **(ח) את האורים.** כְּתָב שֶׁל שֵׁם הַמְפֹרָשׁ:

─── RASHI ELUCIDATED ───

□ וְאֵת פַּר הַחַטָּאת וְגוֹמֵר — AND THE BULL OF THE SIN-OFFERING, ETC. אֵלּוּ הָאֲמוּרִים — These are [the offerings] mentioned בְּעִנְיַן צַוָּאַת הַמִּלּוּאִים — in the topic of the command concerning the inauguration בְּוְאַתָּה תְּצַוֶּה — in *Parashas VeAtah Tetzaveh.*[1] וְעַכְשָׁיו בַּיּוֹם רִאשׁוֹן לַמִּלּוּאִים — Now, on the first day of the inauguration, חָזַר וְזֵרְזוֹ בִּשְׁעַת מַעֲשֶׂה — [God] repeated these commands to spur [Moses] on at the time of the act, i.e., at the time the command is to be carried out.[2]

3. הַקְהֵל אֶל פֶּתַח אֹהֶל מוֹעֵד — GATHER [THE ENTIRE ASSEMBLY] TO THE ENTRANCE OF THE TENT OF MEETING. זֶה אֶחָד מִן הַמְּקוֹמוֹת — This is one of the places mentioned in Scripture שֶׁהֶחֱזִיק מוּעָט אֶת הַמְּרֻבֶּה — where the little held the many.[3]

5. זֶה הַדָּבָר — THIS IS THE THING. דְּבָרִים שֶׁתִּרְאוּ — The things that you will see שֶׁאֲנִי עוֹשֶׂה לִפְנֵיכֶם — that I am to perform before you, צִוַּנִי הַקָּדוֹשׁ בָּרוּךְ הוּא לַעֲשׂוֹת — the Holy One, Blessed is He, commanded me to do. וְאַל תֹּאמְרוּ — Do not say that לִכְבוֹדִי — for my own honor וְלִכְבוֹד אָחִי — and for the honor of my brother אֲנִי עוֹשֶׂה — I am acting.[4] {כָּל הָעִנְיָן הַזֶּה דְּפָרָשַׁת הַמִּלּוּאִים — This entire topic of the chapter on the inauguration פֵּרַשְׁתִּי — I have explained[5] בְּוְאַתָּה תְּצַוֶּה — in *Parashas VeAtah Tetzaveh.*[5]}

8. אֶת הָאוּרִים — THE URIM. כְּתָב שֶׁל שֵׁם הַמְפֹרָשׁ — A writing of the Explicit Name.[6]

---

1. *Exodus* Ch. 29.
2. Rashi (to *Exodus* 19:24) cites the *Mechilta*: "We spur on a person [to follow instructions] prior to the act, and spur him on again at the time of the act."
3. *Vayikra Rabbah* 10:9. The area of the Tent of Meeting miraculously held the entire Israelite nation.

[Some of the other places are *Exodus* 9:8; *Numbers* 20:10; and *Joshua* 3:9.]

4. Rashi explains what Moses' point was in making this seemingly unnecessary introduction (*Gur Aryeh*).
5. *Exodus* 29:1-37.
6. This is a Divine Name which is generally forbidden

and the Tumim. ⁹ He put the Mitznefes upon his head; and upon the Mitznefes, toward his face, he placed the golden Tzitz, the sacred diadem, as Hashem had commanded Moses.

¹⁰ Moses took the oil of anointment and anointed the Tabernacle and everything within it; thus he sanctified them. ¹¹ He sprinkled from it seven times on the Mizbe'ach; he anointed the Mizbe'ach and all its utensils, and the laver and its base, in order to sanctify them. ¹² He poured from the oil of anointment upon Aaron's head, and he anointed him to sanctify him. ¹³ Moses brought the sons of Aaron forward, he dressed them in Kutanos and he bound [each of] them with an Avneit and he bound the Migbaos upon them, as Hashem had commanded Moses.

ט וְאֶת־הַתֻּמִּים: וַיָּשֶׂם אֶת־הַמִּצְנֶפֶת עַל־רֹאשׁוֹ וַיָּשֶׂם עַל־הַמִּצְנֶפֶת אֶל־מוּל פָּנָיו אֵת צִיץ הַזָּהָב נֵזֶר הַקֹּדֶשׁ כַּאֲשֶׁר צִוָּה יהוה אֶת־מֹשֶׁה: י וַיִּקַּח מֹשֶׁה אֶת־שֶׁמֶן הַמִּשְׁחָה וַיִּמְשַׁח אֶת־הַמִּשְׁכָּן וְאֶת־כָּל־אֲשֶׁר־בּוֹ וַיְקַדֵּשׁ אֹתָם: יא וַיַּז מִמֶּנּוּ עַל־הַמִּזְבֵּחַ שֶׁבַע פְּעָמִים וַיִּמְשַׁח אֶת־הַמִּזְבֵּחַ וְאֶת־כָּל־כֵּלָיו וְאֶת־הַכִּיֹּר וְאֶת־כַּנּוֹ לְקַדְּשָׁם: יב וַיִּצֹק מִשֶּׁמֶן הַמִּשְׁחָה עַל רֹאשׁ אַהֲרֹן וַיִּמְשַׁח אֹתוֹ לְקַדְּשׁוֹ: יג וַיַּקְרֵב מֹשֶׁה אֶת־בְּנֵי אַהֲרֹן וַיַּלְבִּשֵׁם כֻּתֳּנֹת וַיַּחְגֹּר אֹתָם אַבְנֵט וַיַּחֲבֹשׁ לָהֶם מִגְבָּעוֹת כַּאֲשֶׁר צִוָּה יהוה אֶת־מֹשֶׁה:

———————— אונקלוס ————————

וְיָת תֻּמַּיָּא: ט וְשַׁוִּי יָת מִצְנֶפְתָּא עַל רֵישֵׁהּ וְשַׁוִּי עַל מִצְנֶפְתָּא לָקֳבֵל אַפּוֹהִי יָת צִיצָא כְּלִילָא דְקוּדְשָׁא כְּמָא דִי פַקִּיד יְיָ יָת מֹשֶׁה: י וּנְסִיב מֹשֶׁה יָת מִשְׁחָא דִרְבוּתָא וְרַבִּי יָת מַשְׁכְּנָא וְיָת כָּל דִּי בֵהּ וְקַדֵּשׁ יָתְהוֹן: יא וְאַדִּי מִנֵּהּ עַל מַדְבְּחָא שְׁבַע זִמְנִין וְרַבִּי יָת מַדְבְּחָא וְיָת כָּל מָנוֹהִי וְיָת כִּיּוֹרָא וְיָת בְּסִיסֵהּ לְקַדָּשׁוּתְהוֹן: יב וַאֲרִיק מִמִּשְׁחָא דִרְבוּתָא עַל רֵישָׁא דְאַהֲרֹן וְרַבִּי יָתֵהּ לְקַדָּשׁוּתֵהּ: יג וְקָרֵיב מֹשֶׁה יָת בְּנֵי אַהֲרֹן וְאַלְבֵּשִׁנּוּן כִּתּוּנִין וְזָרֵז יָתְהוֹן הֶמְיָנִין וַאֲתַקֵּן לְהוֹן כּוֹבְעִין כְּמָא דִי פַקִּיד יְיָ יָת מֹשֶׁה:

———————— רש"י ————————

(ט) וישם על המצנפת. פְּתִילֵי תְכֵלֶת הַקְּבוּעִים בַּצִּיץ נָתַן עַל הַמִּצְנֶפֶת נִמְצָא הַצִּיץ תָּלוּי בַּמִּצְנֶפֶת: (יא) ויז ממנו על המזבח. לֹא יָדַעְתִּי הֵיכָן נִצְטַוָּה בַּהַזָּאוֹת הַלָּלוּ: (יב) ויצק. וימשח. בַּתְּחִלָּה יוֹצֵק עַל רֹאשׁוֹ וְאַחַ"כ נוֹתֵן בֵּין רִיסֵי עֵינָיו וּמוֹשֵׁךְ בְּאֶצְבָּעוֹ מִזֶּה לָזֶה (כריתות ה:): (יג) ויחבש. לְשׁוֹן קְשִׁירָה:

———————— RASHI ELUCIDATED ————————

9. וַיָּשֶׂם עַל הַמִּצְנֶפֶת — AND UPON THE *MITZNEFES*, [TOWARD HIS FACE,] HE PLACED. פְּתִילֵי תְכֵלֶת — The strings of turquoise wool הַקְּבוּעִים בַּצִּיץ — that are set in the *Tzitz*, נָתַן עַל הַמִּצְנֶפֶת — he placed on the *Mitznefes*. נִמְצָא הַצִּיץ תָּלוּי בַּמִּצְנֶפֶת — It is thus found that the *Tzitz* is suspended from the *Mitznefes*.[1]

11. וַיַּז מִמֶּנּוּ עַל הַמִּזְבֵּחַ — HE SPRINKLED FROM IT . . . ON THE *MIZBE'ACH*. לֹא יָדַעְתִּי — I do not know הֵיכָן נִצְטַוָּה — where [Moses] was commanded בַּהַזָּאוֹת הַלָּלוּ — about these sprinklings.[2]

12. וַיִּצֹק . . . וַיִּמְשַׁח — HE POURED . . . AND HE ANOINTED. בַּתְּחִלָּה יוֹצֵק עַל רֹאשׁוֹ — At first he pours on his head, וְאַחַר כָּךְ — and afterwards נוֹתֵן בֵּין רִיסֵי עֵינָיו — he puts oil among his eyelashes,[3] וּמוֹשֵׁךְ בְּאֶצְבָּעוֹ — and draws the oil with his finger מִזֶּה לָזֶה — from one to the other.[4]

13. וַיַּחֲבֹשׁ — AND HE BOUND. לְשׁוֹן קְשִׁירָה — This expresses tying.

---

to be uttered. *Tzeidah LaDerech* maintains that it was the forty-two-letter Name. According to others, it was the seventy-two-letter Name (*Chizkuni; Baal HaTurim*; see also *Zohar, Pekudei*). The *Urim* and the *Tumim* was a writing of this Explicit Name. See *Exodus* 28:30 and Rashi there.

1. Rashi explains the way the *Tzitz* was hung from the *Mitznefes* at length in his comments to *Exodus* 28:37 and 39:31.

2. *Ramban* suggests that the source is *Exodus* 40:10. The phrase, in that verse, "you shall sanctify the *Mizbe'ach* " refers to anointing it with oil just as all the other implements of the *Mishkan*; the added phrase "and the *Mizbe'ach* shall be holy of holies" alludes to an additional procedure, the sprinklings of our verse.

3. The translation of רִיסֵי as "eyelashes" is based on Rashi's comments to *Kiddushin* 31a and *Sanhedrin* 104b.

4. *Kereisos* 5a. See note 7 on page 22.

¹⁴ He brought forward the sin-offering bull; Aaron and his sons leaned their hands upon the head of the sin-offering bull. ¹⁵ He slaughtered it, and Moses took the blood and placed it on the horns of the Mizbe'ach, all around, with his forefinger, and he cleansed the Mizbe'ach; he poured the [remaining] blood upon the base of the Mizbe'ach and he sanctified it to atone upon it.

¹⁶ Then he took all the fat that is upon the innards, and the diaphragm of the liver, and the two kidneys with their fat; and Moses caused them to go up in smoke on the Mizbe'ach. ¹⁷ And the bull, with its hide, its flesh and its waste, he burned in fire outside the camp, as HASHEM had commanded Moses. ¹⁸ Then he brought near the ram for the olah-offering, and Aaron and his sons leaned their hands upon

יד וַיַּגֵּשׁ אֵת פַּר הַחַטָּאת וַיִּסְמֹךְ אַהֲרֹן וּבָנָיו אֶת־יְדֵיהֶם עַל־רֹאשׁ פַּר הַחַטָּאת: טו וַיִּשְׁחָט וַיִּקַּח מֹשֶׁה אֶת־הַדָּם וַיִּתֵּן עַל־קַרְנוֹת הַמִּזְבֵּחַ סָבִיב בְּאֶצְבָּעוֹ וַיְחַטֵּא אֶת־הַמִּזְבֵּחַ וְאֶת־הַדָּם יָצַק אֶל־יְסוֹד הַמִּזְבֵּחַ וַיְקַדְּשֵׁהוּ לְכַפֵּר עָלָיו: טז וַיִּקַּח אֶת־כָּל־הַחֵלֶב אֲשֶׁר עַל־הַקֶּרֶב וְאֵת יֹתֶרֶת הַכָּבֵד וְאֶת־שְׁתֵּי הַכְּלָיֹת וְאֶת־חֶלְבְּהֶן וַיַּקְטֵר מֹשֶׁה הַמִּזְבֵּחָה: יז וְאֶת־הַפָּר וְאֶת־עֹרוֹ וְאֶת־בְּשָׂרוֹ וְאֶת־פִּרְשׁוֹ שָׂרַף בָּאֵשׁ מִחוּץ לַמַּחֲנֶה כַּאֲשֶׁר צִוָּה יְהוָה אֶת־מֹשֶׁה: יח וַיַּקְרֵב אֵת אֵיל הָעֹלָה וַיִּסְמְכוּ אַהֲרֹן וּבָנָיו אֶת־יְדֵיהֶם עַל־

— אונקלוס —

יד וְקָרֵיב יָת תּוֹרָא דְחַטָּאתָא וּסְמַךְ אַהֲרֹן וּבְנוֹהִי יָת יְדֵיהוֹן עַל רֵישׁ תּוֹרָא דְחַטָּאתָא: טו וּנְכֵס וּנְסִיב מֹשֶׁה יָת דְמָא וִיהַב עַל קַרְנַת מַדְבְּחָא סְחוֹר סְחוֹר בְּאֶצְבְּעֵהּ וְדַכִּי יָת מַדְבְּחָא וְיָת דְמָא אֲרֵיק לִיסוֹדָא דְמַדְבְּחָא וְקַדְּשֵׁהּ לְכַפָּרָא עֲלוֹהִי: טז וּנְסִיב יָת כָּל תַּרְבָּא דִי עַל גַּוָּא וְיָת חֲצַר כַּבְדָּא וְיָת תַּרְתֵּין כָּלְיָן וְיָת תַּרְבְּהֶן וְאַסֵּק מֹשֶׁה לְמַדְבְּחָא: יז וְיָת תּוֹרָא וְיָת מַשְׁכֵּהּ וְיָת בִּסְרֵהּ וְיָת אֻכְלֵהּ אוֹקִיד בְּנוּרָא מִבָּרָא לְמַשְׁרִיתָא כְּמָא דִי פַקִּיד יְיָ יָת מֹשֶׁה: יח וְקָרִיב יָת דִּכְרָא דַעֲלָתָא וּסְמַךְ אַהֲרֹן וּבְנוֹהִי יָת יְדֵיהוֹן עַל

— רש"י —

(טו) **ויחטא את המזבח.** חטאו וטהרו מזרות להכנס הכפרות: **(טז) ואת יתרת הכבד** (שמות לקדושה: **ויקדשהו.** בעבודה זו: **לכפר עליו.** מעתה כל כט:יג). לבד הכבד. שהיה נוטל מעט מן הכבד עמה:

— RASHI ELUCIDATED —

15. וַיְחַטֵּא אֶת הַמִּזְבֵּחַ — AND HE CLEANSED THE *MIZBE'ACH*. חִטְּאוֹ — He cleansed it וְטִהֲרוֹ — and purified it מִזָּרוּת — of what is alien, לְהִכָּנֵס לִקְדֻשָּׁה — to enter into holiness,[1]

☐ וַיְקַדְּשֵׁהוּ — AND HE SANCTIFIED IT בַּעֲבוֹדָה זוּ — through this service.[2]

☐ לְכַפֵּר עָלָיו — TO ATONE UPON IT, מֵעַתָּה — from now on, כָּל הַכַּפָּרוֹת — all atonements.[3]

16. וְאֵת יֹתֶרֶת הַכָּבֵד — THE DIAPHRAGM OF THE LIVER. {עַל הַכָּבֵד,[4] — This is similar in meaning to, "with the liver,"[4] that is,} לְבַד הַכָּבֵד — besides some of the liver, שֶׁהָיָה נוֹטֵל — for he would take מְעַט מִן הַכָּבֵד — a bit of the liver עִמָּהּ — along with [the diaphragm].[5]

---

1. In his commentary to *Exodus* 27:3, Rashi explains that certain verb forms "serve both building and destroying," i.e., a thing and its opposite. Here too, the root חטא in its simple form (see Rashi to 1:15 above and note 1 there) means "to sin"; but in its intensive forms it means "to cleanse of sin." Rashi teaches here that the application of blood to the *Mizbe'ach* brings about its purification and is therefore called חטוי (*Be'er Yitzchak*).

2. "And he sanctified it" is not a procedure which followed "and he poured the blood upon the base of the *Mizbe'ach*." It is the result of pouring the blood (*Mesiach Ilmim*).

3. The term לְכַפֵּר עָלָיו could be understood as "to atone *for* it." But that implies that the *Mizbe'ach* had not yet been atoned for. The *Mizbe'ach* had, however, been atoned for at this point, as it says, וַיְחַטֵּא אֶת הַמִּזְבֵּחַ, "and he cleansed the *Mizbe'ach*." Therefore, לְכַפֵּר עָלָיו means "to atone *upon* it," in the future (*Sefer Zikaron*).

4. *Exodus* 29:13.

5. The fact that part of the liver itself is separated with the diaphragm is not derived from our verse. See Rashi to *Exodus* 29:13, and to 3:4 above. See *Yosef Hallel* for a discussion of the various texts of this comment of Rashi.

the head of the ram. ¹⁹ He slaughtered it, and Moses threw its blood upon the Mizbe'ach, all around. ²⁰ He cut the ram into its parts; Moses caused the head, the parts, and the fats to go up in smoke. ²¹ He washed the innards and the feet with water; Moses caused the entire ram to go up in smoke on the Mizbe'ach — it was an olah-offering, for a satisfying aroma; it was a fire-offering to HASHEM, as HASHEM had commanded Moses.

²² Then he brought near the second ram, the inauguration ram, and Aaron and his sons leaned their hands upon the head of the ram. ²³ He slaughtered it, and Moses took some of its blood and placed it upon the middle part of Aaron's right ear, upon the thumb of his right hand, and upon the big toe of his right foot. ²⁴ He brought the sons of Aaron forward, and Moses put some of the blood upon the middle part of their right ear, upon the thumb of their right hand and upon the big toe of their right foot; and Moses threw the [remaining] blood upon the Mizbe'ach, all around. ²⁵ He took the fat, and the tail, and all the fat that was upon the innards, and the diaphragm of the liver, and the two kidneys and their fat,

יט רֹאשׁ הָאָיִל: וַיִּשְׁחָט וַיִּזְרֹק מֹשֶׁה
כ אֶת־הַדָּם עַל־הַמִּזְבֵּחַ סָבִיב: וְאֶת־
הָאַיִל נִתַּח לִנְתָחָיו וַיַּקְטֵר מֹשֶׁה
אֶת־הָרֹאשׁ וְאֶת־הַנְּתָחִים וְאֶת־
כא הַפָּדֶר: וְאֶת־הַקֶּרֶב וְאֶת־הַכְּרָעַיִם
רָחַץ בַּמָּיִם וַיַּקְטֵר מֹשֶׁה אֶת־כָּל־
הָאַיִל הַמִּזְבֵּחָה עֹלָה הוּא לְרֵיחַ־
נִיחֹחַ אִשֶּׁה הוּא לַיהוָה כַּאֲשֶׁר צִוָּה
כב יְהוָה אֶת־מֹשֶׁה: ששי וַיַּקְרֵב אֶת־
הָאַיִל הַשֵּׁנִי אֵיל הַמִּלֻּאִים וַיִּסְמְכוּ
אַהֲרֹן וּבָנָיו אֶת־יְדֵיהֶם עַל־רֹאשׁ
כג הָאָיִל: וַיִּשְׁחָט ׀ וַיִּקַּח מֹשֶׁה מִדָּמוֹ
וַיִּתֵּן עַל־תְּנוּךְ אֹזֶן־אַהֲרֹן הַיְמָנִית
וְעַל־בֹּהֶן יָדוֹ הַיְמָנִית וְעַל־בֹּהֶן
כד רַגְלוֹ הַיְמָנִית: וַיַּקְרֵב אֶת־בְּנֵי אַהֲרֹן
וַיִּתֵּן מֹשֶׁה מִן־הַדָּם עַל־תְּנוּךְ אָזְנָם
הַיְמָנִית וְעַל־בֹּהֶן יָדָם הַיְמָנִית וְעַל־
בֹּהֶן רַגְלָם הַיְמָנִית וַיִּזְרֹק מֹשֶׁה אֶת־
כה הַדָּם עַל־הַמִּזְבֵּחַ סָבִיב: וַיִּקַּח אֶת־
הַחֵלֶב וְאֶת־הָאַלְיָה וְאֶת־כָּל־הַחֵלֶב
אֲשֶׁר עַל־הַקֶּרֶב וְאֵת יֹתֶרֶת הַכָּבֵד
וְאֶת־שְׁתֵּי הַכְּלָיֹת וְאֶת־חֶלְבְּהֶן

───── אונקלוס ─────

רֵישׁ דְּכְרָא: יט וּנְכֵס וְזָרֵק מֹשֶׁה יָת דְּמָא עַל מַדְבְּחָא סְחוֹר סְחוֹר: כ וְיָת דִּכְרָא פַּלֵּיג לְאֶבְרוֹהִי וְאַסֵּק מֹשֶׁה יָת רֵישָׁא וְיָת אֶבְרַיָּא וְיָת תַּרְבָּא: כא וְיָת גַּוָּא וְיָת כְּרָעַיָּא חַלֵּיל בְּמַיָּא וְאַסֵּק מֹשֶׁה יָת כָּל דִּכְרָא לְמַדְבְּחָא עֲלָתָא הוּא לְאִתְקַבָּלָא בְּרַעֲוָא קֻרְבָּנָא הוּא קֳדָם יְיָ כְּמָא דִי פַקֵּיד יְיָ יָת מֹשֶׁה: כב וְקָרֵיב יָת דִּכְרָא תִנְיָנָא דְּכַר קֻרְבָּנַיָּא וּסְמָכוּ אַהֲרֹן וּבְנוֹהִי יָת יְדֵיהוֹן עַל רֵישׁ דִּכְרָא: כג וּנְכֵס וּנְסֵיב מֹשֶׁה מִן דְּמֵהּ וִיהַב עַל רוּם אוּדְנָא דְאַהֲרֹן דְּיַמִּינָא וְעַל אֶלְיוֹן יְדֵהּ דְּיַמִּינָא וְעַל אֶלְיוֹן רַגְלֵהּ דְּיַמִּינָא: כד וְקָרֵיב יָת בְּנֵי אַהֲרֹן וִיהַב מֹשֶׁה מִן דְּמָא עַל רוּם אוּדְנְהוֹן דְּיַמִּינָא וְעַל אֶלְיוֹן יְדֵיהוֹן דְּיַמִּינָא וְעַל אֶלְיוֹן רַגְלֵיהוֹן דְּיַמִּינָא וּזְרַק מֹשֶׁה יָת דְּמָא עַל מַדְבְּחָא סְחוֹר סְחוֹר: כה וּנְסֵיב יָת תַּרְבָּא וְיָת אַלִּיתָא וְיָת כָּל תַּרְבָּא דִּי עַל גַּוָּא וְיָת חֲצַר כַּבְדָּא וְיָת תַּרְתֵּין כָּלְיָן וְיָת תַּרְבְּהֶן

───── רש"י ─────

(כב) **איל המלאים.** השלמים שממלאים ומשלימים את הכהנים בכהונתם (ת"כ מלואים כ): השלמים ל' שלמים

───── RASHI ELUCIDATED ─────

22. אֵיל הַמִּלֻּאִים — This means אֵיל הַשְּׁלָמִים — **the ram of the peace-offering,** שְׁמִּלּוּאִים לְשׁוֹן שְׁלָמִים — for **מִלּוּאִים**, literally, "fillings," **expresses** שְׁלָמִים, "peace-offerings" or "completenesses," שֶׁמְמַלְּאִים — **וּמַשְׁלִימִים אֶת הַכֹּהֲנִים** — **for they fill and complete the Kohanim** בְּכַהֲנָתָם — **in their kehunah.**[1]

---

1. *Toras Kohanim, Miluim* 20. The word מלואים usually means "inauguration." It does not mean that here, however, for there is no reason to label the second ram of the inauguration ceremony "the ram of inauguration" any more than the first. Rashi explains that here the word denotes a peace-offering, and goes on to explain why it is appropriate to refer to this peace-offering as מלואים (*Minchas Yehudah;* see, however, Ramban, who interprets מלואים of our verse as "inauguration," and explains that the second ram is referred to as "the ram of inauguration" because it is the last of the inaugural offerings, and with it, Aaron and his sons fully entered the *kehunah*).

and the right leg. ²⁶ *And from the basket of matzos that was before* HASHEM *he took one matzah loaf, one loaf of oil bread, and one wafer, and placed them on the fats and on the right leg.* ²⁷ *He put it all on Aaron's palms and on the palms of his sons; and he waved them as a wave-service before* HASHEM. ²⁸ *Then Moses took them from on their palms and he caused them to go up in smoke on the Mizbe'ach after the olah-offering; they were inauguration offerings, for a satisfying aroma; it was a fire-offering to* HASHEM. ²⁹ *Moses took the breast and waved it as a wave-service before* HASHEM; *from the ram of the dedication it was a portion for Moses, as* HASHEM *had commanded Moses.*

³⁰ *Moses took from the oil of anointment and some of the blood that was on the Mizbe'ach, and he sprinkled it upon*

כו וְאֵת שׁוֹק הַיָּמִין: וּמִסַּל הַמַּצּוֹת אֲשֶׁר ׀ לִפְנֵי יהוה לָקַח חַלַּת מַצָּה אַחַת וְחַלַּת לֶחֶם שֶׁמֶן אַחַת וְרָקִיק אֶחָד וַיָּשֶׂם עַל־הַחֲלָבִים וְעַל שׁוֹק הַיָּמִין: כז וַיִּתֵּן אֶת־הַכֹּל עַל כַּפֵּי אַהֲרֹן וְעַל כַּפֵּי בָנָיו וַיָּנֶף אֹתָם תְּנוּפָה לִפְנֵי יהוה: כח וַיִּקַּח מֹשֶׁה אֹתָם מֵעַל כַּפֵּיהֶם וַיַּקְטֵר הַמִּזְבֵּחָה עַל־הָעֹלָה מִלֻּאִים הֵם לְרֵיחַ נִיחֹחַ אִשֶּׁה הוּא לַיהוה: כט וַיִּקַּח מֹשֶׁה אֶת־הֶחָזֶה וַיְנִיפֵהוּ תְנוּפָה לִפְנֵי יהוה מֵאֵיל הַמִּלֻּאִים לְמֹשֶׁה הָיָה לְמָנָה כַּאֲשֶׁר צִוָּה יהוה אֶת־מֹשֶׁה:

שביעי ל וַיִּקַּח מֹשֶׁה מִשֶּׁמֶן הַמִּשְׁחָה וּמִן־הַדָּם אֲשֶׁר עַל־הַמִּזְבֵּחַ וַיַּז עַל־

— אונקלוס —

וְיָת שׁוֹקָא דְיַמִּינָא: כו וּמִסַּלָּא דְפַטִּירַיָּא דִּי קֳדָם יְיָ נְסִיב גְּרִצְתָּא פַטִּירְתָּא חֲדָא וּגְרִצְתָּא דִּלְחֵם מְשַׁח חֲדָא וְאֶסְפּוֹג חַד וְשַׁוִּי עַל תַּרְבַּיָּא וְעַל שׁוֹקָא דְיַמִּינָא: כז וִיהַב יָת כֹּלָּא עַל יְדֵי אַהֲרֹן וְעַל יְדֵי בְנוֹהִי וַאֲרֵם יָתְהוֹן אֲרָמָא קֳדָם יְיָ: כח וּנְסִיב מֹשֶׁה יָתְהוֹן מֵעַל יְדֵיהוֹן וְאַסֵּק לְמַדְבְּחָא עַל עֲלָתָא קֻרְבָּנַיָּא אִנּוּן לְאִתְקַבָּלָא בְרַעֲוָא קֻרְבָּנָא הוּא קֳדָם יְיָ: כט וּנְסִיב מֹשֶׁה יָת חֶדְיָא וַאֲרֵמֵהּ אֲרָמָא קֳדָם יְיָ מִדְּכַר קֻרְבָּנַיָּא לְמֹשֶׁה הֲוָה לָחֳלָק כְּמָא דִּי פַקִּיד יְיָ יָת מֹשֶׁה: ל וּנְסִיב מֹשֶׁה מִמִּשְׁחָא דִרְבוּתָא וּמִן דְּמָא דִּי עַל מַדְבְּחָא וְאַדִּי עַל

— רש"י —

(כו) וחלת לחם שמן. היא רבוכה שהיה מרבה בה שמן כנגד החלות משה שמש כל שבעת ימי המלואים בחלוק לבן (ע"ז ל"ד:): **על העולה:** אחר העולה ולא מצינו שוק שלמים קרב בכל מקום חוץ מזה: והרקיקין כך מפורש במנחות (עח.): **(כח) ויקטר המזבחה.**

— RASHI ELUCIDATED —

26. וְחַלַּת לֶחֶם שֶׁמֶן — ONE LOAF OF OIL BREAD. הִיא רְבוּכָה — It is the bread which is scalded.[1] It is called "oil bread" as — שֶׁהָיָה מַרְבֶּה בָהּ שֶׁמֶן — because he would put much oil in it, כְּנֶגֶד הַחַלּוֹת וְהָרְקִיקִין — as much as the *challos* and wafers combined. כָּךְ מְפֹרָשׁ בִּמְנָחוֹת — Thus is it stated explicitly in *Menachos*.[2]

28. וַיַּקְטֵר הַמִּזְבֵּחָה — AND HE CAUSED THEM TO GO UP IN SMOKE ON THE *MIZBE'ACH*. מֹשֶׁה שִׁמֵּשׁ — Moses officiated כָּל שִׁבְעַת יְמֵי הַמִּלּוּאִים — for the entire seven-day period of the inauguration בַּחֲלוּק לָבָן — in a white tunic.[3]

עַל הָעֹלָה — This means אַחַר הָעֹלָה — after the *olah*-offering. וְלֹא מָצִינוּ שׁוֹק שֶׁל שְׁלָמִים קָרֵב — We have not found a leg of a peace-offering offered on the *Mizbe'ach* בְּכָל מָקוֹם — in any place חוּץ מִזֶּה — besides this one.

---

1. Scalding water was poured on the flour. It was then baked, and fried in oil to make it crisp (*Sefer Zikaron* to Exodus 29:2).

2. *Menachos* 78a.

3. *Avodah Zarah* 34a. He did not wear the priestly garments. We find Moses performing parts of the Altar service which are otherwise restricted to Kohanim as early as verse 15, where he receives and sprinkles the blood.

Rashi withholds comment until this verse because he wishes to explain why the thigh of this peace-offering was offered on the *Mizbe'ach*, unlike any other, as he notes in his next comment. It is because the thigh is normally the portion of the Kohen. Here, God wished to show the distinction between Moses, who was a Levite, and the Kohanim, so He has Moses place the thigh on the *Mizbe'ach*, rather than take it as his portion, as a Kohen would (*Minchas Yehudah; Sifsei Chachamim*).

Aaron and his vestments, and upon his sons and upon the vestments of his sons who were with him; thus he sanctified Aaron and his vestments, and his sons, and the vestments of his sons with him.

³¹ Moses said to Aaron and to his sons: Cook the flesh at the entrance of the Tent of the Meeting and there you shall eat it and the bread that is in the basket of the inauguration-offerings, as I have commanded, saying: "Aaron and his sons shall eat it." ³² And whatever is left over of the flesh and of the bread, you shall burn in the fire. ³³ You shall not leave the entrance of the Tent of the Meeting for seven days, until the day when your days of inauguration are completed; for you shall be inaugurated for a seven-day period.

³⁴ As he did on this day, so HASHEM had commanded to be done to atone for you. ³⁵ At the entrance of the Tent of Meeting shall you dwell day and night for a seven-day period, and you shall protect HASHEM's charge

אַהֲרֹן עַל־בְּגָדָיו וְעַל־בָּנָיו וְעַל־בִּגְדֵי בָנָיו אִתּוֹ וַיְקַדֵּשׁ אֶת־אַהֲרֹן אֶת־בְּגָדָיו וְאֶת־בָּנָיו וְאֶת־בִּגְדֵי בָנָיו אִתּוֹ: לא וַיֹּאמֶר מֹשֶׁה אֶל־אַהֲרֹן וְאֶל־בָּנָיו בַּשְּׁלוּ אֶת־הַבָּשָׂר פֶּתַח אֹהֶל מוֹעֵד וְשָׁם תֹּאכְלוּ אֹתוֹ וְאֶת־הַלֶּחֶם אֲשֶׁר בְּסַל הַמִּלֻּאִים כַּאֲשֶׁר צִוֵּיתִי לֵאמֹר אַהֲרֹן וּבָנָיו יֹאכְלֻהוּ: לב וְהַנּוֹתָר בַּבָּשָׂר וּבַלָּחֶם בָּאֵשׁ תִּשְׂרֹפוּ: לג וּמִפֶּתַח אֹהֶל מוֹעֵד לֹא תֵצְאוּ שִׁבְעַת יָמִים עַד יוֹם מְלֹאת יְמֵי מִלֻּאֵיכֶם כִּי שִׁבְעַת יָמִים יְמַלֵּא אֶת־יֶדְכֶם: לד כַּאֲשֶׁר עָשָׂה בַּיּוֹם הַזֶּה צִוָּה יהוה לַעֲשֹׂת לְכַפֵּר עֲלֵיכֶם: לה וּפֶתַח אֹהֶל מוֹעֵד תֵּשְׁבוּ יוֹמָם וָלַיְלָה שִׁבְעַת יָמִים וּשְׁמַרְתֶּם אֶת־מִשְׁמֶרֶת יהוה

──────── אונקלוס ────────

אַהֲרֹן עַל לְבוּשׁוֹהִי וְעַל בְּנוֹהִי וְעַל לְבוּשֵׁי בְנוֹהִי עִמֵּהּ וְקַדִּישׁ יָת אַהֲרֹן יָת לְבוּשׁוֹהִי וְיָת בְּנוֹהִי וְיָת לְבוּשֵׁי בְנוֹהִי עִמֵּהּ: לא וַאֲמַר מֹשֶׁה לְאַהֲרֹן וְלִבְנוֹהִי בַּשִּׁילוּ יָת בִּסְרָא בִּתְרַע מַשְׁכַּן זִמְנָא וְתַמָּן תֵּיכְלוּן יָתֵהּ וְיָת לַחְמָא דִּי בְסַל קֻרְבָּנַיָּא כְּמָא דִי פַקֵּדִית לְמֵימַר אַהֲרֹן וּבְנוֹהִי יֵיכְלֻנֵּהּ: לב וּדְיִשְׁתְּאַר בְּבִסְרָא וּבְלַחְמָא בְּנוּרָא תוֹקְדוּן: לג וּמִתְּרַע מַשְׁכַּן זִמְנָא לָא תִפְּקוּן שִׁבְעָא יוֹמִין עַד יוֹם מִשְׁלַם יוֹמֵי קֻרְבָּנֵיכוֹן אֲרֵי שִׁבְעָא יוֹמִין יְקָרֵב יָת קֻרְבָּנְכוֹן: לד כְּמָא דִי עֲבַד בְּיוֹמָא הָדֵין פַּקִּיד יְיָ לְמֶעְבַּד לְכַפָּרָא עֲלֵיכוֹן: לה וּבִתְרַע מַשְׁכַּן זִמְנָא תֵּיתְבוּן יְמָמָא וְלֵילְיָא שִׁבְעָא יוֹמִין וְתִטְּרוּן יָת מַטְּרַת מֵימְרָא דַיְיָ

──────── רש"י ────────

(לד) **צוה ה' לעשות.** כל שבעת הימים. ורבותינו דרשו, לעשות, זה מעשה פרה. לכפר, זה מעשה יום הכפורים. וללמד שכהן גדול טעון פרישה קודם יום הכפורים שבעת ימים וכן הכהן השורף את הפרה (תורת כהנים שם ל"ז; יומא ג:):

──────── RASHI ELUCIDATED ────────

34. צִוָּה ה' לַעֲשֹׂת — HASHEM HAD COMMANDED TO BE DONE ‖ כָּל שִׁבְעַת הַיָּמִים — for the entire seven-day period.[1] ‖ וְרַבּוֹתֵינוּ דָּרְשׁוּ — And our Rabbis expounded the verse as follows: ‖ "לַעֲשֹׂת" — "to be done," ‖ זֶה מַעֲשֵׂה פָרָה — this refers to **the procedure of the cow**;[2] ‖ "לְכַפֵּר" — "to atone," ‖ זֶה מַעֲשֵׂה יוֹם הַכִּפּוּרִים — this refers to **the procedure of Yom Kippur**.[3] ‖ וּלְלַמֵּד — To teach us ‖ שֶׁכֹּהֵן גָּדוֹל טָעוּן פְּרִישָׁה — that a **Kohen Gadol requires separation** ‖ קוֹדֶם יוֹם הַכִּפּוּרִים שִׁבְעַת יָמִים — **for a seven-day period prior to Yom Kippur,** ‖ וְכֵן הַכֹּהֵן הַשּׂוֹרֵף אֶת הַפָּרָה — **and so, too, the Kohen who burns the cow** requires a seven-day separation before burning the cow.[4]

---

1. "As he did on this day, so HASHEM had commanded to be done" appears to be a statement of the obvious. There is no reason to suspect that the inauguration ceremony performed was anything other than the fulfillment of God's command. Rashi explains that this is an abbreviated verse. Its implicit meaning is, "As he did on this day, so HASHEM commanded to be done all seven days" (*Mizrachi; Sifsei Chachamim*).

2. The procedure of the burning of the red cow. See *Numbers* 19:1-10.

3. The sacrificial service of Yom Kippur. See 16:1-34 below.

4. *Toras Kohanim, Miluim* 37; *Yoma* 3b. The Kohen Gadol and the Kohen who burns the cow must prepare themselves for the ceremonies they are to perform by separating themselves from their families.

so that you will not die; for so have I been commanded. ³⁶ And Aaron and his sons carried out all the matters that HASHEM commanded through Moses.

לֹא תָמֻתוּ כִּי־כֵן צֻוֵּיתִי: וַיַּעַשׂ אַהֲרֹן וּבָנָיו אֵת כָּל־הַדְּבָרִים אֲשֶׁר־צִוָּה יהוה בְּיַד־מֹשֶׁה: ס ס ס

THE HAFTARAH FOR TZAV APPEARS ON PAGE 390.
During non-leap years, Shabbos HaGadol always coincides with Tzav. The regular Haftarah is then replaced with the Haftarah for Shabbas HaGadol, page 415.
During leap years, when Parashas Zachor or Parashas Parah coincides with Tzav, the regular Maftir and Haftarah are replaced with the readings for Parashas Zachor, page 407, or Parashas Parah, page 409.

───────── אונקלוס ─────────
וְלָא תְמוּתוּן אֲרֵי כֵן אִתְפַּקָּדִית: לוּוַעֲבַד אַהֲרֹן וּבְנוֹהִי יָת כָּל פִּתְגָמַיָּא דִּי פַקִּיד יְיָ בִּידָא דְמֹשֶׁה.

───────── רש"י ─────────
(לה) ולא תמותו. הָא אִם לֹא תַעֲשׂוּ כֵן הֲרֵי אַתֶּם חַיָּבִים מִיתָה: (לו) ויעש אהרן ובניו. לְהַגִּיד שִׁבְחָן שֶׁלֹּא הִטּוּ יָמִין וּשְׂמֹאל:

───────── RASHI ELUCIDATED ─────────

הֲרֵי אַתֶּם — But if you do not do so,¹ **הָא אִם לֹא תַּעֲשׂוּ כֵן** — SO THAT YOU WILL NOT DIE. — **וְלֹא תָמֻתוּ .35** **חַיָּבִים מִיתָה** — then you are worthy of death.

36. וַיַּעַשׂ אַהֲרֹן וּבָנָיו — AND AARON AND HIS SONS CARRIED OUT. — **לְהַגִּיד שִׁבְחָן** — To tell their praise, **שֶׁלֹּא הִטּוּ יָמִין וּשְׂמֹאל** — that they veered neither right nor left, but did exactly as they were instructed.²

---

1. *Rashi* often states: מִכְּלַל לָאו אַתָּה שׁוֹמֵעַ הֵן, "from the implication of the negative you infer the positive," and, מִכְּלַל הֵן אַתָּה שׁוֹמֵעַ לָאו, "from the implication of the positive, you infer the negative." See Rashi to *Exodus* 20:12, 28:35, 30:20; *Numbers* 5:19; *Deuteronomy* 11:21 and 17:20.

2. It is obvious that people as saintly as Aaron and his sons would have carried out God's command. The Torah nonetheless tells us this point to inform us that they carried out His instructions *exactly* (*Minchas Yehudah*; *Sifsei Chachamim*). Or, we might say that if all the Torah wished to tell us was that Aaron and his sons carried out God's command, it could have done so briefly by saying, וַיַּעֲשׂוּ כֵן, "and they did so." The lengthier language indicates that they carried out instructions exactly (*Maskil LeDavid*). Carrying out the laws of the Divine service precisely is especially praiseworthy because of the importance of the service and the complexity of its laws. Aaron and his sons did not make a single error throughout the entire service (*Gur Aryeh*).
See also *Rashi* to *Numbers* 8:3.

פרשת שמיני

Parashas Shemini

9 ¹ It was on the eighth day, Moses called to Aaron and his sons, and to the elders of Israel. ² He said to Aaron: Take yourself a calf, a young male of cattle, for a sin-offering and a ram for an olah-offering — unblemished; and offer [them] before HASHEM. ³ And to the Children of Israel speak as follows: Take a he-goat for a sin-offering, and a calf and a sheep in their first year — unblemished — for an olah-offering. ⁴ And a bull and a ram for a peace-offering to sacrifice before HASHEM,

א וַיְהִי בַּיּוֹם הַשְּׁמִינִי קָרָא מֹשֶׁה לְאַהֲרֹן וּלְבָנָיו וּלְזִקְנֵי יִשְׂרָאֵל: ב וַיֹּאמֶר אֶל־אַהֲרֹן קַח־לְךָ עֵגֶל בֶּן־בָּקָר לְחַטָּאת וְאַיִל לְעֹלָה תְּמִימִם וְהַקְרֵב לִפְנֵי יהוה: ג וְאֶל־בְּנֵי יִשְׂרָאֵל תְּדַבֵּר לֵאמֹר קְחוּ שְׂעִיר־עִזִּים לְחַטָּאת וְעֵגֶל וָכֶבֶשׂ בְּנֵי־שָׁנָה תְּמִימִם לְעֹלָה: ד וְשׁוֹר וָאַיִל לִשְׁלָמִים לִזְבֹּחַ לִפְנֵי יהוה

──────── אונקלוס ────────

א וַהֲוָה בְּיוֹמָא תְמִינָאָה קְרָא מֹשֶׁה לְאַהֲרֹן וְלִבְנוֹהִי וּלְסָבֵי יִשְׂרָאֵל: ב וַאֲמַר לְאַהֲרֹן סַב לָךְ עֵגֶל בַּר תּוֹרֵי לְחַטָּאתָא וּדְכַר לַעֲלָתָא שַׁלְמִין וְקָרֵב קֳדָם יְיָ: ג וְעִם בְּנֵי יִשְׂרָאֵל תְּמַלֵּל לְמֵימָר סִיבוּ צְפִיר בַּר עִזִּין לְחַטָּאתָא וְעֵגֶל וְאִמַּר בְּנֵי שְׁנָא שַׁלְמִין לַעֲלָתָא: ד וְתוֹר וּדְכַר לְנִכְסַת קוּדְשַׁיָּא לְדַבָּחָא קֳדָם יְיָ

──────── רש״י ────────

(א) **ויהי ביום השמיני.** שמיני למלואים, הוא ראש חודש ניסן, שהוקם המשכן בו ביום ונטל עשר עטרות השנויות בסדר עולם (פ"ז): ת"כ מכילתא דמלואים שמיני פרשתא א:ח; שבת פז:)**ולזקני** להשמיעם שעל פי הדבור אהרן נכנס ומשמש בכהונה גדולה ולא יאמרו מאליו נכנס (תנחומא ג): (ב) **קח לך עגל.** להודיע שכפר לו הקב"ה ע"י עגל זה על מעשה העגל שעשה (ת"כ)

──────── RASHI ELUCIDATED ────────

9.

1. וַיְהִי בַּיּוֹם הַשְּׁמִינִי — IT WAS ON THE EIGHTH DAY. שְׁמִינִי לַמִּלּוּאִים — The eighth day of the inauguration of Aaron and his sons into the *kehunah*. הוּא רֹאשׁ חֹדֶשׁ נִיסָן — This is the first of the month of Nissan שֶׁהוּקַם הַמִּשְׁכָּן בּוֹ בַּיּוֹם — for on that day the *Mishkan* was erected,¹ וְנָטַל עֶשֶׂר עֲטָרוֹת הַשְּׁנוּיוֹת בְּסֵדֶר — and it took the ten crowns that are recounted in *Seder Olam*.²

□ וּלְזִקְנֵי יִשְׂרָאֵל — AND TO THE ELDERS OF ISRAEL. לְהַשְׁמִיעָם — To let them hear שֶׁעַל פִּי הַדִּבּוּר — that in accordance with the statement of God אַהֲרֹן נִכְנָס — Aaron enters וּמְשַׁמֵּשׁ בִּכְהֻנָּה גְדוֹלָה — and officiates in the office of Kohen Gadol, וְלֹא יֹאמְרוּ — and they should not say that מֵאֵלָיו נִכְנָס — he enters the office of Kohen Gadol **on his own.**³

2. קַח לְךָ עֵגֶל — TAKE YOURSELF A CALF. לְהוֹדִיעַ — To inform Aaron שֶׁכִּפֵּר לוֹ הַקָּדוֹשׁ בָּרוּךְ הוּא — that the Holy One, Blessed is He, grants atonement for him עַל יְדֵי עֵגֶל זֶה — through this calf עַל — for the matter of the Golden **Calf that he made.**⁴ מַעֲשֵׂה הָעֵגֶל שֶׁעָשָׂה —

---

1. See *Exodus* 40:2 and Rashi to *Numbers* 7:1. Moses would erect and dismantle the *Mishkan* each day of the seven days of inauguration. On the first of Nissan, the *Mishkan* was erected and not dismantled at the end of the day (*Toras Kohanim, Tzav, Miluim* 36; *Bamidbar Rabbah* 12:15). Rashi explains that "eighth" here means the eighth day of the inauguration, not the eighth of the month (*Gur Aryeh*).

2. *Seder Olam* 7; *Toras Kohanim, Miluim* 1; *Shabbos* 87b. The ten crowns taken by the first of Nissan of that year are that it is: (i) the first day of Creation, for it was a Sunday; (ii) the first day of the offerings brought by the princes of the tribes in honor of the inauguration of the *Mizbe'ach*; (iii) the first day of the assumption of the *kehunah* by Aaron and his sons; (iv) the first day of the regular *Mizbe'ach* service; (v) the first day that fire descended from Heaven onto the *Mizbe'ach* (see v. 24); (vi) the first day of the restriction that offerings be eaten on the grounds of the *Mishkan* only; (vii) the first day of the prohibition against bringing offerings on altars located outside the grounds of the *Mishkan*; (viii) the first day of the first month of the year; (ix) the first day that the *Shechinah* rested among Israel in the *Mishkan*; (x) the first day that the Kohanim delivered the priestly blessing.

Rashi cites this passage from *Seder Olam* in support of his assertion that the eighth day referred to here does not mean the eighth of the month (*Mesiach Ilmim*; see also *Toras Kohanim, Miluim* 14).

3. *Tanchuma* 3. This explains why the elders were summoned to hear commandments that were addressed to Aaron (*Mesiach Ilmim*).

4. *Toras Kohanim, Miluim* 3; *Tanchuma* 4. That is why Aaron's sin-offering, distinct from any other sin-offering in the Torah, is a calf (see *Chizkuni*). See also Rashi to *Numbers* 19:22, s.v., פָּרָה אֲדֻמָּה, where he explains that the red cow was also a form of atonement for the Golden Calf.

and a meal-offering mixed with oil; for today Hashem *appears to you.*
⁵ *They took what Moses had commanded to the front of the Tent of Meeting; and the entire assembly approached and stood before* Hashem. ⁶ *Moses said: This is the thing that* Hashem *has commanded you to do; then the glory of* Hashem *will appear to you.*
⁷ *Moses said to Aaron: Come near to the Mizbe'ach and perform the service of your sin-offering and your olah-offering and provide atonement for yourself and for the people; then perform the service of the people's*

וּמִנְחָה בְלוּלָה בַשֶּׁמֶן כִּי הַיּוֹם יהוה
נִרְאָה אֲלֵיכֶם: וַיִּקְחוּ אֵת אֲשֶׁר צִוָּה ה
מֹשֶׁה אֶל־פְּנֵי אֹהֶל מוֹעֵד וַיִּקְרְבוּ
כָּל־הָעֵדָה וַיַּעַמְדוּ לִפְנֵי יהוה:
וַיֹּאמֶר מֹשֶׁה זֶה הַדָּבָר אֲשֶׁר־צִוָּה ו
יהוה תַּעֲשׂוּ וְיֵרָא אֲלֵיכֶם כְּבוֹד
יהוה: וַיֹּאמֶר מֹשֶׁה אֶל־אַהֲרֹן קְרַב ז
אֶל־הַמִּזְבֵּחַ וַעֲשֵׂה אֶת־חַטָּאתְךָ
וְאֶת־עֹלָתֶךָ וְכַפֵּר בַּעַדְךָ וּבְעַד
הָעָם וַעֲשֵׂה אֶת־קָרְבַּן הָעָם

― אונקלוס ―

וּמִנְחָתָא דְפִילָא בִמְשַׁח אֲרֵי יוֹמָא דֵין יְקָרָא דַיְיָ מִתְגְּלֵי לְכוֹן: וּנְסִיבוּ יָת דִּי פַקֵּיד מֹשֶׁה לָקֳדָם מַשְׁכַּן זִמְנָא וּקְרִיבוּ כָּל כְּנִשְׁתָּא וְקָמוּ קֳדָם יְיָ: וַאֲמַר מֹשֶׁה דֵין פִּתְגָּמָא דִּי פַקֵּיד יְיָ תַּעְבְּדוּן וְיִתְגְּלֵי לְכוֹן יְקָרָא דַיְיָ: וַאֲמַר מֹשֶׁה לְאַהֲרֹן קְרַב לְמַדְבְּחָא וְעִבֵּד יָת חַטָּאתָךְ וְיָת עֲלָתָךְ וְכַפֵּר עֲלָךְ וְעַל עַמָּא וַעֲבֵד יָת קָרְבַּן עַמָּא

― רש"י ―

שם ג: תנחומא ז): (ד) כי היום ה' נראה אליכם. להשרות שכינתו במעשה ידיכם (ת"כ שם ד) לכך קרבנות הללו באין חובה ליום זה: (ז) קרב אל
המזבח. שהיה אהרן בוש וירא לגשת אמר לו משה למה אתה בוש לכך נבחרת (שם ח): את חטאתך. עגל בן בקר: ואת עולתך. האיל: קרבן העם. שעיר עזים

― RASHI ELUCIDATED ―

4. כִּי הַיּוֹם ה' נִרְאָה אֲלֵיכֶם — FOR TODAY HASHEM APPEARS TO YOU — לְהַשְׁרוֹת שְׁכִינָתוֹ — to rest His *Shechinah* ¹בְּמַעֲשֵׂה יְדֵיכֶם — in the work of your hands.¹ לְכָךְ — For this reason קָרְבָּנוֹת הַלָּלוּ בָּאִין חוֹבָה — these offerings come as an obligation לְיוֹם זֶה — for this day.²

7. קְרַב אֶל הַמִּזְבֵּחַ — COME NEAR TO THE *MIZBE'ACH*. — שֶׁהָיָה אַהֲרֹן בּוֹשׁ — For Aaron was embarrassed וְיָרֵא לָגֶשֶׁת — and afraid to approach. אָמַר לוֹ מֹשֶׁה — Moses said to him, לָמָּה אַתָּה בוֹשׁ — "Why are you embarrassed? ³לְכָךְ נִבְחַרְתָּ — This is what you were selected for."³

☐ אֶת חַטָּאתְךָ — YOUR SIN-OFFERING. This is the עֵגֶל בֶּן בָּקָר — "calf, young male of cattle"⁴ mentioned in verse 2.

☐ וְאֶת עֹלָתֶךָ — AND YOUR *OLAH*-OFFERING. This is הָאַיִל — the ram mentioned in verse 2.⁵

☐ קָרְבַּן הָעָם — THE PEOPLE'S OFFERING. This is the group of animals comprising שְׂעִיר עִזִּים — a

---

1. *Toras Kohanim, Miluim* 4.

2. The verse seems to say that the appearance of the presence of God is the reason for the offerings. But we find that God appears several times to the Israelites in the desert without their having to bring offerings. Rashi explains that this appearance is unique, for it signals that the *Shechinah* is to rest in the *Mishkan* (*Nachalas Yaakov; Sifsei Chachamim*).
    The apparently superfluous הַיּוֹם, "today," indicates that these offerings do not mark an event — the appearance of the *Shechinah*. Rather, they "come as an obligation for this day"; they mark the beginning of a new era characterized by the continuous appearance of the *Shechinah* (*Mishmeres HaKodesh*).

3. *Toras Kohanim, Miluim* 8. Moses could have told Aaron, "Perform the service of your sin-offering and your *olah*-offering," without any introduction. The introductory statement, קְרַב אֶל הַמִּזְבֵּחַ, "come near to the *Mizbe'ach*," indicates that Aaron hesitated to approach the *Mizbe'ach* (*Mizrachi; Sifsei Chachamim*).

4. Unlike the word שֶׂה which is used for the young of more than one species of animal [e.g., שֶׂה כְשָׂבִים וְשֶׂה עִזִּים, "the young of the sheep and the young of the goat" (*Deuteronomy* 14:4)], the word עֵגֶל refers to only one species, the young of cattle. If so, the term בֶּן בָּקָר, "the child of cattle," cannot be construed as defining the species (*Malbim*). Rather, עֵגֶל without further description refers to a calf in its first year (see Rashi below, s.v., קָרְבַּן הָעָם). And עֵגֶל בֶּן בָּקָר refers to a calf that has approached closer to the age of בָּקָר, "mature cattle," that is, its second year. After its second year, it loses the name עֵגֶל completely and is called a פַּר, "bull."

5. The sin-offering and *olah*-offering spoken of by our verse are intended to "effect atonement for yourself and for the people." This could lead one to think that the verse deals with the offerings of the people mentioned in verse 3, rather than the offerings of Aaron mentioned in verse 2, for it is not evident that Aaron's

offering and provide atonement for them, as HASHEM has commanded.

⁸ Aaron came near to the Mizbe'ach, and slaughtered the sin-offering calf that was his. ⁹ The sons of Aaron brought the blood to him. He dipped his finger into the blood and placed it upon the horns of the Mizbe'ach, and he poured the [remaining] blood upon the foundation of the Mizbe'ach. ¹⁰ And the fats, and the kidneys, and the diaphragm, [and] from the liver of the sin-offering, he caused to go up in smoke on the Mizbe'ach, as HASHEM had commanded Moses. ¹¹ And the flesh and the hide

וְכַפֵּר בַּעֲדָם כַּאֲשֶׁר צִוָּה יְהוָה: ⁸ וַיִּקְרַב אַהֲרֹן אֶל־הַמִּזְבֵּחַ וַיִּשְׁחַט אֶת־עֵגֶל הַחַטָּאת אֲשֶׁר־לוֹ: ⁹ וַיַּקְרִבוּ בְּנֵי אַהֲרֹן אֶת־הַדָּם אֵלָיו וַיִּטְבֹּל אֶצְבָּעוֹ בַּדָּם וַיִּתֵּן עַל־קַרְנוֹת הַמִּזְבֵּחַ וְאֶת־הַדָּם יָצַק אֶל־יְסוֹד הַמִּזְבֵּחַ: ¹⁰ וְאֶת־הַחֵלֶב וְאֶת־הַכְּלָיֹת וְאֶת־הַיֹּתֶרֶת מִן־הַכָּבֵד מִן־הַחַטָּאת הִקְטִיר הַמִּזְבֵּחָה כַּאֲשֶׁר צִוָּה יְהוָה אֶת־מֹשֶׁה: ¹¹ וְאֶת־הַבָּשָׂר וְאֶת־הָעוֹר

─── אונקלוס ───

וְכַפַּר עֲלֵיהוֹן כְּמָא דִי פַקִּיד יְיָ: ⁸וּקְרֵב אַהֲרֹן לְמַדְבְּחָא וּנְכֵס יָת עֶגְלָא דְחַטָּאתָא דִי לֵהּ: ⁹וְקָרִיבוּ בְּנֵי אַהֲרֹן יָת דְּמָא לֵהּ וּטְבַל אֶצְבְּעֵהּ בִּדְמָא וִיהַב עַל קַרְנַת מַדְבְּחָא וְיָת דְּמָא אֲרִיק לִיסוֹדָא דְמַדְבְּחָא: ¹⁰וְיָת תַּרְבָּא וְיָת כָּלְיָתָא וְיָת חִצְרָא מִן כַּבְדָּא מִן חַטָּאתָא אַסֵּק לְמַדְבְּחָא כְּמָא דִי פַקִּיד יְיָ יָת מֹשֶׁה: ¹¹וְיָת בִּשְׂרָא וְיָת מַשְׁכָּא

─── רש"י ───

וענל וכבש. כל מקום שנא' עגל בן שנה הוא (ר"ה י:ה **העור וגו'**. לא מצינו חטאת חיצונה נשרפת אלא זו ומכאן אתה למד: (**יא**) **ואת הבשר ואת** וְשֶׁל מִלּוּאִים (שמות כט:יד) וכולן ע"פ הדבור:

─── RASHI ELUCIDATED ───

he-goat, וָעֵגֶל – **and a calf,** וָכֶבֶשׂ – **and a sheep** mentioned in verse 3.¹ כָּל מָקוֹם שֶׁנֶּאֱמַר עֵגֶל – **Wherever it says "calf"** without further description, ² בֶּן שָׁנָה הוּא – **it is within its first year;²** וּמִכָּאן אַתָּה לָמֵד – **and you learn** it **from here.³** 11. וְאֶת הַבָּשָׂר וְאֶת הָעוֹר וְגוֹ׳ – **THE FLESH AND THE HIDE, ETC.** לֹא מָצִינוּ חַטָּאת חִיצוֹנָה נִשְׂרֶפֶת – **We do not find an outer sin-offering,** i.e., one whose blood is sprinkled on the outer *Mizbe'ach,* which is entirely **burned** אֶלָּא זוֹ – **except for this one** ⁴ וְשֶׁל מִלּוּאִים – **and the one of the inauguration.**⁴ וְכֻלָּן עַל פִּי הַדִּבּוּר – **All of them** were burned **in accordance with the statement** of God.⁵

offerings effect atonement for anyone other than himself. The verse would then be calling the offerings "*your* sin-offering" and "*your* olah-offering," not because they are the personal offerings of Aaron, but rather because he is the one who is to perform the sacrificial procedure. Rashi therefore points out that the verse does, in fact, refer to the offerings of Aaron himself (*Gur Aryeh*). The sin-offering effects atonement for the people, as well as for Aaron himself, because, as Rashi has mentioned in his comments to verse 2, it comes as atonement for the sin of the Golden Calf. Although Aaron bore special responsibility for this sin, it was the sin of the nation as a whole, and the entire nation received some degree of atonement through the atonement of Aaron (*Mishmeres HaKodesh*).

1. Although the verse says "the people's *offering,*" in the singular, it refers to this entire group of animals. The peace-offerings mentioned in verse 4 are not included, however, for our verse refers to the offerings that atone on the people's behalf. Peace-offerings do not bring about atonement.

2. *Rosh Hashanah* 10a.

3. By "from here," Rashi means verse 3, where the verse speaks of "a calf [וְעֵגֶל] and a sheep *in their first year.*" Rashi views this phrase as being descriptive of the term עֵגֶל in general (see Rashi to *Rosh Hashanah* 10a, s.v., עגל בן שנה; *Gur Aryeh*). Rashi did not make this point in his

comments to verse 2. He cites it in our verse to explain why the Torah includes both the sin-offering and *olah*-offering of the people in the single term קָרְבַּן הָעָם, whereas it uses two distinct terms — אֶת חַטָּאתְךָ וְאֶת עֹלָתֶךָ — for Aaron's sin-offering and *olah*-offering. This is because the he-goat, sheep, and calf were all alike in that they were all in their first year. Aaron's offerings are mentioned individually, however, because their age requirements were not identical. An עֵגֶל בֶּן בָּקָר, "a young bull," is a calf in the entire second year of its life (see note 4 on p. 95 above). An אַיִל refers to a ram which has entered the second month of the second year of its life (see *Parah* 1:3; see also note 7 on p. 55). Furthermore, once a ram has become an אַיִל, it retains that name even after its second year. An עֵגֶל בֶּן בָּקָר is no longer referred to as such once it enters its third year. At that point it becomes a פַּר (see *Amar N'kei*; see *Yosef Hallel,* however, who suggests that the end of this comment which states that "calf" means a one-year-old was printed here by error, and rightfully belongs in Rashi's commentary to v. 3).

4. See *Exodus* 29:14 and Rashi there. This refers to the sin-offering brought by Moses during the seven days of inauguration.

5. Although we find no explicit command that the calf brought by Aaron be burned entirely as we do in the case of the sin-offering brought by Moses (*Exodus* 29:14), it

9/12-16 — ט/יב-טז

he burned in fire outside the camp. ¹² He slaughtered the olah-offering; the sons of Aaron presented the blood to him and he threw it upon the Mizbe'ach, all around. ¹³ They presented the olah-offering to him in its pieces with the head; and he caused it to go up in smoke on the Mizbe'ach. ¹⁴ He washed the innards and the feet, and caused them to go up in smoke on the olah-offering on the Mizbe'ach.
¹⁵ He brought near the offering of the people: He took the sin-offering goat that was for the people, and slaughtered it and made it into a sin-offering, like the first one. ¹⁶ He brought near the olah-offering and performed its service in accordance with the law.

יב שָׂרַף בָּאֵשׁ מִחוּץ לַמַּחֲנֶה: וַיִּשְׁחַט אֶת־הָעֹלָה וַיַּמְצִאוּ בְּנֵי אַהֲרֹן אֵלָיו אֶת־הַדָּם וַיִּזְרְקֵהוּ עַל־הַמִּזְבֵּחַ סָבִיב: יג וְאֶת־הָעֹלָה הִמְצִיאוּ אֵלָיו לִנְתָחֶיהָ וְאֶת־הָרֹאשׁ וַיַּקְטֵר עַל־הַמִּזְבֵּחַ: יד וַיִּרְחַץ אֶת־הַקֶּרֶב וְאֶת־הַכְּרָעָיִם וַיַּקְטֵר עַל־הָעֹלָה הַמִּזְבֵּחָה: טו וַיַּקְרֵב אֵת קָרְבַּן הָעָם וַיִּקַּח אֶת־שְׂעִיר הַחַטָּאת אֲשֶׁר לָעָם וַיִּשְׁחָטֵהוּ וַיְחַטְּאֵהוּ כָּרִאשׁוֹן: טז וַיַּקְרֵב אֶת־הָעֹלָה וַיַּעֲשֶׂהָ כַּמִּשְׁפָּט:

---- אונקלוס ----

אוקיד בנורא מברא למשריתא: יב ונכס ית עלתא ואמטיאו בני אהרן לה ית דמא וזרקה על מדבחא סחור סחור: יג וית עלתא אמטיאו לה לאברהא וית רישא ואסק על מדבחא: יד וחליל ית גוא וית כרעיא ואסק על עלתא למדבחא: טו וקרב ית קרבן עמא ונסיב ית צפירא דחטאתא די לעמא ונכסה וכפר בדמה כקדמאה: טז וקרב ית עלתא ועבדה כדחזי:

---- רש"י ----

(יב) וימצאו. לשון הושטה והזמנה: (טו) כעגל שלו: (טז) ויעשה במשפט. המפורש ויחטאהו. עשהו כמשפט חטאת: בראשון. בעולת נדבה בויקרא (לעיל פרק א; בילה כ.):

---- RASHI ELUCIDATED ----

12. וַיַּמְצִאוּ — [THEY] PRESENTED. לְשׁוֹן הוֹשָׁטָה וְהַזְמָנָה — This word is **an expression of proffering and preparation.**¹

15. וַיְחַטְּאֵהוּ — AND HE MADE IT INTO A SIN-OFFERING. עֲשָׂהוּ כְּמִשְׁפַּט חַטָּאת — This means **he performed it in accordance with the law of a sin-offering.**²

בָּרִאשׁוֹן — LIKE THE FIRST ONE. כְּעֵגֶל שֶׁלּוֹ — **Like his calf.**³

16. וַיַּעֲשֶׂהָ כַּמִּשְׁפָּט — AND PERFORMED ITS SERVICE IN ACCORDANCE WITH THE LAW — הַמְפֹרָשׁ — **which is stated explicitly**⁴ בְּעוֹלַת נְדָבָה — regarding **a voluntary** *olah*-**offering** ⁵בְּוַיִּקְרָא — **in** Chapter 1 of Parashas **Vayikra.**⁵

---

too, was burned in accordance with God's command.

1. The word is not related to the phrase in 1:15 above, וְנִמְצָה דָמוֹ, "and its blood shall be squeezed out" (*Be'er Mayim Chayim*). According to *Ibn Ezra*, the root of וַיַּמְצִאוּ is מצא, "to find." Aaron's sons proffered and prepared the blood so that their father would "find" it at hand when he needed it during the service.

2. See Rashi to 6:19 above, s.v., הַמְחַטֵּא אוֹתָהּ, and note 4 there.

3. This cannot refer to Aaron's ram discussed in the verses immediately prior, for that was an *olah*-offering, and this verse refers to a sin-offering (*Mizrachi*).

4. The prefixes ב, "in," כ, "like," and ל, "to," are generally vowelized with a *sheva* (־ בְּ־ כְּ־ לְ). However, when they are affixed to a word that is already prefixed with the definite article הַ, the ה is usually dropped and its vowel is shifted to the new prefix. Thus, the word בַּיּוֹם (v. 1 above) is a contraction of בְּהַיּוֹם — the ה is dropped

and its *patach* is taken by the ב. Similarly, לַמַּחֲנֶה (v. 11) and כָּרִאשׁוֹן (v. 15) are shortened from לְהַמַּחֲנֶה and בְּהָרִאשׁוֹן. Our verse does not say כְּמִשְׁפָּט, which means "in accordance with *a* law," but כַּמִּשְׁפָּט, a contraction of כְּהַמִּשְׁפָּט, which means "in accordance with *the* law." The word thus implies a known law stated explicitly in another passage (*Leshon Chayim*). *Rashi* explains that this refers to the law of the voluntary *olah*-offering for the reason given in the following note.

5. *Beitzah* 20a. The preceding verse indicates that the sin-offering of the people was brought in accordance with the procedure of Aaron's sin-offering by using the word כָּרִאשׁוֹן, "as for the first one." The Torah uses a different word with regard to the *olah*-offering of the people, כַּמִּשְׁפָּט, "in accordance with the law," to teach us that it was not brought in exactly the same way as Aaron's *olah*-offering, whose steps are enumerated in verses 12-14, but rather, in accordance with some other law, the law of the voluntary *olah*-offering, which

17 He brought near the meal-offering, and he filled his hand from it, and caused it to go up in smoke on the Mizbe'ach; aside from the olah-offering of the morning. **18** He slaughtered the bull and the ram — the people's sacrifice of the peace-offering; the sons of Aaron presented the blood to him, and he threw it upon the Mizbe'ach, all around. **19** As for the fats from the bull and from the ram, and the tail, and that which covers, and the kidneys, and the diaphragm with the liver, **20** they placed the fats upon the breasts, and caused the fats to go up in smoke on the Mizbe'ach.

יז וַיַּקְרֵב֙ אֶת־הַמִּנְחָ֔ה וַיְמַלֵּ֥א כַפּ֖וֹ מִמֶּ֑נָּה וַיַּקְטֵ֖ר עַל־הַמִּזְבֵּ֑חַ
יח מִלְּבַ֖ד עֹלַ֥ת הַבֹּֽקֶר: וַיִּשְׁחַ֤ט אֶת־הַשּׁוֹר֙ וְאֶת־הָאַ֔יִל זֶ֥בַח הַשְּׁלָמִ֖ים אֲשֶׁ֣ר לָעָ֑ם וַ֠יַּמְצִ֠אוּ בְּנֵ֨י אַהֲרֹ֤ן אֶת־הַדָּם֙ אֵלָ֔יו וַיִּזְרְקֵ֥הוּ עַל־הַמִּזְבֵּ֖חַ סָבִֽיב: וְאֶת־הַחֲלָבִ֖ים
יט מִן־הַשּׁ֑וֹר וּמִן־הָאַ֔יִל הָאַלְיָ֥ה וְהַֽמְכַסֶּ֖ה וְהַכְּלָיֹ֑ת וְיֹתֶ֥רֶת הַכָּבֵֽד:
כ וַיָּשִׂ֥ימוּ אֶת־הַחֲלָבִ֖ים עַל־הֶֽחָז֑וֹת וַיַּקְטֵ֥ר הַחֲלָבִ֖ים הַמִּזְבֵּֽחָה:

— אונקלוס —

יז וְקָרֵב יָת מִנְחָתָא וּמְלָא יְדֵהּ מִנַּהּ וְאַסֵּיק עַל מַדְבְּחָא בַּר מֵעֲלַת צַפְרָא: יח וּנְכַס יָת תּוֹרָא וְיָת דִּכְרָא נִכְסַת קוּדְשַׁיָּא דִי לְעַמָּא וְאַמְטִיאוּ בְּנֵי אַהֲרֹן יָת דְּמָא לֵהּ וּזְרָקֵהּ עַל מַדְבְּחָא סְחוֹר סְחוֹר: יט וְיָת תַּרְבַּיָּא מִן תּוֹרָא וּמִן דִּכְרָא אַלִּיתָא וְחָפֵי גַּוָּא וְכֻלְיָתָא וַחֲצַר כַּבְדָּא: כ וְשַׁוִּיאוּ יָת תַּרְבַּיָּא עַל חֶדְוָתָא וְאַסֵּיק תַּרְבַּיָּא לְמַדְבְּחָא:

— רש"י —

(יז) וימלא כפו. הִיא קְמִיצָה (ת"כ שם יא; מנחות ט:): **מלבד עלת הבקר.** כָּל אֵלֶּה עָשָׂה אַחַר עוֹלַת הַתָּמִיד: **(יט) והמכסה.** חֵלֶב הַמְכַסֶּה אֶת הַקֶּרֶב: **(כ) וישימו את החלבים על החזות.** לְאַחַר הַתְּנוּפָה נְתָנָן כֹּהֵן הַמֵּנִיף לְכֹהֵן אַחֵר לְהַקְטִירָם נִמְצְאוּ הָעֶלְיוֹנִים לְמַטָּה:

— RASHI ELUCIDATED —

17. וַיְמַלֵּא כַפּוֹ — AND HE FILLED HIS HAND [FROM IT]. הִיא קְמִיצָה — This is the scooping of the threefingersful.[1]

מִלְּבַד עֹלַת הַבֹּקֶר — ASIDE FROM THE *OLAH*-OFFERING OF THE MORNING. כָּל אֵלֶּה עָשָׂה — He performed all these אַחַר עוֹלַת הַתָּמִיד — after the continual *olah*-offering of the morning.[2]

19. וְהַמְכַסֶּה — AND THAT WHICH COVERS. This refers to the חֵלֶב הַמְכַסֶּה אֶת הַקֶּרֶב — fat that covers the entrails.[3]

20. וַיָּשִׂימוּ אֶת הַחֲלָבִים עַל הֶחָזוֹת — THEY PLACED THE FATS UPON THE BREASTS. לְאַחַר הַתְּנוּפָה — After the waving, נְתָנָן כֹּהֵן הַמֵּנִיף לְכֹהֵן אַחֵר — the Kohen who waved the fats and the breasts gave them to another Kohen לְהַקְטִירָם — to cause them to go up in smoke. נִמְצְאוּ הָעֶלְיוֹנִים — It is thus found that the upper ones, i.e., those which were previously on top, are now לְמַטָּה — below.[4]

---

includes סְמִיכָה, leaning of hands upon the animal, a step not performed on Aaron's *olah*-offering (see *Be'er Yitzchak*).

Rashi in his comments to *Beitzah* 20a explains our verse as referring to Aaron's *olah*-offering. *Tosafos* there notes that this runs counter to the flow of the text, however, for verse 15 has stated explicitly that we are dealing with the offerings of the people. See *Tosafos* and *P'nei Yehoshua* in *Beitzah* who explain that Rashi agrees that the simple meaning of the text refers to the *olah*-offering of the people, and that the law of the *olah*-offering of Aaron is derived from it.

1. *Toras Kohanim, Miluim* 11; *Menachos* 9b. See Rashi to 2:2 above, s.v., מְלֹא קֻמְצוֹ, for a description of קֹמֶץ, "a threefingersful."

Unlike the expression מְלֹא יַד, "filling a hand," which is used in the figurative sense of inauguration (see, for example, 8:33 above), מִלֵּא כַף is used in the literal sense.

2. The Torah has taught us above (6:5; see Rashi there) that the continual *olah*-offering of the morning is the first offering of the day. Rashi therefore stresses that "aside from the *olah*-offering," i.e., after it, does not apply only to the meal-offering, which was the subject of the beginning of the verse. It applies to "all these" — all of the inaugural offerings brought that day (*Sefer Zikaron*).

3. Elsewhere (above 3:3,9,14; 4:8; 7:3; *Exodus* 29:13,22) the Torah refers to this as הַחֵלֶב הַמְכַסֶּה אֶת הַקֶּרֶב, which Rashi (to *Exodus* 29:13) defines as the membrane that covers the stomach.

4. See Rashi to 7:30 above.

99 / VAYIKRA/LEVITICUS — PARASHAS SHEMINI — 9/21-23

²¹ *Aaron had lifted up the breasts and the right thigh as a wave-service before* HASHEM, *as Moses had commanded.*
²² *Aaron raised his hands toward the people and blessed them; and he descended from having performed the sin-offering, the olah-offering, and the peace-offering.* ²³ *Moses and Aaron came to the Tent of Meeting,*

כא וְאֵת הֶחָזוֹת וְאֵת שׁוֹק הַיָּמִין הֵנִיף אַהֲרֹן תְּנוּפָה לִפְנֵי יהוה כַּאֲשֶׁר צִוָּה מֹשֶׁה: כב וַיִּשָּׂא אַהֲרֹן אֶת־יָדָו אֶל־הָעָם וַיְבָרְכֵם וַיֵּרֶד מֵעֲשֹׂת הַחַטָּאת וְהָעֹלָה וְהַשְּׁלָמִים: כג וַיָּבֹא מֹשֶׁה וְאַהֲרֹן אֶל־אֹהֶל מוֹעֵד

— אונקלוס —

כא וְיָת חֶדְוָתָא וְיָת שׁוֹקָא דְיַמִּינָא אֲרֵים אַהֲרֹן אֲרָמָא קֳדָם יְיָ כְּמָא דִי פַקִּיד מֹשֶׁה: כב וַאֲרֵים אַהֲרֹן יָת יְדוֹהִי עַל עַמָּא וּבָרְכִנּוּן וּנְחַת מִלְמֶעְבַּד חַטָּאתָא וַעֲלָתָא וְנִכְסַת קוּדְשַׁיָּא: כג וְעַל מֹשֶׁה וְאַהֲרֹן לְמַשְׁכַּן זִמְנָא

— רש״י —

(כב) ויברכם. בִּרְכַּת כֹּהֲנִים יְבָרֶכְךָ יָאֵר יִשָּׂא (ת״כ שם ל; סוטה לח.): וירד. מֵעַל הַמִּזְבֵּחַ: (כג) ויבא משה ואהרן וגו׳. לָמָּה נִכְנְסוּ, מָצָאתִי בְּפָ׳ מִלּוּאִים בַּבָּרַיְתָא הַנּוֹסֶפֶת עַל ת״כ שֶׁלָּנוּ, לָמָּה נִכְנַס מֹשֶׁה עִם אַהֲרֹן, לְלַמְּדוֹ עַל מַעֲשֵׂה הַקְּטֹרֶת. אוֹ לֹא נִכְנַס אֶלָּא לְדָבָר אַחֵר לְדָבָר אַחֵר, הֲרֵינִי דָן, יְרִידָה וּבִיאָה טְעוּנוֹת בְּרָכָה, מַה יְרִידָה מֵעֵין עֲבוֹדָה אַף בִּיאָה מֵעֵין עֲבוֹדָה, הָא לָמַדְתָּ, לָמָּה נִכְנַס מֹשֶׁה עִם אַהֲרֹן, לְלַמְּדוֹ עַל מַעֲשֵׂה הַקְּטֹרֶת. דָּבָר אַחֵר, כֵּיוָן שֶׁרָאָה אַהֲרֹן שֶׁקָּרְבוּ כָּל הַקָּרְבָּנוֹת וְנַעֲשׂוּ כָּל הַמַּעֲשִׂים וְלֹא יָרְדָה שְׁכִינָה לְיִשְׂרָאֵל

— RASHI ELUCIDATED —

22. וַיְבָרְכֵם — AND BLESSED THEM. — בִּרְכַּת כֹּהֲנִים — The Priestly Blessing:[1] — ״יְבָרֶכְךָ״ — May [HASHEM] bless you . . . , ״יָאֵר״ — may [HASHEM] illuminate [His face toward you] . . . , ״יִשָּׂא״ — may [HASHEM] raise [His face to you] . . . .[2]

☐ וַיֵּרֶד — AND HE DESCENDED — מֵעַל הַמִּזְבֵּחַ — from on top of the *Mizbe'ach*.[3]

23. וַיָּבֹא מֹשֶׁה וְאַהֲרֹן וְגוֹמֵר — MOSES AND AARON CAME, ETC. — לָמָּה נִכְנְסוּ — Why did they enter? — מָצָאתִי — I found in the section of *Toras Kohanim* about the inauguration, בְּבָרַיְתָא הַנּוֹסֶפֶת — in a *baraisa* that is appended onto our version of *Toras Kohanim*,[4] as follows: עַל תּוֹרַת כֹּהֲנִים שֶׁלָּנוּ — לָמָּה נִכְנַס מֹשֶׁה עִם אַהֲרֹן — Why did Moses enter with Aaron? — לְלַמְּדוֹ עַל מַעֲשֵׂה הַקְּטֹרֶת — To teach him about the procedure of burning the incense. — אוֹ לֹא נִכְנַס אֶלָּא לְדָבָר אַחֵר — Or might he not have entered for something else? — הֲרֵינִי דָן — See that I can reason that he entered to teach Aaron about the incense, as follows: יְרִידָה וּבִיאָה טְעוּנוֹת בְּרָכָה — Both descending and coming require a blessing.[5] — מַה יְרִידָה מֵעֵין עֲבוֹדָה — Just as descending is related to the service of the *Mishkan*,[6] אַף בִּיאָה מֵעֵין עֲבוֹדָה — coming, too, — is related to the service of the *Mishkan*. הָא לָמַדְתָּ — Now, then, you have learned, לָמָּה נִכְנַס מֹשֶׁה עִם אַהֲרֹן — why Moses entered with Aaron,[7] לְלַמְּדוֹ עַל מַעֲשֵׂה הַקְּטֹרֶת — to teach him about the procedure of burning the incense.[7] דָּבָר אַחֵר — Alternatively: — כֵּיוָן שֶׁרָאָה אַהֲרֹן — Once Aaron saw שֶׁקָּרְבוּ כָּל הַקָּרְבָּנוֹת — that all the offerings had been brought, וְנַעֲשׂוּ כָּל הַמַּעֲשִׂים — and all the acts of the *Mishkan* service had been performed, וְלֹא יָרְדָה שְׁכִינָה לְיִשְׂרָאֵל — but the *Shechinah* had not descended to Israel,

---

1. *Numbers* 6:24-26.
2. *Toras Kohanim, Miluim* 30; *Sotah* 38a.
3. Aaron blessed the people from atop a platform, not from the top of the *Mizbe'ach*. "And he descended from having performed the sin-offering, the *olah*-offering, and the peace-offering" might have been understood as, "And he descended from the platform after the blessing, which was the culmination of the performance of the sin-offering, the *olah*-offering, and the peace-offering." But if this were so, the verse would be stating the obvious. Surely, Aaron would not have lingered on the platform forever after having blessed the people. Rashi therefore explains that the verse refers to Aaron's descent from the top of the *Mizbe'ach* after bringing the offerings; his descent preceded the blessing. The verse means to say, "Aaron raised his hands toward the people and blessed them, *upon descending* from having performed the sin-offering, the *olah*-offering, and the peace-offering" (*Nachalas Yaakov; Sifsei Chachamim; Maskil Le-David*).

4. The section of *Toras Kohanim* that discusses the inauguration is called *Miluim* (in full מְכִילְתָּא דְמִלּוּאִים), and appears in most printed editions, but did not appear in all manuscripts.

5. Both Aaron's descending from the *Mizbe'ach* mentioned in the preceding verse and the coming of Moses and Aaron to the *Mishkan* mentioned in this verse are accompanied by a blessing to the people.

6. Aaron's descent immediately follows his performance of the *Mizbe'ach* service.

7. *Toras Kohanim, Miluim* 30.

וַיֵּצְא֥וּ וַֽיְבָרֲכ֖וּ אֶת־הָעָ֑ם וַיֵּרָ֥א כְבוֹד־ and they went out and they blessed the people — and the glory of Hashem appeared to the entire people! יהוה אֶל־כָּל־הָעָֽם: שלישי כד וַתֵּ֤צֵא אֵשׁ֙
מִלִּפְנֵ֣י יהו֔ה וַתֹּ֨אכַל֙ עַל־הַמִּזְבֵּ֔חַ אֶת־הָעֹלָ֖ה וְאֶת־הַחֲלָבִ֑ים וַיַּ֤רְא כָּל־הָעָם֙ וַיָּרֹ֔נּוּ וַֽיִּפְּל֖וּ עַל־פְּנֵיהֶֽם:

²⁴ A fire went forth from before Hashem and consumed upon the Mizbe'ach the olah-offering and the fats; the people saw and they praised and fell upon their faces.

─── אונקלוס ───

וּנְפָקוּ וּבָרִיכוּ יָת עַמָּא וְאִתְגְּלִי יְקָרָא דַיְיָ לְכָל עַמָּא: כד וּנְפָקַת אֶשָּׁתָא מִן קֳדָם יְיָ וַאֲכָלַת עַל מַדְבְּחָא יָת עֲלָתָא וְיָת תַּרְבַּיָּא וַחֲזָא כָל עַמָּא וְשַׁבַּחוּ וּנְפָלוּ עַל אַפֵּיהוֹן:

─── רש״י ───

שֶׁהֱטַמִּיד משה לְמַקֵּם וְשִׁמֵּשׁ בּוֹ וּפוֹרְקוֹ בְּכָל יוֹם שִׁרְפָה בּוֹ שְׁכִינָה, וְהָיוּ יִשְׂרָאֵל נִכְלָמִים וְאוֹמְרִים לְמשׁה רַבֵּינוּ כָל הַטּוֹרַח שֶׁטָּרַחְנוּ שֶׁתִּשְׁרֶה שְׁכִינָה בֵּינֵינוּ וְנֵדַע שֶׁנִּתְכַּפֶּר לָנוּ עֲוֹן הָעֵגֶל. לְכָךְ אָמַר לָהֶם זֶה הַדָּבָר אֲשֶׁר צִוָּה ה' תַּעֲשׂוּ וְיֵרָא אֲלֵיכֶם כְּבוֹד ה'. אַהֲרֹן אָחִי כְדַאי וְחָשׁוּב מִמֶּנִּי, שֶׁעַל יְדֵי קָרְבְּנוֹתָיו וַעֲבוֹדָתוֹ תִּשְׁרֶה שְׁכִינָה בָּכֶם וְתֵדְעוּ שֶׁהַמָּקוֹם בָּחַר בּוֹ: (כד) וַיָּרֹנּוּ. כְּתַרְגּוּמוֹ.
הָיָה מִצְטַעֵר, וְאָמַר יוֹדֵעַ אֲנִי שֶׁכָּעַס הקב"ה עָלַי וּבִשְׁבִילִי לֹא יָרְדָה שְׁכִינָה לְיִשְׂרָאֵל. אָמַר לוֹ לְמשֶׁה, משֶׁה אָחִי כָּךְ עָשִׂיתָ לִי שֶׁנִּכְנַסְתִּי וְנִתְבַּיַּשְׁתִּי, מִיָּד נִכְנַס משֶׁה עִמּוֹ וּבִקְּשׁוּ רַחֲמִים וְיָרְדָה שְׁכִינָה לְיִשְׂרָאֵל (שם יט): וַיֵּצְאוּ וַיְבָרְכוּ אֶת הָעָם. אָמְרוּ וִיהִי נֹעַם ד' אֱלֹהֵינוּ עָלֵינוּ (תהלים צ:יז) יְהִי רָצוֹן שֶׁתִּשְׁרֶה שְׁכִינָה בְּמַעֲשֵׂה יְדֵיכֶם (ת"כ שם טו). לְפִי שֶׁכָּל שִׁבְעַת יְמֵי הַמִּלּוּאִים

─── RASHI ELUCIDATED ───

יוֹדֵעַ אֲנִי – "I know¹ שְׁבַע הַקָּדוֹשׁ בָּרוּךְ הוּא עָלַי – "I know¹ שְׁבַע הַקָּדוֹשׁ בָּרוּךְ הוּא עָלַי that the Holy One, Blessed is He, has become angry with me,¹ וּבִשְׁבִילִי לֹא יָרְדָה שְׁכִינָה לְיִשְׂרָאֵל – and because of me the *Shechinah* did not descend to Israel." אָמַר לוֹ לְמשֶׁה – He said to Moses, מֹשֶׁה אָחִי – "Moses, my brother! כָּךְ עָשִׂיתָ לִי – Thus have you done to me, שֶׁנִּכְנַסְתִּי – that I entered the matter of performing the service because you asked me to,² וְנִתְבַּיַּשְׁתִּי – and I was embarrassed, because the *Shechinah* did not descend." מִיָּד נִכְנַס מֹשֶׁה עִמּוֹ – Thereupon, Moses entered with him וּבִקְּשׁוּ רַחֲמִים – and they sought, i.e., prayed for, mercy,³ וְיָרְדָה שְׁכִינָה לְיִשְׂרָאֵל – and the *Shechinah* descended to Israel.³

□ וַיֵּצְאוּ וַיְבָרְכוּ אֶת הָעָם – AND THEY WENT OUT AND THEY BLESSED THE PEOPLE. אָמְרוּ – They said, וִיהִי – "May the pleasantness of my Lord, our God, be upon us.⁴ יְהִי רָצוֹן שֶׁתִּשְׁרֶה – May the *Shechinah* rest in the work of your hands."⁵ לְפִי שֶׁכָּל שִׁבְעַת יְמֵי הַמִּלּוּאִים – Because for all the seven days of the inauguration, שֶׁהֶעֱמִידוֹ מֹשֶׁה לַמִּשְׁכָּן – during which Moses put up the *Mishkan* וְשִׁמֵּשׁ בּוֹ – and officiated in it וּפֵרְקוֹ – and dismantled it בְּכָל יוֹם – each day, וְהָיוּ יִשְׂרָאֵל נִכְלָמִים – and Israel was ashamed. וְאוֹמְרִים לְמשֶׁה – And they said to Moses, מֹשֶׁה רַבֵּנוּ – "Moses, our master! כָּל הַטֹּרַח שֶׁטָּרַחְנוּ – All the trouble we went to שֶׁתִּשְׁרֶה שְׁכִינָה בֵּינֵינוּ – that the *Shechinah* should rest among us, וְנֵדַע שֶׁנִּתְכַּפֵּר לָנוּ עֲוֹן הָעֵגֶל – and that thus we should know that the sin of the Golden Calf was atoned for on our behalf! Now we see that it was all for nothing." לְכָךְ אָמַר לָהֶם – Therefore, he said to them, זֶה הַדָּבָר אֲשֶׁר צִוָּה ה' תַּעֲשׂוּ – "This is the thing that Hashem has commanded you to do; וְיֵרָא אֲלֵיכֶם כְּבוֹד ה' – then the glory of Hashem will appear to you.⁶ אַהֲרֹן אָחִי כְּדַאי וְחָשׁוּב מִמֶּנִּי – Aaron, my brother, is worthier and more important than I, שֶׁעַל יְדֵי קָרְבְּנוֹתָיו – for through his offerings וַעֲבוֹדָתוֹ – and his service תִּשְׁרֶה שְׁכִינָה בָּכֶם – the *Shechinah* will rest among you, וְתֵדְעוּ שֶׁהַמָּקוֹם בָּחַר בּוֹ – and you will know that the Omnipresent has chosen him."⁷

24. וַיָּרֹנּוּ – This is to be understood כְּתַרְגּוּמוֹ – as the *Targum* Onkelos rendered it, וְשַׁבַּחוּ – "and

---

1. A variant vowelization here reads, שְׁבַע הַקָּדוֹשׁ בָּרוּךְ הוּא עָלַי, "that the anger of the Holy One . . . is upon me."
2. "That I entered" does not refer to entering the *Mishkan*, for all of the services performed by Aaron thus far were performed outside the *Mishkan*.
3. *Toras Kohanim, Miluim* 9.
4. *Psalms* 90:17.
5. *Toras Kohanim, Miluim* 15. In his commentary to *Exodus* 39:43, Rashi cites a similar blessing given by Moses.
6. Above verse 6.
7. Moses promised the people that the *Shechinah* would rest among them only after Aaron would perform the service, not after the seven days that Moses performed the service. Therefore, immediately after Aaron performed the service, they prayed that its acceptance would be manifest through the resting of the *Shechinah* among them.

101 / VAYIKRA/LEVITICUS — PARASHAS SHEMINI — 10/1-3

10 ¹The sons of Aaron, Nadab and Abihu, each took his fire-pan, they put fire in them and placed incense upon it; and they brought before HASHEM an alien fire that He had not commanded them. ² A fire came forth from before HASHEM and consumed them, and they died before HASHEM. ³ Moses said to Aaron: Of this did HASHEM speak, saying: "I will be sanctified through those who are close to Me, they praised."¹

יְ א וַיִּקְחוּ בְנֵי־אַהֲרֹן נָדָב וַאֲבִיהוּא אִישׁ מַחְתָּתוֹ וַיִּתְּנוּ בָהֵן אֵשׁ וַיָּשִׂימוּ עָלֶיהָ קְטֹרֶת וַיַּקְרִיבוּ לִפְנֵי יהוה אֵשׁ זָרָה אֲשֶׁר לֹא צִוָּה אֹתָם: ב וַתֵּצֵא אֵשׁ מִלִּפְנֵי יהוה וַתֹּאכַל אוֹתָם וַיָּמֻתוּ לִפְנֵי יהוה: ג וַיֹּאמֶר מֹשֶׁה אֶל־אַהֲרֹן הוּא אֲשֶׁר־דִּבֶּר יהוה ׀ לֵאמֹר בִּקְרֹבַי אֶקָּדֵשׁ

— אונקלוס —

אוּנְסִיבוּ בְנֵי אַהֲרֹן נָדָב וַאֲבִיהוּא גְבַר מַחְתִּיתֵהּ וִיהָבוּ בְהוֹן אֶשָּׁתָא וְשַׁוִּיאוּ עֲלַהּ קְטֹרֶת (בּוּסְמִין) וְקָרִיבוּ קֳדָם יְיָ אֶשָּׁתָא נוּכְרָיְתָא דִּי לָא פַקִּיד יָתְהוֹן: בוּנְפַקַת אֶשָּׁתָא מִן קֳדָם יְיָ וַאֲכַלַת יָתְהוֹן וּמִיתוּ קֳדָם יְיָ: גוַאֲמַר מֹשֶׁה לְאַהֲרֹן הוּא דִּי מַלִּיל יְיָ לְמֵימַר בִּקְרִיבַי אֶתְקַדָּשׁ

— רש"י —

(ב) **ותצא אש.** רבי אליעזר אומר לא מתו בני אהרן אלא על ידי שהורו הלכה בפני משה רבן (ת"כ שם לב; עירובין סג.). רבי ישמעאל אומר שתויי יין נכנסו למקדש. ותדע, שאחר מיתתן הזהיר הנותרים שלא יכנסו שתויי יין למקדש.] משל למלך שהיה לו בן בית וכו' כדאיתא בויקרא רבה (יב:א): (ג) **הוא אשר דבר וגו'.** היכן דבר, ונועדתי שמה לבני ישראל ונקדש בכבודי (שמות כט:מג) אל תקרי בכבודי אלא בכבודי. אמר לו משה לאהרן אחי

— RASHI ELUCIDATED —

10.

2. וַתֵּצֵא אֵשׁ — A FIRE CAME FORTH. רַבִּי אֱלִיעֶזֶר אוֹמֵר — The *Tanna* R' Eliezer says: לֹא מֵתוּ בְּנֵי אַהֲרֹן — The sons of Aaron did not die ² אֶלָּא עַל יְדֵי שֶׁהוֹרוּ הֲלָכָה בִּפְנֵי מֹשֶׁה רַבָּן — but for the fact that they rendered a halachic decision in the presence of their teacher, Moses.²

רַבִּי יִשְׁמָעֵאל אוֹמֵר — The *Tanna* R' Yishmael says: שְׁתוּיֵי יַיִן — While intoxicated by wine, נִכְנְסוּ לַמִּקְדָּשׁ — they entered the Sanctuary. {תֵּדַע — You can know with certainty that this is the reason for their death, שֶׁאַחַר מִיתָתָן — for after their death, הִזְהִיר הַנּוֹתָרִים — [the Torah] warned the remaining Kohanim שֶׁלֹּא יִכָּנְסוּ שְׁתוּיֵי יַיִן לַמִּקְדָּשׁ — that they should not enter the Sanctuary intoxicated by wine.} מָשָׁל לְמֶלֶךְ — This can be compared to a king שֶׁהָיָה לוֹ בֶּן בַּיִת וְכוּלְּהוּ — who had a household member, etc., ³ כִּדְאִיתָא בְּוַיִּקְרָא רַבָּה — as stated in *Vayikra Rabbah*.³

3. הוּא אֲשֶׁר דִּבֶּר וְגוֹמֵר — OF THIS DID HASHEM SPEAK... הֵיכָן דִּבֵּר — Where did He speak, i.e., where did He say this? ⁴וְנוֹעַדְתִּי שָׁמָּה לִבְנֵי יִשְׂרָאֵל וְנִקְדַּשׁ בִּכְבֹדִי — "I shall meet there with the Children of Israel, and it shall be sanctified through My honor."⁴ אַל תִּקְרֵי בִּכְבֹדִי — Do not read this word as it is vowelized בִּכְבוֹדִי "through My honor," ⁵אֶלָּא — but rather, read it as if it were vowelized בִּכְבוּדַי "through My honored ones."⁵ אָמַר לוֹ מֹשֶׁה לְאַהֲרֹן — Moses said to Aaron, אַהֲרֹן אָחִי — Aaron

---

1. *Targum* and Rashi here disagree with *Ibn Ezra* who translates "they raised their voices" as רָנּוּ, as used in *I Kings* 22:36. See *Targum* and *Ibn Ezra* to *Psalms* 106:44 for a similar disagreement about the meaning of רִנָּתָם.

2. *Toras Kohanim*, *Miluim* 32; *Eruvin* 63a. They reasoned that although fire descended upon the *Mizbe'ach* from Heaven, it was still incumbent upon the Kohanim to light a fire on it. This was a correct ruling (Rashi, *Yoma* 53a). Still, it is referred to as "an alien fire that He had not commanded them" because even though they had arrived at the correct conclusion, they should have consulted Moses before lighting it (*Gur Aryeh*).

3. *Vayikra Rabbah* 12:1. The complete parable there reads: A king had a trusted household member. He once found him standing at the entrance to some stores, and without explanation, had [the household member's] head cut off. He appointed another member of his household in his stead. We would not know why he killed the first one except for the command he gave the second one, "Do not go through the entrances of these stores." Through it we know that this first has been killed for transgressing this command.

4. *Exodus* 29:43.

5. Some editions read בִּמְכֻבָּדַי which has the same basic meaning. See Rashi and *Shittah Mekubetzes* to *Zevachim* 115b. כָּבוֹד is a noun that means "honor" or "glory," as in

וְעַל־פְּנֵי כָל־הָעָם אֶכָּבֵד וַיִּדֹּם *and I will be honored before the entire*
אַהֲרֹן: ד וַיִּקְרָא מֹשֶׁה אֶל־מִישָׁאֵל *people"; and Aaron fell silent.*
וְאֶל אֶלְצָפָן בְּנֵי עֻזִּיאֵל דֹּד אַהֲרֹן **⁴** *Moses summoned Mishael and Elzaphan, sons of Aaron's uncle Uzziel,*

---- אונקלוס ----

וְעַל אַפֵּי כָל עַמָּא אִתְיַקַּר וּשְׁתִיק אַהֲרֹן: ד וּקְרָא מֹשֶׁה לְמִישָׁאֵל וּלְאֶלְצָפָן בְּנֵי עֻזִּיאֵל אַח אֲבוּהִי דְאַהֲרֹן

---- רש"י ----

יודע הייתי שיתקדש הבית במיודעיו של מקום והייתי סבור או בי או (ויק״ר שם): **בקרובי. בנחירי: ועל פני כל העם אכבד.**
בך, עכשיו רואה אני שהם גדולים ממני וממך (ת״כ שם לו; ויק״ר כשהקב״ה עושה דין בצדיקים מתיירא ומתעלה ומתקלס (ונצמים
יב:ב; זבחים קטו:): **וידם אהרן.** קבל שכר על שתיקתו (שם) ומה קטו:): אם כן באלו כ״ש ברשעים וכן הוא אומר נורא אלהים
שכר קבל, שנתייחד עמו הדבור, שנאמרה לו לבדו פרשת שתויי יין ממקדשיך (תהלים סח:לו) אל תקרי ממקדשיך אלא ממקודשיך:

---- RASHI ELUCIDATED ----

"Aaron, my brother. יוֹדֵעַ הָיִיתִי — I knew שֶׁיִּתְקַדֵּשׁ הַבַּיִת — that the House (*Mishkan*) would become sanctified בִּמְיוּדָעָיו שֶׁל מָקוֹם — through those intimate with the Omnipresent. וְהָיִיתִי סָבוּר — I was under the impression that it would become sanctified אוֹ בִּי אוֹ בָךְ — either through me or through you. עַכְשָׁו רוֹאֶה אֲנִי שֶׁהֵם גְּדוֹלִים מִמֶּנִּי וּמִמְּךָ — Now I see that they are greater than I and you."[1]

□ וַיִּדֹּם אַהֲרֹן — AND AARON FELL SILENT.[2] קִבֵּל שָׂכָר — He received reward[3] עַל שְׁתִיקָתוֹ — for his silence.[3] וּמַה שָּׂכָר קִבֵּל — What reward did he receive? שֶׁנִּתְיַחֵד עִמּוֹ הַדִּבּוּר — That the speech of God was directed to him alone, שֶׁנֶּאֶמְרָה לוֹ לְבַדּוֹ — that to him alone was said[4] פָּרָשַׁת שְׁתוּיֵי יַיִן — the section of the Torah that deals with those intoxicated of wine.[4]

□ בִּקְרֹבַי — THROUGH THOSE WHO ARE CLOSE TO ME. This means, בִּבְחִירַי — through those whom I have chosen.[5]

□ וְעַל פְּנֵי כָל הָעָם אֶכָּבֵד — AND I WILL BE HONORED BEFORE THE ENTIRE PEOPLE. כְּשֶׁהַקָּדוֹשׁ בָּרוּךְ הוּא עוֹשֶׂה דִּין בַּצַּדִּיקִים — When the Holy One, Blessed is He, carries out judgment against the righteous, מִתְיָרֵא — He is feared, וּמִתְעַלֶּה — and exalted, וּמִתְקַלֵּס — and lauded.[6] אִם כֵּן בְּאֵלּוּ — If so with these, i.e., if He carries out judgment against the righteous, כָּל שֶׁכֵּן בָּרְשָׁעִים — all the more so against the wicked. וְכֵן הוּא אוֹמֵר — And in a like manner it says:[7] ,,נוֹרָא אֱלֹהִים מִמִּקְדָּשֶׁיךָ" — "God is feared from Your Sanctuary."[7] אַל תִּקְרִי ,,מִמִּקְדָּשֶׁיךָ" — Do not read this word as it is vowelized "from Your Sanctuary," אֶלָּא ,,מִמְּקֻדָּשֶׁיךָ" — but rather read it as if it were vowelized מִמְּקֻדָּשֶׁיךָ "from Your sanctified ones."[8]

9:23 כְּבוֹד (the construct form of כָּבוֹד שֶׁל ה'), "the glory of HASHEM." The word כְּבוֹדִי is the construct form of הַכָּבוֹד שֶׁלִּי and means "my honor." כָּבוֹד (plural כְּבוֹדִים) is an adjective in the masculine (its feminine form כְּבוּדָּה appears in Ezekiel 23:41) and means "honored." When it appears without its noun, it means "honored one." Thus, כְּבוּדֵי (the construct form of כְּבוּדִים שֶׁלִּי) means "my honored ones."

1. *Toras Kohanim, Miluim* 30; *Vayikra Rabbah* 12:2; *Zevachim* 115b.

2. Rashi explains "and Aaron fell silent" before commenting on earlier phrases of the verse, because this phrase is linked to the preceding comment. Aaron fell silent when he heard Moses acknowledge the saintliness of his sons (*Gur Aryeh; Sifsei Chachamim*).

3. We would have assumed that Aaron was silent unless the Torah had quoted him. If the Torah states explicitly that he was silent, it is to imply that he received reward for his silence (*Gur Aryeh; Sifsei Chachamim*).

4. *Vayikra Rabbah* 12:2. A Kohen in a drunken state is forbidden to enter the precincts of the Sanctuary from the *Mizbe'ach* and beyond (see vv. 8-11 below, and Rashi there). Aaron's reward was twofold. Normally, he would not hear even those parts of the Torah addressed to both him and Moses. In those situations, God would speak to Moses, and Moses would convey God's words to Aaron (see Rashi to 1:1). Here, not only did Aaron hear the word of God, but it was addressed primarily to him. Moses, because of his great merit, was privileged to hear this *parashah* from God, as well, but only as a bystander (*Mizrachi; Sifsei Chachamim*).

5. "Those who are close to me" could mean either "those who are geographically close to me," or "my relatives." Neither of these senses of the term is appropriate in the context of the relationship between God and man. Here it means "those whom I have chosen" (*Be'er Yitzchak*).

6. *Zevachim* 115b.

7. *Psalms* 68:36.

8. That is, God is feared through the judgment He carries out against His sanctified ones. The word מְקַדֵּשׁ (as in 12:4 below) is a noun and means

103 / VAYIKRA/LEVITICUS — Parashas Shemini — י/ה־ו — 10/5-6

and said to them, "Approach, carry your brothers out of the Sanctuary to the outside of the camp." ⁵ They approached and carried them in their Kutanos to the outside of the camp, as Moses had spoken.

⁶ Moses said to Aaron and to his sons Elazar and Ithamar, "Do not leave your heads unshorn and do not rend your garments that you do not die and He

וַיֹּאמֶר אֲלֵהֶם קִרְבוּ שְׂאוּ אֶת־אֲחֵיכֶם
מֵאֵת פְּנֵי־הַקֹּדֶשׁ אֶל־מִחוּץ לַמַּחֲנֶה:
ה וַיִּקְרְבוּ וַיִּשָּׂאֻם בְּכֻתֳּנֹתָם אֶל־מִחוּץ
לַמַּחֲנֶה כַּאֲשֶׁר דִּבֶּר מֹשֶׁה: ו וַיֹּאמֶר
מֹשֶׁה אֶל־אַהֲרֹן וּלְאֶלְעָזָר וּלְאִיתָמָר ׀
בָּנָיו רָאשֵׁיכֶם אַל־תִּפְרָעוּ ׀ וּבִגְדֵיכֶם
לֹא־תִפְרֹמוּ וְלֹא תָמֻתוּ וְעַל כָּל־

אונקלוס

וַאֲמַר לְהוֹן קְרִיבוּ טוּלוּ יָת אֲחֵיכוֹן מִן קֳדָם אַפֵּי קוּדְשָׁא לְמִבָּרָא לְמַשְׁרִיתָא: ה וּקְרִיבוּ וּנְטָלוּנוּן בְּכִתּוּנֵיהוֹן לְמִבָּרָא לְמַשְׁרִיתָא כְּמָא דִּי מַלִּיל מֹשֶׁה: ו וַאֲמַר מֹשֶׁה לְאַהֲרֹן וּלְאֶלְעָזָר וּלְאִיתָמָר בְּנוֹהִי רֵישֵׁיכוֹן לָא תְרַבּוֹן וּלְבוּשֵׁיכוֹן לָא תְבַזְעוּן וְלָא תְמוּתוּן וְעַל כָּל

רש"י

(ד) דד אהרן. עֻזִּיאֵל אֲחִי עַמְרָם הָיָה שֶׁנֶּאֱמַר׳ וּבְנֵי קְהָת וְגוֹ' (שמות ו:יח): שאו את אחיכם וגו׳. כְּאָדָם הָאוֹמֵר לַחֲבֵרוֹ הַעֲבֵר אֶת הַמֵּת מִלִּפְנֵי הַכַּלָּה שֶׁלֹּא לְעַרְבֵּב אֶת הַשִּׂמְחָה (ויק"ר כ:ד): (ה) בכתנתם. שֶׁל מֵתִים מְלַמֵּד שֶׁלֹּא נִשְׂרְפוּ בִּגְדֵיהֶם אֶלָּא

נְשָׁמָתָם כְּמִין שְׁנֵי חוּטִין שֶׁל אֵשׁ נִכְנְסוּ לְתוֹךְ חֳטָמֵיהֶם (ת"כ שם כז; סנהדרין נב.): (ו) אל תפרעו. אַל תְּגַדְּלוּ שֵׂעָר מִכָּאן שֶׁאָבֵל אָסוּר בְּתִסְפֹּרֶת (מוֹעֵד קָטָן יד.): אֲבָל אַתֶּם אַל תְּעַרְבְּבוּ שִׂמְחָתוֹ שֶׁל מָקוֹם: ולא תמתו. הָא אִם תַּעֲשׂוּ כֵן תָּמוּתוּ (ת"כ שם מא):

— RASHI ELUCIDATED —

4. דד אהרן — AARON'S UNCLE. — עֻזִּיאֵל אֲחִי עַמְרָם הָיָה — Uzziel was the brother of Amram, Aaron's father, שֶׁנֶּאֱמַר — as it says, וּבְנֵי קְהָת וְגוֹמֵר, "the sons of Kohath, etc."[1]

☐ שְׂאוּ אֶת אֲחֵיכֶם וְגוֹמֵר — CARRY YOUR BROTHERS, ETC. כְּאָדָם הָאוֹמֵר לַחֲבֵרוֹ — Like a man who says to his friend, הַעֲבֵר אֶת הַמֵּת מִלִּפְנֵי הַכַּלָּה — "Remove the corpse from the presence of the bride שֶׁלֹּא לְעַרְבֵּב אֶת הַשִּׂמְחָה — so as not to disturb the rejoicing of the wedding with mourning."[2]

5. בְּכֻתֳּנֹתָם — IN THEIR KUTANOS, that is, in the Kutanos שֶׁל מֵתִים — of the dead.[3] מְלַמֵּד — This teaches us אֶלָּא נִשְׁמָתָם — but only that their garments were not burned, שֶׁלֹּא נִשְׂרְפוּ בִּגְדֵיהֶם — that their garments were not burned, אֶלָּא נִשְׁמָתָם — but only their souls — נִכְנְסוּ לְתוֹךְ חֳטָמֵיהֶם — Something like two threads of fire[4] — entered into their nostrils.[4]

6. אַל תִּפְרָעוּ — DO NOT LEAVE YOUR HEADS UNSHORN. This means אַל תְּגַדְּלוּ שֵׂעָר — do not grow hair. מִכָּאן — From here we have a source for the law שֶׁאָבֵל אָסוּר בְּתִסְפֹּרֶת[6] — that a mourner is forbidden to have a haircut.[5,6] אֲבָל אַתֶּם — But you, אַל תְּעַרְבְּבוּ שִׂמְחָתוֹ שֶׁל מָקוֹם — do not disturb the rejoicing of the Omnipresent.[7]

☐ וְלֹא תָמֻתוּ — THAT YOU DO NOT DIE. הָא אִם תַּעֲשׂוּ כֵן — But if you do so, תָּמוּתוּ[8] — you shall die.[8]

"holy place," thus מִקְדָּשֶׁיךָ (the construct form of מִקְדָּשִׁים שֶׁלָּךְ) means "your holy places," i.e., "Your Sanctuary." The word מְקֻדָּשׁ (as in *Ezekiel* 48:11) is an adjective that means "sanctified." When it appears without its noun, מְקֻדָּשׁ means "sanctified one" or "holy one." Thus מְקֻדָּשֶׁיךָ (the construct form of מְקֻדָּשִׁים שֶׁלָּךְ) means "Your holy ones."

1. *Exodus* 6:18. That verse lists four sons of Kohath: Amram, Izhar, Hebron and Uzziel.

2. *Vayikra Rabbah* 20:4. The verse could have said, "Carry your brothers and bury them." "Carry your brothers out of the Sanctuary to the outside of the camp" implies that the purpose of carrying them out was not primarily to bury them, but because the presence of the corpses inside the Sanctuary was inappropriate (*Mizrachi*; *Sifsei Chachamim*).

3. It must refer to the Kutanos of the dead, for the Kutoness (plural, Kutanos) is one of the priestly garments. Nadab and Abihu were Kohanim, but their cousins, Mishael and Elzaphan, were Levites (*Mizrachi*; *Sifsei Chachamim*).

4. *Toras Kohanim*, *Miluim* 23; *Sanhedrin* 52a. According to *Toras Kohanim*, their souls and bodies were burned. According to the Talmud, their souls but not their bodies were burned.

5. This includes shaving.

6. *Moed Kattan* 14b.

7. If the verse makes a point of forbidding Aaron and his sons to leave their heads unshorn, it must be because normally that is what a mourner must do. An exception is made in the case of Aaron and his sons, because an outward display of mourning on their part would diminish the rejoicing of the inauguration of the *Mishkan* (see Rashi to *Moed Kattan* 14b).

8. *Toras Kohanim*, *Miluim* 41. See note 1 to 8:35 above.

הָעֵדָה יִקְצֹף וְאַחֵיכֶם כָּל־בֵּית יִשְׂרָאֵל יִבְכּוּ אֶת־הַשְּׂרֵפָה אֲשֶׁר שָׂרַף יהוה: ז וּמִפֶּתַח אֹהֶל מוֹעֵד לֹא תֵצְאוּ פֶּן־תָּמֻתוּ כִּי־שֶׁמֶן מִשְׁחַת יהוה עֲלֵיכֶם וַיַּעֲשׂוּ כִּדְבַר מֹשֶׁה: ח־ט וַיְדַבֵּר יהוה אֶל־אַהֲרֹן לֵאמֹר: יַיִן וְשֵׁכָר אַל־תֵּשְׁתְּ ׀ אַתָּה ׀ וּבָנֶיךָ אִתָּךְ בְּבֹאֲכֶם אֶל־אֹהֶל מוֹעֵד וְלֹא תָמֻתוּ חֻקַּת עוֹלָם לְדֹרֹתֵיכֶם:

become wrathful with the entire assembly; and your brothers, the entire House of Israel shall bewail the conflagration that HASHEM ignited. [7] *Do not leave the entrance of the Tent of Meeting lest you die, for the oil of HASHEM's anointment is upon you"; and they carried out Moses' bidding.*

[8] *HASHEM spoke to Aaron saying:* [9] *Do not drink intoxicating wine, you and your sons with you, when you come to the Tent of Meeting, that you not die — this is an eternal decree for your generations.*

───── אונקלוס ─────

בְּנִשְׁתָּא יְהֵא רוּגְזָא וַאֲחֵיכוֹן כָּל בֵּית יִשְׂרָאֵל יִבְכּוּן יָת יְקֵדְתָא דִי אוֹקִיד יְיָ: זוּמִתְּרַע מַשְׁכַּן זִמְנָא לָא תִפְּקוּן דִילְמָא תְמוּתוּן אֲרֵי מְשַׁח רְבוּתָא דַיְיָ עֲלֵיכוֹן וַעֲבָדוּ כִּפִּתְגָמָא דְמֹשֶׁה: חוּמַלִיל יְיָ לְאַהֲרֹן לְמֵימָר: טחֲמַר וּמְרַוֵי לָא תִשְׁתֵּי אַתְּ וּבְנָיךְ עִמָּךְ בְּמֵעַלְכוֹן לְמַשְׁכַּן זִמְנָא וְלָא תְמוּתוּן קְיָם עָלַם לְדָרֵיכוֹן:

───── רש"י ─────

ואחיכם כל בית ישראל. מכאן שצרתן של תלמידי חכמים מוטלת על הכל להתאבל בה (מועד קטן כח:): (ט) **יין ושכר.** יין דרך שכרותו (ת"כ פרשתא א:ב; כריתות יג:): **בבואכם אל אהל מועד.** אין לי אלא בבואם להיכל, בגשתם למזבח מנין. נא' כאן ביאת אהל מועד ונאמר בקידוש ידים ורגלים ביאת אהל מועד (שמות ל:כ) מה להלן עשה גישת מזבח

───── RASHI ELUCIDATED ─────

□ **וַאֲחֵיכֶם כָּל בֵּית יִשְׂרָאֵל** — AND YOUR BROTHERS, THE ENTIRE HOUSE OF ISRAEL. מִכָּאן — From here we see **שֶׁצָּרָתָן שֶׁל תַּלְמִידֵי חֲכָמִים** — that the distress of Torah scholars **מֻטֶּלֶת עַל הַכֹּל** — is placed upon everybody [1] **לְהִתְאַבֵּל בָּהּ** — to mourn it, i.e., the entire community must share in the distress of Torah scholars.[1]

9. **יַיִן וְשֵׁכָר** — INTOXICATING WINE. This means [2] **יַיִן דֶּרֶךְ שִׁכְרוּתוֹ** — wine in a manner in which it intoxicates.[2]

□ **בְּבֹאֲכֶם אֶל אֹהֶל מוֹעֵד** — WHEN YOU COME TO THE TENT OF MEETING. **אֵין לִי אֶלָּא בְּבֹאָם לַהֵיכָל** — I have nothing stated here **but when they come to the Sanctuary.**[3] **בְּגִשְׁתָּם לַמִּזְבֵּחַ מִנַּיִן** — From where do I know that the prohibition applies even **when they come near the** *Mizbe'ach*, which is outside the Sanctuary, to perform the service? **נֶאֱמַר כָּאן בִּיאַת אֹהֶל מוֹעֵד** — Coming to the Tent of Meeting is mentioned here, **וְנֶאֱמַר בְּקִדּוּשׁ יָדַיִם וְרַגְלַיִם בִּיאַת אֹהֶל מוֹעֵד**[4] — and coming to the Tent of Meeting is mentioned with regard to sanctification through ritual washing **of the Kohanim's hands and feet.**[4] **מַה לְהַלָּן** — Just as there regarding the sanctification **עָשָׂה גִּישַׁת מִזְבֵּחַ** — [the Torah] made

---

1. *Moed Kattan* 25a.

2. *Toras Kohanim, parshasa* 1:2; *Kereisos* 13b. But if a Kohen enters the grounds of the *Beis HaMikdash* having drunk less than a *revi'is* (in modern terms, opinions range from 3 to 5.3 fl. oz.) at one time, or if he drank wine that was diluted, he has not committed a transgression. Rashi here follows the opinion of the *Tanna* R' Eliezer (in *Toras Kohanim*) who holds that וְשֵׁכָר modifies יַיִן. He reasons that just as וְשֵׁכָר refers to wine when it appears in the context of the laws of the *nazir* (one who takes a particular vow of abstinence — see *Numbers* 6:1-21), so, too, here. The prefix ו in this case does not serve to connect the two nouns יַיִן, "wine," and שֵׁכָר, "intoxicant." Rather, it serves to turn שֵׁכָר into a modifier of יַיִן, that is, "Do not drink wine and become intoxicated from it." The *Tanna* R' Yehudah, however, holds that יַיִן וְשֵׁכָר means "wine and hard drink," that is, a Kohen may not enter the grounds of the *Beis HaMikdash* after having drunk any intoxicating beverage. But if all intoxicating beverages fall under the same prohibition, why did the Torah have to list wine separately? This teaches that only when one enters the Sanctuary after drinking wine does he incur the death penalty; after drinking other intoxicants, one may not enter the precincts of the Sanctuary, but if one does, he does not incur the death penalty (*Mizrachi*).

3. That is, on the basis of this verse, I have the right to conclude only that the Kohanim may not enter the Sanctuary after they have drunk wine.

4. *Exodus* 30:20 reads: "When they come to the Tent of Meeting, they shall wash with water, that they not die; or when they draw near to the *Mizbe'ach* to serve, to raise up in smoke a fire-offering to HASHEM."

105 / VAYIKRA/LEVITICUS — PARASHAS SHEMINI — **10/10-12**

¹⁰ *To distinguish between the sacred and the profane, and between the impure and the pure,* ¹¹ *and to teach the Children of Israel all the decrees that* HASHEM *had spoken to them through Moses.*

¹² *Moses spoke to Aaron and to Elazar and Ithamar, his remaining sons,*

י וּלֲהַבְדִּיל בֵּין הַקֹּדֶשׁ וּבֵין הַחֹל וּבֵין
יא הַטָּמֵא וּבֵין הַטָּהוֹר: וּלְהוֹרֹת אֶת־
בְּנֵי יִשְׂרָאֵל אֵת כָּל־הַחֻקִּים אֲשֶׁר
דִּבֶּר יהוה אֲלֵיהֶם בְּיַד־מֹשֶׁה:
יב רביעי וַיְדַבֵּר מֹשֶׁה אֶל־אַהֲרֹן וְאֶל
אֶלְעָזָר וְאֶל־אִיתָמָר ׀ בָּנָיו הַנּוֹתָרִים

——— אונקלוס ———

י וּלְאַפְרָשָׁא בֵּין קוּדְשָׁא וּבֵין חֻלָּא וּבֵין מְסָאָבָא וּבֵין דָּכְיָא: יא וּלְאַלָּפָא יָת בְּנֵי יִשְׂרָאֵל יָת כָּל קְיָמַיָּא דִּי מַלִּיל יְיָ לְהוֹן בִּידָא דְמֹשֶׁה: יב וּמַלִּיל מֹשֶׁה עִם אַהֲרֹן וְעִם אֶלְעָזָר וְעִם אִיתָמָר בְּנוֹהִי דְאִשְׁתָּאָרוּ

——— רש"י ———

כְּבִיאַת אֹהֶל מוֹעֵד. אַף כָּאן עָשָׂה גִישַׁת מִזְבֵּחַ כְּבִיאַת אֹהֶל מוֹעֵד (ת"כ שם ד): (י) וּלְהַבְדִּיל. כְּדֵי שֶׁתִּבְדְּלוּ בֵּין עֲבוֹדָה קְדוֹשָׁה לִמְחֻלֶּלֶת. הָא לָמַדְתָּ, שֶׁאִם עָבַד עֲבוֹדָתוֹ פְּסוּלָה (ת"כ שם ח; זבחים יז:): (יא) וּלְהוֹרֹת. לִמֵּד שֶׁאָסוּר שִׁכּוֹר בְּהוֹרָאָה (ת"כ שם ט). יָכוֹל יְהֵא חַיָּב מִיתָה, ת"ל אַתָּה וּבָנֶיךָ אִתְּךָ וְלֹא תָמוּתוּ (לעיל פסוק ט) כֹּהֲנִים בַּעֲבוֹדָתָם בְּמִיתָה, וְאֵין חֲכָמִים בְּהוֹרָאָתָם בְּמִיתָה (ת"כ שם ו־ז): (יב) הַנּוֹתָרִים. מִן הַמִּיתָה, מְלַמֵּד שֶׁאַף עֲלֵיהֶם נִקְנְסָה מִיתָה (ת"כ פרק א:ב; יומא פז.) עַל עֲוֹן הָעֵגֶל. הוּא שֶׁנֶּאֱמַר וּבְאַהֲרֹן הִתְאַנַּף ה' מְאֹד לְהַשְׁמִידוֹ (דברים ט:כ) וְאֵין הַשְׁמָדָה אֶלָּא כִּלּוּי בָּנִים שֶׁנֶּאֱמַר וָאַשְׁמִיד פִּרְיוֹ מִמַּעַל (עמוס ב:ט)

——— RASHI ELUCIDATED ———

approaching the Mizbe'ach בְּבִיאַת אֹהֶל מוֹעֵד — **like coming to the Tent of Meeting**, in that both require sanctification of the hands and feet, אַף כָּאן — **here, too,** עָשָׂה גִישַׁת מִזְבֵּחַ — **[the Torah] made coming near the Mizbe'ach** ¹בְּבִיאַת אֹהֶל מוֹעֵד — **like coming to the Tent of Meeting.**¹

10. וּלְהַבְדִּיל — TO DISTINGUISH. כְּדֵי שֶׁתִּבְדְּלוּ — **So that you shall distinguish** בֵּין עֲבוֹדָה קְדוֹשָׁה — **between holy service** לִמְחֻלֶּלֶת — **and that which has been profaned.**² הָא לָמַדְתָּ — **See, now, that you have learned** שֶׁאִם עָבַד — **that if he performed the service** of the *Beis HaMikdash* while intoxicated, ³עֲבוֹדָתוֹ פְסוּלָה — **his service is invalid.**³

11. וּלְהוֹרֹת — AND TO TEACH. לִמֵּד — [The verse] has taught us ⁴שֶׁאָסוּר שִׁכּוֹר בְּהוֹרָאָה — **that one who is intoxicated is forbidden to teach,** i.e., to render halachic decisions.⁴ יָכוֹל — **One might be able** to think that יְהֵא חַיָּב מִיתָה — **he deserves the death penalty** for rendering a halachic decision while intoxicated.⁵ תַּלְמוּד לוֹמַר — To teach us otherwise, **the verse says,** ⁶"אַתָּה וּבָנֶיךָ אִתְּךָ וְלֹא תָמֻתוּ — **"you and your sons with you . . . that you not die."**⁶ כֹּהֲנִים בַּעֲבוֹדָתָם — **Kohanim who are engaged in their service** while intoxicated are liable בְּמִיתָה — to the **death** penalty, וְאֵין חֲכָמִים — **but scholars** בְּהוֹרָאָתָם בְּמִיתָה⁷ — **in their teaching are not liable** to the **death penalty.**⁷

12. הַנּוֹתָרִים — REMAINING. מִן הַמִּיתָה — **from the death.** מְלַמֵּד — **This teaches us** שֶׁאַף עֲלֵיהֶם — **that** ⁸נִקְנְסָה מִיתָה — **the death penalty was sentenced upon them, as well,**⁸ עַל עֲוֹן הָעֵגֶל — **for the sin of the** Golden Calf.⁹ הוּא שֶׁנֶּאֱמַר — **This is** the idea referred to in **that which it says,** ¹⁰"וּבְאַהֲרֹן הִתְאַנַּף ה' מְאֹד לְהַשְׁמִידוֹ — **"And against Aaron, HASHEM became very enraged, to destroy him."**¹⁰ וְאֵין הַשְׁמָדָה אֶלָּא כִּלּוּי בָּנִים — **"Destruction"** in this context **refers only to annihilation of children,** שֶׁנֶּאֱמַר — **as it says,** ¹¹"וָאַשְׁמִיד פִּרְיוֹ מִמַּעַל — **"I destroyed his fruit from above."**¹¹

---

1. *Toras Kohanim, parshasa* 1:4.
2. The verse appears to say that the Kohanim may not enter the Tent of Meeting while intoxicated so that they will be able to distinguish between the sacred and the profane. But this cannot be the meaning of the verse, for everything in the Tent of Meeting is sacred. The verse thus implies that there is a distinction to be drawn between holy service and service that has been profaned by the intoxication of the officiating Kohen (*Mesiach Ilmim*).
3. *Toras Kohanim, parshasa* 1:8; *Zevachim* 17b.
4. *Toras Kohanim, parshasa* 1:9; *Kereisos* 13b.
5. Just as a Kohen is liable to be punished by death for entering the Tent of Meeting while intoxicated.
6. Above v. 9.
7. *Toras Kohanim, parshasa* 1:6-7. The apparently superfluous "with you" (אִתְּךָ) of "you and your sons with you" is interpreted as limiting the death penalty of this passage to the Kohanim alone (*Minchas Yehudah; Sifsei Chachamim*).
8. *Toras Kohanim,* perek 1:2; *Yoma* 87a.
9. Obviously, Elazar and Ithamar are "remaining sons" for they did not die. The Torah nonetheless states this to teach us that they were *spared* from death (*Devek Tov*).
10. *Deuteronomy* 9:20.
11. *Amos* 2:9. "Fruit" is understood by Rashi as a metaphor for children.

"Take the meal-offering that is left from the fire-offerings of Hashem, and eat it unleavened near the Mizbe'ach; for it is that which is holy of the highest degree. ¹³ You shall eat it in a holy place, for it is your portion and the portion of your sons from the fire-offerings of Hashem, for so have I been commanded.

קְחוּ אֶת־הַמִּנְחָה הַנּוֹתֶרֶת מֵאִשֵּׁי יהוה וְאִכְלוּהָ מַצּוֹת אֵצֶל הַמִּזְבֵּחַ כִּי קֹדֶשׁ קָדָשִׁים הִוא: וַאֲכַלְתֶּם אֹתָהּ בְּמָקוֹם קָדוֹשׁ כִּי חָקְךָ וְחָק־בָּנֶיךָ הִוא מֵאִשֵּׁי יהוה כִּי־כֵן צֻוֵּיתִי:

— אונקלוס —

סִיבוּ יָת מִנְחָתָא דְאִשְׁתָּאֲרַת מִקֻּרְבָּנַיָּא דַּיָי וְאִכְלוּהָ פַטִּיר בִּסְטַר מַדְבְּחָא אֲרֵי קֹדֶשׁ קוּדְשִׁין הִיא: יגוְתֵיכְלוּן יָתַהּ בַּאֲתַר קַדִּישׁ אֲרֵי חֳלָקָךְ וְחֳלָק בְּנָיךְ הִיא מִקֻּרְבָּנַיָּא דַּיָי אֲרֵי כֵן אִתְפַּקָּדִית:

— רש"י —

וּתְפִלָּתוֹ שֶׁל מֹשֶׁה בָּטְלָה מֶחֱצָה שֶׁנֶּאֱמַר וְאֶתְפַּלֵּל גַּם בְּעַד אַהֲרֹן בָּעֵת הַהִיא: **קְחוּ אֶת הַמִּנְחָה.** אַף עַל פִּי שֶׁאַתֶּם אוֹנְנִין וְקָדָשִׁים אֲסוּרִים לְאוֹנֵן: **אֶת הַמִּנְחָה.** זוֹ מִנְחַת שְׁמִינִי וּמִנְחַת נַחְשׁוֹן (במדבר ז,יג; ת"כ פרק א:ב): **וְאִכְלוּהָ מַצּוֹת.** מַה תַּ"ל, לְפִי שֶׁהִיא מִנְחַת צִבּוּר וּמִנְחַת שָׁעָה וְאֵין כַּיּוֹצֵא בָהּ לְדוֹרוֹת הוּצְרַךְ לְפָרֵשׁ בָּהּ דִּין שְׁאָר מְנָחוֹת (ת"כ שָׁם ד): (יג) **וְחָק בָּנֶיךָ.** אֵין לַבָּנוֹת חֹק בַּקָּדָשִׁים (שָׁם ז): **כִּי כֵן צֻוֵּיתִי.** בַּאֲנִינוּת יֹאכְלוּהָ (שָׁם ח; זבחים קא.):

— RASHI ELUCIDATED —

□ וּתְפִלָּתוֹ שֶׁל מֹשֶׁה בָּטְלָה מֶחֱצָה — Moses' prayer nullified half of the decree against Aaron and his sons, שֶׁנֶּאֱמַר as it says, ,,וָאֶתְפַּלֵּל גַּם בְּעַד אַהֲרֹן בָּעֵת הַהִיא'' — "And I prayed for Aaron, too, at that time."[1]

□ קְחוּ אֶת הַמִּנְחָה — TAKE THE MEAL-OFFERING. אַף עַל פִּי שֶׁאַתֶּם אוֹנְנִין — Even though you are *onenim*[2] וְקָדָשִׁים אֲסוּרִים לְאוֹנֵן — and that which is holy is forbidden to be eaten by an *onein*.

□ אֶת הַמִּנְחָה — THE MEAL-OFFERING. זוֹ מִנְחַת שְׁמִינִי — This is the meal-offering of the eighth day of the inauguration[3] וּמִנְחַת נַחְשׁוֹן[4] — and the meal-offering of Nahshon.[4]

□ וְאִכְלוּהָ מַצּוֹת — AND EAT IT UNLEAVENED. מַה תַּלְמוּד לוֹמַר — Why is this stated?[5] לְפִי שֶׁהִיא מִנְחַת צִבּוּר — Because it is a meal-offering of the public וּמִנְחַת שָׁעָה — and a meal-offering of the hour[6] וְאֵין כַּיּוֹצֵא בָהּ לְדוֹרוֹת — and there is nothing like it for future generations; הוּצְרַךְ לְפָרֵשׁ בָּהּ — therefore [the Torah] had to state explicitly with regard to it that its law insofar as being unleavened is like דִּין שְׁאָר מְנָחוֹת[7] — the law of other meal-offerings.[7]

13. וְחָק בָּנֶיךָ — AND THE PORTION OF YOUR SONS. אֵין לַבָּנוֹת חֹק בַּקָּדָשִׁים[8] — Daughters do not have a portion in that which is holy.[8]

□ כִּי כֵן צֻוֵּיתִי — FOR SO HAVE I BEEN COMMANDED. בַּאֲנִינוּת יֹאכְלוּהָ — That they shall eat it in a state

---

1. *Deuteronomy* 9:20.
2. An *onein*, in the sense that the term is used by Scripture, is one of the seven mourners (son, daughter, mother, father, brother, sister, spouse) on the day of the death of a relative.
3. See 9:4 above.
4. *Toras Kohanim*, *perek* 1:3. Nahshon's meal-offering is described in *Numbers* 7:13. The princes of the tribes began to bring their offerings in honor of the inauguration of the *Mizbe'ach* (see *Numbers*, Ch. 7) on the eighth day of the inaugural ceremony. The first prince to bring his offering was Nahshon ben Amminadab of the tribe of Judah (*Minchas Yehudah*; *Sifsei Chachamim*).
5. All meal-offerings are eaten unleavened. See 6:9-10 above.
6. That is, it is a meal-offering the like of which was brought only at that time.
7. *Toras Kohanim*, *perek* 1:4.
8. *Toras Kohanim*, *perek* 1:7. Our verse speaks of the meal-offering, which is an offering of the highest degree of holiness. Therefore, when Rashi says, "Daughters do not have a portion in that which is holy," *Maskil LeDavid* understands him to mean that with regard to this offering, not only are they not allotted a portion, but they may not eat of the portion allotted to their father if he gives it to them. According to *Be'er BaSadeh*, however, Rashi would not use the broad term "that which is holy" if he meant only that which is holy of the highest degree. Thus, *Be'er BaSadeh* understands that Rashi sees our verse as a source for the general rule that daughters of Kohanim are not allotted a share of the offerings. Although the following verse states this principle with regard to peace-offerings, which are of the lesser degree of holiness, had the Torah stated only that verse, we would have said that it applies only where the meat of the offering is not enough for both male Kohanim and their daughters. Then, males take precedence. Our verse teaches us that the daughters never receive a share. [This does not mean that the daughters of the Kohanim may not eat the meat of offerings, only that they do not receive a portion of their own when the Kohanim divide the sacrificial meat among themselves. Thus, a Kohen's wife or

¹⁴ *And the breast of the waving and the thigh of the raising you are to eat in a pure place, you and your sons and your daughters with you; for they have been given as your portion and the portion of your sons from the sacrifices*

יד וְאֵת ׀ חֲזֵה הַתְּנוּפָה וְאֵת ׀ שׁוֹק הַתְּרוּמָה תֹּאכְלוּ בְּמָקוֹם טָהוֹר אַתָּה וּבָנֶיךָ וּבְנֹתֶיךָ אִתָּךְ כִּי־חָקְךָ וְחָק־בָּנֶיךָ נִתְּנוּ מִזִּבְחֵי

— אונקלוס —

יד וְיָת חֶדְיָא דַאֲרָמוּתָא וְיָת שׁוֹקָא דְאַפְרָשׁוּתָא תֵּיכְלוּן בַּאֲתַר דְּכֵי אַתְּ וּבְנָיךְ וּבְנָתָיךְ עִמָּךְ אֲרֵי חֳלָקָךְ וַחֲלָק בְּנָיךְ אִתְיְהִיבוּ מִנִּכְסַת

— רש"י —

(יד) ואת חזה התנופה. של שלמי צבור: תאכלו במקום טהור. וכי את הראשונים אכלו במקום טמא. אלא הראשונים שהם קדשי קדשים הוזקקו אכילתם במקום קדוש, אבל אלו אין צריכים תוך הקלעים, אבל צריכים הם לאכל תוך מחנה

ישראל שהוא טהור מליכנס שם מצורעים. מכאן שקדשים קלים נאכלין בכל העיר (ת"כ שם ט; זבחים נה.): אתה ובניך ובנותיך. אתה ובניך בחלק, אבל בנותיך לא בחלק, אלא אם נתנו להם מתנות רשאות הן לאכול בחזה ושוק.

— RASHI ELUCIDATED —

of day-of-death mourning.¹

14. וְאֵת חֲזֵה הַתְּנוּפָה — **AND THE BREAST OF THE WAVING** שֶׁל שַׁלְמֵי צִבּוּר — of the peace-offerings of the public.²

□ תֹּאכְלוּ בְּמָקוֹם טָהוֹר — **YOU ARE TO EAT IN A PURE PLACE.** וְכִי אֶת הָרִאשׁוֹנִים אָכְלוּ בְּמָקוֹם טָמֵא — **But did they eat those** offerings mentioned **earlier in an impure place?**³ אֶלָּא הָרִאשׁוֹנִים — **But regarding those** mentioned **earlier** שֶׁהֵם קָדְשֵׁי קָדָשִׁים — **which are holy of the highest degree,** הוּזְקְקוּ אֲכִילָתָם — **they were required** to see to it **that their eating** would be done בְּמָקוֹם קָדוֹשׁ — **in a holy place,** i.e., in the Courtyard of the *Mishkan* or *Beis HaMikdash.* אֲבָל אֵלוּ — **But these** which are of the peace-offerings of the public, אֵין צְרִיכִים — **they do not need** to be eaten תּוֹךְ הַקְּלָעִים — **within the curtains** surrounding the Courtyard of the *Mishkan,* אֲבָל צְרִיכִים הֵם לֶאֱכֹל — **but they do need to be** eaten תּוֹךְ מַחֲנֵה יִשְׂרָאֵל — **within the Camp of Israel**⁴ שֶׁהוּא טָהוֹר מִלִּכָּנֵס שָׁם מְצוֹרָעִים — **which is pure with regard to the entry of those suffering from *tzara'as.*⁵** מִכָּאן — **From here** we see נֶאֱכָלִין בְּכָל הָעִיר⁷ — **may be eaten** שֶׁקָּדְשִׁים קַלִּים — **that that which is holy in the lesser degree** throughout the entire city.⁶,⁷

□ אַתָּה וּבָנֶיךָ וּבְנֹתֶיךָ — **YOU AND YOUR SONS AND YOUR DAUGHTERS.** אַתָּה וּבָנֶיךָ בַּחֵלֶק — **You and your sons are** included **in the apportioning,** אֲבָל בְּנוֹתֶיךָ לֹא בַחֵלֶק — **but your daughters are not** included **in the apportioning.** אֶלָּא אִם תִּתְּנוּ לָהֶם מַתָּנוֹת — **But if you give them** food from the **gifts** of the *kehunah,* רַשָּׁאוֹת הֵן לֶאֱכֹל — **they are permitted to eat** בְּחָזֶה וָשׁוֹק — **of the breast** of the waving

---

daughter may eat from her husband's or father's portion of offerings of lesser holiness (see Rashi to v. 14 below, s.v., אַתָּה וּבָנֶיךָ וּבְנֹתֶיךָ, "you and your sons and your daughters").]

1. *Toras Kohanim, perek* 1:8; *Zevachim* 101a. See note 2 on page 106.

2. The only other peace-offerings brought by the public, the two sheep offered on Shavuos, have the status of that which is holy of the highest degree (see 23:20 below and Rashi there), and may only be eaten by male Kohanim on the grounds of the *Beis HaMikdash.* The peace-offering of the public mentioned by our verse, however, has the status of that which is holy of the lesser degree, for it may be eaten by the daughters of the Kohanim, as well. Therefore it may be eaten within a greater area, as Rashi goes on to explain.

The same law applied to the peace-offering brought on that day by Nahshon ben Amminadab. Rashi does not mention it because it is obvious that it had the status of that which is holy of the lesser degree,

as do all peace-offerings brought by individuals (*Be'er BaSadeh*).

Mizrachi understands our verse as granting permission to the Kohanim to eat the peace-offering while in a state of *aninus,* in addition to the meal-offering, which was the subject of the preceding verse.

3. All that is holy must be eaten in a pure place. Why does the verse specify the breast of the waving and the thigh of the raising-up?

4. The area of the Israelite camp in which the tribes other than the tribe of Levi pitched their tents.

5. The Camp of Israel is pure in that one suffering from *tzara'as,* a disease which renders the sufferer impure, may not enter it (see 13:46 below).

6. In the days of the *Beis HaMikdash,* the entire city within the walls of Jerusalem beyond the grounds of the *Beis HaMikdash* had the status of the camp of Israel in the desert.

7. *Toras Kohanim, perek* 1:9; *Zevachim* 55a.

טו שַׁלְמֵי בְּנֵי יִשְׂרָאֵל: שׁוֹק הַתְּרוּמָה וַחֲזֵה הַתְּנוּפָה עַל אִשֵּׁי הַחֲלָבִים יָבִיאוּ לְהָנִיף תְּנוּפָה לִפְנֵי יהוה וְהָיָה לְךָ וּלְבָנֶיךָ אִתְּךָ לְחָק־עוֹלָם כַּאֲשֶׁר צִוָּה יהוה: חמישי טז וְאֵת ׀ שְׂעִיר הַחַטָּאת דָּרֹשׁ דָּרַשׁ מֹשֶׁה וְהִנֵּה

of the peace-offerings of the Children of Israel. ¹⁵ *They are to bring the thigh of the raising and the breast of the waving upon the fire-offering fats to wave as a wave-service before* HASHEM; *and it shall be for you and your sons with you for an eternal decree, as* HASHEM *has commanded."*

¹⁶ *Moses inquired insistently about the he-goat of the sin-offering, for behold,*

────────────── אונקלוס ──────────────

שׁוּקָא דְּאַפְרָשׁוּתָא וְחֶדְיָא דַאֲרָמוּתָא עַל קוּרְבָּנַיָּא טו קוּדְשַׁיָּא דִּבְנֵי יִשְׂרָאֵל: דְתַרְבַּיָּא יֵיתוּן לַאֲרָמָא אֲרָמָא קֳדָם יְיָ וִיהֵי לָךְ וְלִבְנָיךְ עִמָּךְ לִקְיָם עָלָם כְּמָא דִי פַקִּיד יְיָ: טז וְיָת צְפִירָא דְחַטָּאתָא מִתְבַּע תְּבַע מֹשֶׁה וְהָא

────────────── רש"י ──────────────

אוֹ אֵינוֹ אֶלָּא אַף הַבָּנוֹת בַּחֵלֶק, ת"ל כִּי חָקְךָ וְחָק בָּנֶיךָ נִתְּנוּ, חָק לַבָּנִים וְאֵין חֹק לַבָּנוֹת (ת"כ שם י): (טו) שׁוֹק הַתְּרוּמָה וַחֲזֵה הַתְּנוּפָה. לְשׁוֹן אֲשֶׁר הוּנַף וַאֲשֶׁר הוּרָם (שמות כט:כז), תְּנוּפָה מוֹלִיךְ וּמֵבִיא תְּרוּמָה מַעֲלֶה וּמוֹרִיד. וְלָמָּה חִלֵּק הַכָּתוּב תְּרוּמָה בְּשׁוֹק וּתְנוּפָה בֶחָזֶה לֹא יָדַעְנוּ, שֶׁשְּׁנֵיהֶם בַּהֲרָמָה וַהֲנָפָה: [עַל

אִשֵּׁי הַחֲלָבִים. כְּמוֹ עַל חֶלְבֵי הָאִשִּׁים:] **עַל אִשֵּׁי הַחֲלָבִים.** מִכָּאן שֶׁהַחֲלָבִים לְמַטָּה בִּשְׁעַת תְּנוּפָה, וְיִשּׁוּב הַמִּקְרָאוֹת שֶׁלֹּא יַכְחִישׁוּ זֶה אֶת זֶה כְּבָר פֵּרַשְׁתִּי שְׁלָשְׁתָּן בְּצַו אֶת אַהֲרֹן (לְעֵיל ז:ל): **(טז) שְׂעִיר הַחַטָּאת.** שְׂעִיר מוּסְפֵי רֹאשׁ חֹדֶשׁ. וּשְׁלֹשָׁה שְׂעִירֵי חַטָּאוֹת קָרְבוּ בוֹ בַיּוֹם, [קְחוּ] שְׂעִיר עִזִּים (לְעֵיל ט:ג):

────────────── RASHI ELUCIDATED ──────────────

and the thigh of the raising.¹ — אוֹ אֵינוֹ אֶלָּא — *Or perhaps this is not so, but rather* אַף הַבָּנוֹת בַּחֵלֶק — *the daughters, too, are* included *in the apportioning?*² — תַּלְמוּד לוֹמַר — *To teach us otherwise, the verse says,* "כִּי חָקְךָ וְחָק בָּנֶיךָ נִתְּנוּ — *"for they have been given as your portion and the portion of your sons,"* implying חֹק לַבָּנִים — *there is a portion for the sons,* ³ וְאֵין חֹק לַבָּנוֹת — *but there is no portion for the daughters.*³

15. שׁוֹק הַתְּרוּמָה וַחֲזֵה הַתְּנוּפָה — THE THIGH OF THE RAISING AND THE BREAST OF THE WAVING. לְשׁוֹן אֲשֶׁר — ⁴הוּנַף וַאֲשֶׁר הוּרָם — *This expression means "[the breast] that has been waved, and [the thigh] that has been raised."*⁴ תְּנוּפָה — *"Waving"* means מוֹלִיךְ וּמֵבִיא — *he moves back and forth.* תְּרוּמָה — *"Raising"* means מַעֲלֶה וּמוֹרִיד — *he lifts and lowers.* וְלָמָּה חִלֵּק הַכָּתוּב — *But as to why the verse separates them,* juxtaposing תְּרוּמָה בְּשׁוֹק — *raising with the thigh* וּתְנוּפָה בֶחָזֶה — *and waving with the breast,* לֹא יָדַעְנוּ — *we do not know,* שֶׁשְּׁנֵיהֶם — *for both [the thigh and the breast]* בַּהֲרָמָה וַהֲנָפָה — *are* included *in raising and waving.*

{עַל חֶלְבֵי — *UPON THE FIRE-OFFERING FATS.* כְּמוֹ — *This has* the same meaning as עַל חֶלְבֵי הָאִשִּׁים — upon the fats of the fire-offering.⁵}

עַל אִשֵּׁי הַחֲלָבִים — UPON THE FIRE-OFFERING FATS. מִכָּאן — *From here* we see שֶׁהַחֲלָבִים לְמַטָּה — *that the fats are at the bottom* בִּשְׁעַת תְּנוּפָה — *at the time of waving.* וְיִשּׁוּב הַמִּקְרָאוֹת — *And as for the resolution of the verses* which seem to contradict each other regarding this matter, שֶׁלֹּא יַכְחִישׁוּ זֶה אֶת זֶה — *so that they should not contradict each other,* כְּבָר פֵּרַשְׁתִּי שְׁלָשְׁתָּן — *I have already explained the three of them,* i.e., the three relevant verses, ⁶בְּצַו אֶת אַהֲרֹן — in *Parashas Tzav es Aharon*.⁶

16. שְׂעִיר הַחַטָּאת — THE HE-GOAT OF THE SIN-OFFERING. שְׂעִיר מוּסְפֵי רֹאשׁ חֹדֶשׁ — *This refers to the he-goat of the* mussaf-*offerings of the First of the Month.* וּשְׁלֹשָׁה שְׂעִירֵי חַטָּאוֹת — *Three he-goats of sin-offerings* קָרְבוּ בוֹ בַיּוֹם — *were offered on that day:* ⁷ [קְחוּ] שְׂעִיר עִזִּים — {Take} *a he-goat,*⁷

---

1. Although the daughters of the Kohanim are forbidden to eat of that which is holy in the highest degree, such as meal-offerings (see 6:11 above), they may partake of that which is holy in the lesser degree, such as peace-offerings. However, they do not receive their own share when the portions are given out to the Kohanim (Mizrachi).

2. Perhaps our verse equates the daughters to Aaron and his sons not only in that they may eat of that which is of the lesser degree of holiness, but even as far as receiving their own portion of them.

3. *Toras Kohanim, perek* 1:10.

4. *Exodus* 29:27.

5. The literal meaning is "upon the fire-offerings of the fats."

6. See Rashi to 7:30 above.

7. Above 9:3. This refers to the he-goat of the inaugural offering of that day. According to the editions that omit

שָׂרֹף ׀ וַיִּקְצֹף עַל־אֶלְעָזָר וְעַל־ *it had been burned! — and he was wrathful with Elazar and Ithamar, Aaron's remaining sons, [bidding them] to say:* ¹⁷ *"Why did you not eat the* אִיתָמָר בְּנֵי אַהֲרֹן הַנּוֹתָרִם לֵאמֹר: ^{יז} מַדּוּעַ לֹא־אֲכַלְתֶּם אֶת

---- אונקלוס ----

אִתּוֹקַד וּרְגֵז עַל אֶלְעָזָר וְעַל אִיתָמָר בְּנֵי אַהֲרֹן דְּאִשְׁתְּאָרוּ לְמֵימַר: ^{יז} מָדֵין לָא אֲכַלְתּוּן יָת

---- רש"י ----

וּשְׂעִיר נַחְשׁוֹן (בַּמִּדְבָּר ז:טז) וּשְׂעִיר רֹאשׁ חֹדֶשׁ (שָׁם כח:טו): (לְעֵיל פָּס' יב; ת"כ פֶּרֶק ב:ח-י; זְבָחִים קא.): **דָּרֹשׁ דָּרַשׁ.** וּמִכּוּלָן לֹא נִשְׂרַף אֶלָּא זֶה. וְנֶחְלְקוּ בַּדָּבָר חַכְמֵי יִשְׂרָאֵל, יֵשׁ שְׁתֵּי דְרִישׁוֹת, מִפְּנֵי מָה נִשְׂרַף זֶה וּמִפְּנֵי מָה נֶאֶכְלוּ אֵלּוּ. אוֹמְרִים מִפְּנֵי הַטֻּמְאָה שֶׁנָּגְעָה בּוֹ נִשְׂרַף וְיֵשׁ אוֹמְרִים כָּךְ הוּא בַּת"כ (פֶּרֶק ב:ג): **עַל אֶלְעָזָר וְעַל אִיתָמָר.** מִפְּנֵי אֲנִינוּת נִשְׂרַף לְפִי שֶׁהוּא קָדְשֵׁי דוֹרוֹת אֲבָל בְּקָדְשֵׁי בִּשְׁבִיל כְּבוֹדוֹ שֶׁל אַהֲרֹן הָפַךְ פָּנָיו כְּנֶגֶד הַבָּנִים וְכָעַס שָׁעָה סָמְכוּ עַל מֹשֶׁה שֶׁאָמַר לָהֶם בְּמִנְחָה וַאֲכָלוּהָ מַצּוֹת (שָׁם ג): **לֵאמֹר.** אָמַר לָהֶם הֲשִׁיבוּנִי עַל דְּבָרַי (שָׁם):

---- RASHI ELUCIDATED ----

וּשְׂעִיר נַחְשׁוֹן – **and the he-goat of Nahshon,**[1] וּשְׂעִיר רֹאשׁ חֹדֶשׁ[2] – **and the he-goat of the First of the Month.**[2] וּמִכֻּלָּן – **Of them all,** לֹא נִשְׂרַף אֶלָּא זֶה – **only this one was burned** entirely.[3] וְנֶחְלְקוּ בַּדָּבָר חַכְמֵי יִשְׂרָאֵל – **The Sages of Israel were divided** in opinion **about the matter:** יֵשׁ אוֹמְרִים – **There are those who say** that מִפְּנֵי הַטֻּמְאָה שֶׁנָּגְעָה בּוֹ – **because of the impurity which touched it** נִשְׂרַף – **it was burned.**[4] וְיֵשׁ אוֹמְרִים – **And there are those who say** that מִפְּנֵי אֲנִינוּת – **because of the state of day-of-death mourning** which Aaron and his sons were in נִשְׂרַף – **it was burned,** לְפִי שֶׁהוּא קָדְשֵׁי דוֹרוֹת – **because it is that which is holy for generations,**[5] אֲבָל בְּקָדְשֵׁי שָׁעָה – **but** regarding that which is holy for the hour, i.e., that which was holy only at that particular time, סָמְכוּ עַל מֹשֶׁה – **they relied on Moses,** שֶׁאָמַר לָהֶם בְּמִנְחָה – **who said to them with regard to the meal-offering,** ״וַאֲכָלוּהָ מַצּוֹת״[6,7] – **"and eat it unleavened."**[6,7]

☐ דָּרֹשׁ דָּרַשׁ – **INQUIRED INSISTENTLY.** שְׁתֵּי דְרִישׁוֹת – **Two inquiries:**[8] מִפְּנֵי מַה נִשְׂרַף זֶה – **Why was this one burned?** וּמִפְּנֵי מַה נֶאֶכְלוּ אֵלּוּ – **And why were these eaten?**[9] כָּךְ הִיא בְּתוֹרַת כֹּהֲנִים – **Thus is** it interpreted in *Toras Kohanim*.[9]

☐ עַל אֶלְעָזָר וְעַל אִיתָמָר – **WITH ELAZAR AND ITHAMAR.** בִּשְׁבִיל כְּבוֹדוֹ שֶׁל אַהֲרֹן – **Because of,** i.e., to spare, **Aaron's dignity** הָפַךְ פָּנָיו – **[Moses] turned his face** כְּנֶגֶד הַבָּנִים – **toward the sons,** ¹⁰וְכָעַס – **and** displayed his anger.[10]

☐ לֵאמֹר – **[BIDDING THEM] TO SAY.** אָמַר לָהֶם – **He said to them,** ״הֲשִׁיבוּנִי עַל דְּבָרַי״[11] – **"Respond to me with regard to my words."**[11]

---

the word קְחוּ, "take," Rashi merely alludes to that he-goat. According to those that include the word קְחוּ, Rashi is citing the verse verbatim.

1. *Numbers* 7:16. This goat was part of the offering of Nahshon ben Amminadab, the prince of the tribe of Judah.

2. *Numbers* 28:15. Rashi to verse 1 above has stated that the inaugural ceremony discussed here took place on the first of Nissan. Thus, the he-goat sin-offering of Rosh Chodesh was brought on this day.

3. The next verse describes the burned goat as atoning for the people. This description holds true only for the sin-offering of Rosh Chodesh and not for the other two goats (*Mizrachi; Sifsei Chachamim*).

4. Normally, the meat of a sin-offering is eaten by the Kohanim. If this one was burned entirely, it must be because it came into contact with something impure.

5. That offering is of a category of the holy which applies to future generations. Therefore, just as in future generations such meat would be forbidden to an *onein*, so was this meat forbidden to Aaron and his remaining sons.

6. Above verse 12.

7. *Toras Kohanim, perek* 2:8-10; *Zevachim* 101a. According to the first opinion, the sin-offering of Rosh Chodesh was the only he-goat of the three which was burned entirely because it alone came into contact with something impure. According to the second opinion, only the sin-offering of Rosh Chodesh was burned, in accordance with the law that Kohanim who are in a state of *aninus* may not eat that which is holy. It did not apply to the other two goats, for they were exceptional sin-offerings with exceptional laws.

8. Rashi explains the repetition of the verb (*Devek Tov*).

9. *Toras Kohanim, perek* 2:2.

10. *Toras Kohanim, perek* 2:3. Moses was angry at Aaron, also. He, too, was responsible for not eating the sin-offering, and it is Moses who provided justification for that decision (v. 19). But Moses addressed his anger toward Elazar and Ithamar to spare Aaron's dignity (*Mizrachi; Sifsei Chachamim*).

11. *Toras Kohanim, perek* 2:3. The word לֵאמֹר often means, "to say [to others]." Thus, וַיְדַבֵּר ה׳ אֶל מֹשֶׁה לֵּאמֹר, means, "HASHEM spoke to Moses to say [to the Children

הַחַטָּאת֙ בִּמְק֣וֹם הַקֹּ֔דֶשׁ כִּ֛י קֹ֥דֶשׁ קָֽדָשִׁ֖ים הִ֑וא וְאֹתָ֣הּ ׀ נָתַ֣ן לָכֶ֗ם לָשֵׂאת֙ אֶת־עֲוֺ֣ן הָעֵדָ֔ה לְכַפֵּ֥ר עֲלֵיהֶ֖ם לִפְנֵ֥י יְהוָֽה: יח הֵ֚ן לֹא־הוּבָ֣א אֶת־דָּמָ֔הּ אֶל־הַקֹּ֖דֶשׁ פְּנִ֑ימָה

sin-offering in the holy place, for it is that which is holy of the highest degree; and He gave it to you to gain forgiveness for the sin of the assembly and to atone for them before Hashem? ¹⁸ *Behold, its blood was not brought into the Sanctuary within;*

──────── אונקלוס ────────

חַטָּאתָא בַּאֲתַר קַדִּישׁ אֲרֵי קֹדֶשׁ קוּדְשִׁין הִיא וְיָתַהּ יְהַב לְכוֹן לְסַלָּחָא עַל חוֹבֵי כְנִשְׁתָּא לְכַפָּרָא עֲלֵיהוֹן קֳדָם יְיָ: יח הָא לָא אִתָּעַל יָת דְּמַהּ לְבֵית קוּדְשָׁא לְגָו

──────── רש"י ────────

(יז) **מדוע לא אכלתם את החטאת במקום הקדש**. וכי חוץ לקדש אכלוה והלא שרפוה, ומהו אומר במקום הקדש. אלא אמר להם שמא חוץ לקלעים יצאה ונפסלה: **כי קדש קדשים הוא**. ונפסלין ביוצא, והם אמרו לו לאו. אמר להם הואיל ובמקום הקדש היתה מדוע לא אכלתם אותה: **ואותה נתן לכם לשאת וגו'**. שהכהנים אוכלים ובעלים מתכפרים (שם ד): **לשאת את עון העדה**. מכאן למדנו ששעיר ראש חודש הי' שהוא מכפר על עון טומאת מקדש וקדשיו (ת"כ שם ב; זבחים קא:) שחטאת שמיני וחטאת נחשון לא לכפרה באו: (יח) **הן לא הובא וגו'**. שאילו הובא הי' לכם לשרפה כמו שנאמר

──────── RASHI ELUCIDATED ────────

17. מַדּוּעַ לֹא אֲכַלְתֶּם אֶת הַחַטָּאת בִּמְקוֹם הַקֹּדֶשׁ — **WHY DID YOU NOT EAT THE SIN-OFFERING IN THE HOLY PLACE?** — וְכִי חוּץ לַקֹּדֶשׁ אֲכָלוּהָ — **Did they eat it outside the Sanctuary?** וַהֲלֹא שְׂרָפוּהָ — **Did they not burn it?** וּמַהוּ אוֹמֵר — **What is** the meaning of **that which he is saying,** ״בִּמְקוֹם הַקֹּדֶשׁ״ — **"in the holy place"?** אֶלָּא אָמַר לָהֶם — **But, he said to them,** שֶׁמָּא חוּץ לַקְּלָעִים יָצְאָה — **"Perhaps [the flesh of the sin-offering] went beyond the curtains,** i.e., out of the perimeter of the Courtyard of the *Mishkan*, וְנִפְסְלָה — **and thus became disqualified,**[1]
□ כִּי קֹדֶשׁ קָדָשִׁים הִיא — **FOR IT IS THAT WHICH IS HOLY OF THE HIGHEST DEGREE,** וְנִפְסָלִין[2] בְּיוֹצֵא — **and** [such offerings] become disqualified[2] through leaving the grounds of the *Mishkan*."[3] וְהֵם אָמְרוּ לוֹ — **They said to him,** לָאו — **"No."** אָמַר לָהֶם — **He said to them,** הוֹאִיל וּבִמְקוֹם הַקֹּדֶשׁ הָיְתָה — **"Since it was** *in the holy place*, מַדּוּעַ לֹא אֲכַלְתֶּם אוֹתָהּ — **why did you not eat it?"**[4]
□ וְאֹתָהּ נָתַן לָכֶם לָשֵׂאת וְגוֹמֵר — **AND HE GAVE IT TO YOU TO GAIN FORGIVENESS, ETC.** — שֶׁהַכֹּהֲנִים אוֹכְלִים — For the Kohanim eat the meat of the sin-offering, [5] וּבְעָלִים מִתְכַּפְּרִים — **and the owner** of the offering **gains atonement.**[5]
□ לָשֵׂאת אֶת עֲוֺן הָעֵדָה — **TO GAIN FORGIVENESS FOR THE SIN OF THE ASSEMBLY.** — מִכַּאן לָמַדְנוּ — **From here we have learned** שֶׁשָּׂעִיר רֹאשׁ חֹדֶשׁ הָיָה — **that it was the he-goat of the First of the Month** which they did not eat, שֶׁהוּא מְכַפֵּר — **for it atones** [6] עַל עֲוֺן טֻמְאַת מִקְדָּשׁ וְקָדָשָׁיו — **for the sin of the impurity of the Sanctuary and its holies,**[6] i.e., for the sin of entering the Sanctuary or eating that which is holy while impure. שֶׁחַטֹּאת שְׁמִינִי — **For the sin-offering of the eighth** day of the inauguration וְחַטַּאת נַחְשׁוֹן — **and the sin-offering of Nahshon,** the prince of the tribe of Judah, לֹא לְכַפָּרָה בָּאוּ — **did not come for atonement.**[7]

18. הֵן לֹא הוּבָא וְגוֹמֵר — **BEHOLD, [ITS BLOOD] WAS NOT BROUGHT, ETC.** שֶׁאִלּוּ הוּבָא — **For if it had been brought** into the Sanctuary, הָיָה לָכֶם לְשָׂרְפָהּ — **you should have burned it,** כְּמוֹ שֶׁנֶּאֱמַר — **as it says,**

of Israel]." Here, לֵאמֹר cannot mean that Moses expected Elazar and Ithamar to communicate his wrath to others, for Aaron, the only other person toward whom Moses may have been angry, was present, and was aware of Moses' wrath. It means that he expected them "to say to another," namely, to respond to his questions (*Mesiach Ilmim*).

1. Moses' words continue into the next comment.
2. Our text follows that of the first printed edition. Most present-day editions read וְנִפְסְלָה, "and it becomes disqualified."
3. Moses' statement, which began in the previous comment, ends here.
4. Moses did not ask, "Why did you not eat it in the holy place," which would have implied that they ate it elsewhere. He asked, "Why did you not eat it? After all, it had continuously been *in the holy place,* and did not become disqualified" (*Mizrachi*).
5. *Toras Kohanim, perek* 2:4. The owner in this case is the entire Nation of Israel (*Maskil LeDavid*).
6. *Toras Kohanim, perek* 2:2; *Zevachim* 101b.
7. The sin-offerings of the eighth day of the inauguration did, in fact, atone for the people, as stated explicitly in 9:7 above. The calf sin-offering atoned for

111 / VAYIKRA/LEVITICUS — PARASHAS SHEMINI   10/19 — י"ט / י

אָכוֹל תֹּאכְלוּ אֹתָהּ בַּקֹּדֶשׁ כַּאֲשֶׁר
צִוֵּיתִי: יט וַיְדַבֵּר אַהֲרֹן אֶל־מֹשֶׁה הֵן

you should have eaten it in the Holy, as I had commanded!"
[19] *Aaron spoke to Moses: "Was it they*

──────────────── אונקלוס ────────────────

מֵיכַל תֵּיכְלוּן יָתַהּ בְּקוּדְשָׁא כְּמָא דִי פַקֵּדִית: יט וּמַלִּיל אַהֲרֹן עִם מֹשֶׁה הָא

──────────────── רש"י ────────────────

וכל חטאת אשר יובא מדמה וגו' (לעיל וכו.): **אבל תאכלו** | דיבור אלא ל' עז שנאמר וידבר העם וגו' (במדבר כא:ה; ע"כ
אותה. הי' לכם לאכלה אע"פ שאתם אוננים: **כאשר צויתי.** | פרק ב:ז). אפשר משה קצף על אלעזר ועל איתמר ואהרן
לכם במנחה (לעיל פסוק יב): (יט) **וידבר אהרן.** אין לשון | מדבר, הא ידעת שלא היתה אלא מדת כבוד. אמרו, אינו בדין

──────────────── RASHI ELUCIDATED ────────────────

¹ וְגוֹמֵר מִדָּמָהּ יוּבָא אֲשֶׁר חַטָּאת וְכָל,, — **"And any sin-offering from which some blood has been brought** to the Tent of Meeting to effect atonement within the Holy **etc.** shall not be eaten; it shall be burned in fire."[1]

□ אֹתָהּ תֹּאכְלוּ אָכֹל — **This means** לְאָכְלָה לָכֶם הָיָה — **you should have eaten it,**[2] אוֹנְנִים שֶׁאַתֶּם פִּי עַל אַף — **although you are** *onenim*.

□ צִוֵּיתִי כַּאֲשֶׁר — **AS I HAD COMMANDED** ³ בַּמִּנְחָה לָכֶם — **you with regard to the meal-offering.**[3]

19. אַהֲרֹן וַיְדַבֵּר — **AARON SPOKE.** דִּבּוּר The term דִּבּוּר, as used in Scripture, עָז לָשׁוֹן אֶלָּא דִּבּוּר לְשׁוֹן אֵין — **is always a term of force,**[4] שֶׁנֶּאֱמַר — **as it says,** ⁵,⁶ וְגוֹמֵר הָעָם וַיְדַבֵּר,, — **"The people spoke** etc."[5,6] אִיתָמָר וְעַל אֶלְעָזָר עַל מֹשֶׁה קֶצֶף אֶפְשָׁר — **Is it possible that Moses vented his anger on Elazar and on Ithamar** מְדַבֵּר וְאַהֲרֹן — **and Aaron spoke** in response? יָדַעְתָּ הָא — **See, now, that you know** כָּבוֹד מִדַּת[7] אֶלָּא הָיְתָה שֶׁלֹּא — **that [Elazar and Ithamar's failure to respond to Moses] was a measure[7] of respect** toward their father, Aaron.[8] אָמְרוּ — **They said,** בַּדִּין אֵינוּ — **"It**

the sin of the Golden Calf, as Rashi, based on *Toras Kohanim*, mentions in his comment to 9:3. *Toras Kohanim* adds that the he-goat sin-offering atoned for the sin of selling Joseph, for the brothers dipped his coat in the blood of a he-goat. When Rashi says that the sin-offering of the eighth day of the inauguration "did not come for atonement," he means that it did not atone for the sin of the impurity of the Sanctuary and its holies. The term עָוֹן נְשִׂיאַת, "forgiving sin," that appears in our verse in the form of עָוֹן אֶת לָשֵׂאת, connotes forgiveness for that sin specifically, as in *Exodus* 28:38, בְּנֵי יַקְדִּישׁוּ אֲשֶׁר הַקֳּדָשִׁים עֲוֹן אֶת אַהֲרֹן וְנָשָׂא קָדְשֵׁיהֶם מַתְּנֹת לְכָל יִשְׂרָאֵל, "And Aaron shall bear the sin of that which is holy that the Children of Israel consecrate for any gifts of their holy offerings" (see Rashi there; *Maskil LeDavid*).

1. Above 6:23. The sin-offering of Rosh Chodesh is brought on the outer *Mizbe'ach*. Any sin-offering offered on the outer *Mizbe'ach* whose blood is brought inside the *Mishkan* is disqualified and may not be eaten. Moses is telling Elazar and Ithamar that justification for not eating the offering does not apply in their case.

2. Although אֹתָהּ תֹּאכְלוּ אָכֹל seems imperative, it cannot be understood as "you shall eat it," for the offering had already been burned (*Mizrachi*; *Sifsei Chachamim*).

3. Above v. 12. Moses had commanded them to partake of the meal-offering although they were *onenim* (see Rashi to v. 12). *Mizrachi* and *Sifsei Chachamim* raise the question of why Moses mentions only the meal-offering here, when he also commanded them to partake

of the breast and the thigh of the peace-offering. They answer that Rashi mentions only the meal-offering, for it, like the sin-offering, is of the higher degree of holiness; the breast and thigh of the peace-offering are of the lesser degree. Thus, the meal-offering can serve as a precedent for the sin-offering, but the breast and thigh cannot. However, according to our understanding of verse 14 (based on *Be'er BaSadeh*, see note 2 on page 107), Moses did not permit the Kohanim to partake of the peace-offering while they were *onenim*. Thus, Rashi could cite only the meal-offering as a precedent.

4. Of the two verbs for speaking, דבר and אמר, דבר denotes forceful speech unless it is tempered by a form of אמר, as, for example, in לֵאמֹר מֹשֶׁה אֶל ה' וַיְדַבֵּר (*Gur Aryeh*; *Sifsei Chachamim*).

5. *Numbers* 21:5. The verse continues, "against God and against Moses."

6. *Toras Kohanim, perek* 2:7.

7. Most modern editions read כָּבוֹד מִדֶּרֶךְ, "by way of respect." However, many early editions of Rashi read מִדַּת, as does the *Yalkut Shimoni*. The Rome edition, in fact, reads כָּבוֹד מִדַּת אֶלָּא זוֹ מִדָּה וְאֵין, "and this measure is only a measure of respect." *Yosef Hallel* suggest that early copyists may have used the abbreviated form מד׳, which was later misinterpreted as מִדֶּרֶךְ.

8. Although Rashi said above (v. 16) that it was actually Aaron at whom Moses was angry, still, since his words were directed at Elazar and Ithamar, it would seem that it was they who should have responded (*Mizrachi*).

הַיּוֹם הִקְרִיבוּ אֶת־חַטָּאתָם וְאֶת־עֹלָתָם לִפְנֵי יהוה וַתִּקְרֶאנָה אֹתִי כָּאֵלֶּה וְאָכַלְתִּי חַטָּאת הַיּוֹם

who this day offered their sin-offering and their olah-offering before HASHEM? Now that such things befell me — had I eaten the sin-offering this day,

—— אונקלוס ——

יוֹמָא דֵין קָרִיבוּ יָת חַטָּאתְהוֹן וְיָת עֲלָתְהוֹן קֳדָם יְיָ וַעֲרָעָא יָתִי עָקָן כְּאִלֵּין אִלּוּ פוֹן אֲכָלִית חַטָּאתָא יוֹמָא דֵין

—— רש"י ——

שֶׁיְּהֵא אָבִינוּ יוֹשֵׁב וְאָנוּ מְדַבְּרִים לְפָנָיו וְאֵינוֹ בַּדִּין שֶׁיְּהֵא תַלְמִיד מֵשִׁיב אֶת רַבּוֹ. יָכוֹל. מִפְּנֵי שֶׁלֹּא הָיָה בְאֶלְעָזָר לְהָשִׁיב, ת"ל וַיֹּאמֶר אֶלְעָזָר הַכֹּהֵן אֶל אַנְשֵׁי הַצָּבָא וְגוֹ' (שם לא:כא) הֲרֵי כְּשֶׁרָצָה דִבֵּר לִפְנֵי מֹשֶׁה וְלִפְנֵי הַנְּשִׂיאִים. זוֹ מָצָאתִי בְּסִפְרֵי שֶׁל פָּנִים שֵׁנִי: הֵן הַיּוֹם הִקְרִיבוּ. מַהוּ אוֹמֵר, אֶלָּא אָמַר לָהֶם מֹשֶׁה שֶׁמָּא זְרַקְתֶּם דָּמָהּ אוֹנְנִים, שֶׁהָאוֹנֵן שֶׁעָבַד חִלֵּל. אָמַר לוֹ

אַהֲרֹן וְכִי הֵם הִקְרִיבוּ שֶׁהֵם הֶדְיוֹטוֹת, אֲנִי הִקְרַבְתִּי (וּבַחֲמִים קָאֵי). וַתִּקְרֶאנָה אֹתִי כָּאֵלֶּה. אֲפִלּוּ לֹא הָיוּ הַמֵּתִים בָּנַי אֶלָּא שְׁאָר קְרוֹבִים שֶׁאֲנִי חַיָּב לִהְיוֹת אוֹנֵן עֲלֵיהֶם כָּגוֹן כָּל הָאֲמוּרִים בְּפָרָשַׁת כֹּהֲנִים (לְהַלַּן כא:ב-ג) שֶׁהַכֹּהֵן מִטַּמֵּא לָהֶם (ת"כ שם ט): הַיּוֹם. אֲבָל אֲנִינוּת לַיְלָה חַטָּאת. וְאִם אָכַלְתִּי הַיֵּיטַב וְגוֹ'.

—— RASHI ELUCIDATED ——

וְאָנוּ מְדַבְּרִים לְפָנָיו — and would be improper שֶׁיְּהֵא אָבִינוּ יוֹשֵׁב — that our father should sit in silence we should speak in his presence. וְאֵינוֹ בַּדִּין — And it would be improper שֶׁיְּהֵא תַלְמִיד מֵשִׁיב אֶת רַבּוֹ — that a pupil should respond to, i.e., should refute, his teacher.[1] יָכוֹל — One might be able to think that they did not respond[2] מִפְּנֵי שֶׁלֹּא הָיָה בְאֶלְעָזָר לְהָשִׁיב — because Elazar was not capable of responding.[2] תַּלְמוּד לוֹמַר — To teach us otherwise, the verse says, "וַיֹּאמֶר אֶלְעָזָר הַכֹּהֵן אֶל אַנְשֵׁי הַצָּבָא" — "Elazar the Kohen said to the men of the army, etc."[3] וְגוֹמֵר — See, now, that when הֲרֵי כְּשֶׁרָצָה — he wanted to, דִּבֵּר לִפְנֵי מֹשֶׁה — he spoke in the presence of Moses וְלִפְנֵי הַנְּשִׂיאִים — and in the presence of the princes. זוֹ מָצָאתִי בְּסִפְרֵי שֶׁל פָּנִים שֵׁנִי — I found this in a second version of Sifrei.[4]

□ הֵן הַיּוֹם הִקְרִיבוּ — WAS IT THEY WHO THIS DAY OFFERED. מַהוּ אוֹמֵר — What is he saying?[5] אֶלָּא אָמַר — לָהֶם מֹשֶׁה — But, Moses said to them, שֶׁמָּא זְרַקְתֶּם דָּמָהּ אוֹנְנִים — "Perhaps you sprinkled its blood while you were onenim, שֶׁהָאוֹנֵן שֶׁעָבַד — for an onein who performed the service חִלֵּל — has defiled it." אָמַר לוֹ אַהֲרֹן — Aaron said to him, וְכִי הֵם הִקְרִיבוּ — "Is it they who brought the offering; שֶׁהֵם הֶדְיוֹטוֹת — they, who are common Kohanim? אֲנִי הִקְרַבְתִּי — I brought the offering, וּמַקְרִיב אוֹנֵן — and may bring an offering as an onein."[6] שֶׁאֲנִי כֹּהֵן גָּדוֹל — I, who am the Kohen Gadol

□ וַתִּקְרֶאנָה אֹתִי כָּאֵלֶּה — NOW THAT SUCH THINGS BEFELL ME. אֲפִלּוּ לֹא הָיוּ הַמֵּתִים בָּנַי — Even if the dead were not my sons, שֶׁאֲנִי חַיָּב לִהְיוֹת אוֹנֵן עֲלֵיהֶם כָּאֵלּוּ — over whom I am obligated to be an onein as אֶלָּא שְׁאָר קְרוֹבִים — but other relatives for [my sons],[7] כָּגוֹן כָּל הָאֲמוּרִים — for instance, all those who are stated[8] בְּפָרָשַׁת כֹּהֲנִים — in the section of the Torah on the laws of the Kohanim[8] שֶׁהַכֹּהֵן מִטַּמֵּא לָהֶם — for whom a Kohen may become impure.[9]

□ וְאָכַלְתִּי חַטָּאת — HAD I EATEN THE SIN-OFFERING. This means וְאִם אָכַלְתִּי חַטָּאת — and if I ate a sin-offering, "הַיֵּיטַב וְגוֹמֵר" — "would He approve, etc.?"[10]

□ הַיּוֹם — THIS DAY. אֲבָל אֲנִינוּת לַיְלָה — But being an onein at night, i.e., on the night following the death

1. Elazar and Ithamar were students of Moses.
2. Some editions read שֶׁלֹּא הָיָה בְאֶלְעָזָר מַה לְהָשִׁיב, "because Elazar had nothing with which to respond."
3. Numbers 31:21.
4. Sifrei Zuta is apparently the source for Rashi's comment.
5. How is this a response to Moses' complaint that they should have eaten the sin-offering? (Mizrachi; Sifsei Chachamim).
6. Zevachim 101a. Although Elazar and Ithamar were permitted to eat of the extraordinary offerings which pertained to that day only, despite their being onenim, they were nonetheless forbidden to perform the service. From Aaron's response, we can infer that Moses asked him if the reason they burned the sin-offering of Rosh Chodesh rather than eating it was because onenim offered it. Aaron replied that it was he who brought the offering, and the prohibition against an onein performing the service does not apply to the Kohen Gadol (Gur Aryeh; Sifsei Chachamim).
7. See note 2 on page 106.
8. Below 21:2-3.
9. Toras Kohanim, perek 2:9.
10. This is not a declarative sentence — "I ate the sin-offering." The sense being discussed here is the fact that Aaron and his sons did not eat the sin-offering (Kitzur Mizrachi; Sifsei Chachamim). The word אָכַלְתִּי is in the past tense and means "I ate." Following the general rule for past tense, the word is accented on the second root letter — אָכַלְתִּי. When pre-

would HASHEM approve?"
²⁰ Moses heard and he approved.

11 ¹ HASHEM spoke to Moses and to Aaron, to say to them. ² Speak to the Children of Israel, saying: These

כ הַיִּיטַב בְּעֵינֵי יהוה: וַיִּשְׁמַע מֹשֶׁה וַיִּיטַב בְּעֵינָיו:
יא א שׁשׁי וַיְדַבֵּר יהוה אֶל־מֹשֶׁה וְאֶל־אַהֲרֹן ב לֵאמֹר אֲלֵהֶם: דַּבְּרוּ אֶל־בְּנֵי יִשְׂרָאֵל

— אונקלוס —

הֲתַקֵּן קֳדָם יְיָ: כּוּשְׁמַע מֹשֶׁה וְשַׁפַּר בְּעֵינוֹהִי: א וּמַלִּיל יְיָ עִם מֹשֶׁה וּלְאַהֲרֹן לְמֵימַר לְהוֹן: ב מַלִּילוּ עִם בְּנֵי יִשְׂרָאֵל

— רש"י —

לֵאמֹר אֲלֵיהֶם. אָמַר שֶׁיֹּאמַר לְאֶלְעָזָר וּלְאִיתָמָר. אוֹ אֵינוֹ אֶלָּא לוֹמַר לְיִשְׂרָאֵל, כְּשֶׁהוּא אוֹמֵר דַּבְּרוּ אֶל בְּנֵי יִשְׂרָאֵל הֲרֵי דִּבּוּר אָמוּר לְיִשְׂרָאֵל, הָא מָה אֲנִי מְקַיֵּים לֵאמֹר אֲלֵהֶם, לְבָנָיו לְאֶלְעָזָר וּלְאִיתָמָר (ת"כ פרשתא ב:א): **(ב) דַּבְּרוּ אֶל בְּנֵי יִשְׂרָאֵל.** אֶת כֻּלָּם הִשְׁוָה לִהְיוֹת שְׁלוּחִים בְּדִבּוּר זֶה

מוּתָר שֶׁאֵין אוֹנֵן אֶלָּא יוֹם קְבוּרָה (ת"כ שָׁם יח; זְבָחִים שָׁם): **הַיִּיטַב בְּעֵינֵי ה'.** אִם שְׁמַעְתֶּם בְּקָדְשֵׁי שָׁעָה אֵין לָכֶם לְהָקֵל בְּקָדְשֵׁי דוֹרוֹת: **(ב) וַיִּיטַב בְּעֵינָיו.** הוֹדָה וְלֹא בּוֹשׁ לוֹ' לֹא שְׁמַעְתִּי (ת"כ שָׁם יב): **(א) אֶל מֹשֶׁה וְאֶל אַהֲרֹן.** לְמֹשֶׁה אָמַר שֶׁיֹּאמַר לְאַהֲרֹן (ת"כ לְעֵיל פ' וַיִּקְרָא נְדָבָה פֶּרֶק ב:אַ):

— RASHI ELUCIDATED —

of a close relative, מֻתָּר – it is permitted for a Kohen to eat of that which is holy, שֶׁאֵין אוֹנֵן אֶלָּא יוֹם קְבוּרָה¹ – for the law of an *onein* applies only on the *day* of burial.¹

□ הַיִּיטַב בְּעֵינֵי ה' – **WOULD HASHEM APPROVE?** אִם שְׁמַעְתֶּם – **If you heard** that we may partake of the offerings despite our being *onenim* בְּקָדְשֵׁי שָׁעָה – **regarding that which is holy for the hour**, i.e., that which is holy only at that particular time, such as the sin-offering of the Inauguration, and the one brought by Nahshon, אֵין לָךְ לְהָקֵל – **you may not deal leniently** insofar as an *onein* eating בְּקָדְשֵׁי דוֹרוֹת – **that which is holy of generations**, i.e., that which is holy for future generations, such as the sin-offering of the First of the Month.

20. וַיִּיטַב בְּעֵינָיו – **AND HE APPROVED.** הוֹדָה – **He admitted** that Aaron was right וְלֹא בוֹשׁ לוֹמַר – and was not ashamed to say, ²לֹא שָׁמַעְתִּי – **"I had not heard** this law."²

11.

1. אֶל מֹשֶׁה וְאֶל אַהֲרֹן – **TO MOSES AND TO AARON.** לְמֹשֶׁה אָמַר – **He said** it **to Moses** ³שֶׁיֹּאמַר לְאַהֲרֹן – **so that** *he* **should say** it **to Aaron.**³

□ לֵאמֹר אֲלֵהֶם – **TO SAY TO THEM.** אָמַר שֶׁיֹּאמַר לְאֶלְעָזָר וְאִיתָמָר – [HASHEM] said that [Aaron]⁴ should **say to Elazar and Ithamar.**⁵ אוֹ אֵינוֹ אֶלָּא לֵאמֹר לְיִשְׂרָאֵל – **Or perhaps** לֵאמֹר **means only "to say" to Israel?**⁵ כְּשֶׁהוּא אוֹמֵר – **When it says** in the following verse, דַּבְּרוּ אֶל בְּנֵי יִשְׂרָאֵל – **"speak to the Children of Israel,"** הֲרֵי דִּבּוּר אָמוּר לְיִשְׂרָאֵל – **you can see that speaking to Israel has been stated** in *that* verse. הָא מָה אֲנִי מְקַיֵּים לֵאמֹר אֲלֵהֶם – **What, then, do I maintain "to say to them"** of our verse means? לְבָנָיו – **To his sons,** ⁶לְאֶלְעָזָר וּלְאִיתָמָר – **to Elazar and to Ithamar.**⁶

2. דַּבְּרוּ אֶל בְּנֵי יִשְׂרָאֵל – **SPEAK TO THE CHILDREN OF ISRAEL.** אֶת כֻּלָּם הִשְׁוָה – **He made them all equal,** i.e., God drew no distinction between Moses, Aaron, Elazar and Ithamar,⁷ לִהְיוֹת שְׁלוּחִים בְּדִבּוּר זֶה –

---

fixed with a ו, the word has two possible meanings. Either (a) the prefix is the conjunctive ו (וְהַחִבּוּר) which merely adds "and" to the translation – "and I ate"; or (b) the prefix is the conversive ו (וְהַהִפּוּךְ) which converts the tense from past to future – "I will eat." But, with the conversive ו the accent would move to the final syllable – וְאָכַלְתִּי, as in *II Samuel* 13:5, while with the conjunctive ו, it would stay on the second root letter וְאָכַלְתִּי. [Another example of this accent shift is שָׁמַעְתִּי, "I have heard" (*Exodus* 6:5), and וְשָׁמַעְתִּי, "I shall hear" (*Exodus* 22:26).]

Because the cantillation in our verse is on the second root letter – וְאָכַלְתִּי – Rashi interprets the word as being in the past. However, since Aaron did not actually eat the meat under discussion, the word must be in the conditional past – "had I eaten" (*Leshon Chaim*).

1. *Toras Kohanim*, *perek* 2:11; *Zevachim* 101a. For the ha-

lachos of *onein* as they are practiced today, see *Shulchan Aruch*, *Yoreh Deah* 341.

2. *Toras Kohanim*, *perek* 2:12. See *Beiurim LePeirush Rashi Al HaTorah*.

3. *Toras Kohanim* to *Vayikra*, *Nedavah*, *perek* 2:1. God did not speak to Aaron directly. See Rashi to 1:1 (*Mizrachi*; *Sifsei Chachamim*).

4. The interpolation of "Aaron" follows *Nachalas Yaakov*.

5. Some editions read: אוֹ אֵינוֹ אֶלָּא שֶׁיֹּאמַר לְיִשְׂרָאֵל, "or perhaps it means only that he should say to Israel." The basic intent, however, is unchanged.

6. *Toras Kohanim*, *parshasa* 2:1.

7. The imperative דַּבְּרוּ, "Speak!" is in the plural form. The singular is דַּבֵּר. (See also Rashi to *Exodus* 12:3, where Rashi also comments on this usage. Although this form appears in 15:2 below, Rashi makes no comment there.)

לֵאמֹר זֹאת הַחַיָּה אֲשֶׁר תֹּאכְלוּ
מִכָּל־הַבְּהֵמָה אֲשֶׁר עַל־הָאָרֶץ:

are the life forms that you may eat from among all the animals that are upon the earth.

---- אונקלוס ----

לְמֵימַר דָּא חַיְתָא דִּי תֵיכְלוּן מִכָּל בְּעִירָא דִּי עַל אַרְעָא:

---- רש"י ----

לְפִי שֶׁהוּשְׁווּ בִדְמִימָה (ת"כ לעיל פרק א:ח) וְקִבְּלוּ עֲלֵיהֶם גְּזֵירַת הַמָּקוֹם בְּאַהֲבָה: זֹאת הַחַיָּה. לְשׁוֹן חַיִּים. לְפִי שֶׁיִּשְׂרָאֵל דְּבוּקִים בַּמָּקוֹם וּרְאוּיִין לִהְיוֹת חַיִּים, לְפִיכָךְ הִבְדִּילָם מִן הַטֻּמְאָה וְגָזַר עֲלֵיהֶם מִצְווֹת, וְלָאֻמּוֹת הָעוֹלָם לֹא אָמַר [ש"א חסר] כְּלוּם. מָשָׁל לְרוֹפֵא שֶׁנִּכְנַס לְבַקֵּר אֶת הַחוֹלֶה וכו'. כִּדְאִיתָא בְּמִדְרַשׁ רַבִּי תַּנְחוּמָא (ו): זֹאת הַחַיָּה. מְלַמֵּד שֶׁהָיָה מֹשֶׁה אוֹחֵז בַּחַיָּה וּמַרְאֶה אוֹתָהּ לְיִשְׂרָאֵל זֹאת תֹּאכְלוּ וְזֹאת לֹא תֹאכְלוּ. אֶת זֶה תֹּאכְלוּ וְגוֹ' (להלן פסוק ט), אַף בְּשַׁרְצֵי הַמַּיִם אָחַז מִכָּל מִין וָמִין וְהֶרְאָה לָהֶם. וְכֵן בָּעוֹף וְאֶת אֵלֶּה תְּשַׁקְּצוּ מִן הָעוֹף (להלן פסוק יג). וְכֵן בַּשְּׁרָצִים וְזֶה לָכֶם הַטָּמֵא (שם ת"כ שם): מִכָּל הַבְּהֵמָה. מְלַמֵּד שֶׁהַבְּהֵמָה בִּכְלַל חַיָּה (חולין עא.):

---- RASHI ELUCIDATED ----

לְפִי שֶׁהוּשְׁווּ — insofar as being messengers from God to the Children of Israel regarding this statement, בִּדְמִימָה[1] — because they were equal in their silence[1] — וְקִבְּלוּ עֲלֵיהֶם גְּזֵרַת הַמָּקוֹם — and they accepted the decree of the Omnipresent upon themselves בְּאַהֲבָה — with love.

□ זֹאת הַחַיָּה — THESE ARE THE LIFE FORMS. לְשׁוֹן חַיִּים — The word חַיָּה is related to the word חַיִּים "life."[2] וּרְאוּיִין לִהְיוֹת חַיִּים — and are fit to be alive, לְפִי שֶׁיִּשְׂרָאֵל דְּבוּקִים בַּמָּקוֹם — Because Israel cleave to the Omnipresent, לְפִיכָךְ הִבְדִּילָם מִן הַטֻּמְאָה — therefore, He separated them from impurity, וְגָזַר עֲלֵיהֶם — and decreed commandments upon them, i.e., decreed that they perform commandments. מִצְווֹת וְלָאֻמּוֹת הָעוֹלָם — But to the other nations of the world, לֹא אָמַר כְּלוּם[3] — He said[3] nothing. מָשָׁל — This can be compared to a doctor לְרוֹפֵא — שֶׁנִּכְנַס לְבַקֵּר אֶת הַחוֹלֶה וכו' — who went in to visit one who was ill, etc.[4] כִּדְאִיתָא בְּמִדְרַשׁ רַבִּי תַּנְחוּמָא — as stated in *Midrash R' Tanchuma*.[4]

□ זֹאת הַחַיָּה — THESE ARE THE LIFE FORMS. מְלַמֵּד — This teaches us שֶׁהָיָה מֹשֶׁה אוֹחֵז בַּחַיָּה — that Moses would hold the creature וּמַרְאֶה אוֹתָהּ לְיִשְׂרָאֵל — and show it to Israel, and say, זֹאת תֹּאכְלוּ — "This you may eat, וְזֹאת לֹא תֹאכְלוּ[5] — and this you may not eat."[5] And the verse, אֶת זֶה תֹּאכְלוּ — "this may you eat, etc,"[6] teaches us that וְגוֹמֵר[6] — אַף בְּשַׁרְצֵי הַמַּיִם — with the creeping creatures of the water, too, אָחַז מִכָּל מִין וָמִין — he held a specimen of each and every species, וְהֶרְאָה לָהֶם — and showed it to them. וְכֵן בָּעוֹף — Similarly with the birds, as it says, וְאֶת אֵלֶּה תְּשַׁקְּצוּ מִן הָעוֹף[7] — "these shall you abominate from among the birds."[7] וְכֵן בַּשְּׁרָצִים — And so, too, with the creeping things, as it says, וְזֶה לָכֶם הַטָּמֵא[8,9] — "these are for you the impure."[8,9]

□ זֹאת הַחַיָּה . . . מִכָּל הַבְּהֵמָה — THESE ARE THE LIFE FORMS . . . FROM AMONG ALL THE ANIMALS. מְלַמֵּד — This teaches us שֶׁהַבְּהֵמָה בִּכְלַל חַיָּה[10] — that בְּהֵמָה, "animal," is included in the term חַיָּה, which usually means "beast."[10]

---

1. *Toras Kohanim*, perek 1:1. Moses, Elazar, and Ithamar joined Aaron in accepting the decree of the deaths of Nadab and Abihu in silence. See 10:3 above.
2. The word הַחַיָּה appears superfluous, for the verse could have said, זֹאת אֲשֶׁר תֹּאכְלוּ מִכָּל הַבְּהֵמָה, "This is what you may eat from among all the animals . . ." The Torah wrote it to allude to the life-giving quality of its commandments (*Mizrachi; Sifsei Chachamim*).
3. Some editions read, לֹא אָסַר כְּלוּם, "he forbade nothing."
4. *Tanchuma* 6. The following parable is related there:
   A doctor went to visit two patients. He saw that one had a fatal illness. He told that patient's family, "Give him any food he wants." The doctor saw that the other patient had a chance to survive. He said to that patient's family, "He should eat these foods, and not eat those foods." They said to the doctor, "What's going on? Why do you tell this one to eat whatever he pleases, and to the other you forbid so many foods?" The doctor said, "I told the one who will live, 'Eat this and do not eat that,' but I told [the family of] the one who will die, 'Give him whatever he wants, for he

will not live.' " Similarly, the Holy One, Blessed is He, permitted those who worship stars and constellations to eat disgusting creatures and creeping things, but to Israel, who are destined to live, He said, " 'You shall be holy unto Me, for I am holy' (below 20:26). 'Do not make yourselves abominable' (11:43). This shall you eat, and this shall you not eat. 'Do not make yourselves impure through them lest you become impure through them' (11:43)." Why? For they (Israel) are destined to live, as it says, "And you who cleave to Hashem your God are all alive today" (*Deuteronomy* 4:4).

5. *Toras Kohanim, parshasa* 2:2; *Chullin* 42a.
6. Below v. 9.
7. Below v. 13.
8. Below v. 29. The demonstratives "this" and "these" in the verses noted by Rashi indicate that Moses displayed the animals under discussion to the people.
9. *Toras Kohanim, parshasa* 2:2.
10. *Chullin* 71a. The verse begins, "These are the life

³ *Any one among the animals that has a split hoof, which is separated with a split [into] hooves, and that brings up its cud*

ג כֹּל ׀ מַפְרֶסֶת פַּרְסָה וְשֹׁסַעַת שֶׁסַע פְּרָסֹת מַעֲלַת גֵּרָה בַּבְּהֵמָה

— אונקלוס —

ג כֹּל דִּסְדִיקָא פַּרְסָתָא וּמַטִּלְפָא טִלְפִין פַּרְסָתָהּ מַסְקָא פִּשְׁרָא בִּבְעִירָא

— רש"י —

(ג) **מפרסת.** כתרגומו סדיקא: **פרסה.** פלנט"א בלע"ז: **ושסעת שסע.** שמובדלת מלמעלה ומלמטה בשתי צפרנין, שיש שפרסותיו סדוקות מלמעלה ואינן שסועות ומובדלות לגמרי, שמלמטה מחוברות: **מעלת גרה.** מעלה ומקיאה האוכל ממעיה ומחזרת אותו לתוך פיה לכתשו ולטחנו הדק: **גרה.** כך שמו, ויתכן להיות מגזרת מים הנגרים [שמואל ב יד:יד] שהוא [נגררו] אחר הפה, ותרגומו פשרא שע"י הגרה האוכל נפשר ונמוח: **בבהמה.** תיבה זו יתירה היא

— RASHI ELUCIDATED —

□ **3. מַפְרֶסֶת** — This is understood **בְּתַרְגּוּמוֹ** — as *Targum Onkelos* renders it, **סְדִיקָא,,** — "split."[1]

□ **פַּרְסָה** — HOOF. **פלנט"א בלע"ז** — In Old French, *plante*.[1]

□ **וְשֹׁסַעַת שֶׁסַע** — SEPARATED WITH A SPLIT. This means **שֶׁמֻּבְדֶּלֶת מִלְמַעְלָה וּמִלְמַטָּה** — that [the hoof] is divided above and below, i.e., throughout the entire height of the hoof, **בִּשְׁתֵּי צִפָּרְנִין** — into two nails **כְּתַרְגּוּמוֹ** — as the *Targum* renders it, **וּמַטִּלְפָא טִלְפִין,,** — "hoofed with hooves."[2] **שֵׁיֵּשׁ שֶׁפַּרְסוֹתָיו** — **סְדוּקוֹת מִלְמַעְלָה** — For there are [animals] whose hooves are split at the tip, **וְאֵינָן שְׁסוּעוֹת וּמֻבְדָּלוֹת לְגַמְרֵי** — but they are not split and divided completely, **שֶׁמִּלְמַטָּה מְחֻבָּרוֹת** — for behind, i.e., where the hoof meets the bottom of the foot, they are connected.

□ **מַעֲלַת גֵּרָה** — THAT BRINGS UP ITS CUD. **מַעֲלָה וּמְקִיאָה הָאֹכֶל מִמֶּעֶיהָ** — It brings up and regurgitates the food from its innards, **וּמַחֲזֶרֶת אוֹתוֹ לְתוֹךְ פִּיהָ** — and returns it into its mouth **לְכָתְשׁוֹ וּלְטָחֳנוֹ הָדֵק** — to crush it and grind it finely.

□ **גֵּרָה** — CUD. **כָּךְ שְׁמוֹ** — This is its name.[3] **וְיִתָּכֵן לִהְיוֹת מִגִּזְרַת** — It might be of the same root **מַיִם,, שֶׁהוּא {נִגְרָר}[5] אַחַר** — as **הַנִּגָּרִים** in the phrase, **"waters that flow."**[4] The cud flows like water **הַפֶּה** — for it flows[5] toward the mouth. **וְתַרְגּוּמוֹ** — *Targum Onkelos* renders it **פִּשְׁרָא,,** from the root **פשר**, which can mean "dissolve"[6] **שֶׁעַל יְדֵי הַגֵּרָה** — for through the cud-chewing process **הָאֹכֶל נִפְשָׁר וְנִמּוֹחַ** — the food dissolves and is softened.

□ **בַּבְּהֵמָה** — AMONG THE ANIMALS. **תֵּיבָה יְתֵרָה הִיא** — This is a superfluous word which is written forms that you may eat," and begins to enumerate specifics with, "from among all animals that are upon the earth. Any one among the animals that has a split hoof." We may thus conclude that חַיָּה, as it is used here, is a broad term which includes בְּהֵמָה (*Mizrachi*).

1*. See Rashi to *Deuteronomy* 14:6.
1. In both Old and Modern French this word means "sole of the foot." The Modern English word "plantar" means "of the sole of the foot." The related English word "plantigrade" refers to an animal, such as a bear, that walks on its entire sole.

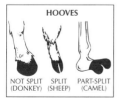

HOOVES

NOT SPLIT (DONKEY) | SPLIT (SHEEP) | PART-SPLIT (CAMEL)

2. The literal meaning of the term וְשֹׁסַעַת שֶׁסַע, "split with a split," does not necessarily mean that the hoof was split all the way through its height. Rashi cites Onkelos who interprets וְשֹׁסַעַת שֶׁסַע as, hoofed with טִלְפִין, "hooves," which denotes that the hoof is split into two distinct parts (*Maskil LeDavid*).
3. Rashi sees גֵּרָה as a noun. He differs in this from other commentators, such as Ibn Ezra, who view גֵּרָה

as an adverb deriving from גָּרוֹן, "throat." According to them, מַעֲלַת גֵּרָה means "that brings up by the throat."

4. *II Samuel* 14:14.
5. Based on the absence of the word נִגְרָר, "flows", from in the first printed edition of Rashi, *Yosef Hallel* suggests another interpretation of this comment: The word גֵּרָה means "throat," for it is after the mouth, i.e., the throat is below the mouth, and the food flows into it, similar to מַיִם הַנִּגָּרִים, "waters that flow." According to this interpretation the flow is from the mouth to the throat. According to the other interpretation, that גֵּרָה means "cud," the flow is toward the mouth.

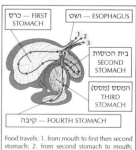

ושט — ESOPHAGUS
כרס — FIRST STOMACH
בית הכוסות — SECOND STOMACH
המסס (מסס) — THIRD STOMACH
קיבה — FOURTH STOMACH

Food travels: 1. from mouth to first then second stomach; 2. from second stomach to mouth; 3. from mouth to third then fourth stomach

6. See, for example, *Bava Kamma* 28b; *Targum Onkelos* to *Exodus* 16:21.

ד אֹתָהּ תֹּאכֵלוּ: אַךְ אֶת־זֶה לֹא תֹאכְלוּ מִמַּעֲלֵי הַגֵּרָה וּמִמַּפְרִיסֵי הַפַּרְסָה אֶת־הַגָּמָל כִּי־מַעֲלֵה גֵרָה הוּא וּפַרְסָה אֵינֶנּוּ מַפְרִיס טָמֵא הוּא לָכֶם: ה וְאֶת־הַשָּׁפָן כִּי־מַעֲלֵה גֵרָה הוּא וּפַרְסָה לֹא יַפְרִיס טָמֵא הוּא לָכֶם: ו וְאֶת־הָאַרְנֶבֶת כִּי־מַעֲלַת גֵּרָה הִוא וּפַרְסָה לֹא הִפְרִיסָה טְמֵאָה הִוא לָכֶם: ז וְאֶת־הַחֲזִיר כִּי־מַפְרִיס פַּרְסָה הוּא וְשֹׁסַע שֶׁסַע פַּרְסָה וְהוּא גֵּרָה לֹא־יִגָּר טָמֵא הוּא לָכֶם: ח מִבְּשָׂרָם לֹא תֹאכֵלוּ

— that one you may eat. ⁴ But this is what you shall not eat from among those that bring up their cud or that have split hooves: the camel, for it brings up its cud, but its hoof is not split — it is impure to you; ⁵ and the hyrax, for it brings up its cud, but its hoof is not split — it is impure to you; ⁶ and the hare, for it brings up its cud, but its hoof is not split — it is impure to you; ⁷ and the pig, for its hoof is split and its hoof is completely separated, but it does not chew its cud — it is impure to you. ⁸ You may not eat of their flesh

―――――― אונקלוס ――――――

יָתַהּ תֵּיכְלוּן: ד בְּרַם יָת דֵּין לָא תֵיכְלוּן מִמַּסְקֵי פִשְׁרָא וּמִסְדִּיקֵי פַרְסָתָא יָת גַּמְלָא אֲרֵי מַסִּיק פִּשְׁרָא הוּא וּפַרְסָתֵהּ לָא סְדִיקָא מְסָאָב הוּא לְכוֹן: ה וְיָת טַפְזָא אֲרֵי מַסִּיק פִּשְׁרָא הוּא וּפַרְסָתֵהּ לָא סְדִיקָא מְסָאָב הוּא לְכוֹן: ו וְיָת אַרְנְבָא אֲרֵי מַסְּקָא פִשְׁרָא הִיא וּפַרְסָתַהּ לָא סְדִיקָא מְסָאֲבָא הִיא לְכוֹן: ז וְיָת חֲזִירָא אֲרֵי סְדִיק פַּרְסָתָא הוּא וּמַטִּלְפָא טִלְפִין פַּרְסָתֵהּ וְהוּא פִשְׁרָא לָא פָשַׁר מְסָאָב הוּא לְכוֹן: ח מִבִּסְרְהוֹן לָא תֵיכְלוּן

―――――― רש"י ――――――

לְדָרְשָׁא לְהַתִּיר אֶת הַשָּׁלִיל הַנִּמְצָא בִּמְעֵי אִמּוֹ (ת"כ שָׁם ט; חוּלִין סט.). **(ח) מִבְּשָׂרָם.** וְלֹא בְּהֵמָה טְמֵאָה. וַהֲלֹא בְּאַזְהָרָה הִיא (להלן פסוק ח) אֶלָּא לַעֲבוֹר עָלֶיהָ בַּעֲשֵׂה ולֹא תַעֲשֶׂה (ת"כ פֶּרֶק ג:א-ב; זְבָחִים לד.): **אוֹתָהּ תֹּאכֵלוּ.** (ת"כ ב:ט שָׁם עו.) וְלֹא תְטֻּשָּׂה אֶת הַשָּׁלִיל הַנִּמְצָא בִּמְעֵי אִמּוֹ אֵין לִי אֶלָּא אֵלּוּ. שְׁאָר בְּהֵמָה טְמֵאָה שֶׁאֵין לָהּ לֹא שׁוּם סִימָן טָהֳרָה בַּעֲשֵׂה מִנַּיִן. אָמַרְתָּ קַל וָחוֹמֶר:

―――――― RASHI ELUCIDATED ――――――

הַנִּמְצָא בִּמְעֵי אִמּוֹ¹ **לְדָרְשָׁא** – to be expounded **לְהַתִּיר אֶת הַשָּׁלִיל** – to permit the eating of **the fetus** — **which is found in the insides of its mother.**¹

וַהֲלֹא **אֹתָהּ תֹּאכֵלוּ** – THAT ONE YOU MAY EAT. **וְלֹא בְּהֵמָה טְמֵאָה** – But not an impure animal. **וַהֲלֹא בְּאַזְהָרָה הִיא²** – But is it not already included in a negative commandment?² **אֶלָּא** – But this verse is needed to make one liable **לַעֲבוֹר עָלֶיהָ בַּעֲשֵׂה ולֹא תַעֲשֶׂה³** – for violating [the prohibition against eating an impure animal] in two ways: with transgression of **a positive commandment** and with transgression of **a negative commandment.**³

8. מִבְּשָׂרָם לֹא תֹאכֵלוּ – YOU MAY NOT EAT OF THEIR FLESH. **אֵין לִי אֶלָּא אֵלּוּ** – All I have is these, i.e., on the basis of this passage, I know only that the specific impure animals mentioned are included in this prohibition. **שְׁאָר בְּהֵמָה טְמֵאָה** – Other impure animals, **שֶׁאֵין לָהּ שׁוּם סִימָן טָהֳרָה** – which have no sign of purity, **מִנַּיִן** – from where do I derive their prohibition? **אָמַרְתָּ קַל וָחוֹמֶר** – You can say a

---

1. *Toras Kohanim, parshasa* 2:9; *Chullin* 69a. The preceding verse has already stated that we are dealing with animals. The apparently superfluous "among the animals" of our verse is interpreted as being connected to "among all the animals" of the preceding verse, as if the preceding verse said, "These are the life forms that you may eat. From among all animals — among — that is to say, *within* — the animals." The verse thus indicates that even a fully formed fetus, which could survive on its own, is allowed to be eaten without ritual slaughter if its mother has been properly slaughtered (Rashi to *Chullin* 69a; *Mizrachi*; *Sifsei Chachamim*).

2. See v. 8 below.

3. *Toras Kohanim, perek* 3:1-2; *Zevachim* 34a. Our verse could have said, "Any one among the animals... and that brings up its cud you may eat." אַךְ, "that one," appears superfluous. Rashi explains that it is meant to imply a prohibition against eating any animal other than the pure ones described here — "that one you may eat — but no other." Rashi goes on to ask why this is necessary, for there is an explicit negative commandment against eating impure animals in verse 4. He answers that the prohibition implied by our verse increases the severity of the sin of eating impure animals. Verse 4 is a negative commandment. Our verse, which is phrased in positive terms, is considered a positive commandment. Now, eating impure animals is a violation of two commandments, one positive and one negative (*Be'er Yitzchak*).

117 / VAYIKRA/LEVITICUS — PARASHAS SHEMINI   11/9 — ט/יא

nor may you touch their carcass — they are impure to you.
⁹ This may you eat from everything that is in the water: everything that has fins and scales

וּבְנִבְלָתָ֖ם לֹ֣א תִגָּ֑עוּ טְמֵאִ֥ים הֵ֖ם לָכֶֽם: ט אֶת־זֶה֙ תֹּֽאכְל֔וּ מִכֹּ֖ל אֲשֶׁ֣ר בַּמָּ֑יִם כֹּ֣ל אֲשֶׁר־ל֣וֹ סְנַפִּ֗יר וְקַשְׂקֶ֛שֶׂת

—————— אונקלוס ——————

וּבְנִבְלָתְהוֹן לָא תִקְרְבוּן מְסָאֲבִין אִנּוּן לְכוֹן: ט יָת דֵּין תֵּיכְלוּן מִכֹּל דִּי בְמַיָּא כֹּל דִּי לֵהּ צִיצִין וְקַלְפִין

—————— רש״י ——————

[Rashi Hebrew text]

—————— RASHI ELUCIDATED ——————

kal vachomer[1] to derive their prohibition as follows: וּמַה אֵלּוּ — **Now, if these** animals mentioned specifically יֵשׁ בָּהֶן קְצָת סִימָנֵי טָהֳרָה — **which have some signs of purity**, i.e., they either chew their cud or have split hooves, ²אֲסוּרוֹת וְכוּלְהוּ — **are forbidden, etc.**[2]

□ מִבְּשָׂרָם — OF THEIR FLESH. עַל בְּשָׂרָם — Concerning eating **their flesh,** the Torah states a prohibition בְּאַזְהָרָה — **with a negative commandment,** וְלֹא עַל עֲצָמוֹת — **but not concerning bones,** וְגִידִין — **and sinews,** {וְקַרְנַיִם — **and horns**,}[3] וּטְלָפַיִם — **and hooves.**[3]

□ וּבְנִבְלָתָם לֹא תִגָּעוּ — NOR MAY YOU TOUCH THEIR CARCASS. יָכוֹל — **One might be able** to think on the basis of this verse יְהוּ יִשְׂרָאֵל מֻזְהָרִים עַל מַגַּע נְבֵלָה — **that Israelites** (non-Kohanim) **are warned against**, i.e., are forbidden, **contact with a carcass** of an impure animal. תַּלְמוּד לוֹמַר — **To teach us** otherwise, **the Torah says,** [4]אֱמֹר אֶל הַכֹּהֲנִים וְגוֹמֵר — **"Say to the Kohanim, etc."**[4] כֹּהֲנִים מֻזְהָרִין — **Kohanim** alone **are prohibited** from making themselves impure through contact with the dead, וְאֵין יִשְׂרָאֵל מֻזְהָרִין — **but Israelites, are not prohibited.** קַל וָחוֹמֶר מֵעַתָּה — **Now, this is** *kal vachomer* as follows: וּמָה טֻמְאַת מֵת — **If** in the case of **impurity caused by contact with the dead,** which is חֲמוּרָה — **more severe,**[5] לֹא הִזְהִיר בָּהּ אֶלָּא כֹּהֲנִים — **[the Torah] prohibited only Kohanim** with regard to it, then with regard to טֻמְאַת נְבֵלָה קַלָּה — **impurity of a carcass,** which is **less severe,** לֹא כָל שֶׁכֵּן — **does it not follow** all the more so that Israelites are not prohibited? וּמַה תַּלְמוּד לוֹמַר — **What** then **does the Torah mean by** ״לֹא תִגָּעוּ — **"nor may you touch"?** בָּרֶגֶל — **It means on the festival.**[6]

9. סְנַפִּיר — FINS. אֵלּוּ שָׁשָׁט בָּהֶם — **These are what it swims with.**

□ קַשְׂקֶשֶׂת — SCALES. אֵלּוּ קְלָפִים — **These are shell-like parts** [7]הַקְּבוּעִים בּוֹ — **which are set into [the fish],**[7] — כְּמוֹ שֶׁנֶּאֱמַר as it says, [8,9]״וְשִׁרְיוֹן קַשְׂקַשִּׂים הוּא לָבוּשׁ — **"and he was wearing armor of scales."**[8,9]

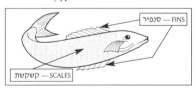

1. A *kal vachomer* is a logical argument which states that if a rule has been stated for a given situation where there is relatively little reason to apply it, all the more so should it apply to a situation in which the rule has not been explicitly stated, but where there is more reason to apply it, even though the rule has not been given explicitly in the second case.
2. *Toras Kohanim, perek* 3:2. The *kal vachomer* continues: All the more so are other impure animals which have no signs of purity.
3. *Toras Kohanim, perek* 4:8. The קְרָנַיִם, "horns," are not mentioned in *Toras Kohanim*.
4. Below 21:1. That verse forbids a Kohen to come into contact with a human corpse.
5. That is, contact with the dead causes a minimum of seven days of impurity, while contact with the carcass of an impure animal causes only a minimum of one day of impurity.
6. *Toras Kohanim, perek* 4:8; *Rosh Hashanah* 16b. All Jewish men must take care not to be impure on the festivals, for they must be present on the grounds of the *Beis HaMikdash* to bring the *olah*-offering of the festival (*Mizrachi*; *Sifsei Chachamim* — see *Rambam*, Hil. *Tum'as Ochlin* 16:10, who says that women, too, must not be impure on the festivals for they also partake of offerings then).
7. *Chullin* 59a.
8. *I Samuel* 17:5. Rashi there describes armor of links covered with scale-like plates.
9. *Chullin* 66b.

in the water, in the seas, and in the streams, those may you eat. **10** And everything that does not have [both] fins and scales in the seas and in the streams — from all the creeping things in the water, and from all living creatures in the water — they are an abomination to you. **11** And they shall be an abomination to you; you shall not eat of their flesh and you shall abominate their carcass. **12** Anything that does not have fins and scales in the water —

— אונקלוס —

בְּמַיָּא בְּיַמְמַיָּא וּבְנַחֲלַיָּא יֵיכְלוּן: י וְכֹל דִּי לֵית לֵהּ צִיצִין וְקַלְפִין בְּיַמְמַיָּא וּבְנַחֲלַיָּא מִכֹּל רַחֲשָׁא דְמַיָּא וּמִכֹּל נַפְשָׁתָא חַיְתָא דִי בְמַיָּא שְׁקָצָא אִנּוּן לְכוֹן: יא וְשִׁקְצָא יְהוֹן לְכוֹן מִבִּסְרְהוֹן לָא תֵיכְלוּן וְיָת נְבֶלְתְּהוֹן תְּשַׁקְּצוּן: יב וְכֹל דִּי לֵית לֵהּ צִיצִין וְקַלְפִין

— רש"י —

(י) שרץ. בכל מקום משמעו דבר נמוך שרוחש ונד על הארץ. **(יא) ושקץ יהיו.** לאסור את עירוביהן אם יש פרס בנותן טעם (ע"כ פרשתא ג:ט). **מבשרם.** אינו מוזהר על הסנפירים ועל העצמות (שם י): **ואת נבלתם תשקצו.** לרבות

יתחושין שסיננן (חולין סז.) יתחושין מושיירונ"ש בלט"ז: **(יב) כל אשר אין לו וגו'.** מה ת"ל, שיכול אין לי שיהא מותר אלא המעלה סימנים שלו ליבשה, השירן במים מנין, תלמוד לומר כל אשר אין לו סנפיר וקשקשת במים, הא אם היו לו במים

— RASHI ELUCIDATED —

10. שֶׁרֶץ — CREEPING THINGS. בְּכָל מָקוֹם — In every place that this word appears, מַשְׁמָעוֹ — its meaning is דָּבָר נָמוּךְ — a low-lying thing שְׁרוֹחֵשׁ וְנָד — which creeps and moves עַל הָאָרֶץ — along the earth, i.e., close to the earth's surface.[1]

11. וְשֶׁקֶץ יִהְיוּ — AND THEY SHALL BE AN ABOMINATION TO YOU. לֶאֱסוֹר אֶת עֵרוּבֵיהֶן — This is stated to forbid their admixtures אִם יֵשׁ בָּהֶם — if there is in [the mixtures] enough of the forbidden matter בְּנוֹתֵן טַעַם[2] — to give flavor to the entire mixture.[2]

□ מִבְּשָׂרָם — OF THEIR FLESH. אֵינוֹ מוּזְהָר — He is not prohibited from eating עַל הַסְּנַפִּירִים — with regard to the fins, וְעַל הָעֲצָמוֹת[3] — and with regard to the bones.[3]

□ וְאֶת נִבְלָתָם תְּשַׁקֵּצוּ — AND YOU SHALL ABOMINATE THEIR CARCASS. This verse comes לְרַבּוֹת יַתּוּשִׁין — to include gnats שֶׁסִּנְּנָן[4] — that he strained out of water.[4] יַתּוּשִׁין — Gnats are מושיירונ"ש בלע"ז — *moucheirons* in Old French.[5]

12. כֹּל אֲשֶׁר אֵין לוֹ וְגוֹמֵר — ANYTHING THAT DOES NOT HAVE, ETC. מַה תַּלְמוּד לוֹמַר — Why does the Torah say this?[6] שֶׁיָּכוֹל — For one might be able to think, אֵין לִי שֶׁיְּהֵא מֻתָּר — I know of nothing to be permitted אֶלָּא הַמַּעֲלֶה סִימָנִין שֶׁלּוֹ לַיַּבָּשָׁה — except for that which brings up its signs of purity to the dry land, i.e., that which retains its fins and scales after it is taken out of water. הִשִּׁירָן בַּמַּיִם מִנַּיִן — If it sheds them in the water, from where do I know that they are nonetheless permitted? תַּלְמוּד לוֹמַר — To provide a source, the Torah says: "כֹּל אֲשֶׁר אֵין לוֹ סְנַפִּיר וְקַשְׂקֶשֶׂת בַּמָּיִם,, — "anything that does not have fins and scales *in the water*." הָא אִם הָיוּ לוֹ בַּמַּיִם — But if it had fins and scales while

---

1. See Rashi to *Genesis* 1:20, s.v., שֶׁרֶץ, and 1:24, s.v., וָרֶמֶשׂ.
2. *Toras Kohanim, parshasa* 3:9. The preceding verse concluded, "they are an abomination to you." This verse thus appears superfluous. Rashi explains that it indicates that not only is the swarming thing itself forbidden, but, so, too, a mixture containing it, providing the forbidden matter gives flavor to the mixture (*Mizrachi; Sifsei Chachamim*).
3. *Toras Kohanim, parshasa* 3:10.
4. *Chullin* 67a. Creatures that breed in stagnant bodies of water such as ditches, or in vessels, may be eaten even if they do not have fins and scales. The apparently superfluous clause, "and you shall abominate their carcass," limits this, however. These creatures may be eaten only while they are still in the water. If, however, they have been removed from the water by straining or the like, they are forbidden (*Mizrachi; Minchas Yehudah; Sifsei Chachamim*).
5. In Modern French, *moucherons*; in English, "midges" or "gnats." The word "mosquito" is derived from the same Latin root.
6. The previous verses have already stated that creeping things that have no fins or scales may not be eaten.

119 / VAYIKRA/LEVITICUS — PARASHAS SHEMINI — 11/13-17

it is an abomination to you.

13 *These shall you abominate from among the fowl, they may not be eaten — they are an abomination: the nesher, the peres, the ozniah;* **14** *the daah and the ayah according to its kind;* **15** *every orev according to its kind;* **16** *the bas hayaanah, the tachmos, the shachaf, and the netz according to its kind;* **17** *the kos, the shalach,*

יג שֶׁקֶץ הוּא לָכֶם: וְאֶת־אֵלֶּה תְּשַׁקְּצוּ מִן־הָעוֹף לֹא יֵאָכְלוּ שֶׁקֶץ הֵם אֶת־הַנֶּשֶׁר וְאֶת־הַפֶּרֶס וְאֵת הָעָזְנִיָּה: יד וְאֶת־הַדָּאָה וְאֶת־הָאַיָּה לְמִינָהּ: אֶת טו כָּל־עֹרֵב לְמִינוֹ: וְאֵת בַּת הַיַּעֲנָה טז וְאֶת־הַתַּחְמָס וְאֶת־הַשָּׁחַף וְאֶת־הַנֵּץ לְמִינֵהוּ: יז וְאֶת־הַכּוֹס וְאֶת־הַשָּׁלָךְ

─── אונקלוס ───

בְּמַיָּא שִׁקְצָא הוּא לְכוֹן: יג וְיָת אִלֵּין תְּשַׁקְּצוּן מִן עוֹפָא לָא יִתְאַכְלוּן שִׁקְצָא אִנוּן נִשְׁרָא וְעָר וְעָזְיָא: יד וְדִיתָא וְטָרָפִיתָא לִזְנַהּ: טו יָת כָּל עוֹרְבָא לִזְנֵהּ: טז וְיָת בַּת נַעֲמִיתָא וְצִיצָא וְצִפַּר שַׁחְפָּא וְנָצָא לִזְנוֹהִי: יז וְקַרְיָא וְשָׁלֵי נוּנָא

─── רש"י ───

אע"פ שֶׁהִשִּׁירָן בַּעֲלִיָּתוֹ מֻתָּר (ת"כ שם כ"א): (יג) לֹא יֵאָכְלוּ. לְחַיֵּב אֶת הַמַּאֲכִילָן לִקְטַנִּים, שֶׁכֵּן מַשְׁמָעוֹ לֹא יְהוּ נֶאֱכָלִין עַל יָדְךָ. אוֹ אֵינוֹ אֶלָּא לְאָסְרָן בַּהֲנָאָה, ת"ל לֹא תֹאכְלוּ (דברים יד:יב) בַּאֲכִילָה אֲסוּרִין, בַּהֲנָאָה מֻתָּרִין (ת"כ פרק ה:א). כָּל עוֹף שֶׁנֶּאֱמַר בּוֹ לְמִינָהּ לְמִינוֹ לְמִינֵהוּ יֵשׁ בְּאוֹתוֹ הַמִּין שֶׁאֵין דּוֹמִין זֶה לָזֶה לֹא בְּמַרְאֵיהֶם וְלֹא בִשְׁמוֹתָם, וְכֻלָּן מִין אֶחָד (ת"כ שם ג:ה; חולין סג:): (טז) הַנֵּץ. אִשְׁפַּרְוִי"ר: (יז) הַשָּׁלָךְ. פֵּירְשׁוּ רַבּוֹתֵינוּ זֶה הַשּׁוֹלֶה דָגִים

─── RASHI ELUCIDATED ───

it was still **in the water,** אַף עַל פִּי שֶׁהִשִּׁירָן בַּעֲלִיָּתוֹ — **even though it shed them in its emergence** from the water, מֻתָּר¹ **— it is permitted.**¹

13. לֹא יֵאָכְלוּ — **THEY MAY NOT BE EATEN.** לְחַיֵּב — **To hold culpable** אֶת הַמַּאֲכִילָן לִקְטַנִּים — **one who feeds them to minors.** שֶׁכֵּן מַשְׁמָעוֹ — **For its implication is as follows:** לֹא יְהוּ נֶאֱכָלִין — **They shall not be eaten** by anybody עַל יָדְךָ — **through you.** אוֹ אֵינוֹ אֶלָּא לְאָסְרָן בַּהֲנָאָה — **Or perhaps this is not so. Rather, it is to forbid them with regard to benefit** not involving eating.² תַּלְמוּד לוֹמַר — **To teach** us otherwise, **the Torah says,** לֹא תֹאכְלוּ,³ — **"You shall not eat."**³ Hence, you must conclude, בַּאֲכִילָה אֲסוּרִין — **they are forbidden with regard to eating,** but בַּהֲנָאָה מֻתָּרִין⁴ — **they are permitted with regard to** other kinds of **benefit.**⁴ כָּל עוֹף שֶׁנֶּאֱמַר בּוֹ — **Any fowl about which it says,** ",לְמִינָהּ — **"to its kind"** in the feminine, ",לְמִינוֹ — **"to its kind"** in the masculine, or ",לְמִינֵהוּ — **"to its kind,"** in another form of the masculine, יֵשׁ בְּאוֹתוֹ הַמִּין — **has within that species** subspecies שֶׁאֵין דּוֹמִין זֶה לָזֶה — **which are not like each other** לֹא בְּמַרְאֵיהֶם וְלֹא בִשְׁמוֹתָם — **neither in their appearance, nor in their name.** וְכֻלָּן מִין אֶחָד⁵ — **Yet they are all one species.**⁵

16. הַנֵּץ — **THE** *NETZ.* אשפרוי"ר — *Esparvier.*⁶

17. הַשָּׁלָךְ — **THE** *SHALACH.* פֵּרְשׁוּ רַבּוֹתֵינוּ — **Our Rabbis explained,** זֶה הַשּׁוֹלֶה דָגִים — **this is [the**

---

1. *Toras Kohanim, parshasa* 3:11.

2. Rashi here gives the opinion of the *Amora* Chizkiyah (*Pesachim* 21b), who holds that a prohibition against eating expressed by the Torah with a passive verb (*nifal*) implies not only a prohibition against eating per se, but a prohibition against any benefit that can cause a savings or profit and thus allows the recipient of the benefit to have money with which he can buy food. Our verse expresses its prohibition with a passive verb, לֹא יֵאָכְלוּ, "they may not be eaten." Thus, Rashi asks, perhaps this is used to indicate a prohibition that includes any form of benefit rather than a prohibition against feeding them to minors.

3. *Deuteronomy* 14:12.

4. *Toras Kohanim, perek* 5:1. Commandments repeated by the Torah in *Deuteronomy* expand or add to what has been expressed earlier in the Torah. If our verse, which expresses the prohibition against eating forbid-den birds in a passive form, were meant to indicate a prohibition against deriving any benefit, the verse in *Deuteronomy* that repeats it would not use an active form, which indicates a prohibition against eating only, because that limits the earlier statement. If, however, our verse uses the passive to indicate that there is a prohibition against feeding to minors, it is valid for the verse in *Deuteronomy* to disregard this point. For eating versus deriving any benefit are two steps on the same scale — deriving benefit directly. But the prohibition against feeding forbidden birds to minors is not a more inclusive form of the prohibition. It is an independent issue that does not relate to derivation of benefit (*Gur Aryeh*).

5. *Toras Kohanim, perek* 5:3-5; *Chullin* 63a.

6. In Modern French, *éprevier*. In English, "sparrow hawk." *Tosafos* to *Chullin* 63a disagrees with Rashi on the translation of נֵץ, but does not offer a different one.

and the yanshuf; ⁱ⁸ the tinshemes, the kaas, and the racham; ¹⁹ the chasidah, the anafah according to its kind, the duchifas,

יח וְאֶת־הַיַּנְשׁוּף: וְאֶת־הַתִּנְשֶׁמֶת וְאֶת־הַקָּאָת וְאֶת־הָרָחָם: יט וְאֶת־הַחֲסִידָה הָאֲנָפָה לְמִינָהּ וְאֶת־הַדּוּכִיפַת

―――――― אונקלוס ――――――

וְקִפּוֹפָא: יח וּבוּתָא וְקָאתָא וִירַקְרְקָא: יט וְחַוָּרִיתָא וְאִבּוּ לִזְנָהּ וְנַגַּר [ס״א וְנַגָּר] טוּרָא

―――――― רש״י ――――――

(יט) הַחֲסִידָה. זוֹ דַיָּה לְבָנָה ציגוני״א וְלָמָּה נִקְרָא שְׁמָהּ חֲסִידָה שֶׁעוֹשָׂה חֲסִידוּת עִם חַבְרוֹתֶיהָ בִּמְזוֹנוֹת (חולין שם): הָאֲנָפָה. הִיא דַיָּה רַגְזָנִית (שם) וְנִרְאֶה לִי שֶׁהִיא שֶׁקּוֹרִין לָהּ הירו״ן: הַדּוּכִיפַת. תַּרְנְגוֹל הַבָּר וְכַרְבָּלְתּוֹ כְּפוּלָה וּבְלַעַז הֵירוּפ״א וְלָמָּה נִקְרָא שְׁמוֹ דּוּכִיפַת שֶׁהוֹדוֹ כָּפוּת וְזוֹ הִיא כַּרְבָּלְתּוֹ [ת״א: וְנַגָּר טוּרָא הִיא כַּרְבָּלְתּוֹ

מִן הַיָּם (חולין שם). וְזֶהוּ שֶׁתִּרְגֵּם אוּנְקְלוֹס וְשָׁלֵי נוּנָא: וְיַנְשׁוּף. הַס צוֹאיטי״ש הַצּוֹעֲקִים בַּלַּיְלָה וְיֵשׁ לָהֶם לְסָתוֹת כְּאָדָם (נדה כג). וְעוֹד אַחֵר דּוֹמֶה לוֹ שֶׁקּוֹרִין יבו״ש: (יח) הַתִּנְשֶׁמֶת. הִיא קלב״א שוריץ וְדוֹמָה לְעַכְבָּר וּפוֹרַחַת בַּלַּיְלָה. וְתִנְשֶׁמֶת הָאֲמוּרָה בִּשְׁרָצִים הִיא בְּשֶׁרָצִים הִיא וְאֵין לָהּ עֵינַיִם וְקוֹרִין לָהּ טלפ״א:

―――――― RASHI ELUCIDATED ――――――

bird] which casts fish out — מִן הַיָּם — of the sea.¹ וְזֶהוּ שֶׁתִּרְגֵּם אוּנְקְלוֹס — This is why Targum Onkelos rendered it, ",וְשָׁלֵי נוּנָא — "that which casts out fish."

□ וְיַנְשׁוּף כּוֹס — THE KOS, ... THE YANSHUF. הַס צוֹאיטי״ש — They are çuetes,² הַצּוֹעֲקִים בַּלַּיְלָה — which cry out at night, וְיֵשׁ לָהֶם לְסָתוֹת כְּאָדָם — and have cheeks like a man,²ᵃ וְעוֹד אַחֵר — and another one דּוֹמֶה לוֹ — similar to it שֶׁקּוֹרִין יבו״ש — which they call ibou.²

18. הַתִּנְשֶׁמֶת — THE TINSHEMES. הִיא קלב״א שוריץ — This is calva sorice.³ וְדוֹמָה לְעַכְבָּר — It is like a mouse וּפוֹרַחַת בַּלַּיְלָה — and flies at night. וְתִנְשֶׁמֶת הָאֲמוּרָה בִּשְׁרָצִים — The tinshemes that is mentioned among the creeping things⁴ הִיא דּוֹמָה לָהּ — is similar to it, וְאֵין לָהּ עֵינַיִם — and has no eyes. וְקוֹרִין לָהּ טלפ״א — They call it talpe.⁵

19. הַחֲסִידָה — THE CHASIDAH. זוֹ דַיָּה לְבָנָה — This is the white dayah.⁶ ציגוני״א — Cegoine.⁷ וְלָמָּה — שֶׁעוֹשָׂה חֲסִידוּת — Why has its name been designated as, literally, "kind one"? נִקְרָא שְׁמָהּ חֲסִידָה — For it does kindness עִם חַבְרוֹתֶיהָ — with its companions בִּמְזוֹנוֹת — with food.⁸

□ הָאֲנָפָה — THE ANAFAH. הִיא דַיָּה רַגְזָנִית⁹ — This is the hot-tempered dayah.⁶,⁹ וְנִרְאֶה לִי — It appears to me שֶׁהִיא שֶׁקּוֹרִין לָהּ הירו״ן — that this is the one they call hairon.¹⁰

□ הַדּוּכִיפַת — THE DUCHIFAS. תַּרְנְגוֹל הַבָּר — The wild rooster. וְכַרְבָּלְתּוֹ כְּפוּלָה — Its comb is doubled over; וּבְלַעַז הירופ״א — and in Old French herupe.¹¹ וְלָמָּה נִקְרָא שְׁמוֹ דּוּכִיפַת — Why has its name been designated as duchifas? שֶׁהוֹדוֹ כָּפוּת — Because its splendor is tied; וְזוֹ הִיא כַּרְבָּלְתּוֹ — [its splendor] is its comb.¹² וְנַגָּר טוּרָא נִקְרָא — It is called "cutter of the mountain" by Targum Onkelos

---

1. Chullin 63a. Rashi there defines this as עוֹרֵב הַמַּיִם, literally, "water raven." Apparently, Rashi means the "cormorant," a name derived from the Latin corvus marinus, "sea raven."
2. In Modern French, çuete is chouette, and ibou is hibou. Both words means "owl" and are onomatopoetic names derived from the owl's hooting sound. The word chouette usually is appended to another word to describe a particular species of owl, e.g., chouette effraie, "screech owl." The word hibou usually stands by itself. It is therefore difficult to determine to which species Rashi refers. Moreover, Rashi is undecided between çuete and ibou as to which is the כּוֹס and which is the יַנְשׁוּף; thus, he explains both in the same comment.
2a. Niddah 23a.
3. In Modern French, chauve-souris, literally, "bald mouse"; in English, "bat."
4. Below v. 30.
5. In Modern French, taupe; in English, "mole." The English word "taupe" is derived from this French word and means "brownish-gray," the color of a mole.

6. A type of impure bird mentioned in Deuteronomy 14:13. According to Rashi there, the ayah of verse 14 here has three names, one of which is dayah.
7. In Modern French, cigogne; in English, "stork."
8. Chullin 63a. It shares its food with its companions (Rashi there).
9. Chullin 63a.
10. In Modern French, héron; in English, "heron."
11. Some translators consider this word a forerunner of the Modern French huppe, which in English means "hoopoe." However, it is difficult to reconcile Rashi's description of this bird's comb with the erect, fan-like comb of the hoopoe. Rashi to Chullin 63a renders poon salvage, in Modern French, paon sauvage, which means "wild peacock."
12. The word דּוּכִיפַת is a combination of הוֹדוֹ and כָּפוּת. Its "splendor is tied" in the sense that its comb does not flap freely as does the comb of other roosters, but is rather folded over and imbedded into its head (Rashi to Chullin 63a).

11/20-21

כ וְאֶת־הָעֲטַלֵּף: כֹּל שֶׁרֶץ הָעוֹף הַהֹלֵךְ עַל־אַרְבַּע שֶׁקֶץ הוּא לָכֶם: כא אַךְ אֶת־זֶה תֹּאכְלוּ מִכֹּל שֶׁרֶץ הָעוֹף הַהֹלֵךְ עַל־אַרְבַּע אֲשֶׁר־לֹא °לוֹ ק׳ כְרָעַיִם מִמַּעַל לְרַגְלָיו לְנַתֵּר בָּהֵן

and the atalef. [20] *Every flying creeping creature that walks on four legs — it is an abomination to you.* [21] *Only this may you eat from among all flying creeping creatures that walk on four: one that has jumping legs above its legs, with which to spring*

— אונקלוס —

וְיָת עֲטַלְפָא: כ כֹּל רִחֲשָׁא דְעוֹפָא דִמְהַלֵּךְ עַל אַרְבַּע שְׁקָצָא הוּא לְכוֹן: כא בְּרַם יָת דֵּין תֵּיכְלוּן מִכֹּל רִחֲשָׁא דְעוֹפָא דִמְהַלֵּךְ עַל אַרְבַּע דִּי לֵהּ קַרְצוּלִין מֵעִלָּוֵי רַגְלוֹהִי לְקַפָּצָא בְהוֹן

— רש״י —

עַל שֵׁם מַטָּשָׂיו, כְּמוֹ שֶׁפֵּירְשׁוּ רַבּוֹתֵינוּ בְּמַסֶּ׳ גִּטִּין בְּפֶרֶק מִי שֶׁאֲחָזוֹ (סח:): (ב) **שֶׁרֶץ הָעוֹף.** הֵם הַדַּקִּים הַנְּמוּכִים הָרוֹחֲשִׁין עַל הָאָרֶץ כְּגוֹן זְבוּבִים וִיתוּשִׁין וַחֲגָבִים: (בא) **עַל אַרְבַּע.** עַל אַרְבַּע רַגְלָיִם: **מִמַּעַל לְרַגְלָיו.** סָמוּךְ לְצַוָּארוֹ יֵשׁ לוֹ כְּמִין שְׁתֵּי רַגְלַיִם לְבַד אַרְבַּע רַגְלָיו וּכְשֶׁרוֹצֶה לָעוּף וְלִקְפֹּץ מִן הָאָרֶץ מִתְחַזֵּק בְּאוֹתָן שְׁתֵּי כְרָעַיִם וּפוֹרֵחַ. וְיֵשׁ הַרְבֵּה כְּאוֹתָן שֶׁקּוֹרִין לנגוש״טא, אֲבָל אֵין אָנוּ בְּקִיאִין בָּהֶן, שֶׁאַרְבָּעָה סִימָנֵי טָהֳרָה נֶאֶמְרוּ בָהֶם, אַרְבַּע רַגְלַיִם וְאַרְבַּע כְּנָפַיִם וְקַרְסוּלִין, אֵלּוּ כְּרָעַיִם הַכְּתוּבִים כָּאן, וּכְנָפָיו חוֹפִין אֶת רוּבּוֹ (חולין נט.). וְכָל סִימָנִין הַלָּלוּ מְצוּיִין בְּאוֹתָן שֶׁבֵּינוֹתֵינוּ אֲבָל יֵשׁ שֶׁרֹאשָׁן אָרוֹךְ וְיֵשׁ {שֶׁאֵין} לָהֶם זָנָב וְצָרִיךְ שֶׁיְּהֵא שְׁמוֹ חָגָב וּבָזֶה אֵין אָנוּ יוֹדְעִים לְהַבְדִּיל בֵּינֵיהֶם:

— RASHI ELUCIDATED —

בְּמַסֶּכֶת גִּטִּין — *in Tractate Gittin,* בְּפֶרֶק מִי שֶׁאֲחָזוֹ — *in Chapter Mi Sheachazo.*[1] כְּמוֹ שֶׁפֵּירְשׁוּ רַבּוֹתֵינוּ — *as our Rabbis explained* עַל שֵׁם מַעֲשָׂיו — *because of its deeds,*

20. שֶׁרֶץ הָעוֹף — FLYING CREEPING CREATURES. הֵם הַדַּקִּים הַנְּמוּכִים — *They are the tiny, low-lying things* הָרוֹחֲשִׁין עַל הָאָרֶץ — *which creep along the earth,*[2] כְּגוֹן זְבוּבִים — *such as flies,* וְצִרְעִין — *and wasps,* וְיַתּוּשִׁין — *and mosquitos,* וַחֲגָבִים — *and grasshoppers.*

21. עַל אַרְבַּע — ON FOUR. עַל אַרְבַּע רַגְלַיִם — *On four legs.*

מִמַּעַל לְרַגְלָיו — ABOVE ITS LEGS. סָמוּךְ לְצַוָּארוֹ — *Near its neck,* יֵשׁ לוֹ כְּמִין שְׁתֵּי רַגְלַיִם — *it has two legs, of a sort,* לְבַד אַרְבַּע רַגְלָיו — *besides its four legs.* וּכְשֶׁרוֹצֶה לָעוּף — *And when it wants to fly* וְלִקְפֹּץ מִן הָאָרֶץ — *and to jump from the ground,* מִתְחַזֵּק בְּאוֹתָן שְׁתֵּי כְרָעַיִם — *it exerts its strength through those two jumping legs,* וּפוֹרֵחַ — *and ascends into flight.* וְיֵשׁ הַרְבֵּה — *There are many such insects,* כְּאוֹתָן שֶׁקּוֹרִין לנגוש״טא — *such as those they call langosta,*[3] אֲבָל אֵין אָנוּ בְּקִיאִין בָּהֶן — *but we are not expert in them,* i.e., we do not have the expertise to determine which of them may be eaten, שֶׁאַרְבָּעָה סִימָנֵי טָהֳרָה נֶאֶמְרוּ בָהֶם — *because there are four signs of purity stated concerning them:* They must have אַרְבַּע רַגְלַיִם — *four legs,* וְאַרְבַּע כְּנָפַיִם — *and four wings,* וְקַרְסֻלִּין — *and joints,* אֵלּוּ כְּרָעַיִם הַכְּתוּבִים כָּאן — *which are the* jumping legs written *of here,*[4] וּכְנָפָיו חוֹפִין אֶת רֻבּוֹ — *and its wings must cover most of its body.*[4] וְכָל סִימָנִין הַלָּלוּ מְצוּיִין — *All of these signs are found* בְּאוֹתָן שֶׁבֵּינוֹתֵינוּ — *in those* grasshoppers *which are among us,* אֲבָל יֵשׁ שֶׁרֹאשָׁן אָרוֹךְ — *but there are* among them *some whose head is long,* וְיֵשׁ {שֶׁאֵין} לָהֶם זָנָב — *and {there are* among them *some that do not} have a tail,*[5] וְצָרִיךְ שֶׁיְּהֵא שְׁמוֹ חָגָב — *and its name must be chagav,*[5] אֵין אָנוּ יוֹדְעִים לְהַבְדִּיל בֵּינֵיהֶם — *we do not know* how *to distinguish between them,* i.e., between those long-headed and tailed grasshoppers that are called *chagav* and those that are not.

---

1. *Gittin* 68b. The *Gemara* relates that the wild rooster would take the *shamir* (a small creature that could miraculously split stone) and put it on rocky mountaintops, to break up their soil and make them fit for cultivation. It would then bring seeds and plant them in the soil. Thus, the wild rooster would fashion the mountains into areas conducive to habitation.

2. See Rashi to verse 10 above.

3. The English word "locust" is cognate with this word, and that was its meaning in Old French. However, in Modern French the word is spelled *langouste* and has come to mean "crayfish." The word for "locust" is *sauterelle,* which is derived from the verb *sauter,* "to jump."

4. *Chullin* 59a.

5. *Chullin* 65b. Although a grasshopper has all the four signs of purity, it is not permitted unless it is of the family called *chagav*.

Our text of Rashi is that quoted by *Ramban* in his comments to *Chullin* 65b. Many editions of Rashi read, וְיֵשׁ שֶׁאֵין לָהֶם זָנָב "and there are [among them] some that do not have a tail."

122 / ויקרא – פרשת שמיני

כב עַל־הָאָֽרֶץ׃ אֶת־אֵ֤לֶּה מֵהֶם֙ תֹּאכֵ֔לוּ אֶת־הָֽאַרְבֶּ֣ה לְמִינ֔וֹ וְאֶת־הַסָּלְעָ֖ם לְמִינֵ֑הוּ וְאֶת־הַחַרְגֹּ֣ל לְמִינֵ֔הוּ וְאֶת־הֶחָגָ֖ב לְמִינֵֽהוּ׃ כג וְכֹל֙ שֶׁ֣רֶץ הָע֔וֹף אֲשֶׁר־ל֖וֹ אַרְבַּ֣ע רַגְלָ֑יִם שֶׁ֥קֶץ ה֖וּא לָכֶֽם׃ כד וּלְאֵ֖לֶּה תִּטַּמָּ֑אוּ כָּל־הַנֹּגֵ֥עַ בְּנִבְלָתָ֖ם יִטְמָ֥א עַד־הָעָֽרֶב׃ כה וְכָל־הַנֹּשֵׂ֖א מִנִּבְלָתָ֑ם יְכַבֵּ֥ס בְּגָדָ֖יו וְטָמֵ֥א עַד־הָעָֽרֶב׃ כו לְכָל־הַבְּהֵמָ֡ה אֲשֶׁ֣ר הִוא֩ מַפְרֶ֨סֶת פַּרְסָ֜ה וְשֶׁ֣סַע ׀ אֵינֶ֣נָּה שֹׁסַ֗עַת

upon the earth. ²² *You may eat these from among them: the* arbeh *according to its kind; the* sal'am *according to its kind, the* chargol *according to its kind, and the* chagav *according to its kind.* ²³ *Every flying creeping thing that has four legs — it is an abomination to you.*

²⁴ *To these you will become impure — anyone who touches their carcass becomes impure until evening;* ²⁵ *and anyone who carries of their carcass shall immerse his clothing and be impure until evening —* ²⁶ *every animal that has split hooves that are not completely split,*

———————— אונקלוס ————————

עַל אַרְעָא׃ כב יָת אִלֵּין מִנְּהוֹן תֵּיכְלוּן יָת גּוּבָא וְיָת רָשׁוֹנָא לִזְנוֹהִי וְיָת חַרְגּוֹלָא לִזְנוֹהִי וְיָת חֲגָבָא לִזְנוֹהִי׃ כג וְכֹל רִחְשָׁא דְעוֹפָא דִּי לֵהּ אַרְבַּע רַגְלִין שִׁקְצָא הוּא לְכוֹן׃ כד וּלְאִלֵּין תִּסְתָּאֲבוּן כָּל דְּיִקְרַב בִּנְבִלְתְּהוֹן יְהֵי מְסָאָב עַד רַמְשָׁא׃ כה וְכָל דִּיטוּל מִנְּבִלְתְּהוֹן יְצַבַּע לְבוּשׁוֹהִי וִיהֵי מְסָאָב עַד רַמְשָׁא׃ כו לְכָל בְּעִירָא דִּי הִיא סְדִיקָא פַרְסָתָא וְטִלְפִין לֵיתְהָא מַטִּלְפָא

———————— רש"י ————————

(כג) וכל שרץ העוף וגו'. בָּא לְלַמֵּד שֶׁאִם יֵשׁ לוֹ חָמֵשׁ טָהוֹר (ת"כ פרק ה:י): **(כד) ולאלה.** הָעֲתִידִין לְהֵאָמֵר לְמַטָּה בָּעִנְיָן (ת"כ פרשתא ד:ח): **תטמאו.** כְּלוֹמַר בְּנְגִיעָתָם יֵשׁ טוּמְאָה: **(כה) וכל הנשא מנבלתם.** כָּל מָקוֹם שֶׁנֶּאֶמְרָה טוּמְאַת מַשָּׂא חֲמוּרָה מְטֻמְאַת מַגָּע שֶׁהִיא טְעוּנָה כִּבּוּס בְּגָדִים:

מטומאת מגע שהיא טעונה כבוס בגדים (ספ ז"ח): (כו) מפרסת פרסה ושסע איננה שוסעת. כְּגוֹן גָּמָל שֶׁפַּרְסָתוֹ סְדוּקָה לְמַעְלָה אֲבָל לְמַטָּה הִיא מְחֻבֶּרֶת. כָּאן לִמַּד שֶׁנִּבְלַת בְּהֵמָה טְמֵאָה מְטַמְּאָה, וּבְעִנְיָן שֶׁבְּסוֹף הַפָּרָשָׁה (לְהַלָּן פְּסוּקִים לט-מ) פֵּי' עַל בְּהֵמָה טְהוֹרָה:

———————— RASHI ELUCIDATED ————————

23. וְכֹל שֶׁרֶץ הָעוֹף וְגוֹמֵר — EVERY FLYING CREEPING THING, ETC. — בָּא לְלַמֵּד — [The verse] came to teach us שֶׁאִם יֵשׁ לוֹ חָמֵשׁ — that if it has five legs, [1] טָהוֹר — it is pure.[1]

24. וּלְאֵלֶּה — TO THESE — הָעֲתִידִין לְהֵאָמֵר — that are going to be stated [2] לְמַטָּה בָּעִנְיָן — below in this topic.[2]

תִּטַּמָּאוּ — YOU WILL BECOME IMPURE. — כְּלוֹמַר — That is to say, בִּנְגִיעָתָם — through contact with them יֵשׁ טֻמְאָה — there is impurity.[3]

25. וְכָל הַנּוֹשֵׂא מִנִּבְלָתָם — AND ANYONE WHO CARRIES OF THEIR CARCASS. — כָּל מָקוֹם שֶׁנֶּאֶמְרָה טֻמְאַת מַשָּׂא — Wherever impurity through carrying is stated in the Torah, חֲמוּרָה מִטֻּמְאַת מַגָּע — it is more stringent than impurity through touching [4] שֶׁהִיא טְעוּנָה כִּבּוּס בְּגָדִים — for it requires washing garments.[4]

26. מַפְרֶסֶת פַּרְסָה וְשֶׁסַע אֵינֶנָּה שֹׁסַעַת — THAT HAS SPLIT HOOVES THAT ARE NOT COMPLETELY SPLIT. — כְּגוֹן גָּמָל — Such as a camel, שֶׁפַּרְסָתוֹ סְדוּקָה לְמַעְלָה — whose hoof is split at its tip, אֲבָל לְמַטָּה — but behind, i.e., where it meets the bottom of the foot, הִיא מְחֻבֶּרֶת — it is connected. כָּאן לִמֵּד — Here [the Torah] has taught you שֶׁנִּבְלַת בְּהֵמָה טְמֵאָה — that the carcass of an impure animal מְטַמְּאָה — transmits impurity.[5] וּבְעִנְיָן שֶׁבְּסוֹף הַפָּרָשָׁה — In the topic at the end of the portion[5] פֵּרֵשׁ — [the Torah] speaks in detail עַל בְּהֵמָה טְהוֹרָה

---

1. *Toras Kohanim*, *perek* 5:10. Verse 20 is a general prohibition against eating four-legged, flying creatures that creep. Verses 21 and 22 deal with exceptions to that rule. Our verse appears to be a repetition of verse 20. But it is necessary, for on the basis of verses 20-22 alone, we might have concluded that any winged, creeping species that has *at least* four legs may not be eaten. Our verse teaches us that the prohibition applies only to creatures which have exactly four legs. Five-legged creatures are permitted (*Gur Aryeh*).

2. *Toras Kohanim, parshasa* 4:1. "These" refers to the animals about to be mentioned, not to those mentioned in the preceding verses (*Mizrachi*).

3. The verse is not to be understood as a commandment to become impure (*Mizrachi*; *Sifsei Chachamim*).

4. *Toras Kohanim, parshasa* 4:7-8. Impurity transmitted through touching is removed by immersing oneself in a spring or in a *mikveh*. Purification of impurity transmitted through carrying requires not only immersion of the one who carries the impurity, but his garments must be immersed as well, for they, too, become impure.

5. Verses 39-40 below.

or does not chew its cud, they are impure to you; whoever touches them becomes impure. ²⁷ And every one that walks on its paws, among all animals that walk on four legs, they are impure to you; whoever touches their carcass shall be impure until evening. ²⁸ One who carries their carcass shall immerse his clothing and be impure until evening; they are impure to you. ²⁹ These are for you the impure among the creeping animals that creep upon the ground: the choled, the achbar, and the tzav according to its kind;	וְגֵרָה אֵינֶנָּה מַעֲלָה טְמֵאִים הֵם לָכֶם כָּל־הַנֹּגֵעַ בָּהֶם יִטְמָא: וְכֹל ׀ הוֹלֵךְ עַל־כַּפָּיו בְּכָל־הַחַיָּה הַהֹלֶכֶת עַל־אַרְבַּע טְמֵאִים הֵם לָכֶם כָּל־הַנֹּגֵעַ בְּנִבְלָתָם יִטְמָא עַד־הָעָרֶב: וְהַנֹּשֵׂא אֶת־נִבְלָתָם יְכַבֵּס בְּגָדָיו וְטָמֵא עַד־הָעָרֶב טְמֵאִים הֵמָּה לָכֶם: וְזֶה לָכֶם הַטָּמֵא בַּשֶּׁרֶץ הַשֹּׁרֵץ עַל־הָאָרֶץ הַחֹלֶד וְהָעַכְבָּר וְהַצָּב לְמִינֵהוּ:

──────── אונקלוס ────────

וּפִשְׁרָא לֵיתָהָא מַסְּקָא מְסָאֲבִין אִנּוּן לְכוֹן כָּל דְּיִקְרַב בְּהוֹן יְהֵי מְסָאָב: (כז) וְכֹל דִּמְהַלֵּךְ עַל יְדוֹהִי בְּכָל חֵיתָא דִּמְהַלְּכָא עַל אַרְבַּע מְסָאֲבִין אִנּוּן לְכוֹן כָּל דְּיִקְרַב בִּנְבִלְתְּהוֹן יְהֵא מְסָאָב עַד רַמְשָׁא: (כח) וּדְיִטּוֹל יָת נְבִלְתְּהוֹן יְצַבַּע לְבוּשׁוֹהִי וִיהֵי מְסָאָב עַד רַמְשָׁא מְסָאֲבִין אִנּוּן לְכוֹן: (כט) וְדֵין לְכוֹן מְסָאֲבָא בְּרִחֲשָׁא דְרָחֵשׁ עַל אַרְעָא חֻלְדָּא וְעַכְבְּרָא וְצָבָא לִזְנוֹהִי:

──────── רש״י ────────

(כז) עַל כַּפָּיו. כְּגוֹן כֶּלֶב וְדוֹב וְחָתוּל: **טְמֵאִים הֵם לָכֶם.** לְמַגָּע: **(כט) וְזֶה לָכֶם הַטָּמֵא.** לְטוּמְאָה מַמָּשׁ לִהְיוֹת טָמֵא בְּמַגָּעָן וְנֶאֱסָר לֶאֱכֹל תְּרוּמָה וְקָדָשִׁים וְלִכָּנֵס בַּמִּקְדָּשׁ: **הַחֹלֶד.** מושטיל״ה: **וְהַצָּב.** פרוויי״ט שֶׁדּוֹמֶה לִצְפַרְדֵּעַ:

──────── RASHI ELUCIDATED ────────

about the unslaughtered carcass of **a pure animal.**

27. עַל כַּפָּיו – ON ITS PAWS. כְּגוֹן כֶּלֶב – Such as a dog, וְדֹב – a bear, וְחָתוּל – or a cat.[1]

□ טְמֵאִים הֵם לָכֶם – THEY ARE IMPURE TO YOU. לְמַגָּע – With regard to touching.[2]

29. וְזֶה לָכֶם הַטָּמֵא – THESE ARE FOR YOU THE IMPURE. כָּל טְמָאוֹת הַלָּלוּ – All these impurities, i.e., all these references to impurity, אֵינָן לְאִסּוּר אֲכִילָה – do not refer to a prohibition against eating, אֶלָּא לְטֻמְאָה מַמָּשׁ – but to impurity in a literal sense,[3] לִהְיוֹת טָמֵא בְּמַגָּעָן – to become impure through contact with [their carcasses], וְנֶאֱסָר – and to become forbidden as a result of the impurity transmitted by the carcass לֶאֱכוֹל תְּרוּמָה – to eat terumah[4] וְקָדָשִׁים – and that which is holy, וּלְהִכָּנֵס בַּמִּקְדָּשׁ – and to enter the Sanctuary.

□ הַחֹלֶד – THE CHOLED. מושטיל״א – Mostele.[5]

□ וְהַצָּב – AND THE TZAV. פרוויי״ט – Froit, שֶׁדּוֹמֶה לִצְפַרְדֵּעַ – which is similar to a frog.[6]

1. The previous verse (26) speaks of hooved animals. This one speaks of animals without hooves (Mizrachi; Sifsei Chachamim).

2. As the verse continues, Rashi does not state מַגָּע, "touching," to the exclusion of מַשָּׂא, "carrying." He means that "impure" here is used in its literal sense, and does not mean "non-kosher," forbidden foods (Be'er BaSadeh).

3. Impurity here is not meant in a borrowed sense, as a prohibition against eating (as it is used in verses 4-7 above), for all creeping animals may not be eaten, not only the eight mentioned here; rather, it is meant in a literal sense.

4. The portion of the yearly crop given to the Kohanim. See Numbers 18:12, 25-30.

5. This word means "weasel." The Modern English word "mustelid," which describes weasels and related animals, is cognate with this Old French word.

6. This has been mistaken for Modern French, furet; English "ferret" (a kind of weasel). However, Rashi to Avodah Zarah 40a, s.v., בֵּיצַת הַשֶּׁרֶץ, states that the צָב lays eggs and looks like a frog and is called בוטרי״ל, "boterel," which is Old French for "a small toad." (The reading boterel is according to manuscripts; the word כוטורי״ל that appears in the printed editions is a corruption of בוכרדרי״ל, "cocodrille," an Old French form of "crocodile.") Rashi to Niddah 56a, s.v., ובוגי, also calls the צָב, "froit," and adds that some people call this animal in French, בוט״א, "bote," which means "toad." The unfamiliarity with the word froit by those who called it bote is what prompted Rashi to note that "it is similar to a frog," ensuring the correct identification.

³⁰ the anakah, the koach, and the leta'ah; and the chomet and the tinshemes. ³¹ Only these are impure to you among all the creeping animals; anyone who touches them when they are dead shall be impure until evening; ³² and when they are dead, anything upon which part of them will fall shall become impure, whether it is a wooden utensil, a garment, leather, or sackcloth — any utensil with which work is done — shall be brought into the water, and remain impure until the evening, and it becomes cleansed. ³³ Any earthenware utensil into whose interior one of them will fall, everything in it shall become impure — and you shall

ל וְהָאֲנָקָה וְהַכֹּחַ וְהַלְּטָאָה וְהַחֹמֶט
לא וְהַתִּנְשָׁמֶת: אֵלֶּה הַטְּמֵאִים לָכֶם
בְּכָל־הַשָּׁרֶץ כָּל־הַנֹּגֵעַ בָּהֶם
לב בְּמֹתָם יִטְמָא עַד־הָעָרֶב: וְכֹל
אֲשֶׁר־יִפֹּל־עָלָיו מֵהֶם ׀ בְּמֹתָם
יִטְמָא מִכָּל־כְּלִי־עֵץ אוֹ בֶגֶד
אוֹ־עוֹר אוֹ שָׂק כָּל־כְּלִי אֲשֶׁר־
יֵעָשֶׂה מְלָאכָה בָּהֶם בַּמַּיִם יוּבָא
לג וְטָמֵא עַד־הָעֶרֶב וְטָהֵר: שביעי וְכָל־
כְּלִי־חֶרֶשׂ אֲשֶׁר־יִפֹּל מֵהֶם אֶל־
תּוֹכוֹ כֹּל אֲשֶׁר בְּתוֹכוֹ יִטְמָא

אונקלוס

ל וְיַלָּא וְכֹחָא וְחִלְטֵיתָא וְחֹמְטָא וְאָשׁוּתָא: לא אִלֵּין דִּמְסָאֲבִין לְכוֹן בְּכָל רִחְשָׁא כָּל דְּיִקְרַב בְּהוֹן בְּמוֹתְהוֹן יְהֵי מְסָאָב עַד רַמְשָׁא: לב וְכֹל דִּי יִפֵּל עֲלוֹהִי מִנְּהוֹן בְּמוֹתְהוֹן יְהֵי מְסָאָב מִכָּל מָאן דְּאָע אוֹ לְבוּשׁ אוֹ מְשַׁךְ אוֹ שַׂק כָּל מָאן דִּי יִתְעֲבֵד עֲבִידָא בְהוֹן בְּמַיָּא יִתָּעַל וִיהֵי מְסָאָב עַד רַמְשָׁא וְיִדְכֵּי: לג וְכָל מָאן דַּחֲסַף דִּי יִפֵּל מִנְּהוֹן לְגַוֵּהּ כֹּל דִּי בְגַוֵּהּ יִסְתָּאָב

רש"י

(ל) אנקה. הירינ"ו: הלטאה. ליישרד"א: חמט. לימצ"א: תנשמת. טלפ"א: (לב) במים יובא. ואף לאחר טבילתו טמא הוא לתרומה. עד הערב. ואחר כך: וטהר. בהערב השמש (יבמות עה.): (לג) אל תוכו. אין כלי חרס מיטמא אלא מאוירו (כלים ב:א; חולין כד:): כל אשר בתוכו יטמא. הכלי חוזר ומטמא מה שבאוירו (ס"א שבתוכו):

RASHI ELUCIDATED
---

30. אֲנָקָה — ANAKAH. הירינצו"ן — Heriçon.[1]

☐ הַלְּטָאָה — THE LETA'AH. ליישרד"א — Laisarde.[2]

☐ חֹמֶט — CHOMET. לימצ"א — Limace.[3]

☐ תִּנְשָׁמֶת — TINSHEMES. טלפ"א — Talpe.[4]

32. בַּמַּיִם יוּבָא — SHALL BE BROUGHT INTO THE WATER. וְאַף לְאַחַר טְבִילָתוֹ — Even after its immersion טָמֵא הוּא — it is impure לִתְרוּמָה — for *terumah*, i.e., in that it renders *terumah* which comes into contact with it impure,

☐ עַד הָעֶרֶב — UNTIL THE EVENING. וְאַחַר כָּךְ — And afterwards,

☐ וְטָהֵר — AND IT BECOMES CLEANSED, בְּהַעֲרֵב הַשֶּׁמֶשׁ[5] — with the setting of the sun.[5]

33. אֶל תּוֹכוֹ — INTO WHOSE INTERIOR. אֵין כְּלִי חֶרֶס מִטַּמֵּא — An earthenware vessel does not become impure [6] אֶלָּא מֵאֲוִירוֹ — except through its interior space.[6]

☐ כֹּל אֲשֶׁר בְּתוֹכוֹ יִטְמָא — EVERYTHING IN IT SHALL BECOME IMPURE. הַכְּלִי — The vessel חוֹזֵר — acts in turn וּמְטַמֵּא — and makes impure מַה שֶּׁבַּאֲוִירוֹ — that which is in its interior space.[7]

---

1. In Modern French, *hérisson*, which means "hedgehog" or "porcupine."
2. In Modern French, *lézard*; in English, "lizard."
3. In Old French, *limace* was used for both "snail" (in Modern French, *limaçon* or *escargot*) and "slug", a snail-like creature which has no shell (M.F., *limace*). Rashi to *Chagigah* 11a describes the *chomet* as a *limace* that grows in a shell; thus, it is the snail.
4. The mole. See note 5 to verse 18 above.
5. *Yevamos* 75a.
6. *Keilim* 2:1; *Chullin* 24b. The verse states that if the impure object enters the interior of an earthenware vessel, the vessel becomes impure. This implies that if the impure object merely comes within the inner space, without even touching the inner walls of the vessel, the vessel becomes impure. If, on the other hand, it touches the outer walls of the vessel, the vessel remains pure (*Mizrachi*; *Sifsei Chachamim*).
7. Some editions read שֶׁבְּתוֹכוֹ, "that which is within it." The meaning, however, is unchanged. The impure object within the interior space of the earthenware vessel makes the vessel impure. The vessel, in turn, makes the foods within its interior space impure even though they do not touch the vessel itself.

break it — ³⁴ *of any food that is edible, upon which water comes, shall become impure; and any liquid that can be drunk in any vessel shall*

לד וְאֹתוֹ תִשְׁבֹּרוּ: מִכָּל־הָאֹכֶל אֲשֶׁר יֵאָכֵל אֲשֶׁר יָבוֹא עָלָיו מַיִם יִטְמָא וְכָל־מַשְׁקֶה אֲשֶׁר יִשָּׁתֶה בְּכָל־כְּלִי

—————————— אונקלוס ——————————

וְיָתֵהּ תִּתְבְּרוּן: לד מִכָּל מֵיכְלָא דְּמִתְאֲכֵל דְּיֵעוֹל עֲלוֹהִי מַיָּא יְהֵי מְסָאָב וְכָל מַשְׁקֶה דִּי יִשְׁתְּתֵי בְּכָל מָאן

—————————— רש"י ——————————

ואתו תשברו. לָמַד שֶׁאֵין לוֹ טָהֳרָה בְּמִקְוֶה (ת"כ פרשתא ז:יג): **(לד) מכל האכל אשר יאכל.** מוּסָב עַל מִקְרָא הָעֶלְיוֹן, אֲשֶׁר בָּאוּ עָלָיו מַיִם, מִכָּל הָאֹכֶל אֲשֶׁר יֵאָכֵל אֲשֶׁר בָּאוּ עָלָיו מַיִם, וְהוּא בְּתוֹךְ כְּלִי חֶרֶס הַטָּמֵא, יִטְמָא. וְכֵן כָּל מַשְׁקֶה אֲשֶׁר יִשָּׁתֶה בְּכָל כְּלִי, וְהוּא בְּתוֹךְ כְּלִי חֶרֶס הַטָּמֵא. לָמַדְנוּ מִכָּאן דְּבָרִים הַרְבֵּה. לָמַדְנוּ שֶׁאֵין אֹכֶל מֻכְשָׁר וּמְתֻקָּן לְקַבֵּל טוּמְאָה עַד שִׁיָּבֹאוּ עָלָיו מַיִם פַּעַם אַחַת, וּמִשֶׁבָּאוּ עָלָיו מַיִם פַּעַם אַחַת מְקַבֵּל טוּמְאָה לְעוֹלָם, וַאֲפִילוּ נָגוּב. וְהַיַּיִן וְהַשֶּׁמֶן וְכָל הַנִּקְרָא מַשְׁקֶה מַכְשִׁיר זְרָעִים לְטוּמְאָה כַּמַּיִם, שֶׁכָּךְ יֵשׁ לִדְרוֹשׁ הַמִּקְרָא, אֲשֶׁר יָבוֹא עָלָיו מַיִם אוֹ כָּל מַשְׁקֶה אֲשֶׁר יִשָּׁתֶה בְּכָל כְּלִי, יִטְמָא הָאוֹכֶל:

—————————— RASHI ELUCIDATED ——————————

□ וְאֹתוֹ תִשְׁבֹּרוּ — AND YOU SHALL BREAK IT. לָמַד — This teaches us שֶׁאֵין לוֹ טָהֳרָה בְּמִקְוֶה — that it has no purification in a *mikveh*.[1]

34. מִכָּל הָאֹכֶל אֲשֶׁר יֵאָכֵל — OF ANY FOOD THAT IS EDIBLE. מוּסָב עַל מִקְרָא הָעֶלְיוֹן — This refers to the preceding verse as follows:[2] ״בָּל אֲשֶׁר בְּתוֹכוֹ יִטְמָא״ — "Everything in it shall become impure," ״מִכָּל הָאֹכֶל אֲשֶׁר יֵאָכֵל״ — "of any food that is edible" אֲשֶׁר בָּאוּ עָלָיו מַיִם — upon which water *has come*, i.e., fallen,[3] וְהוּא בְּתוֹךְ כְּלִי חֶרֶס הַטָּמֵא — and [the food] is *within* the impure earthenware vessel, ״יִטְמָא״ — "[the food] shall become impure." וְכֵן — And similar to water is וְהוּא בְּתוֹךְ כְּלִי חֶרֶס — ״כָּל מַשְׁקֶה אֲשֶׁר יִשָּׁתֶה בְּכָל כְּלִי״ — "any liquid that can be drunk in any vessel," הַטָּמֵא — and [the food] is within an impure earthenware vessel ״יִטְמָא״ — "[the food] shall become impure." לָמַדְנוּ מִכָּאן דְּבָרִים הַרְבֵּה — We have learned from here many things: First, לָמַדְנוּ — we have learned שֶׁאֵין אוֹכֶל מֻכְשָׁר וּמְתֻקָּן — that food does not become ready and prepared, i.e., does not become susceptible, לְקַבֵּל טֻמְאָה — to receive impurity עַד שֶׁיָּבֹאוּ עָלָיו מַיִם פַּעַם אַחַת — until water will have come upon it at some time. וּמִשֶׁבָּאוּ עָלָיו מַיִם פַּעַם אַחַת — And once water has come upon it even only one time, מְקַבֵּל טֻמְאָה לְעוֹלָם — it receives, i.e., it is susceptible to, impurity forever, וַאֲפִילוּ נָגוּב — even if it is presently dry.[4] וְהַיַּיִן — And we have learned a second rule that the wine, וְהַשֶּׁמֶן — and the oil, וְכָל הַנִּקְרָא מַשְׁקֶה — and anything called a liquid[5] מַכְשִׁיר זְרָעִים לְטֻמְאָה — prepares seeds for, i.e., renders seeds susceptible to, impurity, כַּמַּיִם — as does water. שֶׁכָּךְ יֵשׁ לִדְרוֹשׁ הַמִּקְרָא — For the verse can be expounded as follows: ״אֲשֶׁר יָבוֹא עָלָיו מַיִם״ — "upon which water comes" אוֹ ״כָּל מַשְׁקֶה אֲשֶׁר יִשָּׁתֶה בְּכָל כְּלִי״ — "or any liquid that can be drunk in any vessel" ״יִטְמָא הָאוֹכֶל״ — will make the food susceptible to becoming "impure."[6]

---

1. *Toras Kohanim, parshasa* 7:13. It does become pure, however, if it is broken, provided that it becomes unfit for its designated use. For example, if in a vessel used for food, one made a hole big enough for an olive to fall through; or, if in a vessel used for liquids, one made a hole large enough so that liquids could enter the vessel through it, the vessel becomes pure, and remains so even after the hole is repaired (*Mizrachi; Sifsei Chachamim*).

2. This verse expands on "everything in it shall become impure" of the preceding verse. It is not connected to "and you shall break it" which immediately precedes it (*Mizrachi; Sifsei Chachamim*).

3. Although יָבוֹא is in the future tense, Rashi points out that it does not mean that once food has been inside an impure vessel, *future* contact with water renders it impure even after it has left the vessel. Impurity follows the wetting, not the other way around. Impurity is transmitted to food which becomes wet while it is inside the impure vessel, or food which had been wet before it entered the vessel, as indicated by verse 38 which speaks of a situation in which water has fallen upon a seed before the seed enters the situation of potential impurity (*Mizrachi; Sifsei Chachamim*).

4. For the verse says, אֲשֶׁר יָבוֹא עָלָיו מַיִם, "upon which water comes," rather than, אֲשֶׁר יֵשׁ עָלָיו מַיִם, "upon which there *is* water" (*Gur Aryeh*; see also Rashi to v. 38 below, s.v., וְנָפַל מִנִּבְלָתָם עָלָיו).

5. There are seven liquids which are called מַשְׁקֶה: dew, water, wine, oil, blood, milk, and honey (*Machshirin* 6:4).

6. According to the understanding of the verse presented at the beginning of Rashi's comment, "and any drink" is also an elaboration of "everything in it shall become impure." But this interpretation is not satisfied with that, because it does not explain a lack of sym-

רש"י

ועוד למדו רבותינו מכאן שאין ולד הטומאה מטמא כלים. שכך שנינו, יכול יהו כל הכלים מיטמאין מאויר כלי חרס, ת"ל כל אשר בתוכו יטמא מכל האוכל, אוכל ומשקה מיטמאין מאויר כלי חרס ואין כל הכלים מיטמאין מאויר כלי חרס (ת"כ פרק ט:ח; פסחים כ.) לפי שהשרץ אב הטומאה והכלי שנטמא ממנו ולד הטומאה, לפיכך

אינו חוזר ומטמא כלים שבתוכו. ולמדנו עוד שהשרץ שנפל לאויר תנור, והפת בתוכו, ולא נגע השרץ בפת, התנור ראשון והפת שנייה. ולא נאמר רואין את התנור כאילו מלא טומאה ותהא הפת תחלה, שאם אתה אומר כן לא נתמעטו כל הכלים מלטמא מאויר כלי חרס, שהרי טומאה עצמה נגעה בהן מגבן (פסחים שם).

RASHI ELUCIDATED

שֶׁאֵין וְלַד הַטֻּמְאָה מְטַמֵּא — וְעוֹד לָמְדוּ רַבּוֹתֵינוּ מִכָּאן — **And our Rabbis also learned** a third thing **from here,** כֵּלִים — **that an offspring of impurity,** i.e., that which received its impurity from a primary source of impurity, **does not transmit impurity to implements.**[1] שֶׁכָּךְ שָׁנִינוּ — **For we have learned as follows:** יָכוֹל — **One might be able** to think יְהוּ כָּל הַכֵּלִים מִטַּמְּאִין — **that all implements should become impure** מֵאֲוִיר כְּלִי חֶרֶס — **from** being inside **the interior space of an** impure **earthenware vessel,** תַּלְמוּד לוֹמַר — To teach us otherwise, **the Torah says,** ,,כֹּל אֲשֶׁר בְּתוֹכוֹ יִטְמָא'' — **"Everything in it shall become impure...** ,,מִכָּל הָאֹכֶל'' — **of any food."** אֹכֶל וּמַשְׁקֶה — **Food and drink** מִטַּמֵּא מֵאֲוִיר כְּלִי חֶרֶס — become impure from the interior space of an impure **earthenware vessel,** וְאֵין כָּל הַכֵּלִים — but all implements do not become impure[2] מֵאֲוִיר כְּלִי חֶרֶס — **from the interior space of an earthenware vessel.**[2] לְפִי שֶׁהַשֶּׁרֶץ אַב הַטֻּמְאָה — **Because** the carcass of the **creeping animal is a father,** i.e., primary source, **of impurity,** וְהַכְּלִי שֶׁנִּטְמָא מִמֶּנּוּ — **and the** earthenware **vessel which became impure through it** וְלַד הַטֻּמְאָה — **is an offspring of the impurity,** i.e., a lesser degree of impurity, לְפִיכָךְ אֵינוֹ חוֹזֵר וּמְטַמֵּא — **therefore, it cannot in turn defile** כֵּלִים שֶׁבְּתוֹכוֹ — **vessels which are inside it.**[3] וְלָמַדְנוּ עוֹד — **And we have also learned** a fourth thing, שֶׁהַשֶּׁרֶץ — that in the case of **a creeping animal** שֶׁנָּפַל לַאֲוִיר תַּנּוּר — **[whose carcass] fell into an** earthenware **oven's interior space** וְהַפַּת בְּתוֹכוֹ — **and bread is inside** [the oven], וְלֹא נָגַע הַשֶּׁרֶץ בַּפַּת — **and the creeping animal did not touch the bread,** הַתַּנּוּר רִאשׁוֹן — **the oven is an offspring** of impurity **of the first degree,** וְהַפַּת שְׁנִיָּה — **and the bread is an offspring** of impurity **of the second degree.** וְלֹא נֹאמַר — **But we do not say** that וּתְהֵא הַפַּת תְּחִלָּה — **we view the oven as if it were full of impurity,** רוֹאִין אֶת הַתַּנּוּר כְּאִלּוּ מָלֵא טֻמְאָה — **and the bread should be an offspring of the first degree.**[4] שֶׁאִם אַתָּה אוֹמֵר כֵּן — **For if you say this,** מִלְּטַמֵּא מֵאֲוִיר כְּלִי חֶרֶס — from לֹא נִתְמַעֲטוּ כָּל הַכֵּלִים — **all implements have not been excluded** becoming impure from the interior space of an earthenware vessel, שֶׁהֲרֵי טֻמְאָה עַצְמָהּ — for a primary source of **impurity itself**[5] נָגְעָה בָּהֶן מִגַּבָּן — **has touched them on their outer surface.**[5]

---

metry between the references to food and drink in our verse. The verse begins, מִכָּל הָאֹכֶל, "of any food." But it continues, וְכָל מַשְׁקֶה, "and any liquid," rather than וּמִכָּל מַשְׁקֶה, "and of any liquid"; there is no parallel "of" for drink. This means verse 34 contains two ideas: "Of any food..." is a continuation of a phrase of the preceding verse — "Everything in it shall become impure, of any food which can be eaten upon which water shall come it shall be impure," i.e., water prepares the way for possible impurity. "Any liquid that can be drunk will cause impurity" is a second point, i.e., other drinks are like water. The ו ("and") of וְכָל מַשְׁקֶה joins it to מַיִם, "water," not to מִכָּל הָאֹכֶל, "of any food" (*Gur Aryeh*).

1. Here, the earthenware vessel is an "offspring of impurity" because its impurity was transmitted to it from the primary impurity of a carcass of one of the creeping animals enumerated in verses 29-30.

2. *Toras Kohanim, perek* 9:1; *Pesachim* 20a.

3. The earthenware vessel can itself become impure because it receives impurity from a primary source of impurity (אַב הַטֻּמְאָה), namely, the carcass of a creeping animal. Its impurity, however, is of a lesser degree, and can be transmitted only to food and drink which are

mentioned by the verse, not to other implements.

4. Rashi has mentioned in his comments to the preceding verse (see note 6 there) that an earthenware vessel becomes impure if the carcass of a creeping animal was suspended in its interior space, even if it did not touch the vessel. This might be interpreted as implying that the carcass is viewed as if it fills the entire space and touches the vessel, thereby transmitting impurity to it. Were this so, if a primary impurity is within the cavity of an oven, and there is bread in the oven, the bread would be considered an offspring of the first degree, like the oven, for the impurity is viewed as filling the space and thus "touches" the bread, too, so to speak. [An offspring of the first degree transmits impurity to any food or beverage. An offspring of the second degree transmits impurity only to *kodshim* and *terumah*.]

5. *Pesachim* 20a. Implements, even those made of materials other than earthenware and which can therefore receive impurity through their outer surface, do not become impure through contact with the interior space of an impure vessel. This holds true even when there is an impurity within that space. If the impurity were viewed as filling the space and touching the inner surfaces of

become impure. **35** *Anything upon which part of their carcass may fall shall be impure — an oven or a stove shall be smashed —*

לה וְכֹל אֲשֶׁר־יִפֹּל מִנִּבְלָתָם ׀ עָלָיו יִטְמָא תַּנּוּר וְכִירַיִם יֻתָּץ

— אונקלוס —

וְכֹל דִּי יִפֵּל מִנְבִלְתְּהוֹן עֲלוֹהִי יְהֵי מְסָאָב תַּנּוּר וְכִירַיִם יִתְּרְעוּן לה יְהֵי מְסָאָב:

— רש״י —

וְלִמַּדְנוּ עוֹד עַל בִּיאַת מַיִם בַּכְּשֶׁרֶת זְרָעִים שֶׁאֵינָהּ מַכְשֶׁרֶת אֶלָּא ח״כ נָפְלוּ עֲלֵיהֶן מִשֶּׁנִּתְלְשׁוּ (חוּלִין קי״ח:) שֶׁאִם אַתָּה אוֹמֵר מְקַבְּלִין הַכְשֵׁר בִּמְחֻבָּר, אֵין לְךָ שֶׁלֹּא בָּאוּ עָלָיו מַיִם, וּמַהוּ אוֹמֵר אֲשֶׁר יָבוֹא עָלָיו מָיִם. וְלִמַּדְנוּ עוֹד שֶׁאֵין אוֹכֶל מְטַמֵּא אֲחֵרִים אֶלָּא ח״כ יֵשׁ בּוֹ כַבֵּיצָה, שֶׁנֶּאֱמַר אֲשֶׁר יֵאָכֵל אוֹכֶל הַנֶּאֱכָל בְּבַת אַחַת; וְשִׁעֲרוּ חֲכָמִים אֵין בֵּית הַבְּלִיעָה מַחֲזִיק יוֹתֵר מִבֵּיצַת תַּרְנְגֹלֶת (יוֹמָא שם): **(לה) תַּנּוּר וְכִירַיִם.** כֵּלִים הַמְטַלְטְלִים הֵם וְיֵשׁ לָהֶן תּוֹךְ, וְשׁוֹפֵת אֶת הַקְדֵרָה עַל נֶקֶב הֶחָלָל, וּשְׁנֵיהֶם פִּיהֶם לְמַעְלָה.

— RASHI ELUCIDATED —

וְלִמַּדְנוּ עוֹד — And we have also learned a fifth thing, namely, **עַל בִּיאַת מַיִם — about** the act of **coming into contact with water,** **שֶׁאֵינָהּ מַכְשֶׁרֶת זְרָעִים — that it does not ready seeds,** or that which grows from seeds, to make them susceptible to impurity **אֶלָּא אִם כֵּן נָפְלוּ עֲלֵיהֶן — unless it fell on them מִשֶּׁנִּתְלְשׁוּ — once they are detached** from the ground.[1] **שֶׁאִם אַתָּה אוֹמֵר — For if you say** that **מְקַבְּלִין הַכְשֵׁר — they receive readying,** i.e., they are rendered susceptible, **בִּמְחֻבָּר — while they are** still **attached** to the ground, **אֵין לְךָ — you do not have,** i.e., there is no such thing as a seed **שֶׁלֹּא בָּאוּ עָלָיו מַיִם — upon which water has not come, וּמַהוּ אוֹמֵר — and what,** then, **is [the Torah] saying** in the verse, **״אֲשֶׁר יָבוֹא עָלָיו מָיִם״ — "upon which water comes"?**[2] **וְלִמַּדְנוּ עוֹד — And we have also learned** a sixth thing, **שֶׁאֵין אוֹכֶל מְטַמֵּא אֲחֵרִים — that food does not transmit impurity to other [objects] אֶלָּא אִם כֵּן יֵשׁ בּוֹ כְּבֵיצָה — unless there is in it** as much **as the** volume of **an egg, שֶׁנֶּאֱמַר — as it says,** *״אֲשֶׁר יֵאָכֵל״,*[3] **— "that is edible,"**[3] that is, the amount of **אוֹכֶל הַנֶּאֱכָל בְּבַת אַחַת — food which can be eaten** all at once. **וְשִׁעֲרוּ חֲכָמִים — And the Sages calculated** that **אֵין בֵּית הַבְּלִיעָה מַחֲזִיק — the gullet does not hold**[4] **יוֹתֵר מִבֵּיצַת תַּרְנְגֹלֶת — more than** the volume of **a hen's egg.**[4]

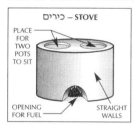

KIRAYIM — STOVE
PLACE FOR TWO POTS TO SIT
OPENING FOR FUEL
STRAIGHT WALLS

35. תַּנּוּר וְכִירַיִם — AN OVEN OR A STOVE. כֵּלִים הַמְטַלְטְלִים הֵם — They are movable appliances,[5] **וְהֵם שֶׁל חֶרֶס — and they are of earthenware, וְיֵשׁ לָהֶן תּוֹךְ — and they have a cavity. וְשׁוֹפֵת אֶת הַקְדֵרָה עַל נֶקֶב הֶחָלָל — He sets the pot on the hole of the hollow space. וּשְׁנֵיהֶם פִּיהֶם לְמַעְלָה — Both [an oven and a stove] have their openings at their top.**

TANUR — OVEN
LID
BREAD BAKING ON OVEN WALL
OPENING FOR FUEL
SLOPED WALLS

the earthenware vessel, it would be viewed as touching the exterior surface of the vessel occupying space within the earthenware vessel, as well. That inner vessel would then be an offspring of the first degree, just as the earthenware vessel is. But the vessel within the earthenware vessel does not become impure; thus the impurity within the interior space of the earthenware vessel is *not* viewed as filling that space. The fact that the carcass transmits impurity to the earthenware vessel is a law particular to earthenware vessels, namely, impurity is transmitted to them through their interior space without direct contact. Any other object in their interior can receive impurity only from the earthenware vessel. Since the earthenware vessel is only an offspring of the first degree, it cannot transmit impurity to other implements. But it does transmit impurity to food, such as bread, making that food an offspring of the second degree.

1. *Chullin* 118b. Contact with water (or any of the other liquids mentioned above) renders plants susceptible to

impurity only if that contact takes place after the plants are detached from the ground. Plants still implanted in the ground do not become susceptible to impurity by being watered.

2. The distinction between food upon which water falls and upon which water does not fall is meaningful within the realm of plant life only with regard to plants which have been detached from the ground, for all plants come into contact with water while they are growing. If the verse makes this distinction, it says that the laws of impurity apply when the distinction has significance — once the plant is detached from the ground (*Mizrachi; Sifsei Chachamim*).

3. *Toras Kohanim, perek* 9:1; *Yoma* 80a.

4. *Yoma* 80a.

5. They are not permanently attached to the ground. Were they permanently attached to the ground, they would not become impure (*Mizrachi; Sifsei Chachamim*).

לו טְמֵאִים הֵם וּטְמֵאִים יִהְיוּ לָכֶם: אַךְ מַעְיָן וּבוֹר מִקְוֵה־מַיִם יִהְיֶה טָהוֹר לז וְנֹגֵעַ בְּנִבְלָתָם יִטְמָא: וְכִי יִפֹּל מִנִּבְלָתָם עַל־כָּל־זֶרַע זֵרוּעַ אֲשֶׁר

they are impure and they shall be impure to you — ³⁶ only a spring or a pit of a gathering of water, shall be pure — but one who touches their carcass shall become impure. ³⁷ And if its carcass will fall upon any seeds of a seeding that has

---------- אונקלוס ----------

מְסָאֲבִין אִנּוּן וּמְסָאֲבִין יְהוֹן לְכוֹן: לו בְּרַם מַעְיָן וְגוֹב בֵּית כְּנִישׁוּת מַיָּא יְהֵי דְכֵי וְדִיקְרַב בִּנְבִלְתְּהוֹן יְהֵי מְסָאָב: לז וַאֲרֵי יִפֹּל מִנִּבְלַתְהוֹן עַל כָּל (בַּר) זְרַע זְרוּעַ דִּי

---------- רש"י ----------

בנבלתם יטמא. אפי' הוא בתוך מעין ובור ונוגע בנבלתם יטמא. שלא תאמר ק"ו, אם מטהר את הטמאים מטומאתם ק"ו שיציל את הטהור מליטמא, לכך נאמר ונוגע בנבלתם יטמא (ת"כ פרשתא ט:ה): **(לז) זרע זרוע.** זריעה של מיני זרעונין. זרוע שם דבר הוא כמו ויתנו לנו מן הזרועים (דניאל א:יב):

יתץ. שאין לכלי חרס טהרה בטבילה: **וטמאים יהיו לכם.** שלא תאמר מצווה אני לנתצם ת"ל וטמאים יהיו לכם אם רצה לקיימן בטומאתן רשאי (ת"כ פרק י"ז): **(לו) אך מעין ובור מקוה מים.** המחוברים לקרקע אין מקבלין טומאה. ועוד יש לך ללמוד, הטובל בהם מטומאתו: **ונוגע**

---------- RASHI ELUCIDATED ----------

□ יֻתָּץ — SHALL BE SMASHED. שֶׁאֵין לִכְלִי חֶרֶס טָהֳרָה — For an earthenware vessel has no purification בִּטְבִילָה — through immersion in a *mikveh* or spring.¹

□ וּטְמֵאִים יִהְיוּ לָכֶם — AND THEY SHALL BE IMPURE TO YOU. שֶׁלֹּא תֹאמַר — This is repeated so that you should not say, מְצֻוֶּה אֲנִי לְנָתְצָם — I am dutybound to smash them. תַּלְמוּד לוֹמַר — To teach us otherwise, the Torah says, "וּטְמֵאִים יִהְיוּ לָכֶם,, — "and they shall be impure *to you,*" implying אִם רָצָה לְקַיְּמָן — if he wishes to keep them בְּטֻמְאָתָן — while they are in their state of impurity, רַשַּׁאי — he is permitted to do so.²

36. אַךְ מַעְיָן וּבוֹר מִקְוֵה מַיִם — ONLY A SPRING OR A PIT OF A GATHERING OF WATER, הַמְחֻבָּרִים לַקַּרְקַע — which are connected to the ground, אֵין מְקַבְּלִין טֻמְאָה — cannot receive impurity. וְעוֹד יֵשׁ לְךָ — Furthermore, you can learn לִלְמוֹד — from this verse that "יִהְיֶה טָהוֹר,, — he who הַטּוֹבֵל בָּהֶם — immerses in them "shall be pure" מִטֻּמְאָתוֹ — of his impurity.³

□ וְנֹגֵעַ בְּנִבְלָתָם יִטְמָא — BUT ONE WHO TOUCHES THEIR CARCASS SHALL BECOME IMPURE. אֲפִלּוּ הוּא בְּתוֹךְ מַעְיָן — Even if he is in a spring וּבוֹר — or a pit of gathered water, וְנוֹגֵעַ בְּנִבְלָתָם — and he touches their carcass, יִטְמָא — he shall become impure.⁴ The Torah must teach us this שֶׁלֹּא תֹאמַר קַל וָחוֹמֶר — so that you should not say a *kal vachomer*⁵ to arrive at the opposite conclusion as follows: אִם — If [a spring or a pit of water] purifies those who are impure מִטֻּמְאָתָם — of their impurity, קַל וָחוֹמֶר — all the more so שֶׁיַּצִּיל אֶת הַטָּהוֹר — that it should save one who is pure מִלִּטַּמֵּא — from becoming impure. לְכָךְ נֶאֱמַר — Therefore it says, "וְנֹגֵעַ בְּנִבְלָתָם יִטְמָא,,⁶ — "but one who touches their carcass shall become impure."⁶

37. זֶרַע זֵרוּעַ — SEEDS OF A SEEDING. זְרִיעָה — A seeding שֶׁל מִינֵי זֵרְעוֹנִין — of varieties of seeds. הַזֵּרוּעִים — like "הַזֵּרוּעִים,, in "and they וַיִּתְּנוּ לָנוּ מִן הַזֵּרוּעִים,, — וְזָרוּעַ — The word זָרוּעַ is a noun,⁷ זְרוּעַ שֵׁם דָּבָר הוּא — shall give us from the seeds."⁷

---

1. See Rashi to verse 33 above and note 1 on page 125.

2. *Toras Kohanim, perek* 10:10. Impure earthenware vessels cannot be made pure while intact. When the verse says that they shall be smashed, it means smashing them to the extent that they are rendered useless, and then repairing them, is the only way that they can be purified of their impurity. However, if one wishes to keep them in their impure state and use them, he may. For though an impure vessel may not come into contact with *terumah* or that which is holy, it may be used for ordinary food.

3. The term יִהְיֶה טָהוֹר literally means, "it shall be pure." Sometimes this is interpreted as, "it shall become pure." In our verse it is used in the sense of "it shall remain pure," i.e., if the carcass falls into water connected to the

ground, the water remains pure. But the Torah expresses this through the positive expression יִהְיֶה טָהוֹר rather than the more direct negative expression לֹא יִטְמָא, "it shall not become impure," to communicate a second message, that which became impure "shall become pure" if immersed in such a body of water (*Gur Aryeh*).

4. Verse 31 has already stated that one who touches the carcass of an impure animal becomes impure. This law is repeated here to teach us that the carcass transmits impurity even to a person in a spring or a pit filled with water (*Mizrachi; Sifsei Chachamim*).

5. See note 1 on page 117 above.

6. *Toras Kohanim, parshasa* 9:5.

7. *Daniel* 1:12. זֶרַע זֵרוּעַ is not the equivalent of זֶרַע זָרוּעַ, "a

11/38-40

לח יִזָּרֵעַ טָהוֹר הוּא: וְכִי יֻתַּן־מַיִם עַל־
זֶרַע וְנָפַל מִנִּבְלָתָם עָלָיו טָמֵא הוּא
לָכֶם: לט וְכִי יָמוּת מִן־
הַבְּהֵמָה אֲשֶׁר־הִיא לָכֶם לְאָכְלָה
הַנֹּגֵעַ בְּנִבְלָתָהּ יִטְמָא עַד־הָעָרֶב:
מ וְהָאֹכֵל מִנִּבְלָתָהּ יְכַבֵּס בְּגָדָיו וְטָמֵא

been planted, it is pure. ³⁸ But if water shall have been placed upon a seed and then their carcass falls upon it, it is impure to you. ³⁹ If an animal that you may eat has died, one who comes in contact with its carcass shall become impure until evening. ⁴⁰ And one who eats from its carcass shall immerse his clothing and remain impure

---

אונקלוס

יִזְדְּרַע דְּכֵי הוּא: לח וַאֲרֵי יִתְיְהֵב מַיָּא עַל (בַּר) זַרְעָא וְיִפֵּל מִנְּבִלַתְהוֹן עֲלוֹהִי מְסָאָב הוּא לְכוֹן: לט וַאֲרֵי יְמוּת מִן בְּעִירָא דִי הִיא לְכוֹן לְמֵיכַל דְּיִקְרַב בִּנְבִלְתַהּ יְהֵי מְסָאָב עַד רַמְשָׁא: מ וּדְיֵכוּל מִנְּבִלְתַהּ יְצַבַּע לְבוּשׁוֹהִי וִיהֵי מְסָאָב

רש"י

טָהוֹר הוּא. לִמְּדָךְ הַכָּתוּב שֶׁלֹּא הוּכְשַׁר וְנִתְקַן לִקְרוֹת אֹכֶל לְקַבֵּל טֻמְאָה עַד שֶׁיָּבֹאוּ עָלָיו מַיִם: **(לח) וְכִי יֻתַּן מַיִם עַל זֶרַע.** לְאַחַר שֶׁנִּתְלַשׁ (חולין קיח:) שֶׁאִם תֹּאמַר יֵשׁ הֶכְשֵׁר בִּמְחֻבָּר אֵין לְךָ זֶרַע שֶׁלֹּא הוּכְשַׁר: **מַיִם עַל זֶרַע.** בֵּין מַיִם בֵּין שְׁאָר מַשְׁקִין בֵּין הֵם עַל הַזֶּרַע בֵּין הַזֶּרַע נָפַל לְתוֹכָן הַכֹּל נִדְרָשׁ בְּתוֹרַת

כֹּהֲנִים (פֶּרֶק יא:ט,יא): **וְנָפַל מִנִּבְלָתָם עָלָיו.** אַף מִשֶּׁנָּגַב מִן הַמַּיִם (ב"מ כב:-כג.) שֶׁלֹּא הִקְפִּידָה תּוֹרָה אֶלָּא לִהְיוֹת עָלָיו שֵׁם אֹכֶל, וּמִשֶּׁיָּרַד לוֹ הֶכְשֵׁר קַבָּלַת טֻמְאָה פַּעַם אַחַת שׁוּב אֵינוֹ נֶעְקָר הֵימֶנּוּ: **(לט) בְּנִבְלָתָהּ.** וְלֹא בַעֲצָמוֹת וְגִידִים וְלֹא בְקַרְנַיִם וּטְלָפַיִם וְלֹא בָעוֹר (ת"כ פרשתא י:ה; חולין קיז:):

RASHI ELUCIDATED

☐ טָהוֹר הוּא — IT IS PURE. לִמְּדָךְ הַכָּתוּב — Scripture teaches you שֶׁלֹּא הֻכְשַׁר וְנִתְקַן — that it is not readied and prepared לִקְרוֹת אֹכֶל — to be termed a food with regard to being susceptible לְקַבֵּל טֻמְאָה — to receive impurity עַד שֶׁיָּבֹאוּ עָלָיו מַיִם — until water has come upon it.[1]

38. וְכִי יֻתַּן מַיִם עַל זֶרַע — BUT IF WATER SHALL HAVE BEEN PLACED UPON A SEED לְאַחַר שֶׁנִּתְלַשׁ — after it had been uprooted.[2] שֶׁאִם תֹּאמַר — For if you will say יֵשׁ הֶכְשֵׁר — there can be readying to receive impurity בִּמְחֻבָּר — while a seed or that which grows from it is still connected to the ground, אֵין לְךָ — you do not have, i.e., there is no such thing as, זֶרַע שֶׁלֹּא הֻכְשַׁר — a seed that has not been readied.[3]

☐ מַיִם עַל זֶרַע — WATER [SHALL HAVE BEEN PLACED] UPON A SEED. בֵּין מַיִם — The same law applies whether it is water בֵּין שְׁאָר מַשְׁקִין — or whether it is another liquid,[4] בֵּין הֵם עַל הַזֶּרַע — whether [the liquids] are on the seed בֵּין זֶרַע נוֹפֵל לְתוֹכָן — or whether the seed falls into [the liquids]. הַכֹּל נִדְרָשׁ בְּתוֹרַת כֹּהֲנִים — All this is derived from the verse in *Toras Kohanim*.[5]

☐ וְנָפַל מִנִּבְלָתָם עָלָיו — AND THEN THEIR CARCASS FALLS UPON IT. אַף מִשֶּׁנָּגַב — Even once it, i.e., the food, has become dry מִן הַמַּיִם — of the water.[6] שֶׁלֹּא הִקְפִּידָה תּוֹרָה אֶלָּא לִהְיוֹת עָלָיו — For the Torah was only concerned that there be on [the object receiving impurity] שֵׁם אֹכֶל — the title "food," i.e., that it be called food. וּמִשֶּׁיָּרַד לוֹ הֶכְשֵׁר קַבָּלַת טֻמְאָה — And once readying to receive impurity has descended upon it by its coming into contact with water and becoming "food" פַּעַם אַחַת — one time, שׁוּב אֵינוֹ נֶעְקָר הֵימֶנּוּ — it is never taken away from it afterwards.[7]

39. בְּנִבְלָתָהּ — [WHO COMES IN CONTACT] WITH ITS CARCASS, i.e., who touches its meat, וְלֹא בַעֲצָמוֹת וְגִידִין — but not its bones or sinews, וְלֹא בְּקַרְנַיִם וּטְלָפַיִם — and not its horns or hooves, וְלֹא בָעוֹר[8] — and not its hide.[8]

---

planted seed." [In this Rashi disagrees with *Ibn Ezra's* first interpretation in which he regards זֵרוּעַ and זֶרַע as identical.] זֶרַע is a noun (זֵרוּעַ is a passive participle used as an adjective), and זֶרַע is in the construct form. The phrase means "seeds of a seeding" (*Be'er Yitzchak*).

1. The next verse states that the seed can become impure once water has come upon it. This verse, which says that the seeds remain pure, must refer to a case where water has not come upon it.

2. *Chullin* 118b.

3. See note 2 on page 127.

4. See note 5 on page 125.

5. *Toras Kohanim, perek* 11:6,9.

6. *Bava Metzia* 22a,b.

7. See the first of Rashi's six points in his commentary to verse 34 above.

8. *Toras Kohanim, parshasa* 10:5; *Chullin* 117b. "Carcass" denotes only the meat. However, if the parts mentioned by Rashi are still connected to the meat of the carcass, they *do* transmit impurity (*Mizrachi*; *Sifsei Chachamim*). See Rashi to verse 8 above for a similar interpretation of מִבְּשָׂרָם.

עַד־הָעֶרֶב וְהַנֹּשֵׂא אֶת־נִבְלָתָהּ
יְכַבֵּס בְּגָדָיו וְטָמֵא עַד־הָעָרֶב: מא וְכָל־
הַשֶּׁרֶץ הַשֹּׁרֵץ עַל־הָאָרֶץ שֶׁקֶץ הוּא

until evening; and one who carries its carcass must immerse his clothing and remain impure until evening.
41 Every creeping creature that creeps upon the ground — it is an abomination,

— אונקלוס —

עַד רַמְשָׁא וְדִיטוֹל יָת נְבֶלְתָּהּ יְצַבַּע לְבוּשׁוֹהִי וִיהֵי מְסָאָב עַד רַמְשָׁא: מא וְכָל רִחֲשָׁא דְרָחֵשׁ עַל אַרְעָא שִׁקְצָא הוּא

— רש"י —

(מ) **והנושא את נבלתה.** חמורה טומאת משא מטומאת מגע, שהנושא מטמא בגדים והנוגע אין בגדיו טמאין, שלא נאמר בו יכבס בגדיו: **והאוכל מנבלתה.** יכול תטמאנו אכילתו, כשהוא או' בנבלת עוף טהור נבלה וטרפה לא יאכל לטמאה בה (להלן כב:ח) בה, אותה מטמאתו בגדים באכילתה ואין נבלת בהמה מטמאתו בגדים באכילתה בלא משא, כגון אם תחבה לו

חבירו בבית הבליעה. ח"כ מה ת"ל האוכל, ליתן שיעור לנושא ולנוגע כדי אכילה, והוא כזית (ת"כ שם ז; נדה מב:): **וטמא עד הערב.** אע"פ שטבל צריך הערב שמש: **(מא) השרץ על הארץ.** להוציא את היתושין שבכליסין ושבפולין ושבעדשים (ת"כ פרק יב:ח; חולין סז:) שהרי לא שרצו על הארץ אלא בתוך האוכל, אבל משיצאו לאויר ושרצו הרי נאסרו.

—— RASHI ELUCIDATED ——

40. וְהַנֹּשֵׂא אֶת נִבְלָתָהּ — AND ONE WHO CARRIES ITS CARCASS. — חֲמוּרָה טֻמְאַת מַשָּׂא מִטֻּמְאַת מַגָּע — The impurity brought about through **carrying is more severe than the impurity** brought about through **touching,** שֶׁהַנּוֹשֵׂא — for he who carries — מְטַמֵּא בְגָדִים — makes his garments impure, וְהַנּוֹגֵעַ — but he who touches, אֵין בְּגָדָיו טְמֵאִין — his garments do not become impure, שֶׁלֹּא נֶאֱמַר בּוֹ — for of him it is not said, "יְכַבֵּס בְּגָדָיו" — "he must immerse his clothing."[1]

□ וְהָאֹכֵל מִנִּבְלָתָהּ — AND ONE WHO EATS FROM ITS CARCASS. — יָכוֹל — One might be able to think on the basis of this verse תְּטַמְּאֶנּוּ אֲכִילָתוֹ — that his eating of [the unslaughtered carcass of a pure animal] would make him impure.[2] But this can be refuted as follows: כְּשֶׁהוּא אוֹמֵר — When it says בְּנִבְלַת עוֹף טָהוֹר — about the unslaughtered carcass of a pure bird, "נְבֵלָה וּטְרֵפָה לֹא יֹאכַל לְטָמְאָה בָהּ"[3] — "A carcass or a mauled animal he shall not eat to become defiled through it," — "בָּהּ" — "through it" implies that אוֹתָהּ מְטַמְּאָה בְגָדִים בַּאֲכִילָתָהּ — it makes garments impure through its being eaten, וְאֵין נִבְלַת בְּהֵמָה מְטַמְּאָה בְגָדִים — but the unslaughtered carcass of an animal does not make garments impure, nor does it make the one who ate it impure, בַּאֲכִילָתָהּ — through its being eaten בְּלֹא מַשָּׂא — without carrying it. כְּגוֹן — For example, אִם תְּחָבָה לוֹ חֲבֵרוֹ בְּבֵית הַבְּלִיעָה — if his friend stuck food into his gullet.[4] אִם כֵּן — If so, מַה תַּלְמוּד לוֹמַר — why does the Torah say, "הָאֹכֵל" — "one who eats"? לִתֵּן שִׁעוּר — To set a minimum measure לַנּוֹשֵׂא — for one who carries וְלַנּוֹגֵעַ — and one who touches as being כְּדֵי אֲכִילָה — the amount of an eating,[5] וְהוּא כְזַיִת — and this is comparable to the volume of an olive.[5]

□ וְטָמֵא עַד הָעָרֶב — AND REMAIN IMPURE UNTIL EVENING. — אַף עַל פִּי שֶׁטָּבַל — Although he immersed himself in a spring or *mikveh*, צָרִיךְ הַעֲרֵב שֶׁמֶשׁ — he requires the setting of the sun after his immersion before he becomes pure.[6]

41. הַשֶּׁרֶץ עַל הָאָרֶץ — THAT CREEPS UPON THE GROUND. — לְהוֹצִיא אֶת הַיַּתּוּשִׁין — To exclude the bugs שֶׁבַּעֲדָשִׁים — that are in lentils,[7] וְשֶׁבַּפּוֹלִין — that are in pods — וְשֶׁבַּכְּלִיסִין — and in beans, וְאֶת הַזִּיזִין — and the mites[7] — עַל הָאָרֶץ — on the ground, שֶׁהֲרֵי לֹא שָׁרְצוּ — for see, now, that they have not crept עַל הָאָרֶץ — on the ground, אֶלָּא בְּתוֹךְ הָאוֹכֶל — but rather, inside the food.[8] אֲבָל מִשֶּׁיָּצְאוּ — But once they have emerged לָאֲוִיר — into the air, i.e., out of the food, וְשָׁרְצוּ — and have crept, הֲרֵי נֶאֶסְרוּ — see, now, that they have become forbidden.

---

1. See Rashi to v. 25 above, and note 4 there.
2. Even in a situation where no touching or carrying is involved, as Rashi will explain.
3. Below 22:8.
4. Contact with unseen parts of the body is considered neither carrying nor touching.
5. *Toras Kohanim, parshasa* 10:7; *Niddah* 42b. Impurity is transmitted by the flesh of a carcass only if the flesh has the volume of an olive, the standard volume wherever the Torah speaks of eating.
6. See note 7 to 12:4 above regarding to *t'vul yom*.
7. *Toras Kohanim, perek* 12:1; *Chullin* 67b.
8. Rashi is speaking of a situation in which the bug first begins moving when the plant it is in has been detached from the ground. Then, as long as the bug is in the fruit it is considered part of the fruit, and is

it shall not be eaten. **⁴²** *All that goes on its belly, and all that walks on four legs, up to those with numerous legs, of every creeping creature that creeps upon the ground, you may not eat them, for they are an abomination.* **⁴³** *Do not make your souls abominable by means of any*

מב לֹא יֵאָכֵל: כֹּל הוֹלֵךְ עַל־גָּחוֹן וְכֹל
ו׳ רבתי הוֹלֵךְ עַל־אַרְבַּע עַד כָּל־מַרְבֵּה
רַגְלַיִם לְכָל־הַשֶּׁרֶץ הַשֹּׁרֵץ עַל־
הָאָרֶץ לֹא תֹאכְלוּם כִּי־שֶׁקֶץ הֵם:
מג אַל־תְּשַׁקְּצוּ אֶת־נַפְשֹׁתֵיכֶם בְּכָל

---- אונקלוס ----

לָא יִתְאֲכֵל: מב כֹּל דִּמְהַלֵּךְ עַל מְעוֹהִי וְכֹל דִּמְהַלֵּךְ עַל אַרְבַּע עַד כָּל סַגִּיאוּת רַגְלַיִן לְכָל
רַחֲשָׁא דְּרָחֵשׁ עַל אַרְעָא לָא תֵיכְלֻנּוּן אֲרֵי שִׁקְצָא אִנּוּן: מג לָא תְשַׁקְּצוּן יָת נַפְשָׁתְכוֹן בְּכָל

---- רש״י ----

לֹא יֵאָכֵל. לְחַיֵּב עַל הַמַּאֲכִיל כָּאוֹכֵל (ת״כ שם) וְאֵין קָרוּי שֶׁרֶץ אֶלָּא דָּבָר נָמוּךְ קְצַר רַגְלַיִם שֶׁאֵינוֹ נִרְאֶה אֶלָּא כְּרוֹחֵשׁ וְנָד: **(מב) הוֹלֵךְ עַל גָּחוֹן.** זֶה נָחָשׁ (ת״כ שם ב; חולין סז:) וּלְשׁוֹן גָּחוֹן שְׁחִיָּה שֶׁהוֹלֵךְ שַׁח וְנוֹפֵל [שם״א] עַל מֵעָיו: **כֹּל הוֹלֵךְ.** לְהָבִיא הַשִּׁלְשׁוּלִין וְאֶת הדומה לדומה (שם): **בֹּל. זה עקרב: הוֹלֵךְ עַל אַרְבַּע.** זה עקרב: **מַרְבֵּה** **רַגְלַיִם.** זה נדל (שם), שרץ שיש לו רגלים מראשו ועד זנבו לכאן ולכאן וקורין לינטפי״י ד: **(מג) אַל תְּשַׁקְּצוּ.** בַּאֲכִילָתָן שהרי כתיב הדומה לדומה (שם): **בַּל.** להביא את החפושית אשקרבו״ט בלע״ז ואת הדומה לדומה (שם): **מַרְבֵּה**

---- RASHI ELUCIDATED ----

□ **לֹא יֵאָכֵל — IT SHALL NOT BE EATEN.** לְחַיֵּב עַל הַמַּאֲכִיל — **To make one who feeds them to others culpable**[1] כָּאוֹכֵל — **like one who eats them.**[1]

וְאֵין קָרוּי שֶׁרֶץ — **There is nothing termed "a creeping thing"** אֶלָּא דָּבָר נָמוּךְ — **except for a low-lying thing** קְצַר רַגְלַיִם — **with short legs** שֶׁאֵינוֹ נִרְאֶה אֶלָּא כְּרוֹחֵשׁ וְנָד — **which looks only as if it slithers and moves.**[2]

42. הוֹלֵךְ עַל גָּחוֹן — **THAT GOES ON ITS BELLY.** זֶה נָחָשׁ[3] — **This is a snake.**[3] וּלְשׁוֹן גָּחוֹן — **The term** גָּחוֹן means שְׁחִיָּה — **bending low,** שֶׁהוֹלֵךְ שַׁח — **for it goes bent low,** וְנוֹפֵל עַל מֵעָיו — **and falling**[4] **on its stomach.**

□ **כֹּל הוֹלֵךְ — ALL THAT GOES.** לְהָבִיא הַשִּׁלְשׁוּלִין — **To include the worms,**[5] וְאֶת הַדּוֹמֶה לַדּוֹמֶה — **and that which is similar to that which is similar.**[5]

□ הוֹלֵךְ עַל אַרְבַּע — **THAT WALKS ON FOUR LEGS.** זֶה עַקְרָב — **This is a scorpion.**

□ **כֹּל — EVERYTHING.** לְהָבִיא אֶת הַחֲפוּשִׁית — **To include the beetle,** אשקרבו״ט בלע״ז — *escharbot* **in Old French,**[6] וְאֶת הַדּוֹמֶה לַדּוֹמֶה — **and that which is similar to that which is similar.**[7]

□ **מַרְבֵּה רַגְלַיִם — THOSE WITH NUMEROUS LEGS.** זֶה נַדָּל[3] — **This is a centipede,**[3] שֶׁרֶץ — **a creeping thing** שֶׁיֵּשׁ לוֹ רַגְלַיִם — **that has legs** מֵרֹאשׁוֹ וְעַד זְנָבוֹ — **from its head to its tail** לְכָאן וּלְכָאן — **on both sides** of its body. וְקוֹרִין צינטפיי״ד — **They call it** *centpied*.[8]

43. אַל תְּשַׁקְּצוּ — **DO NOT MAKE [YOUR SOULS] ABOMINABLE** בַּאֲכִילָתָן — **by eating them.** שֶׁהֲרֵי כְּתִיב

---

not forbidden until it has crept outside the fruit. But as long as the fruit is still attached to the ground it has the status of the ground itself; once a bug begins moving inside such fruit, the bug is no longer considered as part of the fruit and it is forbidden (*Maskil LeDavid*).

1. *Toras Kohanim, perek* 12:1. This is implied by the verse's use of the passive verb rather than the active "you shall not eat them" (*Gur Aryeh*). There is a dispute among the commentators as to whether Rashi and the *Toras Kohanim*, which is apparently his source, refer to feeding other adult Jews or feeding minors. See *Korban Aharon*; *Maskil LeDavid*; *Malbim*.

2. Although it walks, the shortness of its legs makes it appear as if it is slithering.

3. *Toras Kohanim, perek* 12:2; *Chullin* 67b.

4. Some editions read וְנָפוֹל, "and fallen."

5. *Toras Kohanim, perek* 12:2; *Chullin* 67b. "That goes on its belly" means specifically a snake. *All* includes worms, which are similar to a snake in that they have no legs and move by slithering, and "that which is similar to that which is similar," i.e., wormlike creatures with poorly developed legs that appear to slither (*Mizrachi*; *Be'er Yitzchak*).

6. In Modern French, *scarabée* or *escarbot;* in English, "scarab," a type of beetle.

7. *Toras Kohanim, perek* 12:2; *Chullin* 67b. There are creatures with greater and lesser similarity to scorpions just as there are in the case of snakes (*Mizrachi*; *Be'er Yitzchak*).

8. Literally, "a hundred feet." In Modern French, *scolopendre;* in English, "centipede."

הַשֶּׁרֶץ וְלֹא תִטַּמְּאוּ בָּהֶם
וְנִטְמֵתֶם בָּם: כִּי אֲנִי יהוה אֱלֹהֵיכֶם מד
וְהִתְקַדִּשְׁתֶּם וִהְיִיתֶם קְדֹשִׁים כִּי
קָדוֹשׁ אָנִי וְלֹא תְטַמְּאוּ אֶת־
נַפְשֹׁתֵיכֶם בְּכָל־הַשֶּׁרֶץ הָרֹמֵשׂ
עַל־הָאָרֶץ: מפטיר כִּי ׀ אֲנִי מה

creeping thing; and you shall not make yourselves impure through them lest you make yourselves impure through them. **44** For I am Hashem your God — you are to sanctify yourselves and you shall become holy, for I am holy; and you shall not make your souls impure through any creeping thing that creeps on the earth. **45** For I am

---

— אונקלוס —

רִחֲשָׁא דְּרָחֵשׁ וְלָא תְסָאֲבוּן בְּהוֹן וְתִסְתָּאֲבוּן פּוֹן בְּהוֹן: מד אֲרֵי אֲנָא יְיָ אֱלָהֲכוֹן וְתִתְקַדְּשׁוּן וּתְהוֹן
קַדִּישִׁין אֲרֵי קַדִּישׁ אֲנָא וְלָא תְסָאֲבוּן יָת נַפְשָׁתֵיכוֹן בְּכָל רִחֲשָׁא דְּרָחֵשׁ עַל אַרְעָא: מה אֲרֵי אֲנָא

— רש"י —

נפשותיכם ואין שיקוץ נפש במגע, וכן ולא תטמאו באכילתן. וְהִתְקַדִּשְׁתֶּם. קַדֵּשׁוּ עַצְמְכֶם לְמַטָּה (ת"כ פרק יב:ג): וִהְיִיתֶם
וְנִטְמֵתֶם בָּם. אִם אַתֶּם מִטַּמְּאִין בָּהֶם בָּאָרֶץ אַף אֲנִי מְטַמֵּא קְדֹשִׁים. לְפִי שֶׁאֲנִי אֲקַדֵּשׁ אֶתְכֶם לְמַעְלָה וְלָעוֹלָם הַבָּא (יומא
אֶתְכֶם בָּעוֹלָם הַבָּא וּבִישִׁיבָה שֶׁל מַעְלָה (יומא לט.): (מד) כִּי שם): וְלֹא תְטַמְּאוּ וְגוֹ'. לַעֲבוֹר עֲלֵיהֶם בְּלָאוִין הַרְבֵּה, וְכָל
אֲנִי ה' אֱלֹהֵיכֶם. כְּשֵׁם שֶׁאֲנִי קָדוֹשׁ שֶׁאֲנִי ה' אֱלֹהֵיכֶם כָּךְ לָאו מַלְקוּת, וְזֶהוּ שֶׁאָמְרוּ בַּתַּלְמוּד אָכַל פּוּטִיתָא לוֹקֶה אַרְבַּע

RASHI ELUCIDATED

— **For you can see that it is written,** ''נַפְשֹׁתֵיכֶם,'' — **''your souls,''** וְאֵין שִׁקּוּץ נֶפֶשׁ בְּמַגָּע — **and there is no abomination of the soul by touching.**[1] וְכֵן, ''וְלֹא תְטַמְּאוּ'' — Similarly, **''and you shall not make yourselves impure''** means בַּאֲכִילָתָם — **by eating them.**[2]

☐ וְנִטְמֵתֶם בָּם — LEST YOU MAKE YOURSELVES IMPURE THROUGH THEM. אִם אַתֶּם מִטַּמְּאִין בָּהֶם — **If you make yourselves impure through them** בָּאָרֶץ — **on earth,** אַף אֲנִי מְטַמֵּא אֶתְכֶם — **I, too, will make you impure** בָּעוֹלָם הַבָּא — **in the World to Come**[3] וּבִישִׁיבַת מַעְלָה — **and in the Heavenly convocation.**[3]

44. כִּי אֲנִי ה' אֱלֹהֵיכֶם — FOR I AM HASHEM YOUR GOD. כְּשֵׁם שֶׁאֲנִי קָדוֹשׁ — **Just as I am holy,** שֶׁאֲנִי ה' — אֱלֹהֵיכֶם — **for I am Hashem, your God,** כָּךְ, ''וְהִתְקַדִּשְׁתֶּם'' — **likewise, ''you are to sanctify yourselves,''** i.e., קַדְּשׁוּ עַצְמְכֶם — **sanctify yourselves** לְמַטָּה — **below,** i.e., on earth;[4]

☐ וִהְיִיתֶם קְדֹשִׁים — AND YOU SHALL BECOME HOLY, לְפִי[5] שֶׁאֲנִי אֲקַדֵּשׁ אֶתְכֶם — **because I will sanctify you** לְמַעְלָה — **above,** i.e., in Heaven, וּבָעוֹלָם הַבָּא[6] — **and in the World to Come.**[6]

☐ וְלֹא תְטַמְּאוּ וְגוֹמֵר — AND YOU SHALL NOT MAKE [YOUR SOULS] IMPURE, ETC. לַעֲבוֹר עֲלֵיהֶם בְּלָאוִין הַרְבֵּה — **To transgress many negative commandments over them,** וְכָל לָאו — **and each negative commandment** entails מַלְקוּת — **lashes.**[7] וְזֶהוּ שֶׁאָמְרוּ בַּתַּלְמוּד — **This is the basis for what they said in the Talmud,** אָכַל פּוּטִיתָא — **if he ate a** *putisa*, a small aquatic animal, לוֹקֶה אַרְבַּע — **he receives**

---

1. "Abomination of the soul" connotes repugnance. Eating creeping things brings repugnance to the soul, for the life force transmitted to the body through eating forbidden things makes one prone to sin. Any repugnance in touching does not affect the soul (see *Mizrachi*).

2. The phrase וְלֹא תִטַּמְּאוּ בָּהֶם, "and you shall not make yourselves impure through them," of our verse also refers to eating, for the verb טמא, "becoming impure," followed by the prefix ב indicates the impurity of the soul which comes about through eating forbidden things. Impurity of the body is indicated when טמא is followed by the prefix ל (*HaKesav VeHaKabbalah*).

3. *Yoma* 39a. Rashi explains the apparent redundancy of "Do not make yourselves impure through them, lest you become impure through them" (*Devek Tov*).

4. *Toras Kohanim*, *perek* 12:3. Rashi explains the connection between "I am Hashem, your God" and "you are to sanctify yourselves." Because I, Hashem, your God, am holy, you should strive to emulate Me (*Mizrachi*).

5. The first printed edition and some manuscripts read לְפָנַי instead of לְפִי. The meaning is then: "And you shall become holy *before Me*, because..."

6. *Yoma* 39a. The apparent redundancy of "you are to sanctify yourselves and you will become holy" is interpreted to parallel the apparent redundancy concerning impurity in the preceding verse (*Be'er Yitzchak*; see Rashi to the preceding verse and note 3 there).

7. Several negative commandments have already been stated with regard to eating creeping things. This additional negative commandment was given to make the eating of creeping things the violation of an additional commandment, thus making the transgressor liable to additional lashes.

HASHEM *Who brings you up from the land of Egypt to be a God unto you; you shall be holy, for I am holy.* ⁴⁶ *This is the law of the animal, the bird, every living creature that swarms in the water, and for every creature that creeps on the ground;* ⁴⁷ *For distinguishing between*

יְהוָֹה הַמַּעֲלֶה אֶתְכֶם מֵאֶרֶץ מִצְרַיִם לִהְיֹת לָכֶם לֵאלֹהִים וִהְיִיתֶם קְדֹשִׁים כִּי קָדוֹשׁ אָנִי: מו זֹאת תּוֹרַת הַבְּהֵמָה וְהָעוֹף וְכֹל נֶפֶשׁ הַחַיָּה הָרֹמֶשֶׂת בַּמָּיִם וּלְכָל־נֶפֶשׁ הַשֹּׁרֶצֶת עַל־הָאָרֶץ: מז לְהַבְדִּיל בֵּין

---אונקלוס---

יְיָ דְּאַסֵּק יָתְכוֹן מֵאַרְעָא דְמִצְרָיִם לְמֶהֱוֵי לְכוֹן לֶאֱלָהּ וּתְהוֹן קַדִּישִׁין אֲרֵי קַדִּישׁ אֲנָא: מו דָּא אוֹרַיְתָא דִּבְעִירָא וּדְעוֹפָא וְכָל נַפְשָׁתָא חַיְתָא דְרָחֲשָׁא בְּמַיָּא וּלְכָל נְפַשׁ דְּרָחֲשָׁא עַל אַרְעָא: מז לְאַפְרָשָׁא בֵּין

---רש"י---

נְמָלָה לוֹקֶה חָמֵשׁ לְרַעַת לוֹקֶה שָׁם (מכות טז.; פסחים כד.): (מה) **כִּי אֲנִי ה' הַמַּעֲלֶה אֶתְכֶם.** עַל מְנָת שֶׁתְּקַבְּלוּ מִצְוֹתַי מַעֲלֶה אֶתְכֶם (ת"כ שם ד) [ד"א כי אני ה' הַמַּעֲלֶה אֶתְכֶם. בְּכוּלָן כְּתִיב וְהוֹצֵאתִי, וְכָאן כְּתִיב הַמַּעֲלֶה. תָּנָא דְבֵי רַבִּי יִשְׁמָעֵאל אִלְמָלֵי לֹא הֶעֱלֵיתִי אֶת יִשְׂרָאֵל מִמִּצְרַיִם אֶלָּא בִּשְׁבִיל שֶׁאֵין מְטַמְּאִין בִּשְׁרָצִים כִּשְׁאָר אֻמּוֹת [ס"א כְּמוֹ מִצְרִים וּכְנַעֲנִים] דַּיִּי, וּמַעֲלִיּוּתָא הִיא לְגַבַּיְיהוּ זֶהוּ לְשׁוֹן מַעֲלֶה (ב"מ סאּ:)]: (מז) **לְהַבְדִּיל.** לֹא בִּלְבַד הַשּׁוֹנֶה אֶלָּא שֶׁיְּהֵא יוֹדֵעַ וּמַכִּיר וּבָקִי בָּהֶן (ת"כ שם ו):

---RASHI ELUCIDATED---

four sets of lashes.[1] **נְמָלָה** – If he ate an **ant, לוֹקֶה חָמֵשׁ** – **he receives five sets of lashes.**[2] **צִרְעָה** – If he ate a **wasp,** **לוֹקֶה שֵׁשׁ** – **he receives six sets of lashes.**[3,4]

45. **עַל מְנָת** – On the condition **כִּי אֲנִי ה' הַמַּעֲלֶה אֶתְכֶם** – FOR I AM HASHEM WHO BRINGS YOU UP. **הֶעֱלֵיתִי אֶתְכֶם** – I brought you up[5] **שֶׁתְּקַבְּלוּ מִצְוֹתַי** – that you accept my commandments.

{**דָּבָר אַחֵר** – An alternative explanation: **"כִּי אֲנִי ה' הַמַּעֲלֶה אֶתְכֶם,"** – "For I am HASHEM who brings you up." **בְּכוּלָן** – In all verses that refer to God taking Israel out of Egypt **כְּתִיב** – it is written, **"הוֹצֵאתִי,"** – "I brought you *out*," **וְכָאן כְּתִיב** – but here it is written, **"הַמַּעֲלֶה,"** – "Who brings you *up*." **תָּנָא דְבֵי רַ' יִשְׁמָעֵאל** – To explain the unique wording of our verse, it was taught in the House of R' Yishmael that the verse means to say, **אִלְמָלֵי לֹא הֶעֱלֵיתִי אֶת יִשְׂרָאֵל מִמִּצְרַיִם** – had I not brought Israel out of Egypt **אֶלָּא בִּשְׁבִיל שֶׁאֵין מְטַמְּאִין בִּשְׁרָצִים** – for any reason other than that they do not make themselves impure through creeping things **כִּשְׁאָר אֻמּוֹת** – as do the other nations,[6] **דַּיִּי** – it would have been sufficient cause for them to have been redeemed, **וּמַעֲלִיּוּתָא הִיא לְגַבַּיְיהוּ** – and [abstaining from creeping things] is an elevation for them. **זֶהוּ לְשׁוֹן מַעֲלֶה** – This is why the Torah here uses the expression "brings up."[7]}

47. לְהַבְדִּיל – FOR DISTINGUISHING. **לֹא בִּלְבַד הַשּׁוֹנֶה** – The verse refers **not merely to one who can repeat,** i.e., one who has committed the laws to memory, **אֶלָּא שֶׁיְּהֵא יוֹדֵעַ** – but that he should know, **וּמַכִּיר** – and recognize, **וּבָקִי בָּהֶן**[8] – and be expert in them.[8]

---

1. There are four negative commandments that apply to eating creeping things that live in water. Verse 11 of this chapter and *Deuteronomy* 14:10 apply specifically to such creatures. Verse 43 of this chapter contains two negative commandments that apply to all creeping things, including those that live in water (see Rashi to *Pesachim* 24a-b).

2. There are five negative commandments that apply to things that creep on the ground. The commandments of verses 41, 42, and 44 of this chapter apply specifically to those creatures, and the two general statements of verse 43 apply to them as well (see Rashi to *Pesachim* 24a-b).

3. There are six negative commandments that apply to creeping things that fly. The five that apply to things that creep on the ground also apply to creeping things that fly, for they, too, creep on the ground. In addition, the negative commandment of *Deuteronomy* 14:19 applies to them specifically (see Rashi to *Pesachim* 24a-b).

4. *Makkos* 16a; *Pesachim* 24a.

5. *Toras Kohanim, perek* 12:4.

6. Some editions read כְּמוֹ מִצְרִים וּכְנַעֲנִים, "as do Egyptians and Canaanites."

7. *Bava Metzia* 61b. According to the first explanation given by Rashi, the verse gives a reason for keeping the commandments in general, and does not distinguish between "bring up" and "bring out." According to the second explanation, the verse refers specifically to the prohibition against eating creeping things, and puts the emphasis on "bringing up" as distinct from "bringing out" (*Lifshuto shel Rashi*).

8. *Toras Kohanim, perek* 12:6.

134 / ויקרא – פרשת שמיני

הַטָּמֵא וּבֵין הַטָּהֹר וּבֵין הַחַיָּה הַנֶּאֱכֶלֶת וּבֵין הַחַיָּה אֲשֶׁר לֹא תֵאָכֵל: פ פ פ

the impure and the pure, and between the creature that may be eaten and the creature that may not be eaten.

THE HAFTARAH FOR PARASHAS SHEMINI APPEARS ON PAGE 392.
When Erev Rosh Chodesh Iyar coincides with Shemini, the regular Haftarah is replaced with the Haftarah for Shabbas Erev Rosh Chodesh, page 405.
When Parashas Parah coincides with Shemini, the regular Maftir and Haftarah readings are replaced with the readings for Parashas Parah, page 409.

― אונקלוס ―
מְסָאֲבָא וּבֵין דַּכְיָא וּבֵין חַיְתָא דְּמִתְאַכְלָא וּבֵין חַיְתָא דִּי לָא מִתְאַכְלָא:

― רש״י ―
בין הטמא ובין הטהור. צריך לומר בין חמור לפרה, והלא כבר מפורשים הם. אלא בין טמאה לך לטהורה לך, בין נשחט חציו של קנה לנשחט רובו (שם ז): **ובין החיה הנאכלת.** צריך לומר בין צבי לערוד, והלא כבר מפורשים הם. אלא בין שנולדו בה סימני טרפה כשרה לנולדו בה סימני טרפה פסולה (שם ח):

― RASHI ELUCIDATED ―

□ **בֵּין הַטָּמֵא וּבֵין הַטָּהֹר** — BETWEEN THE IMPURE AND THE PURE. **צָרִיךְ לוֹמַר** — Does it need to say that one must be able to distinguish **בֵּין חֲמוֹר לְפָרָה** — between a donkey and a cow? **וַהֲלֹא כְּבָר מְפֹרָשִׁים הֵם** — Are they not already explicit?[1] **אֶלָּא** — Rather, the Torah demands that you be expert in distinguishing **בֵּין טְמֵאָה לְךָ** — between that which is impure *to you,* **לִטְהוֹרָה לְךָ** — and that which is pure *to you*;[2] that is, **בֵּין נִשְׁחַט חֶצְיוֹ שֶׁל קָנֶה** — between one which has half of its windpipe slaughtered, i.e., severed by slaughtering, **לְנִשְׁחַט רֻבּוֹ**[3] — and one which has most of it slaughtered.[3]

□ **וּבֵין הַחַיָּה הַנֶּאֱכֶלֶת** — AND BETWEEN THE CREATURE THAT MAY BE EATEN. **צָרִיךְ לוֹמַר** — Does it need to say that one must be able to distinguish **בֵּין צְבִי לַעֲרוֹד** — between a deer and a wild donkey?[4] **וַהֲלֹא** **כְּבָר מְפֹרָשִׁים הֵם** — Are they not already explicit? **אֶלָּא** — Rather, the Torah demands that you be expert in distinguishing **בֵּין שֶׁנּוֹלְדוּ בָהּ** — between one in which there developed **סִימָנֵי טְרֵפָה** — signs of a defect which is ruled to be **כְּשֵׁרָה** — kosher, **לְנוֹלְדוּ בָהּ** — and one in which there developed **סִימָנֵי טְרֵפָה** — signs of a defect which was ruled to render the animal **פְּסוּלָה**[5] — unfit to be eaten.[5]

1. Has the Torah not already stated explicitly the signs of split hooves and chewing of the cud which distinguish the cow from the donkey? (*Sifsei Chachamim*).
2. One whose purity or impurity is dependent upon an act of yours (*Mizrachi; Sifsei Chachamim*).
3. *Toras Kohanim, perek* 12:7. Distinguishing between species requires no expertise. It is in distinguishing between a properly slaughtered animal of a pure species and an improperly slaughtered one that the Torah demands that we be expert. If only half of the windpipe is severed through slaughtering, the slaughter is invalid. We must be able to determine if half of it has been severed, or more than half of it. See, too, Rashi to 20:25 below and note 4 there.
4. Deer and wild donkeys are species that fall under the category of חַיָּה rather than בְּהֵמָה. The deer has split hooves and chews its cud; the wild donkey does not.
5. *Toras Kohanim, perek* 12:8. An animal that has certain physical defects that will lead to its death is considered a *tereifah* and may not be eaten (see *Exodus* 22:30). The Torah requires us to develop the expertise to distinguish between those signs of defect that indicate a status of *tereifah* and those that do not.

פרשת תזריע
Parashas Tazria

12

12 ¹ Hashem spoke to Moses, saying: ² Speak to the Children of Israel, saying: When a woman conceives and gives birth to a male, she shall be impure for a seven-day period, as during the days of her menstrual infirmity shall she be impure. ³ On the eighth day, the flesh of his foreskin shall be circumcised. ⁴ For thirty-three days she shall stay

יב א-ב וַיְדַבֵּר יְהוָה אֶל־מֹשֶׁה לֵּאמֹר: דַּבֵּר אֶל־בְּנֵי יִשְׂרָאֵל לֵאמֹר אִשָּׁה כִּי תַזְרִיעַ וְיָלְדָה זָכָר וְטָמְאָה שִׁבְעַת יָמִים כִּימֵי נִדַּת דְּוֹתָהּ תִּטְמָא: ג וּבַיּוֹם הַשְּׁמִינִי יִמּוֹל בְּשַׂר עָרְלָתוֹ: ד וּשְׁלֹשִׁים יוֹם וּשְׁלֹשֶׁת יָמִים תֵּשֵׁב

— אונקלוס —

א וּמַלִּיל יְיָ עִם מֹשֶׁה לְמֵימָר: ב מַלֵּל עִם בְּנֵי יִשְׂרָאֵל לְמֵימָר אִתְּתָא אֲרֵי תְעַדֵּי וּתְלִיד דְּכַר וּתְהֵי מְסָאֲבָא שַׁבְעָא יוֹמִין כְּיוֹמֵי רִחוּק סוֹבְתַהּ תְּהֵי מְסָאֲבָא: ג וּבְיוֹמָא תְמִינָאָה יִגְזַר בִּסְרָא דְעָרְלְתֵהּ: ד וּתְלָתִין וּתְלָתָא יוֹמִין תִּתֵּיב

— רש"י —

(ב) אשה כי תזריע. א"ר שמלאי כשם שיצירתו של אדם אחר כל בהמה חיה ועוף במעשה בראשית, כך תורתו נתפרשה אחר תורת בהמה חיה ועוף (ויק"ר יד:א): **כי תזריע.** לרבות שאפילו ילדתו מחוי, שנמחה ונעשה כעין זרע, אמו טמאה לידה (נדה כז:ב): **כימי נדת דותה תטמא.** כסדר כל טומאה האמורה בנדה מטמאה בטומאת לידה, ואפילו נפתח הקבר בלא דם: **דותה.** לשון דבר הזב מגופה. לשון אחר, לשון מדוה וחולי, שאין אשה רואה דם שלא תחלה, וראשה ואבריה כבדין עליה: **(ד) תשב.** אין תשב [ס"א לשון ישיבה] אלא לשון עכבה,

— RASHI ELUCIDATED —

12.

2. אִשָּׁה כִּי תַזְרִיעַ — WHEN A WOMAN CONCEIVES. — אָמַר ר' שִׂמְלָאי — The Amora R' Simlai said: כְּשֵׁם שֶׁיְּצִירָתוֹ שֶׁל אָדָם — Just as the fashioning of man came אַחַר כָּל בְּהֵמָה חַיָּה וָעוֹף — after all cattle, beasts, and fowl בְּמַעֲשֵׂה בְרֵאשִׁית — in the Torah's account of the act of Creation, כָּךְ תּוֹרָתוֹ נִתְפָּרְשָׁה — so is his law explained ¹ אַחַר תּוֹרַת בְּהֵמָה חַיָּה וָעוֹף — after the law of cattle, beast, and fowl.¹

□ כִּי תַזְרִיעַ — WHEN [A WOMAN] CONCEIVES. — לְרַבּוֹת — To include שֶׁאֲפִילוּ יְלָדַתּוּ מָחוּי — even if she gave birth to him dissolved; that is, שֶׁנִּמְחָה — that the features of his body were dissolved, וְנַעֲשָׂה כְּעֵין זֶרַע — and he lost his human form to the point where he became like semen, i.e., he became fluid in appearance, ² אִמּוֹ טְמֵאָה לֵידָה — his mother is nonetheless impure due to childbirth.²

□ כִּימֵי נִדַּת דְּוֹתָהּ תִּטְמָא — AS DURING THE DAYS OF HER MENSTRUANT INFIRMITY SHALL SHE BE IMPURE. כְּסֵדֶר כָּל טֻמְאָה — In the order of all impurity הָאֲמוּרָה בְּנִדָּה — which is stated concerning a woman who is impure due to menstruation מִטַּמְּאָה בְּטֻמְאַת לֵידָה — she becomes impure through the impurity of childbirth, וַאֲפִילוּ נִפְתַּח הַקֶּבֶר בְּלֹא דָם — even if the womb opens without blood.³

□ דְּוֹתָהּ — INFIRMITY.⁴ לְשׁוֹן דָּבָר הַזָּב מִגּוּפָהּ — This word is an expression of something which flows from her body.⁵ לָשׁוֹן אַחֵר — Alternatively, לְשׁוֹן מַדְוֶה — it is an expression of infirmity וָחוֹלִי — and illness, שֶׁאֵין אִשָּׁה רוֹאָה דָם — for a woman does not see blood ⁶ שֶׁלֹּא תֶחֱלֶה — without feeling ill, וְרֹאשָׁהּ וְאֵבָרֶיהָ כְּבֵדִין עָלֶיהָ — her head and her limbs feeling heavy upon her.⁷

4. תֵּשֵׁב — SHE SHALL STAY. אֵין תֵּשֵׁב⁸ אֶלָּא לְשׁוֹן עַכָּבָה — Here, תֵּשֵׁב can mean nothing other than

---

1. *Vayikra Rabbah* 14:1.

2. *Niddah* 27b. The verse could have simply said, "When a woman gives birth to a male." The apparently superfluous word תַזְרִיעַ, "conceives," was added because it is a form of the word זֶרַע, "semen," and implies that the impurity due to childbirth takes effect even if a woman miscarries a dissolved fetus (*Mizrachi*).

3. The laws of this passage had to be stated specifically for a case in which the womb opened without a discharge of blood. If blood had been discharged, these laws would apply to the woman giving birth by virtue of her having the status of a woman who has menstruated (*Mizrachi*).

4. This translation follows Rashi's second explanation

in this comment.

5. *Sefer Zikaron* points out that according to this interpretation the root דוה is similar to the root דבא which means "to flow" (see Rashi's second interpretation of דָּבָא in *Deuteronomy* 33:25). Another pair of words in which the letters ב and ו are interchanged is תַּאֲבָה and תַּאֲוָה which both mean "desire" or "lust" (see *Radak* and *Metzudas Tzion* to *Psalms* 119:20).

6. Some editions read: שֶׁלֹּא תְהֵא תְחִלָּה רֹאשָׁהּ וְאֵבָרֶיהָ כְּבֵדִין עָלֶיהָ, "without at first her head and her limbs feeling heavy upon her."

7. See *Niddah* 63b.

8. Some editions read: . . . אֵין לְשׁוֹן יְשִׁיבָה אֶלָּא, "It is not an expression of 'sitting' but an expression of 'staying.'"

in blood of purity; she may not touch anything sacred and she may not enter the Sanctuary, until the completion of her days of purity. ⁵ *If she gives birth to a female,*

בִּדְמֵי טָהֳרָה בְּכָל־קֹדֶשׁ לֹא־תִגָּע וְאֶל־הַמִּקְדָּשׁ לֹא תָבֹא עַד־מְלֹאת ה יְמֵי טָהֳרָהּ: וְאִם־נְקֵבָה תֵלֵד

— אונקלוס —

בְּדַם דְּכוּ בְּכָל קוּדְשָׁא לָא תִקְרַב וּלְמַקְדְּשָׁא לָא תֵעוֹל עַד מִשְׁלַם יוֹמֵי דָכוּתַהּ: ה וְאִם נֻקְבְּתָא תְלִיד

— רש״י —

כְּמוֹ וַתֵּשֶׁב בְּקָדֵשׁ (דברים א:מו) וַיֵּשֶׁב בְּאֵלֹנֵי מַמְרֵא (בראשית יג:יח): בִּדְמֵי טָהֳרָה. אַף־עַל־פִּי שֶׁרוֹאָה [דָּם] טְהוֹרָה: טָהֳרָה. לֹא מַפִּיק ה״א, וְהוּא שֵׁם דָּבָר כְּמוֹ טֹהַר: יְמֵי טָהֳרָהּ. מַפִּיק ה״א, יְמֵי טֹהַר שֶׁלָּהּ: בְּכָל קֹדֶשׁ. לְרַבּוֹת אֶת הַתְּרוּמָה (יבמות עה.) לְפִי שֶׁזּוֹ טְבוּלַת יוֹם אָרוֹךְ, שֶׁטָּבְלָה לְסוֹף שִׁבְעָה וְאֵין שִׁמְשָׁהּ מַעֲרִיב לְטַהֲרָהּ עַד שְׁקִיעַת הַחַמָּה שֶׁל יוֹם אַרְבָּעִים, שֶׁלְּמָחָר תָּבִיא אֶת כַּפָּרַת טָהֳרָתָהּ: לֹא תִגָּע. אַזְהָרָה לָאוֹכֵל וְכוּ׳ כְּמוֹ שֶׁשְּׁנוּיָה בִּיבָמוֹת (שָׁם):

— RASHI ELUCIDATED —

וַיֵּשֶׁב בְּאֵלֹנֵי מַמְרֵא,"[3] and וַיֵּשֶׁב in, "**he stayed at the plains of Mamre.**"[3] — וַתֵּשֶׁב in, "**you stayed in Kadesh,**"[2] — וַתֵּשֶׁב in, "**you stayed in Kadesh,**"[2] — like וַתֵּשֶׁב — בְּמוֹ ,,וַתֵּשֶׁב בְּקָדֵשׁ[2]" "**staying,**"[1] —

□ בִּדְמֵי טָהֳרָה — IN BLOOD OF PURITY. {דָּם} אַף עַל פִּי שֶׁרוֹאָה — Even though she sees {blood} during this thirty-three-day period, טְהוֹרָה — she is pure.

□ בִּדְמֵי טָהֳרָה — IN BLOOD OF PURITY. לֹא מַפִּיק ה״א — The final letter ה is not pronounced.[4] וְהוּא שֵׁם דָּבָר — [The word] is a noun, כְּמוֹ טֹהַר — like in meaning to טֹהַר, "**purity.**"

□ יְמֵי טָהֳרָהּ — HER DAYS OF PURITY. מַפִּיק ה״א — The final letter ה is pronounced.[4] The word טָהֳרָהּ means, יְמֵי טֹהַר שֶׁלָּהּ — her days of purity.

□ בְּכָל קֹדֶשׁ — ANYTHING SACRED. ⁵לְרַבּוֹת אֶת הַתְּרוּמָה — This is stated **to include** *terumah*.[5] לְפִי שֶׁזּוֹ — since she immersed herself at the end of seven days after childbirth, שֶׁטָּבְלָה לְסוֹף שִׁבְעָה — טְבוּלַת יוֹם אָרוֹךְ — For this [woman] is immersed of an extended day, וְאֵין שִׁמְשָׁהּ מַעֲרִיב — but her sun does not fade into evening לְטַהֲרָהּ — to purify her עַד שְׁקִיעַת הַחַמָּה — until the setting of the sun שֶׁל יוֹם אַרְבָּעִים — of the fortieth day, שֶׁלְּמָחָר — because on the following day תָּבִיא אֶת כַּפָּרַת טָהֳרָתָהּ — she will bring the atonement of her purification.[6]

□ לֹא תִגָּע — SHE MAY NOT TOUCH. אַזְהָרָה לָאוֹכֵל וְכוּלְהוּ — This is a negative commandment for one who eats, etc., ⁷כְּמוֹ שֶׁשְּׁנוּיָה בִּיבָמוֹת — as taught in Tractate *Yevamos*.[7]

---

1. See *Megillah* 21a.
2. *Deuteronomy* 1:46.
3. *Genesis* 13:18. See also Rashi to *Deuteronomy* 9:9.
4. The letters ה, ו, and י are usually silent vowels when they appear at the end of a word (e.g., אוֹ שְׁנֵי בְנֵי־יוֹנָה in v. 8 below). Sometimes these letters are pronounced as consonants at the end of a word (e.g., מִבָּנָיו in 13:3; חַי in 13:10; דְּוֹתָה in v. 2 above). The early grammarians called such letters מַפִּיק, literally, "brought out," i.e., pronounced. A *dagesh* is placed in a *mapik* ה to distinguish it from a silent ה, and the term *mapik* has come to refer to that dot. In most cases the *mapik* ה indicates the possessive pronoun "her." Thus, if טָהֳרָהּ here had been spelled with a *mapik*, the word would have meant "*her* purity" (see Rashi's next comment).
5. *Yevamos* 75a. *Terumah* is the portion given to the *Kohanim* from the yearly crop. See *Numbers* 18:12,25-32.
6. *Makkos* 14b; *Yevamos* 75a. Certain types of impurity require immersion in a spring or *mikveh* on the last day of impurity as one of the steps of the purification procedure. Someone who has undergone immersion has the status of *tevul yom* — literally, "immersed of day" — until sunset. During this period, he transmits impurity only to that which is holy, including *terumah*. After sunset, he may partake of *terumah*. In the case of lesser types of impurity,

he may also partake of offerings at this point. In the case of more severe types of impurity, he must wait until after he has brought an offering the following day before partaking of offerings. During the period between sunset and the time he brings his offering, he is considered a *mechusar kippurim*, "one lacking atonement."

Our verse could have said בְּקֹדֶשׁ לֹא תִגַּע, "she may not touch that which is sacred." This would have implied that she may not eat of offerings. בְּכָל קֹדֶשׁ לֹא תִגַּע, "she may not touch *anything* sacred," implies that she may not eat even that which has a lesser degree of holiness, namely, *terumah*. But this law requires explanation. After the woman who has given birth to a son immerses herself on the seventh day, she has the status of a *tevul yom*. Why is she forbidden to eat *terumah* until sunset of the fortieth day? Why is she not permitted to eat *terumah* after sunset, as is any other *tevul yom*? Rashi explains that she is considered "immersed of an extended day." The Torah decrees that she has *tevul yom* status until sunset of the fortieth day. For the operative sunset is not necessarily the one that follows the immersion; it is the one that precedes the bringing of offerings when such offerings are part of the procedure of purification, as they are here (*Mizrachi*; *Mesiach Ilmim*; *Sifsei Chachamim*).

7. *Yevamos* 75a. Although the verse speaks of touching,

וְטָמְאָה שְׁבֻעַיִם כְּנִדָּתָהּ וְשִׁשִּׁים יוֹם וְשֵׁשֶׁת יָמִים תֵּשֵׁב עַל־דְּמֵי טָהֳרָה: וּבִמְלֹאת ׀ יְמֵי טָהֳרָהּ לְבֵן אוֹ לְבַת תָּבִיא כֶּבֶשׂ בֶּן־שְׁנָתוֹ לְעֹלָה וּבֶן־יוֹנָה אוֹ־תֹר לְחַטָּאת אֶל־פֶּתַח אֹהֶל־מוֹעֵד אֶל־הַכֹּהֵן: וְהִקְרִיבוֹ לִפְנֵי יהוה וְכִפֶּר עָלֶיהָ וְטָהֲרָה מִמְּקֹר דָּמֶיהָ זֹאת תּוֹרַת הַיֹּלֶדֶת לַזָּכָר אוֹ לַנְּקֵבָה: וְאִם־לֹא תִמְצָא יָדָהּ דֵּי שֶׂה וְלָקְחָה שְׁתֵּי־תֹרִים אוֹ שְׁנֵי בְּנֵי יוֹנָה אֶחָד לְעֹלָה וְאֶחָד לְחַטָּאת

she shall be impure for two weeks, as during her menstruation period; and for sixty-six days she shall stay in blood of purity. ⁶ *Upon the completion of the days of her purity for a son or for a daughter, she shall bring a sheep within its first year for an olah-offering, and a young dove or a turtledove for a sin-offering, to the entrance of the Tent of Meeting, to the Kohen.* ⁷ *He shall offer it before* HASHEM *and atone for her, and she shall become purified from the source of her blood; this is the law of one who gives birth to a male or to a female.* ⁸ *But if she cannot afford a sheep, then she shall take two turtledoves or two young doves, one for an olah-offering and one for a sin-offering;*

──────── אונקלוס ────────

וּתְהֵי מְסָאֲבָא אַרְבְּעָה עֲסַר כְּרֻחוּקַהּ וְשִׁתִּין וְשִׁתָּא יוֹמִין תֵּיתֵב עַל דַּם דָּכֵי: וּבְמִשְׁלַם יוֹמֵי דְכוּתַהּ לִבְרָא אוֹ לִבְרַתָּא תַּיְתֵי אִמַּר בַּר שַׁתֵּהּ לַעֲלָתָא וּבַר יוֹנָה אוֹ שַׁפְנִינָא לְחַטָּאתָא לִתְרַע מַשְׁכַּן זִמְנָא לְוָת כַּהֲנָא: וִיקָרְבִנֵּהּ קֳדָם יְיָ וִיכַפַּר עֲלַהּ וְתִדְכֵּי מִסּוֹאֲבַת דְּמַהּ דָּא אוֹרַיְתָא דְמָה דָא אוֹרַיְתָא דִילֵדְתָּא לְדְכַר אוֹ לְנֻקְבָּא: ח וְאִם לָא תַשְׁכַּח יְדַהּ כְּמִסַּת אִמְּרָא וְתִסַּב תַּרְתֵּין שַׁפְנִינִין אוֹ תְרֵין בְּנֵי יוֹנָה חַד לַעֲלָתָא וְחַד לְחַטָּאתָא

──────── רש"י ────────

(ז) **וְהִקְרִיבוֹ.** לִמֵּד שֶׁאֵין מְעַכְּבָה מִלֶּאֱכֹל בַּקֳּדָשִׁים אֶלָּא אֶחָד מֵהֶם, וְאֵי זֶה הוּא, זֶה חַטָּאת שֶׁנֶּאֱמַר וְכִפֶּר עָלֶיהָ הַכֹּהֵן וְטָהֵרָה (פסוק ח), מִי שֶׁהוּא בָּא לְכַפֵּר בּוֹ הַטָּהֳרָה תְלוּיָה (ת"כ תזריע פרק ג:ה): **וְטָהֲרָה.** מִכְּלָל שֶׁעַד כָּאן קְרוּיָה טְמֵאָה (סנהדרין פג:): (ח) **אֶחָד לְעֹלָה וְאֶחָד לְחַטָּאת.** לֹא הִקְדִּימָה הַכָּתוּב אֶלָּא לְמִקְרָאָה, אֲבָל לְהַקְרָבָה חַטָּאת קוֹדֶם לְעוֹלָה (זבחים צ.):

──────── RASHI ELUCIDATED ────────

7. וְהִקְרִיבוֹ — HE SHALL OFFER IT. לִמֵּד — This has taught you שֶׁאֵין מְעַכְּבָה מִלֶּאֱכֹל בַּקֳּדָשִׁים אֶלָּא אֶחָד מֵהֶם — that failure to offer only one of them prevents her from eating that which is holy.[1] וְאֵי זֶה הוּא — And which one is it? זֶה חַטָּאת — This is the sin-offering, שֶׁנֶּאֱמַר — as it says, ,,וְכִפֶּר עָלֶיהָ הַכֹּהֵן וְטָהֵרָה'' — "And the Kohen shall atone for her, and she shall become purified."[2] מִי שֶׁהוּא בָּא — The one which comes to atone, לְכַפֵּר ³בּוֹ הַטָּהֳרָה תְלוּיָה — upon *it* does the purity depend.[3]

□ **וְטָהֲרָה — AND SHE SHALL BECOME PURIFIED.** מִכְּלָל — This implies שֶׁעַד כָּאן — that up to this point[4] קְרוּיָה טְמֵאָה — she is called impure.[4]

8. אֶחָד לְעֹלָה וְאֶחָד לְחַטָּאת — ONE FOR AN *OLAH*-**OFFERING AND ONE FOR A SIN-OFFERING.** לֹא הִקְדִּימָה — Scripture put [the *olah*-offering] first הַכָּתוּב אֶלָּא לְמִקְרָאָה — only with regard to its reading,[5] אֲבָל לְהַקְרָבָה — but for offering, חַטָּאת קוֹדֶם לְעוֹלָה — the sin-offering precedes the *olah*-offering.

the negative commandment here is applied only to eating. This is because our verse juxtaposes "touching" with entering the Sanctuary while impure; just as entering the Sanctuary while impure is a sin punishable by loss of life (see *Numbers* 19:13), so, too, "touching" refers to a sin punishable by *kares* (premature death and childlessness — see Rashi to 7:20 above). Eating *terumah* is also punishable by premature death at the hands of the heavenly court (see 22:6-9 below). Touching either offerings or *terumah* while impure is not punishable by loss of life (see Rashi to *Yevamos* 75a).

1. The previous verse speaks of two offerings, yet our verse states "he shall offer *it*," in the singular, rather than, "he shall offer *them*" (*Mizrachi*; *Sifsei Chachamim*).
2. Below v. 8.
3. *Toras Kohanim*, *perek* 3:5. The verse makes her purification dependent upon her atonement. The offering upon which her purification depends is the sin-offering, for a sin-offering is generally associated with atonement (*Mizrachi*; *Sifsei Chachamim*).
4. *Sanhedrin* 83b; *Zevachim* 19b. Although she has become pure as far as eating *terumah* is concerned on the night after the fortieth day (see Rashi to v. 4 and note 6 there), this verse teaches us that she does not achieve full purity. For she is not permitted to eat of offerings until she brings the offering that atones for her (*Minchas Yehudah*; *Sifsei Chachamim*).
5. It is read in Scripture before the sin-offering (see Rashi to *Zevachim* 90a and *Tosafos* there). The Kohanim would read the section of the Torah that deals with a particular offering before they would bring it. In this case, according

and the Kohen shall atone for her and she shall become purified.

13 ¹ HASHEM spoke to Moses and to Aaron, saying: ² If a person will have on the skin of his flesh a s'eis, or a sapachas, or a baheres, and it will become a tzaraas affliction on the skin of his flesh; he shall be brought to Aaron the Kohen, or to one of his sons the Kohanim. ³ The Kohen shall look at the affliction on the skin of his flesh: If hair in the affliction has turned white, and the affliction's appearance is deeper than the skin of his flesh —

יג א וַיְדַבֵּר יהוה אֶל־מֹשֶׁה וְאֶל־אַהֲרֹן
ב לֵאמֹר: אָדָם כִּי־יִהְיֶה בְעוֹר־בְּשָׂרוֹ
שְׂאֵת אֽוֹ־סַפַּחַת אוֹ בַהֶרֶת וְהָיָה
בְעוֹר־בְּשָׂרוֹ לְנֶגַע צָרָעַת וְהוּבָא
אֶל־אַהֲרֹן הַכֹּהֵן אוֹ אֶל־אַחַד מִבָּנָיו
הַכֹּהֲנִים: ג וְרָאָה הַכֹּהֵן אֶת־הַנֶּגַע
בְּעוֹר־הַבָּשָׂר וְשֵׂעָר בַּנֶּגַע הָפַךְ לָבָן
וּמַרְאֵה הַנֶּגַע עָמֹק מֵעוֹר בְּשָׂרוֹ
וְכִפֶּר עָלֶיהָ הַכֹּהֵן וְטָהֵרָה:

———— אונקלוס ————

וִיכַפֵּר עֲלַהּ כַּהֲנָא וְתִדְכֵּי: א וּמַלִּיל יְיָ עִם מֹשֶׁה וְעִם אַהֲרֹן לְמֵימָר: ב אֱנָשׁ אֲרֵי יְהֵי בִמְשַׁךְ בִּסְרֵהּ עֲמָקָא אוֹ עָדְיָא אוֹ בַהֲרָא וִיהֵי בִמְשַׁךְ בִּסְרֵהּ לְמַכְתַּשׁ סְגִירוּ וְיִתֵּיתֵי לְוָת אַהֲרֹן כַּהֲנָא אוֹ לְוָת חַד מִבְּנוֹהִי כָהֲנַיָּא: ג וְיֶחֱזֵי כַּהֲנָא יָת מַכְתָּשָׁא בִּמְשַׁךְ בִּסְרָא וְשַׂעֲרָא בְמַכְתָּשָׁא אִתְהֲפִיךְ לְמֶחֱוַר וּמֶחֱזֵי מַכְתָּשָׁא עַמִּיק בִּמְשַׁךְ בִּסְרָא

———— רש"י ————

כך שנינו בזבחים (צ.): כל הַתָּדִיר (ל.): (ב) **שאת או ספחת** וגו׳. שמות נגעים הֵם וּלְבָנוֹת זוֹ מִזּוֹ (ת״כ נגעים פרשתא א:ח; שבועות ה.): **בהרת.** חברבורות טק״א בלעז, וכן בהיר הוא בשחקים (איוב לז:כא): **אל אהרן וגו׳.** גזירת הכתוב היא שאין טומאת נגעים וטהרתן אלא ע״פ כהן (ת״כ שם ט): (ג) **ושער בנגע הפך לבן.** מתחלה שחור והפך ללבן בתוך הנגע, ומיעוט שער שנים (ת״כ שם פרק ב:ב-ג): **עמק מעור בשרו.** כל מראה לבן עמוק הוא,

———— RASHI ELUCIDATED ————

בְּפֶרֶק כָּל הַתָּדִיר — in Chapter Kol HaTadir.[1] כָּךְ שָׁנִינוּ בִּזְבָחִים — Thus have we learned in tractate Zevachim.

13.

2. שְׂאֵת אוֹ סַפַּחַת וְגוֹמֵר — A S'EIS OR A SAPACHAS, ETC. שְׁמוֹת נְגָעִים הֵם — These are names of afflictions. וּלְבָנוֹת זוֹ מִזּוֹ² — One is whiter than the other, i.e., they are of varying degrees of whiteness.²

□ בַּהֶרֶת — BAHERES. חֲבַרְבּוּרוֹת — Spots; טק״א בְּלַעַ״ז — tache in Old French.³ וְכֵן — And similarly, בָּהִיר has a related meaning in, "בָּהִיר הוּא בַּשְּׁחָקִים„⁴ — "it is cloudy in the skies."⁴

□ אֶל אַהֲרֹן וְגוֹמֵר — TO AARON [THE KOHEN]. גְּזֵרַת הַכָּתוּב הִיא — It is a decree of Scripture⁵ שֶׁאֵין טֻמְאַת — that there is neither impurity of afflictions of tzara'as נְגָעִים וְטָהֳרָתָן — nor their purification אֶלָּא עַל פִּי כֹהֵן⁶ — except by the word of a Kohen.⁶

3. וְשֵׂעָר בַּנֶּגַע הָפַךְ לָבָן — IF HAIR IN THE AFFLICTION HAS TURNED WHITE. מִתְּחִלָּה שָׁחוֹר — At first it was black, i.e., dark, וְהָפַךְ לְלָבָן — and it turned to white בְּתוֹךְ הַנֶּגַע — inside the area of the affliction. וּמִעוּט שֵׂעָר שְׁנַיִם⁷ — The minimum amount of "hair" is two single hairs.⁷

□ עָמֹק מֵעוֹר בְּשָׂרוֹ — DEEPER THAN THE SKIN OF HIS FLESH. כָּל מַרְאֵה לָבָן — Any white appearance, i.e., anything that looks white, עָמֹק הוּא — is deep, i.e., appears deeper than something dark next to it,

---

to Rashi, they would read the section of the olah-offering before the section of the sin-offering even though the sin-offering is brought first (Likkutei Yehudah citing Imrei Emes and Rechovos HaNahar).

1. Zevachim 90a. The tenth chapter of Tractate Zevachim is called Kol HaTadir.
2. Toras Kohanim, Negaim, parshasa 1:4; Shevuos 5b.
3. In Modern French tacheté, "a colored spot." The modern medical term for the dark spot that results from a tick bite is tache noire.
4. Job 37:21. The term בָּהִיר of the verse in Job is related to בַהֶרֶת of our verse, for it connotes a sky spotted with clouds. See Rashi there and to Taanis 7b.

5. A law of the Torah whose rationale man does not understand is referred to as גְּזֵרַת הַכָּתוּב, "a decree of Scripture." In our case, we might think that decisions regarding the purity or impurity of afflictions of tzaraas would best be rendered by a scholar expert in these laws. But the Torah demands that they be pronounced by a Kohen.

6. Toras Kohanim, Negaim, parshasa 1:9.

7. Toras Kohanim, Negaim, perek 2:2-3. The term שֵׂעָר means a group of hairs (as distinct from a single hair) unless the Torah specifies otherwise. [For one hair, Scripture uses שַׂעֲרָה (R' Shimshon MiShantz).] By using this word, the verse indicates that a minimum of

נֶגַע צָרַעַת הִוא וְרָאָהוּ הַכֹּהֵן וְטִמֵּא אֹתוֹ: וְאִם־בַּהֶרֶת לְבָנָה הִוא בְּעוֹר בְּשָׂרוֹ וְעָמֹק אֵין־מַרְאֶהָ מִן־הָעוֹר וּשְׂעָרָה לֹא־הָפַךְ לָבָן וְהִסְגִּיר הַכֹּהֵן אֶת־הַנֶּגַע שִׁבְעַת יָמִים: ה וְרָאָהוּ הַכֹּהֵן בַּיּוֹם הַשְּׁבִיעִי וְהִנֵּה הַנֶּגַע עָמַד בְּעֵינָיו לֹא־פָשָׂה הַנֶּגַע בָּעוֹר וְהִסְגִּירוֹ הַכֹּהֵן שִׁבְעַת יָמִים שֵׁנִית: ו וְרָאָה הַכֹּהֵן אֹתוֹ

it is a tzara'as affliction; the Kohen shall look at it and make him impure. ⁴ *If it is a white baheres on the skin of his flesh, and its appearance is not deeper than the skin, and the hair has not turned white, then the Kohen shall close off the affliction for a seven-day period.* ⁵ *The Kohen shall look at it on the seventh day, and behold! — the affliction remained in its appearance, and the affliction did not spread on the skin, then the Kohen shall close him off a second time for a seven-day period.* ⁶ *The Kohen shall look at it*

— אונקלוס —

מַכְתַּשׁ סְגִירוּתָא הוּא וִיסָאֲבִנֵּהּ כַּהֲנָא וִיסָאֵב יָתֵהּ: ד וְאִם בַּהֲרָא חִוָּרָא הִיא בִּמְשַׁךְ בִּסְרֵהּ וַעֲמִיק לֵית מֶחֱזַהָא מִן מַשְׁכָא וּשְׂעָרַהּ לָא אִתְהֲפִיךְ לְחִוָּר וְיַסְגַּר כַּהֲנָא יָת מַכְתָּשָׁא שִׁבְעָא יוֹמִין: ה וְיֶחֱזִנֵּהּ כַּהֲנָא בְּיוֹמָא שְׁבִיעָאָה וְהָא מַכְתָּשָׁא קָם כַּד הֲוָה לָא אוֹסִיף מַכְתְּשָׁא בְּמַשְׁכָא וְיַסְגְּרִנֵּהּ כַּהֲנָא שִׁבְעָא יוֹמִין תִּנְיָנוּת: ו וְיֶחֱזֵי כַּהֲנָא יָתֵהּ

— רש״י —

כְּמַרְאֵה חַמָּה עֲמֻקָּה מִן הַצֵּל (ת״כ פרשתא ד:ה; שבועות ו:): **הָעוֹר.** לֹא יָדַעְתִּי פֵּרוּשׁוֹ: **וְהִסְגִּיר.** יַסְגִּירֶנּוּ בְּבַיִת אֶחָד וְלֹא יֵרָאֶה עַד סוֹף הַשָּׁבוּעַ, וְיוֹכִיחוּ סִימָנִים עָלָיו: (ה) **בְּעֵינָיו.** **וְטִמֵּא אֹתוֹ.** יֹאמַר לוֹ טָמֵא אַתָּה, שֶׁשֵּׂעָר לָבָן סִימָן בְּמַרְאֵהוּ וּבְשִׁעוּרוֹ הָרִאשׁוֹן: **וְהִסְגִּירוֹ שֵׁנִית.** הָא אִם פָּשָׂה טֻמְאָה הוּא גְּזֵרַת הַכָּתוּב: (ד) **וְעָמֹק אֵין מַרְאֶה** [מִן

— RASHI ELUCIDATED —

עֲמֻקָּה מִן — **as the appearance of the sun,** i.e., a surface that reflects the light of the sun, הַצֵּל[1] — **is deeper than the shade.**

☐ וְטִמֵּא אֹתוֹ — AND MAKE HIM IMPURE. — יֹאמַר לוֹ — **He shall say to him,** ״טָמֵא אַתָּה,, — "**You are impure,**"[2] שֵׂעָר לָבָן — **for white hair** סִימָן טֻמְאָה הוּא — **is a sign of impurity,** גְּזֵרַת הַכָּתוּב — by decree of Scripture.[3]

4. {וְעָמֹק אֵין מַרְאֶה} {מִן הָעוֹר} — AND ITS APPEARANCE IS NOT DEEPER {THAN THE SKIN} — לֹא יָדַעְתִּי פֵּרוּשׁוֹ — I do not know its meaning.[4]

☐ וְהִסְגִּיר — THEN [THE KOHEN] SHALL CLOSE OFF. — יַסְגִּירֶנּוּ בְּבַיִת אֶחָד — **He shall confine him to one house,**[5] וְלֹא יֵרָאֶה — **and he shall not appear** before the Kohen עַד סוֹף הַשָּׁבוּעַ — **until the end of the week,**[6] וְיוֹכִיחוּ סִימָנִים עָלָיו — **and** then, the **characteristics** of his affliction **will indicate about him** whether he is pure or impure.

5. בְּעֵינָיו — IN ITS APPEARANCE. — בְּמַרְאֵהוּ וּבְשִׁעוּרוֹ הָרִאשׁוֹן — The word בְּעֵינָיו does not mean "in his eyes,"[7] but **in its original appearance and size.**

☐ וְהִסְגִּירוֹ שֵׁנִית — THEN THE KOHEN SHALL CLOSE HIM OFF A SECOND TIME. — הָא אִם פָּשָׂה — **But if it**

---

two hairs must turn white for the affliction to cause impurity (*Ra'avad* to *Toras Kohanim*; *Mishmeres HaKodesh*).

1. *Toras Kohanim, Negaim, parshasa* 1:4; *Shevuos* 6b.
2. "Making him impure" means *declaring* him impure. It does not mean transmitting impurity to him (*Mizrachi*; *Sifsei Chachamim*).
3. See page 139, note 5.
4. Rashi on the preceding verse has stated that that which is light appears deeper than that which is dark. How, then, can the appearance of this white *baheres* not appear deeper than the surrounding, darker, skin? (*Mizrachi*; *Sifsei Chachamim*). For other places in Rashi's commentary where he tells us nothing more than "I do not know . . .," see

Rashi to *Genesis* 28:5 and our note there.
5. According to Rashi, "closing off the affliction" does not mean making a mark around it as some commentators explain (see *Meiri, Megillah* 8b; *Tosafos HaRosh, Moed Kattan* 7a). It means quarantining the afflicted party (*Mizrachi*; *Sifsei Chachamim; Be'er Yitzchak*).
6. Throughout Rashi's commentary on this topic, the word שָׁבוּעַ refers to the seven-day period of confinement, not to the calendar week.
7. The word עַיִן can mean either "eye" or "appearance" (see Rashi to *Exodus* 10:5); the suffix ו can mean either "his" or "its." Rashi understands the word בְּעֵינָיו to mean "in its appearances." In this he differs from *Ramban* who translates "in his eyes," i.e., in the judgment (eyes) of the Kohen (see *Sefer Zikaron*).

13/7-8

again on the seventh day, and behold! — if the affliction has dimmed and the affliction has not spread on the skin, then the Kohen shall declare him pure, it is a mispachas; he shall immerse his garments and become pure. ⁷ But if the mispachas should spread on the skin after it had been shown to the Kohen for its purification, it should be shown to the Kohen again. ⁸ The Kohen shall look, and behold! — the mispachas has spread on the skin; the Kohen shall make him impure; it is tzara'as.

בַּיּוֹם הַשְּׁבִיעִי שֵׁנִית וְהִנֵּה כֵּהָה הַנֶּגַע וְלֹא־פָשָׂה הַנֶּגַע בָּעוֹר וְטִהֲרוֹ הַכֹּהֵן מִסְפַּחַת הִוא וְכִבֶּס בְּגָדָיו וְטָהֵר: ⁷ וְאִם־פָּשֹׂה תִפְשֶׂה הַמִּסְפַּחַת בָּעוֹר אַחֲרֵי הֵרָאֹתוֹ אֶל־הַכֹּהֵן לְטָהֳרָתוֹ וְנִרְאָה שֵׁנִית אֶל־הַכֹּהֵן: ⁸ וְרָאָה הַכֹּהֵן וְהִנֵּה פָּשְׂתָה הַמִּסְפַּחַת בָּעוֹר וְטִמְּאוֹ הַכֹּהֵן צָרַעַת הִוא:

---- אונקלוס ----

בְּיוֹמָא שְׁבִיעָאָה תִנְיָנוּת וְהָא עָמְיָא מַכְתָּשָׁא וְלָא אוֹסִיף מַכְתָּשָׁא בְּמַשְׁכָּא וִידַכִּנֵהּ כַּהֲנָא עֲדִיתָא הִיא וִיצַבַּע לְבוּשׁוֹהִי וְיִדְכֵּי: ⁷ וְאִם אוֹסָפָא תוֹסֵף עֲדִיתָא בְּמַשְׁכָּא בָּתַר דְּאִתַּחֲזִי לְכַהֲנָא לְדַכְיוּתֵהּ וְיִתַּחֲזִי תִנְיָנוּת לְכַהֲנָא: ⁸ וְיֶחֱזֵי כַהֲנָא וְהָא אוֹסֵפַת עֲדִיתָא בְּמַשְׁכָּא וִיסָאֲבִנֵּהּ כַּהֲנָא סְגִירוּתָא הִיא:

---- רש"י ----

בְּשָׁבוּעַ רִאשׁוֹן טָמֵא מוּחְלָט (נגעים ג:ג): (ו) בֵּהָה. סוּכְּהָה מִמַּרְאִיתוֹ, הָא אִם עָמַד בְּמַרְאִיתוֹ אוֹ פָּשָׂה טָמֵא: מִסְפַּחַת. שֵׁם נֶגַע טָהוֹר: וְכִבֶּס בְּגָדָיו וְטָהֵר. הוֹאִיל וְנִזְקַק לְהִסָּגֵר נִקְרָא טָמֵא וְלָרִיךְ טְבִילָה: (ח) וְטִמְּאוֹ הַכֹּהֵן. וּמִשְׁטִמְּאוֹ הֲרֵי הוּא מוּחְלָט וְזָקוּק לְצִפֳּרִים וּלְתִגְלַחַת וּלְקָרְבָּן הָאָמוּר בְּפָּ' זֹאת תִּהְיֶה (לְהַלָּן יד:א־לב; מגילה ח:): צָרַעַת הִוא. הַמִּסְפַּחַת הַזֹּאת:

---- RASHI ELUCIDATED ----

בְּשָׁבוּעַ רִאשׁוֹן – spread **during the first week.**² טָמֵא מוּחְלָט – **he is decidedly impure.**¹,²

6. כֵּהָה – **HAS DIMMED.** הִכְהָה מִמַּרְאִיתוֹ – It became **dimmer than its** original **appearance.**³ הָא אִם עָמַד בְּמַרְאִיתוֹ – **But if it remained in its** original **appearance** אוֹ פָּשָׂה – **or it spread,** טָמֵא – **he is impure.**⁴

□ מִסְפַּחַת – *MISPACHAS.* שֵׁם נֶגַע טָהוֹר – It is **the name of a pure affliction,** i.e., affliction that does not render the sufferer impure.

□ וְכִבֶּס בְּגָדָיו וְטָהֵר – HE SHALL IMMERSE HIS GARMENTS AND BECOME PURE. הוֹאִיל וְנִזְקַק לְהִסָּגֵר – Since he required a quarantine, נִקְרָא טָמֵא – he is called impure וְצָרִיךְ טְבִילָה – and needs immersion.⁵

8. וְטִמְּאוֹ הַכֹּהֵן – THE KOHEN SHALL MAKE HIM IMPURE. וּמִשְׁטִמְּאוֹ – And once he makes him impure, הֲרֵי הוּא מוּחְלָט – behold, he is one who is decidedly impure, וְזָקוּק לְצִפֳּרִים – and is in need of birds, וּלְקָרְבָּן – and an offering, וּלְתִגְלַחַת – and shaving, הָאָמוּר בְּפָרָשַׁת זֹאת תִּהְיֶה⁶,⁷ – which are stated in the portion that begins with the words ⁶זֹאת תִּהְיֶה as elements of the purification procedure of one who has suffered *tzara'as.*⁷

□ צָרַעַת הִוא – IT IS *TZARA'AS.* הַמִּסְפַּחַת הַזֹּאת – This *mispachas.*⁸

---

1. That is, he requires no further quarantine.
2. *Negaim* 3:3.
3. The word כֵּהָה is a verb. It is not an adjective ("the affliction is dim") in our verse as it is in *Isaiah* 42:3, for then it would be feminine and could not modify the masculine noun נֶגַע. If the word were a masculine adjective it would be vowelized כֵּהֶה (*Leket Bahir*; see *Ibn Ezra* to *Isaiah* 42:3).
4. According to Rashi, in order for the affliction to become pure, both conditions mentioned in the verse must be met: It must become dimmer than its original appearance and it must not have spread. *Ramban* notes that this runs counter to *Negaim* 1:3 which implies that if the affliction did not spread, it is pure even if it did not change color. *Divrei David* suggests

that the text of Rashi be emended to read פָּשָׂה, "*and it spread*," rather than אוֹ פָּשָׂה, "or it spread," to make the words of Rashi agree with the Mishnah.

5. The affliction is not one of *tzara'as*. The sufferer does not have to tear his garments and leave his hair unshorn, nor must he undergo the purification procedure of the *metzora*. But the fact that the sufferer had to be quarantined is enough to cause a lesser degree of impurity which requires immersion (*Devek Tov*).

6. Below 14:1-32.
7. *Megillah* 8b.
8. Although וְטִמְּאוֹ has a suffix which indicates a masculine object, the feminine הִוא must refer to something else, מִסְפַּחַת (*Sefer Zikaron*).

⁹ *If a tzara'as affliction will be in a person, he shall be brought to the Kohen.* ¹⁰ *The Kohen shall look, and behold! — it is a white s'eis on the skin, and it has turned hair to white, or there is healthy, live flesh within the s'eis:* ¹¹ *It is an old tzara'as in the skin of his flesh and the Kohen shall make him impure; he shall not close it off for it is impure.*

¹² *If the tzara'as will erupt on the skin, and the tzara'as will cover the entire skin of the affliction from his head to his feet,*

ט נֶגַע צָרַעַת כִּי תִהְיֶה בְּאָדָם וְהוּבָא אֶל־הַכֹּהֵן: י וְרָאָה הַכֹּהֵן וְהִנֵּה שְׂאֵת־לְבָנָה בָּעוֹר וְהִיא הָפְכָה שֵׂעָר לָבָן וּמִחְיַת בָּשָׂר חַי בַּשְׂאֵת: יא צָרַעַת נוֹשֶׁנֶת הִוא בְּעוֹר בְּשָׂרוֹ וְטִמְּאוֹ הַכֹּהֵן לֹא יַסְגִּרֶנּוּ כִּי טָמֵא הוּא: יב וְאִם־פָּרוֹחַ תִּפְרַח הַצָּרַעַת בָּעוֹר וְכִסְּתָה הַצָּרַעַת אֵת כָּל־עוֹר הַנֶּגַע מֵרֹאשׁוֹ וְעַד־רַגְלָיו

———— אונקלוס ————

ט מַכְתַּשׁ סְגִירוּתָא אֲרֵי תְהֵי בֶאֱנָשָׁא וְיִתֵּיתֵי לְוָת כַּהֲנָא: י וְיֶחֱזֵי כַהֲנָא וְהָא עֲמִיקָא חִוְּרָא בְּמַשְׁכָא וְהִיא הֲפָכַת שְׂעַר לְחִוָּר וְרֹשֶׁם בִּסְרָא חַיָּא בְּעַמִּיקְתָּא: יא סְגִירוּת עַתִּיקָא הִיא בְּמַשְׁךְ בִּסְרֵהּ וִיסָאֲבִנֵּהּ כַּהֲנָא לָא יַסְגְּרִנֵּהּ אֲרֵי מְסָאָב הוּא: יב וְאִם אַסְגָּאָה תַסְגֵּי סְגִירוּתָא בְּמַשְׁכָא וּתְחַפֵּי סְגִירוּתָא יָת כָּל מְשַׁךְ מַכְתָּשָׁא מֵרֵישֵׁהּ וְעַד רַגְלוֹהִי

———— רש"י ————

צרעת. לשון נקבה. נגע, לשון זכר: (י) **ומחית.** שנימ"י ט בלעז שנהפך מקצת הלובן שבתוך השאת למראה בשר, אף הוא סימן טומאה. שער לבן בלא מחיה, ומחיה בלא שער לבן. ואע"פ שלא נאמרה מחיה אלא בשאת, אף בכל המראות ותולדותיהן הוא סימן טומאה (ת"כ פרשתא ג:ח): (יא) **צרעת נושנת הוא.** מכה ישנה היא תחת המחיה, ומבורא זו נראית בריאה מלמעלה ותחתיה מלאה לחה, שלא תאמר הואיל ועלתה מחיה אטהרנה: (יב) **מראשו.** של אדם ועד רגליו:

———— RASHI ELUCIDATED ————

□ צָרַעַת — *TZARA'AS* — לְשׁוֹן נְקֵבָה — is feminine. נֶגַע — "**Affliction**" — לְשׁוֹן זָכָר — is masculine.[1]

10. וּמִחְיַת — **HEALTHY FLESH.** — שנימ"י ט בְּלַעַ"ז — *Sanement* in Old French.[2] שֶׁנֶּהֱפַךְ מִקְצָת הַלֹּבֶן — that part of the whiteness within the *s'eis* changed לְמַרְאֵה בָשָׂר — to the appearance of flesh.[3] שֶׁבְּתוֹךְ הַשְּׂאֵת — *within the s'eis* אַף הוּא — This, too, סִימָן טֻמְאָה — is a sign of impurity. שֵׂעָר לָבָן בְּלֹא — שֵׂעָר לָבָן בְּלֹא מִחְיָה — White hair without healthy flesh, וּמִחְיָה בְּלֹא שֵׂעָר לָבָן — or healthy flesh without white hair, is each a sign of impurity.[4] וְאַף עַל פִּי שֶׁלֹּא נֶאֶמְרָה מִחְיָה — Although healthy flesh was not stated as a sign of impurity אֶלָּא בַשְׂאֵת — except with regard to *s'eis*, אַף בְּכָל הַמַּרְאוֹת וְתוֹלְדוֹתֵיהֶן — regarding all appearances of an affliction of *tzara'as* and their offspring,[5] הוּא סִימָן טֻמְאָה — it is a sign of impurity.[6]

11. צָרַעַת נוֹשֶׁנֶת הִוא — *IT IS AN OLD TZARA'AS.* — מַכָּה יְשָׁנָה הִיא — It is an old wound תַּחַת הַמִּחְיָה — underneath the healthy flesh, וַחֲבוּרָה זוֹ — and this bruise נִרְאֵית בְּרִיאָה מִלְמַעְלָה — appears healthy on its upper surface, וְתַחְתֶּיהָ — but on its underside מְלֵאָה לֵחָה — it is full of fluid. The verse states this so שֶׁלֹּא תֹאמַר — that you should not say, הוֹאִיל וְעָלְתָה מִחְיָה — since healthy flesh has arisen on the affliction, אֲטַהֲרֶנָּה — I will purify it, i.e., declare it pure.

12. מֵרֹאשׁוֹ — **FROM HIS HEAD** — שֶׁל אָדָם — From the head **of the** afflicted **person** וְעַד רַגְלָיו — **to his feet.**[7]

---

1. Thus, the subject of the feminine verb תִהְיֶה of the following verse must be the feminine noun צָרַעַת, not the masculine noun נֶגַע (*Mizrachi; Sifsei Chachamim*).
2. "A healing." The related English word "sanitary" means "providing healthy cleanliness."
3. According to Rashi מִחְיַת is related to healing, and not to blotting out, as *Abarbanel* understands. Nor is it related to בָּשָׂר חַי, "raw meat," as it means in *I Samuel* 2:15.
4. The ו of וּמִחְיַת is understood as "or," not "and" — either white hair or healthy flesh makes the affliction impure (*Sefer Zikaron; Be'er Yitzchak*).
5. *S'eis* and *baheres*, which are first mentioned in verse 2, are the two whitest afflictions, and are considered the primary appearances of *tzara'as*. *Sapachas* which is also mentioned in that verse, is interpreted as teaching us that both *s'eis* and *baheres* have an offspring, an appearance of a lesser degree of whiteness, which is also an impure affliction. See *Negaim* 1:1.
6. *Toras Kohanim, parshasa* 3:1. Verse 9 uses נֶגַע צָרַעַת, "an affliction of *tzara'as*," when צָרַעַת alone should have been sufficient. The additional נֶגַע teaches us that the laws of verses 9-10 apply to any affliction of *tzara'as*, not only to *s'eis* (*Minchas Yehudah; Sifsei Chachamim*).
7. The term מֵרֹאשׁוֹ וְעַד רַגְלָיו does not refer to הַנֶּגַע, "the affliction," which immediately precedes it in the verse, in which case it would have meant "from its top to its bottom." It refers to the person who has the affliction (*Sefer Zikaron; Mizrachi; Sifsei Chachamim*).

יג לְכָל־מַרְאֵה עֵינֵי הַכֹּהֵן: וְרָאָה
הַכֹּהֵן וְהִנֵּה כִסְּתָה הַצָּרַעַת אֶת־
כָּל־בְּשָׂרוֹ וְטִהַר אֶת־הַנֶּגַע כֻּלּוֹ
יד הָפַךְ לָבָן טָהוֹר הוּא: וּבְיוֹם הֵרָאוֹת
טו בּוֹ בָּשָׂר חַי יִטְמָא: וְרָאָה הַכֹּהֵן

wherever the eyes of the Kohen can see — ¹³ *the Kohen shall look, and behold! — the affliction has covered his entire flesh, then he shall declare the affliction to be pure; having turned completely white, it is pure.* ¹⁴ *And on the day healthy flesh appears in it, it shall be impure.* ¹⁵ *The Kohen shall look*

---- אונקלוס ----

לְכָל חֵיזוּ עֵינֵי כַהֲנָא: יגוְיֶחֱזֵי כַהֲנָא וְהָא חֲפַת סְגִירוּתָא יָת כָּל בִּסְרֵהּ וִידַכֵּי יָת מַכְתָּשָׁא כֻּלֵּהּ אִתְהֲפִיךְ לְמֶחְוָר דְּכֵי הוּא: ידוּבְיוֹמָא דְּאִתַּחֲזֵי בֵהּ בִּסְרָא חַיָּא יְהֵי מְסָאָב: טווְיֶחֱזֵי כַהֲנָא

---- רש"י ----

לכל מראה עיני הכהן. פרט לכהן שחשך מאורו (שם פרק ד:ד):
(יד) וביום הראות בו בשר חי. אם צמחה בו מחיה הרי כבר פי' שהמחיה סימן טומאה. אלא הרי שהי' הנגע בא' מכ"ד ראשי איברים שאין מטמאין משום מחיה, לפי שאין נראה הנגע כולו כאחד

שנופט (ס"א שנופטין) אילך ואילך, וחזר ראש האבר ונתגלה שפוטו ע"י שומן כגון שהבריא ונעשה רחב ונרחית בו המחיה, למדנו הכתוב שתטמא (שם פרק ה:א): **וביום.** מה תלמוד לומר. יש יום שאתה רואה בו ויש יום שאין אתה רואה בו. מכאן אמרו,

---- RASHI ELUCIDATED ----

□ לְכָל מַרְאֵה עֵינֵי הַכֹּהֵן — **WHEREVER THE EYES OF THE KOHEN CAN SEE.** פְּרָט לְכֹהֵן — **To the exclusion of a Kohen** שֶׁחָשַׁךְ מְאוֹרוֹ¹ — **whose power of vision is impaired.**¹

14. וּבְיוֹם הֵרָאוֹת בּוֹ בָּשָׂר חַי — **AND ON THE DAY HEALTHY FLESH APPEARS IN IT.** אִם צָמְחָה בּוֹ מִחְיָה — **If healthy flesh had grown in it,** הֲרֵי כְּבָר פֵּרֵשׁ — **[the Torah] has already stated explicitly**² שֶׁהַמִּחְיָה סִימַן טֻמְאָה — **that healthy flesh is a sign of impurity,** and this verse would not need to repeat it. אֶלָּא — **Rather,** our verse teaches us the following: הֲרֵי שֶׁהָיָה הַנֶּגַע בְּאֶחָד מֵעֶשְׂרִים וְאַרְבָּעָה רָאשֵׁי אֵבָרִים — **Now, then, if [the affliction] was on one of the twenty-four tips of limbs,**³ שֶׁאֵין מְטַמְּאִין מִשּׁוּם מִחְיָה — **which do not cause impurity due to** the appearance of the sign of **healthy flesh,** לְפִי שֶׁאֵין נִרְאֶה הַנֶּגַע — **because the affliction cannot be seen** כֻּלּוֹ — **in its entirety** כְּאֶחָד — **at once,** i.e. with a single look, שֶׁשּׁוֹפֵעַ⁴ — **because it slants**⁴ אֵילָךְ וְאֵילָךְ — **to this side and to that,** וְחָזַר רֹאשׁ הָאֵבָר — **and then the tip of the limb underwent a change** וְנִתְגַּלָּה שִׁפּוּעוֹ — **and its inclination was exposed,** i.e., the area which previously could not be seen in its entirety at once, became visible as a whole, עַל יְדֵי שׁוּמָן — **through fat,** i.e., because an accumulation of fat eliminated the incline, כְּגוֹן שֶׁהִבְרִיא — **for example, [the area of the affliction] became fat** וְנַעֲשָׂה רָחָב — **and it became broader,** וְנִרְאֵית בּוֹ הַמִּחְיָה — **and the healthy flesh became visible** in its entirety **in it,** לִמְּדָנוּ הַכָּתוּב — **the verse teaches us** שֶׁתְּטַמֵּא⁵ — **that it makes** him **impure.**⁵

□ וּבְיוֹם — **AND ON THE DAY.** מַה תַּלְמוּד לוֹמַר — **Why is this stated?** לְלַמֵּד — **To teach** us that יֵשׁ יוֹם שֶׁאַתָּה רוֹאֶה בּוֹ — **there is a day on which you look** at afflictions to determine whether they are pure, שֶׁאֵין אַתָּה רוֹאֶה בּוֹ — **on which you do not look.**⁶ מִכָּאן אָמְרוּ — **From** וְיֵשׁ יוֹם — **and there is a day**

---

1. *Toras Kohanim, Negaim, perek* 4:4.
2. Verses 10-11.
3. The twenty-four tips of limbs are: the twenty fingers and toes, the two ears, the nose, and the tip of the male organ (*Kiddushin* 25a; see also *Rashi* to *Exodus* 21:26).
4. "It" may refer to either the affliction or the limb. Some editions read שֶׁשּׁוֹפְעָין, "because they slant," with "the tips of limbs" as the subject.
5. *Toras Kohanim, perek* 5:1. Verse 3 says, וְרָאָהוּ הַכֹּהֵן, "the Kohen shall look at it." The verse could have said וְרָאָה הַכֹּהֵן, "the Kohen shall look," and "at it" would have been understood. The Torah adds the ו suffix which means "at it" to teach us that the Kohen must be able to see the entire affliction in one glance in order to declare the sufferer impure. If the affliction is on one of the twenty-four tips of limbs (see below), which are slanted, however, the Kohen would not be able to see it all at once. In this situation, although the affliction might be larger than the minimum size, the sufferer is not impure. Our verse deals with a case in which the Kohen originally declared the sufferer pure because he could not view the entire affliction with one glance, and subsequently the tip of the limb became visible as a whole, because the limb became broader. Although the affliction he has is the same one once declared pure, now that it is visible in its entirety, the sufferer becomes impure (*Mizrachi*; *Sifsei Chachamim*).

6. The verse could have said, בְּהֵרָאוֹת בּוֹ בָּשָׂר חַי, "when healthy flesh appears in it." "On the day" implies that the affliction is to be viewed only on certain days (*Gur Aryeh*; *Sifsei Chachamim*).

at the healthy flesh and make him impure; the healthy flesh is impure; it is tzara'as. ¹⁶ But if the healthy flesh changes again and turns white, he shall come to the Kohen. ¹⁷ The Kohen shall look at it, and behold! — the affliction has turned white, the Kohen shall declare the affliction pure; it is pure.

¹⁸ If flesh will have had an inflammation on its skin, and it will have healed, ¹⁹ and on the place of the inflammation there will be a white s'eis or a reddish-white baheres, it shall be shown to the Kohen.

אֶת־הַבָּשָׂר הַחַי וְטִמְּאוֹ הַבָּשָׂר
טו הַחַי טָמֵא הוּא צָרַעַת הִוא: אוֹ כִי
יָשׁוּב הַבָּשָׂר הַחַי וְנֶהְפַּךְ לְלָבָן
יז וּבָא אֶל־הַכֹּהֵן: וְרָאָהוּ הַכֹּהֵן וְהִנֵּה
נֶהְפַּךְ הַנֶּגַע לְלָבָן וְטִהַר הַכֹּהֵן
אֶת־הַנֶּגַע טָהוֹר הוּא:
יח שלישי וּבָשָׂר כִּי־יִהְיֶה בוֹ־בְעֹרוֹ
יט שְׁחִין וְנִרְפָּא: וְהָיָה בִּמְקוֹם
הַשְּׁחִין שְׂאֵת לְבָנָה אוֹ בַהֶרֶת
לְבָנָה אֲדַמְדָּמֶת וְנִרְאָה אֶל־הַכֹּהֵן:

— אונקלוס —

יָת בִּסְרָא חַיָּא וִיסָאֲבִנֵּהּ בִּסְרָא חַיָּא מְסָאָב הוּא סְגִירוּת הוּא: טז אוֹ אֲרֵי יְתוּב בִּסְרָא חַיָּא וְיִתְהַפֵּךְ לְמִחְוָר וְיֵיתֵי לְוָת כָּהֲנָא: יז וְיֶחֱזִנֵּהּ כַּהֲנָא וְהָא אִתְהַפֵּךְ מַכְתָּשָׁא לְמִחְוַר וִידַכֵּי כַהֲנָא יָת מַכְתָּשָׁא דְּכֵי הוּא: יח וֶאֱנָשׁ אֲרֵי יְהֵי בֵהּ בְּמַשְׁכֵּהּ שִׁחֲנָא וְיִתַּסֵּי: יט וִיהֵי בַּאֲתַר שִׁחֲנָא עֲמַק חִוָּר אוֹ בַהֲרָא חִוְרָא סָמְקָא וְיִתַּחֲזֵי לְכַהֲנָא:

— רש"י —

חַתָּן נוֹתְנִין לוֹ כָל שִׁבְעַת יְמֵי הַמִּשְׁתֶּה לוֹ וּלְאִצְטְלִיתוֹ וּלְכִסוּתוֹ וּלְבֵיתוֹ, וְכֵן בָּרֶגֶל נוֹתְנִין לוֹ כָּל יְמֵי הָרֶגֶל (מו"ק ז:) בְּכוֹרוֹת לד:): (טו) צָרַעַת הוּא. הַבָּשָׂר הַהוּא. בָּשָׂר לְשׁוֹן זָכָר: (יח) שְׁחִין. לְשׁוֹן חֲמוּם, שֶׁנִּתְחַמֵּם הַבָּשָׂר בְּלִקּוּי הַבָּא לוֹ מֵחֲמַת מַכָּה שֶׁלֹּא מֵחֲמַת הָאוּר (חולין ח.): וְנִרְפָּא. הַשְּׁחִין הֶעֱלָה אֲרוּכָה וּבִמְקוֹמוֹ הֶעֱלָה נֶגַע אַחֵר: (יט) אוֹ בַהֶרֶת לְבָנָה אֲדַמְדָּמֶת. שֶׁאֵין הַנֶּגַע לָבָן חָלָק אֶלָּא פָתוּךְ וּמְעֹרָב בִּשְׁתֵּי מַרְאוֹת לֹבֶן וְאֹדֶם (נגעים א:ב; שבועות ו.):

— RASHI ELUCIDATED —

here, i.e., on the basis of this source, [the Sages] said, regarding חָתָן – a bridegroom, נוֹתְנִין לוֹ כָּל שִׁבְעַת יְמֵי הַמִּשְׁתֶּה – that they grant him the entire seven days of his celebration; לוֹ – for him,¹ וּלְאִצְטְלִיתוֹ – and for his robe, וְלִכְסוּתוֹ – and for his garment,² וּלְבֵיתוֹ – and for his house.³ וְכֵן בָּרֶגֶל – Similarly, on a festival,⁴ נוֹתְנִין לוֹ כָּל יְמֵי הָרֶגֶל – they grant him all of the days of the festival.⁴

15. צָרַעַת הוּא – IT IS TZARA'AS. הַבָּשָׂר הַהוּא – That flesh. בָּשָׂר לְשׁוֹן זָכָר – The word בָּשָׂר is masculine.⁵

18. שְׁחִין – AN INFLAMMATION. This word לְשׁוֹן חִמּוּם – means "heating,"⁶ שֶׁנִּתְחַמֵּם הַבָּשָׂר – for the flesh became hot בְּלִקּוּי הַבָּא לוֹ – through infection which came to it מֵחֲמַת מַכָּה – due to a blow; שֶׁלֹּא מֵחֲמַת הָאוּר – not due to fire.⁷

וְנִרְפָּא – AND IT WILL HAVE HEALED. הַשְּׁחִין – The inflammation הֶעֱלָה אֲרוּכָה – grew better, וּבִמְקוֹמוֹ – and in its place הֶעֱלָה נֶגַע אַחֵר – another affliction developed.⁸

19. אוֹ בַהֶרֶת לְבָנָה אֲדַמְדָּמֶת – OR A REDDISH-WHITE BAHERES. This means שֶׁאֵין הַנֶּגַע לָבָן חָלָק – that the affliction is not solid white, אֶלָּא פָתוּךְ – but rather streaked וּמְעֹרָב – and mixed בִּשְׁתֵּי מַרְאוֹת – by two appearances; לֹבֶן וְאֹדֶם⁹ – whiteness and redness, i.e., it is a blend of two colors, white and red.⁹

1. If he develops an affliction of *tzara'as*, the Kohen will not view the affliction during the seven days of his wedding celebration, so as not to mar his joy through a pronouncement of impurity.
2. If his garment develops an affliction. See below verses 47-58.
3. If his house develops an affliction. See 14:33-53.
4. *Moed Kattan* 7b; *Bechoros* 34b. This law applies to anyone, not only a bridegroom, so as not to mar the joy of the festival (*Sifsei Chachamim*).
5. Although צָרַעַת is feminine, the masculine הוּא follows

it, because הוּא refers to the masculine הַבָּשָׂר (*Mizrachi*).
6. Rashi explains that although in everyday language the word שְׁחִין is used to describe the boil and the fluid that oozes from it, the precise meaning of the word שְׁחִין is "heat" (*Mizrachi* to *Exodus* 9:9).
7. *Toras Kohanim, perek* 6:6; *Chullin* 8a.
8. "It" of "it will have healed" refers to the inflammation, not to the flesh. The flesh cannot be said to have healed if there is still an affliction on it (*Mizrachi*; *Sifsei Chachamim*).
9. *Negaim* 1:2; *Shevuos* 6a.

²⁰ *The Kohen shall look, and behold! — its appearance is lower than the skin, and its hair has turned white: The Kohen shall make him impure; it is a tzara'as affliction that erupted on the inflammation.* ²¹ *But if the Kohen looks at it, and behold! — there is no white hair in it, and it is not lower than the skin, and it is dim; the Kohen shall close it off for a seven-day period.* ²² *If it spreads on the skin, the Kohen shall make him impure; it is an affliction.* ²³ *But if the baheres remains in its place without spreading, it is a scarring of the inflammation;*

כ וְרָאָה הַכֹּהֵן וְהִנֵּה מַרְאֶהָ שָׁפָל מִן־הָעוֹר וּשְׂעָרָהּ הָפַךְ לָבָן וְטִמְּאוֹ הַכֹּהֵן נֶגַע־צָרַעַת הִוא בַּשְּׁחִין פָּרָחָה: כא וְאִם ׀ יִרְאֶנָּה הַכֹּהֵן וְהִנֵּה אֵין־בָּהּ שֵׂעָר לָבָן וּשְׁפָלָה אֵינֶנָּה מִן־הָעוֹר וְהִיא כֵהָה וְהִסְגִּירוֹ הַכֹּהֵן שִׁבְעַת יָמִים: כב וְאִם־פָּשֹׂה תִפְשֶׂה בָּעוֹר וְטִמֵּא הַכֹּהֵן אֹתוֹ נֶגַע הִוא: כג וְאִם־תַּחְתֶּיהָ תַעֲמֹד הַבַּהֶרֶת לֹא פָשָׂתָה צָרֶבֶת הַשְּׁחִין הִוא

---------- אונקלוס ----------

כ וְיֶחֱזֵי כַהֲנָא וְהָא מֶחֱזַהָא מַכִּיךְ מִן מַשְׁכָּא וְשַׂעְרַהּ אִתְהֲפִיךְ לְמֶחְוַר וִיסָאֲבִנֵּהּ כַהֲנָא מַכְתָּשׁ סְגִירוּתָא הִיא בְּשִׁחֲנָא סְגִיאַת: כא וְאִם יֶחֱזִנַּהּ כַּהֲנָא וְהָא לֵית בַּהּ שְׂעַר חִוַּר וּמַכִּיכָא לֵיתָהָא מִן מַשְׁכָּא וְהִיא עַמְיָא וְיַסְגְּרִנֵּהּ כַּהֲנָא שַׁבְעָא יוֹמִין: כב וְאִם אוֹסָפָא תוֹסִף בְּמַשְׁכָּא וִיסָאֵב כַּהֲנָא יָתֵהּ מַכְתָּשָׁא הִיא: כג וְאִם בְּאַתְרָהָא קָמַת בְּהֶרְתָּא לָא אוֹסֵפַת רֹשֶׁם שִׁחֲנָא הִיא

---------- רש"י ----------

(ב) מראה שפל. ואין ממשו שפל אלא מתוך לבנוניתו הוא נראה שפל ועמוק, כמראה חמה עמוקה מן הצל (ת"כ נגעים פרשתא ח:ד; שבועות ו.): (כב) נגע הוא. השאת הזאת או הבהרת: (כג) תחתיה. במקומה: צרבת השחין. כתרגומו רשם שיחנא, אינו אלא רושם החמום הניכר בבשר. כל לרבת לשון רגיעת עור הנרגע מחמת חימום, כמו ונלרבו בה כל פנים (יחזקאל כא:ג) רייטרי"ר בלע"ז: צרבת. רייטרישמנ"ט בלע"ז:

---------- RASHI ELUCIDATED ----------

20. שָׁפָל מַרְאֵהוּ — ITS APPEARANCE IS LOWER. שָׁפָל מַמָּשׁוּ אֵין — But its substance is not lower, וְעָמוֹק — הוּא נִרְאֶה שָׁפָל — it appears low אֶלָּא מִתּוֹךְ לַבְנוּנִיתוֹ — but because of its whiteness and deep, כְּמַרְאֵה חַמָּה — as the appearance of sun, i.e., the appearance of a surface which reflects the sun's light, עֲמוּקָה מִן הַצֵּל — is deeper than the shade, i.e., it appears to be lower than the shade.[1]

22. נֶגַע הוּא — IT IS AN AFFLICTION. הַשְּׂאֵת הַזֹּאת — This *s'eis*[2] אוֹ הַבַּהֶרֶת — or *baheres*.

23. תַּחְתֶּיהָ — This means בִּמְקוֹמָהּ — in its place.[3]

□ צָרֶבֶת הַשְּׁחִין — A SCARRING OF THE INFLAMMATION. This is to be understood כְּתַרְגּוּמוֹ — as *Targum Onkelos* renders it, "רֹשֶׁם שִׁחֲנָא,, — "a mark of the inflammation," i.e., its scar. אֵינוֹ אֶלָּא רוֹשֶׁם הַנִּכָּר בַּבָּשָׂר — It is nothing but a mark of the heating, i.e., the inflammation, הַחִמּוּם — that is discernible in the flesh. כָּל צָרֶבֶת — Any use of צָרֶבֶת — לְשׁוֹן רְגִיעַת עוֹר — is an expression of wrinkling of skin הַנִּרְגָּע מֵחֲמַת חִמּוּם — which wrinkles because of heating, כְּמוֹ ,,וְנִצְרְבוּ בָהּ כָּל — like in, "and all faces shall be shriveled by it."[4] פָּנִים,, — רייטרי"ר בלע"ז — *Retraire* in Old French.[5]

□ צָרֶבֶת — This means רייטרישמנ"ט בלע"ז — *rétréciment* in Old French.[6]

---

1. *Toras Kohanim, Negaim, parshasa* 1:4; *Shevuos* 6b.

2. Although נֶגַע is masculine, as Rashi has mentioned in his comments to verse 8, the verse here uses the feminine הִיא because it refers to the feminine שְׂאֵת and בַּהֶרֶת (*Sefer Zikaron*).

3. The word does not mean "underneath it," as it does in *Joshua* 7:21. Rather, it means "in its place," as it does in *Job* 28:15.

4. *Ezekiel* 21:3.

5. The Old French verbs *retraire* (also spelled *retraite*, see Rashi to *Shabbos* 120a; in Modern French, *retirer*) and *rétrécir* (same in Modern French; see next note), when used in reference to cloth or skin, mean "to shrink" or "to shrivel."

6. Some editions read רייטריאמנ"ט, *retraiement* (in Modern French *rétraction*). That word and *rétréciment* (in Modern French *rétrécissement*) are the respective noun forms of *retraire* and *rétrécir* (see previous note) and mean "shrinkage" or "shriveling."

the Kohen shall declare him pure. ²⁴ If a person will have a burn from fire on his skin, and the healed skin of the burn is a reddish-white baheres or is all white; ²⁵ the Kohen shall look, and behold! — hair has turned white in the baheres, and its appearance is deeper than the skin, it is tzara'as that erupted on the burn, the Kohen shall make him impure; it is a tzara'as affliction. ²⁶ And if the Kohen looks at it and behold! — there is no white hair in the baheres, and it is not lower than the skin, and it is dim; the Kohen shall close him off for a seven-day period. ²⁷ The Kohen shall look at it on the seventh day: If it has spread on the skin, the Kohen shall make him impure; it is a tzara'as affliction. ²⁸ But if the baheres remains in its place, not spreading on the skin, and it is dim, it is a s'eis of the burn; the Kohen shall declare him pure, for it is the scarring of the burn.

²⁹ A man or a woman in whom there will be an affliction, on the scalp or in the beard: ³⁰ The Kohen shall look at the

כד וְטִהֲרוֹ הַכֹּהֵן: רביעי [שני] אוֹ בָשָׂר כִּי־יִהְיֶה בְעֹרוֹ מִכְוַת־אֵשׁ וְהָיְתָה מִחְיַת הַמִּכְוָה בַּהֶרֶת לְבָנָה אֲדַמְדֶּמֶת אוֹ לְבָנָה: כה וְרָאָה אֹתָהּ הַכֹּהֵן וְהִנֵּה נֶהְפַּךְ שֵׂעָר לָבָן בַּבַּהֶרֶת וּמַרְאֶהָ עָמֹק מִן־הָעוֹר צָרַעַת הִוא בַּמִּכְוָה פָּרָחָה וְטִמֵּא אֹתוֹ הַכֹּהֵן נֶגַע צָרַעַת הִוא: כו וְאִם ׀ יִרְאֶנָּה הַכֹּהֵן וְהִנֵּה אֵין־בַּבֶּהֶרֶת שֵׂעָר לָבָן וּשְׁפָלָה אֵינֶנָּה מִן־הָעוֹר וְהִוא כֵהָה וְהִסְגִּירוֹ הַכֹּהֵן שִׁבְעַת יָמִים: כז וְרָאָהוּ הַכֹּהֵן בַּיּוֹם הַשְּׁבִיעִי אִם־פָּשֹׂה תִפְשֶׂה בָּעוֹר וְטִמֵּא הַכֹּהֵן אֹתוֹ נֶגַע צָרַעַת הִוא: כח וְאִם־תַּחְתֶּיהָ תַעֲמֹד הַבַּהֶרֶת לֹא־פָשְׂתָה בָעוֹר וְהִוא כֵהָה שְׂאֵת הַמִּכְוָה הִוא וְטִהֲרוֹ הַכֹּהֵן כִּי־צָרֶבֶת הַמִּכְוָה הִוא:

חמישי כט וְאִישׁ אוֹ אִשָּׁה כִּי־יִהְיֶה בוֹ נָגַע בְּרֹאשׁ אוֹ בְזָקָן: ל וְרָאָה הַכֹּהֵן אֶת־

אונקלוס

וִידַכִּנֵּהּ כַּהֲנָא: כד אוֹ אֱנַשׁ אֲרֵי יְהֵי בְמַשְׁכֵּהּ כְּוָאָה דְּנוּר וּתְהֵי רֹשֶׁם כְּוָאָה בַּהֲרָא חִוָּרָא סַמְקָא אוֹ חִוָּרָא: כה וְיֶחֱזֵי יָתַהּ כַּהֲנָא וְהָא אִתְהַפִּיךְ שְׂעַר חִוָּר בְּבַהֲרָתָא וּמֶחֱזַהּ מִן מַשְׁכָּא סַגְיָא סְגִירוּתָא הִיא בִּכְוָאָה סְגִיאַת וִיסָאֵב יָתֵהּ כַּהֲנָא מַכְתַּשׁ סְגִירוּתָא הִיא: כו וְאִם יֶחֱזִנַּהּ כַּהֲנָא לֵית בְּבַהֲרָתָא שְׂעַר חִוָּר וּמוּכִיכָא לֵיתַהָא מִן מַשְׁכָּא וְהִיא עֲמִיָא וְיַסְגְּרִנֵּהּ כַּהֲנָא שִׁבְעָא יוֹמִין: כז וְיֶחֱזִנֵּהּ כַּהֲנָא בְּיוֹמָא שְׁבִיעָאָה אִם אוֹסָפָא תוֹסַף בְּמַשְׁכָּא וִיסָאֵב כַּהֲנָא יָתֵהּ מַכְתַּשׁ סְגִירוּתָא הִיא: כח וְאִם בְּאַתְרַהָא קָמַת בַּהֲרָתָא לָא אוֹסֵפַת בְּמַשְׁכָּא וְהִיא עֲמִיָא עֲמִיק כְּוָאָה הִיא וִידַכִּנֵּהּ כַּהֲנָא אֲרֵי רֹשֶׁם כְּוָאָה הִיא: כט וּגְבַר אוֹ אִתְּתָא אֲרֵי יְהֵי בֵהּ מַכְתָּשָׁא בְּרֵישָׁא אוֹ בְדִקְנָא: ל וְיֶחֱזֵי כַהֲנָא יָת

רש"י

(כד) מחית המכוה. שנימי"ט בלע"ז כשחיתה המכוה נהפכה לבהרת פתוכה או לבנה חלקה. וסימני מכוה וסימני שחין שוים הם, ולמה חלקן הכתוב, לומר שאין מצטרפין זה עם זה, נולד חצי גריס בשחין וחצי גריס במכוה לא ידונו כגריס (חולין ח.): (כט) בראש או בזקן. בא הכתוב לחלק בין נגע שבמקום שער לנגע שבמקום בשר, שזה סימנו

RASHI ELUCIDATED

24. מִחְיַת הַמִּכְוָה — THE HEALED SKIN OF THE BURN. — שנימי"ט בלע"ז — *Sanement* in Old French.[1] פְּתוּכָה — a mixture of white and red אוֹ לְבָנָה חֲלָקָה — or solid white. וְסִימָנֵי מִכְוָה — The signs of impurity of a burn וְסִימָנֵי שְׁחִין — and the signs of impurity of an inflammation שָׁוִים הֵם — are identical. וְלָמָּה — כְּשֶׁחָיְתָה הַמִּכְוָה — When the burn healed, נֶהְפְּכָה לְבַהֶרֶת — it turned into a *baheres*, חִלְּקָן הַכָּתוּב — Why, then, did Scripture divide them, i.e., present them separately? לוֹמַר — To say שֶׁאֵין מִצְטָרְפִין זֶה עִם זֶה — that they do not combine with each other; that is, נוֹלַד חֲצִי גְרִיס בַּשְּׁחִין — if there developed half a *g'ris*[2] of *baheres* in the inflammation where it healed, וַחֲצִי גְרִיס בַּמִּכְוָה — and half a *g'ris* of *baheres* in the burn where it healed, לֹא יִדּוֹנוּ כִּגְרִיס — they are not to be considered as a full *g'ris* of *baheres*, and the combined afflictions do not cause impurity.[3]

29. בְּרֹאשׁ אוֹ בְזָקָן — ON THE SCALP OR IN THE BEARD. בָּא הַכָּתוּב לְחַלֵּק — Scripture comes to distinguish לְגֶנַע שֶׁבִּמְקוֹם שֵׂעָר — between an affliction that is in a hairy place בֵּין נֶגַע שֶׁבִּמְקוֹם שֵׂעָר — – and an affliction that is in a place of flesh, שֶׁזֶּה סִימָנוֹ — for this one, i.e., the affliction in a

---

1. See verse 10, note 2 above.
2. A type of large bean; its size is the minimum size for an affliction to cause impurity.
3. *Chullin* 8a.

13 *affliction, and behold! — its appearance is deeper than the skin, and in it is yellowish, weak, hair; the Kohen shall make him impure; it is a nesek, a tzara'as of the head or the beard.* ³¹ *But if the Kohen looks at the nesek affliction, and behold! — its appearance is not deeper than the skin, but there is no dark hair in it; the Kohen shall close off the nesek affliction for seven days.* ³² *The Kohen shall look at the affliction on the seventh day and behold! — the nesek had not spread and no yellowish hair was in it,*

הַנֶּגַע וְהִנֵּה מַרְאֵהוּ עָמֹק מִן־הָעוֹר וּבוֹ שֵׂעָר צָהֹב דָּק וְטִמֵּא אֹתוֹ הַכֹּהֵן נֶתֶק הוּא צָרַעַת הָרֹאשׁ אוֹ הַזָּקָן הוּא: לא וְכִי־יִרְאֶה הַכֹּהֵן אֶת־נֶגַע הַנֶּתֶק וְהִנֵּה אֵין־מַרְאֵהוּ עָמֹק מִן־ הָעוֹר וְשֵׂעָר שָׁחֹר אֵין בּוֹ וְהִסְגִּיר הַכֹּהֵן אֶת־נֶגַע הַנֶּתֶק שִׁבְעַת יָמִים: לב וְרָאָה הַכֹּהֵן אֶת־הַנֶּגַע בַּיּוֹם הַשְּׁבִיעִי וְהִנֵּה לֹא־פָשָׂה הַנֶּתֶק וְלֹא־הָיָה בוֹ שֵׂעָר צָהֹב

— אונקלוס —

מַכְתָּשָׁא וְהָא מֶחְזוֹהִי עַמִּיק מִן מַשְׁכָּא וּבֵהּ שְׂעַר סַמַּק דַּעֲדַק וִיסָאֵב יָתֵהּ כַּהֲנָא נִתְקָא הוּא סְגִירוּת רֵישָׁא אוֹ דְקָנָא הוּא: לא וַאֲרֵי יֶחֱזֵי כַּהֲנָא יָת מַכְתַּשׁ נִתְקָא וְהָא לֵית מֶחְזוֹהִי עַמִּיק מִן מַשְׁכָּא וּשְׂעַר אֻכָּם לֵית בֵּהּ וְיַסְגַּר כַּהֲנָא יָת מַכְתַּשׁ נִתְקָא שִׁבְעָא יוֹמִין: לב וְיֶחֱזֵי כַהֲנָא יָת מַכְתָּשָׁא בְּיוֹמָא שְׁבִיעָאָה וְהָא לָא אוֹסִיף נִתְקָא וְלָא הֲוָה בֵהּ שְׂעַר סַמָּק

— רש"י —

(ל) **וּבוֹ שֵׂעָר צָהֹב.** שֶׁנֶּהְפַּךְ שְׂעַר שָׁחוֹר שֶׁבּוֹ לְצָהוֹב: **נֶתֶק הוּא.** כָּךְ שְׁמוֹ שֶׁל נֶגַע שֶׁבִּמְקוֹם שֵׂעָר: **(לא) וְשֵׂעָר שָׁחֹר אֵין בּוֹ.** הָא אִם הָיָה בוֹ שֵׂעָר שָׁחֹר בְּשִׂמָּנוֹ בְּשֵׂעָר לָבָן (ת"כ פרשתא ה:ה): שָׁחוֹר, טָהוֹר, וְאֵין צָרִיךְ לְהַסְגִּיר, שֶׁשְּׂעָר שָׁחוֹר סִימָן טָהֳרָה הוּא בִּנְתָקִים כְּמוֹ שֶׁנֶּאֱמַר וְשֵׂעָר שָׁחוֹר לָמָח בּוֹ וְגוֹ' (להלן פסוק לז; ת"כ פרק ח:ט): **(לב) וְהִנֵּה לֹא פָשָׂה** **וְגוֹ'.** הָא אִם פָּשָׂה אוֹ הָיָה בוֹ שֵׂעָר צָהֹב, טָמֵא:

— RASHI ELUCIDATED —

place of flesh, discussed in the previous passages, **its sign** of impurity בְּשֵׂעָר לָבָן – **is in white hair**, וְזֶה סִימָנוֹ – **and this one**, i.e., the affliction in a hairy place, **its sign** of impurity ¹בְּשֵׂעָר צָהֹב – **is in yellowish hair.**¹

30. וּבוֹ שֵׂעָר צָהֹב – **AND IN IT IS YELLOWISH, [WEAK,] HAIR.** ²שֶׁנֶּהְפַּךְ שֵׂעָר שָׁחוֹר שֶׁבּוֹ לְצָהוֹב – **That the dark hair in it turned yellowish.**²

נֶתֶק הוּא – **IT IS A** *NESEK.* כָּךְ שְׁמוֹ – **Such is the name** שֶׁל נֶגַע – **of an affliction** שֶׁבִּמְקוֹם שֵׂעָר – **that is in a hairy place.**

31. וְשֵׂעָר שָׁחֹר אֵין בּוֹ – **BUT THERE IS NO DARK HAIR IN IT.** הָא אִם הָיָה בּוֹ שֵׂעָר שָׁחוֹר – **But if there was in it dark hair,** טָהוֹר – **it is pure,** וְאֵין צָרִיךְ לְהַסְגִּיר – **and he does not have to be closed off,**³ שֶׁשְּׂעָר שָׁחוֹר – **because dark hair** סִימָן טָהֳרָה הוּא – **is a sign of purity** בִּנְתָקִים – **in afflictions of the hairy parts,** כְּמוֹ שֶׁנֶּאֱמַר – **as it says,** ⁴,⁵״וְשֵׂעָר שָׁחֹר צָמַח בּוֹ וְגוֹמֵר,, – **"and dark hair has sprouted in it, etc."**⁴,⁵

32. וְהִנֵּה לֹא פָשָׂה וְגוֹמֵר – **AND BEHOLD! – THE** *NESEK* **HAD NOT SPREAD, ETC.** הָא אִם פָּשָׂה – **But if it spread,** אוֹ הָיָה בוֹ שֵׂעָר צָהֹב – **or there was in it yellowish hair,** טָמֵא – **it is impure.**⁶

---

1. *Toras Kohanim, parshasa* 5:5.

2. *Toras Kohanim, perek* 8:1. Yellowish hair is a sign of impurity only if the hair turned yellowish due to the affliction. If the hair was originally yellowish, it is not a sign of impurity (see *Mizrachi*).

3. See verse 4 above.

4. Below v. 37. That verse continues, "the *nesek* has healed — it is pure."

5. *Toras Kohanim, perek* 8:9. Our verse says that if the Kohen examines the affliction and there is no dark hair in it, the affliction is to be quarantined. This could be taken to imply that if there *is* dark hair in it, the affliction is decidedly impure, with no need for quarantine and further examination. Rashi shows that this is not the case by citing verse 37 which says that dark hair is a sign of purity. Thus, our verse is saying that if dark hair remained in the *nesek*, he is pure without need for further quarantine and examination (*Mizrachi*; *Sifsei Chachamim*).

6. "The *nesek* had not spread and no yellowish hair was in it" could be understood as implying that both conditions are necessary for declaring impurity. Rashi explains that either the spread of the *nesek* or the presence of yellowish hair alone is sufficient to declare the *nesek* impure (*Mizrachi*).

/ ויקרא – פרשת תזריע

and the appearance of the nesek is not deeper than the skin — ³³ then he shall shave himself, but he shall not shave that which is with the nesek; and the Kohen shall close off the nesek for a second seven-day period. ³⁴ The Kohen shall look at the nesek on the seventh day, and behold! — the nesek had not spread on the skin, and its appearance is not deeper than the skin; the Kohen shall declare him pure, and he shall immerse his clothing and he is pure. ³⁵ But if the nesek shall spread on the skin after it has been declared pure, ³⁶ the Kohen shall look at it, and behold! — the nesek has spread on the skin: The Kohen need not examine it for a yellowish hair, it is impure. ³⁷ But if the nesek has retained its appearance, and dark hair has sprouted in it,

וּמַרְאֵה הַנֶּתֶק אֵין עָמֹק מִן־הָעוֹר: לג וְהִתְגַּלָּח וְאֶת־הַנֶּתֶק לֹא יְגַלֵּחַ וְהִסְגִּיר הַכֹּהֵן אֶת־הַנֶּתֶק שִׁבְעַת יָמִים שֵׁנִית: לד וְרָאָה הַכֹּהֵן אֶת־הַנֶּתֶק בַּיּוֹם הַשְּׁבִיעִי וְהִנֵּה לֹא־פָשָׂה הַנֶּתֶק בָּעוֹר וּמַרְאֵהוּ אֵינֶנּוּ עָמֹק מִן־הָעוֹר וְטִהַר אֹתוֹ הַכֹּהֵן וְכִבֶּס בְּגָדָיו וְטָהֵר: לה וְאִם־פָּשֹׂה יִפְשֶׂה הַנֶּתֶק בָּעוֹר אַחֲרֵי טָהֳרָתוֹ: לו וְרָאָהוּ הַכֹּהֵן וְהִנֵּה פָּשָׂה הַנֶּתֶק בָּעוֹר לֹא־יְבַקֵּר הַכֹּהֵן לַשֵּׂעָר הַצָּהֹב טָמֵא הוּא: לז וְאִם־בְּעֵינָיו עָמַד הַנֶּתֶק וְשֵׂעָר שָׁחֹר צָמַח־בּוֹ

אונקלוס

וּמֶחְזֵי נִתְקָא לֵית עַמִּיק מִן מַשְׁכָּא: לג וִיגַלַּח סָחֲרָנֵי נִתְקָא וּדְעִם נִתְקָא לָא יְגַלַּח וְיַסְגַּר כַּהֲנָא יָת נִתְקָא שִׁבְעָא יוֹמִין תִּנְיָנוּת: לד וְיֶחֱזֵי כַהֲנָא יָת נִתְקָא בְּיוֹמָא שְׁבִיעָאָה וְהָא לָא אוֹסִיף נִתְקָא בְּמַשְׁכָּא וּמֶחְזוֹהִי לֵיתוֹהִי עַמִּיק מִן מַשְׁכָּא וִידַכֵּי יָתֵהּ כַּהֲנָא וִיצַבַּע לְבוּשׁוֹהִי וְיִדְכֵּי: לה וְאִם אוֹסָפָא יוֹסִיף נִתְקָא בְּמַשְׁכָּא בָּתַר דְּכוּתֵהּ: לו וְיַחְזִנֵּהּ כַּהֲנָא וְהָא אוֹסִיף נִתְקָא בְּמַשְׁכָּא לָא יְבַקַּר לְשַׂעַר כַּהֲנָא סַמַּק סְאִב הוּא: לז וְאִם בְּעֵינוֹהִי קָם נִתְקָא וּשְׂעַר אוּכָּם צְמַח בֵּהּ

רש"י

(לג) **והתגלח.** סְבִיבוֹת הַנֶּתֶק (נגעים י׳:ה׳): **ואת הנתק לא יגלח.** מֵנִיחַ שְׁתֵּי שְׂעָרוֹת סָמוּךְ לוֹ סָבִיב כְּדֵי שֶׁיְּהֵא נִכָּר אִם פָּשָׂה (שם): (לה) **אחרי טהרתו.** אֵין לִי אֶלָּא פּוֹשֶׂה לְאַחַר הַפְּטוֹר, מִנַּיִן אַף בְּסוֹף שָׁבוּעַ רִאשׁוֹן וּבְסוֹף שָׁבוּעַ שֵׁנִי, ת"ל פָּשֹׂה יִפְשֶׂה (ת"כ פרק ט:ט): (לז) **ושער שחר.** מִנַּיִן אַף הַיָּרוֹק

RASHI ELUCIDATED

33. וְהִתְגַּלָּח – THEN HE SHALL SHAVE HIMSELF¹ סְבִיבוֹת הַנֶּתֶק – around the *nesek*.¹

וְאֶת הַנֶּתֶק לֹא יְגַלֵּחַ – BUT HE SHALL NOT SHAVE THAT WHICH IS WITH THE *NESEK*. מֵנִיחַ שְׁתֵּי שְׂעָרוֹת סָמוּךְ לוֹ – He leaves two hairs next to it סָבִיב – all around it, i.e., he leaves a belt two hairs wide around the affliction, כְּדֵי שֶׁיְּהֵא נִכָּר – so that it will be discernible ²אִם פָּשָׂה – if [the *nesek*] spread.² שֶׁאִם יִפְשֶׂה – For if it will spread, יַעֲבוֹר הַשְּׂעָרוֹת – it will pass beyond the hairs וְיֵצֵא לִמְקוֹם הַגִּלּוּחַ – and go out to the shaved area.³

35. אַחֲרֵי טָהֳרָתוֹ – AFTER IT HAS BEEN DECLARED PURE. אֵין לִי אֶלָּא פּוֹשֶׂה – I have nothing but [a *nesek*] which spreads לְאַחַר הַפְּטוֹר – after the dismissal by the Kohen.⁴ מִנַּיִן – From where do I know that אַף בְּסוֹף שָׁבוּעַ רִאשׁוֹן – even at the end of the first week וּבְסוֹף שָׁבוּעַ שֵׁנִי – and at the end of the second week if the *nesek* spreads it is impure? תַּלְמוּד לוֹמַר – The verse says, ״פָּשֹׂה ⁵יִפְשֶׂה״ – literally, "spread shall it spread," using the double verb form which includes the infinitive.⁵

37. וְשֵׂעָר שָׁחֹר – AND DARK HAIR. מִנַּיִן – From where do we know that אַף הַיָּרוֹק – even yellow⁶

---

1. *Negaim* 10:5. See also *Targum Onkelos* who interpolates the words סָחֲרָנֵי נִתְקָא, the Aramaic form of Rashi's words סְבִיבוֹת הַנֶּתֶק.

Rashi teaches that shaving here does not involve the entire body as it does in 14:8-9 below.

2. *Negaim* 10:5.

3. The term וְאֶת הַנֶּתֶק לֹא יְגַלֵּחַ could be understood as, "but he shall not shave the *nesek*." The *nesek* itself, however, cannot be shaved, for it does not have any hair in it. Therefore, אֶת here should be understood as *Targum Onkelos* understands it, in the sense of "and that which is with," akin to its meaning in, *I Samuel* 30:21, for example. The verse thus tells us that "that which is with, or next to, the affliction" shall not be shaved (*Ramban*).

4. That is, on the basis of this verse alone, I know only that a *nesek* that spreads after the sufferer has been declared pure and dismissed by the Kohen is impure.

5. *Toras Kohanim, perek* 9:9.

6. The term יָרוֹק is a term used for different colors in different contexts (see *Tosafos, Succah* 31b; see *Rashi* to v. 49 below and note 6 there).

נִרְפָּא הַנֶּתֶק טָהוֹר הוּא וְטִהֲרוֹ הַכֹּהֵן: לח וְאִישׁ אוֹ־אִשָּׁה כִּי־יִהְיֶה בְעוֹר־בְּשָׂרָם בֶּהָרֹת בֶּהָרֹת לְבָנֹת: לט וְרָאָה הַכֹּהֵן וְהִנֵּה בְעוֹר־בְּשָׂרָם בֶּהָרֹת כֵּהוֹת לְבָנֹת בֹּהַק הוּא פָּרַח בָּעוֹר טָהוֹר הוּא: ששי [שלישי] מ וְאִישׁ כִּי יִמָּרֵט רֹאשׁוֹ קֵרֵחַ הוּא טָהוֹר הוּא:

the nesek has healed — it is pure; the Kohen shall declare it pure. ³⁸ *If a man or woman has spots in the skin of their flesh, white spots;* ³⁹ *the Kohen shall look, and behold! — on the skin of their flesh are dim white spots, it is a bohak that has erupted on the skin, it is pure.* ⁴⁰ *If the hair of a man's head falls out: He is bald at the back of the head, he is pure.*

---- אונקלוס ----

אִתַּסִּי נִתְקָא דְּכֵי הוּא וִידַכִּנֵּהּ כַּהֲנָא: לח וּגְבַר אוֹ אִתְּתָא אֲרֵי יְהֵי בִמְשַׁךְ בִּסְרְהוֹן בַּהֲרָן חִוָּרָן: לט וְיֶחֱזֵי כַהֲנָא וְהָא בִמְשַׁךְ בִּסְרְהוֹן בַּהֲרָן עַמְיָן חִוָּרָן בָּהֲקָא הוּא סְגִי בְמַשְׁכָּא דְּכֵי הוּא: מ וּגְבַר אֲרֵי יִתַּר שְׂעַר רֵישֵׁהּ קָרַח הוּא דְּכֵי הוּא:

---- רש"י ----

והאדום שאינו צהוב, ת"ל ושער (פסוק י) ולמדו [ס"א ולשון] צהוב דומה לתבנית הזהב (שם פרשתא הי"ז) צהוב כמו זהוב אורפל"א בלע"ז: **טהור הוא וטהרו הכהן**. הא טמא שטיהרו הכהן לא טהור (שם פרק ט:ט"ז): (לח) **בהרת**. חברבורות: (לט) **כהות לבנות**. שאין לובן שלהן עז אלא כהה. כמו [ס"א כמין] לובן הנראה בבשר אדם אדום שקורין רו"ש בין חברבורות אדמימותו, קרוי בהק. כאיש עדשן שבין עדשה לעדשה מבהיק הבשר בלובנו לח: (מ) **קרח הוא טהור הוא**. טהור מטומאת נתקין, שאינו נדון בסימני ראש וזקן

---- RASHI ELUCIDATED ----

וְהָאָדֹם – *and red* hairs שֶׁאֵינוֹ צָהֹב – *which are not yellowish* are a sign of purity?[1] תַּלְמוּד לוֹמַר *The verse says*, "וְשֵׂעָר,"[2] – *"and [dark] hair."*[2] וּלְמָה צָהֹב דּוֹמֶה – *To what is*[3] *"yellowish"* similar? לְתַבְנִית הַזָּהָב[4] – *To the appearance of gold.*[4] צָהֹב כְּמוֹ זָהֹב – *The word* צָהֹב *is similar to the word* זָהֹב, *which means "golden"*;[5] אורפל"א בְּלַעַ"ז – *or pale in Old French.*[6]

טָהוֹר הוּא וְטִהֲרוֹ הַכֹּהֵן – *IT IS PURE; THE KOHEN SHALL DECLARE IT PURE.* □ הָא טָמֵא – *But an impure* affliction שֶׁטִּהֲרוֹ הַכֹּהֵן – *which the Kohen declares pure* לֹא טָהוֹר[7] – *is not pure.*[7]

38. בֶּהָרֹת – *This means* חֲבַרְבּוּרוֹת – *spots.*[8]

39. אֶלָּא כֵהָה – בֵּהוֹת לְבָנֹת – *DIM WHITE.* שֶׁאֵין לוֹבֶן שֶׁלָּהֶן עַז – *That their whiteness is not intense,* but dim.

□ בֹּהַק – *BOHAK.* כְּמוֹ[9] לוֹבֶן – *Like a white patch,* הַנִּרְאָה בִּבְשַׂר אָדָם אָדֹם – *which can be seen on the flesh of a red-complexioned man* שֶׁקּוֹרִין רוֹ"ש – *which they call ros in Old French;*[10] בֵּין חֲבַרְבּוּרוֹת – *between the spots* אֲדַמִימוּתוֹ – *of his redness* קָרוּי בֹּהַק – *is called bohak.* כְּאִישׁ עַדְשָׁן – *Like a freckled person* שֶׁבֵּין עֲדָשָׁה לַעֲדָשָׁה – *upon whom between one freckle and another* מַבְהִיק הַבָּשָׂר בְּלוֹבְנוֹ צַח – *the flesh shines with a gleaming whiteness.*

40. טָהוֹר מִטֻּמְאַת נְתָקִין – He *is pure of the impurity of nesakin,* שֶׁאֵינוֹ נִדּוֹן – *for he is not judged* בְּסִימָנֵי רֹאשׁ וְזָקָן – *by the*

---

1. From where do we know that any hair that is not yellowish is a sign of purity, even if it is not dark?

2. *Toras Kohanim, perek* 9:14. The ו prefix which means "and" is apparently unnecessary. It was written to include hair which is not dark as a sign of purity (*Mesiach Ilmim*).

3. The standard printed editions read וּלְשׁוֹן צָהֹב, "and the expression 'yellowish'..." Our text is based on the first printed edition (see *Yosef Hallel*).

4. *Toras Kohanim, parshasa* 5:5.

5. The two words are spelled identically except for their first letter. The two first letters are related because they are both formed by the teeth, with the tongue low in the mouth. See *Sefer Yetzirah* 2:3.

6. "Pale gold." Many manuscripts read אורבל"א, "*orable*," which means "golden."

7. *Toras Kohanim, perek* 9:16. Although the declaration of the Kohen is a necessary condition for the impurity of *tzara'as* to take effect, the Kohen's declaration cannot render an impure affliction pure (*Mizrachi*; *Sifsei Chachamim*).

8. See Rashi to v. 2 above.

9. Some editions read כְּמִין לוֹבֶן, "like a kind of white patch."

10. In Modern French, *roux*; in English, "rosy." This refers to the complexion of the person, not to the color of the *bohak*.

⁴¹ And if his hair falls out toward his face, he is frontally bald, he is pure. ⁴² And if in the posterior or frontal baldness there shall be a reddish-white affliction: It is an eruption of tzara'as on his posterior or frontal baldness. ⁴³ The Kohen shall look at it, and behold! — there is a s'eis affliction that is reddish-white, in his posterior or frontal baldness, like the appearance of tzara'as on the skin of the flesh.

מא וְאִם מִפְּאַת פָּנָיו יִמָּרֵט רֹאשׁוֹ גִּבֵּחַ הוּא טָהוֹר הוּא: מב וְכִי־יִהְיֶה בַקָּרַחַת אוֹ בַגַּבַּחַת נֶגַע לָבָן אֲדַמְדָּם צָרַעַת פֹּרַחַת הִוא בְּקָרַחְתּוֹ אוֹ בְגַבַּחְתּוֹ: מג וְרָאָה אֹתוֹ הַכֹּהֵן וְהִנֵּה שְׂאֵת־הַנֶּגַע לְבָנָה אֲדַמְדֶּמֶת בְּקָרַחְתּוֹ אוֹ בְגַבַּחְתּוֹ כְּמַרְאֵה צָרַעַת עוֹר בָּשָׂר:

―――――――――― אונקלוס ――――――――――

מא וְאִם מִלְקֳבֵל אַפּוֹהִי יִתַּר שְׂעַר רֵישֵׁהּ גְּלוֹשׁ הוּא דְּכֵי הוּא: מב וַאֲרֵי יְהֵי בְקָרַחוּתֵהּ אוֹ בִגְלוֹשׁוּתֵהּ מַכְתַּשׁ חִוָּר סָמוֹק סְגִירוּת סַגְיָא הִיא בְּקָרַחוּתֵהּ אוֹ בִגְלוֹשׁוּתֵהּ: מג וְיֶחֱזֵי יָתֵהּ כַּהֲנָא וְהָא עֲמִיק מַכְתָּשָׁא חִוָּר סָמוֹק בְּקָרַחוּתֵהּ אוֹ בִגְלוֹשׁוּתֵהּ כְּמֶחֱזֵי סְגִירוּתָא מְשַׁךְ בִּסְרָא:

―――――――――― רש"י ――――――――――

ת"ל נגע (שם פרק יא:ד'ג): (מג) כמראה צרעת עור בשר. כמראה הצרעת האמור בפרשת עור בשר, אדם כי יהיה בעור בשרו (לעיל פסוק ב) ומה אמור בו, שמטמא בארבעה מראות ונדון בב' שבועות, ולא כמראה צרעת האמור בשחין ומכוה שהוא נדון בשבוע א', ולא כמראה נתקין של מקום שער

שהם מקום שער אלא בסימני גנעי עור בשר, [בסעָר לבן ומחיה ופשיון (שם פרק יא:ד'ב; נגעים ג:ו, י'ו)]: (מא) ואם מפאת פניו. משפוט קדקד כלפי פניו קרוי גבחת, ואף הצדעין שמכאן ושמכאן בכלל, ומשפוט קדקד כלפי אחוריו קרוי קרחת (ת"כ פרק י'ז:ה): (מב) נגע לבן אדמדם. פתוך. מנין שאר המראות.

―――――――――― RASHI ELUCIDATED ――――――――――

שֶׁהֵם מְקוֹם שֵׂעָר — which are places of hair, אֶלָּא — but rather, {בְּשֵׂעָר לָבָן ו}מִחְיָה — {by white hair¹ and} healthy flesh ²וּפִשְׂיוֹן — and spreading.²

41. וְאִם מִפְּאַת פָּנָיו — AND IF [HIS HAIR FALLS OUT] TOWARD HIS FACE. מִשִּׁפּוּעַ קָדְקֹד — Absence of hair from where the crown of the head slopes כְּלַפֵּי פָנָיו — toward his face קָרוּי גַּבַּחַת — is called frontal baldness. וְאַף הַצְּדָעִין שֶׁמִּכָּאן וּמִכָּאן בִּכְלָל — And the temples on both sides, too, are included. וּמִשִּׁפּוּעַ קָדְקֹד — Absence of hair from where the crown of the head slopes כְּלַפֵּי אֲחוֹרָיו — toward his back ³קָרוּי קָרַחַת — is called posterior baldness.³

42. נֶגַע לָבָן אֲדַמְדָּם — A WHITISH-RED AFFLICTION. This means that it is פָּתוּךְ — streaked with the colors white and red. מִנַּיִן — From where do we know that שְׁאָר הַמַּרְאוֹת — other appearances which are impure in afflictions of the skin also are impure in afflictions of the skin of the head when they come in a blend of red and white? תַּלְמוּד לוֹמַר — The verse says, ⁴"נֶגַע" — "affliction."⁴

43. כְּמַרְאֵה — כְּמַרְאֵה צָרַעַת עוֹר בָּשָׂר — LIKE THE APPEARANCE OF TZARA'AS ON THE SKIN OF THE FLESH. הַצָּרַעַת — Like the appearance of the tzara'as הָאָמוּר — which is stated בְּפָרָשַׁת — in the section of the Torah of, i.e., that deals with, עוֹר בָּשָׂר — the flesh of the skin: ⁵"אָדָם כִּי יִהְיֶה בְעוֹר בְּשָׂרוֹ — "if a person will have on the skin of his flesh."⁵ וּמַה אָמוּר בּוֹ — And what is stated with regard to it? שֶׁמְּטַמֵּא בְּאַרְבָּעָה מַרְאוֹת — That it causes impurity by four appearances, i.e., four shades of white, וְנִדּוֹן בִּשְׁנֵי שָׁבוּעוֹת — and it is judged in two weeks, i.e., two weeks may be required to determine if the sufferer is definitely impure. וְלֹא כְּמַרְאֵה צָרַעַת הָאָמוּר בִּשְׁחִין וּמִכְוָה — And the affliction of the head is not judged like the appearance of tzara'as which is stated with regard to an inflammation and a burn, וְלֹא כְּמַרְאֵה נְתָקִין שֶׁל מְקוֹם שֵׂעָר — nor — שֶׁהוּא נִדּוֹן בְּשָׁבוּעַ אֶחָד — which is judged in one week,

1. This phrase is problematic. For white hair is not a sign of impurity in afflictions of the bald parts of the head, as can be seen from *Negaim* 10:10. *Yosef Hallel* and the Berliner edition of Rashi note that the words בְּשֵׂעָר לָבָן, "by white hair," and the conjunctive *vav* prefix of וּמִחְיָה do not appear in many early editions of Rashi.

2. *Toras Kohanim, perek* 11:1-2; *Negaim* 3:6, 10:10.
3. *Toras Kohanim, perek* 10:7.
4. *Toras Kohanim, perek* 11:1-3. By referring to discoloration of the skin of the head as an affliction, the Torah indicates that it shares laws in common with the afflictions of the skin — the shades of solid white which are signs of impurity (*Lifshuto shel Rashi*).

Our text follows the first printed edition and is based on *Toras Kohanim*. In most printed editions of Rashi, this comment and the next appear as one, with the word נֶגַע, "affliction," and the verse number מג, "43," omitted.

5. Above v. 2.

44 *He is a person with tzara'as, he is impure; the Kohen shall make him impure; his affliction is upon his head.* **45** *And the person with tzara'as in whom there is the affliction — his garments shall be rent, the hair of his head shall be unshorn, and he shall cloak himself to his mustache; he is to call out, "Impure! Impure!"* **46** *All the days that the affliction is upon him he shall remain impure;*

מד אִישׁ־צָרוּעַ הוּא טָמֵא הוּא טָמֵא יְטַמְּאֶנּוּ הַכֹּהֵן בְּרֹאשׁוֹ נִגְעוֹ: מה וְהַצָּרוּעַ אֲשֶׁר־בּוֹ הַנֶּגַע בְּגָדָיו יִהְיוּ פְרֻמִים וְרֹאשׁוֹ יִהְיֶה פָרוּעַ וְעַל־שָׂפָם יַעְטֶה וְטָמֵא ׀ טָמֵא יִקְרָא: מו כָּל־יְמֵי אֲשֶׁר הַנֶּגַע בּוֹ יִטְמָא

—————— אונקלוס ——————

מד גְּבַר סְגִיר הוּא מְסָאָב הוּא סָאֲבָא יְסָאֲבִנֵּהּ כַּהֲנָא בְּרֵישֵׁהּ מַכְתָּשֵׁהּ: מה וּסְגִירָא דִי בֵהּ מַכְתָּשָׁא לְבוּשׁוֹהִי יְהוֹן מְבַזְּעִין וְרֵישֵׁהּ יְהֵי פְרִיעַ וְעַל שָׂפָם כַּאֲבֵלָא יִתְעַטָּף וְלָא תִסְתָּאֲבוּן וְלָא תִסְתָּאֲבוּן יִקְרֵי: מו כָּל יוֹמֵי דִי מַכְתָּשָׁא בֵהּ יְהֵי מְסָאָב

—————— רש"י ——————

שְׁאֵין מְטַמְּאִין בְּאַרְבָּעָה מַרְאוֹת [שְׂאֵת וְתוֹלַדְתָּהּ בַּהֶרֶת וְתוֹלַדְתָּהּ] (ת"כ פרק יב:ב־ג): (מד) בְּרֹאשׁוֹ נִגְעוֹ. אֵין לִי אֶלָּא נְתָקִין, מִנַּיִן לְרַבּוֹת שְׁאָר הַמְנֻגָּעִים, ת"ל טָמֵא יְטַמְּאֶנּוּ לְרַבּוֹת אֶת כֻּלָּן (ת"כ פרק יב:ב־ג). עַל כֻּלָּן הוּא אוֹמֵר בְּגָדָיו יִהְיוּ פְרוּמִים וְגוֹ' (שם ו): (מה) פְּרֻמִים. קְרוּעִים. פָּרוּעַ. מְגוּדָּל שֵׂעָר [ס"א פרע] (שם): וְעַל שָׂפָם יַעְטֶה. כְּאָבֵל: שָׂפָם. שְׂעַר הַשְּׂפָתַיִם גרנו"ן בְּלַעַ"ז. וְטָמֵא יִקְרָא. מַשְׁמִיעַ שֶׁהוּא טָמֵא וְיִפְרְשׁוּ מִמֶּנּוּ (מו"ק ה.):

—————— RASHI ELUCIDATED ——————

מַרְאוֹת בְּאַרְבָּעָה מְטַמְּאִין שֶׁאֵין – which do not cause impurity by four appearances, namely, {שְׂאֵת וְתוֹלַדְתָּהּ – *s'eis* and its offspring, and בַּהֶרֶת וְתוֹלַדְתָּהּ – *baheres* and its offspring.}[1]

44. בְּרֹאשׁוֹ נִגְעוֹ – HIS AFFLICTION IS UPON HIS HEAD. אֵין לִי אֶלָּא נְתָקִין – I have nothing but *nesakin.* מִנַּיִן לְרַבּוֹת שְׁאָר הַמְנֻגָּעִים – From where do we know that we include others suffering from afflictions of *tzara'as?*[2] תַּלְמוּד לוֹמַר – The verse says, ״טָמֵא יְטַמְּאֶנּוּ״ – "[he] shall make him impure," using the double verb form that includes an infinitive, לְרַבּוֹת אֶת כֻּלָּן[3] – to include all of them.[3] עַל כֻּלָּן הוּא אוֹמֵר – About all of them it says, [4]״בְּגָדָיו יִהְיוּ פְרוּמִים וְגוֹמֵר״ – "his garments shall be rent, etc."[4]

45. פְּרֻמִים – RENT, that is, קְרוּעִים[5] – torn.[5]

□ פָּרוּעַ – UNSHORN. This means [6]מְגוּדָּל שֵׂעָר – with hair grown long.[6]

□ וְעַל שָׂפָם יַעְטֶה – AND HE SHALL CLOAK HIMSELF TO HIS MUSTACHE [7]כְּאָבֵל – like a mourner.[7]

□ שָׂפָם – MUSTACHE. This means שְׂעַר הַשְּׂפָתַיִם – hair of the lips; גרנו"ן בְּלַעַ"ז – *gernon* in Old French.[8]

□ וְטָמֵא טָמֵא יִקְרָא – HE IS TO CALL OUT, "IMPURE! IMPURE!" מַשְׁמִיעַ שֶׁהוּא טָמֵא – He informs others that he is impure[9] [10]וְיִפְרְשׁוּ מִמֶּנּוּ – and they keep away from him.[10]

---

1. *Toras Kohanim, perek* 11:3-6; *Negaim* 3:6; 10:10. See verse 10 above and note 5 there. The *nesek* is impure even if it is not white as are *s'eis, baheres,* and their offsprings.

2. The laws of rending garments and leaving the head unshorn of the following verses are stated explicitly in the context of an affliction on the bald parts of the head. The apparently superfluous phrase "his affliction is upon his head" allows us to apply the laws to *nesakin* — afflictions of the hairy parts of the head. But it does not allow us to extend the law to afflictions of other parts of the body, because it says specifically "upon his head." What tells us that they apply to all afflictions? (*Mizrachi; Sifsei Chachamim*).

3. *Toras Kohanim, perek* 12:2-3.

4. *Toras Kohanim, perek* 12:5-9.

5. *Toras Kohanim, perek* 12:6; *Moed Katan* 15a. The *Mishnah* in *Sotah* 7a contrasts פְּרִימָה with קְרִיעָה. There, Rashi (s.v., ואם נפרמו) explains that קְרִיעָה means "tearing," and פְּרִימָה means "tattering." Here, where the Torah mentions only one verb form, the word פְּרֻמִים is synonymous with קְרוּעִים.

6. *Toras Kohanim, perek* 12:6; see Rashi to 10:6 above, s.v., אַל תִּפְרָעוּ, and 21:10 below. Some editions of Rashi here read מְגַדֵּל פֶּרַע, but the meaning is the same.

7. *Toras Kohanim, perek* 12:7.

8. This Old French word for "mustache" is also spelled *grenon.* It has no modern derivative in French or English.

9. The verse could have been understood as saying that he calls others impure (*Mizrachi; Sifsei Chachamim*).

10. *Toras Kohanim, perek* 12:7; *Moed Katan* 5a.

טָמֵא הוּא בָּדָד יֵשֵׁב מִחוּץ לַמַּחֲנֶה מוֹשָׁבוֹ: מז וְהַבֶּגֶד כִּי־יִהְיֶה בוֹ נֶגַע צָרָעַת בְּבֶגֶד צֶמֶר אוֹ בְּבֶגֶד פִּשְׁתִּים: מח אוֹ בִשְׁתִי אוֹ בְעֵרֶב לַפִּשְׁתִּים וְלַצָּמֶר אוֹ בְעוֹר אוֹ בְּכָל־מְלֶאכֶת עוֹר: מט וְהָיָה הַנֶּגַע יְרַקְרַק ׀ אוֹ אֲדַמְדָּם

he is impure. He shall stay in isolation; his dwelling shall be outside the camp. [47] If there shall be a tzara'as affliction in a garment, in a woolen garment or a linen garment, [48] or in the warp or the woof of the linen or of the wool; or in leather or in anything fashioned of leather; [49] and the affliction shall be deep green or deep red,

---
— אונקלוס —

מְסָאָב הוּא בִּלְחוֹדוֹהִי יְתֵב מִבָּרָא לְמַשְׁרִיתָא מוֹתְבֵהּ: מז וּלְבוּשָׁא אֲרֵי יְהֵי בֵהּ מַכְתַּשׁ סְגִירוּ בִּלְבוּשׁ עֲמַר אוֹ בִלְבוּשׁ כִּתָּן: מח אוֹ בְשִׁתְיָא אוֹ בְעַרְבָא לְכִתָּנָא וּלְעַמְרָא אוֹ בְמַשְׁכָא אוֹ בְּכָל עֲבִידַת מְשָׁךְ: מט וִיהֵי מַכְתָּשָׁא יָרוֹק סַמּוֹק

— רש"י —

(מו) בדד ישב. שֶׁלֹּא יִהְיוּ שְׁאָר טְמֵאִים יוֹשְׁבִים עִמּוֹ. וְאָמְרוּ רַבּוֹתֵינוּ מַה נִּשְׁתַּנָּה מִשְּׁאָר טְמֵאִים שֶׁיֵּשֵׁב בָּדָד, הוֹאִיל וְהוּא הִבְדִּיל בִּלְשׁוֹן הָרַע בֵּין אִישׁ לְאִשְׁתּוֹ וּבֵין אִישׁ לְרֵעֵהוּ, אַף הוּא יִבָּדֵל (ערכין טז:): **מחוץ למחנה.** חוּץ לְשָׁלֹשׁ מַחֲנוֹת (ת"כ שם

יד; פסחים סז.): **(מח) לפשתים ולצמר.** שֶׁל פִּשְׁתִּים אוֹ שֶׁל צֶמֶר: **או בעור.** זֶה עוֹר שֶׁלֹּא נַעֲשָׂה בּוֹ מְלָאכָה: **מלאכת עור.** זֶה עוֹר שֶׁנַּעֲשָׂה בּוֹ מְלָאכָה: **(מט) ירקרק.** יָרוֹק שֶׁבִּירוֹקִין: **אדמדם.** אָדֹם שֶׁבָּאֲדוּמִים (ת"כ פרק יד:ב):

—— RASHI ELUCIDATED ——

46. בָּדָד יֵשֵׁב – **HE SHALL STAY IN ISOLATION.** שֶׁלֹּא יִהְיוּ שְׁאָר טְמֵאִים יוֹשְׁבִים עִמּוֹ – That others who are impure are not to stay with him.[1] וְאָמְרוּ רַבּוֹתֵינוּ – Our Rabbis have said: מַה נִּשְׁתַּנָּה – Why is [the one who suffers from *tzara'as*] different מִשְּׁאָר טְמֵאִים – from others who are impure that he should לֵישֵׁב בָּדָד – stay in isolation? הוֹאִיל וְהוּא הִבְדִּיל – Since he caused a parting בִּלְשׁוֹן הָרַע – through malicious talk[2] בֵּין אִישׁ לְאִשְׁתּוֹ – between a man and his wife וּבֵין אִישׁ לְרֵעֵהוּ – and between a man and his colleague,[3] אַף הוּא יִבָּדֵל – he, too, shall be set apart.[3]

□ מִחוּץ לַמַּחֲנֶה – **OUTSIDE THE CAMP.** חוּץ לְשָׁלֹשׁ מַחֲנוֹת[4] – Outside three camps.[4]

48. לַפִּשְׁתִּים וְלַצָּמֶר – This means שֶׁל פִּשְׁתִּים אוֹ שֶׁל צָמֶר – of the **linen or** of the **wool**.[5]

□ אוֹ בְעוֹר – **OR IN LEATHER.** זֶה עוֹר – This is leather שֶׁלֹּא נַעֲשָׂה בּוֹ מְלָאכָה – in which no work has been done, i.e., it has not been fashioned into a completed garment or vessel.

□ אוֹ בְּכָל מְלֶאכֶת עוֹר – **OR IN ANYTHING FASHIONED OF LEATHER.** זֶה עוֹר – This is leather שֶׁנַּעֲשָׂה בּוֹ מְלָאכָה – in which work has been done, i.e., it has been fashioned into a completed garment or vessel.

49. יְרַקְרַק – **DEEP GREEN.** יָרוֹק שֶׁבִּירוֹקִין[7] – The greenest of greens.[6,7]

□ אֲדַמְדָּם – **DEEP RED.** אָדֹם שֶׁבָּאֲדוּמִים[7] – The reddest of reds.[7]

---

1. "Outside the camp" would have been sufficient if the verse had only intended that he dwell outside the Israelite camp. The additional "he shall stay in isolation" implies that others who are impure are not to stay with him (*Mesiach Ilmim; Be'er BaSadeh*). The commentators disagree as to who those impure ones are. Some say that Rashi means others who are in an intense state of impurity, such as those who are impure through contact with the dead; they do not have to be outside all three camps (see Rashi's following comment), as do the sufferers of *tzara'as*. Others say Rashi means that the sufferers of *tzara'as* may not stay together outside the three camps. See *Be'er Mayim Chaim, Malbim, Torah Temimah, Leket Bahir*.

2. See Rashi to 14:4 below, s.v., טָהֳרוֹת.

3. *Arachin* 16b.

4. *Toras Kohanim, perek* 12:14; *Pesachim* 67a. The Israelites had three camps in the desert. The grounds of the Tabernacle were the Camp of the *Shechinah*. The Camp of the Levites was located around the perimeter of the grounds of the Tabernacle. Around it was the Camp of Israel.

5. The ל prefix here means "of" and not "to" or "for" as it generally does (*Mizruchi, Sifsei Chachamim*). Also, the prefix ו means "or" and not "and."

6. See note 6 on page 148. In translating יְרַקְרַק as deep green, we have followed the opinion of the *Tanna* Sumchos, who states that it is the color of "a peacock wing and a palm leaf." According to the *Tanna* R' Elazar, it is the color of "wax and egg yolk," that is, "deep yellow" (see *Tosefta Negaim* 1:3 with *Hagahos HaGra*). The translation "green" was chosen because: (a) it concurs with the halachah as decided by the *Rambam* (*Hil. Tzaraas* 12:1); and (b) *Lo'azei Rashi BaTanach* cites a manuscript Rashi that contains the Old French טרי"ו וירי"ט, "tres vert," which means "very green."

7. *Toras Kohanim, perek* 14:2.

in the garment or the leather, or the warp or the woof, or in any leather utensil: It is a tzaraas affliction, and it shall be shown to the Kohen. ⁵⁰ *The Kohen shall look at the affliction; and he shall close off the affliction for a seven-day period.* ⁵¹ *He shall look at the affliction on the seventh day: If the affliction has spread in the garment or in the warp or in the woof or in the leather — for whatever purpose the leather has been fashioned — the affliction is a degenerative tzaraas; it is impure.* ⁵² *He shall burn the garment, or the warp or the woof, of the wool or of the linen, or any leather utensil*

RASHI ELUCIDATED

51. צָרַעַת מַמְאֶרֶת — **A DEGENERATIVE TZARA'AS.** לָשׁוֹן, סִלּוֹן מַמְאִיר — The word מַמְאֶרֶת is related to מַמְאִיר in, **"a piercing thorn";**[1] פּוֹינְיְי"ט בְּלַעַ"ז — *poiniant* in Old French.[2] וּמִדְרָשׁוֹ — Its aggadic interpretation is, תֵּן בּוֹ מְאֵרָה — **put a curse on it,** שֶׁלֹּא תַהֲנֶה הֵימֶנּוּ — **that you should not enjoy any benefit from it.**[3]

52. בַּצֶּמֶר אוֹ בַפִּשְׁתִּים — This means שֶׁל צֶמֶר — **of wool** אוֹ שֶׁל פִּשְׁתִּים — **or of linen.**[4] זֶהוּ פְּשׁוּטוֹ — **This is [the verse's] simple meaning.** וּמִדְרָשׁוֹ — **And its midrashic interpretation** is as follows: יָכוֹל — **One might be able** to think that יָבִיא גִּזֵּי צֶמֶר — **he should bring shearings of wool** וַאֲנִיצֵי פִשְׁתָּן — **and bundles of flax stalks** וְיִשְׂרְפֵם עִמּוֹ — **and burn them with [the afflicted garment].**[5] תַּלְמוּד לוֹמַר — To teach us otherwise, **the Torah says,** הוּא בָּאֵשׁ תִּשָּׂרֵף — *"it* **shall be burned in fire."** אֵינָהּ צְרִיכָה — **It does not require** דָּבָר אַחֵר עִמָּהּ — anything else to be burned **with it.** אִם כֵּן — **If so,** מַה תַּלְמוּד לוֹמַר — **why does the verse say,** ,,בַּצֶּמֶר אוֹ בַפִּשְׁתִּים,, — *"in* **the wool or** *in* **the linen"?**[6] לְהוֹצִיא אֶת הָאִמְרִיּוֹת שֶׁבּוֹ — **To exclude the borders on [the afflicted garment]** [7] שֶׁהֵן מִמִּין אַחֵר — **which are of a different variety** of textile.[7]

---

1. *Ezekiel* 28:24.
2. "Sharp, piercing." The Modern French and English "poignant" is derived from this word.
3. *Toras Kohanim, perek* 12:11. According to the simple interpretation, מַמְאֶרֶת connotes pain. The *tzara'as*, like a thorn, causes pain to the owner of the garment by making his garment unfit for use. According to the aggadic interpretation, מַמְאֶרֶת is related to the word for curse or malediction (מְאֵרָה) — see, for example, *Proverbs* 3:33; *Sefer Zikaron*; see also Rashi to *Deuteronomy* 28:20).
4. The ב prefix more commonly means "in" or "with." Here it is understood as "of."
5. One might think that the ב prefix means "with" here — "He shall burn the garment, or the warp or the woof, with the wool or with the linen."
6. If the ב prefix were understood as "with," the verse would be telling us a law it had not informed us of before — that the garment must be burned together with wool and flax. This cannot be so, however, for the verse indicates that the garment is burned by itself. The ב is thus taken as "in"; the burning of the garment takes place "*in* the wool or *in* the linen," i.e., in the woolen or linen parts of the garments, to the exclusion of the hem, which is of some other material (*Malbim; Be'er BaSadeh*).
7. *Toras Kohanim, perek* 15:1-3. If the afflicted woolen or linen garment had a border of some other variety of textile, the border may be removed before the rest of the garment is burned (*Be'er BaSadeh*).

אֲשֶׁר־יִהְיֶה בּוֹ הַנֶּגַע כִּי־צָרַעַת
מַמְאֶרֶת הִוא בָּאֵשׁ תִּשָּׂרֵף: נג וְאִם
יִרְאֶה הַכֹּהֵן וְהִנֵּה לֹא־פָשָׂה הַנֶּגַע
בַּבֶּגֶד אוֹ בַשְּׁתִי אוֹ בָעֵרֶב אוֹ בְּכָל־
כְּלִי־עוֹר: נד וְצִוָּה הַכֹּהֵן וְכִבְּסוּ אֵת
אֲשֶׁר־בּוֹ הַנָּגַע וְהִסְגִּירוֹ שִׁבְעַת־
יָמִים שֵׁנִית: [רביעי] שביעי וְרָאָה הַכֹּהֵן
אַחֲרֵי | הֻכַּבֵּס אֶת־הַנֶּגַע וְהִנֵּה לֹא־
הָפַךְ הַנֶּגַע אֶת־עֵינוֹ וְהַנֶּגַע לֹא־
פָשָׂה טָמֵא הוּא בָּאֵשׁ תִּשְׂרְפֶנּוּ

in which the affliction may be; for it is a degenerative tzara'as, it shall be burned in fire. **53** *But if the Kohen shall look, and behold! — the affliction had not spread in the garment, or the warp or the woof; or in any leather utensil,* **54** *the Kohen shall command; and they wash that which contains the affliction; and he shall close it off for a second seven-day period.* **55** *The Kohen shall look after the affliction has been washed, and behold! — the affliction has not changed its color and the affliction has not spread, it is impure, you shall burn it in fire;*

----- אונקלוס -----

דִּי יְהֵי בֵהּ מַכְתָּשָׁא אֲרֵי סְגִירוּת מְחַזְּרַת הִיא בְּנוּרָא תִּתּוֹקַד: נג וְאִם יֶחֱזֵי כַהֲנָא וְהָא לָא
אוֹסִיף מַכְתָּשָׁא בִּלְבוּשָׁא אוֹ בְשִׁתְיָא אוֹ בְעַרְבָּא אוֹ בְכָל מָאן דִּמְשָׁךְ: נד וִיפַקֵּד כַּהֲנָא
וִיחַוְּרוּן יָת דִּי בֵהּ מַכְתָּשָׁא וְיַסְגְּרִנֵּהּ שַׁבְעָא יוֹמִין תִּנְיָנוּת: נה וְיֶחֱזֵי כַהֲנָא בָּתַר דְּחַוָּרוּ יָת
מַכְתָּשָׁא וְהָא לָא שְׁנָא מַכְתָּשָׁא מִן כַּד הֲוָה וּמַכְתָּשָׁא לָא אוֹסִיף מְסָאָב הוּא בְּנוּרָא תּוֹקְדִנֵּהּ

----- רש"י -----

(שם ה:) **(נה) אחרי הכבס.** לְשׁוֹן הֵעָשׂוֹת: **לֹא הָפַךְ הַנֶּגַע
אֶת עֵינוֹ.** לֹא הֻכְּהָה מִמַּרְאִיתוֹ: **וְהַנֶּגַע לֹא פָשָׂה.** שָׁמַעְנוּ
שֶׁאִם לֹא הָפַךְ וְלֹא פָשָׂה טָמֵא, וְאֵין צָ"ל הָפַךְ וּפָשָׂה. הָפַךְ

טו:א-ג.) אִימָרַיּוֹת לְשׁוֹן שָׂפָה כְּמוֹ אִימְרָא: **(נד) אֶת אֲשֶׁר בּוֹ
הַנָּגַע.** יָכוֹל מְקוֹם הַנֶּגַע בִּלְבַד, תַּ"ל אֵת אֲשֶׁר בּוֹ הַנָּגַע. יָכוֹל כָּל
הַבֶּגֶד כֻּלּוֹ טָעוּן כִּבּוּס, תַּ"ל הַנֶּגַע. הָא כֵיצַד, יְכַבֵּס מִן הַבֶּגֶד עִמּוֹ

----- RASHI ELUCIDATED -----

אִמְרִיּוֹת — The word אִמְרִיּוֹת used here in the quotation from *Toras Kohanim* לְשׁוֹן שָׂפָה — means "hem," כְּמוֹ אִמְרָא — as does the more familiar word, אִמְרָא.

54. אֶת אֲשֶׁר בּוֹ הַנָּגַע — THAT WHICH CONTAINS THE AFFLICTION. יָכוֹל מְקוֹם הַנֶּגַע בִּלְבַד — One might be able to think that they must wash **the place of the affliction alone.** תַּלְמוּד לוֹמַר — To teach us otherwise, **the verse says,** ״אֶת אֲשֶׁר בּוֹ הַנָּגַע״ — "that which contains the affliction."[1] On the basis of this phrase, יָכוֹל — one might be able to think that כָּל הַבֶּגֶד כֻּלּוֹ טָעוּן כִּבּוּס — the entire garment requires washing. תַּלְמוּד לוֹמַר — To teach us otherwise, **the verse says,** ״הַנֶּגַע״ — "the affliction."[2] הָא כֵּיצַד — How is this to be fulfilled?[3] יְכַבֵּס מִן הַבֶּגֶד עִמּוֹ — He shall wash part of the garment along with [the affliction].[3]

55. אַחֲרֵי הֻכַּבֵּס — AFTER [THE AFFLICTION] HAS BEEN WASHED. לְשׁוֹן הֵעָשׂוֹת — This expresses "having been done," i.e., it is a passive verb form.[4]

□ לֹא הָפַךְ הַנֶּגַע אֶת עֵינוֹ — THE AFFLICTION HAS NOT CHANGED ITS COLOR. לֹא הֻכְהָה — It has not become dimmer מִמַּרְאִיתוֹ — than its original appearance.[5]

□ וְהַנֶּגַע לֹא פָשָׂה — AND THE AFFLICTION HAS NOT SPREAD. שָׁמַעְנוּ — We have heard, i.e., we can infer from this, שֶׁאִם לֹא הָפַךְ — that **if it did not change** in color וְלֹא פָשָׂה — and it did not spread, טָמֵא — it is impure. וְאֵין צָרִיךְ לוֹמַר — And it is not necessary to say, i.e., it goes without saying, that if לֹא הָפַךְ — it did not change color וּפָשָׂה — and it spread that it is impure.[6] הָפַךְ — If it changed

1. Had the Torah simply said, "and they shall wash the affliction," we would have thought that the affliction alone must be washed (*Mizrachi*).
2. Had the Torah meant that the entire garment be washed, it would have said, "and they shall wash the garment." "And they shall wash that which contains the affliction" implies that less than the entire garment need be washed (*Mizrachi*).
3. *Toras Kohanim, perek* 15:5.
4. The word הֻכַּבֵּס is in the *hufal*, while הֵעָשׂוֹת is in

the *nifal*. Rashi wishes to note only that הֻכַּבֵּס, like הֵעָשׂוֹת, is a passive verb in the infinitive form (*Be'er Yitzchak*).
5. The change in color referred to here does not include an intensification of the green or the red. Since green and red are signs of impurity, it stands to reason that their intensification should not be viewed as a sign of purity (*Mizrachi; Sifsei Chachamim*).
6. Because spreading is a greater cause for impurity than not spreading (*Mizrachi; Sifsei Chachamim*).

פְּחֶתֶת הִוא בְּקָרַחְתּוֹ אוֹ בְגַבַּחְתּוֹ: *it is a penetrating affliction in his worn garment or in his new garment.*

— אונקלוס —

תַּבְרָא הִיא בִּשְׁחִיקוּתַהּ אוֹ בְחַדְתּוּתֵהּ:

— רש"י —

ולא פשה איני יודע מה יעשה לו, ת"ל והסגיר את הנגע [והסגירו שבעת ימים לעיל פסוק נד)] מכל מקום, דברי רבי יהודה. וחכמים אומרים וכו' כדאיתא בתורת כהנים (שם ז) ורמזתיה כאן ליישב המקרא על אפניו: **פחתת היא.** לשון גומא, כמו באחת הפחתים (שמואל ב' יז:ט) כלומר שפלה היא, נגע שמראיו שוקעין (שם ער): **בקרחתו או בגבחתו.** כתרגומו בשחיקותיו או בחדתותיה: **קרחתו.** שחקים, ישנים (שם) ומפני המדרש שהוצרך לגזרה שוה, מנין לפריחה בבגדים שהיא טהורה, נאמרה קרחת וגבחת באדם (לעיל פסוק מב) ונאמרה קרחת וגבחת בבגדים, מה להלן פרח בכולו טהור (לעיל פסוק יג) אף כאן פרח בכולו טהור (נדה יט.) לכך אחז הכתוב לשון קרחת וגבחת. ולענין פירושו ותרגומו זהו משמעו,

— RASHI ELUCIDATED —

וְלֹא פָשָׂה – **but did not spread,** **אֵינִי יוֹדֵעַ מַה יֵּעָשֶׂה לּוֹ** – **I do not yet know what shall be done to it.**[1] **תַּלְמוּד לוֹמַר** – **To provide this information, the verse says,** **״וְהִסְגִּיר אֶת הַנֶּגַע״** – **"and he shall close off the affliction,"**[2] **מִכָּל מָקוֹם** – **in any additional case.**[3] **דִּבְרֵי רַבִּי יְהוּדָה** – These are **the words of** the *Tanna* **R' Yehudah.** **וַחֲכָמִים אוֹמְרִים וְכוּלֵהּ** – **But the Sages say, etc.,**[4] **כִּדְאִיתָא בְּתוֹרַת כֹּהֲנִים** – **as stated in** *Toras Kohanim*.[5] **וּרְמַזְתִּיהָ כָּאן** – **I have alluded to it here** **לְיַשֵּׁב הַמִּקְרָא עַל אָפְנָיו** – to **put the verse in its proper setting.**

☐ **פְּחֶתֶת הִוא** – **IT IS A PENETRATING AFFLICTION.** **לְשׁוֹן גּוּמָא** – The word **פְּחֶתֶת** **means an indentation,** **כְּמוֹ ״בְּאַחַת הַפְּחָתִים״** – **like הַפְּחָתִים** in, **"in one of the ditches."**[6] **כְּלוֹמַר** – **That is to say,** **שְׁפָלָה הִיא** – **it is something low,** **נֶגַע שֶׁמַּרְאָיו שׁוֹקְעִין** – **an affliction whose appearance is sunken.**[7]

☐ **בְּקָרַחְתּוֹ אוֹ בְגַבַּחְתּוֹ** – **This is to be understood** **כְּתַרְגּוּמוֹ** – **as the** *Targum* **renders it:** **בִּשְׁחִיקוּתַהּ** – **In his worn garment** **אוֹ בְחַדְתּוּתֵהּ** – **or in his new garment.**[8]

☐ **קָרַחְתּוֹ** – **The word קָרַחְתּוֹ** means **שְׁחָקִים יְשָׁנִים**[9] – **old, worn, clothes.**[9] **וּמִפְּנֵי הַמִּדְרָשׁ** – **The terms** **קָרַחַת** and **גַּבַּחַת** are used here **because of the Scriptural interpretation,** **שֶׁהוּצְרַךְ לִגְזֵרָה שָׁוָה** – **for it is required for** the following *gezeirah shavah*:[10] **מִנַּיִן** – **From where do we know** **לִפְרִיחָה בִּבְגָדִים** – **that an eruption in garments,** i.e., an affliction which covers the entire garment, **שֶׁהִיא טְהוֹרָה** – **is pure?** **נֶאֶמְרָה קָרַחַת וְגַבַּחַת בָּאָדָם** – **The terms** **קָרַחַת** and **גַּבַּחַת** **are stated with regard to man,**[11] **וְנֶאֶמְרָה קָרַחַת וְגַבַּחַת בַּבְּגָדִים** – **and the terms** **קָרַחַת** and **גַּבַּחַת** **are stated with regard to garments.** **מַה לְהַלָּן** – **Just as above** with regard to man **פָּרַח בְּכֻלּוֹ** – if **[the affliction] erupted on his entirety,** i.e., on his entire body, [12]**טָהוֹר** – **he is pure,**[12] **אַף כָּאן** – **here, too,** with regard to garments, **פָּרַח** **בְּכֻלּוֹ** – if **it erupted in its entirety** [13]**טָהוֹר** – **it is pure.**[13] **לְכָךְ אָחַז הַכָּתוּב** – **That is why Scripture took hold of,** i.e., chose to use, **לְשׁוֹן קָרַחַת וְגַבַּחַת** – **the terms** **קָרַחַת** and **גַּבַּחַת**. **וּלְעִנְיַן פֵּירוּשׁוֹ** – **On the subject of its explanation** **וְתַרְגּוּמוֹ** – **and its translation,**[14] **זֶהוּ מַשְׁמָעוֹ** – **this**

---

1. The change here does not refer to dimming in color, for the following verse says explicitly that if it became dimmer, it is pure. Rather, it refers to a change from green to red, or vice versa. We have not yet been informed if a change of this sort is cause for impurity or not (*Gur Aryeh*).
2. Above v. 50. Some editions adduce from verse 54, וְהִסְגִּירוֹ שִׁבְעַת יָמִים שֵׁנִית, "and he shall close it off for a second seven-day period."
3. The verse could have used the shorter וְהִסְגִּירוֹ, "and he shall close it off." The apparently superfluous "the affliction" indicates that there is an additional affliction to be included within the category of those which must be quarantined — one which has changed color but has not spread (*Mizrachi*; *Leket Bahir*).
4. The Sages are of the opinion that a change from green to red or vice versa is not considered a change which leads to purity, for both are equally signs of impurity (*Mizrachi*).
5. *Toras Kohanim, perek* 15:7.
6. *II Samuel* 17:9.
7. *Toras Kohanim, perek* 15:9.
8. In verse 40 above, these words referred to posterior and frontal baldness.
9. *Toras Kohanim, perek* 15:9.
10. Literally, "identical cutting" (*Klalei HaGemara*). A method of applying information stated explicitly in one verse to another verse by virtue of an identical word or phrase appearing in both verses. This only applies when such association of two contexts is a matter of received tradition. It is not a procedure which is rooted in logical criteria that can be used at one's own initiative.
11. Above v. 42.
12. See v. 13 above.
13. *Niddah* 19a.
14. Rashi explains how the word which has been used for posterior baldness also expresses worn garments, and

ויקרא – פרשת תזריע

נו וְאִם־רָאָה הַכֹּהֵן וְהִנֵּה כֵּהָה הַנֶּגַע אַחֲרֵי הֻכַּבֵּס אֹתוֹ וְקָרַע אֹתוֹ מִן־הַבֶּגֶד אוֹ מִן־הָעוֹר אוֹ מִן־הַשְּׁתִי אוֹ מִן־הָעֵרֶב: מפטיר נז וְאִם־תֵּרָאֶה עוֹד בַּבֶּגֶד אוֹ־בַשְּׁתִי אוֹ־בָעֵרֶב אוֹ בְכָל־כְּלִי־עוֹר פֹּרַחַת הִוא בָּאֵשׁ תִּשְׂרְפֶנּוּ אֵת אֲשֶׁר־בּוֹ הַנָּגַע: נח וְהַבֶּגֶד אוֹ־הַשְּׁתִי אוֹ־הָעֵרֶב אוֹ־כָל־כְּלִי הָעוֹר אֲשֶׁר תְּכַבֵּס וְסָר מֵהֶם הַנָּגַע

56 But if the Kohen shall look, and behold! — the affliction grew dimmer after it was laundered, he shall rip it from the garment or from the leather, or from the warp or from the woof. **57** If it appears again in the garment or in the warp or in the woof, or in any leather utensil, it is an eruption; you shall burn in fire that which contains the affliction. **58** But if the garment or the warp or the woof or any leather utensil had been laundered and then the affliction left them,

— אונקלוס —

נו וְאִם חֲזָא כַהֲנָא וְהָא עֲמָא מַכְתָּשָׁא בָּתַר דְּחַוָּרוּ יָתֵהּ וִיבְזַע יָתֵהּ מִן לְבוּשָׁא אוֹ מִן מַשְׁכָּא אוֹ מִן שְׁתָיָא אוֹ מִן עַרְבָא: נז וְאִם תִּתְחֲזֵי עוֹד בִּלְבוּשָׁא אוֹ בְשְׁתָיָא אוֹ בְעַרְבָא אוֹ בְכָל מַאן דְּמַשַׁךְ סַגִּיאָה הִיא בְּנוּרָא תוֹקְדִנֵּהּ יָת דִּי בֵהּ מַכְתָּשָׁא: נח וּלְבוּשָׁא אוֹ שְׁתָיָא אוֹ עַרְבָא אוֹ כָל מַאן דְּמַשַׁךְ דִּי יִתְחַוָּר (נ"א תְחַוַּר) וְיֶעְדֵּי מִנְּהוֹן מַכְתָּשָׁא

— רש"י —

קָרַחַת לְשׁוֹן יְשָׁנִים וְגַבַּחַת לְשׁוֹן חֲדָשִׁים, כְּאִלּוּ נִכְתַּב בְּאַחֲרִיתוֹ אוֹ בְקַדְמוּתוֹ, שֶׁהַקָּרַחַת לְשׁוֹן אֲחוֹרַיִּם וְהַגַּבַּחַת לְשׁוֹן פָּנִים, כְּמוֹ שֶׁכָּתוּב וְאִם מִפְּאַת פָּנָיו וְגוֹ' (לעיל פסוק מא) וְהַקָּרַחַת כָּל שֶׁשּׁוֹפֵעַ וְיוֹרֵד מִן הַקָּדְקֹד וּלְאַחֲרָיו. כָּךְ מְפֹרָשׁ בְּתוֹרַת כֹּהֲנִים: (נו) **וְקָרַע אֹתוֹ.** יִקְרַע מְקוֹם הַנֶּגַע מִן הַבֶּגֶד וְיִשְׂרְפֶנּוּ (שם): (נז) **פֹּרַחַת הִוא.** דָּבָר הַחוֹזֵר וְצוֹמֵחַ: **בָּאֵשׁ תִּשְׂרְפֶנּוּ.** אֶת כָּל הַבֶּגֶד: (נח) **וְסָר מֵהֶם הַנָּגַע.** אִם כְּשֶׁכִּבְּסוּהוּ בַּתְּחִלָּה עַל פִּי כֹהֵן סָר מִמֶּנּוּ הַנֶּגַע לְגַמְרֵי:

RASHI ELUCIDATED

וְגַבַּחַת לְשׁוֹן חֲדָשִׁים – and the term גַּבַּחַת means new ones, קָרַחַת – The term קָרַחַת means old ones, is its meaning: בְּאַחֲרִיתוֹ – "at its end," i.e., at the end of the life of the garment, אוֹ בְקַדְמוּתוֹ – "or at its beginning," כְּאִלּוּ נִכְתַּב – as if it had been written שֶׁהַקָּרַחַת לְשׁוֹן אֲחוֹרַיִּם – for קָרַחַת means the back, וְהַגַּבַּחַת לְשׁוֹן פָּנִים – and גַּבַּחַת means the face, כְּמוֹ שֶׁכָּתוּב – as it is written, וְאִם מִפְּאַת פָּנָיו וְגוֹמֵר – "and if his hair falls out toward his face, etc."[1] וְהַקָּרַחַת – And קָרַחַת means כָּל שֶׁשּׁוֹפֵעַ וְיוֹרֵד – any baldness which slopes downward מִן הַקָּדְקֹד וּלְאַחֲרָיו – from the crown of the head toward his back.[2] כָּךְ מְפֹרָשׁ בְּתוֹרַת כֹּהֲנִים[3] – Thus is it explained in Toras Kohanim.[3]

56. וְקָרַע אֹתוֹ – HE SHALL RIP IT. יִקְרַע מְקוֹם הַנֶּגַע – He shall rip the place of the affliction מִן הַבֶּגֶד – from the garment וְיִשְׂרְפֶנּוּ[4] – and burn it.[4]

57. פֹּרַחַת הִוא – IT IS AN ERUPTION. This means דָּבָר הַחוֹזֵר וְצוֹמֵחַ – something that grows recurringly. בָּאֵשׁ תִּשְׂרְפֶנּוּ – YOU SHALL BURN [IT] IN FIRE. אֶת כָּל הַבֶּגֶד – The entire garment.[5]

58. וְסָר מֵהֶם הַנָּגַע – AND THEN THE AFFLICTION LEFT THEM. אִם כְּשֶׁכִּבְּסוּהוּ בַּתְּחִלָּה – If when they washed it at first עַל פִּי כֹהֵן – by the word of the Kohen,[6] סָר מִמֶּנּוּ הַנֶּגַע – the affliction left it לְגַמְרֵי – entirely.

---

how the word which has been used for frontal baldness also expresses new garments.

1. Above v. 41. This phrase continues, "he is frontally bald."

2. Thus קָרַחַת and גַבַּחַת connote "end" and "beginning" in the context of the bald parts of the head, as well as in the context of the ages of garments.

3. Toras Kohanim, perek 15:9.

4. Toras Kohanim, perek 16:2. Not only shall he rip it, but he shall burn it, as well, as stated in verse 52

above (Mizrachi; Sifsei Chachamim).

5. Rashi in his comments to verse 54 said that אֵת אֲשֶׁר בּוֹ הַנֶּגַע, "that which contains the affliction," of verse referred only to the part of the garment which had the affliction on it and its surrounding area. In our verse it means the entire garment (Nachalas Yaakov).

6. Washing here refers only to washing it "at first" at the instruction of the Kohen, as mentioned in verse 54, before the affliction developed into an eruption (Sefer Zikaron; Be'er Yitzchak).

it shall be washed again and it shall become pure. ⁵⁹ *This is the law of the tzara'as affliction, a garment of wool or linen, or the warp or the woof, or any leather utensil; to declare it pure or to declare it impure.*

נט וְכֻבַּס שֵׁנִית וְטָהֵר: זֹאת תּוֹרַת נֶגַע־צָרַעַת בֶּגֶד הַצֶּמֶר ׀ אוֹ הַפִּשְׁתִּים אוֹ הַשְּׁתִי אוֹ הָעֵרֶב אוֹ כָּל־כְּלִי־עוֹר לְטַהֲרוֹ אוֹ לְטַמְּאוֹ:

פ פ פ

THE HAFTARAH FOR TAZRIA APPEARS ON PAGE 394.
During non-leap years, Tazria is always read together with Metzora.
The Haftarah of Tazria is omitted during those years.
The following rules apply during leap years:
When Rosh Chodesh Nissan coincides with Tazria, Tazria is divided into six aliyos;
the Rosh Chodesh reading, page 405, is the seventh aliyah;
and the readings for Parashas HaChodesh, page 412, follow.
When Parashas HaChodesh coincides with Tazria (on a day other than Rosh Chodesh), the regular Maftir and Haftarah are replaced with the readings for Parashas HaChodesh, page 412.

──────────── אונקלוס ────────────

וְיִצְטַבַּע תִּנְיָנוּת וְיִדְכֵּי: נט דָּא אוֹרַיְתָא דְמַכְתָּשׁ סְגִירוּ בִּלְבוּשׁ עֲמַר אוֹ כִתָּנָא אוֹ שְׁתְיָא אוֹ עַרְבָּא אוֹ כָל מַאן דִּמְשַׁךְ לְדַכָּיוּתֵהּ אוֹ לְסָאָבוּתֵהּ:

──────────── רש"י ────────────

וכבס שנית. ל' טבילה. תרגום של כבוסין שבפרשה זו תרגומו ויטטבע. וכן כל כבוסי בגדים שהן לטבילה מתורגמין לשון לבון, ויתחוור, חוץ מזה שאינו ללבון אלא לטבול, לכך ויטטבע:

──────────── RASHI ELUCIDATED ────────────

□ וְכֻבַּס שֵׁנִית – **IT SHALL BE WASHED AGAIN.** לְשׁוֹן טְבִילָה – "Washing" here **means immersion.**[1] שֶׁבְּפָרָשָׁה זוֹ – **which are in this section** תַּרְגּוּם שֶׁל כִּבּוּסִין – Targum Onkelos' **translations of words with the root** כבס לְשׁוֹן לִבּוּן וְ,,יִתְחַוַּר'' – **mean laundering** such as יִתְחַוַּר which he used for תְּכַבֵּס earlier in the verse, חוּץ מִזֶּה – **except for this one,** שֶׁאֵינוֹ לְלִבּוּן – **which is not,** i.e., which does not mean, **laundering,** אֶלָּא לִטְבּוֹל – **but rather, to immerse.** לְכָךְ תַּרְגּוּמוֹ ,,וְיִצְטַבַּע'' – **Therefore,** Targum Onkelos' **rendering of it is** וְיִצְטַבַּע, **"and it shall be immersed."** וְכֵן – **Similarly,** כָּל כִּבּוּסֵי בְגָדִים – any "washings" of garments שֶׁהֵן לִטְבִילָה – **which are for** the purpose of ritual **immersion** מִתַּרְגְּמִין ,,וְיִצְטַבַּע'' – **are translated by** Targum Onkelos with a word of the same root (צבע) as וְיִצְטַבַּע.

───────────────────────────

1. It does not mean washing here, for the stain of the affliction has already been washed out (*Be'er Yitzchak*).

פרשת מצורע
Parashas Metzora

14. ¹ **H**ASHEM spoke to Moses, saying: ² This shall be the law of the metzora on the day of his purification: He shall be brought to the Kohen. ³ The Kohen shall go forth to the outside of the camp; the Kohen shall look, and behold! — the tzara'as affliction had been healed from the metzora. ⁴ The Kohen shall command; and for the person being purified there shall be taken two live, pure birds, cedarwood,

א וַיְדַבֵּר יהוה אֶל־מֹשֶׁה לֵּאמֹר: ²זֹאת תִּהְיֶה תּוֹרַת הַמְּצֹרָע בְּיוֹם טָהֳרָתוֹ וְהוּבָא אֶל־הַכֹּהֵן: ³ וְיָצָא הַכֹּהֵן אֶל־מִחוּץ לַמַּחֲנֶה וְרָאָה הַכֹּהֵן וְהִנֵּה נִרְפָּא נֶגַע־הַצָּרַעַת מִן־הַצָּרוּעַ: ⁴ וְצִוָּה הַכֹּהֵן וְלָקַח לַמִּטַּהֵר שְׁתֵּי־ צִפֳּרִים חַיּוֹת טְהֹרוֹת וְעֵץ אֶרֶז

אונקלוס

א וּמַלִּיל יְיָ עִם מֹשֶׁה לְמֵימָר: ב דָּא תְּהֵי אוֹרַיְתָא דִּסְגִירָא בְּיוֹמָא דְדָכוּתֵהּ וְיִתֵּיתִי לְוָת כַּהֲנָא: ג וְיִפּוֹק כַּהֲנָא לְמִבָּרָא לְמַשְׁרִיתָא וְיֶחֱזֵי כַּהֲנָא וְהָא אִתַּסִּי מַכְתָּשׁ סְגִירוּתָא מִן סְגִירָא: ד וִיפַקֵּד כַּהֲנָא וְיִסַּב לְדְמִדְּכֵּי תַּרְתֵּין צִפֳּרִין חַיִּין דָּכְיָן וְאָעָא דְאַרְזָא

רש"י

(ב) **זאת תהיה [וגו'] תורת המצורע ביום טהרתו.** מלמד שאין מטהרין אותו בלילה (ת"כ מצורע פרשתא א׳:ב׳; מגילה כ״א.): (ג) **אל מחוץ למחנה.** חוץ לשלשה מחנות שנשתלח שם בימי חלוטו: (ד) **חיות.** פרט לטרפות (חולין ק"מ.): **טהורות.** פרט לעוף טמא (ת"כ שם י"ב; חולין קמ:). לפי שהנגעים באין על לשון הרע (ערכין ט"ו:) שהוא מעשה פטפוטי דברים, לפיכך הוזקקו לטהרתו צפרים שמפטפטין תמיד בצפצוף קול (תנחומא מצורע ג׳): **ועץ ארז.** לפי שהנגעים באין על גסות הרוח (תנחומא מצורע ג׳):

RASHI ELUCIDATED

14.

2. זֹאת תִּהְיֶה תּוֹרַת הַמְּצֹרָע בְּיוֹם טָהֳרָתוֹ — THIS SHALL BE THE LAW OF THE *METZORA* ON THE DAY OF HIS PURIFICATION. מְלַמֵּד — This teaches us שֶׁאֵין מְטַהֲרִין אוֹתוֹ — that they do not purify him בַּלַּיְלָה — at night.[1]

3. אֶל מִחוּץ לַמַּחֲנֶה — TO THE OUTSIDE OF THE CAMP. חוּץ לִשְׁלֹשָׁה מַחֲנוֹת — To the area outside of three camps שֶׁנִּשְׁתַּלַּח שָׁם — where he was sent בִּימֵי חֲלוּטוֹ — in the days of his absoluteness, i.e., the days in which he had been declared decidedly impure.[2]

4. חַיּוֹת — LIVE.[3] פְּרָט לִטְרֵפוֹת — To the exclusion of *tereifos*.[3]

☐ טְהֹרוֹת — PURE.[4] פְּרָט לְעוֹף טָמֵא — To the exclusion of an impure fowl, i.e., a fowl of a non-kosher species.[4] לְפִי שֶׁהַנְּגָעִים — Since afflictions of *tzara'as* בָּאִין עַל לְשׁוֹן הָרַע — come about because of malicious talk,[5] שֶׁהוּא מַעֲשֵׂה[6] פִּטְפוּטֵי דְּבָרִים — which is an act of[6] verbal twittering, לְפִיכָךְ הֻזְקְקוּ — therefore, there was required for [the sufferer's] purification, לְטָהֳרָתוֹ — צִפֳּרִים שֶׁמְּפַטְפְּטִין תָּמִיד — birds that constantly twitter בְּצִפְצוּף קוֹל — with the chirping of sound.[7]

☐ וְעֵץ אֶרֶז — CEDARWOOD. לְפִי שֶׁהַנְּגָעִים — Because afflictions of *tzara'as* בָּאִין עַל גַּסּוּת הָרוּחַ — come because of haughtiness.[8]

---

1. *Toras Kohanim, parshasa* 1:3; *Megillah* 21a. This is derived from the apparently superfluous בְּיוֹם, "on the day" (*Mizrachi*).

2. See above 13:46 and note 1 there.

3. *Chullin* 140a. *Tereifos*, literally, "torn ones," are birds or animals that are alive, but have certain physical defects that will inevitably lead to their death.
It is obvious that the birds the verse speaks of must be alive, for verse 5 states that one of them shall be slaughtered, and verse 7 states that the other shall be set loose. "Live" of our verse therefore indicates that they should not be suffering from mortal defects (*Minchas Yehudah; Sifsei Chachamim*).

4. *Toras Kohanim, parshasa* 1:12; *Chullin* 139b-140a. Although the *Gemara* says that צִפּוֹר, the word used by our verse for bird, applies exclusively to pure species, Rashi here is based on *Toras Kohanim*, which is of the opinion that צִפּוֹר embraces both pure and impure species. Therefore, טְהֹרוֹת must be stated to limit צִפּוֹר to the pure species (*Mizrachi*). Alternatively, although צִפּוֹר normally refers only to pure birds, here we may have thought that it can include impure birds, as well, for the bird represents the impure action of the one bringing it, as Rashi goes on to say. Thus, even according to the *Gemara*, in this case טְהֹרוֹת is necessary to teach us that the birds must be pure (*Minchas Yehudah; Sifsei Chachamim*).

5. *Arachin* 15b.

6. Some editions add פַּטִּיט, "a garrulous person."

7. *Arachin* 16b.

8. *Tanchuma* 3. The cedar, a tall and beautiful tree, serves to remind the sinner that he considered himself high and glorious (*Minchas Yehudah; Sifsei Chachamim*).

a crimson [tongue of] wool, and hyssop. ⁵ The Kohen shall command; and the one bird shall be slaughtered into an earthenware vessel over spring water. ⁶ The live bird, he shall take it and the cedar wood and the crimson [tongue of] wool and the

ה וּשְׁנִ֥י תוֹלַ֖עַת וְאֵזֹֽב: וְצִוָּה֙ הַכֹּהֵ֔ן וְשָׁחַ֖ט אֶת־הַצִּפּ֣וֹר הָאֶחָ֑ת אֶל־כְּלִי־חֶ֖רֶשׂ עַל־מַ֥יִם חַיִּֽים: ו אֶת־הַצִּפֹּ֥ר הַֽחַיָּ֖ה יִקַּ֣ח אֹתָ֑הּ וְאֶת־עֵ֤ץ הָאֶ֙רֶז֙ וְאֶת־שְׁנִ֣י הַתּוֹלַ֔עַת וְאֶת־

---- אונקלוס ----

וּצְבַע זְהוֹרִי וְאֵזוֹבָא: ה וִיפַקֵּד כַּהֲנָא וְיִכּוֹס יָת צִפְּרָא חֲדָא לְמָאן דַּחֲסַף עַל מֵי מַבּוּעַ: ו יָת צִפְּרָא חַיְתָא יִסַּב יָתַהּ וְיָת אָעָא דְאַרְזָא וְיָת צְבַע זְהוֹרִי וְיָת

---- רש״י ----

וּשְׁנִי תוֹלַעַת וְאֵזֹב. מַה תַּקָּנָתוֹ וְיִתְרַפֵּא, יַשְׁפִּיל עַצְמוֹ מִגַּאֲוָתוֹ כְּתוֹלַעַת וּכְאֵזוֹב (שם): **עֵץ אֶרֶז.** מַקֵּל שֶׁל אֶרֶז: **שְׁנִי תוֹלַעַת.** לְשׁוֹן שֶׁל צֶמֶר צָבוּעַ זְהוֹרִית: **(ה) עַל מַיִם חַיִּים.** נוֹתֵן אוֹתָם תְּחִלָּה בִּכְלִי כְּדֵי שֶׁיְּהֵא דַם הַצִּפּוֹר נִיכָּר בָּהֶם, וְכַמָּה הֵם, רְבִיעִית (ת״כ פרק א:ה; סוטה טז:): **(ו) אֶת הַצִּפּוֹר הַחַיָּה יִקַּח אֹתָהּ.** מְלַמֵּד שֶׁאֵינוֹ אוֹגְדָהּ עִמָּהֶם אֶלָּא מַפְרִישָׁהּ לְעַצְמָהּ. אֲבָל הָעֵץ וְהָאֵזוֹב כְּרוּכִין יַחַד

---- RASHI ELUCIDATED ----

□ וּשְׁנִי תוֹלַעַת וְאֵזֹב — CRIMSON [TONGUE OF] WOOL, AND HYSSOP. מַה תַּקָּנָתוֹ וְיִתְרַפֵּא — **What is his remedy,** i.e., what is the remedy of one who is guilty of malicious talk or haughtiness, **that he should be cured** of his affliction? יַשְׁפִּיל עַצְמוֹ מִגַּאֲוָתוֹ — **He should lower himself from his arrogance** כְּתוֹלַעַת — **like a worm**[1] וּכְאֵזוֹב — **and like hyssop.**[2]

□ עֵץ אֶרֶז — CEDAR WOOD. מַקֵּל שֶׁל אֶרֶז — **A stick of cedar.**[3]

□ שְׁנִי תוֹלַעַת — CRIMSON WOOL. This refers to לְשׁוֹן שֶׁל צֶמֶר — **a tongue of wool** צָבוּעַ זְהוֹרִית — **dyed crimson.**[4]

5. עַל מַיִם חַיִּים — OVER SPRING WATER. נוֹתֵן אוֹתָם תְּחִלָּה — **He puts [the water] first** בִּכְלִי — **into a vessel,**[5] כְּדֵי שֶׁיְּהֵא דַם צִפּוֹר — **so that the blood of the bird should be** נִכָּר בָּהֶם — **discernible in them.**[6] וְכַמָּה הֵם — **How much is [this quantity of water]?** [7] רְבִיעִית — **A revi'is.**[7]

6. אֶת הַצִּפּוֹר הַחַיָּה יִקַּח אֹתָהּ — THE LIVE BIRD, HE SHALL TAKE IT. מְלַמֵּד — **This teaches us** שֶׁאֵינוֹ אוֹגְדָהּ עִמָּהֶם — **that he does not join it together with them,** אֶלָּא מַפְרִישָׁהּ לְעַצְמָהּ — **but he sets it apart, by itself.**[8] {אֲבָל הָעֵץ} — **But the** cedarwood וְהָאֵזוֹב — **and the hyssop** כְּרוּכִין יַחַד — **are bound**

---

1. תּוֹלַעַת means both "dyed wool," as in our verse (see note 4 below), and "worm," as in *Exodus* 16:20 (see Rashi there) and *Deuteronomy* 28:39.

2. The hyssop is an herb which, in contrast to the cedar, does not grow tall. This cure applies not only to arrogance, but to malicious talk, as well. See *Arachin* 15b. Ibn Ezra points out that these two species, the lofty cedar and the lowly hyssop, are also contrasted in the Prophet's description of Solomon's wisdom (see *I Kings* 5:13 with Rashi).
   It should be noted that the word "hyssop" is a distorted Greek transliteration of the word אֵזוֹב. According to the verse in *Kings*, it grows out of walls (like moss or lichen). It is almost certain that the native European plant of the mint family known as hyssop is not the same plant. In his medical writings, *Rambam* (Maimonides) states that it is the herb called *za'atar* that is native to Eretz Yisrael.

3. עֵץ means both "tree" (23:40 below) and "wood" (11:32 above). Rashi explains that the purification does not require an entire cedar tree (*Mizrachi; Sifsei Chachamim*). He must bring a stick, at least one-*amah* long with leaves on it (*Toras Kohanim, parshasa* 1:12-13).

4. Wool which has been combed but not yet spun is called לָשׁוֹן ("tongue") because it was the practice to comb it into long, tonguelike, strips (*Sefer Zikaron*). צֶמֶר is undyed wool; תּוֹלָע or תּוֹלַעַת is dyed wool. שָׁנִי (or, in the construct form, שְׁנִי) is the color crimson (*Rashbam* to *Exodus* 25:4).

5. "Over spring water" does not modify כְּלִי חֶרֶשׂ, "an earthenware vessel," which immediately precedes it in the verse; the vessel need not be over spring water. "Over spring water" modifies וְשָׁחַט, "and one shall slaughter." The water must be inside the vessel, and the act of slaughter takes place over the water in the vessel (*Mishmeres HaKodesh*).

6. The water must be small enough in quantity so that even the blood of a small bird will cause it to change its appearance.

7. *Toras Kohanim, perek* 1:5; *Sotah* 16b. Opinions regarding the modern-day equivalent of a *revi'is* range from slightly more than three fluid ounces to almost five and a half fluid ounces. The water must be exactly a *revi'is* (see *Sotah* 16b and Rashi, s.v., אף דם צפור, and s.v., בצפור דרור).

8. אֶת הַצִּפֹּר הַחַיָּה, "the live bird," mentioned at the beginning of the verse, appears superfluous, for the verse goes on to say, "he shall dip them *and the live bird.*" It is stated to teach us that it is not tied together with the other objects (*Sefer Zikaron*). Alternatively, the verse could have written, אֶת הַצִּפֹּר הַחַיָּה וְאֶת עֵץ הָאֶרֶז וְגוֹמֵר, "he shall take the live bird with the cedarwood, etc." The word אֹתָהּ, "it," appears superfluous. It is written to set the bird apart from the other items, indicating that it is not tied in the bundle composed of the other items (*Mizrachi*).

הָאֵזֹב וְטָבַל אוֹתָם וְאֵת ׀ הַצִּפֹּר הַחַיָּה בְּדַם הַצִּפֹּר הַשְּׁחֻטָה עַל הַמַּיִם הַחַיִּים: וְהִזָּה עַל הַמִּטַּהֵר מִן־הַצָּרַעַת שֶׁבַע פְּעָמִים וְטִהֲרוֹ וְשִׁלַּח אֶת־הַצִּפֹּר הַחַיָּה עַל־פְּנֵי הַשָּׂדֶה: וְכִבֶּס הַמִּטַּהֵר אֶת־בְּגָדָיו וְגִלַּח אֶת־כָּל־שְׂעָרוֹ וְרָחַץ בַּמַּיִם וְטָהֵר וְאַחַר יָבוֹא אֶל־הַמַּחֲנֶה וְיָשַׁב מִחוּץ לְאָהֳלוֹ שִׁבְעַת יָמִים: וְהָיָה בַיּוֹם הַשְּׁבִיעִי יְגַלַּח אֶת־כָּל־שְׂעָרוֹ אֶת־רֹאשׁוֹ וְאֶת־זְקָנוֹ

hyssop, and he shall dip them and the live bird into the blood of the bird that was slaughtered over the spring water. **⁷** *Then he shall sprinkle seven times upon the person being purified from the tzara'as; he shall purify him, and he shall set the live bird free upon the open field.* **⁸** *The person being purified shall immerse his clothing, shave off all his hair, and immerse himself in the water and become pure. Thereafter he may enter the camp; but he shall dwell outside of his tent for seven days.*
⁹ *On the seventh day he shall shave off all his hair — his head, his beard,*

———— אונקלוס ————

אֵזוֹבָא וְיִטְבּוֹל יָתְהוֹן וְיָת צִפְּרָא חַיְתָא בִּדְמָא דְצִפְּרָא דְנְכִיסָא עַל מֵי מַבּוּעַ: וְיַדֵּי עַל דְמִדַּכֵּי מִן סְגִירוּתֵהּ שְׁבַע זִמְנִין וִידַכִּנֵהּ וִישַׁלַּח יָת צִפְּרָא חַיְתָא עַל אַפֵּי חַקְלָא: חוִיצְבַּע דְמִדַּכֵּי יָת לְבוּשׁוֹהִי וִיגַלַּח יָת כָּל שַׂעֲרֵהּ וְיַסְחֵי בְמַיָּא וְיִדְכֵּי וּבָתַר כֵּן יֵעוֹל לְמַשְׁרִיתָא וִיתֵב מִבָּרָא לְמַשְׁכְּנֵהּ שַׁבְעָא יוֹמִין: טוִיהֵי בְּיוֹמָא שְׁבִיעָאָה יְגַלַּח יָת כָּל שַׂעֲרֵהּ יָת רֵישֵׁהּ וְיָת דִּקְנֵהּ

———— רש"י ————

הכשר לכלל טבילה (ת"כ שם ו): (ח) **וישב מחוץ לאהלו.** מלמד שאסור בתשמיש המטה (ת"כ פרשתא ב:י"ח; מו"ק ז:): (ט) **את כל שערו וגו׳.** כלל ופרט וכלל, להביא כל מקום כנוס שער

בלשון הזהורית, כעניין שנאמר ואת עץ הארז ואת שני תולעת ואת האזוב, קיחה אחת לשלשתן.] יכול כשם שאינה בכלל אגודה כך לא תהיה בכלל טבילה, ת"ל וטבל אותם ואת הצפור החיה, החזיר את

———— RASHI ELUCIDATED ————

בְּלָשׁוֹן הַזְּהוֹרִית — **with the tongue of crimson wool**,[1] כָּעִנְיָן שֶׁנֶּאֱמַר — **as that which is stated together**, וְאֵת עֵץ הָאֶרֶז וְאֵת שְׁנֵי הַתּוֹלַעַת וְאֶת הָאֵזוֹב — "**and the cedar wood, and the crimson wool, and the hyssop.**" This phrase implies קִיחָה אַחַת לִשְׁלָשְׁתָּן — **one taking for the three of them.**[2]} יָכוֹל — **One might be able to think that** כְּשֵׁם שֶׁאֵינָה בְּאַגֻדָּה — **just as [the bird] is not included in the joining** with the cedarwood, crimson strip, and hyssop, כָּךְ לֹא תִהְיֶה בִּכְלַל טְבִילָה — **so, too, it should not be included in dipping** into the water.[3] תַּלְמוּד לוֹמַר — **To teach us otherwise, the verse says,** וְטָבַל אוֹתָם וְאֵת הַצִּפֹּר הַחַיָּה — "**and he shall dip them and the live bird.**" הֶחֱזִיר אֶת הַצִּפּוֹר — **[The verse] has reinstated the bird** לִכְלַל טְבִילָה — **into the category of dipping,** i.e., into the category of objects that are dipped.[4]

8. וְיָשַׁב מִחוּץ לְאָהֳלוֹ — **BUT HE SHALL DWELL OUTSIDE OF HIS TENT.** מְלַמֵּד — **This teaches us** שֶׁאָסוּר בְּתַשְׁמִישׁ הַמִּטָּה — **that he is forbidden to have sexual relations.**[5]

9. אֶת כָּל שְׂעָרוֹ וְגוֹמֵר — **ALL HIS HAIR, ETC.** כְּלָל וּפְרָט וּכְלָל — This verse includes **a broad statement** followed by **a statement of particulars,** and this is followed by **a second broad statement,** לְהָבִיא כָּל מְקוֹם כִּנּוּס שֵׂעָר — **to include any place of collection of hair,** i.e., any place on the body which has a

---

1. The crimson strip is longer than the pieces of cedar-wood and hyssop. It is bunched together with them, and the part that extends beyond the cedar and hyssop is used to tie the bunch together (Negaim 14:1).
2. The verse states, אֶת הַצִּפֹּר הַחַיָּה יִקַּח אֹתָהּ, "the live bird: He shall take it," with reference to the bird, and then adds, . . . וְאֶת עֵץ הָאֶרֶז, "and the cedarwood . . ." It could have written: וְיִקַּח אֶת הַצִּפֹּר הַחַיָּה וְאֶת עֵץ הָאֶרֶז, "He shall take the living bird, the cedarwood, the crimson wool, and the hyssop," with all of the objects grouped together. Since the last three objects follow the verb while the first precedes it, these last three constitute a distinct group (see Nachalas Yaakov).

3. According to Mizrachi, were it not for אֶת הַצִּפֹּר הַחַיָּה, "and the live bird," we would have thought that the bird is not dipped altogether. According to Nachalas Yaakov and Sifsei Chachamim, we would have thought that the bird is dipped, but not with the other objects.

4. Toras Kohanim, perek 1:6.

5. Toras Kohanim, parshasa 2:11; Moed Katan 7b. The word אָהֳלוֹ, "his tent," is a euphemism for "his wife." The verse is not to be understood literally; the metzora is permitted to enter his tent. The expression בֵּיתוֹ, literally, "his house" (as used in 16:6 below), is also explained as meaning "his wife" (Yoma 2a).

163 / VAYIKRA/LEVITICUS — PARASHAS METZORA — 14/10 — יד/י

his eyebrows, and all his hair shall he shave off; he shall immerse his clothing and immerse his flesh in water, and become pure.

¹⁰ On the eighth day, he shall take two unblemished male lambs and one unblemished ewe in its first year; three tenth-ephahs of fine flour as a meal-offering mixed with oil; and one log of oil.

וְאֵת גַּבֹּת עֵינָיו וְאֶת־כָּל־שְׂעָרוֹ יְגַלֵּחַ וְכִבֶּס אֶת־בְּגָדָיו וְרָחַץ אֶת־בְּשָׂרוֹ בַּמַּיִם וְטָהֵר: וּבַיּוֹם הַשְּׁמִינִי יִקַּח שְׁנֵי־כְבָשִׂים תְּמִימִם וְכַבְשָׂה אַחַת בַּת־שְׁנָתָהּ תְּמִימָה וּשְׁלֹשָׁה עֶשְׂרֹנִים סֹלֶת מִנְחָה בְּלוּלָה בַשֶּׁמֶן וְלֹג אֶחָד שָׁמֶן:

—————————— אונקלוס ——————————

וְיָת גְּבִינֵי עֵינוֹהִי וְיָת כָּל שַׂעֲרֵהּ יְגַלַּח וִיצַבַּע יָת לְבוּשׁוֹהִי וְיַסְחֵי יָת בִּסְרֵהּ בְּמַיָּא וְיִדְכֵּי: יוּבְיוֹמָא תְמִינָאָה יִסַּב תְּרֵין אִמְּרִין שַׁלְמִין וְאִמַּרְתָּא חֲדָא בַּת שַׁתַּא שְׁלֶמְתָא וּתְלָתָא עֶשְׂרוֹנִין סָלְתָּא מִנְחָתָא דְפִילָא בִמְשַׁח וְלֻגָּא חַד דְּמִשְׁחָא:

—————————— רש״י ——————————

וְנִרְאֶה (סוטה טז.): **(י) וּבְכַשְׂבָּה אַחַת.** לְחַטָּאת: שְׁחִיטָתוֹ וַאֲשָׁמוֹ שֶׁל מְצֹרָע טְעוּנִין נְסָכִים (מנחות צא.): **וּשְׁלֹשָׁה עֶשְׂרוֹנִים.** לְנִסְכֵּי שְׁלֹשָׁה כְבָשִׂים הַלָּלוּ. **וְלֹג אֶחָד שָׁמֶן.** לְהַזּוֹת [עָלָיו] שֶׁבַע

—————————— RASHI ELUCIDATED ——————————

dense covering of hair, וְנִרְאֶה — **which is visible.**[1]

10. וְכַבְשָׂה אַחַת — **AND ONE [UNBLEMISHED] EWE.** לְחַטָּאת — **For a sin-offering.**[2]

□ וּשְׁלֹשָׁה עֶשְׂרוֹנִים — **THREE TENTH-EPHAHS.** לְנִסְכֵּי שְׁלֹשָׁה כְבָשִׂים הַלָּלוּ — **For the poured-offerings of** these three lambs, שְׁחִיטָתוֹ וַאֲשָׁמוֹ שֶׁל מְצֹרָע — **for the sin-offering and guilt-offering of one who suffers from** *tzara'as* [3] טְעוּנִין נְסָכִים — **require poured-offerings.**[3]

□ וְלֹג אֶחָד שָׁמֶן — **AND ONE *LOG* OF OIL.** לְהַזּוֹת {עָלָיו} שֶׁבַע — **To sprinkle {upon him} seven** times,[4]

1. *Sotah* 16a. כְּלָל וּפְרָט וּכְלָל, "a broad statement and a statement of particulars and a broad statement," is a technical term used for one of the thirteen principles by which the Sages expounded the Torah. That principle declares that the apparent contradiction between the two broad statements (which include everything applicable) and the statement of particulars (which excludes anything not mentioned) is resolved as follows: The broad statements include everything that is essentially similar to the items mentioned in the statement of particulars.

Here we have an example of that principle. The verse begins by telling us that he should shave אֶת כָּל שְׂעָרוֹ, "all his hair," a broad statement which implies that all the hair, without exception, must be shaved. The next phrase, אֶת רֹאשׁוֹ וְאֶת זְקָנוֹ וְאֵת גַּבֹּת עֵינָיו, "his head, his beard, and his eyebrows," is a statement of particulars and implies that only those three areas must be shaved. The next phrase, וְאֶת כָּל שְׂעָרוֹ, "and all his hair," is another broad statement. According to the principle of כְּלָל וּפְרָט וּכְלָל, the verse is interpreted as follows: Just as the head, beard, and eyebrows are areas of the body which have a dense covering of hair and are visible, so, too, other areas of the body that are essentially similar, i.e., they also have a dense covering of hair and are visible, must be shaved. This, however, excludes hair such as that on the arms, for the arms are not densely covered with hair.

Gur Aryeh notes that according to *Sotah* 16a, R' Yishmael, who views our verse as a כְּלָל וּפְרָט וּכְלָל, "a broad statement and a statement of particulars and a broad statement," the verse excludes hair of the nostrils and the armpits as not being visible, but not pubic hair. R' Akiva there, however, interprets our verse differently and excludes only hair of the nostrils. Rashi here explains the verse in accordance with the opinion of R' Yishmael.

2. Verse 12 says that one of the male lambs is brought as a guilt-offering. Verses 19 and 20 say that the remaining two animals are brought as a sin-offering and an *olah*-offering, but does not state which animal is used for which offering. Rashi concludes that the ewe is brought as the sin-offering, because *olah*-offerings can only be brought from male animals (see 1:10 above; *Mizrachi; Sifsei Chachamim*).

3. *Menachos* 91a. *Olah*-offerings and peace-offerings are accompanied by an offering of wine and an offering of meal ("poured-offering"); guilt-offerings and sin-offerings usually are not (see *Numbers* 15:1-16). The meal-offering that accompanies a lamb *olah*-offering has a volume of one tenth-*ephah*. But our verse requires one who comes to purify himself from *tzara'as* to bring three tenth-*ephahs* and three lambs — one for an *olah*-offering, one for a guilt-offering, and one for a sin-offering. We might have concluded that one of the three tenth-*ephahs* of meal mentioned in our verse is to accompany the *olah*-offering, and the other two are for meal-offerings brought independently of animal offerings. Rashi explains that this is not so. Rather, unlike other sin- and guilt-offerings, the guilt- and sin-offerings of one who comes to purify himself from *tzara'as* require poured-offerings. It is for these offerings that the meal is brought (*Mizrachi; Sifsei Chachamim*).

4. The oil is not sprinkled on the purificant, but rather in the direction of the Holy of Holies (see verse 16 and Rashi there). *Yosef Hallel* therefore concludes that the text of the first printed edition of Rashi, which does not include the word עָלָיו, "upon him," is more accurate than the common editions.

11 The Kohen who purifies shall place the person being purified along with them before HASHEM at the entrance of the Tent of Meeting. **12** The Kohen shall take the one lamb and bring it near for a guilt-offering, with the log of oil; and he shall wave them as a wave-service before HASHEM.

13 He shall slaughter the lamb in the place where he will slaughter the sin-offering

יא וְהֶעֱמִיד הַכֹּהֵן הַמְטַהֵר אֵת הָאִישׁ הַמִּטַּהֵר וְאֹתָם לִפְנֵי יהוה פֶּתַח אֹהֶל מוֹעֵד: יב וְלָקַח הַכֹּהֵן אֶת־הַכֶּבֶשׂ הָאֶחָד וְהִקְרִיב אֹתוֹ לְאָשָׁם וְאֶת־לֹג הַשָּׁמֶן וְהֵנִיף אֹתָם תְּנוּפָה לִפְנֵי יהוה: שני יג וְשָׁחַט אֶת־הַכֶּבֶשׂ בִּמְקוֹם אֲשֶׁר יִשְׁחַט אֶת־הַחַטָּאת

---------- אונקלוס ----------

יא וִיקִים כַּהֲנָא דִמְדַכֵּי יָת גַּבְרָא דְמִדַּכֵּי וְיָתְהוֹן קֳדָם יְיָ בִּתְרַע מַשְׁכַּן זִמְנָא: יב וְיִסַּב כַּהֲנָא יָת אִמְּרָא חַד וִיקָרֵב יָתֵהּ לַאֲשָׁמָא וְיָת לֻגָּא דְמִשְׁחָא וִירִים יָתְהוֹן אֲרָמָא קֳדָם יְיָ: יג וְיִכּוֹס יָת אִמְּרָא בְּאַתְרָא דִי יִכּוֹס יָת חַטָּאתָא

---------- רש"י ----------

וְיִתֵּן מִמֶּנּוּ עַל תְּנוּךְ אָזְנוֹ וּמַתַּן בְּהוֹנוֹת: **(יא) לִפְנֵי ה'**. בְּשַׁעַר נִקָנוֹר (ת"כ פרשתא ג:ו; סוטה ז.) וְלֹא בָעֲזָרָה עַצְמָהּ לְפִי שֶׁהוּא מְחֻסַּר כִּפּוּרִים: **(יב) וְהִקְרִיב אֹתוֹ לְאָשָׁם**. יַקְרִיבֶנּוּ לְתוֹךְ הָעֲזָרָה לְשֵׁם אָשָׁם: **לְהָנִיף**. שֶׁהוּא טָעוּן תְּנוּפָה חַי (מנחות סב.): **וְהֵנִיף אֹתָם**. אֵת הָאָשָׁם וְאֵת הַלֹּג (ת"כ שָׁם ז; מנחות סא.): **(יג) בִּמְקוֹם אֲשֶׁר יִשְׁחַט וְגוֹ'**. עַל יֶרֶךְ הַמִּזְבֵּחַ בַּצָּפוֹן. וּמַה תַּ"ל, וַהֲלֹא כְבָר נֶאֱמַר בְּתוֹרַת אָשָׁם בְּפָרָשַׁת צַו אֶת אַהֲרֹן (ויקרא ז:ב) שֶׁהָאָשָׁם טָעוּן שְׁחִיטָה בַצָּפוֹן. לְפִי שֶׁיָּצָא זֶה

---------- RASHI ELUCIDATED ----------

וּמַתַּן בְּהוֹנוֹת – **and for** applications on the purificant's **thumb and big toe.**[2] **11.** לִפְנֵי ה' – BEFORE HASHEM.[3] בְּשַׁעַר נִקָנוֹר – **At the Gate of Nikanor.**[3] וְלֹא בָעֲזָרָה עַצְמָהּ – **But not in the Courtyard itself,** לְפִי שֶׁהוּא מְחֻסַּר כִּפּוּרִים – **because he is lacking atonement.**[4] **12.** וְהִקְרִיב אֹתוֹ לְאָשָׁם – AND BRING IT NEAR FOR A GUILT-OFFERING. יַקְרִיבֶנּוּ – **He shall bring it near,** לְתוֹךְ הָעֲזָרָה – **into the Courtyard,** לְשֵׁם אָשָׁם – **for the sake of** its being offered as **a guilt-offering.**[5] לְהָנִיף – TO WAVE. This teaches us שֶׁהוּא טָעוּן תְּנוּפָה חַי[6] – **that it requires waving** while it is still **alive.**[6] וְהֵנִיף אֹתָם – AND HE SHALL WAVE THEM.[7] אֵת הָאָשָׁם וְאֵת הַלֹּג – **The guilt-offering and the** *log* of oil.[7] **13.** בִּמְקוֹם אֲשֶׁר יִשְׁחַט וְגוֹמֵר – IN THE PLACE WHERE HE WILL SLAUGHTER, ETC. This means עַל יֶרֶךְ הַמִּזְבֵּחַ – **at the side of the Altar,** בַּצָּפוֹן – **on the north.** וּמַה תַּלְמוּד לוֹמַר – **Why did the Torah have to say this?** וַהֲלֹא כְבָר נֶאֱמַר – **Has it not already been stated** בְּתוֹרַת אָשָׁם – **in the law of the guilt-offering** בְּפָרָשַׁת צַו אֶת אַהֲרֹן[8] – in *Parashas Tzav Es Aharon*[8] שֶׁהָאָשָׁם – **that the guilt-offering** טָעוּן שְׁחִיטָה – **requires slaughtering** בַּצָּפוֹן – **on the north?** לְפִי שֶׁיָּצָא זֶה – **Since**

---

1. See Rashi to *Exodus* 29:20 and to verse 14 below, s.v., תנוך.

2. The *log* of oil mentioned here is not the oil mentioned earlier in the verse which is used for the meal-offering (*Minchas Yehudah; Sifsei Chachamim*).

A *log* (plural לֻגִּין) contains six times the volume of a בֵּיצָה, "chicken egg." Halachic authorities differ widely regarding the modern-day equivalents of these measures. Opinions regarding the בֵּיצָה range from 2 to 3.5 fluid ounces. Thus, the volume of a *log* is approximately 12 to 21 fluid ounces.

3. *Toras Kohanim, parshasa* 3:6; *Sotah* 7a.

4. The Gate of Nikanor was at the eastern entrance of the Courtyard. Whoever stands there can be said to be "before HASHEM" because he faces the entrance of the *Beis HaMikdash* (*Minchas Yehudah; Sifsei Chachamim*). The purificant could approach no closer at this stage for he was "lacking atonement" (see page 73, note 6) — he had not yet brought the offerings that atone for him and are the final stage of the process of his purification.

5. וְהִקְרִיב אֹתוֹ לְאָשָׁם could have been understood as, "he shall offer, i.e. slaughter, it as a guilt-offering." It does not mean this in our verse, however, for the next verse speaks of slaughtering the guilt-offering. Our verse refers to an earlier stage. He must bring the animal into the Courtyard with the conscious intent that it be offered as a guilt-offering (*Mizrachi; Sifsei Chachamim*).

6. *Menachos* 62b. This is in contrast to the law of the peace-offering. There, those parts of the offering that are to be burnt upon the Altar are waved *after* the animal is slaughtered (*Divrei David*).

7. *Toras Kohanim, parshasa* 3:7; *Menachos* 61a. "Them" of "he shall wave them" refers only to the guilt-offering and the *log* of oil mentioned in this verse, not to all that is mentioned in verse 10 which includes two other lambs and flour. This is clearly so for verse 24 below states explicitly with regard to the offering of a poor purificant that only the guilt-offering and *log* of oil are waved (*Mizrachi; Sifsei Chachamim*).

8. See above 7:2 and 1:11.

and the olah-offering, in the holy place; for like the sin-offering, the guilt-offering is to the Kohen, it is most holy. ¹⁴ *The Kohen shall take from the blood of the* וְאֶת־הָעֹלָה בִּמְקוֹם הַקֹּדֶשׁ כִּי כַחַטָּאת הָאָשָׁם הוּא לַכֹּהֵן קֹדֶשׁ קָדָשִׁים הוּא: יד וְלָקַח הַכֹּהֵן מִדַּם

— אונקלוס —

וְיָת עֲלָתָא בַּאֲתַר קַדִּישׁ אֲרֵי כְּחַטָּאתָא אֲשָׁמָא הוּא לְכַהֲנָא קֹדֶשׁ קוּדְשִׁין הוּא: יד וְיִסַּב כַּהֲנָא מִדְּמָא

— רש"י —

מכלל אשמות לידון בהעמדה, יכול תהא שחיטתו במקום העמדתו, לכך נאמר ושחט במקום אשר ישחט וגו' (ת"כ שם ח): **כי בחטאת.** כי ככל התחטאות האשם הזה הוא לכהן. שלא בכל עבודות התלויות בכהן אשם זה לחטאת. תאמר הואיל ויצא דמו מכלל שאר אשמות לנתן על תנוך ובהונות, לא יהא טעון מתן דמים ואימורים לגבי מזבח, לכך נאמר כי כחטאת האשם הוא לכהן. יכול יהא דמו ניתן למעלה כחטאת, ת"ל וכו'. בתורת כהנים (פרק ג:ח):

——— RASHI ELUCIDATED ———

לְדוּן – this guilt-offering **has gone out** מִכְּלָל אֲשָׁמוֹת – of the general category of guilt-offerings בְּהַעֲמָדָה – **to fall under the law of being placed,**[1] יָכוֹל – one might be able to think that תְּהֵא – שְׁחִיטָתוֹ **– its slaughtering should be** בִּמְקוֹם הַעֲמָדָתוֹ – **at the location of its placing,** at the eastern side of the Courtyard, near the gate of Nikanor. לְכָךְ נֶאֱמַר – **Therefore it says,** ",וְשָׁחַט בִּמְקוֹם אֲשֶׁר יִשְׁחַט וְגוֹמֵר"[2] – **"he shall slaughter** the lamb **in the place where he will slaughter** the sin-offering, etc.," i.e., on the north.[2]

□ כִּי כַחַטָּאת – **FOR LIKE THE SIN-OFFERING.** כִּי בְּכָל הַחַטָּאוֹת – For like all sin-offerings, הָאָשָׁם הַזֶּה – this הוּא לַכֹּהֵן – **is to the Kohen.** בְּכָל עֲבוֹדוֹת הַתְּלוּיוֹת בַּכֹּהֵן – In all services that are dependent upon a Kohen, i.e., which must be performed by a Kohen, הֻשְׁוָה אָשָׁם זֶה – this guilt-offering has been made equal לְחַטָּאת – **to a sin-offering.** שֶׁלֹּא תֹאמַר – So that you should not say, הוֹאִיל וְיָצָא דָמוֹ – since its blood has gone out מִכְּלָל שְׁאָר אֲשָׁמוֹת – of the general category of guilt-offerings לְנָתֵן עַל תְּנוּךְ – to be put on the cartilage of the ear וּבְהוֹנוֹת – and the thumb and big toe, לֹא יְהֵא טָעוּן מַתַּן דָּמִים – it should not require application of blood וְאֵמוּרִים – and stated parts[4] לְגַבֵּי מִזְבֵּחַ – upon the Altar. לְכָךְ נֶאֱמַר – **Therefore it says,** כִּי כַחַטָּאת. יָכוֹל – One might be able to think that הָאָשָׁם הוּא לַכֹּהֵן" – **"for like the sin-offering the guilt-offering is to the Kohen."**[5] יְהֵא דָמוֹ נָתָן לְמַעְלָה – **its blood should be put above** the midpoint of the Altar כַּחַטָּאת – like the blood of **a sin-offering.**[6] תַּלְמוּד לוֹמַר וְכַלֵּה – To teach us otherwise, **the verse says ["this is the teaching of the guilt-offering,] etc.,"**[7] to include all guilt-offerings, and the guilt-offering of the one who comes to purify himself of *tzaraas* among them, in the law of having their blood applied to the lower part of the Altar, בְּתוֹרַת כֹּהֲנִים[8] – as stated in ***Toras Kohanim.***[8]

1. Verse 11 states that the Kohen shall place the purificant and his offerings "before HASHEM." No other guilt-offering has such a requirement.

2. *Toras Kohanim, parshasa* 3:8.

3. See end of note 5 below.

4. These are those parts of guilt-offerings that the Torah has stated must be burned on the Altar.

5. This guilt-offering is different from all other guilt-offerings in that some of its blood is applied to the body of the one who brings it. Since we might have thought that this application comes in place of the application of blood to the Altar and the offering of parts of the animal upon the Altar, Scripture compares this guilt-offering to a sin-offering: Both are "to the Kohen" with respect to the application of blood on the Altar and burning of the stated parts. These are services which may be performed only by the Kohanim, and are part of the procedure of the guilt-offering of one who comes to purify himself of *tzaraas*, just as they are part of the procedure of the sin-offering. Rashi stresses that the comparison is only between *this* guilt-offering and the sin-offering, for there is no reason to think that applications of blood and burning of stated parts does not apply to any other guilt-offering (*Mizrachi; Sifsei Chachamim*).

6. The blood of a sin-offering is applied to the upper half of the Altar (see 4:30 above), while the blood of other offerings, including the guilt-offering, is applied to its lower half. One might think that the comparison of this guilt-offering to a sin-offering extends to the place where the blood is applied, as well.

7. Above 7:1.

8. *Toras Kohanim, perek* 3:1. The word תּוֹרָה, or, as it appears in 7:1 in its construct form, תּוֹרַת, is an inclusory term. Here it includes the guilt-offering of the *metzora* within the general category of guilt-offerings. That is why the blood is applied to the lower part of the Altar, despite the comparison made by our verse between the guilt-offering of the *metzora* and the sin-offering, whose blood is applied to the upper part (*Mizrachi; Sifsei Chachamim*).

guilt-offering, and the Kohen shall place it on the tenuch of the right ear of the person being purified and on the thumb of his right hand and the big toe of his right foot. *15* The Kohen shall take from the log of oil and he shall pour it upon the Kohen's left palm. *16* The Kohen shall dip his right forefinger into the oil that is in his left palm; and he shall sprinkle from the oil with his finger seven times before HASHEM. *17* Some of the oil remaining on his palm, the Kohen shall put on the tenuch of the right ear of the man being purified, on the thumb of his right hand and on the big toe of his right foot; on the blood of the guilt-offering.

הָאָשָׁם֙ וְנָתַן֙ הַכֹּהֵ֔ן עַל־תְּנ֛וּךְ אֹ֥זֶן הַמִּטַּהֵ֖ר הַיְמָנִ֑ית וְעַל־בֹּ֤הֶן יָדוֹ֙ הַיְמָנִ֔ית וְעַל־בֹּ֥הֶן רַגְל֖וֹ הַיְמָנִֽית: טו וְלָקַ֥ח הַכֹּהֵ֖ן מִלֹּ֣ג הַשָּׁ֑מֶן וְיָצַק֙ עַל־כַּ֥ף הַכֹּהֵ֖ן הַשְּׂמָאלִֽית: טז וְטָבַ֤ל הַכֹּהֵן֙ אֶת־אֶצְבָּע֣וֹ הַיְמָנִ֔ית מִן־הַשֶּׁ֕מֶן אֲשֶׁ֥ר עַל־כַּפּ֖וֹ הַשְּׂמָאלִ֑ית וְהִזָּ֨ה מִן־הַשֶּׁ֧מֶן בְּאֶצְבָּע֛וֹ שֶׁ֥בַע פְּעָמִ֖ים לִפְנֵ֥י יְהֹוָֽה: יז וּמִיֶּ֨תֶר הַשֶּׁ֜מֶן אֲשֶׁ֣ר עַל־כַּפּ֗וֹ יִתֵּ֤ן הַכֹּהֵן֙ עַל־תְּנ֨וּךְ֙ אֹ֣זֶן הַמִּטַּהֵ֔ר הַיְמָנִ֔ית וְעַל־בֹּ֤הֶן יָדוֹ֙ הַיְמָנִ֔ית וְעַל־בֹּ֥הֶן רַגְל֖וֹ הַיְמָנִ֑ית עַ֖ל דַּ֥ם הָאָשָֽׁם:

———————— אונקלוס ————————

דַאֲשָׁמָא וְיִתֵּן כַּהֲנָא עַל רוּם אוּדְנָא דְמִדַּכֵּי דְיַמִּינָא וְעַל אֶלְיוֹן יְדֵהּ דְיַמִּינָא וְעַל אֶלְיוֹן רַגְלֵהּ דְיַמִּינָא: טו וְיִסַּב כַּהֲנָא מִלֹּגָא דְמִשְׁחָא וִירִיק עַל יְדָא דְכַהֲנָא דִסְמָאלָא: טז וְיִטְבּוֹל כַּהֲנָא יָת אֶצְבְּעֵהּ דְיַמִּינָא מִן מִשְׁחָא דִי עַל יְדֵהּ דִסְמָאלָא וְיַדִּי מִן מִשְׁחָא בְּאֶצְבְּעֵהּ שְׁבַע זִמְנִין קֳדָם יְיָ: יז וּמִדְּאִשְׁתְּאַר מִשְׁחָא דִי עַל יְדֵהּ יִתֵּן כַּהֲנָא עַל רוּם אוּדְנָא דְמִדַּכֵּי דְיַמִּינָא וְעַל אֶלְיוֹן יְדֵהּ דְיַמִּינָא וְעַל אֶלְיוֹן רַגְלֵהּ דְיַמִּינָא עַל דְּמָא דַאֲשָׁמָא:

———————— רש"י ————————

(יד) תנוך. גדר אמצעי שבאוזן (שם פרק ג:ה). ולשון תנוך לא נודע לי והפותרים קורים לו טנדרו"ן. **(טז) לפני ה'.** כנגד בית קדש הקדשים (שם טו): **(יז) על דם האשם.** שיקדים הדם לשמן, ולעכב (מנחות ה.)]

———————— RASHI ELUCIDATED ————————

14. תְּנוּךְ — THE *TENUCH*. This means ¹גֶּדֶר אֶמְצָעִי שֶׁבָּאוֹזֶן — the middle section of the ear.[1] וּלְשׁוֹן תְּנוּךְ — The etymology of תְּנוּךְ is not known to me.[2] וְהַפּוֹתְרִים קוֹרִים לוֹ טנדרו"ן — The interpreters[3] call it *tendron*.[4]

בֹּהֶן — This means גּוּדָל — thumb/big toe.[5]

16. לִפְנֵי ה' — BEFORE HASHEM. ⁶כְּנֶגֶד בֵּית קָדְשֵׁי הַקֳּדָשִׁים — Toward the Holy of Holies.[6]

{**17.** עַל דַּם הָאָשָׁם — ON THE BLOOD OF THE GUILT-OFFERING. This teaches us שֶׁיַּקְדִּים הַדָּם לַשֶּׁמֶן — that he should do the service of **the blood before** the service of **the oil.** ⁷וּלְעַכֵּב — And it teaches that **this prevents,** i.e., that if it is not done in this order the service is invalid.[7]}

1. *Toras Kohanim, perek* 3:5.
2. The etymology of תְּנוּךְ is discussed by *Tosafos Yom Tov, Negaim* 14:9.
3. "The interpreters" were teachers of *Chumash*. The notebooks they kept provided a source for the definitions of words and the meanings of verses. See A.M. Lifshitz in *Sefer Rashi, Mossad HaRav Kook,* Jerusalem, 5716.
4. This word means "cartilage," and should not be confused with "tendon." The word *tendron* is used today in cookery to describe the gristle of veal.
5. בֹּהֶן and גּוּדָל are synonyms to either the "thumb" or the "big toe." English has no single word that refers to both digits.
6. *Toras Kohanim, perek* 3:9. In verse 11, "before HASHEM" meant at the Gate of Nikanor, for there the verse was discussing one who was "lacking atonement" and was not permitted to enter the Courtyard (see v. 11, note 4 above). Our verse refers to a point after the offerings have been brought, when the *metzora* is permitted to enter the Courtyard. "Before HASHEM," then, means toward the entrance of the Holy of Holies, rather than at the Gate of Nikanor. Nor do we find any instance of sprinkling which is performed at the Gate of Nikanor (*Minchas Yehudah; Sifsei Chachamim*).

Yosef Hallel and *Leket Bahir* both take issue with this explanation, however, for the purificant maintains the status of one who is lacking atonement and may not enter the Courtyard until *after* the sprinkling of the oil and its application upon his right ear, thumb and big toe, and upon his head. They say that in verse 11, "before HASHEM" refers to an action performed by the purificant. As he is still impure at that stage, Rashi says that "before HASHEM" must refer to a place outside the Courtyard — the Gate of Nikanor. In our verse, however, "before HASHEM" refers to an action performed by the Kohen within; thus Rashi says that "before HASHEM," within, means opposite the Holy of Holies.

7. *Menachos* 5a.

18 And the rest of the oil that is on the Kohen's palm, he shall place upon the head of the person being purified; and the Kohen shall provide him atonement before HASHEM. **19** The Kohen shall perform the sin-offering service and provide atonement for the person being purified from his impurity; after that he shall slaughter the olah-offering. **20** The Kohen shall bring the olah-offering and the meal-offering up to the Mizbe'ach; and the Kohen shall provide him atonement, and he becomes pure.

21 If he is poor and his means are not sufficient, then he shall take one male lamb as a guilt-offering for a wave-service to provide atonement for him; and one tenth-ephah of fine flour mixed with oil for a meal-offering, and a log of oil. **22** And two turtledoves or two young doves — for whichever his means are sufficient — one shall be a sin-offering

וְהַנּוֹתָר בַּשֶּׁמֶן אֲשֶׁר עַל־כַּף הַכֹּהֵן יִתֵּן עַל־רֹאשׁ הַמִּטַּהֵר וְכִפֶּר עָלָיו הַכֹּהֵן לִפְנֵי יהוה: וְעָשָׂה הַכֹּהֵן אֶת־הַחַטָּאת וְכִפֶּר עַל־הַמִּטַּהֵר מִטֻּמְאָתוֹ וְאַחַר יִשְׁחַט אֶת־הָעֹלָה: וְהֶעֱלָה הַכֹּהֵן אֶת־הָעֹלָה וְאֶת־הַמִּנְחָה הַמִּזְבֵּחָה וְכִפֶּר עָלָיו הַכֹּהֵן וְטָהֵר: שלישי [חמישי] וְאִם־דַּל הוּא וְאֵין יָדוֹ מַשֶּׂגֶת וְלָקַח כֶּבֶשׂ אֶחָד אָשָׁם לִתְנוּפָה לְכַפֵּר עָלָיו וְעִשָּׂרוֹן סֹלֶת אֶחָד בָּלוּל בַּשֶּׁמֶן לְמִנְחָה וְלֹג שָׁמֶן: וּשְׁתֵּי תֹרִים אוֹ שְׁנֵי בְּנֵי יוֹנָה אֲשֶׁר תַּשִּׂיג יָדוֹ וְהָיָה אֶחָד חַטָּאת

— אונקלוס —

יח וּדְאִשְׁתְּאַר בְּמִשְׁחָא דִּי עַל יְדָא דְכַהֲנָא יִתֵּן עַל רֵישׁ דְּמִדַּכֵּי וִיכַפֵּר עֲלוֹהִי כַהֲנָא קֳדָם יְיָ: יט וְיַעְבֵּד כַּהֲנָא יָת חַטָּאתָא וִיכַפֵּר עַל דְּמִדַּכֵּי מִסּוֹאֲבֵתֵיהּ וּבָתַר כֵּן יִכּוֹס יָת עֲלָתָא: כ וְיַסֵּק כַּהֲנָא יָת עֲלָתָא וְיָת מִנְחָתָא לְמַדְבְּחָא וִיכַפֵּר עֲלוֹהִי כַהֲנָא וְיִדְכֵּי: כא וְאִם מִסְכֵּן הוּא וְלֵית יְדֵהּ מַדְבְּקָא וְיִסַּב אִמַּר חַד אֲשָׁמָא לַאֲרָמָא לְכַפָּרָא עֲלוֹהִי וְעֶשְׂרוֹנָא סָלְתָּא חַד דְּפִיל בִּמְשַׁח לְמִנְחָתָא וְלֻגָּא דְמִשְׁחָא: כב וְתַרְתֵּין שַׁפְנִינִין אוֹ תְרֵין בְּנֵי יוֹנָה דִּי תַדְבֵּק יְדֵהּ וִיהֵי חַד חַטָּאתָא

— רש"י —

(כ) וְאֵת הַמִּנְחָה. מִנְחַת נְסָכִים שֶׁל בְּהֵמָה (מנחות צ"א): יָבִיא עִשָּׂרוֹן אֶחָד לִנְסָכָיו: **וְלֹג שָׁמֶן.** לָתֵת מִמֶּנּוּ עַל בְּהוֹנוֹת. וְשֶׁמֶן שֶׁל נִסְכֵּי הַמִּנְחָה לֹא הֻזְקַק הַכָּתוּב לִפְרֵשׁ: (כא) **וְעִשָּׂרוֹן סֹלֶת אֶחָד.** לְכֶבֶשׂ זֶה שֶׁהוּא ה' הַבְּהוֹנוֹת. וְשֶׁמֶן שֶׁל נִסְכֵּי הַמִּנְחָה לֹא הֻזְקַק הַכָּתוּב לִפְרֵשׁ:

— RASHI ELUCIDATED —

20. וְאֵת הַמִּנְחָה — AND THE MEAL-OFFERING. מִנְחַת נְסָכִים — A meal-offering of poured-offerings שֶׁל בְּהֵמָה — of animal offerings.[1]

21. וְעִשָּׂרוֹן סֹלֶת אֶחָד — AND ONE TENTH-*EPHAH* OF FINE FLOUR. לְכֶבֶשׂ זֶה — For this lamb שֶׁהוּא אֶחָד — which is one, יָבִיא עִשָּׂרוֹן אֶחָד — he shall bring one tenth-*ephah* לִנְסָכָיו — for its poured-offerings.[2]

וְלֹג שָׁמֶן — AND A *LOG* OF OIL. לָתֵת מִמֶּנּוּ — To apply from it עַל הַבְּהוֹנוֹת — on the thumb and big toe. וְשֶׁמֶן שֶׁל נִסְכֵּי הַמִּנְחָה — With respect to **the oil of the meal-offering that accompanies the poured-offering,** לֹא הֻזְקַק הַכָּתוּב לְפָרֵשׁ — Scripture did not feel the necessity to state it explicitly.[3]

---

1. *Menachos* 91a. It is not a meal-offering brought independently of animal offerings. Such meal-offerings have only a *kometz* of flour taken from them to be burned on the Altar. The meal-offering of our verse is juxtaposed to the *olah*-offering to teach us that it is burned in its entirety, like the *olah*-offering. This is characteristic of meal-offerings along with the poured-offerings that accompany animal offerings (*Mizrachi*; *Sifsei Chachamim*).

2. Our verse had to say כֶּבֶשׂ אֶחָד, "*one* male lamb," to contrast the one lamb brought by the poor purificant with the three lambs brought by the rich one. But why does the verse say עִשָּׂרוֹן סֹלֶת אֶחָד, "*one* tenth-*ephah* of fine flour"? Couldn't the verse have said, "*a* tenth-*ephah* of flour," without using אֶחָד? The verse uses this word to stress that the אֶחָד of the fine flour parallels the אֶחָד of the sheep. The meal-offering of fine flour mentioned here accompanies the poured-offering for the one sheep. Without this אֶחָד, we might have thought that the tenth-*ephah* of flour and the *log* of oil mentioned at the end of the verse compose a meal-offering independent of the guilt-offering and any other offerings that might accompany it (*Gur Aryeh*; *Divrei David*; *Sifsei Chachamim*).

3. Once the verse has referred to "one tenth-*ephah* of fine flour," it may be assumed that the tenth-*ephah* is mixed with the standard quarter-*hin* (three *logs*) of oil, as stated in *Numbers* 15:4. The single *log* mentioned by our verse must therefore be for the applications of oil, as in verse 10 above (see Rashi there; *Divrei David*).

and one an olah-offering. ²³ **He shall bring them to the Kohen, on the eighth day of his purification, to the entrance of the Tent of Meeting, before** HASHEM. ²⁴ **The Kohen shall take the guilt-offering lamb and the log of oil; and the Kohen shall wave them as a wave-service before** HASHEM. ²⁵ **He shall slaughter the guilt-offering lamb and the Kohen shall take some of the guilt-offering's blood and place it on the middle part of the right ear of the man being purified and on the thumb of his right hand and on the big toe of his right foot.** ²⁶ **From the oil, the Kohen shall pour upon the Kohen's left palm.** ²⁷ **The Kohen shall sprinkle with his right forefinger some of the oil that is in his left palm seven times before** HASHEM. ²⁸ **The Kohen shall place some of the oil that is on his palm upon the middle of the right ear of the person being purified, on the thumb of his right hand and on the big toe of his right foot — on the place of the guilt-offering's blood.** ²⁹ **And the rest of the oil that is on the Kohen's palm, he shall place upon the head of**	כג וְהָאֶחָ֣ד עֹלָ֑ה: וְהֵבִ֨יא אֹתָ֤ם בַּיּ֣וֹם הַשְּׁמִינִ֔י לְטָהֳרָת֖וֹ אֶל־הַכֹּהֵ֑ן אֶל־ כד פֶּ֥תַח אֹֽהֶל־מוֹעֵ֖ד לִפְנֵ֥י יהוֹה: וְלָקַ֣ח הַכֹּהֵ֞ן אֶת־כֶּ֤בֶשׂ הָֽאָשָׁם֙ וְאֶת־לֹ֣ג הַשָּׁ֔מֶן וְהֵנִ֨יף אֹתָ֧ם הַכֹּהֵ֛ן תְּנוּפָ֖ה כה לִפְנֵ֥י יהוֹה: וְשָׁחַט֙ אֶת־כֶּ֣בֶשׂ הָֽאָשָׁ֔ם וְלָקַ֤ח הַכֹּהֵן֙ מִדַּ֣ם הָֽאָשָׁ֔ם וְנָתַ֛ן עַל־ תְּנ֛וּךְ אֹֽזֶן־הַמִּטַּהֵ֖ר הַיְמָנִ֑ית וְעַל־ בֹּ֤הֶן יָדוֹ֙ הַיְמָנִ֔ית וְעַל־בֹּ֥הֶן רַגְל֖וֹ כו הַיְמָנִֽית: וּמִן־הַשֶּׁ֖מֶן יִצֹ֣ק הַכֹּהֵ֑ן עַל־ כז כַּ֥ף הַכֹּהֵ֖ן הַשְּׂמָאלִֽית: וְהִזָּ֨ה הַכֹּהֵ֜ן בְּאֶצְבָּע֤וֹ הַיְמָנִית֙ מִן־הַשֶּׁ֔מֶן אֲשֶׁ֥ר עַל־כַּפּ֖וֹ הַשְּׂמָאלִ֑ית שֶׁ֤בַע פְּעָמִים֙ כח לִפְנֵ֥י יהוֹה: וְנָתַ֣ן הַכֹּהֵן֮ מִן־הַשֶּׁ֣מֶן ׀ אֲשֶׁ֣ר עַל־כַּפּוֹ֒ עַל־תְּנ֞וּךְ אֹ֤זֶן הַמִּטַּהֵר֙ הַיְמָנִ֔ית וְעַל־בֹּ֤הֶן יָדוֹ֙ הַיְמָנִ֔ית וְעַל־בֹּ֥הֶן רַגְל֖וֹ הַיְמָנִ֑ית עַל־ כט מְק֖וֹם דַּ֥ם הָֽאָשָֽׁם: וְהַנּוֹתָ֗ר מִן־הַשֶּׁ֨מֶן֙ אֲשֶׁר֙ עַל־כַּ֣ף הַכֹּהֵ֔ן יִתֵּ֖ן עַל־רֹ֣אשׁ

אונקלוס

וְחַד עֲלָתָא: כגוְיַיְתֵי יָתְהוֹן בְּיוֹמָא תְמִינָאָה לְדַכְיוּתֵיהּ לְוָת כַּהֲנָא לִתְרַע מַשְׁכַּן זִמְנָא קֳדָם יְיָ: כדוְיִסַּב כַּהֲנָא יָת אִמַּר אֲשָׁמָא וְיָת לֻגָּא דְמִשְׁחָא וִירִים יָתְהוֹן כַּהֲנָא אֲרָמָא קֳדָם יְיָ: כהוְיִכּוֹס יָת אִמְּרָא דַאֲשָׁמָא וְיִסַּב כַּהֲנָא מִדְּמָא דַאֲשָׁמָא וְיִתֵּן עַל רוּם אוּדְנָא דְמִטַהֵר דְּיַמִּינָא וְעַל אֶלְיוֹן יְדֵיהּ דְּיַמִּינָא וְעַל אֶלְיוֹן רַגְלֵיהּ דְּיַמִּינָא: כווּמִן מִשְׁחָא יְרִיק כַּהֲנָא עַל יְדָא דְכַהֲנָא דִשְׂמָאלָא: כזוְיַדֵּי כַהֲנָא בְּאֶצְבְּעֵהּ דְּיַמִּינָא מִן מִשְׁחָא דִּי עַל יְדֵהּ דִשְׂמָאלָא שְׁבַע זִמְנִין קֳדָם יְיָ: כחוְיִתֵּן כַּהֲנָא מִן מִשְׁחָא דִּי עַל יְדֵהּ עַל רוּם אוּדְנָא דְמִטַהֵר דְּיַמִּינָא וְעַל אֶלְיוֹן יְדֵיהּ דְּיַמִּינָא וְעַל אֶלְיוֹן רַגְלֵיהּ דְּיַמִּינָא עַל אֲתַר דְּמָא דַאֲשָׁמָא: כטוּדְיִשְׁתָּאַר מִן מִשְׁחָא דִּי עַל יְדָא דְכַהֲנָא יִתֵּן עַל רֵישָׁא

רש"י

(כג) **ביום השמיני לטהרתו.** שמיני לצפרים ולהזאת עץ ארז ואזוב ושני תולעת: [(כח)] **על מקום דם האשם.** אפי' נתקנח הדם.

RASHI ELUCIDATED

23. בַּיּוֹם הַשְּׁמִינִי לְטָהֳרָתוֹ — ON THE EIGHTH DAY OF HIS PURIFICATION. שְׁמִינִי — The **eighth** day לַצִּפֳּרִים — **to the birds,** i.e., after the slaughter of one of the two birds brought by the purificant and the "sending away" of the other, וּלְהַזָּאַת עֵץ אֶרֶז — **and to,** i.e., after, **the sprinkling** upon the purificant by means **of cedarwood** וְאֵזוֹב — **and hyssop** — וּשְׁנִי תוֹלַעַת — **and crimson wool.**[1]

28. עַל מְקוֹם דַּם הָאָשָׁם — ON THE PLACE OF THE GUILT-OFFERING'S BLOOD. אֲפִילוּ נִתְקַנַּח הַדָּם — Even if

---

1. When the purificant shaves off all his hair on the seventh day after bringing the birds, he is said to be pure (see v. 9 above). Our verse, however, means the eighth day after the bringing of the birds. For the Torah also says that the offerings of the rich purificant must be brought on the eighth day (v. 10 above). There, it is clear that the verse means the eighth day after the bringing of the birds, for the verse immediately preceding said the shaving of the purificant takes place on the seventh day. If the offerings of the rich purificant are brought on the eighth day after the slaughter of the birds, it stands to reason that when the Torah says that the offerings of the poor purificant must be brought on the eighth day, it also means the eighth day after the bringing of the birds. "The eighth day of his purification" means the eighth day from the beginning of the process of purification (*Gur Aryeh*).

the person being purified; to provide him atonement before HASHEM.
³⁰ He shall then perform the service of one of the turtledoves or of the young doves, for whichever his means are sufficient. ³¹ Of whichever his means are sufficient — one is a sin-offering and one is an olah-offering — along with the meal-offering; and the Kohen shall provide atonement for the one being purified, before HASHEM. ³² This is the law of one in whom there is a tzara'as affliction — whose means are not sufficient — for his purification.
³³ HASHEM spoke to Moses and Aaron, saying: ³⁴ When you arrive in the land of Canaan that I give you as a possession, and I will place a tzara'as affliction upon a house in the land of your possession; ³⁵ the one to whom the house belongs shall come and declare to the Kohen, saying: Something like an affliction has appeared to me in the house.

הַמִּטַּהֵר לְכַפֵּר עָלָיו לִפְנֵי יהוה׃
ל וְעָשָׂה אֶת־הָאֶחָד מִן־הַתֹּרִים אוֹ
לא מִן־בְּנֵי הַיּוֹנָה מֵאֲשֶׁר תַּשִּׂיג יָדוֹ׃ אֵת
אֲשֶׁר־תַּשִּׂיג יָדוֹ אֶת־הָאֶחָד חַטָּאת
וְאֶת־הָאֶחָד עֹלָה עַל־הַמִּנְחָה
וְכִפֶּר הַכֹּהֵן עַל הַמִּטַּהֵר לִפְנֵי יהוה׃
לב זֹאת תּוֹרַת אֲשֶׁר־בּוֹ נֶגַע צָרָעַת
אֲשֶׁר לֹא־תַשִּׂיג יָדוֹ בְּטָהֳרָתוֹ׃
לג רביעי [ששי] וַיְדַבֵּר יהוה אֶל־מֹשֶׁה
לד וְאֶל־אַהֲרֹן לֵאמֹר׃ כִּי תָבֹאוּ
אֶל־אֶרֶץ כְּנַעַן אֲשֶׁר אֲנִי נֹתֵן
לָכֶם לַאֲחֻזָּה וְנָתַתִּי נֶגַע צָרַעַת
לה בְּבֵית אֶרֶץ אֲחֻזַּתְכֶם׃ וּבָא
אֲשֶׁר־לוֹ הַבַּיִת וְהִגִּיד לַכֹּהֵן
לֵאמֹר כְּנֶגַע נִרְאָה לִי בַּבָּיִת׃

— אונקלוס —

דְּמִדַּכֵּי לְכַפָּרָא עֲלוֹהִי קֳדָם יְיָ: ל וְיַעֲבֵד יָת חַד מִן שַׁפְנִינַיָּא אוֹ מִן בְּנֵי יוֹנָה מִדִּי תַדְבֵּק יְדֵהּ: לא יָת דִּי תַדְבֵּק יְדֵהּ חַד חַטָּאתָא וְיָת חַד עֲלָתָא עַל מִנְחָתָא וִיכַפַּר כַּהֲנָא עַל דְּמִדַּכֵּי קֳדָם יְיָ: לב דָּא אוֹרַיְתָא דִּי בֵהּ מַכְתַּשׁ סְגִירוּ דִּי לָא תַדְבֵּק יְדֵהּ בִּדְכוּתֵהּ: לג וּמַלִּיל יְיָ עִם מֹשֶׁה וְעִם אַהֲרֹן לְמֵימָר: לד אֲרֵי תֵעֲלוּן לְאַרְעָא דִכְנַעַן דִּי אֲנָא יָהֵב לְכוֹן לְאַחֲסָנָא וְאֶתֵּן מַכְתַּשׁ סְגִירוּ בְּבֵית אַרְעָא אַחֲסַנְתְּכוֹן: לה וְיֵיתֵי דְּדִילֵהּ בֵּיתָא וִיחַוֵּי לְכַהֲנָא לְמֵימַר כְּמַכְתָּשָׁא אִתְחֲזִי לִי בְּבֵיתָא:

— רש"י —

למד שאין הדם גורם אלא המקום גורם (מנחות י.): (לד) **ונתתי נגע צרעת.** בשורה היא להם שהנגעים באים עליהם (ת"כ פרשתא ה:ד). אפי' תלמיד חכם שיודע נגע ודאי, (לה) **כנגע נראה לי בבית.** בקירות בתיהם כל ארבעתים שנה שהיו ישראל במדבר, וט"י הנגע נותן הבית ומוצאן (ויק"ר יז:ו):

— RASHI ELUCIDATED —

the blood has been wiped off.[1] לָמַד – [The verse] has taught us שֶׁאֵין הַדָּם גּוֹרֵם – that the blood does not cause, i.e., that it is not the actual presence of blood which determines where the oil is to be applied; אֶלָּא – rather, ²הַמָּקוֹם גּוֹרֵם – the place where the blood was initially put causes, i.e., determines where the oil is to be applied.²}

34. וְנָתַתִּי נֶגַע צָרַעַת – AND I WILL PLACE A *TZARA'AS* AFFLICTION. בְּשׂוֹרָה הִיא לָהֶם – This is a good tiding to them ³שֶׁהַנְּגָעִים בָּאִים עֲלֵיהֶם – that afflictions are to come upon them,[3] אֱמוֹרִיִּים – because the Amorites hid מַטְמוֹנִיּוֹת שֶׁל זָהָב – treasures of gold בְּקִירוֹת בָּתֵּיהֶם – in the walls of their houses כָּל אַרְבָּעִים שָׁנָה – all forty years שֶׁהָיוּ יִשְׂרָאֵל בַּמִּדְבָּר – that Israel were in the desert, וְעַל יְדֵי הַנֶּגַע – and as a result of the affliction, נוֹתֵץ הַבַּיִת – he breaks down the house וּמוֹצְאָן – and finds them.[4]

35. כְּנֶגַע נִרְאָה לִי בַּבָּיִת – SOMETHING LIKE AN AFFLICTION HAS APPEARED TO ME IN THE HOUSE. The verse implies that אֲפִילוּ תַּלְמִיד חָכָם – even if he is a Torah scholar, שֶׁיּוֹדֵעַ נֶגַע וַדַּאי – ⁵who knows[5]

---

1. This is implied by the verse's use of עַל מְקוֹם דַּם הָאָשָׁם, "on the *place of the* guilt-offering's blood," rather than simply, עַל דַּם הָאָשָׁם, "on the guilt-offering's blood," as in verse 17 (*Mizrachi*).
2. *Menachos* 10a.
3. *Toras Kohanim, parshasa* 5:4.
4. *Vayikra Rabbah* 17:6. Rashi explains the verse's use

of וְנָתַתִּי נֶגַע צָרַעַת, "and I will place a *tzara'as* affliction," a definite statement, rather than כִּי תִהְיֶה נֶגַע צָרַעַת, "if there will be a *tzaraas* affliction," the form used above in 13:2,9,29,42,49, in reference to afflictions on people or garments (*Mizrachi*; *Sifsei Chachamim*).
5. Some editions read שֶׁאֲפִילוּ חָכָם הוּא וְיוֹדֵעַ, "[The verse implies] that even if he is a scholar and knows ..."

36 The Kohen shall command, and they shall clear the house when the Kohen has not yet come to look at the affliction, so that everything in the house should not become impure; and afterward shall the Kohen come to look at the house. **37** He shall look at the affliction and behold! —

לו וְצִוָּה הַכֹּהֵן וּפִנּוּ אֶת־הַבַּיִת בְּטֶרֶם יָבֹא הַכֹּהֵן לִרְאוֹת אֶת־הַנֶּגַע וְלֹא יִטְמָא כָּל־אֲשֶׁר בַּבָּיִת וְאַחַר כֵּן יָבֹא הַכֹּהֵן לִרְאוֹת אֶת־ לז הַבָּיִת: וְרָאָה אֶת־הַנֶּגַע וְהִנֵּה

───────── אונקלוס ─────────

לו וִיפַקֵּד כַּהֲנָא וִיפַנּוּן יָת בֵּיתָא עַד לָא עֵיל כַּהֲנָא לְמֶחֱזֵי יָת מַכְתָּשָׁא וְלָא יִסְתָּאַב כָּל דִּי בְבֵיתָא וּבָתַר כֵּן עֵיל כַּהֲנָא לְמֶחֱזֵי יָת בֵּיתָא: לז וְיֶחֱזֵי יָת מַכְתָּשָׁא וְהָא

───────── רש"י ─────────

לֹא יִפְסוֹק דָּבָר בָּרוּר לוֹמַר נֶגַע נִרְאָה לִי, אֶלָּא כְּנֶגַע נִרְאָה לִי (ת"כ): שָׁם ; נְגָעִים יב:ה): (לוֹ) **בְּטֶרֶם יָבֹא הַכֹּהֵן.** שֶׁכָּל זְמַן שֶׁאֵין כֹּהֵן נִזְקָק לוֹ אֵין שָׁם תּוֹרַת טוּמְאָה: **וְלֹא יִטְמָא כֹּל אֲשֶׁר בַּבָּיִת.** שֶׁאִם לֹא יְפַנֶּהוּ וְיָבֹא הַכֹּהֵן וְיִרְאֶה אֶת הַנֶּגַע, נִזְקַק לְהַסְגֵּר, וְכֹל מַה שֶּׁבְּתוֹכוֹ יִטָּמֵא. וְעַל מַה חָסָה תּוֹרָה, אִם עַל כְּלֵי שֶׁטֶף, יַטְבִּילֵם וְיִטְהֲרוּ. וְאִם עַל אוֹכָלִין וּמַשְׁקִין, יֹאכְלֵם בִּימֵי טוּמְאָתוֹ.

───────── RASHI ELUCIDATED ─────────

לֹא יִפְסֹק דָּבָר בָּרוּר — he should not render judgment with a definite statement, לוֹמַר — by saying, נֶגַע נִרְאָה לִי — "An affliction has appeared to me"; אֶלָּא — rather, he should say, כְּנֶגַע נִרְאָה לִי — "*Something like* an affliction has appeared to me."[1]

36. בְּטֶרֶם יָבֹא הַכֹּהֵן — WHEN THE KOHEN HAS NOT YET COME. שֶׁכָּל זְמַן — For all the while שֶׁאֵין כֹּהֵן — that a Kohen אֵין שָׁם — does not become involved with it, i.e., does not render a decision, נִזְקָק לוֹ תּוֹרַת טֻמְאָה — there is no law of impurity there, i.e., the law of impurity does not take effect, even if the affliction is an impure one.[2]

☐ וְלֹא יִטְמָא כָּל אֲשֶׁר בַּבַּיִת — SO THAT EVERYTHING IN THE HOUSEHOLD SHOULD NOT BECOME IMPURE. וְיִרְאֶה אֶת — שֶׁאִם לֹא יְפַנֵּהוּ — For if he will not clear it out, וְיָבֹא הַכֹּהֵן — and the Kohen will come, הַנֶּגַע — and see the affliction, נִזְקָק לְהַסְגֵּר — [the house] will need to be closed off, וְכָל מַה שֶּׁבְּתוֹכוֹ יִטְמָא — and everything that is inside it will become impure. וְעַל מַה חָסָה תּוֹרָה — Upon what is it that the Torah had pity, i.e., what property inside the house was the Torah concerned about? אִם עַל כְּלֵי שֶׁטֶף — If the Torah were concerned **about implements of rinsing**, i.e., those which need only to be immersed in a *mikveh* in order to become pure, such as those of wood and metal, יַטְבִּילֵם — let him immerse them וְיִטְהֲרוּ — and they will become pure. These, therefore, cannot be the objects of the Torah's concern. וְאִם עַל אֳכָלִין וּמַשְׁקִין — If the Torah is concerned **over foods and beverages**, יֹאכְלֵם — let him eat them בִּימֵי טֻמְאָתוֹ — in the days of his

───────────────

1. *Toras Kohanim, parshasa* 5:4; *Negaim* 12:5. There are several reasons why one should not make a definitive statement with regard to the affliction: (a) One should train himself to admit to the limitations of his knowledge, even in a situation where he is certain (*Mizrachi*). (b) It is not technically an "affliction" until the Kohen declares it to be such (see Rashi's next comment); to call it an affliction before then has a taint of falsehood (*Gur Aryeh*). (c) One should try to avoid speaking of unfortunate events. If speaking of them is unavoidable, one should try to speak of them in a circumspect manner whenever possible; for to speak of that which is menacing can cause it to happen (*Tosafos Yom Tov* to *Negaim* 12:5).

2. Our verse reads, וְצִוָּה הַכֹּהֵן וּפִנּוּ אֶת הַבַּיִת בְּטֶרֶם יָבֹא הַכֹּהֵן לִרְאוֹת אֶת הַנֶּגַע וְלֹא יִטְמָא כָּל אֲשֶׁר בַּבַּיִת, "The Kohen shall command, and they shall clear the house when the Kohen has not yet come to look at the affliction, so that everything in the house should not become impure."

The word הַכֹּהֵן in בְּטֶרֶם יָבֹא הַכֹּהֵן, "when the Kohen has not yet come," appears superfluous. The verse could have said only בְּטֶרֶם יָבֹא, "when *he* has not yet come," and it would have been clear that "he" refers to the Kohen. Furthermore, וְלֹא יִטְמָא כָּל אֲשֶׁר בַּבַּיִת, "so that everything in the house should not become impure," could be understood to imply that it is only the contents of the house that are not yet impure, but the house itself is impure already.

Rashi here deals with these problems. The apparently superfluous הַכֹּהֵן is meant to teach us that "all the while that a Kohen does not take it in charge, there is no law of impurity there"; until the Kohen makes his pronouncement neither the house nor its contents are impure. "So that everything in the house should not become impure" is not meant to teach us that the house itself is already impure. It implies only that the contents of the house can be saved from the impurity resulting from the Kohen's declaration. The house itself cannot (*Mishmeres HaKodesh*).

the affliction is in the walls of the house, depressed, deep greens or deep reds; and their appearance is lower than the wall. **38** The Kohen shall exit from the house to the entrance of the house; and he shall close off the house for a seven-day period. **39** The Kohen shall return on the seventh day; he shall look and behold! — the affliction had spread in the walls of the house. **40** The Kohen shall command, and they shall remove the stones that contain the affliction, and they shall cast them outside the city onto an impure place.

הַנֶּגַע בְּקִירֹת הַבַּיִת שְׁקַעֲרוּרֹת יְרַקְרַקֹּת אוֹ אֲדַמְדַּמֹּת וּמַרְאֵיהֶן שָׁפָל מִן־הַקִּיר: לח וְיָצָא הַכֹּהֵן מִן־הַבַּיִת אֶל־פֶּתַח הַבָּיִת וְהִסְגִּיר אֶת־הַבַּיִת שִׁבְעַת יָמִים: לט וְשָׁב הַכֹּהֵן בַּיּוֹם הַשְּׁבִיעִי וְרָאָה וְהִנֵּה פָּשָׂה הַנֶּגַע בְּקִירֹת הַבָּיִת: מ וְצִוָּה הַכֹּהֵן וְחִלְּצוּ אֶת־הָאֲבָנִים אֲשֶׁר בָּהֵן הַנָּגַע וְהִשְׁלִיכוּ אֶתְהֶן אֶל־מִחוּץ לָעִיר אֶל־מָקוֹם טָמֵא:

— אונקלוס —

מַכְתָּשָׁא בְּכָתְלֵי בֵיתָא פַּחֲתִין יַרְקָן אוֹ סָמְקָן וּמֶחֱזֵיהוֹן מַכִּיךְ מִן כָּתְלָא: לח וְיִפּוֹק כַּהֲנָא מִן בֵּיתָא לִתְרַע בֵּיתָא וְיַסְגַּר יָת בֵּיתָא שַׁבְעָא יוֹמִין: לט וִיתוּב כַּהֲנָא בְּיוֹמָא שְׁבִיעָאָה וְיֶחֱזֵי וְהָא אוֹסִיף מַכְתָּשָׁא בְּכָתְלֵי בֵיתָא: מ וִיפַקֵּד כַּהֲנָא וִישַׁלְּפוּן יָת אַבְנַיָּא דִי בְהֵן מַכְתָּשָׁא וְיִרְמוֹן יָתְהֵן לְמִבָּרָא לְקַרְתָּא לַאֲתַר מְסָאָב:

— רש"י —

הָא לֹא חָסָה הַתּוֹרָה אֶלָּא עַל כְּלֵי חֶרֶס, שֶׁאֵין לָהֶם טׇהֳרָה בְּמִקְוֶה (ספ' יב): (לז) שְׁקַעֲרוּרֹת. שׁוֹקְעוֹת בְּמַרְאֵיהֶן (שם פרשתא ה:ו): (מ) וְחִלְּצוּ אֶת הָאֲבָנִים. כְּתַרְגּוּמוֹ וִישַׁלְּפוּן, יִעְלָם

משם, כמו וחלצה נעלו (דברים כה:ט) לשון הסרה: אֶל מָקוֹם טָמֵא. מָקוֹם שֶׁאֵין טׇהֳרוֹת מִשְׁתַּמְּשׁוֹת שָׁם. לִמֶּדְךָ הַכָּתוּב שֶׁהָאֲבָנִים הַלָּלוּ מְטַמְּאוֹת מְקוֹמָן בְּעוֹדָן בּוֹ (ת"כ פרק ד:ד):

— RASHI ELUCIDATED —

עַל כְּלֵי חֶרֶס – on earthenware vessels שֶׁאֵין לָהֶם טׇהֳרָה – which have no purification by being immersed ¹בְּמִקְוֶה – in a *mikveh*.[1] הָא לֹא חָסָה הַתּוֹרָה אֶלָּא – The Torah, then, had pity only impurity.

37. שְׁקַעֲרוּרֹת – DEPRESSED. This is formed from the words[2] שׁוּקעוֹת – sunken ³בְּמַרְאֵיהֶן – in their appearance.[3]

40. וְחִלְּצוּ אֶת הָאֲבָנִים – AND THEY SHALL REMOVE THE STONES. This is to be understood כְּתַרְגּוּמוֹ – as the *Targum* Onkelos renders it, וִישַׁלְּפוּן – which means, יִטְּלֵם מִשָּׁם – he shall take away [the stones] from there, ⁴"וְחָלְצָה נַעֲלוֹ" – like וְחָלְצָה means in, **"and she shall take off his shoe,"**[4] לְשׁוֹן הֲסָרָה – an expression of removal.[5]

□ אֶל מָקוֹם טָמֵא – ONTO AN IMPURE PLACE. מָקוֹם שֶׁאֵין טׇהֳרוֹת מִשְׁתַּמְּשׁוֹת שָׁם – A place where things which must be kept pure are not used.[6] לִמֶּדְךָ הַכָּתוּב – Scripture has taught you שֶׁהָאֲבָנִים הַלָּלוּ – that these stones מְטַמְּאוֹת מְקוֹמָן – make their location impure ⁷בְּעוֹדָן בּוֹ – while they are in [that place].[7]

---

1. *Toras Kohanim, parshasa* 5:12. Although one can use impure earthenware vessels while he himself is impure (see *Rashi* to 11:35, s.v., וּטְמֵאִים יִהְיוּ לָכֶם) the Torah prefers that impure earthenware vessels not be kept around the house lest they come into contact with offerings or *terumah*, which are forbidden to be made impure (*Minchas Yehudah; Sifsei Chachamim*).

2. This interpolation is based on *Sefer Zikaron*.

3. *Toras Kohanim, parshasa* 6:5. Rashi here follows the opinion of *Toras Kohanim*. Other commentators (see *Rashbam, Radak*) understand שְׁקַעֲרוּרֹת as a color, like יְרַקְרַקֹּת and אֲדַמְדַּמֹּת which follow it. *Mizrachi* points out that according to *Toras Kohanim*, the end of the verse, וּמַרְאֵיהֶן שָׁפָל מִן הַקִּיר, "and their appearance is lower than the wall," seems redundant, for it appears to be a repetition of שְׁקַעֲרוּרֹת. *Malbim* answers that מַרְאֵיהֶן, as used by Rashi here, means "their color," and not "their appearance," as it means later in this verse. Thus, שְׁקַעֲרוּרֹת does not mean that the affliction *looks* deeper than the wall, as does the end of the verse, but that the color of the affliction penetrates the wall beyond its outer surface.

4. *Deuteronomy* 25:9.

5. The root חלץ sometimes means "to save" or "to rescue" (e.g., *Psalms* 91:15; *Proverbs* 11:8).

6. The verse does not mean that the place was impure before the stones were brought there, for ground does not become impure (*Sefer Zikaron*).

7. *Toras Kohanim, perek* 4:4. Although the afflicted stones transmit impurity to people or vessels in a covered, enclosed space above them, as does a corpse, once the source of impurity is removed, no impurity remains in its previous location (*Levush HaOrah*).

41 And the house shall be scraped from within, all around; the mortar that they have scraped at the edges they are to pour outside the city onto an impure place. **42** They shall take other stones and bring them in place of the stones; and they shall take other mortar and plaster the house.

43 If the affliction returns and erupts in the house after he has removed the stones, after the house has been scraped at the edges

מא וְאֶת־הַבַּיִת יַקְצִעַ מִבַּיִת סָבִיב וְשָׁפְכוּ אֶת־הֶעָפָר אֲשֶׁר הִקְצוּ אֶל־מִחוּץ לָעִיר אֶל־מָקוֹם טָמֵא: מב וְלָקְחוּ אֲבָנִים אֲחֵרוֹת וְהֵבִיאוּ אֶל־תַּחַת הָאֲבָנִים וְעָפָר אַחֵר יִקַּח וְטָח אֶת־הַבָּיִת:
מג וְאִם־יָשׁוּב הַנֶּגַע וּפָרַח בַּבַּיִת אַחַר חִלֵּץ אֶת־הָאֲבָנִים וְאַחֲרֵי הִקְצוֹת

──── אונקלוס ────

מא וְיָת בֵּיתָא יְקַלְפוּן מִגָּיו סְחוֹר סְחוֹר וְיִרְמוֹן יָת עַפְרָא דִּי קַלִּיפוּן לְמִבָּרָא לְקַרְתָּא לַאֲתַר מְסָאָב: מב וְיִסְּבוּן אַבְנַיָּא אַחֲרָנְיָן וְיָעֵלוּן בַּאֲתַר אַבְנַיָּא וַעֲפַר אָחֳרָן יִסַּב וִישׁוּעַ יָת בֵּיתָא: מג וְאִם יְתוּב מַכְתָּשָׁא וְיִסְגֵּי בְּבֵיתָא בָּתַר דִּשַׁלְפוּן יָת אַבְנַיָּא וּבָתַר דִּיקַלְפוּן

──── רש"י ────

(מא) **יקצע**. רוויי"ר בלע"ז, ובלשון משנה יש הרבה: **מבית**. מבפנים: (שם ה): **סביב**. סביבות הנגע. בת"כ נדרש כן (שם). **הקצו**. שקלוף הטיח סביב אבני הנגע: קיה, אשר קלטו בקצות הנגע סביב: (מג) **הקצות**. לשון העשות, וכן הטוח, אבל חלץ את האבנים מוסב הלשון אל האדם שחלצן, והוא משקל לשון כבד, כמו כפר דבר:

──── RASHI ELUCIDATED ────

41. יַקְצֵעַ — SHALL BE SCRAPED. This means רוויי"ר בְּלַעַ"ז — *rooignier* in Old French.[1] וּבִלְשׁוֹן מִשְׁנָה – In the language of the Mishnah יֵשׁ הַרְבֵּה — there are many related words.[2]

□ מִבַּיִת — FROM WITHIN. This means מִבִּפְנִים[3] — on the inside.[3]

□ סָבִיב — ALL AROUND. סְבִיבוֹת הַנֶּגַע — Around the affliction, בְּתוֹרַת כֹּהֲנִים נִדְרָשׁ כֵּן[4] — in *Toras Kohanim* it is explained thus;[4] שֶׁיְקַלֵּף הַטִּיחַ — that he should peel away the plaster שֶׁסָּבִיב אַבְנֵי הַנֶּגַע — that is around the stones of the affliction.[5]

□ הִקְצוּ — THEY HAVE SCRAPED AT THE EDGES. This word לְשׁוֹן קָצֶה — is related to end/edge. In context it means אֲשֶׁר קָצְעוּ — that they have scraped away בִּקְצוֹת הַנֶּגַע — at the edges of the affliction, סָבִיב — all around it.[6]

43. הִקְצוֹת — HAS BEEN SCRAPED AT THE EDGES. This word לְשׁוֹן הֵעָשׂוֹת — is of the same form as "being done," וְכֵן ,,הַטּוֹחַ'' — and similarly, "been plastered,"[7] which appears at the end of the verse. אֲבָל ,,חִלֵּץ אֶת הָאֲבָנִים'' — But with regard to the clause, "he has removed the stones," מוּסָב הַלָּשׁוֹן אֶל הָאָדָם שֶׁחִלְּצָן — the expression, i.e., the verb חִלֵּץ, refers to the man who removed them.[8] וְהוּא מִשְׁקַל לָשׁוֹן כָּבֵד — It is in the form of intensive language,[9] כְּמוֹ כִּפֶּר דָּבָר — like "he

---

1. In Modern French, *rogner*, "to trim."
2. See, for example, *Keilim* 27:4,5. See, too, Rashi to *Bava Kamma* 66b, s.v., שקעו.
3. *Toras Kohanim, perek* 4:5. The most common meaning of בַּיִת is "house." מִבַּיִת of our verse cannot mean "from the house," for it does not have the definite article. "From the house" would be expressed by מֵהַבַּיִת. Here it means "inside," as it does in *Genesis* 6:14 (*Mizrachi; Sifsei Chachamim*). The word מִבַּיִת also has the meaning "on the inside" in *Exodus* 25:11 and 37:2. Rashi in these places need not explain מִבַּיִת, for *Genesis* speaks of Noah's ark and *Exodus* speaks of the Holy Ark. In neither case can the word mistakenly be translated "from the house," for no house is mentioned.
4. *Toras Kohanim, perek* 4:5.
5. Had the verse said only, "And the house shall be scraped within," we would have understood that all the inner surfaces of the house should be scraped. Now that the verse adds סָבִיב, "all around," it indicates that the scraping is to be done only around the afflicted area (*Mizrachi; Sifsei Chachamim*).
6. הִקְצוֹ is from the root קצה, unlike יַקְצֵעַ at the beginning of the verse which is from the root קצע. Rashi disagrees with *Onkelos* who appears to be of the opinion that both words are forms of the verb for scraping (see *Rashbam; Ibn Ezra; Lifshuto shel Rashi; Shaarei Aharon*).
7. הַקְצוֹת and הַטּוֹחַ are passive infinitives, in the *nifal*. The difference in vowelization is because of the different form of the roots. The root of הַקְצוֹת is קצה, which is in the form נַחֵי ל"ה (the third root letter is a ה and is omitted or changed to ו in some conjugations). The root of הַטּוֹחַ is טיח, which is a ע"י נָחֵי verb (the second root letter is a י and is omitted or changed to ו in some conjugations).
8. חִלֵּץ is an active verb with a subject, the person who removes the stones.
9. The word חִלֵּץ is in the intensive *piel*, rather than the simple *kal* (חָלַץ). The intensive form often indicates intensity of action.

173 / VAYIKRA/LEVITICUS — PARASHAS METZORA — 14/44 — יד/מד

and after it has been plastered; **44** *the Kohen shall come and look, and behold! — the affliction has spread in the house:*

מד אֶת־הַבַּיִת וְאַחֲרֵי הִטּוֹחַ: וּבָא הַכֹּהֵן וְרָאָה וְהִנֵּה פָּשָׂה הַנֶּגַע בַּבָּיִת

─────────── אונקלוס ───────────

יָת בֵּיתָא וּבָתַר דְּיִתְּשַׁע: מד וְיֵיעוּל כָּהֲנָא וְיֶחֱזֵי וְהָא אוֹסִיף מַכְתָּשָׁא בְּבֵיתָא

─────────── רש"י ───────────

ואם ישוב הנגע וגו'. יכול חזר בו ביום יהא טמא, ת"ל ושב הכהן, ואם ישוב, מה שיבה האמורה להלן בסוף שבוע, אף שיבה האמורה כאן בסוף שבוע (ת"כ פרשתא ז.י): **(מד) ובא הכהן וראה והנה פשה.** יכול לא יהא החוזר טמא אלא אם כן פשה, נאמר צרעת ממארת בבתים ונאמר צרעת ממארת בבגדים (לעיל יג:נא-נב) מה להלן טמא את החוזר אע"פ שאינו פושה (שם נז) אף כאן טמא את החוזר אע"פ שאינו פושה. אם כן מה ת"ל והנה פשה, אין כאן מקומו של מקרא זה, אלא ונתץ את הבית היה לו לכתוב אחר ואם ישוב הנגע. וראה והנה פשה, הא לא בא ללמד אלא על נגע העומד בעיניו

─────────── RASHI ELUCIDATED ───────────

atoned"[1] and *"he spoke."*[2]

☐ **יָכוֹל — One might be able** to think that if **וְאָם יָשׁוּב הַנֶּגַע וְגוֹמֵר — IF THE AFFLICTION RETURNS, ETC.**, **חָזַר בּוֹ בַּיּוֹם — it returned on that day**, **יְהֵא טָמֵא — it should be impure**. **תַּלְמוּד לוֹמַר — To teach us** otherwise, **the verse says,** [3]**"וְשָׁב הַכֹּהֵן — "the Kohen shall return** on the seventh day,"[3] and it says in our verse, **"וְאִם יָשׁוּב, — "if the affliction returns."** **מַה שִׁיבָה — Just as** the **returning הָאֲמוּרָה** **שִׁיבָה הָאֲמוּרָה כָּאן — so, too,** the **returning which is stated here** **בְּסוֹף שָׁבוּעַ — is at the end of a week**,[4] **אַף — so, too,** **שִׁיבָה הָאֲמוּרָה כָּאן — so, too,** the **returning which is stated here** **בְּסוֹף שָׁבוּעַ — is at the end of a week**.[4]

44. וּבָא הַכֹּהֵן וְרָאָה וְהִנֵּה פָּשָׂה — THE KOHEN SHALL COME AND LOOK, AND BEHOLD! — [THE AFFLICTION] HAS SPREAD. **יָכוֹל — One might be able** to think that **לֹא יְהֵא הַחוֹזֵר טָמֵא — that which returns, i.e.,** an affliction that returns after the originally afflicted stones have been removed, **should not be impure אֶלָּא אִם כֵּן — unless פָּשָׂה — it has spread,** as our verse says, "the affliction has spread in the house . . . it is impure." To teach us otherwise, **נֶאֱמַר — בְּבָתִּים — "degenerative** *tzara'as"* **is** mentioned here **with regard to houses,** **וְנֶאֱמַר ,,צָרַעַת מַמְאֶרֶת בִּבְגָדִים — and "degenerative** *tzaraas"* **is** mentioned with regard to garments.[5] **מַה לְּהַלָּן — Just as above טִמֵּא אֶת הַחוֹזֵר — [the** Torah] made impure that which returns, [6]**אַף עַל פִּי שֶׁאֵינוֹ פּוֹשֶׂה — even though it does not spread,**[6] **אַף כָּאן — here, too, טִמֵּא אֶת הַחוֹזֵר — [the Torah] made impure that which returns, אַף עַל פִּי שֶׁאֵינוֹ פּוֹשֶׂה — even though it does not spread.** **אִם כֵּן מַה תַּלְמוּד לוֹמַר — If so, why does the Torah say, ,,וְהִנֵּה פָּשָׂה — "and behold! — [the affliction] has spread"?** **אֵין כָּאן מְקוֹמוֹ שֶׁל מִקְרָא זֶה — This is not the** place for this verse which speaks of the spreading of the affliction.[7] **אֶלָּא — Rather, ,,וְנָתַץ אֶת הַבַּיִת — [the Torah] should have written** the passage that begins **"He shall demolish the house,"**[8] **אַחַר ,,וְאִם יָשׁוּב הַנֶּגַע — immediately after the verse that begins, "If the affliction returns."**[9] As for the verse, **,,וְרָאָה וְהִנֵּה פָּשָׂה הַנֶּגַע — "[The Kohen shall come] and look, and behold! — the affliction has spread,"** **הָא לֹא בָּא לְלַמֵּד אֶלָּא — this comes to teach only עַל נֶגַע הָעוֹמֵד בְּעֵינָיו — about**

---

1. For example, see verse 18 above. (The word there is prefaced by a ו׳ ההפוך which changes the tense from past to future.)
2. As in 10:11 above.
3. Above verse 39.
4. *Toras Kohanim, parshasa* 7:6. Rashi here is using a *gezeirah shavah*, a method of deriving information in which that which is stated explicitly in one context is applied to another context, as well, by virtue of similar words or phrases appearing in the two contexts. This only applies when such association of two contexts is a matter of received tradition. It is not a procedure which is rooted in logical criteria that can be used at one's own initiative. In our verse, as in verse 39, a form of the word שוב, "returning," is used. This teaches us that just as the return of the Kohen mentioned in verse 39 takes place after a week has elapsed, so, too, the return of the
affliction that renders the house impure takes place after a week. If the affliction returns the day that the afflicted stones are removed, or at any other time before a week has passed, the house remains pure if the affliction disappears by the seventh day (*Mizrachi*).
5. Above 13:51-52. This is a *gezeirah shavah* (see previous note). It allows an analogy to be made between *tzara's* of garments and *tzara'as* of houses.
6. Above 13:57.
7. Rashi means that the verses do not refer to the events in sequence.
8. Verse 45. Rashi means verses 45-47, as he states explicitly below.
9. Verse 43. Thus, if the affliction returns after the originally afflicted stones have been removed, as described in verse 43, even if it does not spread, he shall demolish the house, as described in verse 45.

רש"י

בשבוע ראשון ובא בסוף שבוע שני ומלאו שפשה, שלא פירש בו הכתוב למעלה (פסוק לו) כלום בעומד בעיניו בשבוע ראשון, ולמדת כאן בפשיון זה שאינו מדבר אלא בעומד בראשון ופשה בשני. ומה יעשה לו, יכול יתצנו כמו שסמך לו ונתץ את הבית, ת"ל ושב הכהן (לעיל פסוק לט) ובא הכהן (כאן) נלמד ביאה מישיבה, מה

שיבה חולץ וקוצה וטח ונותן לו שבוע [ואם חוזר נותץ], אף מנין חולץ וקוצה וטח ונותן לו שבוע, ואם חוזר נותץ, לא חזר טהור. ומנין שאם עמד בזה ובזה חולץ וקוצה וטח ונותן לו שבוע, ת"ל {ובא}, ואם בא יבא (להלן פסוק מח) [וכו']. במה הכתוב מדבר, אם בפושה בראשון, הרי כבר אמור. אם בפושה בשני, הרי כבר אמור.

RASHI ELUCIDATED

an affliction which stands unchanged **in its appearance,** בְּשָׁבוּעַ רִאשׁוֹן – **at** the end of **the first week** after it has been closed off, וּבָא בְּסוֹף שָׁבוּעַ שֵׁנִי – **and [the Kohen] came at the end of the second week** וּמָצְאוּ שֶׁפָּשָׂה – **and found that it had spread;** שֶׁלֹּא פֵּרַשׁ בּוֹ הַכָּתוּב לְמַעְלָה[1] כְּלוּם – **for Scripture has not stated anything explicitly above**[1] בְּעוֹמֵד בְּעֵינָיו – **about that which stands** unchanged **in its appearance** בְּשָׁבוּעַ רִאשׁוֹן – **at** the end of **the first week.**[2] וְלִמֶּדְךָ כָּאן – **It has taught you** about that situation **here,** בְּפִשְׂיוֹן זֶה – **with this** mention **of spreading,** שֶׁאֵינוֹ מְדַבֵּר אֶלָּא בְּעוֹמֵד בָּרִאשׁוֹן – **which speaks of nothing but [an affliction] which stands** unchanged **at the end of the first** week וּפָשָׂה בַּשֵּׁנִי – **and has spread at the end of the second** week. וּמַה יַּעֲשֶׂה לוֹ – **What should he do to it?** יָכוֹל יִתְּצֶנּוּ – **One might be able** to think that **he should demolish [the afflicted house]** כְּמוֹ שֶׁסָּמַךְ לוֹ – **as [the Torah] puts adjacent to [this mention of spreading]** the verse, [3]וְנָתַץ אֶת הַבַּיִת – **"he shall demolish the house."**[3] תַּלְמוּד לוֹמַר – **To teach us otherwise, the Torah says,** וְשָׁב הַכֹּהֵן[4] – **"the Kohen shall return,"**[4] and [5]וּבָא הַכֹּהֵן – **"the Kohen shall come."**[5] נִלְמוֹד בִּיאָה – **We shall derive** the law of the case spoken of in terms of **coming**[6] מִישִׁיבָה – **from** the law of the case spoken of in terms of **returning.**[7] מַה שִּׁיבָה – **Just as** in the case spoken of in terms of **returning,** חוֹלֵץ – **he removes** the afflicted stones, וְקוֹצֶה – **and scrapes the edges** around them, וְטָח – **and plasters** the house, וְנוֹתֵן לוֹ שָׁבוּעַ – **and gives it a week** to see if the affliction will return, {וְאִם חוֹזֵר – **and if it returns** at the end of that week,} נוֹתֵץ – **he demolishes** the house,} אַף בִּיאָה – **so, too,** in the case spoken of in terms of **coming,** חוֹלֵץ – **he removes** the afflicted stones, וְקוֹצֶה – **and scrapes the edges** around them, וְטָח – **and plasters** the house, וְנוֹתֵן לוֹ שָׁבוּעַ – **and gives it a week** to see if the affliction will return. וְאִם חוֹזֵר – **If it returns** at the end of that week, נוֹתֵץ – **he demolishes** the house; לֹא חָזַר – **if it did not return,** טָהוֹר – **it is pure.** וּמִנַּיִן – **And from where do we know** שֶׁאִם עָמַד בָּזֶה וּבָזֶה – **that if it stood** unchanged **in this one and in this one,** i.e., after both the first week and the second week, that חוֹלֵץ – **he removes** the afflicted stones, וְקוֹצֶה – **and scrapes the edges** around them, וְטָח – **and plasters** the house, וְנוֹתֵן לוֹ שָׁבוּעַ – **and gives it** yet another **week** to see if the affliction will return?[8] תַּלְמוּד לוֹמַר – **The Torah says,** וְאִם בֹּא יָבֹא,, – **"if [the Kohen] is to come"**[9] וְכוּלְהוּ – **{**"the Kohen shall come,"**}** etc.}.[10] בַּמֶּה הַכָּתוּב מְדַבֵּר – **What** situation **is the verse speaking about?** אִם בְּפוֹשֶׂה בָּרִאשׁוֹן – **If** you wish to say that the verse speaks **of [an affliction] that spreads by** the end of **the first** week, הֲרֵי כְּבָר אָמוּר – **that has already been stated.**[11] אִם בְּפוֹשֶׂה בַּשֵּׁנִי – **If** you wish to say that the verse speaks **of [an affliction] that spreads by** the end of **the second** week, הֲרֵי כְּבָר אָמוּר – **that has already been**

---

1. Above v. 39.
2. Verse 39 which begins the discussion of what happens at the end of the first week speaks only of a case in which the affliction has spread.
3. Below v. 45.
4. Above v. 39.
5. Our verse.
6. The case of our verse which speaks of an affliction which remains unchanged after the first week but spreads after the second.
7. The case of verse 39, where the affliction spread after the first week. The terms וְשָׁב הַכֹּהֵן of verse 39 and וּבָא הַכֹּהֵן of our verse are similar enough to be used for a *gezeirah shavah* (see note 4 on page 173).
8. Verses 39-43 tell us the law of an affliction that spread by the end of the first week. Verse 44 tells us the law of an affliction that did not spread by the end of the first week, but spread by the end of the second week. What is the source for the law of an affliction that remained unchanged even at the end of the second week?
9. Below v. 48.
10. There is a confusion in many modern texts here. Some ancient texts cite the entire passage as it appears in *Toras Kohanim*. The first printed edition stops at this point, adds the word וְכוּלְהוּ, "etc.," then omits the remainder of the discussion, until בִּבְרַיְתָא בְּתוֹרַת כֹּהֲנִים, "as stated in Toras Kohanim." Some modern editions have combined both versions, i.e., after citing the entire passage from *Toras Kohanim*, they add the meaningless "etc."
11. In verses 39-43.

175 / VAYIKRA/LEVITICUS — PARASHAS METZORA — יד/מד — 14/44

רש״י

הא אינו אומר [ובּא,] ואם בא יבא אלא את שבא בסוף שבוע ראשון ובא בסוף שבוע שני וראה והנה לא פשה, זה העומד מה יעשה לו, יכול יפטר וילך כמו שכתוב כאן וטהר את הבית, ת״ל כי נרפא הנגע, לא טהרתי אלא את הרפוי, מה יעשה לו, ביאה אמורה למעלה (כאן) וביאה אמורה למטה (להלן פסוק מח) מה בעליונה חולץ וקוצה וטח ונותן לו שבוע, דגמר לה זהו שיבה זהו ביאה, אף בתחתונה כן כדאיתא בתורת כהנים (שם ד׳ט). גמרו של דבר, אין נתילה אלא בנגע החוזר אחר חליצה וקוצי וטיחה, ואין החוזר צריך פשיון. וסדר המקראות כך הוא. ואם ישוב, ונתץ. והבא אל הבית, והאוכל בבית, ובא הכהן וראה והנה פשה. ודבר הכתוב בעומד בראשון שנותן לו שבוע שני להסגרו, ובסוף שבוע שני להסגרו בא וראהו שפשה. ומה יעשה לו, חולץ וקוצה וטח ונותן לו שבוע. חזר נותץ, לא חזר טעון לפרים, שאין בנגעים יותר משלשה שבועות.

RASHI ELUCIDATED

stated.[1] הָא אֵינוֹ אוֹמֵר — See, then, that [the Torah] does not say, {וּבָא,,} — "the Kohen shall come,"} וְאִם בֹּא יָבֹא,, — "if [the Kohen] is to come" about any case אֶלָּא אֶת שֶׁבָּא בְּסוֹף שָׁבוּעַ רִאשׁוֹן — but that in which he comes at the end of the first week and finds the affliction unchanged, וּבָא בְּסוֹף שָׁבוּעַ שֵׁנִי — and he comes at the end of the second week, וְרָאָה וְהִנֵּה לֹא פָשָׂה,, — "and look and behold! [it] has not spread." זֶה הָעוֹמֵד — This affliction which stands unchanged, מַה יַּעֲשֶׂה לוֹ what should he do to it? יָכוֹל — One might be able to think that יִפָּטֵר וְיֵלֵךְ — he may depart and go off, and not declare the house impure, כְּמוֹ שֶׁכָּתוּב כָּאן — as it is written here, וְטִהַר אֶת הַבַּיִת,, — "And [the Kohen] shall declare the house to be pure."[2] תַּלְמוּד לוֹמַר — To teach us otherwise, the verse says, כִּי נִרְפָּא הַנָּגַע,, — "for the affliction has healed," which implies, לֹא טִהַרְתִּי אֶלָּא אֶת הָרָפוּי — I have made pure only that which has healed, but not that which remains unchanged. מַה יַּעֲשֶׂה לוֹ — What, then, should he do to it? בִּיאָה אֲמוּרָה לְמַעְלָה — "Coming" has been stated above,[3] וּבִיאָה אֲמוּרָה לְמַטָּה — and "coming" has been stated below.[4] מַה בָּעֶלְיוֹנָה — Just as in the upper one, i.e., in the earlier verse, חוֹלֵץ — he removes the afflicted stones, וְקוֹצֶה — and he scrapes the edges around them, וָטָח — and he plasters the house, וְנוֹתֵן לוֹ שָׁבוּעַ — and he gives it a week to see if the affliction returns, דְּגָמַר לָהּ — for it[5] is a tradition that for the purpose of a gezeirah shavah זֶהוּ שִׁיבָה זֶהוּ בִּיאָה — the word שׁוב is considered the same word as בֹּא, אַף בַּתַּחְתּוֹנָה כֵּן — so, too, in the lower one, i.e., in the later verse, he does so, כִּדְאִיתָא בְּתוֹרַת כֹּהֲנִים — as stated in Toras Kohanim.[6] גְּמָרוֹ שֶׁל דָּבָר — The summing up of the matter is, אֵין נְתִיצָה — there is no obligation of demolishing a house with an affliction אֶלָּא בְּנֶגַע הַחוֹזֵר — except in the case of an affliction that returns אַחַר חֲלִיצָה — after removal of the afflicted stones, וְקִצּוּי — and scraping of the edges around them, וְטִיחָה — and plastering the house. וְאֵין הַחוֹזֵר צָרִיךְ פִּשְׂיוֹן — And [an affliction] which returns does not require spreading to be considered impure. וְסֵדֶר הַמִּקְרָאוֹת כָּךְ הוּא — The order of the verses which reflects the actual laws of the affliction is the following: וְאִם יָשׁוּב,, — "If [the affliction] returns";[7] וְנָתַץ,, — "He shall demolish";[8] וְהַבָּא אֶל הַבַּיִת,, — "Anyone who comes into the house";[9] וְהָאוֹכֵל בַּבָּיִת,, — "And one who eats in the house."[10] וּבָא הַכֹּהֵן וְרָאָה וְהִנֵּה פָשָׂה,, — Then the verse, "The Kohen shall come and look and behold! [the affliction] has spread,"[11] וְדִבֶּר הַכָּתוּב — and this verse speaks בְּעוֹמֵד בָּרִאשׁוֹן — of [an affliction] that stands unchanged at the end of the first week, שֶׁנּוֹתֵן לוֹ שָׁבוּעַ שֵׁנִי לְהֶסְגֵּרוֹ — to which he gives a second week for its being closed off, וּבְסוֹף שָׁבוּעַ שֵׁנִי לְהֶסְגֵּרוֹ — and at the end of the second week of its being closed off, בָּא וְרָאָהוּ שֶׁפָּשָׂה — he came and saw that it had spread. וּמַה יַּעֲשֶׂה לוֹ — What should he do to it? חוֹלֵץ — He removes the afflicted stones, וְקוֹצֶה — and scrapes the edges around them, וָטָח — and plasters the house, וְנוֹתֵן לוֹ שָׁבוּעַ — and gives it a week to see if the affliction returns. חָזַר נוֹתֵץ — If it returned, he demolishes it. לֹא חָזַר — If it did not return, טָעוּן צִפֳּרִים — it requires birds,[12] שֶׁאֵין בַּנְּגָעִים יוֹתֵר מִשְּׁלֹשָׁה שָׁבוּעוֹת — for there are no more than three weeks in afflictions, i.e., the status of an affliction is always determined

---

1. In our verse.
2. Below v. 48.
3. In our verse, וּבָא הַכֹּהֵן.
4. Below v. 48, וְאִם בֹּא יָבֹא.
5. The fact that the law of removing, scraping and plastering applies to the affliction that spread by the end of the second week and which is the subject of verse 44.
6. Toras Kohanim, parshasa 7:4-9.
7. Verse 43.
8. Verse 45.
9. Verse 46.
10. Verse 47. The verses listed by Rashi up to this point deal with the laws of an affliction that spread by the end of the first week, and returned by the end of the second.
11. Verse 44.
12. This refers to the process of purification that requires birds. See verses 49-53 below.

It is a degenerative tzara'as in the house, it is impure. **45** *He shall demolish the house — its stones, its timber, and all the mortar of the house; they shall take it to the outside of the city, to an impure place.* **46** *Anyone who comes into the house during all the days he has closed it off shall be impure until evening.*

צָרַ֨עַת מַמְאֶ֧רֶת הִ֛וא בַּבַּ֖יִת טָמֵ֥א
הֽוּא: וְנָתַ֣ץ אֶת־הַבַּ֗יִת אֶת־אֲבָנָיו֙
וְאֶת־עֵצָ֔יו וְאֵ֖ת כָּל־עֲפַ֣ר הַבָּ֑יִת
וְהוֹצִיא֙ אֶל־מִח֣וּץ לָעִ֔יר אֶל־מָק֖וֹם
טָמֵֽא: וְהַבָּא֙ אֶל־הַבַּ֔יִת כָּל־יְמֵ֖י
הִסְגִּ֣יר אֹת֑וֹ יִטְמָ֖א עַד־הָעָֽרֶב:

—— אונקלוס ——

סגירות מחזרא היא בביתא מסאב הוא: מה וִיתָרֵע יָת בֵּיתָא יָת אַבְנוֹהִי וְיָת אָעוֹהִי וְיָת כָּל עֲפַר בֵּיתָא וְיַפֵּק לְמִבָּרָא לְקַרְתָּא לַאֲתַר מְסָאָב: מו וּדְיֵעוֹל לְבֵיתָא כָּל יוֹמִין דְּיַסְגַּר יָתֵהּ יְהֵי מְסָאָב עַד רַמְשָׁא:

—— רש"י ——

וְאִם בֹּא יָבֹא לְסוֹף שָׁבוּעַ שֵׁנִי. וְרָאָה וְהִנֵּה לֹא פָשָׂה, מִקְרָא זֶה בָּא לְלַמֵּד בְּטוּחַ בְּעֵינָיו וּבְשֵׁנִי. מַה יַּעֲשֶׂה לּוֹ, יָכוֹל יְטַהֲרֶנּוּ, כְּמַשְׁמָעוֹ שֶׁל מִקְרָא וְטִהַר הַכֹּהֵן אֶת הַבַּיִת, ת"ל כִּי נִרְפָּא הַנֶּגַע, לֹא טִהַרְתִּי אֶלָּא אֶת הַרְפוּי, וְאֵין רָפוּי אֶלָּא הַבַּיִת שֶׁהוּקְצָה וְהוּטַח וְלֹא חָזַר הַנֶּגַע, אֲבָל זֶה טָעוּן חֲלִיצָה וּקְצִיצָה וּטִיחָה וּשְׁבוּעַ שְׁלִישִׁי. וְכֵן הַמִּקְרָא נִדְרַשׁ, וְאִם בֹּא יָבֹא בַּשֵּׁנִי, וְנִרְאָה וְהִנֵּה לֹא פָשָׂה יְטִיחֶנּוּ, וְאֵין טִיחָה בְּלֹא חִלּוּף וּקְצִיצָה וְאַחֲרֵי הִטּוֹחַ אֶת הַבַּיִת וְטִהַר הַכֹּהֵן אֶת הַבַּיִת, אִם לֹא חָזַר, כְּבָר פֵּרַשׁ עַל הַחוֹזֵר שֶׁטָּעוּן נְתִיצָה (שם יב:): (מו) **כָּל יְמֵי הִסְגִּיר אֹתוֹ.** וְלֹא יְמֵי שִׁקְלוּף אֶת נִגְעוֹ. יָכוֹל שֶׁאֲנִי מוֹצִיא

—— RASHI ELUCIDATED ——

within a period of three weeks.[1] וְרָאָה ,, — "If the Kohen is to come" — לְסוֹף שָׁבוּעַ שֵׁנִי — at the end of the second week. ,,וְהִנֵּה לֹא פָשָׂה — "and look, and behold! — [the affliction] has not spread." מִקְרָא זֶה — This verse בָּא לְלַמֵּד — comes to teach us בְּעוֹמֵד בְּעֵינָיו — about [an affliction] which stands unchanged in its appearance בָּרִאשׁוֹן — at the end of the first week, וּבַשֵּׁנִי — and at the end of the second week. וּמַה יַּעֲשֶׂה לּוֹ — What should he do to it? יָכוֹל יְטַהֲרֶנּוּ — One might be able to think that he should declare it pure, כְּמַשְׁמָעוֹ שֶׁל מִקְרָא — as is the implication of the verse, which says, וְטִהַר הַכֹּהֵן אֶת הַבַּיִת — "and the Kohen shall declare the house to be pure." תַּלְמוּד לוֹמַר — To teach us otherwise, the verse says, ,,כִּי נִרְפָּא הַנֶּגַע — "for the affliction has healed," which implies, לֹא טִהַרְתִּי אֶלָּא אֶת הָרְפוּי — I have made pure only that which has healed, but not that which remains unchanged. וְאֵין רָפוּי אֶלָּא — That which has healed is only הַבַּיִת שֶׁהוּקְצָה — the house which has had the edges of the affliction scraped, וְהוּטַח — and has been plastered, וְלֹא חָזַר הַנֶּגַע — and the affliction did not return. אֲבָל זֶה טָעוּן — But this one whose appearance did not change requires חֲלִיצָה — removal of afflicted stones, וּקְצִיצָה — and scraping of the edges around them, וְטִיחָה — and plastering, וְשָׁבוּעַ שְׁלִישִׁי — and waiting a third week to see if the affliction returns. וְכֵן הַמִּקְרָא נִדְרַשׁ — And this is how the verse is expounded: ,,וְאִם בֹּא יָבֹא בַּשֵּׁנִי — "If [he] is to come" at the end of the second week, ,,וְנִרְאָה וְהִנֵּה לֹא פָשָׂה — "and look, and behold! — [it] did not spread," יְטִיחֶנּוּ — he shall plaster it, בְּלֹא חִלּוּף — without removal of afflicted stones, וּקְצִיצָה — and וְאֵין טִיחָה — and there is no plastering scraping the edges. ,,וְאַחֲרֵי הִטּוֹחַ אֶת הַבַּיִת וְטִהַר הַכֹּהֵן אֶת הַבַּיִת — And the phrase, "after he has plastered the house, and the Kohen shall declare the house to be pure," applies אִם לֹא חָזַר — if the [affliction] did not return, לְסוֹף הַשָּׁבוּעַ — at the end of the third week, ,,כִּי נִרְפָּא הַנֶּגַע — "for the affliction has healed." וְאִם חָזַר — But if it returned, i.e., with respect to an affliction which returns, עַל הַחוֹזֵר — about [an affliction] which returns כְּבָר פֵּרַשׁ — [the Torah] has already stated explicitly שֶׁטָּעוּן נְתִיצָה — that [the house] requires demolition.[2]

שֶׁקִּלֵּף אֶת נִגְעוֹ — But not days **46.** כָּל יְמֵי הִסְגִּיר אֹתוֹ — ALL THE DAYS HE HAS CLOSED IT OFF. וְלֹא יְמֵי — in which he peeled away its affliction.[3] יָכוֹל — One might be able to think שֶׁאֲנִי מוֹצִיא — that

---

1. Many modern editions insert Rashi's comments to verse 46 at this point, then set off the remainder of the present comment as commentary to verse 48. We have followed the text of the first printed edition and other early editions of Rashi (see *Yosef Hallel*). This is also the order followed in *Toras Kohanim*, where *parashah* 7 comes before *perek* 5.

2. *Toras Kohanim, parshasa* 7:12.

3. Rashi follows the wording of *Toras Kohanim*. The *Toras Kohanim* may be interpreted as follows: It is forbidden to peel away the affliction during the days in which the house is closed off. Nonetheless, if it is removed, one who enters the house does not become impure (*Ra'avad* in his commentary to *Toras Ko-*

⁴⁷ **But one who reclines in the house shall immerse his garments; and one who eats in the house shall immerse his garments.** ⁴⁸ **If the Kohen is to come and look and behold! — the affliction has not spread in the house after he has plastered**

מז וְהַשֹּׁכֵב בַּבַּיִת יְכַבֵּס אֶת־בְּגָדָיו וְהָאֹכֵל בַּבַּיִת יְכַבֵּס אֶת־בְּגָדָיו: מח וְאִם־בֹּא יָבֹא הַכֹּהֵן וְרָאָה וְהִנֵּה לֹא־פָשָׂה הַנֶּגַע בַּבַּיִת אַחֲרֵי הִטֹּחַ

— אונקלוס —

מז וּדְיִשְׁכּוּב בְּבֵיתָא יְצַבַּע יָת לְבוּשׁוֹהִי וּדְיֵיכוּל בְּבֵיתָא יָת צְבַע יָת לְבוּשׁוֹהִי:
מח וְאִם מֵעַל יֵעוּל כַּהֲנָא וְיֶחֱזֵי וְהָא לָא אוֹסִיף מַכְתָּשָׁא בְּבֵיתָא בָּתַר דְּיִתְשַׁע

— רש"י —

יטמא עד הערב. מלמד שאין מטמא בגדים. יכול אפי׳ שהה בכדי אכילת פרס, ת"ל והאוכל בבית יכבס את בגדיו (פסוק מז). אין לי אלא אוכל, שוכב מנין, ת"ל ל כל ימי (שם פרק הו:ד): **המוחלט** שקלף את נגעו, ת"ל כל ימי (שם פרק הו:ד): אוכל, שוכב מנין, ת"ל והשוכב. אין לי אלא אוכל ושוכב, לא אוכל ולא שוכב מנין, ת"ל יכבס יכבס ריבה. אם כן למה נא' אוכל ושוכב, ליתן שיעור לשוכב כדי אכילת פרס (ת"כ שם ה-ח):

— RASHI ELUCIDATED —

I also exclude from this law הַמֻּחְלָט — that which is decidedly impure שֶׁקִּלֵּף אֶת נִגְעוֹ — whose affliction he has peeled away.[1] **תַּלְמוּד לוֹמַר — To teach us otherwise, the verse says,** "כָּל יְמֵי,, —[2] **"all the days."**[2]

□ **יִטְמָא עַד הָעָרֶב — SHALL BE IMPURE UNTIL EVENING. מְלַמֵּד — This teaches us שֶׁאֵין מְטַמֵּא בְּגָדִים — that it does not make the clothes of one who enters impure.**[3] **יָכוֹל — One might be able to think that it does not make clothes impure אֲפִילוּ שֶׁהָה — even if he stayed inside the afflicted house בִּכְדֵי אֲכִילַת פְּרָס — time enough for the eating of half a loaf.**[4] **We reject this conclusion as follows: תַּלְמוּד לוֹמַר — The verse says,** ⁵"וְהָאוֹכֵל בַּבַּיִת יְכַבֵּס אֶת בְּגָדָיו,, **— "and one who eats in the house shall immerse his garments."**[5] **אֵין לִי אֶלָּא — I have only, i.e., on the basis of this verse, I know only, that אוֹכֵל — one who eats in the afflicted house must immerse his garments. שׁוֹכֵב מִנַּיִן — From where do we know that one who reclines in the afflicted house must immerse his garments, even if he does not eat? תַּלְמוּד לוֹמַר — The verse says,** "וְהַשּׁוֹכֵב,, — **"but one who reclines." אֵין לִי אֶלָּא — I have only, i.e., on the basis of this verse, I know only, that אוֹכֵל וְשׁוֹכֵב — one who eats or one who reclines in the afflicted house must immerse his garments, even if he does not eat. לֹא אוֹכֵל — One who neither eats וְלֹא שׁוֹכֵב — nor reclines, מִנַּיִן — from where do we know that he, too, must immerse his garments? תַּלְמוּד לוֹמַר — The verse says,** "יְכַבֵּס . . . יְכַבֵּס,, — **"[He] shall immerse . . . [he] shall immerse."**[6] **רִבָּה — It has thus included even one who neither eats nor reclines among those who must immerse their garments. אִם כֵּן — If so, לָמָה נֶאֱמַר אוֹכֵל וְשׁוֹכֵב — why are "one who eats" and "one who reclines" stated? לִתֵּן שִׁעוּר — To assign a measure of time לַשּׁוֹכֵב — for one who reclines as** ⁷כִּדֵי אֲכִילַת פְּרָס — **time enough for the eating of half a loaf.**[7]

hanim). Alternatively, Toras Kohanim might be saying that one who enters the house becomes impure only during the days it is closed off, not the days in which he removes the afflicted stones, scrapes the edges around them, and plasters the house (Mizrachi; Sifsei Chachamim, Sefer Zikaron; Malbim).

1. If a house was to be demolished because it is impure and the afflicted area was removed before it is torn down, we might have thought that whoever enters such a house would not become impure, for there is no actual affliction present.

2. Toras Kohanim, perek 5:4. The apparently superfluous "all" includes that which is decidedly impure.

3. This verse, unlike the following one that deals with a person who eats or reclines in an afflicted house, does not say יְכַבֵּס אֶת בְּגָדָיו, "shall immerse his garments" (Gur Aryeh).

4. Half a loaf is the volume of four eggs (see note 2 on p. 164), enough for a medium-sized meal (Rashi to Eruvin 4a, s.v., פרס; see also Rashi to Eruvin 82b, s.v., חציה לבית המנוגע).

5. Below v. 47.

6. Verse 47 reads וְהַשּׁכֵב בַּבַּיִת יְכַבֵּס אֶת בְּגָדָיו וְהָאֹכֵל בַּבַּיִת יְכַבֵּס אֶת בְּגָדָיו, "But one who reclines in the house shall immerse his garments; and one who eats in the house shall immerse his garments," with separate verbs for reclining and for eating. The verse could have said, וְהַשּׁכֵב וְהָאֹכֵל בַּבַּיִת יְכַבֵּס אֶת בְּגָדָיו, "But one who reclines in the house and one who eats in the house shall immerse his garments." יְכַבֵּס, "he shall immerse," appears to be repeated unnecessarily.

7. Toras Kohanim, perek 5:5-8. If he reclines long enough to eat half a loaf or remains in the house in any other posture for that length of time, he must immerse his clothes (Sefer Zikaron).

the house; then the Kohen shall declare the house to be pure, for the affliction has healed. ⁴⁹ To cleanse the house, he shall take two birds, cedar wood, crimson [tongue of] wool, and hyssop. ⁵⁰ He shall slaughter the one bird into an earthenware vessel over spring water. ⁵¹ He shall take the cedarwood, the hyssop, the crimson [tongue of] wool, and the live bird, and he shall dip them into the blood of the slaughtered bird and into the fresh water; and he shall sprinkle upon the house seven times. ⁵² He shall cleanse the house with the blood of the bird and with the fresh water; and with the live bird, with the cedarwood, with the hyssop, and with the crimson [tongue of] wool. ⁵³ He shall set the live bird free toward the outside of the city upon the open field; thus he shall provide atonement for the house, and it shall become purified.

⁵⁴ This is the law for every tzara'as affliction and the nesek; ⁵⁵ and tzara'as of the garment and of the house; ⁵⁶ and of the s'eis, of the sapachas, and of the baheres; ⁵⁷ to rule about the impure day and on which day it is purified; this is the law of tzaraas.

15 ¹ HASHEM spoke to Moses and Aaron, saying, ² Speak to the Children of Israel and say to them: Any man

---

אֶת־הַבַּיִת וְטָהֵר הַכֹּהֵן אֶת־הַבַּיִת כִּי נִרְפָּא הַנָּגַע: וְלָקַח לְחַטֵּא אֶת־הַבַּיִת שְׁתֵּי צִפֳּרִים וְעֵץ אֶרֶז וּשְׁנִי תוֹלַעַת וְאֵזֹב: וְשָׁחַט אֶת־הַצִּפֹּר הָאֶחָת אֶל־כְּלִי־חֶרֶשׂ עַל־מַיִם חַיִּים: וְלָקַח אֶת־עֵץ־הָאֶרֶז וְאֶת־הָאֵזֹב וְאֵת ׀ שְׁנִי הַתּוֹלַעַת וְאֵת הַצִּפֹּר הַחַיָּה וְטָבַל אֹתָם בְּדַם הַצִּפֹּר הַשְּׁחוּטָה וּבַמַּיִם הַחַיִּים וְהִזָּה אֶל־הַבַּיִת שֶׁבַע פְּעָמִים: וְחִטֵּא אֶת־הַבַּיִת בְּדַם הַצִּפּוֹר וּבַמַּיִם הַחַיִּים וּבַצִּפֹּר הַחַיָּה וּבְעֵץ הָאֶרֶז וּבָאֵזֹב וּבִשְׁנִי הַתּוֹלָעַת: וְשִׁלַּח אֶת־הַצִּפֹּר הַחַיָּה אֶל־מִחוּץ לָעִיר אֶל־פְּנֵי הַשָּׂדֶה וְכִפֶּר עַל־הַבַּיִת וְטָהֵר: חמישי זֹאת הַתּוֹרָה לְכָל־נֶגַע הַצָּרַעַת וְלַנָּתֶק: וּלְצָרַעַת הַבֶּגֶד וְלַבָּיִת: וְלַשְׂאֵת וְלַסַּפַּחַת וְלַבֶּהָרֶת: לְהוֹרֹת בְּיוֹם הַטָּמֵא וּבְיוֹם הַטָּהֹר זֹאת תּוֹרַת הַצָּרָעַת:

טו ¹ וַיְדַבֵּר יהוה אֶל־מֹשֶׁה וְאֶל־אַהֲרֹן לֵאמֹר: ² דַּבְּרוּ אֶל־בְּנֵי יִשְׂרָאֵל וַאֲמַרְתֶּם אֲלֵהֶם אִישׁ אִישׁ

— אונקלוס —

יָת בֵּיתָא וִידַכֵּי כַהֲנָא יָת בֵּיתָא אֲרֵי אִתַּסִּי מַכְתָּשָׁא: מטוְיִסַּב לְדַכָּאָה יָת בֵּיתָא תַּרְתֵּין צִפֳּרִין וְאָעָא דְאַרְזָא וּצְבַע זְהוֹרִי וְאֵזוֹבָא: נוְיִכּוֹס יָת צִפְּרָא חֲדָא לְמָאן דַּחֲסַף עַל מֵי מַבּוּעַ: נאוְיִסַּב יָת אָעָא דְאַרְזָא וְיָת אֵזוֹבָא וְיָת צְבַע זְהוֹרִי וְיָת צִפְּרָא חַיְתָא וְיִטְבּוֹל יָתְהוֹן בִּדְמָא דְצִפְּרָא דִּנְכִיסָא וּבְמֵי מַבּוּעַ וְיַדֵּי לְבֵיתָא שְׁבַע זִמְנִין: נבוִידַכֵּי יָת בֵּיתָא בִּדְמָא דְצִפְּרָא וּבְמֵי מַבּוּעַ וּבְצִפְּרָא חַיְתָא וּבְאָעָא דְאַרְזָא וּבְאֵזוֹבָא וּבִצְבַע זְהוֹרִי: נגוִישַׁלַּח יָת צִפְּרָא חַיְתָא לְמִבָּרָא לְקַרְתָּא לְאַפֵּי חַקְלָא וִיכַפֵּר עַל בֵּיתָא וְיִדְכֵּי: נדדָּא אוֹרַיְתָא לְכָל מַכְתַּשׁ סְגִירוּתָא וּלְנִתְקָא: נהוְלִסְגִירוּת לְבוּשָׁא וּלְבֵיתָא: נווְלַעֲמָקָא וּלְכַדְבָּנָא וּלְבַהֲרָא: נזלְאַלָּפָא בְּיוֹמָא מְסָאָבָא וּבְיוֹמָא דָּכְיָא דָּא אוֹרַיְתָא דִסְגִירוּתָא: אוּמַלִּיל יְיָ עִם מֹשֶׁה וְעִם אַהֲרֹן לְמֵימָר: בּמַלִּילוּ עִם בְּנֵי יִשְׂרָאֵל וְתֵימְרוּן לְהוֹן גְּבַר גְּבַר

— רש"י —

(נז) להורת ביום הטמא וגו'. איזה יום מטהרו ואיזה יום מטמאו:

RASHI ELUCIDATED

57. אֵיזֶה יוֹם מְטַהֲרוֹ — TO RULE ABOUT THE IMPURE DAY, ETC. — לְהוֹרֹת בְּיוֹם הַטָּמֵא וְגוֹמֵר — Which day renders him pure, וְאֵיזֶה יוֹם מְטַמְּאוֹ — and which day renders him impure.[1]

---

1. The ב of בְּיוֹם is understood as "about." It does not mean "on." The verse is not teaching us *when* he will rule, but rather what he will rule about (*Mizrachi; Sifsei Chachamim*).

who will have a discharge from his flesh, his discharge is impure. ³ *Thus shall be his impurity through his discharge:*

בְּ֣י יִהְיֶה֙ זָ֣ב מִבְּשָׂר֔וֹ זוֹב֖וֹ טָמֵ֥א הֽוּא: ג וְזֹ֛את תִּהְיֶ֥ה טֻמְאָת֖וֹ בְּזוֹבֽוֹ

———————————— אונקלוס ————————————

אֲרֵי יְהֵי דְיֵאב מִבִּשְׂרֵהּ דּוֹבֵהּ מְסָאָב הוּא: ג וְדָא תְּהֵי סוֹבְתֵהּ בְּדוֹבֵהּ

———————————— רש"י ————————————

(ב) **כי יהיה זב.** יכול מכל מקום יהא טמא, ת"ל מבשרו ולא כל בשרו. אחר שחלק הכתוב בין בשר לבשר זכיתי לדין. טמא בזב וטמא בזבה, מה זבה ממקום שהיא מטמאה טומאה קלה, נדה,

מטמאה טומאה חמורה, זיבה, אף הזב ממקום שמטמא טומאה קלה, קרי, מטמא טומאה חמורה, זיבה (ת"כ זבים פרשתא א:ג-ה): **זובו טמא.** למד על הטפה שהיא מטמאה (שם ט).

———————————— RASHI ELUCIDATED ————————————

15.

2. **כִּי יִהְיֶה זָב** — WHO WILL HAVE A DISCHARGE. **יָכוֹל** — One might be able to think that if **זָב** — he had a discharge **מִכָּל מָקוֹם** — from any place on his body[1] **יְהֵא טָמֵא** — he will be impure. **תַּלְמוּד לוֹמַר** — To teach us otherwise, **the verse says,** **"מִבְּשָׂרוֹ,"** — **"from his flesh,"** **וְלֹא כָּל בְּשָׂרוֹ** — but not all of his flesh.[2] **אַחַר שֶׁחִלֵּק הַכָּתוּב** — Once the verse has drawn a distinction **בֵּין בָּשָׂר לְבָשָׂר** — between flesh from which a discharge renders a man impure **and flesh** from which a discharge does not render a man impure, **זָכִיתִי לָדִין** — I have the right to use reasoning to determine from which part of the body a discharge renders one impure. Thus, I reason as follows: **טִמֵּא בְזָב** — [The Torah] made a man who had a discharge impure, **וְטִמֵּא בְזָבָה** — and it made a woman who had a discharge impure; **מַה זָּבָה** — just as with regard to a *zavah*, her impurity came through a discharge **מִמָּקוֹם** — from a place **שֶׁהִיא מִטַּמְּאָה טֻמְאָה קַלָּה** — from which she becomes impure with a lesser impurity, that is, **נִדָּה** — the impurity of a *niddah*,[3] **מְטַמְּאָה טֻמְאָה חֲמוּרָה** — she becomes impure with a more severe impurity, that is, **זִיבָה** — the impurity of *zivah*,[4] **אַף הַזָּב** — so, too, with regard to a man who had a discharge, **מִמָּקוֹם** — through a discharge from a place **שֶׁמְּטַמֵּא טֻמְאָה קַלָּה** — from which he becomes impure with a lesser impurity, that is, **קֶרִי** — the impurity caused by the emission of semen, **מְטַמֵּא טֻמְאָה חֲמוּרָה** — he becomes impure with a more severe impurity, that is, ⁵**זִיבָה** — the impurity of *zivah*.⁵

□ **זוֹבוֹ טָמֵא** — HIS DISCHARGE IS IMPURE. **לִמֵּד עַל הַטִּפָּה** — This teaches us about the droplet of the discharge ⁶**שֶׁהִיא מְטַמְּאָה** — that it transmits impurity to that which it comes into contact with or that which bears its weight.[6]

---

1. Even from the nose or mouth or ear (*Mizrachi; Sifsei Chachamim*).

2. *Niddah* 43a. The word מִן, as well as its prefixed form מ, means "from," and is considered a limitation on the noun to which it is connected. In our verse, "from" limits the broad term "his flesh" and implies that a discharge from *some* part or parts of his body renders him impure, but not from every part (*Mizrachi*).

3. A *zavah* is a woman who has had a menstrual flow during a certain specified period of time (see note 7 on p. 188) in her personal cycle, and who has not yet purified herself by immersion in a *mikveh* (see vv. 25-30 below). A *niddah* is a woman who has had a bloody discharge at any time outside of the specified period mentioned above, and who has not yet purified herself (see vv. 19-24 below). The term *zivah* refers to the discharge of a *zav* (the subject of our verse) and of a *zavah*.

4. The impurity of a *zavah* is more severe than the impurity of a *niddah* in two respects. [The first difference is based on the law as stated in the Torah. However, over the centuries, rabbinic law and Jewish custom have adapted the semi-stringencies (of the waiting period before purification) on the *niddah* as on the *zavah*.] (a) A *zavah* must wait seven discharge-free days before she can undergo purification, whereas a *niddah* can undergo purification the day after she stops menstruating if seven days have elapsed since her flow began. (b) A *zavah* must bring offerings as part of her purification procedure, whereas a *niddah* does not (*Mizrachi; Sifsei Chachamim*).

5. *Toras Kohanim, Zavim, parshasa* 1:3-5. The impurity of discharging is more severe than the impurity brought on by the emission of semen in a number of respects. A man who had two or more discharges is called a *zav* and is impure for at least seven days, whereas a man who has had emissions of semen can immerse himself in a *mikveh* that very day and become pure with the evening which follows. A *zav* sometimes must bring offerings as part of his purification procedure (see note 7 on p. 180), whereas a man who had an emission of semen does not (*Mizrachi; Sefer Zikaron*).

6. *Toras Kohanim, Zavim, parshasa* 1:9. Although we know that one who has a discharge becomes impure, without the apparently superfluous זוֹבוֹ of our verse we would have thought that the fluid of the discharge itself is not impure, just as the goat which is sent off to Azazel (see 16:10 below) renders the one who sends it off impure, while it itself is not impure (*Mizrachi; Sifsei Chachamim*).

ויקרא / 180 — פרשת מצורע

רָר בְּשָׂרוֹ אֶת־זוֹבוֹ אוֹ־הֶחְתִּים
בְּשָׂרוֹ מִזּוֹבוֹ טֻמְאָתוֹ הִוא: ד כָּל־
הַמִּשְׁכָּב אֲשֶׁר יִשְׁכַּב עָלָיו הַזָּב

whether his flesh runs with his discharge or whether his flesh is stopped up because of his discharge, that is his impurity. [4] Any bedding upon which the zav will

---- אונקלוס ----

רָר בְּשָׂרֵהּ יָת דּוֹבֵהּ אוֹ חָתִים בִּשְׂרֵהּ מִדּוֹבֵהּ סוֹבְתָהּ הִיא: ד כָּל מִשְׁכְּבָא דִּי יִשְׁכּוּב עֲלוֹהִי דוֹבָנָא

---- רש"י ----

זוֹב דּוֹמֶה לְמֵי בָצֵק שֶׁל שְׂעוֹרִין, וְדָחוּי, וְדוֹמֶה לְלוֹבֶן בֵּיצָה
הַמּוּזֶרֶת. שִׁכְבַת זֶרַע קָשׁוּר כְּלוֹבֶן בֵּיצָה שֶׁאֵינָהּ מוּזֶרֶת (נדה
לה:): (ג) רָר. לְשׁוֹן רִיר, שֶׁזָּב בְּשָׂרוֹ אֶת זוֹבוֹ. כְּמוֹ רִיר שֶׁיּוֹצֵא
צָלוּל: אוֹ הֶחְתִּים. שִׁיּוֹצֵא עָב וְסוֹתֵם אֶת פִּי הָאַמָּה, וְנִסְתַּם
בְּשָׂרוֹ מִטִּפַּת זוֹבוֹ. זֶהוּ פְשׁוּטוֹ. וּמִדְרָשׁוֹ, מָנָה הַכָּתוּב הָרִאשׁוֹן

רְאִיּוֹת שְׁתַּיִם וּקְרָאוֹ טָמֵא, שֶׁנֶּאֱמַר ״זָב מִבְּשָׂרוֹ״ ״זוֹבוֹ״ טָמֵא הוּא.
וּמָנָה הַכָּתוּב הַשֵּׁנִי שָׁלֹשׁ רְאִיּוֹת וּקְרָאוֹ טָמֵא, שֶׁנֶּאֱמַר ״רָר בְּשָׂרוֹ
אֶת זוֹבוֹ אוֹ הֶחְתִּים בְּשָׂרוֹ מִזּוֹבוֹ״ ״טֻמְאָתוֹ הִוא״. הָא כֵּיצַד,
שְׁתַּיִם לְטֻמְאָה וְהַשְּׁלִישִׁית מַזְקִיקָתוֹ לְקָרְבָּן (מגילה ח.; נדה מג:): (ד) כָּל הַמִּשְׁכָּב. הָרָאוּי לְמִשְׁכָּב.

---- RASHI ELUCIDATED ----

זוֹב — The **discharge** discussed in this passage דּוֹמֶה — **is similar** לְמֵי בָצֵק שֶׁל שְׂעוֹרִין — **to water** which exudes **from dough** made **of barley,** וְדָחוּי — **and is thin,** not viscous, וְדוֹמֶה — **and is similar** לְלוֹבֶן בֵּיצָה — **to the white of an egg** הַמּוּזֶרֶת — **which is spoiled** and so cannot be fertilized. שִׁכְבַת זֶרַע קָשׁוּר — **Semen is viscous** כְּלוֹבֶן בֵּיצָה — **like the white of an egg**[1] שֶׁאֵינָהּ מוּזֶרֶת — **which is not spoiled** and so can be fertilized.[1]

3. רָר — **RUNS.** This word is לְשׁוֹן רִיר — **related to** "**spittle.**"[2] It means שֶׁזָּב בְּשָׂרוֹ אֶת זוֹבוֹ — **that his flesh discharged** *his discharge* כְּמוֹ רִיר — **like spittle,** שֶׁיּוֹצֵא צָלוּל — **which comes out** of the body **clear.**[3]

□ אוֹ הֶחְתִּים — **OR [WHETHER HIS FLESH] IS STOPPED UP,** שֶׁיּוֹצֵא עָב — **for it comes out thick** וְסוֹתֵם אֶת פִּי הָאַמָּה — **and clogs the opening of the male organ,** וְנִסְתַּם בְּשָׂרוֹ — **and his flesh becomes clogged** מִטִּפַּת זוֹבוֹ — **from the droplet of his discharge.** זֶהוּ פְשׁוּטוֹ — **This is** [the verse's] **simple meaning.** וּמִדְרָשׁוֹ — **It is expounded** as follows: מָנָה הַכָּתוּב הָרִאשׁוֹן — **The first,** i.e., preceding, **verse counts** רְאִיּוֹת שְׁתַּיִם — **two perceptions** of a discharge וּקְרָאוֹ טָמֵא — **and calls him impure,** שֶׁנֶּאֱמַר — **as it says,** ״זָב מִבְּשָׂרוֹ״ — "**a discharge from his flesh,**" and, ״זוֹבוֹ״ — "**his discharge,**" then, טָמֵא הוּא — "[it] **is impure.**"[4] וּמָנָה הַכָּתוּב הַשֵּׁנִי — **The second verse,** i.e., our verse, **counts** רְאִיּוֹת שָׁלֹשׁ — **three perceptions** of a discharge וּקְרָאוֹ טָמֵא — **and calls him impure,** שֶׁנֶּאֱמַר — **as it says,** ״רָר בְּשָׂרוֹ אֶת זוֹבוֹ״ — "**whether his flesh runs with his discharge,**" and ״אוֹ הֶחְתִּים בְּשָׂרוֹ מִזּוֹבוֹ״ — "**or whether his flesh is stopped up because of his discharge,**" then, ״טֻמְאָתוֹ הִוא״ — "**that is his impurity.**"[5] הָא כֵּיצַד — **How is this?**[6] שְׁתַּיִם לְטֻמְאָה — **Two** discharges are necessary **for impurity,**[7] וְהַשְּׁלִישִׁית מַזְקִיקָתוֹ לְקָרְבָּן — **and the third requires him to** bring **an offering.**[7]

4. כָּל הַמִּשְׁכָּב — **ANY BEDDING.** הָרָאוּי לְמִשְׁכָּב — **That which is fit for reclining.**[8] יָכוֹל — **One might**

---

1. *Niddah* 35b. See Rashi there.
2. See Rashi to *I Samuel* 21:14 and *Job* 6:6.
3. The text presented here is based on the first printed edition of Rashi and other early editions. The text as it appears in most modern editions seemed to be confused.
4. The preceding verse contains the words זָב and זוֹבוֹ; this is taken to indicate two discharges. The verse ends with טָמֵא הוּא, "[it] is impure"; this shows that impurity takes effect after two discharges.
5. This verse contains בְּזוֹב, זוֹבוֹ, and מִזּוֹבוֹ; these are taken to indicate three discharges. The verse ends with טֻמְאָתוֹ הִוא, "that is his impurity"; this shows that impurity takes effect after three discharges.
6. How are we to reconcile the preceding verse, which indicates that the impurity takes effect after two discharges, with our verse, which indicates that the impurity takes effect after three discharges?
7. *Megillah* 8a; *Niddah* 43b. A man who has only one discharge is impure, but he has the same impurity as one who has an emission of semen, rather than one who is impure because of two or more discharges (see verse 16 below). He can immerse himself in the *mikveh* that same day and become pure that evening. He transmits impurity only to food, and only by touching it, not by merely bearing its weight. A man who has two discharges becomes impure with the impurity of *zivah* and cannot become pure for at least seven days. He transmits impurity not only to that which he touches, but even through carrying an object. A man who has three discharges follows the same rule but must also bring an offering as part of his purification procedure; see verse 14 below (*Mizrachi; Sifsei Chachamim*).
8. The word מִשְׁכָּב, literally, "bed" or "couch," and here translated "bedding," refers to anything that is made to

recline shall be impure and any vessel upon which he will sit shall become impure. *⁵ A person who will touch his bedding shall immerse his garments and immerse himself in the water, and he remains impure until the evening. ⁶ And one who sits upon an article upon which the zav will sit, shall immerse*

יִטְמָא וְכָל־הַכְּלִי אֲשֶׁר־יֵשֵׁב עָלָיו יִטְמָא: ה וְאִישׁ אֲשֶׁר יִגַּע בְּמִשְׁכָּבוֹ יְכַבֵּס בְּגָדָיו וְרָחַץ בַּמַּיִם וְטָמֵא עַד־הָעָרֶב: ו וְהַיֹּשֵׁב עַל־הַכְּלִי אֲשֶׁר־יֵשֵׁב עָלָיו הַזָּב יְכַבֵּס

—————— אונקלוס ——————

יְהֵי מְסָאָב וְכָל מָנָא דְיֵיתֵב עֲלוֹהִי יְהֵי מְסָאָב: ה וּגְבַר דִּי יִקְרַב בְּמִשְׁכְּבֵהּ יְצַבַּע לְבוּשׁוֹהִי וְיִסְחֵי בְמַיָּא וִיהֵי מְסָאָב עַד רַמְשָׁא: ו וּדְיֵיתֵב עַל מָנָא דְיֵיתֵב עֲלוֹהִי דּוּבָנָא יְצַבַּע

—————— רש"י ——————

אפי' מיוחד למלאכה אחרת, ת"ל אשר ישכב. אשר שכב לא נאמר, אלא אשר ישכב, המיוחד תמיד לכך, יצא זה שאומרים לו עמוד ונעשה מלאכתנו (ת"כ פרק ב:ג): אשר ישב. ישב לא נאמר אלא אשר ישב עליו הזב, במיוחד תמיד לכך (שם ד; שבת נט.): (ה) ואיש אשר יגע במשכבו. לימד על המשכב שחמור מן המגע, שזה נעשה אב הטומאה לטמא אדם לטמא בגדים, והמגע שאינו משכב אינו אלא ולד הטומאה, ואינו מטמא אלא אוכלין ומשקין): (ו) והישב על הכלי. אפילו לא נגע ואפי' עשרה כלים זה על זה

—————— RASHI ELUCIDATED ——————

be able to think that he transmits impurity **אֲפִילוּ מְיֻחָד לִמְלָאכָה אַחֶרֶת** — **even** to that which **is designated for another function.**[1] **תַּלְמוּד לוֹמַר** — To teach us otherwise, **the verse says,** **"אֲשֶׁר שָׁכַב" לֹא נֶאֱמַר** — **It does not say,** **"[upon] which** [the *zav*] **has reclined,"** **אֶלָּא "אֲשֶׁר יִשְׁכַּב"** — **but rather, "[upon] which** [the *zav*] **will recline,"** implying, **הַמְיֻחָד תָּמִיד לְכָךְ** — **that which is always designated for that purpose.**[2] **יָצָא זֶה** — **To the exclusion of this** object **שֶׁאוֹמְרִים לוֹ** — **about which they say to him** who reclines upon it, **עֲמוֹד** — **"Get up** from it,**[3] וְנַעֲשֶׂה מְלַאכְתֵּנוּ** — **so that we may do our work** with it."[3]

☐ **אֲשֶׁר יֵשֵׁב** — [UPON] WHICH HE WILL SIT. **"יָשַׁב" לֹא נֶאֱמַר** — It does not say, "he sat," **אֶלָּא** — but **rather, "אֲשֶׁר יֵשֵׁב עָלָיו"** — **"upon which he will sit."** The verse thus speaks **בִּמְיֻחָד תָּמִיד לְכָךְ**[4] — about that which is always designated for that purpose.[4]

5. וְאִישׁ אֲשֶׁר יִגַּע בְּמִשְׁכָּבוֹ — A PERSON WHO WILL TOUCH HIS BEDDING. **לִמֵּד עַל הַמִּשְׁכָּב** — This has **taught** us **about the bedding שֶׁחָמוּר מִן הַמַּגָּע** — **that its** impurity **is more severe than the** impurity transmitted through **touching** a *zav*, i.e., than the impurity of an object which has been touched by a *zav*, **שֶׁזֶּה** — for this bedding **נַעֲשֶׂה אַב הַטֻּמְאָה** — **becomes a primary source of impurity לְטַמֵּא אָדָם** — to **transmit impurity to man,** who in turn **לְטַמֵּא בְגָדִים** — **transmits impurity to garments** while he is still in contact with them; **וְהַמַּגָּע** — **but the touching,** i.e., the object that has been touched, **שֶׁאֵינוֹ מִשְׁכָּב** — **that is not bedding אֵינוֹ אֶלָּא וְלַד הַטֻּמְאָה** — **is only an offspring of impurity, וְאֵינוֹ מְטַמֵּא אֶלָּא אֳכָלִין {וּמַשְׁקִין}** — **and transmits impurity only** to **foods {and liquids}.**[5]

6. וְהַיּוֹשֵׁב עַל הַכְּלִי — AND ONE WHO SITS UPON AN ARTICLE. **אֲפִילוּ לֹא נָגַע** — Even if he did not **touch** the article that the *zav* sat on, **וַאֲפִילוּ עֲשָׂרָה כֵלִים** — and even if there are ten articles **זֶה עַל זֶה** — one on top of the other, and the one the *zav* had sat on is the lowest layer,

---

1. One might think that a *zav* transmits impurity even if he reclines on an object which is not meant for bedding but for some other purpose, such as a baker's platter or a large kneading trough (*Sefer Zikaron*).
2. The future tense can be used to indicate an action often repeated. See, for example, Rashi to *Exodus* 15:1, *Numbers* 9:8, and *Job* 1:5 (*Be'er Rechovos*).
3. *Toras Kohanim, Zavim, perek* 2:3.
4. *Toras Kohanim, Zavim, perek* 2:4; *Shabbos* 59a. See note 2 above.
5. Our verse, which speaks of a man and his garments becoming impure, refers specifically to one who

be reclined upon, such as a bed, mattress or bedsheet.
touches the bedding of a *zav*. This implies that it is only the bedding of the *zav* that transmits impurity to man and, in turn, to his garments. This is a characteristic of a primary source of impurity. Other objects that the *zav* touches have the status of an offspring of impurity and transmit impurity only to food and liquids (*Mizrachi; Sifsei Chachamim*).

The unique impurity of the bedding applies only if the *zav* sits, lays, or stands on it, or if he has been suspended from it, or if he has supported himself on it. If the *zav* touches it in some other manner, it becomes an offspring of impurity like any other object the *zav* touches (*Sefer Zikaron* from *Zavim* 2:4).

his garments and immerse himself in the water, and he remains impure until the evening. ⁷ One who touches the flesh of the zav shall immerse his garments and immerse himself in the water, and he remains impure until the evening. ⁸ If the zav will spit upon a pure person, he shall immerse his garments and immerse himself in the water, and he remains impure until the evening. ⁹ Any riding equipment upon which the zav will ride shall become impure. ¹⁰ And whoever touches anything that will be beneath him shall become impure until

בְּגָדָיו וְרָחַץ בַּמַּיִם וְטָמֵא עַד־הָעָרֶב: ⁷ וְהַנֹּגֵעַ בִּבְשַׂר הַזָּב יְכַבֵּס בְּגָדָיו וְרָחַץ בַּמַּיִם וְטָמֵא עַד־הָעָרֶב: ⁸ וְכִי־יָרֹק הַזָּב בַּטָּהוֹר וְכִבֶּס בְּגָדָיו וְרָחַץ בַּמַּיִם וְטָמֵא עַד־הָעָרֶב: ⁹ וְכָל־הַמֶּרְכָּב אֲשֶׁר יִרְכַּב עָלָיו הַזָּב יִטְמָא: ¹⁰ וְכָל־הַנֹּגֵעַ בְּכֹל אֲשֶׁר יִהְיֶה תַחְתָּיו יִטְמָא עַד־

אונקלוס

לבושוהי ויסחי במיא ויהי מסאב עד רמשא: ⁷ודיקרב בבסר דובנא יצבע לבושוהי ויסחי במיא ויהי מסאב עד רמשא: ⁸וארי ירוק דובנא בדכיא ויצבע לבושוהי ויסחי במיא ויהי מסאב עד רמשא: ט וכל מרכבא די ירכוב עלוהי דובנא יהי מסאב: י וכל דיקרב בכל די יהי תחותוהי יהי מסאב עד

רש״י

כולן מטמאין משום מושב (ת״כ פרק ג:א) וכן במסכת (נדה נה:): **הזב בטהור.** וגע בו או נשאו, שהרוק מטמא במשא (נדה נה:): (ט) **ובל המרכב.** אע״פ שלא ישב עליו, כגון התפוס של סרגא שקורין ארצו״ן, טמא משום מרכב, והאוכף שקורין סיל״א [וס״א אלו״ש] טמא טומאת מושב: (י) **ובל הנוגע בכל אשר יהיה תחתיו.** של זב (ת״כ פרק ד:א) בא ולימד על המרכב שיהא הנוגע בו טמא

RASHI ELUCIDATED

כֻּלָּן מְטַמְּאִין — **all of them transmit impurity** to one who sits on the topmost layer ¹ **מִשּׁוּם מוֹשָׁב** — **as a seat** of a zav,¹ **וְכֵן בְּמַסֶּכֶת** — **and the law is the same with regard to** his **bedding**.

8. **וְכִי יָרֹק הַזָּב בַּטָּהוֹר** — IF THE ZAV WILL SPIT UPON A PURE PERSON **וְנָגַע בּוֹ** — **and [the spittle] touched [the pure person], אוֹ נְשָׂאוֹ** — **or [the pure person] carries it**s weight, the person will become impure² **שֶׁהָרוֹק מְטַמֵּא בְּמַשָּׂא** — **for spittle transmits impurity when carried**.²

9. **וְכָל הַמֶּרְכָּב** — ANY RIDING EQUIPMENT. **אַף עַל פִּי שֶׁלֹּא יָשַׁב עָלָיו** — **Even though he did not sit on it**, but merely used it to give him support, **כְּגוֹן הַתְּפוֹס שֶׁל סַרְגָּא** — **such as the saddlebow שֶׁקּוֹרִין ארצו״ן** — **which they call** arçon,³ **טָמֵא מִשּׁוּם מֶרְכָּב** — **it is impure because of the law of riding equipment**, **וְהָאֻכָּף** — **But the saddle** upon which the rider actually sits, **שֶׁקּוֹרִין סיל״א** — **that they call** selle,⁴ **טָמֵא טֻמְאַת מוֹשָׁב** — **is impure with the impurity of a seat**.⁵

10. **וְכָל הַנֹּגֵעַ בְּכֹל אֲשֶׁר יִהְיֶה תַחְתָּיו** — AND WHOEVER TOUCHES ANYTHING THAT WILL BE BENEATH HIM, i.e., beneath **שֶׁל זָב** — **the** zav.⁶ **בָּא** — **[This verse] comes וְלִמֵּד** — **and teaches** us **עַל הַמֶּרְכָּב** — **about riding equipment**,⁷ **שֶׁיְּהֵא הַנּוֹגֵעַ בּוֹ טָמֵא** — **that one who touches it should be impure**,

---

1. *Toras Kohanim, Zavim, perek* 3:1. All of them, as long as they are on top of the seat, allow the impurity of the seat to be transmitted through them to the one who sits on top of them. This holds true even if an object that cannot receive impurity, such as a stone, is on top of the seat (*Sefer Zikaron; Be'er Yitzchak*).

2. *Niddah* 55b. The verse could have expressed "upon a pure person" with the words עַל טָהוֹר. But that would have implied physical contact with the saliva. בַּטָּהוֹר implies that the pure person bears the weight of the saliva, but does not necessarily touch it (*Malbim*).

3. In Modern French, *arçon de selle*, the rounded upward projecting front part of a saddle onto which a rider holds (see Rashi to *Eruvin* 27a).

4. In both Old and Modern French this word means "saddle." Most Modern editions of Rashi read אלווי״ש, "*alves*," which refers to the "girth" of the saddle, a metal or leather band that passes underneath the horse to hold the saddle in place.

5. See v. 6 above.

6. *Toras Kohanim, Zavim, perek* 4:1. תַּחְתָּיו is to be understood as "beneath him," that is, beneath the *zav*, not "beneath it," as the masculine suffix can also refer to the riding equipment. If the verse were read "beneath it," it would mean that riding equipment transmits impurity to that which bears its weight, even if there is no direct contact. This cannot be so, for a *zav* himself transmits impurity in this fashion only to bedding and to a seat, but not to any other objects (*Mizrachi*).

7. Verses 5 and 6 above have already spoken of one who touches the bedding or the seat of a *zav*, and said that he is impure until evening and must immerse his garments. It stands to reason, then, that our verse which speaks of "that which is beneath" the *zav*, and makes

15/11-12

הָעֶרֶב וְהַנּוֹשֵׂא אוֹתָם יְכַבֵּס בְּגָדָיו וְרָחַץ בַּמַּיִם וְטָמֵא עַד־הָעָרֶב: יא וְכֹל אֲשֶׁר יִגַּע־בּוֹ הַזָּב וְיָדָיו לֹא־שָׁטַף בַּמָּיִם וְכִבֶּס בְּגָדָיו וְרָחַץ בַּמַּיִם וְטָמֵא עַד־הָעָרֶב: יב וּכְלִי־חֶרֶשׂ אֲשֶׁר־יִגַּע־בּוֹ הַזָּב יִשָּׁבֵר וְכָל־כְּלִי־עֵץ יִשָּׁטֵף בַּמָּיִם:

evening; and whoever carries them shall immerse his garments and immerse himself in the water, and he remains impure until the evening. [11] *Whomever the zav touches without having rinsed his hands in the water shall immerse his garments and immerse himself in the water, and he remains impure until the evening.* [12] *Pottery that the zav will touch shall be broken; and any wooden utensil shall be rinsed in water.*

אונקלוס

רִמְשָׁא וּדְיִטּוֹל יָתְהוֹן יְצַבַּע לְבוּשׁוֹהִי וְיִסְחֵי בְמַיָּא וִיהֵי מְסָאָב עַד רַמְשָׁא: יא וְכֹל דִּי יִקְרַב בֵּהּ דּוֹבָנָא וִידוֹהִי לָא שְׁטַף בְּמַיָּא וִיצַבַּע לְבוּשׁוֹהִי וְיִסְחֵי בְמַיָּא וִיהֵי מְסָאָב עַד רַמְשָׁא: יב וּמָאן דַּחֲסַף דִּי יִקְרַב בֵּהּ דּוֹבָנָא יִתָּבַר וְכָל מַאן דְּאָע יִשְׁתַּטַּף בְּמַיָּא:

רש"י

וְאֵין טָעוּן כִּבּוּס בְּגָדִים, וְהוּא חֹמֶר בְּמִשְׁכָּב מִבְּמֶרְכָּב: **וְהַנּוֹשֵׂא אוֹתָם.** כָּל הָאָמוּר בְּעִנְיַן הַזָּב, זוֹבוֹ וְרוּקוֹ וְשִׁכְבַת זַרְעוֹ וּמֵימֵי רַגְלָיו וְהַמִּשְׁכָּב וְהַמֶּרְכָּב, מִשָּׂאָן מְטַמֵּא אָדָם לְטַמֵּא בְגָדִים (שם ד): (יא) **וְיָדָיו לֹא שָׁטַף בַּמָּיִם.** בְּעוֹד שֶׁלֹּא טָבַל מִטּוּמְאָתוֹ, וַאֲפִלּוּ פָסַק מִזּוֹבוֹ וְסָפַר שִׁבְעָה וּמְחֻסַּר טְבִילָה, מְטַמֵּא בְכָל טוּמְאוֹתָיו. וְזֶה שֶׁהוֹצִיא הַכָּתוּב טְבִילַת גּוּפוֹ שֶׁל זָב בִּלְשׁוֹן שְׁטִיפַת יָדַיִם, לְלַמֶּדְךָ שֶׁאֵין בֵּית הַסְּתָרִים טָעוּן בִּיאַת מַיִם אֶלָּא אֵבֶר הַגָּלוּי כְּמוֹ הַיָּדַיִם (שם ה): (יב) **וּכְלִי חֶרֶשׂ אֲשֶׁר יִגַּע בּוֹ הַזָּב.** יָכוֹל אֲפִלּוּ נָגַע בּוֹ מֵאֲחוֹרָיו וְכוּ׳, כְּדַאֲמָרִינַן בְּת"כ, עַד מֵיחֲזוֹ מַגְּעוֹ שֶׁהוּא כְּכֻלּוֹ [ס"א בְּכֻלּוֹ] הֱוֵי אוֹמֵר

RASHI ELUCIDATED

וְהוּא חֹמֶר בְּמִשְׁכָּב — It is a stricture of the laws that apply to a seat — מִבְּמֶרְכָּב — over the laws that apply to riding equipment.

□ וְהַנּוֹשֵׂא אוֹתָם — AND WHOEVER CARRIES THEM. כָּל הָאָמוּר בְּעִנְיַן הַזָּב — All the sources of impurity that have been mentioned in the topic of the zav,: זוֹבוֹ — the fluid of his discharge, וְרֻקּוֹ — his spittle, וְשִׁכְבַת זַרְעוֹ — his semen, וּמֵימֵי רַגְלָיו — his urine, וְהַמִּשְׁכָּב — the bedding and seat, וְהַמֶּרְכָּב — and the riding equipment.[1] מַשָּׂאָן — Their being carried מְטַמֵּא אָדָם — makes a person impure, and he in turn [2] לְטַמֵּא בְגָדִים — makes his garments impure.[2]

11. וְיָדָיו לֹא שָׁטַף בַּמָּיִם — WITHOUT HAVING RINSED HIS HANDS IN THE WATER. This means בְּעוֹד שֶׁלֹּא טָבַל מִטּוּמְאָתוֹ — as long as he has not yet immersed himself in a *mikveh* and thereby purified himself from his impurity, וַאֲפִלּוּ פָסַק מִזּוֹבוֹ — even if he has ceased from his discharging, וְסָפַר שִׁבְעָה — and has counted seven consecutive days without a discharge, וּמְחֻסַּר טְבִילָה — but is lacking immersion, מְטַמֵּא — he transmits impurity בְּכָל טֻמְאוֹתָיו — with all of his impurities, i.e., by all manner of transmission noted above. וְזֶה שֶׁהוֹצִיא הַכָּתוּב — And [the fact] that Scripture expressed טְבִילַת גּוּפוֹ שֶׁל זָב — immersion of the body of the *zav* בִּלְשׁוֹן שְׁטִיפַת יָדַיִם — through the expression of "rinsing hands" is meant לְלַמֶּדְךָ — to teach you שֶׁאֵין בֵּית הַסְּתָרִים טָעוּן בִּיאַת מַיִם — that the inner parts of organs such as the cavities of the nose or the mouth do not require coming of water, i.e., do not have to come in contact with the water of the *mikveh* during immersion; אֶלָּא אֵבֶר הַגָּלוּי — only an exposed limb [3] כְּמוֹ הַיָּדַיִם — like the hands must actually touch the water.[3]

12. וּכְלִי חֶרֶשׂ אֲשֶׁר יִגַּע בּוֹ הַזָּב — POTTERY THAT THE ZAV WILL TOUCH. יָכוֹל — "One might be able to think that אֲפִילוּ נָגַע בּוֹ — even if he touched it מֵאֲחוֹרָיו וְכוּלְהוּ — on its outside, etc.," כִּדְאִיתָא בְּתוֹרַת כֹּהֲנִים — as stated in *Toras Kohanim* עַד — until the words, אֵיזֶהוּ מַגָּעוֹ שֶׁהוּא כְּכֻלּוֹ — "What is 'touching it' which is like touching all of it?[4] הֱוֵי אוֹמֵר — You should say

---

no mention of immersion of garments, speaks of something other than the bedding and the seat, namely, riding equipment (*Sefer Zikaron*).
1. Although one who touches riding equipment does not have to immerse his garments, one who carries its weight does (*Be'er Yitzchak*).
2. *Toras Kohanim, Zavim, perek* 4:4.

3. *Toras Kohanim, Zavim, perek* 4:5. Nevertheless, they must be cleaned of any imposition, such as food between the teeth, so that the water would be able to touch them if it entered the cavity (*Niddah* 66b).
4. According to *Sefer Zikaron* and the first printed edition of Rashi, the text should read אֵיזֶהוּ מַגָּעוֹ שֶׁהוּא בְּכֻלּוֹ, "What is touching which is [touching] all of it"

ויקרא – פרשת מצורע

יג וְכִי־יִטְהַ֤ר הַזָּב֙ מִזּוֹב֔וֹ וְסָ֥פַר ל֛וֹ שִׁבְעַ֥ת יָמִ֖ים לְטָהֳרָת֑וֹ וְכִבֶּ֣ס בְּגָדָ֗יו וְרָחַ֧ץ בְּשָׂר֛וֹ בְּמַ֥יִם חַיִּ֖ים וְטָהֵֽר: יד וּבַיּ֣וֹם הַשְּׁמִינִ֗י יִֽקַּֽח־לוֹ֙ שְׁתֵּ֣י תֹרִ֔ים א֥וֹ שְׁנֵ֖י בְּנֵ֣י יוֹנָ֑ה וּבָ֣א ׀ לִפְנֵ֣י יהו֗ה אֶל־פֶּ֙תַח֙ אֹ֣הֶל מוֹעֵ֔ד וּנְתָנָ֖ם אֶל־הַכֹּהֵֽן: טו וְעָשָׂ֤ה אֹתָם֙ הַכֹּהֵ֔ן אֶחָ֖ד

---אונקלוס---

יג וַאֲרֵי יִדְכֵּי דּוֹבָנָא מִדּוֹבֵהּ וְיִמְנֵי לֵהּ שִׁבְעָא יוֹמִין לְדָכוּתֵהּ וִיצַבַּע לְבוּשׁוֹהִי וְיַסְחֵי בִשְׂרֵהּ בְּמֵי מַבּוּעַ וְיִדְכֵּי: יד וּבְיוֹמָא תְמִינָאָה יִסַּב לֵהּ תַּרְתֵּין שַׁפְנִינִין אוֹ תְרֵין בְּנֵי יוֹנָה וְיֵיתֵי לָקֳדָם יְיָ לִתְרַע מַשְׁכַּן זִמְנָא וְיִתְּנִנּוּן לְכַהֲנָא: טו וְיַעְבֵּד יָתְהוֹן כַּהֲנָא חַד

---רש"י---

זה הסיטו (שם פרשתא ג:א"ב-ב): (יג) וכי שבעת ימים טהורים מטומאת זיבה שלא יטהר. כְּסִפְסוֹק: שבעת ימים לטהרתו. יראה זוב, וכולן רצופין (שם פרק ה:ד"ו):

---RASHI ELUCIDATED---

זֶה הֱסִיטוֹ[1] – this is moving it.[1]

13. וְכִי יִטְהַר – This means כְּפִשְׁפּוּט – when he will cease having discharges.[2] שִׁבְעַת יָמִים לְטָהֳרָתוֹ – A SEVEN-DAY PERIOD FROM HIS CESSATION. שִׁבְעַת יָמִים – A seven-day period טְהוֹרִים מִטֻּמְאַת זִיבָה – pure of the impurity of discharging, שֶׁלֹּא יִרְאֶה זוֹב – that he will not see a discharge during those seven days,[3] וְכֻלָּן רְצוּפִין[4] – and they must all be consecutive.[4]

(see *Yosef Hallel*). The standard text, however, appears in Rashi to *Shabbos* 83a, s.v., בְּרַע הזב טמאין, and in Rashi to *Pesachim* 67b, s.v., וּמטמא כלי חרס.

1. The passage in *Toras Kohanim* (*Zavim, parshasa* 3:1-2) reads as follows: [The verse states,] "that the *zav* will touch." One might be able to think that even if the *zav* touched it on its outer surface it should be impure. It can be derived logically [that this is not so, as follows]: If a corpse, whose impurity is more severe [than that of a *zav*, in that one who becomes impure through contact with the dead must undergo sprinkling (see *Numbers* 19:19) while a *zav* does not, and in that a corpse transmits impurity to those under the same roof with it, while a *zav* does not], does not transmit impurity to pottery through its outer surface, does it not stand to reason that a *zav*, who has a lesser impurity, should not transmit impurity to pottery through its outer surface? No! If you say [that a corpse does not transmit impurity to pottery through its outer surface, it could be attributed to the fact] that if it rests on bedding or a seat it does not make them a primary source of impurity. Could you say this about a *zav*, who *does* make bedding or a seat a primary source? Since he makes [other objects impure with the status of] bedding and a seat, he might [also] make pottery impure through its outer surface.

[To teach us otherwise], the Torah says here, אֲשֶׁר יִגַּע בּוֹ, "that [the *zav*] will touch," and it says above [with reference to pottery that has absorbed the juices of a sin-offering], אֲשֶׁר תְּבֻשַּׁל בּוֹ, "in which it was cooked" (6:21). Just as בּוֹ of the above verse refers to the inside [of the vessel, for absorption of the juices comes about through the sin-offering being cooked inside the vessel of pottery], so, too, בּוֹ here refers to the inside. Once we have learned that [pottery] can only become impure through its inner air space, why does the Torah say, "that [the *zav*] will touch" [without specifying from the inside]? This refers to a touch which affects all of it [as implied by אֲשֶׁר יִגַּע בּוֹ rather than אֲשֶׁר יִגַּע בְּתוֹכוֹ (*Malbim*)]. Say that this is moving it [even indirectly, for example, by pushing it with a stick, for this affects the entire vessel].

2. וְכִי יִטְהַר הַזָּב, literally, "when the *zav* will become pure." This sounds as if it refers to the culmination of the purification procedure, when his impurity ceases. It cannot mean that here, however. Since the verse concludes, "He shall ... immerse his flesh in spring water, and become purified," the beginning of the verse must refer to an earlier stage; it refers to the cause of his eventual purity — the cessation of his discharge (*Mizrachi; Sifsei Chachamim*).

3. The verse does not mean that he must count seven days from the day that he is purified (as *Ibn Ezra*, for example, understands it). טָהֳרָה is used here in the same sense as in וְכִי יִטְהַר of the beginning of the verse, which Rashi interpreted as cessation of discharge.

4. *Toras Kohanim, Zavim, perek* 5:4-6. The construct form שִׁבְעַת indicates a period of seven consecutive days (see Rashi to *Exodus* 10:22, 29:30). In his comments to *Shabbos* 11b, however, Rashi cites the *Toras Kohanim*, which derives that the days must be consecutive from לְטָהֳרָתוֹ, "for his purification," which implies a single, unbroken, period of purification.

as a sin-offering and one as an olah-offering — thus the Kohen shall provide him atonement before Hashem *from his discharge.*

¹⁶ *A man from whom there is an emission of semen shall immerse his entire flesh in the water and remain impure until evening.* ¹⁷ *Any garment or anything of leather, upon which there shall be semen, shall be immersed in the water and remain impure until evening.* ¹⁸ *A woman with whom a man will have carnal relations, they shall immerse in the water and they shall remain impure until evening.*

¹⁹ *When a woman has a discharge — her discharge from her flesh being blood — she shall be in her state of separation for a seven-*

חַטָּאת וְהָאֶחָד עֹלָה וְכִפֶּר עָלָיו הַכֹּהֵן לִפְנֵי יהוה מִזּוֹבוֹ: ששי [שביעי] טז וְאִישׁ כִּי־תֵצֵא מִמֶּנּוּ שִׁכְבַת־זָרַע וְרָחַץ בַּמַּיִם אֶת־כָּל־בְּשָׂרוֹ וְטָמֵא עַד־הָעָרֶב: יז וְכָל־בֶּגֶד וְכָל־עוֹר אֲשֶׁר־יִהְיֶה עָלָיו שִׁכְבַת־זָרַע וְכֻבַּס בַּמַּיִם וְטָמֵא עַד־הָעָרֶב: יח וְאִשָּׁה אֲשֶׁר יִשְׁכַּב אִישׁ אֹתָהּ שִׁכְבַת־זָרַע וְרָחֲצוּ בַמַּיִם וְטָמְאוּ עַד־הָעָרֶב: יט וְאִשָּׁה כִּי־תִהְיֶה זָבָה דָּם יִהְיֶה זֹבָהּ בִּבְשָׂרָהּ שִׁבְעַת יָמִים תִּהְיֶה בְנִדָּתָהּ

──────── אונקלוס ────────

חַטָּאתָא וְחַד עֲלָתָא וִיכַפַּר עֲלוֹהִי כַהֲנָא קֳדָם יְיָ מִדּוֹבֵהּ: טז וּגְבַר אֲרֵי תִפּוֹק מִנֵּהּ שִׁכְבַת זַרְעָא וְיַסְחֵי בְמַיָּא יָת כָּל בִּסְרֵהּ וִיהֵי מְסָאָב עַד רַמְשָׁא: יז וְכָל לְבוּשׁ וְכָל מְשַׁךְ דִּי יְהֵי עֲלוֹהִי שִׁכְבַת זַרְעָא וְיִצְטַבַּע בְּמַיָּא וִיהֵי מְסָאָב עַד רַמְשָׁא: יח וְאִתְּתָא דִּי יִשְׁכּוּב גְּבַר יָתַהּ שִׁכְבַת זַרְעָא וְיִסְחוּן בְּמַיָּא וִיהוֹן מְסָאֲבִין עַד רַמְשָׁא: יט וְאִתְּתָא אֲרֵי תְהֵי דָיְבָא דַּם יְהֵי דוֹבַהּ בְּבִסְרַהּ שִׁבְעָא יוֹמִין תְּהֵי בְרִחוּקַהּ

──────── רש"י ────────

(יח) ורחצו במים. גְּזֵרַת מֶלֶךְ הִיא שֶׁתִּטַּמֵּא הָאִשָּׁה בְּבִיאָה, וְאֵין הַטַּעַם מִשּׁוּם נוֹגֵעַ בְּשִׁכְבַת זֶרַע שֶׁהֲרֵי מַגַּע בֵּית הַסְּתָרִים הוּא (שם פרק ו'י'): **(יט) כי תהיה זבה.** יָכוֹל מֵאֶחָד מִכָּל אֵיבָרֶיהָ, ת"ל וְהִיא גִּלְּתָה אֶת מְקוֹר דָּמֶיהָ ד:ב, אֵין דָּם מְטַמֵּא אֶלָּא הַבָּא מִן הַמָּקוֹר (ת"כ פרשתא ד:ב): **דם יהיה זובה.** אֵין זוֹבָהּ קָרוּי זוֹב לְטַמֵּא אֶלָּא אִם כֵּן הוּא אָדוֹם (נדה יט.):

──────── RASHI ELUCIDATED ────────

18. וְרָחֲצוּ בַמַּיִם — THEY SHALL IMMERSE THEMSELVES IN THE WATER. גְּזֵרַת מֶלֶךְ הִיא — **It is a decree of the King,**[1] שֶׁתִּטַּמֵּא הָאִשָּׁה — **that a woman becomes impure** בְּבִיאָה — **through intercourse.** וְאֵין הַטַּעַם — **The reason** for her impurity **is not** מִשּׁוּם נוֹגֵעַ בְּשִׁכְבַת זֶרַע — **because of** the impurity of **one who comes into contact with semen,** שֶׁהֲרֵי מַגַּע בֵּית הַסְּתָרִים הוּא[2] — **for [the contact with semen which comes about through intercourse] is contact of the unseen parts of organs.**[2]

19. כִּי תִהְיֶה זָבָה — WHEN [A WOMAN] HAS A DISCHARGE. יָכוֹל — **One might be able** to think that a discharge מֵאֶחָד מִכָּל אֵיבָרֶיהָ — **from one among any of her limbs** renders her impure. תַּלְמוּד לוֹמַר — To teach us otherwise, **the verse says:** ״וְהִיא גִּלְּתָה אֶת מְקוֹר דָּמֶיהָ״[3] — **"and she has bared the source of her blood,"**[3] implying אֵין דָּם מְטַמֵּא — that a discharge of **blood does not cause impurity** אֶלָּא הַבָּא מִן הַמָּקוֹר[4] — **except for that which comes from the uterus.**[4]

☐ דָּם יִהְיֶה זֹבָהּ — HER DISCHARGE FROM HER FLESH BEING BLOOD. אֵין זוֹבָהּ קָרוּי זוֹב — Her discharge is not called a discharge לְטַמֵּא — insofar as rendering her impure אֶלָּא אִם כֵּן — unless הוּא אָדוֹם[5] — it is red.[5]

---

1. A decree of God the rationale of which man cannot comprehend.

2. *Toras Kohanim, perek* 6:10. Such contact with semen does not cause impurity. Thus it is the act of consummated intercourse itself that brings about the woman's impurity.

3. Below 20:18. That verse speaks of the punishment for having relations with a woman who is impure due to menstruation.

4. *Toras Kohanim, Zavim, parshasa* 4:2. The verse could have said, וְהִיא גִּלְּתָה אֶת דָּמֶיהָ, "and she bared her blood." The apparently superfluous מְקוֹר, "source" or "uterus," teaches us that only blood that comes from the uterus makes a woman impure (*Mizrachi; Malbim; Be'er Yitzchak*).

5. *Niddah* 19a. "Blood" connotes redness, as it says, "Moab saw the waters, red as blood" (*II Kings* 3:22). Although the halachah is that there are five different colors of blood which can render a woman impure (*Yoreh Deah* 188), all fall into the category of red (see Rashi to *Niddah* 19a, s.v., דמיה דמיה).

day period and anyone who touches her shall remain impure until the evening. ²⁰ *Anything upon which she may recline during her state of separation shall become impure; and anything upon which she sits shall become impure.* ²¹ *Anyone who touches her bedding shall immerse his garments and immerse himself in the water, and he remains impure until evening.* ²² *Anyone who touches any utensil upon which she will sit shall immerse his garments and immerse himself in the water, and he remains impure until evening.* ²³ *And if someone is on the bedding or on*

וְכָל־הַנֹּגֵעַ בָּהּ יִטְמָא עַד־הָעָרֶב: כ וְכֹל אֲשֶׁר תִּשְׁכַּב עָלָיו בְּנִדָּתָהּ יִטְמָא וְכֹל אֲשֶׁר־תֵּשֵׁב עָלָיו יִטְמָא: כא וְכָל־הַנֹּגֵעַ בְּמִשְׁכָּבָהּ יְכַבֵּס בְּגָדָיו וְרָחַץ בַּמַּיִם וְטָמֵא עַד־הָעָרֶב: כב וְכָל־הַנֹּגֵעַ בְּכָל־כְּלִי אֲשֶׁר־תֵּשֵׁב עָלָיו יְכַבֵּס בְּגָדָיו וְרָחַץ בַּמַּיִם וְטָמֵא עַד־הָעָרֶב: כג וְאִם עַל־הַמִּשְׁכָּב הוּא אוֹ עַל

אונקלוס

וְכָל דְּיִקְרַב בַּהּ יְהֵי מְסָאָב עַד רַמְשָׁא: כ וְכֹל דִּי תִשְׁכּוּב עֲלוֹהִי בְּרַחוּקַהּ יְהֵי מְסָאָב וְכֹל דִּי תֵיתֵב עֲלוֹהִי יְהֵי מְסָאָב: כא וְכָל דְּיִקְרַב בְּמִשְׁכְּבַהּ יְצַבַּע לְבוּשׁוֹהִי וְיִסְחֵי בְמַיָּא וִיהֵי מְסָאָב עַד רַמְשָׁא: כב וְכָל דְּיִקְרַב בְּכָל מָנָא דִּי תֵיתֵב עֲלוֹהִי יְצַבַּע לְבוּשׁוֹהִי וְיִסְחֵי בְמַיָּא וִיהֵי מְסָאָב עַד רַמְשָׁא: כג וְאִם עַל מִשְׁכְּבָא הוּא אוֹ עַל

רש"י

בנדתה. כְּמוֹ וּמִתַּבֵּל יְנִידוּהוּ (איוב יח:יח) שֶׁהִיא מְנֻדָּה מִמַּגַּע כָּל אָדָם: תהיה בנדתה. אֲפִלּוּ לֹא רָאֲתָה אֶלָּא רְאִיָּה רִאשׁוֹנָה (ת"כ שם ה:): (כג) ואם. הָאֲמוּרָה בְמִקְרָא הָעֶלְיוֹן, שְׁטוּן כִּבּוּס בְּגָדִים: על המשכב הוא. הַשּׁוֹכֵב אוֹ הַיּוֹשֵׁב עַל מִשְׁכָּבָהּ אוֹ עַל מוֹשָׁבָהּ אֲפִלּוּ לֹא נָגַע בּוֹ [ס"א אף בּהּ] אַף הוּא בְּדַת טוּמְאָה הָאֲמוּרָה בְמִקְרָא הָעֶלְיוֹן, שְׁטוּן כִּבּוּס בְּגָדִים:

RASHI ELUCIDATED

☐ בְּנִדָּתָהּ — IN HER STATE OF SEPARATION. This word is כְּמוֹ ,,וּמִתֵּבֵל יְנִדֻּהוּ״ — like יְנִדֻּהוּ¹ in the phrase, "and from the universe they will banish him."¹ She is referred to in this way שֶׁהִיא מְנֻדָּה — because she is banished מִמַּגַּע כָּל אָדָם — from touching any person.²

☐ תִּהְיֶה בְנִדָּתָהּ — SHE SHALL BE IN HER STATE OF SEPARATION אֲפִילוּ לֹא רָאֲתָה — even if she did not see anything³ אֶלָּא רְאִיָּה רִאשׁוֹנָה — but the first perception of a discharge of blood.³

23. וְאִם עַל הַמִּשְׁכָּב הוּא — AND IF SOMEONE IS ON THE BEDDING.⁴ הַשּׁוֹכֵב — One who lies אוֹ הַיּוֹשֵׁב — or who sits עַל מִשְׁכָּבָהּ — on her bedding אוֹ עַל מוֹשָׁבָהּ — or on her seat, ⁵אֲפִילוּ לֹא נָגַע בּוֹ — even if he did not make direct **contact with it**,⁵ אַף הוּא בְּדַת טֻמְאָה — he, too, is included in the law of impurity הָאֲמוּרָה בַמִּקְרָא הָעֶלְיוֹן — which is stated in the verse above, שֶׁטָּעוּן כִּבּוּס בְּגָדִים — that he requires immersion of garments.⁶

---

1. *Job* 18:18.
2. She is barred from touching her husband. Furthermore, in the days of the *Beis HaMikdash*, her contact with others was limited due to her state of impurity, lest she transmit her impurity to other objects.
3. *Toras Kohanim, Zavim, parshasa* 4:5. Had the verse meant that the flow of blood must last for seven days for there to be impurity, it would have said שִׁבְעַת יָמִים תִּטְמָא, "She will have an impurity by her state of separation for a seven-day period." Verbs of being such as תִּהְיֶה connote continuous states. Thus, שִׁבְעַת יָמִים תִּהְיֶה בְנִדָּתָהּ, "She shall be in her state of separation for a seven-day period," implies that the state of separation always lasts for at least seven days, even if it was brought on by only a single discharge (*Malbim*).
4. See note 8 on page 180.
5. Our text reads בּוֹ, "with it," using the masculine pronominal suffix. The antecedent of "it" is then מִשְׁכָּב or מוֹשָׁב, since these are masculine nouns. Rashi, then, is repeating what he stated in his commentary to

verse 6 above. Some editions read בָּהּ, using the feminine pronominal suffix. If so, the word cannot be translated "with it" for there is no feminine antecedent. Rashi teaches that even if he doesn't have contact "with her," he nevertheless becomes impure.
6. Our verse appears to deal with the same subject as verses 21 and 22 — one who touches the bedding or the seat of a woman impure because of menstruation — but states a different law in that situation, for while verses 21 and 22 require immersion of garments, our verse does not. Rashi, based on *Toras Kohanim*, therefore interprets our verse as referring to cases not mentioned in the above verses. The first phrase of the verse, וְאִם עַל הַמִּשְׁכָּב הוּא, "and if someone is on the bedding," is a continuation of the preceding verses. Not only does one who actually touches the bedding and the seat require immersion of himself and his garments, but even someone who is merely "*on* the bedding," without touching it. Rashi, in his next comment, interprets וְכָל הַכְּלִי, which refers to a situation where immersion of garments is

the utensil upon which she is sitting, when he touches it, he shall become impure until evening. ²⁴ *If a man lies with her, and her state of separation will be upon him and he will be impure for a seven-day period; any bedding upon which he may recline shall become impure.*
²⁵ *If a woman's blood flows for many days outside of her period of separation,*

הַכְּלִ֛י אֲשֶׁר־הִ֥וא יֹשֶֽׁבֶת־עָלָ֖יו
בְּנָגְעוֹ־ב֑וֹ יִטְמָ֖א עַד־הָעָֽרֶב: וְאִ֡ם
שָׁכֹב֩ יִשְׁכַּ֨ב אִ֜ישׁ אֹתָ֗הּ וּתְהִ֤י
נִדָּתָהּ֙ עָלָ֔יו וְטָמֵ֖א שִׁבְעַ֣ת יָמִ֑ים
וְכָל־הַמִּשְׁכָּ֛ב אֲשֶׁר־יִשְׁכַּ֥ב עָלָ֖יו
יִטְמָֽא: וְאִשָּׁ֞ה כִּֽי־יָז֣וּב ז֗וֹב
דָּמָ֞הּ יָמִ֤ים רַבִּים֙ בְּלֹ֣א עֶת־נִדָּתָ֔הּ

――― אונקלוס ―――

מָנָא דִּי הִיא יָתְבָא עֲלוֹהִי בְּמִקְרְבֵהּ בֵּהּ יְהֵי מְסָאָב עַד רַמְשָׁא: ^{כד}וְאִם מִשְׁכַּב יִשְׁכּוּב גְּבַר יָתַהּ וּתְהֵי רְחוּקַהּ עֲלוֹהִי וִיהֵי מְסָאָב שַׁבְעָא יוֹמִין וְכָל מִשְׁכְּבָא דִּי יִשְׁכּוּב עֲלוֹהִי יְהֵי מְסָאָב: ^{כה}וְאִתְּתָא אֲרֵי יְדוּב דּוֹב דְּמַהּ יוֹמִין סַגִּיאִין בְּלָא עִדַּן רְחוּקַהּ

――― רש"י ―――

עַל הַכְּלִי. לְרַבּוֹת אֶת הַמֶּרְכָּב (שם טו): **בְּנָגְעוֹ בוֹ.** אֵינוֹ מְדַבֵּר אֶלָּא עַל הַמֶּרְכָּב שֶׁנִּתְרַבָּה מֵעַל הַכְּלִי. **בְּנָגְעוֹ בוֹ יִטְמָא.** וְאֵינוֹ טָעוּן כִּבּוּס בְּגָדִים, שֶׁהַמֶּרְכָּב אֵין מְגַעוֹ מְטַמֵּא אָדָם לְטַמֵּא בְגָדִים (שם): (כד) **וּתְהִי נִדָּתָהּ עָלָיו.** יָכוֹל יַעֲלֶה לְרַגְלָהּ, שֶׁאִם בָּא עָלֶיהָ בַּחֲמִישִׁי לְנִדָּתָהּ לֹא יִטַּמֵּא אֶלָּא שְׁלֹשָׁה יָמִים כְּמוֹתָהּ, ת"ל וְטָמֵא שִׁבְעַת יָמִים. וּמַה ת"ל וּתְהִי נִדָּתָהּ עָלָיו, מַה הִיא מְטַמְּאָה אָדָם וּכְלִי חֶרֶס אַף הוּא מְטַמֵּא אָדָם וּכְלִי חֶרֶס (ת"כ פרק ז'; נדה לג.): **(כה) יָמִים** **רַבִּים.** שְׁלֹשָׁה יָמִים. **בְּלֹא עֶת נִדָּתָהּ.** אַחַר שֶׁיָּצְאוּ שִׁבְעַת יְמֵי נִדָּתָהּ (ת"כ פרשתא ה' ע':; נדה עב:-עג.):

――― RASHI ELUCIDATED ―――

☐ **עַל הַכְּלִי** — ON THE UTENSIL. This is stated **לְרַבּוֹת אֶת הַמֶּרְכָּב** — to include the riding equipment.[1]
☐ **בְּנָגְעוֹ בוֹ** — WHEN HE TOUCHES IT. **אֵינוֹ מְדַבֵּר אֶלָּא עַל הַמֶּרְכָּב** — This[2] refers only to the riding equipment **שֶׁנִּתְרַבָּה מֵ...עַל הַכְּלִי** — which has been included from the words **"on the utensil."**[3]
☐ **בְּנָגְעוֹ בוֹ יִטְמָא** — WHEN HE TOUCHES IT, HE SHALL BECOME IMPURE. **וְאֵינוֹ טָעוּן** — But he does not require **כִּבּוּס בְּגָדִים** — immersion of garments, **שֶׁהַמֶּרְכָּב אֵין מַגָּעוֹ מְטַמֵּא אָדָם** — for with respect to riding equipment, touching it does not make a man impure[4] **לְטַמֵּא בְגָדִים** — to, in turn, make garments impure.[4]

24. וּתְהִי נִדָּתָהּ עָלָיו — AND HER STATE OF SEPARATION WILL BE UPON HIM. **יָכוֹל** — One might be able to think **יַעֲלֶה לְרַגְלָהּ** — that he should ascend from his impurity when her time of separation has ended, that is, **שֶׁאִם בָּא עָלֶיהָ** — that if he had relations with her **בַּחֲמִישִׁי לְנִדָּתָהּ** — on the fifth day of her state of separation **לֹא יִטַּמֵּא אֶלָּא שְׁלֹשָׁה יָמִים** — he should be impure for only three days, the fifth, sixth, and seventh days of her state of impurity, **כְּמוֹתָהּ** — like her.[5] **תַּלְמוּד לוֹמַר** — To teach us otherwise, the verse says, **וְטָמֵא שִׁבְעַת יָמִים** — "and he will be impure for a seven-day period." **וּמַה תַּלְמוּד לוֹמַר** — Why then does the Torah say, **וּתְהִי נִדָּתָהּ עָלָיו** — "and her state of separation will be upon him"? To teach us, **מַה הִיא מְטַמְּאָה אָדָם וּכְלִי חֶרֶס** — just as she transmits impurity to people and pottery, **אַף הוּא מְטַמֵּא אָדָם וּכְלִי חֶרֶס** — he too transmits impurity to people and pottery.[6]

25. יָמִים רַבִּים — MANY DAYS. This means [7] **שְׁלֹשָׁה יָמִים** — three days.[7]

☐ **בְּלֹא עֶת נִדָּתָהּ** — OUTSIDE OF HER PERIOD OF SEPARATION, that is [8] **אַחַר שֶׁיָּצְאוּ שִׁבְעַת יְמֵי נִדָּתָהּ** — immediately after the seven days of her separation have elapsed.[8]

---

1. *Toras Kohanim, Zavim, parshasa* 4:15. See preceding note.
2. This part of the verse, which speaks of one who receives impurity through touching without the impurity extending to his clothing, refers . . .
3. As mentioned in Rashi's preceding comment.
4. *Toras Kohanim, Zavim, parshasa* 4:15.
5. Since the verse says, *"her state of separation* shall be upon him," one might think that his impurity is not only of the same type as hers, but matches that of the particular woman he had relations with in every detail (*Sefer Zikaron*).
6. *Toras Kohanim, perek* 7:3; *Niddah* 33a.
7. *Toras Kohanim, Zavim, parshasa* 5:9-10. When the Torah uses a plural noun without specifying a number, the implication is two, for that is the minimum amount for which the plural is used. Thus, יָמִים, "days," implies two days. The addition of רַבִּים, "many," implies an additional day (*Mizrachi; Sifsei Chachamim*).
8. *Toras Kohanim, perek* 8:1-2; *Niddah* 72b-73a.

or if she has a flow beyond her separation, all the days of her impure flow shall be like the days of her separation; she is impure. ²⁶ *Any bedding upon which she may lie throughout the days of her flow shall be to her like the bedding of her state of separation; any vessel upon which she may sit shall be impure, like the impurity of her state of separation.*

אוֹ כִי־תָזוּב עַל־נִדָּתָהּ כָּל־יְמֵי זוֹב טֻמְאָתָהּ כִּימֵי נִדָּתָהּ תִּהְיֶה טְמֵאָה הִוא: כו כָּל־הַמִּשְׁכָּב אֲשֶׁר־תִּשְׁכַּב עָלָיו כָּל־יְמֵי זוֹבָהּ כְּמִשְׁכַּב נִדָּתָהּ יִהְיֶה־לָהּ וְכָל־הַכְּלִי אֲשֶׁר תֵּשֵׁב עָלָיו טָמֵא יִהְיֶה כְּטֻמְאַת נִדָּתָהּ:

— אונקלוס —

אוֹ אֲרֵי תְדוֹב עַל רְחוּקַהּ כָּל יוֹמֵי דוֹב סוֹבְתַהּ תְּהֵי מְסָאָבָא הִיא: כו כָּל מִשְׁכְּבָא דִי תִשְׁכּוּב עֲלוֹהִי כָּל יוֹמֵי דוֹבַהּ כְּמִשְׁכַּב רְחוּקַהּ יְהֵי לַהּ וְכָל מָנָא דִי תֵיתֵב עֲלוֹהִי מְסָאָב יְהֵי כְּסוֹאֲבַת רְחוּקַהּ:

— רש"י —

או כי תזוב. אֶת שְׁלֹשֶׁת הַיָּמִים הַלָּלוּ: **על נדתה.** מוּפְלָג מִנִּדָּתָהּ יוֹם אֶחָד זוּ הִיא זָבָה (שם) וּמִשְׁפָּטָהּ חֲרוּץ בְּפָרָשָׁה זוֹ. וְלֹא כְּדַת הַנִּדָּה, שֶׁזּוֹ טְעוּנָה סְפִירַת שִׁבְעָה נְקִיִּים וְקָרְבָּן, וְהַגָּדָה אֵינָהּ טְעוּנָה סְפִירַת שִׁבְעָה נְקִיִּים אֶלָּא שִׁבְעַת יָמִים תִּהְיֶה בְנִדָּתָהּ בֵּין רוֹאָה בֵּין שְׁאֵינָהּ רוֹאָה. וְדָרְשׁוּ בְּפָרָשָׁה זוֹ אַחַד עָשָׂר יוֹם שֶׁבֵּין סוֹף נִדָּה לִתְחִלַּת נִדָּה, שֶׁכָּל שְׁלֹשָׁה רְצוּפִין שֶׁתִּרְאֶה בְּאֶחָד עָשָׂר יוֹם הַלָּלוּ תְּהֵא זָבָה (ת"כ שם ב'/ד'; נדה שם):

— RASHI ELUCIDATED —

אֶת שְׁלֹשֶׁת הַיָּמִים הַלָּלוּ — **these three days.**[1] אוֹ כִי תָזוּב — OR IF SHE HAS A FLOW ☐ עַל נִדָּתָה — BEYOND HER SEPARATION, מֻפְלָג — which is **distant** in time מִנִּדָּתָהּ — **from her period of separation** by יוֹם אֶחָד — **one day** or more, [2] זוֹ הִיא זָבָה — **this**, i.e., either of these cases, **is a case** of *zavah*.[2] וּמִשְׁפָּטָהּ חָרוּץ — **Her law is ruled upon** בְּפָרָשָׁה זוֹ — **in this portion** of the Torah.[3] וְלֹא כְּדַת הַנִּדָּה — **It is not like the law of a woman impure due to menstruation**,[4] שֶׁזּוּ — **for** in order to become pure, **this** [*zavah*], who has a discharge after the seventh day from the onset of her menstrual flow, טְעוּנָה — **requires** סְפִירַת שִׁבְעָה נְקִיִּים — **a count of seven clean** days without a discharge, וְקָרְבָּן — **and an offering.** וְהַנִּדָּה — But the *niddah* אֵינָהּ טְעוּנָה — **does not require** סְפִירַת שִׁבְעָה נְקִיִּים — **a count of seven clean** days, אֶלָּא — **but rather,** "שִׁבְעַת יָמִים תִּהְיֶה בְנִדָּתָהּ — **"she shall be in her state of separation for a seven-day period"**[5] בֵּין רוֹאָה — **whether she sees** blood beyond her initial flow, בֵּין שֶׁאֵינָהּ רוֹאָה — **or whether she does not see** any more blood.[6] וְדָרְשׁוּ בְּפָרָשָׁה זוֹ — [The Sages] interpreted this portion of the Torah as indicating אַחַד עָשָׂר יוֹם — **the eleven days** שֶׁבֵּין סוֹף נִדָּה — **that** intervene **between the end of** one period of separation לִתְחִלַּת נִדָּה — **and the beginning of** the next **period of separation,** שֶׁכָּל שְׁלֹשָׁה רְצוּפִין — **that any three consecutive days** שֶׁתִּרְאֶה — **in which she will see** a discharge of blood בְּאַחַד עָשָׂר יוֹם הַלָּלוּ — **during these eleven days,** [7] תְּהֵא זָבָה — **she will become a** *zavah*.[7]

---

1. Although יָמִים רַבִּים, "many days," at the beginning of the verse was not stated explicitly with reference to the flow which is עַל נִדָּתָהּ, "beyond her separation," it applies to that phrase, as well as to the flow which is בְּלֹא עֵת נִדָּתָהּ, "outside of her period of separation" (*Mizrachi; Sifsei Chachamim*).
2. *Toras Kohanim, perek* 8:1-2; *Niddah* 72b-73a.
3. Beginning with verse 25 above.
4. Discussed in verses 19-24.
5. Above v. 19.
6. At the end of seven days she can purify herself through immersion, without bringing offerings. According to contemporary halachic practice, however, a woman who has any uterine discharge of blood at any time must wait for a period of at least five days or longer, until her discharge has stopped, and then have seven days free of discharge before immersion.
7. *Toras Kohanim, perek* 8:2-4; *Niddah* 73a. The first time a woman has a flow of blood, she becomes impure by the law of *niddah*, a woman in a state of separation. She remains in this state for seven days. If her flow has ended by the end of the seventh day, she can purify herself by immersion in a *mikveh*. If she has a flow of blood during the next eleven days she is subject to the laws of *zivah*, the impurity brought on by discharging. If that flow lasts only one day, or for not more than two consecutive days of those eleven, she may immerse herself on the day after the flow ceases. If she has no flow on that day, she is pure. If she has a flow for three or more consecutive days during those eleven, she cannot immerse herself until she has seven days free of any flow. If she has no flow during those eleven days, or if she had a flow of no more than two days, or even if she had a flow of three consecutive days, but her seven clean days after *zivah* elapsed after the eleven-day period, she is again subject to the law of *niddah*.

²⁷ *Anyone who touches them shall become impure; he shall immerse his garments and immerse himself in the water, and he remains impure until evening.* ²⁸ *If she ceases her flow, she must count seven days for herself, and afterwards she can be purified.* ²⁹ *On the eighth day she shall take for herself two turtledoves or two young doves; she shall bring them to the Kohen, to the entrance of the Tent of Meeting.* ³⁰ *The Kohen shall make one a sin-offering and one an olah-offering; the Kohen shall provide atonement for her before* HASHEM *from her impure flow.*
³¹ *You shall separate the Children of Israel from their impurity; and they shall not die as a result of their impurity if they make impure My Tabernacle that is among them.* ³² *This is the law concerning the zav, and from whom*

כז וְכָל־הַנּוֹגֵעַ בָּם יִטְמָא וְכִבֶּס בְּגָדָיו וְרָחַץ בַּמַּיִם וְטָמֵא עַד־הָעָרֶב:
כח וְאִם־טָהֲרָה מִזּוֹבָהּ וְסָפְרָה לָהּ שִׁבְעַת יָמִים וְאַחַר תִּטְהָר:
כט שביעי וּבַיּוֹם הַשְּׁמִינִי תִּקַּח־לָהּ שְׁתֵּי תֹרִים אוֹ שְׁנֵי בְּנֵי יוֹנָה וְהֵבִיאָה אוֹתָם אֶל־הַכֹּהֵן אֶל־פֶּתַח אֹהֶל מוֹעֵד:
ל וְעָשָׂה הַכֹּהֵן אֶת־הָאֶחָד חַטָּאת וְאֶת־הָאֶחָד עֹלָה וְכִפֶּר עָלֶיהָ הַכֹּהֵן לִפְנֵי יהוה מִזּוֹב טֻמְאָתָהּ:
לא מפטיר וְהִזַּרְתֶּם אֶת־בְּנֵי־יִשְׂרָאֵל מִטֻּמְאָתָם וְלֹא יָמֻתוּ בְּטֻמְאָתָם בְּטַמְּאָם אֶת־מִשְׁכָּנִי אֲשֶׁר בְּתוֹכָם: לב זֹאת תּוֹרַת הַזָּב וַאֲשֶׁר

— אונקלוס —

כזוְכָל דְּיִקְרַב בְּהוֹן יְהֵי מְסָאָב וִיצַבַּע לְבוּשׁוֹהִי וְיִסְחֵי בְמַיָּא וִיהֵי מְסָאָב עַד רַמְשָׁא: כחוְאִם דְּכִיאַת מִדּוֹבַהּ וְתִמְנֵי לַהּ שַׁבְעָא יוֹמִין וּבָתַר כֵּן תִּדְכֵּי: כטוּבְיוֹמָא תְמִינָאָה תִסַּב לַהּ תַּרְתֵּין שַׁפְנִינִין אוֹ תְרֵין בְּנֵי יוֹנָה וְתַיְתִי יָתְהוֹן לְוָת כַּהֲנָא לִתְרַע מַשְׁכַּן זִמְנָא: לוְיַעְבֵּד כַּהֲנָא יָת חַד חַטָּאתָא וְיָת חַד עֲלָתָא וִיכַפֵּר עֲלַהּ כַּהֲנָא קֳדָם יְיָ מִדּוֹב סוֹבְתַהּ: לאוְתַפְרְשׁוּן יָת בְּנֵי יִשְׂרָאֵל מִסּוֹאֲבָתְהוֹן וְלָא יְמוּתוּן בְּסוֹאֲבָתְהוֹן בְּסָאָבוּתְהוֹן יָת מַקְדְּשִׁי דִּי בֵינֵיהוֹן: לבדָּא אוֹרַיְתָא דְדוֹבָנָא

— רש"י —

(לא) **וְהִזַּרְתֶּם.** אֵין נְזִירָה אֶלָּא פְּרִישָׁה, וְכֵן נְזֹרוּ אָחוֹר (ישעיה א:ד) וְכֵן נְזִיר אֶחָיו (בראשית מט:כו): **וְלֹא יָמֻתוּ בְטֻמְאָתָם.** הֲרֵי הַכָּרֵת שֶׁל מְטַמֵּא מִקְדָּשׁ קָרוּי מִיתָה (ספרי חקת קכה): (לב) **זֹאת תּוֹרַת הַזָּב.** בַּעַל רְאִיָּה אַחַת, וּמַהוּ תוֹרָתוֹ:

— RASHI ELUCIDATED —

31. וְהִזַּרְתֶּם — YOU SHALL SEPARATE. אֵין נְזִירָה אֶלָּא פְּרִישָׁה — The term נְזִירָה, from נזר, the root of וְהִזַּרְתֶּם, means nothing but setting apart. ¹״וְכֵן ,,נָזֹרוּ אָחוֹר — Similarly נזרו in the phrase, **"They separated themselves to the rear"**;[1] ²״וְכֵן ,,נְזִיר אֶחָיו — similarly נְזִיר in the phrase, **"the one separated from his brothers."**[2]

□ וְלֹא יָמֻתוּ בְּטֻמְאָתָם — AND THEY SHALL NOT DIE AS A RESULT OF THEIR IMPURITY. הֲרֵי הַכָּרֵת — See, now, that the *kares*[3] שֶׁל מְטַמֵּא מִקְדָּשׁ — of one who makes the Sanctuary impure, i.e., one who enters the grounds of the *Beis HaMikdash* or the Tabernacle while impure, קָרוּי מִיתָה — is called **"death."**[4]

32. זֹאת תּוֹרַת הַזָּב — THIS IS THE LAW CONCERNING THE ZAV, בַּעַל רְאִיָּה אֶחָת — one who had one perception of a discharge.[5] וּמַהוּ תוֹרָתוֹ — And what is his law? ...

---

1. *Isaiah* 1:4; see Rashi there.
2. *Genesis* 49:26; see Onkelos and Rashi there.
3. Literally, "excision." According to Rashi (*Genesis* 17:14, *Leviticus* 17:9) this means that the sinner dies childless and suffers premature death.
4. *Sifrei, Chukas* 125. When the Torah speaks of a punishment of "death" without further specification, it could be understood as מִיתָה בִּידֵי שָׁמַיִם, "death by the hands of heaven," by which the sinner himself dies prematurely, but does not involve his children. *Numbers* 19:20 has stated explicitly, however, that the punishment for entering the grounds of the *Beis HaMikdash* while impure is *kares*, by which not only does he die prematurely, but his offspring die, as well (see Rashi to *Kesubos* 30a). "Dying" of our verse thus refers to *kares*. It, too, can properly be referred to by Scripture as "dying," for it is a punishment by which the sinner dies (see *Mizrachi; Sifsei Chachamim*).

5. "A person who has his discharge" is mentioned again in the following verse. The apparently superfluous הַזָּב, "the man impure due to discharge," of our verse, is used to teach us the law of a person who has a discharge on only one day, which has not yet been given by Scripture (*Sefer Zikaron*).

| *there is an emission of semen, through which he becomes impure.* ³³ *and concerning a woman who suffers through her separation, and a person who has his discharge, whether male or female, and concerning a man who lies with an impure woman.* | תֵּצֵא מִמֶּנּוּ שִׁכְבַת־זֶרַע לְטָמְאָה־ בָהּ: וְהַדָּוָה בְּנִדָּתָהּ וְהַזָּב אֶת־זוֹבוֹ לַזָּכָר וְלַנְּקֵבָה וּלְאִישׁ אֲשֶׁר יִשְׁכַּב עִם־טְמֵאָה: פ פ פ | לג |

THE HAFTARAH FOR METZORA APPEARS ON PAGE 395.
When Rosh Chodesh Iyar coincides with Metzora, the regular Maftir and Haftarah
are replaced with the reading for Shabbas Rosh Chodesh, page 405.
When Shabbas HaGadol coincides with Metzora, the regular Haftarah is replaced
with the Haftarah for Shabbas HaGadol, page 415.

אונקלוס

וְדִי תִפּוֹק מִנֵּהּ שִׁכְבַת זַרְעָא לְסָאָבָא בַהּ: לגּ וְלִדְסוֹבַתְהָּא בְרִחוּקַהּ וּלְדָאִיב יָת דּוֹבֵהּ לִדְכַר וּלְנֻקְבָא וְלִגְבַר דִּי יִשְׁכּוּב עִם מְסָאֲבָא:

רש"י

וַאֲשֶׁר תֵּצֵא מִמֶּנּוּ שִׁכְבַת זֶרַע. הֲרֵי הוּא כְּבַעַל קֶרִי, שְׁתֵּי רְאִיּוֹת וּבַעַל שָׁלֹשׁ רְאִיּוֹת, שֶׁתּוֹרָתָן מְפוֹרֶשֶׁת לְמַעְלָה (שם טמאת ערב (ת"כ שם ח): (לג) **וְהַזָּב אֶת זוֹבוֹ.** בַּעַל ט):

RASHI ELUCIDATED

□ וַאֲשֶׁר תֵּצֵא מִמֶּנּוּ שִׁכְבַת זֶרַע — AND FROM WHOM THERE IS AN EMISSION OF SEMEN. — הֲרֵי הוּא כְּבַעַל קֶרִי See, now, that [he who had only one perception of a discharge] is like one who is impure due to an emission of semen. ¹טָמֵא טֻמְאַת עָרֶב — He is impure with the impurity of evening.¹

33. וְהַזָּב אֶת זוֹבוֹ — AND A PERSON WHO HAS HIS DISCHARGE. בַּעַל שְׁתֵּי רְאִיּוֹת — One who had two perceptions וּבַעַל שָׁלֹשׁ רְאִיּוֹת — and one who had three perceptions ³שֶׁתּוֹרָתָן מְפוֹרֶשֶׁת לְמַעְלָה whose law has been stated explicitly above.²,³

---

1. *Toras Kohanim, perek* 8:8. Though he may immerse himself in the *mikveh* the same day as the discharge, and his impurity ends with the arrival of the evening which follows his immersion.
2. Verses 2 and 3. See Rashi to v. 3.
3. *Toras Kohanim, perek* 8:9.

פרשת אחרי

Parashas Acharei

16 ¹ HASHEM spoke to Moses after the death of Aaron's two sons, when they approached before HASHEM, and they died. ² And HASHEM said to Moses: Speak to Aaron, your brother — he may not come at all times into the Sanctuary, within the Curtain, in front of the Cover that is upon the Ark, and he will not die; for with a cloud I appear upon the Ark-cover.

טז א וַיְדַבֵּר יהוה אֶל־מֹשֶׁה אַחֲרֵי מוֹת שְׁנֵי בְּנֵי אַהֲרֹן בְּקָרְבָתָם לִפְנֵי־יהוה וַיָּמֻתוּ: ב וַיֹּאמֶר יהוה אֶל־מֹשֶׁה דַּבֵּר אֶל־אַהֲרֹן אָחִיךָ וְאַל־יָבֹא בְכָל־עֵת אֶל־הַקֹּדֶשׁ מִבֵּית לַפָּרֹכֶת אֶל־פְּנֵי הַכַּפֹּרֶת אֲשֶׁר עַל־הָאָרֹן וְלֹא יָמוּת כִּי בֶּעָנָן אֵרָאֶה עַל־הַכַּפֹּרֶת:

— אונקלוס —

א וּמַלִּיל יְיָ עִם מֹשֶׁה בָּתַר דְּמִיתוּ תְּרֵין בְּנֵי אַהֲרֹן בְּקָרוֹבֵיהוֹן אֶשָּׁתָא נוּכְרֵיתָא קֳדָם יְיָ וּמִיתוּ: ב וַאֲמַר יְיָ לְמֹשֶׁה מַלֵּל עִם אַהֲרֹן אָחוּךְ וְלָא יְהֵי עָלֵל בְּכָל עִדָּן לְקוּדְשָׁא מִגָּיו לְפָרֻכְתָּא לָקֳדָם כַּפֻּרְתָּא דִּי עַל אֲרוֹנָא וְלָא יְמוּת אֲרֵי בַּעֲנָנָא אֲנָא מִתְגְּלֵי עַל בֵּית כַּפֻּרְתָּא:

— רש"י —

(א) **וידבר ה' אל משה אחרי מות שני בני אהרן וגו'.** מַה תַּ"ל. [ס"א אֵין אָנוּ יוֹדְעִים מַה נֶּאֱמַר לוֹ בַּדִּבּוּר רִאשׁוֹן.] הָיָה רַבִּי אֶלְעָזָר בֶּן עֲזַרְיָה מוֹשְׁלוֹ מָשָׁל, לְחוֹלֶה שֶׁנִּכְנַס אֶצְלוֹ רוֹפֵא, אָמַר לוֹ אַל תֹּאכַל צוֹנֵן וְאַל תִּשְׁכַּב בְּטַחַב. בָּא אַחֵר וְאָמַר לוֹ אַל תֹּאכַל צוֹנֵן וְאַל תִּשְׁכַּב בְּטַחַב, שֶׁלֹּא תָמוּת כְּדֶרֶךְ שֶׁמֵּת פְּלוֹנִי. זֶה זֵרְזוֹ יוֹתֵר מִן הָרִאשׁוֹן. לְכָךְ נֶאֱמַר אַחֲרֵי מוֹת שְׁנֵי בְּנֵי אַהֲרֹן. וַיֹּאמֶר ה' אֶל מֹשֶׁה דַּבֵּר אֶל אַהֲרֹן אָחִיךְ וְאַל יָבֹא, (ב) **ולא ימות.** שֶׁאִם בָּא הוּא מֵת (שָׁם): **כי בענן אראה.** כִּי תָמִיד אֲנִי נִרְאֶה שָׁם עִם עַמּוּד עֲנָנִי, וּלְפִי שֶׁגִּלּוּי שְׁכִינָתִי שָׁם יִזָּהֵר שֶׁלֹּא יַרְגִּיל לָבֹא.

— RASHI ELUCIDATED —

16.

1. וַיְדַבֵּר ה' אֶל מֹשֶׁה אַחֲרֵי מוֹת שְׁנֵי בְּנֵי אַהֲרֹן וְגוֹמֵר — HASHEM SPOKE TO MOSES AFTER THE DEATH OF AARON'S TWO SONS, ETC. ² מַה תַּלְמוּד לוֹמַר — Why did the Torah say this?[1,2] הָיָה רַבִּי אֶלְעָזָר בֶּן עֲזַרְיָה מוֹשְׁלוֹ מָשָׁל — The Tanna R' Elazar ben Azaryah would explain it with a parable. לְחוֹלֶה — It can be compared to a sick person שֶׁנִּכְנַס אֶצְלוֹ רוֹפֵא — to whom a doctor entered to treat. אָמַר לוֹ — [The doctor] said to him, אַל תֹּאכַל צוֹנֵן — "Do not eat cold food, וְאַל תִּשְׁכַּב בַּטַּחַב — and do not lie in a damp, chilly place." בָּא אַחֵר — Another doctor came וְאָמַר לוֹ — and said to him, אַל תֹּאכַל צוֹנֵן — "Do not eat cold food, וְאַל תִּשְׁכַּב בַּטַּחַב — and do not lie in a damp, chilly place, שֶׁלֹּא תָמוּת — so that you will not die כְּדֶרֶךְ שֶׁמֵּת פְּלוֹנִי — the way that So-and-so died." זֶה זֵרְזוֹ — This second doctor roused him to follow his instructions יוֹתֵר מִן הָרִאשׁוֹן — more than the first. לְכָךְ נֶאֱמַר — This is why it says, "אַחֲרֵי מוֹת שְׁנֵי בְּנֵי אַהֲרֹן" — "after the death of Aaron's two sons."[3] וַיֹּאמֶר ה' אֶל מֹשֶׁה דַּבֵּר אֶל אַהֲרֹן "אָחִיךָ וְאַל יָבֹא" — And HASHEM said to Moses: Speak to Aaron, your brother — he may not come..." שֶׁלֹּא יָמוּת — so that he will not die כְּדֶרֶךְ שֶׁמֵּתוּ בָּנָיו — the way that his sons died.[4,5]

2. וְלֹא יָמוּת — AND HE WILL NOT DIE. שֶׁאִם בָּא — For if he comes into the Holy of Holies when he is not allowed to, ⁶הוּא מֵת — he will die.⁶

כִּי בֶּעָנָן אֵרָאֶה — FOR WITH A CLOUD I APPEAR. כִּי תָמִיד אֲנִי נִרְאֶה שָׁם — For I always appear there עִם עַמּוּד עֲנָנִי — with My pillar of cloud.⁷ וּלְפִי שֶׁגִּלּוּי שְׁכִינָתִי שָׁם — And because the Revelation of My Shechinah (immanent presence) is there, יִזָּהֵר — he should take care שֶׁלֹּא יַרְגִּיל לָבֹא — that he

---

1. Since our verse begins, "HASHEM spoke to Moses...," we would expect to be told what was said. The next verse, however, begins, "And HASHEM said to Moses...," indicating a new statement, without having told us what the first statement said. Thus, Rashi questions the purpose of our verse (see *Sefer Zikaron, Maskil LeDavid, Be'er Mayim Chaim, Devek Tov*, et al.).

Alternatively, Rashi's question is: Why did the Torah state when this command was given? (see *Maskil LeDavid*).

2. According to *Mizrachi*, the text of Rashi's question reads: אֵין אָנוּ יוֹדְעִים מַה נֶּאֱמַר לוֹ בַּדִּבּוּר רִאשׁוֹן, "We do not know what was said to him in the first statement!" This is the way it appears in *Toras Kohanim*, Rashi's source

for this comment.

3. In most editions this comment ends here, and the remainder appears as a separate comment. Merging the two comments into one is based on *Sefer Zikaron* and *Be'er Yitzchak*.

4. Similarly, Moses drew upon the example of Nadab and Abihu to rouse Aaron to deal carefully with matters having to do with the sanctity of the Tabernacle (*Sefer Zikaron*).

5. *Toras Kohanim, parshasa* 1:3-4.

6. *Toras Kohanim, parshasa* 1:4.

7. Rashi explains that בֶּעָנָן is understood as "with a cloud" rather than "in a cloud." If the verse had meant

16/3

³ With this shall Aaron come into the Sanctuary: with a bull, a young male of cattle, for a sin-offering and a ram for an olah-offering.

ג בְּזֹאת יָבֹא אַהֲרֹן אֶל־הַקֹּדֶשׁ בְּפַר
בֶּן־בָּקָר לְחַטָּאת וְאַיִל לְעֹלָה:

──── אונקלוס ────

ג בְּדָא יְהֵי עָלֵל אַהֲרֹן לְקוּדְשָׁא בְּתוֹר בַּר תּוֹרֵי לְחַטָּאתָא וּדְכַר לַעֲלָתָא:

──── רש"י ────

זהו פשוטו. ורבותינו דרשוהו, אל יבא כי אם בענן הקטרת ביום הכפורים (שם ו"ז; יומא נג.): **(ג) בזאת.** גימטריא שלו ארבע מאות ועשר רמז לבית [ס"א לבני בית] ראשון (ויק"ר כא:ז): **בזאת יבא אהרן וגו'.** ואף זו לא בכל עת כי אם ביום הכפורים, כמו שמפורש בסוף הפרשה, בחדש השביעי בעשור לחדש (להלן פסוק כט):

──── RASHI ELUCIDATED ────

should not come there regularly.[1] — זֶהוּ פְּשׁוּטוֹ — This is [the verse's] simple meaning. וְרַבּוֹתֵינוּ דְּרָשׁוּהוּ[2] — And our Rabbis interpreted it:[2] אַל יָבֹא — He may not come into the Sanctuary כִּי אִם בַּעֲנַן הַקְּטֹרֶת — except with the cloud of incense which he is to offer up there בְּיוֹם הַכִּפּוּרִים — on Yom Kippur.[3]

3. בְּזֹאת — WITH THIS. גִּימַטְרִיָּא שֶׁלּוֹ — Its gematria[4] is אַרְבַּע מֵאוֹת וָעֶשֶׂר — four hundred and ten, רֶמֶז לְבַיִת רִאשׁוֹן[5] — an allusion to the first Beis HaMikdash which stood for four hundred and ten years.[5]

□ בְּזֹאת יָבֹא אַהֲרֹן וְגוֹמֵר — WITH THIS SHALL AARON COME, ETC. וְאַף זוֹ לֹא בְּכָל עֵת — And even this is not to be done at any time, כִּי אִם בְּיוֹם הַכִּפּוּרִים — except on Yom Kippur, כְּמוֹ שֶׁמְּפֹרָשׁ — as stated explicitly בְּסוֹף הַפָּרָשָׁה — at the end of the portion, ,,בַּחֹדֶשׁ הַשְּׁבִיעִי בֶּעָשׂוֹר לַחֹדֶשׁ"[6] — "in the seventh month, on the tenth of the month."[6]

"in a cloud," then the words "upon the Ark-cover" would refer to the cloud, and the verse would have stated, שֶׁעַל הַכַּפֹּרֶת, "that is upon the Ark-cover" (Mizrachi).

א	ב	ג	ד	ה	ו	ז	ח	ט	י	כ	ל	מ	נ	ס	ע	פ	צ	ק	ר	ש	ת
1	2	3	4	5	6	7	8	9	10	20	30	40	50	60	70	80	90	100	200	300	400

1. The verse could be understood to imply that the fact that God appears in a cloud is the cause of the death penalty for entering the Holy of Holies without permission, but if He were to appear without the cloud there would be no death penalty. Rashi explains that it is the presence of the Shechinah which causes the death penalty, not the cloud. Rashi also explains that אֶרָאֶה in our verse does not indicate the simple future, but rather, an ongoing action (Mizrachi). Rashi also notes this verb form in his comments to Exodus 15:6,7.

2. Some editions read וּמִדְרָשׁוֹ, "the interpretation derived from it is."

3. Toras Kohanim, parshasa 1:6-13; Yoma 53a. According to this interpretation, the verse is understood, "He may not come at any time to the Sanctuary ... except for when I will appear with a cloud of smoke"; the cloud of the verse is not the pillar of cloud which regularly accompanied the presence of the Shechinah as it is according to the first interpretation, but rather the smoke cloud of incense burned in the Sanctuary by the Kohen Gadol on Yom Kippur (Mizrachi; Sifsei Chachamim). Furthermore, according to this interpretation, כִּי of our verse means "except," whereas according to the first interpretation it means "because" (Mizrachi; Sifsei Chachamim). Additionally, in this interpretation, אֶרָאֶה is a simple future, not a verb that indicates ongoing action.

4. גִּימַטְרִיָּא, gematria, refers to the numerical equivalent of Hebrew letters. Every letter corresponds to a number. The sum of the values of a word's letters form the gematria of that word. (See chart for letter values.)

5. Some early editions read לִשְׁנֵי בַיִת רִאשׁוֹן, "to the years of the first Beis HaMikdash."

Vayikra Rabbah 21:9. The verse says that Aaron is to come into the Sanctuary with two animals as offerings. Why then does it use בְּזֹאת, "with this," rather than בְּאֵלֶּה, "with these"? The Torah uses בְּזֹאת to allude to the fact that the first Beis HaMikdash would stand for 410 years (Minchas Yehudah; Sifsei Chachamim). The verse does not mean to imply that the prohibition against entering the Sanctuary at times other than Yom Kippur applies only to the period of the first Beis HaMikdash. Rather, the verse implies that the eighteen Kohanim who succeeded Aaron as Kohen Gadol during the period of the first Beis HaMikdash were all righteous men who carried on the tradition of their ancestor, Aaron. In this respect, Aaron is considered to have come into the Sanctuary for that entire 410-year period (Maskil LeDavid).

6. Below v. 29. Rashi in his comment to the preceding verse already stated that Aaron may come into the Sanctuary only when there is a smoke cloud of incense there on Yom Kippur. Still, he says that our verse also refers to Yom Kippur, so that it should not be understood as an additional situation in which entry to the Sanctuary is permitted; that is, he may come to the Sanctuary either with the smoke cloud of incense on Yom Kippur, or with a young bull for a sin-offering and a ram for an olah-offering during the rest of the year (Mizrachi; Sifsei Chachamim).

Alternatively, Vayikra Rabbah 21:7 cites an opinion that our verse refers to any day of the year. Aaron — but no other Kohen Gadol — was allowed to enter the Holy of Holies at any time, as long as he brought the offerings

⁴ *He shall don a sacred linen Kutoness; linen Michnasaim shall be upon his flesh, he shall gird himself with a linen Avneit, and cover his head with a linen Mitznefes; they are sacred garments —*

ד כְּתֹנֶת־בַּד קֹדֶשׁ יִלְבָּשׁ וּמִכְנְסֵי־בַד יִהְיוּ עַל־בְּשָׂרוֹ וּבְאַבְנֵט בַּד יַחְגֹּר וּבְמִצְנֶפֶת בַּד יִצְנֹף בִּגְדֵי־קֹדֶשׁ הֵם

―――――― אונקלוס ――――――

ד כִּתּוּנָא דְבוּצָא קוּדְשָׁא יִלְבַּשׁ וּמִכְנְסִין דְּבוּץ יְהוֹן עַל בִּסְרֵהּ וּבְהֶמְיָנָא דְבוּצָא יֵסַר וּמִצְנֶפְתָּא דְבוּצָא יָחֵת בְּרֵישֵׁהּ לְבוּשֵׁי קוּדְשָׁא אִנּוּן

―――――― רש"י ――――――

(ד) כתנת בד וגו'. מַגִּיד שֶׁאֵינוֹ מְשַׁמֵּשׁ לִפְנִים בִּשְׁמוֹנָה בְגָדִים שֶׁהוּא מְשַׁמֵּשׁ בָּהֶם בַּחוּץ שֶׁיֵּשׁ בָּהֶם זָהָב, לְפִי שֶׁאֵין קַטֵּיגוֹר נַעֲשֶׂה סָנֵיגוֹר (ר"ה כו.) אֶלָּא בְאַרְבָּעָה כְּכֹהֵן הֶדְיוֹט, וְכֻלָּן שֶׁל בּוּץ: **הדיוט, וכולן של בוץ** (ת"כ פרק א:ה): **קדש ילבש.** שֶׁיִּהְיוּ מִשֶּׁל הַקֹּדֶשׁ (שם י): **יצנף.** כְּתַרְגּוּמוֹ יַחֵת בְּרֵישֵׁיהּ, כְּמוֹ וַתַּנַּח בִּגְדוֹ (בראשית לט:טז) וַאֲחִתְּתֵהּ:

―――――― RASHI ELUCIDATED ――――――

4. כְּתֹנֶת בַּד וְגוֹמֵר — A [SACRED] LINEN *KUTONESS*, ETC. מַגִּיד — **This tells us** שֶׁאֵינוֹ מְשַׁמֵּשׁ לִפְנִים — **that he does not serve within the Holy of Holies**[1] בִּשְׁמוֹנָה בְגָדִים — **in the eight garments** שֶׁהוּא מְשַׁמֵּשׁ בָּהֶם — **in which he serves** בַּחוּץ — **outside of the Holy of Holies**[1] שֶׁיֵּשׁ בָּהֶם זָהָב — **which have gold in them.**[2] ³ לְפִי שֶׁאֵין קַטֵּיגוֹר נַעֲשֶׂה סָנֵיגוֹר — **For a prosecutor does not become a defense counselor.**[3] אֶלָּא — **Rather,** he serves בְּאַרְבָּעָה — **in four** garments כְּכֹהֵן הֶדְיוֹט — **like an ordinary Kohen,** וְכֻלָּן שֶׁל בּוּץ⁴ — **and all of them are** made **of linen.**[4]

□ קֹדֶשׁ יִלְבָּשׁ — HE SHALL DON A SACRED [LINEN *KUTONESS*]. This teaches ⁵שֶׁיְּהֵא מִשֶּׁל הַקֹּדֶשׁ — **that it shall belong to** *hekdesh*, i.e., it shall be the property of the *Beis HaMikdash*.[5]

□ יִצְנֹף — [HE SHALL] COVER HIS HEAD. This word is to be understood כְּתַרְגּוּמוֹ — as *Targum Onkelos* renders it, ״יַחֵת בְּרֵישֵׁהּ״ — which means, יַנִּיחַ בְּרֹאשׁוֹ — "he shall place upon his head,"[6] כְּמוֹ ״וַתַּנַּח בִּגְדוֹ״[7] — just as *Targum Onkelos* renders וַתַּנַּח in, "and she put his garment,"[7] ״וַאֲחִתְּתֵהּ״ — a verb of the same root as יָחֵת.

enumerated here. Rashi here presents a different view. He explains that the permission granted to Aaron to enter the Holy of Holies mentioned by our verse applies only on Yom Kippur. See the Gaon of Vilna in *Kol Eliyahu* for an elaboration of the opinion cited in *Vayikra Rabbah*.

1. לִפְנִים means, "inside." The term עֲבוֹדַת פְּנִים, "inside service," refers to the service performed by the Kohen Gadol in the Holy of Holies. By extension, it also includes certain services that are unique to Yom Kippur, such as the sprinklings in the Holy (see vv. 16,18 below) and the casting of lots for the goats (see v. 8 below).

בַּחוּץ, literally, "outside," refers to the entire *Beis HaMikdash* and the Courtyard except for the Holy of Holies. The term עֲבוֹדַת חוּץ, "outside service," refers to the services that are not unique to Yom Kippur.

2. These garments are described in *Exodus*, ch. 28.

3. *Rosh Hashanah* 26a. Gold brings to mind the sin of the Golden Calf. Thus, it is said to speak against Israel, to act as a prosecutor. It should not appear on the Kohen Gadol when he performs the special Yom Kippur service within the Holy of Holies, for this service is meant to defend Israel and gain them forgiveness.

4. *Toras Kohanim*, perek 1:5. These are the same four garments that an ordinary Kohen wears (see *Exodus* 28:40,42). However, unlike an ordinary Kohen — whose *Avneit* (sash), according to one opinion, contained wool — the Kohen Gadol's four garments were all of pure linen.

5. *Toras Kohanim*, perek 1:10. We know that these garments are sacred for the verse goes on to say, "they are sacred garments." The apparently superfluous קֹדֶשׁ, "sacred," is juxtaposed with יִלְבָּשׁ, "he shall don," to teach us that they must already be sacred at the time that he dons them, that is, they must be purchased from the funds of the *Beis HaMikdash*, not from Aaron's money (see *Devek Tov*; *Ho'il Moshe*). According to the Mishnah in *Yoma* 34b, a set amount was used from the sacred funds for these garments. If the Kohen Gadol desired, he could donate his own money to the *Beis HaMikdash* treasury so that more expensive garments could be made for him.

6. The verb צנף can mean covering something in a way that encompasses it entirely (see Rashi to *Isaiah* 22:18). But it cannot have that meaning here, for the *Mitznefes* did not cover and encompass the entire head of the Kohen Gadol. As Rashi notes in his comments to *Exodus* 28:37, the *Mitznefes* rested on the crown of his head. Rashi therefore cites *Targum Onkelos* to show that in our verse, צנף means "placing upon the head" (*Devek Tov; Nesinah LaGer; Be'er Rechovos*). Alternatively, צנף can be used as the verb for wrapping something around one's head in the manner of a turban. Rashi cites *Targum Onkelos* to show that the *Mitznefes* was *placed* upon the head, not wrapped around it (see *Amar N'kei*).

7. *Genesis* 39:16.

16/5-7 — טז/ה-ז

he shall immerse his flesh in the water and then don them. ⁵ *From the assembly of the Children of Israel he shall take two he-goats for a sin-offering and one ram for an olah-offering.* ⁶ *Aaron shall bring near his own sin-offering bull, and atone for himself and for his household.* ⁷ *He shall take the two he-goats*

וְרָחַץ בַּמַּיִם אֶת־בְּשָׂרוֹ וּלְבֵשָׁם: ה וּמֵאֵת עֲדַת בְּנֵי יִשְׂרָאֵל יִקַּח שְׁנֵי־שְׂעִירֵי עִזִּים לְחַטָּאת וְאַיִל אֶחָד לְעֹלָה: ו וְהִקְרִיב אַהֲרֹן אֶת־פַּר הַחַטָּאת אֲשֶׁר־לוֹ וְכִפֶּר בַּעֲדוֹ וּבְעַד בֵּיתוֹ: ז וְלָקַח אֶת־שְׁנֵי הַשְּׂעִירִם

───── אונקלוס ─────

וְיַסְחֵי בְמַיָּא יָת בִּסְרֵהּ וְיִלְבְּשִׁנּוּן: ה וּמִן כְּנִשְׁתָּא דִּבְנֵי יִשְׂרָאֵל יִסַּב תְּרֵין צְפִירֵי עִזִּין לְחַטָּאתָא וּדְכַר חַד לַעֲלָתָא: ו וִיקָרֵב אַהֲרֹן יָת תּוֹרָא דְחַטָּאתָא דִּי לֵהּ וִיכַפַּר עֲלוֹהִי וְעַל אֱנַשׁ בֵּיתֵהּ: ז וְיִסַּב יָת תְּרֵין צְפִירִין

───── רש"י ─────

ורחץ במים. אותו היום טעון טבילה בכל חליפותיו (ת"כ שם יא"ב; יומא לב.) וחמש פעמים היה מחליף מעבודת פנים לעבודת חוץ ומחוץ לפנים, ומשנה מבגדי זהב לבגדי לבן ומבגדי לבן לבגדי זהב, ובכל חליפה טעון טבילה ושני קדוש ידים ורגלים מן

הכיור (ת"כ פרק ו:ה"ו; יומא שם): **(ו) את פר החטאת אשר לו.** [הוא] האמור למעלה (פסוק ג), ולמדך כאן שמשלו הוא בא ולא משל צבור (ת"כ פרשתא ב:ב; יומא ג:): **ובכפר בעדו ובעד ביתו.** מתודה עליו עוונותיו ועונות ביתו (ת"כ שם ב"ג; יומא לז:):

───── RASHI ELUCIDATED ─────

□ וְרָחַץ בַּמַּיִם — HE SHALL IMMERSE [HIS FLESH] IN THE WATER. אוֹתוֹ הַיּוֹם — On that day, Yom Kippur, טָעוּן טְבִילָה — he requires immersion בְּכָל חֲלִיפוּתָיו¹ — each time he changes clothing.¹ חָמֵשׁ פְּעָמִים – Five times הָיָה מַחֲלִיף – he would change clothing: when he would go מֵעֲבוֹדַת פְּנִים – from service of the inside, i.e., from performing parts of the service which are done inside the Holy of Holies, לַעֲבוֹדַת חוּץ – to service of the outside;² וּמִחוּץ לִפְנִים – and from the outside service to the inside service. וּמְשַׁנֶּה – He would change מִבִּגְדֵי זָהָב – from garments of gold,³ used for the parts of the service performed outside the Holy of Holies, לְבִגְדֵי לָבָן – to garments of white linen, used for the parts of the service performed inside the Holy of Holies, וּמִבִּגְדֵי לָבָן – and from garments of white back לְבִגְדֵי זָהָב – to garments of gold. וּבְכָל חֲלִיפָה – At each change of clothing טָעוּן טְבִילָה – he required immersion וּשְׁנֵי קִדּוּשֵׁי יָדַיִם וְרַגְלַיִם – and two sanctifications of hands and feet⁴ מִן הַכִּיוֹר⁵ – from the *Kiyyor*.⁵

6. אֶת פַּר הַחַטָּאת אֲשֶׁר לוֹ – HIS OWN SIN-OFFERING BULL. ⁶{הוּא} הָאָמוּר לְמַעְלָה – {it is} that which was mentioned above.⁶ וְלִמֶּדְךָ כָּאן – [The Torah] teaches you here שֶׁמִּשֶּׁלּוֹ הוּא בָא – that it comes from his own, i.e., that it is purchased with his own money, ⁷וְלֹא מִשֶּׁל צִבּוּר – and not from that of the public funds.⁷

□ וְכִפֶּר בַּעֲדוֹ וּבְעַד בֵּיתוֹ — AND ATONE FOR HIMSELF AND FOR HIS HOUSEHOLD. מִתְוַדֶּה עָלָיו – He confesses over it עֲוֹנוֹתָיו – his sins ⁸וַעֲוֹנוֹת בֵּיתוֹ – and the sins of his household.⁸

---

1. *Toras Kohanim, perek* 1:11-12; *Yoma* 32a. Anyone entering the Courtyard had to immerse in a *mikveh* first. Therefore all Kohanim, including the Kohen Gadol, would immerse themselves before they would enter the Courtyard each day. Our verse does not refer to that immersion, however. Since the verse says וְרָחַץ בְּשָׂרוֹ בַּמַּיִם וּלְבֵשָׁם, "He shall wash his flesh in water and then don them," it refers to an immersion which is a precondition for donning his garments. From here we learn that the Kohen Gadol immersed himself every time he changed garments on Yom Kippur (*Mizrachi*; *Sifsei Chachamim*).

2. See note 1 on page 194.

3. That is, garments that contained gold in their composition.

4. See *Exodus* 30:19 and Rashi there for the sanctification procedure.

5. *Toras Kohanim, perek* 6:5-6; *Yoma* 32a. The *Kiyyor* was a water-filled vessel from which the Kohanim washed ("sanctified") their hands and feet. See *Exodus* 30:17-21. The Kohen Gadol performed the sanctification procedure twice with each change of garments: once before removing the ones he was wearing and once after donning the fresh ones (*Yoma* 34b).

6. Above v. 3.

7. *Toras Kohanim, parshasa* 2:2; *Yoma* 3b. The only bull of a sin-offering that has been mentioned is the one Aaron is commanded to bring in verse 3. The Torah must be referring to that bull. But by saying אֲשֶׁר לוֹ, "[that is] his own," the Torah teaches us that the bull is Aaron's, not only in the sense that he performs its service, but also in the sense that it must be purchased with his funds (*Mizrachi*; *Sifsei Chachamim*). This is in contrast to his garments, which were not bought with his funds (see *Gur Aryeh*; *Sifsei Chachamim* to v. 4; see note 5 to v. 4 above).

8. *Toras Kohanim, parshasa* 2:2-3; *Yoma* 36b. Offerings bring about full atonement for those who bring them only

and stand them before Hashem, at the entrance of the Tent of Meeting. [8] Aaron shall place lots upon the two he-goats: one lot "to Hashem" and one lot "to Azazel." [9] Aaron shall bring near the he-goat designated by lot to Hashem, and he shall make it a sin-offering. [10] And the he-goat designated by lot to Azazel shall be stood alive before

וְהֶעֱמִיד אֹתָם֙ לִפְנֵ֣י יהוה פֶּ֔תַח אֹ֖הֶל מוֹעֵֽד: ח וְנָתַ֧ן אַהֲרֹ֛ן עַל־שְׁנֵ֥י הַשְּׂעִירִ֖ם גֹּרָל֑וֹת גּוֹרָ֤ל אֶחָד֙ לַֽיהוה וְגוֹרָ֥ל אֶחָ֖ד לַעֲזָאזֵֽל: ט וְהִקְרִ֤יב אַהֲרֹן֙ אֶת־הַשָּׂעִ֔יר אֲשֶׁ֨ר עָלָ֥ה עָלָ֛יו הַגּוֹרָ֖ל לַיהוה וְעָשָׂ֥הוּ חַטָּֽאת: י וְהַשָּׂעִ֗יר אֲשֶׁר֩ עָלָ֨ה עָלָ֜יו הַגּוֹרָ֣ל לַעֲזָאזֵ֗ל יָֽעֳמַד־חַ֛י לִפְנֵ֥י

― אונקלוס ―

וִיקִים יָתְהוֹן קֳדָם יְיָ בִּתְרַע מַשְׁכַּן זִמְנָא: ח וְיִתֵּן אַהֲרֹן עַל תְּרֵין צְפִירִין עַדְבִין עַדְבָּא חַד לִשְׁמָא דַיְיָ וְעַדְבָּא חַד לַעֲזָאזֵל: ט וִיקָרֵב אַהֲרֹן יָת צְפִירָא דִּי סְלִיק עֲלוֹהִי עַדְבָּא לִשְׁמָא דַיְיָ וְיַעְבְּדִנֵּהּ חַטָּאתָא: י וּצְפִירָא דִּי סְלִיק עֲלוֹהִי עַדְבָּא לַעֲזָאזֵל יִתָּקַם כַּד חַי קֳדָם

― רש״י ―

(ח) **ונתן אהרן על שני השעירים גרלות.** מעמיד אחד לימין ואחד לשמאל, ונותן שתי ידיו בקלפי, ונוטל גורל בימין וחברו בשמאל ונותן עליהם. את שכתוב בו לשם הוא לשם, ואת שכתוב בו לעזאזל משתלח לעזאזל (יומא לט.): **עזאזל.** הוא הר עז וקשה, צוק גבוה, שנא׳ ארץ גזרה (להלן פסוק כב) חתוכה (יומא סז:): (ט) **ועשהו חטאת.** כשמניח הגורל עליו קורא לו שם ואומר לה׳ חטאת (יומא לט.): (י) **יעמד חי.** כמו יועמד חי, על ידי אחרים,

― RASHI ELUCIDATED ―

8. מַעֲמִיד אֶחָד — וְנָתַן אַהֲרֹן עַל שְׁנֵי הַשְּׂעִירִים גֹּרָלוֹת — AARON SHALL PLACE LOTS UPON THE TWO HE-GOATS. לַיָמִין — He has one goat **stand to the right** וְאֶחָד לַשְּׂמֹאל — and one to the left. וְנוֹתֵן שְׁתֵּי יָדָיו בְּקַלְפֵּי — He puts his two hands into a lottery box, וְנוֹטֵל גּוֹרָל בַּיָמִין — and draws a lot in the right hand וַחֲבֵרוֹ בַשְּׂמֹאל — and draws the other lot in the left hand. וְנוֹתֵן עֲלֵיהֶם — He puts the lots on the [goats].[1] אֶת שֶׁכָּתוּב בּוֹ לַשֵּׁם — The one about which, i.e., on whose lot, is written "to Hashem" הוּא לַשֵּׁם — is offered to Hashem, וְאֶת שֶׁכָּתוּב בּוֹ לַעֲזָאזֵל — and the one about which, i.e., on whose lot, is written "to Azazel" מִשְׁתַּלֵּחַ לַעֲזָאזֵל[2] — is sent to Azazel.[2]

עֲזָאזֵל — AZAZEL. הוּא הַר עַז וְקָשֶׁה — It is an austere and harsh mountain,[3] צוּק גָּבוֹהַּ — a high cliff, שֶׁנֶּאֱמַר — as it says, "אֶרֶץ גְּזֵרָה"[4] — "a cut land,"[4] for the word גְּזֵרָה means חֲתוּכָה[5] — cut.[5]

9. וְעָשָׂהוּ חַטָּאת — AND HE SHALL MAKE IT A SIN-OFFERING. כְּשֶׁמַּנִּיחַ הַגּוֹרָל עָלָיו — When he puts the lot on it, קוֹרֵא לוֹ שֵׁם — he calls it a name, i.e., he declares it an offering, וְאוֹמֵר — by saying, "לַה׳, חַטָּאת"[6] — "to Hashem, a sin-offering."[6]

10. יָעֳמַד חַי — SHALL BE STOOD ALIVE. כְּמוֹ יָעֳמַד חַי — This has the same meaning as "shall be made to stand, alive," עַל יְדֵי אֲחֵרִים — by others, i.e., it means "the goat shall be

---

after their blood has been sprinkled on the *Mizbe'ach*. Our verse cannot refer to that, for this "atonement" precedes the slaughter of the offering (see v. 11). It must refer to an earlier stage in the process of atonement, namely, confession (*Mizrachi; Sifsei Chachamim*).

1. The lot in his right hand on the goat standing at his right, and the lot in his left hand on the goat standing at his left.

2. *Yoma* 39a.

3. The term עֲזָאזֵל is a combination of עַז, "severe" or "austere," and אֵל, "strong" or "harsh" (*Mizrachi; Sifsei Chachamim*). See *Genesis* 31:29 and Rashi there for a similar example of אֵל as "strong."

4. Below v. 22.

5. *Yoma* 67b. The Talmud cites three interpretations for the word גְּזֵרָה: (a) It is an adjective meaning חֲתוּכָה, "cut," and modifies אֶרֶץ, "land" (see next paragraph); (b) it is a

noun meaning something "cut to bits" and refers to the carcass of the goat as it falls down the side of the cliff; and (c) it is a noun meaning "decree" and refers to the phenomenon of atonement being achieved through the goat service — "I have issued a 'decree' and you are not authorized to call it into question."

Rashi here follows the first opinion. In his commentary to *Yoma*, Rashi explains חֲתוּכָה [see (a) above] as a reference to the terrain: "a mountaintop that has been cut vertically and is not a gradual slope," i.e., land that looks as if part of it has been cut off — a cliff. In this, Rashi differs with others who explain חֲתוּכָה as cut off from human habitation (*Targum Onkelos*) or from the ability to grow crops (*Rashbam*).

6. *Yoma* 39a, 40b. "He shall make it a sin-offering" does not mean that he shall offer it upon the *Mizbe'ach* as a sin-offering, for our verse deals with a stage in the sacrificial procedure prior to the animal's slaughter. It means

HASHEM, to atone upon it, to send it to Azazel to the wilderness. **11** Aaron shall bring near his own sin-offering bull and he shall atone for himself and for his household; then he shall slaughter his own sin-offering bull.

יְהוָה לְכַפֵּר עָלָיו לְשַׁלַּח אֹתוֹ
לַעֲזָאזֵל הַמִּדְבָּרָה: יא וְהִקְרִיב
אַהֲרֹן אֶת־פַּר הַחַטָּאת אֲשֶׁר־
לוֹ וְכִפֶּר בַּעֲדוֹ וּבְעַד בֵּיתוֹ וְשָׁחַט
אֶת־פַּר הַחַטָּאת אֲשֶׁר־לוֹ:

──────────── אונקלוס ────────────

יְיָ לְכַפָּרָא עֲלוֹהִי לְשַׁלָּחָא יָתֵהּ לַעֲזָאזֵל לְמַדְבְּרָא: יא וִיקָרֵב אַהֲרֹן יָת תּוֹרָא
דְחַטָּאתָא דִּי לֵהּ וִיכַפַּר עֲלוֹהִי וְעַל אֱנַשׁ בֵּיתֵהּ וְיִכּוֹס יָת תּוֹרָא דְחַטָּאתָא דִּי לֵהּ:

──────────── רש"י ────────────

וְתַרְגּוּמוֹ יִתָּקַס חַי. מַה תַּ"ל, לְפִי שֶׁנֶּא' לְשַׁלַּח אֹתוֹ לַעֲזָאזֵל וְאֵינִי יוֹדֵעַ שִׁלּוּחוֹ אִם לְמִיתָה אִם לְחַיִּים, לְכָךְ נֶאֱמַר עֳמִידָתוֹ חַי, עֲמִידָתוֹ חַי עַד שִׁשְׁתַּלַּח, מִכָּאן שֶׁשִּׁלּוּחוֹ לְמִיתָה (ת"כ פרשתא ב:ו): **לְכַפֵּר** בּוֹ (ת"כ פרשתא ג:ח) שֶׁיִּ' **עָלָיו.** שִׁיתוּדֶה עָלָיו (שם ז; יומא לו:, מו:) כדכתיב וְהִתְוַדָּה עָלָיו (להלן פסוק כא): **(יא) וְכִפֶּר בַּעֲדוֹ וגו'.** וִדּוּי שֵׁנִי עָלָיו וְעַל אֶחָיו הַכֹּהֲנִים (יומא מא:) שֶׁהֵם כֻּלָּם קְרוּיִים בֵּיתוֹ (ת"כ פרשתא ג:ח) שֶׁנֶּ':

──────────── RASHI ELUCIDATED ────────────

placed."[1] וְתַרְגּוּמוֹ — *Targum Onkelos* therefore **renders it** with a passive Aramaic verb form: ",יִתָּקַם ",כַּד חַי — "**shall be made to stand while alive.**" מַה תַּלְמוּד לוֹמַר — **Why does the Torah say this?**[2] לְפִי שֶׁנֶּאֱמַר — **Because it says,** ",לְשַׁלַּח אֹתוֹ לַעֲזָאזֵל — "**to send it to Azazel,**" וְאֵינִי יוֹדֵעַ — **and I do not know** שִׁלּוּחוֹ אִם לְמִיתָה — **if its sending is for death** אִם לְחַיִּים — **or for life**, i.e., if it is sent to Azazel to its death, or if it is to survive after it is sent.[3] לְכָךְ נֶאֱמַר — **Therefore, it says,** ",יַעֲמַד חַי — "[**it**] **shall be stood alive**," which implies עֲמִידָתוֹ חַי — its standing takes place while it **is alive,** עַד שֶׁיִּשְׁתַּלַּח — **until it is sent away.** מִכָּאן — **From here** we learn [4] שֶׁשִּׁלּוּחוֹ לְמִיתָה — **that its sending is for death**, i.e., that it is sent to Azazel to its death.[4]

☐ לְכַפֵּר עָלָיו — **TO ATONE UPON IT.** [5]שֶׁיִּתְוַדֶּה עָלָיו — **That he should confess over it,**[5] כְּדִכְתִיב — **as it is written,** ",וְהִתְוַדָּה עָלָיו וְגוֹמֵר — "**and confess upon it, etc.**"[6]

11. וְכִפֶּר בַּעֲדוֹ וְגוֹמֵר — **AND HE SHALL ATONE FOR HIMSELF, ETC.** וִדּוּי שֵׁנִי — **A second confession**, in addition to the confession mentioned in verse 6, עָלָיו — **over himself,** i.e., over his own sins,[7] וְעַל אֶחָיו הַכֹּהֲנִים — **and over his brothers, the Kohanim,** i.e., over the sins of the other Kohanim,[7] [8]שֶׁהֵם כֻּלָּם קְרוּיִים בֵּיתוֹ — **for they are all called his household,**[8] שֶׁנֶּאֱמַר — **as it says,**

---

he shall verbally designate it as a sin-offering (*Mizrachi; Sifsei Chachamim*).

1. The passive form of verbs in the *hifil* is usually the *hufal*. The passive form of יַעֲמִיד would thus have been יָעֳמַד. However, since the first letter of the root of יַעֲמִיד is ע, a guttural, the passive of the *hifil* is the *hofal*, יָעֳמַד (*Mesiach Ilmim*). The only difference between the *hufal* and the *hofal* is in the vowelization. In the *hufal* the prefix takes a *kubutz* (יֻ), while in the *hofal* it takes a *kamatz* (יָ). In either case, the first root letter takes a *sheva* (here a *chataf patach* or a *chataf kamatz* due to the ע) and the second root letter takes a *patach*.

2. If the he-goat is standing, it is obvious that it is alive. Why does the Torah have to say חַי, "alive" (*Minchas Yehudah; Sifsei Chachamim*)?

3. The Torah does not state explicitly what becomes of the goat once it is sent to Azazel.

4. *Toras Kohanim, parshasa* 2:6. "It shall be stood alive before HASHEM" implies that it is kept alive as long as it is "before HASHEM," i.e., in the Courtyard of the *Beis HaMikdash*. Once it is sent off to Azazel, it is on its way to death (*Mizrachi*).

5. *Toras Kohanim, parshasa* 2:7; *Yoma* 36b, 40b.

6. Below v. 21. The atonement here cannot refer to that brought about by sprinkling of the blood (see note 8 to v. 6 above), as there is no sprinkling of the blood for the goat sent to Azazel (*Mizrachi; Sifsei Chachamim*).

7. *Yoma* 41b.

8. *Toras Kohanim, parshasa* 3:1. Verse 6 has already stated וְכִפֶּר בַּעֲדוֹ וּבְעַד בֵּיתוֹ, "and atone for himself and for his household." In that verse, בֵּיתוֹ, "his household," means his wife. Before placing the lots on the goats the Kohen Gadol would confess on his own behalf and on behalf of his wife. In our verse, בֵּיתוֹ, "his household," refers to the entire order of Kohanim. After placing the lots on the goats, the Kohen Gadol would confess on his own behalf and on behalf of all of his fellow Kohanim. It was to the benefit of the entire order of Kohanim that the Kohen Gadol did not confess on their behalf in his first confession, for the confession of one who has already attained atonement, as the Kohen Gadol did through his first confession, is more effective than that of one who has not. The Kohen Gadol nonetheless included himself while confessing on behalf of the other Kohanim to atone for any sins he may have committed in the interim between the two confessions (*Gur Aryeh; Sifsei Chachamim*).

198 / ויקרא – פרשת אחרי

¹² He shall take a shovelful of fiery coals from atop the Mizbe'ach from before Hashem, and his cupped handsful of finely ground incense-spices, and bring it within the Curtain. ¹³ He shall place the incense

יב וְלָקַח מְלֹא־הַמַּחְתָּה גַּחֲלֵי־אֵשׁ מֵעַל הַמִּזְבֵּחַ מִלִּפְנֵי יהוה וּמְלֹא חָפְנָיו קְטֹרֶת סַמִּים דַּקָּה וְהֵבִיא מִבֵּית לַפָּרֹכֶת: יג וְנָתַן אֶת־הַקְּטֹרֶת

――――― אונקלוס ―――――

יב וְיִסַּב מְלֵי מַחְתִּיתָא גּוּמְרִין דְּאֶשָּׁא מֵעֲלָוֵי מַדְבְּחָא מִן קֳדָם יְיָ וּמְלֵי חָפְנוֹהִי קְטֹרֶת בּוּסְמִין דַּקִּיקִין וְיָעֵיל מִגָּיו לְפָרֻכְתָּא: יג וְיִתֵּן יָת קְטֹרֶת בּוּסְמַיָּא

――――― רש"י ―――――

בֵּית אַהֲרֹן בָּרְכוּ אֶת ה' וְגוֹ' (תהלים קלה:יט) מִכָּאן שֶׁהַכֹּהֲנִים מִתְכַּפְּרִים בּוֹ. וְכֹל כַּפָּרָתוֹ [ס"א כַּפָּרָתָן] אֵינָהּ אֶלָּא עַל טֻמְאַת מִקְדָּשׁ וְקָדָשָׁיו, כְּמוֹ שֶׁנֶּאֱמַר וְכִפֶּר עַל הַקֹּדֶשׁ מִטֻּמְאֹת וְגוֹ' (לְהַלָּן פָּסוּק טז): מִלִּפְנֵי ה'. מִצַּד שֶׁלִּפְנֵי הַפֶּתַח וְהוּא לַד מַעֲרָבִי (ת"כ פֶּרֶק ג:ו; יוֹמָא מה:): דַּקָּה. מַה ת"ל דַּקָּה וַהֲלֹא כָּל הַקְּטֹרֶת דַּקָּה הִיא, שֶׁנֶּאֱמַר וְשָׁחַקְתָּ מִמֶּנָּה הָדֵק, אֶלָּא שֶׁתְּהֵא דַקָּה מִן הַדַּקָּה, שֶׁבְּעֶרֶב יוֹם הַכִּפּוּרִים הָיָה מַחֲזִירָהּ לַמַּכְתֶּשֶׁת (ת"כ שָׁם ע"ז; כְּרִיתוּת וֹ:):

――――― RASHI ELUCIDATED ―――――

בֵּית אַהֲרֹן בָּרְכוּ אֶת ה' וְגוֹ' – "House of Aaron, bless Hashem! etc."[1] מִכָּאן – From here we learn שֶׁהַכֹּהֲנִים מִתְכַּפְּרִים בּוֹ – that the Kohanim gain atonement through [the sin-offering of the Kohen Gadol]. ² וְכָל כַּפָּרָתָן – Their entire atonement,[2] i.e., the entire atonement gained by the Kohanim through the sin-offering of the Kohen Gadol, אֵינָהּ אֶלָּא עַל טֻמְאַת מִקְדָּשׁ וְקָדָשָׁיו – is only for impurity of the Sanctuary and its holies,³ כְּמוֹ שֶׁנֶּאֱמַר – as it says, וְכִפֶּר עַל הַקֹּדֶשׁ מִטֻּמְאֹת וְגוֹ' – "Thus shall he bring atonement upon the Sanctuary for the impurities, etc."[4,4a]

12. מֵעַל הַמִּזְבֵּחַ – FROM ATOP THE *MIZBE'ACH*. This refers to ⁵הַחִיצוֹן – the outer one.[5]

□ מִלִּפְנֵי ה' – FROM BEFORE HASHEM. מִצַּד שֶׁלִּפְנֵי הַפֶּתַח – From the side of the *Mizbe'ach* that faces the entrance of the *Beis HaMikdash*, ⁶וְהוּא צַד מַעֲרָבִי – and that is the west side.[6]

□ דַּקָּה – FINELY GROUND. מַה תַּלְמוּד לוֹמַר "דַּקָּה" – Why does the verse say "finely ground"? וַהֲלֹא – Isn't כָּל הַקְּטֹרֶת דַּקָּה הִיא – all of the incense finely ground, שֶׁנֶּאֱמַר – as it says, ⁷וְשָׁחַקְתָּ מִמֶּנָּה הָדֵק – "you shall grind of it finely"?[7] אֶלָּא – But the Torah writes this to teach us שֶׁתְּהֵא דַקָּה מִן הַדַּקָּה – that it should be the finest of the fine, שֶׁבְּעֶרֶב יוֹם הַכִּפּוּרִים – that on the eve of Yom Kippur הָיָה מַחֲזִירָהּ – he would return it ⁸לַמַּכְתֶּשֶׁת – to the mortar to be reground.[8]

---

1. *Psalms* 135:19-20. The verse cannot be referring to Aaron's wife, for it was written centuries after Aaron's death. It is referring to the entire order of Kohanim, just as the parallel verses in that Psalm, "House of Levi" and "House of Israel," refer to large groups within the Jewish people.

2. According to our interpretation, the antecedent of the plural pronominal suffix ן is "the Kohanim," and כַּפָּרָתָן refers to the atonement gained by the Kohanim. Alternatively, the antecedent may be the bull and goat sin-offerings, in which case כַּפָּרָתָן refers to the atonement brought about by these sin-offerings (*Yosef Hallel*, based on *Shevuos* 4b). In some early editions, the word reads כַּפָּרָתוֹ, "its atonement," and refers to the atonement brought about by the bull sin-offering.

3. That is: entering the grounds of the *Beis HaMikdash* or eating that which is holy, while in a state of impurity; or eating that which is holy and has become impure, even though the one who eats it is pure.

4. Below v. 16. Although that verse refers to the goat sin-offering, Rashi cites it because it sheds light on the bull, as well. For about the goat, verse 15 says, אֶת וְשָׁחַט שְׂעִיר הַחַטָּאת אֲשֶׁר לָעָם, "He shall slaughter the sin-offering he-goat of the people," about which Rashi there says, "That for which the bull atones on behalf of the Kohanim, the he-goat atones for on behalf of the rest of Israel" (see v. 15 below and note 6 there as to how this is derived from that verse). Thus, since the verse says that the goat atones for the impurity of the Sanctuary and its holies on behalf of the rest of Israel, it must be that it is for this sin as well that the bull atones on behalf of the Kohanim (*Mesiach Ilmim*).

4a. *Shevuos* 12b,13b.

5. *Yoma* 45b. The next words of the verse, "from before Hashem," indicate that it refers to a *Mizbe'ach* of which part is in a holier location than the rest of it, as Rashi explains in his following comment. This is only true of the Outer *Mizbe'ach*, for the *Mizbe'ach* of Gold stood inside the Sanctuary in its entirety (*Mizrachi*; *Sifsei Chachamim*). Verse 18 describes it as הַמִּזְבֵּחַ אֲשֶׁר לִפְנֵי ה' "in its entirety (*Maskil LeDavid*).

6. *Toras Kohanim, perek* 3:6; *Yoma* 45b; *Zevachim* 58b. The verse has already stated that he takes the coals from atop the *Mizbe'ach*. "From before Hashem" would thus be redundant if it referred to the entire *Mizbe'ach*. It refers specifically to the side of the *Mizbe'ach* that faces the *Beis HaMikdash* (*Gur Aryeh*).

7. *Exodus* 30:36.

8. *Toras Kohanim, perek* 3:9-10; *Kereisos* 6b; *Yoma* 45a.

upon the fire before Hashem — so that the cloud of the incense shall blanket the Ark-cover that is atop the [Tablets of the] Testimony — so that he shall not die. ¹⁴ He shall take some of the blood of the bull and sprinkle with his finger upon the eastern front of the Ark-cover; and in front of the Ark-cover he shall sprinkle seven times from the blood with his finger. ¹⁵ He shall slaughter the sin-offering he-goat of the people, and bring its blood within the Curtain; he shall do with its blood as

עַל־הָאֵשׁ לִפְנֵי יהוה וְכִסָּה ׀ עֲנַן
הַקְּטֹרֶת אֶת־הַכַּפֹּרֶת אֲשֶׁר עַל־
הָעֵדוּת וְלֹא יָמוּת: ^{יד} וְלָקַח מִדַּם
הַפָּר וְהִזָּה בְאֶצְבָּעוֹ עַל־פְּנֵי
הַכַּפֹּרֶת קֵדְמָה וְלִפְנֵי הַכַּפֹּרֶת יַזֶּה
שֶׁבַע־פְּעָמִים מִן־הַדָּם בְּאֶצְבָּעוֹ:
^{טו} וְשָׁחַט אֶת־שְׂעִיר הַחַטָּאת אֲשֶׁר
לָעָם וְהֵבִיא אֶת־דָּמוֹ אֶל־מִבֵּית
לַפָּרֹכֶת וְעָשָׂה אֶת־דָּמוֹ כַּאֲשֶׁר

─────── אונקלוס ───────

עַל אֶשָּׁתָא לָקֳדָם יְיָ וִיחַפֵּי עֲנָנָא קְטָרְתָּא יָת כַּפֻּרְתָּא דִּי עַל סָהֲדוּתָא וְלָא יְמוּת: ^{יד} וְיִסַּב מִדְּמָא דְתוֹרָא וְיַדִּי בְאֶצְבְּעֵהּ עַל אַפֵּי כַפֻּרְתָּא קִדּוּמָא וְלָקֳדָם כַּפֻּרְתָּא יַדִּי שְׁבַע זִמְנִין מִן דְּמָא בְּאֶצְבְּעֵהּ: ^{טו} וְיִכּוֹס יָת צְפִירָא דְחַטָּאתָא דִּי לְעַמָּא וְיָעֵל יָת דְּמֵהּ לְמִגָּיו לְפָרֻכְתָּא וְיַעְבֵּד יָת דְּמֵהּ כְּמָא

─────── רש"י ───────

(יג) עַל הָאֵשׁ. שֶׁבְּתוֹךְ הַמַּחְתָּה: **וְלֹא יָמוּת.** הָא אִם לֹא עֲשָׂאָהּ כְּתִקְנָהּ חַיָּב מִיתָה (ת"כ שם יח; יומא נג.): **(יד) וְהִזָּה בְאֶצְבָּעוֹ.** הַזָּאָה אַחַת בְּמַשְׁמָע: **וְלִפְנֵי הַכַּפֹּרֶת יַזֶּה שֶׁבַע.** הֲרֵי אַחַת לְמַעְלָה וְשֶׁבַע לְמַטָּה (שם נה.): **(טו) אֲשֶׁר לָעָם.** מַה שֶּׁהַפָּר מְכַפֵּר עַל הַכֹּהֲנִים מְכַפֵּר הַשָּׂעִיר עַל יִשְׂרָאֵל (שם סא.) וְהוּא הַשָּׂעִיר שֶׁעָלָה עָלָיו הַגּוֹרָל לַשֵּׁם:

─────── RASHI ELUCIDATED ───────

13. עַל הָאֵשׁ — UPON THE FIRE שֶׁבְּתוֹךְ הַמַּחְתָּה — that is in the fire-pan.[1]

□ וְלֹא יָמוּת — SO THAT HE SHALL NOT DIE. הָא אִם לֹא עֲשָׂאָהּ — But if he did not do it כְּתִקְנָהּ — according to its regulations ²חַיָּב מִיתָה — he is subject to the death penalty.[2]

14. וְהִזָּה בְאֶצְבָּעוֹ — AND SPRINKLE WITH HIS FINGER. הַזָּאָה אַחַת בְּמַשְׁמָע — One sprinkling is implied.[3]

□ וְלִפְנֵי הַכַּפֹּרֶת יַזֶּה שֶׁבַע — AND IN FRONT OF THE ARK-COVER HE SHALL SPRINKLE SEVEN. הֲרֵי אַחַת לְמַעְלָה — See, now, that there is one sprinkling above ⁴וְשֶׁבַע לְמַטָּה — and seven below.[4]

15. אֲשֶׁר לָעָם — OF THE PEOPLE. מַה שֶּׁהַפָּר מְכַפֵּר עַל הַכֹּהֲנִים — That for which the bull atones on behalf of the Kohanim[5] מְכַפֵּר הַשָּׂעִיר — the he-goat atones for ⁶עַל יִשְׂרָאֵל — on behalf of the rest of Israel.[6] וְהוּא הַשָּׂעִיר — It is the he-goat שֶׁעָלָה עָלָיו הַגּוֹרָל לַשֵּׁם — upon which the lot "to Hashem"[7] fell.

---

1. Although the fire-pan contained hot coals rather than flames, the term "fire" applies to it. Our verse refers to the coals of the fire-pan, not the flames of the Mizbe'ach (Gur Aryeh).

2. Toras Kohanim, perek 3:11; Yoma 53a.

3. The verse here says, "and sprinkle with his finger," without specifying how many times he should sprinkle, in contrast to the end of the verse which states explicitly that he should sprinkle seven times in front of the Ark-cover. The verse's silence here implies that he sprinkles the minimum number of times, one (Gur Aryeh).

4. Yoma 55a. None of the blood of the sprinklings mentioned in our verse actually touched the Ark-cover. The sprinkling described in our verse as being "upon the eastern front of the Ark-cover" is "above," in that it was aimed higher than the other seven which were "below."

5. Those sins for which the sin-offering mentioned above in verse 11 atones on behalf of the Kohanim, namely, for entering the grounds of the Beis HaMikdash in a state of impurity or for eating that which is holy while impure, or for eating that which is holy that has become impure (Minchas Yehudah; Sifsei Chachamim).

6. Yoma 61a. The phrase אֲשֶׁר לָעָם, "of the people," appears superfluous, for only "the people" bring a he-goat, as stated in verse 5. It is meant to teach us what the bull brought as a sin-offering atones for. The following verse states explicitly that the goat atones for sins involving impurity of the Sanctuary. "Of the people" implies a comparison between that sin-offering and the bull sin-offering of the Kohanim, as if to say, what the goat atones for on behalf of the people, the bull atones for on behalf of the Kohanim (Mishmeres HaKodesh).

7. See verse 8 above and Rashi there.

he had done with the blood of the bull, and sprinkle it upon the Ark-cover and in front of the Ark-cover. ¹⁶ Thus shall he bring atonement upon the Sanctuary for the impurities of the Children of Israel, and for their willful sins among all their sins; and so

עָשָׂה לְדַם הַפָּר וְהִזָּה אֹתוֹ עַל־הַכַּפֹּרֶת וְלִפְנֵי הַכַּפֹּרֶת: וְכִפֶּר עַל־הַקֹּדֶשׁ מִטֻּמְאֹת בְּנֵי יִשְׂרָאֵל וּמִפִּשְׁעֵיהֶם לְכָל־חַטֹּאתָם וְכֵן

— אונקלוס —

דִּי עֲבַד לִדְמָא דְתוֹרָא וְיַדִּי יָתֵהּ עַל כַּפֻּרְתָּא וְלָקֳדָם כַּפֻּרְתָּא: טז וִיכַפַּר עַל קוּדְשָׁא מִסּוֹאֲבַת בְּנֵי יִשְׂרָאֵל וּמִמָּרְדֵיהוֹן לְכָל חֲטָאֵיהוֹן וְכֵן

— רש"י —

כאשר עשה לדם הפר. אחת למעלה ושבע למטה (יומא נג:): נודע להם בסוף, שנאמר לכל חטאתם, וחטאת הוא שוגג (שבועות ז:): **(טז) מטמאת בני ישראל.** על הנכנסין למקדש בטומאה ולא **ומפשעיהם.** אף הנכנסין מזיד בטומאה (שם):

— RASHI ELUCIDATED —

□ כַּאֲשֶׁר עָשָׂה לְדַם הַפָּר — AS HE HAD DONE WITH THE BLOOD OF THE BULL. אַחַת לְמַעְלָה — One sprinkling above ¹ וְשֶׁבַע לְמַטָּה — and seven below.¹

16. מִטֻּמְאֹת בְּנֵי יִשְׂרָאֵל — FOR THE IMPURITIES OF THE CHILDREN OF ISRAEL. עַל הַנִּכְנָסִין לַמִּקְדָּשׁ — For those who enter the *Beis HaMikdash* בְּטֻמְאָה — in a state of impurity וְלֹא נוֹדַע לָהֶם בַּסּוֹף — and it was not known to them in the end, שֶׁנֶּאֱמַר — as it says, ״לְכָל חַטֹּאתָם״ — "among all their sins," וְחַטָּאת — and the word חַטָּאת, "sin," ² הִיא שׁוֹגֵג — means [a sin] which is unintentional.²

□ וּמִפִּשְׁעֵיהֶם — AND FOR THEIR WILLFUL SINS. The he-goat atones ³ אַף הַנִּכְנָסִין מֵזִיד בְּטֻמְאָה — even for those who enter the *Beis HaMikdash* intentionally in a state of impurity.³

---

1. *Yoma* 53b. See verse 14 above and Rashi there.

2. *Shevuos* 7b. Those who enter the *Beis HaMikdash* unintentionally in a state of impurity can be divided into categories: (a) those who were aware that they were impure, forgot their impurity and entered the *Beis HaMikdash*, and subsequently realized that they had entered wrongfully; (b) those who were aware that they were impure, forgot their impurity and entered the *Beis HaMikdash*, and have not yet remembered their impurity; (c) those who had not been aware that they were impure, entered the *Beis HaMikdash* in their state of impurity, but subsequently learned of their impurity; (d) those who had not been aware of their impurity prior to their entering the *Beis HaMikdash*, nor did they learn of it afterwards.

The unintentional sin for which the goat sin-offering on Yom Kippur atones cannot be category (a), because in that situation, the one who entered the *Beis HaMikdash* in a state of impurity must bring his own personal sin-offering (see 5:3 above). It also does not atone for categories (c) and (d) because the verse refers to the unintentional sin of our verse as חַטָּאת, a term which also means "sin-offering." This implies that the goat discussed here atones for a sin to which a sin-offering of an individual can also apply. This excludes categories (c) and (d), because an individual brings a sin-offering for entering the *Beis HaMikdash* unintentionally while impure only if he had been aware of his impurity beforehand (see *Shevuos* 8b). Category (c) and, according to one opinion in the Mishnah (*Shevuos* 2a-b), category (d) are atoned for by the he-goat brought as a *mussaf*-offering on Yom Kippur. According to other opinions, category (d) is atoned for by the *mussaf*-offerings of the Festivals or of the New Moon. Thus, the goat sin-offering mentioned in our verse atones only for category (b), those who were aware that they were impure, forgot their impurity and entered the *Beis HaMikdash*, and have not yet remembered their impurity. In this case, the goat sin-offering brings temporary atonement until they discover their sin. At that point, they are obligated to bring their own sin-offering (*Maskil LeDavid*).

3. *Shevuos* 7b. The phrase מִטֻּמְאֹת בְּנֵי יִשְׂרָאֵל וּמִפִּשְׁעֵיהֶם, appears to mean, "for the impurities of the Children of Israel and for their willful sins." "Willful sins" would then be a category distinct from "the impurities of the Children of Israel." The verse would then be saying that the goat sin-offering atones for impurities and willful sins. The next phrase of the verse, לְכָל חַטֹּאתָם, "[and] for all their sins," would imply that the goat atones for unintentional sins, as well. But if this were the meaning of the verse, חַטֹּאתָם, "unintentional sins," should have been mentioned before פִּשְׁעֵיהֶם, "willful sins," for once the verse has stated that the goat atones for willful sins, it goes without saying that it atones for unintentional sins. The verse puts פִּשְׁעֵיהֶם before חַטֹּאתָם to indicate that the entire verse deals only with sins of impurity and that פִּשְׁעֵיהֶם qualifies חַטֹּאתָם. That is, פִּשְׁעֵיהֶם refers to one who enters the *Beis HaMikdash* intentionally while in a state of impurity. Just as he does not bring an offering for his sin, so, too, the specific unintentional sin of חַטֹּאתָם is one for which the sinner does not bring an offering, namely, when he is not yet aware that he entered the *Beis HaMikdash* in a state of impurity. Rashi identifies מִטֻּמְאֹת בְּנֵי יִשְׂרָאֵל with לְכָל חַטֹּאתָם, and defines חַטֹּאתָם before he defines פִּשְׁעֵיהֶם, in ascending order of severity, to indicate that neither לְכָל חַטֹּאתָם nor פִּשְׁעֵיהֶם are categories distinct from מִטֻּמְאֹת בְּנֵי יִשְׂרָאֵל (*Be'er BaSadeh*).

16/17-18

shall he do for the Tent of Meeting that dwells with them amid their impurity. ¹⁷ **Any person shall not be in the Tent of Meeting when he comes to provide atonement in the Sanctuary until his departure; he shall provide atonement for himself, for his household, and for the entire congregation of Israel.**

¹⁸ **He shall go out to the Mizbe'ach that is**

יַעֲשֶׂה לְאֹהֶל מוֹעֵד הַשֹּׁכֵן אִתָּם
בְּתוֹךְ טֻמְאֹתָם: וְכָל־אָדָם לֹא־
יִהְיֶה ׀ בְּאֹהֶל מוֹעֵד בְּבֹאוֹ לְכַפֵּר
בַּקֹּדֶשׁ עַד־צֵאתוֹ וְכִפֶּר בַּעֲדוֹ
וּבְעַד בֵּיתוֹ וּבְעַד כָּל־קְהַל יִשְׂרָאֵל:
יח שני וְיָצָא אֶל־הַמִּזְבֵּחַ אֲשֶׁר

—— אונקלוס ——

יַעֲבֵד לְמַשְׁכַּן זִמְנָא דְּשָׁרֵי עִמְּהוֹן בְּגוֹ סוֹאֲבָתְהוֹן: יּ וְכָל אֱנָשׁ לָא יְהֵי בְּמַשְׁכַּן זִמְנָא בְּמֵעֲלֵהּ לְכַפָּרָא בְּקוּדְשָׁא עַד מִפְּקֵהּ וִיכַפַּר עֲלוֹהִי וְעַל אֱנַשׁ בֵּיתֵהּ וְעַל כָּל קְהָלָא דְיִשְׂרָאֵל: יח וְיִפּוֹק לְמַדְבְּחָא דִּי

—— רש"י ——

(יח) אל המזבח אשר לפני ה'. זה מזבח הזהב שהוא לפני ה' בהיכל. ומה ת"ל ויצא, לפי שהוא הזאות על הפרוכת ועמד מן המזבח ולפנים והזה, וכמתנות המזבח הזקיקו לצאת מן המזבח ולחוץ, ויתחיל מקרן מזרחית לפונית (ת"כ פרק ד:ז-י; יומא נח:).

וכן יעשה לאהל מועד. כשם שהזה משניהם בפנים אחת למעלה ושבע למטה, כך מזה על הפרוכת מבחוץ משניהם אחת למעלה ושבע למטה (יומא נו:): **השכן אתם בתוך טומאותם.** אף על פי שהם טמאים שכינה ביניהם (שם נז.):

—— RASHI ELUCIDATED ——

□ וְכֵן יַעֲשֶׂה לְאֹהֶל מוֹעֵד — AND SO SHALL HE DO FOR THE TENT OF MEETING. כְּשֵׁם שֶׁהִזָּה מִשְּׁנֵיהֶם — **Just as he sprinkled from both** [the blood of the bull and the he-goat] בִּפְנִים — **inside** the Holy of Holies, אַחַת לְמַעְלָה — **one above** וְשֶׁבַע לְמַטָּה — **and seven below,**[1] כָּךְ מַזֶּה — **so does he sprinkle** עַל הַפָּרֹכֶת — **on the** *Paroches*[2] מִבַּחוּץ — **from the outside,** i.e., on the side facing the Sanctuary and not the Holy of Holies, מִשְּׁנֵיהֶם — **from both** [the blood of the bull and the he-goat], אַחַת לְמַעְלָה — **one above**[3] וְשֶׁבַע לְמַטָּה — **and seven below.**[3]

□ הַשֹּׁכֵן אִתָּם בְּתוֹךְ טֻמְאֹתָם — THAT DWELLS WITH THEM AMID THEIR IMPURITY. אַף עַל פִּי שֶׁהֵם טְמֵאִים — **Even though they are impure,**[4] שְׁכִינָה בֵּינֵיהֶם[5] — the *Shechinah* **is among them.**[5]

18. אֶל הַמִּזְבֵּחַ אֲשֶׁר לִפְנֵי ה' — TO THE *MIZBE'ACH* THAT IS BEFORE HASHEM. זֶה מִזְבַּח הַזָּהָב — **This is the Gold** *Mizbe'ach* שֶׁהוּא ,,לִפְנֵי ה'" — **which is "before HASHEM"** בַּהֵיכָל — **in the Sanctuary.**[6] וּמַה תַּלְמוּד לוֹמַר ,,וְיָצָא" — **Why,** then, **does the Torah say, "he shall go out,"** which could imply that he goes out of the Sanctuary? לְפִי שֶׁהֵזָּה הַהַזָּאוֹת — **Because he had sprinkled sprinklings** עַל הַפָּרֹכֶת — **on the** *Paroches,* וְעָמַד מִן הַמִּזְבֵּחַ וְלִפְנִים — **and** at that time **he had stood** in the area which extends **from the Gold** *Mizbe'ach* **and within** וְהִזָּה — **and had sprinkled,** וּבְמַתְּנוֹת הַמִּזְבֵּחַ — **and at the applications of** blood to the *Mizbe'ach* הִזְקִיקוֹ — [the Torah] **required him** לָצֵאת — **to go out** into the area which extends מִן הַמִּזְבֵּחַ וְלַחוּץ — **from the** *Mizbe'ach* **and beyond,** וְיַתְחִיל — **that he may begin** to put blood on the *Mizbe'ach* מִקֶּרֶן מִזְרָחִית צְפוֹנִית[7] — **from the northeastern corner.**[7]

---

1. See Rashi to verses 14 and 15 above.

2. The curtain that serves as a partition between the Holy of Holies and the rest of the Sanctuary.

3. *Yoma* 56b.

4. The verse, "for the Tent of Meeting that dwells with them amid their impurity," could be understood to imply that the possibility of the presence of impurity is the cause of the Tent of Meeting dwelling among them. But this is not so. The verse means to say that the *Shechinah* (immanent presence of God) rests among them in the Tent of Meeting despite their impurity (*Mesiach Ilmim*).

5. *Yoma* 57a. The term שכן, "dwelling," is a verb which applies only to living things. It seems inappropriate when used with reference to inanimate objects such as the Tent of Meeting, as in our verse. Rashi explains that it applies to the *Shechinah*, which is present in the Tent of Meeting (*Be'er Yitzchak*).

6. As opposed to the Copper Altar which was located in the Courtyard, outside the Sanctuary.

7. *Toras Kohanim, perek* 4:7-10; *Yoma* 58b. The Holy of Holies was at the western end of the Sanctuary. The *Paroches* separated it from the rest of the Sanctuary. The Golden *Mizbe'ach* stood between the *Paroches* and the entrance at the eastern end of the Sanctuary. When the Kohen Gadol sprinkled the blood in the direction of the *Paroches,* he stood between the *Mizbe'ach* and the *Paroches,* inward from the *Mizbe'ach.* When the Torah says, וְיָצָא, "he shall go out," it does not mean that he should leave the Sanctuary. Rather, it means that he should leave the area between the *Mizbe'ach* and the *Paroches.* He shall go outward, i.e., in the direction of the entrance, before he places blood on the *Mizbe'ach.* He begins putting blood on the *Mizbe'ach* from the northeastern corner, which faces the entrance on the east side of the Sanctuary (see *Mizrachi; Sifsei Chachamim*).

before Hashem, and make atonement upon it: He shall take from the blood of the bull and from the blood of the he-goat and place it on the horns of the Mizbe'ach all around. [19] He shall sprinkle upon it from the blood with his finger seven times; and he shall purify it and sanctify it from the impurities of the Children of Israel.

[20] When he is finished atoning for the Sanctuary, the Tent of Meeting, and the Mizbe'ach, he shall bring the living he-goat near. [21] Aaron shall lean his two hands upon the head of the living he-goat and confess upon it all the iniquities of the Children of Israel, and all their rebellious sins among all their sins, and place them upon

לִפְנֵי־יְהוָה וְכִפֶּר עָלָיו וְלָקַח מִדַּם הַפָּר וּמִדַּם הַשָּׂעִיר וְנָתַן עַל־קַרְנוֹת הַמִּזְבֵּחַ סָבִיב: וְהִזָּה עָלָיו מִן־הַדָּם בְּאֶצְבָּעוֹ שֶׁבַע פְּעָמִים וְטִהֲרוֹ וְקִדְּשׁוֹ מִטֻּמְאֹת בְּנֵי יִשְׂרָאֵל: [19]

וְכִלָּה מִכַּפֵּר אֶת־הַקֹּדֶשׁ וְאֶת־אֹהֶל מוֹעֵד וְאֶת־הַמִּזְבֵּחַ וְהִקְרִיב אֶת־הַשָּׂעִיר הֶחָי: וְסָמַךְ אַהֲרֹן אֶת־שְׁתֵּי יָדָיו עַל־רֹאשׁ הַשָּׂעִיר הַחַי וְהִתְוַדָּה עָלָיו אֶת־כָּל־עֲוֺנֹת בְּנֵי יִשְׂרָאֵל וְאֶת־כָּל־פִּשְׁעֵיהֶם לְכָל־חַטֹּאתָם וְנָתַן אֹתָם עַל־ [20] [21]

─── אונקלוס ───

קֳדָם יְיָ וִיכַפַּר עֲלוֹהִי וְיִסַּב מִדְּמָא דְתוֹרָא וּמִדְּמָא דִצְפִירָא וְיִתֵּן עַל קַרְנַת מַדְבְּחָא סְחוֹר סְחוֹר: [יט] וְיַדֵּי עֲלוֹהִי מִן דְּמָא בְּאֶצְבְּעֵהּ שְׁבַע זִמְנִין וִידַכִּנֵּהּ וִיקַדְּשִׁנֵּהּ מִסּוֹאֲבַת בְּנֵי יִשְׂרָאֵל: [כ] וִישֵׁיצֵי מִלְּכַפָּרָא יָת קוּדְשָׁא וְיָת מַשְׁכַּן זִמְנָא וְיָת מַדְבְּחָא וִיקָרֵב יָת צְפִירָא חַיָּא: [כא] וְיִסְמוֹךְ אַהֲרֹן יָת תַּרְתֵּין יְדוֹהִי עַל רֵישׁ צְפִירָא חַיָּא וִיוַדֵּי עֲלוֹהִי יָת כָּל עֲוָיָת בְּנֵי יִשְׂרָאֵל וְיָת כָּל חוֹבֵיהוֹן לְכָל חֲטָאֵיהוֹן וְיִתֵּן יָתְהוֹן עַל

─── רש"י ───

וכפר עליו. ומה היא כפרתו, **ולקח מדם הפר ומדם השעיר**, מעורבין זה לתוך זה (ת"כ שם יב; יומא נז:-נח.): **וטהרו.** ממה שעבר: **וקדשו.** לעתיד לבא (ת"כ שם יג): שנקן מתנות באצבעו על קרנותיו מזה שבע הזאות על גגו (ת"כ שם יב; יומא נח.):

─── RASHI ELUCIDATED ───

☐ **וְכִפֶּר עָלָיו** — AND MAKE ATONEMENT UPON IT. וּמַה הִיא כַּפָּרָתוֹ — What is its atonement? . . .

☐ **וְלָקַח מִדַּם הַפָּר וּמִדַּם הַשָּׂעִיר** — HE SHALL TAKE FROM THE BLOOD OF THE BULL AND FROM THE BLOOD OF THE HE-GOAT[1] — מְעֹרָבִין זֶה לְתוֹךְ זֶה — intermingled with each other.[2]

19. וְהִזָּה עָלָיו מִן הַדָּם — HE SHALL SPRINKLE UPON IT FROM THE BLOOD. אַחַר שֶׁנָּתַן מַתָּנוֹת — After he has put applications בְּאֶצְבָּעוֹ — with his finger עַל קַרְנוֹתָיו — on its horns, מַזֶּה שֶׁבַע הַזָּאוֹת — he sprinkles seven sprinklings[3] עַל גַּגּוֹ — on its top.[3]

☐ **וְטִהֲרוֹ** — AND HE SHALL PURIFY IT מִמַּה שֶּׁעָבַר — from that which has passed,

☐ **וְקִדְּשׁוֹ** — AND SANCTIFY IT לֶעָתִיד לָבֹא[4] — for that which is destined to come, i.e., for the future.[4]

---

1. In verses 6 and 11, וְכִפֶּר was used with reference to confession. Here the verse speaks of a stage that takes place after the confession. Hence, וְכִפֶּר refers to the intermingling of blood and its application which follows in the verse (Mizrachi; Sifsei Chachamim). According to Rashi, both וְכִפֶּר and וְלָקַח refer to the same act. This is unlike Targum Yonasan, who interprets וְכִפֶּר of our verse as also referring to confession (see Mesiach Ilmim).

2. Toras Kohanim, perek 4:7-10; Yoma 53b. Previously, the blood of the bull and that of the he-goat were offered separately in the sprinkling before the Cover of the Ark (כַּפֹּרֶת) and the dividing Curtain (פָּרֹכֶת); see verses 14-16 and Rashi there. Here the blood of the one is mixed with that of the other (see Yoma 57b-58a).

3. Toras Kohanim, perek 4:12; Yoma 58b-59a. Rashi explains that "he shall sprinkle upon it," is not meant as an explanation of "and place it on the horns of the Mizbe'ach," of the preceding verse (Mizrachi). He also explains that עָלָיו, "on it," is understood as "on top of it" (Mizrachi; Sifsei Chachamim).

4. Toras Kohanim, perek 4:13. He shall purify it of impurities of the past and sanctify it to take care not to profane it in the future (Mizrachi; Sifsei Chachamim). Alternatively, the purification referred to here removes any impurity from the Mizbe'ach. However, in addition to purification, the implements of the Mishkan were also sanctified before they were used (see Exodus 40:9). The sprinkling of the blood constituted not only a purification of the Mizbe'ach, but a re-sanctification, as well (Maskil LeDavid).

the head of the he-goat, and send it with a timely man to the desert. ²² *The he-goat will bear upon itself all their iniquities to a cut land, and he should send away the he-goat to the desert.*

²³ *Aaron shall come to the Tent of Meeting — he shall remove the linen garments that he had worn when he entered the*

רֹאשׁ הַשָּׂעִיר וְשִׁלַּח בְּיַד־אִישׁ
כב עִתִּי הַמִּדְבָּרָה: וְנָשָׂא הַשָּׂעִיר עָלָיו
אֶת־כָּל־עֲוֹנֹתָם אֶל־אֶרֶץ גְּזֵרָה
כג וְשִׁלַּח אֶת־הַשָּׂעִיר בַּמִּדְבָּר: וּבָא
אַהֲרֹן אֶל־אֹהֶל מוֹעֵד וּפָשַׁט אֶת־
בִּגְדֵי הַבָּד אֲשֶׁר לָבַשׁ בְּבֹאוֹ אֶל־

———— אונקלוס ————

רֵישׁ צְפִירָא וִישַׁלַּח בְּיַד גְּבַר דְּזַמִּין לְמֵהַךְ לְמַדְבְּרָא: כב וְיִטּוֹל צְפִירָא עֲלוֹהִי יָת כָּל חוֹבֵיהוֹן לְאַרְעָא דְלָא יָתְבָא וִישַׁלַּח יָת צְפִירָא לְמַדְבְּרָא (נ״א בְּמַדְבְּרָא): כג וְיֵיעוֹל אַהֲרֹן לְמַשְׁכַּן זִמְנָא וְיַשְׁלַח יָת לְבוּשֵׁי בּוּצָא דִּי לְבַשׁ בְּמֵעֲלֵהּ

———— רש״י ————

(בא) **איש עתי.** המוכן לכך מיום אתמול (שם פרשתא ד:ה; יומא סו:): (כג) **ובא אהרן אל אהל מועד.** אמרו רבותינו שאין זה מקומו של מקרא זה, ונתנו טעם לדבריהם במסכת יומא (לב.) ואמרו כל הפרשה כולה נאמרה על הסדר, חוץ מביאה זו שהיא אחר עשיית עולתו ועולת העם והקטרת

אימורי פר ושעיר שנעשים בחוץ בבגדי זהב, וטובל ומקדש ופושטן ולובש בגדי לבן, ובא אל אהל מועד להוציא את הכף ואת המחתה שהקטיר בה הקטורת לפני ולפנים (ת״כ פרק ו:ב; יומא שם): **ופשט את בגדי הבד.** אחר שהוציאם, ולובש בגדי זהב לתמיד של בין הערבים. וזהו סדר העבודות.

———— RASHI ELUCIDATED ————

21. עִתִּי אִישׁ — A TIMELY MAN הַמּוּכָן לְכָךְ — who has been prepared for this task [1] מִיּוֹם אֶתְמוֹל — from the preceding day.[1]

23. וּבָא אַהֲרֹן אֶל אֹהֶל מוֹעֵד — AARON SHALL COME TO THE TENT OF MEETING. אָמְרוּ רַבּוֹתֵינוּ — Our Rabbis said שֶׁאֵין זֶה מְקוֹמוֹ — that this is not the sequential position שֶׁל מִקְרָא זֶה — of this verse. וְנָתְנוּ טַעַם לְדִבְרֵיהֶם — They gave reason for their words, i.e., for their opinion, בְּמַסֶּכֶת יוֹמָא[2] — in Tractate *Yoma*.[2] וְאָמְרוּ — They said: כָּל הַפָּרָשָׁה כֻּלָּהּ — The entire portion נֶאֶמְרָה עַל הַסֵּדֶר — is stated in the Torah according to the order in which the service of Yom Kippur was performed חוּץ מִבִּיאָה זוֹ — except for this "coming," i.e., except for this statement that Aaron shall come to the Tent of Meeting, שֶׁהִיא אַחַר עֲשִׂיַּת עוֹלָתוֹ — for it takes place after the performance of the service of his *olah*-offering וְעוֹלַת הָעָם — and the *olah*-offering of the people,[3] וְהַקְטָרַת אֵמוּרֵי פַר וְשָׂעִיר — and the burning of the specified parts of the bull and the he-goat, שֶׁנַּעֲשִׂים בַּחוּץ — all of which were performed outside the Sanctuary בְּבִגְדֵי זָהָב — in garments of which gold was one of the materials. After performing these services, וְטוֹבֵל — he immerses himself in a *mikveh*, וּמְקַדֵּשׁ — and sanctifies his hands and feet by pouring water from the *Kiyyor* on them,[4] וּפוֹשְׁטָן — and takes them off, וְלוֹבֵשׁ בִּגְדֵי לָבָן — and puts on garments of white linen, וּבָא אֶל אֹהֶל מוֹעֵד — and comes to the Tent of Meeting לְהוֹצִיא אֶת הַכַּף — to take out the ladle with which he brought the incense into the Holy of Holies וְאֶת הַמַּחְתָּה — and the coal-pan upon which he poured the incense, שֶׁהִקְטִיר בָּהּ הַקְּטֹרֶת — with which he raised the fumes of the incense [5] לִפְנֵי וְלִפְנִים — in the very interior, i.e., in the Holy of Holies.[5]

☐ וּפָשַׁט אֶת בִּגְדֵי הַבָּד — HE SHALL REMOVE THE LINEN GARMENTS אַחַר שֶׁהוֹצִיאָם — after he will have taken out [the ladle and the coal-pan] וְלוֹבֵשׁ בִּגְדֵי זָהָב — and put on the garments of gold לְתָמִיד שֶׁל בֵּין הָעַרְבַּיִם — for the service of the continual *olah*-offering of the evening. וְזֶהוּ סֵדֶר הָעֲבוֹדוֹת — The order of the services of Yom Kippur (and the five changes of garments) is as

---

1. *Toras Kohanim, parshasa* 4-8; *Yoma* 66b. The term עִתִּי, "timely," means that he has been told to be ready for a particular time — he was told the day before Yom Kippur to be ready to perform his task on Yom Kippur (*Gur Aryeh*). Alternatively, עַת can denote a full day. עִתִּי implies a person who has undergone a process of preparation which takes a full day (*Maskil LeDavid*).

2. *Yoma* 32a.

3. See v. 24 below.

4. See *Exodus* 30:17-21.

5. *Toras Kohanim, perek* 6:2; *Yoma* 32a. Although the verse seems to be saying that Aaron entered the Sanctuary in order to change his clothes, he would not have undressed there, nor would he have left his clothes there indefinitely as שָׁם וְהִנִּיחָם, "and he shall leave them there," appears to imply (*Ramban*). That is why the Sages explain that this verse speaks about two events performed at different times: (a) While wearing his white linen garments, the Kohen Gadol entered the Sanctuary for a purpose not specified by the verse; and, (b) after having done so and having left the Holy of

ויקרא – פרשת אחרי

—— רש"י ——

תמיד של שחר בבגדי זהב, ועבודת פר ושעיר הפנימים וקטורת של מחתה בבגדי לבן, ואילו ואיל העם ומקלת המוספין בבגדי זהב, והוצאת כף ומחתה בבגדי לבן, ושירי המוספין ותמיד של בין הערבים וקטורת ההיכל שעל מזבח הפנימי בבגדי זהב

(ת"כ שם ה; יומא שם). וסדר המקראות לפי סדר העבודות הוא. ושלח את השעיר במדבר. ורחץ את בשרו במים וגו' ויצא ועשה את עולתו וגו' ואת חלב החטאת וגו'. ועד הפרשה עד ואחרי כן יבא אל המחנה, ואחר כך ובא אהרן:

—— RASHI ELUCIDATED ——

follows: **תָּמִיד שֶׁל שַׁחַר בְּבִגְדֵי זָהָב** — (a) **the continual** *olah-***offering of the morning in garments of gold;** **וַעֲבוֹדַת פַּר וְשָׂעִיר הַפְּנִימִים** — (b) **the service of the interior bull and he-goat,** i.e., the bull of the Kohen Gadol and the he-goat designated by lot "to HASHEM, a sin-offering," both of whose service was performed inside the Sanctuary,[1] **וּקְטֹרֶת שֶׁל מַחְתָּה** — **and the incense of the coal-pan,** i.e., the incense whose fumes were raised on the coal-pan,[2] **בְּבִגְדֵי לָבָן** — **in garments of white** linen; **וְאֵילוֹ וְאֵיל הָעָם** — (c) **the ram of [the Kohen Gadol] and the ram of the people**[3] **וּמִקְצָת הַמּוּסָפִין** — **and some of the** *mussaf-***offerings**[4] **בְּבִגְדֵי זָהָב** — **in garments of gold;** **וְהוֹצָאַת כַּף וּמַחְתָּה** — (d) **the removal of the ladle and the coal-pan** **בְּבִגְדֵי לָבָן** — **in garments of white** linen; **וּשְׁיָרֵי הַמּוּסָפִין** — (e) **and the rest of the** *mussaf-***offerings,**[5] **וְתָמִיד שֶׁל בֵּין הָעַרְבַּיִם** — **and the continual** *olah-***offering of the evening** **וּקְטֹרֶת הַהֵיכָל** — **and the incense of the Sanctuary,** **שֶׁעַל מִזְבַּח הַפְּנִימִי** — **which was** burned **on the inner Altar**[6] **בְּבִגְדֵי זָהָב**[7] — **in garments of gold.**[7] **וְסֵדֶר הַמִּקְרָאוֹת** — **The order of the verses** **לְפִי סֵדֶר הָעֲבוֹדוֹת** — **in accordance with the order** of the performance of the services **כָּךְ הוּא** — **is as follows:** ",,וְשִׁלַּח אֶת הַשָּׂעִיר בַּמִּדְבָּר" — **"He should send away the he-goat to the desert."**[8] ",,וְרָחַץ אֶת בְּשָׂרוֹ בַמַּיִם וְגוֹמֵר" — **"He shall immerse his flesh in the water, etc."**[9] ",,וְיָצָא וְעָשָׂה אֶת עֹלָתוֹ וְגוֹמֵר" — **"He shall go out and offer his own** *olah-***offering, etc."**[9] ",,וְאֵת חֵלֶב הַחַטָּאת וְגוֹמֵר" — **"The fat of the sin-offering** [he shall burn], **etc."**[10] **וְכָל הַפָּרָשָׁה** — **and** all of the steps of the service mentioned in **the entire** remainder **of the portion** **עַד ",,וְאַחֲרֵי כֵן** — **until, "thereafter he may enter the camp."**[11] ",,יָבוֹא אֶל הַמַּחֲנֶה" — **And afterwards,** ",,וּבָא אַהֲרֹן" — **"Aaron shall come."**[12]

Holies, he removed the white garments and put them away, as described by Rashi below.

Why did he enter the Sanctuary? Previously, upon leaving the Holy of Holies after offering the incense (verse 18), he had left the coal-pan and ladle behind while the incense burned; the first part of this verse tells us that he returned there — wearing his white garments — to remove those utensils.

The Talmud (*Yoma* 32a) proves that he could not have done this immediately after having dispatched the goat to Azazel (verse 22), for the following reason: There is a tradition taught to Moses at Sinai (הֲלָכָה לְמֹשֶׁה מִסִּינַי) that the Kohen Gadol immerses himself five times on Yom Kippur, once for each change of garments — but if he were to enter the Holy of Holies immediately after having sent away the goat, he would still be wearing his white garments; if so, he would not be making five changes of garments and so would not be immersing himself five times. It is imperative, therefore, that after sending away the goat, the Kohen Gadol immerse himself and change back to his garments of gold. Later, he would once more immerse himself and don his white garments to perform the service of removing the coal-pan and ladle. He would not do this until later in the day, when he had finished the services described in verses 24-28; thus, this verse is not in its chronological sequence. After his removal of the coal-pan and ladle, he would undress and dispose of his white garments, in the manner described by Rashi below.

The Torah departs from the chronological sequence of the day's service because it prefers to continue to list all parts of the service that were performed by the Kohen Gadol in his white garments. All the services described from verse 4 to this one were done in the white garments, including the entry into the Holy of Holies to remove the coal-pan and ladle. Thus, rather than describe the day's service in strict chronological order, the Torah completes the description of everything done in the special Yom Kippur garments, and then, in verse 25, proceeds to what the Kohen Gadol did in his regular eight garments of gold (see *Mizrachi; Sifsei Chachamim*).

1. Above vv. 6-11, 14-20.
2. Above vv. 12-13.
3. Verses 3,5,22.
4. The seven *olah-*offerings of sheep. See *Numbers* 29:8.
5. The bull and ram brought as *olah-* offerings (see *Numbers* 29:8) and the he-goat brought as a sin-offering (see *Numbers* 29:11).
6. The incense whose fumes were raised in the Sanctuary twice daily (see *Exodus* 30:34-36), as opposed to the incense of the coal-pan referred to by Rashi above whose fumes were raised in the Holy of Holies only on Yom Kippur.
7. *Toras Kohanim, perek* 6:5; *Yoma* 32a.
8. Verse 22.
9. Verse 24. After dispatching the he-goat to Azazel (v. 22), the Kohen Gadol changes into the garments of gold and performs the service of the rams brought as *olah-* offerings for himself and for the people.
10. Verse 25.
11. Verse 28.
12. Verse 23.

16/24 — טז/כד

Sanctuary, and he shall leave them there. ²⁴ **He shall immerse his flesh in the water in a sacred place and don his garments;**

כד הַקֹּדֶשׁ וְהִנִּיחָם שָׁם: וְרָחַץ אֶת־בְּשָׂרוֹ בַמַּיִם בְּמָקוֹם קָדוֹשׁ וְלָבַשׁ אֶת־בְּגָדָיו

— אונקלוס —

לְקוּדְשָׁא וְיַצְנְעִנּוּן תַּמָּן: כד וְיַסְחֵי יָת בִּסְרֵהּ בְּמַיָּא בַּאֲתַר קַדִּישׁ וְיִלְבַּשׁ יָת לְבוּשׁוֹהִי

— רש"י —

וְהִנִּיחָם שָׁם. מְלַמֵּד שֶׁטְּעוּנִין גְּנִיזָה וְלֹא יִשְׁתַּמֵּשׁ בְּאוֹתָן אַרְבָּעָה בְּגָדִים לְיוֹם כִּפּוּרִים אַחֵר (ת"כ שם ז; יומא כד.): **(כד) וְרָחַץ אֶת בְּשָׂרוֹ וְגוֹ'.** לְמַעְלָה לִמְּדָנוּ מוֹרְחָץ אֶת בְּשָׂרוֹ וּלֹבֵשׁ (לְטִיל פסוק ד) כְּשֶׁהוּא מְשַׁנֶּה מִבִּגְדֵי זָהָב לְבִגְדֵי לָבָן טָעוּן טְבִילָה, וְשֶׁבְּאוֹתָהּ טְבִילָה פָּשַׁט בִּגְדֵי זָהָב שֶׁעָבַד בָּהֶן עֲבוֹדַת תָּמִיד שֶׁל שַׁחַר וְלוֹבֵשׁ בִּגְדֵי לָבָן לַעֲבוֹדַת הַיּוֹם. וְכָאן לִמְּדָנוּ שֶׁכְּשֶׁהוּא מְשַׁנֶּה מִבְּגָדִים לְבָנִים לְבִגְדֵי זָהָב טְבִילָה בֵּינֵיהֶם: **בְּמָקוֹם קָדוֹשׁ.** הַמְקוּדָשׁ בִּקְדֻשַּׁת עֲזָרָה, וְהִיא הָיְתָה בְּגַג בֵּית הַפַּרְוָה וְכֵן אַרְבַּע טְבִילוֹת הַבָּאוֹת חוֹבָה לַיּוֹם, אֲבָל הָרִאשׁוֹנָה הָיְתָה בְּחֹל (וס"א בַּחֵיל) [ת"כ שָׁם ח; יומא ל.]: **וְלָבַשׁ אֶת בְּגָדָיו.** שְׁמוֹנָה בְגָדִים שֶׁהוּא עוֹבֵד בָּהֶן כָּל יְמוֹת הַשָּׁנָה:

— RASHI ELUCIDATED —

☐ וְהִנִּיחָם שָׁם — AND HE SHALL LEAVE THEM THERE. מְלַמֵּד — This teaches us שֶׁטְּעוּנִין גְּנִיזָה — that they require permanent storage, וְלֹא יִשְׁתַּמֵּשׁ בְּאוֹתָן אַרְבָּעָה בְּגָדִים — and he should not use those four linen garments ¹לְיוֹם הַכִּפּוּרִים אַחֵר — on another Yom Kippur.[1]

24. וְרָחַץ אֶת בְּשָׂרוֹ וְגוֹמֵר — HE SHALL IMMERSE HIS FLESH, ETC. לְמַעְלָה לָמַדְנוּ — We learned above, ²מִ,,וְרָחַץ אֶת בְּשָׂרוֹ וּלְבָשָׁם'' — from "he shall immerse his flesh in water and then don them,"[2] שֶׁכְּשֶׁהוּא מְשַׁנֶּה — that when he changes מִבִּגְדֵי זָהָב — from garments of gold, לְבָן לְבָן — to garments of white linen טָעוּן טְבִילָה — he requires immersion, {שֶׁבְּאוֹתָהּ טְבִילָה} — for in that immersion פָּשַׁט בִּגְדֵי זָהָב — he took off the garments of gold שֶׁעָבַד בָּהֶן עֲבוֹדַת תָּמִיד שֶׁל שַׁחַר — in which he performed the service of the continual *olah*-offering of the morning וְלוֹבֵשׁ בִּגְדֵי לָבָן — and put on the garments of white linen לַעֲבוֹדַת הַיּוֹם — for the performance of the service unique to the day of Yom Kippur}. וְכָאן לָמַדְנוּ — And here we learned שֶׁכְּשֶׁהוּא מְשַׁנֶּה — that when he changes מִבִּגְדֵי לָבָן — from garments of white linen לְבִגְדֵי זָהָב — to garments of gold ³טָעוּן טְבִילָה — he also requires immersion.[3]

☐ בְּמָקוֹם קָדוֹשׁ — IN A SACRED PLACE. A place הַמְקֻדָּשׁ — which has been consecrated בִּקְדֻשַּׁת עֲזָרָה — with the sanctity of the Courtyard of the *Beis HaMikdash*. וְהִיא הָיְתָה בְּגַג בֵּית הַפַּרְוָה — It was on the roof of the House of Parvah.[4] וְכֵן אַרְבַּע טְבִילוֹת — And likewise all four immersions, including the one mentioned here, הַבָּאוֹת חוֹבָה לַיּוֹם — which come as a specific obligation for the day of Yom Kippur were done on the roof of the House of Parvah.[5] אֲבָל הָרִאשׁוֹנָה — But the first immersion, which was done every day, not only on Yom Kippur,[5] ⁶הָיְתָה בְחֹל — took place in an unconsecrated area.[6]

☐ וְלָבַשׁ אֶת בְּגָדָיו — AND DON HIS GARMENTS. שְׁמוֹנָה בְגָדִים — The eight garments שֶׁהוּא עוֹבֵד בָּהֶן — in which he serves כָּל יְמוֹת הַשָּׁנָה — all the days of the year.[7]

---

1. *Toras Kohanim*, *perek* 6:7; *Yoma* 24a. It is inconceivable that the Kohen Gadol should leave his garments in the Tent of Meeting indefinitely as the verse seems to say. Rather, he leaves his garments there in the sense that they are never to be used again (*Ramban*).

2. Above v. 4.

3. *Toras Kohanim*, *perek* 6:4-5; *Yoma* 32b.

4. The House of Parvah was a building on the grounds of the *Beis HaMikdash*. The Talmud (*Yoma* 35a) explains that Parvah was an אֲמָגוּשָׁא, "magus," a Persian sorcerer. Rashi (there) adds that Parvah built the chamber that bore his name. According to *Rabbeinu Chananel*, Parvah so desired to observe the Kohen Gadol perform the Yom Kippur service that he tunneled under and into the *Beis HaMikdash*. When the Kohanim discovered Parvah in the tunnel, they killed him for having trespassed the Temple. Nevertheless, [in recognition of his misplaced devotion,] they named one of the chambers after him. (See *Peirush HaRosh*,

Peirush HaRambam and *Rashash* to *Middos* 5:3.)

5. See verse 4 above and note 1 on page 195.

6. *Toras Kohanim*, *perek* 6:8; *Yoma* 31a. The immersion that preceded the Kohen Gadol's entry into the Courtyard in the morning took place in a *mikveh* located on the roof of one of the gates of the Courtyard called the Gate of the Water. This roof, unlike the roof of the House of Parvah, was not consecrated (*Yoma* 31a).

Many modern editions read בְּחֵיל, "in the *cheil*," instead of בְּחוֹל, "in an unconsecrated area." The *cheil* was a ten-*amah*-wide band around the Courtyard walls that was demarcated by a low fence. However, there is nowhere in the Talmud or Midrash that mentions a *mikveh* in the *cheil*. Indeed, as noted above, the Talmud and *Sifra* state that the first immersion took place on the roof of the Gate of the Water which was not consecrated (*Yosef Hallel*).

7. These are the garments of gold.

וַיָּצָ֗א וְעָשָׂ֤ה אֶת־עֹֽלָתוֹ֙ וְאֶת־עֹלַ֣ת
הָעָ֔ם וְכִפֶּ֥ר בַּֽעֲד֖וֹ וּבְעַ֥ד הָעָֽם:
כה וְאֵ֛ת חֵ֥לֶב הַֽחַטָּ֖את יַקְטִ֥יר
הַמִּזְבֵּֽחָה: כו וְהַֽמְשַׁלֵּ֤חַ אֶת־הַשָּׂעִיר֙
לַֽעֲזָאזֵ֔ל יְכַבֵּ֣ס בְּגָדָ֔יו וְרָחַ֥ץ אֶת־
בְּשָׂר֖וֹ בַּמָּ֑יִם וְאַֽחֲרֵי־כֵ֖ן יָב֥וֹא אֶל־
הַֽמַּחֲנֶֽה: כז וְאֵת֩ פַּ֨ר הַֽחַטָּ֜את וְאֵ֣ת ׀
שְׂעִ֣יר הַֽחַטָּ֗את אֲשֶׁ֨ר הוּבָ֤א אֶת־
דָּמָם֙ לְכַפֵּ֣ר בַּקֹּ֔דֶשׁ יוֹצִ֖יא אֶל־
מִח֣וּץ לַֽמַּחֲנֶ֑ה וְשָֽׂרְפ֣וּ בָאֵ֔שׁ אֶת־
עֹֽרֹתָ֥ם וְאֶת־בְּשָׂרָ֖ם וְאֶת־פִּרְשָֽׁם:

he shall go out and offer his own olah-offering and the olah-offering of the people, and shall provide atonement for himself and for the people. ²⁵ And the fat of the sin-offering he shall burn on the *Mizbe'ach*. ²⁶ The one who dispatched the he-goat to Azazel shall immerse his clothing and immerse himself in the water; thereafter he may enter the camp. ²⁷ The sin-offering bull and the sin-offering he-goat, whose blood had been brought to provide atonement in the Sanctuary, someone shall remove to the outside of the camp; and they shall burn in fire their hides, their flesh, and their waste.

— אונקלוס —

וְיִפּוֹק וְיַעֲבֵד יָת עֲלָתֵהּ וְיָת עֲלַת עַמָּא וִיכַפֵּר עֲלוֹהִי וְעַל עַמָּא: כה וְיָת תַּרְבָּא דְחַטָּאתָא יַסֵּק לְמַדְבְּחָא: כו וּדְמוֹבִיל יָת צְפִירָא לַעֲזָאזֵל יְצַבַּע לְבוּשׁוֹהִי וְיַסְחֵי יָת בִּסְרֵהּ בְּמַיָּא וּבָתַר כֵּן יֵעוֹל לְמַשְׁרִיתָא: כז וְיָת תּוֹרָא דְחַטָּאתָא וְיָת צְפִירָא דְחַטָּאתָא דִּי אִתָּעַל מִדִּמְהוֹן לְכַפָּרָא בְקוּדְשָׁא יִתַּפְּקוּן לְמִבָּרָא לְמַשְׁרִיתָא וְיוֹקְדוּן בְּנוּרָא יָת מַשְׁכֵּיהוֹן וְיָת בִּסְרְהוֹן וְיָת אֻכְלֵיהוֹן:

— רש"י —

ויצא. מן ההיכל אל החצר שמזבח העולה שם: **ועשה את עולתו.** ואיל לעולה האמור למעלה, בזאת יבא אהרן וגו' (פסוק ג): **ואת עולת העם.** ואיל אחד לעולה האמור למעלה, ומאת עדת בני ישראל וגו' (פסוק ה):

(כה) ואת חלב החטאת. אימורי פר ושעיר: **יקטיר המזבחה.** על מזבח החיצון, דאילו בפנימי כתיב לא תעלו עליו קטרת זרה ועולה ומנחה (שמות ל:ט): **(כז) אשר הובא את דמם.** להיכל ולפני ולפנים:

— RASHI ELUCIDATED —

☐ וַיָּצָא — HE SHALL GO OUT — מִן הַהֵיכָל — of the Sanctuary — אֶל הֶחָצֵר — to the Courtyard,¹ שֶׁמִּזְבֵּחַ הָעוֹלָה שָׁם — where the *Mizbe'ach* of the *Olah*-offering stands.

☐ וְעָשָׂה אֶת עֹלָתוֹ — AND OFFER HIS OWN *OLAH*-OFFERING. This refers to the phrases, "וְאַיִל לְעֹלָה" — "And the ram for an *olah*-offering," הָאָמוּר לְמַעְלָה — that is stated above in the verse, "בְּזֹאת יָבֹא" — אַהֲרֹן וְגוֹמֵר"² — "with this shall Aaron come into the Sanctuary, etc."²

☐ וְאֶת עֹלַת הָעָם — AND THE *OLAH*-OFFERING OF THE PEOPLE. This refers to "וְאַיִל אֶחָד לְעֹלָה" — "and one ram for an *olah*-offering" הָאָמוּר לְמַעְלָה — which is stated above as being "וּמֵאֵת עֲדַת בְּנֵי יִשְׂרָאֵל וְגוֹמֵר"³ — "from the assembly of the Children of Israel, etc."³

25. וְאֵת חֵלֶב הַחַטָּאת — AND THE FAT OF THE SIN-OFFERING. אֵמוּרֵי פַר וְשָׂעִיר — The specified parts of the bull and the he-goat, i.e., the parts which the Torah says must be burned on the *Mizbe'ach*.⁴

☐ יַקְטִיר הַמִּזְבֵּחָה — HE SHALL BURN ON THE *MIZBE'ACH*. עַל מִזְבֵּחַ הַחִיצוֹן — On the outer *Mizbe'ach*. דְּאִלּוּ בִּפְנִימִי — For of the inner *Mizbe'ach* — כְּתִיב — it is written, "לֹא תַעֲלוּ עָלָיו קְטֹרֶת זָרָה וְעֹלָה וּמִנְחָה"⁵ — "You shall not bring up on it foreign incense, or *olah*-offering or meal-offering."⁵

27. אֲשֶׁר הוּבָא אֶת דָּמָם — WHOSE BLOOD HAD BEEN BROUGHT — לַהֵיכָל — into the Sanctuary, וְלִפְנֵי וְלִפְנִים — and into the very interior, i.e., the Holy of Holies.⁶

---

1. The term וַיָּצָא, "he shall go out," is used in a different sense than it was in verse 18. See Rashi there (Mizrachi).

2. Above v. 3.

3. Above v. 5.

4. The singular הַחַטָּאת, "the sin-offering," is used to refer to both the bull and the he-goat since they are both sin-offerings (Mizrachi; Sifsei Chachamim).

5. *Exodus* 30:9. Although the blood of the sin-offerings is sprinkled on the *Mizbe'ach* of Gold that was inside the Sanctuary, the parts of the offerings may not be burned on it (*Lifshuto shel Rashi*). Rashi understands "*olah*-offering" of the verse quoted to be representative of all animal offerings (*Nachalas Yaakov*).

6. In other contexts, הַקֹּדֶשׁ means "the Sanctuary" (see, for example, *Exodus* 26:33). Here it also refers to the Holy of Holies (*Mizrachi; Sifsei Chachamim*).

VAYIKRA/LEVITICUS — PARASHAS ACHAREI — 16/28-32

28 The one who burns them shall immerse his clothing and wash his flesh in the water; thereafter he may enter the camp. **29** This shall remain for you an eternal decree: In the seventh month, on the tenth of the month, you shall afflict yourselves and you shall not do any work, neither the native nor the proselyte who dwells among you. **30** For on this day he shall provide atonement for you to cleanse you; from all your sins before HASHEM shall you be cleansed.
31 It is a Sabbath of complete rest for you, and you shall afflict yourselves; an eternal decree. **32** The Kohen, who has been anointed or who has been given the authority to serve in place of his father, shall atone;

כח וְהַשֹּׂרֵף אֹתָם יְכַבֵּס בְּגָדָיו וְרָחַץ אֶת־בְּשָׂרוֹ בַּמָּיִם וְאַחֲרֵי־כֵן יָבוֹא אֶל־הַמַּחֲנֶה: כט וְהָיְתָה לָכֶם לְחֻקַּת עוֹלָם בַּחֹדֶשׁ הַשְּׁבִיעִי בֶּעָשׂוֹר לַחֹדֶשׁ תְּעַנּוּ אֶת־נַפְשֹׁתֵיכֶם וְכָל־מְלָאכָה לֹא תַעֲשׂוּ הָאֶזְרָח וְהַגֵּר הַגָּר בְּתוֹכְכֶם: ל כִּי־בַיּוֹם הַזֶּה יְכַפֵּר עֲלֵיכֶם לְטַהֵר אֶתְכֶם מִכֹּל חַטֹּאתֵיכֶם לִפְנֵי יְהוָה תִּטְהָרוּ: לא שַׁבַּת שַׁבָּתוֹן הִיא לָכֶם וְעִנִּיתֶם אֶת־נַפְשֹׁתֵיכֶם חֻקַּת עוֹלָם: לב וְכִפֶּר הַכֹּהֵן אֲשֶׁר־יִמְשַׁח אֹתוֹ וַאֲשֶׁר יְמַלֵּא אֶת־יָדוֹ לְכַהֵן תַּחַת אָבִיו

─── אונקלוס ───

כח וּדְמוֹקִיד יָתְהוֹן יְצַבַּע לְבוּשׁוֹהִי וְיַסְחֵי יָת בִּסְרֵהּ בְּמַיָּא וּבָתַר כֵּן יֵיעוֹל לְמַשְׁרִיתָא: כט וּתְהֵא לְכוֹן לִקְיָם עָלָם בְּיַרְחָא שְׁבִיעָאָה בְעַסְרָא לְיַרְחָא תְּעַנּוּן יָת נַפְשָׁתֵיכוֹן וְכָל עֲבִידָא לָא תַעְבְּדוּן יַצִּיבָא וְגִיּוֹרָא דְיִתְגַּיַּר בֵּינֵיכוֹן: ל אֲרֵי בְיוֹמָא הָדֵין יְכַפַּר עֲלֵיכוֹן לְדַכָּאָה יָתְכוֹן מִכֹּל חוֹבֵיכוֹן קֳדָם יְיָ תִּדְכּוּן: לא שַׁבָּא שַׁבְּתָא הִיא לְכוֹן וּתְעַנּוּן יָת נַפְשָׁתֵיכוֹן קְיָם עָלָם: לב וִיכַפַּר כָּהֲנָא דִּי יְרַבֵּי יָתֵהּ וְדִי יְקָרֵב יָת קֻרְבָּנֵהּ לְשַׁמָּשָׁא תְּחוֹת אֲבוּהִי

─── רש״י ───

חל(ד): **וכפר הכהן אשר ימשח וגו'**. כפרה זו של יום הכפורים אינה כשרה אלא בכהן גדול, לפי שנאמרה כל הפרשה באהרן. הוצרך לומר בכהן גדול הבא אחריו שיהא כמוהו (ת"כ פרק ח): **(לב): ואשר ימלא את ידו**. [שיכול] אין לי אלא המשוח בשמן המשחה, מרובה בגדים מנין, ת"ל ואשר ימלא את ידו וגו' (ת"כ שם) והם כל הכהנים הגדולים שעמדו מאחריו ואילך,

─── RASHI ELUCIDATED ───

כפרה זו 32. וְכִפֶּר הַכֹּהֵן אֲשֶׁר יִמְשַׁח וְגוֹמֵר — THE KOHEN, WHO HAS BEEN ANOINTED... SHALL ATONE, ETC. שֶׁל יוֹם הַכִּפּוּרִים — This atonement service of Yom Kippur [1] אֵינָהּ כְּשֵׁרָה אֶלָּא בְּכֹהֵן גָּדוֹל — is valid only if performed **by the Kohen Gadol.**[1] לְפִי שֶׁנֶּאֶמְרָה כָּל הַפָּרָשָׁה בְּאַהֲרֹן — Since the entire portion has been stated about Aaron, performing the service, הֻצְרַךְ לוֹמַר — it was necessary for [the Torah] to say בְּכֹהֵן גָּדוֹל הַבָּא אַחֲרָיו — about the Kohen Gadol who succeeds him שֶׁיְּהֵא כָּמוֹהוּ [2] — that he will be like [Aaron], i.e., he, too, will be allowed to perform the service of Yom Kippur.[2]

□ **וַאֲשֶׁר יְמַלֵּא אֶת יָדוֹ — OR WHO HAS BEEN GIVEN THE AUTHORITY.** {שֶׁיָּכוֹל — For one might have been able to think} on the basis of "the Kohen who has been anointed" alone: אֵין לִי אֶלָּא — I have nothing but, i.e., I know only that, הַמָּשׁוּחַ בְּשֶׁמֶן הַמִּשְׁחָה — [the Kohen Gadol] who was anointed with the oil of anointing may perform the service of Yom Kippur. מְרֻבֵּה בְּגָדִים מִנַּיִן — From where do we know that one whose garments were increased may perform the service?[3] תַּלְמוּד לוֹמַר — The Torah says, ״וַאֲשֶׁר יְמַלֵּא אֶת יָדוֹ וְגוֹמֵר״ [4] — "or who has been given the authority, etc."[4] וְהֵם כָּל הַכֹּהֲנִים הַגְּדוֹלִים — [Those whose garments were increased] are all of the Kohanim Gedolim שֶׁעָמְדוּ מֵאַחֲרָיו וְאֵילָךְ

---

1. *Yoma* 73a.
2. *Toras Kohanim, perek* 8:4.
3. In the period of the Tabernacle and the first *Beis HaMikdash* until the reign of Josiah, Kohanim Gedolim were anointed with the oil of anointing (see *Exodus* 30:30). Josiah hid the oil and other sacred objects of the *Beis HaMikdash* because he foresaw that Israel was destined to go into exile, and he did not want the sacred objects of the *Beis HaMikdash* to go into exile with them (*Yoma* 52b). From the reign of Josiah on, there was no oil of anointing. Then, Kohanim Gedolim were distinguished from ordinary Kohanim only through their wearing eight garments, while ordinary Kohanim wore four. The inauguration to the office of Kohen Gadol was accomplished by the new Kohen Gadol performing the service in his eight garments. (See Rashi to *Yoma* 12a, s.v., אמר אביי.)
4. *Toras Kohanim, perek* 8:4. The term מִלּוּי יָדַיִם, "giving authority," or, literally, "filling of hands," is associated by the Torah with wearing the garments of the priesthood. See *Exodus* 29:8-9.

he shall don the linen vestments, the sacred vestments. ³³ He shall bring atonement upon the Holy of Holies, and he shall bring atonement upon the Tent of Meeting and the Mizbe'ach; and upon the Kohanim and upon all the people of the congregation shall he bring atonement. ³⁴ This shall be to you an eternal decree to bring atonement upon the Children of Israel for all their sins once a year; and [Aaron] did as HASHEM commanded Moses.

17 ¹ HASHEM spoke to Moses, saying: ² Speak to Aaron and to his sons and to all the Children of Israel, and say to them: This is the matter that HASHEM has commanded, saying: ³ Any man from the House of Israel who will slaughter an ox, or a sheep, or a goat in the camp, or

וְלָבַשׁ אֶת־בִּגְדֵי הַבָּד בִּגְדֵי הַקֹּֽדֶשׁ׃ לג וְכִפֶּר אֶת־מִקְדַּשׁ הַקֹּדֶשׁ וְאֶת־אֹהֶל מוֹעֵד וְאֶת־הַמִּזְבֵּחַ יְכַפֵּר וְעַל הַכֹּהֲנִים וְעַל־כָּל־עַם הַקָּהָל יְכַפֵּר׃ לד וְהָיְתָה־זֹּאת לָכֶם לְחֻקַּת עוֹלָם לְכַפֵּר עַל־בְּנֵי יִשְׂרָאֵל מִכָּל־חַטֹּאתָם אַחַת בַּשָּׁנָה וַיַּעַשׂ כַּאֲשֶׁר צִוָּה יְהוָה אֶת־מֹשֶֽׁה׃

יז א רביעי וַיְדַבֵּר יְהוָה אֶל־מֹשֶׁה לֵּאמֹֽר׃ ב דַּבֵּר אֶל־אַהֲרֹן וְאֶל־בָּנָיו וְאֶל כָּל־בְּנֵי יִשְׂרָאֵל וְאָמַרְתָּ אֲלֵיהֶם זֶה הַדָּבָר אֲשֶׁר־צִוָּה יְהוָה לֵאמֹֽר׃ ג אִישׁ אִישׁ מִבֵּית יִשְׂרָאֵל אֲשֶׁר יִשְׁחַט שׁוֹר אוֹ־כֶשֶׂב אוֹ־עֵז בַּמַּחֲנֶה אוֹ

─── אונקלוס ───

וְיִלְבַּשׁ יָת לְבוּשֵׁי בוּצָא לְבוּשֵׁי קוּדְשָׁא: לג וִיכַפַּר יָת מַקְדְּשָׁא קוּדְשָׁא וְיָת מַשְׁכַּן זִמְנָא וְיָת מַדְבְּחָא יְכַפַּר וְעַל כָּהֲנַיָּא וְעַל כָּל עַמָּא דִקְהָלָא יְכַפַּר: לד וּתְהֵי דָא לְכוֹן לִקְיַם עָלַם לְכַפָּרָא עַל בְּנֵי יִשְׂרָאֵל מִכָּל חוֹבֵיהוֹן חֲדָא בְשַׁתָּא וַעֲבַד כְּמָא דִי פַקִּיד יְיָ יָת מֹשֶׁה: א וּמַלִּיל יְיָ עִם מֹשֶׁה לְמֵימָר: ב מַלֵּל עִם אַהֲרֹן וְעִם בְּנוֹהִי וְעִם כָּל בְּנֵי יִשְׂרָאֵל וְתֵימַר לְהוֹן דֵּין פִּתְגָּמָא דִי פַקִּיד יְיָ לְמֵימַר: ג גְּבַר גְּבַר מִבֵּית יִשְׂרָאֵל דִּי יִכּוֹס תּוֹר אוֹ אִמַּר אוֹ עִזָּא בְּמַשְׁרִיתָא אוֹ

─── רש"י ───

שבימיו נגנזה צלוחית של שמן המשחה (יומא נב:): **לכהן תחת אביו.** ללמד שאם בנו ממלא את מקומו הוא קודם לכל אדם (ת"כ שם ה): (לד) **ויעש כאשר צוה ה' וגו'.** כשהגיע יום הכפורים עשה כסדר הזה, ולהגיד שבחו של אהרן שלא היה לובש לגדולתו אלא כמקיים גזירת המלך (שם י): (ג) **אשר ישחט שור או כשב.** במוקדשין הכתוב מדבר,

─── RASHI ELUCIDATED ───

who held office from the reign of **Josiah on,** שֶׁבְּיָמָיו – **for in his days,** נִגְנְזָה צְלוֹחִית שֶׁל שֶׁמֶן הַמִּשְׁחָה¹ — **the flask of the oil of anointing** which remained from the days of Moses **was hidden away.**¹

☐ לְכֹהֵן תַּחַת אָבִיו – **TO SERVE IN PLACE OF HIS FATHER.** לְלַמֵּד – **To teach us** שֶׁאִם בְּנוֹ מְמַלֵּא אֶת מְקוֹמוֹ — **that if [the Kohen Gadol's] son can fill [his father's] place,** ² הוּא קוֹדֵם לְכָל אָדָם – **he takes precedence over any** other man to succeed his father.²

34. וַיַּעַשׂ כַּאֲשֶׁר צִוָּה ה' וְגוֹמֵר – **AND [AARON] DID AS HASHEM COMMANDED, ETC.** כְּשֶׁהִגִּיעַ יוֹם הַכִּפּוּרִים – **When Yom Kippur arrived,** עָשָׂה כַּסֵּדֶר הַזֶּה – **he performed** the service **according to this order.**³ וּלְהַגִּיד שִׁבְחוֹ שֶׁל אַהֲרֹן – And the Torah mentions this **to tell the praise of Aaron,** שֶׁלֹּא הָיָה לוֹבֵשׁ – **that he did not wear [the garments]** ⁴לִגְדֻלָּתוֹ – **for his own greatness,**⁴ אֶלָּא כִּמְקַיֵּם גְּזֵרַת הַמֶּלֶךְ – **but rather, as one who fulfills the decree of the king.**

17.

3. אֲשֶׁר יִשְׁחַט שׁוֹר אוֹ כֶשֶׂב – **WHO WILL SLAUGHTER A BULL, OR A SHEEP.** בְּמֻקְדָּשִׁין הַכָּתוּב מְדַבֵּר – **The**

---

1. *Yoma* 52b.
2. *Toras Kohanim, perek* 8:5.
3. Aaron was given the commandments of this chapter on the day after the death of his sons, Nadab and Avihu. "And [Aaron] did as HASHEM commanded Moses" does not mean that Aaron carried out the commandments immediately after he was given them. He carried them out in their proper time — on Yom Kippur (*Mizrachi; Sifsei Chachamim*).
4. *Toras Kohanim, perek* 8:10. There are many commandments addressed to Aaron or the Children of Israel about which the Torah presumes that we understand that they were carried out, without saying so explicitly. If the Torah makes a point of telling us that Aaron carried out the commandments of Yom Kippur, it is to teach us that he carried them out with the sublimest of intentions (*Mizrachi*).

who will slaughter outside the camp, **4** *and he has not brought it to the entrance of the Tent of Meeting to bring it as an offering to* HASHEM *before the Tabernacle of* HASHEM *— it shall be considered as blood for that man, he has spilled blood, and that man shall be cut off from his people.* **5** *So that the Children of Israel will bring their sacrifices that they slaughter on the open field, and they shall bring them to* HASHEM *to the entrance of the Tent of Meeting to the Kohen; and they shall slaughter them as sacrifices of peace-offerings to* HASHEM.

ד אֲשֶׁר יִשְׁחָט מִחוּץ לַמַּחֲנֶה: וְאֶל־
פֶּתַח אֹהֶל מוֹעֵד לֹא הֱבִיאוֹ
לְהַקְרִיב קָרְבָּן לַיהוה לִפְנֵי מִשְׁכַּן
יהוה דָּם יֵחָשֵׁב לָאִישׁ הַהוּא דָּם
שָׁפָךְ וְנִכְרַת הָאִישׁ הַהוּא מִקֶּרֶב
ה עַמּוֹ: לְמַעַן אֲשֶׁר יָבִיאוּ בְּנֵי יִשְׂרָאֵל
אֶת־זִבְחֵיהֶם אֲשֶׁר הֵם זֹבְחִים
עַל־פְּנֵי הַשָּׂדֶה וֶהֱבִיאֻם לַיהוה
אֶל־פֶּתַח אֹהֶל מוֹעֵד אֶל־הַכֹּהֵן
וְזָבְחוּ זִבְחֵי שְׁלָמִים לַיהוה אוֹתָם:

———————— אונקלוס ————————

דִּי יִכּוֹס מִבָּרָא לְמַשְׁרִיתָא: ד וְלִתְרַע מַשְׁכַּן זִמְנָא לָא אַיְתְיֵהּ לְקָרָבָא קָרְבָּנָא קֳדָם יְיָ קֳדָם מַשְׁכְּנָא דַּיָּי דְּמָא יִתְחַשֵּׁב לְגַבְרָא הַהוּא דְּמָא אֲשַׁד וְיִשְׁתֵּיצֵי אֱנָשָׁא הַהוּא מִגּוֹ עַמֵּהּ: ה בְּדִיל דִּי יַיְתוֹן בְּנֵי יִשְׂרָאֵל יָת דִּבְחֵיהוֹן דִּי אִנּוּן דָּבְחִין עַל אַפֵּי חַקְלָא וְיַיְתִנּוּן קֳדָם יְיָ לִתְרַע מַשְׁכַּן זִמְנָא לְוָת כַּהֲנָא וְיִדְבְּחוּן דִּבְחֵי קוּדְשִׁין קֳדָם יְיָ יָתְהוֹן:

———————— רש"י ————————

שֶׁנֶּאֱמַר לְהַקְרִיב קָרְבָּן (ת"כ פרשתא ו:ה): **בַּמַּחֲנֶה.** חוּץ לָעֲזָרָה: **בְּנֶפֶשׁ: דָּם שָׁפָךְ.** לְרַבּוֹת אֶת הַזּוֹרֵק דָּמִים בַּחוּץ (זבחים קז.): (ת"כ שם ג:) (ד) **דָּם יֵחָשֵׁב.** כְּשׁוֹפֵךְ דַּם הָאָדָם שֶׁמִּתְחַיֵּב (ה) **אֲשֶׁר הֵם זֹבְחִים.** אֲשֶׁר הֵם רְגִילִים לִזְבּוֹחַ (שם קו:):

———————— RASHI ELUCIDATED ————————

לְהַקְרִיב ,, – שֶׁנֶּאֱמַר – as it says, לְהַקְרִיב קָרְבָּן – "to bring [it] as an offering."[1,2]

□ בַּמַּחֲנֶה – IN THE CAMP. חוּץ לָעֲזָרָה[3] – Outside the Courtyard of the *Beis HaMikdash* or the Tabernacle.[3]

4. דָּם יֵחָשֵׁב – IT SHALL BE CONSIDERED AS BLOOD. כְּשׁוֹפֵךְ דַּם הָאָדָם – As one who shed the blood of a human being, שֶׁמִּתְחַיֵּב בְּנַפְשׁוֹ – for which one pays with his life.[4]

□ דָּם שָׁפָךְ – HE HAS SPILLED BLOOD. לְרַבּוֹת – To include in the punishment stated by this verse אֶת הַזּוֹרֵק דָּמִים בַּחוּץ[5] – one who sprinkles blood of an offering outside the grounds of the *Beis HaMikdash*.[5]

5. אֲשֶׁר הֵם זֹבְחִים – THAT THEY SLAUGHTER. That is, אֲשֶׁר הֵם רְגִילִים לִזְבּוֹחַ[6] – that they are in the habit of slaughtering.[6]

---

1. Verse 4. Rashi explains our verse in accordance with the opinion of the *Tanna* R' Akiva in *Chullin* 17a. The *Tanna* R' Ishmael there, however, understands that our verse applies even to animals which have not been consecrated. According to him, no meat was allowed to be eaten during the forty years that the Israelites sojourned in the desert unless it was slaughtered in the grounds of the Tabernacle as an offering on the *Mizbe'ach*. Accordingly, the verse says that no man may slaughter a bull, a sheep, or a goat, unless he does so as an offering.

2. *Toras Kohanim, parshasa*, 6:5.

3. *Toras Kohanim, parshasa* 6:3.

4. "It shall be considered as blood" cannot be taken literally, for it is obvious that the blood of an animal slaughtered outside the Tabernacle grounds is considered blood. The verse means that the blood of this animal is considered somewhat like the blood of a man; just as one is punished with death for killing a man, so, too, is one punished with *kares* (premature death) for slaughtering this animal outside the Courtyard (*Mizrachi; Sifsei Chachamim*).

5. *Zevachim* 107a. The verse speaks of one who slaughters an animal. Of necessity he spills its blood. However, this apparently superfluous fact is stated to make the sprinkling of the blood of the offering outside of the grounds of the *Beis HaMikdash*, as well as its slaughter, a sinful act (*Devek Tov; Ho'il Moshe*).

6. *Zevachim* 106b. The literal meaning of אֲשֶׁר הֵם זֹבְחִים is "that they are slaughtering." However, the verse cannot refer to offerings that are actually slaughtered in the open field. Those can no longer be brought to the Tent of Meeting as peace-offerings. The verse must mean that the Children of Israel should bring those offerings that they are in the habit of slaughtering in the open field (but are not slaughtering now), to the Tent of Meeting instead (*Mizrachi; Gur Aryeh*).

⁶ The Kohen shall throw the blood upon the Mizbe'ach of Hashem, at the entrance of the Tent of Meeting; and he shall cause the fats to go up in smoke for a satisfying aroma to Hashem. ⁷ They shall no longer slaughter their sacrifices to the demons after whom they stray; this shall be an eternal decree to them for their generations.

⁸ And to them you shall say: Any man of the House of Israel and of the proselyte who shall dwell among you who will offer an olah-offering or a sacrifice [of a peace-offering], ⁹ and he will not bring it to the entrance of the Tent of Meeting to perform its service to Hashem — that man shall be cut off from his people.

וְזָרַק הַכֹּהֵן אֶת־הַדָּם עַל־מִזְבַּח יהוה פֶּתַח אֹהֶל מוֹעֵד וְהִקְטִיר הַחֵלֶב לְרֵיחַ נִיחֹחַ לַיהוה: ז וְלֹא־יִזְבְּחוּ עוֹד אֶת־זִבְחֵיהֶם לַשְּׂעִירִם אֲשֶׁר הֵם זֹנִים אַחֲרֵיהֶם חֻקַּת עוֹלָם תִּהְיֶה־זֹּאת לָהֶם לְדֹרֹתָם:

ח חמישי [שלישי] וַאֲלֵהֶם תֹּאמַר אִישׁ אִישׁ מִבֵּית יִשְׂרָאֵל וּמִן־הַגֵּר אֲשֶׁר־יָגוּר בְּתוֹכָם אֲשֶׁר־יַעֲלֶה עֹלָה אוֹ־זָבַח: ט וְאֶל־פֶּתַח אֹהֶל מוֹעֵד לֹא יְבִיאֶנּוּ לַעֲשׂוֹת אֹתוֹ לַיהוה וְנִכְרַת הָאִישׁ הַהוּא מֵעַמָּיו:

— אונקלוס —

ו וְיִזְרוֹק כַּהֲנָא יָת דְּמָא עַל מַדְבְּחָא דַייָ בִּתְרַע מַשְׁכַּן זִמְנָא וְיַסֵּק תַּרְבָּא לְאִתְקַבָּלָא בְרַעֲוָא קֳדָם יְיָ: ז וְלָא יְדַבְּחוּן עוֹד יָת דִּבְחֵיהוֹן לְשֵׁדִין דִּי אִנּוּן טָעַן בַּתְרֵיהוֹן קְיָם עָלַם תְּהֵי דָא לְהוֹן לְדָרֵיהוֹן: ח וּלְהוֹן תֵּימַר גְּבַר גְּבַר מִבֵּית יִשְׂרָאֵל וּמִן גִּיּוֹרָא דְּיִתְגַּיַּר בֵּינֵיכוֹן דִּי יַסֵּק עֲלָתָא אוֹ נִכְסַת קוּדְשַׁיָּא: ט וְלִתְרַע מַשְׁכַּן זִמְנָא לָא יַיְתִנֵּהּ לְמֶעְבַּד יָתֵהּ קֳדָם יְיָ וְיִשְׁתֵּיצֵי אֲנָשָׁא הַהוּא מֵעַמֵּהּ:

— רש"י —

(ז) לשעירם. לשדים, כמו ושעירים ירקדו שם (ישעיה יג:כא), ת"כ: בחוץ כשוחט בחוץ, שאם שחט אחד והעלה חבירו שניהם חייבין (ת"כ פרק י:ו; זבחים קו.): (ט) ונכרת. זרעו נכרת וימיו נכרתין:

(ח) אשר יעלה עולה. לחייב על המקטיר אברים

— RASHI ELUCIDATED —

7. לַשְּׂעִירִם — This means לַשֵּׁדִים — to the demons,¹ כְּמוֹ ,,וּשְׂעִירִים יְרַקְּדוּ שָׁם‏‏‏‎" — like וּשְׂעִירִים in, "and demons will dance there."²,³

8. אֲשֶׁר יַעֲלֶה עֹלָה — WHO WILL OFFER AN OLAH-OFFERING. לְחַיֵּב עַל הַמַּקְטִיר אֲבָרִים בַּחוּץ — This verse serves **to make the one who burns the limbs or organs** of an offering **outside** the grounds of the *Beis HaMikdash* liable to punishment כְּשׁוֹחֵט בַּחוּץ — **like one who slaughters** an offering **outside** the grounds of the *Beis HaMikdash*, to teach us שֶׁאִם שָׁחַט אֶחָד — **that if one man slaughtered,** וְהֶעֱלָה חֲבֵרוֹ — **and his fellow offered up** the limbs or organs, שְׁנֵיהֶם חַיָּבִין — **both of them are held liable.**⁴

9. וְנִכְרַת — SHALL BE CUT OFF. זַרְעוֹ נִכְרָת — **His seed is cut off,** i.e., his children die,⁵ וְיָמָיו נִכְרָתִין — **and his days are cut off,** i.e., he dies prematurely.

---

1. In the preceding chapter, שָׂעִיר was used several times for "he-goat." Rashi points out that in this verse it means "demon." Demons are referred to by the word for "he-goat" because that is how they are visualized by those who believe in them (*Ibn Ezra* here; *Radak* to *Isaiah* 13:21). Alternatively, because they share the he-goat's restless nature (see *Abarbanel; Haamek Davar*).

2. *Isaiah* 13:21.

3. *Toras Kohanim, perek* 9:8.

4. *Toras Kohanim, perek* 10:6; *Zevachim* 106a. The term אֲשֶׁר יַעֲלֶה, "who will offer," of our verse does not refer to slaughtering, for the prohibition against slaughtering offerings outside the Courtyard has already been dealt with in the preceding verses. Rather, it refers to offering up the limbs and organs on an altar (*Minchas Yehudah; Sifsei Chachamim*). Rashi goes so far as to say that this prohibition extends even to offerings which have been disqualified by being slaughtered outside the Courtyard, although it could have been viewed as referring to offerings which are as yet valid; he understands that "and to them you shall say," of the beginning of this verse, links this verse to the subject of slaughtering outside the Courtyard with which the preceding verses dealt (*Mizrachi; Gur Aryeh*).

5. According to *Tosafos* (*Shabbos* 25a, s.v., כרת), "his seed is cut off" refers exclusively to young children. Many of the supercommentaries (to Rashi to 20:20 below) hold that Rashi agrees with that view (*Gur Aryeh*; *Tzeidah LaDerech*; *Nachalas Yaakov*). However, *Be'er BaSadeh* (based on Rashi to *Genesis* 15:2, s.v., הוֹלֵךְ עֲרִירִי), states that adult children are also included.

¹⁰ Any man of the House of Israel and of the proselyte who dwells among them who will consume any blood — I shall direct my face upon the soul consuming the blood, and I will cut it off from its people. ¹¹ For the soul of the flesh is in the blood and I have assigned it for you upon the Mizbe'ach to provide atonement for your souls; for it is the blood that atones for the soul. ¹² Therefore I have said to the Children of Israel: "Any person from among you may not consume blood;

י וְאִישׁ אִישׁ מִבֵּית יִשְׂרָאֵל וּמִן־הַגֵּר הַגָּר בְּתוֹכָם אֲשֶׁר יֹאכַל כָּל־דָּם וְנָתַתִּי פָנַי בַּנֶּפֶשׁ הָאֹכֶלֶת אֶת־הַדָּם וְהִכְרַתִּי אֹתָהּ מִקֶּרֶב עַמָּהּ: יא כִּי־נֶפֶשׁ הַבָּשָׂר בַּדָּם הִוא וַאֲנִי נְתַתִּיו לָכֶם עַל־הַמִּזְבֵּחַ לְכַפֵּר עַל־נַפְשֹׁתֵיכֶם כִּי־הַדָּם הוּא בַּנֶּפֶשׁ יְכַפֵּר: יב עַל־כֵּן אָמַרְתִּי לִבְנֵי יִשְׂרָאֵל כָּל־נֶפֶשׁ מִכֶּם לֹא־תֹאכַל דָּם

──────── אונקלוס ────────

י וּגְבַר גְּבַר מִבֵּית יִשְׂרָאֵל וּמִן גִּיּוֹרַיָּא דְיִתְגַּיַּר בֵּינֵיהוֹן דִּי יֵיכוּל כָּל דָּם וְאֶתֵּן רוּגְזִי בֶּאֱנָשָׁא דְּיֵיכוּל יָת דְּמָא וֶאֱשֵׁיצֵי יָתֵהּ מִגּוֹ עַמֵּהּ: יא אֲרֵי נְפַשׁ בִּסְרָא בִּדְמָא הִיא וַאֲנָא יְהַבְתֵּהּ לְכוֹן עַל מַדְבְּחָא לְכַפָּרָא עַל נַפְשָׁתֵיכוֹן אֲרֵי דְמָא הוּא בִּנְפַשָׁא מְכַפֵּר: יב עַל כֵּן אֲמָרִית לִבְנֵי יִשְׂרָאֵל כָּל אֱנַשׁ מִנְּכוֹן לָא יֵיכוּל דְּמָא

──────── רש"י ────────

(י) כל דם. לפי שנאמר בנפש יכפר (פסוק יא), יכול לא יהא חייב אלא על דם המוקדשים, ת"ל כל דם (ת"כ פרשתא ח:ב): ונתתי פני. פנאי שלי פונה אני מכל עסקי ועוסק בו (שם ז): (יא) כי נפש הבשר. של כל בריה בדם היא תלויה, ולפיכך נתתיו על המזבח לכפר על נפש האדם. תבוא נפש ותכפר על הנפש: (יב) כל נפש מכם. להזהיר גדולים על הקטנים (שם ו:):

──────── RASHI ELUCIDATED ────────

יָכוֹל — "atones for the soul,"[1] בַּנֶּפֶשׁ יְכַפֵּר — Since it says, לְפִי שֶׁנֶּאֱמַר — לְפִי שֶׁנֶּאֱמַר 10. כָּל דָּם — ANY BLOOD. — one might be able to think that לֹא יְהֵא חַיָּב — he shall not be held liable אֶלָּא עַל דַּם הַמֻּקְדָּשִׁים — except for consuming the blood of those animals that have been consecrated as offerings, for it is only their blood that brings atonement. תַּלְמוּד לוֹמַר — To teach us otherwise, the verse says, ‏,,כָּל דָּם"[2] — "any blood."[2]

□ וְנָתַתִּי פָנַי — I SHALL DIRECT MY FACE. פְּנַאי שֶׁלִּי — My attention. פּוֹנֶה אֲנִי מִכָּל עֲסָקַי — I turn aside from all My concerns וְעוֹסֵק בּוֹ[3] — and deal with him.[3]

11. כִּי נֶפֶשׁ הַבָּשָׂר — FOR THE SOUL OF THE FLESH שֶׁל כָּל בְּרִיָּה — of every creature[4] — בַּדָּם הִיא תְלוּיָה — depends upon the blood,[5] וּלְפִיכָךְ נְתַתִּיו — therefore,[6] I assigned it, i.e., I decreed that it should be placed, עַל הַמִּזְבֵּחַ — upon the Mizbe'ach, לְכַפֵּר עַל נֶפֶשׁ הָאָדָם — to atone for man's soul. תָּבוֹא נֶפֶשׁ — Let a soul of an animal come וּתְכַפֵּר עַל הַנֶּפֶשׁ — and atone for the soul of man.

{12. כָּל נֶפֶשׁ מִכֶּם — ANY PERSON FROM AMONG YOU. לְהַזְהִיר גְּדוֹלִים — To warn adults עַל הַקְּטַנִּים[7] — with respect to minors.[7]}

---

1. Below v. 11.
2. Toras Kohanim, parshasa 8:2.
3. Toras Kohanim, parshasa 8:4. God's direction of His face whenever someone can have a benign connotation. Rashi explains that "My face" in our verse is not to be understood in this sense. It is to be understood as "My attention." In this sense it has no benign connotation (Minchas Yehudah; Sifsei Chachamim). According to Sefer Zikaron, Rashi is saying that פָּנַי of our verse is not to be understood as "My face" at all, but is rather a form of the word פְּנַאי, attention, but without the א. According to Leket Bahir, Rashi understands the word as "My face," but explains how "My face" is to be interpreted in this context. He uses פְּנַאי, a word similar to פָּנַי, in his explanation, for aesthetic reasons only.
4. בָּשָׂר generally refers to the flesh of a dead animal. But "the soul of the flesh is in the blood" here does not refer to the meat of the dead animal whose blood is being eaten.

Because that animal is dead, its meat is no longer linked to its soul. "The flesh" here refers to living creatures in general (Be'er BaSadeh).
5. "In the blood" does not mean "inside the blood." The soul is not a physical entity which can be inside something else. Rather, it means that the animal's soul — its life — depends on its blood (Mizrachi; Sifsei Chachamim).
6. Rashi explains that "and" of "and I have assigned it" does not introduce an independent reason for the prohibition against eating blood which follows in verse 12. It is related to "for the soul of the flesh is in the blood" (Mizrachi; Sifsei Chachamim).
7. Toras Kohanim, parshasa 8:6. The verse could have said "you shall not eat blood." The lengthier, "any person among you shall not eat blood," is used to imply that care should be taken that any person among the people of Israel, even minors, should not eat blood (Korban Aharon).

וְהַגֵּר הַגָּר בְּתוֹכְכֶם לֹא־יֹאכַל דָּם:
יג וְאִישׁ אִישׁ מִבְּנֵי יִשְׂרָאֵל וּמִן־הַגֵּר הַגָּר בְּתוֹכָם אֲשֶׁר יָצוּד צֵיד חַיָּה אוֹ־עוֹף אֲשֶׁר יֵאָכֵל וְשָׁפַךְ אֶת־דָּמוֹ וְכִסָּהוּ בֶּעָפָר: יד כִּי־נֶפֶשׁ כָּל־בָּשָׂר דָּמוֹ בְנַפְשׁוֹ הוּא וָאֹמַר לִבְנֵי יִשְׂרָאֵל דַּם כָּל־בָּשָׂר לֹא תֹאכֵלוּ כִּי נֶפֶשׁ כָּל־בָּשָׂר דָּמוֹ הִוא כָּל־אֹכְלָיו יִכָּרֵת: טו וְכָל־נֶפֶשׁ אֲשֶׁר תֹּאכַל נְבֵלָה וּטְרֵפָה בָּאֶזְרָח וּבַגֵּר

and the proselyte who dwells among you may not consume blood." ¹³ Any man of the Children of Israel and of the proselyte who dwells among them who will trap a catch of a beast or bird that may be eaten, he shall pour out its blood and cover it with earth. ¹⁴ For the life of any flesh is — its blood represents its life, so I say to the Children of Israel, "You shall not consume the blood of any flesh; for the life of any flesh is its blood, whoever consumes it will be cut off." ¹⁵ Any person who will eat that which died or was mauled — the native or the proselyte

───────── אונקלוס ─────────

וְגִיּוֹרָא דְּיִתְגַּיְּרוּן בֵּינֵיכוֹן לָא יֵיכוּל דְּמָא: יג וּגְבַר מִן בְּנֵי יִשְׂרָאֵל וּמִן גִּיּוֹרַיָּא דְּיִתְגַּיְּרוּן בֵּינֵיכוֹן דִּי יָצוּד צֵיד חַיְתָא אוֹ עוֹפָא דִּי מִתְאֲכֵל וְיֵישׁוֹד יָת דְּמֵהּ וִיכַסְּנֵהּ בְּעַפְרָא: יד אֲרֵי נֶפֶשׁ כָּל בִּסְרָא דְּמֵהּ בְּנַפְשֵׁהּ הוּא וַאֲמָרִית לִבְנֵי יִשְׂרָאֵל דַּם כָּל בִּסְרָא לָא תֵיכְלוּן אֲרֵי נֶפֶשׁ כָּל בִּסְרָא דְּמֵהּ הִיא כָּל דְּיֵיכְלִנַּהּ יִשְׁתֵּיצֵי: טו וְכָל אֱנָשׁ דִּי יֵיכוּל נְבִילָא וּתְבִירָא בְּיַצִּיבָא וּבְגִיּוֹרָא

───────── רש"י ─────────

(יג) **אשר יצוד.** אֵין לִי אֶלָּא הַצָּד, [נִגְדָּלִין וְעוֹמְדִים כְּגוֹן] אַוָּזִין וְתַרְנְגוֹלִין מִנַּיִן, תַּ"ל צֵיד, מִכָּל מָקוֹם וְאִם כֵּן לָמָּה נֶאֱמַר אֲשֶׁר יָצוּד, שֶׁלֹּא יֹאכַל בָּשָׂר אֶלָּא בַּהַזְמָנָה זֹאת (ת"כ פרק יא:ב; חולין פד.): **אשר יאכל.** פְּרָט לִטְמֵאִים (ת"כ שם ג):

דמו בנפשו הוא. דָּמוֹ הוּא לוֹ בִּמְקוֹם הַנֶּפֶשׁ, שֶׁהַנֶּפֶשׁ תְּלוּיָה בּוֹ: **כי נפש כל בשר דמו הוא.** הַנֶּפֶשׁ הִיא הַדָּם. דָּם וּבָשָׂר לְשׁוֹן זָכָר, נֶפֶשׁ לְשׁוֹן נְקֵבָה: (טו) **אשר תאכל נבלה וטרפה.** בְּנִבְלַת עוֹף טָהוֹר דִּבֶּר הַכָּתוּב, שֶׁאֵין לָהּ טֻמְאָה

───────── RASHI ELUCIDATED ─────────

13. אֲשֶׁר יָצוּד — WHO WILL TRAP. אֵין לִי אֶלָּא הַצָּד — On the basis of this phrase **I know only** that the commandment to cover the blood applies to **one who traps** an animal. {נִצּוֹדִין וְעוֹמְדִין, כְּגוֹן אַוָּזִין וְתַרְנְגוֹלִין מִנַּיִן — From where do we know** that it also applies to domestic animals {which are considered **already trapped, such as} geese and chickens?** — תַּלְמוּד לוֹמַר — **The verse says,** ״צֵיד״ — **"a catch,"** which implies מִכָּל מָקוֹם — **in any sort of circumstance.**[1] {אִם כֵּן — **If so,** that the commandment applies to animals taken by any means, לָמָּה נֶאֱמַר — **why does it say,** ״אֲשֶׁר יָצוּד״ — "**who will trap**"? To teach us שֶׁלֹּא יֹאכַל בָּשָׂר — **that one should not eat meat** אֶלָּא בַּהֲזְמָנָה זֹאת — **unless it is with this preparation.**}[2]

□ אֲשֶׁר יֵאָכֵל — THAT MAY BE EATEN.[3] פְּרָט לִטְמֵאִים — **To the exclusion of non-kosher [animals].**[3]

14. דָּמוֹ בְנַפְשׁוֹ הוּא — ITS BLOOD REPRESENTS ITS LIFE. דָּמוֹ הוּא לוֹ — **Its blood serves it** בִּמְקוֹם הַנֶּפֶשׁ — **in the role of its life,** שֶׁהַנֶּפֶשׁ תְּלוּיָה בּוֹ — **for life depends upon it.**[4]

□ כִּי נֶפֶשׁ כָּל בָּשָׂר דָּמוֹ הוּא — FOR THE LIFE OF ANY FLESH IS ITS BLOOD. הַנֶּפֶשׁ הִיא הַדָּם — **The life is the blood.** דָּם וּבָשָׂר לְשׁוֹן זָכָר — "**Blood**" **and** "**flesh**" **are masculine terms.** נֶפֶשׁ לְשׁוֹן נְקֵבָה — "**Life**" **is a feminine term.**[5]

15. אֲשֶׁר תֹּאכַל נְבֵלָה וּטְרֵפָה — WHO WILL EAT THAT WHICH DIED OR WAS MAULED. בְּנִבְלַת עוֹף טָהוֹר דִּבֶּר — **The verse speaks of the unslaughtered carcass of a kosher bird,** שֶׁאֵין לָהּ טֻמְאָה — **which**

---

1. The apparently superfluous צֵיד, "a catch," includes animals that do not need to be actively hunted, but rather allow themselves to be caught (*Mizrachi*; *Gur Aryeh*).

2. *Toras Kohanim*, *perek* 11:2.; *Chullin* 84a. One should not eat meat regularly. It should be viewed as a thing that has to be trapped, i.e., as something not readily attainable (see Rashi to *Chullin* 84a).

3. *Toras Kohanim*, *perek* 11:3.

4. The phrase דָּמוֹ בְנַפְשׁוֹ הוּא could have been understood as, "its blood depends upon its life." But this cannot be the meaning of the verse, for life depends on the blood, not blood upon the life. Therefore Rashi explains that the verse means "the blood is in the role of its life," i.e., it represents its life (*Mesiach Ilmim*; *Mizrachi*; *Sifsei Chachamim*).

5. The feminine pronoun הִוא in our verse refers to the feminine noun נֶפֶשׁ; the masculine pronoun הוּא in our verse refers to the masculine noun דָּמוֹ (*Mizrachi*).

17/16 — טז/יז

וְכִבֶּס בְּגָדָיו וְרָחַץ בַּמַּיִם וְטָמֵא
עַד־הָעָרֶב וְטָהֵר: וְאִם לֹא
יְכַבֵּס וּבְשָׂרוֹ לֹא יִרְחָץ וְנָשָׂא
עֲוֹנוֹ:

— he shall immerse his garments and immerse himself in the water; he shall remain impure until evening and then become pure. ¹⁶ But if he does not immerse [his garments] and does not immerse his flesh, he shall bear his iniquity.

אונקלוס

וִיצַבַּע לְבוּשׁוֹהִי וְיַסְחֵי בְמַיָא וִיהֵי מְסָאָב עַד רַמְשָׁא וְיִדְכֵּי: טז וְאִם לָא יְצַבַּע וּבִסְרֵהּ לָא יַסְחֵי וִיקַבֵּל חוֹבָהּ:

רש"י

אלא בשעה שנבלעת בבית הבליעה. ולמדך כאן שמטמאה
באכילתה [וחיבה מטמאה במגע]. וטרפה האמורה כאן לא
נכתב אלא לדרוש. וכן שנינו יכול תהא נבלת עוף טמא מטמאה
בבית הבליעה, ת"ל וטרפה, מי שיש במינו טרפה, יצא עוף
טמא שאין במינו טרפה (ת"כ שם פרק יב:ג): (טז) וְנָשָׂא
עֲוֹנוֹ. אם יאכל קדש או יכנס למקדש חייב על טומאה זו ככל
שאר טומאות (שם יד): וּבְשָׂרוֹ לֹא יִרְחָץ וְנָשָׂא עֲוֹנוֹ. על
רחיצת גופו ענוש כרת, ועל כבוס בגדים במלקות (שם יג):

RASHI ELUCIDATED

שֶׁנִּבְלַעַת — that it is has, i.e., transmits, no impurity אֶלָּא בְּשָׁעָה — other than at the time שֶׁמְּטַמְּאָה — [The Torah] teaches you here וְלִמֶּדְךָ כָּאן — in the throat.¹ בְּבֵית הַבְּלִיעָה — swallowed — that it transmits impurity בַּאֲכִילָתָהּ — by its being eaten, {וְאֵינָהּ מְטַמְּאָה בְּמַגָּע} — and it does not transmit impurity through touching it}. וּטְרֵפָה״ הָאֲמוּרָה כָאן — The mauled animal mentioned here לֹא נִכְתַּב אֶלָּא לִדְרוֹשׁ — is written only to be expounded.² וְכֵן שָׁנִינוּ — We have learned how it is expounded as follows: יָכוֹל — One might be able to think that תְּהֵא נִבְלַת עוֹף טָמֵא מְטַמְּאָה — the unslaughtered carcass of a bird of a non-kosher species should transmit impurity בְּבֵית הַבְּלִיעָה — through being swallowed in the throat. תַּלְמוּד לוֹמַר — To teach us otherwise, the verse says, ״וּטְרֵפָה״ — "mauled," to imply that such impurity applies only to מִי שֶׁיֵּשׁ בְּמִינוֹ — one which has in its species a halachic class of טְרֵפָה — a "mauled" animal.³ יָצָא עוֹף טָמֵא — This excludes a non-kosher bird, שֶׁאֵין בְּמִינוֹ טְרֵפָה⁴ — in whose species there is no halachic class of "mauled" animal.⁴

16. וְנָשָׂא עֲוֹנוֹ — HE SHALL BEAR HIS INIQUITY. אִם יֹאכַל קֹדֶשׁ — If he will eat that which is holy אוֹ יִכָּנֵס לַמִּקְדָּשׁ — or enter the Beis HaMikdash, חַיָּב עַל טֻמְאָה זוֹ — he is liable to suffer kares for this impurity ⁵כְּכָל שְׁאָר טֻמְאוֹת — just as for all other impurities.⁵

□ וּבְשָׂרוֹ לֹא יִרְחָץ וְנָשָׂא עֲוֹנוֹ — AND DOES NOT IMMERSE HIS FLESH, HE SHALL BEAR HIS INIQUITY. עַל רְחִיצַת גּוּפוֹ — For not immersing his body עָנוּשׁ כָּרֵת — he is punished by kares, וְעַל כִּבּוּס בְּגָדִים — and for not washing, i.e., immersing, garments he is punished ⁶בְּמַלְקוֹת — by lashes.⁶

---

1. The meat of the carcass does not transmit impurity to one who eats it while it is in his mouth. It transmits impurity only while it is in the throat. So, too, if one immerses himself in a *mikveh* after having swallowed the meat of the carcass, he becomes purified even if there is a chunk of the meat of the carcass still in his stomach.

2. There is a dispute in the Gemara (*Zevachim* 69b) as to whether an animal that has one of the twenty-four mortal defects which render it a *tereifah* ("a mauled animal," i.e., an animal that has a mortal defect and therefore cannot become kosher even if it is slaughtered in accordance with halachah) is considered legally dead or not. According to either opinion, וּטְרֵפָה of our verse appears superfluous. If such an animal is considered dead, it falls under the category of נְבֵלָה, "an unslaughtered, dead animal," which was already mentioned in the verse. If it is considered to be living, it would not transmit impurity. וּטְרֵפָה is therefore interpreted as modifying נְבֵלָה which precedes it — "any person who will eat that which has died, if it is of a species to which the law of טְרֵפָה applies" (see Rashi to *Zevachim* 69b, s.v., אם טריפה חיה, and 69a, s.v., אלא תלמוד לומר טריפה; and *Mesiach Ilmim*).

3. A species of which members suffering certain organic defects may not be eaten even after they are slaughtered, i.e., a kosher species, as opposed to a species of which no members may be eaten, regardless of whether they were suffering organic defects or not, i.e., a non-kosher species.

4. *Toras Kohanim, perek* 12:7.

5. *Toras Kohanim, perek* 12:14; see *Numbers* 19:20. Becoming impure by eating the bird's carcass is in itself not a sin. The iniquity referred to by the verse is eating that which is holy or entering the *Beis HaMikdash* while in a state of impurity (*Mizrachi*; *Sefer Zikaron*).

6. *Toras Kohanim, perek* 12:13. The word בְשָׂרוֹ, "[and] his flesh," of our verse appears superfluous, for the verse could have written, וְלֹא יִרְחָץ, "and he will not immerse himself." וּבְשָׂרוֹ is written to teach us that only for the sin of eating that which is holy or entering the *Beis HaMikdash*, i.e., failure to immerse himself before eating that which is holy or entering the *Beis HaMikdash*, is he punished by kares (*Gur Aryeh*; *Sifsei Chachamim*). If, however, he throws his impure garments into the grounds of the *Beis HaMikdash*, he is punished only by lashes (*Mizrachi*).

18

¹ Hashem spoke to Moses, saying: **²** Speak to the Children of Israel and say to them: I am Hashem, your God. **³** Like the practice of the land of Egypt in which you dwelled do not do; and do not perform the practice of the land of Canaan

יח א־ב וַיְדַבֵּר יהוה אֶל־מֹשֶׁה לֵּאמֹר: דַּבֵּר אֶל־בְּנֵי יִשְׂרָאֵל וְאָמַרְתָּ אֲלֵהֶם אֲנִי יהוה אֱלֹהֵיכֶם: ג כְּמַעֲשֵׂה אֶרֶץ־מִצְרַיִם אֲשֶׁר יְשַׁבְתֶּם־בָּהּ לֹא תַעֲשׂוּ וּכְמַעֲשֵׂה אֶרֶץ־כְּנַעַן

— אונקלוס —

א וּמַלִּיל יְיָ עִם מֹשֶׁה לְמֵימָר: ב מַלֵּיל עִם בְּנֵי יִשְׂרָאֵל וְתֵימַר לְהוֹן אֲנָא יְיָ אֱלָהֲכוֹן: ג כְּעוֹבָדֵי עַמָּא דְאַרְעָא דְמִצְרַיִם דִּי יְתֶבְתּוּן בַּהּ לָא תַעְבְּדוּן וּכְעוֹבָדֵי עַמָּא דְאַרְעָא דִכְנָעַן

— רש״י —

(ב) אני ה׳ אלהיכם. אֲנִי הוּא שֶׁאָמַרְתִּי בְּסִינַי אָנֹכִי ה׳ אֱלֹהֶיךָ (שמות כ:ב) וְקִבַּלְתֶּם עֲלֵיכֶם מַלְכוּתִי, מֵעַתָּה קַבְּלוּ גְזֵרוֹתַי (ת״כ פרק יג:ג). רַבִּי אוֹמֵר, גָּלוּי וְיָדוּעַ לְפָנָיו שֶׁסּוֹפָן לִנָּתֵק בַּעֲרָיוֹת (שם ד) בִּימֵי עֶזְרָא, לְפִיכָךְ בָּא עֲלֵיהֶם בִּגְזֵרָה, אֲנִי ה׳ אֱלֹהֵיכֶם, דְּעוּ מִי גּוֹזֵר עֲלֵיכֶם, דַּיָּן לִפָּרַע וְנֶאֱמָן לְשַׁלֵּם שָׂכָר (שם ה): (ג) כמעשה ארץ מצרים. מַגִּיד שֶׁמַּעֲשֵׂיהֶם שֶׁל מִצְרִיִּים וְשֶׁל כְּנַעֲנִים מְקֻלְקָלִים מִכָּל הָאֻמּוֹת, וְאוֹתוֹ מָקוֹם שֶׁיָּשְׁבוּ בוֹ יִשְׂרָאֵל מְקֻלְקָל מִן הַכֹּל (שם ו):

— RASHI ELUCIDATED —

18.

2. אֲנִי ה׳ אֱלֹהֵיכֶם — I AM HASHEM, YOUR GOD. אֲנִי הוּא — I am the One שֶׁאָמַרְתִּי בְּסִינַי — Who said at Sinai, "אָנֹכִי ה׳ אֱלֹהֶיךָ" — "I am Hashem, your God,"[1] וְקִבַּלְתֶּם עֲלֵיכֶם — and you accepted upon yourselves מַלְכוּתִי — My sovereignty. מֵעַתָּה — Now, קַבְּלוּ גְזֵרוֹתַי — accept My decrees.[2] רַבִּי אוֹמֵר — Rabbi[3] says: גָּלוּי וְיָדוּעַ לְפָנָיו — It is known and revealed before Him שֶׁסּוֹפָן לִנָּתֵק — that in the future [Israel] is going to rebel[4] בַּעֲרָיוֹת[5] — by sexual immorality[5] בִּימֵי עֶזְרָא — in the days of Ezra.[6] לְפִיכָךְ בָּא עֲלֵיהֶם — Therefore, He confronted them בִּגְזֵרָה — with a decree that begins with, "אֲנִי ה׳ אֱלֹהֵיכֶם" — "I am Hashem, your God," as if to say, דְּעוּ מִי גּוֹזֵר עֲלֵיכֶם — know Who it is Who decrees upon you, דַּיָּן לִפָּרַע — a judge Who exacts punishment[7] וְנֶאֱמָן לְשַׁלֵּם שָׂכָר[7] — and is faithful to pay reward.[7]

3. כְּמַעֲשֵׂה אֶרֶץ מִצְרַיִם — LIKE THE PRACTICE OF THE LAND OF EGYPT. מַגִּיד — [This verse] tells us שֶׁמַּעֲשֵׂיהֶם שֶׁל מִצְרִיִּים — that the practices of the Egyptians וְשֶׁל כְּנַעֲנִים — and the Canaanites מְקֻלְקָלִים מִכָּל הָאֻמּוֹת — are the most degenerate of all nations, וְאוֹתוֹ מָקוֹם — and that place שֶׁיָּשְׁבוּ — בּוֹ יִשְׂרָאֵל — in which Israel dwelled[8] מְקֻלְקָל מִן הַכֹּל — is the most degenerate of all, i.e., the Egyptians in Goshen were the most degenerate of all Egyptians.[8]

---

1. *Exodus* 20:2.

2. *Toras Kohanim, perek* 13:3. The statement "I am Hashem your God" seems unnecessary here. Rashi explains that our verse and those that follow serve as an introduction to prohibitions against sexual immorality. Since it is very difficult at times to keep these prohibitions, God reminds us here of His relationship with us, that He is our God, and we are bound to keep His decrees even under the most difficult circumstances (*Be'er Yitzchak*).

3. The *Tanna* R' Yehudah HaNasi, compiler of the Mishnah, is often referred to only by the title "Rabbi." See *Yevamos* 45a.

4. This translation of לִינָּתֵק is based on its usage in *Sifra* (*Shelach* 115; in *Malbim* edition, 73). Others interpret the word as, "to be scourged," related to נֶתֶק, a type of *tzara'as* (see 13:30 above; *Sefer Zikaron*); or (based on *Psalms* 2:3) as, "to be drawn after," as in the Talmudic expression לָאו הֲנִיתָּק לַעֲשֵׂה, "a negative commandment attached to a positive commandment" (*Minchas Yehudah*).

5. *Toras Kohanim, perek* 13:4.

6. *Toras Kohanim*, the source for the opinion of Rabbi which Rashi quotes, does not include the words בִּימֵי עֶזְרָא, "in the days of Ezra." It does, however, cite *Malachi* 2:13, "And this second thing you do covers the *Mizbe'ach* of Hashem with tears, [with] weeping and moaning; it prevents [My] turning any longer to the meal-offering, and taking tribute from your hands." Rashi in his comments to that verse and to *Malachi* 2:11 says (on the basis of *Megillah* 15a) that Malachi is Ezra, and that the sin the verse refers to is that of Jewish men marrying non-Jewish women, as mentioned in *Ezra* 9:1-2, 10:2-3,11-12.

7. *Toras Kohanim, perek* 13:5. ה׳, "Hashem," is the name that connotes God's attribute of mercy. אֱלֹהִים, "God," connotes His attribute of judgment. The use of both names here implies that He can be trusted to mete out both reward and punishment (*Mizrachi; Sifsei Chachamim*).

8. *Toras Kohanim, perek* 13:6. The phrase אֲשֶׁר יְשַׁבְתֶּם בָּהּ, "in which you dwelled," indicates that the non-Jewish inhabitants of the area of Egypt in which Israel dwelled, the land of Goshen (see *Genesis* 47:27, *Exodus* 8:18), were the most degenerate of all (*Mizrachi; Sifsei Chachamim*).

אֲשֶׁר אֲנִי מֵבִיא אֶתְכֶם שָׁמָּה לֹא *to which I bring you, and do not*
תַעֲשׂוּ וּבְחֻקֹּתֵיהֶם לֹא תֵלֵכוּ: אֶת־ *follow their statutes.* ⁴ *Carry out My*
מִשְׁפָּטַי תַּעֲשׂוּ וְאֶת־חֻקֹּתַי תִּשְׁמְרוּ *judgments and observe My decrees*

―――――― אונקלוס ――――――

דִּי אֲנָא מָעֵל יָתְכוֹן תַּמָּן לָא תַעַבְדּוּן וּבְנִימוֹסֵיהוֹן לָא תְהָכוּן: דּ יָת דִּינַי תַּעַבְדּוּן וְיָת קְיָמַי תִּטְּרוּן

―――――― רש"י ――――――

אשר אני מביא אתכם שמה. מַגִּיד שֶׁאוּתָן עַמְּמִין שֶׁכָּבְשׁוּ יִשְׂרָאֵל מְקֻלְקָלִים [יוֹתֵר] מִכֻּלָּם (שם ז): **ובחקתיהם לא תלכו.** מַה הִנִּיחַ הַכָּתוּב שֶׁלֹּא אָמַר, אֶלָּא אֵלּוּ נִמוּסוֹת שֶׁלָּהֶן, דְּבָרִים הַחֲקוּקִין לָהֶם, כְּגוֹן טַרְטִיָאוֹת וְאִצְטַדִיָאוֹת. רַבִּי מֵאִיר אוֹמֵר אֵלּוּ דַרְכֵי הָאֱמוֹרִי שֶׁמָּנוּ חֲכָמִים (ת"כ שם ט, שבת סז:א'־ב): **(ד) את משפטי תעשו.** אֵלּוּ דְּבָרִים הָאֲמוּרִים בַּתּוֹרָה בְּמִשְׁפָּט, שֶׁאִלּוּ לֹא נֶאֶמְרוּ הָיוּ כְדַאי לְאָמְרָן: **ואת חקותי תשמרו.** דְּבָרִים שֶׁהֵם גְּזֵרַת הַמֶּלֶךְ, שֶׁיֵּצֶר הָרַע מֵשִׁיב עֲלֵיהֶם לָמָּה לָנוּ לְשָׁמְרָן, וְאֻמּוֹת הָעוֹלָם מְשִׁיבִין עֲלֵיהֶם, כְּגוֹן אֲכִילַת חֲזִיר וּלְבִישַׁת שַׁעַטְנֵז, לְכָךְ נֶאֱמַר אֲנִי ה' גָּזַרְתִּי עֲלֵיכֶם, אִי אַתֶּם רַשָּׁאִים לִפָּטֵר [וס"א אֲנִי גָּזַרְתִּי עֲלֵיכֶם, אִי אַתָּה רַשַּׁאי לִפָּטֵר] (ת"כ שם י):

―――――― RASHI ELUCIDATED ――――――

□ אֲשֶׁר אֲנִי מֵבִיא אֶתְכֶם שָׁמָּה – TO WHICH I BRING YOU. מַגִּיד – [This verse] tells us שֶׁאוּתָן עַמְּמִין – that those nations שֶׁכָּבְשׁוּ יִשְׂרָאֵל – whom Israel conquered מְקֻלְקָלִים מִכֻּלָּם – are the most degenerate among all of them.[1]

□ וּבְחֻקֹּתֵיהֶם לֹא תֵלֵכוּ – AND DO NOT FOLLOW THEIR STATUTES. מַה הִנִּיחַ הַכָּתוּב – What did Scripture leave over שֶׁלֹּא אָמַר – that it did not state?[2] אֶלָּא אֵלּוּ נִמוּסוֹת שֶׁלָּהֶן – But these are their traditions, דְּבָרִים הַחֲקוּקִין לָהֶם – matters that are etched for them in their ways as if they were laws, כְּגוֹן טַרְטִיָאוֹת – such as theaters וְאִצְטַדִיָאוֹת – and stadiums,[3] i.e., (days set aside for) attendance at theaters or stadiums. רַבִּי מֵאִיר אוֹמֵר – The *Tanna* Rabbi Meir says: אֵלּוּ דַרְכֵי הָאֱמוֹרִי – These are the ways of the Amorites, ⁴שֶׁמָּנוּ חֲכָמִים – which the Sages have enumerated.[4]

4. אֶת מִשְׁפָּטַי תַּעֲשׂוּ – CARRY OUT MY JUDGMENTS. אֵלּוּ דְּבָרִים הָאֲמוּרִים בַּתּוֹרָה – These are matters that are stated in the Torah בְּמִשְׁפָּט – in judgment, i.e., laws which accord with human reason, שֶׁאִלּוּ לֹא נֶאֶמְרוּ – of such a sort that if they had not been stated by the Torah, הָיוּ כְדַאי לְאָמְרָן – they would have been worthy of having been stated by man.

□ וְאֶת חֻקֹּתַי תִּשְׁמְרוּ – AND OBSERVE MY DECREES. דְּבָרִים שֶׁהֵם גְּזֵרַת הַמֶּלֶךְ – These are matters that are a decree of the King, שֶׁיֵּצֶר הָרַע מֵשִׁיב עֲלֵיהֶם – concerning which the evil inclination reacts, by asking לָמָּה לָנוּ לְשָׁמְרָן – why we should observe them. וְאֻמּוֹת הָעוֹלָם מְשִׁיבִין עֲלֵיהֶם – And the non-Jewish nations of the world likewise react concerning them. כְּגוֹן – For example, אֲכִילַת חֲזִיר – the prohibitions against eating pork, וּלְבִישַׁת שַׁעַטְנֵז – and wearing *shaatnez*,[5] וְטָהֳרַת מֵי חַטָּאת – and the purification of the waters of the sprinkling.[6] לְכָךְ נֶאֱמַר – Therefore it says, ״אֲנִי ה׳״ – "I am HASHEM," which implies, גָּזַרְתִּי עֲלֵיכֶם – My decree is upon you; אִי אַתֶּם רַשָּׁאִים ⁷לִפָּטֵר – you are not permitted to be exempt from it.[7]

1. *Toras Kohanim, perek* 3:7. While Israel dwelled in Egypt, the Egyptians, and especially those who lived in the land of Goshen, were the most degenerate, because they steeped themselves in the immoral practices of their pagan cult in the hope that their pagan gods would thereby keep Israel in bondage. When Israel was conquering the land of Canaan, it was the Canaanites who were the most degenerate, because they engaged in immoral pagan practices in the hope that they would fend off the Israelite conquest (*Be'er BaSadeh*).
Our text follows the first printed editions. Later editions read, מְקֻלְקָלִים יוֹתֵר מִכֻּלָּם, "are more degenerate than any of them."

2. What prohibitions are referred to here other than those explicitly forbidden below?

3. Rashi to *Avodah Zarah* 18b defines טַרְטִיָאוֹת as palaces where people would gather for entertainment, and אִצְטַדִיָאוֹת as bullrings.

4. *Toras Kohanim, perek* 13:9. *Shabbos* 67a-b enumerates various superstitious practices that fall into this category.

5. A garment made of a combination of wool and linen. See 19:19 below and *Deuteronomy* 22:11.

6. Whoever has become impure through contact with the dead must be sprinkled with water containing the ashes of a red cow in order to become purified. See *Numbers*, Chapter 19.

7. *Toras Kohanim, perek* 13:10. Some editions of Rashi read, אֲנִי גָּזַרְתִּי עֲלֵיהֶם, "I have decreed regarding them i.e., these statutes," אֵין אַתָּה רַשַּׁאי לִפָּטֵר, "you (singular) are not permitted to be exempt from it."

to follow them; I am HASHEM, your God. **⁵** You shall observe My decrees and My judgments, which man shall carry out and live by them — I am HASHEM.

⁶ Any man shall not approach his close relative to uncover nakedness; I am HASHEM.

⁷ The nakedness of your father and the

לָלֶכֶת בָּהֶם אֲנִי יהוה אֱלֹהֵיכֶם: ה וּשְׁמַרְתֶּם אֶת־חֻקֹּתַי וְאֶת־מִשְׁפָּטַי אֲשֶׁר יַעֲשֶׂה אֹתָם הָאָדָם וָחַי בָּהֶם אֲנִי יהוה: ששי אִישׁ אִישׁ אֶל־כָּל־שְׁאֵר בְּשָׂרוֹ לֹא תִקְרְבוּ לְגַלּוֹת עֶרְוָה אֲנִי יהוה: ז עֶרְוַת אָבִיךָ

―――――――― אונקלוס ――――――――

לִמְהַךְ בְּהוֹן אֲנָא יְיָ אֱלָהֲכוֹן: ה וְתִטְּרוּן יָת קְיָמַי וְיָת דִּינַי דִּי יַעֲבֵּד יָתְהוֹן אֱנָשָׁא וְיֵיחֵי בְהוֹן חַיֵּי עָלְמָא אֲנָא יְיָ: ו גְּבַר גְּבַר לְכָל קָרִיב בִּסְרֵהּ לָא תִקְרְבוּן לְגַלָּאָה עֶרְיְתָא אֲנָא יְיָ: ז עֶרְיַת אֲבוּךְ

―――――――― רש"י ――――――――

ללכת בהם. אל תפטר מתוכם. שלא תאמר למדתי חכמת ישראל, אלך ואלמד חכמת האומות (שם יא): **(ה) ושמרתם את חקותי וגו'.** לרבות שאר דקדוקי הפרשה שלא פרט הכתוב [בהם] (שם יב). דבר אחר, ליתן שמירה ועשייה לחוקים, ושמירה ועשייה למשפטים (שם פרשתא ט:י) לפי שלא נתן אלא עשייה

למשפטים ושמירה לחוקים (לעיל פסוק ד): **וחי בהם.** לעוה"ב, שאם תאמר בעוה"ז והלא סופו הוא מת (ת"כ שם): **אני ה'.** נאמן לשלם שכר: **(ו) לא תקרבו.** להזהיר הנקבה כזכר לכך נאמר לשון רבים (שם פרק יג:א): **אני ה'.** נאמן לשלם שכר (שם ב): **(ז) ערות אביך.** זו אשת אביך. או אינו

―――――――― RASHI ELUCIDATED ――――――――

□ לָלֶכֶת בָּהֶם – TO FOLLOW THEM. אַל תִּפָּטֵר מִתּוֹכָם – Do not take leave of them, שֶׁלֹּא תֹאמַר – that you should not say, אֵלֵךְ וְאֶלְמַד – "I have learned the wisdom of Israel. אֵלֵךְ וְאֶלְמַד – I will go and I will learn ¹חָכְמַת הָאֻמּוֹת – the wisdom of the other nations."[1]

5. וּשְׁמַרְתֶּם אֶת חֻקֹּתַי וְגוֹמֵר – YOU SHALL OBSERVE MY DECREES, ETC. לְרַבּוֹת שְׁאָר דִּקְדּוּקֵי הַפָּרָשָׁה – To include other fine points of the portion {בָּהֶם}[2] – שֶׁלֹּא פֵּרַט הַכָּתוּב – {about which} Scripture did not specify explicitly.[2]

דָּבָר אַחֵר – Alternatively, לִתֵּן שְׁמִירָה וַעֲשִׂיָּה לַחֻקִּים – to assign "observing" and "carrying out" to decrees, וּשְׁמִירָה וַעֲשִׂיָּה לַמִּשְׁפָּטִים[3] – and "observing" and "carrying out" to judgments,[3] לְפִי שֶׁלֹּא – since [the Torah] had only assigned "carrying out" to judgments נָתַן אֶלָּא עֲשִׂיָּה לַמִּשְׁפָּטִים – and "observing" to decrees in the preceding verse.[4]

□ וָחַי בָּהֶם – AND LIVE BY THEM לָעוֹלָם הַבָּא – in the World to Come, שֶׁאִם תֹּאמַר – for if you should say that our verse refers to life בָּעוֹלָם הַזֶּה – in this world, וַהֲלֹא סוֹפוֹ הוּא מֵת[3] – is it not man's destiny to die?[3]

□ אֲנִי ה' – I AM HASHEM, Who is ³נֶאֱמָן לְשַׁלֵּם שָׂכָר – faithful to pay reward.[3,5]

6. לֹא תִקְרְבוּ – SHALL NOT APPROACH. This phrase is stated לְהַזְהִיר הַנְּקֵבָה – to prohibit the female כַּזָּכָר – like the male; לְכָךְ נֶאֱמַר לְשׁוֹן רַבִּים[6] – this is why it is stated in the plural.[6]

□ אֲנִי ה' – I AM HASHEM, Who is נֶאֱמָן לְשַׁלֵּם שָׂכָר – faithful to pay reward.[7]

7. עֶרְוַת אָבִיךָ – THE NAKEDNESS OF YOUR FATHER. זוּ אֵשֶׁת אָבִיךָ – This is your father's wife. אוֹ אֵינוֹ

―

1. Toras Kohanim, perek 13:11. The verse has already said, אֶת חֻקֹּתַי תִּשְׁמֹרוּ, "observe My decrees." The apparently superfluous לָלֶכֶת בָּהֶם, "to follow them," implies that just as one is never free to abandon observance of the commandments, so too, he is never free to abandon their study (Mizrachi; Sifsei Chachamim).

2. Toras Kohanim, perek 13:12.

3. Toras Kohanim, parshasa 9:10.

4. Verse 4 used "carrying out" with reference to judgments and "observing" with reference to decrees. Our seemingly redundant verse applies "carrying out" and "observing" to both decrees and judgments (Mizrachi; Sifsei Chachamim). "Carrying out" refers to performance of the commandments; "observing"

refers to their study (Gur Aryeh; see, too, Rashi to 22:31 below).

5. See Exodus 6:2 and v. 2 above, and Rashi there.

6. Toras Kohanim, perek 13:1. The subject of this clause, אִישׁ אִישׁ, "any man," normally takes a singular verb. The plural תִקְרְבוּ is used by our verse to teach us that the prohibitions which follow apply to women as well as men (Mizrachi; Sifsei Chachamim).

7. Toras Kohanim, perek 13:2. Our verse repeats this to teach us that not only is God faithful to pay reward for actively carrying out His commandments, He is just as faithful to pay reward for passively refraining from sins such as "you shall not approach" of our verse (Mizrachi; Sifsei Chachamim).

nakedness of your mother you shall not uncover; she is your mother, you shall not uncover her nakedness.

⁸ The nakedness of your father's wife you shall not uncover; it is your father's nakedness.

⁹ The nakedness of your sister — whether your father's daughter or your mother's daughter, whether born in the home or born outside — you shall not uncover their nakedness.

¹⁰ The nakedness of your son's daughter or

וְעֶרְוַת אִמְּךָ לֹא תְגַלֵּה אִמְּךָ הִוא לֹא תְגַלֵּה עֶרְוָתָהּ: ח אֶשֶׁת־אָבִיךָ לֹא תְגַלֵּה עֶרְוַת אָבִיךָ הִוא: ט עֶרְוַת אֲחוֹתְךָ בַת־אָבִיךָ אוֹ בַת־אִמְּךָ מוֹלֶדֶת בַּיִת אוֹ מוֹלֶדֶת חוּץ לֹא תְגַלֵּה עֶרְוָתָן: י עֶרְוַת בַּת־בִּנְךָ אוֹ

—————— אונקלוס ——————

וְעֶרְיַת אִמָּךְ לָא תְגַלֵּי אִמָּךְ הִיא לָא תְגַלֵּי עֶרְיְתַהּ: ח עֶרְיַת אִתַּת אָבוּךְ לָא תְגַלֵּי עֶרְיְתַהּ: ט עֶרְיַת אֲחָתָךְ בַּת אָבוּךְ אוֹ בַּת אִמָּךְ דִּילִידָא מִן אָבוּךְ אוֹ מִן אָחֳרָן לְגָבַר אָחֳרָן לָא תְגַלֵּי עֶרְיָתְהֶן: י עֶרְיַת בַּת בְּנָךְ אוֹ

—————— רש"י ——————

אֶלָּא כְּמַשְׁמָעוֹ, נֶאֱמַר כָּאן עֶרְוַת אָבִיךְ וְנֶאֱמַר לְהַלָּן עֶרְוַת אָבִיו גִּלָּה (כ:יא) מַה לְּהַלָּן אֵשֶׁת אָבִיו אַף כָּאן אֵשֶׁת אָבִיו (סַנְהֶדְרִין נד.): **וְעֶרְוַת אִמְּךָ.** לְהָבִיא אִמּוֹ שֶׁאֵינָהּ אֵשֶׁת אָבִיו (שם): **(ח) עֶרְוַת אֵשֶׁת אָבִיךָ.** לְרַבּוֹת לְאַחַר מִיתָה (שם): **(ט) בַּת אָבִיךָ.** אַף בַּת אֲנוּסָה בְּמַשְׁמָע: בַּת אֲנוּסָה בְּמַשְׁמָע (יבמות כג:): **מוֹלֶדֶת בַּיִת אוֹ מוֹלֶדֶת חוּץ.** בֵּין שֶׁאוֹמְרִים לוֹ לְאָבִיךָ קַיֵּם אֶת אִמָּהּ וּבֵין שֶׁאוֹמְרִים לוֹ הוֹצֵא אֶת אִמָּהּ כְּגוֹן מַמְזֶרֶת אוֹ נְתִינָה (יבמות כג.) כְּבַת מְאֻנֶּסֶת מֵאִשְׁתּוֹ אוֹ נְתִינָה: **(י) עֶרְוַת בַּת בִּנְךָ וְגוֹ'.**

—————— RASHI ELUCIDATED ——————

אֶלָּא כְּמַשְׁמָעוֹ – Or perhaps it means nothing but the way it sounds, i.e., perhaps it means having relations with your father? To teach us otherwise, נֶאֱמַר כָּאן ,,עֶרְוַת אָבִיךָ״ – "the nakedness of your father" is stated here, ¹וְנֶאֱמַר לְהַלָּן ,,עֶרְוַת אָבִיו גִּלָּה״ – and it says further on, "he will have uncovered his father's nakedness."[1] מַה לְּהַלָּן אֵשֶׁת אָבִיו – Just as further on the verse refers to one's father's wife, ²אַף כָּאן אֵשֶׁת אָבִיו – here, too, the verse refers to one's father's wife.[2]

□ וְעֶרְוַת אִמְּךָ – AND THE NAKEDNESS OF YOUR MOTHER. This verse is needed לְהָבִיא אִמּוֹ – to include one's mother ²שֶׁאֵינָהּ אֵשֶׁת אָבִיו – who is not the wife of his father.[2,3]

8. עֶרְוַת אֵשֶׁת אָבִיךָ – THE NAKEDNESS OF YOUR FATHER'S WIFE. This verse is needed לְרַבּוֹת – to enlarge the scope of the prohibition to include ²לְאַחַר מִיתָה – after death.[2,4]

9. בַּת אָבִיךָ – YOUR FATHER'S DAUGHTER. ⁵אַף בַּת אֲנוּסָה בְּמַשְׁמָע – The daughter of a woman who was raped by one's father or fathered by him through other non-marital relations is also implied.[5]

□ מוֹלֶדֶת בַּיִת אוֹ מוֹלֶדֶת חוּץ – BORN IN THE HOME OR BORN OUTSIDE. בֵּין שֶׁאוֹמְרִים לוֹ לְאָבִיךָ – Whether they say to your father, קַיֵּם אֶת אִמָּהּ – "You may maintain this woman who is the mother of [your daughter] as your wife," וּבֵין שֶׁאוֹמְרִים לוֹ – or whether they say to him, ⁶הוֹצֵא אֶת אִמָּהּ – "Send away her mother,"[6] כְּגוֹן מַמְזֶרֶת – for instance, the mother of a mamzeres[7] אוֹ נְתִינָה – or a nesinah.[8]

10. עֶרְוַת בַּת בִּנְךָ וְגוֹמֵר – THE NAKEDNESS OF YOUR SON'S DAUGHTER [OR YOUR DAUGHTER'S DAUGHTER]. בְּבִתּוֹ מֵאֲנוּסָתוֹ – About his daughter from a woman he raped, or from any woman to whom he was not

---

1. Below 20:11. The full sentence in that verse reads, "A man who shall lie with his father's wife will have uncovered his father's nakedness."

2. *Sanhedrin* 54a.

3. If, for instance, the child was conceived as the result of rape or seduction (*Minchas Yehudah; Sifsei Chachamim*).

4. The apparent repetition of the prohibition stated in the preceding verse extends it to a woman who had been married to his father but no longer is; i.e., his widow. The same holds true for a woman divorced by his father.

5. *Yevamos* 22b. "Your father's daughter" seems superfluous, for it seems to say no more than "sister," and "sister" has just been stated. The Torah, however, states this to teach us that even a child conceived from a rape committed by one's father is included. She is not excluded on the basis of "your father's wife's daughter" (v. 11), which excludes one's sister from a mother who is a slave-woman or a non-Jew (see Rashi there; *Mesiach Ilmim*).

6. *Yevamos* 23a.

7. A *mamzer* (feminine, *mamzeres*) is a child born of a forbidden union which is punishable by *kares* (see note 8 on page 8) or a court-imposed death penalty.

8. A descendant of the Gibeonites, a Canaanite nation that converted to Judaism under false pretenses in the days of Joshua (see *Joshua* 9:27). It is forbidden for Jews of unblemished pedigree to intermarry with them. Rashi

בַּת־בִּתְּךָ֖ לֹ֣א תְגַלֶּ֣ה עֶרְוָתָ֑ן כִּ֥י
עֶרְוָתְךָ֖ הֵֽנָּה: יא עֶרְוַ֨ת
בַּת־אֵ֣שֶׁת אָבִ֗יךָ מוֹלֶ֣דֶת אָבִ֔יךָ
אֲחוֹתְךָ֖ הִ֑וא לֹ֥א תְגַלֶּ֖ה

your daughter's daughter — you shall not uncover their nakedness; for they are your own shame. ¹¹ *The nakedness of your father's wife's daughter who was born to your father — she is your sister; you shall not uncover her*

―――――― אונקלוס ――――――

בַּת בְּרַתָּךְ לָא תְגַלֵּי עֶרְיַתְהֵן אֲרֵי עֶרְיָתָךְ אִנִּין: יא עֶרְיַת בַּת אִתַּת אֲבוּךְ דִּילִידָא מִן אֲבוּךְ אֲחָתָךְ הִיא לָא תְגַלֵּי

―――――― רש"י ――――――

הכתוב מדבר (סנהדרין עו.), ובת בתו ובת בנו מאשתו אנו למדין מערות אשה ובתה, שנאמר בהן לא תגלה בין שהיא ממנו בין שהיא מאיש אחר (יבמות כב:): **ערות בת בנך.** קל וחומר לבתך, אלא לפי שאין מזהירין מן הדין למדוה מגזרה שוה במסכת יבמות (ג.) [וס"א כריתות (ה.)]: **(יא) ערות בת אשת אביך.** למד שאינו חייב על אחותו משפחה ונכרית. ולפי שאמר למעלה

―――――― RASHI ELUCIDATED ――――――

וּבַת – **married,** הַכָּתוּב מְדַבֵּר[1] – **the verse speaks** when it refers to "your daughter's daughter."[1] That relations with **his daughter** וּבַת בִּתּוֹ – **and the daughter of his daughter** מֵאִשְׁתּוֹ – **from his wife** are forbidden אָנוּ לְמֵדִין – **we learn** מֵעֶרְוַת אִשָּׁה וּבִתָּהּ – **from "the nakedness of a woman and her daughter,"**[2] שֶׁנֶּאֱמַר בָּהֶן – **about whom it says,** "לֹא תְגַלֶּה" – **"you shall not uncover,"** בֵּין שֶׁהִיא מִמֶּנּוּ – **whether she is** the woman's daughter **from him,** בֵּין שֶׁהִיא מֵאִישׁ אַחֵר[3] – **or whether** she is the woman's daughter **from another man.**[3]

עֶרְוַת בַּת בִּנְךָ – **THE NAKEDNESS OF YOUR SON'S DAUGHTER.** קַל וָחוֹמֶר לְבִתְּךָ – **All the more so**[4] your own **daughter.**[5] אֶלָּא – **But,** לְפִי שֶׁאֵין מַזְהִירִין מִן הַדִּין – **since they do not derive a negative prohibition by means of reasoning,**[6] לְמָדוּהָ – **they learned [the negative commandment for your own daughter]** מִגְּזֵרָה שָׁוָה[7] – **from a** *gezeirah shavah*[7] בְּמַסֶּכֶת יְבָמוֹת – **in Tractate Yevamos.**[8]

11. עֶרְוַת בַּת אֵשֶׁת אָבִיךָ – **THE NAKEDNESS OF YOUR FATHER'S WIFE'S DAUGHTER.** לִמֵּד – **This teaches** us שֶׁאֵינוֹ חַיָּב – **that he is not liable** to punishment עַל אֲחוֹתוֹ – **for his sister** born מִשִּׁפְחָה – **from** a Canaanite **slavewoman** וְנָכְרִית – **or a non-Jew.** לְפִי שֶׁאָמַר לְמַעְלָה – **Since it says above,**

---

uses the mother of a *nesinah* as an example of a woman with whom relations are forbidden by force of a negative commandment that carries with it no penalty of death or *kares*. In this case, "send away her mother" means "divorce her mother," because the bond of matrimony (תְּפִיסַת קִדּוּשִׁין) can exist with such a woman. In the case of the mother of a *mamzeres*, with whom marriage cannot take effect, "send her away" is understood literally (see *Mizrachi*).

"Whether born in the home or born outside" does not refer to the location of the birth of your sister. It means, "Whether born of a woman who may remain in the home of your father as his wife, or of a woman who should be sent away from his home" (*Yevamos* 23a).

1. *Sanhedrin* 76a. The same holds true for "son's" in בַּת בִּנְךָ, "your son's daughter"; the son is by a woman to whom he was not married.
2. Below v. 17.
3. *Yevamos* 22b.
4. For the meaning of קַל וָחוֹמֶר see note 8 on page 2.
5. If the Torah forbids the daughter of your daughter who was conceived as a result of rape, all the more so is your daughter who was conceived as a result of rape forbidden. "Daughter" here means specifically a daughter who was conceived out of wedlock, not a child

of a marriage, for, as Rashi has just stated, relations with a daughter who is a child of a legitimate marriage is prohibited by verse 17 (*Mizrachi*; *Sifsei Chachamim*).

6. There appears to be more reason to forbid a daughter than a granddaughter, and if the Torah forbids a granddaughter, the prohibition which applies to a daughter would appear to go without saying. However, the Torah does not allow for the derivation of negative commandments, which are punishable by flogging or other punishments, through such reasoning, for human reasoning is subject to error. Negative prohibitions must therefore be stated explicitly by the Torah, or derived through one of the principles by which the Torah is expounded which are based on tradition handed down from Sinai, and are not the product of human logic (*Sefer Zikaron*).

7. For the meaning of *gezeirah shavah*, see note 10 on page 155.

8. *Yevamos* 3a; *Kereisos* 5a.

The word הֵנָּה, "they," appears both in our verse and in verse 17 below. There the verse speaks of "a woman and her daughter." The *gezeirah shavah* teaches us that just as verse 17 speaks of a parent-daughter relationship, so does our verse include a parent-daughter relationship.

219 / VAYIKRA/LEVITICUS — PARASHAS ACHAREI — 18/12-17 — יח/יב-יז

nakedness.
12 *The nakedness of your father's sister you shall not uncover; she is your father's flesh.*
13 *The nakedness of your mother's sister you shall not uncover; for she is your mother's flesh.*
14 *The nakedness of your father's brother you shall not uncover; do not approach his wife, she is your aunt.*
15 *The nakedness of your daughter-in-law you should not uncover; she is your son's wife, you shall not uncover her nakedness.*
16 *The nakedness of your brother's wife you shall not uncover; it is your brother's shame.*
17 *The nakedness of a woman and her daughter you shall not uncover; you shall not take her son's daughter or her daughter's daughter to uncover her nakedness —*

יב עֶרְוַ֨ת אֲחוֹת־אָבִ֜יךָ לֹ֣א תְגַלֵּ֗ה שְׁאֵ֥ר אָבִ֛יךָ הִֽוא׃ יג עֶרְוַ֥ת אֲחוֹת־אִמְּךָ֖ לֹ֣א תְגַלֵּ֑ה כִּֽי־שְׁאֵ֥ר אִמְּךָ֖ הִֽוא׃ יד עֶרְוַ֥ת אֲחִֽי־אָבִ֖יךָ לֹ֣א תְגַלֵּ֑ה אֶל־אִשְׁתּוֹ֙ לֹ֣א תִקְרָ֔ב דֹּדָֽתְךָ֖ הִֽוא׃ טו עֶרְוַ֥ת כַּלָּֽתְךָ֖ לֹ֣א תְגַלֵּ֑ה אֵ֤שֶׁת בִּנְךָ֙ הִ֔וא לֹ֥א תְגַלֶּ֖ה עֶרְוָתָֽהּ׃ טז עֶרְוַ֥ת אֵֽשֶׁת־אָחִ֖יךָ לֹ֣א תְגַלֵּ֑ה עֶרְוַ֥ת אָחִ֖יךָ הִֽוא׃ יז עֶרְוַ֥ת אִשָּׁ֛ה וּבִתָּ֖הּ לֹ֣א תְגַלֵּ֑ה אֶֽת־בַּת־בְּנָ֞הּ וְאֶת־בַּת־בִּתָּ֗הּ לֹ֥א תִקַּ֛ח לְגַלּ֥וֹת עֶרְוָתָ֖הּ

───── אונקלוס ─────

עֶרְיְתָהּ: יב עֶרְיַת אֲחָת אֲבוּךְ לָא תְגַלֵּי קְרִיבַת אֲבוּךְ הִיא: יג עֶרְיַת אֲחָת אִמָּךְ לָא תְגַלֵּי אֲרֵי קְרִיבַת אִמָּךְ הִיא: יד עֶרְיַת אֲחִי אֲבוּךְ לָא תְגַלֵּי לְאִתְּתֵהּ לָא תִקְרָב אִתַּת אַח אֲבוּךְ הִיא: טו עֶרְיַת כַּלָּתָךְ לָא תְגַלֵּי אִתַּת בְּרָךְ הִיא לָא תְגַלֵּי עֶרְיְתַהּ: טז עֶרְיַת אִתַּת אֲחוּךְ לָא תְגַלֵּי עֶרְיַת אֲחוּךְ הִיא: יז עֶרְיַת אִתְּתָא וּבְרַתַּהּ לָא תְגַלֵּי יָת בַּת בְּרַהּ וְיָת בַּת בְּרַתַּהּ לָא תִסַּב לְגַלָּאָה עֶרְיְתַהּ

───── רש"י ─────

מוֹלַדְתָּ חוּץ, שֶׁאוֹמְרִים לְאָבִיךָ הוֹצִיא, יָכוֹל אַף מִשְׁפַּחַת וְנָכְרִית,] לְכָךְ נֶאֱמַר בַּת אֵשֶׁת אָבִיךָ בִּרְאוּיָה לְקִדּוּשִׁין (יבמות כג.): (יד) **עֶרְוַת אֲחִי אָבִיךָ לֹא תְגַלֵּה.** וּמַה הִיא עֶרְוָתוֹ, אֶל אִשְׁתּוֹ לֹא תִקְרָב:
(טו) **אֵשֶׁת בִּנְךָ הִיא.** לֹא אָמַרְתִּי אֶלָּא בְּשֶׁיֵּשׁ לְבִנְךָ אִישׁוּת בָּהּ, פְּרָט לַאֲנוּסָה וְשִׁפְחָה וְנָכְרִית (סנהדרין נב:): (יז) **עֶרְוַת אִשָּׁה וּבִתָּהּ.** לֹא אָסַר הַכָּתוּב אֶלָּא

───── RASHI ELUCIDATED ─────

מוֹלֶדֶת חוּץ — **"born outside,"** which means, שֶׁאוֹמְרִים לְאָבִיךָ הוֹצֵא — **they say to your father, "Send her away,"** יָכוֹל — **one would be able to think** that this applies אַף מִשְׁפָּחָה וְנָכְרִית — **even from a** Canaanite **slavewoman or a non-Jew,**} לְכָךְ נֶאֱמַר בַּת אֵשֶׁת אָבִיךָ — **this is why it says: "your father's wife's daughter,"** to imply that the prohibition applies only בִּרְאוּיָה לְקִדּוּשִׁין — **about** the daughter of one who is fit for marriage.[1]

14. עֶרְוַת אֲחִי אָבִיךָ לֹא תְגַלֵּה — **THE NAKEDNESS OF YOUR FATHER'S BROTHER YOU SHALL NOT UNCOVER.** אֶל — **And what is his nakedness** which is meant here? The verse goes on to explain, וּמַה הִיא עֶרְוָתוֹ — אִשְׁתּוֹ לֹא תִקְרָב[2] — **"do not approach his wife."**[2]

15. אֵשֶׁת בִּנְךָ הִיא — **SHE IS YOUR SON'S WIFE.** לֹא אָמַרְתִּי — **I did not say** this אֶלָּא בְּשֶׁיֵּשׁ לְבִנְךָ אִישׁוּת בָּהּ — **except** in a case **where your son is in a state of matrimony with her.** פְּרָט לַאֲנוּסָה[3] — **This excludes a woman who was raped** by your son, or who had non-marital relations with him in any way,[3] וְשִׁפְחָה — **and a** Canaanite **slavewoman** with whom your son has had relations, וְנָכְרִית[4] — **and a non-Jewish woman** with whom your son has had relations.[4]

17. עֶרְוַת אִשָּׁה וּבִתָּהּ — **THE NAKEDNESS OF A WOMAN AND HER DAUGHTER.** לֹא אָסַר הַכָּתוּב אֶלָּא

---

1. *Yevamos* 23a. The bond of marriage (תְּפִיסַת קִדּוּשִׁין) cannot exist between a Jewish man and a non-Jewish woman or a Canaanite slavewoman. If a man has a daughter by such a woman, that daughter does not fall under the prohibition of our verse. Nevertheless, the prohibition *does* include a woman with whom one's father cannot enter into the bond of marriage, but who can be married to another Jew, such as close relatives (see *Mizrachi* to v. 10).

2. *Sanhedrin* 54a. Rashi explains the verse according to the opinion of the *Tanna* R' Yehudah there, unlike the Sages who hold that the verse refers to sodomizing one's father's brother.

3. *Yevamos* 97a.

4. *Toras Kohanim, Kedoshim, perek* 10:10.

they are kin, it is a suggestion, a sinful advice. ¹⁸ *You shall not take a wife to her sister, to make them rivals, to uncover the nakedness of one upon the other in her lifetime.* ¹⁹ *You shall not approach a woman in her time of menstruant impurity, to uncover*

יח שַׁאֲרָה הֵנָּה זִמָּה הִוא: וְאִשָּׁה אֶל־
אֲחֹתָהּ לֹא תִקָּח לִצְרֹר לְגַלּוֹת
עֶרְוָתָהּ עָלֶיהָ בְּחַיֶּיהָ: וְאֶל־אִשָּׁה יט
בְּנִדַּת טֻמְאָתָהּ לֹא תִקְרַב לְגַלּוֹת

───── אונקלוס ─────

קָרִיבָן אִנִּין עֲצַת חֶטְאִין הִיא: יח וְאִתְּתָא עִם אֲחָתַהּ לָא תִסַּב לְאַעָקָא
לְגַלָּאָה עֶרְיְתַהּ עֲלַהּ בְּחַיֵּיהָא: יט וּלְאִתְּתָא בְּרִחוּק סוֹבְתַהּ לָא תִקְרַב לְגַלָּאָה

───── רש"י ─────

ע"י נְשׂוּאֵי הָרִאשׁוֹנָה, לְכָךְ נֶאֱמַר לֹא תִקָּח, לְשׁוֹן קִיחָה.
וְכֵן לְעִנְיַן הָעֹנֶשׁ, אֲשֶׁר יִקַּח אֶת אִשָּׁה וְאֶת אִמָּהּ (לְהַלָּן
כ,יד) לְשׁוֹן קִיחָה. אֲבָל אָנַס אִשָּׁה מֻתָּר לִשָּׂא בִּתָּהּ
(יבמות צז.): [שַׁאֲרָה הֵנָּה. קְרוֹבוֹת זוֹ לָזוֹ: זִמָּה. עֵצָה,

כְּתַרְגּוּמוֹ עֲצַת חֶטְאִין, שֵׂיצֶרְךָ יוֹעֶצְךָ לַחֲטוֹא:]
(יח) אֶל אֲחֹתָהּ. שְׁתֵּיהֶן כְּאַחַת (קדושין נ.): לִצְרֹר.
לְשׁוֹן צָרָה, לַעֲשׂוֹת אֶת זוֹ צָרָה לָזוֹ: בְּחַיֶּיהָ. לִמֶּדְךָ שֶׁאִם
גֵּרְשָׁהּ לֹא יִשָּׂא אֶת אֲחוֹתָהּ כָּל זְמַן שֶׁהִיא בַּחַיִּים:

───── RASHI ELUCIDATED ─────

עַל יְדֵי נְשׂוּאֵי הָרִאשׁוֹנָה — **The verse forbade only through the marriage of the first one,** i.e., the prohibition referred to by the verse applies only when you are married to the mother. לְכָךְ נֶאֱמַר ,,לֹא תִקַּח'' — **This is why** further on in the verse **it says, "you shall not take,"** which is לְשׁוֹן קִיחָה — **an expression of "taking" in wedlock.**[1] וְכֵן לְעִנְיַן הָעֹנֶשׁ — **Similarly,** in the verse **on the subject of the punishment** for the prohibition given in our verse, it says, ,,אֲשֶׁר יִקַּח אֶת אִשָּׁה וְאֶת אִמָּהּ'' — **"a man who shall take a woman and her mother,"**[2] using לְשׁוֹן קִיחָה — **an expression of "taking in wedlock."** אֲבָל אָנַס אִשָּׁה — **But if he raped a woman,** or had other non-marital relations with her, מֻתָּר לִשָּׂא בִּתָּהּ[3] — **he is allowed to marry her daughter,** if she is not his own.[3]

□ {שַׁאֲרָה הֵנָּה — **THEY ARE KIN,** — קְרוֹבוֹת זוֹ לָזוֹ — **closely related to each other.**}

□ {זִמָּה — **A SUGGESTION.** עֵצָה — The word זִמָּה means **advice,** כְּתַרְגּוּמוֹ — **as the** *Targum Onkelos* **renders it,** ,,עֲצַת חֶטְאִין'' — **"sinful advice."**[4] The term "advice" is appropriate here, even though it appears to have nothing to do with the sin referred to by the verse, שֵׂיצֶרְךָ יוֹעֶצְךָ לַחֲטוֹא — **for your evil inclination advises you to sin.**}

18. אֶל אֲחֹתָהּ — **TO HER SISTER.** שְׁתֵּיהֶן כְּאַחַת[5] — **The two of them at once.**[5]

□ לִצְרֹר — **TO MAKE THEM RIVALS.** לְשׁוֹן צָרָה — The word לִצְרֹר is **related to** צָרָה, **"co-wife."**[6] It means לַעֲשׂוֹת אֶת זוֹ צָרָה לָזוֹ — **to make one the co-wife of the other.**

□ בְּחַיֶּיהָ — **IN HER LIFETIME.** לִמֶּדְךָ — **This has taught you** שֶׁאִם גֵּרְשָׁהּ — **that if he divorced her** לֹא יִשָּׂא אֶת אֲחוֹתָהּ — **he may not marry her sister** כָּל זְמַן — **all the while** שֶׁהִיא בַּחַיִּים[7] — **that she is alive.**[7]

---

1. The Torah uses the verb לקח to express marriage; e.g., *Deuteronomy* 22:13, 24:1. It uses the phrase לֹא תִקַּח, "do not take . . . to uncover her nakedness" in this verse to imply that the prohibition takes effect only if he married the first woman of the pair.
2. Below 20:14.
3. *Yevamos* 97a.
4. Rashi to *Avodah Zarah* 17b (s.v., זימה ומתרגמי׳ עצת חטאין) explains that *Targum Onkelos'* עֵצָה, "advice," is his translation of זִמָּה. He adds חֶטְאִין, "sinful," or "of sins," by way of explanation.
5. *Kiddushin* 50b. Our verse could have said אֲחוֹת אִשָּׁה לֹא תִקַּח, "do not take a wife's sister." But that would have implied that it is forbidden to take a wife's sister even after the wife has died. The verse uses instead וְאִשָּׁה אֶל אֲחֹתָהּ לֹא תִקַּח, "do not take a woman to her sister," to imply that the prohibition applies only to "the two of them at once," i.e., while they are both alive (*Nachalas Yaakov*).
6. The word צָרָה, "co-wife," appears in *I Samuel* 1:6. *Metzudas* there explains that the word is related to צַר, "enemy," for co-wives are natural enemies, who rival each other for their husband's affection.
7. "You shall not take a wife to her sister" alone, which implies, "do not take the two of them at once," could have been understood to mean that one may not be married to the two of them at once, but if he divorces one, he may marry the other. "In her lifetime" implies that the prohibition applies as long as the first sister he married is alive, even if he has divorced her (*Nachalas Yaakov*).

18/20-25

וְאֶל־אֵשֶׁת עֲמִיתְךָ֔ לֹא־תִתֵּ֥ן שְׁכָבְתְּךָ֖ לְזָ֑רַע לְטָמְאָה־בָֽהּ׃ כ
וּמִֽזַּרְעֲךָ֥ לֹא־תִתֵּ֖ן לְהַעֲבִ֣יר לַמֹּ֑לֶךְ וְלֹ֧א תְחַלֵּ֛ל אֶת־שֵׁ֥ם אֱלֹהֶ֖יךָ אֲנִ֥י יְהוָֽה׃ כא
[רביעי] [שביעי] וְאֶ֨ת־זָכָ֔ר לֹ֥א תִשְׁכַּ֖ב מִשְׁכְּבֵ֣י אִשָּׁ֑ה תּוֹעֵבָ֖ה הִֽוא׃ כב
וּבְכָל־בְּהֵמָ֛ה לֹא־תִתֵּ֥ן שְׁכָבְתְּךָ֖ לְטָמְאָה־בָ֑הּ וְאִשָּׁ֗ה לֹֽא־תַעֲמֹ֞ד לִפְנֵ֧י בְהֵמָ֛ה לְרִבְעָ֖הּ תֶּ֥בֶל הֽוּא׃ כג אַל־תִּֽטַּמְּא֖וּ בְּכָל־אֵ֑לֶּה כִּ֤י בְכָל־אֵ֙לֶּה֙ נִטְמְא֣וּ הַגּוֹיִ֔ם אֲשֶׁר־אֲנִ֥י מְשַׁלֵּ֖חַ מִפְּנֵיכֶֽם׃ כד וַתִּטְמָ֣א הָאָ֔רֶץ וָאֶפְקֹ֥ד כה

her nakedness. [20] *You shall not lie carnally with your fellow's wife, to make yourself impure with her.*
[21] *You shall not present any of your children to pass through for Molech, and do not profane the Name of your God — I am* HASHEM.
[22] *You shall not lie with a man as one lies with a woman, it is an abomination.* [23] *Do not lie with any animal to be made impure with it; a woman shall not stand before an animal for mating, it is a perversion.*
[24] *Do not become impure through any of these; for through all of these the nations that I expel before you became impure.* [25] *The Land became impure and I recalled*

---- אונקלוס ----

עֶרְיָתַהּ: כּוּלְאִתַּת חַבְרָךְ לָא תִתֵּן שְׁכָבְתָּךְ לְאִסְתָּאָבָא בַהּ: כאוּמִבְּנָיךְ לָא תִתֵּן לְאַעְבָּרָא לְמֹלֶךְ וְלָא תְחַלֵּל יָת שְׁמָא דֶאֱלָהָךְ אֲנָא יְיָ: כבוְיָת דְּכוּרָא לָא תִשְׁכּוּב מִשְׁכְּבֵי אִתְּתָא תּוֹעֵבְתָא הִיא: כגוּבְכָל בְּעִירָא לָא תִתֵּן שְׁכָבְתָּךְ לְאִסְתָּאָבָא בַהּ וְאִתְּתָא לָא תְקוּם קֳדָם בְּעִירָא לְמִשְׁלַט בַּהּ תֶּבֶלָא הוּא: כדלָא תִסְתָּאֲבוּן בְּכָל אִלֵּין אֲרֵי בְכָל אִלֵּין אִסְתָּאָבוּ עַמְמַיָּא דִּי אֲנָא מְגַלֵּי מִן קֳדָמֵיכוֹן: כהוְאִסְתָּאֲבַת אַרְעָא וְאַסְעָרִית

---- רש"י ----

(כא) למלך. עֲבוֹדַת זָרָה הִיא שֶׁשְּׁמָהּ מֹלֶךְ (סנהדרין ס״ד.), וְזוֹ הִיא עֲבוֹדָתָהּ, שֶׁמּוֹסֵר בְּנוֹ לַכְּמָרִים וְעוֹשִׂין שְׁתֵּי מְדוּרוֹת גְּדוֹלוֹת וּמַעֲבִירִין אֶת הַבֵּן בְּרַגְלָיו בֵּין שְׁתֵּי מְדוּרוֹת הָאֵשׁ (שם ס״ד:): **לֹא תִתֵּן.** זוֹ הִיא מְסִירָתוֹ לַכְּמָרִים (שם): **לְהַעֲבִיר לַמֹּלֶךְ.** זוֹ הַעֲבָרַת הָאֵשׁ. **(בג) תֶּבֶל הוּא.** לְשׁוֹן קֹדֶשׁ וְעֶרְוָה, וְכֵן וְאַפִּי עַל תַּבְלִיתָם (ישעיה י׳:כ״ה), [ד"א], תֶּבֶל הוּא לְשׁוֹן בְּלִילָה וְעִרְבּוּב, זֶרַע אָדָם וְזֶרַע בְּהֵמָה:

---- RASHI ELUCIDATED ----

21. לַמֹּלֶךְ — FOR MOLECH. עֲבוֹדָה זָרָה הִיא — This is a pagan deity[1] שֶׁשְּׁמָהּ מֹלֶךְ — whose name is Molech.[1] וְזוֹ הִיא עֲבוֹדָתָהּ — This is its worship: שֶׁמּוֹסֵר בְּנוֹ לַכְּמָרִים — that he hands over his son or daughter **to the priests** of Molech, וְעוֹשִׂין שְׁתֵּי מְדוּרוֹת גְּדוֹלוֹת — and they make two big bonfires, וּמַעֲבִירִין אֶת הַבֵּן — and they make the son or daughter pass {בְּרַגְלָיו — on foot} בֵּין שְׁתֵּי מְדוּרוֹת הָאֵשׁ[2] — between the two blazing bonfires.[2]
□ לֹא תִתֵּן — YOU SHALL NOT PRESENT. [3] זוֹ הִיא מְסִירָתוֹ לַכְּמָרִים — This is, i.e. refers to, **giving him over to the priests.**[3]
□ לְהַעֲבִיר לַמֹּלֶךְ — TO PASS THROUGH FOR MOLECH. [4] זוֹ הַעֲבָרַת הָאֵשׁ — This is the passing through of the fire.[4]

23. תֶּבֶל הוּא — IT IS A PERVERSION. לְשׁוֹן קָדֵשׁ — The term תֶּבֶל is an expression of "harlotry," וְעֶרְוָה — and "nakedness," וְנִאוּף — and "adultery," [5] וְכֵן ״וְאַפִּי עַל תַּבְלִיתָם״ — Similarly, תַּבְלִיתָם in, "and My wrath over their perversion."[5] {Alternatively,[6] דָּבָר אַחֵר — תֶּבֶל הוּא לְשׁוֹן בְּלִילָה — the term תֶּבֶל הוּא means mixture וְעִרְבּוּב — and mingling זֶרַע אָדָם — of seed of man וְזֶרַע בְּהֵמָה — and seed of animal.

---

1. *Sanhedrin* 64a.
2. *Sanhedrin* 64b. According to Rashi there (s.v., שרגא דלבני), the child passes through the fire but is not burned. In this, Rashi differs from *Aruch* (s.v., שוור) and *Ramban* (to our verse) who write that the child is burned to death.
3. *Sanhedrin* 64b. The verb נתן can mean "allow," as in *Numbers* 22:13, for example. Thus our verse could have been understood, "You shall not allow your children to pass through for Molech." Rashi explains that לא תתן of our verse means actively giving the child over to the priests of Molech. Merely allowing the child to pass through for Molech does not constitute a violation of the commandment of our verse (*Lifshuto shel Rashi*).
4. *Sanhedrin* 64b.
5. *Isaiah* 10:25.
6. This phrase does not appear in the first printed edition. See Rashi to 20:12 below and our note there.

its iniquity upon it; and the Land vomited out its inhabitants. **26** But you shall safeguard My decrees and My judgments, and not commit any of these abominations — the native or the proselyte who lives among you. **27** For the inhabitants of the Land who are before you committed all these abominations, and the Land became impure. **28** Let not the Land vomit you out for having made it impure, as it vomited out the nation that was before you. **29** For if anyone commits any of these abominations, the people doing so will be cut off from among their people.

30 You shall safeguard My charge that

עֹנָהּ עָלֶיהָ וַתָּקִא הָאָרֶץ אֶת־
כו יֹשְׁבֶיהָ: וּשְׁמַרְתֶּם אַתֶּם אֶת־חֻקֹּתַי
וְאֶת־מִשְׁפָּטַי וְלֹא תַעֲשׂוּ מִכֹּל
הַתּוֹעֵבֹת הָאֵלֶּה הָאֶזְרָח וְהַגֵּר הַגָּר
כז בְּתוֹכְכֶם: כִּי אֶת־כָּל־הַתּוֹעֵבֹת הָאֵל
עָשׂוּ אַנְשֵׁי־הָאָרֶץ אֲשֶׁר לִפְנֵיכֶם
כח וַתִּטְמָא הָאָרֶץ: מפטיר וְלֹא־תָקִיא
הָאָרֶץ אֶתְכֶם בְּטַמַּאֲכֶם אֹתָהּ
כַּאֲשֶׁר קָאָה אֶת־הַגּוֹי אֲשֶׁר לִפְנֵיכֶם:
כט כִּי כָּל־אֲשֶׁר יַעֲשֶׂה מִכֹּל הַתּוֹעֵבֹת
הָאֵלֶּה וְנִכְרְתוּ הַנְּפָשׁוֹת הָעֹשֹׂת
ל מִקֶּרֶב עַמָּם: וּשְׁמַרְתֶּם אֶת־מִשְׁמַרְתִּי

---------- אונקלוס ----------

חוֹבַהּ עֲלַהּ וְרוֹקִינַת אַרְעָא יָת יָתְבָהָא: כוּ וְתִטְּרוּן אַתּוּן יָת קְיָמַי וְיָת דִּינַי וְלָא תַעְבְּדוּן מִכֹּל תּוֹעֲבָתָא הָאִלֵּין יַצִּיבָא וְגִיּוֹרָא דְיִתְגַּיְּרוּן בֵּינֵיכוֹן: כז אֲרֵי יָת כָּל תּוֹעֲבָתָא הָאִלֵּין עֲבַדוּ אֱנָשֵׁי אַרְעָא דִּי קֳדָמֵיכוֹן וְאִסְתָּאָבַת אַרְעָא: כח וְלָא תְרוֹקֵן אַרְעָא יָתְכוֹן בְּסָאֲבוּתְכוֹן יָתַהּ כְּמָא דְרוֹקִינַת יָת עַמְמַיָּא דִּי קֳדָמֵיכוֹן: כט אֲרֵי כָל דִּי יַעְבֵּד מִכֹּל תּוֹעֲבָתָא הָאִלֵּין וְיִשְׁתֵּיצוּן נַפְשָׁתָא דְּיַעְבְּדוּן מִגּוֹ עַמְּהוֹן: ל וְתִטְּרוּן יָת מַטְּרַת מֵימְרִי

---------- רש"י ----------

(כח) ולא תקיא הארץ אתכם. משל לבן מלך שהאכילוהו דבר מאוס, שאין עומד במעיו אלא מקיאו. כך ארץ ישראל אינה מקיימת עוברי עבירה (ת"כ קדושים פרק יב:יד) ותרגומו **ולא** **תרוקן,** לשון ריקון, מריקה עצמה מהם: **(כט) הנפשות העשת.** הזכר והנקבה במשמע (ת"כ פרשתא ט:כ): **(ל) ושמרתם** **את משמרתי.** להזהיר בית דין על כך (ת"כ פרק יג:כב):

---------- RASHI ELUCIDATED ----------

28. וְלֹא תָקִיא הָאָרֶץ אֶתְכֶם — LET NOT THE LAND VOMIT YOU OUT. מָשָׁל לְבֶן מֶלֶךְ — This can be compared to the son of a king שֶׁהֶאֱכִילוּהוּ דָּבָר מָאוּס — whom they fed something repulsive שֶׁאֵין עוֹמֵד בְּמֵעָיו — which cannot stay in his stomach, אֶלָּא מְקִיאוֹ — but rather, he vomits it out. כָּךְ אֶרֶץ יִשְׂרָאֵל — Similarly, the Land of Israel אֵינָהּ מְקַיֶּמֶת עוֹבְרֵי עֲבֵירָה — does not abide transgressors.[1] וְתַרְגּוּמוֹ וְלֹא תָקִיא as וְלָא תְרוֹקֵן, לְשׁוֹן רִקּוּן — The *Targum Onkelos* renders וְלֹא תָקִיא as וְלָא תְרוֹקֵן, an expression of "emptying," because מְרִיקָה עַצְמָהּ מֵהֶם — it empties itself of them when it expels them.

29. הַנְּפָשׁוֹת הָעֹשׂוֹת — THE PEOPLE DOING SO.[2] הַזָּכָר וְהַנְּקֵבָה בְּמַשְׁמָע — Both the male and the female are implied.[2]

30. וּשְׁמַרְתֶּם אֶת מִשְׁמַרְתִּי — YOU SHALL SAFEGUARD MY CHARGE. לְהַזְהִיר בֵּית דִּין — To enjoin the court עַל כָּךְ — regarding this.[3]

---

1. *Toras Kohanim, Kedoshim, perek* 12:14. The verse could have been read, "The Land will not vomit you out for having made it impure, as it vomited out the nation that was before you." This would not have been a threat, but rather an assurance that Israel would not suffer punishment for having sinned, as did the nation which preceded them. Rashi brings the parable of the son of the king to teach us that the verse is a threat, "Let not the Land vomit you out" (*Minchas Yehudah*; *Sifsei Chachamim*). The Land is like a prince of delicate constitution, who cannot abide food which disagrees with him, and vomits it out (*Be'er BaSadeh*).

2. *Toras Kohanim, parshasa* 9:20. Although the *Gemara* (*Kiddushin* 35a) derives the general rule that punishments for sins apply equally to men and women, there is a specific source to that effect given here for sins of incest and adultery. For in all other cases, the sinful act is identical for both men and women. But here, the act of the man differs from that of the woman. Nonetheless, the Torah tells us that their punishment is the same (see Rashi to v. 6 with *Mizrachi* and *Sifsei Chachamim* there).

3. *Toras Kohanim, perek* 13:22. The Torah says, "But you shall safeguard My decrees and My judgments, and not commit any of these abominations, [neither] the native, [n]or the proselyte who lives among you" (v. 26). That verse commands every individual not to commit the abominations. Our apparently redundant verse which says, "You shall safeguard My charge that these abominable traditions that were done before you

223 / VAYIKRA/LEVITICUS — PARASHAS ACHAREI — 18/30 — יח/ל

לְבִלְתִּ֞י עֲשׂ֤וֹת מֵחֻקּוֹת֙ הַתּ֣וֹעֵבֹ֔ת אֲשֶׁ֥ר נַעֲשׂ֖וּ לִפְנֵיכֶ֑ם וְלֹ֥א תִֽטַּמְּא֖וּ בָּהֶ֑ם אֲנִ֖י יהוה אֱלֹהֵיכֶֽם: פ פ פ

these abominable traditions that were done before you not be done, and not make yourselves impure through them; I am Hashem, *your God.*

THE HAFTARAH FOR ACHAREI APPEARS ON PAGE 397.
During non-leap years Acharei is always read together with Kedoshim. The Haftarah for Acharei is then read.
During leap years when Erev Rosh Chodesh Iyar coincides with Acharei, the regular Haftarah is replaced with the Haftarah for Shabbas Erev Rosh Chodesh, page 403.
When Shabbas HaGadol coincides with Acharei, the regular Haftarah is replaced with the Haftarah for Shabbas HaGadol, page 415.
See note on page 397 for further exceptions.

─────────── אונקלוס ───────────

בְּדִיל דְּלָא לְמֶעְבַּד מִנִּימוּסֵי תּוֹעֲבָתָא דְּאִתְעֲבִידוּ קֳדָמֵיכוֹן וְלָא תִסְתָּאֲבוּן בְּהוֹן אֲנָא יְיָ אֱלָהֲכוֹן:

─────────── רש"י ───────────

ולא תטמאו בהם אני ה' אלהיכם. הָא אִם תִּטַּמְּאוּ בְּכַס וְאַתֶּם מִתְחַיְּבִים כְּלָיָה. לְכָךְ נֶאֱמַר אֵינִי אֱלֹהֵיכֶם וְאַתֶּם נִפְסָלִים מֵאַחֲרַי, וּמַה הֲנָאָה יֵשׁ לִי (שם):

─────────── RASHI ELUCIDATED ───────────

□ וְלֹא תִטַּמְּאוּ בָּהֶם אֲנִי ה' אֱלֹהֵיכֶם — AND NOT MAKE YOURSELVES IMPURE THROUGH THEM; I AM HASHEM, YOUR GOD. אֵינִי אֱלֹהֵיכֶם — I am not your God, הָא אִם תִּטַּמְּאוּ — But if you make yourselves impure וְאַתֶּם נִפְסָלִים מֵאַחֲרַי — and you become unfit to be My followers, וּמַה הֲנָאָה יֵשׁ לִי בָּכֶם — for what benefit do I have from you, וְאַתֶּם מִתְחַיְּבִים כְּלָיָה — when you deserve annihilation? לְכָךְ נֶאֱמַר — This is why it says, אֲנִי ה' אֱלֹהֵיכֶם,, — "I am Hashem, your God."[1]

---

not be done," implies that there is an obligation to see to it that these abominable traditions not be done by others. This is an obligation that falls on the courts (*Mizrachi; Sifsei Chachamim*).

1. *Toras Kohanim*, perek 13:22. "I am Hashem, your God" generally connotes that God can be trusted to reward observance of His commandments and punish their transgression. But here it cannot mean that for the phrase has already been used in this portion in that sense [v. 2, see Rashi there] (see *Gur Aryeh*).

פרשת קדושים
Parashas Kedoshim

19 ¹ Hashem spoke to Moses, saying: ² Speak to the entire assembly of the Children of Israel and say to them: You shall be holy, for holy am I, Hashem, your God.

³ Every man shall revere his mother and his father and you shall observe My Sabbaths —

יט א־ב וַיְדַבֵּר יהוה אֶל־מֹשֶׁה לֵּאמֹר: דַּבֵּר אֶל־כָּל־עֲדַת בְּנֵי־יִשְׂרָאֵל וְאָמַרְתָּ אֲלֵהֶם קְדֹשִׁים תִּהְיוּ כִּי קָדוֹשׁ אֲנִי יהוה אֱלֹהֵיכֶם: ג אִישׁ אִמּוֹ וְאָבִיו תִּירָאוּ וְאֶת־שַׁבְּתֹתַי תִּשְׁמֹרוּ

אונקלוס

א וּמַלִּיל יְיָ עִם מֹשֶׁה לְמֵימָר: ב מַלֵּל עִם כָּל כְּנִשְׁתָּא דִבְנֵי יִשְׂרָאֵל וְתֵימַר לְהוֹן קַדִּישִׁין תְּהוֹן אֲרֵי קַדִּישׁ אֲנָא יְיָ אֱלָהֲכוֹן: ג גְּבַר מִן אִמֵּיהּ וּמִן אֲבוּהִי תְּהוֹן דָּחֲלִין וְיָת יוֹמֵי שַׁבַּיָּא דִילִי תִּטְּרוּן

רש"י

(ב) דבר אל כל עדת בני ישראל. מלמד שנאמרה פרשה זו בהקהל מפני שרוב גופי תורה תלויין בה (ת"כ פרשתא א:א; ויק"ר כד:ה): קדשים תהיו. הוו פרושים מן העריות ומן העבירה, שכל מקום שאתה מוצא גדר ערוה אתה מוצא קדושה, אשה זונה וחללה וגו' (להלן כא:ז) אני ה' מקדשכם (שם טו), וקדושים יהיו (שם ו), ולא יחלל זרעו, אני ה' מקדשו (שם טו), אשה זונה וחללה (שם ו־ח): (ג) איש אמו ואביו תיראו. כל אחד מכם תירְאוּ אביו ואמו. זהו פשוטו.

RASHI ELUCIDATED

19.

2. דַּבֵּר אֶל כָּל עֲדַת בְּנֵי יִשְׂרָאֵל — SPEAK TO THE ENTIRE ASSEMBLY OF THE CHILDREN OF ISRAEL. — מְלַמֵּד — This teaches us שֶׁנֶּאֶמְרָה פָּרָשָׁה זוּ — that this portion of the Torah was said בְּהַקְהֵל — at a gathering of the entire assembly of Israel[1] מִפְּנֵי שֶׁרוֹב גּוּפֵי תוֹרָה — because the majority of the essentials of the Torah ²תְּלוּיִין בָּהּ — depend upon it.[2]

□ קְדֹשִׁים תִּהְיוּ — YOU SHALL BE HOLY. — הֱווּ פְרוּשִׁים מִן הָעֲרָיוֹת — Be removed from arayos[3] וּמִן הָעֲבֵירָה — and from sin,[4] שֶׁכָּל מָקוֹם שֶׁאַתָּה מוֹצֵא גֶּדֶר עֶרְוָה — for wherever you find restriction of sexual immorality mentioned in the Torah, אַתָּה מוֹצֵא קְדֻשָּׁה — you find holiness juxtaposed with it. For example, after the Torah says, ⁵אִשָּׁה זֹנָה וַחֲלָלָה וְגוֹ׳,, — "[They (the Kohanim) shall not marry] a woman who is a zonah or a chalalah etc.,"[5] it goes on to say, ⁶אֲנִי ה׳ מְקַדִּשְׁכֶם,, — "[For holy am] I, Hashem, Who sanctifies you."[6] And after the Torah says, ⁷וְלֹא יְחַלֵּל זַרְעוֹ,, — [A Kohen] shall not defile his offspring"[7] by fathering a child from a woman forbidden to him, the verse concludes, ,,אֲנִי ⁷ה׳ מְקַדְּשׁוֹ — "I am Hashem Who sanctifies him."[7] {And after the Torah says: ⁸,,קְדֹשִׁים יִהְיוּ — "[The Kohanim] shall be holy,"[8] it says, ⁹,,אִשָּׁה זֹנָה וַחֲלָלָה — "[They shall not marry] a woman who is a zonah or a chalalah."[9]}[10]

3. אִישׁ אִמּוֹ וְאָבִיו תִּירָאוּ — EVERY MAN SHALL REVERE HIS MOTHER AND HIS FATHER. — כָּל אֶחָד מִכֶּם — Every one of you תִּירְאוּ אָבִיו וְאִמּוֹ — shall revere his father and his mother. זֶהוּ פְּשׁוּטוֹ — This is

---
1. The other portions of the Torah were also taught by Moses to the entire people of Israel, as Rashi describes in detail in his comments to *Exodus* 34:32. The apparently superfluous כָּל עֲדַת, "the entire assembly of," implies that when Moses taught this portion, every individual had to be present. When he taught other portions, individuals had the right to absent themselves if they so wished (*Sefer Zikaron*; *Gur Aryeh*).

2. *Toras Kohanim*, *parshasa* 1:1; *Vayikra Rabbah* 24:5. Maharzav to *Vayikra Rabbah* enumerates the "essentials" referred to here: honoring parents (v. 3), observing the Sabbath (v. 3), desisting from robbery (v. 13), not taking revenge or bearing a grudge (v. 18), and the commandment to love your fellow as yourself (v. 18). Rashi here follows the opinion of the *Amora* R' Chiya (in *Vayikra Rabbah*). According to the *Amora* R' Levi (there) this portion's *mitzvos* parallel the Ten Commandments. Therefore, just as the Ten Commandments were given to the entire assembly, so did this portion require everyone's presence (*Yefeh To'ar*).

3. This refers to the most serious sins of sexual immorality, including incest, adultery, and relations with a woman impure due to menstruation.

4. The term sin is used here for sin of a sexual nature (*Minchas Yehudah*; *Sifsei Chachamim*). It is used in this sense in *Yoma* 29a (see Rashi there, s.v., הרהורי עבירה) and *Sotah* 3a (see Rashi there, s.v., אדם עובר עבירה).

5. Below 21:7. See notes there for definitions of *zonah* and *chalalah*.

6. Below 21:8.

7. Below 21:15.

8. Below 21:6.

9. Below 21:7.

10. The Torah's conception of holiness is separation from materialistic desires, and attachment to that which is spiritual. The urge for forbidden sex is the most mundane of man's desires. Thus, when the Torah says, "Be holy," it means, remove yourself from the most materialistic aspect of your life (*Gur Aryeh*).

I am Hashem, *your God.* ⁴ *Do not turn to* — ד אֲנִי יהוה אֱלֹהֵיכֶם: אַל־תִּפְנוּ אֶל־

———— אונקלוס ————
אֲנָא יְיָ אֱלָהֲכוֹן: ד לָא תִתְפְּנוּן בָּתַר

———— רש"י ————

ומדרשו, אין לי אלא איש, אשה מנין, כשהוא אומר תיראו הרי כאן שנים. אם כן למה נאמר איש, שהאיש סיפק בידו לעשות אבל אשה רשות אחרים עליה (ת"כ שם ג; קידושין ל:): אמו ואביו תיראו. כאן הקדים אם לאב לפי שגלוי לפניו שהבן ירא את אביו יותר מאמו, ובכבוד הקדים אב לאם לפי שגלוי לפניו שהבן מכבד את אמו יותר מאביו, מפני שמשדלתו

בדברים (קידושין ל:לא.): ואת שבתתי תשמרו. סמך שמירת שבת למורא אב, לומר, אע"פ שהזהרתיך על מורא אב, אם יאמר לך חלל את השבת אל תשמע לו, וכן בשאר כל המצות (ת"כ שם י; יבמות ה:ו.; ב"מ לב.): אני ה' אלהיכם. אתה ואביך חייבים בכבודי (שם) לפיכך לא תשמע לו לבטל את דברי. איזהו מורא לא ישב במקומו

———— RASHI ELUCIDATED ————

[the verse's] simple meaning.[1] **וּמִדְרָשׁוֹ — And its exegetical interpretation is as follows:** אֵין לִי אֶלָּא **אִישׁ — On the basis of the word** **אִישׁ** alone, **I have only a statement that a man** must revere his parents. **אִשָּׁה מִנַּיִן — From where do I know that a woman** is also included in this commandment? **כְּשֶׁהוּא אוֹמֵר — When [the verse] says, "you** (in the plural) **... shall revere,"** **״תִּירָאוּ״ הֲרֵי כָאן שְׁנַיִם — see, then, that there are two here** whom the verse is addressing, both a man and a woman. אִם כֵּן **— If so,** that a woman is also included in the commandment, לָמָּה נֶאֱמַר ״אִישׁ״ **— why does [the verse] say** *man* , which could be misinterpreted to exclude a woman? שֶׁהָאִישׁ סִפֵּק בְּיָדוֹ לַעֲשׂוֹת **— Because a man** generally **has the wherewithal to perform** this commandment, אֲבָל אִשָּׁה רְשׁוּת אֲחֵרִים עָלֶיהָ[2] **— but a woman** often **is subject to the authority of others.**[2]

□ **אִמּוֹ וְאָבִיו תִּירָאוּ — SHALL REVERE HIS MOTHER AND HIS FATHER.** כָּאן הִקְדִּים אֵם לְאָב **— Here [the verse] put "mother" ahead of "father,"** לְפִי שֶׁגָּלוּי לְפָנָיו **— because it is revealed before Him** שֶׁהַבֵּן יָרֵא אֶת אָבִיו **— that the son reveres his father** יוֹתֵר מֵאִמּוֹ **— more than** he reveres **his mother;** therefore, the verse needed to emphasize revering the mother. וּבְכָבוֹד **— But with regard to honoring** parents, הִקְדִּים אָב לְאֵם **— [the verse] put "father" ahead of "mother,"**[3] לְפִי שֶׁגָּלוּי לְפָנָיו **— because it is revealed before Him** שֶׁהַבֵּן מְכַבֵּד אֶת אִמּוֹ **— that the son honors his mother** יוֹתֵר מֵאָבִיו **— more than** he honors **his father** מִפְּנֵי שֶׁמְּשַׁדַּלְתּוֹ בִּדְבָרִים **— because she wins him over with** pleasant **words.**[4]

□ **וְאֶת שַׁבְּתֹתַי תִּשְׁמֹרוּ — AND YOU SHALL OBSERVE MY SABBATHS.** סָמַךְ שְׁמִירַת שַׁבָּת **— [The verse]** juxtaposed observance of the Shabbos לְמוֹרָא אָב **— to reverence for** one's **father,** i.e., parent, לוֹמַר **— to say,** אַף עַל פִּי שֶׁהִזְהַרְתִּיךָ **— although I enjoined you** עַל מוֹרָא אָב **— about revering a** father, אִם יֹאמַר לְךָ **— if [your father] should say to you,** חַלֵּל אֶת הַשַּׁבָּת **— "Desecrate the** Shabbos," אַל תִּשְׁמַע לוֹ **— do not listen to him.**[5] וְכֵן בִּשְׁאָר כָּל הַמִּצְווֹת **— And so, too, with regard to other commandments.**[5]

□ **אֲנִי ה' אֱלֹהֵיכֶם — I AM HASHEM, YOUR GOD.**[5] אַתָּה וְאָבִיךָ חַיָּבִים בִּכְבוֹדִי **— You and your father are** both **obligated in** upholding **My honor;**[5] לְפִיכָךְ **— therefore,** לֹא תִשְׁמַע לוֹ **— do not listen to him** לְבַטֵּל אֶת דְּבָרַי **— to cancel,** i.e., transgress, **My words.**[6]

אֵיזֶהוּ מוֹרָא **— What constitutes reverence** of a parent? לֹא יֵשֵׁב בִּמְקוֹמוֹ **— One may not sit in** [his

---

1. Although the subject of this sentence, אִישׁ, literally, "a man," is singular, the predicate, תִּירָאוּ, literally, "you (plural) shall revere," uses the plural form of the pronoun. Rashi explains that אִישׁ does not refer to a single individual, but to each of the members of a group. Thus, the plural verb is appropriate when the members are taken as a sum total (*Mizrachi; Sifsei Chachamim*).

2. *Toras Kohanim, parshasa* 1:3; *Kiddushin* 30b. "Man" indicates a greater involvement by men than by women in the obligation to revere parents. A woman is exempt from the commandment while she is under the authority of others, i.e., while she is married, if honoring her parents conflicts with her husband's wishes (see *Shulchan Aruch, Yoreh Deah*, 240:17, and

Sifsei Kohen , ad loc., note 19).

3. *Exodus* 20:12 and *Deuteronomy* 5:16 (the fifth of the Ten Commandments) begin: כַּבֵּד אֶת אָבִיךָ וְאֶת אִמֶּךָ, "Honor your father and your mother."

4. *Kiddushin* 30b-31a.

5. *Toras Kohanim, parshasa* 1:10; *Yevamos* 5b-6a; *Bava Metzia* 32a. See Rashi's next comment for the rationale of this rule.

6. In his preceding comment Rashi explained that the juxtaposition of the commandments to revere one's parents and to observe the Shabbos teach us that one must not obey a parent who asks him to violate a law of the Torah. But how do we know that this is how the

הָאֱלִילִם וֵאלֹהֵי מַסֵּכָה לֹא תַעֲשׂוּ לָכֶם אֲנִי יהוה אֱלֹהֵיכֶם: — *the idols, and molten gods you shall not make for yourselves — I am* HASHEM, *your God.*

―――― אונקלוס ――――
טַעֲוָן וְדַחֲלָן דְּמַתְּכָא לָא תַעְבְּדוּן לְכוֹן אֲנָא יְיָ אֱלָהֲכוֹן:

―――― רש"י ――――
(ד) **אל תפנו אל האלילם.** לַעֲבֹד (ת"כ שם) אֱלִילִים לְשׁוֹן אַל, כְּלֹא הוּא חָשׁוּב: **ואלהי מסכה.** תְּחִלָּתָן אֱלִילִים הֵם, וְאִם אַתָּה פּוֹנֶה אַחֲרֵיהֶם סוֹפְךָ לַעֲשׂוֹתָן אֱלוֹהוּת (שם יא): **לא תעשו לכם.** לֹא תַּעֲשׂוּ לַאֲחֵרִים וְלֹא אֲחֵרִים לָכֶם, וְאִ"תּ לֹא תַעֲשׂוּ לְעַצְמְכֶם אֲבָל אֲחֵרִים עוֹשִׂין לָכֶם, הֲרֵי כְּבָר נֶאֱמַר לֹא יִהְיֶה לְךָ (שמות כ״ג:ג) לֹא שֶׁלְּךָ וְלֹא שֶׁל אֲחֵרִים:

―――― RASHI ELUCIDATED ――――

וְלֹא יִסְתּוֹר אֶת — *parent's] place,* וְלֹא יְדַבֵּר בִּמְקוֹמוֹ — nor may he speak in [his parent's] place,[1] דְּבָרָיו — nor may he contradict [his parent's] words. וְאֵיזֶהוּ כָּבוֹד — What constitutes honoring a parent? מַאֲכִיל — Feeding him מַשְׁקֶה — and giving him drink, מַלְבִּישׁ — dressing him, וּמַנְעִיל — and putting on his shoes, מַכְנִיס — escorting him in [2]וּמוֹצִיא — and escorting him out.[2]

4. אַל תִּפְנוּ אֶל הָאֱלִילִם — DO NOT TURN TO THE IDOLS [3]לְעָבְדָם — to worship them.[3] אֱלִילִים לְשׁוֹן אַל — The word אֱלִילִים is related to אַל, "not," because כְּלֹא הוּא חָשׁוּב — [an idol] is considered as a non-entity.[4]

❑ וֵאלֹהֵי מַסֵּכָה — AND MOLTEN GODS. תְּחִלָּתָן אֱלִילִים הֵם — At first they are "non-entities," וְאִם אַתָּה פּוֹנֶה אַחֲרֵיהֶם — but if you turn to follow them, [5]סוֹפְךָ לַעֲשׂוֹתָן אֱלוֹהוּת — your end shall be to make them gods.[5]

❑ לֹא תַעֲשׂוּ לָכֶם — YOU SHALL NOT MAKE FOR YOURSELVES. לֹא תַעֲשׂוּ לַאֲחֵרִים — Do not make them for others, [6]וְלֹא אֲחֵרִים לָכֶם — nor should others make them for you.[6] וְאִם תֹּאמַר — If you will say that the verse means לֹא תַעֲשׂוּ לְעַצְמְכֶם — do not make them for yourselves אֲבָל אֲחֵרִים עוֹשִׂין לָכֶם — but others may make them for you, הֲרֵי כְּבָר נֶאֱמַר — see, then, that it has already been said, לֹא יִהְיֶה לְךָ[7] — "there shall not be to you [gods of others before Me],"[7] which implies that you may have לֹא שֶׁלְּךָ — neither yours, i.e., neither idols which you have made for yourself, וְלֹא שֶׁל אֲחֵרִים — nor of others, i.e., idols made by others.[8]

―――――――――――

juxtaposition is to be interpreted? Perhaps the Torah means to tell us that one should obey a parent even to desecrate the Shabbos? For in his comments to *Exodus* 35:2, Rashi says that the Torah put the commandment to observe the Shabbos before the commandment to build the Tabernacle to teach us that the construction of the Tabernacle does not override the observance of the Shabbos. By that line of reasoning, if the commandment to revere a parent is stated before the commandment to observe the Shabbos, this should teach us that revering a parent supersedes observing the Shabbos. The Torah therefore adds the apparently superfluous "I am HASHEM, your God" to teach us that obeying the word of God takes precedence over obeying a parent (*Minchas Yehudah; Sifsei Chachamim*).

1. In a situation where people are expecting a statement from the parent, the child should not speak (see *Minchas Yehudah; Sifsei Chachamim*).

2. *Toras Kohanim, parshasa* 1:10; *Kiddushin* 31b.

3. *Toras Kohanim, parshasa* 1:10. "Do not turn to the idols" does not mean "do not worship the idols," for the Torah has already prohibited idol worship in

Exodus 20:3-5 and *Exodus* 22:19. "Do not turn to the idols" means "do not turn to worship them," i.e., do not even consider worshiping them (*Mizrachi; Gur Aryeh; Sifsei Chachamim*).

4. Rashi explains that אֱלִילִים is not related to אַל, "god," but to אַל, "not." See also Rashi to *Job* 13:4.

5. *Toras Kohanim, parshasa* 1:11. This explains why the verse begins by referring to idols as אֱלִילִים, "non-entities," yet goes on to call them אֱלֹהֵי מַסֵּכָה, "molton gods" (*Mizrachi; Sifsei Chachamim*).

6. *Toras Kohanim, parshasa* 1:12.

7. *Exodus* 20:3.

8. The phrase "do not make for yourselves" could have been interpreted as forbidding only the making of idols for yourselves, but not idols that others made for you. But this cannot be so, for *Exodus* 20:3 implies that the prohibition applies to any idol you possess, no matter who made it. Therefore, our verse is interpreted as implying two prohibitions: לֹא תַעֲשׂוּ, "you shall not *make* idols for others," and לָכֶם, "you shall not *have* idols for *yourselves*," even if they are made by others (*Mizrachi; Sifsei Chachamim*).

⁵ **When you slaughter a sacrifice of a peace-offering to** H‍ASHEM**, you shall slaughter it to appease for you.** ⁶ **It must be eaten on your day of slaughter and on the next day, and whatever remains until the third day shall be burned in fire.** ⁷ **But if it will be eaten on the third day, it is rejected** —

ה וְכִי תִזְבְּחוּ זֶבַח שְׁלָמִים לַיהוה
לִרְצֹנְכֶם תִּזְבָּחֻהוּ: ו בְּיוֹם זִבְחֲכֶם
יֵאָכֵל וּמִמָּחֳרָת וְהַנּוֹתָר עַד־יוֹם
הַשְּׁלִישִׁי בָּאֵשׁ יִשָּׂרֵף: ז וְאִם הֵאָכֹל
יֵאָכֵל בַּיּוֹם הַשְּׁלִישִׁי פִּגּוּל הוּא

───────────────── אונקלוס ─────────────────

ה וַאֲרֵי תִכְסוּן נִכְסַת קוּדְשַׁיָּא קֳדָם יְיָ לְרַעֲוָא לְכוֹן תִּכְסֻנֵּהּ: ו בְּיוֹמָא דְיִתְנְכֵס לְכוֹן יִתְאֲכַל וּמִיּוֹמָא דְבַתְרוֹהִי וּדְאִשְׁתָּאַר עַד יוֹמָא תְלִיתָאָה בְּנוּרָא יִתּוֹקָד: ז וְאִם אִתְאֲכָלָא יִתְאֲכַל בְּיוֹמָא תְלִיתָאָה מְרָחָק הוּא

───────────────── רש"י ─────────────────

(ה) וְכִי תִזְבָּחוּ וְגו'. לֹא נֶאֶמְרָה פָּרָשָׁה זוֹ אֶלָּא לְלַמֵּד שֶׁלֹּא תְהֵא זְבִיחָתָן אֶלָּא עַל מְנָת לְהֵאָכֵל בְּתוֹךְ הַזְּמַן הַזֶּה (ת"כ פרק אב:א). שֶׁאִם לִקְבֹּעַ לָהֶם זְמַן אֲכִילָה הֲרֵי כְּבָר נֶאֱמַר וְאִם נֶדֶר אוֹ נְדָבָה זֶבַח קָרְבָּנוֹ וְגוֹ' (לעיל ז:טז): **לִרְצֹנְכֶם תִּזְבָּחֻהוּ.** תְּחִלַּת זְבִיחָתוֹ תְּהֵא עַל מְנַת נַחַת רוּחַ שֶׁיְּהֵא לָכֶם לְרָצוֹן, שֶׁאִם תַּחְשְׁבוּ עָלָיו מַחֲשֶׁבֶת פָּסוּל לֹא יְרַצֶּה עֲלֵיכֶם **לִרְצֹנְכֶם.** אפיימנ"ט, זֶהוּ לְפִי פְשׁוּטוֹ. וְרַבּוֹתֵינוּ לָמְדוּ מִכָּאן לַמִּתְעַסֵּק בְּקָדָשִׁים שֶׁפָּסוּל, שֶׁצָּרִיךְ שֶׁיִּתְכַּוֵּן לִשְׁחוֹט (חולין י"ג.): **(ו) בְּיוֹם זִבְחֲכֶם יֵאָכֵל.** כְּשֶׁתִּזְבָּחוּהוּ תִּשְׁחֲטוּהוּ עַל מְנָת זְמַן זֶה שֶׁקָּבַעְתִּי לָכֶם כְּבָר: **(ז) וְאִם הֵאָכֹל יֵאָכֵל וְגו'.** אִם אֵינוֹ עִנְיָן לְחוּץ לִזְמַנּוֹ, שֶׁהֲרֵי כְּבָר נֶאֱמַר

───────────────── RASHI ELUCIDATED ─────────────────

5. וְכִי תִזְבְּחוּ וְגוֹמֵר — WHEN YOU SLAUGHTER, ETC. לֹא נֶאֶמְרָה פָּרָשָׁה זוֹ אֶלָּא לְלַמֵּד — This portion was said only to teach us שֶׁלֹּא תְהֵא זְבִיחָתָן אֶלָּא — that the slaughter [of peace-offerings] should be only עַל מְנַת לְהֵאָכֵל — with the intent that they be eaten ¹בְּתוֹךְ הַזְּמַן הַזֶּה — within this time, i.e., the time stated in the following verse.¹ שֶׁאִם לִקְבֹּעַ לָהֶם זְמַן אֲכִילָה — For if the verse only means **to fix a time period of eating for them**, i.e., to set a time limit within which they must be eaten, הֲרֵי כְּבָר נֶאֱמַר — see, then, that it has already been said, ״וְאִם נֶדֶר אוֹ נְדָבָה זֶבַח קָרְבָּנוֹ וְגוֹמֵר,, — "**but if the sacrifice of his offering is for a vow or a donation, etc.**"²

□ לִרְצֹנְכֶם תִּזְבָּחֻהוּ — **YOU SHALL SLAUGHTER IT TO APPEASE FOR YOU.** תְּחִלַּת זְבִיחָתוֹ — The outset of its slaughter תְּהֵא עַל מְנַת — should be with intent נַחַת רוּחַ — of contentment, i.e., to bring contentment to God, שֶׁיְּהֵא לָכֶם לְרָצוֹן — that it should be an appeasement before God on your behalf. שֶׁאִם תַּחְשְׁבוּ עָלָיו מַחֲשֶׁבֶת פָּסוּל — For if you shall think a thought of invalidation, with regard to [the offering],³ לֹא יְרַצֶּה עֲלֵיכֶם — it will not appease for you לְפָנַי — before Me.

□ לִרְצֹנְכֶם — **TO APPEASE FOR YOU.** The root of this word is רָצוֹן, which means אפיימנ"ט — *apaiement* in Old French.⁴ זֶהוּ לְפִי פְשׁוּטוֹ — This is [the word's meaning] according to its simple explanation. וְרַבּוֹתֵינוּ לָמְדוּ מִכָּאן — And our Rabbis learned from here לַמִּתְעַסֵּק בְּקָדָשִׁים — regarding one who performs an unintentional act upon that which is holy שֶׁפָּסוּל — that [the act] is invalid, שֶׁצָּרִיךְ שֶׁיִּתְכַּוֵּן לִשְׁחוֹט⁵ — for he must have intention to slaughter.⁵

6. בְּיוֹם זִבְחֲכֶם יֵאָכֵל — **IT MUST BE EATEN ON YOUR DAY OF SLAUGHTER.** כְּשֶׁתִּזְבָּחוּהוּ — When you slaughter it, תִּשְׁחֲטוּהוּ — you shall slaughter it עַל מְנַת זְמַן זֶה — with intent for eating it within this period, שֶׁקָּבַעְתִּי לָכֶם כְּבָר — that I have already fixed for you.⁶

7. וְאִם הֵאָכֹל יֵאָכֵל וְגוֹמֵר — **BUT IF IT WILL BE EATEN, ETC.** אִם אֵינוֹ עִנְיָן — If [the verse] is not applicable לְחוּץ לִזְמַנּוֹ — to the thought of eating it **beyond its time**,⁷ שֶׁהֲרֵי כְּבָר נֶאֱמַר — for see, then, that it has

---

1. *Toras Kohanim*, perek 1:1.
2. Above 7:16. That verse continues: "it must be eaten on the day he offered his sacrifice; and on the next day, what is left over from it may be eaten."
3. That is, if it is slaughtered with the intention that its meat would be eaten (or its blood service would be performed) beyond its prescribed time period or outside its prescribed location.
4. In Modern French, *apaisement*; in English, "appeasement."
5. *Chullin* 13a. It teaches us that if a person performs the act of slaughter or any other act of the sacrificial procedure without realizing that he is performing the act, the act is invalid; for instance, if he waved a knife and it happened to cut the throat of an animal designated as an offering, the offering is invalid (*Sefer Zikaron*). According to this interpretation of the Rabbis, לִרְצֹנְכֶם is understood as "with your will." The word רָצוֹן has a similar meaning in 1:3 above.
6. See Rashi to the preceding verse, s.v., תִּזְבָּחֻהוּ.
7. Which is the apparent subject of this verse.

ח לֹא יֵרָצֶה: וְאֹכְלָיו עֲוֹנוֹ יִשָּׂא כִּי־
אֶת־קֹדֶשׁ יהוה חִלֵּל וְנִכְרְתָה
ט הַנֶּפֶשׁ הַהִוא מֵעַמֶּיהָ: וּבְקֻצְרְכֶם
אֶת־קְצִיר אַרְצְכֶם לֹא תְכַלֶּה פְּאַת

it shall not be considered pleasing. **8** Whosoever eats it will bear his sin, for what is sacred to HASHEM has he desecrated; and that soul will be cut off from its people.
9 When you reap the harvest of your land, you shall not finish off the corner of

---

אונקלוס

לָא יְהֵי לְרַעֲוָא: ח וּדְיֵיכְלִנֵּהּ חוֹבֵהּ יְקַבֵּל אֲרֵי יָת קוּדְשָׁא דַייָ יָת אַחֵל וְיִשְׁתֵּיצֵי אֱנָשָׁא הַהוּא מֵעַמֵּהּ: ט וּבְמֶחְצָדְכוֹן יָת חֲצָדָא דְאַרְעֲכוֹן לָא תְשֵׁיצֵי פָּאתָא

רש"י

ואם האכל יאכל מבשר זבח שלמיו וגו' (לעיל ז:יח) תנה ענין לחוץ למקומו (ת"כ שם ד; זבחים כח.-כח:). יכול יהו חייבין כרת על אכילתו, ת"ל והנפש האוכלת ממנו עונה תשא (לעיל ז:יח) ממנו ולא מחבירו, יצא הנשחט במחשבת חוץ למקומו (זבחים כט.): **פגול.** מתועב כמו ומרק פגולים כליהם (ישעיה סה:ד): **(ח) ואכליו עונו ישא.** בנותר גמור הכתוב מדבר. [ואינו ענוש כרת על הנשחט חוץ לזמנו שכבר מיעטו הכתוב. וזה בנותר גמור מדבר,] ובמסכת כריתות (ה.) למדוהו מגזרה שוה: **(ט) לא תכלה פאת שדך.** שיניח פאה בסוף שדהו (ת"כ שם י; פאה א:ב):

RASHI ELUCIDATED

□ already been said, ¹וְגוֹמֵר שְׁלָמָיו זֶבַח מִבְּשַׂר יֵאָכֵל הָאָכֹל וְאִם – "and if there will be eaten some of the flesh of his peace-offering, etc."¹ — תְּנֵהוּ לְעִנְיָן חוּץ לִמְקוֹמוֹ — learn it as applying to the thought of eating it **outside of its** designated **place**.² יָכוֹל יְהוּ חַיָּבִין כָּרֵת — One might be able to think that **they deserve kares** ³ עַל אֲכִילָתוֹ — **for eating it.** ⁴ תַּלְמוּד לוֹמַר — To teach us otherwise, **the verse says,** ⁵ ״וְהַנֶּפֶשׁ הָאֹכֶלֶת מִמֶּנּוּ עֲוֹנָהּ תִּשָּׂא״ — **"and the soul that eats of it shall bear its sin."**⁵ ״מִמֶּנּוּ״ — **"Of it,"** וְלֹא מֵחֲבֵרוֹ — **but not of that which is related to it.**⁶ יָצָא הַנִּשְׁחָט בְּמַחֲשֶׁבֶת חוּץ לִמְקוֹמוֹ — **That which has been slaughtered with a thought of "outside its place"** has thus **left** the category of that which is punished by *kares*.⁷

□ פִּגּוּל — IT IS REJECTED. The word פִּגּוּל means מְתֹעָב — **repulsive,** ⁸״וּמְרַק פִּגֻּלִים כְּלֵיהֶם״ — **like** פִּגֻּלִים in the phrase, **"And the gravy of that which is repulsive is [in] their vessels."**⁸

8. וְאֹכְלָיו עֲוֹנוֹ יִשָּׂא — WHOSOEVER EATS IT WILL BEAR HIS SIN. בְּנוֹתָר גָּמוּר הַכָּתוּב מְדַבֵּר — The verse **speaks of absolute** *nosar*.⁹ וְאֵינוֹ עָנוּשׁ כָּרֵת — **He is not punished by** *kares* עַל הַנִּשְׁחָט חוּץ לִמְקוֹמוֹ — **for that which has been slaughtered outside of its place,**¹⁰ שֶׁכְּבָר מִעֲטוֹ הַכָּתוּב — **for the verse has already excluded it** from the punishment of *kares*.¹¹ וְזֶהוּ בְּנוֹתָר גָּמוּר מְדַבֵּר — **This** verse **speaks of absolute** *nosar*.} וּבְמַסֶּכֶת כְּרִיתוֹת¹² לְמָדוּהוּ מִגְּזֵרָה שָׁוָה — **In Tractate** *Kereisos*¹² **they learned this from a** *gezeirah shavah*.¹³

9. לֹא תְכַלֶּה פְּאַת שָׂדֶךָ — YOU SHALL NOT FINISH OFF THE CORNER OF YOUR FIELD. This means שֶׁיַּנִּיחַ — **that he should leave aside** for the poor ¹⁴שָׂדֵהוּ בְּסוֹף פֵּאָה — **a corner at the end of his field.**¹⁴

---

1. Above 7:18. Rashi, in his comments to that verse, explains that it refers to slaughtering the offering with intent to eat it beyond the time set for it by the Torah.
2. *Toras Kohanim*, *perek* 1:4; *Zevachim* 28a-b.
3. Literally, "excision." See Rashi to 17:9 above.
4. One might think that the penalty of *kares* mentioned in the next verse applies even to eating from an offering that was slaughtered with the intent of eating it outside of the area set for it by the Torah, for this is the subject of the verse as Rashi has just explained.
5. Above 7:18.
6. The apparently superfluous מִמֶּנּוּ, "of it," implies that the punishment referred to by the verse applies only to the subject of the verse, an offering slaughtered with intent to eat it beyond the time limit set by the Torah, but not to that which is related to it, an offering slaughtered with intent to eat it outside the area set for it by the Torah.
7. *Zevachim* 29a.
8. *Isaiah* 65:4.

9. *Nosar*, literally, "left over," is meat of an offering that has remained uneaten beyond the time the Torah set for it to be eaten. By absolute *nosar*, Rashi means meat that has actually been left over, as distinct from פִּגּוּל, meat of an offering that was slaughtered with the intention of leaving it over after its fixed time, or of eating it after its fixed time.
10. That is, meat of an offering that was slaughtered with intent that it be eaten outside the area within which the Torah said that it must be eaten; it is the subject of the preceding verse.
11. See Rashi to v. 7, s.v. וְאִם הָאָכֹל יֵאָכֵל וְגוֹמֵר.
12. *Kereisos* 5a.
13. For the definition of *gezeirah shavah* see p. 155 note 10. Here, our verse uses the word קֹדֶשׁ as does *Exodus* 29:34 which speaks of *nosar*. Hence, our verse, too, is understood to refer to *nosar*.
14. *Toras Kohanim*, *perek* 1:10; *Pe'ah* 1:3. The corner to be left aside for the poor must be left aside at the

your field to reap [it]; and you shall not gather the gleanings of your harvest. ¹⁰ You shall not harvest the young grapes of your vineyard; and you shall not gather the fallen fruit of your vineyard; for the poor and the proselyte shall you leave them — I am HASHEM, your God.

¹¹ You shall not steal, and you shall not

שָׂדְךָ לִקְצֹר וְלֶקֶט קְצִירְךָ לֹא תְלַקֵּט: וְכַרְמְךָ לֹא תְעוֹלֵל וּפֶרֶט כַּרְמְךָ לֹא תְלַקֵּט לֶעָנִי וְלַגֵּר תַּעֲזֹב אֹתָם אֲנִי יהוה אֱלֹהֵיכֶם: יא לֹא תִּגְנֹבוּ וְלֹא־

───── אונקלוס ─────

דְּחַקְלָךְ לְמֶחֱצַד וּלְקָטָא דַחֲצָדָךְ לָא תְלַקֵּט: יְכַרְמָךְ לָא תְעַלֵּל וְנִתְרָא דְכַרְמָךְ לָא תְלַקֵּט לְעַנְיֵי וּלְגִיּוֹרֵי תִּשְׁבּוֹק יָתְהוֹן אֲנָא יְיָ אֱלָהֲכוֹן: יא לָא תִּגְנְבוּן וְלָא

───── רש״י ─────

ולקט קצירך. שבלים הנושרים בשעת קצירה אחת או שתים, אבל שלש אינן לקט (פאה ו:ה): **(י) לא תעולל.** לא תטול עוללות שבה והן ניכרות איזהו עוללות כל שאין לה כתף ולא נטף (ת״כ פרק ג:ב; פאה ז:ד): **ופרט כרמך.** גרגרי ענבים הנושרים בשעת בצירה (ת״כ שם ב; פאה שם ג): **אני ה׳**

אלהיכם. דיין להפרע, ואיני גובה מכם אלא נפשות, שנאמר אל תגזל דל וגו׳ כי ה׳ יריב ריבם וקבע את קבעיהם נפש (משלי כב:כב-כג): ת״כ שם ז): **(יא) לא תגנבו.** אזהרה לגונב ממון, אבל לא תגנוב שבעשרת הדברות אזהרה לגונב נפשות, דבר הלמד מעניינו, דבר שחייבין עליו מיתת ב״ד (מכילתא בחדש ח):

───── RASHI ELUCIDATED ─────

□ **וְלֶקֶט קְצִירְךָ** — AND [YOU SHALL NOT GATHER] THE GLEANINGS OF YOUR HARVEST. **שִׁבֳּלִים הַנּוֹשְׁרִים** — Stalks that fall away **בִּשְׁעַת קְצִירָה** — at the time of reaping, **אַחַת אוֹ שְׁתַּיִם** — one or two at a time. **אֲבָל שָׁלֹשׁ** — But three that fall away together ¹**אֵינָן לֶקֶט** — are not considered gleanings and may be gathered by the landowner.¹

10. לֹא תְעוֹלֵל — YOU SHALL NOT HARVEST THE YOUNG GRAPES. **לֹא תִטֹּל** — Do not take **עוֹלֵלוֹת שֶׁבָּהּ** — young grapes that are in [a vineyard]. **וְהֵן נִכָּרוֹת** — They are identifiable. **אֵיזֶהוּ עוֹלֵלוֹת** — Which are young grapes? **כֹּל שֶׁאֵין לוֹ לֹא כָתֵף** — Any which have neither "shoulder" ²**וְלֹא נָטָף** — nor "drops."²

□ **וּפֶרֶט כַּרְמְךָ** — AND [YOU SHALL NOT GATHER] THE FALLEN FRUIT OF YOUR VINEYARD. This refers to **גַּרְגְּרֵי עֲנָבִים** — single grapes **הַנּוֹשְׁרִים** — that fall off the clusters ³**בִּשְׁעַת בְּצִירָה** — at the time of picking.³

□ **אֲנִי ה׳ אֱלֹהֵיכֶם** — I AM HASHEM, YOUR GOD. **דַּיָּן לְהִפָּרַע** — A judge who exacts punishment, **וְאֵינִי** — **שֶׁנֶּאֱמַר** — as it says, **גּוֹבֶה מִכֶּם אֶלָּא נְפָשׁוֹת** — and I take as payment from you nothing but lives, **״כִּי ה׳ יָרִיב רִיבָם וְקָבַע אֶת קֹבְעֵיהֶם נָפֶשׁ״** — **״אַל תִּגְזָל דַּל וְגוֹמֵר״** — "Do not rob a poor man, etc." ⁴,⁵**for** "for HASHEM will fight their fight, and despoil the lives of those who despoil them."⁴,⁵

11. לֹא תִגְנֹבוּ — YOU SHALL NOT STEAL. **אַזְהָרָה** — This is a negative commandment **לְגוֹנֵב מָמוֹן** — for one who steals money. ⁶**אֲבָל ״לֹא תִגְנֹב״** — But the verse, "You shall not steal,"⁶ **שֶׁבַּעֲשֶׂרֶת** — **הַדִּבְּרוֹת** — which is in the Ten Commandments, **אַזְהָרָה לְגוֹנֵב נְפָשׁוֹת** — is a negative commandment for one who steals people, i.e., kidnaps. **דָּבָר הַלָּמֵד מֵעִנְיָנוֹ** — This is so because it is **a matter which is learned from its context,** ⁷**דָּבָר שֶׁחַיָּבִין עָלָיו מִיתַת בֵּית דִּין** — a matter for which one is liable to a court-imposed death penalty.⁷

end of the reaping. One may not designate a corner beforehand (*Mizrachi; Sifsei Chachamim*). If one does set aside a portion of his field as *pe'ah* before he has reaped the rest of the field, that portion is considered *pe'ah* and belongs to the poor, but he must nevertheless leave another "corner" when he has completed reaping the rest of the field (*Toras Kohanim, perek* 1:9).

1. *Pe'ah* 6:5.

2. *Toras Kohanim, perek* 3:3; *Pe'ah* 7:4. A mature cluster of grapes is formed by many smaller clusters growing on small branches of a main shoot. The upper clusters weigh down on one another like a man leaning on his friend's "shoulder." The lowest clusters hang straight down and resemble "drops" dripping from the

bunch (*Rav* to *Peah* 7:4).

3. *Toras Kohanim, perek* 3:2; *Peah* 7:3.

4. *Proverbs* 22:22-23.

5. *Toras Kohanim, perek* 3:7. "I am HASHEM, your God" connotes God as judge (see Rashi to 18:2 above). The verse uses this phrase after commanding us to allow the poor to take parts of our produce, because God's judgment is especially severe with regard to these commandments — the transgressor pays with his life (see *Gur Aryeh; Sifsei Chachamim*). See Rashi to 23:22 and note 7 there.

6. *Exodus* 20:13; *Deuteronomy* 5:17.

7. *Mechilta, BaChodesh* 8. "You shall not steal" of the

תְּכַחֲשׁוּ וְלֹא־תְשַׁקְּרוּ אִישׁ בַּעֲמִיתוֹ: יב וְלֹא־תִשָּׁבְעוּ בִשְׁמִי לַשָּׁקֶר וְחִלַּלְתָּ אֶת־שֵׁם אֱלֹהֶיךָ אֲנִי יהוה: יג לֹא־

deny falsely, and you shall not lie, one man to his fellow. **12** *And you shall not swear falsely by My Name, thereby desecrating the Name of your God — I am* HASHEM. **13** *You shall not*

──── אונקלוס ────

תְכַדְּבוּן וְלָא תְשַׁקְּרוּן אֱנָשׁ בְּחַבְרֵהּ: יב וְלָא תִשְׁתַּבְּעוּן בִּשְׁמִי לְשִׁקְרָא וְתַחֵל יָת שְׁמָא דֶאֱלָהָךְ אֲנָא יְיָ: יג לָא

──── רש״י ────

ולא תכחשו. לפי שנא׳ (לעיל ה:כב) וכחש בה משלם קרן וחומש למדנו עונש, אזהרה מנין, ת״ל ולא תכחשו (ת״כ פרשתא ב:ג): **ולא תשקרו.** לפי שנאמר ונשבע על שקר ישלם קרן וחומש למדנו עונש, אזהרה מנין, ת״ל ולא תשקרו: **לא תגנבו**

ולא תכחשו ולא תשקרו ולא תשבעו. אם גנבת סופך לכחש, סופך לשקר, סופך לישבע לשקר (ת״כ שם ה:ג): **(יב) ולא תשבעו בשמי.** למה נאמר, לפי שנא׳ לא תשא את שם ה׳ אלהיך לשוא (שמות כ:ז) יכול לא יהא חייב אלא על שם המיוחד,

──── RASHI ELUCIDATED ────

☐ וְלֹא תְכַחֲשׁוּ — AND YOU SHALL NOT DENY FALSELY. — לְפִי שֶׁנֶּאֱמַר — Since it has been said, ״וְכִחֶשׁ בָּהּ וְגוֹמֵר״[1] — "and [he] denied it, etc.,"[1] {קֶרֶן וְחוֹמֶשׁ מְשַׁלֵּם — that he pays {the principal plus a fifth},[2] לָמַדְנוּ עֹנֶשׁ — we have learned the punishment. אַזְהָרָה מִנַּיִן — From where do we know the negative commandment? תַּלְמוּד לוֹמַר — The verse says, ״וְלֹא תְכַחֲשׁוּ״,[3] — "and you shall not deny falsely."[3]

☐ וְלֹא תְשַׁקְּרוּ — AND YOU SHALL NOT LIE. — לְפִי שֶׁנֶּאֱמַר — Since it has been said, ״וְנִשְׁבַּע עַל שֶׁקֶר״[4] — "and he swore falsely,"[4] יְשַׁלֵּם קֶרֶן וָחֹמֶשׁ — that he should pay the principal plus a fifth,[5] לָמַדְנוּ עֹנֶשׁ — we have learned the punishment. אַזְהָרָה מִנַּיִן — From where do we know the negative commandment? תַּלְמוּד לוֹמַר — The verse says, ״וְלֹא תְשַׁקְּרוּ״, — "and you shall not lie."

☐ לֹא תִגְנֹבוּ וְלֹא תְכַחֲשׁוּ וְלֹא תְשַׁקְּרוּ וְלֹא תִשָּׁבְעוּ — YOU SHALL NOT STEAL, AND YOU SHALL NOT DENY FALSELY, AND YOU SHALL NOT LIE ... AND YOU SHALL NOT SWEAR [FALSELY BY MY NAME]. אִם גָּנַבְתָּ — If you have stolen, סוֹפְךָ לְכַחֵשׁ — your end will be to deny falsely; and then סוֹפְךָ לְשַׁקֵּר — your end will be to lie;[6] and then סוֹפְךָ לִשָּׁבַע לַשֶּׁקֶר — your end will be to swear falsely.[7]

12. וְלֹא תִשָּׁבְעוּ בִשְׁמִי — AND YOU SHALL NOT SWEAR [FALSELY] BY MY NAME. לָמָּה נֶאֱמַר — Why was this said? לְפִי שֶׁנֶּאֱמַר — Because it says, ״לֹא תִשָּׂא אֶת שֵׁם ה׳ אֱלֹהֶיךָ לַשָּׁוְא״,[8] — "You shall not take the name of HASHEM, your God, in vain,"[8] יָכוֹל לֹא יְהֵא חַיָּב — one might be able to think that he should not be liable for swearing falsely in God's name אֶלָּא עַל שֵׁם הַמְיֻחָד — except for swearing by the

---

Ten Commandments is stated in the context of other commandments, such as murder and adultery, for which the violation is punished by a court-imposed death penalty. Hence, it, too, must be a commandment punishable by death, namely, kidnaping (see *Deuteronomy* 24:7), not stealing money. See, too, Rashi to *Exodus* 20:13, s.v., לא תגנב.

1. Above 5:22.
2. According to *Mizrachi*, the words קֶרֶן וָחֹמֶשׁ, "the principal plus a fifth," do not belong in the text of Rashi, for here Rashi refers to a situation in which one swears falsely in denying a claim, but is contradicted by valid witnesses. The punishment referred to by Rashi according to *Mizrachi* is that he is responsible for anything that may happen to the stolen object until he has returned it in accordance with 5:23 above. The additional fifth is not paid unless he admits on his own to having sworn falsely. Rashi's following comment, which deals with one who swore falsely and then admitted his guilt, correctly refers to the principal and a fifth. (But see *Gur Aryeh*, who defends the text as it stands.)

3. *Toras Kohanim, parshasa* 2:3.
4. Above 5:22.
5. Verse 5:24 states that one must pay the principal plus a fifth if he swears falsely to a claim made against him.
6. After you have stolen, first you will "deny falsely" when your victim claims payment from you. Then you will "lie," i.e., weave a web of lies in support of your false denial (*Maskil LeDavid*).
7. *Toras Kohanim, parshasa* 2:5. Verses 11 and 12 echo *Exodus* 20:13 in their listing of several negative commandments in quick succession. But the verse in *Exodus* does not link each negative commandment with the conjunctive ו prefix. Rashi explains that they are joined here because one who violates the first commandment is prone to violate the next; this, in turn, leads to the next transgression (see *Korban Aharon*).
8. *Exodus* 20:7.

cheat your fellow and you shall not rob; payment for the work of a hired worker shall not stay overnight with you until morning. ¹⁴ You shall not curse a deaf person, and

תַעֲשֹׁק אֶת־רֵעֲךָ וְלֹא תִגְזֹל לֹא־תָלִין פְּעֻלַּת שָׂכִיר אִתְּךָ עַד־בֹּקֶר: יד לֹא־תְקַלֵּל חֵרֵשׁ

―――――― אונקלוס ――――――

תַעֲשׁוֹק יָת חַבְרָךְ וְלָא תָנִיס לָא תְבִית אֲגַר אֲגִירָא עִמָּךְ עַד צַפְרָא: יד לָא תְלוּט דְּלָא שָׁמַע

―――――― רש"י ――――――

מִנַּיִן לְרַבּוֹת כָּל הַכִּנּוּיִין, ת"ל וְלֹא תִשָּׁבְעוּ בִשְׁמִי לַשָּׁקֶר, כָּל שֵׁם שֶׁיֵּשׁ לִי (ת"כ שָׁם ו): (יג) לֹא תַעֲשֹׁק. זֶה הַכּוֹבֵשׁ שְׂכַר שָׂכִיר (שָׁם ט): לֹא תָלִין. לְשׁוֹן נְקֵבָה מוּסָב עַל הַפְּעֻלָּה: עַד בֹּקֶר. בִּשְׂכִיר יוֹם הַכָּתוּב מְדַבֵּר, שֶׁיְּצִיאָתוֹ מִשֶּׁשִּׁקְעָה חַמָּה, לְפִיכָךְ זְמַן גְּבוּי שְׂכָרוֹ כָּל הַלַּיְלָה. וּבְמָקוֹם אַחֵר הוּא אוֹמֵר וְלֹא תָבוֹא עָלָיו

הַשֶּׁמֶשׁ (דְּבָרִים כד:טו) מְדַבֵּר בִּשְׂכִיר לַיְלָה, שֶׁהַשְׁלָמַת פְּעֻלָּתוֹ מַעֲלַת עַמּוּד הַשַּׁחַר, לְפִיכָךְ זְמַן גְּבוּי שְׂכָרוֹ כָּל הַיּוֹם (ת"כ שָׁם יב; ב"מ קי:) לְפִי שֶׁנָּתְנָה תּוֹרָה זְמַן לְבַעַל הַבַּיִת עוֹנָה לְבַקֵּשׁ מָעוֹת: (יד) לֹא תְקַלֵּל חֵרֵשׁ. אֵין לִי אֶלָּא חֵרֵשׁ, מִנַּיִן לְרַבּוֹת כָּל אָדָם, ת"ל בְּעַמְּךָ לֹא תָאֹר (שְׁמוֹת כב:כז) אִם כֵּן

―――――― RASHI ELUCIDATED ――――――

Special Name.[1] מִנַּיִן לְרַבּוֹת – **From where do we know that we should include** כָּל הַכִּנּוּיִין – **all of the alternative Names of God** in the prohibition against swearing falsely in His Name? תַּלְמוּד לוֹמַר – To provide this source, **the verse says,** ״וְלֹא תִשָּׁבְעוּ בִשְׁמִי לַשֶּׁקֶר״ – **"And you shall not swear falsely by My Name,"** which implies ²כָּל שֵׁם שֶׁיֵּשׁ לִי – **every Name that I have.**[2]

13. לֹא תַעֲשֹׁק – YOU SHALL NOT CHEAT.[3] זֶה הַכּוֹבֵשׁ שְׂכַר שָׂכִיר – **This refers to one who withholds the wages of a hired worker.**[3]

□ לֹא תָלִין – [IT] SHALL NOT STAY OVERNIGHT. לְשׁוֹן נְקֵבָה – This is **a feminine verb,** מוּסָב עַל הַפְּעֻלָּה – **which refers to "the work."**[4]

□ עַד בֹּקֶר – UNTIL MORNING. בִּשְׂכִיר יוֹם הַכָּתוּב מְדַבֵּר – **The verse speaks of a worker hired for a day,** i.e., the daylight hours, שֶׁיְּצִיאָתוֹ – **whose departure** from his work מִשֶּׁשִּׁקְעָה חַמָּה – **is when the sun has set,** i.e., his workday ends with sunset. לְפִיכָךְ – **Therefore,** זְמַן גְּבוּי שְׂכָרוֹ – **the time for the collection of his wages is** כָּל הַלַּיְלָה – **the entire night.** וּבְמָקוֹם אַחֵר הוּא אוֹמֵר – **Elsewhere it says,** ⁵״וְלֹא תָבוֹא עָלָיו הַשֶּׁמֶשׁ״ – **"the sun should not set over him,"**[5] i.e., he should not have to wait until sunset to collect his wages. מְדַבֵּר בִּשְׂכִיר לַיְלָה – **[That verse] speaks of a worker hired for a night,** שֶׁהַשְׁלָמַת פְּעֻלָּתוֹ – **the completion of whose work** מַעֲלַת עַמּוּד הַשַּׁחַר – **is at the break of dawn.** לְפִיכָךְ – **Therefore,** זְמַן גְּבוּי שְׂכָרוֹ – **the time for the collection of his wages** ⁶כָּל הַיּוֹם – **is the entire day.**[6] לְפִי שֶׁנָּתְנָה תּוֹרָה זְמַן לְבַעַל הַבַּיִת – **For the Torah gave time to the householder,** i.e., the employer, עוֹנָה – **a period of a day or a night** לְבַקֵּשׁ מָעוֹת – **to seek money** to pay his worker.

14. לֹא תְקַלֵּל חֵרֵשׁ – YOU SHALL NOT CURSE A DEAF PERSON. אֵין לִי אֶלָּא חֵרֵשׁ – On the basis of this verse alone, **I have only a deaf man,** i.e., I know only that it is forbidden to curse a deaf man. מִנַּיִן לְרַבּוֹת כָּל אָדָם – **From where do I know that I should include** cursing **any person** in this prohibition? תַּלְמוּד לוֹמַר – To provide this source, **the verse says,** ⁷״בְּעַמְּךָ לֹא תָאֹר״ – **"You shall not curse** [a leader] **among your people."**[7] אִם כֵּן – **If it is so** that the prohibition is not limited to cursing a deaf person,

---

1. The Tetragrammaton, i.e., the Name consisting of the four letters י-ה and ה.

2. *Toras Kohanim, parshasa* 2:6. Had the verse said, לֹא תִשָּׂא שְׁמִי לַשָּׁקֶר, "You shall not take My Name falsely," it could have been understood as referring to the Special Name alone. Its use of בִשְׁמִי, "*by* My Name," implies "by any word which is used for My Name" (*Biurei Maharia*). Alternatively, had the Torah referred to the Special Name, as it did in *Exodus* 20:7, quoted by Rashi above, it used שֵׁם ה' אֱלֹקֶיךָ, "the Name of Hashem, your God." Here the Torah uses בִשְׁמִי, "by My Name," without further qualification, to include any of God's names (*Malbim*).

3. *Toras Kohanim, parshasa* 2:9. Since "you shall not cheat" appears here in the context of a verse that explicitly mentions withholding the wages of a hired worker, it, too, is understood as referring to withhold-ing wages (*Minchas Yehudah*).

4. The ת of תָלִין could have been understood to indicate the masculine, second person, singular form of the verb, in which case the verse would have said, "You shall not keep overnight [payment for] a hired worker's work." But if this were so, אִתָּךְ, "with you," which follows would be superfluous, for it is implicit in "you shall not keep overnight." Therefore, Rashi understands the ת to indicate the feminine, third person, singular. Its subject is the feminine פְּעֻלַּת. The verse says, "[Payment for] the work of a hired worker shall not stay overnight with you until morning" (*Minchas Yehudah; Sifsei Chachamim*).

5. *Deuteronomy* 24:15.

6. *Toras Kohanim, parshasa* 2:12; *Bava Metzia* 110b.

7. *Exodus* 22:27. The apparently superfluous בְּעַמְּךָ, "among your people," implies that the prohibition

וְלִפְנֵי עִוֵּר לֹא תִתֵּן מִכְשֹׁל וְיָרֵאתָ מֵּאֱלֹהֶיךָ אֲנִי יְהוָה׃

you shall not place a stumbling block in front of a blind person; and you shall have fear of your God — I am HASHEM.

— אונקלוס —

וְקֳדָם דְּלָא חָזֵי לָא תְשִׁים תַּקְלָא וְתִדְחַל מֵאֱלָהָךְ אֲנָא יְיָ׃

— רש"י —

וְלִפְנֵי עִוֵּר לֹא תִתֵּן מִכְשֹׁל. לִפְנֵי הַסּוּמָא בְדָבָר לֹא תִּתֵּן עֵצָה שֶׁאֵינָהּ הוֹגֶנֶת לוֹ. אַל תֹּאמַר מְכֹר שָׂדְךָ וְקַח לְךָ חֲמוֹר וְאַתָּה עוֹקֵף עָלָיו וְנוֹטְלָהּ הֵימֶנּוּ: **וְיָרֵאתָ מֵאֱלֹהֶיךָ.** לְפִי שֶׁהַדָּבָר הַזֶּה אֵינוֹ מָסוּר לַבְּרִיּוֹת לֵידַע אִם דַּעְתּוֹ שֶׁל זֶה לְטוֹבָה אוֹ לְרָעָה, וְיָכוֹל לְהִשָּׁמֵט וְלוֹמַר לְטוֹבָה נִתְכַּוַּנְתִּי, לְפִיכָךְ נֶאֱמַר בּוֹ וְיָרֵאתָ מֵאֱלֹהֶיךָ, הַמַּכִּיר מַחְשְׁבוֹתֶיךָ. וְכֵן כָּל דָּבָר הַמָּסוּר לְלִבּוֹ שֶׁל אָדָם הָעוֹשֵׂהוּ, וְאֵין שְׁאָר הַבְּרִיּוֹת מַכִּירוֹת בּוֹ, נֶאֱמַר בּוֹ וְיָרֵאתָ מֵאֱלֹהֶיךָ (שָׁם פֶּרֶק ז:יד):

— RASHI ELUCIDATED —

just as מַה חֵרֵשׁ מְיֻחָד שֶׁהוּא בַחַיִּים – לָמָּה נֶאֱמַר חֵרֵשׁ – *why does it say, "a deaf person"? To teach us* **a deaf person has the distinct quality of being alive,** אַף – *so, too,* does the prohibition apply to cursing כָּל שֶׁהוּא בַחַיִּים – *anyone who is alive.* יָצָא הַמֵּת – *A dead person has* thus **left the category** of those whom the verse forbids cursing¹ שֶׁאֵינוֹ בַחַיִּים – *for he is not alive.*¹

☐ וְלִפְנֵי עִוֵּר לֹא תִתֵּן מִכְשֹׁל – AND YOU SHALL NOT PLACE A STUMBLING BLOCK IN FRONT OF A BLIND PERSON. לִפְנֵי הַסּוּמָא בְדָבָר – **In front of one who is blind about the** particular **matter,** לֹא תִּתֵּן עֵצָה – Do not give him advice שֶׁאֵינָהּ הוֹגֶנֶת לוֹ – *that is not appropriate for him.*² אַל תֹּאמַר – Do not say, ״מְכֹר שָׂדְךָ וְקַח לְךָ חֲמוֹר״ – *"Sell your field, and buy yourself a donkey,"* וְאַתָּה עוֹקֵף עָלָיו – and you thereby twist him to your advantage ³וְנוֹטְלָהּ הֵימֶנּוּ – *and take [the field] from him.*³

☐ וְיָרֵאתָ מֵאֱלֹהֶיךָ – AND YOU SHALL HAVE FEAR OF YOUR GOD. לְפִי שֶׁהַדָּבָר הַזֶּה – Since this matter אֵינוֹ מָסוּר לַבְּרִיּוֹת – is not given to people לֵידַע – to know, i.e., since people are unable to determine, אִם דַּעְתּוֹ שֶׁל זֶה – if the intent of this person who gives the bad advice לְטוֹבָה – is for the good of the person he advises אוֹ לְרָעָה – or for bad, וְיָכוֹל לְהִשָּׁמֵט – and he is able to escape blame, וְלוֹמַר – and to say, ״לְטוֹבָה נִתְכַּוַּנְתִּי״ – *"I meant well,"* לְפִיכָךְ – therefore, נֶאֱמַר בּוֹ – it is said about him, ״וְיָרֵאתָ מֵאֱלֹהֶיךָ״ – *"and you shall have fear of your God"* – Who הַמַּכִּיר מַחְשְׁבוֹתֶיךָ – recognizes the nature of your thoughts. וְכֵן – And so, too, כָּל דָּבָר הַמָּסוּר לְלִבּוֹ שֶׁל אָדָם הָעוֹשֵׂהוּ – anything that is given over to the heart of the person who does it, i.e., any act, of which the intention can be known with certainty only by the person who performs it, וְאֵין שְׁאָר הַבְּרִיּוֹת מַכִּירוֹת בּוֹ – and the nature of **which other people cannot recognize,** נֶאֱמַר בּוֹ – of it, it is said, ⁴״וְיָרֵאתָ מֵאֱלֹהֶיךָ״ – *"and you shall have fear of your God."*⁴,⁵

applies to cursing anyone among your people (*Mizrachi; Sifsei Chachamim*).

1. *Toras Kohanim, parshasa* 2:13. If cursing the dead had not been eliminated from the prohibition, we would have thought that it was forbidden, just as it is forbidden to curse a parent even after his death (see Rashi to 20:9 below; *Mizrachi; Sifsei Chachamim*).

2. Had the verse referred only to a blind man in the literal sense, it would have said וְלִפְנֵי עִוֵּר לֹא תָשִׂים מִכְשֹׁל. The verse expresses "you shall not place" with לֹא תִתֵּן, literally, "you shall not give," to include a situation where one is giving something which is ostensibly of value – advice (*Korban Aharon; Mishmeres HaKodesh*). Alternatively, putting an obstacle in front of a blind person is an action which can be identified as a sin by a third party. The conclusion of the verse, וְיָרֵאתָ מֵאֱלֹהֶיךָ, "You shall have fear of your God," however, is a phrase which is used in the context of commandments which only the transgressor knows that he has trespassed as Rashi states in the following comment. This applies to the giving of advice, for only the one advising knows what his intentions are. Therefore, the verse is interpreted in a figurative sense (*Gur Aryeh*). Nevertheless, the verse does not refer *only* to giving bad advice; putting a stumbling block in front of one who is blind in the literal sense is also included (*Mesiach Ilmim*).

3. *Toras Kohanim, parshasa* 2:14. You tell him to sell the field so that you will eventually be able to take possession of it.

4. *Toras Kohanim, perek* 7:14. We refrain from transgressing *all* negative commandments out of fear of God. If the Torah states, "You shall have fear of your God" only in the context of some of them, it is because they involve a unique dimension of fear of God; one can evade blame for them in the eyes of man, but not before God (*Mesiach Ilmim*).

5. This phrase appears five times in Scripture, all in *Leviticus*. In addition to our verse, it appears in 19:32; 25:17, 36 and 43 below. Rashi repeats his comment each time this phrase appears.

15 *You shall not do wrong in justice; you shall not favor a destitute man and you shall not honor a great man; with righteousness shall you judge your fellow.*

טו לֹא־תַעֲשׂוּ עָוֶל בַּמִּשְׁפָּט לֹא־תִשָּׂא פְנֵי־דָל וְלֹא תֶהְדַּר פְּנֵי גָדוֹל בְּצֶדֶק תִּשְׁפֹּט עֲמִיתֶךָ:

— אונקלוס —

טו לָא תַעְבְּדוּן שְׁקַר בְּדִינָא לָא תִסַּב אַפֵּי מִסְכֵּנָא וְלָא תֶהְדַּר אַפֵּי רַבָּא בְּקוּשְׁטָא תְדִינֵהּ לְחַבְרָךְ:

— רש"י —

(טו) **לא תעשו עול במשפט.** מְלַמֵּד שֶׁהַדַּיָּן הַמְקַלְקֵל אֶת הַדִּין קָרוּי עַוָּל, שָׂנוּא וּמְשֻׁקָּץ, חֵרֶם וְתוֹעֵבָה (שם פרק ד:א). שֶׁהֶעָוֶל קָרוּי תּוֹעֵבָה שֶׁנֶּאֱמַר כִּי תוֹעֲבַת ה' וְגוֹ' כֹּל עוֹשֵׂה עָוֶל (דברים כה:טז) וְהַתּוֹעֵבָה קָרוּי שֶׁקֶץ וְחֵרֶם שֶׁנֶּ' וְלֹא תָבִיא תוֹעֵבָה אֶל בֵּיתֶךָ וְהָיִיתָ חֵרֶם כָּמוֹהוּ שַׁקֵּץ תְּשַׁקְּצֶנּוּ וְגוֹ' (שם ז:כו): **לא תשא פני דל.** שֶׁלֹּא תֹאמַר עָנִי הוּא זֶה וְהֶעָשִׁיר חַיָּיב לְפַרְנְסוֹ, אֲזַכֶּנּוּ בַּדִּין וְנִמְצָא מִתְפַּרְנֵס בִּנְקִיּוּת (ת"כ שם ב): **ולא תהדר פני גדול.** שֶׁלֹּא תֹאמַר עָשִׁיר הוּא זֶה, בֶּן גְּדוֹלִים הוּא זֶה, הֵיאַךְ אֲבַיְּשֶׁנּוּ וְאֶרְאֶה בְּבוּשְׁתּוֹ, עוֹנֶשׁ יֵשׁ בַּדָּבָר. לְכָךְ נֶאֱמַר וְלֹא תֶהְדַּר פְּנֵי גָדוֹל (ת"כ שם ג): **בצדק תשפט עמיתך.** כְּמַשְׁמָעוֹ. דָּבָר אַחֵר, הֱוֵי דָן אֶת חֲבֵרְךָ לְכַף זְכוּת (שם ד):

— RASHI ELUCIDATED —

15. לֹא תַעֲשׂוּ עָוֶל בַּמִּשְׁפָּט — YOU SHALL NOT DO WRONG IN JUSTICE. מְלַמֵּד — This teaches us שֶׁהַדַּיָּן — that a judge הַמְקַלְקֵל אֶת הַדִּין — who perverts the judgment קָרוּי עַוָּל — is called a wrongdoer, שָׂנוּא — hateful וּמְשֻׁקָּץ — and repulsive, חֵרֶם — banned [1] וְתוֹעֵבָה — and an abomination.[1] שֶׁהֶעָוֶל — For a wrongdoer is called "an abomination," שֶׁנֶּאֱמַר ,,כִּי תוֹעֲבַת ה' וְגוֹמֵר כֹּל עֹשֵׂה עָוֶל,, — as it says, "for it is an abomination to HASHEM, etc., any who do wrong."[2] וְהַתּוֹעֵבָה — And an abomination קָרוּי ,,שֶׁקֶץ,, — is called "repulsive" וְ,,חֵרֶם,, — and "banned," שֶׁנֶּאֱמַר ,,וְלֹא תָבִיא תוֹעֵבָה אֶל בֵּיתֶךָ — as it says, "Do not bring an abomination to your house, וְהָיִיתָ חֵרֶם כָּמֹהוּ — lest you be banned like it; שַׁקֵּץ תְּשַׁקְּצֶנּוּ וְגוֹמֵר,, — treat it with repulsion, etc."[3]

☐ לֹא תִשָּׂא פְנֵי דָל — YOU SHALL NOT FAVOR A DESTITUTE MAN. שֶׁלֹּא תֹאמַר — This means that you should not say, עָנִי הוּא זֶה — "This is a poor man, וְהֶעָשִׁיר חַיָּב לְפַרְנְסוֹ — and the rich man is obligated to provide him with his livelihood. אֲזַכֶּנּוּ בַּדִּין — I will pronounce the verdict in his favor in judgment, וְנִמְצָא — and it will thus be found מִתְפַּרְנֵס בִּנְקִיּוּת [5] — that he gains his livelihood in cleanliness, i.e., without shame and without resorting to dishonesty."[4,5]

☐ וְלֹא תֶהְדַּר פְּנֵי גָדוֹל — AND YOU SHALL NOT HONOR A GREAT MAN. שֶׁלֹּא תֹאמַר — That you should not say, עָשִׁיר הוּא זֶה — "This is a rich man. בֶּן גְּדוֹלִים הוּא זֶה — This is the son of great people, i.e., a man of noble ancestry. הֵיאַךְ אֲבַיְּשֶׁנּוּ — How can I humiliate him by ruling against him וְאֶרְאֶה בְּבוּשְׁתּוֹ — and see his humiliation? עֹנֶשׁ יֵשׁ בַּדָּבָר — There is punishment for the matter, i.e., I would be punished for doing such a thing." לְכָךְ נֶאֱמַר — This is why it says, ,,וְלֹא תֶהְדַּר פְּנֵי גָדוֹל,, [6] — "and you shall not honor a great man."[4,6]

☐ בְּצֶדֶק תִּשְׁפֹּט עֲמִיתֶךָ — WITH RIGHTEOUSNESS SHALL YOU JUDGE YOUR FELLOW. This is to be understood לְכַף זְכוּת [7] judge your friend הֱוֵי דָן אֶת חֲבֵרְךָ — Alternatively, דָּבָר אַחֵר — as it sounds. כְּמַשְׁמָעוֹ — toward the scale of merit, i.e., when the nature of his conduct is questionable, give him the benefit of the doubt.[7]

---

1. *Toras Kohanim*, perek 4:1.
2. *Deuteronomy* 25:16.
3. *Deuteronomy* 7:26. Among the terms Rashi applies to a judge who perverts judgment is "hateful," yet he does not adduce support from Scripture for that term as he does for the others. *Yosef Da'as* cites a text of Rashi which concludes with the verse אֲשֶׁר שָׂנֵא ה' כִּי כָל תוֹעֲבַת , "for every abomination unto HASHEM which He hates" (*Deuteronomy* 12:31), which equates "abomination" with "hateful." *Sefer Zikaron* maintains that once Rashi has brought support from Scripture that such a judge is a wrongdoer, repulsive, banned, and an abomination, it can be presumed that he is hateful, even without a source from Scripture. In one manuscript of Rashi, "hateful" does not appear at all among the terms that describe a judge who perverts justice (*Yosef Hallel*).
See Rashi to v. 35 below, where he repeats these five negative attributes then adds that a judge who prevents judgment causes five evils to befall the nation.

4. "You shall not do wrong in justice" includes any miscarriage of justice, be it in favor of a destitute man or a great man. Scripture nonetheless gives these two specific examples because in each case there is a particular rationalization by which a judge might justify a perversion of justice (*Gur Aryeh; Sifsei Chachamim*).

5. *Toras Kohanim*, perek 4:2.
6. *Toras Kohanim*, perek 4:3.
7. *Toras Kohanim*, perek 4:4. According to the simple meaning of the verse, "with righteousness" refers to the judge — he should be fair in judging any case that comes before him. According to the second interpretation, "with righteousness" refers to the one being judged — when you have to judge the conduct of another, try to attribute

16 You shall not go about gossiping among your people, you shall not stand

טז לֹא־תֵלֵךְ רָכִיל בְּעַמֶּיךָ לֹא תַעֲמֹד

―――――― אונקלוס ――――――

טז לָא תֵיכוּל קוּרְצִין בְּעַמָּךְ לָא תְקוּם

―――――― רש"י ――――――

(טז) לא תלך רכיל. אני אומר על שם שכל משלחי מדנים ומספרי לשון הרע הולכים בבתי רעיהם לרגל מה יראו רע או מה ישמעו רע לספר בשוק, נקראים הולכי רכיל, הולכי רגילה אישפיי"מנט בלעז. וראיה לדברי, שלא מצינו רכילות שאין כתוב בלשון הליכה. לא תלך רכיל, הולכי רכיל נחשת וברזל (ירמיה ו:כח), [והולך רכיל מגלה סוד (משלי יא:יג)]. ושאר לשון הרע אין כתוב בו הליכה, מלשני בסתר רעהו (תהלים קא:ה), לשון רמיה (שם קכ:ב-ג), לשון מדברת גדולות (שם יב:ד). לכך אני אומר שהלשון [לשון] הולך ומרגל, שהכ"ף נחלפת בגימ"ל, שכל האותיות שמוצאיהם ממקום אחד מתחלפות זו בזו.

―――――― RASHI ELUCIDATED ――――――

16. לֹא תֵלֵךְ רָכִיל – **YOU SHALL NOT GO ABOUT GOSSIPING.** אֲנִי אוֹמֵר – **I say,** עַל שֵׁם שֶׁכָּל מְשַׁלְּחֵי מְדָנִים – that **because all who instigate bad will** וּמְסַפְּרֵי לָשׁוֹן הָרָע – **and who relate malicious talk** הוֹלְכִים בְּבָתֵּי רֵעֵיהֶם – **go to their fellows' houses** לְרַגֵּל מַה יִּרְאוּ רָע – **to spy out what bad they may see** אוֹ מַה יִּשְׁמְעוּ רָע – **or what bad they may hear** לְסַפֵּר בַּשּׁוּק – **to relate** the bad which they saw or heard **in the market,** i.e., to spread it among the public, נִקְרָאִים הוֹלְכֵי רָכִיל – **they are called "those who go about gossiping,"** which is linguistically related to הוֹלְכֵי רְגִילָה – **"those who go about spying,"** אישפיימנ"ט בלע"ז – *espiement* **in Old French.**[1] וּרְאָיָה לִדְבָרַי – **There is proof to my words** שֶׁלֹּא מָצִינוּ רְכִילוּת – **for we have not found** the word רְכִילוּת used for **"gossiping"** שֶׁאֵין כָּתוּב בִּלְשׁוֹן הֲלִיכָה – **which is not written along with terms of** הֲלִיכָה, "going," for example, our verse, "לֹא תֵלֵךְ רָכִיל" – **"you shall not go about gossiping,"** and, "הֹלְכֵי רָכִיל נְחֹשֶׁת וּבַרְזֶל"[2] – **"who go gossip as strong as copper and iron."**[2] וּשְׁאָר לְשׁוֹן הָרָע – **Other** terms for **malicious talk** mentioned in Scripture אֵין כָּתוּב בּוֹ הֲלִיכָה – **do not have "going"** written with them, for example, "מְלָשְׁנִי בַסֵּתֶר רֵעֵהוּ"[3] – **"one who slanders his fellow in secrecy";**[3] "לָשׁוֹן רְמִיָּה"[4] – **"a treacherous tongue";**[4] "לָשׁוֹן מְדַבֶּרֶת גְּדֹלוֹת"[5] – **"a tongue that speaks haughtily."**[5] לְכָךְ אֲנִי אוֹמֵר – **Therefore I say** שֶׁהַלָּשׁוֹן {לְשׁוֹן} הוֹלֵךְ וּמְרַגֵּל – **that this expression,** {is related to} הוֹלֵךְ רָכִיל **"goes and spies."**[6] שֶׁהַכַּ"ף נֶחְלֶפֶת בַּגִּימֶ"ל – **For the letter כ is interchangeable with the letter ג,** שֶׁכָּל הָאוֹתִיּוֹת – **because all the letters** שֶׁמּוֹצָאֵיהֶם מִמָּקוֹם אֶחָד – **that have their source from the same place,** i.e., they are formed by the same organs of speech,[7] מִתְחַלְּפוֹת זוֹ בָּזוֹ – **are**

righteousness to him.
The simple meaning of this part of the verse is compatible with the subject matter of the rest of the verse, which is addressed to judges. On the other hand, it does not take עֲמִיתֶךָ, "your fellow," into account, for a judge must judge everyone with righteousness. The second interpretation accounts for "your fellow," for it is only a Jew who observes the commandments of the Torah to whom you must give the benefit of the doubt. You are not required to do so for a sinner (see *Maskil LeDavid*).

1. In Modern French, *espionnage*; in English, "espionage" or "the act of spying."

2. *Jeremiah* 6:28. The verse means that the gossipers stand behind their lies as strongly as copper and iron (Rashi to that verse).
 Some editions adduce another verse here: הוֹלֵךְ רָכִיל מְגַלֶּה סוֹד, "He goes in gossip, who reveals a secret" (*Proverbs* 11:13).
 Other verses in which רָכִיל is juxtaposed with הֲלִיכָה are *Jeremiah* 9:3 and *Proverbs* 20:19. In each of the verses cited, רָכִיל appears as part of a verbal phrase, with הֲלִיכָה as the verb. *Ezekiel* 22:9 reads: אַנְשֵׁי רָכִיל

הָיוּ בָךְ, "Slanderous men were among you." Although רָכִיל appears in that verse without a form of הֲלִיכָה, this does not pose a contradiction to Rashi. For there רָכִיל is used as an adjective to modify אַנְשֵׁי, "men," and is not part of a verbal phrase (*Lifshuto shel Rashi*).

3. *Psalms* 101:5.

4. *Psalms* 120:2-3.

5. *Psalms* 12:4.

6. See *Judges* 18:14.

7. The twenty-two letters of the *aleph-beis* are classified according to the speech organs used in their pronunciation. Thus, the letters אהח"ע have their origin in the throat and are called אוֹתִיּוֹת הַגָּרוֹן, "letters of the throat" or "gutturals"; גיכ"ק are אוֹתִיּוֹת הַחֵךְ, "letters of the palate" or "palatals"; דטלנ"ת are אוֹתִיּוֹת הַלָּשׁוֹן, "letters of the tongue (with its tip at the teeth)" or "dentals"; זסרש"ץ are אוֹתִיּוֹת הַשִּׁנַּיִם, "letters of the teeth" or "sibilants"; and בומ"פ are אוֹתִיּוֹת הַשְּׂפָתַיִם, "letters of the lips" or "labials" (*Sefer Yetzirah* 2:3).
 Until this point Rashi has shown the similarity of spelling and pronunciation that connects the roots רכל and רגל. From here on, he shows the similarity of their meanings.

over the blood of your friend — I am HASHEM. עַל־דַּם רֵעֶךָ אֲנִי יְהוָה:

──────── אונקלוס ────────
עַל דְּמָא דְחַבְרָךְ אֲנָא יְיָ:

──────── רש״י ────────

בי״ת בפ״א [ובו״ו], וגימ״ל בכ״ף וקו״ף [בכ״ף], ונו״ן בלמ״ד, [ורי״ש] וזי״ן בלד״י, וכן וירגל בעבדך (שמואל ב יט:כח) רגל במרמה לאמר עלי רעה. וכן לא רגל על לשונו (תהלים טו:ג) וכן רוכל, הסוחר ומרגל אחר כל סחורה, וכל [וס"ם וכן] המוכר בשמים להתקשט בהם הנשים, על שם שמחזר תמיד בעיירות נקרא רוכל לשון נכיל. ותרגומו לא תיכול קורצין, כמו ואכלו קרציהון די יהודיא (דניאל ג:ח) אכל ביה קורצא בי מלכא (ברכות נח.) נראה בעיני שהיה משפטם לאכול בבית המקבל דבריהם שום הלעטה, והוא גמר חזוק שדבריו מקויימים ועומידם על האמת. ואותה הלעטה נקראת אכילת קורצין, לשון קורץ בעיניו (משלי ו:יג) שכן דרך כל הולכי רכיל לקרוץ בעיניהם ולרמוז דברי רכילותן שלא יבינו שאר השומעים: **לא תעמוד על דם רעך.** לראות במיתתו

──────── RASHI ELUCIDATED ────────

interchangeable with one another; for example, {וּבְנִי״א בֵּי״ת – ב with פ {and with ו},[1] {וְרֵי״שׁ} וְזַיִ״ן – and נ with ל,[3] {בְּכָ״ף וְקוֹ״ף בְּכָ״ף},[2] וְגִימֶ״ל בְּכָ״ף – and ג with כ and ק {with כ}, and ז with צ.[4] {וְ} and {ד} – ברד״י. 5וְכֵן, וַיְרַגֵּל בַּעֲבָדֶּךָ – So, too, וַיְרַגֵּל in, "and he slurred your slave,"[5] reflects the similarity of the roots רכל and רגל; for that verse speaks of malicious talk, and means, רִגֵּל בְּמִרְמָה – he spied treacherously לֵאמֹר עָלַי רָעָה – so as to say evil about me.[6] וְכֵן – Similarly, we find that רָגַל is like in meaning to רָכִיל in the phrase, 7"לֹא רָגַל עַל לְשׁנוֹ – "he did not slander with his tongue."[7] וְכֵן – And similarly, רוֹכֵל הַסּוֹחֵר וּמְרַגֵּל אַחַר כָּל סְחוֹרָה – a peddler, who goes around and spies out any merchandise.[8] וְכָל הַמּוֹכֵר בְּשָׂמִים – And anyone[9] who sells spices לְהִתְקַשֵּׁט בָּהֶם הַנָּשִׁים – for women to adorn themselves, עַל שֵׁם שֶׁמְּחַזֵּר תָּמִיד – because he is always circulating בָּעֲיָרוֹת – in the towns, נִקְרָא רוֹכֵל – he is called a *rocheil,* לְשׁוֹן רוֹגֵל – which is related to "going on foot."[10] וְתַרְגּוּמוֹ – The *Targum Onkelos* renders רָכִיל, as לָא תֵכַל קוּרְצִין "לָא תֵיכוֹל קוּרְצִין,, – which means literally, "do not eat of winking," כְּמוֹ – similar in meaning to, 11"וַאֲכַלוּ קַרְצֵיהוֹן דִּי יְהוּדָיֵא,, – "they 'ate the winking' of the Jews,"[11] i.e., they slandered the Jews, and to, 12"אֲכַל בֵּה קוּרְצָא בֵּי מַלְכָּא,, – "he 'ate winking' against him, i.e., he slandered him, **in the house of the king."**[12] נִרְאֶה בְעֵינַי – It appears in my eyes שֶׁהָיָה מִשְׁפָּטָם – that their practice was לֶאֱכוֹל – to eat בְּבֵית הַמְקַבֵּל דִּבְרֵיהֶם שׁוּם הַלְעָטָה – some mouthful in the house of the one who received their words of gossip, וְהוּא גְמַר חִזּוּק – and it was a sign of **final affirmation** שֶׁדְּבָרָיו מְקוּיָּמִים – that his words were authentic, וַיְעַמִידָם עַל הָאֱמֶת – and he could vouch for their truth.[13] וְאוֹתָהּ הַלְעָטָה – That mouthful נִקְרֵאת – is called אֲכִילַת קוּרְצִין – "eating of winking," 14"קוֹרֵץ בְּעֵינָיו,, – לְשׁוֹן – an expression related to "he winks with his eyes,"[14] שֶׁכֵּן דֶּרֶךְ כָּל הוֹלְכֵי רָכִיל – for such is the way of all who go gossip, לִקְרוֹץ בְּעֵינֵיהֶם – to wink with their eyes וְלִרְמוֹז דִּבְרֵי רְכִילוּתָן – and to communicate by means of **gesture the words of their gossip,** שֶׁלֹּא יָבִינוּ שְׁאָר הַשּׁוֹמְעִים – so that the other listeners should not understand.

לִרְאוֹת בְּמִיתָתוֹ – to YOU SHALL NOT STAND OVER THE BLOOD OF YOUR FRIEND, לֹא תַעֲמֹד עַל דַּם רֵעֶךָ □

---

1. For examples, see Rashi to *Menachos* 27b, s.v., למעוט משופש דרך; Rashi and *Radak* to *Psalms* 68:31 regarding the word בֹּזֵר; and Rashi to *Daniel* 11:24, s.v., יְבַזּוֹר.

2. For examples, see Rashi to *Isaiah* 19:4, s.v., וְסִכַּרְתִּי; *Metzudas Tzion* to *Psalms* 63:12, s.v., יִסָּכֵר; and *Metzudas Tzion* to *Malachi* 3:3, s.v., וְזִקֵּק.

3. For examples, see Rashi to *Chagigah* 12b, s.v., עליית אגלים; and to *Genesis* 25:4, s.v., וּלְטוּשִׁם.

4. For examples, see Rashi to 13:37 above, s.v., וְשַׁעַר שָׁחֹר.

5. *II Samuel* 19:28.

6. Some early editions read, רִגֵּל וְתָר מַה לֵאמֹר עָלַי רָעָה, "He spied and explored what evil to say about me."

7. *Psalms* 15:3. See *Targum* there.

8. Rashi explains the similarity of רכל in the sense of "peddling" to רגל in the sense of "spying."

9. Some editions of Rashi read, וְכֵן הַמּוֹכֵר בְּשָׂמִים – "And similarly one who sells spices."

10. Rashi brings another illustration of how the roots רכל and רגל are related.

Ibn Ezra explains that just as the peddler transfers merchandise by buying from one and selling to another, so does the gossip [and the spy] transfer information by hearing from one and repeating to another.

11. *Daniel* 3:8.

12. *Berachos* 58a.

13. The recipient of the gossip would give the gossiper food to show that he believed what the gossiper told him (*Ramban*).

14. *Proverbs* 6:13.

ויקרא – פרשת קדושים

יז לֹא־תִשְׂנָא אֶת־אָחִיךָ בִּלְבָבֶךָ הוֹכֵחַ תּוֹכִיחַ אֶת־עֲמִיתֶךָ וְלֹא־תִשָּׂא עָלָיו חֵטְא: יח לֹא־תִקֹּם וְלֹא־תִטֹּר אֶת־בְּנֵי עַמֶּךָ וְאָהַבְתָּ לְרֵעֲךָ כָּמוֹךָ אֲנִי יהוה: יט אֶת־חֻקֹּתַי תִּשְׁמֹרוּ בְּהֶמְתְּךָ לֹא־תַרְבִּיעַ כִּלְאַיִם שָׂדְךָ לֹא־תִזְרַע כִּלְאָיִם

¹⁷ You shall not hate your brother in your heart; you shall reprove your fellow and you shall not bear a sin because of him. **¹⁸** You shall not take revenge and you shall not bear a grudge against the members of your people; you shall love your fellow as yourself — I am Hashem.

¹⁹ You shall observe My statutes: you shall not mate your animal with another species, you shall sow your field with mixed seed;

──────── אונקלוס ────────

יז לָא תִשְׂנֵי יָת אֲחוּךְ בְּלִבָּךְ אוֹכָחָא תוֹכַח יָת חַבְרָךְ וְלָא תְקַבֵּל עַל דִּילֵהּ חוֹבָא: יח לָא תִקּוֹם וְלָא תִטַּר דְּבָבוּ לִבְנֵי (נ״א לִבְנֵי) עַמָּךְ וְתִרְחַם לְחַבְרָךְ כְּוָתָךְ אֲנָא יְיָ: יט יָת קְיָמַי תִּטְּרוּן בְּעִירָךְ לָא תַרְכֵּב עֵרוּבִין חַקְלָךְ לָא תִזְרַע עֵרוּבִין

──────── רש"י ────────

ואתה יכול להצילו, כגון טובע בנהר, וחיה או לסטים באים עליו (ת"כ פרק ד:ח; סנהדרין עג.): **אני ה':** נאמן לשלם שכר ונאמן לפרע: (יז) **ולא תשא עליו חטא.** לא תלבין את פניו ברבים (ת"כ שם, ערכין טז:): (יח) **לא תקום.** אמר לו השאילני מגלך, אמר לו לאו. למחר אמר לו השאילני קרדומך, אמר לו איני משאילך, כדרך שלא השאלתני, זו היא נקימה.

ואיזו היא נטירה, אמר לו השאילני קרדומך, אמר לו לאו. למחר אמר לו השאילני מגלך, אמר לו הא לך, ואיני כמותך שלא השאלתני, זו היא נטירה, שנוטר האיבה בלבו אף על פי שאינו נוקם (ת"כ שם יח; יומא כג.): **ואהבת לרעך כמוך.** אמר רבי עקיבא זה כלל גדול בתורה (ת"כ שם יב): (יט) **את חקתי תשמרו.** ואלו הן בהמתך לא תרביע כלאים וגו'.

──────── RASHI ELUCIDATED ────────

בְּגוֹן – for instance, you must save טוֹבֵעַ בְּנָהָר – one who is drowning in a river, וְחַיָּה – or if an animal אוֹ לִסְטִים – or bandits בָּאִים עָלָיו – are coming upon him.[1]

אֲנִי ה׳ □ – I AM HASHEM. נֶאֱמָן לְשַׁלֵּם שָׂכָר – Faithful to pay reward, וְנֶאֱמָן לִפָּרֵעַ – and faithful to exact payment.[2]

17. וְלֹא תִשָּׂא עָלָיו חֵטְא – AND YOU SHALL NOT BEAR A SIN BECAUSE OF HIM. לֹא תַלְבִּין אֶת פָּנָיו – Do not make his face pale[3] by reproving him בָּרַבִּים – in public.[4]

18. לֹא תִקֹּם – YOU SHALL NOT TAKE REVENGE. אָמַר לוֹ – [One man] said to [another], הַשְׁאִילֵנִי מַגָּלְךָ – "Lend me your sickle," אָמַר לוֹ – [the second] said to [the first], לָאו – "No." לְמָחָר – The next day, אָמַר לוֹ – [the second] said to [the first], הַשְׁאִילֵנִי קַרְדֻּמְּךָ – "Lend me your hatchet," אָמַר לוֹ – [the first] said to [the second], אֵינִי מַשְׁאִילְךָ – "I am not lending it to you כְּדֶרֶךְ שֶׁלֹּא הִשְׁאַלְתַּנִי – just as you did not lend me your sickle." זוֹ הִיא נְקִימָה – This is taking revenge.

וְאֵיזוֹ הִיא נְטִירָה – And what is bearing a grudge? אָמַר לוֹ – [One man] said to [another], הַשְׁאִילֵנִי אֶת קַרְדֻּמְּךָ – "Lend me your hatchet," אָמַר לוֹ – [the second] said to [the first], לָאו – "No." לְמָחָר – The next day, אָמַר לוֹ – [the second] said to [the first], הַשְׁאִילֵנִי מַגָּלְךָ – "Lend me your sickle," אָמַר לוֹ – [the first] said to [the second], הֵא לְךָ – "Here it is for you, וְאֵינִי כְּמוֹתְךָ – and I am not like you, שֶׁלֹּא הִשְׁאַלְתַּנִי – for you did not lend me your hatchet." זוֹ הִיא נְטִירָה – This is bearing a grudge, literally, "keeping" or "guarding," שֶׁנּוֹטֵר הָאֵיבָה בְּלִבּוֹ – for he keeps the enmity in his heart[5] אַף עַל פִּי שֶׁאֵינוֹ נוֹקֵם – even though he does not take revenge.[5]

וְאָהַבְתָּ לְרֵעֲךָ כָּמוֹךָ □ – YOU SHALL LOVE YOUR FELLOW AS YOURSELF. אָמַר רַבִּי עֲקִיבָא – The Tanna R' Akiva said,[6] זֶה כְּלָל גָּדוֹל בַּתּוֹרָה – "This is a great rule in the Torah."[6]

19. אֶת חֻקֹּתַי תִּשְׁמֹרוּ – YOU SHALL OBSERVE MY STATUTES. וְאֵלּוּ הֵן – They are the following: ,,בְּהֶמְתְּךָ לֹא תַרְבִּיעַ כִּלְאַיִם וְגוֹמֵר׳׳ – "You shall not mate your animal with another species, etc."

---

1. Toras Kohanim, perek 4:8; Sanhedrin 73a.
2. See Rashi to v. 10 above, s.v., אֲנִי ה׳ אֱלֹהֵיכֶם, and note 6 there.
3. That is, do not make him blush; do not make his face turn red and then turn pale (see Bava Metzia 58b and Tosafos there).
4. Toras Kohanim, perek 4:8; Arachin 16b.
5. Toras Kohanim, perek 4:11; Yoma 23a.
6. Toras Kohanim, perek 4:12.

239 / VAYIKRA/LEVITICUS — PARASHAS KEDOSHIM — 19/20 — יט/כ

וּבֶ֤גֶד כִּלְאַ֙יִם֙ שַֽׁעַטְנֵ֔ז לֹ֥א יַעֲלֶ֖ה עָלֶֽיךָ: כ וְ֠אִ֠ישׁ כִּֽי־יִשְׁכַּ֨ב אֶת־אִשָּׁ֜ה שִׁכְבַת־זֶ֗רַע וְהִ֤וא שִׁפְחָה֙ נֶחֱרֶ֣פֶת

and a garment that is a mixture of combined fibers shall not come upon you.
²⁰ *If a man lies carnally with a woman, and she is a slavewoman who has been designated*

— אונקלוס —

וּלְבוּשׁ עֵרוּבִין שַׁעַטְנֵזָא לָא יִסַּק עֲלָךְ: כּג וּגְבַר אֲרֵי יִשְׁכּוּב עִם אִתְּתָא שִׁכְבַת זַרְעָא וְהִיא אַמְתָא אֲחִידָא

— רש"י —

ובגד כלאים וגו': למה נאמר, לפי שנאמר (דברים כב:יא) לא תלבש שעטנז צמר ופשתים יחדו, יכול לא ילבש גיזי צמר ואניצי פשתן, ת"ל בגד. מנין לרבות הלבדים, ת"ל שעטנז, דבר שהוא שוע טווי ונוז (מו"ק יב:) שאלו מפרשין לשון כמום, פליישט"א. ולשון שעטנו פי' מנחם מחברת צמר ופשתים: (כ) **נחרפת לאיש.** מיועדת ומיוחדת לאיש ואיני יודע לו דמיון במקרא ובשפחה כנענית שחציה שפחה וחציו בת חורין המאורסת לעבד עברי שמותר בשפחה הכתוב מדבר (ת"כ פרק ה:ב; כריתות יא.):

חקים אלו גזרות מלך שאין טעם לדבר: חזיין לנמלי דאית בהון נוז לשון לחברו, מישטי"ר בלע"ז, כמו נוז לשון דבר הגמול וחזור זה עם זה לחברו, מישטי"ר בלע"ז, כמו

— RASHI ELUCIDATED —

חֻקִּים אֵלּוּ – **These statutes** **גְּזֵרַת מֶלֶךְ** – **are a decree of the King,** **שֶׁאֵין טַעַם לַדָּבָר** – **for there is no rationale to the matter** which man can see.

□ **וּבֶגֶד כִּלְאַיִם וְגוֹמֵר** – AND A GARMENT THAT IS A MIXTURE, ETC. **לָמָּה נֶאֱמַר** – **Why was this stated?** **לְפִי שֶׁנֶּאֱמַר** – **Because it says,** **"לֹא תִלְבַּשׁ שַׁעַטְנֵז** – **"You shall not wear combined fibers,** **צֶמֶר וּפִשְׁתִּים יַחְדָּו"**[1] – **wool and linen together,"**[1] **יָכוֹל** – **one might be able** to think that **לֹא יִלְבַּשׁ** – **he may not wear** **גִּזֵּי צֶמֶר** – **shearings of wool** **וַאֲנִיצֵי פִשְׁתָּן** – **and bundles of linen fibers.** **תַּלְמוּד לוֹמַר** – **To teach us otherwise, the verse says** here, **"בֶּגֶד"** – **"a garment."** **מִנַּיִן** – **From where do we have a source** **לְרַבּוֹת הַלְּבָדִים** – **to include felts** in the prohibition?[2] **תַּלְמוּד לוֹמַר** – **To provide** this source, **the verse says,** **"שַׁעַטְנֵז"** – **"combined fibers,"** which implies **דָּבָר שֶׁהוּא שׁוּעַ טָווּי וְנוּז** – anything **which is carded,** or **spun, or twined.**[3] **וְאוֹמֵר אֲנִי** – **I say** that **נוּז** – **"twined"** **לְשׁוֹן דָּבָר** – means something **הַנִּגְמָל וְשָׁזוּר זֶה עִם זֶה** – **which is rolled and twisted together** **לְחַבְּרוֹ** – **to bind it,** **מִישְׁטִי"ר בְּלַעַ"ז** – *misture* in Old French.[4] **כְּמוֹ** – It is like **"לִנְוָאֵי** in, "they are **חָזְיָן לְנַוְאֵי דְּאִית בְּהוֹן"**[5] – fit for the withered ones that are inside them,"[5] **שֶׁאָנוּ מְפָרְשִׁין לְשׁוֹן כְּמוּשׁ** – **which we interpret as** related to "withering,"[6] **פלייישטר"א** – *flestre* in Old French.[7] **וּלְשׁוֹן שַׁעַטְנֵז** – **And the meaning of the word** **שַׁעַטְנֵז,** **פֵּרֵשׁ מְנַחֵם** – **Menachem**[8] **explained** as meaning **מַחְבֶּרֶת צֶמֶר וּפִשְׁתִּים** – **a combination of wool and linen.**

20. נֶחֱרֶפֶת לְאִישׁ – DESIGNATED TO A MAN. **מְיֻעֶדֶת** – **She has been assigned** **וּמְיֻחֶדֶת** – **and specified** **לְאִישׁ** – **to** another **man.** **וְאֵינִי יוֹדֵעַ לוֹ דִּמְיוֹן בַּמִּקְרָא** – **I do not know any word akin to** [**נֶחֱרֶפֶת**] in Scripture. **וּבְשִׁפְחָה כְּנַעֲנִית** – It is about a Canaanite slavewoman **שֶׁחֶצְיָהּ שִׁפְחָה** – **who is half slavewoman** **וְחֶצְיָהּ בַּת חוֹרִין** – **and half freewoman** **הַמְאֹרֶסֶת לְעֶבֶד עִבְרִי** – **who is married to a Hebrew servant** **שֶׁמֻּתָּר בְּשִׁפְחָה** – **who** (the Hebrew servant) **is permitted** to have relations **with** a Canaanite **slavewoman** **הַכָּתוּב מְדַבֵּר**[9] – **that the verse speaks.**[9]

---

1. *Deuteronomy* 22:11.
2. Felt is cloth that is carded, but not spun or twined. Rashi refers to cloth of linen and wool that were carded together.
3. The term שַׁעַטְנֵז is a combination of the words שׁוּעַ טָווּי נוּז. This implies that anything which has undergone one of the three processes, carding, spinning or twining, falls under the prohibition. Hence, felts are also forbidden (see *HaKesav VeHaKabbalah*).
4. The English word "mixture" is derived from this Old French word. Both have the same meaning.
5. *Moed Katan* 12b.
6. Withered sesame plants, the subject of the quotation from *Moed Katan,* are bent and twisted, and in that sense are similar to twisted threads (based on Rashi from manuscript to *Moed Katan* 12b, Efraim Kupfer, ed., Jerusalem, 5721, s.v., לנוייתא דאית בהו, who appears to understand that "the withered ones" referred to by the *Gemara* are the sesame plants; *Sifsei Chachamim,* based on *Minchas Yehudah,* who understands that "the withered ones" refers to the sesame seeds, follows the commentary erroneously attributed to Rashi printed in the standard edition of the Talmud).
7. In Modern French, *"flétri,"* "withered."
8. Menachem ben Saruk (Spain, c. 920-980) compiled *Machberes,* a dictionary of the Hebrew language frequently quoted by Rashi.
9. *Toras Kohanim, perek* 5:2; *Kereisos* 11a. A Canaanite slavewoman cannot enter a bond of marriage. No Jew, except a servant owned by a fellow Jew, may have relations with her. Such a Jewish servant may be assigned a Canaanite slavewoman by his master (see *Exodus* 21:4). Our verse (see next note) speaks of a woman who is half Canaanite slavewoman and half free Jew, e.g., a

to a man, and who has not been redeemed, or freedom has not been granted her; there shall be an investigation — they shall not

לְאִישׁ וְהָפְדֵּה֙ לֹ֣א נִפְדָּ֔תָה א֥וֹ חֻפְשָׁ֖ה לֹ֣א נִתַּן־לָ֑הּ בִּקֹּ֧רֶת תִּהְיֶ֛ה לֹ֥א

— אונקלוס —

לִגְבַר וְאִתְפְּרָקָא לָא אִתְפְּרִיקַת בְּכַסְפָּא אוֹ חֵרוּתָא לָא אִתְיְהִיבַת לַהּ בִּשְׁטַר בִּקַּרְתָּא תְּהִי לָא

— רש"י —

והפדה לא נפדתה. פדויה ואינה פדויה. וסתם פדיון בכסף (ת"כ שם ג; גיטין לט:): **או חפשה.** בשטר (שם): **בקרת תהיה.** היא לוקה ולא הוא (ת"כ שם ד; כריתות שם). יש על בית דין לבקר את הדבר שלא לחייבה מיתה, כי לא חפשה, ואין קידושיה קידושין גמורין. ורבותינו למדו מכאן שמי שהוא במלקות תהא בקריאה, שהדיינים המלקין קורין על הלוקה אם לא תשמור לעשות וגו' והפלא ה' את מכותך וגו' (דברים כח:נח־נט):

— RASHI ELUCIDATED —

☐ **וְהָפְדֵּה לֹא נִפְדָּתָה — AND WHO HAS NOT BEEN REDEEMED.** This means פְּדוּיָה — **redeemed,** וְאֵינָהּ פְּדוּיָה — **and not redeemed.**[1] וּסְתָם פִּדְיוֹן — **Redemption, when stated without further qualification,** בְּכֶסֶף — **is through money.**[2]

☐ **אוֹ חֻפְשָׁה — OR FREEDOM.** [2]בִּשְׁטָר — **Through a document.**[2,3]

☐ **בִּקֹּרֶת תִּהְיֶה — THERE SHALL BE AN INVESTIGATION.** הִיא לוֹקָה — **She gets lashes,** [4]וְלֹא הוּא — **but not he.**[4] יֵשׁ עַל בֵּית דִּין — **It is incumbent upon the court** לְבַקֵּר אֶת הַדָּבָר — **to investigate the matter** שֶׁלֹּא לְחַיְּבָהּ מִיתָה — **so as not to impose the death penalty upon her**[5] like a married woman who commits adultery,[6] ,,כִּי לֹא חֻפָּשָׁה״ — **"for she has not been freed,"** וְאֵין קִדּוּשֶׁיהָ קִדּוּשִׁין גְּמוּרִין — and therefore **her marriage is not a complete marriage.**

וְרַבּוֹתֵינוּ לָמְדוּ מִכָּאן — **Our Rabbis learned from here** [7]שֶׁמִּי שֶׁהוּא בְּמַלְקוּת — **that someone who is subject to the penalty of lashes**[7] תְּהֵא בִּקְרִיאָה — **shall be in reciting;** that is, שֶׁהַדַּיָּנִים הַמַּלְקִין — **that the judges who carry out the lashing** קוֹרִין עַל הַלּוֹקֶה — **recite over the one who is being lashed,** ,,אִם לֹא תִשְׁמוֹר לַעֲשׂוֹת וְגוֹמֵר״ — **"If you do not take care to carry out, etc.,"** וְהִפְלָא ה' אֶת מַכֹּתְךָ ,,וְגוֹמֵר״[8] — **"Hashem will make your punishments** [and the punishments of your children] **extraordinary, etc."**[8]

---

slavewoman who was owned by two Jewish partners, one of whom freed her with respect to his share in her. [A freed Canaanite slave is no longer a Canaanite, but takes on the status of a free Jew. Since this woman was only freed by one of her masters, she is in the unique position of being both a Canaanite slavewoman and a free Jew.] Such a woman may not have relations with a Canaanite slave, for she is half free, and that liberated side of her may not have relations with a Canaanite slave. Nor may she have relations with a free Jew, because of the slave side of her. She can enter into a relationship with a Jewish servant of a fellow Jew, however. He can marry the free side of her, and he is permitted to have relations with the slave side of her.

מְאֹרֶסֶת, the word used here by Rashi for "married," denotes that she has entered the first stage of marriage, which is effected by the marriage transaction (מַעֲשֵׂה קִדּוּשִׁין), and by which she becomes forbidden as a married woman to all but her husband. She enters the household of her husband with the second stage of marriage, נִשּׂוּאִין.

1. The two-verb unit which includes an apparently unnecessary infinitive is common in the Torah and is usually not interpreted as two separate verbs. Here, however, if we were to take וְהָפְדֵּה לֹא נִפְדָּתָה, "and who has not been redeemed," at face value, it would be stating the obvious; if the Torah refers to a שִׁפְחָה, "a slavewoman," it goes without saying that she has not been redeemed. וְהָפְדֵּה לֹא נִפְדָּתָה is therefore separated into two distinct and opposed verbal effects, "she has been redeemed; she has not been redeemed." It is from here that we know that the verse discusses a woman who is half free and half slave (*Maskil LeDavid*).

2. *Toras Kohanim, perek* 5:3; *Gittin* 39b.

3. "Who has not been redeemed, or freedom has not been granted her" sounds redundant. Rashi explains that "who has not been redeemed" refers to attaining freedom from slavery by payment of money, while "or freedom has not been granted her" refers to attaining freedom through a document of manumission (שְׁטָר שִׁחְרוּר).

4. *Toras Kohanim, perek* 5:4; *Kereisos* 11a. In the first printed edition of Rashi and other early editions, the words הִיא לוֹקָה וְלֹא הוּא appear as a separate comment on תִּהְיֶה, which appears after Rashi's comment on בִּקֹּרֶת תִּהְיֶה (see *Yosef Hallel*; see note 8 below for an explanation of these words of Rashi).

5. Some editions read לְחַיְּבוֹ מִיתָה, "to impose the death penalty upon him" (see *Ramban*).

6. In some editions, the comment ends here and a new comment, s.v., כִּי לֹא חֻפָּשָׁה, begins.

7. The first printed edition reads, שֶׁהִיא בְּמַלְקוּת, "that she is [subject to the penalty] of lashes"; תְּהֵא בִּקְרִיאָה, "she shall be in reciting."

8. *Deuteronomy* 28:58-59. The Torah uses the word בִּקֹּרֶת for the penalty of lashes, because of its similarity to בִּקְרִיאָה, "in reciting." It alludes to lashes, for during the administration of lashes, the head of the court *recites*

be put to death, for she has not been freed. [21] *He shall bring his guilt-offering to* HASHEM, *to the entrance of the Tent of the Meeting, a ram guilt-offering.* [22] *The Kohen shall provide him atonement with the ram guilt-offering before* HASHEM *for the sin that he had committed; and the sin that he had committed shall be forgiven him.*

[23] *When you shall come to the Land and you shall plant any food tree, you shall treat its fruit as* orlah; *for three years it shall be* orlah *to you, they shall*

──────────── אונקלוס ────────────

יוּמְתוּן אֲרֵי לָא אִתְחֲרָרַת: כא וְיַיְתִי יָת אֲשָׁמֵהּ קֳדָם יְיָ לִתְרַע מַשְׁכַּן זִמְנָא דְּכַר לַאֲשָׁמָא: כב וִיכַפֵּר עֲלוֹהִי כַהֲנָא בְּדִכְרָא דַאֲשָׁמָא קֳדָם יְיָ עַל חוֹבְתֵהּ דִּי חָב וְיִשְׁתְּבֵק לֵהּ מֵחוֹבְתֵהּ דִּי חָב: כג וַאֲרֵי תֵעֲלוּן לְאַרְעָא וְתִצְּבוּן כָּל אִילָן דְּמֵיכַל וּתְרַחֲקוּן רַחָקָא יָת אִבֵּהּ תְּלַת שְׁנִין יְהֵי לְכוֹן מְרַחַק לַאֲבָדָא

──────────── רש"י ────────────

כי לא חפשה. לפיכך אין חייב עליה מיתה שאין קדושיה קדושין, הא אם חופשה קדושיה קדושין וחייבין] מיתה (ת"כ שם ה): **(כב) ונסלח לו מחטאתו אשר חטא.** לרבות את המזיד כשוגג (ת"כ שם ז): **(כג) וערלתם ערלתו.** ואטמתם אטימתו. יהא אטום ונסתם מליהנות ממנו: **שלש שנים יהיה לכם ערלים.** מאימתי מונה לו, משעת נטיעתו (ת"כ פרשתא ג:ג):

──────────── RASHI ELUCIDATED ────────────

□ **כִּי לֹא חֻפָּשָׁה** — **FOR SHE HAS NOT BEEN FREED.** **לְפִיכָךְ** — **Therefore,** **אֵין חַיָּב עָלֶיהָ מִיתָה** — **he is not liable to** being punished by **death for** committing adultery with **her,** **שֶׁאֵין קִדּוּשֶׁיהָ קִדּוּשִׁין** — **for her marriage is not a** valid marriage. **הָא אִם חֻפָּשָׁה** — **But if she had been freed,** **קִדּוּשֶׁיהָ קִדּוּשִׁין** — **her marriage would be a** valid marriage, [1,2] **וְחַיָּב מִיתָה** — **and he would be subject to the death penalty**[1] if he had relations with her.[2]

22. וְנִסְלַח לוֹ מֵחַטָּאתוֹ אֲשֶׁר חָטָא — **AND THE SIN THAT HE HAD COMMITTED SHALL BE FORGIVEN HIM.** **לְרַבּוֹת אֶת הַמֵּזִיד** — **To include the intentional** transgression [3] **כְּשׁוֹגֵג** — **like the unintentional.**[3]

23. וַעֲרַלְתֶּם עָרְלָתוֹ — **YOU SHALL TREAT ITS FRUIT AS** ORLAH. These words mean literally, **וַאֲטַמְתֶּם אֲטִימָתוֹ** — **you shall block its blockage;** **יְהֵא אָטוּם וְנִסְתָּם** — **it shall be blocked and closed off** **מִלֵּיהָנוֹת מִמֶּנּוּ** — **from deriving benefit from it.**[4]

□ **שָׁלֹשׁ שָׁנִים יִהְיֶה לָכֶם עֲרֵלִים** — **THREE YEARS IT SHALL BE** ORLAH **TO YOU.** **מֵאֵימָתַי מוֹנֶה לוֹ** — **From when does he** begin to **count** the three years **for it?** [5] **מִשְּׁעַת נְטִיעָתוֹ** — **From the time of its planting,**[5]

verses that discuss punishment.

This interpretation of the Rabbis understands בקרת תהיה as, "she will be in reciting." According to the variant of Rashi mentioned above in note 4, Rashi comments at this point, after citing the interpretation of the Rabbis, "she gets lashes but not he." For if בקרת תהיה means, "she will be in reciting," the Torah could have used בקרת יהיה, "he will be in reciting," using a masculine verb, which normally implies that the law stated applies equally to men and women. The feminine verb teaches us that it is only *she* who receives lashes. The man who sinned with her must bring an offering (*Be'er Yitzchak*).

1. Some editions read וְחַיָּבִין מִיתָה, "and they would be subject to the death penalty."

2. *Toras Kohanim, perek* 5:5.

3. *Toras Kohanim, perek* 5:7; *Kereisos* 9a. The verse could apparently have said only, וְנִסְלַח לוֹ, "and it shall

be forgiven him," with "it" referring to "the sin that he had committed" which immediately precedes it in the verse. The Torah repeats מֵחַטָּאתוֹ אֲשֶׁר חָטָא, "the sin that he had committed," to teach us that not only must one who has relations with the "designated slavewoman" without being aware of her status bring a guilt-offering; even one who does so with full knowledge must bring the offering. Had the Torah not repeated this phrase, we would have thought that the guilt-offering must be brought only by the unintentional transgressor for two reasons: (a) sin- and guilt-offerings are generally not brought for intentional sins, and (b) חָטָא, the term used by our verse for sin, usually refers to an unintentional sin (see *Gur Aryeh*).

4. Rashi also discusses the meaning of עָרֵל, both as used in this verse and elsewhere, in his comments to *Exodus* 6:12.

5. *Toras Kohanim, parshasa* 3:3.

not be eaten. ²⁴ *In the fourth year, all its fruit shall be sanctified lauding to* HASHEM. ²⁵ *And in the fifth year you may eat its fruit — in order to increase its crop for you — I am* HASHEM*, your God.*

כד לֹא יֵאָכֵל: וּבַשָּׁנָה הָרְבִיעִת יִהְיֶה כָּל־פִּרְיוֹ קֹדֶשׁ הִלּוּלִים לַיהוָה: כה וּבַשָּׁנָה הַחֲמִישִׁת תֹּאכְלוּ אֶת־פִּרְיוֹ לְהוֹסִיף לָכֶם תְּבוּאָתוֹ אֲנִי יהוה אֱלֹהֵיכֶם:

— אונקלוס —

לָא יִתְאֲכֵל: כד וּבְשַׁתָּא רְבִיעֵתָא יְהֵי כָּל אִבֵּהּ קֹדֶשׁ תֻּשְׁבְּחָן קֳדָם יְיָ: כה וּבְשַׁתָּא חֲמִישֵׁתָא תֵּיכְלוּן יָת אִבֵּהּ לְאוֹסָפָא לְכוֹן עֲלַלְתֵּהּ אֲנָא יְיָ אֱלָהֲכוֹן:

— רש"י —

(כה) **להוסיף לכם תבואתו.** המצוה הזאת שתשמרו תהיה להוסיף לכם תבואתו, שבשכרה אני מברך לכם פירות הנטיעות. היה רבי עקיבא אומר דברה תורה כנגד יצר הרע, שלא יאמר אדם הרי ארבע שנים אני מלטער בו חנם, לפיכך נאמר להוסיף לכם תבואתו (ת"כ שם): **אני ה'.** אני ה' המבטיח על כך ונאמן לשמור הבטחתי:

יכול אם הצניעו לאחר שלש שנים יהא מותר, ת"ל יהיה, בהוייתו יהא (קידושין נד:): (כד) **יהיה כל פריו קדש.** כמעשר שני, שכתוב בו וכל מעשר הארץ וגו' קדש לה' (להלן כז:ל) מה מעשר שני אינו נאכל חוץ לחומת ירושלים אלא בפדיון אף זה כן. ודבר זה הלולים לה' הוא, שנושאו שם לשבח ולהלל לשמים (ת"כ שם ט; ברכות לה.):

— RASHI ELUCIDATED —

i.e., *from the time that it was planted.* יָכוֹל אִם הִצְנִיעוֹ — **One might be able** to think that **if he stored** [the fruit of the first three years] away, לְאַחַר שָׁלֹשׁ שָׁנִים — **after three years** יְהֵא מֻתָּר — **it would be permitted** to derive benefit from them. תַּלְמוּד לוֹמַר — **To teach us otherwise, the verse says,** ״יִהְיֶה״ — **"it shall be,"** which implies, ¹בַּהֲוָיָתוֹ יְהֵא — **it shall remain in its state** of being forbidden.¹

24. יִהְיֶה כָּל פִּרְיוֹ קֹדֶשׁ — **ALL ITS FRUIT SHALL BE SANCTIFIED** ²כְּמַעֲשֵׂר שֵׁנִי — **like the second tithe,²** שֶׁכָּתוּב בּוֹ — **about which it is written,** ״וְכָל מַעְשַׂר הָאָרֶץ וְגוֹמֵר קֹדֶשׁ לַה׳ ״³ — **"Any tithe of the land, etc., is holy to** HASHEM."³ מַה מַּעֲשֵׂר שֵׁנִי — **Just as the second tithe** אֵינוֹ נֶאֱכָל — **may not be eaten** חוּץ לְחוֹמַת יְרוּשָׁלַיִם — **outside the wall of Jerusalem** אֶלָּא בְּפִדְיוֹן — **except after its redemption,⁴** אַף זֶה כֵּן — **this, too, is so.** וְדָבָר זֶה ״הִלּוּלִים לַה׳ ״ הוּא — **And this matter is "lauding to** HASHEM," שֶׁנּוֹשְׂאוֹ שָׁם — **because he carries** [the fruit of the fourth year] **there,** to Jerusalem, לְשַׁבֵּחַ וּלְהַלֵּל לַשָּׁמַיִם — **to praise and to laud Heaven.⁵**

25. לְהוֹסִיף לָכֶם תְּבוּאָתוֹ — [IN ORDER] TO INCREASE ITS CROP FOR YOU. הַמִּצְוָה הַזֹּאת שֶׁתִּשְׁמְרוּ — **This commandment that you will observe** תִּהְיֶה — **shall be** לְהוֹסִיף לָכֶם תְּבוּאָתוֹ — **"[in order] to increase its crop for you."** שֶׁבִּשְׂכָרָהּ — **For as its reward** אֲנִי מְבָרֵךְ לָכֶם פֵּרוֹת הַנְּטִיעוֹת — **I bless the fruit of the plantings for you.** הָיָה רַבִּי עֲקִיבָא אוֹמֵר — **The** *Tanna* **R' Akiva used to say:** דִּבְּרָה תוֹרָה — **The Torah spoke** כְּנֶגֶד יֵצֶר הָרַע — **against the evil inclination,** שֶׁלֹּא יֹאמַר אָדָם — **that a person should not say,** הֲרֵי אַרְבַּע שָׁנִים — **"Now, then, for four years** אֲנִי מִצְטַעֵר בּוֹ — **I am troubling myself over [this tree]** חִנָּם — **without any gain!** How can the Torah expect me to keep the laws of *orlah* and the planting of the fourth year?"⁶ לְפִיכָךְ נֶאֱמַר — **Therefore it says,** ⁷״לְהוֹסִיף לָכֶם תְּבוּאָתוֹ״ — **"[in order] to increase its crop for you."**⁷

□ אֲנִי ה׳ — **I AM** HASHEM. אֲנִי ה׳ — **I am** HASHEM הַמַּבְטִיחַ עַל כָּךְ — **Who makes the promise about this,** וְנֶאֱמָן לִשְׁמוֹר הַבְטָחָתִי — **and am trustworthy to keep My promise.⁸**

1. *Toras Kohanim, parshasa* 3:4.
2. *Kiddushin* 54b.
3. *Below* 27:30.
4. See *Deuteronomy* 14:22-26. The comparison between the planting of the fourth year and the second tithe is derived from a *gezeirah shavah* (for definition see note 10 page 155) based on the presence of the word קֹדֶשׁ in both contexts (see *Minchas Yehudah; Sifsei Chachamim*).
5. *Toras Kohanim, parshasa* 3:9; *Berachos* 35a.

6. The evil inclination would make a person exaggerate his loss; even though he is to enjoy the fruit of the fourth year, since it is enjoyment with restrictions, he will refer to it as being "without gain."
7. *Toras Kohanim, parshasa* 3:9.
8. The statement, "I am HASHEM," appears incongruous in the context of our verse. Rashi explains that it is meant as an assurance that the promise of increased crops which precedes it will be kept. Rashi explains "I am HASHEM" similarly in his comments to verse 16 above and to *Exodus* 6:2.

243 / VAYIKRA/LEVITICUS — PARASHAS KEDOSHIM — 19/26-27 — יט/כו־כז

²⁶ *You shall not eat over the blood; you shall not practice divination and you shall not believe in lucky times.* ²⁷ *You shall not round off the edge of your scalp and you shall not destroy*

כו לֹא תֹאכְלוּ עַל־הַדָּם לֹא
תְנַחֲשׁוּ וְלֹא תְעוֹנֵנוּ: כז לֹא תַקִּפוּ
פְּאַת רֹאשְׁכֶם וְלֹא תַשְׁחִית

───── אונקלוס ─────

כו לָא תֵיכְלוּן עַל דְּמָא לָא תְנַחֲשׁוּן וְלָא תְעוֹנְנוּן: כז לָא תַקְּפוּן פָּאתָא דְרֵישְׁכוֹן וְלָא תְחַבֵּל

───── רש"י ─────

(כו) לא תאכלו על הדם. להרבה פנים נדרש בסנהדרין (סג.):
ת"כ פרק ו:א) אזהרה שלא יאכל מבשר קדשים לפני זריקת דמים,
ואזהרה לאוכל מבהמת חולין טרם שתצא נפשה, ועוד הרבה: **לא
תנחשו.** כגון אלו המנחשין בחולדה ובעופות (ת"כ שם ב) פתו

נפלה מפיו צבי הפסיקו בדרך (סנהדרין סה:)‎: **ולא תעוננו.** ל'
עונות ושעות שאומר יום פלוני יפה להתחיל מלאכה, שעה פלונית
קשה לצאת (סנהדרין שם): **(כז) לא תקיפו פאת ראשכם.** זה
המשוה לדעיו לאחורי אזנו ולפדחתו (מכות כ:) ונמלא הקף ראשו

───── RASHI ELUCIDATED ─────

26. לֹא תֹאכְלוּ עַל הַדָּם — **YOU SHALL NOT EAT OVER THE BLOOD.** לְהַרְבֵּה פָנִים נִדְרָשׁ — [This verse] is expounded as having many facets ¹בְּסַנְהֶדְרִין — in Tractate *Sanhedrin*;[1] אַזְהָרָה — as a negative commandment שֶׁלֹּא יֹאכַל — that one should not eat מִבְּשַׂר קָדָשִׁים — from the flesh of that which is holy, i.e., from the flesh of offerings, לִפְנֵי זְרִיקַת דָּמִים — before the sprinkling of blood;[2] וְאַזְהָרָה — and as a negative commandment לָאוֹכֵל — for one who eats מִבֶּהֱמַת חֻלִּין — from an animal that has not been consecrated טֶרֶם שֶׁתֵּצֵא נַפְשָׁהּ — while its life has not yet departed.[3] וְעוֹד הַרְבֵּה — And it is interpreted in **many more** ways.[4]

□ לֹא תְנַחֲשׁוּ — **YOU SHALL NOT PRACTICE DIVINATION.** כְּגוֹן — For instance, אֵלּוּ הַמְנַחֲשִׁין — those who engage in divination ⁵בְּחֻלְדָּה וּבְעוֹפוֹת — with a weasel or with birds.[5] Or he views as omens events such as, פִּתּוֹ נָפְלָה מִפִּיו — his bread fell from his mouth, or ⁶צְבִי הִפְסִיקוֹ בַּדֶּרֶךְ — a deer crossed his path.[6]

□ וְלֹא תְעוֹנֵנוּ — **AND YOU SHALL NOT BELIEVE IN LUCKY TIMES.** [תְעוֹנֵנוּ] [The word] לְשׁוֹן עוֹנוֹת וְשָׁעוֹת — denotes seasons and hours.[7] The prohibition of our verse applies to a case שֶׁאוֹמֵר — in which one says שָׁעָה פְּלוֹנִית קָשָׁה — a certain hour is inauspicious יוֹם פְּלוֹנִי יָפֶה — a certain day is auspicious לְהַתְחִיל מְלָאכָה — for beginning work; [8]לָצֵאת — for embarking on a journey.[8]

27. לֹא תַקִּפוּ פְּאַת רֹאשְׁכֶם — **YOU SHALL NOT ROUND OFF THE EDGE OF YOUR SCALP.**[9] זֶה הַמַּשְׁוֶה צְדָעָיו — This is one who makes his temples even לַאֲחוֹרֵי אָזְנָיו — with the area behind his ears, ¹⁰וּלְפַדַּחְתּוֹ — and his forehead.[10] וְנִמְצָא הֶקֵּף רֹאשׁוֹ — It is thus found that the circumference of his head

---

1. *Sanhedrin* 63a; see also *Toras Kohanim, perek* 6:1.

2. The phrase, "you shall not eat over the blood," is interpreted to mean "you shall not eat the flesh of the offering while the blood that must be sprinkled is present."

3. This refers to eating the flesh of an animal that has been ritually slaughtered but is still in its last spasms (מְפַרְכֶּסֶת). Once it has been slaughtered, the prohibition against eating the meat of a live animal (see *Genesis* 9:4 and Rashi there) does not apply to it. But our verse forbids its consumption until life has departed completely (*Mizrachi*). According to this interpretation, "blood" is interpreted as "life." "You shall not eat over the blood" means "do not eat of the animal while signs of life are still present."

4. Had the verse said לֹא תֹאכְלוּ הַדָּם, "you shall not eat the blood," we would have taken it literally as a prohibition against eating blood. However, the cryptic עַל הַדָּם, "over the blood," lends itself to many interpretations, two of which are quoted by Rashi (*Ho'il Moshe* citing *Chidushei HaRashba* [to *Berachos* 10b, printed with *Ein Yaakov*]).

5. *Toras Kohanim, perek* 6:2; *Sanhedrin* 66a. Encountering a weasel was viewed as an omen. The chirping of birds was also interpreted as an augur for the future. *Toras Kohanim* adds וּבְכוֹכָבִים, "or with the stars"; *Sanhedrin* adds וּבְדָגִים, "or with fish."

6. *Sanhedrin* 65b. The Gemara there gives many other examples.

7. The verb תְעוֹנֵנוּ is cognate with עוֹנָה, "season."

8. *Sanhedrin* 65b. Rashi here cites the opinion of the *Tanna* R' Akiva there. In his comments to *Deuteronomy* 18:10 (s.v., מְעוֹנֵן), Rashi cites the opinion of the Sages also.

9. According to *Mizrachi* (and *Sifsei Chachamim*), the "edge of the scalp" is the line around "the hair of the head (רֹאשׁ)," as opposed to "the hair of the back of the head (עֹרֶף)," and the hair of the beard. This line runs across the forehead, down to where the temple meets the jawbone, and up around the ear, to the back of the head. One who "rounds off the edge of the scalp" breaks this line by removing the hair of the temples, thus forming a new, straight, hairline, going from behind one ear to behind the other.

According to *Gur Aryeh,* פְּאַת רֹאשׁ might more precisely be rendered "the corner of your scalp" than "the edge of your head." It is the hair of the temple above the point where it meets the jawbone. "Rounding off the corner of the head" means removing that hair. For the head is composed of two parts: the face and beard are one part, and the scalp is the other. The junction of the two parts at the temple is "the corner of the head."

10. *Makkos* 20a. There is a separate punishment of

the edge of your beard. [28] *You shall not make in your flesh a scratch over a soul, and you shall not place a tattoo upon yourselves — I am* H<small>ASHEM</small>.

כח אֶת־פְּאַת זְקָנֶךָ: וְשֶׂרֶט לָנֶפֶשׁ לֹא תִתְּנוּ בִּבְשַׂרְכֶם וּכְתֹבֶת קַעֲקַע לֹא תִתְּנוּ בָּכֶם אֲנִי יְהוָה:

— אונקלוס —

יָת פָּאתָא דְדִקְנָךְ: כח וְחִבּוּל עַל מִית לָא תִתְּנוּן בְּבִסְרְכוֹן וְרוּשְׁמִין חֲרִיתִין לָא תִתְּנוּן בְּכוֹן אֲנָא יְיָ:

— רש"י —

עָגוֹל סָבִיב, שֶׁעַל אֲחוֹרֵי אָזְנָיו עִקְּרֵי שְׂעָרוֹ לְמַעְלָה מִלְּדָעָיו. הַרְבֵּה: **פְּאַת זְקָנֶךָ.** סוֹף הַזָּקָן וּגְבוּלָיו. וְהֵן חָמֵשׁ, שְׁתַּיִם בְּכָל לֶחִי וּלְחִי לְמַעְלָה אֵצֶל הָרֹאשׁ שֶׁהוּא רָחָב וְיֵשׁ בּוֹ שְׁתֵּי פֵאוֹת, וְאַחַת לְמַטָּה בַּסַּנְטֵר מְקוֹם חִבּוּר שְׁנֵי הַלְּחָיַיִם יַחַד (שם כ.): **(כח) וְשֶׂרֶט לַנָּפֶשׁ.** כֵּן דַּרְכָּן שֶׁל אֱמוֹרִיִּים לִהְיוֹת מְשָׂרְטִין בִּבְשָׂרָם כְּשֶׁמֵּת לָהֶם מֵת: **וּכְתֹבֶת קַעֲקַע.** כְּתָב הַמְחֻקֶּה וְשָׁקוּעַ שֶׁאֵינוֹ נִמְחָק לְעוֹלָם, שֶׁמְּקַעְקְעוֹ בְּמַחַט וְהוּא מַשְׁחִיר לְעוֹלָם (ת"כ שם י; מכות כא.):

— RASHI ELUCIDATED —

עָגוֹל – **is rounded off** סָבִיב – **perimetrically.**[1] שֶׁעַל אַחוֹרֵי אָזְנָיו – **For on the area behind his ears** עִקְּרֵי שְׂעָרוֹ – **the roots of his hair** לְמַעְלָה מִצְּדָעָיו הַרְבֵּה – **are much higher than his temples.**[2]

☐ פְּאַת זְקָנֶךָ – **THE EDGE OF YOUR BEARD.** This refers to סוֹף הַזָּקָן – **the end of the beard,** וּגְבוּלָיו – **and its extremities.** וְהֵן חָמֵשׁ – **They are five:** שְׁתַּיִם בְּכָל לֶחִי וּלְחִי – **two on each cheek** לְמַעְלָה – **at the top,** אֵצֶל הָרֹאשׁ – **next to the head,** שֶׁהוּא רָחָב – **for [the cheek] is wide,** וְיֵשׁ בּוֹ שְׁתֵּי פֵאוֹת – **and it has two edges;**[3] וְאַחַת לְמַטָּה – **and one below,** בַּסַּנְטֵר – **at his chin,** מְקוֹם חִבּוּר שְׁנֵי הַלְּחָיַיִם – **the place where the two jaws connect with each other.**[4] יַחַד[4] –

28. וְשֶׂרֶט לַנָּפֶשׁ – **A SCRATCH OVER A SOUL.** כֵּן דַּרְכָּן שֶׁל אֱמוֹרִיִּים – **Such is the practice of the Amorites** כְּשֶׁמֵּת לָהֶם מֵת – **when someone among them dies,**[5] לִהְיוֹת מְשָׂרְטִין בִּבְשָׂרָם – **to scratch into their flesh**

☐ וּכְתֹבֶת קַעֲקַע – **AND [YOU SHALL NOT PLACE] A TATTOO.** כְּתָב – **Writing** הַמְחֻקֶּה – **which is engraved** וְשָׁקוּעַ – **and embedded,** שֶׁאֵינוֹ נִמְחָק לְעוֹלָם – **which cannot ever be erased.** שֶׁמְּקַעְקְעוֹ – **For he tattoos it** בְּמַחַט – **with a needle,**[6] וְהוּא מַשְׁחִיר לְעוֹלָם – **and it stays dark permanently.**[6]

THE TWO EDGES

According to *Nimukei Yosef*

According to *Mizrachi*

lashes for shaving each temple.
According to *Mizrachi* and *Sifsei Chachamim,* the verse speaks of one who shaves his temples so that his head is hairless from behind one ear, across the forehead, to behind the other ear.
According to *Gur Aryeh,* the verse speaks of one who shaves either of his temples so that his head is hairless from behind an ear across the forehead. Rashi to *Shavuos* 2b, s.v., על הראש, appears to conform to *Gur Aryeh*'s understanding.

1. According to *Mizrachi,* the back of the head is not referred to as ראש, but rather as עורף. Hair which grows there is not called "hair of the head," but rather, "hair of the back of the head." Hair of the beard and temples, however, does fall under the category of hair of the head. By removing the hair at the temples, the main area of the hair of the head, the top of the head, ends in a rounded hairline, along the perimeter of the scalp.
According to *Gur Aryeh,* the hairless parts of the head — the forehead and the area behind the ear — become joined by removing the hair at the temple, thus "rounding off" the head with a band of bare skin stretching from the forehead "perimetrically" to behind the ear.
2. It might appear that the hair behind the ear is even with the hair at the temples when the hair at the temples is not removed. Rashi explains that this is not so in reality. The hair behind the ear might grow to a length where the ends of the hair appear to be even with the hair at the temple. But this is irrelevant, for we are concerned with the roots of the hair, and the roots of the hair behind the ear are higher than those of the hair

temple (*Mechokekei Yehudah*).
3. The cheek ends at the top of the jawbone, where it meets the temple. The hair of the beard at this point is wide enough for the beard to be considered to have two edges, the outer edge next to the ear, and the inner edge, on the side of the beard nearer the eye (see *Nimukei Yosef* to *Rif* on *Makkos,* 4b in the pages of the *Rif,* in the name of Rashi).
Alternatively, the entire top edge of the beard, where it meets the temple, is considered one of the edges. The side of the beard at the front of the cheek, where the beard is widest on the cheek, is the second edge (*Mizrachi; Sifsei Chachamim*).
4. *Makkos* 20a.
5. Rashi explains why the Torah forbids making scratches in one's flesh in mourning over the dead, but does not forbid the same act as an expression of grief over some other loss. It was only over the dead that the Amorites would perform this ritual, not over other misfortunes (*Mishmeres HaKodesh*).
6. *Toras Kohanim, perek* 6:10; *Makkos* 21a. He punctures his skin with a needle and inserts a pigment that remains indelibly embedded in the skin.

²⁹ **Do not profane your daughter to prostitute her, lest the earth prostitute itself, if the Land become filled with depravity.** ³⁰ **You shall observe My Sabbaths and revere My Sanctuary — I am Hashem.**

כט אַל־תְּחַלֵּל אֶת־בִּתְּךָ לְהַזְנוֹתָהּ וְלֹא־תִזְנֶה הָאָרֶץ וּמָלְאָה הָאָרֶץ זִמָּה: ל אֶת־שַׁבְּתֹתַי תִּשְׁמֹרוּ וּמִקְדָּשִׁי תִּירָאוּ אֲנִי יהוה:

— אונקלוס —

כט לָא תָחֵל יָת בְּרַתָּךְ לְאַטְעָיוּתַהּ וְלָא תִטְעֵי אַרְעָא וְתִתְמְלֵי אַרְעָא עֲצַת חֲטָאִין: ל יָת יוֹמֵי שַׁבַּיָּא דִילִי תִּטְּרוּן וּלְבֵית מַקְדְּשִׁי תְּהוֹן דָּחֲלִין אֲנָא יְיָ:

— רש״י —

קַעֲקַע. ל׳ וְהוֹקַע אוֹתָם (במדבר כה:ד) וְהוֹקַעֲנוּם (שמואל ב כא:ו), תּוֹחֲבִין עֵץ בָּאָרֶץ וְתוֹלִין אוֹתָם עֲלֵיהֶם וְנִמְלְאוּ מְחוּקִין וּתְחוּבִין בַּקַּרְקַע, פורפוינ״ט בלעז: **(כט) אַל תְּחַלֵּל אֶת בִּתְּךָ לְהַזְנוֹתָהּ.** בְּמוֹסֵר בִּתּוֹ פְּנוּיָה לְבִיאָה שֶׁלֹּא לְשֵׁם קִדּוּשִׁין (ת״כ פרק ז:ה; סנהדרין עו.): **וְלֹא תִזְנֶה הָאָרֶץ.** אִם אַתָּה עוֹשֶׂה כֵּן הָאָרֶץ מְזַנָּה אֶת פֵּרוֹתֶיהָ

לַעֲשׂוֹתָן בְּמָקוֹם אַחֵר וְלֹא בְּאַרְצְכֶם, וְכֵן הוּא אוֹמֵר וַיִּמָּנְעוּ רְבִיבִים וְגוֹ׳ (ירמיה ג:ג; ת״כ שם ג־ד): **(ל) וּמִקְדָּשִׁי תִּירָאוּ.** לֹא יִכָּנֵס בְּמַקְלוֹ וְלֹא בְמִנְעָלוֹ וּבַאֲפוּנְדָּתוֹ וּבְאָבָק שֶׁעַל רַגְלָיו (ת״כ שם ט; ברכות נד.): **וְאַף** עַל פִּי שֶׁאֲנִי מַזְהִירְכֶם עַל הַמִּקְדָּשׁ אֶת שַׁבְּתוֹתַי תִּשְׁמֹרוּ אֵין בִּנְיַן בֵּית הַמִּקְדָּשׁ דּוֹחֶה שַׁבָּת (ת״כ שם ז; יבמות ו.):

—— RASHI ELUCIDATED ——

□ **קַעֲקַע** — **TATTOO.** ¹וְהוֹקַע אוֹתָם — לְשׁוֹן — This is related to וְהוֹקַע in, "and hang them,"¹ and, ²וְהוֹקַעֲנוּם — "and we will hang them."² Tattooing is related to hanging for the following reason: תּוֹחֲבִין עֵץ בָּאָרֶץ — They stick a wooden pole into the ground וְתוֹלִין אוֹתָם עֲלֵיהֶם — and hang them on [the poles]. וְנִמְצְאוּ מְחוּקִין — They, like the poles, are thus found to be embedded וּתְחוּבִין — and stuck, בַּקַּרְקַע — into the ground;³ פורפוינ״ט בלע״ז — *porpoint* in Old French.⁴

29. אַל תְּחַלֵּל אֶת בִּתְּךָ לְהַזְנוֹתָהּ — **DO NOT PROFANE YOUR DAUGHTER TO PROSTITUTE HER.** The verse speaks בְּמוֹסֵר בִּתּוֹ פְּנוּיָה — of one who gives his unmarried daughter over לְבִיאָה — for intercourse, שֶׁלֹּא ⁵לְשֵׁם קִדּוּשִׁין — not for the sake of marriage.⁵

□ וְלֹא תִזְנֶה הָאָרֶץ — **LEST THE EARTH PROSTITUTE ITSELF.** אִם אַתָּה עוֹשֶׂה כֵּן — If you do so, הָאָרֶץ מְזַנָּה — the earth "prostitutes" its fruits⁶ אֶת פֵּרוֹתֶיהָ — by producing them elsewhere לַעֲשׂוֹתָן בְּמָקוֹם אַחֵר וְלֹא בְּאַרְצְכֶם — and not in your land. וְכֵן הוּא אוֹמֵר — And so it says, ⁷,⁸וַיִּמָּנְעוּ רְבִיבִים וְגוֹמֵר — "showers were withheld, etc."⁷,⁸

30. וּמִקְדָּשִׁי תִּירָאוּ — **AND REVERE MY SANCTUARY.** לֹא יִכָּנֵס — He should not enter the grounds of the Temple בְּמַקְלוֹ — neither with his staff, וְלֹא בְמִנְעָלוֹ — nor with his shoes on his feet, וּבַאֲפוּנְדָּתוֹ — nor with his moneybelt, וּבְאָבָק שֶׁעַל רַגְלָיו⁹ — nor with the dust that is on his feet, i.e., he should not enter with dirty feet.⁹ וְאַף עַל פִּי שֶׁאֲנִי מַזְהִירְכֶם — And although I enjoin you to have reverence עַל הַמִּקְדָּשׁ — with regard to the *Beis HaMikdash,* nonetheless, ״אֶת שַׁבְּתוֹתַי תִּשְׁמֹרוּ״ — "you shall observe My Sabbaths"; ¹⁰אֵין בִּנְיַן בֵּית הַמִּקְדָּשׁ דּוֹחֶה שַׁבָּת — the construction of the *Beis HaMikdash* does not override the Sabbath.¹⁰

---

1. *Numbers* 25:4.
2. *II Samuel* 21:6.
3. Just as the poles and those hung on them are embedded in the ground, so, too, the pigment of the tattoo is embedded into the flesh.
4. This word means "pierced." In Modern French and Modern English, "pourpoint" is a garment made of layered (i.e., quilted) fabrics that are held together by the repeated piercings of a threaded needle.
5. *Toras Kohanim, perek* 7:1; *Sanhedrin* 76a.
6. The verse could have said, וְלֹא תִזְנֶה הָאָרֶץ וּמָלְאָה זִמָּה without repeating the word הָאָרֶץ. The repetition indicates that the two appearances of the word have different meanings. The first is understood as "the earth," i.e., that which produces fruit — "lest the earth prostitute itself. The second is understood as "the Land," i.e., the inhabitants of the Land of Israel — "if the Land will become filled with depravity" (*Malbim*).
7. *Jeremiah* 3:3. That verse reads in its entirety: "Showers were withheld, and there was no late rain, yet you have the brazen forehead of a prostitute; you refused to be ashamed."
8. *Toras Kohanim, perek* 7:3-4.
9. *Toras Kohanim, perek* 7:9; *Berachos* 54a.
10. *Toras Kohanim, perek* 7:7; *Yevamos* 6a. The Torah juxtaposes the commandment to observe the Sabbath with the commandment to revere the Sanctuary, and places the observance of the Sabbath first to teach us that when they clash it has primacy over the commandment to build the *Beis HaMikdash* (*Levush HaOrah*). See also Rashi's comments to verse 3 above (and note 6 there) and to *Exodus* 35:2.

³¹ **Do not turn to [the necromancy of] the Ovos and Yid'onim, and do not seek to become impure through them — I am HASHEM, your God.**

לֹא אַל־תִּפְנוּ אֶל־הָאֹבֹת וְאֶל־הַיִּדְּעֹנִים אַל־תְּבַקְשׁוּ לְטָמְאָה בָהֶם אֲנִי יהוה אֱלֹהֵיכֶם:

— אונקלוס —

לָא לָא תִתְפְּנוּן בָּתַר בִּדִּין וּדְכוּרוּ לָא תִתְבְּעוּן לְאִסְתָּאָבָא בְהוֹן אֲנָא יְיָ אֱלָהֲכוֹן:

— רש"י —

(לא) אל תפנו אל האובות. אזהרה לבעל אוב וידעוני. בעל אוב זה פיתום המדבר משחיו. וידעוני המכניס עצם חיה ששמה ידוע לתוך פיו והעצם מדבר (ת"כ שם י: סנהדרין סה.-סה:): אל תבקשו. להיות עסוקים בם שאם תעסקו בם אתם מיטמאין לפני ואני מתעב אתכם (ת"כ שם יא): אני ה' אלהיכם. דעו את מי אתם מחליפין במי (שם):

— RASHI ELUCIDATED —

31. אַל תִּפְנוּ אֶל הָאֹבֹת — DO NOT TURN TO [THE NECROMANCY OF] THE *OVOS*. אַזְהָרָה — This is a negative commandment לְבַעַל אוֹב — for one who practices the necromancy of *ov* וְיִדְּעוֹנִי — or *yid'oni*.¹ בַּעַל אוֹב זֶה פִּיתוֹם — One who practices the necromancy of *ov* is the one who is called *"Pisom,"* הַמְדַבֵּר מִשֶּׁחְיוֹ — who speaks through his armpit.² וְיִדְּעוֹנִי — *Yid'oni* is one הַמַּכְנִיס — who inserts עֶצֶם חַיָּה שֶׁשְּׁמָהּ יָדוּעַ — a bone of an animal whose name is *yadua*³ לְתוֹךְ פִּיו — into his mouth, וְהָעֶצֶם מְדַבֵּר⁴ — and the bone speaks.⁴

□ אַל תְּבַקְשׁוּ — DO NOT SEEK לִהְיוֹת עֲסוּקִים בָּם — to be involved with them, שֶׁאִם תַּעַסְקוּ בָם — for if you become involved with them, אַתֶּם מִטַּמְּאִין לְפָנַי — you make yourselves impure before Me, וַאֲנִי מְתַעֵב אֶתְכֶם⁵ — and I abhor you.⁵

□ אֲנִי ה' אֱלֹהֵיכֶם — I AM HASHEM, YOUR GOD. דְּעוּ אֶת מִי אַתֶּם מַחֲלִיפִין בְּמִי⁶ — Know Whom you are exchanging for whom.⁶

---

1. "Do not turn to the necromancy of the *ovos*" does not mean "do not turn your thoughts to contemplate that necromancy" (*Mizrachi*), nor does it mean "do not consult one who practices that necromancy" (*Gur Aryeh*; *Sifsei Chachamim*). It is a negative commandment against the practice of that particular type of necromancy.

Rashi here stands in apparent contradiction to his comment on the Mishnah (*Sanhedrin* 65a) where he says that our verse is a prohibition against *consulting* one who practices the necromancy of *ov*. See *Yad David*, and *Maharsha's* comments on *Tosafos* there, as well as *Nachalas Yaakov's* comments here.

2. He raises the souls of the dead, and they speak through his armpit (Rashi to *Sanhedrin* 65a).

3. The name of this form of necromancy, יִדְעֹנִי, is derived from the name of the animal used, יָדוּעַ.

4. *Toras Kohanim, perek* 7:10; *Sanhedrin* 65a-b.

5. *Toras Kohanim, perek* 7:11. "Do not seek to become impure through them" cannot be taken at face value. People conjure up the dead in order to divine the future, not to become impure. Rashi explains that "to become involved in them" is implicit in our verse. The verse is saying, "Do not seek to become involved in them, lest you become impure through them" (*Mizrachi; Sifsei Chachamim*).

6. *Toras Kohanim, perek* 7:11. The identical phrase appears above in verse 10. There Rashi explained that it implies that God is a judge who is sure to carry out judgment. That interpretation is appropriate to that verse, for it deals with gifts to the poor. That verse says that one should not think that he can successfully cheat the poor of the gifts that are their due, for God will surely judge him. In our verse, however, which does not involve an issue of deceit, the phrase must be interpreted differently.

A similar phrase appears above in verse 16. There Rashi explained that it implies that God can be relied upon to mete out both reward and punishment. That interpretation is appropriate to that verse, for it deals with the prohibition against refraining from helping another Jew in a life-threatening situation. That prohibition does not apply if attempting to save the life of another would endanger one's own life. There are situations in which only the individual who could save a life knows whether his own life would be endangered in the attempt. "I am HASHEM" of that verse is interpreted as an exhortation to judge such situations honestly — God is sure to reward you for fulfilling His commandment if you do, and sure to punish you if you do not. Such an interpretation is inappropriate to our verse, for conjuring up the dead is an act in which the sin is evident to all.

"I am HASHEM" appears again in verse 25. There Rashi interprets it as an assurance that the promise of a reward which was mentioned earlier in that verse will come true. Our verse, however, contains no promise of reward or punishment.

Therefore, Rashi explains that here "I am HASHEM, your God" is used to stress the grave results of conjuring up the dead. By doing so, one attempts to exchange the Providence of God, in a sense, for the guidance of lesser forces of His creation.

32 You shall rise in the presence of an old person and you shall honor the presence of an elder and you shall have fear of your God — I am HASHEM. **33** When a proselyte dwells among you in your land, do not harass him. **34** The proselyte who dwells with you shall be like a native among you, and you shall love him like yourself, for you have been aliens in the

לב מִפְּנֵי שֵׂיבָה תָּקוּם וְהָדַרְתָּ פְּנֵי זָקֵן וְיָרֵאתָ מֵּאֱלֹהֶיךָ אֲנִי לג יְהוָה: רביעי [ששי] וְכִי־יָגוּר אִתְּךָ לד גֵּר בְּאַרְצְכֶם לֹא תוֹנוּ אֹתוֹ: כְּאֶזְרָח מִכֶּם יִהְיֶה לָכֶם הַגֵּר ׀ הַגָּר אִתְּכֶם וְאָהַבְתָּ לוֹ כָּמוֹךָ כִּי־גֵרִים הֱיִיתֶם

— אונקלוס —

— רש"י —

— RASHI ELUCIDATED —

32. מִפְּנֵי שֵׂיבָה תָּקוּם — YOU SHALL RISE IN THE PRESENCE OF AN OLD PERSON. יָכוֹל — One might be able to think that this commandment applies even to זָקֵן אַשְׁמַאי — a condemnable elder.[1] תַּלְמוּד לוֹמַר — To teach us otherwise, **the verse says,** "זָקֵן״ — "an elder." אֵין זָקֵן אֶלָּא — "An elder" implies only שֶׁקָּנָה חָכְמָה — one who has acquired wisdom.[2]

□ וְהָדַרְתָּ פְּנֵי זָקֵן — AND YOU SHALL HONOR THE PRESENCE OF AN ELDER. אֵיזֶהוּ הָדוּר — What is honor? לֹא יֵשֵׁב בִּמְקוֹמוֹ — He should not sit in [an elder's] place, {וְלֹא יְדַבֵּר בִּמְקוֹמוֹ — nor should he speak in his place,} וְלֹא יִסְתּוֹר אֶת דְּבָרָיו — nor should he contradict his words. יָכוֹל יַעֲצִים עֵינָיו — One might be able to think that he may close his eyes כְּמִי שֶׁלֹּא רָאָהוּ — as if he did not see [the old person], and thereby avoid rising before him. לְכָךְ נֶאֱמַר — This is why it says, "וְיָרֵאתָ מֵּאֱלֹהֶיךָ״ — "and you shall have fear of your God." שֶׁהֲרֵי דָּבָר זֶה — For this matter מָסוּר לְלִבּוֹ שֶׁל עוֹשֵׂהוּ — is given over to the heart of the one who does it, שֶׁאֵין מַכִּיר בּוֹ אֶלָּא הוּא — for none can discern it but he, i.e., no one but he knows if he truly did not notice the old person or if he is dissembling. וְכָל דָּבָר — And of anything which is given over to the heart it says, "וְיָרֵאתָ מֵּאֱלֹהֶיךָ״[3] — "You shall have fear of your God," for He knows your true intention.[3]

33. לֹא תוֹנוּ — DO NOT HARASS. This refers to אוֹנָאַת דְּבָרִים — verbal harassment. לֹא תֹּאמַר לוֹ — Do not say to him, אֶמֶשׁ הָיִיתָ עוֹבֵד עֲבוֹדָה זָרָה — "Last night, i.e., in the past, you were an idolater, וְעַכְשָׁיו אַתָּה בָּא — and now you come לִלְמֹד תּוֹרָה — to learn Torah[4] שֶׁנִּתְּנָה מִפִּי הַגְּבוּרָה — which was given from the mouth of the Almighty?"[4]

34. כִּי־גֵרִים הֱיִיתֶם — FOR YOU HAVE BEEN ALIENS. מוּם שֶׁבְּךָ — An imperfection that exists in you, אַל תֹּאמַר לַחֲבֵרְךָ[5] — do not say to your friend, i.e., do not taunt another with a flaw you share with him in common.[5]

---

1. An old person who is wicked and ignorant (Rashi to *Kiddushin* 32b); one who is ignorant in Torah (Rashi to *Eruvin* 11a, s.v., פיתחי שימאי).

2. *Toras Kohanim*, perek 7:12; *Kiddushin* 32b. זָקֵן is interpreted as a combination of the words זֶה שֶׁקָּנָה חָכְמָה, "this one who has acquired wisdom."
   Although none of the letters of חָכְמָה, appear in the word זָקֵן, wisdom is the acquisition *par excellence*. For in Chapter 8 of *Proverbs*, the Torah, personified as חָכְמָה, "Wisdom," gives a lengthy description of its attributes, among them: "קָנָנִי רֵאשִׁית דַּרְכּוֹ״, HASHEM acquired me prior to His way [of Creation]." And, as the Talmud (*Nedarim* 41a) states regarding knowledge: דָּא קְנֵי מַה חָסֵר, "If he has acquired this, what is he missing?" דָּא לָא קְנֵי, "If he has not acquired this," מָה קְנֵי, "what has he acquired?"

3. *Toras Kohanim*, perek 7:14. See also Rashi to verse 14 above.

4. *Toras Kohanim*, perek 8:2; *Bava Metzia* 58b.

5. *Bava Metzia* 59b.

land of Egypt — I am HASHEM, your God. ³⁵ You shall not do wrong in justice, in measurement, in weight, or in the mesurah. ³⁶ You shall have correct scales,

בְּאֶרֶץ מִצְרָיִם אֲנִי יהוה אֱלֹהֵיכֶם:
לה לֹא־תַעֲשׂוּ עָוֶל בַּמִּשְׁפָּט בַּמִּדָּה
לו בַּמִּשְׁקָל וּבַמְּשׂוּרָה: מֹאזְנֵי צֶדֶק

── אונקלוס ──
בְּאַרְעָא דְמִצְרָיִם אֲנָא יְיָ אֱלָהֲכוֹן: לה לָא תַעְבְּדוּן שְׁקַר בְּדִין בִּמְשַׁחְתָּא בְּמַתְקְלָא וּבִמְכַלְתָּא: לו מאזְנָן דִּקְשׁוֹט

── רש"י ──

אני ה' אלהיכם. אֱלֹהֵי וֵאלֹהָיו אֲנִי: **(לה) לֹא תַעֲשׂוּ עָוֶל בַּמִּשְׁפָּט.** אִם לַדִּין הֲרֵי כְּבָר נֶאֱמַר לֹא תַעֲשׂוּ עָוֶל בַּמִּשְׁפָּט (לְעֵיל פָּסוּק טו) וּמַהוּ מִשְׁפָּט הַשָּׁנוּי כָּאן, הוּא הַמִּדָּה וְהַמִּשְׁקָל וְהַמְּשׂוּרָה. מְלַמֵּד שֶׁהַמּוֹדֵד נִקְרָא דַיָּן, שֶׁאִם שִׁקֵּר בַּמִּדָּה הֲרֵי הוּא כִּמְקַלְקֵל אֶת הַדִּין, וְקָרְאוּי עָוֶל שָׂנוּי וּמְשֻׁקָּץ חֵרֶם וְתוֹעֵבָה, וְגוֹרֵם לַחֲמִשָּׁה דְּבָרִים כָּאֲמוּרִים בְּדַיָּן, מְטַמֵּא אֶת הָאָרֶץ וּמְחַלֵּל אֶת הַשֵּׁם וּמְסַלֵּק אֶת הַשְּׁכִינָה וּמַפִּיל אֶת יִשְׂרָאֵל בַּחֶרֶב וּמַגְלֶה אוֹתָם מֵאַרְצָם: **בַּמִּדָּה.** הִיא מִדַּת הָאָרֶץ (ת"כ שָׁם ו; ב"מ סא:): **בַּמִּשְׁקָל.** כְּמַשְׁמָעוֹ: **וּבַמְּשׂוּרָה.** הִיא מִדַּת הַלַּח [וְהַיָּבֵשׁ] (ת"כ שָׁם):

── RASHI ELUCIDATED ──

□ אֲנִי ה' אֱלֹהֵיכֶם — I AM HASHEM, YOUR GOD. — אֱלֹהֶיךָ וֵאלֹהָיו אֲנִי — I am your God and his God.[1]

35. לֹא תַעֲשׂוּ עָוֶל בַּמִּשְׁפָּט — YOU SHALL NOT DO WRONG IN JUSTICE. — אִם לַדַּיָּן — If this commandment is addressed **to a judge,** הֲרֵי כְּבָר נֶאֱמַר — **see, now, that it has already been said,** "לֹא תַעֲשׂוּ עָוֶל בַּמִּשְׁפָּט" — "and you shall not do wrong in justice."[2] וּמַהוּ מִשְׁפָּט הַשָּׁנוּי כָּאן — **What**, then, **is "justice" which is stated here?** הוּא הַמִּדָּה וְהַמִּשְׁקָל וְהַמְּשׂוּרָה — **It is** the calculation of **the measurement, the weight, and the volume** with which the verse concludes. מְלַמֵּד — **[The verse] teaches** us שֶׁהַמּוֹדֵד — **that one who measures** that which is to be sold נִקְרָא דַיָּן — **is called a judge,** שֶׁאִם שִׁקֵּר בַּמִּדָּה — **that if he lied in measurement,** הֲרֵי הוּא כִּמְקַלְקֵל אֶת הַדִּין — **see, now, he is like one who perverts the judgment,** וְקָרְאוּי עָוֶל — **and is called a wrongdoer,** שָׂנוּי — **hateful,** וּמְשֻׁקָּץ — **and repulsive,** חֵרֶם — **banned,** וְתוֹעֵבָה — **and an abomination.**[3] וְגוֹרֵם לַחֲמִשָּׁה דְּבָרִים — **And he causes the five things** הָאֲמוּרִים בְּדַיָּן — **which are stated with regard to a judge** who perverts judgment: מְטַמֵּא אֶת הָאָרֶץ — **He contaminates the Land;** וּמְחַלֵּל אֶת הַשֵּׁם — **and profanes the Name** of God; וּמְסַלֵּק אֶת הַשְּׁכִינָה — **and causes the Shechinah** (God's immanent Presence) **to depart;** וּמַפִּיל אֶת יִשְׂרָאֵל בַּחֶרֶב — **and causes Israel to fall by the sword** of their enemies; [4] וּמַגְלֶה אוֹתָם מֵאַרְצָם — **and causes them to be exiled from their land.**[4]

□ בַּמִּדָּה — IN MEASUREMENT. — זוֹ מִדַּת הָאָרֶץ — This is the measure of the area or length of **land.**[5]

□ בַּמִּשְׁקָל — IN WEIGHT. This is to be understood כְּמַשְׁמָעוֹ — **as it sounds.**[6]

□ וּבַמְּשׂוּרָה — OR IN THE *MESURAH.* — [וְהִיא בֵשׁ] הִיא מִדַּת הַלַּח [7] — It is a measure of the volume **of that which is liquid {and that which is dry}.**[7]

---

1. The plural form of the pronominal suffix כֶ־, "your," in "I am HASHEM, your God" here provides a rationale for the prohibition against taunting a proselyte: HASHEM is just as much his God as He is yours.
2. Above v. 15. Rashi there explained that the verse referred to a judge who perverts justice.
3. See Rashi to v. 15 above.
4. *Toras Kohanim, perek* 4:1 and 8:5. Rashi has mentioned above that a judge who perverts judgment is called תּוֹעֵבָה, "an abomination." This indicates a kinship between such a judge and an idol, which is also referred to as תּוֹעֵבָה in *Deuteronomy* 7:26. Thus, descriptions with which the Torah characterizes idolatry can also apply to a judge who perverts judgment. With regard to Molech worship, a form of idolatry, the Torah says, "to defile that which is sacred to Me, and to desecrate My holy Name" (20:3 below). We see from here that idolatry and, by extension, perversion of judgment by a judge, contaminate the Land and profane the Name of God ("that which is sacred to Me" is taken as the Land of Israel according to this interpretation.

Departure of the Divine Presence as a result of idolatry is alluded to in 26:30 below: "I will cast your carcasses upon the carcasses of your *idols*, and *My spirit will reject you.*" In the same context, the Torah says, "I will unsheathe the sword after you" (26:33 below), which indicates that because of idolatry, Israel falls by the sword of their enemies. The same verse also says, "and you, I will scatter among the nations," which indicates that idolatry causes Israel to be exiled from their land (Glosses of the Vilna Gaon to *Toras Kohanim* 4:1).
5. *Toras Kohanim, perek* 8:6; *Bava Metzia* 61b; *Bava Basra* 89b.
6. "Weight" in this verse does not refer to the stone with which one weighs. The commandment to have accurate weights is the subject of the following verse, as Rashi notes there. Here מִשְׁקָל, "weight," means "weighing" (*Mesiach Ilmim*).
7. *Toras Kohanim, perek* 8:6. The *mesurah* was the smallest commonly used measure of volume, one thirty-sixth of a *log*, or one-sixth of a *beitzah*; in modern-day terms, two or three teaspoonfuls. By specifying it, the

correct stones, a correct ephah, and a correct hin — I am HASHEM, your God, Who brought you forth from the land of Egypt. ³⁷ You shall observe all My decrees and all My ordinances, and you shall perform them — I am HASHEM.

20 ¹ HASHEM spoke to Moses, saying: ² And to the Children of Israel you shall say: Any man from the Children of Israel and from the proselyte who lives with Israel, who shall give of his seed to Molech,

אַבְנֵי־צֶדֶק אֵיפַת צֶדֶק וְהִין צֶדֶק יִהְיֶה לָכֶם אֲנִי יהוה אֱלֹהֵיכֶם אֲשֶׁר־הוֹצֵאתִי אֶתְכֶם מֵאֶרֶץ מִצְרָיִם: לזּ וּשְׁמַרְתֶּם אֶת־כָּל־חֻקֹּתַי וְאֶת־כָּל־מִשְׁפָּטַי וַעֲשִׂיתֶם אֹתָם אֲנִי יהוה:

כ א וַיְדַבֵּר יהוה אֶל־מֹשֶׁה לֵּאמֹר: ב וְאֶל־בְּנֵי יִשְׂרָאֵל תֹּאמַר אִישׁ אִישׁ מִבְּנֵי יִשְׂרָאֵל וּמִן־הַגֵּר ׀ הַגָּר בְּיִשְׂרָאֵל אֲשֶׁר יִתֵּן מִזַּרְעוֹ לַמֹּלֶךְ

——— אונקלוס ———

אַבְנִין דִּקְשׁוֹט מְכִילָן דִּקְשׁוֹט וְהִינִין דִּקְשׁוֹט יְהוֹן לְכוֹן אֲנָא יְיָ אֱלָהֲכוֹן דִּי אַפֵּקִית יָתְכוֹן מֵאַרְעָא דְמִצְרָיִם: לז וְתִטְּרוּן יָת כָּל קְיָמַי וְיָת כָּל דִּינַי וְתַעְבְּדוּן יָתְהוֹן אֲנָא יְיָ: א וּמַלִּיל יְיָ עִם מֹשֶׁה לְמֵימָר: ב וְעִם בְּנֵי יִשְׂרָאֵל תְּמַלֵּל (נ״א וְלִבְנֵי יִשְׂרָאֵל תֵּימַר) גְּבַר גְּבַר מִבְּנֵי יִשְׂרָאֵל וּמִן גִּיּוֹרָא דְיִתְגַּיֵּר בְּיִשְׂרָאֵל דִּי יִתֵּן מִזַּרְעֵהּ לְמֹלֶךְ

——— רש"י ———

(לו) אבני צדק. הם המשקולות ששוקלין כנגדן (שם): **איפה.** היא מדת היבש: **והין.** זו היא מדת הלח: **אשר הוצאתי אתכם.** על מנת כן (שם י). ד"א אני הבחנתי במצרים בין טפה של בכור לטפה שאינה של בכור ואני הנאמן להפרע ממי שטומן משקלותיו במלח להונות את הבריות מכירים שאין בהם (בבא מציעא סא:): **(ב) ואל בני ישראל תאמר.** עונשין על האזהרות:

——— RASHI ELUCIDATED ———

36. אַבְנֵי צֶדֶק — CORRECT STONES. הֵם הַמִּשְׁקוֹלוֹת — They are the weights שֶׁשּׁוֹקְלִין כְּנֶגְדָּן — against which they weigh.¹

□ אֵיפָה — EPHAH. הִיא מִדַּת הַיָּבֵשׁ — That is a dry measure.

□ וְהִין — AND A [CORRECT] HIN. זוּ הִיא מִדַּת הַלַּח — That is a liquid measure.

□ אֲשֶׁר הוֹצֵאתִי אֶתְכֶם — WHO BROUGHT YOU FORTH ²עַל מְנָת כֵּן — on this condition, that you keep honest weights and measures.² דָּבָר אַחֵר — Alternatively, אֲנִי הִבְחַנְתִּי — I distinguished בְּמִצְרַיִם — in Egypt לְטִפָּה — between a droplet which caused the conception of a firstborn בֵּין טִפָּה שֶׁל בְּכוֹר — שֶׁאֵינָהּ שֶׁל בְּכוֹר — and a droplet which was not the cause of conception of a firstborn, וַאֲנִי הַנֶּאֱמָן — and I am the One Who can be trusted לְהִפָּרַע — to exact punishment מִמִּי שֶׁטּוֹמֵן מִשְׁקְלוֹתָיו בְּמֶלַח — from one who stores his weights in salt לְהוֹנוֹת אֶת הַבְּרִיּוֹת — to cheat the people שֶׁאֵין מַכִּירִים בָּהֶם³ — who do not know about them.³

20.

2. וְאֶל בְּנֵי יִשְׂרָאֵל תֹּאמַר — AND TO THE CHILDREN OF ISRAEL YOU SHALL SAY עֳנָשִׁין עַל הָאַזְהָרוֹת — punishments for the negative commandments.⁴

Torah says that one may not cheat even with regard to small amounts (see *Shaarei Aharon*). Our text follows the first printed edition of Rashi, and several other early editions. Some commentators have deleted the word וְהַיָּבֵשׁ. See *Yosef Hallel*.

1. *Toras Kohanim, perek* 8:6.
2. *Toras Kohanim, perek* 8:10. Rashi explains why the verse mentions the Exodus from Egypt at this point.
3. *Bava Metzia* 61b; *Bava Basra* 89b. Weights stored in salt absorb some of it and thereby increase in weight. Using such weights would be to the advantage of the buyer (Rashi to *Bava Metzia*). In this explanation, Rashi follows *Rabbeinu Gershom*. According to *Rabbeinu Tam* (*Tosafos* to *Bava Basra*), the salt has the opposite effect. It eats away at the weight and lightens it. Using such a weight would be to the advantage of the seller.

Thus, according to *Rabbeinu Tam*, the verse addresses the seller; according to Rashi, it addresses the buyer.

4. The most common phrase which follows וַיְדַבֵּר ה' אֶל מֹשֶׁה לֵּאמֹר, "HASHEM spoke to Moses, saying," when it introduces a commandment or laws concerning a commandment is דַּבֵּר אֶל בְּנֵי יִשְׂרָאֵל, "Speak to the Children of Israel" (e.g., below 23:1,2, 27:1,2). Our verse begins with וְאֶל בְּנֵי יִשְׂרָאֵל, "and to the Children of Israel," because it is linked to an earlier section of the Torah; it states the punishments for transgression of the negative commandments in Chapter 18 above (*Be'er BaSadeh*).

מוֹת יוּמָת עַם הָאָרֶץ יִרְגְּמֻהוּ בָאָבֶן: ג וַאֲנִי אֶתֵּן אֶת־פָּנַי בָּאִישׁ הַהוּא וְהִכְרַתִּי אֹתוֹ מִקֶּרֶב עַמּוֹ כִּי מִזַּרְעוֹ נָתַן לַמֹּלֶךְ לְמַעַן טַמֵּא

shall be put to death; the people of the land shall pelt him with stones. ³ I shall direct My face at that man, and I shall cut him off from among his people, for he has given of his offspring to the Molech in order to defile

— אונקלוס —

יִתְקְטָלָא יִתְקְטֵיל עַמָּא בֵית יִשְׂרָאֵל יִרְגְּמֻנֵּהּ בְּאַבְנָא: ג וַאֲנָא אֶתֵּן יָת רוּגְזִי בְּגַבְרָא הַהוּא וֶאֱשֵׁיצֵי יָתֵהּ מִגּוֹ עַמֵּהּ אֲרֵי מִזַּרְעֵהּ יְהַב לְמֹלֶךְ בְּדִיל לְסָאָבָא

— רש"י —

מוֹת יוּמָת. בְּבֵית דִּין, וְאִם אֵין כֹּחַ לְבֵית דִּין **עַם הָאָרֶץ** מְסַיְּעִין אוֹתָן (ת"כ פרשתא יד:ג): **עַם הָאָרֶץ.** עַם שֶׁבִּגְלָלוֹ נִבְרֵאת הָאָרֶץ. דָּבָר אַחֵר, עַם שֶׁעֲתִידִין לִירַשׁ אֶת הָאָרֶץ ע"י מִצְוֹת הַלָּלוּ (שם): (ג) **אֶתֵּן אֶת פָּנַי.** פְּנַאי שֶׁלִּי, פּוּנֶה אֲנִי מִכָּל עֲסָקַי **וְאֶעֱסוֹק בּוֹ: בָּאִישׁ.** וְלֹא בַּצִּבּוּר (שם) שֶׁאֵין כָּל הַצִּבּוּר נִכְרָתִין. **לְפִי שֶׁנֶּאֱמַר כִּי מִזַּרְעוֹ נָתַן לַמֹּלֶךְ**, מִנַּיִן עַל הַמַּעֲבִיר בְּנוֹ וּבִתּוֹ וּבֶן בְּנוֹ וּבֶן בִּתּוֹ, ת"ל **כִּי מִזַּרְעוֹ נָתַן לַמֹּלֶךְ**. זֶרַע פָּסוּל מִנַּיִן, ת"ל

— RASHI ELUCIDATED —

☐ **מוֹת יוּמָת** — **SHALL BE PUT TO DEATH** — בְּבֵית דִּין — **by the court.** וְאִם אֵין בֹּחַ לְבֵית דִּין — **And if the court does not have the power** to put him to death,¹ ²עַם הָאָרֶץ מְסַיְּעִין אוֹתָן — **the people of the land assist them.**²

☐ **עַם הָאָרֶץ** — **THE PEOPLE OF THE LAND.** עַם שֶׁבִּגְלָלוֹ — **The people on whose account** נִבְרֵאת הָאָרֶץ — **the land,** i.e., the world, **was created.** {דָּבָר אַחֵר — **Alternatively,**} עַם שֶׁעֲתִידִין לִירַשׁ אֶת הָאָרֶץ — **the people who are destined to inherit the land** עַל יְדֵי מִצְוֹת הַלָּלוּ³ — **by means of these commandments.**³

3. אֶתֵּן אֶת פָּנַי — **I SHALL DIRECT MY FACE.** פְּנַאי שֶׁלִּי — **My attention,**⁴ פּוּנֶה אֲנִי מִכָּל עֲסָקַי — **I turn aside from all My concerns** וְעוֹסֵק בּוֹ⁵ — **and deal with him.**⁵

☐ **בָּאִישׁ** — **AT [THAT] MAN.** ⁵וְלֹא בַּצִּבּוּר — **But not at the community,**⁵,⁶ שֶׁאֵין כָּל הַצִּבּוּר נִכְרָתִין — **for the entire community cannot be cut off.**⁷

☐ **כִּי מִזַּרְעוֹ נָתַן לַמֹּלֶךְ** — **FOR HE HAS GIVEN OF HIS OFFSPRING TO THE MOLECH.** לְפִי שֶׁנֶּאֱמַר — **Since it says,** ⁸״מַעֲבִיר בְּנוֹ וּבִתּוֹ בָּאֵשׁ״ — **"one who makes his son or daughter pass through the fire,"**⁸ בֶּן בְּנוֹ וּבֶן בִּתּוֹ מִנַּיִן — **from where do we know** that the prohibition applies also to **the son of his son and the son of his daughter?** תַּלְמוּד לוֹמַר — **To provide this source, the verse says,** ״כִּי מִזַּרְעוֹ נָתַן לַמֹּלֶךְ״ — **"for he has given of his offspring to the Molech."**⁹ זֶרַע פָּסוּל מִנַּיִן — **From where do we know** that **unfit offspring** are included in the prohibition?¹⁰ תַּלְמוּד לוֹמַר — **To provide this source, the verse**

---

1. For example, if the sinner is a powerful and violent person who might threaten the lives of the court should they attempt to execute him (*Be'er BaSadeh*).

2. *Toras Kohanim, parshasa* 10:4. "The people of the land shall pelt him with stones" is not the verse's explanation of "shall be but to death." If it were, "shall be put to death" would be superfluous. Rather, the verse says that optimally, the sinner should be put to death by the court. If this cannot be done by the court themselves, others should assist them (*Mizrachi; Sifsei Chachamim*).

3. *Toras Kohanim, parshasa* 10:4. The term עַם הָאָרֶץ does not mean "the people who inhabit the land," for in that case, the verse could have stated הָעָם "the people," and omitted הָאָרֶץ, "of the land" (*Gur Aryeh; Sifsei Chachamim*).
  According to Rashi's first interpretation, הָאָרֶץ refers to the entire world. According to his second interpretation, it refers to the World to Come (see Rashi to *Kiddushin* 39b, s.v., ונוחל את הארץ).

4. See Rashi to 17:10 and note there.

5. *Toras Kohanim, parshasa* 10:5.

6. The verse could have used בּוֹ, "at him." The lengthier "at that man" indicates that the punishment mentioned in the verse applies only to the transgression of an individual (*Leket Bahir*).

7. We may have thought that the entire community is held responsible if one of its members commits Molech worship (see Commentary of R' Shimshon of Sens [רי"שמשאנ"ץ] to *Toras Kohanim, Tzav, perek* 14:7, s.v., הנפס ולא הציבור). Alternatively, the verse teaches us that *kares* does not apply if an entire community commits Molech worship (*Nachalas Yaakov; Sifsei Chachamim*).

8. Deuteronomy 18:10.

9. The preceding verse has stated explicitly that we are discussing one who commits Molech worship. The apparently superfluous כִּי מִזַּרְעוֹ נָתַן לַמֹּלֶךְ, which uses the broad term "offspring" instead of בָּנָיו, "his children," is stated to teach us that the prohibition applies to grandchildren as well as children (*Mizrachi; Sifsei Chachamim*, based on Rashi to *Sanhedrin* 64b).

10. "Unfit offspring" includes *chalalim* — children born of unions forbidden to Kohanim — and *mamzerim* — children born of incestuous or adulterous unions.

| that which is sacred to me and to desecrate My holy Name. **⁴** But if the people of the land avert their eyes from that man when he gives from his offspring to Molech, not to put him to death — **⁵** then I shall concentrate My attention upon that man and upon his family; I will cut off | אֶת־מִקְדָּשִׁי וּלְחַלֵּל אֶת־שֵׁם קָדְשִׁי: ד וְאִם הַעְלֵם יַעְלִימוּ֮ עַם הָאָ֒רֶץ אֶת־עֵינֵיהֶם֙ מִן־הָאִ֣ישׁ הַה֔וּא בְּתִתּ֥וֹ מִזַּרְע֖וֹ לַמֹּ֑לֶךְ לְבִלְתִּ֖י הָמִ֥ית אֹתֽוֹ: ה וְשַׂמְתִּ֨י אֲנִ֧י אֶת־פָּנַ֛י בָּאִ֥ישׁ הַה֖וּא וּבְמִשְׁפַּחְתּ֑וֹ וְהִכְרַתִּ֨י אֹת֜וֹ |

---------- אונקלוס ----------

יָת מַקְדְּשִׁי וּלְאַחֲלָא יָת שְׁמָא דְקוּדְשִׁי: ד וְאִם מִכְבָּשׁ יִכְבְּשׁוּן עַמָּא בֵית יִשְׂרָאֵל יָת עֵינֵיהוֹן מִן גַּבְרָא הַהוּא בִּדְיָהֵב מִזַּרְעֵהּ לְמֹלֶךְ בְּדִיל דְּלָא לְקַטָּלָא יָתֵהּ: ה וֶאֱשַׁוֵּי אֲנָא יָת רוּגְזִי בְּגַבְרָא הַהוּא וּבְסִעְדָדוֹהִי וֶאֱשֵׁיצֵי יָתֵהּ

---------- רש"י ----------

בתתו מזרעו למולך (ת"כ ו"ז; סנהדרין סד:): **(ד) ואם העלם יעלימו.** אם העלימו בדבר אחד שיעלימו בדברים הרבה (ת"כ שם י'). אם העלימו סנהדרי קטנה סוף שיעלימו סנהדרי גדולה (שם יא'):
(ה) ובמשפחתו. אמר ר"ש וכי משפחה מה חטאה, אלא ללמדך שאין לך משפחה שיש בה מוכס שאין כולם מוכסין, שכולן מחפין עליו (שם י"ג; שבועות לט:): **והכרתי אותו.** למה נא', לפי שנא' ובמשפחתו יכול יהיו כל המשפחה בהכרת, ת"ל אותו, אותו בהכרת ולא כל המשפחה בהכרת אלא ביסורין (שם י"ד):

למען טמא את מקדשי. את כנסת ישראל שהיא מקודשת לי, כלשון ולא יחלל את מקדשי (להלן כא:כג): **(ד) ואם העלם יעלימו.** אם העלימו בדבר אחד סוף שיעלימו בדברים הרבה (ת"כ שם י).

---------- RASHI ELUCIDATED ----------

says, **בְּתִתּוֹ מִזַּרְעוֹ לַמֹּלֶךְ,** – **"when he gives from his offspring to Molech."**[1,2]

{ **לְמַעַן טַמֵּא אֶת מִקְדָּשִׁי** – IN ORDER TO DEFILE THAT WHICH IS SACRED TO ME. – The אֶת כְּנֶסֶת יִשְׂרָאֵל – **The Assembly of Israel** שֶׁהִיא מְקֻדֶּשֶׁת לִי, – **which is sanctified unto Me.**[3] מִקְדָּשִׁי is used here בְּלָשׁוֹן ,,וְלֹא – in a similar manner as the term מִקְדָּשִׁי in the verse, **"he shall not desecrate that of Mine which is holy."**[4]}[5]

4. וְאִם הַעְלֵם יַעְלִימוּ – BUT IF [THE PEOPLE OF THE LAND] AVERT. – **אִם הֶעֱלִימוּ בְּדָבָר אֶחָד** – **If they avert their eyes in one matter,** [6]סוֹף שֶׁיַּעֲלִימוּ בִּדְבָרִים הַרְבֵּה – the end will be **that they will avert** their eyes **in many matters.**[6] **סוֹף שֶׁיַּעֲלִימוּ** – **אִם הֶעֱלִימוּ סַנְהֶדְרֵי קְטַנָּה** – **If a lesser Sanhedrin averted** their eyes, [7]סַנְהֶדְרֵי גְדוֹלָה – the end will be **that the Great Sanhedrin** will avert their eyes.[7]

5. וּבְמִשְׁפַּחְתּוֹ – AND UPON HIS FAMILY. – **אָמַר רַבִּי שִׁמְעוֹן** – The *Tanna* **R' Shimon said: וְכִי מִשְׁפָּחָה מֶה חָטְאָה** – **In what did the family sin?** Why should they be punished? – **אֶלָּא** – **But,** this verse is meant **לְלַמֶּדְךָ** – **to teach you שֶׁאֵין לְךָ מִשְׁפָּחָה** – **that you have,** i.e., that there is, **no family שֶׁיֵּשׁ בָּהּ מוֹכֵס** – **which has in it an** unjust **tax collector שֶׁאֵין כֻּלָּם מוֹכְסִין** – **in which they are all not** unjust **tax collectors,** [8]שֶׁכֻּלָּן מְחַפִּין עָלָיו – **for they all cover up for him,** and thereby support him in his sin.[8]

□ **וְהִכְרַתִּי אֹתוֹ** – I WILL CUT OFF [FROM AMONG THEIR PEOPLE,] HIM. – **לָמָּה נֶאֱמַר** – **Why is this stated?** Has it not already been stated in verse 3? – **לְפִי שֶׁנֶּאֱמַר** – **Because it says, ,,וּבְמִשְׁפַּחְתּוֹ"** – **"and upon his family,"** – **יָכוֹל יִהְיוּ כָל הַמִּשְׁפָּחָה בְּהִכָּרֵת** – **one might be able** to think that **the entire family shall be** included in the punishment of *kares*. – **תַּלְמוּד לוֹמַר** – To teach us otherwise, **the verse says,** **,,אֹתוֹ"** – **"him,"** to imply, **אֹתוֹ בְהִכָּרֵת** – **he is** included in the punishment of *kares*, **וְלֹא כָל הַמִּשְׁפָּחָה בְּהִכָּרֵת** – **but the entire family is not** included in the punishment of *kares*. **אֶלָּא בְיִסּוּרִין**[9] – **Rather,** they are punished **by torments.**[9]

---

1. Verse 4. This, too, is an apparently superfluous phrase (*Mizrachi; Sifsei Chachamim* based on Rashi to *Sanhedrin* 64b).
2. *Toras Kohanim, parshasa* 10:6-7; *Sanhedrin* 64b.
3. מִקְדָּשִׁי here does not mean "My sanctuary," i.e., the *Beis HaMikdash* or the Tabernacle (as it does in 19:30 above), for committing Molech worship does not affect them (*Mizrachi; Sifsei Chachamim*).
4. Below 21:23. מִקְדָּשִׁי there does not refer to the *Beis HaMikdash* or the Tabernacle, for the verse speaks of sacrificial service performed by a blemished *Kohen*. Such service defiles only the offering, but not the *Beis HaMikdash* or Tabernacle (see Rashi, *Mizrachi*, and *Sifsei Chachamim* there).
5. This comment does not appear in the first printed edition.
6. *Toras Kohanim, parshasa* 10:10.
7. *Toras Kohanim, parshasa* 10:11. The two-verb unit which includes a *makor* (an infinitive, הַעְלֵם) indicates that if the people avert their eyes from one sinner, it will lead to a general breakdown of the judicial system (*Be'er BaSadeh; Maskil LeDavid*).
8. *Toras Kohanim, parshasa* 10:13; *Shevuos* 39a.
9. *Toras Kohanim, parshasa* 10:14.

from among their people, him and all who stray after him to stray after the Molech. **⁶ And the person who shall turn to the sorcery of the Ovos and the Yid'onim to stray after them — I shall concentrate My attention upon that person and cut him off from among his people.**

⁷ You shall sanctify yourselves and you will be holy, for I am HASHEM**, your God.**

⁸ You shall observe My decrees and perform them — I am HASHEM**, Who sanctifies you. ⁹ For any man who will curse his father or mother shall be put to death; his father or his mother has he cursed, his blood is upon him.**

וְאֵת ׀ כָּל־הַזֹּנִים אַחֲרָ֑יו לִזְנ֛וֹת אַחֲרֵ֥י הַמֹּ֖לֶךְ מִקֶּ֣רֶב עַמָּֽם: וְהַנֶּ֗פֶשׁ אֲשֶׁ֨ר תִּפְנֶ֤ה אֶל־הָֽאֹבֹת֙ וְאֶל־הַיִּדְּעֹנִ֔ים לִזְנ֖וֹת אַֽחֲרֵיהֶ֑ם וְנָֽתַתִּ֤י אֶת־פָּנַי֙ בַּנֶּ֣פֶשׁ הַהִ֔וא וְהִכְרַתִּ֥י אֹת֖וֹ מִקֶּ֥רֶב עַמּֽוֹ:
ז וְהִ֨תְקַדִּשְׁתֶּ֔ם וִֽהְיִיתֶ֖ם קְדֹשִׁ֑ים כִּ֛י אֲנִ֥י יְהוָ֖ה אֱלֹֽהֵיכֶֽם: [שביעי] ח וּשְׁמַרְתֶּם֙ אֶת־חֻקֹּתַ֔י וַעֲשִׂיתֶ֖ם אֹתָ֑ם אֲנִ֥י יְהוָ֖ה מְקַדִּשְׁכֶֽם: ט כִּֽי־אִ֣ישׁ אִ֗ישׁ אֲשֶׁ֨ר יְקַלֵּ֧ל אֶת־אָבִ֛יו וְאֶת־אִמּ֖וֹ מ֣וֹת יוּמָ֑ת אָבִ֧יו וְאִמּ֛וֹ קִלֵּ֖ל דָּמָ֥יו בּֽוֹ:

— אונקלוס —

וְיָת כָּל דְּטָעַן בַּתְרוֹהִי לְמִטְעֵי בָּתַר מֹלֶךְ מִגּוֹ עַמְּהוֹן: ו וֶאֱנָשׁ דִּי יִתְפְּנֵי בָּתַר בִּדִּין וּדְכוּרוּ לְמִטְעֵי בַּתְרֵיהוֹן וְאֶתֵּן יָת רוּגְזִי בְּגַבְרָא הַהוּא וֶאֱשֵׁיצֵי יָתֵיהּ מִגּוֹ עַמֵּהּ: ז וְתִתְקַדְּשׁוּן וּתְהוֹן קַדִּישִׁין אֲרֵי אֲנָא יְיָ אֱלָהֲכוֹן: ח וְתִטְּרוּן יָת קְיָמַי וְתַעְבְּדוּן יָתְהוֹן אֲנָא יְיָ מְקַדִּשְׁכוֹן: ט אֲרֵי גְבַר גְּבַר דִּי יְלוּט יָת אֲבוּהִי וְיָת אִמֵּהּ אִתְקְטָלָא יִתְקְטֵיל אֲבוּהִי וְאִמֵּהּ לָט קְטָלָא חַיָּב:

— רש"י —

לזנות אחרי המולך. לרבות שאר עבודה זרה שעבדה בכך ואפילו אין זו עבודתה (סנהדרין סד.): **(ז) והתקדשתם.** זו פרישות עבודה זרה (ספרי פרק י"ב): **(ט) אביו ואמו קלל.** לרבות לאחר מיתה (שם טו): **דמיו בו.** זו סקילה וכן כל מקום שנאמר [דמיו בו] דמיהם בם, ולמדנו מאוב וידעוני שנאמר בהם באבן ירגמו אותם

— RASHI ELUCIDATED —

לִזְנוֹת אַחֲרֵי הַמֹּלֶךְ — **TO STRAY AFTER THE MOLECH.** This is stated ¹ לְרַבּוֹת שְׁאָר עֲבוֹדָה זָרָה — **to include other** forms of **idolatry**,¹ שֶׁעֲבָדָהּ בְּכָךְ — **which he worshiped in such a manner,** וַאֲפִילוּ אֵין זוֹ עֲבוֹדָתָהּ — **even if this is not its** standard manner of **worship.²**

7. וְהִתְקַדִּשְׁתֶּם — **YOU SHALL SANCTIFY YOURSELVES.** ³ זוֹ פְּרִישׁוּת עֲבוֹדָה זָרָה — **This is separation from idolatry.³**

9. אָבִיו וְאִמּוֹ קִלֵּל — **HIS FATHER OR HIS MOTHER HAS HE CURSED.** This is stated ⁴ לְרַבּוֹת לְאַחַר מִיתָה — **to include** cursing a parent **after** the parent's **death.⁴**

דָּמָיו בּוֹ — **HIS BLOOD IS UPON HIM.** ⁵ זוֹ סְקִילָה — **This is** execution by **stoning,⁵** וְכֵן — **and similarly,** this is the meaning כָּל מָקוֹם שֶׁנֶּאֱמַר — **any place where [the Torah] says,** {דָּמָיו בּוֹ} — **"his blood is upon him,"** or⁶ דְּמֵיהֶם בָּם — **"their blood is upon them."⁷** וְלָמַדְנוּ — **We have learned** this מֵאוֹב וְיִדְּעוֹנִי — **from ov and yid'oni⁸** שֶׁנֶּאֱמַר בָּהֶם — **about which it says,** ״בָּאֶבֶן יִרְגְּמוּ אֹתָם,,

---

1. *Toras Kohanim, parshasa* 10:15.

2. It is obvious from the context that our verse speaks of Molech worship; thus, "to stray after Molech" appears superfluous. It is written to teach us that one who worships a different pagan deity in the manner in which Molech is worshiped, by passing his offspring through two bonfires, is subject to *kares*, even though that deity is usually worshiped in a different manner. Normally, one receives *kares* for idolatry only for worshiping a pagan deity in its standard fashion, with the exception of certain other universally forbidden forms of worship listed in the Mishnah in *Sanhedrin* 60a (*Mizrachi*; *Be'er Yitzchak*).

3. *Toras Kohanim, perek* 10:2. This is indicated by the context of the phrase (*Be'er Yitzchak*). Although Rashi (19:2 above) stated that "holiness" or "sanctity" indicates refraining from sexual immorality, there are exceptions to this rule where the context indicates otherwise. See, for example, 11:44 above where it is used with regard to refraining from eating creeping animals (*Gur Aryeh*).

4. *Sanhedrin* 85b. This phrase appears superfluous, for the verse has already said, "for any man who will curse his father or mother" (*Gur Aryeh*). It is written to teach us that the prohibition against cursing a parent applies even after the parent's death. We might have thought it applies only during the parent's lifetime, just as the prohibition against striking a parent applies only during his lifetime (*Mizrachi*; *Sifsei Chachamim*).

5. *Toras Kohanim, perek* 10:7.

6. Most early editions omit this phrase because ours is the only verse in the Torah in which it appears. Those editions that include the phrase allude to *Ezekiel* 18:13 which can be interpreted as a reference to stoning (see *Yosef Hallel*).

7. Verses 11,12,13,16, and 27 below.

8. Types of necromancy. See 19:31 below.

¹⁰ A man who will commit adultery with a man's wife, who will commit adultery with the wife of his fellow; the adulterer and the adulteress shall be put to death. ¹¹ A man who shall lie with his father's wife will have uncovered his father's nakedness; the two of them shall be put to death, their blood is upon them. ¹² A man who shall lie with his daughter-in-law, the two of them shall be put to death; they have committed a perversion, their blood is upon them.

וְאִישׁ אֲשֶׁר יִנְאַף אֶת־אֵשֶׁת אִישׁ אֲשֶׁר יִנְאַף אֶת־אֵשֶׁת רֵעֵהוּ מוֹת־יוּמַת הַנֹּאֵף וְהַנֹּאָפֶת: וְאִישׁ אֲשֶׁר יִשְׁכַּב אֶת־אֵשֶׁת אָבִיו עֶרְוַת אָבִיו גִּלָּה מוֹת־יוּמְתוּ שְׁנֵיהֶם דְּמֵיהֶם בָּם: וְאִישׁ אֲשֶׁר יִשְׁכַּב אֶת־כַּלָּתוֹ מוֹת יוּמְתוּ שְׁנֵיהֶם תֶּבֶל עָשׂוּ דְּמֵיהֶם בָּם:

────── אונקלוס ──────

י וּגְבַר דִּי יְגוּף יָת אִתַּת גְּבַר דִּי יְגוּף יָת אִתַּת חַבְרֵהּ אִתְקְטָלָא יִתְקְטֵל גַּיָּפָא וְגַיָּפְתָא: יא וּגְבַר דִּי יִשְׁכּוּב עִם אִתַּת אֲבוּהִי עֶרְיְתָא דַאֲבוּהִי גַּלִּי אִתְקְטָלָא יִתְקְטְלוּן תַּרְוֵיהוֹן קְטָלָא חַיָּבִין: יב וּגְבַר דִּי יִשְׁכּוּב עִם כַּלְּתֵהּ אִתְקְטָלָא יִתְקְטְלוּן תַּרְוֵיהוֹן תֶּבְלָא עֲבַדוּ קְטָלָא חַיָּבִין:

────── רש"י ──────

דמיהם בם (להלן פסוק כז; ת"כ פרק ט:יב; כריתות ה.). ופשוטו של מקרא כמו דמו בראשו (יהושע ב:יט) אין נענש על מיתתו אלא הוא, שהוא גרס לעצמו שיהרג: (י) ואיש. פרט לקטן (ת"כ שם ח; סנהדרין נב:): אשר ינאף את אשת איש. פרט לאשת קטן (שם). למדנו שאין לקטן קידושין. ועל איזו אשת איש חייבתי לך, אשר ינאף את אשת רעהו, פרט לאשת גוי (שם). למדנו שאין קידושין לגוי: מות יומת הנואף והנואפת. כל מיתה האמורה בתורה סתם אינה אלא חנק (שם): (יב) תבל עשו. גנאי. ל"א מבלבלין זרע האב

────── RASHI ELUCIDATED ──────

דְּמֵיהֶם בָּם [2,1] — "They shall pelt them with stones; their blood is upon them."[1,2] דָּמוּ בְרֹאשׁוֹ [3] — literally, "his blood is on his head,"[3] which means, אֵין נֶעֱנָשׁ עַל מִיתָתוֹ — no one is to be punished for his death אֶלָּא הוּא — but himself, שֶׁהוּא גָּרַם לְעַצְמוֹ שֶׁיֵּהָרֵג — for he will have caused himself to be killed.[4] וּפְשׁוּטוֹ שֶׁל מִקְרָא — But the simple meaning of the verse is כְּמוֹ — like that of

10. וְאִישׁ – A MAN, פְּרָט לְקָטָן[5] – to the exclusion of a minor.[5]

□ אֲשֶׁר יִנְאַף אֶת אֵשֶׁת אִישׁ – WHO WILL COMMIT ADULTERY WITH A MAN'S WIFE. פְּרָט לְאֵשֶׁת קָטָן[6] – To the exclusion of the wife of a minor.[6] לִמְּדָנוּ – [The verse] has taught us שֶׁאֵין לְקָטָן קִדּוּשִׁין – that there exists no state of matrimony for a male minor. וְעַל אֵיזוֹ אֵשֶׁת אִישׁ חִיַּבְתִּי לָךְ – And for which "man's wife" have I obligated you, i.e., for adultery with whose wife have I prescribed death? אֲשֶׁר יִנְאַף אֶת אֵשֶׁת רֵעֵהוּ – For one "who will commit adultery with the wife of his fellow." פְּרָט לְאֵשֶׁת גּוֹי[7] – To the exclusion of the wife of a non-Jew.[7] לִמְּדָנוּ – [The verse] has taught us שֶׁאֵין קִדּוּשִׁין לְגוֹי – that there exists no state of matrimony for a non-Jew.

□ מוֹת יוּמַת הַנֹּאֵף וְהַנֹּאָפֶת – THE ADULTERER AND THE ADULTERESS SHALL BE PUT TO DEATH. כָּל מִיתָה – Any "death" הָאֲמוּרָה בַּתּוֹרָה סְתָם – which is stated in the Torah without further specification אֵינָהּ אֶלָּא חֶנֶק[7] – is nothing other than strangulation.[7]

12. תֶּבֶל עָשׂוּ – THEY HAVE COMMITTED A PERVERSION. לָשׁוֹן אַחֵר – תֶּבֶל means shame. גְּנַאי Alternatively, תֶּבֶל is related to the word for "mixture";[8] מְבַלְבְּלִין – they mix זֶרַע הָאָב – the seed

---

1. Below v. 27.
2. *Toras Kohanim*, perek 9:12; *Kereisos* 5a.
3. *Joshua* 2:19; *Ezekiel* 33:4. See Rashi's comments to those verses and to *Niddah* 17a, s.v., דמו בראשו.
4. Unlike Rashi's first interpretation, according to the simple meaning of the verse, "his blood is upon him" does not connote stoning any more than any other form of execution (*Maskil LeDavid*).
5. *Toras Kohanim*, perek 9:8; *Sanhedrin* 52b. Minors are never punished by the court for sins they have committed. We might have thought that minors are

executed for adultery, however, not as a punishment, but as a response to the state of "impurity of the Land" that results from it (see 18:24-28 above), just as an ox that gores a person to death is killed to atone for "impurity of the Land." See Rashi to *Exodus* 21:12 and our note 4 there; Rashi to *Arachin* 16a, s.v., אהנו מעשיו.

6. *Toras Kohanim*, perek 9:8; *Sanhedrin* 52b; *Kiddushin* 19a.
7. *Toras Kohanim*, perek 9:8; *Sanhedrin* 52b.
8. See Rashi to 18:23 above.

וְאִ֗ישׁ אֲשֶׁ֨ר יִשְׁכַּ֤ב אֶת־זָכָר֙ מִשְׁכְּבֵ֣י אִשָּׁ֔ה תּוֹעֵבָ֥ה עָשׂ֖וּ שְׁנֵיהֶ֑ם מ֥וֹת יוּמָ֖תוּ דְּמֵיהֶ֥ם בָּֽם: וְאִ֗ישׁ אֲשֶׁ֨ר יִקַּ֧ח אֶת־אִשָּׁ֛ה וְאֶת־אִמָּ֖הּ זִמָּ֣ה הִ֑וא בָּאֵ֞שׁ יִשְׂרְפ֤וּ אֹתוֹ֙ וְאֶתְהֶ֔ן וְלֹא־תִֽהְיֶ֥ה זִמָּ֖ה בְּתֽוֹכְכֶֽם: וְאִ֗ישׁ אֲשֶׁ֨ר יִתֵּ֧ן שְׁכָבְתּ֛וֹ בִּבְהֵמָ֖ה מ֣וֹת יוּמָ֑ת וְאֶת־הַבְּהֵמָ֖ה תַּהֲרֹֽגוּ:

13 A man who lies with a man as one lies with a woman, they have both done an abomination; they shall be put to death, their blood is upon them.

14 A man who shall take a woman and her mother, it is a depraved plot; they shall burn him and them in fire, and there shall not be depravity among you.

15 A man who shall lie with an animal shall be put to death; and you shall kill the animal.

— אונקלוס —

יג וּגְבַר דִּי יִשְׁכּוּב עִם דְּכוּרָא מִשְׁכְּבֵי אִתְּתָא תּוֹעֶבְתָּא עֲבַדוּ תַּרְוֵיהוֹן אִתְקְטָלָא יִתְקַטְּלוּן קְטָלָא חַיָּבִין: יד וּגְבַר דִּי יִסַּב יָת אִתְּתָא וְיָת אִמַּהּ עֲצַת חֶטְאִין הִיא בְּנוּרָא יוֹקְדוּן יָתֵהּ וְיָתְהֶן וְלָא תְהֵי עֲצַת חֶטְאִין בֵּינֵיכוֹן: טו וּגְבַר דִּי יִתֵּן שְׁכָבְתֵּהּ בִּבְעִירָא אִתְקְטָלָא יִתְקְטֵל וְיָת בְּעִירָא תִּקְטְלוּן:

— רש"י —

בְּזֶרַע הַבֵּן: (יג) **מִשְׁכְּבֵי אִשָּׁה.** מַכְנִיס כְּמִכְחוֹל בִּשְׁפוֹפֶרֶת: (יד) **יִשְׂרְפוּ אֹתוֹ וְאֶתְהֶן.** אִי אַתָּה יָכוֹל לוֹמַר אִשְׁתּוֹ הָרִאשׁוֹנָה יִשְׂרְפוּ, שֶׁהֲרֵי נְשָׂאָהּ בְּהֶתֵּר וְלֹא נֶאֶסְרָה עָלָיו, אֶלָּא אִשָּׁה וְאִמָּהּ הַכְּתוּבוֹת כָּאן שְׁתֵּיהֶן לְאִסּוּר, שֶׁנָּשָׂא אֶת חֲמוֹתוֹ וְאִמָּהּ. וְיֵשׁ מֵרַבּוֹתֵינוּ שֶׁאוֹמְרִים אֵין כָּאן אֶלָּא חֲמוֹתוֹ, וּמַהוּ אֶתְהֶן, אֶת אַחַת מֵהֶן, וּלְשׁוֹן יְוָנִי הוּא, הֵן אַחַת: (טו) **וְאֶת הַבְּהֵמָה תַּהֲרֹגוּ.** אִם אָדָם חָטָא, בְּהֵמָה מֶה חָטְאָה, אֶלָּא מִפְּנֵי שֶׁבָּאָה לְאָדָם תַּקָּלָה עַל יָדָהּ לְפִיכָךְ אָמַר הַכָּתוּב תִּסָּקֵל, קַל וָחֹמֶר לְאָדָם, שֶׁיּוֹדֵעַ לְהַבְחִין בֵּין טוֹב לְרַע וְגוֹרֵם רָעָה לַחֲבֵרוֹ לַעֲבֹר עֲבֵרָה. כַּיּוֹצֵא בַדָּבָר אַתָּה אוֹמֵר אַבֵּד תְּאַבְּדוּן אֶת כָּל הַמְּקוֹמוֹת (דברים יב:ב):

RASHI ELUCIDATED

בְּזֶרַע הַבֵּן — with the seed of the son of the father.

13. מִשְׁכְּבֵי אִשָּׁה — AS ONE LIES WITH A WOMAN. מַכְנִיס — He inserts, כְּמִכְחוֹל — like an applicator בִּשְׁפוֹפֶרֶת — into a tube of cosmetics.

14. יִשְׂרְפוּ אֹתוֹ וְאֶתְהֶן — THEY SHALL BURN HIM AND THEM. אִי אַתָּה יָכוֹל לוֹמַר — You cannot say אִשְׁתּוֹ הָרִאשׁוֹנָה יִשְׂרְפוּ — that they should burn his first wife, שֶׁהֲרֵי נְשָׂאָהּ בְּהֶתֵּר — for he married her with permission, וְלֹא נֶאֶסְרָה עָלָיו — and she did not become forbidden to him at the time he married the second.[1] אֶלָּא אִשָּׁה וְאִמָּהּ הַכְּתוּבוֹת כָּאן — But "a woman and her mother" who are written of here שְׁתֵּיהֶן לְאִסּוּר — are both forbidden to the man who is marrying them, שֶׁנָּשָׂא אֶת חֲמוֹתוֹ וְאִמָּהּ — for he married his mother-in-law, who was already forbidden to him because he had married her daughter, and her mother, i.e., the mother of the mother-in-law. וְיֵשׁ מֵרַבּוֹתֵינוּ שֶׁאוֹמְרִים — There are those among our Rabbis who say, אֵין כָּאן אֶלָּא חֲמוֹתוֹ — there is no one here but his mother-in-law.[2] וּמַהוּ אֶתְהֶן — What is meant by the plural אֶתְהֶן, "them"? אֶתְהֶן here is not a plural. It means אֶת אַחַת מֵהֶן[3] — one of them. וּלְשׁוֹן יְוָנִי הוּא — It is in the Greek language, in which הֵן אַחַת — the word הֵן means "one."[3]

15. וְאֶת הַבְּהֵמָה תַּהֲרֹגוּ — AND YOU SHALL KILL THE ANIMAL. אִם אָדָם חָטָא — If man sinned, בְּהֵמָה מֶה חָטְאָה — what sin did the animal commit? Why should it be killed? אֶלָּא — But it is killed מִפְּנֵי שֶׁבָּאָה — because ruination came to man through it. לְאָדָם תַּקָּלָה עַל יָדָהּ — לְפִיכָךְ — This is why אָמַר הַכָּתוּב — Scripture said תִּסָּקֵל — that it should be stoned. קַל וָחֹמֶר לְאָדָם — How much more so is there punishment **for man** שֶׁיּוֹדֵעַ לְהַבְחִין בֵּין טוֹב לְרַע — who knows how to distinguish between good and evil וְגוֹרֵם רָעָה לַחֲבֵרוֹ — and causes evil to befall his fellow man[4] לַעֲבוּר עֲבֵרָה — by leading him to commit a sin.[4] כַּיּוֹצֵא בַדָּבָר — In a similar vein אַתָּה אוֹמֵר — you say, i.e., the Torah says, אַבֵּד ,, תְּאַבְּדוּן אֶת כָּל הַמְּקוֹמוֹת — "You shall destroy all of the places [where the nations from whom[5]

---

1. The verse says "him and them," implying that both the mother and the daughter are put to death. But the death penalty cannot apply to whichever of the two he married first, for the first woman was not forbidden to him.

2. According to these Rabbis, when the verse says, "they shall burn him and them," it does not mean that the daughter, whom he married first, should be put to death,

for he married her permissibly and she does not become forbidden, as Rashi has pointed out. The death penalty applies only to the mother-in-law, whom he married later.

3. *Sanhedrin* 76b. The word הֵן (*Job* 28:13) is also translated in this way (*Shabbos* 31b).

4. *Toras Kohanim*, *perek* 11:5.

5. *Deuteronomy* 12:2.

16 And a woman who approaches any animal for it to mate with her, you shall kill the woman and the animal; they shall be put to death, their blood is upon them.

17 A man who shall take his sister, the daughter of his father or the daughter of his mother, and he shall see her nakedness and she shall see his nakedness, it is a disgrace and they shall be cut off in the sight of the members of their people; he will have uncovered the nakedness of his sister, he shall bear his iniquity.

18 A man who shall lie with a woman in her affliction and has uncovered her nakedness, he has bared her source and she has

טז וְאִשָּׁה אֲשֶׁר תִּקְרַב אֶל־כָּל־בְּהֵמָה לְרִבְעָה אֹתָהּ וְהָרַגְתָּ אֶת־הָאִשָּׁה וְאֶת־הַבְּהֵמָה מוֹת יוּמָתוּ דְּמֵיהֶם בָּם: יז וְאִישׁ אֲשֶׁר־יִקַּח אֶת־אֲחֹתוֹ בַּת־אָבִיו אוֹ בַת־אִמּוֹ וְרָאָה אֶת־עֶרְוָתָהּ וְהִיא־תִרְאֶה אֶת־עֶרְוָתוֹ חֶסֶד הוּא וְנִכְרְתוּ לְעֵינֵי בְּנֵי עַמָּם עֶרְוַת אֲחֹתוֹ גִּלָּה עֲוֹנוֹ יִשָּׂא: יח וְאִישׁ אֲשֶׁר־יִשְׁכַּב אֶת־אִשָּׁה דָּוָה וְגִלָּה אֶת־עֶרְוָתָהּ אֶת־מְקֹרָהּ הֶעֱרָה וְהִוא

אונקלוס

טז וְאִתְּתָא דִּי תִקְרַב לְכָל בְּעִירָא לְמִשְׁלַט בַּהּ וְתִקְטוֹל יָת אִתְּתָא וְיָת בְּעִירָא אִתְקְטָלָא יִתְקַטְּלוּן קְטָלָא חַיָּבִין: יז וּגְבַר דִּי יִסַּב יָת אֲחָתֵיהּ בַּת אֲבוּהִי אוֹ בַת אִמֵּיהּ וְיֶחֱזֵי יָת עֶרְיְתַהּ וְהִיא תֶחֱזֵי יָת עֶרְיְתֵיהּ קְלָנָא הוּא וְיִשְׁתֵּיצוּן לְעֵינֵי בְּנֵי עַמְּהוֹן עֶרְיַת אֲחָתֵיהּ גַּלִּי חוֹבֵיהּ יְקַבֵּל: יח וּגְבַר דִּי יִשְׁכּוּב עִם אִתְּתָא מְסָאָבָא וִיגַלֵּי יָת עֶרְיְתַהּ יָת קְלָנַהּ גַּלִּי וְהִיא

רש"י

הרי דברים ק"ו. ומה אילנות שאינן רואין ואינן שומעין, על שבאת תקלה על ידם אמרה תורה השחת שרוף וכלה, המטה את חבירו מדרך חיים לדרכי מיתה על אחת כמה וכמה (ת"כ שם י; סנהדרין נה.). **(יז) חֶסֶד הוּא.** לשון ארמי חרפה חסודא. ומדרשו, אם

תאמר קין נשא את אחותו, חסד עשה המקום לבנות עולמו ממנו, שנא' עולם חסד יבנה (תהלים פט:ג; ת"כ שם יח; סנהדרין נח:): **(יח) הֶעֱרָה.** גלה, וכן כל לשון ערוה גלוי הוא, והו"ו יורדת בתיבה לשם דבר, כמו זעוה מגזרת (וְלֹא קָם) ולא זָע (אסתר ה:ט):

RASHI ELUCIDATED
---

you shall take possession worshiped their gods, upon the high mountains and upon the hills, and under every flourishing tree]."[1] וּמַה – See, now, that the matter is a *kal vachomer*.[2] הֲרֵי דְּבָרִים קַל וָחֹמֶר – אֵינָן שׁוֹמְעִין and do not hear, וְאֵינָן רוֹאִין – which do not see שֶׁאֵינָן רוֹאִין – Now, if trees אִילָנוֹת – because ruination came about through them תַּקָּלָה עַל יָדָם – the Torah has said, אָמְרָה תוֹרָה – destroy, burn, and obliterate them. הַשְׁחֵת שְׂרוֹף וְכַלֵּה – One who turns his fellow הַמַּטֶּה אֶת חֲבֵרוֹ – from the way of life מִדֶּרֶךְ חַיִּים – to ways of death, לְדַרְכֵי מִיתָה – how much more so should he be destroyed.[3] עַל אַחַת כַּמָּה וְכַמָּה

17. חֶסֶד הוּא – IT IS A DISGRACE. לְשׁוֹן אֲרַמִּי – In the Aramaic language, "חֶרְפָּה"[4] – "disgrace" is חִסּוּדָא.[4] וּמִדְרָשׁוֹ – Its midrashic interpretation is: אִם תֹּאמַר – If you will say, קַיִן נָשָׂא אֶת אֲחוֹתוֹ – Cain married his sister, and thus argue that it is permitted to have relations with one's sister, I will refute you by saying that חֶסֶד עָשָׂה הַמָּקוֹם – the Omnipresent did kindness so as לִבְנוֹת עוֹלָמוֹ מִמֶּנּוּ – to build His world from [Cain], שֶׁנֶּאֱמַר – as it says, [5,6] "עוֹלָם חֶסֶד יִבָּנֶה" – "the world will be built through kindness."[5,6]

18. הֶעֱרָה – HE HAS BARED. גִּלָּה – This means exposed. וְכֵן כָּל לְשׁוֹן עֶרְוָה – Similarly, any word related to עֶרְוָה גִּלּוּי הוּא – connotes exposing. וְהַוָּי"ו יוֹרֶדֶת בַּתֵּבָה – And the ו descends into the word לְשֵׁם דָּבָר – to form a noun;[7] כְּמוֹ "זְוָעָה" – similarly, the noun זְוָעָה, "terror,"[8] מִגִּזְרַת "{וְלֹא קָם} וְלֹא זָע"[9] – which is of the same root as זָע in, "{and he did not rise,} nor did he tremble,"[9]

---

1. *Deuteronomy* 12:2.
2. For a definition of *kal vachomer* see note 8 on page 2 above.
3. *Toras Kohanim*, perek 11:6; *Sanhedrin* 55a.
4. See *Targum Onkelos* to *Genesis* 30:23 and 34:14. חֶסֶד usually means "kindness." But that does not fit our verse. Here it is understood in the Aramaic sense of the word, "disgrace."
5. *Psalms* 89:3.
6. *Toras Kohanim*, perek 11:11; *Sanhedrin* 58b. One cannot use Cain as a precedent for relations with a sister. His case was a "kindness" — a unique dispensation from God.
7. This is why the verb הֶעֱרָה has no ו, while the noun עֶרְוָה does.
8. As in *Deuteronomy* 28:25.
9. *Esther* 5:9. The verb זָע, like הֶעֱרָה, has no ו, while the noun זְוָעָה does.

bared the source of her blood; the two of them will be cut off from the midst of their people.

¹⁹ The nakedness of your mother's sister or your father's sister shall you not uncover, for that is baring one's own flesh; they shall bear their iniquity. ²⁰ And a man who will lie with his aunt will have uncovered the nakedness of his uncle; they shall bear their sin, they shall die childless. ²¹ A man who shall take

גִּלְּתָה אֶת־מְקוֹר דָּמֶיהָ וְנִכְרְתוּ שְׁנֵיהֶם מִקֶּרֶב עַמָּם: יט וְעֶרְוַת אֲחוֹת אִמְּךָ וַאֲחוֹת אָבִיךָ לֹא תְגַלֵּה כִּי אֶת־שְׁאֵרוֹ הֶעֱרָה עֲוֺנָם יִשָּׂאוּ: כ וְאִישׁ אֲשֶׁר יִשְׁכַּב אֶת־דֹּדָתוֹ עֶרְוַת דֹּדוֹ גִּלָּה חֶטְאָם יִשָּׂאוּ עֲרִירִים יָמֻתוּ: כא וְאִישׁ אֲשֶׁר יִקַּח

— אונקלוס —

תְגַלֵי יָת סוֹאֲבַת דְּמָהָא וְיִשְׁתֵּיצוּן תַּרְוֵיהוֹן מִגּוֹ עַמְּהוֹן: יט וְעֶרְיַת אֲחַת אִמָּךְ וַאֲחַת אֲבוּךְ לָא תְגַלֵי אֲרֵי יָת קָרִיבֵהּ גַּלִי חוֹבְהוֹן יְקַבְּלוּן: כ וּגְבַר דִּי יִשְׁכּוּב יָת אִתַּת אַח אֲבוּהִי עֶרְיַת אַח אֲבוּהִי גַּלִי חוֹבְהוֹן יְקַבְּלוּן בְּלָא וְלָד יְמוּתוּן: כא וּגְבַר דִּי יִסַּב

— רש"י —

(כ) אֲשֶׁר יִשְׁכַּב אֶת דֹּדָתוֹ. הַמִּקְרָא הַזֶּה בָּא לְלַמֵּד עַל כָּרֵת הָאָמוּר לְמַעְלָה שֶׁהוּא בַּעֹנֶשׁ הֲלִיכַת עֲרִירִי: עֲרִירִים. כְּתַרְגּוּמוֹ, בְּלָא וָלָד. וְדוֹמֶה לוֹ וְאָנֹכִי הוֹלֵךְ עֲרִירִי (בראשית טו:ב); יֵשׁ לוֹ בָּנִים קוֹבְרָן, אֵין לוֹ בָּנִים מֵת בְּלֹא

אָבִיו לֹא הוּזְהַר אֶלָּא עַל אֵשֶׁת אֲחִי אָבִיו מִן הָאָב. וְכֵן אָחוֹת מְגֻזֶּרֶת אַחַת. וְהַטְרָאָה זוֹ נֶחְלְקוּ בָהּ רַבּוֹתֵינוּ, יֵשׁ אוֹמְרִים זוֹ נְשִׁיקַת שַׁמָּשׁ וְיֵשׁ אוֹמְרִים זוֹ הַכְנָסַת עֲטָרָה (יבמות נה:). שָׁנָה הַכָּתוּב בְּאַזְהָרָתָן לוֹמַר שֶׁהֻזְהַר עֲלֵיהֶן בֵּין עַל אֲחוֹת אָבִיו וְאִמּוֹ מִן הָאָב בֵּין עַל אֲחִיּוֹתֵיהֶן מִן הָאֵם, אֲבָל עַל עֶרְוַת אֵשֶׁת אֲחִי

— RASHI ELUCIDATED —

וְכֵן אַחֲוָה – similarly, the noun אַחֲוָה, **"brotherhood,"**[1] מִגְּזֵרַת אָח – is related to אָח, **"brother."** 19. וְעֶרְוַת אֲחוֹת אִמֵּךְ – THE NAKEDNESS OF YOUR MOTHER'S SISTER. וְהַעְרָאָה זוֹ נֶחְלְקוּ בָהּ רַבּוֹתֵינוּ – Our Rabbis have disagreed about the definition of **this "baring"** mentioned in our verse. יֵשׁ אוֹמְרִים – **There are those who say** זוֹ נְשִׁיקַת שַׁמָּשׁ – **this is mere contact with the male organ,** וְיֵשׁ אוֹמְרִים – **and there are those who say** זוֹ הַכְנָסַת עֲטָרָה[2] – **this is insertion of the tip of the male organ.**[2]

19. וְעֶרְוַת אֲחוֹת אִמֵּךְ – THE NAKEDNESS OF YOUR MOTHER'S SISTER. שָׁנָה הַכָּתוּב בְּאַזְהָרָתָן – Scripture repeated the negative commandment of [having relations with a mother's sister or a father's sister][3] לוֹמַר – **to say** שֶׁהֻזְהַר עֲלֵיהֶן – **that one has been given a prohibition against them** בֵּין עַל אֲחוֹת אָבִיו וְאִמּוֹ מִן הָאָב – **both against the paternal sister of his father or his mother** בֵּין אַחְיוֹתֵיהֶן מִן הָאֵם – **as well as against their maternal sisters.** אֲבָל עַל עֶרְוַת אֵשֶׁת אֲחִי אָבִיו – **But regarding the nakedness of the wife of a father's brother,** לֹא הֻזְהַר אֶלָּא עַל אֵשֶׁת אֲחִי אָבִיו מִן הָאָב[4] – **one has been given a prohibition only regarding the wife of his father's paternal brother.**[4]

20. אֲשֶׁר יִשְׁכַּב אֶת דֹּדָתוֹ – WHO WILL LIE WITH HIS AUNT. הַמִּקְרָא הַזֶּה בָּא לְלַמֵּד עַל כָּרֵת – **This verse comes to teach** us about "cutting off" הָאָמוּר לְמַעְלָה – **which was stated above**[5] שֶׁהוּא בָעֹנֶשׁ הֲלִיכַת עֲרִירִי – **that it is in the punishment of going childless.**[6]

עֲרִירִים – CHILDLESS. כְּתַרְגּוּמוֹ – This word is to be understood as Targum Onkelos renders it, בְּלָא וְלָד – **"without child."** וְדוֹמֶה לוֹ – **Similar to it** is עֲרִירִי in the verse, וְאָנֹכִי הוֹלֵךְ עֲרִירִי[7] – **"and I go childless."**[7]

יֵשׁ לוֹ בָּנִים – If **he has children** at the time that he commits the sin for which he is "cut off," קוֹבְרָן – **he buries them** in his lifetime. אֵין לוֹ בָּנִים – **If he has no children,** מֵת בְּלֹא

---

1. As in *Zechariah* 11:14.
2. *Yevamos* 55b.
3. Our chapter lists the punishments for the relationships for which negative commandments were given in Chapter 18 above. A mother's sister and a father's sister are the only relationships for which a negative commandment was stated there (vv. 12,13) and is repeated in this chapter. The negative commandments were given above 18:12,13.
4. *Yevamos* 54b.

5. Verse 18:29 above reads, "For if anyone commits any of these abominations [the forbidden relationships mentioned earlier in the chapter], the people doing so will be *cut off* from among their people."
6. The punishment of "cutting off (*kares*)" includes dying before one's time (see Rashi to 17:9 above). Without our verse, we would have thought that those who sinned would be "cut off," but that the punishment would not affect their children (*Gur Aryeh*).
7. *Genesis* 15:2.

אֶת־אֵשֶׁת אָחִיו נִדָּה הִוא עֶרְוַת אָחִיו גִּלָּה עֲרִירִים יִהְיוּ: וּשְׁמַרְתֶּם אֶת־כָּל־חֻקֹּתַי וְאֶת־כָּל־מִשְׁפָּטַי וַעֲשִׂיתֶם אֹתָם וְלֹא־תָקִיא אֶתְכֶם הָאָרֶץ אֲשֶׁר אֲנִי מֵבִיא אֶתְכֶם שָׁמָּה לָשֶׁבֶת בָּהּ: שביעי וְלֹא תֵלְכוּ בְּחֻקֹּת הַגּוֹי אֲשֶׁר־אֲנִי מְשַׁלֵּחַ מִפְּנֵיכֶם כִּי אֶת־כָּל־אֵלֶּה עָשׂוּ וָאָקֻץ בָּם: וָאֹמַר

his brother's wife, it is proscribed; he will have uncovered his brother's nakedness, they shall be childless. **22** *You shall observe all My decrees and all My ordinances and perform them; then the Land to which I bring you to dwell will not disgorge you.* **23** *Do not follow the traditions of the nation that I expel from before you, for they did all of these and I was disgusted with them.* **24** *So I said*

---- אונקלוס ----

יָת אִתַּת אֲחוּהִי מְרַחֲקָא הִיא עֶרְיְתָא דַּאֲחוּהִי גַּלִי בְּלָא וְלָד יְהוֹן: כבוְתִטְּרוּן יָת כָּל קְיָמַי וְיָת כָּל דִּינַי וְתַעְבְּדוּן יָתְהוֹן וְלָא תְרוֹקֵן יָתְכוֹן אַרְעָא דִּי אֲנָא מָעֵל יָתְכוֹן תַּמָּן לְמִתַּב בַּהּ: כגוְלָא תְהָכוּן בְּנִימוּסֵי עַמְמַיָּא דִּי אֲנָא מַגְלֵי מִן קֳדָמֵיכוֹן אֲרֵי יָת כָּל אִלֵּין עֲבָדוּ וְרָחֵיק מֵימְרִי בְּהוֹן: כדוַאֲמָרִית

---- רש"י ----

בָּנִים (ת"כ פרק יב:ז) לכך שנה בשני מקראות אלו, עֲרִירִים יָמוּתוּ, עֲרִירִים יִהְיוּ. עֲרִירִים יָמוּתוּ, אִם יִהְיוּ לוֹ בִּשְׁעַת עֲבֵירָה לֹא יִהְיוּ לוֹ כְּשֶׁיָּמוּת, לְפִי שֶׁקּוֹבְרָן בְּחַיָּיו. עֲרִירִים יִהְיוּ, שֶׁאִם אֵין לוֹ בִּשְׁעַת עֲבֵירָה יִהְיֶה [כָּל יָמָיו] כְּמוֹ שֶׁהוּא עַכְשָׁיו (ע' יבמות נה.): (כא) **נִדָּה הִוא.** הַשְּׁכִיבָה הַזֹּאת מְנֻדָּה הִיא וּמְאוּסָה. וְרַבּוֹתֵינוּ דָּרְשׁוּ לֶאֱסוֹר הָעֲרָאָה בָּהּ כְּנִדָּה, שֶׁהָעֲרָאָה מְפֹרֶשֶׁת בָּהּ, אֶת מְקוֹרָהּ הֶעֱרָה (לְעֵיל פָּסוּק יח; יבמות נד.): **וָאָקֻץ.** לְשׁוֹן מִיאוּס, כְּמוֹ קַצְתִּי בְחַיַּי (בראשית כז:מו) כְּאָדָם שֶׁהוּא קָץ בִּמְזוֹנוֹ (ת"כ פרק ט:ד):

---- RASHI ELUCIDATED ----

בָּנִים — **he dies without children.**[1] לְכָךְ שָׁנָה — **This is why [the Torah] repeated the word** עֲרִירִי בִּשְׁנֵי מִקְרָאוֹת אֵלּוּ — **in these two verses,** our verse and the one which follows, "עֲרִירִים יָמוּתוּ," — **"they shall die childless,"** and, "עֲרִירִים יִהְיוּ" — **"they shall be childless,"** so that they should be interpreted as follows: "עֲרִירִים יָמוּתוּ" — **"They shall die childless"** implies אִם יִהְיוּ לוֹ — **that if he will have** children בִּשְׁעַת עֲבֵירָה — **at the time of the sin,** לֹא יִהְיוּ לוֹ — **he will not have** them כְּשֶׁיָּמוּת — **when he dies,** לְפִי שֶׁקּוֹבְרָן בְּחַיָּיו — **because he buries them in his lifetime.** The next verse, "עֲרִירִים יִהְיוּ" — **"they shall be childless,"** implies שֶׁאִם אֵין לוֹ — **that if he does not have** children בִּשְׁעַת עֲבֵירָה — **at the time of the sin,** יִהְיֶה — **he will be** {כָּל יָמָיו — **all his days**}[2] כְּמוֹ שֶׁהוּא עַכְשָׁיו — **as he is now,** childless.[2]

21. נִדָּה הִוא — **IT IS PROSCRIBED.** הַשְּׁכִיבָה הַזֹּאת — **This lying** מְנֻדָּה הִיא — **is put under ban** וּמְאוּסָה — **and is repulsive.**[3] וְרַבּוֹתֵינוּ דָּרְשׁוּ — **Our Rabbis interpreted** the verse's use of נִדָּה which can also mean "a woman impure due to menstruation" לֶאֱסוֹר הָעֲרָאָה בָּהּ — **to forbid "baring"**[4] **with regard to [a brother's wife]** כְּנִדָּה — **as** the Torah did with regard to **a woman impure due to menstruation** שֶׁהָעֲרָאָה מְפֹרֶשֶׁת בָּהּ — **about whom "baring" has been stated explicitly,** "אֶת מְקוֹרָהּ הֶעֱרָה" — **"he has bared her source."**[5,6]

23. וָאָקֻץ — **AND I WAS DISGUSTED.** {לְשׁוֹן מֵאוּס — **This means repulsion,**} כְּמוֹ "קַצְתִּי בְחַיַּי"[7] — **like** קַצְתִּי in, **"I am disgusted with my life";**[7] [8]כְּאָדָם שֶׁהוּא קָץ בִּמְזוֹנוֹ — **like a person who is nauseated by his food.**[8]

---

1. *Toras Kohanim, perek* 12:7.
2. Cf. *Yevamos* 55a.
3. נִדָּה is commonly used for "a woman impure due to menstruation" (see, for example, *Ezekiel* 18:6; related words with this meaning appear above 12:2,5, 15:19-20,24-26,33). Our verse could have been understood as, "She is a woman impure due to menstruation." This would have implied either that one's brothers' wives are to be considered to him as if they were impure due to menstruation, or that a brother's wife is forbidden only when she is impure due to menstruation, both erroneous conclusions. Rashi explains that נִדָּה here does not mean a woman impure due to menstruation, but rather, "put under ban and repulsive." According to this, the feminine pronoun הִוא of our verse does not mean "she," but rather, "it," and refers to "this lying" — forbidden relations with a brother's wife.
4. See v. 18 above and Rashi there.
5. Above v. 18.
6. *Yevamos* 54a.
7. *Genesis* 27:46.
8. *Toras Kohanim, perek* 9:4. Rashi adds this seemingly superfluous phrase to link our verse with the preceding one. God's "nausea," so to speak, leads to the Land of

to you: You shall inherit their land, and I will give it to you to inherit it, a land flowing with milk and honey — I am HASHEM, your God, Who has separated you from the peoples. **25** You shall distinguish between the pure animal and the impure, and between the pure bird and the impure; and you shall not render your souls abominable through such animals and birds, and through anything that creeps on the ground, which I have set apart for you to render impure. **26** You shall be holy for Me, for I HASHEM am holy; and I have separated you from among the peoples to be Mine.

לָכֶ֗ם אַתֶּם֙ תִּֽירְשׁ֣וּ אֶת־אַדְמָתָ֔ם וַאֲנִ֞י אֶתְּנֶ֤נָּה לָכֶם֙ לָרֶ֣שֶׁת אֹתָ֔הּ אֶ֛רֶץ זָבַ֥ת חָלָ֖ב וּדְבָ֑שׁ אֲנִי֙ יהוה אֱלֹ֣הֵיכֶ֔ם אֲשֶׁר־הִבְדַּ֥לְתִּי אֶתְכֶ֖ם מִן־הָֽעַמִּֽים: כה מפטיר וְהִבְדַּלְתֶּ֞ם בֵּֽין־הַבְּהֵמָ֤ה הַטְּהֹרָה֙ לַטְּמֵאָ֔ה וּבֵֽין־הָע֥וֹף הַטָּמֵ֖א לַטָּהֹ֑ר וְלֹֽא־תְשַׁקְּצ֨וּ אֶת־נַפְשֹֽׁתֵיכֶ֜ם בַּבְּהֵמָ֣ה וּבָע֗וֹף וּבְכֹל֙ אֲשֶׁ֣ר תִּרְמֹ֣שׂ הָֽאֲדָמָ֔ה אֲשֶׁר־הִבְדַּ֥לְתִּי לָכֶ֖ם לְטַמֵּֽא: כו וִהְיִ֤יתֶם לִי֙ קְדֹשִׁ֔ים כִּ֥י קָד֖וֹשׁ אֲנִ֣י יהוה וָאַבְדִּ֥ל אֶתְכֶ֛ם מִן־הָֽעַמִּ֖ים לִֽהְי֥וֹת לִֽי:

— אונקלוס —

לְכוֹן אַתּוּן תֵּירְתוּן יָת אַרְעֲהוֹן וַאֲנָא אֶתְּנִנַּהּ לְכוֹן לְמֵירַת יָתָהּ אַרְעָא עָבְדָא חֲלָב וּדְבָשׁ יְיָ אֱלָהֲכוֹן דִּי אַפְרֵשִׁית יָתְכוֹן מִן עַמְמַיָּא: כהוְתַפְרְשׁוּן בֵּין בְּעִירָא דַכְיָא לִמְסָאֲבָא וּבֵין עוֹפָא מְסָאֲבָא לְדָכֵי וְלָא תְשַׁקְּצוּן יָת נַפְשָׁתֵיכוֹן בִּבְעִירָא וּבְעוֹפָא וּבְכֹל דִּי תַרְחֵשׁ אַרְעָא דִּי אַפְרֵשִׁית לְכוֹן לְסָאָבָא: כווּתְהוֹן קֳדָמַי קַדִּישִׁין אֲרֵי קַדִּישׁ אֲנָא יְיָ וְאַפְרֵשׁ יָתְכוֹן מִן עַמְמַיָּא לְמֶהֱוֵי פָלְחִין קֳדָמַי:

— רש"י —

(כה) והבדלתם בין הבהמה הטהורה לטמאה. אֵין צָרִיךְ לוֹמַר בֵּין פָּרָה לַחֲמוֹר, שֶׁהֲרֵי מֻבְדָּלִין וְנִכָּרִין הֵם, אֶלָּא בֵּין טְהוֹרָה לְךָ לִטְמֵאָה לָךְ, בֵּין שֶׁנִּשְׁחַט רֻבּוֹ שֶׁל סִימָן לְנִשְׁחַט חֶצְיוֹ. וְכַמָּה בֵּין רֻבּוֹ לְחֶצְיוֹ, מְלֹא שַׂעֲרָה (שם ז'): **אשר הבדלתי לכם לטמא.** לֶאֱסוֹר (שם ח'): **(כו) ואבדל אתכם מן העמים להיות לי.** אִם אַתֶּם מֻבְדָּלִים מֵהֶם הֲרֵי אַתֶּם שֶׁלִּי,

— RASHI ELUCIDATED —

25. וְהִבְדַּלְתֶּם בֵּין הַבְּהֵמָה הַטְּהֹרָה לַטְּמֵאָה — YOU SHALL DISTINGUISH BETWEEN THE PURE ANIMAL AND THE IMPURE. אֵין צָרִיךְ לוֹמַר — [The Torah] does not need to say that one must be able to distinguish בֵּין — פָּרָה לַחֲמוֹר — between a cow and a donkey, שֶׁהֲרֵי מֻבְדָּלִין וְנִכָּרִין הֵם — for they are distinct and obvious.[1] אֶלָּא — Rather, the Torah demands that you be expert in distinguishing בֵּין טְהוֹרָה לְךָ — between that which is pure to *you,* לִטְמֵאָה לָךְ — and that which is impure to *you*;[2] that is, בֵּין שֶׁנִּשְׁחַט רֻבּוֹ שֶׁל סִימָן — between one which has the greater part of a sign[3] slaughtered, i.e., severed by slaughtering, לְנִשְׁחַט חֶצְיוֹ — and one which has half of it slaughtered. וְכַמָּה — And how much is the difference בֵּין רֻבּוֹ — between the greater part of it לְחֶצְיוֹ — and half of it?[4] מְלֹא שַׂעֲרָה — A hairsbreadth.[4]

□ אֲשֶׁר הִבְדַּלְתִּי לָכֶם לְטַמֵּא — WHICH I HAVE SET APART FOR YOU TO RENDER IMPURE, that is, לֶאֱסוֹר[5] — to prohibit.[5]

26. וָאַבְדִּל אֶתְכֶם מִן הָעַמִּים לִהְיוֹת לִי — AND I HAVE SEPARATED YOU FROM AMONG THE PEOPLES TO BE MINE. אִם אַתֶּם מֻבְדָּלִים מֵהֶם — If you are separated from [the other peoples], הֲרֵי אַתֶּם שֶׁלִּי — see, then, you

Israel "vomiting out" sinful inhabitants like a person who is nauseated by his food (see *Lifshuto shel Rashi*; see also Rashi to *Exodus* 1:12, where he gives an alternative interpretation for a similar phrase).

1. Distinguishing between a cow and a donkey demands no expertise for the differences between them are obvious — a cow chews its cud and has split hooves, while a donkey does not.

2. One whose purity or impurity is dependent upon an act of yours (*Mizrachi; Sifsei Chachamim*).

3. The "signs" are the organs that must be severed by the act of slaughtering, the trachea and the esophagus.

4. *Toras Kohanim, perek* 9:7. Rashi cited an identical interpretation by *Toras Kohanim* above 11:47. The two verses are not redundant, however. Our verse teaches us that most of both signs must be slaughtered to render the animal permissible to be eaten. The above verse, which appears in the context of the laws of ritual impurity, teaches us that the same standard applies to the impurity of the carcass of an unslaughtered animal; if one of the signs was only half severed, the impurity of a carcass applies because the animal has died unslaughtered (*Maskil LeDavid*).

5. *Toras Kohanim, perek* 9:8. As mentioned above, our verse does not deal with ritual impurity, but rather with the prohibition against eating animals that have not been slaughtered properly (*Mizrachi; Gur Aryeh*).

27 Any man or woman in whom there shall be the necromancy of Ov or of Yid'oni, they shall be put to death; they shall pelt them with stones, their blood is upon them.

כז וְאִישׁ אוֹ־אִשָּׁה כִּי־יִהְיֶה בָהֶם אוֹב אוֹ יִדְּעֹנִי מוֹת יוּמָתוּ בָּאֶבֶן יִרְגְּמוּ אֹתָם דְּמֵיהֶם בָּם: פ פ פ

THE HAFTARAH FOR KEDOSHIM APPEARS ON PAGE 398.
When Acharei and Kedoshim are read together, the Haftarah for Acharei, page 397, is read.
When Rosh Chodesh Iyar coincides with Kedoshim, the regular Maftir and Haftarah are replaced with the readings for Shabbas Rosh Chodesh, page 405.

— אונקלוס —

כז וּגְבַר אוֹ אִתְּתָא אֲרֵי יְהֵי בְהוֹן בִּדִּין אוֹ דְכוּרוּ אִתְקְטָלָא יִתְקַטְלוּן בְּאַבְנָא יִרְגְּמוּן יָתְהוֹן קְטָלָא חַיָּבִין:

— רש"י —

ואם לאו הרי אתם של נבוכדנצר וחביריו. רבי אלעזר בן עזריה אומר, מנין שלא יאמר אדם נפשי קצה בבשר חזיר, אי אפשי ללבוש כלאים, אבל יאמר אפשי, ומה אעשה ואבי שבשמים וגזר עלי, ת"ל ואבדיל אתכם מן העמים להיות לי, שתהא הבדלתכם מהם לשמי. פורש מן העבירה ומקבל עליו עול מלכות שמים (שם י): (בז) כי יהיה בהם אוב וגו'. כאן נאמר בהם מיתה ולמעלה (פסוק ו) כרת. עדים והתראה בסקילה, מזיד בלא התראה בהכרת, ושגגתם חטאת. וכן בכל חייבי מיתות שנאמר בהם כרת:

— RASHI ELUCIDATED —

are Mine. וְאִם לָאו — But if not, הֲרֵי אַתֶּם שֶׁל נְבוּכַדְנֶצַּר וַחֲבֵרָיו — see, then, you belong to Nebuchadnezzar and his colleagues.

רַבִּי אֶלְעָזָר בֶּן עֲזַרְיָה אוֹמֵר — The *Tanna* R' Elazar ben Azaryah says: מִנַּיִן — From where do we know שֶׁלֹּא יֹאמַר אָדָם — that a person should not say, נַפְשִׁי קָצָה בִּבְשַׂר חֲזִיר — "I am nauseated by pork," or, אִי אֶפְשִׁי לִלְבּוֹשׁ כִּלְאַיִם — "I do not wish to wear clothes made of a mixture of wool and linen," אֲבָל יֹאמַר — but rather, he should say, אֶפְשִׁי — "I wish to eat pork and wear the forbidden mixture, וּמָה אֶעֱשֶׂה — but what can I do? וְאָבִי שֶׁבַּשָּׁמַיִם גָּזַר עָלַי — My Father Who is in Heaven has decreed upon me not to"? תַּלְמוּד לוֹמַר — To provide this source, the verse says, "וָאַבְדִּל אֶתְכֶם מִן הָעַמִּים — ...and I have separated you from among the peoples לִהְיוֹת לִי — to be Mine"; that is, שֶׁתְּהֵא — הַבְדָּלַתְכֶם מֵהֶם — that your separation from them shall be לִשְׁמִי — for My sake. פּוֹרֵשׁ מִן הָעֲבֵרָה — He stays away from sin, וּמְקַבֵּל עָלָיו — and accepts upon himself[1] עוֹל מַלְכוּת שָׁמַיִם — the yoke of the Kingdom of Heaven.[1]

27. כִּי יִהְיֶה בָהֶם אוֹב וְגוֹמֵר — IN WHOM THERE SHALL BE [THE NECROMANCY OF] *OV*, ETC. כָּאן נֶאֱמַר בָּהֶם מִיתָה — Here the death penalty is stated with regard to them, וּלְמַעְלָה[2] כָּרֵת — and above[2] *kares* ("cutting off") was given as their punishment. This apparent contradiction can be resolved as follows: עֵדִים וְהַתְרָאָה — If there were witnesses to the sin and warning given to the sinner before he committed the sin, בִּסְקִילָה — he is punished by stoning as stated by our verse. מֵזִיד — If he sinned intentionally בְּלֹא הַתְרָאָה — but without warning, or without witnesses, בְּהִכָּרֵת — he is punished by being cut off. וְשִׁגְגָתָם חַטָּאת — Their unintentional violation is atoned for by a sin-offering. וְכֵן בְּכָל חַיָּבֵי מִיתוֹת — So, too, with all those who are subject to execution שֶׁנֶּאֱמַר בָּהֶם כָּרֵת — about whom *kares* is also stated.[3]

---

1. *Toras Kohanim, perek* 9:10. According to the first explanation, the verse says that Israel belongs to God, that is, is not subject to the domination of other nations, only if they separate themselves from the other nations. According to R' Elazar ben Azaryah, the verse says that the commandments that God gave us to distinguish us from other nations are to be fulfilled with intent "to be Mine" — as an expression of the subjugation of our will to God.
2. Above v. 6.
3. Execution by the court applies when there are witnesses and warning, *kares* applies in the absence of either, and a sin-offering applies for unintentional violation.

פרשת אמור
Parashas Emor

21

21. ¹ HASHEM said to Moses: Say to the Kohanim, the sons of Aaron, and you shall say to them: to a [dead] person he shall not become impure among his people;

וַיֹּאמֶר יהוה אֶל־מֹשֶׁה אֱמֹר אֶל־הַכֹּהֲנִים בְּנֵי אַהֲרֹן וְאָמַרְתָּ אֲלֵהֶם לְנֶפֶשׁ לֹא־יִטַּמָּא בְּעַמָּיו:

אונקלוס

א וַאֲמַר יְיָ לְמֹשֶׁה אֱמַר לְכָהֲנַיָּא בְּנֵי אַהֲרֹן וְתֵימַר לְהוֹן עַל מִית לָא יִסְתָּאַב בְּעַמֵּהּ:

רש"י

(א) **אמור אל הכהנים.** אמור ואמרת להזהיר גדולים על הקטנים (יבמות קיד.): **בני אהרן.** יכול חללים, תלמוד לומר הכהנים (ת"כ אמור פרשתא א:ח): **בני אהרן.** אף בעלי מומין במשמע (שם): **ולא בנות אהרן.** (שם; סוטה כג.; סוטה קידושין לה:): **לא יטמא בעמיו.** בעוד שהמת בתוך עמיו יצא מת מצוה (ת"כ שם ג:): (ב) **כי אם לשארו.** אין שארו אלא אשתו (שם ד):

RASHI ELUCIDATED

21.

1. אָמֹר אֶל הַכֹּהֲנִים — SAY TO THE KOHANIM. ״אֱמֹר״, ״וְאָמַרְתָּ״ — The Torah uses the redundant wording of **"say,"** followed by **"and you shall say"** לְהַזְהִיר גְּדוֹלִים — to enjoin adults ¹עַל הַקְּטַנִּים — with regard to minors.¹

□ בְּנֵי אַהֲרֹן — THE SONS OF AARON. יָכוֹל חֲלָלִים — **One might be able** to think that the prohibition to the Kohanim not to defile themselves through the dead applies also to ***chalalim***.² תַּלְמוּד לוֹמַר — To teach us otherwise, **the verse says:** ³״הַכֹּהֲנִים״ — **"the Kohanim."**³

□ בְּנֵי אַהֲרֹן — THE SONS OF AARON. ⁵אַף בַּעֲלֵי מוּמִין בְּמַשְׁמָע — **Those who are blemished,** and therefore may not perform the service,⁴ **are also implied.**⁵

□ בְּנֵי אַהֲרֹן — THE SONS OF AARON. ⁶וְלֹא בְּנוֹת אַהֲרֹן — **But not the daughters of Aaron.**⁶

□ לֹא יִטַּמָּא בְּעַמָּיו — HE SHALL NOT BECOME IMPURE AMONG HIS PEOPLE. בְּעוֹד שֶׁהַמֵּת בְּתוֹךְ עַמָּיו — While **the dead person is in the midst of his people.**⁷ ⁹יָצָא מֵת מִצְוָה — A ***mes mitzvah***⁸ has thus been excluded.⁹

2. כִּי אִם לִשְׁאֵרוֹ — EXCEPT FOR HIS RELATIVE. ¹⁰אֵין ״שְׁאֵרוֹ״ אֶלָּא אִשְׁתּוֹ — The term שְׁאֵרוֹ, **"his relative,"** in this verse **is none but his wife.**¹⁰

---

1. *Yevamos* 114a. "Say" indicates that adult Kohanim are forbidden to make themselves impure through the dead. "And you shall say" indicates that they are commanded to see to it that Kohanim who are minors not make themselves impure (*Minchas Yehudah; Sifsei Chachamim*; see Rashi to *Yevamos* 114a).
   The first "say" is addressed to Moses. The additional, "and you shall say to them," is the beginning of the words that Moses is to say to the Kohanim. Thus, the verse means: "[You, Moses,] say to the Kohanim ... 'And you [Kohanim] shall say to [your children] ... '" (*Mizrachi*).
2. *Chulalim* are children born from unions specifically forbidden to Kohanim (see v. 7), and the descendants of male children born from such unions. Although *chalalim* are disqualified from performing the Temple service, the phrase בְּנֵי אַהֲרֹן, "sons of Aaron," need not exclude them, for they, too, are descendants of Aaron.
3. *Toras Kohanim, parshasa* 1:1.
4. See vv. 16-23 below.
5. *Toras Kohanim, parshasa* 1:1. Had the Torah only written "the Kohanim," we would have said it implies only those Kohanim who are fit to perform the Temple service, for the word Kohanim comes from the word for "service" (see Rashi to *Exodus* 28:3). The apparently superfluous "the sons of Aaron" is written to include other "sons of Aaron," Kohanim who are blemished and may not perform the service, in the prohibition against becoming impure through contact with the dead (*Mizrachi*).
6. *Toras Kohanim, parshasa* 1:1; *Sotah* 23b; *Kiddushin* 35b. The daughters of Kohanim are not prohibited from becoming impure through contact with the dead.
7. The apparently superfluous "among his people" implies that the prohibition of our verse applies only to a dead person who has people to attend to his burial (*Mizrachi; Sifsei Chachamim*).
8. Literally, "a dead person of a commandment," a corpse whose burial is not being attended to. It is a *mitzvah* (the fulfillment of a commandment) to bury the corpse. A Kohen is not forbidden to become impure through caring for a *mes mitzvah*. On the contrary, he is obligated to do so.
9. *Toras Kohanim, parshasa* 1:3.
10. *Toras Kohanim, parshasa* 1:4; *Yevamos* 22b. The word שְׁאֵר usually means "flesh" or "relative." Its gender is masculine, which explains why it is modified by the masculine adjective הַקָּרֹב rather than the feminine form הַקְּרוֹבָה, as "his sister" is in the next verse.

² except for his relative who is closest to him, to his mother and to his father, to his son, to his daughter, and to his brother; ³ and to his virgin sister who is close to him, who has not been unto a man; for her he shall make himself impure. ⁴ A husband among his people shall not make himself impure to defile him.

ב כִּי אִם־לִשְׁאֵרוֹ הַקָּרֹב אֵלָיו לְאִמּוֹ וּלְאָבִיו וְלִבְנוֹ וּלְבִתּוֹ וּלְאָחִיו: ג וְלַאֲחֹתוֹ הַבְּתוּלָה הַקְּרוֹבָה אֵלָיו אֲשֶׁר לֹא־הָיְתָה לְאִישׁ לָהּ יִטַּמָּא: ד לֹא יִטַּמָּא בַּעַל בְּעַמָּיו לְהֵחַלּוֹ:

──── אונקלוס ────

ב אֶלָהֵן לְקָרִיבֵהּ דְּקָרִיב לֵהּ לְאִמֵּהּ וְלַאֲבוּהִי וְלִבְרֵהּ וְלִבְרַתֵּהּ וְלַאֲחוּהִי: ג וְלַאֲחָתֵהּ בְּתֻלְתָּא דְּקָרִיבָא לֵהּ דִּי לָא הֲוַת לִגְבַר לַהּ יִסְתָּאָב: ד לָא יִסְתָּאָב גַּבְרָא בְּעַמֵּהּ לְאַחֲלוּתֵהּ:

──── רש"י ────

(ג) הַקְּרוֹבָה. לְרַבּוֹת אֶת הָאֲרוּסָה (שם יב; יבמות ס.): אֲשֶׁר לֹא הָיְתָה לְאִישׁ. לְמִשְׁכָּב (ת"כ שם יא; יבמות שם): לָהּ יִטַּמָּא. מִצְוָה (שם יב; זבחים ק.): (ד) לֹא יִטַּמָּא בַּעַל בְּעַמָּיו לְהֵחַלּוֹ. לֹא יִטַּמָּא לְאִשְׁתּוֹ פְּסוּלָה שֶׁהוּא מְחַלֵּל בָּהּ בַּעֲבוֹדָתוֹ עִמּוֹ. וְכֵן פְּשׁוּטוֹ שֶׁל מִקְרָא, לֹא יִטַּמָּא בַּעַל בְּשֶׁאֵרוֹ בְּעוֹד שֶׁהִיא בְּתוֹךְ עַמָּיו שֶׁיֵּשׁ לָהּ קוֹבְרִין שֶׁאֵינָהּ מֵת מִצְוָה, וּבְאֵיזוֹ שְׁאֵר אָמַרְתִּי, בְּאוֹתוֹ שֶׁהוּא פְּסוּלָה לְהֵחַלּוֹ, לְהִתְחַלֵּל הוּא מִכְּהֻנָּתוֹ (ת"כ שם טו-טז):

──── RASHI ELUCIDATED ────

3. הַקְּרוֹבָה – **WHO IS CLOSE.** ¹לְרַבּוֹת אֶת הָאֲרוּסָה – **To include an** *arusah*.¹

□ אֲשֶׁר לֹא הָיְתָה לְאִישׁ – **WHO HAS NOT BEEN UNTO A MAN.** ²לְמִשְׁכָּב – **For relations.**²

□ לָהּ יִטַּמָּא – **FOR HER HE SHALL MAKE HIMSELF IMPURE.** ³מִצְוָה – **It is an obligation.**³

4. לֹא יִטַּמָּא בַּעַל בְּעַמָּיו לְהֵחַלּוֹ – **A HUSBAND AMONG HIS PEOPLE SHALL NOT MAKE HIMSELF IMPURE TO DEFILE HIM.** לֹא יִטַּמָּא – He shall not make himself impure לְאִשְׁתּוֹ פְּסוּלָה – for his unfitting wife שֶׁהוּא מְחַלֵּל בָּהּ – through whom he is defiled בַּעֲבוֹדָה עִמּוֹ – while she is with him as his wife.⁴ וְכֵן – A פְּשׁוּטוֹ שֶׁל מִקְרָא – Accordingly, **the simple meaning of the verse is as follows:** לֹא יִטַּמָּא בַּעַל – A husband shall not make himself impure בִּשְׁאֵרוֹ – through his wife⁵ בְּעוֹד שֶׁהִיא בְּתוֹךְ עַמָּיו – as long as she is "among his people," that is, שֶׁיֵּשׁ לָהּ קוֹבְרִין – that there are those who can bury her other than her husband, שֶׁאֵינָהּ מֵת מִצְוָה – that she is not a *mes mitzvah*.⁶ וּבְאֵיזוֹ שְׁאֵר אָמַרְתִּי – And of which wife have I said [that the husband may not make himself impure]? בְּאוֹתוֹ שֶׁהוּא – Of the one who is "לְהֵחַלּוֹ„ – "to defile him"; that is, ⁷לְהִתְחַלֵּל הוּא מִכְּהֻנָּתוֹ – to make him defiled of his *kehunah*.⁷

1. *Toras Kohanim*, *parshasa* 1:12; *Yevamos* 60a. An *arusah* is a woman who has undergone אֵרוּסִין, *eirusin* (also called קִדּוּשִׁין, *kiddushin*), the first stage of marriage, which is usually transacted by the groom giving the bride a ring, or some other object of value. At this stage, she is a married woman insofar as being forbidden to other men, but remains in her father's house, and does not yet live with her husband. The second stage of marriage is נִשּׂוּאִין, *nisuin*, at which time she moves into her husband's domain and is considered married in all respects. In contemporary practice *nisuin* follows immediately after *kiddushin*.

The apparently superfluous "who is close to him" teaches us that although the end of the verse eliminates a married sister from those for whom a Kohen may make himself impure, he may make himself impure for a married, yet virgin, sister "who is close to him," i.e., who has not yet left the family home (*Be'er BaSadeh*).

2. *Toras Kohanim*, *parshasa* 1:11; *Yevamos* 60a. The verb הָיְתָה can denote *eirusin*; see, for example, *Deuteronomy* 24:2. Here, however, it does not mean that, for the preceding phrase has allowed a Kohen to become impure for a sister who is an *arusah*. "Who has not yet been unto a man" of our verse therefore connotes a woman who has not yet had relations (*Mizrachi*;

Sifsei Chachamim; see Rashi to *Yevamos* 60a).

3. *Toras Kohanim*, *parshasa* 1:12; *Zevachim* 100a. If he refuses to allow himself to become impure, *beis din* (the court) may force him to do so (*Toras Kohanim*).

לָהּ יִטַּמָּא of our verse could have been understood as, "for her he *may* make himself impure." Verse 2, however, has already granted that permission by stating that the prohibition against a Kohen making himself impure through the dead applies "except for" the relatives whom that verse and ours go on to mention. לָהּ יִטַּמָּא is therefore understood as an obligation; a Kohen must make himself impure by engaging in the burial of those relatives listed (*Mizrachi*; *Sifsei Chachamim*).

4. If a Kohen marries a woman forbidden to him, he is defiled and is prohibited from performing the *avodah* (Temple service) until he divorces her or takes a non-nullifiable oath that he will never again have relations with her (see *Berachos* 45b). A Kohen may not make himself impure for such a wife.

5. See v. 2 above and Rashi there.

6. See note 8 on page 262.

7. *Toras Kohanim*, *parshasa* 1:15-16. Although the offspring of this union do not have the status of Kohanim, the Kohen himself is defiled of his *kehunah* only while

5 They shall not make a bald spot on their heads, and they shall not shave the edge of their beard; and in their flesh

ה לֹא־יִקְרְח֤וּ קָרְחָה֙ בְּרֹאשָׁ֔ם וּפְאַ֥ת זְקָנָ֖ם לֹ֣א יְגַלֵּ֑חוּ וּבִבְשָׂרָ֕ם

°יִקְרְחוּ ק׳

אונקלוס

ה לָא יִמְרְטוּן מְרַט בְּרֵישְׁהוֹן וּפָאתָא דְדִקְנְהוֹן לָא יְגַלְּחוּן וּבְבִשְׂרְהוֹן

רש"י

(ה) לא יקרחו קרחה וגו׳. עַל מֵת. וַהֲלֹא אַף יִשְׂרָאֵל הֻזְהֲרוּ עַל כָּךְ, אֶלָּא לְפִי שֶׁנֶּאֱמַר בְּיִשְׂרָאֵל בֵּין עֵינֵיכֶם (דברים י״ד:א׳) יָכוֹל לֹא יְהֵא חַיָּב עַל כָּל הָרֹאשׁ, ת״ל בְּרֹאשָׁם. וְיִלָּמְדוּ יִשְׂרָאֵל מִכֹּהֲנִים בִּגְזֵרָה שָׁוָה, נֶאֱמַר כָּאן קָרְחָה וְנֶאֱמַר לְהַלָּן בְּיִשְׂרָאֵל קָרְחָה (שם) מַה כָּאן כָּל הָרֹאשׁ אַף לְהַלָּן כָּל הָרֹאשׁ בְּמַשְׁמַע, כָּל מָקוֹם שֶׁיִּקְרַח בָּרֹאשׁ, וּמַה לְהַלָּן עַל מֵת אַף כָּאן עַל מֵת (ת״כ פרק א:ב-ג; מכות כ.; קידושין לו.): **ופאת זקנם לא יגלחו.** לְפִי שֶׁנֶּאֱמַר בְּיִשְׂרָאֵל וְלֹא תַשְׁחִית (לעיל יט:כז) יָכוֹל לִקְטוֹ בְמַלְקֵט וּרְהִיטָנִי

RASHI ELUCIDATED

5. לֹא יִקְרְחוּ קָרְחָה וְגוֹמֵר — **THEY SHALL NOT MAKE A BALD SPOT, ETC.,** עַל מֵת — as a sign of mourning over a dead person. וַהֲלֹא אַף יִשְׂרָאֵל הֻזְהֲרוּ עַל כָּךְ — **But were not non-Kohanim** (literally, Israelites) **also enjoined regarding this?**[1] אֶלָּא — **But,** the commandment is repeated לְפִי שֶׁנֶּאֱמַר בְּיִשְׂרָאֵל — **because it says in** the commandment addressed to **non-Kohanim,** ״בֵּין עֵינֵיכֶם״,[1] — "**You shall not put a bald spot between your eyes.**"[1] יָכוֹל — **One might be able** to think on the basis of that verse alone that לֹא יְהֵא חַיָּב עַל כָּל הָרֹאשׁ — **he would not be liable for** making a bald spot **anywhere** else **on the head,** for that verse says specifically, "between your eyes." תַּלְמוּד לוֹמַר — **To teach us otherwise, the verse says** here, ״בְּרֹאשָׁם״, — "**on their heads.**" וְיִלָּמְדוּ יִשְׂרָאֵל מִכֹּהֲנִים — **And let** the law of non-Kohanim stated in *Deuteronomy* without mention of the entire head **be derived from** the law of Kohanim בִּגְזֵרָה שָׁוָה — **by a** *gezeirah shavah*,[2] as follows: נֶאֱמַר כָּאן ״קָרְחָה״ — the word קָרְחָה, "**bald spot,**" **is stated here,** in the context of the commandment to the Kohanim, וְנֶאֱמַר לְהַלָּן בְּיִשְׂרָאֵל ״קָרְחָה״,[1] — **and** קָרְחָה **is stated below** in the context of the commandment to **non-Kohanim.**[1] מַה כָּאן כָּל הָרֹאשׁ — **Just as here** the prohibition applies **anywhere on the head,** אַף לְהַלָּן — **so, too, below,** in *Deuteronomy* כָּל הָרֹאשׁ בְּמַשְׁמַע — **anywhere on the head is meant,** כָּל מָקוֹם שֶׁיִּקְרַח בָּרֹאשׁ — wherever he may make a bald spot on the head. וּמַה לְהַלָּן — **And just as below** the verse states explicitly that the prohibition applies only when the bald spot is made עַל מֵת — **over a dead person,** אַף כָּאן — **so, too, here,** regarding the prohibition addressed to the Kohanim, it applies only עַל מֵת[3] — **over a dead person.**[3]

□וּפְאַת זְקָנָם לֹא יְגַלֵּחוּ — **AND THEY SHALL NOT SHAVE THE EDGE OF THEIR BEARD.** לְפִי שֶׁנֶּאֱמַר — **Since it says** בְּיִשְׂרָאֵל — **in** the prohibition against shaving the edge of the beard which was addressed to non-Kohanim, ״וְלֹא תַשְׁחִית״,[4] — "**and you shall not destroy,**"[4] יָכוֹל לִקְטוֹ — **one might be able** to think that **if he plucked [an edge of the beard] out** בְּמַלְקֵט וּרְהִיטָנִי — **with a** *malkeit* **or a** *rehitani*[5]

---

he still is married to his forbidden spouse. If she dies or if he divorces her [or even if he swears in court that they will no longer derive any benefit one from the other until after they are divorced (*Bechoros* 45b; *Gittin* 35b)], he regains his status of *kehunah*.

1. See *Deuteronomy* 14:1.
2. *Gezeirah shavah* is defined on p. 155, note 10.
3. *Toras Kohanim, perek* 1:2-3; *Makkos* 20a; *Kiddushin* 36a.
4. Above 19:27.
5. These are two implements used for smoothing the skin by removing the hair. Rashi (to *Kiddushin* 35b) describes the *malkeit* as "the sword sharpeners' *plaine* with which they smooth out the sword's sheath," and the *rehitani* as "the shield makers' *plaine*." Elsewhere, Rashi broadens his description of the *rehitani*: "A *plaine* with which they smooth the shields. They place the iron [blade] in a wooden form prepared for it and, when they have finished using it, they remove it"

(*Shabbos* 48b, s.v., איזמל של רהיטני); and, "A shield makers' *plaine* into which they place a blade between two boards made for that purpose . . ." (*Shabbos* 58b, s.v., ואיזמל של רהיטני). However, in his comments to *Shabbos* 97a (s.v., לפי שאי אפשר), Rashi describes the *malkeit* and *rehitani* as "*plaine* in Old French; they are two types of wooden utensils into which a sharp [piece of] iron is embedded, and they are used to even out the face of a plank and make it smooth." From these sources, it seems that Rashi identifies both the *malkeit* and *rehitani* as plane-like instruments used by various artisans in their work. Yet, it is difficult to imagine that the plane used by the carpenter on wood is the same plane used to smooth a leather sheath or shield.

Moreover, a plane would remove hair in the same way as a razor, except that a razor blade is held in the hand and the blade of a plane is held in a wooden form. Additionally, as *Sefer Zikaron* points out, Rashi's use of לקטו, "plucked," does not describe the action of a plane.

In truth, however, the Old French word *plaine*

they shall not scratch a scratch. ⁶ *They shall be holy to their God and they shall not desecrate the Name of their God; for the fire-offerings of H<small>ASHEM</small>, the food of their God, they offer, so they must remain holy.*

לֹ֥א יִשְׂרְט֖וּ שָׂרָ֑טֶת: ⁶ קְדֹשִׁ֤ים יִהְיוּ֙ לֵאלֹ֣הֵיהֶ֔ם וְלֹ֣א יְחַלְּל֔וּ שֵׁ֖ם אֱלֹהֵיהֶ֑ם כִּי֩ אֶת־אִשֵּׁ֨י יְהוָ֜ה לֶ֧חֶם אֱלֹהֵיהֶ֛ם הֵ֥ם מַקְרִיבִ֖ם וְהָ֥יוּ קֹֽדֶשׁ:

— אונקלוס —

לָא יְחַבְּלוּן חִבּוּל: ⁶ קַדִּישִׁין יְהוֹן קֳדָם אֱלָהֲהוֹן וְלָא יְחַלּוּן שְׁמָא דֶאֱלָהֲהוֹן אֲרֵי יָת קֻרְבָּנַיָּא דַיְיָ קֻרְבַּן אֱלָהֲהוֹן אִנּוּן מַקְרִיבִין וִיהוֹן קַדִּישִׁין:

— רש"י —

יהא חייב, לכך נאמר לא יגלחו, שאינו חייב אלא על דבר הקרוי גלוח ויש בו השחתה, וזהו תער (ת"כ קדושים פרק ו:ד; מכות כא.): **ובבשרם לא ישרטו שרטת.** לפי שנאמר בישראל ושרט לנפש לא תתנו (לעיל יט:כח) יכול שרט חמש שריטות

יהא חייב אלא אחת, ת"ל לא ישרטו שרטת, לחייב על כל שריטה ושריטה (ת"כ פרק א:ד; מכות כ:) שתיבה זו יתירה היא לדרוש, שהיה לו לכתוב לא ישרטו ואני יודע שהיא שרטת: (ו) **קדושים יהיו.** על כרחם יקדישום בית דין בכך (ת"כ שם ו):

— RASHI ELUCIDATED —

יְהֵא חַיָּב – *that he should be liable* for violation of this commandment.[1] **לְכָךְ נֶאֱמַר** – *This is why it says,* **"לֹא יְגַלֵּחוּ,"** – *"they shall not shave,"* to teach us that **שֶׁאֵינוֹ חַיָּב** – *he is not liable,* **אֶלָּא** – *but* **עַל דָּבָר** – *for a matter* **הַקָּרוּי גִּלּוּחַ** – *which is termed "shaving,"* **וְיֵשׁ בּוֹ הַשְׁחָתָה** – *and has in it destruction* of the hair. ²**וְזֶהוּ תַעַר** – *This is shaving with a razor.*²

□ **וּבִבְשָׂרָם לֹא יִשְׂרְטוּ שָׂרָטֶת** – AND IN THEIR FLESH THEY SHALL NOT SCRATCH A SCRATCH. **לְפִי שֶׁנֶּאֱמַר** **בְּיִשְׂרָאֵל** – *Since it says in* the commandment addressed to non-Kohanim, ³**"וְשֶׂרֶט לָנֶפֶשׁ לֹא תִתְּנוּ,"** *"You shall not make* [in your flesh] *a scratch over a soul,"*³ **יָכוֹל** – *one might be able* to think that **שָׂרַט חָמֵשׁ שְׂרִיטוֹת** – *if he made five scratches* for one dead person **לֹא יְהֵא חַיָּב אֶלָּא אַחַת** – *he would be liable for only one* sin. **תַּלְמוּד לוֹמַר** – To teach us otherwise, *the verse says,* **"לֹא יִשְׂרְטוּ שָׂרָטֶת,"** – *"they shall not scratch a scratch,"* ⁴**לְחַיֵּב עַל כָּל שְׂרִיטָה וּשְׂרִיטָה** – *to make one liable for each and every scratch,*⁴ **שֶׁתֵּיבָה זוֹ יְתֵרָה הִיא** – *for this word,* **שָׂרָטֶת**, *is superfluous,* **לִדְרוֹשׁ** – *and is meant for us to expound,* **שֶׁהָיָה לוֹ לִכְתּוֹב** – *for it should have written,* **"לֹא יִשְׂרְטוּ,"** – *"they shall not scratch,"*⁵ **וַאֲנִי יוֹדֵעַ** – *and I would know* **שֶׁהִיא שָׂרָטֶת** – *that* [what the verse refers to] *is a scratch.*

6. קְדֹשִׁים יִהְיוּ – THEY SHALL BE HOLY. **עַל כָּרְחָם** – *Against their will* **יַקְדִּישׁוּם בֵּית דִּין** – *the court shall sanctify them* ⁶**בְּכָךְ** – *in this matter.*⁶

does not refer exclusively to the modern "plane." That instrument is called *rabot* in both Modern and Old French, probably because of its rabbit-like (in some Old French dialects, *rabotte*) appearance. "*Plaine,*" on the other hand, was a generic term for any instrument used to smooth a surface. Thus, it may also be used to describe tweezers used to pluck hair or scissors used to cut hair from leather in order to smooth its surface.

According to *Sefer Zikaron, malkeit* means "tweezers" and *rehitani* means "small scissors" (but see the next two notes which contradict this definition of *rehitani*).

According to *Rambam (Makkos* 3:5) and *Meiri (Kiddushin* 35b), both these instruments are types of tweezers, which, if our analysis above is correct, may be Rashi's opinion also.

1. "Destroying" implies removing the hair near the roots. The *malkeit* and the *rehitani* remove hair in this manner, as does a razor, but scissors do not (Rashi in *Makkos* 21a).

2. *Toras Kohanim, Kedoshim, perek* 6:4; *Makkos* 21a. The *malkeit* and the *rehitani* meet the qualification of "destroying" but not of "shaving." Scissors meet the qualification of "shaving" but not of "destroying."

Only a razor meets both qualifications.

3. Above 19:28.

4. *Toras Kohanim, perek* 1:4; *Makkos* 20b.

5. Omitting the word שָׂרָטֶת would make יִשְׂרְטוּ the last word in the verse. In that position the vowelization would change to יִשְׂרְטוּ. The meaning, however, is the same for both vowelizations.

6. *Toras Kohanim, perek* 1:6. The holiness referred to is refraining from becoming impure through the dead *(Be'er BaSadeh).*

Our verse could have said, קְדֹשִׁים הֵם, "they *are* holy." "They *shall* be holy" implies that it is the responsibility of the community, represented by the court, to see to it that the Kohanim be holy (*Minchas Yehudah; Sifsei Chachamim*).

Alternatively, our verse refers to the Kohanim in the third person, in contrast to קְדֹשִׁים תִּהְיוּ, "you shall be holy," of 19:2 above, to teach us that the holiness of the Kohanim is a responsibility which is not theirs alone (*Malbim*).

Alternatively, above the Torah explains what is implied by קְדֹשִׁים תִּהְיוּ by going on to enumerate the commandments that express that holiness. Here, however, קְדֹשִׁים יִהְיוּ follows the commandment that expresses

7-8

אִשָּׁ֨ה זֹנָ֤ה וַחֲלָלָה֙ לֹ֣א יִקָּ֔חוּ וְאִשָּׁ֛ה גְּרוּשָׁ֥ה מֵאִישָׁ֖הּ לֹ֣א יִקָּ֑חוּ כִּֽי־קָדֹ֥שׁ ה֖וּא לֵֽאלֹהָֽיו: וְקִדַּשְׁתּ֔וֹ כִּֽי־אֶת־לֶ֥חֶם אֱלֹהֶ֖יךָ ה֣וּא מַקְרִ֑יב קָדֹשׁ֙ יִֽהְיֶה־לָּ֔ךְ כִּ֣י קָד֔וֹשׁ אֲנִ֥י יהו֖ה מְקַדִּשְׁכֶֽם:

7 They shall not marry a woman who is a zonah or a chalalah, and they shall not marry a woman who has been divorced by her husband; for each one is holy to his God. **8** You shall sanctify him, for he offers the food of your God; he shall be holy to you, for holy am I, Hashem, Who sanctifies you.

— אונקלוס —

ז אִתְּתָא מַטְעְיָא וּמְחַלְלָא לָא יִסְּבוּן וְאִתְּתָא דִּמְתָרְכָא מִבַּעְלַהּ לָא יִסְּבוּן אֲרֵי קַדִּישׁ הוּא קֳדָם אֱלָהֵהּ: ח וּתְקַדְּשִׁנֵּהּ אֲרֵי יָת קֻרְבַּן אֱלָהָךְ הוּא מְקָרֵב קַדִּישׁ יְהֵא לָךְ אֲרֵי קַדִּישׁ אֲנָא יְיָ מְקַדִּשְׁכוֹן:

— רש"י —

(ז) זונה. שֶׁנִּבְעֲלָה בְּעִילַת יִשְׂרָאֵל הָאָסוּר לָהּ, כְּגוֹן חַיָּבֵי כְרִיתוּת (שם ו; יבמות סא.) אוֹ נָתִין אוֹ מַמְזֵר: **חללה.** שֶׁנּוֹלְדָה מִן הַפְּסוּלִים שֶׁבַּכְּהוּנָה, כְּגוֹן בַּת אַלְמָנָה מִכֹּהֵן גָּדוֹל אוֹ בַת גְּרוּשָׁה [וַחֲלוּצָה] מִכֹּהֵן הֶדְיוֹט, וְכֵן שֶׁנִּתְחַלְּלָה מִן הַכְּהוּנָה עַל יְדֵי בִיאַת אֶחָד מִן הַפְּסוּלִים לַכְּהוּנָה: **(ח) וְקִדַּשְׁתּוֹ.** עַל כָּרְחוֹ, שֶׁאִם לֹא רָצָה לְגָרֵשׁ הַלְקֵהוּ וְיַסְּרֵהוּ עַד שֶׁיְּגָרֵשׁ (ת"כ שם יג; יבמות פח:): **קָדֹשׁ יִהְיֶה לָּךְ.** נְהוֹג בּוֹ קְדוּשָּׁה, לִפְתֹּחַ רִאשׁוֹן בְּכָל דָּבָר וּלְבָרֵךְ רִאשׁוֹן

RASHI ELUCIDATED

7. זֹנָה – *ZONAH.* הָאֲסוּרָה לָהּ – [A woman] who has had relations with a Jew – שֶׁנִּבְעֲלָה בְּעִילַת יִשְׂרָאֵל – who is forbidden to her;[1] כְּגוֹן – for example, חַיָּבֵי כְרִיתוֹת – those with whom relations carry the punishment of *kares*,[2] אוֹ נָתִין – or a *nasin*,[3] אוֹ מַמְזֵר – or a *mamzer*.[4,5]

□ חֲלָלָה – *A CHALALAH.* שֶׁנּוֹלְדָה מִן הַפְּסוּלִים שֶׁבַּכְּהֻנָּה – A woman who was born from those unions unfit for the *kehunah*, כְּגוֹן – for example, בַּת אַלְמָנָה מִכֹּהֵן גָּדוֹל – the daughter of a widow from a Kohen Gadol, אוֹ בַת גְּרוּשָׁה [וַחֲלוּצָה] מִכֹּהֵן הֶדְיוֹט – or the daughter of a divorced woman {or a *chalutzah*[6]} from an ordinary Kohen. וְכֵן – Similarly, *chalalah*, literally, "defiled one," also includes שֶׁנִּתְחַלְּלָה מִן הַכְּהֻנָּה – one who has been defiled from the *kehunah* עַל יְדֵי בִיאַת אֶחָד מִן הַפְּסוּלִים לַכְּהֻנָּה – through having relations which are forbidden to the *kehunah*.[7]

8. וְקִדַּשְׁתּוֹ – *YOU SHALL SANCTIFY HIM.* עַל כָּרְחוֹ – Against his will. שֶׁאִם לֹא רָצָה לְגָרֵשׁ – That if [a Kohen] does not wish to divorce a forbidden woman to whom he is married, הַלְקֵהוּ – give him lashes וְיַסְּרֵהוּ – and chastise him עַד שֶׁיְּגָרֵשׁ – until he divorces her.[8]

□ קָדֹשׁ יִהְיֶה לָּךְ – *HE SHALL BE HOLY TO YOU.* נְהוֹג בּוֹ קְדֻשָּׁה – Treat him with holiness, לִפְתֹּחַ – that he should take priority to commence in all matters,[9] וּלְבָרֵךְ רִאשׁוֹן – ראשון

---

1. See *Yevamos* 61a.

2. *Kares* is literally "cutting off." According to Rashi (*Genesis* 17:14, *Leviticus* 17:9) this means premature death of the sinner and the loss of his offspring. For examples of relations that carry the punishment of *kares* see Chapter 18 above.

3. One of the Gibeonites, a Canaanite tribe who tricked Joshua into accepting them as converts (see *Joshua*, Chapter 9). King David decreed that they have the status of slaves and may not marry other Jews (see *Yevamos* 78b and Rashi there).

4. This includes children born from forbidden unions that bear the penalty of *kares*, and their descendants.

5. *Toras Kohanim, perek* 1:7; *Yevamos* 61b.

6. If a man dies childless, by Torah law, one of his brothers should take his widow as his wife. This process is called יִבּוּם, *yibbum*. Should he refuse, he and the widow must follow the procedure called חֲלִיצָה, *chalitzah*, whose effects are comparable in certain ways to those of divorce; see *Deuteronomy* 25:5-10. A rabbinic decree does not allow the practice of *yibbum* nowadays, so that *chalitzah* is the only possible procedure. A woman who has undergone this procedure is called a *chalutzah* and, by rabbinic decree, is forbidden to a Kohen. Since the prohibition against a Kohen marrying a *chalutzah* is only a rabbinic decree, many editions (including the first printed edition of Rashi) do not include the word וַחֲלוּצָה.

7. *Kiddushin* 77a-b. If a widow, for example, has relations with a Kohen Gadol, to whom she is forbidden, she thereby becomes a *chalalah* and is forbidden to all Kohanim. Similarly, if a *zonah* (as per Rashi's previous comment) has relations with a Kohen, she becomes a *chalalah* in addition to being a *zonah*. If she subsequently has relations with a Kohen again, she and the Kohen violate two prohibitions (*Mizrachi*; *Sefer Zikaron*; *Sifsei Chachamim*).

8. *Toras Kohanim, perek* 1:13; *Yevamos* 88b.

9. In all matters in which it is an honor to speak first, whether it is a matter of Torah or some other convocation, the Kohen speaks first (Rashi, *Gittin* 59b, s.v., לפתוח ראשון).

that holiness, and thus appears superfluous. It is therefore understood as a commandment to the court to enforce the holiness of the Kohanim (*Divrei David*; *Be'er BaSadeh*).

267 / VAYIKRA/LEVITICUS — PARASHAS EMOR — 21/9-10 — כא/ט־י

⁹ *If the daughter of a man who is a Kohen will be defiled through having illicit relations, she defiles her father — she shall be burned by the fire.*
¹⁰ *The Kohen who is exalted above his brethren, upon whose head the anointment oil has been poured or who has been inaugurated to don the vestments, shall not allow the hair on his head to grow long and shall not rend his garments.*

ט וּבַת֙ אִ֣ישׁ כֹּהֵ֔ן כִּ֥י תֵחֵ֖ל לִזְנ֑וֹת
אֶת־אָבִ֨יהָ֙ הִ֣יא מְחַלֶּ֔לֶת בָּאֵ֖שׁ
תִּשָּׂרֵֽף: וְהַכֹּהֵן֩
הַגָּד֨וֹל מֵאֶחָ֜יו אֲשֶׁר־יוּצַ֥ק עַל־
רֹאשׁ֣וֹ ׀ שֶׁ֤מֶן הַמִּשְׁחָה֙ וּמִלֵּ֣א אֶת־
יָד֔וֹ לִלְבֹּ֖שׁ אֶת־הַבְּגָדִ֑ים אֶת־
רֹאשׁוֹ֙ לֹ֣א יִפְרָ֔ע וּבְגָדָ֖יו לֹ֥א יִפְרֹֽם:

אונקלוס

ט וּבַת גְּבַר כָּהֵן אֲרֵי תִתְחַל לְמִטְעֵי מִקְדְּשַׁת אֲבוּהָא הִיא מִתַּחֲלָא בְּנוּרָא תִּתּוֹקָד: י וְכַהֲנָא דְּאִתְרַבָּא מֵאֲחוֹהִי דִּי יִתְרַק עַל רֵישֵׁהּ מִשְׁחָא דְרַבוּתָא וְיָקָרֵב יָת קֻרְבָּנֵהּ לְמִלְבַּשׁ יָת לְבוּשַׁיָּא יָת רֵישֵׁהּ לָא יְרַבֵּי פֵרוּעַ וּלְבוּשׁוֹהִי לָא יְבַזַּע:

רש"י

בסעודה (גיטין נט:) **(ט) כי תחל לזנות.** כשתתחלל על ידי זנות, שהיתה בה זיקת בעל [או] מן האירוסין או מן הנשואין. ורבותינו נחלקו בדבר (סנהדרין נא.) יש מרבותינו שאומרים אינה במיתה זו אלא מן הנישואין, ויש מהן שאומרים בין מן האירוסין בין מן הנשואין: **את אביה היא מחללת.** חללה ובזתה את כבודו, שאומרים עליו ארור שזו ילד ארור שזו גדל (שם כב.): **(י) לא יפרע.** לא יגדל פרע

RASHI ELUCIDATED

בִּסְעוּדָה¹ — *and take priority to bless at a meal.*¹

9. כִּי תָחֵל לִזְנוֹת — IF [THE DAUGHTER OF A MAN WHO IS A KOHEN] WILL BE DEFILED THROUGH HAVING ILLICIT RELATIONS. כְּשֶׁתִּתְחַלֵּל — *When she will become defiled*² עַל יְדֵי זְנוּת — *through having illicit relations;* שֶׁהָיְתָה בָּהּ זִיקַת בַּעַל — *that she was subject to the bond of a husband* וְזָנְתָה — *and she had illicit relations.* {אוֹ} מִן הָאֵרוּסִין — {Either} *from eirusin*³ אוֹ מִן הַנִּשּׂוּאִין — *or from nisuin.*³ וְרַבּוֹתֵינוּ נֶחְלְקוּ בַדָּבָר⁴ — *Our Rabbis were divided in their opinions about the matter,*⁴ וְהַכֹּל מוֹדִים — *but all agree* שֶׁלֹּא דִבֶּר הַכָּתוּב — *that the verse does not speak* בִּפְנוּיָה — *of an unmarried woman.*

□ אֶת אָבִיהָ הִיא מְחַלֶּלֶת — SHE DEFILES HER FATHER. חִלְּלָה — *She defiled* וּבִזְּתָה — *and disgraced* אֶת כְּבוֹדוֹ — *his honor,* שֶׁאוֹמְרִים עָלָיו — *for they say about him,* אָרוּר שֶׁזּוּ יָלַד — *"Cursed be the one who fathered this one";* ⁵ אָרוּר שֶׁזּוּ גִדֵּל — *"Cursed be the one who raised this one."*⁵

10. לֹא יִפְרָע — [HE] SHALL NOT ALLOW THE HAIR ON [HIS HEAD] TO GROW LONG לֹא יְגַדֵּל פֶּרַע — *He shall*

---
1. *Gittin* 59b. Verse 6 has already said קְדשִׁים יִהְיוּ, "they shall be holy," and the beginning of our verse has already said וְקִדַּשְׁתּוֹ, "you shall sanctify him." Our apparently redundant verse teaches us that you must accord a Kohen honor because of his holiness (*Mizrachi*).

The commentators note that Rashi's comment stands in apparent contradiction to the *Gemara* (*Gittin* 59b) which derives this law from וְקִדַּשְׁתּוֹ. But Rashi there reads, וְקִדַּשְׁתּוֹ כִּי אֶת וְגוֹמֵר, "you shall sanctify him, for etc.," directing the reader to look further on in the verse. This shows that Rashi felt that the *Gemara*, too, derives this law from קָדשׁ יִהְיֶה לָּךְ, but that it quotes וְקִדַּשְׁתּוֹ because it is the first word of the verse in which that phrase appears (*Aderes Eliyahu*).

"To take priority to bless at a meal" refers to both leading those present in saying Grace and in reciting the blessing over bread (see *Shulchan Aruch, Orach Chaim* 201:2, 167:14).

2. כִּי תָחֵל לִזְנוֹת could have been understood as, "when [the daughter of a man who is a Kohen] *will begin* to have illicit relations," with תָחֵל as a form of הַתְחָלָה, "beginning." Rashi explains that כִּי תָחֵל means כְּשֶׁתִּתְחַלֵּל, "when she will be defiled," to indicate that תָחֵל is related to חִלּוּל, "defilement" (*Mizrachi; Sifsei Chachamim*).

Rashi teaches that the verb תָחֵל is a passive *nifal* form. It does not mean "when she will defile," but "when she will be defiled" (*Gur Aryeh*; *Meira Dachya*; *Havanas HaMikra*).

3. *Toras Kohanim*, *perek* 1:14-16. *Eirusin* and *nisuin* are defined in note 1 on page 263.

4. *Sanhedrin* 51b. The *Tanna* R' Yishmael holds that death by fire mentioned in our verse applies only to the daughter of a Kohen who commits adultery after *eirusin*, but before *nisuin*. The *Tanna* R' Akiva holds that it applies even after *nisuin*. Thus, Rashi means "either from *eirusin*," according to all opinions, "or (even) from *nisuin*," according to R' Akiva. The text of Rashi cited by *Mizrachi* reads וְזָנְתָה מִן הָאֵרוּסִין אוֹ מִן הַנִּשּׂוּאִין (without the word אוֹ preceding מִן הָאֵרוּסִין), "and she had illicit relations from *eirusin* or from *nisuin*." According to this version, Rashi explains the verse in accordance with the opinion of R' Akiva.

5. *Sanhedrin* 52a. The verse does not mean that she makes her father a *chalal*, a defiled Kohen, to whom the privileges and strictures of the *kehunah* do not apply (see note 2 on page 262; *Nachalas Yaakov*).

¹¹ *He shall not come to any souls of the dead; he shall not make himself impure for his father or his mother.* ¹² *He shall not leave the Sanctuary and he will not defile*

יא וְעַ֛ל כָּל־נַפְשֹׁ֥ת מֵ֖ת לֹ֣א יָבֹ֑א לְאָבִ֥יו וּלְאִמּ֖וֹ לֹ֥א יִטַּמָּֽא: יב וּמִן־הַמִּקְדָּשׁ֙ לֹ֣א יֵצֵ֔א וְלֹ֣א יְחַלֵּ֔ל אֵ֖ת

— אונקלוס —

יא וְעַל כָּל נַפְשַׁת מֵתָא לָא יֵיעוֹל לַאֲבוּהִי וּלְאִמֵּהּ לָא יִסְתָּאָב: יב וּמִן מַקְדְּשָׁא לָא יִפּוֹק וְלָא יַחֵל יָת

— רש״י —

(סנהדרין כב:): **(יא) וְעַל כָּל נַפְשֹׁת מֵת.** בְּאֹהֶל הַמֵּת: **נַפְשֹׁת מֵת.** לְהָבִיא רְבִיעִית דָּם מִן הַמֵּת שֶׁמְּטַמֵּא בְּאֹהֶל (ת״כ שָׁם ה; **סנהדרין ד.):** **לְאָבִיו וּלְאִמּוֹ לֹא יִטַּמָּא.** לֹא בָא אֶלָּא לְהַתִּיר לוֹ מֵת מִצְוָה (ת״כ שָׁם; נָזִיר מז:): **(יב) וּמִן הַמִּקְדָּשׁ לֹא יֵצֵא.** אֵינוֹ הוֹלֵךְ אַחַר הַמִּטָּה (ת״כ שָׁם ה; סנהדרין יח.) וְעוֹד

על אֶבֶל (ת״כ פַּרְשְׁתָא ב:ג) וְאֵיזֶהוּ גִּדּוּל פֶּרַע יוֹתֵר מִשְּׁלֹשִׁים יוֹם

— RASHI ELUCIDATED —

וְאֵיזֶהוּ גִּדּוּל פֶּרַע — **What constitutes growth of long hair?** ²**יוֹתֵר מִשְּׁלֹשִׁים יוֹם** — Not having his hair cut for **more than thirty days.**²

11. וְעַל כָּל נַפְשֹׁת מֵת — [HE SHALL NOT COME] TO ANY SOULS OF THE DEAD. **בְּאֹהֶל הַמֵּת** — **In the tent of the dead person,** i.e., under the same roof as a corpse.³

☐ **נַפְשֹׁת מֵת** — SOULS OF THE DEAD. This is stated **לְהָבִיא רְבִיעִית דָּם** — **to include a** *revi'is* ⁴ **of blood מִן הַמֵּת** — **from the dead,** i.e., from a corpse, ⁵**שֶׁמְּטַמֵּא בְּאֹהֶל** — **that it transmits impurity in a roofed area.**⁵

☐ **לְאָבִיו וּלְאִמּוֹ לֹא יִטַּמָּא** — HE SHALL NOT MAKE HIMSELF IMPURE FOR HIS FATHER OR HIS MOTHER. **לֹא בָא אֶלָּא** — [This verse] came only ⁶**לְהַתִּיר לוֹ מֵת מִצְוָה** — to permit him to become impure for **a mes mitzvah.**⁶

12. וּמִן הַמִּקְדָּשׁ לֹא יֵצֵא — HE SHALL NOT LEAVE THE SANCTUARY. ⁷**אֵינוֹ הוֹלֵךְ אַחַר הַמִּטָּה** — **He does not follow the bier,** i.e., he does not participate in his parent's funeral.⁷ **וְעוֹד** — **And furthermore,**

---

1. *Toras Kohanim, parshasa* 2:3.

2. *Sanhedrin* 22b.

3. The word עַל here cannot mean upon. *HaKesav VehaKabbalah* cites numerous verses in which עַל means "within" [e.g., בְּסַל אֶחָד, "in one basket" (*Exodus* 29:3)]. Thus, our verse speaks of an enclosed area. But if the Torah meant to describe an area enclosed by walls, it would have used a form of one of the more common terms בַּיִת or פָּנִים. By using עַל, which can mean "above," the Torah indicates that the area is enclosed only by a roof, not walls.

4. The measures of volume are:

EPHAH	SE'AH	KAV	LOG	BEITZAH
1 אֵיפָה	= 3 סְאָה	= 18 קַב	= 72 לֹג	= 432 בֵּיצָה
	1 סְאָה	= 6 קַב	= 24 לֹג	= 144 בֵּיצָה
		1 קַב	= 4 לֹג	= 24 בֵּיצָה
			1 לֹג	= 6 בֵּיצָה
¹⁄₄₃₂ אֵיפָה	= ¹⁄₁₄₄ סְאָה	= ¹⁄₂₄ קַב	= ¹⁄₆ לֹג	= 1 בֵּיצָה
¹⁄₇₂ אֵיפָה	= ¹⁄₂₄ סְאָה	= ¹⁄₄ קַב	= 1 לֹג	
¹⁄₁₈ אֵיפָה	= ¹⁄₆ סְאָה	= 1 קַב		
¹⁄₃ אֵיפָה	= 1 סְאָה			

A *revi'is*, which is one-fourth of a *log*, is thus a *beitzah* and a half.

Halachic authorities differ widely regarding the modern-day equivalents of these measures. Opinions regarding the basic *beitzah* range from 2 to 3.5 fluid ounces. Thus the volume of a *revi'is* is equivalent to approximately 3 – 5.3 fluid ounces.

5. *Toras Kohanim, parshasa* 2:4; *Sanhedrin* 4a. The verse could have said וְעַל כָּל מֵת לֹא יָבֹא, "he shall not come to any dead person." נֶפֶשׁ, "souls," teaches us that impurity is transmitted even if one is in the same roofed area as a *revi'is* of blood from a corpse, for the minimum quantity of blood necessary to sustain the life or "soul" of the smallest infant is a *revi'is* (see Rashi to *Sotah* 5a, s.v., אדם שאין בו אלא רביעית אחת; Commentary of Rambam to *Ohalos* 2:2). Furthermore, the word נֶפֶשׁ, "soul," is associated with blood, as in *Deuteronomy* 12:23, כִּי הַדָּם הוּא הַנֶּפֶשׁ, "for the blood is the soul" (see *Mizrachi*; *Sefer Zikaron*).

6. *Toras Kohanim, parshasa* 2:4; *Nazir* 47b. (For the definition of *mes mitzvah*, see note 8 on p. 262.) The broad statement at the beginning of the verse, "he shall not come to any souls of the dead," includes a prohibition against the Kohen Gadol making himself impure through any corpse, including those of his parents. That statement cannot apply to any one other than his parents, for it would not be necessary to state such a prohibition. We would assume that the prohibition against becoming impure through the corpses of non-relatives which applies to all Kohanim applies to the Kohen Gadol, too. "He shall not make himself impure for his father or his mother," thus appears to be superfluous. It was stated for us to infer that there is a case in which the Kohen Gadol may become impure, namely, a *mes mitzvah* (*Mizrachi*; *Sifsei Chachamim*).

7. *Toras Kohanim, parshasa* 2:5; *Sanhedrin* 18a. The Tannaim R' Meir and R' Yehudah argue about the meaning of this verse. R' Meir holds that the Kohen Gadol may not be part of the funeral procession, but may follow it from a distance. According to this view,

the Sanctuary of his God; for a crown — the oil of his God's anointment — is upon him; I am HASHEM. ¹³ *He shall marry a woman in her virginity.* ¹⁴ *A widow, and a divorcee, and a chalalah, a zonah — he shall not marry these; only a virgin of his people shall he take as a wife.* ¹⁵ *And he shall not defile his offspring among his people; for*

מִקְדַּשׁ אֱלֹהָיו כִּי נֵזֶר שֶׁמֶן מִשְׁחַת
יג אֱלֹהָיו עָלָיו אֲנִי יהוה: וְהוּא
יד אִשָּׁה בִבְתוּלֶיהָ יִקָּח: אַלְמָנָה
וּגְרוּשָׁה וַחֲלָלָה זֹנָה אֶת־אֵלֶּה לֹא
יִקָּח כִּי אִם־בְּתוּלָה מֵעַמָּיו יִקַּח
טו אִשָּׁה: וְלֹא־יְחַלֵּל זַרְעוֹ בְּעַמָּיו כִּי

――― אונקלוס ―――

מַקְדְּשָׁא דֶאֱלָהֵיהּ אֲרֵי כְּלִיל מְשַׁח רְבוּתָא דֶאֱלָהֵיהּ עֲלוֹהִי אֲנָא יְיָ: יג וְהוּא אִתְּתָא בִּבְתוּלְתָהָא יִסָּב: יד אַרְמְלָא
וּמְתָרְכָא וְחַלָּלָא מַטְעֲיָא יָת אִלֵּין לָא יִסָּב אֱלָהֵן בְּתֻלְתָּא מֵעַמֵּיהּ יִסַּב אִתְּתָא: טו וְלָא יַחֵל זַרְעֵהּ בְּעַמֵּהּ אֲרֵי

――― רש״י ―――

מכאן למדו רבותינו שכהן גדול מקריב אונן (זבחים צט.) וכן | אֶת הָעֲבוֹדָה. שֶׁהִתִּיר לוֹ הַכָּתוּב, הָא כֹּהֵן הֶדְיוֹט שֶׁעָבַד אוֹנֵן
מַשְׁמָעוֹ, אַף אִם מֵתוּ אָבִיו וְאִמּוֹ אֵינוֹ צָרִיךְ לָצֵאת מִן הַמִּקְדָּשׁ, | חִלֵּל (ת״כ שם ו׳; יד) וַחֲלָלָה. שְׁנוֹלְדָה מִפְּסוּלֵי כְהֻנָּה: (טו)
אֶלָּא עוֹבֵד עֲבוֹדָה: ולא יחלל את מקדש. שֶׁאֵינוֹ מְחַלֵּל בְּכָךְ | ולא יחלל זרעו. הָא אִם נָשָׂא אַחַת מִן הַפְּסוּלוֹת זַרְעוֹ הֵימֶנָּה

――― RASHI ELUCIDATED ―――

שֶׁכֹּהֵן גָּדוֹל מַקְרִיב אוֹנֵן — that a **Kohen Gadol** מִכָּאן לָמְדוּ רַבּוֹתֵינוּ — our **Rabbis learned from here performs** the Temple service even while he is an *onein*.[1] וְכֵן מַשְׁמָעוֹ — **This is implied** by the verse as follows: אַף אִם מֵתוּ אָבִיו וְאִמּוֹ — **Even if his father and mother have died,** אֵינוֹ צָרִיךְ לָצֵאת מִן הַמִּקְדָּשׁ — **he is not required to leave the Sanctuary,** אֶלָּא עוֹבֵד עֲבוֹדָה — **but rather, he performs the service.**[2]

שֶׁאֵינוֹ מְחַלֵּל בְּכָךְ אֶת □ וְלֹא יְחַלֵּל אֵת מִקְדָּשׁ — **AND HE WILL NOT DEFILE THE SANCTUARY OF [HIS GOD].** הָעֲבוֹדָה — **For he does not defile the service** thereby, i.e., by performing it while an *onein*, שֶׁהִתִּיר לוֹ הַכָּתוּב — **for Scripture has permitted it for him.**[3] הָא — **But,** we can infer from here that כֹּהֵן הֶדְיוֹט — **an ordinary Kohen** who performs the service while an *onein* חִלֵּל[4] — **has defiled it.**[4]

14. וַחֲלָלָה — **AND A *CHALALAH* —** שֶׁנּוֹלְדָה — **who was born** מִפְּסוּלֵי כְהֻנָּה — **from those** unions **unfit for the** *kehunah*.[5]

15. וְלֹא יְחַלֵּל זַרְעוֹ — **AND HE SHALL NOT DEFILE HIS OFFSPRING.** הָא אִם נָשָׂא — **But if he married אַחַת מִן הַפְּסוּלוֹת** — **one of the women who are unfit** for a Kohen Gadol,[6] זַרְעוֹ הֵימֶנָּה — **his offspring from**

"he shall not leave the Sanctuary" is not to be taken literally, for he may neither eat his meals nor sleep there (*Maskil LeDavid*). Rather, מִקְדָּשׁ here is to be understood as "sanctity" — he shall not leave his sanctified status by participating in the funeral procession of a parent lest he make himself impure by coming into contact with the corpse (Rashi to *Sanhedrin* 18a, s.v., כהן גדול אינו יוצא אחר המטה). R' Yehudah takes מִקְדָּשׁ of our verse literally, and holds that the Kohen Gadol may not leave the *Beis HaMikdash* during the funeral of a parent. According to *Mizrachi*, this comment of Rashi lends itself to either interpretation.

1. *Zevachim* 99a. For the definition of *onein* see note 2 on page 106.

2. According to this interpretation of the Rabbis, like that of R' Yehudah mentioned above, מִקְדָּשׁ is taken in its literal sense, "Sanctuary."

3. וְלֹא יְחַלֵּל אֵת מִקְדָּשׁ אֱלֹהָיו is not a negative commandment — "he shall not desecrate the Sanctuary of his God." Rather, it provides the reason for "he shall not leave the Sanctuary" of the beginning of the verse, as if to say, "he is not on obligation to leave the Sanctuary, for he will not desecrate the Sanctuary of his God by performing the service" (*Mizrachi*; *Sefer Zikaron*).

4. *Toras Kohanim, parshasa* 2:6.

5. In his comments to verse 7 above, Rashi defined *chalalah* as he does here, but gave an additional definition as well — a woman who had relations that are forbidden to the *kehunah* (see note 7 there). For there the verse was speaking of an ordinary Kohen who is not commanded to marry a virgin. Our verse, however, speaks of a Kohen Gadol who may marry only a virgin, as stated in the preceding verse. Therefore, a woman who has had any relations does not enter the discussion. *Chalalah* here applies only to a virgin. This distinction is preserved in *Targum Onkelos*. In verse 7, *Targum Onkelos* renders וּמְחַלְּלָא, treating וַחֲלָלָה as an adjective modifying the word אִשָּׁה חַלָּלָה "woman," that preceded it. He understands אִשָּׁה חַלָּלָה there as "a woman, defiled," which can connote a woman who became defiled by an action, namely, her having forbidden relations. Here *Targum Onkelos* treats חֲלָלָה as a noun, חַלָּלָא, "a defiled woman," which connotes a woman who is inherently defiled from birth (*Nefesh HaGer*).

6. "And he shall not defile his offspring" is not an independent negative commandment. It is linked to the previous verse, as if to say, ". . . he shall not take these; only a virgin of his people shall he take as his wife, *and thereby* he shall not defile his offspring" (*Ramban*).

I am Hashem *Who sanctifies him.*

16 Hashem *spoke to Moses, saying:* **17** *Speak to Aaron, saying: Any man of your offspring throughout their generations in whom there will be a blemish shall not come near to offer the bread of his God.* **18** *For any man in whom there is a blemish shall not approach: a man who is blind or lame or disfigured, or one who has an enlargement;* **19** *or in whom there will be a broken leg or a broken arm;*

טו אֲנִ֥י יְהוָ֖ה מְקַדְּשֽׁוֹ׃ שני טז וַיְדַבֵּ֥ר יְהוָ֖ה אֶל־מֹשֶׁ֥ה לֵּאמֹֽר׃ יז דַּבֵּ֥ר אֶֽל־אַהֲרֹ֖ן לֵאמֹ֑ר אִ֣ישׁ מִֽזַּרְעֲךָ֞ לְדֹרֹתָ֗ם אֲשֶׁ֨ר יִהְיֶ֥ה ב֛וֹ מ֖וּם לֹ֣א יִקְרַ֔ב לְהַקְרִ֖יב לֶ֥חֶם אֱלֹהָֽיו׃ יח כִּ֥י כָל־אִ֛ישׁ אֲשֶׁר־בּ֥וֹ מ֖וּם לֹ֣א יִקְרָ֑ב אִ֤ישׁ עִוֵּר֙ א֣וֹ פִסֵּ֔חַ א֥וֹ חָרֻ֖ם א֥וֹ שָׂרֽוּעַ׃ יט א֣וֹ אִ֔ישׁ אֲשֶׁר־יִהְיֶ֥ה ב֖וֹ שֶׁ֣בֶר רָ֑גֶל א֖וֹ שֶׁ֥בֶר יָֽד׃

— אונקלוס —

אֲנָא יְיָ מְקַדְּשֵׁהּ: טז וּמַלֵּיל יְיָ עִם מֹשֶׁה לְמֵימָר: יז מַלֵּל עִם אַהֲרֹן לְמֵימַר גְּבַר מִבְּנָיךְ לְדָרֵיהוֹן דִּי יְהֵי בֵהּ מוּמָא לָא יִקְרַב לְקָרָבָא קֻרְבָּנָא קֳדָם אֱלָהֵהּ: יח אֲרֵי כָל גְּבַר דִּי בֵהּ מוּמָא לָא יִקְרַב גְּבַר עֲוִיר אוֹ חֲגִיר אוֹ חָרִים אוֹ שָׂרוּעַ: יט אוֹ גְבַר דִּי יְהֵי בֵהּ תְּבַר רַגְלָא אוֹ תְבַר יְדָא:

— רש״י —

חֲלַל מִדִּין קְדֻשַּׁת כְּהֻנָּה (קידושין עז.): **(יז) לֶחֶם אֱלֹהָיו.** מַאֲכַל אֱלֹהָיו. כָּל (יח)סְעוּדָה קְרוּיָה לֶחֶם, כְּמוֹ עֲבַד לְחֶם רַב (דניאל ה:א): **(יח) כִּי כָל אִישׁ אֲשֶׁר בּוֹ מוּם לֹא יִקְרָב.** אֵינוֹ דִין שֶׁיִּקְרָב, כְּמוֹ הַקְרִיבֵהוּ נָא לְפֶחָתֶךָ (מלאכי א:ח): **חָרֻם.** שֶׁחוּטְמוֹ שָׁקוּעַ בֵּין שְׁתֵּי הָעֵינַיִם שְׂכוֹחֵל שְׁתֵּי עֵינָיו כְּאַחַת (ת״כ פרשתא ג:ח; בכורות מג:): **שָׂרוּעַ.** שֶׁאֶחָד מֵאֵבָרָיו גָּדוֹל מֵחֲבֵירוֹ. עֵינוֹ אַחַת גְּדוֹלָה וְעֵינוֹ אַחַת קְטַנָּה, אוֹ שׁוֹקוֹ אַחַת אֲרוּכָּה מֵחֲבֶרְתָּהּ (בכורות מ:-מ״א):

— RASHI ELUCIDATED —

חֲלַל מִדִּין קְדֻשַּׁת כְּהֻנָּה — **her** [1] — **are defiled from** being included in **the law of sanctity of the** *kehunah.*[1]

17. לֶחֶם אֱלֹהָיו — THE BREAD OF HIS GOD. This means מַאֲכַל אֱלֹהָיו — **the food of his God.** כָּל סְעוּדָה [2] — **Any meal** [2] קְרוּיָה לֶחֶם — **is referred to as "bread,"** כְּמוֹ — **as** לֶחֶם in the phrase, עֲבַד לְחֶם רַב [3] — **"made a great feast."** [3]

18. כִּי כָל אִישׁ אֲשֶׁר בּוֹ מוּם לֹא יִקְרָב — FOR ANY MAN IN WHOM THERE IS A BLEMISH SHALL NOT APPROACH. אֵינוֹ בַּדִּין שֶׁיִּקְרַב — **It is not proper that he should approach.** כְּמוֹ ״הַקְרִיבֵהוּ נָא לְפֶחָתֶךָ״ [4] — **It is like** the idea of the verse, **"Go offer it to your ruler!"** [4]

חָרֻם — DISFIGURED. שֶׁחוּטְמוֹ שָׁקוּעַ — **That his nose is sunken** בֵּין שְׁתֵּי הָעֵינַיִם — **between the two eyes,** [5] שְׁבּוֹחֵל שְׁתֵּי עֵינָיו כְּאַחַת — **so much** **that he applies color to his two eyes at once,** i.e., in one unbroken movement, since the bridge of the nose does not stand in the way.[5]

שָׂרוּעַ — ONE WHO HAS AN ENLARGEMENT. שֶׁאֶחָד מֵאֵבָרָיו — **That one of the** external **parts of his body** which come in pairs גָּדוֹל מֵחֲבֵרוֹ — **is larger than its fellow,** for example, עֵינוֹ אַחַת גְּדוֹלָה — **one of his eyes is large** וְעֵינוֹ אַחַת קְטַנָּה — **and one of his eyes is small,** אוֹ שׁוֹקוֹ אַחַת — **or one of his legs** אֲרוּכָה מֵחֲבֶרְתָּהּ [6] — **is longer than its fellow.** [6]

---

1. *Kiddushin* 77b. "And he shall not defile his offspring" does not refer to a punishment; the verse does not mean that if the Kohen Gadol marries a woman unfit for him he will father unrighteous children. It suggests a halachic inference; the children he will father from such a union will be defiled and barred from the *kehunah* (*Gur Aryeh*).

2. Some editions read כָּל הַסְּעוּדָה, "the entire meal."

3. *Daniel* 5:1. "Bread" of our verse could have been understood as referring to the meal-offerings alone (*Maskil LeDavid*). See Rashi to 3:11 above and verse 21 below; see *Yosef Hallel* to our verse for an exposition of the difference between Rashi's comments.

4. *Malachi* 1:8. That verse in its entirety reads,

"When you present that which is blind for slaughter, is that not evil? When you present that which is lame or ill, is that not evil? Go offer it to your ruler! Would he be pleased with you? Or would he favor you? ..."

Verse 17 has already said that a Kohen with a physical blemish may not perform the service. Our verse is giving a rationale for that prohibition; it is unbefitting for a blemished person to serve before the King (*Mizrachi; Sifsei Chachamim*). This is also indicated by the language of the beginning of the verse. "For any man ..." sounds like a reason for that which was stated before it (*Mizrachi*).

5. *Toras Kohanim, parshasa* 3:8; *Bechoros* 43b.

6. *Bechoros* 40a-b.

271 / VAYIKRA/LEVITICUS — PARASHAS EMOR — 21/20

[20] *or one who has unusual eyebrows, or one who has a cataract, or a mixing in his eye, or a garav, or a yalefes, or has crushed testicles.*

ב אוֹ־גִבֵּ֣ן אוֹ־דַ֔ק אוֹ תְּבַלֻּ֖ל בְּעֵינ֑וֹ אוֹ גָרָב֙ אוֹ יַלֶּ֔פֶת אוֹ מְר֖וֹחַ אָֽשֶׁךְ׃

— אונקלוס —

כ אוֹ גְבִין אוֹ דְקָא אוֹ חִלִּיז בְּעֵינֵהּ אוֹ גַרְבָּן אוֹ חֲזָזָן אוֹ מְרַס פַּחֲדִין:

— רש"י —

(ב) **אוֹ גִבֵּן.** שורצי"ל"ש בלע"ז שגביני עיניו שערן ארוך ושוכב (שם מג:): **אוֹ דַק.** שיש לו בעיניו דוק שקורין טייל"א, כמו הנוטה כדוק (ישעיה מ:כב): **אוֹ תְבַלֻּל.** דבר המבלבל את העין, כגון חוט לבן הנמשך מן הלבן ופוסק בסירא, שהוא עוגל המקיף את השחור שקוראים פרוניל"א, והחוט הזה פוסק את העוגל ונכנס בשחור. ותרגום תבלול חיליז לשון חלזון שהוא דומה לתולעת אותו החוט, וכן כינוהו חכמי ישראל במומי הבכור חלזון נחש עינב (בכורות לח:-לח.): **גָרָב אוֹ יַלֶּפֶת.** מיני שחין הם (שם מא.). גרב זו החרס, שחין היבש מבפנים ומבחוץ. ילפת היא חזית המצרית, ולמה נקראת ילפת שמלפפת והולכת עד יום המיתה, והוא לח מבחון ויבש מבפנים, ובמקום אחר קורא גרב לשחין הלח מבחון ויבש מבפנים,

— RASHI ELUCIDATED —

20. אוֹ גִבֵּן — OR ONE WHO HAS UNUSUAL EYEBROWS. שׁוּרְצִילִ"ש בְּלַעַ"ז — *Sorcilles* in Old French.[1] וְשׁוֹכֵב — and droops.[2] שֶׁגְּבִינֵי עֵינָיו שְׂעָרָן אָרֹךְ — That the hair of his eyebrows is unusually long,[2] וְשׁוֹכֵב — and droops.[2]

□ אוֹ דַק — OR ONE WHO HAS A CATARACT. שֶׁיֵּשׁ לוֹ בְּעֵינָיו דַק — That he has a film on his eyes שֶׁקּוֹרִין טיל"א — which they call *toile* in Old French.[3] כְּמוֹ ,,הַנּוֹטֶה כַדֹק" — דַק of our verse is similar to כַדֹק in the verse, "*who spreads out* [the heavens] *like a film.*"[4]

□ אוֹ תְבַלֻּל — OR A MIXING. דָּבָר הַמְבַלְבֵּל אֶת הָעַיִן — A thing which mixes the colors of the eye, כְּגוֹן חוּט לָבָן — such as a white stripe הַנִּמְשָׁךְ מִן הַלֹּבֶן — which extends from the white of the eye וּפוֹסֵק בְּסִירָא — and cuts into the iris, שֶׁהוּא עוּגָל — which is the circle הַמַּקִּיף אֶת הַשָּׁחוֹר — that surrounds the black part of the eye, i.e., the pupil, שֶׁקּוֹרִים פרוניל"א — which they call *prunele* in Old French.[5] וְהַחוּט הַזֶּה — This stripe פּוֹסֵק אֶת הָעוּגָל — cuts the circle וְנִכְנָס בַּשָּׁחוֹר — and enters the black. וְתַרְגּוּם ,,תְּבַלֻּל" ,,חִלִּיז" — And *Targum Onkelos'* translation of תְּבַלֻּל is ,,חִלִּיז" לְשׁוֹן ,,חִלָּזוֹן" — It is related to *chilazon*, a type of sea creature, שֶׁהוּא דוֹמֶה לְתוֹלַעַת אוֹתוֹ הַחוּט — because that stripe is similar in its shape to a worm, as is the *chilazon*. וְכֵן כִּנּוּהוּ חַכְמֵי יִשְׂרָאֵל — The Sages of Israel named it so (as did *Targum Onkelos*), בְּמוּמֵי הַבְּכוֹר — among the blemishes of the firstborn: חִלָּזוֹן נָחָשׁ עֵינָב[6] — "the *chilazon* which is also known as 'the snake,' 'the grape.'"[6]

□ גָרָב אוֹ יַלֶּפֶת — A *GARAV* OR A *YALEFES*. מִינֵי שְׁחִין הֵם — They are types of boils:[7] גָּרָב זוֹ הַחֶרֶס — *garav* is the one known as *cheres*,[8] שְׁחִין הַיָּבֵשׁ מִבִּפְנִים וּמִבַּחוּץ — a boil that is dry on the inside and on the outside; יַלֶּפֶת הִיא — *yalefes* is חֲזָזִית הַמִּצְרִית — the Egyptian rash.[9] וְלָמָּה נִקְרֵאת יַלֶּפֶת — Why is it called *yalefes*? שֶׁמְּלַפֶּפֶת וְהוֹלֶכֶת — For it progressively becomes more closely bound to the sufferer עַד יוֹם הַמִּיתָה — until the day of his death.[10] וְהוּא לַח מִבַּחוּץ — It is moist on the outside וְיָבֵשׁ מִבִּפְנִים — and dry on the inside. וּבְמָקוֹם אַחֵר — Elsewhere, קוֹרֵא ,,גָּרָב" — [Scripture] uses the term *garav* לִשְׁחִין הַלַּח מִבַּחוּץ — for a boil that is moist on the outside וְיָבֵשׁ מִבִּפְנִים — and dry

---

1. In Modern French, *sourcils*. This French word is a contraction of the Latin *supercilia*, which means "eyebrows," literally, "above the eyelashes." The related English word "superciliary" means "pertaining to the eyebrows," and "supercilious" means "with raised eyebrows," i.e., "haughty."

2. *Bechoros* 43b. His eyebrows are so long that they droop over his eyes (Rashi as emended by *Shitah Mekubetzes* to *Bechoros*).

3. This word means "web" in both Old and Modern French. In Modern English "toile" means "thin, almost-transparent cloth."

4. *Isaiah* 40:22.

5. In Modern French, *prunelle* [literally, "sloe, a deep purple plum"], which means "the pupil (of the eye)."

6. *Bechoros* 38a-b. According to the *Gemara*, "the snake" is a synonym for *chilazon*. תְּבַלֻּל of our verse refers to the *chilazon*/snake defect. עֵינָב, "the grape," is an additional blemish listed by the Mishnah. It is characterized by a grapelike spot in the eye (*Bertinoro* to *Bechoros* 6:2).

7. *Bechoros* 41a.

8. Literally, "earthenware." This type of boil is known as "earthenware" because, like earthenware, it is hard (Rashi to *Bechoros* 41a).

9. The type of rash the Egyptians suffered during the Plague of Boils (*Mizrachi* based on Rashi to *Bechoros* 41a).

10. יַלֶּפֶת is related to לפף, "to be attached or bound" (see *Sefer Zikaron*).

21 Any man in whom there is a blemish from among the offspring of Aaron the Kohen shall not approach to offer the fire-offerings of Hashem; there is in him a blemish — the bread of his God he shall not approach to offer. **22** The bread of his God from the holy of holies and from the holies may he eat. **23** But

כא כָּל־אִ֞ישׁ אֲשֶׁר־בּ֣וֹ מ֗וּם מִזֶּ֙רַע֙ אַהֲרֹ֣ן הַכֹּהֵ֔ן לֹ֣א יִגַּ֔שׁ לְהַקְרִ֖יב אֶת־אִשֵּׁ֣י יְהוָ֑ה מ֣וּם בּ֔וֹ אֵ֚ת לֶ֣חֶם אֱלֹהָ֔יו לֹ֥א יִגַּ֖שׁ לְהַקְרִֽיב:
כב לֶ֣חֶם אֱלֹהָ֔יו מִקָּדְשֵׁ֥י הַקֳּדָשִׁ֖ים
כג וּמִן־הַקֳּדָשִׁ֥ים יֹאכֵֽל: אַ֣ךְ אֶל־

― אונקלוס ―

כא כָּל גְּבַר דִּי בֵהּ מוּמָא מִזַּרְעָא דְּאַהֲרֹן כַּהֲנָא לָא יִקְרַב לְקָרָבָא יָת קֻרְבָּנַיָּא דַּייָ מוּמָא בֵהּ יָת קֻרְבַּן אֱלָהֵהּ לָא יִקְרַב לְקָרָבָא: כב קֻרְבַּן אֱלָהֵהּ מִקֹּדֶשׁ קוּדְשַׁיָּא וּמִן קוּדְשַׁיָּא יֵיכוּל: כג בְּרַם

― רש"י ―

מום. לרבות שאר מומין (ת"כ פרק ג:ה): **מום בו.** בעוד מומו בו פסול הא אם עבר מומו כשר (שם ו): **לחם אלהיו.** כל מאכל קרוי לחם: (**כב**) **מקדשי הקדשים.** אלו קדשי הקדשים: **ומן הקדשים יאכל.** אלו קדשים קלים. ואם נאמרו קדשי הקדשים למה נאמר קדשים קלים

שנאמר ובגרב ובחרס (דברים כח:כז). כשסמוך גרב אצל חרס קורא ליבפת גרב, וכשהוא סמוך אצל יבפת קורא לחרס גרב, כך מפורש בבכורות (מא.): **מרוח אשך.** לפי התרגום מריס פחדין שפחדיו מרוססין שבילים שלו כתותין. פחדין כמו גידי פחדיו ישורגו (איוב מ:יז): (**כא**) **כל איש אשר בו**

― RASHI ELUCIDATED ―

on the inside, שֶׁנֶּאֱמַר – for it says, וּבַגָּרָב וּבֶחָרֶס,,[1] – "and with *garav* and with *cheres*."[1] This apparent inconsistency can be explained as follows: כְּשֶׁסָּמַךְ גָּרָב אֵצֶל חָרֶס – When [Scripture] juxtaposes *garav* with *cheres*, קוֹרֵא לְיַלֶּפֶת גָּרָב – it calls *yalefes*, which is moist on the outside and dry on the inside, "*garav*," וּכְשֶׁהוּא סָמוּךְ אֵצֶל יַלֶּפֶת – but when [*garav*] is juxtaposed with *yalefes*, קוֹרֵא לַחָרֶס גָּרָב – [Scripture] calls *cheres* "*garav*." כָּךְ מְפוֹרָשׁ בִּבְכוֹרוֹת – Thus is it explained in *Bechoros*.[2]

☐ מְרוֹחַ אָשֶׁךְ – HAS CRUSHED TESTICLES. לְפִי הַתַּרְגּוּם מְרִיס פַּחֲדִין – According to *Targum* Onkelos this is rendered מְרִיס פַּחֲדִין, which means שֶׁפַּחֲדָיו מְרֻסָּסִין – that his testicles are crushed, שְׁבִיצִים שֶׁלּוֹ כְּתוּתִין – that his testicles are squashed.[3] פַּחֲדִין, פַּחֲדִין כְּמוֹ – *pachadin*, the word used here by *Targum Onkelos* for testicles, is used in the same sense as פַּחֲדָיו in, גִּידֵי פַחֲדָיו יְשׂרָגוּ,, – "the ducts of his testicles are interwoven."[4]

21. כָּל אִישׁ אֲשֶׁר בּוֹ מוּם – ANY MAN IN WHOM THERE IS A BLEMISH. The verse is written לְרַבּוֹת שְׁאָר מוּמִין[5] – to include other blemishes.[5]

☐ מוּם בּוֹ – IN WHOM THERE IS A BLEMISH. בְּעוֹד מוּמוֹ בּוֹ פָּסוּל – While his blemish is still in him, he is disqualified, הָא אִם עָבַר מוּמוֹ – but if his blemish has passed, כָּשֵׁר[6] – he is fit to perform the service.[6]

☐ לֶחֶם אֱלֹהָיו – THE BREAD OF HIS GOD. כָּל מַאֲכָל – All food קָרוּי לֶחֶם – is called "bread."[7]

22. מִקָּדְשֵׁי הַקֳּדָשִׁים – FROM THE HOLY OF HOLIES. אֵלוּ קָדְשֵׁי הַקֳּדָשִׁים – This refers to **those of the higher degree** of holiness.

☐ וּמִן הַקֳּדָשִׁים יֹאכֵל – AND FROM THE HOLY MAY HE EAT. אֵלוּ קָדָשִׁים קַלִּים – This refers to **those of the lesser degree of holiness.** וְאִם נֶאֶמְרוּ קָדְשֵׁי הַקֳּדָשִׁים – If those of the higher degree of holiness have been stated as permitted to be eaten by a blemished Kohen, לָמָּה נֶאֱמַר קָדָשִׁים קַלִּים – why are those

---

1. *Deuteronomy* 28:27; see p. 271 note 8 regarding *cheres*.
2. *Bechoros* 41a.
3. Rashi cites the opinion of *Targum* Onkelos because the definition of מְרוֹחַ אָשֶׁךְ is a matter of dispute among the Sages. In addition to the opinion cited by Rashi, there are those who say that it denotes a man who is missing one or both testicles, one whose testicles are swollen, or one whose complexion is exceedingly dark (*Sefer Zikaron* based on *Toras Kohanim, parshasa* 3:15 and *Bechoros* 7:5).
4. *Job* 40:17.
5. *Toras Kohanim, perek* 3:1. Verse 17 has already stated that a blemished Kohen may not perform the service. Our apparently superfluous verse includes physical defects other than those mentioned in the preceding verses (*Mizrachi*; *Sifsei Chachamim*).
6. *Toras Kohanim, perek* 3:6.
7. Although Rashi has already interpreted "bread" as "food" in his comments to verse 17, he repeats it here after the Torah has prohibited a Kohen with even a transitory blemish from performing the service. For we might have thought that the temporary disqualification of such a Kohen applies only to "bread," only to offerings of the highest degree of sanctity, such as meal-offerings (*Nachalas Yaakov*; *Maskil LeDavid*).

he shall not come to the Paroches, and he shall not approach the Mizbe'ach, for he has a blemish; and he shall not defile My holy services, for I am HASHEM, *Who sanctifies them.*

הַפָּרֹכֶת לֹא יָבֹא וְאֶל־הַמִּזְבֵּחַ לֹא יִגַּשׁ כִּי־מוּם בּוֹ וְלֹא יְחַלֵּל אֶת־מִקְדָּשַׁי כִּי אֲנִי יהוה מְקַדְּשָׁם:

———————— אונקלוס ————————

לְפָרֻכְתָּא לָא יֵיעוֹל וּלְמַדְבְּחָא לָא יִקְרַב אֲרֵי מוּמָא בֵהּ וְלָא יַחֵל יָת מַקְדְּשַׁי אֲרֵי אֲנָא יְיָ מְקַדְּשְׁהוֹן:

———————— רש"י ————————

אִם לֹא נֶאֱמַר הָיִיתִי אוֹמֵר בְּקָדְשֵׁי הַקֳּדָשִׁים יֹאכַל בַּעַל מוּם שֶׁמָּצִינוּ שֶׁהוּתְּרוּ לְזָר שֶׁאָכַל מֹשֶׁה בְּשַׂר הַמִּלּוּאִים, אֲבָל בַּחֲזֶה וְשׁוֹק שֶׁל קָדָשִׁים קַלִּים לֹא יֹאכַל שֶׁלֹּא מָצִינוּ זָר חוֹלֵק בָּהֶן, לְכָךְ נֶאֶמְרוּ קָדָשִׁים קַלִּים. כַּךְ מְפֹרָשׁ בִּזְבָחִים (קא.):

(כג) אַךְ אֶל הַפָּרֹכֶת. לְהַזּוֹת שֶׁבַע הַזָּאוֹת שֶׁעַל הַפָּרֹכֶת: **וְאֶל הַמִּזְבֵּחַ.** הַחִיצוֹן, וּשְׁנֵיהֶם הֻצְרְכוּ לְהִכָּתֵב וּמְפֹרָשׁ בַּת״כ (שם י): **וְלֹא יְחַלֵּל אֶת מִקְדָּשָׁי.** שֶׁאִם עָבַד עֲבוֹדָתוֹ מְחֻלֶּלֶת לְהִפָּסֵל (שם יח; בכורות מג:):

———————— RASHI ELUCIDATED ————————

of the lesser degree of holiness stated? Could we not have reasoned that they are permitted even if it had not been stated? אִם לֹא נֶאֱמַר – **Had it not been stated** הָיִיתִי אוֹמֵר – **I would have said,** בְּקָדְשֵׁי הַקֳּדָשִׁים יֹאכַל בַּעַל מוּם – **"A blemished** Kohen **may eat of those of the higher degree of holiness,** שֶׁמָּצִינוּ שֶׁהוּתְּרוּ לְזָר – **for we have found** a precedent where **they were permitted to a non-Kohen;** שֶׁאָכַל מֹשֶׁה בְּשַׂר הַמִּלּוּאִים – **for Moses,** who was not a Kohen, **ate the flesh,** i.e., the breast, **of the inaugural offerings,**[1] אֲבָל בְּחָזֶה וָשׁוֹק – **but the breast and leg,** the Kohen's portion, שֶׁל קָדָשִׁים קַלִּים – **of those of the lesser degree of holiness** לֹא יֹאכַל – **[a blemished Kohen] may not eat,** שֶׁלֹּא מָצִינוּ זָר חוֹלֵק בָּהֶן – **for we have not found a non-Kohen taking a portion of them."** לְכָךְ נֶאֶמְרוּ קָדָשִׁים קַלִּים – **This is why those of the lesser degree of holiness were stated** as being permitted to a blemished Kohen. [2]כַּךְ מְפֹרָשׁ בִּזְבָחִים – **Thus is it explained in** *Zevachim.*[2]

23. אַךְ אֶל הַפָּרֹכֶת – BUT HE SHALL NOT COME TO THE *PAROCHES*. לְהַזּוֹת שֶׁבַע הַזָּאוֹת – To sprinkle seven sprinklings of blood שֶׁעַל הַפָּרֹכֶת – that are sprinkled on the *Paroches*.[3]

☐ וְאֶל הַמִּזְבֵּחַ – AND [HE SHALL NOT APPROACH] THE *MIZBE'ACH*.[4] הַחִיצוֹן – This refers to the outer one. וּשְׁנֵיהֶם – Both of them, i.e., both statements, the one about the outer *Mizbe'ach* and the other about the *Paroches*, הֻצְרְכוּ לְהִכָּתֵב – had to be written, and one could not have been derived from the other, וּמְפֹרָשׁ בְּתוֹרַת כֹּהֲנִים – and it is explained in *Toras Kohanim*.[5]

☐ וְלֹא יְחַלֵּל אֶת מִקְדָּשַׁי – AND HE SHALL NOT DEFILE MY HOLY SERVICES. שֶׁאִם עָבַד – For if he performed the service, עֲבוֹדָתוֹ מְחֻלֶּלֶת – his service is defiled לְהִפָּסֵל[6] – in that it becomes disqualified.[6]

---

1. The inaugural offerings were holy of the highest degree for they were allowed to be eaten only within the Courtyard of the Tabernacle, and only for one day and one night (Rashi to *Zevachim* 101b, s.v., שהרי הותרו לזר ולהן).

2. *Zevachim* 101b.

3. This is part of the sacrificial procedure of (a) the sin-offering of the Kohen Gadol (see 4:6 above); (b) the sin-offering brought on behalf of the entire nation of Israel when, due to an incorrect ruling by the Sanhedrin, there occurred mass unintentional transgression of a sin whose intentional violation is punished by *kares* (4:17); and (c) the bull and he-goat brought as a sin-offering on Yom Kippur (16:14-16; see, too, Rashi to 16:16).

"Coming to the *Paroches*," as opposed to touching the *Paroches*, implies entering the Sanctuary. But if this were the intent of the verse, it should have said so directly – אֶל אֹהֶל מוֹעֵד לֹא יָבֹא, "he shall not enter the Tent of Meeting." Therefore, "he shall not come to the *Paroches*" is taken to mean, "he shall not perform the service that involves the *Paroches*" (*Maskil LeDavid*).

4. The verse uses הַגָּשָׁה, "approaching," with regard to the *Mizbe'ach*, and בִּיאָה, "coming," with regard to the *Paroches*, to indicate that it refers to the Outer *Mizbe'ach*, which is outside the Sanctuary in a different area from the *Paroches*, and not to the Inner *Mizbe'ach*, which stood inside the Sanctuary together with the *Paroches* (*Maskil LeDavid*).

5. *Toras Kohanim*, *perek* 3:10. Had the verse mentioned only the prohibition against the blemished Kohen sprinkling blood on the *Paroches*, we could not have derived the prohibition against performing the service on the Outer *Mizbe'ach* from it, for the *Paroches* is inside the Sanctuary, in a holier area than the Outer *Mizbe'ach*. Similarly, had the verse mentioned only the prohibition against performing the service on the Outer *Mizbe'ach* we could not have derived the prohibition against sprinkling blood on the *Paroches* from it, for the actual offering takes place on the *Mizbe'ach*, while the *Paroches* is involved only with the sprinkling of the blood (*Toras Kohanim*). The prohibition that applies to the *Paroches* includes performing the service on the Gold *Mizbeach*, for it, like the *Paroches*, is inside the Sanctuary (*Mizrachi*).

6. *Toras Kohanim, perek* 3:11; *Bechoros* 43b. Rashi understands מִקְדָּשַׁי as "My holy services," not "My Sanctuaries" (*Mizrachi; Sifsei Chachamim*).

²⁴ Moses spoke to Aaron and to his sons, and to all the Children of Israel.

22 ¹ Hashem spoke to Moses, saying: ² Speak to Aaron and to his sons, that they shall withdraw from that which is holy of the Children of Israel — that which they consecrate to Me — so as not to defile My holy Name, I am Hashem. ³ Say to them: Throughout your generations, any man from among any of your offspring who shall come near

כד וַיְדַבֵּר מֹשֶׁה אֶל־אַהֲרֹן וְאֶל־בָּנָיו וְאֶל־כָּל־בְּנֵי יִשְׂרָאֵל:
כב א־ב וַיְדַבֵּר יְהֹוָה אֶל־מֹשֶׁה לֵּאמֹר: דַּבֵּר אֶל־אַהֲרֹן וְאֶל־בָּנָיו וְיִנָּזְרוּ מִקָּדְשֵׁי בְנֵי־יִשְׂרָאֵל וְלֹא יְחַלְּלוּ אֶת־שֵׁם קָדְשִׁי אֲשֶׁר הֵם מַקְדִּשִׁים לִי אֲנִי יְהֹוָה: ג אֱמֹר אֲלֵהֶם לְדֹרֹתֵיכֶם כָּל־אִישׁ ׀ אֲשֶׁר־יִקְרַב מִכָּל־זַרְעֲכֶם

— אונקלוס —

כד וּמַלִּיל מֹשֶׁה עִם אַהֲרֹן וְעִם בְּנוֹהִי וְעִם כָּל בְּנֵי יִשְׂרָאֵל: א וּמַלִּיל יְיָ עִם מֹשֶׁה לְמֵימָר: ב מַלֵּל עִם אַהֲרֹן וְעִם בְּנוֹהִי וְיִפְרְשׁוּן מְקוּדְשַׁיָּא דִּבְנֵי יִשְׂרָאֵל וְלָא יְחַלּוּן יָת שְׁמָא דְקוּדְשִׁי דִּי אִנּוּן מְקַדְּשִׁין קֳדָמַי אֲנָא יְיָ: ג אֱמַר לְהוֹן לְדָרֵיכוֹן כָּל גְּבַר דִּי יִקְרַב מִכָּל בְּנֵיכוֹן

— רש"י —

(כד) וידבר משה. המצוה הזאת: **אל אהרן ואל בניו ואל כל בני ישראל.** להזהיר בית דין על הכהנים (ת"כ שם יב): **(ב) וינזרו.** אין נזירה אלא פרישה וכן הוא אומר וינזר מאחרי (יחזקאל יד:ז) נזורו אחור (ישעיה א:ד; ת"כ פרשתא ד:ח) ויכרי מקדשי בני ישראל אשר הם מקדישים לי ולא יחללו את שם קדשי סרס המקרא ודרשהו: **אשר הם מקדישים לי.** לרבות קדשי כהנים עצמן (ת"כ שם): **(ג) כל איש אשר יקרב.** אין

— RASHI ELUCIDATED —

24. וַיְדַבֵּר מֹשֶׁה — MOSES SPOKE הַמִּצְוָה הַזֹּאת — this commandment.[1] אֶל אַהֲרֹן וְאֶל בָּנָיו וְאֶל כָּל בְּנֵי יִשְׂרָאֵל — TO AARON AND TO HIS SONS, AND TO ALL THE CHILDREN OF ISRAEL. לְהַזְהִיר בֵּית דִּין — To alert the court, i.e., to make the court responsible, ²עַל הַכֹּהֲנִים — with regard to the Kohanim keeping the commandments that apply to them alone.[2]

22.

2. וְיִנָּזְרוּ — THAT THEY SHALL WITHDRAW. אֵין נְזִירָה אֶלָּא פְּרִישָׁה — נְזִירָה means only "separation." וְכֵן הוּא אוֹמֵר — And similarly it says, ³"וַיִּנָּזֵר מֵאַחֲרַי" — "and who separated himself from Me,"[3] ⁴'⁵נָזוֹרוּ אָחוֹר, — "they withdrew toward the rear."[4,5] In our verse, וְיִנָּזְרוּ means יִפְרְשׁוּ מִן הַקֳּדָשִׁים — they shall separate from that which is holy בִּימֵי טֻמְאָתָן — in the days of their impurity. The verse is thus to be interpreted as if it were written, וְיִנָּזְרוּ⁶ מִקָּדְשֵׁי בְנֵי יִשְׂרָאֵל — "that they shall withdraw from that which is holy of the Children of Israel אֲשֶׁר הֵם מַקְדִּשִׁים — which they consecrate to me, וְלֹא יְחַלְּלוּ — so as not to defile אֶת שֵׁם קָדְשִׁי — My holy Name." סָרֵס הַמִּקְרָא וְדָרְשֵׁהוּ — Invert the verse and explain it.[7]

□ אֲשֶׁר הֵם מַקְדִּשִׁים לִי — THAT WHICH THEY CONSECRATE TO ME. ⁸לְרַבּוֹת קָדְשֵׁי כֹהֲנִים עַצְמָן — To include that which is holy of the Kohanim themselves, i.e., that which the Kohanim themselves consecrate.[8]

3. אֵין כָּל אִישׁ אֲשֶׁר יִקְרַב — ANY MAN [FROM AMONG ANY OF YOUR OFFSPRING] WHO SHALL COME NEAR. אֵין

---

1. The verse says that Moses spoke to Aaron, his sons, and the Children of Israel, but does not tell us what he said. Rashi supplies the content of the speech mentioned in the verse (*Sefer Zikaron*).
2. *Toras Kohanim, perek* 3:12. This explains why Moses related these commandments, which apply only to the Kohanim, to the entire nation of Israel (*Mizrachi; Sifsei Chachamim*).
3. *Ezekiel* 14:7.
4. *Isaiah* 1:4.
5. *Toras Kohanim, parshasa* 4:1.
6. Many editions of Rashi have the words דָּבָר אַחֵר before the words וְיִנָּזְרוּ מִקָּדְשֵׁי בְּנֵי יִשְׂרָאֵל. The commentators have noted that these words are incongruous, for Rashi does not go on to present an alternative to the explanation that he gave before. *Maskil LeDavid* and *Levush Ha-Orah* are of the opinion that these words should be deleted from the text of Rashi. *Yosef Hallel* points out that this is supported by the fact that דָּבָר אַחֵר does not appear in the first printed edition of Rashi.
7. As the verse stands, it is not clear what "which they consecrate to Me" refers to. Rashi explains that the phrases of the verse must be inverted. The verse means to say, "They shall withdraw from that which is holy of the Children of Israel which they consecrate to Me, so as not to defile My holy Name" (*Gur Aryeh*).
8. *Toras Kohanim, parshasa* 4:1. We may have thought that that which the Kohanim themselves consecrate is

275 / VAYIKRA/LEVITICUS – PARASHAS EMOR   22/3 – כב/ג

───────────────── רש״י ─────────────────

קְרֵבָה זוֹ אֵלָא אֲכִילָה, וְכֵן מָצִינוּ שֶׁנֶּאֶמְרָה אַזְהָרַת אֲכִילַת קָדָשִׁים   הָאֲכִילָה בּוֹ אֶת אַהֲרֹן שְׁתֵּי כְרִיתוֹת זוֹ אֵצֶל זוֹ (לְעֵיל ז:כ-כא) וְאִם
בְּטוּמְאָה בִּלְשׁוֹן נְגִיעָה, בְּכָל קֹדֶשׁ לֹא תִגָּע (לְעֵיל יב:ד) אַזְהָרָה לָאוֹכֵל   עַל הַנְּגִיעָה חַיָּב לֹא הֻצְרַךְ לְחַיְּבוֹ עַל הָאֲכִילָה. וְכֵן נִדְרַשׁ בְּת״כ
וּלְמָדוּהוּ רַבּוֹתֵינוּ מִגְּזֵרָה שָׁוָה [ס״א מֵהֶקֵּשָׁא] (יְבָמוֹת עה.; זְבָחִים   (פָּרָשְׁתָא ד:ז) וְכִי יֵשׁ נוֹגֵעַ חַיָּב, אִם כֵּן מַה ת״ל יִקְרָב, מִשֶּׁיֻּכְשַׁר
מג:) וַאֲנִי אֶפְשָׁר לוֹמַר שֶׁחִיָּב עַל הַנְּגִיעָה, שֶׁהֲרֵי נֶאֱמַר כָּרֵת עַל   לְהִקָּרֵב, שֶׁאֵין חַיָּבִין עָלָיו מִשּׁוּם טוּמְאָה אֶלָּא אִם כֵּן קְרֵבוּ מַתִּירָיו.

─────────────── RASHI ELUCIDATED ───────────────

קְרֵבָה זוֹ אֵלָא אֲכִילָה – This "coming near" means nothing but eating. **וְכֵן מָצִינוּ** – Similarly, we have found **שֶׁנֶּאֶמְרָה אַזְהָרַת אֲכִילַת קָדָשִׁים בְּטוּמְאָה** – that the negative commandment against eating that which is holy while in a state of impurity was stated **בִּלְשׁוֹן נְגִיעָה** – in terms of "touching," in the verse, **בְּכָל קֹדֶשׁ לֹא תִגָּע,** – "she may not touch anything sacred,"[1] **אַזְהָרָה לָאוֹכֵל** – which is a negative commandment for one who eats, i.e., not to eat, that which is holy while impure. **וּלְמָדוּהוּ רַבּוֹתֵינוּ מִגְּזֵרָה שָׁוָה** – Our Rabbis derived [the fact that the above verse refers to eating rather than touching] from a *gezeirah shavah.*[2] **וַאֲנִי אֶפְשָׁר לוֹמַר** – It is impossible to say regarding our verse **שֶׁחִיָּב עַל הַנְּגִיעָה** – that he is subject to *kares* for touching **שֶׁהֲרֵי נֶאֱמַר כָּרֵת עַל הָאֲכִילָה** – because, see, now, *kares* has been stated with regard to eating that which is sacred while in a state of impurity **בְּצַו אֶת אַהֲרֹן** – in *Parashas Tzav es Aharon,* **שְׁתֵּי כְרִיתוֹת** – two mentions of *kares* **זוֹ אֵצֶל זוֹ** – one next to the other,[3] **וְאִם עַל הַנְּגִיעָה חַיָּב** – and if he would be subject to *kares* for the mere touching, **לֹא הֻצְרַךְ** – it would not be necessary **לְחַיְּבוֹ** – to make him subject to *kares,* i.e., to state his punishment explicitly, **עַל הָאֲכִילָה** – for the eating.[4] **וְכֵן נִדְרַשׁ בְּתוֹרַת כֹּהֲנִים**[5] – [Our verse] which speaks of eating in terms of "coming near" is expounded in *Toras Kohanim*[5] as follows: **וְכִי יֵשׁ נוֹגֵעַ חַיָּב** – Can there be one who touches that which is sacred while in a state of impurity who is subject to *kares,* as "any man . . . *who shall come near*" implies? **אִם כֵּן** – If so, that there is no *kares* for touching, **מַה תַּלְמוּד לוֹמַר** – why does the verse say, ",יִקְרָב" – "who shall come near"? To teach us that he is subject to *kares* only **מִשֶּׁיֻּכְשַׁר לִקָּרֵב** – once it has been rendered fit to be brought near, i.e., to be offered up on the *Mizbe'ach,* **שֶׁאֵין חַיָּבִין עָלָיו** – for one is not subject to *kares* on account of it **מִשּׁוּם טֻמְאָה** – because of impurity **אֶלָּא אִם כֵּן קְרֵבוּ מַתִּירָיו** – unless those things which permit it to be eaten have been brought near,[6] i.e., offered up.

---

so holy that impurity would not affect it as it does that which is consecrated by non-Kohanim (*Be'er BaSadeh*). "That which is holy of the Children of Israel . . . which they consecrate to Me" appears redundant, for that which is holy is obviously consecrated. The apparently superfluous "which they consecrate to Me" includes that which the Kohanim consecrate (*Maskil LeDavid*).

1. Above 12:4.

2. *Yevamos* 75a; *Zevachim* 43b. (For the definition of *gezeirah shavah,* see note 10 on page 155.)

Mizrachi and *Sifsei Chachamim* suggest that an error has crept into the text of Rashi, which should read מֵהֶקֵּשָׁא, "from a *hekesh* (הֶקֵּשׁ), comparison," rather than *gezeirah shavah.* A *hekesh* is a method of deriving information in which that which is stated explicitly with regard to one context is applied to another context, as well, by virtue of the two topics appearing in the same verse. The fact that בְּכָל קֹדֶשׁ לֹא תִגָּע refers to eating that which is holy is derived by the *Gemara* in *Yevamos* 75a from a הֶקֵּשׁ. The verse reads, בְּכָל קֹדֶשׁ לֹא תִגָּע וְאֶל הַמִּקְדָּשׁ לֹא תָבֹא, "She may not eat anything sacred, and she may not come to the Sanctuary." Just as the negative commandment with regard to the Sanctuary mentioned by the verse refers to a sin punishable by *kares,* so, too, the negative commandment regarding "touching" that which is sacred must refer to a sin punishable by *kares.* Although it is forbidden, one does not get *kares* for merely touching that which is sacred while in a state of impurity. There is *kares,* however, for eating that which is sacred while one is in a state of impurity. Thus, that verse refers to eating but put it in terms of touching.

However, some authorities are of the opinion that *hekesh* is a sub-category of *gezeirah shavah.* If this is Rashi's opinion, there is no reason to emend our text. See אנציקלופדיה תלמודית under הֶקֵּשׁ.

3. In verses 7:20 and 7:21 above.

4. Because one must touch the food in order to eat it (*Mizrachi*). Alternatively, because eating by its nature is a more severe transgression than mere touching (*Nachalas Yaakov*). Therefore, if the Torah states that one is subject to *kares* for eating, it must be that he is not subject to *kares* for touching.

5. *Toras Kohanim, parshasa* 4:7.

6. "Coming near" of our verse refers to eating rather than touching. *Kares* applies only to one who eats while impure, not to one who touches. But eating is expressed here as "coming near" to teach us that the punishment of *kares* for eating applies only at a particular stage of the sacrificial process — when parts of the offering have been "brought near," i.e., offered up, thus rendering the rest of the offering permissible to be eaten by those who are commanded to eat it. In the case of the meat of animal offerings, this refers to the sprinkling of the blood on the *Mizbe'ach*; in the case of the meal of

אֶל־הַקֳּדָשִׁים֙ אֲשֶׁ֨ר יַקְדִּ֤ישׁוּ בְנֵֽי־יִשְׂרָאֵל֙ לַֽיהֹוָ֔ה וְטֻמְאָת֖וֹ עָלָ֑יו וְנִכְרְתָ֞ה הַנֶּ֧פֶשׁ הַהִ֛וא מִלְּפָנַ֖י אֲנִ֥י יְהֹוָֽה׃

ד אִ֣ישׁ אִ֞ישׁ מִזֶּ֣רַע אַהֲרֹ֗ן וְה֤וּא צָר֙וּעַ֙ א֣וֹ זָ֔ב בַּקֳּדָשִׁים֙ לֹ֣א יֹאכַ֔ל עַ֖ד אֲשֶׁ֥ר יִטְהָ֑ר וְהַנֹּגֵ֙עַ֙

the holies that the Children of Israel may sanctify to HASHEM with his impurity upon him — that person shall be cut off from before Me, I am HASHEM. *4* Any man from the offspring of Aaron and he is a metzora or a person who is impure due to a discharge shall not eat from the holies until he becomes purified; and one who touches

─────────────── אונקלוס ───────────────

לְקוּדְשַׁיָּא דִּי יַקְדְּשׁוּן בְּנֵי יִשְׂרָאֵל קֳדָם יְיָ וְסוֹאֲבְתֵהּ עֲלוֹהִי וְיִשְׁתֵּיצֵי אֲנָשָׁא הַהוּא מִן קֳדָמַי אֲנָא יְיָ: ד גְּבַר גְּבַר מִזַּרְעָא דְאַהֲרֹן וְהוּא סְגִיר אוֹ דָאִיב בְּקוּדְשַׁיָּא לָא יֵיכוּל עַד דִּי יִדְכֵּי וּדְיִקְרַב

─────────────── רש"י ───────────────

וְאִם תֹּאמַר שָׁלֹשׁ כְּרִיתוֹת בְּטוּמְאַת קָדָשִׁים [ס"א ד' כהנים] לָמָּה, כְּבָר נִדְרְשׁוּ בְּמַסֶּ' שְׁבוּעוֹת (ז.) אַחַת לִכְלָל וְאַחַת לִפְרָט וְכוּ':
וְטֻמְאָתוֹ עָלָיו. וְטֻמְאָתוֹ הָאָדָם עָלָיו. יָכוֹל בַּבָּשָׂר הַכָּתוּב מְדַבֵּר, וְטֻמְאָתוֹ שֶׁל בָּשָׂר עָלָיו, וּבְטָהוֹר שֶׁאָכַל אֶת הַטָּמֵא הַכָּתוּב

מְדַבֵּר, עַל כָּרְחֲךָ מִמַּשְׁמָעוֹ אַתָּה לָמֵד, בְּמִי שֶׁטֻּמְאָתוֹ פּוֹרַחַת מִמֶּנּוּ הַכָּתוּב מְדַבֵּר (ת"כ שם ט; זבחים מג:) וְזֶהוּ הָאָדָם שֶׁיֵּשׁ לוֹ טָהֳרָה בִּטְבִילָה: **וְנִכְרְתָה וְגוֹ'.** יָכוֹל מִצַּד זֶה לְצַד זֶה, יִכָּרֵת מִמְּקוֹמוֹ וְיִתְיַשֵּׁב בְּמָקוֹם אַחֵר, ת"ל אֲנִי ה', בְּכָל מָקוֹם אֲנִי (ת"כ שם י):

─────────────── RASHI ELUCIDATED ───────────────

שָׁלֹשׁ כְּרִיתוֹת בְּטֻמְאַת קָדָשִׁים לָמָּה — why are there three statements of the punishment of *kares* made with regard to the impurity of that which is holy, i.e., with regard to the prohibition against eating that which is holy while they are impure?[1] וְאִם תֹּאמַר — **If you will say,** כְּבָר נִדְרְשׁוּ בְּמַסֶּכֶת שְׁבוּעוֹת — They have already been explained in Tractate *Shevuos:*[2] אַחַת לִכְלָל — **One is for a broad statement,** וְאַחַת לִפְרָט וְכוּלְהוּ — **and one is for a statement of particulars ...**[3]

וְטֻמְאָתוֹ עָלָיו — WITH HIS IMPURITY UPON HIM. The verse means, וְטֻמְאַת הָאָדָם עָלָיו — **with the impurity of the person upon him.** יָכוֹל בַּבָּשָׂר הַכָּתוּב מְדַבֵּר — **One might be able** to think that **the verse speaks of the flesh** of an offering, and means וְטֻמְאָתוֹ שֶׁל בָּשָׂר עָלָיו — **with the impurity of the flesh upon** *it,* וּבְטָהוֹר שֶׁאָכַל אֶת הַטָּמֵא הַכָּתוּב מְדַבֵּר — **and the verse would be speaking of one who is pure who ate** meat of an offering that became **impure.** עַל כָּרְחֲךָ — **You must of necessity** say that מִמַּשְׁמָעוֹ אַתָּה לָמֵד — **from** [the verse's] **implication you learn** בְּמִי שֶׁטֻּמְאָתוֹ פּוֹרַחַת מִמֶּנּוּ הַכָּתוּב מְדַבֵּר — that **the verse speaks of one whose impurity can depart from him,**[4] וְזֶהוּ הָאָדָם — **and this is the man** שֶׁיֵּשׁ לוֹ טָהֳרָה בִּטְבִילָה — **who has purification through immersion** in a *mikveh.*[5]

וְנִכְרְתָה וְגוֹמֵר — SHALL BE CUT OFF, ETC. יָכוֹל — **One might be able** to think that he is cut off מִצַּד זֶה לְצַד זֶה — **from this side to that side;** יִכָּרֵת מִמְּקוֹמוֹ — **he shall be cut off from his place** וְיִתְיַשֵּׁב בְּמָקוֹם אַחֵר — **and settle in another place.**[6] תַּלְמוּד לוֹמַר — **To teach us otherwise,** the verse says, אֲנִי ה' — **"I am HASHEM,"** which implies, בְּכָל מָקוֹם אֲנִי — **I am every-where.**[7]

---

meal-offerings, it refers to the burning of the handful of meal on the *Mizbe'ach*. As for those parts of offerings that may not be eaten, such as the frankincense and the handful of meal of the meal-offering, and the parts of animal offerings burned on the *Mizbe'ach*, the law against eating that which is sacred while impure takes effect once they have been placed in the כְּלֵי הַשָּׁרֵת, "sanctified vessels," used in the service (*Mizrachi*).

1. Several editions of Rashi have בְּטֻמְאַת כֹּהֲנִים, "with regard to the impurity of the Kohanim," rather than בְּטֻמְאַת קָדָשִׁים. That text is problematic, for the prohibition against eating that which is holy while in a state of impurity applies to all Jews, not only to Kohanim. Our text follows that of *Mizrachi*.

2. *Shevuos* 7a.

3. See 7:20 above and Rashi there.

4. *Toras Kohanim, parshasa* 4:9; *Zevachim* 43b.

5. "With his impurity upon him" or "with its impurity upon it" implies that the impurity is transitory. This is true of the impurity of man, which departs after he undergoes purification. But meat of offerings that become impure can never be purified (*Mizrachi; Sifsei Chachamim*).

6. We may have thought that by "cutting off," the Torah means exile.

7. *Toras Kohanim, parshasa* 4:10. He is cut off wherever God is present; he is cut off from the entire world through premature death (*Be'er BaSadeh*).

22/5-6

בְּכָל־טְמֵא־נֶפֶשׁ אוֹ אִישׁ אֲשֶׁר־
תֵּצֵא מִמֶּנּוּ שִׁכְבַת־זָרַע: אוֹ־ ה
אִישׁ אֲשֶׁר יִגַּע בְּכָל־שֶׁרֶץ
אֲשֶׁר יִטְמָא־לוֹ אוֹ בְאָדָם אֲשֶׁר
יִטְמָא־לוֹ לְכֹל טֻמְאָתוֹ: נֶפֶשׁ ו

anyone impure by a soul, or a man from whom there is a seminal emission; [5] *or a man who touches any creeping animal through which he can become impure, or a human through whom he can become impure, whatever his impurity.* [6] *The person*

---- אונקלוס ----

בְּכָל מְסָאָב נַפְשָׁא אוֹ גְבַר דִּי תִפּוֹק מִנֵּהּ שִׁכְבַת זַרְעָא: ה אוֹ גְבַר דִּי יִקְרַב
בְּכָל רִחֲשָׁא דִּי יִסְתָּאַב לֵהּ אוֹ בֶאֱנָשָׁא דִּי יִסְתָּאַב לֵהּ לְכֹל סְאוֹבְתֵהּ: ו אֱנָשׁ

---- רש"י ----

(ד) [מִזֶּרַע אַהֲרֹן. הַכֹּהֵן. אֵין לִי אֶלָּא זַרְעוֹ, גּוּפוֹ מִנַּיִן, ת"ל] אַף כַּאן בִּיאַת שֶׁמֶשׁ (שָׁם ב; בְּרָכוֹת ב:): בְּכָל טְמֵא נֶפֶשׁ.
וְהוּא לָרוּעַ. שִׁיכּוֹל הוֹאִיל וּמַקְרִיב אוֹנֵן יַקְרִיב לָרוּעַ וְזָב, בְּמֵי שֶׁנִּטְמָא בְּמֵת (ת"כ שָׁם ג): (ה) בְּכָל שֶׁרֶץ אֲשֶׁר
ת"ל וְהוּא (ת"כ פֶּרֶק ד:א): עַד אֲשֶׁר יִטְהָר. בִּיאַת יִטְמָא לוֹ. בַּשִּׁעוּר הָרָאוּי לְטַמֵּא (שָׁם ד) בְּכַעֲדָשָׁה (חֲגִיגָה יא.):
הַשֶּׁמֶשׁ, אוֹ אֵינוֹ אֶלָּא טְבִילָה, נֶאֱמַר כַּאן יִטְהָר וְנֶאֱמַר לְמַטָּה אוֹ בָאָדָם. בְּמֵת: אֲשֶׁר יִטְמָא לוֹ. כְּשִׁעוּרוֹ לְטַמֵּא וְזֶהוּ כְזַיִת
וְטָהֵר, וּבָא הַשֶּׁמֶשׁ וְטָהֵר (לְהַלָּן פָּסוּק ז), מַה לְּהַלָּן בִּיאַת הַשֶּׁמֶשׁ (אֹהָלוֹת ב:א): לְכָל טֻמְאָתוֹ. לְרַבּוֹת נוֹגֵעַ בְּזָב וְזָבָה

---- RASHI ELUCIDATED ----

4. {¹מִזֶּרַע אַהֲרֹן} — **FROM THE OFFSPRING OF AARON**¹ הַכֹּהֵן — **the Kohen.** From this phrase אֵין לִי אֶלָּא זַרְעוֹ — **I know only of his offspring.** גּוּפוֹ מִנַּיִן — **From where do I know of himself,** i.e., from where do we know that the law of our verse applies to Aaron himself? תַּלְמוּד לוֹמַר — **To provide this source, the verse says,** וְהוּא צָרוּעַ — "**and he is a** *metzora*." שֶׁיָּכוֹל הוֹאִיל וּמַקְרִיב אוֹנֵן — **For one might have thought, since [a Kohen Gadol] may perform the service while he is an** *onein***,** יַקְרִיב צָרוּעַ וְזָב — **he may [also] perform the service while he is a** *metzora* **or a** *zav***.** תַּלְמוּד לוֹמַר — **To teach otherwise, the verse says,** ²"וְהוּא", — "**and he.**"²

□ עַד אֲשֶׁר יִטְהָר — **UNTIL HE BECOMES PURIFIED.** בִּיאַת הַשֶּׁמֶשׁ — **This means with the sunset,** after his immersion. אוֹ אֵינוֹ אֶלָּא טְבִילָה — **Or perhaps it means only immersion?** נֶאֱמַר כַּאן, "יִטְהָר" — **It says** here, יִטְהָר, "**he becomes purified,**" וְנֶאֱמַר לְמַטָּה — **and it says below,** וְטָהֵר, "**and he will become purified,**" in the verse ³"וּבָא הַשֶּׁמֶשׁ וְטָהֵר", — "**after the sun has set, and he will become purified.**"³ מַה לְּהַלָּן בִּיאַת הַשֶּׁמֶשׁ — **Just as below [the verse refers to] sunset,** אַף כַּאן בִּיאַת שֶׁמֶשׁ — **here, too, [the verse refers to] sunset.**⁴}

□ בְּכָל טְמֵא נֶפֶשׁ — **ANYONE WHO IS IMPURE BY A SOUL.** ⁴בְּמִי שֶׁנִּטְמָא בְּמֵת — **One who became impure through** contact with **the dead.**⁵

5. בְּכָל שֶׁרֶץ אֲשֶׁר יִטְמָא לוֹ — **ANY CREEPING ANIMAL THROUGH WHICH HE CAN BECOME IMPURE.** בַּשִּׁעוּר הָרָאוּי לְטַמֵּא — **Through the quantity fit to transmit impurity,**⁶ i.e., ⁷בְּכַעֲדָשָׁה — **through the volume of a lentil.**⁷

□ אוֹ בְאָדָם — **OR A HUMAN.** בְּמֵת — **A corpse.**⁸

□ אֲשֶׁר יִטְמָא לוֹ — **THROUGH WHOM HE CAN BECOME IMPURE.** כְּשִׁעוּרוֹ לְטַמֵּא — **According to its** minimum **quantity for transmitting impurity,** ⁹וְזֶהוּ כְזַיִת — **and this is the volume of an olive.**⁹

□ לְכָל טֻמְאָתוֹ — **WHATEVER HIS IMPURITY.** לְרַבּוֹת נוֹגֵעַ בְּזָב וְזָבָה — **To include one who touches a**

---

1. *Yosef Hallel* notes that Rashi's next two comments appeared in the Alkabetz edition of Rashi (ca. 1482) but have not appeared in subsequent editions.
2. *Toras Kohanim, perek* 4:1.
3. Below v. 7.
4. *Toras Kohanim, perek* 4:2; *Berachos* 2b.
5. *Toras Kohanim, perek* 4:3.
6. *Toras Kohanim, perek* 4:4.
7. *Chagigah* 11a. The verse could have said only בְּכָל שֶׁרֶץ, "any creeping animal," and we would have assumed that it refers to those creeping animals that transmit impurity. The apparently superfluous אֲשֶׁר יִטְמָא לוֹ, "through

which he can become impure," teaches us that not only does one become impure by touching an intact carcass of a creeping animal, but that there also exists a minimum fixed volume that transmits impurity, even if it is only a part of a carcass (*Mizrachi*).
8. One who touches a corpse is impure for at least seven days. Thus, when the following verse says, "the person who touches it shall be impure until evening" with regard to touching a corpse, it means that he shall be impure until the evening of the seventh day. It is not enough that he remain in his impurity for merely part of the seventh day (*Minchas Yehudah; Sifsei Chachamim*).
9. *Ohalos* 2:1. The apparently superfluous אֲשֶׁר יִטְמָא לוֹ,

who touches it shall be impure until evening; he shall not eat from the holies unless he has immersed his flesh in the water. ⁷ *After the sun has set and he will become purified; thereafter, he may eat from that which is holy, for it is his food.* ⁸ *A carcass or a mauled animal he shall not eat, to become impure through it — I am HASHEM.*

אֲשֶׁ֣ר יִגַּע־בּ֔וֹ וְטָמְאָ֖ה עַד־הָעָ֑רֶב וְלֹ֤א יֹאכַל֙ מִן־הַקֳּדָשִׁ֔ים כִּ֛י אִם־רָחַ֥ץ בְּשָׂר֖וֹ בַּמָּֽיִם׃ ⁷ וּבָ֥א הַשֶּׁ֖מֶשׁ וְטָהֵ֑ר וְאַחַר֙ יֹאכַ֣ל מִן־הַקֳּדָשִׁ֔ים כִּ֥י לַחְמ֖וֹ הֽוּא׃ ⁸ נְבֵלָ֧ה וּטְרֵפָ֛ה לֹ֥א יֹאכַ֖ל לְטָמְאָה־בָ֑הּ אֲנִ֖י יְהוָֽה׃

―――――――――――― אונקלוס ――――――――――――

דִּי יִקְרַב בֵּיהּ וִיהֵי מְסָאָב עַד רַמְשָׁא וְלָא יֵיכוּל מִן קוּדְשַׁיָּא אֱלָהֵן אַסְחִי בִשְׂרֵיהּ בְּמַיָּא: ⁷וּבִמְעַל שִׁמְשָׁא וְיִדְכֵּי וּבָתַר כֵּן יֵיכוּל מִן קוּדְשַׁיָּא אֲרֵי לַחְמֵהּ הוּא: ⁸נְבֵילָא וּתְבִירָא לָא יֵיכוּל לְאִסְתָּאָבָא בַהּ אֲנָא יְיָ:

―――――――――――― רש"י ――――――――――――

נדה ויולדת (ת"כ שם ד'): (ו) נפש אשר תגע בו. באחד מן הטמאים הללו: כי אם רחץ בשרו. יכול אבר אבר, ת"ל ובא השמש, מה ביאת שמש כאחת אף טבילה כולה כאחת (שם ז':): (ז) ואחר יאכל מן הקדשים. נדרש ביבמות בתרומה שמותר לאכלה בהערב השמש. ולא כל הקדשים: (ח) נבלה וטרפה לא יאכל לטמאה בה. לענין הטומאה הזהיר כאן,

―――――――――――― RASHI ELUCIDATED ――――――――――――

zav[1] or a *zavah*,[2] — נִדָּה — a *niddah*[3] — וְיוֹלֶדֶת[5] — or a woman who has given birth.[4,5]

6. נֶפֶשׁ אֲשֶׁר תִּגַּע בּוֹ — **THE PERSON WHO TOUCHES IT.** בְּאֶחָד מִן הַטְּמֵאִים הַלָּלוּ — **One of these** people or things **which are impure.**[6]

{כִּי אִם רָחַץ בְּשָׂרוֹ} — **UNLESS HE HAS IMMERSED HIS FLESH.**[7] יָכוֹל אֵבֶר אֵבֶר — **One might be able to** think that he can immerse himself **limb by limb.** תַּלְמוּד לוֹמַר — **To teach us otherwise, the next verse says,** וּבָא הַשֶּׁמֶשׁ — **"after the sun has set";** מַה בִּיאַת שֶׁמֶשׁ כְּאֶחָת — **just as the setting of the sun is as one,** i.e., just as the sun sets in its entirety, not part by part, ⁸אַף טְבִילָה כֻּלָּהּ כְּאַחַת — **so immersion is** to be performed **as one,** i.e., he must immerse his entire body at once.[8]}

7. וְאַחַר יֹאכַל מִן הַקֳּדָשִׁים — **THEREAFTER, HE MAY EAT FROM THAT WHICH IS HOLY.** נִדְרָשׁ בִּיבָמוֹת[9] — [This verse] is interpreted in *Yevamos*[9] בִּתְרוּמָה — as speaking about *terumah*,[10] שֶׁמֻּתָּר לְאָכְלָהּ בְּהֶעֱרֵב הַשֶּׁמֶשׁ — that it is permitted to eat it after the setting of the sun.[11]

{מִן הַקֳּדָשִׁים} — **FROM THAT WHICH IS HOLY.** וְלֹא כָּל הַקֳּדָשִׁים — **But not** from **all that is holy.**[12]}[13]

8. נְבֵלָה וּטְרֵפָה לֹא יֹאכַל לְטָמְאָה בָהּ — **HE SHALL NOT EAT FROM AN UNSLAUGHTERED CARCASS OR FROM A MAULED ANIMAL, TO BECOME IMPURE THROUGH IT.** לְעִנְיַן הַטֻּמְאָה הִזְהִיר כָּאן — **[The Torah] states a**

"through whom he can become impure," teaches us that not only does one become impure by touching an intact corpse, but that there also exists a minimum fixed volume that transmits impurity, even if it is only a part of a corpse (*Mizrachi; Sifsei Chachamim*).

1. See 15:2ff above.
2. See 15:25ff above.
3. See 15:19ff above.
4. See Chapter 12 above.
5. *Toras Kohanim, perek* 4:4. The broad term "whatever his impurity" refers back to, "a man who touches," not to the corpse which is the topic of "a human through whom he can become impure" that immediately precedes it. It includes all impurities not mentioned specifically in this verse and the previous one (*Be'er Yitzchak*).
6. Since our verse refers back to all of the sources of impurity mentioned in the two preceding verses, we would have expected it to say, נֶפֶשׁ אֲשֶׁר תִּגַּע בָּהֶם, "a person who touches *them*." The use of the singular בּוֹ "it," is not meant to indicate that the verse refers to only one of the above. It refers to any of the above

(*Minchas Yehudah; Sifsei Chachamim*).

7. *Yosef Hallel* notes that this comment appeared in the Alkabetz edition of Rashi (1476), but has not appeared in subsequent editions.
8. *Toras Kohanim, perek* 4:7.
9. *Yevamos* 74b.
10. The portion of the yearly crop which is given to the Kohanim. See *Numbers* 18:12.
11. Even in situations where the process of purification culminates in an offering, e.g., that of a woman who has given birth, a *metzora*, or a *zav*, the *terumah* may be eaten after sunset, following immersion. The offering that is brought the next day is a necessary requirement only to allow the eating of offerings.
12. מִן, "from," implies that the setting of the sun allows him to eat from that which is holy — *terumah*, but not all that is holy – not offerings (*Mizrachi; Sifsei Chachamim*).
13. This comment does not appear in the first printed edition of Rashi. In the aforementioned Alkabetz edition, it is linked to the previous comment with the phrase לְכָךְ כְּתִיב, "therefore it is written" (see *Yosef Hallel*).

9 They shall guard My safekeeping and they shall not bear sin over it and die because of it, for they will have defiled it —

ט וְשָׁמְרוּ אֶת־מִשְׁמַרְתִּי וְלֹא־יִשְׂאוּ עָלָיו חֵטְא וּמֵתוּ בוֹ כִּי יְחַלְּלֻהוּ

—————— אונקלוס ——————

ט וְיִטְּרוּן יָת מַטְּרַת מֵימְרִי וְלָא יְקַבְּלוּן עֲלוֹהִי חוֹבָא וִימוּתוּן בֵּהּ אֲרֵי יְחַלְּנַהּ

—————— רש"י ——————

שֶׁאִם אָכַל נִבְלַת עוֹף טָהוֹר שֶׁאֵין שֶׁאֵין טוּמְאַת מַגַּע וּמַשָּׂא אֶלָּא טוּמְאַת אֲכִילָה בְּבֵית הַבְּלִיעָה (ת"כ שָׁם יב/יג) אָסוּר לֶאֱכוֹל בַּקֳּדָשִׁים [וְצָרִיךְ לוֹמַר וּטְרֵפָה מִי שֶׁיֵּשׁ בְּמִינוֹ טְרֵפָה יָצָא נִבְלַת עוֹף טָמֵא שֶׁאֵין בְּמִינוֹ טְרֵפָה (ת"כ אַחֲרֵי פֶּרֶק יב:ז)]: **(ט) וְשָׁמְרוּ אֶת מִשְׁמַרְתִּי.** מִלֶּאֱכוֹל תְּרוּמָה בְּטוּמְאַת הַגּוּף: **וּמֵתוּ בוֹ.** לִמְּדוּ שֶׁהִיא מִיתָה בִּידֵי שָׁמַיִם (סַנְהֶדְרִין פג.):

—————— RASHI ELUCIDATED ——————

prohibition here with regard to the impurity, שֶׁאִם אָכַל נִבְלַת עוֹף טָהוֹר – that if he ate the unslaughtered carcass of a pure, i.e., kosher, **fowl,** שֶׁאֵין לָהּ טֻמְאַת מַגַּע וּמַשָּׂא – which does not have impurity of contact and carrying, i.e., which, unlike the carcasses of other animals, does not transmit impurity to a person by his touching it or bearing its weight, אֶלָּא טֻמְאַת אֲכִילָה – but it has **only impurity of eating,** i.e., impurity transmitted only through eating it, when it is בְּבֵית הַבְּלִיעָה[1] – in the **throat** of the one eating it,[1] אָסוּר לֶאֱכֹל בַּקֳּדָשִׁים – he is **forbidden to eat that which is holy.** וְצָרִיךְ לוֹמַר ,,וּטְרֵפָה'' – [The Torah] had to say "mauled animal," although the flesh of a mauled animal does not transmit impurity when it is eaten, מִי שֶׁיֵּשׁ בְּמִינוֹ טְרֵפָה – to teach us that the verse speaks of **that which has in its species a "mauled" animal,** i.e., a species to which "mauled" applies. יָצָא נִבְלַת עוֹף טָמֵא – This excludes the unslaughtered **carcass of an impure fowl,** i.e., of a non-kosher species, [2] שֶׁאֵין בְּמִינוֹ טְרֵפָה – which does not have a "mauled" animal in its species, i.e., it is a species to which "mauled" does not apply.[2]}

9. וְשָׁמְרוּ אֶת מִשְׁמַרְתִּי – **THEY SHALL GUARD MY SAFEKEEPING** מִלֶּאֱכוֹל תְּרוּמָה – from eating *terumah* בְּטֻמְאַת הַגּוּף – while in a state of **impurity of the body.**[3]

□ וּמֵתוּ בוֹ – **AND DIE BECAUSE OF IT.** לִמְּדָנוּ – This has taught us[4] שֶׁהִיא מִיתָה בִּידֵי שָׁמַיִם – **that it is death by the hands of Heaven.**[4]

---

1. *Toras Kohanim, perek* 4:12-13. Our verse states לֹא יֹאכַל לְטָמְאָה, "he shall not eat ... to become impure." This implies that the verse speaks of a carcass that imparts impurity only through eating, but not through touching or carrying. The carcass that fits this description is that of a kosher species of fowl. One might then reason that although the verse refers only to a fowl, the same law would apply *a fortiori* (*kal vachomer*) to an animal carcass. [If a fowl carcass, which does not impart impurity through touching and carrying, imparts impurity through eating, certainly an animal carcass, which does impart impurity through touching and carrying, also imparts impurity through eating.] To teach us otherwise, the verse states, בָּהּ, "through it," implying that a person becomes impure through eating *it*, but not through eating the carcass of an animal.

2. *Toras Kohanim, Acharei, perek* 12:7. A "mauled" animal is an animal that has one of eight types of mortal physical defects. Such an animal may not be eaten even if it is slaughtered properly. The fact that our verse speaks of a mauled animal appears to run counter to Rashi's assertion that it refers to a prohibition that applies only as the result of impurity, for the flesh of a properly slaughtered "mauled" animal transmits no impurity. Rashi explains that the verse mentions a "mauled" animal to teach us which unslaughtered fowl carcass it refers to. It refers to the unslaughtered carcass of fowl of a kosher species, a species to which the law of the "mauled" animal applies. The carcass of fowl of a non-kosher species does not transmit impurity. We know that the verse does not refer to the unslaughtered carcass of an animal, for the verse speaks in terms of eating. The unslaughtered carcass of an animal transmits impurity not only through eating it, but through touching it or bearing its weight, as well. But the carcass of an unslaughtered fowl transmits impurity only through contact with the throat of one who eats it (see *Mizrachi*).

3. *Sanhedrin* 83a. The verse could have said וְלֹא יִשְׂאוּ חֵטְא, "They shall not bear sin." וְלֹא יִשְׂאוּ עָלָיו חֵטְא "they shall not bear sin *over it*," implies that the verse refers back to *terumah*, which was the subject of verse 7 (see Rashi to *Sanhedrin*; *Nachalas Yaakov*).

4. *Sanhedrin* 83a. "Death at the hands of Heaven" is indicated by death before the age of sixty. Although Rashi has mentioned previously that when the Torah speaks of the death penalty without further elaboration, it refers to death by strangulation (see *Exodus* 21:16), this cannot be the intent of our verse. For eating *terumah* while impure is a lesser sin than eating offerings while impure, and eating offerings while impure does not carry with it a penalty as severe as execution by strangulation (*Minchas Yehudah; Sifsei Chachamim*).

אֲנִי יהוה מְקַדְּשָׁם: וְכָל־זָר לֹא־יֹאכַל קֹדֶשׁ תּוֹשַׁב כֹּהֵן וְשָׂכִיר לֹא־יֹאכַל קֹדֶשׁ: יא וְכֹהֵן כִּי־יִקְנֶה נֶפֶשׁ קִנְיַן כַּסְפּוֹ הוּא יֹאכַל בּוֹ וִילִיד בֵּיתוֹ

I am HASHEM, *Who sanctifies them.*
¹⁰ *Any outsider shall not eat of the holy; a Kohen's resident or a hired worker shall not eat of the holy.* ¹¹ *If a Kohen shall acquire a person, an acquisition of his money, he may eat of it; and someone born in his household*

──────── אונקלוס ────────

אֲנָא יְיָ מְקַדְּשְׁהוֹן: וְכָל חִלּוֹנַי לָא יֵיכוֹל קוּדְשָׁא תּוֹתָבָא דְכַהֲנָא וַאֲגִירָא לָא יֵיכוֹל קוּדְשָׁא: יא וְכָהֵן אֲרֵי יִקְנֵי נְפַשׁ קִנְיַן כַּסְפֵּהּ הוּא יֵיכוֹל בֵּהּ וִילִיד בֵּיתֵהּ

──────── רש"י ────────

(י) לֹא יֹאכַל קֹדֶשׁ. בִּתְרוּמָה הַכָּתוּב מְדַבֵּר שֶׁכָּל הָעִנְיָן דִּבֶּר בָּהּ (שם פג:): **תּוֹשָׁב כֹּהֵן וְשָׂכִיר.** תּוֹשָׁבוֹ שֶׁל כֹּהֵן וּשְׂכִירוֹ, לְפִיכָךְ תּוֹשָׁב זֶה נָקוּד פַּתָּח לְפִי שֶׁהוּא דָבוּק. וְאֵיזֶהוּ תּוֹשָׁב, זֶהוּ נִרְצָע שֶׁהוּא קָנוּי לוֹ עַד הַיּוֹבֵל. וְאֵיזֶהוּ שָׂכִיר, זֶה קְנוּי קִנְיַן שָׁנִים שֶׁיּוֹצֵא בְשֵׁשׁ (ת"כ שם יז; יבמות ע.), בָּא הַכָּתוּב וְלִמֶּדְךָ כָּאן שֶׁאֵין גּוּפוֹ קָנוּי לַאֲדוֹנָיו לֶאֱכוֹל בִּתְרוּמָתוֹ (יא): **וְכֹהֵן כִּי יִקְנֶה נֶפֶשׁ.** עֶבֶד כְּנַעֲנִי שֶׁקָּנוּי לְגוּפוֹ (ת"כ פַּרְשְׁתָא ה:א): **וִילִיד בֵּיתוֹ.** אֵלּוּ בְּנֵי הַשְּׁפָחוֹת. וְאֵשֶׁת כֹּהֵן אוֹכֶלֶת בִּתְרוּמָה מִן הַמִּקְרָא הַזֶּה (ת"כ שם; כתובות נז:) שֶׁאַף הִיא קִנְיַן כַּסְפּוֹ, וְעוֹד לָמַד מִמִּקְרָא אַחֵר (במדבר יח:יא) בְּסִפְרֵי (קרח קיז):

──────── RASHI ELUCIDATED ────────

10. לֹא יֹאכַל קֹדֶשׁ — SHALL NOT EAT OF THE HOLY. בִּתְרוּמָה הַכָּתוּב מְדַבֵּר — The verse speaks of *terumah*, שֶׁכָּל הָעִנְיָן דִּבֶּר בָּהּ — for the entire topic speaks of it.[1] □ תּוֹשַׁב כֹּהֵן וְשָׂכִיר — A KOHEN'S RESIDENT OR A HIRED WORKER. תּוֹשָׁבוֹ שֶׁל כֹּהֵן — A resident of a Kohen וּשְׂכִירוֹ — or his hired worker.[2] לְפִיכָךְ תּוֹשָׁב זֶה נָקוּד פַּתָּח — This is why this word[3] תּוֹשָׁב is vowelized with a *patach*, לְפִי שֶׁהוּא דָבוּק — because it is in the construct form.[4] וְאֵיזֶהוּ תּוֹשָׁב — And who is a "resident"? זֶה נִרְצָע — This is a *nirtza*.[5] He is called a "resident" שֶׁהוּא קָנוּי לוֹ — for he has been acquired by [the master] עַד הַיּוֹבֵל — until the *yovel* year.[6] וְאֵיזֶהוּ שָׂכִיר — And who is a "hired worker"? זֶהוּ קְנוּי קִנְיַן שָׁנִים — This is a [Hebrew servant] who has been acquired as an acquisition for a fixed number of years,[7] שֶׁיּוֹצֵא בְשֵׁשׁ[8] — who goes out of slavery at the end of a six-year term.[8] בָּא הַכָּתוּב — Scripture has come וְלִמֶּדְךָ כָּאן — and taught you here שֶׁאֵין גּוּפוֹ קָנוּי לַאֲדוֹנָיו — that his body is not acquired by his master which would allow him לֶאֱכוֹל בִּתְרוּמָתוֹ — to eat of [the master's] *terumah*.[9]

11. וְכֹהֵן כִּי יִקְנֶה נֶפֶשׁ — IF A KOHEN SHALL ACQUIRE A PERSON. This refers to עֶבֶד כְּנַעֲנִי — a Canaanite slave שֶׁקָּנוּי לְגוּפוֹ[10] — who is acquired for his body, i.e., whose person becomes the property of the master.[10] □ וִילִיד בֵּיתוֹ — AND SOMEONE BORN IN HIS HOUSEHOLD. אֵלּוּ בְּנֵי הַשְּׁפָחוֹת — These are the children of Canaanite slavewomen. וְאֵשֶׁת כֹּהֵן — We also learn that the wife of a Kohen אוֹכֶלֶת בִּתְרוּמָה — may eat *terumah* מִן הַמִּקְרָא הַזֶּה[11] — from this verse,[11] שֶׁאַף הִיא קִנְיַן כַּסְפּוֹ — for she, too, is "an acquisition of his money." וְעוֹד לָמַד מִמִּקְרָא אַחֵר — [This law] is also derived from another verse, ,,כָּל טָהוֹר בְּבֵיתְךָ וְגוֹמֵר"[12] — "anyone who is pure in your household, etc.,"[12] [13]בְּסִפְרֵי — in *Sifrei*.[13]

---

1. *Sanhedrin* 83b; see Rashi to vv. 7 and 9.
2. The verse could have been understood, "a resident who is a Kohen, or a hired worker [who is a Kohen]." It would then have forbidden a Kohen who is a Hebrew servant to eat *terumah*. But this is not a satisfactory interpretation of the verse, for there is no reason to deprive a Kohen of the privileges of the *kehunah* just because he has become a Hebrew servant (*Mizrachi*; *Sifsei Chachamim*).
3. This is the only instance of תּוֹשַׁב with a *patach* in Scripture. In every other appearance it is spelled תּוֹשָׁב, with a *kamatz* (see, e.g., 25:47 below).
4. Had it not been in the construct form, it would have been vowelized with a *kamatz*, תּוֹשָׁב. Had the Torah written, תּוֹשָׁב כֹּהֵן would have been an adjective describing — תּוֹשָׁב — "a priestly resident," i.e., a resident who is a Kohen.
5. Literally, "one who has been bored." This refers to a Jewish manservant who has refused his freedom when his term of service has ended. See *Exodus* 21:5-6.
6. See *Exodus* 21:6 and Rashi there.
7. A Hebrew servant is acquired for a standard six-year term (*Exodus* 21:2). A *nirtza*, however, serves until the onset of the *yovel* year. Thus, the term of a *nirtza* is not reckoned by a standard number of years, but varies by each individual.
8. *Toras Kohanim, perek* 4:17; *Yevamos* 70a.
9. Only his services have been acquired. This is in contrast to the Canaanite slave of the following verse who may eat *terumah* if his master is a Kohen.
10. *Toras Kohanim, parshasa* 5:1.
11. *Toras Kohanim, parshasa* 5:1; *Kesubos* 57b.
12. *Numbers* 18:11. That verse continues, "may eat it."
13. *Sifrei* to *Numbers* 18:13 (*Korach* 117). Had our verse alone been written, we would have construed it as referring only to a slave, for he is "an acquisition of his money."

— they may eat of his bread. ¹² If a Kohen's daughter shall be married to an outsider, she may not eat of the separated holies. ¹³ And a Kohen's daughter who will become a widow or a divorcee, and not have offspring, she may return to her father's home, as in her youth, she may eat from her father's bread; but any outsider may not eat of it. ¹⁴ If a man

יב הֵם יֹאכְלוּ בְלַחְמוֹ: וּבַת־כֹּהֵן כִּי תִהְיֶה לְאִישׁ זָר הִוא בִּתְרוּמַת הַקֳּדָשִׁים לֹא תֹאכֵל: יג וּבַת־כֹּהֵן כִּי תִהְיֶה אַלְמָנָה וּגְרוּשָׁה וְזֶרַע אֵין לָהּ וְשָׁבָה אֶל־בֵּית אָבִיהָ כִּנְעוּרֶיהָ מִלֶּחֶם אָבִיהָ תֹּאכֵל וְכָל־זָר לֹא־יֹאכַל בּוֹ: יד וְאִישׁ כִּי־

──────── אונקלוס ────────

אִנּוּן יֵיכְלוּן בְּלַחְמֵהּ: יב וּבַת כָּהֵן אֲרֵי תְהֵי לִגְבַר חִלּוֹנַי הִיא בְּאַפְרָשׁוּת קוּדְשַׁיָּא לָא תֵיכוּל: יג וּבַת כָּהֵן אֲרֵי תְהֵי אַרְמְלָא וּמְתָרְכָא וּבַר לֵית לַהּ וּתְתוּב לְבֵית אֲבוּהָא כִּרְבִיּוּתָהּ מִלַּחְמָא דַאֲבוּהָא תֵּיכוּל וְכָל חִלּוֹנַי לָא יֵיכוּל בֵּהּ: יד וּגְבַר אֲרֵי

──────── רש"י ────────

(יב) לאיש זר. ללוי וישראל (ת"כ שם ז): **(יג) אלמנה וגרושה.** ממנו אסורה בתרומה כל זמן שהזרע קיים (יבמות פו:-פז.): **ובל** מן האיש הזר: **וזרע אין לה.** ממנו: **ושבה.** הא אם יש לה זרע **זר לא יאכל בו.** לא בא אלא להוציא את האונן שמותר בתרומה,

──────── RASHI ELUCIDATED ────────

12. לְאִישׁ זָר — TO AN OUTSIDER. לְלֵוִי וְיִשְׂרָאֵל — To a Levite or an Israelite,[1] i.e., a Jew who is not a Kohen.[1]

13. אַלְמָנָה וּגְרוּשָׁה — A WIDOW OR A DIVORCEE מִן הָאִישׁ הַזָּר — from the outsider,

וְזֶרַע אֵין לָהּ — AND she does NOT HAVE OFFSPRING מִמֶּנּוּ — from him.[2]

וְשָׁבָה — SHE MAY RETURN. הָא אִם יֵשׁ לָהּ זֶרַע מִמֶּנּוּ — But if she has offspring from him אֲסוּרָה בִּתְרוּמָה — she is forbidden to partake of terumah, כָּל זְמַן שֶׁהַזֶּרַע קַיָּם — all the while that the offspring is alive.[3]

וְכָל זָר לֹא יֹאכַל בּוֹ — ANY OUTSIDER MAY NOT EAT OF IT. לֹא בָא אֶלָּא לְהוֹצִיא אֶת הָאוֹנֵן — [The verse] comes only to exclude an onein[4] from the prohibition, שֶׁמֻּתָּר בִּתְרוּמָה — for he is permitted to

in a sense that a wife is not, i.e., the slave is the property of the owner. The verse in *Numbers* is thus the true source of the law that the wife of a Kohen may eat *terumah*. However, in light of that verse, we see that a wife, too, is included in "an acquisition of his money" (*Maskil LeDavid*).

Alternatively, the verse in *Numbers* alone would be insufficient, for "in your household" of that verse could be taken to imply that the wife of a Kohen may eat *terumah* only after *nisuin* (see definition in note 1 on page 263), for only then does she enter his husband's household. "An acquisition of his money," on the other hand, includes *eirusin*, for that is when the woman is acquired through the initial marriage transaction. But our verse, too, would have been insufficient alone, for "an acquisition of *his* money" could have been taken to exclude a *yevamah*, a wife attained through *yibbum* (see definition in note 6 on page 266), who was acquired by his brother. "*Anyone* who is pure in your household" includes such a wife (*Gur Aryeh*; see also Rashi to *Kiddushin* 10b, s.v., כספה מאכילתה, and s.v., זו שביאתה מאכילתה).

1. *Toras Kohanim*, *parshasa* 5:7. An outsider could have been taken to mean a *mamzer* — one born of a forbidden union punishable by *kares* or execution by the courts, or his descendant. A *mamzer* is "outside" because he or she may not marry a Jew of unblemished ancestry. But had the Torah meant that the daughter of a Kohen may not eat *terumah* only if she marries a *mamzer*, it would have said, וּבַת כֹּהֵן כִּי תִהְיֶה לְזָר, "if a Kohen's daughter shall be married to an outsider." לְאִישׁ זָר, literally, "to an outside man," connotes any Jew who is not a Kohen (*Mizrachi*).

2. Even if she has children from a Kohen, as long as she has no living children from a non-Kohen, she may eat *terumah* (*Mizrachi; Sifsei Chachamim*).

3. *Yevamos* 86b-87a. Our verse speaks in terms of when it is permitted for a widowed or divorced daughter of a Kohen to eat *terumah*. But no explicit verse is necessary to teach us that she is permitted to eat *terumah* once her non-Kohen husband dies, because it stands to reason that if the marriage causes the prohibition, the termination of the marriage would nullify it. The point of our verse is to teach us the prohibition that it implies through its statement of permission — if she has no offspring she may eat *terumah*, but if she has offspring she may not (*Mizrachi; Sifsei Chachamim; Be'er BaSadeh*).

Furthermore, Rashi explains that "and not have offspring" refers to the physical existence of the child, not to having given birth to a child. If the child ceases to exist, she returns to her former state just as she does if her marriage is terminated and she has not borne children (*Gur Aryeh*)

4. A mourner on the day of the death of a relative for whom he is required to mourn.

will eat that which is holy inadvertently, he shall add its fifth to it and he shall give that which is holy to the Kohen. **15** They shall not defile the holy things of the Children of Israel, which they set aside to HASHEM; **16** and they will cause them to bear the sin of guilt when they eat their holy things —

יֹאכַל קֹדֶשׁ בִּשְׁגָגָה וְיָסַף חֲמִשִׁיתוֹ עָלָיו וְנָתַן לַכֹּהֵן אֶת־הַקֹּדֶשׁ: וְלֹא יְחַלְּלוּ אֶת־קָדְשֵׁי בְּנֵי יִשְׂרָאֵל אֵת אֲשֶׁר־יָרִימוּ לַיהוה: וְהִשִּׂיאוּ אוֹתָם עֲוֹן אַשְׁמָה בְּאָכְלָם אֶת־קָדְשֵׁיהֶם

———————— אונקלוס ————————

יֵיכוּל קוּדְשָׁא בְּשָׁלוּ וְיוֹסֵף חוּמְשֵׁהּ עֲלוֹהִי וְיִתֵּן לְכָהֲנָא יָת קוּדְשָׁא: טו וְלָא יְחַלוּן יָת קוּדְשַׁיָּא דִּבְנֵי יִשְׂרָאֵל יָת דִּי יַפְרְשׁוּן קֳדָם יְיָ: טז וִיקַבְּלוּן עֲלֵיהוֹן עֲוָיָן וְחוֹבִין בְּמֵיכָלְהוֹן בְּסוֹאֲבָא יָת קוּדְשֵׁיהוֹן

———————— רש״י ————————

לוזרים: (טז) וְהִשִּׂיאוּ אוֹתָם. אֵת עַצְמָם יִטְעֲנוּ עָוֹן בַּאֲכְלָם אֶת קָדְשֵׁיהֶם שֶׁהוּבְדְּלוּ לְשֵׁם תְּרוּמָה וְקָדְשׁוּ עֲלֵיהֶם וְאוּנְקְלוֹס שֶׁתִּרְגֵּם בְּמֵיכָלְהוֹן בְּסוֹאֲבָא שֶׁלֹּא לְצוֹרֶךְ תִּרְגְּמוֹ כֵן: **וְהִשִּׂיאוּ אוֹתָם.** זֶה אֶחָד מִג' אַתִים שֶׁהָיָה רַבִּי יִשְׁמָעֵאל דּוֹרֵשׁ

זָרוֹת אָמַרְתִּי לָךְ וְלֹא אֲנִינוּת (שָׁם ע״ג): **(יד) בִּי יֹאכַל קֹדֶשׁ. תְּרוּמָה: וְנָתַן לַכֹּהֵן אֶת הַקֹּדֶשׁ.** דָּבָר הָרָאוּי לִהְיוֹת קֹדֶשׁ (ת״כ פֶּרֶק י:ה), שֶׁאֵינוֹ פּוֹרֵעַ לוֹ מָעוֹת אֶלָּא פֵּרוֹת שֶׁל חוּלִּין וְהֵן נַעֲשִׂין תְּרוּמָה (פסחים לב:): **(טו) וְלֹא יְחַלְּלוּ וְגוֹ'.** לְהַאֲכִילָם

———————— RASHI ELUCIDATED ————————

זָרוֹת אָמַרְתִּי לָךְ – **The state of being an** **partake of** *terumah*. This is implied by our verse as follows: **outsider is what I told you,** ¹וְלֹא אֲנִינוּת – **but not** *aninus,* **the state of mourning of an** *onein*.[1]

14. כִּי יֹאכַל קֹדֶשׁ – IF [A MAN] WILL EAT THAT WHICH IS HOLY. This refers to תְּרוּמָה – *terumah*.[2]

□ וְנָתַן לַכֹּהֵן אֶת הַקֹּדֶשׁ – HE SHALL GIVE THAT WHICH IS HOLY TO THE KOHEN. דָּבָר הָרָאוּי לִהְיוֹת קֹדֶשׁ – Something which is fit to be holy,[3] שֶׁאֵינוֹ פּוֹרֵעַ לוֹ מָעוֹת – for he does not pay [the Kohen] money, אֶלָּא פֵּרוֹת שֶׁל חוּלִּין – but rather, fruits which have no sanctity, וְהֵן נַעֲשִׂין תְּרוּמָה – and they become *terumah*.[4]

15. וְלֹא יְחַלְּלוּ וְגוֹמֵר – THEY SHALL NOT DEFILE, ETC. לְהַאֲכִילָם לְזָרִים – by feeding them to non-Kohanim.[5]

16. וְהִשִּׂיאוּ אוֹתָם – AND THEY WILL CAUSE THEM TO BEAR. אֶת עַצְמָם יִטְעֲנוּ עָוֹן – They will burden themselves with sin בְּאָכְלָם אֶת קָדְשֵׁיהֶם – "when they eat their holy things" שֶׁהוּבְדְּלוּ לְשֵׁם תְּרוּמָה – which had been set aside for the sake of *terumah* וְקָדְשׁוּ – and had become holy וְנֶאֶסְרוּ עֲלֵיהֶם – and forbidden to them.[6] וְאוּנְקְלוֹס שֶׁתִּרְגֵּם – And Targum Onkelos, who rendered "בְּמֵיכָלְהוֹן בְּסוֹאֲבָא" – "when they eat [their holy things] while in a state of impurity," as בְּאָכְלָם שֶׁלֹּא לְצוֹרֶךְ תִּרְגְּמוֹ כֵן – translated it so needlessly.[7]}

□ וְהִשִּׂיאוּ אוֹתָם – AND THEY WILL CAUSE THEM TO BEAR. זֶה אֶחָד מִשְּׁלֹשָׁה אַתִים שֶׁהָיָה רַבִּי יִשְׁמָעֵאל דּוֹרֵשׁ

---

1. *Yevamos* 70b. The prohibition that a non-Kohen is forbidden to eat *terumah* appears redundant; it has already been stated above in verse 10. It is repeated so that we should infer that although not being a Kohen is a state which causes this prohibition, there is another state which does not cause the same prohibition – *aninus*. Since an *onein* may not even eat *ma'aser sheni* (see Deuteronomy 26:14 and Rashi there), and a Kohen who is an *onein* may not partake of offerings (see 10:19 above and Rashi there), we may have thought that this holds true for *terumah*, too. Therefore, our verse teaches us that nevertheless he may eat *terumah* (see *Nachalas Yaakov*).

2. It stands to reason that our verse refers to *terumah* because, as Rashi has mentioned in his comments to verse 10 above, the context deals with *terumah* (*Minchas Yehudah; Sifsei Chachamim*).

3. *Toras Kohanim, perek* 6:5 (in some editions).

4. *Pesachim* 32b. "That which is holy" cannot refer to the *terumah* here, for he has already eaten the *terumah* and cannot return it to the Kohen. Rather, the verse means that he shall repay the Kohen something that is fit to be *terumah* (*Minchas Yehudah; Sifsei Chachamim*).

5. The verse must be addressing the Kohanim, for it says, "They shall not defile the holy things of the Children of Israel." If it is the non-Kohanim who are addressed, such phrasing would be awkward. We would expect קָדְשֵׁיהֶם, "their holy things" (*Gur Aryeh* to v. 16).

6. According to *Maskil LeDavid*, Rashi means, "The Kohanim will burden themselves with sin when *the non-Kohanim* eat *the Kohanim's* holy things." According to *Be'er BaSadeh*, Rashi means, "The non-Kohanim will burden themselves with sin when *the non-Kohanim* eat *their own* holy things, before having given them to the Kohanim." According to both opinions, Rashi obviates the possibility that the verse means, "The Kohanim will burden *the non-Kohanim* with sin when *the non-Kohanim* eat *the Kohanim's* holy things."

7. *Targum Onkelos* appears to understand that "they will cause them to bear the sin of guilt when they eat their holy things" refers back to the prohibition against eating that

for I am Hashem Who sanctifies them. ¹⁷ Hashem spoke to Moses, saying: ¹⁸ Speak to Aaron and to his sons and to all the Children of Israel and say to them: Any man of the House of Israel and of the proselytes among Israel who will bring his offering for any of their vows or their voluntary offerings that they will bring to Hashem for an olah-offering; ¹⁹ to be an appeasement for you: unblemished, male, from the cattle, from the sheep, or from the goats.

כִּי אֲנִי יהוה מְקַדְּשָׁם:
יז שלישי וַיְדַבֵּר יהוה אֶל־מֹשֶׁה לֵּאמֹר:
יח דַּבֵּר אֶל־אַהֲרֹן וְאֶל־בָּנָיו וְאֶל כָּל־בְּנֵי יִשְׂרָאֵל וְאָמַרְתָּ אֲלֵהֶם אִישׁ אִישׁ מִבֵּית יִשְׂרָאֵל וּמִן־הַגֵּר בְּיִשְׂרָאֵל אֲשֶׁר יַקְרִיב קָרְבָּנוֹ לְכָל־נִדְרֵיהֶם וּלְכָל־נִדְבוֹתָם אֲשֶׁר־יַקְרִיבוּ לַיהוה לְעֹלָה: יט לִרְצֹנְכֶם תָּמִים זָכָר בַּבָּקָר בַּכְּשָׂבִים וּבָעִזִּים:

──────────── אונקלוס ────────────

אֲרֵי אֲנָא יְיָ מְקַדְּשְׁהוֹן: יזוּמַלִּיל יְיָ עִם מֹשֶׁה לְמֵימָר: יחמַלֵּל עִם אַהֲרֹן וְעִם בְּנוֹהִי וְעִם כָּל בְּנֵי יִשְׂרָאֵל וְתֵימַר לְהוֹן גְּבַר גְּבַר מִבֵּית יִשְׂרָאֵל וּמִן גִּיּוֹרַיָּא בְיִשְׂרָאֵל דִּי יְקָרֵב קֻרְבָּנֵהּ לְכָל נִדְרֵיהוֹן וּלְכָל נִדְבָתְהוֹן דִּי יְקָרְבוּן קֳדָם יְיָ לַעֲלָתָא: יטלְרַעֲוָא לְכוֹן שְׁלִים דְּכוּרָא בְּתוֹרֵי בְּאִמְּרַיָּא וּבְעִזַּיָּא:

──────────── רש"י ────────────

בתורה שמדברים באדם עצמו וכן ביום מלאות ימי נזרו יביא אותו (במדבר ו:יג) הוא יביא את עצמו, וכן ויקבור אותו בגי (דברים לד:ו) הוא קבר את עצמו. כך נדרש בספרי (נשא לב): (יח) נדריהם. הרי עלי: נדבותם. הרי זו (מגילה ח.) לרצונכם. הביאו דבר הראוי לרצות אתכם לפני שיהא לכם לרצון, אפיימנ"ט בלע"ז. ואיזהו הראוי לרצון, תמים זכר בבקר בכשבים ובעזים.

──────────── RASHI ELUCIDATED ────────────

בַּתּוֹרָה – This is one of the three instances of forms of the word אֶת in the Torah that the Tanna R' Yishmael would interpret שֶׁמְּדַבְּרִים בָּאָדָם עַצְמוֹ – as speaking of the person himself, i.e., it is reflexive, the object that follows אֶת is the same as the subject of the verb that precedes it: וְכֵן – Similarly אתו in, ¹"בְּיוֹם מְלֹאת יְמֵי נִזְרוֹ יָבִיא אֹתוֹ" – "on the day of the completion of his term of being a nazir, he shall bring him,"[1] in its context means הוּא יָבִיא אֶת עַצְמוֹ – he shall bring himself. וְכֵן – Similarly, אתו in, ²"וַיִּקְבֹּר אֹתוֹ בַגַּי" – "and he buried him in the valley,"[2] means הוּא קָבַר אֶת עַצְמוֹ – he buried himself. ³כָּךְ נִדְרָשׁ בְּסִפְרֵי – Thus it is expounded in Sifrei.[3]

18. נִדְרֵיהֶם – THEIR VOWS. This refers to pledges made by using the formula, "הֲרֵי עָלַי" – "Behold, it is incumbent upon me to bring an offering."

נִדְבֹתָם – THEIR VOLUNTARY OFFERINGS. This refers to pledges made by using the formula, "הֲרֵי זוֹ"[4] – "Behold, this animal, or meal, or wine is consecrated as an offering."[4]

19. לִרְצֹנְכֶם – TO BE AN APPEASEMENT FOR YOU. הָבִיאוּ דָבָר – Bring something הָרָאוּי – which is fitting שֶׁיְּהֵא לָכֶם לְרָצוֹן – that it shall be an appeasement for you before Me, לְרַצוֹת אֶתְכֶם לְפָנַי – to appease for you before Me, אפיימנ"ט בלע"ז – Apaiement in Old French.[6] וְאֵיזֶהוּ הָרָאוּי לְרָצוֹן – And what animal is fitting as an appeasement? "תָּמִים זָכָר בַּבָּקָר בַּכְּשָׂבִים וּבָעִזִּים" – One that is "unblemished, male, from the cattle, from the sheep, or from the goats."[7]

───────────────────────────────

which is holy while in a state of impurity, mentioned in verse 2. But to Rashi this is unnecessary, for the verse refers to the prohibition against non-Kohanim eating that which is holy, mentioned in the preceding verse (Mizrachi; Sifsei Chachamim).

1. Numbers 6:13. See Rashi there.
2. Deuteronomy 34:6. See Rashi there.
3. Sifrei, Naso 32.
4. Megillah 8a. When one makes a נֶדֶר, "a vow," if the animal designated for the offering becomes blemished or is lost, the one who made the vow must replace it, for he said, "It is incumbent upon me," i.e., he has a personal obligation to bring an offering, whatever may happen. When one makes a נְדָבָה, "a voluntary offering," if the

animal designated for the offering becomes blemished or is lost, the owner is not obligated to replace it, for he pledged only that specific animal.
5. לִרְצֹנְכֶם could have been understood as "by your will," or "as you wish" (Gur Aryeh).
6. See note 4 on page 229.
7. The words תָּמִים זָכָר בַּבָּקָר בַּכְּשָׂבִים וּבָעִזִּים, "unblemished, male, from the cattle, from the sheep, or from the goats," appear to stand by themselves in the verse, without being part of any clause. By inserting the question, "And what animal is fitting as an appeasement?" Rashi indicates that "unblemished . . ." explains "to be an appeasement."
In some editions these five words, תָּמִים . . . וּבָעִזִּים, form the heading of a new comment.

ויקרא / פרשת אמור

כ כֹּל אֲשֶׁר־בּוֹ מוּם לֹא תַקְרִיבוּ כִּי־לֹא לְרָצוֹן יִהְיֶה לָכֶם: כא וְאִישׁ כִּי־יַקְרִיב זֶבַח־שְׁלָמִים לַיהוָה לְפַלֵּא־נֶדֶר אוֹ לִנְדָבָה בַּבָּקָר אוֹ בַצֹּאן תָּמִים יִהְיֶה לְרָצוֹן כָּל־מוּם לֹא יִהְיֶה־בּוֹ: כב עַוֶּרֶת אוֹ שָׁבוּר אוֹ־חָרוּץ אוֹ־יַבֶּלֶת אוֹ

20 Any in which there is a blemish you shall not offer, for it will not be an appeasement for you. 21 And a man who will bring a sacrifice of a peace-offering to HASHEM, *setting aside as a vow or as a voluntary offering from the cattle or the flock, it shall be unblemished for an appeasement, there shall not be any blemish in it. 22 There shall not be in it any blemish: blindness or broken or with a cut eyelid or a wart or a*

אונקלוס

כ כֹּל דִי בֵהּ מוּמָא לָא תְקָרְבוּן אֲרֵי לָא לְרַעֲוָא יְהֵי לְכוֹן: כא וּגְבַר אֲרֵי יְקָרֵב נִכְסַת קוּדְשַׁיָּא קֳדָם יְיָ לְפָרָשָׁא נִדְרָא אוֹ לִנְדַבְתָּא בְּתוֹרֵי אוֹ בְעָנָא שְׁלִים יְהֵי לְרַעֲוָא כָּל מוּמָא לָא יְהֵי בֵהּ: כב עַוִיר אוֹ תְבִיר אוֹ פְסִיק אוֹ יַבְּלָן אוֹ

רש"י

אֲבָל בְּעוֹלַת הָעוֹף אֵין צָרִיךְ תַּמּוּת וְזַכְרוּת, וְאֵינוֹ נִפְסָל בְּמוּם אֶלָּא בְּחֶסְרוֹן אֵבֶר (ת"כ פרשתא ז:ב; קידושין כד:): (כא) **לְפַלֵּא [נֶדֶר]**. לְהַפְרִישׁ בְּדִבּוּרוֹ: (כב) **עַוֶּרֶת**. שֵׁם דָּבָר שֶׁל מוּם עִוָּרוֹן בִּלְשׁוֹן נְקֵבָה, שֶׁלֹּא יְהֵא בוֹ מוּם שֶׁל עַוֶּרֶת: **אוֹ שָׁבוּר**. לֹא יִהְיֶה: **חָרוּץ**. רִיס שֶׁל עַיִן שֶׁנִּסְדַּק אוֹ שֶׁנִּפְגַּם (ת"כ שם יב; בכורות לח.) וְכֵן שְׂפָתוֹ שֶׁנִּסְדְּקָה אוֹ נִפְגְּמָה (שם לט.): **יַבֶּלֶת**. ויר"וא בלע"ז:

RASHI ELUCIDATED

אֲבָל בְּעוֹלַת הָעוֹף — **But with regard to an** *olah*-**offering of fowl,** אֵין צָרִיךְ — **it does not require** תַּמּוּת — **wholeness,** i.e., the state of being unblemished, וְזַכְרוּת — **and maleness.** וְאֵינוֹ נִפְסָל בְּמוּם — **It does not become disqualified through a** mere **blemish,** אֶלָּא — **but rather,**[1] בְּחֶסְרוֹן אֵבֶר — **through the lack of a limb.**[1]

21. {לְפַלֵּא [נֶדֶר] — SETTING ASIDE {AS A VOW}, that is} לְהַפְרִישׁ בְּדִבּוּרוֹ — **to set aside** an animal as an offering **through his statement.**[2]

22. עַוֶּרֶת — BLINDNESS. שֵׁם דָּבָר שֶׁל מוּם עִוָּרוֹן — This is **a noun denoting the blemish of blindness,** בִּלְשׁוֹן נְקֵבָה — **in the feminine form.**[3] שֶׁלֹּא יְהֵא בוֹ — **The beginning of our verse is linked to** לֹא יִהְיֶה בּוֹ of the preceding verse to say **that there shall not be in it** מוּם שֶׁל עַוֶּרֶת — **a blemish of blindness.**

□ אוֹ שָׁבוּר — OR BROKEN. לֹא יִהְיֶה — **it shall not be.**[4]

□ חָרוּץ — CUT. רִיס שֶׁל עַיִן שֶׁנִּסְדַּק — It has **an eyelid that is split**[5] אוֹ שֶׁנִּפְגַּם — **or marred,**[5] וְכֵן — **and likewise,** it falls under this category if שְׂפָתוֹ שֶׁנִּסְדְּקָה — **its lip has been split**[6] אוֹ נִפְגְּמָה — **or marred.**[6]

□ יַבֶּלֶת — A WART. ויר"וא בלע"ז — *Verue* in Old French.[7]

---

1. *Toras Kohanim, parshasa* 7:2; *Kiddushin* 24b. See 1:14 above and Rashi there.

2. The verb פלא is used by the Torah for the declaration of vows, oaths, or pledges. This sense of the word derives from its basic meaning of "separating" (see Rashi to 27:2 below, *Exodus* 34:10, *Numbers* 6:2, and *Deuteronomy* 17:8), for one who makes an oath or vow imbues a person or an object with a quality of sanctity or prohibition that makes it distinct from other things. Rashi stresses that the "setting aside" must be verbal (see *Minchas Yehudah; Sifsei Chachamim*).

Rashi here is interested only in defining לְפַלֵּא. The word נֶדֶר does not appear in the heading in the first printed edition of Rashi.

3. עַוֶּרֶת cannot be a feminine adjective, for some of the other blemishes in the beginning of this verse are given as masculine adjectives. If עַוֶּרֶת were a feminine adjective, it would not agree with the other adjectives of the verse (*Gur Aryeh*). Furthermore, the feminine adjective meaning "blind" would be vowelized עִוֶּרֶת, with a *chirik* under the ע, not a *patach* (*Sefer Zikaron*).

4. Rashi in his preceding comment used לֹא יְהֵא בוֹ, "there shall not be in it," with reference to the noun "blindness" to indicate that it is a continuation of the final clause of the preceding verse — "there shall not be in it any blemish: blindness." But an adjective such as שָׁבוּר, "broken," cannot conclude a clause that begins לֹא יִהְיֶה בּוֹ, "there shall not be in it," in Hebrew, an adjective does not follow בּוֹ. Rashi supplies the beginning of an implicit clause of which שָׁבוּר is part and which does not contain the word בּוֹ, namely, לֹא יִהְיֶה (see *Mizrachi; Sifsei Chachamim*).

5. *Toras Kohanim, parshasa* 7:12; *Bechoros* 38a.

6. *Bechoros* 39a.

7. This word and its Modern French counterpart, *"verrue,"* mean "wart." The present-day medical term for wart is *"verruca,"* and is derived from the same Latin word as Rashi's French word.

a breaking-out or an eruption — you shall not offer these to Hashem, and you shall not place any of them as a fire-offering on the Mizbe'ach for Hashem. ²³ *An ox or a sheep, one which has an enlargement or is undivided — you may make it a voluntary offering, but it shall not appease for a vow.* ²⁴ *One whose testicles are mashed, squashed, disconnected, or cut, you shall not offer*

גָּרָב אוֹ יַלֶּפֶת לֹא־תַקְרִיבוּ אֵלֶּה
לַיהוָה וְאִשֶּׁה לֹא־תִתְּנוּ מֵהֶם
עַל־הַמִּזְבֵּחַ לַיהוָה: וְשׁוֹר וָשֶׂה כג
שָׂרוּעַ וְקָלוּט נְדָבָה תַּעֲשֶׂה
אֹתוֹ וּלְנֵדֶר לֹא יֵרָצֶה: וּמָעוּךְ כד
וְכָתוּת וְנָתוּק וְכָרוּת לֹא תַקְרִיבוּ

— אונקלוס —

גַּרְבָן אוֹ חֲזָזָן לָא תְקָרְבוּן אִלֵּין קֻרְבָּנָא יְיָ וְקֻרְבָּנָא לָא תִתְּנוּן מִנְּהוֹן עַל מַדְבְּחָא קֳדָם יְיָ: כג וְתוֹר וְאִמַּר יַתִּיר וְחַסִּיר נְדַבְתָּא תַעְבֵּד יָתֵהּ וּלְנִדְרָא לָא יְהֵי לְרַעֲוָא: כד וְדִי מְרִיס וְדִי רְסִיס וְדִי שְׁלִיף וְדִי גְזִיר לָא תְקָרְבוּן

— רש"י —

גָּרָב. מִין חֲזָזִית וְכֵן יַלֶּפֶת. וּלְשׁוֹן יַלֶּפֶת כְּמוֹ וַיִּלְפֹּת שִׁמְשׁוֹן (שופטים טז:כט) שֶׁאֲחוּזָה בּוֹ עַד יוֹם מִיתָה, שֶׁאֵין לָהּ רְפוּאָה: **לֹא תַקְרִיבוּ.** שָׁלֹשׁ פְּעָמִים, לְהַזְהִיר עַל הַקְדָּשָׁתָן וְעַל שְׁחִיטָתָן וְעַל זְרִיקַת דָּמָן (תמורה ו.): **וְאִשֶּׁה לֹא תִתְּנוּ.** אַזְהָרַת הַקְטָרָתָן (שם): **שָׂרוּעַ. (כג)** אֵבֶר גָּדוֹל מֵחֲבֵרוֹ (שם): **וְקָלוּט.** פַּרְסוֹתָיו קְלוּטוֹת (שם): **נְדָבָה תַּעֲשֶׂה אֹתוֹ.** לְבֶדֶק הַבַּיִת: **וּלְנֵדֶר.** לַמִּזְבֵּחַ: **לֹא יֵרָצֶה.** אֵי זֶה הַקֹּדֶשׁ בָּא לִרְצוֹת הֱוֵי אוֹמֵר זֶה הַקֹּדֶשׁ הַמִּזְבֵּחַ (ת"כ פרק ז:ו): **(כד) וּמָעוּךְ וְכָתוּת וְנָתוּק וְכָרוּת.** בַּבֵּיצִים אוֹ בַגִּיד (שם ט; בכורות לט:): **מָעוּךְ.** בֵּיצָיו מְעוּכִין בְּיָד:

— RASHI ELUCIDATED —

□ גָּרָב — A BREAKING-OUT. מִין חֲזָזִית — A type of rash, וְכֵן יַלֶּפֶת — and so, too, "an eruption."[1] וּלְשׁוֹן ,,יַלֶּפֶת" — The term *"yalefes"* כְּמוֹ — is related to וַיִּלְפֹּת in, ,,וַיִּלְפֹּת שִׁמְשׁוֹן" — "and Samson took hold."[2] It describes the eruption of our verse שֶׁאֲחוּזָה בּוֹ — for it has taken hold of him עַד יוֹם מִיתָה — until the day of his death, שֶׁאֵין לָהּ רְפוּאָה — for it has no cure.

□ לֹא תַקְרִיבוּ — YOU SHALL NOT OFFER. שָׁלֹשׁ פְּעָמִים — The phrase "you shall not offer" is mentioned three times[3] לְהַזְהִיר — to state a negative commandment עַל הַקְדָּשָׁתָן — against the consecration [of blemished animals], וְעַל שְׁחִיטָתָן — against their slaughter, וְעַל זְרִיקַת דָּמָן[4] — and against the sprinkling of their blood upon the *Mizbe'ach*.[4]

□ וְאִשֶּׁה לֹא תִתְּנוּ — AND YOU SHALL NOT PLACE [ANY OF THEM] AS A FIRE-OFFERING. אַזְהָרַת הַקְטָרָתָן[4] — This is a negative commandment against their being burned upon the *Mizbe'ach*.[4]

23. שָׂרוּעַ — ONE WHICH HAS AN ENLARGEMENT. אֵבֶר גָּדוֹל מֵחֲבֵרוֹ[5] — An external part of the body is larger than its fellow, i.e., the other part of the body which is its pair, for example, one eye is larger than the other.[5]

□ וְקָלוּט — OR IS UNDIVIDED. פַּרְסוֹתָיו קְלוּטוֹת[6] — Its hooves are joined.[6]

□ נְדָבָה תַּעֲשֶׂה אֹתוֹ — YOU MAY MAKE IT A VOLUNTARY-OFFERING לְבֶדֶק הַבַּיִת — for the upkeep of the *Beis HaMikdash*,[7]

□ וּלְנֵדֶר — BUT FOR A VOW לַמִּזְבֵּחַ — to offer upon the *Mizbe'ach*,

□ לֹא יֵרָצֶה — IT SHALL NOT APPEASE. אֵי זֶה הַקֹּדֶשׁ — What kind of holy object בָּא לְרַצוֹת — comes to appease? הֱוֵי אוֹמֵר — You should say that זֶה הַקֹּדֶשׁ הַמִּזְבֵּחַ[8] — it is that which is holy for offering upon the *Mizbe'ach*.[8]

24. וּמָעוּךְ וְכָתוּת וְנָתוּק וְכָרוּת — MASHED, SQUASHED, DISCONNECTED, OR CUT. בַּבֵּיצִים אוֹ בַגִּיד[9] — These descriptions all refer to the testicles or to the male organ.[9]

□ מָעוּךְ — MASHED. בֵּיצָיו מְעוּכִין בְּיָד — Its testicles are mashed by hand.

---

1. See Rashi to 21:20 above.
2. *Judges* 16:29.
3. In our verse, in verse 20, and in verse 24.
4. *Temurah* 6b.
5. *Bechoros* 40a. See Rashi to 21:18 above.
6. *Bechoros* 40a.
7. It may be consecrated, and the money received through its redemption used for the upkeep of the *Beis HaMikdash*.
8. *Toras Kohanim*, *perek* 7:6. Since the verse speaks of appeasement, we may conclude that the "vow" referred to is a vow to bring the animal as an offering.
9. *Toras Kohanim*, *perek* 7:9; *Bechoros* 39b.

כה לַיהוה וּבְאַרְצְכֶם לֹא תַעֲשׂוּ: וּמִיַּד בֶּן־
נֵכָר לֹא תַקְרִיבוּ אֶת־לֶחֶם אֱלֹהֵיכֶם

to HASHEM, nor shall you do in your land. **²⁵ From the hand of a stranger you shall not offer the bread of your God**

אונקלוס

קֳדָם יְיָ וּבְאַרְעֲכוֹן לָא תַעְבְּדוּן: כהוּמִן בַּר עַמְמִין לָא תְקָרְבוּן יָת קֻרְבַּן אֱלָהֲכוֹן

רש"י

כתות. כתושים יותר ממעוך: **נתוק.** תלושים ביד עד שנפסקו חוטים שתלויים בהן אבל נתונים הם בתוך הכיס והכיס לא נתלש: **וכרות.** כרותין בכלי ועודן בכיס: **[ומעוך.** תרגומו ודי מריס. [מעוך ומרוח] זה לשונו בארמית, לשון כתישה. וכתתום, תרגומו ודי רסיס, כמו הבית הגדול רסיסים (עמוס ו:יא) בקיעות דקות, וכן קנה המרוסם (שבת פ:): **ובארצכם לא תעשו.** דבר זה

לסרס שום בהמה וחיה ואפילו טמאה, לכך נאמר בארצכם (חגיגה יד:) לרבות כל אשר בארצכם. שאי אפשר לומר לא נצטוו על הסרוס אלא בארץ, שהרי סרוס חובת הגוף היא, וכל חובת הגוף נוהגת בין בארץ בין בחוצה לארץ (קידושין לו:): **(כה) ומיד בן נכר.** שהביא קרבן ביד [ס"א ליד] כהן להקריבו לשמים, לא תקריבו לו בעל מום. ואע"פ שלא נאסרו בעלי מומין

RASHI ELUCIDATED

☐ **כָּתוּת – SQUASHED.** – **כְּתוּשִׁים יוֹתֵר מִמָעוּךְ** – The word כָּתוּת, "squashed," implies **more** severely **crushed than** מָעוּךְ, "mashed," implies.[1]

☐ **נָתוּק – DISCONNECTED.** – **תְּלוּשִׁים בַּיָּד** – Torn by hand – **עַד שֶׁנִּפְסְקוּ חוּטִים שֶׁתְּלוּיִים בָּהֶן** – until the ducts by which they are suspended have been severed, – **אֲבָל נְתוּנִים הֵם** – but they are still situated – **בְּתוֹךְ הַכִּיס** – inside the scrotum, – **וְהַכִּיס לֹא נִתְלַשׁ** – and the scrotum is not torn off.

☐ **וְכָרוּת – OR CUT.** – **כְּרוּתִין בִּכְלִי** – They are cut off by an implement – **וְעוֹדָן בַּכִּיס** – and they are still in the scrotum. {**וּמָעוּךְ** ,, וּמָעוּךְ,, **תַּרְגּוּמוֹ** ,, וְדִי מְרִיס,, – is rendered by *Targum* Onkelos as וְדִי מְרִיס. – **זֶה לְשׁוֹנוּ[2] בָּאֲרָמִית** – This is the word for it in Aramaic. – **לְשׁוֹן כְּתִישָׁה** – It denotes "crushing." – **וְכָתוּת** ,, וְכָתוּת,, **תַּרְגּוּמוֹ** – The word וְכָתוּת is rendered by *Targum* Onkelos as ,, וְדִי רְסִיס,, – **כְּמוֹ** ,, רְסִיסִים,,[3] – which is related to רְסִיסִים in, – **הַבַּיִת הַגָּדוֹל רְסִיסִים** – "he will smash the great house to smithereens."[3] – **רְסִיסִים** there means, **בְּקִיעוֹת דַּקּוֹת** – fine splinters. – **וְכֵן** – Similarly, **הַמְרֻסָּס** has a related meaning in ,, קָנֶה הַמְרֻסָּס,,[4] – the reference to **"a shattered reed."**[4]}

☐ **וּבְאַרְצְכֶם לֹא תַעֲשׂוּ – NOR SHALL YOU DO IN YOUR LAND** – **דָּבָר זֶה** – this thing – **לְסָרֵס שׁוּם בְּהֵמָה** – to castrate[5] any domestic animal – **וְחַיָּה** – or wild beast,[6] – **וַאֲפִילוּ טְמֵאָה** – even if it is of **a non-kosher species.** [7] **בְּאַרְצְכֶם** ,, בְּאַרְצְכֶם,, – **לְכָךְ נֶאֱמַר** – This is why it says, "in your land,"[7] – **לְרַבּוֹת כָּל אֲשֶׁר בְּאַרְצְכֶם** – to include anything that is in your land, even a non-kosher species. – **שֶׁאִי אֶפְשָׁר לוֹמַר** – For it is impossible to say – **לֹא נִצְטַוּוּ עַל הַסֵּרוּס** – that they were not commanded with regard to castration – **אֶלָּא בָּאָרֶץ** – other than in the Land of Israel, – **שֶׁהֲרֵי סֵרוּס חוֹבַת הַגּוּף הִיא** – for the prohibition against castration is an obligation of the body, i.e., a personal obligation, in contrast to an obligation that falls upon the land, – **וְכָל חוֹבַת הַגּוּף** – and any personal obligation – **נוֹהֶגֶת** – applies – **בֵּין בָּאָרֶץ בֵּין בְּחוּצָה** – **לָאָרֶץ**[8] – both in the Land of Israel and outside the Land.[8]

25. **וּמִיַּד בֶּן נֵכָר – FROM THE HAND OF A STRANGER** – **שֶׁהֵבִיא קָרְבָּן** – who brought an offering – **בְּיַד**[9] **כֹּהֵן** – through[9] the hand of a Kohen – **לְהַקְרִיבוֹ לַשָּׁמַיִם** – to offer it to God, – ,, לֹא תַקְרִיבוּ לוֹ,, – **"you shall not offer"** – **בַּעַל מוּם** – a blemished animal. – **וְאַף עַל פִּי** – Even though – **שֶׁלֹּא נֶאֶסְרוּ בַּעֲלֵי מוּמִין** –

---

1. Rashi (to *Bechoros* 39b, s.v., כתות) states that כָּתוּת, "squashed," denotes crushed with stones. This is in contrast to מָעוּךְ, "mashed," which according to Rashi (here) denotes crushed by hand.

2. Some editions insert the word וּמֵרוּחַ מָעוּךְ here, to indicate that although מָעוּךְ, "mashed," and מָרוּחַ, "crushed" (21:20), are different words in Hebrew, the Aramaic language of Onkelos uses the same word for both.

3. *Amos* 6:11.

4. *Shabbos* 80b.

5. עשה, the root of תַּעֲשׂוּ, is a transitive verb and requires a direct object. Rashi supplies the implicit direct object, דָּבָר זֶה, "this thing," and then explains it, לְסָרֵס שׁוּם בְּהֵמָה וְחַיָּה, "to castrate any animal or beast." Furthermore,

"nor shall you do in your land" could have been understood as forbidding the offering of the blemished cattle mentioned in the verse, for the entire passage has been discussing offerings. Rashi explains that it refers to castration: first, because the verse has already said, "you shall not offer to HASHEM," and second, because "in your land" would then be superfluous – offerings are never brought outside the Land of Israel (see *Be'er Yitzchak*; *Leket Bahir*).

6. The translations of בְּהֵמָה and חַיָּה are based on *Malbim* (*Vayikra* 11:2, §66).

7. *Chagigah* 14b.

8. *Kiddushin* 36b.

9. Some editions read לְיַד, "to the hand of."

from any of these, for their corruption is in them, a blemish is in them, they will not appease for you.

²⁶ HASHEM spoke to Moses, saying: ²⁷ When an ox or a sheep or a goat is born, it shall remain under its mother for seven days; and from the eighth day on, it will appease for a fire-offering to HASHEM. ²⁸ But an ox or a lamb/kid, you may not slaughter it and its offspring on the same day. ²⁹ When you slaughter

מִכָּל־אֵלֶּה כִּי מָשְׁחָתָם בָּהֶם מוּם בָּם לֹא יֵרָצוּ לָכֶם: כו וַיְדַבֵּר יְהוָה אֶל־מֹשֶׁה לֵּאמֹר: כז שׁוֹר אוֹ־כֶשֶׂב אוֹ־עֵז כִּי יִוָּלֵד וְהָיָה שִׁבְעַת יָמִים תַּחַת אִמּוֹ וּמִיּוֹם הַשְּׁמִינִי וָהָלְאָה יֵרָצֶה לְקָרְבַּן אִשֶּׁה לַיהוָה: כח וְשׁוֹר אוֹ־שֶׂה אֹתוֹ וְאֶת־בְּנוֹ לֹא תִשְׁחֲטוּ בְּיוֹם אֶחָד: כט וְכִי־תִזְבְּחוּ

——— אונקלוס ———

מִכָּל אִלֵּין אֲרֵי חִבּוּלְהוֹן בְּהוֹן מוּמָא בְּהוֹן לָא לְרַעֲוָא יְהֵי לְכוֹן: כווּמַלִּיל יְיָ עִם מֹשֶׁה לְמֵימָר: כזתּוֹר אוֹ אִמַּר אוֹ עִזָּא אֲרֵי יִתְיְלִיד וִיהֵי שַׁבְעַת יוֹמִין בָּתַר אִמֵּיהּ וּמִיּוֹמָא תְמִינָאָה וּלְהָלָּא יִתְרְעֵי לְקָרָבָא קֻרְבָּנָא קֳדָם יְיָ: כחוְתוֹרְתָא אוֹ שֵׂיתָא לַהּ וְלִבְרַהּ לָא תִכְּסוּן בְּיוֹמָא חַד: כטוַאֲרֵי תִכְּסוּן

——— רש״י ———

לקרבן בני נח אלא אם כן מחוסרי אבר, וזאת נוהגת בבמה שבשדות, אבל על המזבח שבמשכן לא תקריבו (תמורה ז.) אבל תמימה תקבלו מהם, לכך נאמר למעלה איש איש (פסוק יח), לרבות את הנכרים שנודרים נדרים ונדבות כישראל (חולין יג:): (בז) כי יולד. פרט ליוצא דופן (ת״כ פרשתא חז; חולין לח:): (בח) אתו ואת בנו. נוהג בנקבה, שאסור לשחוט האם והבן או הבת, ואינו נוהג בזכרים, ומותר לשחוט האב והבן

משחתם. חבולהון: לא ירצו לבם. לכפר עליכם (ת״כ שם יב):

——— RASHI ELUCIDATED ———

לְקָרְבַּן בְּנֵי נֹחַ — as an offering of a son of Noah, i.e., a non-Jew, — blemished animals were not forbidden אֶלָּא אִם כֵּן מְחֻסְּרֵי אֵבֶר — unless they were missing an entire limb, וְזֹאת נוֹהֶגֶת בְּבָמָה שֶׁבַּשָּׂדוֹת — that law applies to a platform which is in the fields, i.e., an altar other than that in the Beis HaMikdash or Tabernacle, אֲבָל עַל הַמִּזְבֵּחַ שֶׁבַּמִּשְׁכָּן — but on the Mizbe'ach that is in the Tabernacle, ״לֹא תַקְרִיבוּ״ — "you shall not offer" any blemished animal.¹ אֲבָל תְּמִימָה — But an unblemished one תְּקַבְּלוּ מֵהֶם — you shall accept as an offering from [non-Jews]. לְכָךְ נֶאֱמַר לְמַעְלָה — This is why it says above, ״אִישׁ אִישׁ״, — "any man" [of the House of Israel and of the proselytes among Israel who will bring his offering],"² לְרַבּוֹת אֶת הַנָּכְרִים — to include the non-Jews, שֶׁנּוֹדְרִים נְדָרִים וּנְדָבוֹת — that they can pledge vows and voluntary offerings כְּיִשְׂרָאֵל — like members of the nation of Israel.³

□ מָשְׁחָתָם — THEIR CORRUPTION. ״חִבּוּלְהוֹן״, — This is rendered by Targum Onkelos as "their injury."⁴

□ לֹא יֵרָצוּ לָכֶם — THEY WILL NOT APPEASE FOR YOU ⁵לְכַפֵּר עֲלֵיכֶם — to atone on your behalf.⁵

27. כִּי יִוָּלֵד — WHEN [AN OX OR A SHEEP OR A GOAT] IS BORN. ⁶פְּרָט לְיוֹצֵא דֹפֶן — To the exclusion of one that emerges from the womb by Caesarean section.⁶

28. אֹתוֹ וְאֶת בְּנוֹ — IT AND ITS OFFSPRING. נוֹהֵג — [This law] applies בִּנְקֵבָה — to the female parent,⁷ שֶׁאָסוּר לִשְׁחוֹט — for it is forbidden to slaughter הָאֵם — the mother וְהַבֵּן אוֹ הַבַּת — and the son or the daughter on the same day.⁸ וְאֵינוֹ נוֹהֵג — But it does not apply בִּזְכָרִים — to males, i.e., to the male parent, וּמֻתָּר לִשְׁחוֹט — and it is permitted to slaughter הָאָב וְהַבֵּן — the father and the

---

1. *Temurah* 7a.
2. Above v. 18. The apparently unnecessary repetition of איש includes non-Jews.
3. *Chullin* 13b.
4. "Their corruption" could have been understood as corruption in a moral sense, in which case "their" would have referred to the "stranger" of the beginning of the verse. Rashi cites *Targum Onkelos* to show that "corruption" is used in a physical sense. "Their" thus refers to the blemished animals.
5. *Toras Kohanim, perek* 7:12. The verse does not mean, "they would not appease you" (*Gur Aryeh*).
6. *Toras Kohanim, parshasa* 8:3; *Chullin* 38b. An animal born by Caesarean section is not merely excluded from the law of waiting until the eighth day from birth until it may be offered, it is excluded from being offered at all.
7. The masculine pronoun אתו refers to the species שׁוֹר, which is a masculine noun, and שֶׂה, which can be considered masculine (as in *Psalms* 119:176). Nevertheless, the verse refers to the mother.
8. Although the literal meaning of בְּנוֹ is "its *son*," the word refers to both male and female offspring.

זֶבַח־תּוֹדָה לַיהוָה לִרְצֹנְכֶם תִּזְבָּחֻהוּ: בַּיּוֹם הַהוּא יֵאָכֵל לֹא־

a sacrifice of a thanksgiving-offering to HASHEM, you shall slaughter it to be an appeasement for you. *30* It must be eaten on that same day, you shall not

---
אונקלוס

נִכְסַת תּוֹדְתָא קֳדָם יְיָ לְרַעֲוָא לְכוֹן תִּכְּסֻנֵּהּ: בְּיוֹמָא הַהוּא יִתְאֲכֵל לָא

רש"י

(ת"כ שם יא-יב; חולין עח.): **אֹתוֹ וְאֶת בְּנוֹ**. אַף בְּנוֹ וְאוֹתוֹ בְּמַשְׁמָע (ת"כ פרק ח:ג-ד; חולין פב.): **(כט) לִרְצֹנְכֶם תִּזְבָּחֻהוּ.** תְּחִלַּת זְבִיחַתְכֶם הִזָּהֲרוּ שֶׁתְּהֵא לְרָצוֹן לָכֶם. וּמַהוּ הָרָצוֹן, **בַּיּוֹם הַהוּא יֵאָכֵל.** לֹא בָא לְהַזְהִיר אֶלָּא שֶׁתְּהֵא שְׁחִיטָה עַל מְנָת כֵּן, אַל תִּשְׁחָטוּהוּ עַל מְנָת לְאָכְלוֹ לְמָחָר, שֶׁאִם תַּחְשְׁבוּ בּוֹ מַחֲשֶׁבֶת פְּסוּל לֹא יְהֵא לָכֶם לְרָצוֹן (ת"כ פרק ט:א). דָּבָר אַחֵר לִרְצֹנְכֶם לְדַעְתְּכֶם, מִכָּאן לַמִּתְעַסֵּק בִּשְׁחִיטַת קָדָשִׁים שֶׁפָּסוּל (חולין יג.). וְאַף עַל פִּי שֶׁפֵּרֵט בַּנֶּאֱכָלִים לִשְׁנֵי יָמִים, חָזַר וּפֵרֵט בַּנֶּאֱכָלִין לְיוֹם אֶחָד שֶׁתְּהֵא זְבִיחָתָן עַל מְנָת לְאָכְלָן בִּזְמָנָן: **(ל) בַּיּוֹם הַהוּא יֵאָכֵל.** לֹא בָא לְהַזְהִיר אֶלָּא שֶׁתְּהֵא שְׁחִיטָה עַל מְנָת כֵּן, שֶׁאִם לִקְבּוֹעַ לָהּ זְמַן אֲכִילָה

RASHI ELUCIDATED

offspring on the same day.[1]

אֹתוֹ וְאֶת בְּנוֹ — IT AND ITS OFFSPRING. [2] אַף בְּנוֹ וְאוֹתוֹ בְּמַשְׁמָע — Slaughtering its offspring first and then it is also implied.[2]

29. לִרְצֹנְכֶם תִּזְבָּחֻהוּ — TO GAIN FAVOR ON YOUR BEHALF. תְּחִלַּת זְבִיחַתְכֶם — At the outset of your slaughter of the thanksgiving-offering, הִזָּהֲרוּ שֶׁתְּהֵא לְרָצוֹן לָכֶם — take care that it should be fit for acceptance on your behalf. וּמַהוּ הָרָצוֹן — And what is the condition for gaining favor? בַּיּוֹם הַהוּא יֵאָכֵל — "It must be eaten on that same day."[3] לֹא בָא לְהַזְהִיר אֶלָּא — [The verse] came to enjoin only שֶׁתְּהֵא שְׁחִיטָה עַל מְנָת כֵּן — that the slaughter of the offering should be on this condition, as if to say, אַל תִּשְׁחָטוּהוּ — "Do not slaughter it עַל מְנָת לְאָכְלוֹ לְמָחָר — on condition to eat it the following day, שֶׁאִם תַּחְשְׁבוּ בּוֹ — for if you will think about it at the time of its slaughter מַחֲשֶׁבֶת פְּסוּל — a thought of disqualification, i.e., a thought that the offering should be eaten beyond the time limit set for it, לֹא יְהֵא לָכֶם לְרָצוֹן — it shall not gain favor on your behalf."[4] דָּבָר אַחֵר — Alternatively, לִרְצֹנְכֶם לְדַעְתְּכֶם — the word לִרְצֹנְכֶם here means, "with your awareness." מִכָּאן — From here we learn לַמִּתְעַסֵּק — regarding one who performs an action inadvertently שֶׁפָּסוּל — that it is invalid[5] בִּשְׁחִיטַת קָדָשִׁים — with respect to slaughtering that which is holy, i.e., offerings.[5] וְאַף עַל פִּי — Even though שֶׁפֵּרֵט — [Scripture] has stated specifically that an offering is not valid if the slaughterer has in mind that it will be eaten beyond the time limit set for it, בַּנֶּאֱכָלִים לִשְׁנֵי יָמִים — with regard to those offerings that may be eaten for two days,[6] חָזַר וּפֵרֵט — it stated it specifically again here, בַּנֶּאֱכָלִין לְיוֹם אֶחָד — with regard to those offerings that may be eaten for only one day, שֶׁתְּהֵא זְבִיחָתָן — that their slaughter too should be בִּזְמַנָּן — within their time limit.

30. בַּיּוֹם הַהוּא יֵאָכֵל — IT MUST BE EATEN ON THAT SAME DAY. לֹא בָא לְהַזְהִיר אֶלָּא — It comes to enjoin only שֶׁתְּהֵא שְׁחִיטָה עַל מְנָת כֵּן — that the slaughter should take place on this condition, that it be eaten within one day, שֶׁאִם לִקְבּוֹעַ לָהּ זְמַן אֲכִילָה — for if it is meant to set a time limit for it for eating,

---

1. *Toras Kohanim, parshasa* 8:11-12; *Chullin* 78b. Other halachic authorities are in doubt as to whether the prohibition applies to the father, as well as the mother. See *Shulchan Aruch, Yoreh Deah,* 16:2.

2. *Toras Kohanim, perek* 8:3-4; *Chullin* 82a. The plural לֹא תִשְׁחֲטוּ indicates that the prohibition against slaughtering "it and its offspring" can refer to an instance involving more than one individual. The plural is not needed to allude to a case where an animal has two offspring and two men slaughter the offspring after the mother. Then, it is self-evident that each is liable. So, too, if one man slaughters the mother, a second her offspring, and a third the offspring of the offspring, we do not need a plural verb to tell us that the last two have violated the prohibition. The plural is needed to teach us that when one man slaughters a mother, a second the mother of that mother, and a third the offspring of the mother (three generations of animals), the last two men have violated the prohibition. In this instance an offspring (the "mother" — the second-generation animal) was slaughtered before its mother, the first-generation animal.

3. In some editions this phrase is the rubric for a new comment, rather than a continuation of the previous one.

4. *Toras Kohanim, perek* 9:1.

5. *Chullin* 13a.

6. See 7:18 above and Rashi there.

leave any of it until morning; I am Hashem. [31] *You shall guard My commandments and do them; I am* Hashem. [32] *You shall not defile My holy Name, and I shall be sanctified among the Children of Israel; I am* Hashem *Who sanctifies you,*

לא וּשְׁמַרְתֶּם מִצְוֹתַי וַעֲשִׂיתֶם אֹתָם אֲנִי יהוה: לב אֲנִי יהוה: וְלֹא תְחַלְּלוּ אֶת־שֵׁם קָדְשִׁי וְנִקְדַּשְׁתִּי בְּתוֹךְ בְּנֵי יִשְׂרָאֵל אֲנִי יהוה מְקַדִּשְׁכֶם:

תּוֹתִירוּ מִמֶּנּוּ עַד־בֹּקֶר אֲנִי יהוה:

───── אונקלוס ─────

תִשְׁאֲרוּן מִנֵּהּ עַד צַפְרָא אֲנָא יְיָ: לא וְתִטְּרוּן פִּקּוֹדַי וְתַעְבְּדוּן יָתְהוֹן אֲנָא יְיָ: לב וְלָא תְחַלְּלוּן יָת שְׁמָא דְקוּדְשִׁי וְאֶתְקַדַּשׁ בְּגוֹ בְּנֵי יִשְׂרָאֵל אֲנָא יְיָ מְקַדִּשְׁכוֹן:

───── רש"י ─────

כְּבָר כְּתִיב וּבְשַׂר זֶבַח תּוֹדַת שְׁלָמָיו וְגוֹ'. דַּע מִי גָזַר עַל הַדָּבָר וְאַל יֵקַל בְּעֵינֶיךָ: (לא) וּשְׁמַרְתֶּם. זוֹ הַמִּשְׁנָה (ת"כ שם ג): וַעֲשִׂיתֶם. זֶה הַמַּעֲשֶׂה (שם): (לב) וְלֹא תְחַלְּלוּ. לַעֲבוֹר עַל דְּבָרַי מְזִידִין. מִמַּשְׁמָע שֶׁנֶּאֱמַר וְלֹא תְחַלְּלוּ מַה תַּ"ל וְנִקְדַּשְׁתִּי, מְסוֹר עַצְמְךָ וְקַדֵּשׁ שְׁמִי. יָכוֹל בְּיָחִיד, תַּ"ל בְּתוֹךְ בְּנֵי יִשְׂרָאֵל. וּכְשֶׁהוּא מוֹסֵר עַצְמוֹ יִמְסוֹר עַצְמוֹ עַל מְנָת לָמוּת, שֶׁכָּל הַמּוֹסֵר עַצְמוֹ עַל מְנָת הַנֵּס אֵין עוֹשִׂין לוֹ נֵס, שֶׁכֵּן מָצִינוּ בַּחֲנַנְיָה מִישָׁאֵל וַעֲזַרְיָה שֶׁלֹּא מָסְרוּ עַצְמָן עַל מְנָת הַנֵּס, שֶׁנֶּאֱמַר וְהֵן לָא יְדִיעַ לֶהֱוֵא לָךְ מַלְכָּא וְגוֹ' (דניאל ג:יח) מַצִּיל וְלֹא מַצִּיל, יְדִיעַ לֶהֱוֵא לָךְ וְגוֹ':

───── RASHI ELUCIDATED ─────

"*and the flesh of his* וּבְשַׂר זֶבַח תּוֹדַת שְׁלָמָיו וְגוֹמֵר,, – *thanksgiving peace-offering, etc.*"[1] כְּבָר כְּתִיב – *that has already been written,*

אֲנִי ה' – I AM HASHEM. דַּע מִי גָזַר – Know Who issued the decree עַל הַדָּבָר – regarding the matter, וְאַל יֵקַל בְּעֵינֶיךָ – and let it not be taken lightly in your eyes.[2]

31. וּשְׁמַרְתֶּם – YOU SHALL GUARD, זוֹ הַמִּשְׁנָה[3] – this is the study of the commandments;[3]

וַעֲשִׂיתֶם – AND DO, זֶה הַמַּעֲשֶׂה[3] – this is the performance of the commandments.[3]

32. וְלֹא תְחַלְּלוּ – YOU SHALL NOT DEFILE, לַעֲבוֹר עַל דְּבָרַי – by violating My words מְזִידִין – intentionally. מִמַּשְׁמָע שֶׁנֶּאֱמַר – From the implication of that which it says, ,,וְלֹא תְחַלְּלוּ'' – "you shall not defile," I can infer that the opposite state, God's sanctification, will exist, if there is no defilement. מַה תַּלְמוּד לוֹמַר – Why then does the verse say explicitly, ,,וְנִקְדַּשְׁתִּי'' – "*and I shall be sanctified*"? It means, מְסוֹר עַצְמְךָ – surrender yourself, וְקַדֵּשׁ שְׁמִי – and sanctify My Name.[4] יָכוֹל בְּיָחִיד – One might be able to think on the basis of this verse that there is an obligation to submit to death rather than to violate a commandment of the Torah even in the presence of a single individual.[5] תַּלְמוּד לוֹמַר – To teach us otherwise, the verse says, ,,בְּתוֹךְ בְּנֵי יִשְׂרָאֵל'' – "*among the Children of Israel,*" which implies many witnesses to the sin.[6] וּכְשֶׁהוּא מוֹסֵר עַצְמוֹ – And when he surrenders himself, יִמְסוֹר עַצְמוֹ – he should surrender himself עַל מְנָת לָמוּת – on condition to die, i.e., with the understanding that he might die, שֶׁכָּל הַמּוֹסֵר עַצְמוֹ – for whoever surrenders himself עַל מְנָת הַנֵּס – on condition of the miracle, i.e., with the understanding that God will miraculously save him, אֵין עוֹשִׂין לוֹ נֵס – will have no miracle performed for him. שֶׁכֵּן מָצִינוּ בַּחֲנַנְיָה מִישָׁאֵל וַעֲזַרְיָה – For so have we found concerning Hananiah, Mishael, and Azariah, שֶׁלֹּא מָסְרוּ עַצְמָן – that they did not surrender themselves עַל מְנָת הַנֵּס – on condition of the miracle, שֶׁנֶּאֱמַר – as it says, [7],,וְהֵן לָא'' – "*and if not,* i.e., if He will not save us, *let it be known to you, O King, etc.*"[7] They said, מַצִּיל וְלֹא מַצִּיל – "Whether He saves us or He does not

---

1. Above 7:15. That verse continues, "must be eaten on the day of its offering."
2. See v. 33 below and note 3 there.
3. *Toras Kohanim, perek* 9:3. "Guarding" refers to the study of the commandments, for it denotes keeping something in mind, and an awareness that it has yet to be fulfilled. The performance is the outcome of that awareness, implemented in its proper time (*Mizrachi; Sifsei Chachamim*).
4. Violation of a commandment under threat of death is not a desecration of God's Name. Our verse teaches us that it is not enough to avoid desecrating God's Name. One must sanctify His Name in a positive fashion by refraining from the violation of a commandment even if it means suffering death (*Malbim*).
5. "A single individual" means even the sinner himself, i.e., privately. See *Rambam, Hilchos Yesodei HaTorah,* 5:2.
6. From this phrase, the Talmud learns that suffering martyrdom in public means in the presence of at least ten Jews (see *Sanhedrin* 74b).
7. *Daniel* 3:18. That verse continues, "that we will not worship your god, nor will we bow to the gold image you have erected."

³³ Who takes you out of the land of Egypt to be a God unto you; I am Hashem.

23 ¹ Hashem spoke to Moses, saying: ² Speak to the Children of Israel and say to them: Hashem's appointed festivals which you shall designate as callings of holiness — these are My appointed festivals. ³ For a six-day period labor may be done,

לג הַמּוֹצִיא אֶתְכֶם מֵאֶרֶץ מִצְרַיִם לִהְיוֹת לָכֶם לֵאלֹהִים אֲנִי יהוה:

כג א וַיְדַבֵּר יהוה אֶל־מֹשֶׁה לֵּאמֹר: ב דַּבֵּר אֶל־בְּנֵי יִשְׂרָאֵל וְאָמַרְתָּ אֲלֵהֶם מוֹעֲדֵי יהוה אֲשֶׁר־תִּקְרְאוּ אֹתָם מִקְרָאֵי קֹדֶשׁ אֵלֶּה הֵם מוֹעֲדָי: ג שֵׁשֶׁת יָמִים תֵּעָשֶׂה מְלָאכָה

— אונקלוס —

לגדְּאַפֵּיק יָתְכוֹן מֵאַרְעָא דְמִצְרַיִם לְמֶהֱוֵי לְכוֹן לֶאֱלָהָא אֲנָא יְיָ: א וּמַלִּיל יְיָ עִם מֹשֶׁה לְמֵימָר: ב מַלֵּל עִם בְּנֵי יִשְׂרָאֵל וְתֵימַר לְהוֹן זִמְנַיָּא דַּייָ דִּי תְעָרְעוּן יָתְהוֹן אִנּוּן אֲגַן זִמְנָי: ג שִׁתָּא יוֹמִין תִּתְעֲבֵד עֲבִידָא

— רש״י —

ידיע להוי לך וגו' (ת"כ שם ד"ה): (לג) **המוציא אתכם.** על מנת כן (שם ו): **אני ה'.** נאמן לשלם שכר (שם): (ב) **דבר אל בני ישראל וגו' מועדי ה'.** עשה מועדות שיהיו ישראל בהם, מלמד שמעברים [ס"א שיהיו ישראל מלומדין בהם שמעברים] את

השנה על גליות שנעקרו ממקומן לעלות לרגל ועדיין לא הגיעו לירושלים (ת"כ פרשתא ט:א; סנהדרין י"א; ירושלמי סנהדרין א:ב): (ג) **ששת ימים.** מה ענין שבת אצל מועדות, ללמדך שכל המחלל את המועדות מעלין עליו כאלו חלל את השבתות

— RASHI ELUCIDATED —

יָדִיעַ לֶהֱוֵי לָךְ וְגוֹמֵר — save us, "let it be known to you, etc."[1]

33. הַמּוֹצִיא אֶתְכֶם — WHO TAKES YOU OUT עַל מְנָת כֵּן — on this condition, that you sanctify Me.[2]

אֲנִי ה׳ — I AM HASHEM נֶאֱמָן לְשַׁלֵּם שָׂכָר — faithful to pay reward.[3]

23.

2. דַּבֵּר אֶל בְּנֵי יִשְׂרָאֵל וְגוֹמֵר מוֹעֲדֵי ה׳ — SPEAK TO THE CHILDREN OF ISRAEL, ETC., HASHEM'S APPOINTED FESTIVALS. עֲשֵׂה מוֹעֲדוֹת — Make appointed festivals שֶׁיִּהְיוּ יִשְׂרָאֵל — so that Israel should be present בָּהֶם — in them. מְלַמֵּד — This teaches us[4] שֶׁמְּעַבְּרִים אֶת הַשָּׁנָה — that they intercalate a month in the year, i.e., they add a month to make a leap year of thirteen months, עַל גָּלֻיּוֹת — because of exiles, i.e., Jews living in the Diaspora, שֶׁנֶּעֶקְרוּ מִמְּקוֹמָן — who have been uprooted from their place, i.e., who have left their homes, לַעֲלוֹת לָרֶגֶל — to ascend to Jerusalem for the festival, וַעֲדַיִן לֹא הִגִּיעוּ לִירוּשָׁלַיִם — and have not yet arrived in Jerusalem.[5]

3. שֵׁשֶׁת יָמִים — FOR A SIX-DAY PERIOD. מַה עִנְיַן שַׁבָּת אֵצֶל מוֹעֲדוֹת — Why is the subject of Shabbos put here next to the subject of the festivals?[6] לְלַמֶּדְךָ — To teach you שֶׁכָּל הַמְחַלֵּל אֶת הַמּוֹעֲדוֹת — that whoever desecrates the festivals מַעֲלִין עָלָיו — is considered כְּאִלּוּ חִלֵּל אֶת הַשַּׁבָּתוֹת — as if he

---

1. Toras Kohanim, perek 9:4-5.
2. Toras Kohanim, perek 9:6.
3. Toras Kohanim, perek 9:6. When "I am Hashem" appeared above in verse 30, Rashi interpreted it, "Know Who issued the decree... and let it not be taken lightly in your eyes." There "I am Hashem" followed a negative commandment which might have been taken lightly. But here it follows the most difficult of positive commandments, the obligation to sacrifice one's life for God. Thus, here "I am Hashem" connotes assurance that whoever makes this offering will be amply rewarded (Be'er Yitzchak).
4. Our texts follows the Rome edition of Rashi (ca. 1470 C.E.; the Reggio deCalabria edition [ca. 1475], usually called "the first printed edition" has a similar text). In contemporary editions, this comment begins, שֶׁיִּהְיוּ יִשְׂרָאֵל ..., "מְלַמְּדִין בָּהֶם שֶׁמְעַבְּרִים", "so that Israel should be habituated in them, that they add a month..." (Yosef Hallel).
5. Toras Kohanim, parshasa 9:1; Sanhedrin 11a; Yerushalmi Sanhedrin 1:2. The matter of fixing the calendar is the responsibility of the courts alone, not of the entire nation of Israel. Yet the Torah has Moses address the issue to "the Children of Israel," the entire nation, to teach us that the court should fix the calendar in such a way as to allow for the maximum representation of the nation of Israel in Jerusalem at the time of the festivals by postponing them, if necessary, through the addition of a thirteenth month to the year (Malbim).

This is one of the reasons for which the court may intercalate a thirteenth month. For the other reasons, see Sanhedrin 11a.
6. We cannot say that Shabbos falls within the category of festivals, for the verse says of them, "that you are to designate as callings of holiness," which implies that they are fixed by man. This holds true of the festivals, for they are set in terms of the day of the month, which depends upon the court's declaration of the New Moon. Shabbos, on the other hand, is in no sense "designated" by man, for it is

וּבַיּוֹם֙ הַשְּׁבִיעִ֔י שַׁבַּ֥ת שַׁבָּתוֹן֙ מִקְרָא־
קֹ֔דֶשׁ כָּל־מְלָאכָ֖ה לֹ֣א תַעֲשׂ֑וּ שַׁבָּ֥ת
הִוא֙ לַיהוָ֔ה בְּכֹ֖ל מוֹשְׁבֹתֵיכֶֽם׃
ד אֵ֚לֶּה מוֹעֲדֵ֣י יְהוָ֔ה מִקְרָאֵ֖י קֹ֑דֶשׁ
אֲשֶׁר־תִּקְרְא֥וּ אֹתָ֖ם בְּמוֹעֲדָֽם׃
ה בַּחֹ֣דֶשׁ הָרִאשׁ֗וֹן בְּאַרְבָּעָ֥ה
עָשָׂ֛ר לַחֹ֖דֶשׁ בֵּ֣ין הָעַרְבָּ֑יִם
פֶּ֖סַח לַיהוָֽה׃ ו וּבַחֲמִשָּׁה֩ עָשָׂ֨ר י֜וֹם
לַחֹ֣דֶשׁ הַזֶּ֗ה חַ֧ג הַמַּצּ֛וֹת לַיהוָ֖ה
שִׁבְעַ֣ת יָמִ֖ים מַצּ֥וֹת תֹּאכֵֽלוּ׃ ז בַּיּוֹם֙
הָֽרִאשׁ֔וֹן מִקְרָא־קֹ֖דֶשׁ יִהְיֶ֣ה לָכֶ֑ם
כָּל־מְלֶ֥אכֶת עֲבֹדָ֖ה לֹ֥א תַעֲשֽׂוּ׃

and the seventh day is a day of complete rest, a calling of holiness, you shall not do any work; it is a Sabbath for HASHEM in all your settled places.

⁴ These are the appointed festivals of HASHEM, the callings of holiness, which you shall designate in their appropriate time. ⁵ In the first month on the fourteenth of the month toward evening it is a Pesach to HASHEM. ⁶ And on the fifteenth day of this month is the Festival of Matzos to HASHEM; you shall eat matzos for a seven-day period. ⁷ On the first day there shall be a calling of holiness for you; you shall do no work of labor.

———————————— אונקלוס ————————————

וּבְיוֹמָא שְׁבִיעָאָה שְׁבַת שְׁבָתָא מְעָרַע קַדִּישׁ כָּל עֲבִידָא לָא תַעְבְּדוּן שַׁבְּתָא הִיא קֳדָם יְיָ בְּכֹל מוֹתְבָנֵיכוֹן: ד אִלֵּין זִמְנַיָּא דַּיָּי מְעָרְעֵי קַדִּישׁ דִּי תְעָרְעוּן יָתְהוֹן בְּזִמְנֵיהוֹן: ה בְּיַרְחָא קַדְמָאָה בְּאַרְבְּעַת עַשְׂרָא לְיַרְחָא בֵּין שִׁמְשַׁיָּא פִּסְחָא קֳדָם יְיָ: ו וּבְחַמְשַׁת עַשְׂרָא יוֹמָא לְיַרְחָא הָדֵין חַגָּא דְפַטִּירַיָּא קֳדָם יְיָ שַׁבְעָא יוֹמִין פַּטִּיר תֵּיכְלוּן: ז בְּיוֹמָא קַדְמָאָה מְעָרַע קַדִּישׁ יְהֵי לְכוֹן כָּל עֲבִידַת פָּלְחָן לָא תַעְבְּדוּן:

———————————— רש"י ————————————

וכל המקיים את המועדות מעלין עליו כאלו קיים את השבתות (ת"כ) **(ה) בין הערבים.** משש שעות ומעלה **פסח לה׳.** הקרבת קרבן ששמו פסח: **מדבר בקדוש החדש (שם פרק יא:א): שם ז):** **(ד) אלה מועדי ה׳.** למעלה מדבר בעבור שנה וכאן

———————————— RASHI ELUCIDATED ————————————

מַעֲלִין — and whoever upholds the festivals וְכָל הַמְקַיֵּם אֶת הַמּוֹעֲדוֹת — desecrated the Shabbos days, עָלָיו — is considered ¹כְּאִלּוּ קִיֵּם אֶת הַשַּׁבָּתוֹת — as if he upheld the Shabbos days.¹

4. אֵלֶּה מוֹעֲדֵי ה׳ — THESE ARE THE APPOINTED FESTIVALS OF HASHEM. לְמַעְלָה מְדַבֵּר — Above it speaks בְּעִבּוּר שָׁנָה — of adding a month to the year, וְכָאן מְדַבֵּר — and here it speaks בְּקִדּוּשׁ הַחֹדֶשׁ — of sanctifying the New Moon.²

5. בֵּין הָעַרְבָּיִם — TOWARD EVENING. ³מִשֵּׁשׁ שָׁעוֹת וּלְמַעְלָה — From six hours and onward.³

שֶׁשְּׁמוֹ פֶּסַח — פֶּסַח לַה׳ — IT IS A *PESACH* TO HASHEM. הַקְרָבַת קָרְבָּן — The bringing of the offering whose name is *pesach*.⁴

set in terms of the day of the week, the immutable cycle of which was put into effect at the time of Creation, and in which man has no say (*Nachalas Yaakov*). Furthermore, verses 37-38 below ("these are the appointed festivals . . . aside from HASHEM'S Sabbaths . . .") treat Shabbos as being outside of the category of "appointed festivals."

1. *Toras Kohanim, parshasa* 9:7. Earthly courts treat festivals more leniently than Shabbos. Doing forbidden work on Shabbos is punished by being stoned to death, while doing forbidden work on the festivals is punished by lashes. But the Heavenly Court views them with equal gravity (*Nachalas Yaakov*).

2. *Toras Kohanim, perek* 10:1. Our verse appears to be a repetition of verse 2. But אֲשֶׁר תִּקְרְאוּ אֹתָם, "which you shall designate," of verse 2 teaches us that a month can be added to the year only by the declaration of the court, while אֲשֶׁר תִּקְרְאוּ אֹתָם of our verse teaches us that sanctification of the New Moon can be performed only by the court (*Mizrachi; Sifsei Chachamim*).

Although the common translation of רֹאשׁ חֹדֶשׁ is "New Moon," it should be noted that the dictionary's definition of "new moon" is different from the halachic concept. The English term "new moon" refers to the period when the moon is invisible, but רֹאשׁ חֹדֶשׁ refers to the re-appearance of the moon in its crescent shape after its invisible period.

3. *Toras Kohanim, perek* 11:1. See, too, Rashi to *Exodus* 12:6. The daytime period is divided into twelve equal units, each of which is a halachic hour. Since the length of these hours varies with the length of the daylight period, they are called שָׁעוֹת זְמַנִיּוֹת, "seasonal hours." "From six hours and onward" means "from the end of the sixth hour," i.e., midday.

4. The verse does not mean that the fourteenth is called Pesach, for the festival does not begin until the fifteenth. It means that it is the time of the offering of the *pesach*-offering (*Mesiach Ilmim*; *Devek Tov*).

8 You shall bring a fire-offering to Hashem for a seven-day period; on the seventh day shall be a calling of holiness; you shall do no work of labor.

ח וְהִקְרַבְתֶּ֨ם אִשֶּׁ֤ה לַֽיהוָה֙ שִׁבְעַ֣ת יָמִ֔ים בַּיּ֥וֹם הַשְּׁבִיעִ֖י מִקְרָא־קֹ֑דֶשׁ כָּל־מְלֶ֥אכֶת עֲבֹדָ֖ה לֹ֥א תַעֲשֽׂוּ׃

— אונקלוס —

ח וּתְקָרְבוּן קֻרְבָּנָא קֳדָם יְיָ שַׁבְעָא יוֹמִין בְּיוֹמָא שְׁבִיעָאָה מְעָרַע קַדִּישׁ כָּל עֲבִידַת פָּלְחָן לָא תַעַבְּדוּן:

— רש״י —

(ח) **והקרבתם אשה וגו׳.** הם המוספין האמורים בפרשת פנחס ולמה נאמרו כאן לומר לך שאין המוספין מעכבין זה את זה, והקרבתם אשה לה׳, מכל מקום, אם אין פרים הבא אילים ואם אין פרים ואילים הבא כבשים (שם ה): **שבעת ימים.** כל מקום שנאמר שבעת שם דבר הוא,

שבוע של ימים שטיינ״א בלע״ז. וכן כל לשון שמונת ששת חמשת שלשת: **מלאכת עבודה.** אפילו מלאכות החשובות לכם עבודה וצורך, שיש חסרון כיס בבטלה שלהן כגון דבר האבד. כך הבנתי מתורת כהנים (פרשתא יב:ח), דקתני יכול אף חולו של מועד יהא אסור במלאכת עבודה וכו׳:

— RASHI ELUCIDATED —

8. וְהִקְרַבְתֶּם אִשֶּׁה וְגוֹמֵר — YOU SHALL BRING A FIRE-OFFERING, ETC. — הֵם הַמּוּסָפִין — These are the *mussaf* offerings הָאֲמוּרִים בְּפָרָשַׁת פִּינְחָס — which are stated in detail in *Parashas Pinchas*.[1] וְלָמָּה נֶאֶמְרוּ כָאן — Why are they mentioned here? לוֹמַר לָךְ — To say to you שֶׁאֵין הַמּוּסָפִין מְעַכְּבִין זֶה אֶת זֶה — that the *mussaf* offerings do not obstruct one another,[2] as the verse goes on to imply, ,,וְהִקְרַבְתֶּם אִשֶּׁה לַה׳׳׳[3] — "You shall bring a fire-offering to Hashem,"[3] מִכָּל מָקוֹם — in all circumstances; אִם אֵין פָּרִים — if there are no bulls, still, הָבֵא אֵילִים — bring the rams which are part of the *mussaf* offering, וְאִם אֵין פָּרִים וְאֵילִים — and if there are neither bulls nor rams, still,[4] הָבֵא כְבָשִׂים — bring the **sheep** which are part of the offering.[4]

□ שִׁבְעַת יָמִים — A SEVEN-DAY PERIOD. — כָּל מָקוֹם שֶׁנֶּאֱמַר שִׁבְעַת — Wherever the word שִׁבְעַת is used, שֵׁם — דָּבָר הוּא — it is a noun which means שָׁבוּעַ שֶׁל יָמִים — a septet of days; שְׁטֵיינַ״א בְּלַעַ״ז — in Old French *seteine*.[5] וְכֵן — And, so, too, כָּל לְשׁוֹן — any instance of the terms שְׁמוֹנַת שֵׁשֶׁת חֲמֵשֶׁת שְׁלֹשֶׁת — mean **an octet of, a sextet of, a quintet of, a triad of.**[6]

□ מְלֶאכֶת עֲבֹדָה — WORK OF LABOR. — אֲפִילוּ מְלָאכוֹת — Even tasks הַחֲשׁוּבוֹת לָכֶם עֲבוֹדָה וָצֹרֶךְ — which are considered labor and necessity by you[7] שֶׁיֵּשׁ חֶסְרוֹן כִּיס בְּבַטָּלָה שֶׁלָּהֶן — which have financial loss in abstaining from them, כְּגוֹן דְּבַר הָאָבֵד — such as "a matter which is lost."[8] כָּךְ הֲבִנוֹתִי מִתּוֹרַת — Thus have I understood from *Toras Kohanim*,[9] דְּקָתָנֵי — as we have learned there: יָכוֹל — כְּהָנִים[9] — One might be able to think that אַף חֻלּוֹ שֶׁל מוֹעֵד יְהֵא אָסוּר בִּמְלֶאכֶת עֲבוֹדָה וְכֻלֵּיהּ — even on *chol hamoed* (the intermediate days of the Festival) **work of labor would be forbidden, etc.**[10]

---

1. *Numbers* 28:19-24.
2. Failure or inability to bring some of the *mussaf* offerings does not prevent the rest of the offerings from being brought.
3. In some editions this is the rubric for a new comment.
4. *Toras Kohanim, perek* 10:5. Since our verse does not specify which offerings are to be brought for the seven-day period of Pesach, we may presume that they are the *mussaf* offering, which the Torah states explicitly are to be brought on each of the seven days. The Torah makes reference to this offering twice to teach us that even if the entire set of *mussaf* offerings cannot be brought, the part that can be brought should be (*Devek Tov*).
5. In Modern French *septénaire*; in English, "septet" or "heptad," a group of seven.
6. In his commentary to *Exodus* 29:30, Rashi explains that when this numerical noun form is used in conjunction with days, it implies consecutive days. See also Rashi to *Exodus* 10:22 for further discussion of this numerical noun form.
7. "Work of labor" could have been understood as "hard work." The verse would then have been forbidding hard labor, but allowing easy work. Rashi explains that difficulty is not a factor. By "work of labor," the verse forbids labor which is viewed as a necessity. All the more so that which is not (*Mesiach Ilmim*).
8. A situation in which financial loss will occur if action is not taken immediately.
9. *Toras Kohanim, parshasa* 12:8.
10. The complete *baraisa* in *Toras Kohanim* reads: One might be able to think that even on *chol hamoed* work of labor would be forbidden. [To teach us otherwise] the verse says, "*It* is a restraining" (v. 36 below), [which implies], *it* [*yom tov*] is forbidden in work of labor, but *chol hamoed* is not forbidden in work of labor.

The verse does not permit all work to be done on *chol hamoed*, only "work of labor," work that must be done to avoid loss.

⁹ Hashem spoke to Moses, saying: **¹⁰** Speak to the Children of Israel and say to them: When you shall enter the Land that I give you and you reap its harvest, you shall bring the omer of the first of your harvest to the Kohen. **¹¹** He shall wave the omer before Hashem to be an appeasement for you; on the morrow of the rest day the Kohen shall wave it.

ט וַיְדַבֵּר יְהוָה אֶל־מֹשֶׁה לֵּאמֹר: י דַּבֵּר אֶל־בְּנֵי יִשְׂרָאֵל וְאָמַרְתָּ אֲלֵהֶם כִּי־תָבֹאוּ אֶל־הָאָרֶץ אֲשֶׁר אֲנִי נֹתֵן לָכֶם וּקְצַרְתֶּם אֶת־קְצִירָהּ וַהֲבֵאתֶם אֶת־עֹמֶר רֵאשִׁית קְצִירְכֶם אֶל־הַכֹּהֵן: יא וְהֵנִיף אֶת־הָעֹמֶר לִפְנֵי יְהוָה לִרְצֹנְכֶם מִמָּחֳרַת הַשַּׁבָּת יְנִיפֶנּוּ הַכֹּהֵן:

— אונקלוס —

ט וּמַלִּיל יְיָ עִם מֹשֶׁה לְמֵימָר: י מַלֵּל עִם בְּנֵי יִשְׂרָאֵל וְתֵימַר לְהוֹן אֲרֵי תַעֲלוּן לְאַרְעָא דִי אֲנָא יָהֵב לְכוֹן וְתַחְצְדוּן יָת חֲצָדַהּ וְתַיְתוּן יָת עוּמְרָא רֵישׁ חֲצָדְכוֹן לְוָת כַּהֲנָא: יא וִירִים יָת עוּמְרָא קֳדָם יְיָ לְרַעֲוָא לְכוֹן מִבָּתַר יוֹמָא טָבָא יְרִימִנֵּהּ כַּהֲנָא:

— רש"י —

(י) רֵאשִׁית קְצִירְכֶם. שֶׁתְּהֵא רִאשׁוֹנָה לַקָּצִיר (ת"כ פרשתא יג:): **עֹמֶר.** עֲשִׂירִית הָאֵיפָה כָּךְ הָיָה שְׁמָהּ, כְּמוֹ וַיָּמֹדּוּ בָעֹמֶר (שמות טז:יח): **(יא) וְהֵנִיף.** כָּל תְּנוּפָה מוֹלִיךְ וּמֵבִיא מַעֲלֶה וּמוֹרִיד. מוֹלִיךְ וּמֵבִיא לַעֲצֹר רוּחוֹת רָעוֹת, מַעֲלֶה וּמוֹרִיד לַעֲצֹר טְלָלִים רָעִים (מנחות סב.): **לִרְצֹנְכֶם.** אִם תַּקְרִיבוּ כַמִּשְׁפָּט הַזֶּה יִהְיֶה לָרָצוֹן לָכֶם: **מִמָּחֳרַת הַשַּׁבָּת.** מִמָּחֳרַת יוֹם טוֹב הָרִאשׁוֹן שֶׁל פֶּסַח, שֶׁאִם אַתָּה אוֹמֵר שַׁבַּת בְּרֵאשִׁית אִי אַתָּה יוֹדֵעַ אֵיזֶהוּ (ת"כ פרק יב:ד; מנחות סו.):

— RASHI ELUCIDATED —

10. רֵאשִׁית קְצִירְכֶם — THE FIRST OF YOUR HARVEST. שֶׁתְּהֵא רִאשׁוֹנָה לַקָּצִיר[1] — That it should be the first one of the harvest.[1]

□ עֹמֶר — OMER. עֲשִׂירִית הָאֵיפָה — A tenth of an *ephah*. כָּךְ הָיָה שְׁמָהּ — This was its name, כְּמוֹ ,,וַיָּמֹדּוּ בָעֹמֶר" — as in the verse, "and they measured with an *omer*."[2,3]

11. וְהֵנִיף — HE SHALL WAVE. כָּל תְּנוּפָה — Every "waving" mentioned in the Torah means, מוֹלִיךְ — he moves the object being waved **back and forth** מַעֲלֶה וּמוֹרִיד — and **he lifts and lowers** that object. מוֹלִיךְ וּמֵבִיא — He moves the object **back and forth** לַעֲצֹר רוּחוֹת רָעוֹת — to restrain harmful winds. מַעֲלֶה וּמוֹרִיד — He lifts and lowers it לַעֲצֹר טְלָלִים רָעִים[4] — to restrain harmful dews.[4]

□ לִרְצֹנְכֶם — TO BE AN APPEASEMENT FOR YOU. אִם תַּקְרִיבוּ — If you will bring offerings כַּמִּשְׁפָּט הַזֶּה — in accordance with this law, יִהְיֶה לָרָצוֹן לָכֶם — it will be an appeasement for you.

□ מִמָּחֳרַת הַשַּׁבָּת — ON THE MORROW OF THE REST DAY. This means מִמָּחֳרַת יוֹם טוֹב הָרִאשׁוֹן שֶׁל פֶּסַח — the morrow of the first festival day of Pesach, שֶׁאִם אַתָּה אוֹמֵר — for if you say that it means שַׁבַּת בְּרֵאשִׁית — the Sabbath of Creation, i.e., if הַשַּׁבָּת here is taken in its usual sense as the seventh day of the week, אִי אַתָּה יוֹדֵעַ אֵיזֶהוּ — you do not know which Sabbath of the year the verse refers to.[5]

---

1. *Toras Kohanim, parshasa* 10:3. Had the verse said רֵאשִׁית הַקָּצִיר, "the first of *the* harvest," we might have understood the verse to refer to the area of the field from which the *omer* must be taken, from the first section of the field to be harvested. "The first of *your* harvest," using the plural form of "your," indicates that the *omer* must be the first of the harvest of the entire Jewish people; i.e., no Jew in the Land of Israel may harvest his field before the *omer* is harvested (*Mizrachi*; *Sifsei Chachamim*; *Be'er Yitzchak*).
Alternatively, the word רֵאשִׁית is sometimes used in the sense of "the best," e.g., וְרֵאשִׁית שְׁמָנִים יִמְשָׁחוּ, "and they are anointed with the finest of oils" (*Amos* 6:6; see Rashi there). It is also used in the sense of that which precedes something else, but not necessarily the very outset of an activity, e.g., רֵאשִׁית עֲרִיסֹתֵכֶם חַלָּה תָרִימוּ תְרוּמָה, "The first part of your kneading troughs you shall separate as an offering of *challah*" (*Numbers* 15:20). Rashi there explains that *challah* is רֵאשִׁית, "the first part," in that one may not eat before it is separated. Rashi explains that רֵאשִׁית is being used in neither of these senses here. It does not mean "the best," nor does it mean that we may not eat from the new crop until the *omer* is offered, as in the case of *challah*. It means that the *omer* must be the first grain harvested; we may not harvest other grain before it.
2. *Exodus* 16:18. Rashi cites this verse which is the first time the amount of each daily portion of manna is mentioned. The final verse of that section states explicitly, "The *omer* is a tenth of an *ephah*" (*Exodus* 16:36).
Rashi repeats this fact here because עֹמֶר also means "sheaf," e.g., *Deuteronomy* 24:19 (*Sefer Zikaron*).
3. See chart on p. 268.
4. *Menachos* 62a.
5. *Toras Kohanim, perek* 12:4; *Menachos* 66a. These sources give a variety of reasons to support the view that שַׁבָּת here means the first day of Pesach.

¹² On the day you wave the omer, you shall perform the service of an unblemished lamb in its first year as an olah-offering to HASHEM. ¹³ Its meal-offering shall be two tenth-ephahs of fine flour mixed with oil, a fire-offering to HASHEM, a satisfying aroma; and its poured-offering, wine, a quarter of a hin. ¹⁴ You shall not eat bread and parched meal and plump kernels until this very day, until you bring the offering of your God; it is an eternal decree for your generations

יב וַעֲשִׂיתֶ֕ם בְּי֥וֹם הֲנִֽיפְכֶ֖ם אֶת־הָעֹ֑מֶר כֶּ֣בֶשׂ תָּמִ֧ים בֶּן־שְׁנָת֛וֹ לְעֹלָ֖ה לַיהוָֽה: יג וּמִנְחָתוֹ֩ שְׁנֵ֨י עֶשְׂרֹנִ֜ים סֹ֣לֶת בְּלוּלָ֥ה בַשֶּׁ֛מֶן אִשֶּׁ֥ה לַיהוָ֖ה רֵ֣יחַ נִיחֹ֑חַ וְנִסְכֹּ֥ה יַּ֛יִן רְבִיעִ֥ת הַהִֽין: יד וְלֶ֩חֶם֩ וְקָלִ֨י וְכַרְמֶ֜ל לֹ֣א תֹֽאכְל֗וּ עַד־עֶ֙צֶם֙ הַיּ֣וֹם הַזֶּ֔ה עַ֚ד הֲבִ֣יאֲכֶ֔ם אֶת־קָרְבַּ֖ן אֱלֹהֵיכֶ֑ם חֻקַּ֤ת עוֹלָם֙ לְדֹרֹ֣תֵיכֶ֔ם

— אונקלוס —

יב וְתַעְבְּדוּן בְּיוֹמָא דַאֲרָמוּתְכוֹן יָת שְׁתֵּה בַּר שַׁתֵּהּ שְׁלִים אִמַּר עוּמְרָא יָת קֳדָם יְיָ: יג וּמִנְחָתֵהּ תְּרֵין עֶשְׂרוֹנִין סֻלְתָּא דְּפִילָא בִּמְשַׁח קָרְבָּנָא קֳדָם יְיָ לְאִתְקַבָּלָא בְרַעֲוָא וְנִסְכֵּהּ חַמְרָא רַבְעוּת הִינָא: יד וּלְחֵם וְקָלֵי וּפֵרוּכָן לָא תֵיכְלוּן עַד כְּרַן יוֹמָא הָדֵין עַד אַיְתָיוּתְכוֹן יָת קָרְבַּן אֱלָהֲכוֹן קְיָם עָלַם לְדָרֵיכוֹן

— רש"י —

(יב) ועשיתם. בכש. חובה לעומר הוא בא: (יג) ט"ו שמנחתו כפולה אין נסכיו כפולים (שם ח; מנחות ומנחתו. מנחת נסכיו: שני עשרונים. כפולה היתה: פט:): (יד) וקלי. קמח עשוי מכרמל רך שמייבשין אותו בתנור: וכרמל. הן קליות שקורין גרייל"ש:

— RASHI ELUCIDATED —

12. ... וַעֲשִׂיתֶם ... כֶּבֶשׂ — YOU SHALL PERFORM THE SERVICE OF AN [UNBLEMISHED] LAMB. חוֹבָה לָעוֹמֶר הוּא בָּא — It comes as an obligation for the *omer*.[1]

13. וּמִנְחָתוֹ — ITS MEAL-OFFERING. מִנְחַת נְסָכָיו — The meal-offering of its poured-offerings.[2]

☐ שְׁנֵי עֶשְׂרֹנִים — TWO TENTH-*EPHAHS*.[3] כְּפוּלָה הָיְתָה — It was double the standard meal-offering that accompanies a burnt-offering of sheep.[3]

☐ וְנִסְכֹּה יַיִן רְבִיעִת הַהִין — AND ITS POURED-OFFERING, WINE, A QUARTER OF A HIN. אַף עַל פִּי שֶׁמִּנְחָתוֹ כְּפוּלָה — Even though its meal-offering is double, אֵין נְסָכָיו כְּפוּלִים[5] — its poured-offerings[4] are not double.[5]

14. וְקָלִי — AND PARCHED MEAL. קֶמַח עָשׂוּי מִכַּרְמֶל רַךְ שֶׁמְּיַבְּשִׁין אוֹתוֹ בְּתַנּוּר — Meal made of soft, plump, kernels that they dry in an oven.[6]

☐ וְכַרְמֶל — AND PLUMP KERNELS. הֵן קָלִיּוֹת — They are parched kernels שֶׁקּוֹרִין גרניילי"ש — which they call *grenailles*[7] in Old French.[8]

---

1. This lamb is not mentioned in *Numbers*, Ch. 28, among the animals of the *mussaf* offering of Pesach. Unlike the *mussaf* offerings which are brought each day of the festival, this lamb is brought only on the day that the *omer* is offered (*Mizrachi*; *Sifsei Chachamim*). According to *Nachalas Yaakov*'s view of Rashi, it is offered only if the *omer* is actually offered. According to *Be'er BaSadeh*'s view, Rashi agrees with *Toras Kohanim* (parshasa 10:6) that the lamb is offered even if the *omer* is not. Still, it is the obligation to offer the *omer* which dictates that the lamb be brought. This is unlike the *mussaf* offerings which are brought because of the sanctity of the festival.

2. All burnt-offerings are accompanied by a meal-offering and an offering of wine. The standard meal-offering that accompanies a sheep consists of one tenth-*ephah* of meal (*Numbers* 15:4-5). Since this meal-offering consists of two tenth-*ephahs*, double the usual measure (see Rashi's next comment), we might have thought that the extra tenth-*ephah* is a separate meal-offering brought in addition to a standard meal-offering of one tenth-*ephah*. But since the verse refers to it as "*its* meal-offering," i.e., the meal-offering that accompanies the *olah*-offering of the preceding verse, we may conclude that despite its double measure of flour, this meal-offering is the one that accompanies this *olah*-offering (*Gur Aryeh*).

3. *Toras Kohanim, parshasa* 10:7; *Menachos* 89b. The standard meal-offering to accompany a sheep is one tenth-*ephah*. See *Numbers* 15:4-5.

4. Rashi uses the plural "poured-offerings" because he is referring not only to the wine-offering that accompanies the meal-offering. He refers also to the oil with which the meal is mixed. Although the quantity of meal in this offering is twice the standard tenth of an *ephah*, the quantity of oil remains the standard quarter of a *hin* (*Nachalas Yaakov* based on *Menachos* 89b).

5. *Toras Kohanim, parshasa* 10:8; *Menachos* 89b.

6. See Rashi to 2:14 above, s.v., קָלוּי בָּאֵשׁ.

7. It is not clear what Rashi means by this Old French word which can mean either "small kernels" (related to "granules") or "all sorts of grains." Some editions read גרינו"ש, "*graines*," which means "grains." However, none of these fit Rashi's description of כַּרְמֶל in 2:14.

8. For further discussion of the word כַּרְמֶל, see Rashi to 2:14 above.

in all your settled places. ¹⁵ *You shall count for yourselves — from the morrow of the rest day, from the day when you bring the omer of the waving — seven weeks, they shall be complete.* ¹⁶ *Until the morrow of the seventh week you shall count,*

בְּכֹל מֹשְׁבֹתֵיכֶם: וּסְפַרְתֶּם טו לָכֶם מִמָּחֳרַת הַשַּׁבָּת מִיּוֹם הֲבִיאֲכֶם אֶת־עֹמֶר הַתְּנוּפָה שֶׁבַע שַׁבָּתוֹת תְּמִימֹת תִּהְיֶינָה: עַד טז מִמָּחֳרַת הַשַּׁבָּת הַשְּׁבִיעִת תִּסְפְּרוּ

─── אונקלוס ───

בְּכָל מוֹתְבָנֵיכוֹן: טו וְתִמְנוּן לְכוֹן מִבָּתַר יוֹמָא טָבָא מִיּוֹם אַיְתוֹאֵיכוֹן יָת עוּמְרָא דַאֲרָמוּתָא שְׁבַע שָׁבוּעִין שַׁלְמִין יְהֶוְיָן: טז עַד מִבָּתַר שָׁבוּעֲתָא שְׁבִיעֲתָא תִמְנוּן

─── רש"י ───

בכל משבתיכם. נחלקו בו חכמי ישראל, יש שלמדו מכאן שהחדש נוהג בחוצה לארץ, ויש אומרים לא בא אלא ללמד שלא נצטוו על החדש אלא לאחר ירושה וישיבה משכבשו וחלקו (קידושין ל,ז.): (טו) **ממחרת השבת.** ממחרת יום טוב (ת"כ פרק יב:א):

תמימות תהיינה. מלמד שמתחיל ומונה מבערב שאם לא כן אין תמימות (שם ו; מנחות סו.): (טז) **השבת השביעית.** כתרגומו שבועתא שביעתא: עד ממחרת השבת השביעית **תספרו.** ולא עד בכלל, והן ארבעים ותשעה יום:

─── RASHI ELUCIDATED ───

□ בְּכֹל מֹשְׁבֹתֵיכֶם — IN ALL YOUR SETTLED PLACES. נֶחְלְקוּ בוֹ חַכְמֵי יִשְׂרָאֵל — The Sages of Israel were in dispute about this. יֵשׁ שֶׁלָּמְדוּ מִכָּאן — There were those who learned from here שֶׁהֶחָדָשׁ נוֹהֵג בְּחוּצָה לָאָרֶץ — that *chadash*[1] applies in the area outside of the Land of Israel.[2] וְיֵשׁ אוֹמְרִים — And there are those who say that שֶׁלֹּא נִצְטַוּוּ עַל — [the verse] came only to teach us לֹא בָא אֶלָּא לְלַמֵּד הֶחָדָשׁ אֶלָּא — that they were only commanded with regard to observing the law of *chadash* לְאַחַר יְרֻשָּׁה — after taking possession of the Land of Israel וִישִׁיבָה — and settling it מִשֶּׁכְּבָשׁוּ — once they conquered it וְחִלְּקוּ — and divided it among the Tribes.[3]

15. מִמָּחֳרַת הַשַּׁבָּת — FROM THE MORROW OF THE REST DAY. מִמָּחֳרַת יוֹם טוֹב[4] — From the morrow of the festival.[4]

□ תְּמִימֹת תִּהְיֶינָה — THEY SHALL BE COMPLETE. מְלַמֵּד — This teaches us שֶׁמַּתְחִיל וּמוֹנֶה מִבָּעֶרֶב — that he begins to count from the evening following the fifteenth of Nissan, שֶׁאִם לֹא כֵן — for if this is not so, [5]אֵינָן תְּמִימוֹת — they are not complete.[5]

16. □ הַשַּׁבָּת הַשְּׁבִיעִית — THE SEVENTH WEEK. This is to be understood כְּתַרְגּוּמוֹ — as *Targum* Onkelos renders it, שָׁבוּעֲתָא שְׁבִיעֲתָא — "the seventh week."[6]

□ עַד מִמָּחֳרַת הַשַּׁבָּת הַשְּׁבִיעִית תִּסְפְּרוּ — UNTIL THE MORROW OF THE SEVENTH WEEK YOU SHALL COUNT. וְלֹא עַד בִּכְלָל — But the limit denoted by "until," i.e., the morrow itself, **is not included** in the counting.[7] וְהֵן אַרְבָּעִים וְתִשְׁעָה יוֹם — They, i.e., the days to be counted, **are forty-nine days.**

---

1. Literally, "new"; the term refers to the produce of the current year, before the *omer* is offered; in contradistinction to the produce of earlier years (and of the current year, after the *omer* is offered) which is called יָשָׁן, literally, "old." The Torah uses these two words to refer to the "old" and "new" crops (see 26:10 below). Rashi here uses *chadash* as an abbreviated form for the prohibition against eating *chadash*.
   It should be noted that in non-Temple times, *chadash* is not permitted until after the sixteenth of Nissan, the day on which the *omer* would have been offered, had the *Beis HaMikdash* been standing.

2. "All your settled places" implies even those which are outside the Land of Israel.

3. *Kiddushin* 37a. According to this opinion, "all your settled places" teaches that settling the entire Land of Israel is a necessary condition for the law of *chadash* to apply. It does not teach us that *chadash* applies to settlements outside the Land of Israel.

4. *Toras Kohanim, perek* 12:1. See Rashi to verse 11 above.

5. *Toras Kohanim, perek* 12:6; *Menachos* 66a. Since the day begins with the evening, the seven weeks would not be "complete" unless the counting begins from its outset, on the evening of the first day of the count, i.e., the evening that ends the fifteenth and begins the sixteenth.

6. In verses 11 and 15, *Targum* Onkelos rendered שַׁבָּת as יוֹמָא טָבָא, "festival"; here, however, he renders it שָׁבוּעֲתָא, "week" (*Mizrachi*).

7. Sometimes, as here, the word עַד, "until," is interpreted as עַד וְלֹא עַד בִּכְלָל, "until [a given point], but not including that point." At other times, it is interpreted as עַד וָעַד בִּכְלָל, "until [a given point], and including that point" (see Rashi to *Deuteronomy* 3:16).
   The context of our verse indicates that עַד should be understood as not including the fiftieth day, for if the fiftieth day were included, the term "seven weeks" of verse 15 would be inexact (*Gur Aryeh; Be'er Mayim Chaim*).

חֲמִשִּׁים יוֹם וְהִקְרַבְתֶּם מִנְחָה חֲדָשָׁה לַיהוה: יז מִמּוֹשְׁבֹתֵיכֶם תָּבִיאוּ ׀ לֶחֶם תְּנוּפָה שְׁתַּיִם שְׁנֵי עֶשְׂרֹנִים סֹלֶת תִּהְיֶינָה חָמֵץ תֵּאָפֶינָה בִּכּוּרִים לַיהוה:

fifty days; and you shall offer a new meal-offering to H<small>ASHEM</small>. *17 From your settled places you shall bring bread of elevation, two loaves made of two tenth-ephahs, they shall be fine flour, they shall be baked leavened; first fruits to* H<small>ASHEM</small>.

― אונקלוס ―

חַמְשִׁין יוֹמִין וּתְקָרְבוּן מִנְחָתָא חֲדָתָּא קֳדָם יְיָ: יז מִמּוֹתְבָנֵיכוֹן תַּיְתוּן לְחֵם אֲרָמוּתָא תַּרְתֵּין (גְרִיצָן) תְּרֵין עֶשְׂרוֹנִין סֻלְתָּא יְהֶוְיָן חֲמִיעַ יִתְאַפְיָן בִּכּוּרִין קֳדָם יְיָ:

― רש"י ―

(יז) חמשים יום והקרבתם מנחה חדשה לה'. בַּיּוֹם הַחֲמִשִּׁים תַּקְרִיבוּהוּ. וְאוֹמֵר אֲנִי זֶהוּ מִדְרָשׁוֹ, אֲבָל פְּשׁוּטוֹ עַד מִמָּחֳרַת הַשַּׁבָּת הַשְּׁבִיעִית שֶׁהוּא יוֹם חֲמִשִּׁים תִּסְפְּרוּ, וּמִקְרָא מְסֹרָס הוּא: **מנחה חדשה.** הִיא הַמִּנְחָה הָרִאשׁוֹנָה שֶׁהוּבְאָה מִן הֶחָדָשׁ. וְאִם תֹּאמַר הֲרֵי קָרְבָה מִנְחַת הָעוֹמֶר, **ממושבותיכם.** וְלֹא מְחוּצָה לָאָרֶץ (ת"כ פרק יג:א): **לחם תנופה.** לֶחֶם תְּרוּמָה הַמּוּרָם לְשֵׁם גָּבוֹהַּ, וְזוֹ הִיא הַמִּנְחָה הַחֲדָשָׁה הָאֲמוּרָה לְמַעְלָה: **בכורים.** רִאשׁוֹנָה לְכָל הַמְּנָחוֹת, אַף לְמִנְחַת קְנָאוֹת הַבָּאָה מִן הַשְּׂעוֹרִים, לֹא תִקְרַב מִן הֶחָדָשׁ

― RASHI ELUCIDATED ―

□ חֲמִשִּׁים יוֹם וְהִקְרַבְתֶּם מִנְחָה חֲדָשָׁה לַה' ― **FIFTY DAYS; AND YOU SHALL OFFER A NEW MEAL-OFFERING TO** H<small>ASHEM</small>. בַּיּוֹם הַחֲמִשִּׁים ― **On the fiftieth day** תַּקְרִיבוּהוּ ― **you shall offer it.**[1] וְאוֹמֵר אֲנִי ― **I say that** זֶהוּ מִדְרָשׁוֹ ― **this is its midrashic interpretation,** אֲבָל פְּשׁוּטוֹ ― **but its simple meaning is,** עַד מִמָּחֳרַת הַשַּׁבָּת הַשְּׁבִיעִית ― **until the morrow of the seventh week,** שֶׁהוּא יוֹם חֲמִשִּׁים ― **which is the fiftieth day,** תִּסְפְּרוּ ― **you shall count,** וּמִקְרָא מְסֹרָס הוּא ― **and it is an inverted verse.**[2] □ מִנְחָה חֲדָשָׁה ― **A NEW MEAL-OFFERING.** הִיא הַמִּנְחָה הָרִאשׁוֹנָה ― **It is the first meal-offering** שֶׁהוּבְאָה מִן הֶחָדָשׁ ― **which is brought from the new** crop. וְאִם תֹּאמַר ― **And if you will say** by way of objection, הֲרֵי קָרְבָה מִנְחַת הָעוֹמֶר ― **see, now, that the meal-offering of the** *omer* **has** already **been offered** from the new crop. How then can this meal-offering be termed "new," which implies the first? אֵינָה כְּשְׁאָר ― We can answer, **[the** *omer***] is not like all the other meal-offerings** שֶׁהִיא בָּאָה מִן הַשְּׂעוֹרִים ― **for it comes from barley.**[3]

□ **17.** מִמּוֹשְׁבֹתֵיכֶם ― **FROM YOUR SETTLED PLACES.** וְלֹא מְחוּצָה לָאָרֶץ[4] ― **But not from outside the Land** of Israel.[4]

□ לֶחֶם תְּנוּפָה ― **BREAD OF ELEVATION.** לֶחֶם תְּרוּמָה ― **Bread of raising,** הַמּוּרָם לְשֵׁם גָּבוֹהַּ ― **which is raised up** out of the rest of the crop **for the sake of** He Who is on **High.**[5] וְזוֹ הִיא הַמִּנְחָה הַחֲדָשָׁה ― **This is the "new meal-offering"** הָאֲמוּרָה לְמַעְלָה ― **which is mentioned above,** in the preceding verse.

□ בִּכּוּרִים ― **FIRST FRUITS.** רִאשׁוֹנָה לְכָל הַמְּנָחוֹת ― **First of all the meal-offerings,** אַף לְמִנְחַת קְנָאוֹת ― even prior to **"the meal-offering of jealousies,"**[6] הַבָּאָה מִן הַשְּׂעוֹרִים ― **which comes from barley,** i.e., it must even precede any "meal-offering of jealousies" which comes from the new crop, even though that offering is from barley meal. לֹא תִקְרַב מִן הֶחָדָשׁ ― **[A "meal-offering of jealousies"] may not be**

---

1. The verse appears to command us to count fifty days. But this cannot be so, for the verse has told us to count *until* the morrow of the seventh week, but not the morrow itself ― a total of only forty-nine days. Therefore, חֲמִשִּׁים יוֹם, "fifty days," is understood as if it were written יוֹם הַחֲמִשִּׁים, "[on] the fiftieth day," and is connected to the clause that follows it, "on the fiftieth day you shall offer a new meal-offering" (*Mizrachi; Sifsei Chachamim*).

2. According to the simple meaning, it is as if the verse were written: תִּסְפְּרוּ חֲמִשִּׁים יוֹם . . . , "Until [but not including (see previous Rashi)] the morrow of the seventh week, [i.e.,] the fiftieth day, you shall count." Understood this way, the verse does not say that you shall count for fifty days.

3. *Menachos* 84b. It is "new" in that it is the first meal-offering of wheat from the new crop (*Minchas Yehudah; Sifsei Chachamim*).

4. *Toras Kohanim, perek* 13:1. In verse 14, Rashi interpreted בְּכָל מֹשְׁבֹתֵיכֶם, "in *all* your settled places," as including settlements outside the Land of Israel. The absence of כָּל here limits the offering to flour from the produce of the Land of Israel.

5. תְּנוּפָה does not refer to waving here, as וְהֵנִיף does in verse 11, for waving is a procedure which takes place after an offering is brought to the *Beis HaMikdash*, while our verse refers to an earlier stage. Here it denotes elevation of status and setting aside (*Mizrachi; Sifsei Chachamim*).

6. The meal-offering brought by a woman suspected of adultery. See *Numbers* 5:15.

23/18-19

יח וְהִקְרַבְתֶּם עַל־הַלֶּחֶם שִׁבְעַת כְּבָשִׂים תְּמִימִם בְּנֵי שָׁנָה וּפַר בֶּן־בָּקָר אֶחָד וְאֵילִם שְׁנַיִם יִהְיוּ עֹלָה לַיהוה וּמִנְחָתָם וְנִסְכֵּיהֶם אִשֵּׁה רֵיחַ־נִיחֹחַ לַיהוה: יט וַעֲשִׂיתֶם שְׂעִיר־עִזִּים אֶחָד לְחַטָּאת וּשְׁנֵי כְבָשִׂים בְּנֵי שָׁנָה לְזֶבַח שְׁלָמִים:

18 *On account of the bread you shall offer seven unblemished lambs in their first year, one bull, a young male of cattle, and two rams; they shall be an olah-offering to* HASHEM, *and their meal-offering and their poured-offerings — a fire-offering, a satisfying aroma to* HASHEM. **19** *You shall offer one he-goat as a sin-offering, and two lambs in their first year as a sacrifice of a peace-offering.*

────── אונקלוס ──────

יח וּתְקָרְבוּן עַל לַחְמָא שַׁבְעָא אִמְּרִין שַׁלְמִין בְּנֵי שְׁנָא וְתוֹר בַּר תּוֹרֵי חַד וְדִכְרִין תְּרֵין יְהוֹן עֲלָתָא קֳדָם יְיָ וּמִנְחָתְהוֹן וְנִסְכֵּיהוֹן קֻרְבַּן דְּמִתְקַבֵּל בְּרַעֲוָא קֳדָם יְיָ:
יט וְתַעְבְּדוּן צְפִיר בַּר עִזֵּי חַד לְחַטָּאתָא וּתְרֵין אִמְּרִין בְּנֵי שְׁנָא לְנִכְסַת קוּדְשַׁיָּא:

────── רש"י ──────

קֹדֶם לִשְׁתֵּי הַלֶּחֶם: (יח) **עַל הַלֶּחֶם**. בִּגְלַל הַלֶּחֶם (מְנָחוֹת מה:), חוֹבָה לַלֶּחֶם (ת"כ שם ד): **וּמִנְחָתָם וְנִסְכֵּיהֶם**. כְּמִשְׁפָּט מִנְחָה וּנְסָכִים הַמְפֹרָשִׁים בְּכָל בְּהֵמָה בְּפָרָשַׁת נְסָכִים (במדבר טו/טז): שְׁלֹשָׁה עֶשְׂרוֹנִים לַפָּר וּשְׁנֵי עֶשְׂרוֹנִים לָאַיִל וְעִשָּׂרוֹן לַכֶּבֶשׂ, זוֹ הִיא הַמִּנְחָה. וְהַנְּסָכִים חֲצִי הַהִין לַפָּר וּשְׁלִישִׁית הַהִין לָאַיִל וּרְבִיעִית הַהִין לַכֶּבֶשׂ: (יט) **וַעֲשִׂיתֶם שְׂעִיר עִזִּים**. יָכוֹל

────── RASHI ELUCIDATED ──────

offered from the new crop — קוֹדֶם לִשְׁתֵּי הַלָּחֶם — **before the Two Breads,** the meal-offering of our verse.[1]

18. עַל הַלֶּחֶם — ON ACCOUNT OF THE BREAD. בִּגְלַל הַלֶּחֶם[2] — **Because of the bread;**[2] חוֹבָה לַלֶּחֶם[3] — **an obligation for the bread.**[3]

וּמִנְחָתָם וְנִסְכֵּיהֶם — AND THEIR MEAL-OFFERING AND THEIR POURED-OFFERINGS. כְּמִשְׁפַּט מִנְחָה וּנְסָכִים — **In accordance with the standard rule of a meal-offering and poured-offerings** הַמְפֹרָשִׁים בְּכָל בְּהֵמָה — **which are stated explicitly with regard to each** kind of animal[4] בְּפָרָשַׁת נְסָכִים — **in the section of the Torah which deals with drink-offerings:**[4] שְׁלֹשָׁה עֶשְׂרוֹנִים לַפָּר — **three tenth-*ephahs* for a bull,** וּשְׁנֵי עֶשְׂרוֹנִים לָאַיִל — **and two tenth-*ephahs* for a ram,** וְעִשָּׂרוֹן לַכֶּבֶשׂ — **and a tenth-*ephah* for a sheep.** זוֹ הִיא הַמִּנְחָה — **This is the meal-offering.** וְהַנְּסָכִים — **And the poured-offerings** are חֲצִי הַהִין לַפָּר — **half a *hin* of wine for a bull,** וּשְׁלִישִׁית הַהִין לָאַיִל — **and a third of a *hin* for a ram,** וּרְבִיעִית הַהִין לַכֶּבֶשׂ — **and a quarter *hin* for a sheep.**

19. וַעֲשִׂיתֶם שְׂעִיר עִזִּים — YOU SHALL OFFER [ONE] HE-GOAT. יָכוֹל — **One might be able** to think that

---

1. Although the meal-offering of the *omer* is the first meal-offering of the new crop, the meal-offering of our verse is "first fruits" in that it is the first meal-offering of wheat brought from the new crop. But this cannot be all the verse means to teach us, for this can be inferred from the fact that the preceding verse calls it "a new meal-offering." Our verse calls it "first fruits" to teach us that it must even precede any "meal offering of jealousies" brought from the new crop, even though, like the *omer*, that meal-offering is of barley (*Mizrachi*).

2. *Menachos* 45b. It is clear from the context that עַל here is not used in the sense of its most common meaning, "on" (*Mizrachi*; *Sifsei Chachamim*). For another example of עַל meaning "because of," see *Targum Yonasan* and *Ibn Ezra* to Exodus 17:7.

3. *Toras Kohanim, perek* 13:4. According to *Mizrachi* and *Sifsei Chachamim*, it is an obligation to bring the animal offering of our verse only when the meal-offering is brought. The animal offerings are not brought on the festival of Shavuos if for some reason the meal-offering is not. *Nachalas Yaakov*, however, on the basis of *Menachos* 45b, says that the animal offerings are brought even if the meal-offering is not. By "an obligation for the bread," Rashi means that it is the obligation to bring the meal-offering which dictates that the animal offerings be brought, not the sanctity of the festival. *Be'er BaSadeh*, in defense of *Mizrachi*, asserts that *Mizrachi* refers to the historical period during which there was no obligation to bring the meal-offering, i.e., while the Israelites were in the desert before they conquered the Land of Israel, they had no obligation to bring the animal offerings of our verse, but once the obligation to bring the meal-offering came into effect, they had to bring the animal offerings regardless of whether they brought the meal-offering. See also note 1 to verse 12 above.

4. *Numbers* 15:1-16. Rashi refers to this passage as פָּרָשַׁת נְסָכִים in his comments to *Kiddushin* 37a, s.v., ללמדך שב"מ כו'. *Numbers* 28:12-14, which also delineate the meal-offerings and poured-offering that accompany each type of animal, is not called פָּרָשַׁת נְסָכִים rather it is called פָּרָשַׁת מוּסָפִים.

20 The Kohen shall wave them upon the first fruits breads as a waving before HASHEM — upon two sheep — they shall be holy, for HASHEM and for the Kohen. **21** You shall convoke on this very day — there shall be a calling of holiness for yourselves — you shall do no work of labor; it is an eternal decree in your settled places for your generations.

22 When you reap the harvest of your land, you shall not remove completely the corner of your field as you reap

כ וְהֵנִיף הַכֹּהֵן ׀ אֹתָם עַל לֶחֶם הַבִּכֻּרִים תְּנוּפָה לִפְנֵי יְהוָֹה עַל־שְׁנֵי כְּבָשִׂים קֹדֶשׁ יִהְיוּ לַיהוָֹה לַכֹּהֵן: כא וּקְרָאתֶם בְּעֶצֶם ׀ הַיּוֹם הַזֶּה מִקְרָא־קֹדֶשׁ יִהְיֶה לָכֶם כָּל־מְלֶאכֶת עֲבֹדָה לֹא תַעֲשׂוּ חֻקַּת עוֹלָם בְּכָל־מוֹשְׁבֹתֵיכֶם לְדֹרֹתֵיכֶם: כב וּבְקֻצְרְכֶם אֶת־קְצִיר אַרְצְכֶם לֹא־תְכַלֶּה פְּאַת שָׂדְךָ בְּקֻצְרֶךָ

─── אונקלוס ───

כ וִירִים כַּהֲנָא יָתְהוֹן עַל לְחֵם בִּכּוּרַיָּא אֲרָמוּתָא קֳדָם יְיָ עַל תְּרֵין אִמְּרִין קוּדְשָׁא יְהוֹן קֳדָם יְיָ לְכַהֲנָא: כא וּתְעָרְעוּן בִּכְרַן יוֹמָא הָדֵין מְעָרַע קַדִּישׁ יְהֵי לְכוֹן כָּל עִבִידַת פָּלְחָן לָא תַעְבְּדוּן קְיָם עָלָם בְּכָל מוֹתְבָנֵיכוֹן לְדָרֵיכוֹן: כב וּבְמֶחְצַדְכוֹן יָת חֲצָדָא דְאַרְעֲכוֹן לָא תְשֵׁיצֵי פָּאתָא דְחַקְלָךְ בְּמֶחְצְדָךְ

─── רש״י ───

(ב) והניף הכהן אותם תנופה. מלמד שטעונין תנופה מחיים. יכול כולם, ת"ל על שני כבשים (ת"כ שם ח; מנחות סב.-סב:): **קדש יהיו.** לפי שלמי יחיד קדשים קלים הוזקק לומר בשלמי צבור שהם קדשי קדשים: **(כב) ובקצרכם.** חזר ושנה

שבעת הכבשים והשעיר האמורים כאן הם שבעת הכבשים והשעיר האמורים בחומש הפקודים (שם כח:כו,כז), כשאתה מגיע אצל פרים ואילים אינן הם. אמור מעתה, אלו לעצמן ואלו לעצמן. אלו קרבו בגלל הלחם, ואלו למוספין (ת"כ שם ו; מנחות מה:):

─── RASHI ELUCIDATED ───

הֵם — **the seven sheep and the he-goat which are stated here** שִׁבְעַת הַכְּבָשִׂים וְהַשָּׂעִיר הָאֲמוּרִים כָּאן — **are the seven sheep and the he-goat stated in** *the Book of Numbers*.[1] שִׁבְעַת הַכְּבָשִׂים וְהַשָּׂעִיר הָאֲמוּרִים בְּחוּמַשׁ הַפְּקוּדִים — But **when you reach** the passage of **bulls and rams** you see that אֵינָן הֵם — **they are not the same.**[2] אָמוּר מֵעַתָּה — **Now you should say,** i.e., therefore you should conclude, אֵלּוּ לְעַצְמָן וְאֵלוּ לְעַצְמָן — **these are by themselves and these are by themselves,** i.e., our passage and the passage in *Numbers* speak of different sets of offerings. אֵלוּ קָרְבוּ בִגְלַל הַלֶּחֶם — [The ones mentioned here] were offered because of the bread, i.e., the meal-offering,[3] וְאֵלוּ לְמוּסָפִין — and [the ones mentioned in *Numbers*] were for the *mussaf* offerings.[3]

20. וְהֵנִיף הַכֹּהֵן אֹתָם תְּנוּפָה — THE KOHEN SHALL WAVE THEM ... AS A WAVING. מְלַמֵּד — This teaches us שֶׁטְּעוּנִין תְּנוּפָה — that they require waving מֵחַיִּים — while still alive.[4] יָכוֹל כֻּלָּם — One might be able to think that waving while alive applies to **all of them,** including the seven mentioned in verse 18. תַּלְמוּד לוֹמַר — To teach us otherwise, **the verse says,** [5] עַל שְׁנֵי כְּבָשִׂים — **"upon two sheep,"** which limits the waving to the two sheep of the peace-offering.[5]

קֹדֶשׁ יִהְיוּ — THEY SHALL BE HOLY. לְפִי שֶׁשַּׁלְמֵי יָחִיד — Since peace-offerings of individuals קֳדָשִׁים קַלִּים — are holy of the lesser degree, הֻזְקַק לוֹמַר — [the Torah] had to say בְּשַׁלְמֵי צִבּוּר — about peace-offerings of the public שֶׁהֵם קָדְשֵׁי קָדָשִׁים — that they are holy of the higher degree.[6]

22. וּבְקֻצְרְכֶם — WHEN YOU REAP. חָזַר וְשָׁנָה — [The Torah] returned to and repeated the command-

---

1. See *Numbers* 28:27,30. Among the animals listed there for the *mussaf* offering of Shavuos are seven sheep and a he-goat. We might have thought that the sheep and goat mentioned here in verses 18-19 are the sheep and goat of the *mussaf* offering.

2. Our verses speak of one bull and two rams, while the *mussaf* offering mentioned there (*Numbers* 28:27) includes two bulls and one ram.

3. *Toras Kohanim, parshasa* 13:6; *Menachos* 45b.

4. Verse 7:30 above has already taught us that parts of the peace-offering must be waved. Our verse repeats the commandment of waving to teach us that these sheep require a different sort of waving — waving while they are still alive (*Gur Aryeh*).

5. *Toras Kohanim, perek* 13:8; see *Menachos* 62a-b.

6. It stands to reason that the peace-offerings of our verse which are brought by the public are no less holy than those of individuals. If the verse nonetheless states, "they shall be holy," it is to teach us that their holiness is of a higher degree (*Mizrachi; Sifsei Chachamim*).

299 / VAYIKRA/LEVITICUS — PARASHAS EMOR — 23/23-24

וְלֶ֣קֶט קְצִֽירְךָ֙ לֹ֣א תְלַקֵּ֔ט לֶעָנִ֥י
וְלַגֵּ֖ר תַּעֲזֹ֣ב אֹתָ֑ם אֲנִ֖י יְהוָ֥ה
אֱלֹהֵיכֶֽם׃
^{חמישי} ^{כג} וַיְדַבֵּ֥ר יְהוָ֖ה אֶל־מֹשֶׁ֥ה לֵּאמֹֽר׃
^{כד} דַּבֵּ֛ר אֶל־בְּנֵ֥י יִשְׂרָאֵ֖ל לֵאמֹ֑ר
בַּחֹ֨דֶשׁ הַשְּׁבִיעִ֜י בְּאֶחָ֣ד לַחֹ֗דֶשׁ
יִהְיֶ֤ה לָכֶם֙ שַׁבָּת֔וֹן זִכְר֥וֹן תְּרוּעָ֖ה

and you shall not gather the gleanings of your harvest; for the poor and the proselyte shall you leave them; I am HASHEM, *your God.*

²³ HASHEM *spoke to Moses, saying:* ²⁴ *Speak to the Children of Israel, saying: In the seventh month, on the first of the month, there shall be a rest day for you, a mention of shofar blasts,*

--- ONKELOS ---

וּלְקָטָא דַחֲצָדָךְ לָא תְלַקֵּט לְעַנְיָא וּלְגִיּוֹרֵי תִשְׁבּוֹק יָתְהוֹן אֲנָא יְיָ אֱלָהֲכוֹן: ^{כג} וּמַלִּיל יְיָ עִם מֹשֶׁה לְמֵימָר: ^{כד} מַלֵּל עִם בְּנֵי יִשְׂרָאֵל לְמֵימָר בְּיַרְחָא שְׁבִיעָאָה בְּחַד לְיַרְחָא יְהֵי לְכוֹן נְיָחָא דּוּכְרָן יַבָּבָא

--- RASHI ---

לַעֲבוֹר עֲלֵיהֶם בִּשְׁנֵי לָאוִין. אָמַר אֲוַרְדִּימָס בְּרַבִּי יוֹסֵי [ס"א רבי אבדימי ברבי יוסף] מָה רָאָה הַכָּתוּב לִיתְּנָם בְּאֶמְצַע הָרְגָלִים, פֶּסַח וַעֲצֶרֶת מִכָּאן וְרֹאשׁ הַשָּׁנָה וְיוֹם הַכִּפּוּרִים וְחַג מִכָּאן, לְלַמֶּדְךָ שֶׁכָּל הַנּוֹתֵן לֶקֶט שִׁכְחָה וּפֵאָה לֶעָנִי כָּרָאוּי מַעֲלִין עָלָיו כְּאִלּוּ בָּנָה בֵּית הַמִּקְדָּשׁ וְהִקְרִיב קָרְבְּנוֹתָיו בְּתוֹכוֹ (ת"כ פרק יג:יב): תַּעֲזֹב. הַנַּח לִפְנֵיהֶם וְהֵם יְלַקְּטוּ (פאה ד:א) וְאֵין לְךָ לְסַיֵּעַ לְאֶחָד מֵהֶם (ת"כ קדושים פרק ג:ה; פאה ה:א): אֲנִי ה' אֱלֹהֵיכֶם. נֶאֱמָן לְשַׁלֵּם שָׂכָר: (כד) זִכְרוֹן תְּרוּעָה. זִכְרוֹן פְּסוּקֵי זִכְרוֹנוֹת

--- RASHI ELUCIDATED ---

ment to leave aside a corner of the field when reaping,[1] **לַעֲבוֹר עֲלֵיהֶם בִּשְׁנֵי לָאוִין — to transgress two negative commandments over them,** i.e., so that one who transgresses it will be guilty of violating two negative commandments.

מָה רָאָה הַכָּתוּב לִתְּנָם — אָמַר אֲוַרְדִּימָס בְּרַבִּי יוֹסֵי — The *Tanna* **Avardimas**[2] **the son of R' Yose said: What did Scripture see to put,** i.e., why did Scripture place, **[these commandments] בְּאֶמְצַע הָרְגָלִים — among the festivals, פֶּסַח וַעֲצֶרֶת מִכָּאן — with Pesach and Shavuos placed on one side of the** commandment, i.e., immediately before it, **וְרֹאשׁ הַשָּׁנָה וְיוֹם הַכִּפּוּרִים וְחַג מִכָּאן — and Rosh Hashanah, Yom Kippur, and Succos on the other side** of it, i.e., immediately after it? **לְלַמֶּדְךָ — To teach you שֶׁכָּל הַנּוֹתֵן לֶקֶט שִׁכְחָה וּפֵאָה לֶעָנִי — that whoever gives gleanings, "forgetting,"**[3] **and the corner** of the harvested field **to a poor person כָּרָאוּי — properly, מַעֲלִין עָלָיו — is considered כְּאִלּוּ בָּנָה בֵּית הַמִּקְדָּשׁ — as if he built the** *Beis HaMikdash*[4] **וְהִקְרִיב קָרְבְּנוֹתָיו בְּתוֹכוֹ — and brought his offerings inside it.**[4]

□ **תַּעֲזֹב — SHALL YOU LEAVE. הַנַּח לִפְנֵיהֶם — Leave it before them, וְהֵם יְלַקְּטוּ**[5] **— and** *they* **shall gather it,**[5] **וְאֵין לְךָ לְסַיֵּעַ לְאֶחָד מֵהֶם — and you may not assist** any **one of them in gathering.**[6]

□ **אֲנִי ה' אֱלֹהֵיכֶם — I AM HASHEM, YOUR GOD. נֶאֱמָן לְשַׁלֵּם שָׂכָר — Trustworthy to pay reward.**[7]

24. זִכְרוֹן תְּרוּעָה — A MENTION OF SHOFAR BLASTS. זִכְרוֹן פְּסוּקֵי זִכְרוֹנוֹת — A mentioning of verses of remembrances, i.e., verses which refer to God's remembrance of His mercy toward Creation

---

1. See 19:9 above.
2. Most editions of Rashi read רַבִּי אַבְדִּימִי בְּרַבִּי יוֹסֵף, "R' Avidimi the son of R' Yosef"; however, *Seder HaDoros*, which gives an exhaustive listing of all the *Tannaim* and *Amoraim*, does not mention anyone named רַבִּי אַבְדִּימִי בְּרַבִּי יוֹסֵי. Our reading, אֲוַרְדִּימָס בְּרַבִּי יוֹסֵי, "Avardimas the son of R' Yose," appears in *Toras Kohanim*, Rashi's source for this quote. The Rome edition of Rashi reads אַבְרְדִּימָס; other ancient editions have variant spellings of this name. *Yosef Hallel* suggests that this *Tanna* is really R' Menachem the son of R' Yose who (according to *Shabbos* 118b) was nicknamed וַרְדִּימָס, literally, "roselike," for his countenance was like a rose.
3. See *Deuteronomy* 24:19. שִׁכְחָה is included here even though it is not mentioned in our verse, because, like לֶקֶט and פֵאָה, it is a gift to the poor from the produce of the field.
4. *Toras Kohanim*, *perek* 13:12.
5. *Pe'ah* 4:1. The owner of the field may not apportion the gifts to the poor, even if his absence will result in the aggressive getting more, and the meek getting less.
6. *Toras Kohanim*, *Kedoshim*, *perek* 3:5; *Pe'ah* 5:6. It is necessary for Rashi to stress this point because elsewhere, e.g., *Exodus* 23:5, עזב means "to assist" (*Devek Tov*).
7. The identical phrase appeared above 19:10 with reference to these commandments, yet there Rashi explained it as implying that God can be counted on to mete out punishment to those who fail to keep them. For, according to Rashi, our verse stresses how praiseworthy fulfillment of these commandments is. As he mentioned in his earlier comment on this verse, "It is considered as if he built the *Beis HaMikdash* and brought offerings inside it." It thus stands to reason that "I am HASHEM, your

כה מִקְרָא־קֹדֶשׁ כָּל־מְלֶאכֶת עֲבֹדָה
לֹא תַעֲשׂוּ וְהִקְרַבְתֶּם אִשֶּׁה
לַיהוָה: כו וַיְדַבֵּר יהוה אֶל־
מֹשֶׁה לֵּאמֹר: כז אַךְ בֶּעָשׂוֹר לַחֹדֶשׁ
הַשְּׁבִיעִי הַזֶּה יוֹם הַכִּפֻּרִים הוּא
מִקְרָא־קֹדֶשׁ יִהְיֶה לָכֶם וְעִנִּיתֶם אֶת־
נַפְשֹׁתֵיכֶם וְהִקְרַבְתֶּם אִשֶּׁה לַיהוָה:
כח וְכָל־מְלָאכָה לֹא תַעֲשׂוּ בְּעֶצֶם
הַיּוֹם הַזֶּה כִּי יוֹם כִּפֻּרִים הוּא לְכַפֵּר
עֲלֵיכֶם לִפְנֵי יהוה אֱלֹהֵיכֶם: כט כִּי כָל־
הַנֶּפֶשׁ אֲשֶׁר לֹא־תְעֻנֶּה בְּעֶצֶם הַיּוֹם
הַזֶּה וְנִכְרְתָה מֵעַמֶּיהָ: ל וְכָל־הַנֶּפֶשׁ
אֲשֶׁר תַּעֲשֶׂה כָּל־מְלָאכָה בְּעֶצֶם
הַיּוֹם הַזֶּה וְהַאֲבַדְתִּי אֶת־הַנֶּפֶשׁ

a calling of holiness. **25** *You shall not do any work of labor, and you shall offer a fire-offering to* HASHEM.

26 HASHEM *spoke to Moses, saying:* **27** *But on the tenth day of this month it is the Day of Atonement; there shall be a calling of holiness for you, and you shall afflict yourselves; you shall offer a fire-offering to* HASHEM. **28** *You shall not do any work on this very day, for it is the Day of Atonement to provide you atonement before* HASHEM, *your God.* **29** *For any soul who will not be afflicted on this very day will be cut off from its people.* **30** *And any soul who will do any work on this very day, I will destroy that soul*

אונקלוס

מְעָרַע קַדִּישׁ: כה כָּל עֲבִידַת פָּלְחָנָא לָא תַעְבְּדוּן וּתְקָרְבוּן קָרְבָּנָא קֳדָם יְיָ: כו וּמַלִּיל יְיָ עִם מֹשֶׁה לְמֵימָר: כז בְּרַם בְּעַשְׂרָא לְיַרְחָא שְׁבִיעָאָה הָדֵין יוֹמָא דְכִפּוּרַיָּא הוּא מְעָרַע קַדִּישׁ יְהֵי לְכוֹן וּתְעַנּוּן יָת נַפְשָׁתֵיכוֹן וּתְקָרְבוּן קָרְבָּנָא קֳדָם יְיָ: כח וְכָל עֲבִידָא לָא תַעְבְּדוּן בִּכְרַן יוֹמָא הָדֵין אֲרֵי יוֹמָא דְכִפּוּרַיָּא הוּא לְכַפָּרָא עֲלֵיכוֹן קֳדָם יְיָ אֱלָהֲכוֹן: כט אֲרֵי כָל אֱנָשָׁא דִי לָא יִתְעַנֵּי בִּכְרַן יוֹמָא הָדֵין וְיִשְׁתֵּיצֵי מֵעַמֵּהּ: ל וְכָל אֱנָשָׁא דִי יַעְבֵּד כָּל עֲבִידָא בִּכְרַן יוֹמָא הָדֵין וְאוֹבֵד יָת אֱנָשָׁא

רש"י

וּפְסוּקֵי שׁוֹפְרוֹת (ר"ה לב.) לִזְכּוֹר לָכֶם עֲקֵדַת יִצְחָק שֶׁקָּרַב תַּחְתָּיו אַיִל (שם טז.): **(כה) וְהִקְרַבְתֶּם אִשֶּׁה.** הַמּוּסָפִים הָאֲמוּרִים בְּחֻמַּשׁ הַפְּקוּדִים (במדבר כט:א-ו): **(כז) אַךְ.** כָּל אַכִין וְרַקִּין שֶׁבַּתּוֹרָה מִעוּטִין הֵן לְשָׁבִים וְאֵינוֹ מְכַפֵּר עַל שֶׁאֵינָם שָׁבִים (שבועות יג.): **(ל) וְהַאֲבַדְתִּי.** לְפִי שֶׁהוּא אוֹמֵר כָּרֵת בְּכָל מָקוֹם

RASHI ELUCIDATED

לִזְכּוֹר — **and verses of shofars,**[1] i.e., verses which refer to the shofar, the ram's horn,[1] שֶׁקָּרֵב תַּחְתָּיו אַיִל — **in** לָכֶם — **to remember on your behalf** עֲקֵדַת יִצְחָק — **the binding of Isaac**[2] **whose stead a ram was offered.**[2]

25. וְהִקְרַבְתֶּם אִשֶּׁה — AND YOU SHALL OFFER A FIRE-OFFERING. הַמּוּסָפִים — The *musaf*-offerings הָאֲמוּרִים בְּחֻמַּשׁ הַפְּקוּדִים — **which are stated in the** *Book of Numbers*.[3]

27. אַךְ — BUT. כָּל אַכִין וְרַקִּין שֶׁבַּתּוֹרָה — All instances of the words אַךְ, "but," and רַק, "only," in the Torah, מִעוּטִין הֵן — are words which imply exclusion.[4] Here the exclusion is the following: מְכַפֵּר — הוּא לְשָׁבִים — It atones for those who repent, וְאֵינוֹ מְכַפֵּר — but it does not atone[5] עַל שֶׁאֵינָם שָׁבִים — for those who do not repent.[5]

30. וְהַאֲבַדְתִּי — I WILL DESTROY. לְפִי שֶׁהוּא אוֹמֵר כָּרֵת בְּכָל מָקוֹם — Since [the Torah] mentions *kares*,

---

God" of our verse teaches us something about reward. To avoid redundancy, Rashi concludes that the identical phrase in the earlier verse teaches us about punishment.

1. *Rosh Hashanah* 32a. *Numbers* 29:1 refers to Rosh Hashanah as יוֹם תְּרוּעָה, "a day of shofar blasts." That verse refers to it as "a mention of shofar blasts" to teach us that on Rosh Hashanah, we not only blow the shofar, but, in our prayers we also recite verses that refer to shofar blowing. In addition, זִכְרוֹן is interpreted here as both "mention" and "remembrance"; then, we also recite verses of "remembrance" (*Mizrachi*; *Sifsei* *Chachamim*; *Be'er Yitzchak*). The obligation to recite these verses is of rabbinic origin. Our verse is an *asmachta*, a verse containing an allusion to a rabbinic law (*Sefer Zikaron*). Verses of מַלְכֻיּוֹת, "sovereignties," i.e., verses that proclaim God's sovereignty over the universe, are also recited in the Rosh Hashanah liturgy. These are alluded to in *Numbers* 10:10 (see Rashi there).

2. *Rosh Hashanah* 16a.

3. *Numbers* 29:1-6.

4. *Yerushalmi Berachos* 9:7.

5. *Shevuos* 13a.

301 / VAYIKRA/LEVITICUS — PARASHAS EMOR

from among its people. ³¹ *You shall not do any work; it is an eternal decree throughout your generations in all your settled places.* ³² *It is a day of complete rest for you and you shall afflict yourselves; on the ninth of the month in the evening — from evening to evening — shall you rest on your rest day.*

³³ HASHEM *spoke to Moses, saying:* ³⁴ *Speak to the Children of Israel, saying: On the fifteenth day of this seventh month is the Festival of Succos, a seven-day period for* HASHEM. ³⁵ *On the first day is a calling of holiness,*

לא הַהִוא מִקֶּרֶב עַמָּהּ: כָּל־מְלָאכָה
לֹא תַעֲשׂוּ חֻקַּת עוֹלָם לְדֹרֹתֵיכֶם
לב בְּכֹל מֹשְׁבֹתֵיכֶם: שַׁבַּת שַׁבָּתוֹן
הוּא לָכֶם וְעִנִּיתֶם אֶת־נַפְשֹׁתֵיכֶם
בְּתִשְׁעָה לַחֹדֶשׁ בָּעֶרֶב מֵעֶרֶב עַד־
עֶרֶב תִּשְׁבְּתוּ שַׁבַּתְּכֶם:
לג ששי וַיְדַבֵּר יהוה אֶל־מֹשֶׁה לֵּאמֹר:
לד דַּבֵּר אֶל־בְּנֵי יִשְׂרָאֵל לֵאמֹר
בַּחֲמִשָּׁה עָשָׂר יוֹם לַחֹדֶשׁ הַשְּׁבִיעִי
הַזֶּה חַג הַסֻּכּוֹת שִׁבְעַת יָמִים
לה לַיהוה: בַּיּוֹם הָרִאשׁוֹן מִקְרָא־קֹדֶשׁ

—————— אונקלוס ——————

הַהוּא מִגּוֹ עַמֵּהּ: לא כָּל עֲבִידָא לָא תַעְבְּדוּן קְיָם עָלַם לְדָרֵיכוֹן בְּכֹל מוֹתְבָנֵיכוֹן: לב שַׁבַּת שַׁבָּתָא הוּא לְכוֹן וּתְעַנּוּן יָת נַפְשָׁתֵיכוֹן בְּתִשְׁעָה לְיַרְחָא בְּרַמְשָׁא מֵרַמְשָׁא עַד רַמְשָׁא תְּנוּחוּן נְיָחֵיכוֹן: לג וּמַלִּיל יְיָ עִם מֹשֶׁה לְמֵימָר: לד מַלֵּל עִם בְּנֵי יִשְׂרָאֵל לְמֵימַר בְּחַמְשָׁא עַשְׂרָא יוֹמָא לְיַרְחָא שְׁבִיעָאָה הָדֵין חַגָּא דִמְטַלַּיָּא שַׁבְעַת יוֹמִין קֳדָם יְיָ: לה בְּיוֹמָא קַדְמָאָה מְעָרַע קַדִּישׁ

—————— רש״י ——————

וְאֵינִי יוֹדֵעַ מַה הוּא, כְּשֶׁהוּא אוֹמֵר וְהַאֲבַדְתִּי לָמַד עַל הַכָּרֵת שֶׁאֵינוֹ אֶלָּא אִבְדָּן (ת״כ פרק יד:ד): (לא) כָּל מְלָאכָה וְגוֹ׳. לַעֲבוֹר עָלָיו בְּלָאוִין הַרְבֵּה אוֹ לְהַזְהִיר עַל מְלֶאכֶת לַיְלָה כִּמְלֶאכֶת יוֹם (יוֹמָא פא.): (לה) מִקְרָא קֹדֶשׁ. קַדְּשֵׁהוּ בִּכְסוּת נְקִיָּה וּבִתְפִלָּה וּבְיוֹם הַכִּפּוּרִים, וּבִשְׁאָר יָמִים טוֹבִים בְּמַאֲכָל וּבְמִשְׁתֶּה וּבִכְסוּת נְקִיָּה וּבִתְפִלָּה (ת״כ פרשתא יב:ד):

—————— RASHI ELUCIDATED ——————

"excision," **in all,** i.e., many, **places,** וְאֵינִי יוֹדֵעַ מַה הוּא — and I do not know what it is, for the Torah does not explain what it is in the other places where *kares* is mentioned, כְּשֶׁהוּא אוֹמֵר — **when it says** here, "וְהַאֲבַדְתִּי" — "**I will destroy,**" לָמַד עַל הַכָּרֵת — **it has taught** us **about *kares*,** שֶׁאֵינוֹ אֶלָּא אָבְדָן — that it is nothing other than destruction.[1]

31. כָּל מְלָאכָה וְגוֹמֵר — [YOU SHALL NOT DO] ANY WORK. The prohibition against doing work on Yom Kippur is repeated many times[2] לַעֲבוֹר עָלָיו בְּלָאוִין הַרְבֵּה — to make one guilty of transgressing many negative commandments on account of it, אוֹ לְהַזְהִיר עַל מְלֶאכֶת לַיְלָה — or to enjoin against work of night ³כִּמְלֶאכֶת יוֹם — just as work of day.[3]

35. ⁴מִקְרָא קֹדֶשׁ — A CALLING OF HOLINESS.[4] קַדְּשֵׁהוּ — Sanctify it בִּכְסוּת נְקִיָּה — with clean clothing, וּבִתְפִלָּה — and with its own prayer[5] בְּיוֹם הַכִּפּוּרִים — on Yom Kippur}.[6] וּבִשְׁאָר יָמִים טוֹבִים — And on other festivals, besides the fast of Yom Kippur, sanctify them בְּמַאֲכָל — with food, וּבְמִשְׁתֶּה — and with drink, וּבִכְסוּת נְקִיָּה — and with clean clothing, ⁷וּבִתְפִלָּה — and with their own prayers.[7]

---

1. *Toras Kohanim, perek* 14:4. For more elaboration on the definition of *kares*, see Rashi to 17:9 and 22:3 above.

2. See verse 28 and 16:29 above, and *Numbers* 29:7.

3. *Yoma* 81a. בְּעֶצֶם הַיּוֹם הַזֶּה, "On this very day," which the preceding verse uses with regard to the prohibition against work on Yom Kippur, refers specifically to the daylight hours in other contexts, e.g., *Genesis* 7:13 and 17:23 (see Rashi to those verses). Our apparently superfluous verse can be understood to extend the prohibition to the night (*Mizrachi; Sifsei Chachamim*).

According to some early editions of Rashi, this comment belongs to verse 28, and its rubric reads וְכָל instead of כָּל (see *Yosef Hallel*).

4. According to some early editions of Rashi, this comment belongs to verse 27 (see *Yosef Hallel*).

5. מִקְרָא קֹדֶשׁ implies that mention of the festival must be made in the *Shemoneh Esrei* (*Amidah*) prayer (see *Rosh Hashanah* 32a; Rashi to *Shevuos* 13a, s.v., לא קרא מִקְרָא קֹדֶשׁ; *Be'er BaSadeh*).

6. According to the editions that place this comment in verse 27, the words "on Yom Kippur" are superfluous, for that verse speaks of Yom Kippur. However, according to the editions that place this comment in verse 35, which speaks of Succos, the words "on Yom Kippur" must be inserted.

7. *Toras Kohanim, parshasa* 12:4.

you shall not do any work of labor. ³⁶ For a seven-day period you shall offer a fire-offering to HASHEM; on the eighth day there shall be a calling of holiness for you and you shall offer a fire-offering to HASHEM, it is a restraining, you shall not do any work of labor.

³⁷ These are the appointed festivals of HASHEM that you shall proclaim as callings of holiness, to offer a fire-offering to HASHEM: an olah-offering and a meal-offering, a sacrifice [of a peace-offering] and poured-offerings each day's requirement on its day. ³⁸ Aside from

כָּל־מְלֶאכֶת עֲבֹדָה לֹא תַעֲשׂוּ: לו שִׁבְעַת יָמִים תַּקְרִיבוּ אִשֶּׁה לַיהוָה בַּיּוֹם הַשְּׁמִינִי מִקְרָא־קֹדֶשׁ יִהְיֶה לָכֶם וְהִקְרַבְתֶּם אִשֶּׁה לַיהוָה עֲצֶרֶת הִוא כָּל־מְלֶאכֶת עֲבֹדָה לֹא תַעֲשׂוּ: אֵלֶּה מוֹעֲדֵי יְהוָה אֲשֶׁר־ תִּקְרְאוּ אֹתָם מִקְרָאֵי קֹדֶשׁ לְהַקְרִיב אִשֶּׁה לַיהוָה עֹלָה וּמִנְחָה זֶבַח וּנְסָכִים דְּבַר־יוֹם בְּיוֹמוֹ: מִלְּבַד לח

אונקלוס

כָּל עֲבִידַת פָּלְחָן לָא תַעְבְּדוּן: לו שִׁבְעָא יוֹמִין תְּקָרְבוּן קָרְבָּנָא קֳדָם יְיָ בְּיוֹמָא תְּמִינָאָה מְעָרַע קַדִּישׁ יְהֵי לְכוֹן וּתְקָרְבוּן קָרְבָּנָא קֳדָם יְיָ כְּנֵשׁ הִיא (נ״א בְּנִישִׁין תְּהוֹן) כָּל עֲבִידַת פָּלְחָן לָא תַעְבְּדוּן: לז אִלֵּין זִמְנַיָּא דַּיְיָ דִּי תְעָרְעוּן יָתְהוֹן מְעָרְעֵי קַדִּישׁ לְקָרָבָא קָרְבָּנָא קֳדָם יְיָ עֲלָתָא וּמִנְחָתָא נִכְסַת קוּדְשִׁין וְנִסּוּכִין פִּתְגָם יוֹם בְּיוֹמֵהּ: לח בַּר מִן

רש"י

(לו) **עצרת הוא.** עֲצַרְתִּי אֶתְכֶם אֶצְלִי. כְּמֶלֶךְ שֶׁזִּמֵּן אֶת בָּנָיו לִסְעוּדָה לְכָךְ וְכָךְ יָמִים, כֵּיוָן שֶׁהִגִּיעַ זְמַנָּן לְהִפָּטֵר אָמַר, בְּנֵי בְּבַקָּשָׁה מִכֶּם, עַכְּבוּ עִמִּי עוֹד יוֹם אֶחָד, קָשָׁה עָלַי פְּרִידַתְכֶם: **כָּל מְלֶאכֶת עֲבוֹדָה.** אֲפִלּוּ מְלָאכָה שֶׁהִיא עֲבוֹדָה לָכֶם, שֶׁאִם לֹא תַעֲשׂוּהָ יֵשׁ חֶסְרוֹן כִּיס בַּדָּבָר: **לֹא תַעֲשׂוּ.** יָכוֹל אַף חֻלּוֹ שֶׁל מוֹעֵד יְהֵא אָסוּר בִּמְלֶאכֶת עֲבוֹדָה, תַּלְמוּד לוֹמַר הוּא: (לז) **עֹלָה וּמִנְחָה.** מִנְחַת נְסָכִים הַקְּרֵבָה עִם הָעוֹלָה: **דְּבַר יוֹם בְּיוֹמוֹ.** חֹק הַקָּצוּב בְּחוּמַשׁ הַפְּקוּדִים (במדבר כ"ח-כ"ט): **דְּבַר יוֹם בְּיוֹמוֹ.** הָא אִם עָבַר יוֹמוֹ בָּטֵל קָרְבָּנוֹ (ת"כ שם ט; ברכות כו.):

RASHI ELUCIDATED
---

36. עֲצֶרֶת הִוא — IT IS A RESTRAINING. עֲצַרְתִּי אֶתְכֶם — I have held you back, אֶצְלִי — next to Me, כְּמֶלֶךְ שֶׁזִּמֵּן אֶת בָּנָיו לִסְעוּדָה — like a king who invited his sons to a banquet לְכָךְ וְכָךְ יָמִים — for a certain number of days. כֵּיוָן שֶׁהִגִּיעַ זְמַנָּן לְהִפָּטֵר — Once their time to depart arrived, אָמַר — [the king] said, בְּנֵי — "My sons, בְּבַקָּשָׁה מִכֶּם — I request of you, עַכְּבוּ עִמִּי — linger with me עוֹד יוֹם אֶחָד — one more day. קָשָׁה עָלַי פְּרִידַתְכֶם — Your departure is hard for me."[1]

☐ כָּל מְלֶאכֶת עֲבֹדָה — ANY WORK OF LABOR. אֲפִילוּ מְלָאכָה שֶׁהִיא עֲבוֹדָה לָכֶם — Even a task that is labor for you שֶׁאִם לֹא תַעֲשׂוּהָ — in that if you do not do it יֵשׁ חֶסְרוֹן כִּיס בַּדָּבָר — there is financial loss in the matter.[2]

☐ לֹא תַעֲשׂוּ — YOU SHALL NOT DO. יָכוֹל אַף חֻלּוֹ שֶׁל מוֹעֵד — One might be able to think that even the intermediate days of the festival יְהֵא אָסוּר — should be forbidden בִּמְלֶאכֶת עֲבֹדָה — in "work of labor." תַּלְמוּד לוֹמַר — To teach us otherwise, the verse says, "הוּא"[3] — "it," which implies "it" is forbidden, but not the intermediate days.[3]

37. עֹלָה וּמִנְחָה — AN OLAH-OFFERING AND A MEAL-OFFERING. מִנְחַת נְסָכִים — The meal-offering of the poured-offering הַקְּרֵבָה עִם הָעוֹלָה[4] — which is brought with the olah-offering.[4]

☐ דְּבַר יוֹם בְּיוֹמוֹ — EACH DAY'S REQUIREMENT ON ITS DAY. חֹק הַקָּצוּב — The amount fixed בְּחוּמַשׁ הַפְּקוּדִים[5] — in The Book of Numbers.[5]

☐ דְּבַר יוֹם בְּיוֹמוֹ — EACH DAY'S REQUIREMENT ON ITS DAY. הָא אִם עָבַר יוֹמוֹ — But if its day has passed, בָּטֵל קָרְבָּנוֹ[6] — its offering is canceled.[6] No substitute is brought the next day.

---

1. This parable is found in *Succah* 55b in a slightly different form.
2. See 8 above and Rashi there.
3. *Toras Kohanim, perek* 14:8.
4. *Menachos* 44b. Although our verse does not refer to a *olah*-offering and *its* meal-offering, as did verse 13, the meal-offering of our verse is nonetheless the one that accompanies the *olah*- offering. For "each day's requirement on its day" is an allusion to the list of

mussaf-offerings in the *Book of Numbers* which Rashi mentions in his following comment. There, no mention is made of any specific meal-offering. The meal-offering referred to here must therefore be one which is implied by the other offerings mentioned there explicitly — the meal-offerings that accompany the *olah*-offerings (*Be'er BaSadeh*).

5. Chapters 28 and 29.
6. *Toras Kohanim, perek* 12:9; *Berachos* 26a.

VAYIKRA/LEVITICUS — PARASHAS EMOR — 23/39

שַׁבְּתֹת יהוה וּמִלְּבַד מַתְּנוֹתֵיכֶם וּמִלְּבַד כָּל־נִדְרֵיכֶם וּמִלְּבַד כָּל־נִדְבֹתֵיכֶם אֲשֶׁר תִּתְּנוּ לַיהוה: אַךְ בַּחֲמִשָּׁה עָשָׂר יוֹם לַחֹדֶשׁ הַשְּׁבִיעִי בְּאָסְפְּכֶם אֶת־תְּבוּאַת הָאָרֶץ תָּחֹגּוּ אֶת־חַג־יהוה שִׁבְעַת יָמִים

HASHEM's *Sabbaths, and aside from your gifts, aside from all your vows, and aside from all your voluntary offerings, which you will present to* HASHEM. **39** *But on the fifteenth day of the seventh month, when you bring in the crop of the Land, you shall celebrate* HASHEM's *festival for a seven-day period;*

—————— אונקלוס ——————

שַׁבַּיָּא דַיְיָ וּבַר מִן מַתְּנָתֵיכוֹן וּבַר מִן כָּל נִדְרֵיכוֹן וּבַר מִן כָּל נִדְבָתֵיכוֹן דִּי תִתְּנוּן קֳדָם יְיָ: לט בְּרַם בְּחַמְשָׁא עֲשַׂר יוֹמָא לְיַרְחָא שְׁבִיעָאָה בְּמִכְנָשֵׁיכוֹן יָת עֲלַלַּת אַרְעָא תְּחַגּוּן יָת חַגָּא דַייָ קֳדָם יְיָ שִׁבְעָא יוֹמִין

—————— רש"י ——————

(לט) **אך בחמשה עשר יום תחגו.** קרבן שלמים לחגיגה.
שבעת ימים. חוגג ואם לא חג יום טוב ראשון של חג יכול יחגוג את כולן, ת"ל אך, חלק. ומנין שאם לא חג יביא בז"ה. יכול יהא מביאן כל שבעה, ת"ל אך, חלק. יכול יביא בז"ה. ת"ל ובאספכם את תבואת הארץ (שם פרק טו:ה). שיהא חדש שביעי זה בא בזמן אסיפה. מכאן שנצטוו לעבר את השנים, שאם אין העבור, פעמים שהוא באמצע הקיץ או החורף.

—————— RASHI ELUCIDATED ——————

39. אַךְ בַּחֲמִשָּׁה עָשָׂר יוֹם תָּחֹגּוּ — BUT ON THE FIFTEENTH DAY ... YOU SHALL CELEBRATE by bringing קָרְבַּן שְׁלָמִים — a peace-offering לַחֲגִיגָה — for a festival offering.[1] יָכוֹל — One might be able to think that תִּדְחֶה אֶת הַשַּׁבָּת — [the slaughter of the festival peace-offering] should override the Sabbath. תַּלְמוּד לוֹמַר — To teach us otherwise, **the verse says,** ",אַךְ" — "but."[2] It does not override the Sabbath הוֹאִיל וְיֵשׁ לָהּ תַּשְׁלוּמִין — since it has repayment [3] כָּל שִׁבְעָה — all seven days of the festival.[3] □ בְּאָסְפְּכֶם אֶת תְּבוּאַת הָאָרֶץ — WHEN YOU BRING IN THE CROP OF THE LAND. שֶׁיְּהֵא חֹדֶשׁ שְׁבִיעִי זֶה — That this seventh month בָּא בִּזְמַן אֲסִיפָה — should come at the time of bringing in the crops.[4] מִכָּאן — From here we learn שֶׁנִּצְטַוּוּ לְעַבֵּר אֶת הַשָּׁנִים — that they were commanded to add months to the years, שֶׁאִם אֵין הָעִבּוּר — for if there is no adding additional months, פְּעָמִים — there would be times שֶׁהוּא בְּאֶמְצַע הַקַּיִץ — that [the fifteenth day of the seventh month] would be in the middle of the summer [5] אוֹ הַחֹרֶף — or the winter.[5]

□ תָּחֹגּוּ — YOU SHALL CELEBRATE by bringing שַׁלְמֵי חֲגִיגָה — festival peace-offerings.[6]

□ שִׁבְעַת יָמִים — FOR A SEVEN-DAY PERIOD. אִם לֹא הֵבִיא בָּזֶה — If he did not bring [the festival peace-offering] on this day, יָבִיא בָּזֶה — he may bring it on this day, i.e., on another day, during the seven-day period. יָכוֹל — On the basis of "for a seven-day period," one might be able to think that יְהֵא מְבִיאָן — one should bring [festival peace-offerings] כָּל שִׁבְעָה — all seven days of the festival. תַּלְמוּד לוֹמַר — To teach us otherwise, **the verse says,** ",וְחַגֹּתֶם אֹתוֹ"[7] — "you shall celebrate *it*";[7] יוֹם אֶחָד בְּמַשְׁמָע — one day is implied וְלֹא יוֹתֵר — and no more.[8] וְלָמָּה נֶאֱמַר שִׁבְעָה — Why, then, does

---

1. תָחֹגּוּ connotes celebrating by bringing offerings, as in *Exodus* 5:1 (*Gur Aryeh*).

2. אַךְ, "but," connotes limitation (see Rashi to v. 27 above). In our verse, it eliminates the Sabbath from the commandment to bring the festival peace-offering.

3. *Toras Kohanim, perek* 15:5. If one fails to bring a festival peace-offering on the first day of the festival, he can make up for it on the following six days of the festival, as well as on *Shemini Atzeres*. Hence, the Torah is not as insistent that the festival peace-offering be brought on its proper day as it is with regard to the *mussaf* offerings referred to in the preceding verse. Therefore, the Torah does not let it override the prohibition against doing work on the Sabbath.

4. The verse does not mean that the crops should be brought in on the fifteenth, for that day is a festival when such activity is forbidden (*Nachalas Yaakov*). See Rashi to *Exodus* 34:22 and note 1 on p. 481 there.

5. *Toras Kohanim, perek* 15:6. The seasons follow the cycle of the solar year of 365 days. The Jewish calendar is based on the lunar year of 354 days. Our verse insists that the fifteenth day of the seventh month fall at the time of the harvesting of the crops. This can be assured only if an extra month is sometimes added to the standard twelve; otherwise there could be no overall consistent relationship between the dates of the lunar calendar and the seasons of the solar year.

6. See note 1 above.

7. Below v. 41.

8. The verse uses the singular אֹתוֹ, "it," and not the plural אֹתָם, "them."

the first day is a rest day and the eighth day is a rest day. **40** You shall take for yourselves on the first day the fruit of a tree of splendor, fronds of date palms, and branches of a cordlike tree, and brook willows; and you shall rejoice before HASHEM, your God, for a seven-day period. **41** You shall celebrate it as a festival for HASHEM, a seven-day period in the year, an eternal decree for your generations; in the seventh month shall you celebrate it. **42** You shall dwell in booths for a seven-day period; every native

בַּיּוֹם הָרִאשׁוֹן שַׁבָּתוֹן וּבַיּוֹם הַשְּׁמִינִי שַׁבָּתוֹן: מ וּלְקַחְתֶּם לָכֶם בַּיּוֹם הָרִאשׁוֹן פְּרִי עֵץ הָדָר כַּפֹּת תְּמָרִים וַעֲנַף עֵץ־עָבֹת וְעַרְבֵי־נָחַל וּשְׂמַחְתֶּם לִפְנֵי יהוה אֱלֹהֵיכֶם שִׁבְעַת יָמִים: מא וְחַגֹּתֶם אֹתוֹ חַג לַיהוה שִׁבְעַת יָמִים בַּשָּׁנָה חֻקַּת עוֹלָם לְדֹרֹתֵיכֶם בַּחֹדֶשׁ הַשְּׁבִיעִי תָּחֹגּוּ אֹתוֹ: מב בַּסֻּכֹּת תֵּשְׁבוּ שִׁבְעַת יָמִים כָּל־הָאֶזְרָח

אונקלוס

בְּיוֹמָא קַדְמָאָה נְיָחָא וּבְיוֹמָא תְמִינָאָה נְיָחָא: מ וְתִסְּבוּן לְכוֹן בְּיוֹמָא קַדְמָאָה פֵּרֵי אִילָנָא אֶתְרוֹגִין וְלוּלְבִין וַהֲדַסִּין וְעַרְבִין דְּנַחַל וְתֶחֱדוּן קֳדָם יְיָ אֱלָהֲכוֹן שִׁבְעָה יוֹמִין: מא וּתְחַגּוּן יָתֵהּ חַגָּא קֳדָם יְיָ שִׁבְעָה יוֹמִין בְּשַׁתָּא קְיָם עָלַם לְדָרֵיכוֹן בְּיַרְחָא שְׁבִיעָאָה תֵּחֲגוּן יָתֵהּ: מב בִּמְטַלַּיָּא תֵּיתְבוּן שִׁבְעָה יוֹמִין כָּל יַצִּיבָא

רש"י

לְתַשְׁלוּמִין (שם פרק יח:א"ב; חגיגה ט.): (מ) **פְּרִי עֵץ הָדָר.** עֵץ שֶׁטַּעַם עֵצוֹ וּפִרְיוֹ שָׁוֶה: **הָדָר.** הַדָּר בְּאִילָנוֹ מִשָּׁנָה לְשָׁנָה [הוּא אֶתְרוֹג.] **הָדָר.** וְזֶהוּ אֶתְרוֹג (ת"כ פרק טז:ד; סוכה לה.): **כַּפֹּת תְּמָרִים.** חָסֵר וי"ו לָמַד שֶׁאֵינָהּ אֶלָּא אַחַת (סוכה לב.): **וַעֲנַף עֵץ עָבֹת.** שֶׁעֲנָפָיו קְלוּעִים כְּעֲבוֹתוֹת וְכַחֲבָלִים וְזֶהוּ הֲדַס הֶעָשׂוּי כְּמִין קְלִיעָה (שם לב:): (מב) **הָאֶזְרָח.** זֶה אֶזְרָח הָאֶזְרָח לְהוֹצִיא אֶת הַנָּשִׁים שֶׁלֹּא תִלְמַד מֵחֲמִשָּׁה עָשָׂר בְּנִיסָן לְחַיְּבָן בְּנִיסִין מט"ו (ת"כ פרק יז:ט; סוכה כח.):

RASHI ELUCIDATED

it say seven? — **לְתַשְׁלוּמִין**[1] — **For repayment.**[1]

40. **פְּרִי עֵץ הָדָר** — THE FRUIT OF A TREE OF SPLENDOR. — **עֵץ שֶׁטַּעַם עֵצוֹ וּפִרְיוֹ שָׁוֶה** — A tree, the taste of whose wood and fruit are alike.[2]

{□ **הָדָר** — SPLENDOR.} The word הָדָר is interpreted as if it were vowelized הַדָּר. **הַדָּר בְּאִילָנוֹ** — The fruit of a tree **that dwells on its tree** **מִשָּׁנָה לְשָׁנָה** — **from year to year,** i.e., from one year to the next, **וְזֶהוּ אֶתְרוֹג**[3] — **and this is the citron.**[3]

{□ **כַּפֹּת תְּמָרִים** — FRONDS OF DATE PALMS. **חָסֵר וָי"ו** — **כַּפֹּת** is spelled here **without a ו. לָמַד שֶׁאֵינָהּ אֶלָּא אַחַת**[4] — **This teaches** as that it is only one.[4]

{□ **וַעֲנַף עֵץ עָבֹת** — AND BRANCHES OF A CORDLIKE TREE. — **שֶׁעֲנָפָיו קְלוּעִים** — A tree whose branches are plaited **כַּעֲבוֹתוֹת** — like cords **וְכַחֲבָלִים** — and like ropes, **וְזֶהוּ הֲדַס** — and this is myrtle, **הֶעָשׂוּי כְּמִין קְלִיעָה**[5] — which is formed in a braidlike configuration.[5]

42. **הָאֶזְרָח** — NATIVE. — **זֶה אֶזְרָח** — This is a native, i.e., a Jew by birth. {**הָאֶזְרָח** — "The native," **לְהוֹצִיא אֶת הַנָּשִׁים**[6] — to exclude the women;[6] **שֶׁלֹּא תִלְמַד** — that you should not learn the laws of the fifteenth of Tishrei, i.e., Succos, **מֵחֲמִשָּׁה עָשָׂר בְּנִיסָן** — from a comparison with the laws of **the fifteenth of Nissan, לְחַיְּבָן בְּסֻכָּה** — to obligate [women] in the commandment of **succah** — **כְּמַצָּה** — as they

---

1. *Toras Kohanim,* perek 17:12; *Chagigah* 9a. If he does not bring the offering on the day of the festival, he may bring it within the next seven days.

2. *Toras Kohanim,* perek 16:4; *Succah* 35a. Fruit of a tree can be expressed as פְּרִי הָעֵץ, e.g., *Exodus* 10:15. The Torah uses פְּרִי עֵץ here, without the prefix ה, to indicate that there is a unique similarity between the tree and its fruit, that they have the same flavor (*Gur Aryeh*).

The Torah could have said פְּרִי הָדָר, and we would have known that it refers to the citron, a fruit which remains on the tree for a few years (see Rashi's next comment). By using the additional word עֵץ, it gives us another way of identifying the fruit, one whose taste is the same as that of its tree (*Mizrachi; Sheima Shlomo*).

3. *Toras Kohanim,* perek 16:4; *Succah* 35a. The citron can remain on the tree two or three years (Rashi to *Succah* 35a, s.v., ה"ג עד שבאים קטנים כו').

4. *Succah* 32a. כַּפֹּת is a plural, and is normally spelled with a ו, כַּפּוֹת. It is spelled here without the ו, in a way which could be vowelized as the singular כַּפַּת. This is to teach us that the Torah speaks of only one frond.

5. *Succah* 32b. The myrtle has a braidlike form in that its leaves "overlap" one another (Rashi to *Succah* 32b, s.v., בעניין עבות).

6. *Toras Kohanim,* perek 17:9; *Succah* 28a.

305 / VAYIKRA/LEVITICUS — PARASHAS EMOR — 23/43-24/2 — כג/מג-כד/ב

in Israel shall dwell in booths. ⁴³ So that your generations will know that I caused the Children of Israel to dwell in booths when I took them from the land of Egypt; I am HASHEM, your God.

⁴⁴ And Moses declared the appointed festivals of HASHEM to the Children of Israel.

24 ¹ HASHEM spoke to Moses, saying: ² Command the Children of Israel that they take to you clear olive oil, crushed, for illu-

מג בְּיִשְׂרָאֵל יֵשְׁבוּ בַסֻּכֹּת: לְמַעַן יֵדְעוּ דֹרֹתֵיכֶם כִּי בַסֻּכּוֹת הוֹשַׁבְתִּי אֶת־בְּנֵי יִשְׂרָאֵל בְּהוֹצִיאִי אוֹתָם מֵאֶרֶץ מִצְרָיִם אֲנִי יהוה אֱלֹהֵיכֶם: מד וַיְדַבֵּר מֹשֶׁה אֶת־מֹעֲדֵי יהוה אֶל־בְּנֵי יִשְׂרָאֵל:

כד א שביעי וַיְדַבֵּר יהוה אֶל־מֹשֶׁה לֵּאמֹר: ב צַו אֶת־בְּנֵי יִשְׂרָאֵל וְיִקְחוּ אֵלֶיךָ שֶׁמֶן זַיִת זָךְ כָּתִית לַמָּאוֹר

────── אונקלוס ──────

בְּיִשְׂרָאֵל יֵתְבוּן בִּמְטַלַּיָּא: מג בְּדִיל דְּיִדְּעוּן דָּרֵיכוֹן אֲרֵי בִּמְטַלַּת עֲנָנִי אוֹתֵבִית יָת בְּנֵי יִשְׂרָאֵל בְּאַפָּקוּתִי יָתְהוֹן מֵאַרְעָא דְמִצְרָיִם אֲנָא יְיָ אֱלָהֲכוֹן: מד וּמַלִּיל מֹשֶׁה יָת סִדְרֵי מוֹעֲדַיָּא דַּיְיָ וְאַלֵּפִנּוּן לִבְנֵי יִשְׂרָאֵל:

א וּמַלִּיל יְיָ עִם מֹשֶׁה לְמֵימַר: ב פַּקֵּד יָת בְּנֵי יִשְׂרָאֵל וְיִסְבוּן לָךְ מְשַׁח זֵיתָא דַכְיָא כָּתִישָׁא לְאַנְהָרָא

────── רש"י ──────

בישראל. לרבות את הגרים (ת"כ פרק יז:ט): **(מג) כי בסכות הושבתי.** ענני כבוד (שם יא; סוכה יא:): **(ב) צו את בני ישראל.** זו פרשת מצות הנרות, ופרשת ואתה תצוה (שמות כז:כ) לא נאמרה אלא על סדר מלאכת המשכן לפרש צורך המנורה. וכן משמע, ואתה סוף לצוות את בני ישראל על כך: **שמן זית זך.** שלשה שמנים יוצאים מן הזית,

────── RASHI ELUCIDATED ──────

are obligated in the commandment of **matzah**.}¹

☐ בְּיִשְׂרָאֵל — IN ISRAEL. ² לְרַבּוֹת אֶת הַגֵּרִים — To include the converts.²

43. כִּי בַסֻּכּוֹת הוֹשַׁבְתִּי — THAT I CAUSED [THE CHILDREN OF ISRAEL] TO DWELL IN BOOTHS, i.e., ³עַנְנֵי כָּבוֹד — the Clouds of Glory.³

24.

2. צַו אֶת בְּנֵי יִשְׂרָאֵל — COMMAND THE CHILDREN OF ISRAEL. זוֹ פָּרָשַׁת מִצְוַת הַנֵּרוֹת — This is the section of the Torah that gives the commandment of the lamps, ⁴וּפָרָשַׁת וְאַתָּה תְּצַוֶּה — and the section in *Parashas Ve'atah Tetzaveh* that also deals with the lamps⁴ לֹא נֶאֶמְרָה אֶלָּא — was stated only עַל סֵדֶר מְלֶאכֶת הַמִּשְׁכָּן — with regard to the order of the work of the construction of the Tabernacle and its implements, לְפָרֵשׁ צוֹרֶךְ הַמְּנוֹרָה — to explain the necessity of the Menorah.⁵ וְכֵן מַשְׁמַע — And this is its meaning: וְאַתָּה — You, סוֹפְךָ — your destiny is לְצַוּוֹת אֶת בְּנֵי יִשְׂרָאֵל — to command the Children of Israel עַל כָּךְ — about this.⁶

☐ שֶׁמֶן זַיִת זָךְ — CLEAR OLIVE OIL. שְׁלֹשָׁה שְׁמָנִים — There are **three oils** יוֹצְאִים מִן הַזַּיִת — which come

---

1. The interpolated passage appears in the Alkabetz edition (1476) and is also the version that was before *Ramban* and *Sefer Zikaron*. Contemporary editions have only הָאֶזְרָח זֶה, omitting the main point of Rashi. See *Yosef Hallel*.

2. *Toras Kohanim, perek* 17:9.

3. *Toras Kohanim, perek* 17:11; *Succah* 11b. Rashi here follows the opinion of the *Tanna* R' Akiva, as does *Targum Onkelos* and the *Shulchan Aruch* (*Orach Chaim* 625:1). The *Tanna* R' Eliezer takes "booths" of our verse literally. According to *Ramban*, R' Akiva's explanation more easily fits the verse, for the Clouds of Glory are more likely deserving of commemoration than the booths in which the Israelites dwelled during their sojourn in the desert.

4. *Exodus* 27:20. That verse is identical to ours except that it begins וְאַתָּה תְּצַוֶּה, "you shall command," instead

of the imperative צַו, "Command!" See note 6 below.

5. The matter of the lamps was mentioned in *Ve'atah Tetzaveh* only to explain why it was necessary to make a Menorah, a candelabrum, among the implements of the Tabernacle.

6. *Exodus* 27:20 reads, "And you shall command the Children of Israel, that they shall take for you clear olive oil, crushed for illumination, to light a lamp continually." Rashi explains that תְּצַוֶּה, "you shall command," of that verse, is to be understood as a simple future, "you will command," not as an imperative, for it is our section of the Torah rather than that one which contains the commandment of the lamps of the Menorah.

Ramban takes issue with Rashi, for *Exodus* 40:25 states, "He lit the lamps before HASHEM, as HASHEM had commanded Moses," indicating that the com-

ג לְהַעֲלֹת נֵר תָּמִיד: ³ מִחוּץ לְפָרֹכֶת הָעֵדֻת בְּאֹהֶל מוֹעֵד יַעֲרֹךְ אֹתוֹ אַהֲרֹן

mination, to light a lamp continually. ³ *Outside of the Paroches of the Testimony, in the Tent of Meeting, Aaron shall arrange it,*

───── אונקלוס ─────

לְאַדְלָקָא בּוֹצִינַיָּא תְדִירָא: ג מִבָּרָא לְפָרֻכְתָּא דְסַהֲדוּתָא בְּמַשְׁכַּן זִמְנָא יַסְדַּר יָתֵהּ אַהֲרֹן

───── רש"י ─────

הָרִאשׁוֹן קָרוּי זָךְ, וְהֵם מְפוֹרָשִׁין בִּמְנָחוֹת (פו.) וּבְת"כ (פרשתא יג:א): **תָּמִיד**. מַלִּילָה לְלַיְלָה כְּמוֹ עוֹלַת תָּמִיד (שמות כט:מב) שֶׁאֵינָהּ אֶלָּא מִיּוֹם לְיוֹם: (ג) **לְפָרֹכֶת הָעֵדֻת**. שֶׁלִּפְנֵי הָאָרוֹן שֶׁהוּא קָרוּי עֵדוּת. וְרַבּוֹתֵינוּ דָרְשׁוּ עַל נֵר מַעֲרָבִי שֶׁהוּא עֵדוּת לְכָל בָּאֵי עוֹלָם שֶׁהַשְּׁכִינָה שׁוֹרָה בְּיִשְׂרָאֵל וְט"ש שֶׁהוּא עֵדוּת לְכָל בָּאֵי עוֹלָם שֶׁהַשְּׁכִינָה שׁוֹרָה בְּיִשְׂרָאֵל שֶׁנּוֹתֵן בָּהּ שֶׁמֶן כְּמִדַּת חַבְרוֹתֶיהָ וּמִמֶּנָּה הָיָה מַתְחִיל

───── RASHI ELUCIDATED ─────

וְהֵם מְפֹרָשִׁין בִּמְנָחוֹת — *out of the olive.* "זָךְ", **הָרִאשׁוֹן קָרוּי** — *The first* of them *is called "clear."*[1] *They are explained in Menachos*[1] ² **וּבְתוֹרַת כֹּהֲנִים** — *and in Toras Kohanim.*[2]

□ **תָּמִיד** — CONTINUALLY. **מִלַּיְלָה לְלַיְלָה** — *From night to night,* i.e., the Menorah must be kindled every night. ³ **תָּמִיד כְּמוֹ "עוֹלַת תָּמִיד** here is used in **the same** sense **as** it is used in, **"a continual olah-offering,"**[3] **שֶׁאֵינָהּ אֶלָּא מִיּוֹם לְיוֹם** — which is offered *only from day to day.*[4]

3. **לְפָרֹכֶת הָעֵדֻת**. — OF THE *PAROCHES* OF THE TESTIMONY. **שֶׁלִּפְנֵי הָאָרוֹן** — This refers to the *Paroches* that is in front of the Ark **שֶׁהוּא קָרוּי "עֵדוּת"** — which is called "Testimony."[5] **וְרַבּוֹתֵינוּ דָרְשׁוּ** — But our Rabbis expounded this phrase as speaking **עַל נֵר מַעֲרָבִי** — about the western lamp of the Menorah[6] **שֶׁהַשְּׁכִינָה שׁוֹרָה** — for it is testimony **לְכָל בָּאֵי עוֹלָם** — to all the inhabitants of the world **שֶׁהַשְּׁכִינָה שׁוֹרָה בְּיִשְׂרָאֵל,**[7] — that the Divine Presence rests among Israel,[7] **שֶׁנּוֹתֵן בָּהּ שֶׁמֶן** — for [the Kohen] would put oil into it **בְּמִדַּת חַבְרוֹתֶיהָ** — in the same measure as its fellow [lamps], **וּמִמֶּנָּה הָיָה מַתְחִיל** — and

mandment to light the Menorah had already been given by that earlier point. *Nachalas Yaakov* says in defense of Rashi that *Exodus* 40:25 refers to an exceptional instance of kindling the Menorah which was performed by Moses, who officiated during the service of the inauguration of the Tabernacle referred to in the verse cited by Ramban. Rashi means that the commandment of kindling the lamps given to the Kohanim is the subject of our verse.

1. *Menachos* 86a. It is not enough that the oil not have sediments at the time it is used in the Menorah. It must be oil which never had sediments in it. The Mishnah in *Menachos* explains that the olive tree is harvested three times a year. The first harvest is for the earliest ripening olives at the top of the tree. The second is for the olives on the middle branches which ripen later. Finally, a third harvest is for the fruit of the lowest branches that never receive the full sunlight and so do not ripen until after they have been harvested and left to stand packed tightly together in a vessel. Oil is extracted from the olives of each harvest through three consecutive methods: First, they are crushed in a mortar; then, they are pressed with a beam; finally, they are ground with millstones. The Mishnah that Rashi refers to says that only the oil extracted from each of the three harvests by crushing the olives in a mortar is fit for use in the Menorah.

2. *Toras Kohanim, parshasa* 13:1.

3. *Exodus* 29:42.

4. תָּמִיד here does not mean "continuous" or "constant," as it does in *Exodus* 28:29, for the Menorah did not burn by day. It means "continually." The *olah-* offering, too, is offered "continually," i.e., daily, at particular times, not "continuously," i.e., throughout the twenty-four hours of the day (*Mizrachi; Sifsei Chachamim,* to *Exodus* 27:20).

5. The *Paroches,* the curtain that divided the Holy of Holies from the rest of the Tabernacle, is referred to as "the *Paroches* of the Testimony" because the *Paroches* stood before the *Aron,* which is referred to as "the *Aron* of the Testimony" (e.g., *Exodus* 25:22, 26:33) since it contained the Tablets of the Ten Commandments which are called "the Tablets of the Testimony" (e.g., *Exodus* 31:18).

6. According to the opinion that the lamps of the Menorah ran on an east-west line, perpendicular to the *Paroches,* "the western lamp" is the lamp next to the one furthest east, the first lamp one encounters when moving from the easternmost lamp toward the west. According to the opinion that the lamps of the Menorah ran on a north-south line, parallel to the *Paroches,* "the western lamp" was the one in the middle. It was called by this name because the wicks of the three southern lamps pointed northward, while the wicks of the three northern lamps pointed southward; the wick of the middle lamp pointed westward (see Rashi to *Shabbos* 22b).

7. *Toras Kohanim, parshasa* 13:9.

מֵעֶ֧רֶב עַד־בֹּ֛קֶר לִפְנֵ֥י יהוָ֖ה תָּמִ֑יד חֻקַּ֥ת עוֹלָ֖ם לְדֹרֹֽתֵיכֶֽם: ד עַ֚ל הַמְּנֹרָ֣ה הַטְּהֹרָ֔ה יַעֲרֹ֛ךְ אֶת־הַנֵּר֖וֹת לִפְנֵ֥י יהוָ֖ה תָּמִֽיד:
ה וְלָקַחְתָּ֣ סֹ֔לֶת וְאָפִיתָ֣ אֹתָ֔הּ שְׁתֵּ֥ים עֶשְׂרֵ֖ה חַלּ֑וֹת שְׁנֵי֙ עֶשְׂרֹנִ֔ים יִהְיֶ֖ה הַֽחַלָּ֥ה הָאֶחָֽת: ו וְשַׂמְתָּ֥ אוֹתָ֛ם שְׁתַּ֥יִם מַֽעֲרָכ֖וֹת שֵׁ֣שׁ הַֽמַּעֲרָ֑כֶת עַ֛ל

from evening until morning, before HASHEM, *continually; an eternal decree for your generations.* [4] *On the pure Menorah shall he arrange the lamps, before* HASHEM, *continually.*

[5] *You shall take fine flour and bake it into twelve loaves; each loaf shall be two tenth-ephahs.* [6] *You shall place them in two stacks, six the stack, upon*

———————— אונקלוס ————————

מֵרַמְשָׁא עַד צַפְרָא קֳדָם יְיָ תְּדִירָא קְיָם עָלַם לְדָרֵיכוֹן: ד עַל מְנָרְתָּא דָכִיתָא יְסַדַּר יָת בּוֹצִינַיָּא קֳדָם יְיָ תְּדִירָא: ה וְתִסַּב סֻלְתָּא וְתֵיפֵי יָתַהּ תַּרְתָּא עֶשְׂרֵי גְרִיצָן תְּרֵין עֶשְׂרוֹנִין תְּהֵי גְרִיצְתָּא חֲדָא: ו וּתְשַׁוֵּי יָתְהוֹן תַּרְתֵּין סִדְרִין שִׁית סִדְרָא

———————— רש"י ————————

ובה היה מסיים (שבת כב:): **יערוך אתו אהרן מערב עד בוקר.** יערוך אותו עריכה הראויה למדת כל הלילה (ת"כ שם יא). ושיערו חכמים חצי לוג לכל נר וכו', והן כדאי אף לילי תקופת טבת, ומדה זו הוקצעה להם (מנחות פט.): **(ד) המנורה הטהורה.** שהיא זהב טהור. ד"א על טהרה של מנורה (ת"כ שם יב) שמטהרה ומדשנה תחלה מן האפר: **(ו) שש המערכת.** שש חלות המערכת האחת:

———————— RASHI ELUCIDATED ————————

from it he would begin the kindling, [1] **וּבָהּ הָיָה מְסַיֵּים** — **and with it he would conclude** the cleaning of the lamps.[1]

□ **יַעֲרֹךְ אֹתוֹ** — **יַעֲרֹךְ אֹתוֹ אַהֲרֹן מֵעֶרֶב עַד בֹּקֶר** — AARON SHALL ARRANGE IT FROM EVENING TO MORNING. **עֲרִיכָה** — **an arranging**[2] **הָרְאוּיָה לְמִדַּת כָּל הַלַּיְלָה** — **He shall arrange it** which is fit for the measure of the entire night.[2] **וְשִׁעֲרוּ חֲכָמִים** — The Sages set the measure at **חֲצִי לוֹג** — half a *log*[3] **לְכָל נֵר** — for each lamp. **וְהֵן כְּדַאי** — It is sufficient **אַף לְלֵילֵי תְּקוּפַת טֵבֵת** — even for the nights of the winter season. **וּמִדָּה זוּ** — This measure **הֻקְבְּעָה לָהֶם** — was fixed for them for all nights of the year.[4]

4. הַמְּנֹרָה הַטְּהֹרָה — THE PURE MENORAH. **שֶׁהִיא זָהָב טָהוֹר** — For it is made of pure gold. **דָּבָר אַחֵר** — Alternatively, the verse means, [5] **עַל טָהֳרָהּ שֶׁל מְנוֹרָה** — on the purity of the Menorah,[5] i.e., on the pure, clean, surface of the Menorah, directly on it, **שֶׁמְּטַהֲרָהּ וּמְדַשְּׁנָהּ תְּחִלָּה מִן הָאֵפֶר** — that first, before kindling it, he cleans it and clears it of the ashes.

6. שֵׁשׁ הַמַּעֲרָכֶת — SIX, THE STACK. **שֵׁשׁ חַלּוֹת הַמַּעֲרֶכֶת הָאֶחָת** — Six loaves per one stack.

---

1. *Shabbos* 22b. The other lamps would be lit at night, and go out by the following morning, when they would be cleaned. The western lamp would continue burning throughout the day. It would be cleaned in the evening, at which time it would be lit again, before the other lamps. This lamp's burning time, which lasted so much longer than the others yet used the same amount of oil, was a miracle that testified to the Divine Presence among Israel (*Nachalas Yaakov; Sifsei Chachamim*).

Had our verse meant only to tell us that the *Paroches* stood in front of the *Aron*, it would have referred to it as הַפָּרֹכֶת אֲשֶׁר עַל הָעֵדָה, "the *Paroches* which is over the Testimony," as it does in the parallel verse in *Exodus* 27:21. The verse uses the apparently less precise פָּרֹכֶת הָעֵדֻת, "*Paroches* of the Testimony," to indicate that the words of the verse are to be read in a manner that will yield the interpretation expounded by the Rabbis: מִחוּץ לַפָּרֹכֶת, "outside the *Paroches*,"

הַעֵדֻת בְּאֹהֶל מוֹעֵד יַעֲרֹךְ, "he shall arrange the testimony, i.e., the western lamp, in the Tent of Meeting." Had the verse included the stylistically preferable עַל אֲשֶׁר, it could not have been read this way (*Nachalas Yaakov*).

2. *Toras Kohanim, parshasa* 13:11; *Menachos* 89a. The verse does not mean that Aaron should be actively engaged in the arranging from evening to morning (*Sefer Zikaron*).

3. See table of measurements on page 268.

4. *Menachos* 89a. The Sages set a measure which would be sufficient for the Menorah to burn throughout the night, even on the longest nights of the year. Although the Menorah would burn far into the day when the nights were shorter, this does not constitute a problem (*Mizrachi* to *Exodus* 27:21).

5. *Toras Kohanim, parshasa* 13:12.

the pure Table, before HASHEM. *⁷ You shall put pure frankincense on the stack, and it shall be for a remembrance for the bread, a fire-offering for* HASHEM. *⁸ Each and every Sabbath day*

זהַשֻּׁלְחָן הַטָּהֹר לִפְנֵי יהוה: וְנָתַתָּ עַל־הַמַּעֲרֶכֶת לְבֹנָה זַכָּה וְהָיְתָה לַלֶּחֶם לְאַזְכָּרָה אִשֶּׁה לַיהוה: חבְּיוֹם הַשַּׁבָּת

---— אונקלוס ——
עַל פָּתוּרָא דַכְיָא קֳדָם יְיָ: זוְתִתֵּן עַל סִדְרָא לְבוֹנְתָא דָכִיתָא וּתְהֵי לְלַחְמָא לְאַדְכָּרְתָּא קֻרְבָּנָא קֳדָם יְיָ: חבְּיוֹמָא דְשַׁבְּתָא

---— רש"י ——

הַשֻּׁלְחָן הַטָּהֹר. שֶׁל זָהָב טָהוֹר. דָּ"אַ עַל טָהֳרוֹ שֶׁל שֻׁלְחָן שֶׁלֹּא יִהְיוּ הַסְּנִיפִין מַגְבִּיהִין אֶת הַלֶּחֶם מֵעַל גַּבֵּי הַשֻּׁלְחָן (ס"אַ פרק יח"ד; מנחות צ"ז.): **(ז) וְנָתַתָּ עַל הַמַּעֲרָכֶת.** עַל כָּל אַחַת מִשְׁתֵּי הַמַּעֲרָכוֹת. הָיוּ [ס"אַ הֲרֵי] שְׁנֵי בָּזִיכֵי לְבוֹנָה, מְלֹא קוֹמֶץ לְכָל אַחַת (שָׁם ה"ה): **וְהָיְתָה.** הַלְּבוֹנָה הַזֹּאת: **לַלֶּחֶם לְאַזְכָּרָה.** שֶׁאֵין מִן הַלֶּחֶם לַגָּבוֹהַ כְּלוּם אֶלָּא הַלְּבוֹנָה נִקְטֶרֶת כְּשֶׁמְּסַלְּקִין אוֹתוֹ

---— RASHI ELUCIDATED ——

□ הַשֻּׁלְחָן הַטָּהֹר — THE PURE TABLE. שֶׁל זָהָב טָהוֹר — For it is made of **pure gold.** דָּבָר אַחֵר — **Alternatively,** the verse means to say, עַל טָהֳרוֹ שֶׁל שֻׁלְחָן — **on the purity of the Table,** i.e., directly on the Table, שֶׁלֹּא יִהְיוּ הַסְּנִיפִין מַגְבִּיהִין אֶת הַלֶּחֶם — **that the branches should not raise the bread** מֵעַל גַּבֵּי הַשֻּׁלְחָן — **above the Table.**[1]

7. וְנָתַתָּ עַל הַמַּעֲרֶכֶת — YOU SHALL PUT [PURE FRANKINCENSE] ON THE STACK, that is, עַל כָּל אַחַת מִשְׁתֵּי הַמַּעֲרָכוֹת — **on each one of the two stacks.**[2] הָיוּ[3] שְׁנֵי בָּזִיכֵי לְבוֹנָה — There were[3] **two ladles of frankincense** [5] מְלֹא קוֹמֶץ לְכָל אַחַת — which held **a** *kometz*[4] **each.**[5]

□ וְהָיְתָה — AND IT SHALL BE, i.e. הַלְּבוֹנָה הַזֹּאת — **this frankincense.**[6]

□ לַלֶּחֶם לְאַזְכָּרָה — FOR A REMEMBRANCE FOR THE BREAD. שֶׁאֵין מִן הַלֶּחֶם לַגָּבוֹהַּ כְּלוּם — **For none of the bread at all** is offered **to** Him Who is **on High.** אֶלָּא — **Rather,** הַלְּבוֹנָה נִקְטֶרֶת — **the frankincense is made to go up in smoke** on the *Mizbe'ach* כְּשֶׁמְּסַלְּקִין אוֹתוֹ — **when they remove [the bread]**

---

1. *Toras Kohanim, perek* 18:4; *Menachos* 97a. The "branches" were poles that stood two on either side of the Table. They held "tubes" that formed shelves upon which the Bread of Surfaces rested (see Rashi to *Exodus* 25:29, s.v., וּקְשׂוֹתָיו and וּמְנַקִּיֹּתָיו). According to this explanation, our verse teaches us that the lowest pair of loaves is to rest directly upon the surface of the table, not upon the "tubes."

2. "On the stack" is not meant to imply that frankincense is put only on one stack. It means, "on each stack" (*Be'er BaSadeh*).

3. Some editions read ... הֲרֵי שְׁנֵי בָּזִיכֵי, "thus, [there were] two ladles ..."

4. The word קוֹמֶץ, "*kometz*," is defined in Rashi to 2:2 above, s.v., מְלֹא קֻמְצוֹ.

5. *Toras Kohanim, perek* 18:5-7. The translation follows *Nachalas Yaakov*, whose text of Rashi had אֶחָד where ours has אַחַת. The masculine אֶחָד agrees with the masculine בָּזִיכֵי. Although אַחַת is feminine, our translation maintains *Nachalas Yaakov*'s understanding of Rashi, for the gender of words has been corrupted in many places in Rashi's commentaries, especially where it is a matter of variance of only one letter. If our text which reads אַחַת is taken precisely, אַחַת refers to הַמַּעֲרָכוֹת. With מְלֹא קוֹמֶץ לְכָל אַחַת Rashi says there was a *kometz* of frankincense for each stack.

6. "And it shall be for a remembrance" refers to the frankincense itself, not the act of putting the frankincense on the stacks. Had the Torah meant the act of putting, it would have used the masculine form of "and it shall be," וְהָיָה. Rashi stresses that לְבוֹנָה, "frankincense," is feminine, and thus agrees with the verse's וְהָיְתָה, by using the feminine demonstrative adjective הַזֹּאת, and not the masculine הַזֶּה, with regard to it.

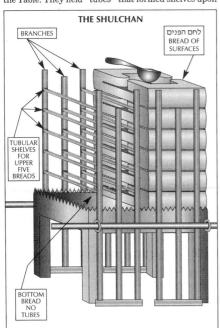

THE SHULCHAN
BRANCHES
לחם הפנים
BREAD OF SURFACES
TUBULAR SHELVES FOR UPPER FIVE BREADS
BOTTOM BREAD NO TUBES

he shall arrange it before HASHEM continually, from the Children of Israel as an eternal covenant. ⁹ And it shall belong to Aaron and his sons, and they shall eat it in a holy place; for it is most holy for him, from the fire-offerings of HASHEM, an eternal decree.

¹⁰ The son of an Israelite woman went out

בְּיוֹם הַשַּׁבָּת יַעַרְכֶנּוּ לִפְנֵי יהוה תָּמִיד מֵאֵת בְּנֵי־יִשְׂרָאֵל בְּרִית עוֹלָם: ט וְהָיְתָה לְאַהֲרֹן וּלְבָנָיו וַאֲכָלֻהוּ בְּמָקוֹם קָדֹשׁ כִּי קֹדֶשׁ קָדָשִׁים הוּא לוֹ מֵאִשֵּׁי יהוה חָק־עוֹלָם: י וַיֵּצֵא בֶּן־אִשָּׁה יִשְׂרְאֵלִית

———— אונקלוס ————

בְּיוֹמָא דְשַׁבְּתָא יְסַדְּרִנֵּהּ קֳדָם יְיָ תְּדִירָא מִן קֳדָם בְּנֵי יִשְׂרָאֵל קְיָם עָלָם: ט וּתְהֵי לְאַהֲרֹן וְלִבְנוֹהִי וְיֵיכְלֻנַּהּ בַּאֲתַר קַדִּישׁ אֲרֵי קֹדֶשׁ קוּדְשִׁין הוּא לֵהּ מִקֻּרְבָּנַיָּא דַיְיָ קְיָם עָלָם: י וּנְפַק בַּר אִתְּתָא בַת יִשְׂרָאֵל

———— רש"י ————

וַיֵּצֵא בֶּן אִשָּׁה יִשְׂרְאֵלִית. מֵהֵיכָן יָצָא, רַבִּי לֵוִי אוֹמֵר מֵעוֹלָמוֹ יָצָא, רַבִּי בְּרֶכְיָה אוֹמֵר מִפָּרָשָׁה שֶׁלְמַעְלָה יָצָא, לִגְלֵג וְאָמַר בְּיוֹם הַשַּׁבָּת יַעַרְכֶנּוּ, דֶּרֶךְ הַמֶּלֶךְ לֶאֱכוֹל פַּת חַמָּה בְּכָל יוֹם, שֶׁמָּא פַּת צוֹנֶנֶת שֶׁל תִּשְׁעָה יָמִים,

בְּכָל שַׁבָּת וְשַׁבָּת, וְהִיא לְזִכָּרוֹן לַלֶּחֶם שֶׁעַל יְדָהּ הוּא נִזְכָּר לְמַעְלָה, כְּקוֹמֶץ שֶׁהוּא אַזְכָּרָה לַמִּנְחָה: **(ט) וְהָיְתָה.** הַמִּנְחָה הַזֹּאת שֶׁכָּל דָּבָר הַבָּא מִן הַתְּבוּאָה בִּכְלַל מִנְחָה הוּא: **וַאֲכָלֻהוּ.** מוּסָב עַל הַלֶּחֶם שֶׁהוּא לְשׁוֹן זָכָר: **(י)**

———— RASHI ELUCIDATED ————

בְּכָל שַׁבָּת וְשַׁבָּת – **every Shabbos.** וְהִיא לְזִכָּרוֹן לַלֶּחֶם – **[The frankincense] serves as a remembrance for the bread,** שֶׁעַל יְדָהּ – **for through it** הוּא נִזְכָּר לְמַעְלָה – **[the bread] is remembered Above.** כַּקוֹמֶץ – In this respect, it is **like the handful** שֶׁהוּא אַזְכָּרָה לַמִּנְחָה – **which is a remembrance for the meal-offering.**[1]

9. וְהָיְתָה – AND IT SHALL BELONG, i.e., הַמִּנְחָה הַזֹּאת – **this meal-offering.**[2] שֶׁכָּל דָּבָר הַבָּא מִן הַתְּבוּאָה – For anything, i.e., any offering, **that comes from grain** בִּכְלַל מִנְחָה הוּא – **is included in** the term מִנְחָה.[3]

וַאֲכָלֻהוּ – AND THEY SHALL EAT IT. מוּסָב עַל הַלֶּחֶם – [It] refers to "the bread," שֶׁהוּא לְשׁוֹן זָכָר – which is a masculine term.[4]

10. וַיֵּצֵא בֶּן אִשָּׁה יִשְׂרְאֵלִית – THE SON OF AN ISRAELITE WOMAN WENT OUT. מֵהֵיכָן יָצָא – From where did he go out?[5] רַבִּי לֵוִי אוֹמֵר – R' Levi says: מֵעוֹלָמוֹ יָצָא – He went out of his world.[6] רַבִּי בְּרֶכְיָה אוֹמֵר – R' Berechyah says: מִפָּרָשָׁה שֶׁלְמַעְלָה יָצָא – He went out of the passage above.[7] לִגְלֵג – He scoffed, וְאָמַר – and said, "בְּיוֹם הַשַּׁבָּת יַעַרְכֶנּוּ" – "On the Sabbath day he shall arrange it."[8] דֶּרֶךְ הַמֶּלֶךְ – It is the practice of the king לֶאֱכוֹל פַּת חַמָּה – to eat warm, fresh bread בְּכָל יוֹם – every day. שֶׁמָּא פַּת צוֹנֶנֶת שֶׁל תִּשְׁעָה יָמִים – Might a king eat cold, nine-day-old bread?"[9]

1. See 2:2 above and Rashi there.

2. "It shall belong" does not refer to the masculine noun, לֶחֶם, "bread," mentioned above, for in that case the verse would have used the masculine וְהָיָה instead of the feminine וְהָיְתָה (Sefer Zikaron). Nor does it refer to the feminine noun מַעֲרָכוֹת, stacks, for then it would have used the plural וְהָיוּ (Mesiach Ilmim). Rather, if refers to the implicit feminine noun מִנְחָה, "meal-offering." (See note 4 below.)

3. Although מִנְחָה does not appear in our passage, it is not unreasonable that "it" of our verse refers to it. For our passage speaks of an offering made from grain, and מִנְחָה applies to any such offering (Mizrachi; Sefer Zikaron; Nachalas Yaakov).

4. Rashi explains why the verse shifts from the feminine וְהָיְתָה, which referred to the implicit מִנְחָה, to וַאֲכָלֻהוּ, an abridged form of אָכְלוּ אתוֹ, "they shall eat it," using אתוֹ, the masculine objective pronoun, for "it." Thus, the antecedent of the objective pronoun

must be with a masculine noun, in this case הַלֶּחֶם, "the bread" (Mesiach Ilmim).

5. What does the verse tell us by mentioning this "going out"? It could have begun by stating that the son of an Israelite woman fought with an Israelite man (Sefer Zikaron).

6. He left this world, i.e., he committed a sin for which he would die (Sefer Zikaron). Alternatively, he left the World to Come, i.e., he committed a sin for which he lost his portion in the World to Come (Ho'il Moshe).

7. That is, he concluded his study of the above passage which deals with the bread that is put on the Table in the Tabernacle (Be'er Yitzchak).

8. Above v. 8.

9. The bread was baked on Friday, and eaten two Sabbaths later. Hence, the bread was eaten a full week and parts of two days (the Friday on which it was baked and the Sabbath on which it was eaten) after it was baked — nine days (see Menachos 100b).

וְהוּא֙ בֶּן־אִ֣ישׁ מִצְרִ֔י בְּת֖וֹךְ בְּנֵ֣י יִשְׂרָאֵ֑ל וַיִּנָּצוּ֙ בַּֽמַּחֲנֶ֔ה בֶּ֚ן הַיִּשְׂרְאֵלִ֔ית וְאִ֖ישׁ הַיִּשְׂרְאֵלִֽי:

— and he was the son of an Egyptian man — among the Children of Israel; they contended in the camp, the son of the Israelite woman and the Israelite man.

---- אונקלוס ----

וְהוּא בַּר גְּבַר מִצְרַי בְּגוֹ בְּנֵי יִשְׂרָאֵל וּנְצוֹ בְּמַשְׁרִיתָא בַּר אִתְּתָא בַּת יִשְׂרָאֵל וְגַבְרָא בַּר יִשְׂרָאֵל:

---- רש"י ----

בְּתַמְיָה (תנחומא כג; ויק"ר לב:ג). ומתניתא אמרה (ת"כ פרשתא יד:א; תנחומא כד; ויק"ר שם) מבית דינו של משה יצא מחויב. בא ליטע אהלו בתוך מחנה דן, אמרו לו מה טיבך לכאן, אמר להם מבני דן אני. אמרו לו איש על דגלו באותות לבית אבותם כתיב (במדבר ב:ב) נכנס לבית דינו של משה ויצא מחויב, עמד וגדף: **בֶּן אִישׁ מִצְרִי.** הוא המצרי שהרג משה (תנחומא שם; ויק"ר שם ד): **בְּתוֹךְ בְּנֵי יִשְׂרָאֵל.** מלמד שנתגייר (שם): **וַיִּנָּצוּ בַּמַּחֲנֶה.** על עסקי המחנה (שם): **וְאִישׁ הַיִּשְׂרְאֵלִי.** זה שכנגדו:

---- RASHI ELUCIDATED ----

בְּתַמְיָה¹ — He said this **in astonishment.** This irreverent remark was the cause of the fight between him and the Israelite.¹ ² וּמַתְנִיתָא אָמְרָה — **A** *baraisa*² **says:** מִבֵּית דִּינוֹ שֶׁל מֹשֶׁה יָצָא מְחֻיָּב — **He went out of the court of Moses at fault** in the following case: בָּא לִטַּע אָהֳלוֹ — **He came to pitch his tent** בְּתוֹךְ מַחֲנֵה דָן — **in the camp of** the tribe of **Dan.** אָמְרוּ לוֹ — **They said to him,** מַה טִּיבְךָ לְכָאן — **"What is your connection here,** i.e., by what right do you come to pitch your tent here?" אָמַר לָהֶם — **He said to them,** מִבְּנֵי דָן אֲנִי³ — **"I am of the sons of** the tribe of **Dan."**³ אָמְרוּ לוֹ — **They said to him,** ",אִישׁ עַל דִּגְלוֹ בְּאֹתֹת לְבֵית אֲבֹתָם"⁴ — **" 'Each man at his banner, by signs, to their paternal house,** shall the Children of Israel encamp,'**⁴ כְּתִיב — is written.**⁵ נִכְנַס לְבֵית דִּינוֹ שֶׁל מֹשֶׁה — **He entered the court of Moses** to claim the right to pitch his tent in the camp of Dan, וְיָצָא מְחֻיָּב — **and went out** of the court **wanting,** i.e., he lost the case. עָמַד וְגִדֵּף — **He got up and blasphemed.**

☐ בֶּן אִישׁ מִצְרִי — **THE SON OF AN EGYPTIAN MAN.** הוּא הַמִּצְרִי — **He is the Egyptian** שֶׁהָרַג מֹשֶׁה⁶ — whom Moses killed.⁶

☐ בְּתוֹךְ בְּנֵי יִשְׂרָאֵל — **AMONG THE CHILDREN OF ISRAEL.** מְלַמֵּד — **This teaches us** ⁷שֶׁנִּתְגַּיֵּיר — **that he converted.**⁷

☐ וַיִּנָּצוּ בַּמַּחֲנֶה — **THEY CONTENDED IN THE CAMP.**⁸ עַל עִסְקֵי הַמַּחֲנֶה — **Over matters of the camp,** i.e., over his claim to be allowed to pitch his tent in the camp of the tribe of Dan.⁸

☐ וְאִישׁ הַיִּשְׂרְאֵלִי — **AND THE ISRAELITE MAN.** זֶה שֶׁכְּנֶגְדּוֹ — **This [Israelite man] who opposed him,**

---

1. *Midrash Tanchuma* 23; *Vayikra Rabbah* 32:3.

2. *Toras Kohanim, parshasa* 14:1; *Tanchuma* 24; *Vayikra Rabbah* 32:3. A *baraisa* (literally, "outside") is Tannaitic material left out of the Mishnah. In *Toras Kohanim* this *baraisa* is cited anonymously; in *Vayikra Rabbah* it is attributed to the *Tanna* R' Chiya; in *Midrash Tanchuma*, it appears as an Amoraic statement by R' Chama bar Abba.

3. Some early editions read מִבְּנוֹת דָן, "of the daughters of (the tribe of) Dan" (see v. 11; see *Yosef Hallel*). That is also the reading in *Toras Kohanim* and *Vayikra Rabbah*.

4. *Numbers* 2:2.

5. "To their paternal house" implies that only those whose relationship to a tribe derives from their father's side have the right to encamp with that tribe. This individual's claim to membership in the tribe of Dan came only through his mother (*Sefer Zikaron*).

6. *Midrash Tanchuma* 24, *Vayikra Rabbah* 32:4. The Hebrew word מִצְרִי means "Egyptian" and implies a male; an Egyptian woman is called מִצְרִית. The word אִישׁ, "man," in the phrase אִישׁ מִצְרִי is then redundant. Rashi therefore explains that the Torah has previously used this term with reference to the Egyptian killed by Moses. By using בֶּן אִישׁ מִצְרִי, "the son of an Egyptian *man,*" here, the verse teaches that it is referring to the son of that Egyptian (*Gur Aryeh*).

7. *Toras Kohanim, parshasa* 14:1. The verse means to say that although he was "the son of an Egyptian man," he was nonetheless "among the Children of Israel," a Jew (*Be'er Yitzchak*). The child of a Jewish mother and a non-Jewish father is halachically considered a Jew. *Ramban* therefore understands that when Rashi says that this individual converted, it means that he took part in the mass national circumcision and *mikveh* immersion prior to entering the Covenant at Sinai. *Ramban* also cites the opinion of the French Torah sages who hold that the law of matrilineal descent came into effect only after the Torah had been given. Therefore, this individual who was born before the Torah was given was not Jewish until he had converted. *Ramban* himself, however, disagrees with their opinion and holds that this law came into effect at the time of Abraham's circumcision.

8. *Toras Kohanim, parshasa* 14:1. The location of the quarrel seems irrelevant. The verse uses בַּמַּחֲנֶה to teach us the issue over which they quarreled (see *Be'er Yitzchak*).

11 *The son of the Israelite woman pronounced the Name and blasphemed — so they brought him to Moses; the name of his mother was Shelomith the daughter of Dibri, of the tribe of Dan.* **12** *They placed him under guard to clarify*

יא וַיִּקֹּב בֶּן־הָאִשָּׁה הַיִּשְׂרְאֵלִית אֶת־הַשֵּׁם וַיְקַלֵּל וַיָּבִיאוּ אֹתוֹ אֶל־מֹשֶׁה וְשֵׁם אִמּוֹ שְׁלֹמִית בַּת־דִּבְרִי לְמַטֵּה־דָן: יב וַיַּנִּיחֻהוּ בַּמִּשְׁמָר לִפְרֹשׁ

——— אונקלוס ———

יא וּפָרֵשׁ בַּר אִתְּתָא בַּת יִשְׂרָאֵל יָת שְׁמָא וְאַרְגֵּז וְאַיְתִיאוּ יָתֵהּ לְוָת מֹשֶׁה וְשׁוּם אִמֵּהּ שְׁלֹמִית בַּת דִּבְרִי לְשִׁבְטָא דְדָן: יב וְאַסָּרוֹהִי בְּבֵית מַטְּרָא עַד דְּיִתְפָּרַשׁ

——— רש״י ———

שָׂמְחָה בּוֹ מַטֵּה אָהֳלוֹ (שָׁם): (יא) וַיִּקֹּב. כְּתַרְגּוּמוֹ וּפָרֵשׁ, שֶׁנָּקַב שֵׁם הַמְּיֻחָד וְגִדֵּף (סנהדרין נ״ו.), וְהוּא שֵׁם הַמְפֹרָשׁ שֶׁשָּׁמַע מִסִּינַי (ת״כ שָׁם ב׳): וְשֵׁם אִמּוֹ שְׁלֹמִית בַּת דִּבְרִי. שִׁבְחָן שֶׁל יִשְׂרָאֵל שֶׁפִּרְסְמָהּ הַכָּתוּב לוֹמַר שֶׁהִיא לְבַדָּהּ הָיְתָה זוֹנָה (וַיִּקְרָא רַבָּה ל״ב:ה׳): שְׁלֹמִית. דַּהֲוַת פַּטְפְּטָה שְׁלָם עֲלָךְ [שְׁלָם עֲלָךְ] שְׁלָם עֲלֵיכוֹן, מְפַטְפֶּטֶת בְּדִבְרֵי, מְפַטְפֶּטֶת בִּדְבָרִים שׁוֹאֶלֶת בִּשְׁלוֹם הַכֹּל: בַּת דִּבְרִי. דַּבְּרָנִית הָיְתָה, מְדַבֶּרֶת עִם כָּל אָדָם, לְפִיכָךְ קִלְקְלָה: לְמַטֵּה דָן. מַגִּיד שֶׁהָרָשָׁע גּוֹרֵם גְּנַאי לוֹ, גְּנַאי לְאָבִיו, גְּנַאי לְשִׁבְטוֹ. כַּיּוֹצֵא בוֹ אָהֳלִיאָב בֶּן אֲחִיסָמָךְ לְמַטֵּה דָן (שְׁמוֹת לֹא:ו׳) שֶׁבַח לוֹ, שֶׁבַח לְאָבִיו, שֶׁבַח לְשִׁבְטוֹ (ת״כ שָׁם ד׳): (יב) וַיַּנִּיחֻהוּ. לְבַדּוֹ, וְלֹא הִנִּיחוּ מְקֹשֵׁשׁ עִמּוֹ,

——— RASHI ELUCIDATED ———

שָׂמְחָה בּוֹ מַטֵּה אָהֳלוֹ¹ — **who objected against his pitching his tent** in the camp of Dan.¹

11. וַיִּקֹּב — PRONOUNCED. This word is to be understood כְּתַרְגּוּמוֹ — as **Targum** Onkelos **renders it,** וּפָרֵשׁ — "**and he said explicitly,**" שֶׁנָּקַב שֵׁם הַמְּיֻחָד — **for he pronounced the Special Name,** וְגִדֵּף² **— and he cursed.²** וְהוּא שֵׁם הַמְפֹרָשׁ — **It was the Explicit Name** ³שֶׁשָּׁמַע מִסִּינַי — **that he heard at Sinai.**³

□ וְשֵׁם אִמּוֹ שְׁלֹמִית בַּת דִּבְרִי — THE NAME OF HIS MOTHER WAS SHELOMITH DAUGHTER OF DIBRI. Her name is stated to teach שִׁבְחָן שֶׁל יִשְׂרָאֵל — **the praise of Israel,** שֶׁפִּרְסְמָהּ הַכָּתוּב לָזוֹ — for **Scripture publicized this one** לוֹמַר — to say ⁴שֶׁהִיא לְבַדָּהּ הָיְתָה זוֹנָה — **that she alone was a prostitute.**⁴

□ שְׁלֹמִית — SHELOMITH. She is called by this name דַּהֲוַת פַּטְפְּטָה — **for she would chatter,** שְׁלָם עֲלָךְ — **"Peace unto you,"** {שְׁלָם עֲלָךְ} — **"Peace unto you,"**} שְׁלָם עֲלֵיכוֹן — **"Peace unto you";** מְפַטְפֶּטֶת בִּדְבָרִים — **chattering with words,** ⁵שׁוֹאֶלֶת בִּשְׁלוֹם הַכֹּל — **inquiring after everyone's welfare.**⁵

□ בַּת דִּבְרִי — DAUGHTER OF DIBRI. דַּבְּרָנִית הָיְתָה — **She was a chatterbox.** מְדַבֶּרֶת עִם כָּל אָדָם — **She would speak with everybody.** לְפִיכָךְ קִלְקְלָה — **This is why she behaved immorally.**}

□ לְמַטֵּה דָן {בַּת דִּבְרִי} — {DAUGHTER OF DIBRI} OF THE TRIBE OF DAN. מַגִּיד — **This tells us** שֶׁהָרָשָׁע — **that a wicked person** גּוֹרֵם גְּנַאי לוֹ — **causes disgrace to himself,** גְּנַאי לְאָבִיו — **disgrace to his father,** גְּנַאי לְשִׁבְטוֹ — **and disgrace to his tribe.** כַּיּוֹצֵא בוֹ — **In a similar vein we find,** אָהֳלִיאָב בֶּן אֲחִיסָמָךְ — **"Oholiab the son of Ahisamach** ⁶לְמַטֵּה דָן — **of the tribe of Dan.**"⁶ שֶׁבַח לוֹ — **Praise for him,** שֶׁבַח לְאָבִיו — **praise for his father,** ⁷שֶׁבַח לְשִׁבְטוֹ — **praise for his tribe.**⁷

12. וַיַּנִּיחֻהוּ — THEY PLACED HIM לְבַדּוֹ — **by himself.**⁸ וְלֹא הִנִּיחוּ מְקֹשֵׁשׁ עִמּוֹ — **But they did not place**

---

1. *Toras Kohanim, parshasa* 14:1. The verse could have said וְאִישׁ יִשְׂרְאֵלִי, "and *an* Israelite man." It says וְאִישׁ הַיִּשְׂרְאֵלִי, "and *the* Israelite man," to teach us that it was an individual who had a role in the incident prior to the fight.

2. *Sanhedrin* 55b 56a.

3. *Toras Kohanim, parshasa* 14:2. This was the Tetragrammaton. We pronounce it as a form of the word אֲדֹנָי, "Lord," but this is not its authentic pronunciation. The son of the Egyptian heard the authentic pronunciation "at Sinai" (see *Nachalas Yaakov*; see also Rashi to v. 16 below and note 7 there).

4. *Vayikra Rabbah* 32:5. Shelomith bas Dibri was not a prostitute by occupation, nor did she have relations with the Egyptian intentionally, as Rashi has stated in his comments to *Exodus* 2:11. She is referred to as "a prostitute" because the Egyptian who had relations with her desired her due to her immodest behavior, which Rashi describes in his following comment (*Levush HaOrah*).

5. *Vayikra Rabbah* 32:5. Rashi interprets the name Shelomith daughter of Dibri as indicating the flaw in her behavior that led to her unwitting sin. Shelomith is related to שָׁלוֹם, the greeting "peace." Dibri is related to דְּבָרִים, "words" (see Rashi's next comment). As her name suggests, she was guilty of speaking with too many men, and being too free with her greetings. See *Kesubos* 72a, where the Mishnah condemns such behavior. See also Rashi to *Hosea* 1:3, where he interprets the name of an immoral woman in a similar manner.

6. *Exodus* 31:6. This verse mentions Oholiab's appointment as Bezalel's assistant in the construction of the Tabernacle.

7. *Toras Kohanim, parshasa* 14:4.

8. "They placed him under guard" could have been expressed by וַיִּתְּנֻהוּ בַּמִּשְׁמָר (as *II Kings* 22:9). The verb וַיַּנִּיחֻהוּ carries with it the connotation of abandonment in

for them through H‑ASHEM. לָהֶם עַל־פִּי יהוה:

¹³ HASHEM *spoke to Moses, saying:* ¹⁴ *Re‑* יג וַיְדַבֵּר יהוה אֶל־מֹשֶׁה לֵּאמֹר:
move the blasphemer to the outside of the יד הוֹצֵא אֶת־הַמְקַלֵּל אֶל־מִחוּץ
camp, and all those who heard shall lean לַמַּחֲנֶה וְסָמְכוּ כָל־הַשֹּׁמְעִים

— אונקלוס —

לְהוֹן עַל גְּזֵרַת מֵימְרָא דַיָי: יג וּמַלִּיל יְיָ עִם מֹשֶׁה לְמֵימָר: יד אַפֵּק יָת
דְּאַרְגֵּז לְמִבָּרָא לְמַשְׁרִיתָא וְיִסְמְכוּן כָּל דְּשָׁמְעִין (נ״א דִּשְׁמָעוּ)

— רש״י —

שֶׁשְּׁנֵיהֶם הָיוּ בְּפֶרֶק אֶחָד, וְיוֹדְעִים הָיוּ שֶׁהַמְקוֹשֵׁשׁ בְּמִיתָה שֶׁנֶּאֱמַר   בַּמְקַלֵּל הוּא אוֹמֵר לִפְרֹשׁ לָהֶם, שֶׁלֹּא הָיוּ יוֹדְעִים אִם חַיָּב
מְחַלְלֶיהָ מוֹת יוּמָת (שמות לא:יד) אֲבָל לֹא פּוֹרַשׁ לָהֶם בְּאֵיזוֹ   מִיתָה אִם לָאו (ת״כ שם ה; סנהדרין עח:): (יד) הַשֹּׁמְעִים. אֵלּוּ
מִיתָה, לְכָךְ נֶאֱמַר כִּי לֹא פֹרַשׁ מַה יֵּעָשֶׂה לוֹ (במדבר טו:לד). אֲבָל   הָעֵדִים (שם פרק יט:א): כָּל. לְהָבִיא אֶת הַדַּיָּנִין (שם):

— RASHI ELUCIDATED —

the one who gathered wood on Shabbos¹ under guard *with him* שֶׁשְּׁנֵיהֶם הָיוּ בְּפֶרֶק אֶחָד — *for both of [the incidents] occurred at the same time.*² שֶׁהַמְקוֹשֵׁשׁ בְּמִיתָה — *They were aware* וְיוֹדְעִים הָיוּ — *that the one who gathered* wood was to receive the death penalty, שֶׁנֶּאֱמַר — *as it says,* ,,מְחַלְלֶיהָ מוֹת יוּמָת'',³ — *"those who desecrate it shall be put to death,"*³ אֲבָל לֹא פּוֹרַשׁ לָהֶם — *but it had not been made clear to them* בְּאֵיזוֹ מִיתָה — *through which death penalty* he should be put to death.⁴ לְכָךְ נֶאֱמַר — *This is why it says,* ,,כִּי לֹא פֹרַשׁ מַה יֵּעָשֶׂה לוֹ'',⁵ — *"for what was to be done to him had not been clarified."*⁵ אֲבָל בַּמְקַלֵּל הוּא אוֹמֵר — *But with regard to the one who cursed, it says* in our verse, ,,לִפְרֹשׁ לָהֶם'', — *"to clarify for them,"* שֶׁלֹּא הָיוּ יוֹדְעִים — *for they did not know* אִם חַיָּב מִיתָה⁶ — *if he deserved the death penalty* אִם לָאו — *or not.*⁶

14. הַשֹּׁמְעִים — THOSE WHO HEARD. ⁷אֵלּוּ הָעֵדִים — *These are the witnesses.*⁷

□ כָּל — ALL. לְהָבִיא אֶת הַדַּיָּנִין — *To include the judges.*⁸

---

solitude (*Be'er BaSadeh*; compare to *Genesis* 39:20, 40:3, 42:17).

1. See *Numbers* 15:32-36.

2. "For both of [the incidents] occurred at the same time" explains why we may have thought that they had been imprisoned together. Rashi goes on to explain why they were not.

3. *Exodus* 31:14.

4. At the time that the wood gatherer committed his sin, the nation had already been informed that desecration of Shabbos carries the death penalty. Although any death penalty given by the Torah without further specification is taken to mean strangulation (see Rashi to 20:10 above), there was nonetheless doubt in this situation. For implicit in desecration of Shabbos is denial that God created the universe; hence, it might be seen as a form of idolatry, and idolatry is punished by death through stoning (*Tosafos* to *Sanhedrin* 78b, s.v., לא היו יודעין באיזה מיתה; *Minchas Yehudah; Sifsei Chachamim*).

5. *Numbers* 15:34.

6. *Toras Kohanim*, *parshasa* 14:5; *Sanhedrin* 78b. "For what was to be done to him had not been clarified" implies that they knew that *something* had to be done, but they did not know *what* had to be done. "To clarify for them" implies that they did not know if any punishment was to be administered at all (*Be'er Yitzhak*). This difference between the two cases explains why the two sinners were not confined together.

If the one who cursed were not subject to the death penalty, he would suffer unnecessary worry if he were confined together with the one who gathered wood on Shabbos, for he might fear that he would share the same fate as his companion (*Minchas Yehudah; Sifsei Chachamim*).

Alternatively, one who is not subject to the death penalty is not imprisoned with one who is, for just as evildoers of different degrees are not buried together (see *Sanhedrin* 46a), so too, evildoers of different degrees are not imprisoned together (*Nachalas Yaakov*). Similarly, the generation of the Exodus (דּוֹר הַמִּדְבָּר) was buried in the same desert as Moses and Aaron. Moses requested that each time his or his brother's death is mentioned, their sin should be mentioned also, lest they be suspected of having joined in the sin of their generation (see Rashi to *Numbers* 27:13).

7. *Toras Kohanim*, *perek* 19:1. "Those who heard" means those who actually heard the curse, not those who heard of the incident (*Be'er Yitzhak*).

8. *Toras Kohanim*, *perek* 19:1. The placing of hands is accompanied by a statement of their own blamelessness for the death of the sinner, as Rashi mentions in his following comment. Had it not been for כָּל, we would have said that the witnesses must state that they are blameless, for the death of the sinner is the direct result of their evidence, but the judges, who are not involved in the same measure, need not. כָּל teaches us that the judges, too, must make this statement.

their hands upon his head: The entire assembly shall stone him. ¹⁵ *And to the Children of Israel you shall speak, saying: Any man who will blaspheme his God shall bear his sin;* ¹⁶ *and one who pronounces blasphemously the Name of* HASHEM *shall be put to death, the entire assembly shall surely pelt him with stones; proselyte and native alike, when he blasphemes the Name, he shall be put to death.*

אֶת־יְדֵיהֶ֖ם עַל־רֹאשׁ֑וֹ וְרָגְמ֥וּ
אֹת֖וֹ כָּל־הָעֵדָֽה: טו וְאֶל־בְּנֵ֥י יִשְׂרָאֵ֖ל
תְּדַבֵּ֣ר לֵאמֹ֑ר אִ֣ישׁ אִ֗ישׁ כִּֽי־
יְקַלֵּ֥ל אֱלֹהָ֖יו וְנָשָׂ֥א חֶטְאֽוֹ: טז וְנֹקֵ֤ב שֵׁם־יְהוָֹה֙ מ֣וֹת יוּמָ֔ת
רָג֥וֹם יִרְגְּמוּ־ב֖וֹ כָּל־הָעֵדָ֑ה
כַּגֵּר֙ כָּֽאֶזְרָ֔ח בְּנָקְבוֹ־שֵׁ֖ם יוּמָֽת:

— אונקלוס —

יָת יְדֵיהוֹן עַל רֵישֵׁהּ וְיִרְגְּמוּן יָתֵהּ כָּל כְּנִשְׁתָּא: טו וְעִם בְּנֵי יִשְׂרָאֵל תְּמַלֵּל לְמֵימָר גְּבַר גְּבַר דִּי יְרַגֵּז קֳדָם אֱלָהֵהּ וִיקַבֵּל חוֹבֵהּ: טז וְדִיפָרֵשׁ שְׁמָא דַּיְיָ אִתְקְטָלָא יִתְקְטֵל מִרְגַם יִרְגְּמוּן בֵּהּ כָּל כְּנִשְׁתָּא כְּגִיּוֹרָא כְּיַצִּיבָא בְּפָרָשׁוּתֵהּ שְׁמָא יִתְקְטֵל:

— רש"י —

אֶת יְדֵיהֶם. אוֹמְרִים לוֹ דָּמְךָ בְרֹאשְׁךָ וְאֵין אָנוּ נֶעֱנָשִׁים בְּמִיתָתְךָ שֶׁאַתָּה גָּרַמְתָּ לָךְ (שם ב): **כָּל הָעֵדָה.** בְּמַעֲמַד כָּל הָעֵדָה (שם ג) [מִכָּאן] שֶׁשְּׁלוּחוֹ שֶׁל אָדָם כְּמוֹתוֹ (קידושין מא.): (טו) **וְנָשָׂא חֶטְאוֹ.** בְּכָרֵת (ת"כ שם ו) כְּשֶׁאֵין הַתְרָאָה: (טז) **וְנֹקֵב שֵׁם.** אֵינוֹ חַיָּב עַד שֶׁיְּפָרֵשׁ אֶת הַשֵּׁם, וְלֹא הַמְקַלֵּל בְּכִנּוּי (שם ה; סנהדרין נו.): **וְנֹקֵב.** לְשׁוֹן קְלָלָה, כְּמוֹ מָה אֶקֹּב (במדבר כג:ח):

— RASHI ELUCIDATED —

□ אֶת יְדֵיהֶם — THEIR HANDS. אוֹמְרִים לוֹ — They say to him, דָּמְךָ בְרֹאשְׁךָ — "Your blood is on your head, i.e., you are to blame for your own death, וְאֵין אָנוּ נֶעֱנָשִׁים — and we do not suffer punishment בְּמִיתָתְךָ — through your death, שֶׁאַתָּה גָּרַמְתָּ לָךְ — for you caused it to yourself."[1]

□ כָּל הָעֵדָה — THE ENTIRE ASSEMBLY. בְּמַעֲמַד כָּל הָעֵדָה[2] — In a convocation of the entire assembly.[2] כְּמוֹתוֹ[3] — From here we have a source for the rule} שֶׁשְּׁלוּחוֹ שֶׁל אָדָם — that a person's agent — is like him.[3]

15. וְנָשָׂא חֶטְאוֹ — SHALL BEAR HIS SIN. בְּכָרֵת[4] — Through kares[4] כְּשֶׁאֵין הַתְרָאָה — when there is no warning immediately prior to the sin.[5]

16. וְנֹקֵב שֵׁם — ONE WHO PRONOUNCES BLASPHEMOUSLY THE NAME. אֵינוֹ חַיָּב — He is not liable to stoning עַד שֶׁיְּפָרֵשׁ אֶת הַשֵּׁם — unless he makes explicit mention of the Name,[6] וְלֹא הַמְקַלֵּל בְּכִנּוּי[7] — but not one who curses with an alternative name of God.[7]

□ {וְנֹקֵב} — ONE WHO PRONOUNCES BLASPHEMOUSLY. לְשׁוֹן קְלָלָה — This word means "cursing," כְּמוֹ — like אֶקֹּב in, "How can I curse?"[8] מָה אֶקֹּב,,

---

1. *Toras Kohanim*, perek 19:2.

2. *Toras Kohanim*, perek 19:3.

3. *Kiddushin* 41b. Rashi's comment appears self-contradictory. He starts by saying that "the entire assembly" means before a convocation of the entire assembly, because the entire assembly did not do the stoning. He then goes on to say that our verse is based on the principle that a person's agent is considered as himself, implying that in a legal sense, the entire assembly *did* do the stoning. Yosef Hallel notes that various sources and alternative texts of Rashi contain either "in a convocation of the entire assembly," or "that a person's agent is like him," but not both, indicating that these are two alternative interpretations presented by Rashi, probably originally set off from each other by דָּבָר אַחֵר.

4. *Toras Kohanim*, perek 19:6. Rashi defines *kares* in his comments to 17:9 above.

5. See Rashi to 20:27 above.

6. But if he hears someone else pronounce God's Name, and he curses it, he is exempt from the death penalty (Rashi to *Sanhedrin* 55b, s.v., עד שיפרש את השם).

7. *Toras Kohanim*, perek 19:5; *Sanhedrin* 56a. It is only for cursing the Tetragrammaton with the Tetragrammaton, i.e., if one says, "May [that Name] curse [that Name]," for which the Torah assigns the punishment of stoning. Cursing with other Divine Names, although they may be forbidden to be erased, does not carry this punishment. This is implied by the term שֵׁם ה׳, "Name of HASHEM." When God spoke to Moses of His Name in *Exodus* 3:15, He referred to the Tetragrammaton (see Rashi to that verse and to *Sanhedrin* 56a, s.v., על שם המיוחד).

8. *Numbers* 23:8. Rashi here explains וְנֹקֵב as "cursing," in line with the interpretation of the *Amora* Shmuel in *Sanhedrin* 56a. This is unlike Targum Onkelos here who sees it as having the same meaning as וַיִּקֹּב in verse 11 above, "to pronounce explicitly." In that verse, the word וַיְקַלֵּל, which can only refer to cursing, also

¹⁷ And a man, if he strikes mortally any human life, he shall be put to death. ¹⁸ And a man who strikes mortally an animal life shall make restitution, a life for a life. ¹⁹ And if a man inflicts a wound in his fellow, as he did, so shall be done to him: ²⁰ a break for a break, an eye for an eye, a tooth for a tooth; just as he will have inflicted a wound on a person, so shall be inflicted upon him. ²¹ One who strikes an animal shall make restitution for it, and one who strikes a person shall be put to death.

יז וְאִישׁ כִּי יַכֶּה כָּל־נֶפֶשׁ אָדָם מוֹת
יח יוּמָת: וּמַכֵּה נֶפֶשׁ־בְּהֵמָה יְשַׁלְּמֶנָּה
יט נֶפֶשׁ תַּחַת נָפֶשׁ: וְאִישׁ כִּי־יִתֵּן מוּם
בַּעֲמִיתוֹ כַּאֲשֶׁר עָשָׂה כֵּן יֵעָשֶׂה
כ לּוֹ: שֶׁבֶר תַּחַת שֶׁבֶר עַיִן תַּחַת עַיִן
שֵׁן תַּחַת שֵׁן כַּאֲשֶׁר יִתֵּן מוּם
כא בָּאָדָם כֵּן יִנָּתֶן בּוֹ: מפטיר וּמַכֵּה
בְהֵמָה יְשַׁלְּמֶנָּה וּמַכֵּה אָדָם יוּמָת:

──────── אונקלוס ────────

יז וּגְבַר אֲרֵי יִקְטוֹל כָּל נַפְשָׁא דַאֲנָשָׁא אִתְקְטָלָא יִתְקְטֵל: יח וּדְיִקְטוֹל נֶפֶשׁ בְּעִירָא יְשַׁלְּמִנַּהּ נַפְשָׁא חֲלָף נַפְשָׁא:
יט וּגְבַר אֲרֵי יִתֵּן מוּמָא בְחַבְרֵהּ כְּמָא דִי עֲבַד כֵּן יִתְעֲבֵד לֵהּ: כ תַּבְרָא חֲלָף תַּבְרָא עֵינָא חֲלָף עֵינָא שִׁנָּא חֲלָף
שִׁנָּא כְּמָא דְיִתֵּן מוּמָא בֶאֱנָשָׁא כֵּן יִתְיְהֵב בֵּהּ: כא וּדְיִקְטוֹל בְּעִירָא יְשַׁלְּמִנַּהּ וּדְיִקְטוֹל אֲנָשָׁא יִתְקְטֵל:

──────── רש"י ────────

(יז) וְאִישׁ כִּי יַכֶּה. לְפִי שֶׁנֶּאֱמַר מַכֵּה אִישׁ וְגוֹ' (שמות כא:יב) אֵין לִי מִיַּד לְיַד (ב"ק פד.): (כא) וּמַכֵּה בְהֵמָה יְשַׁלְּמֶנָּה. לְמַעְלָה דִבֵּר
אֶלָּא שֶׁהָרַג אֶת אִישׁ, אִשָּׁה וְקָטָן מִנַּיִן, ת"ל כָּל נֶפֶשׁ אָדָם (ת"כ פרק בַּהֲרִיגָה בִבְהֵמָה וְכָאן בַּעֲשִׂיַּת בָּהּ חַבּוּרָה: וּמַכֵּה אָדָם יוּמָת.
כ:ח): (כ) בֵּן יִנָּתֶן בּוֹ. פֵּרְשׁוּ רַבּוֹתֵינוּ שֶׁאֵינוֹ נְתִינַת מוּם מַמָּשׁ אֶלָּא אֲפִלּוּ לֹא הֲרָגוֹ אֶלָּא עָשָׂה בּוֹ חַבּוּרָה, שֶׁלֹּא נֶאֱמַר כָּאן נֶפֶשׁ. וּמַכֵּה
תַּשְׁלוּמֵי מָמוֹן, שָׁמִין אוֹתוֹ כְּעֶבֶד, לְכָךְ כָּתוּב בּוֹ לְשׁוֹן נְתִינָה, דָּבָר הַנִּתּוֹן אָבִיו וְאִמּוֹ וְאָמַר דָּבָר הַכָּתוּב, וּבָא לְהַקִּישׁ לְמַכֵּה בְהֵמָה, מַה מַכֵּה בְהֵמָה

──────── RASHI ELUCIDATED ────────

17. וְאִישׁ כִּי יַכֶּה — AND A MAN, IF HE STRIKES. — לְפִי שֶׁנֶּאֱמַר — Since it says,[1] "מַכֵּה אִישׁ וְגוֹמֵר״ — "one who strikes a man, etc.,"[1] — אֵין לִי אֶלָּא — I know only — שֶׁהָרַג אֶת אִישׁ — that if he killed **a man** he is put to death. אִשָּׁה וְקָטָן מִנַּיִן — From where do we know that he is put to death if he killed **a woman or a minor?** — תַּלְמוּד לוֹמַר — To provide this source, **the verse says,** [2] ״כָּל נֶפֶשׁ אָדָם״ — **"any human life."**[2]

20. כֵּן יִנָּתֶן בּוֹ — SO SHALL BE INFLICTED UPON HIM. — פֵּרְשׁוּ רַבּוֹתֵינוּ — Our Rabbis explained שֶׁאֵינוֹ נְתִינַת מוּם מַמָּשׁ — that it is not, i.e., that this does not mean, **actually inflicting a blemish,** אֶלָּא תַּשְׁלוּמֵי מָמוֹן — but, rather, **monetary payment.** שָׁמִין אוֹתוֹ — **They assess [the injured party]** כְּעֶבֶד — **as a slave,** and estimate how much his value as a slave decreased as a result of his injury. לְכָךְ כָּתוּב בּוֹ לְשׁוֹן נְתִינָה — **That is why** יִנָּתֶן, an expression of נְתִינָה, whose most common meaning is "giving," **was written with regard to it,** to suggest [3] דָּבָר הַנִּתּוֹן מִיַּד לְיָד — **a thing which is given from hand to hand,** i.e., money.[3]

21. וּמַכֵּה בְהֵמָה יְשַׁלְּמֶנָּה — ONE WHO STRIKES AN ANIMAL SHALL MAKE RESTITUTION FOR IT. — לְמַעְלָה — Above,[4] דִּבֵּר בַּעֲשִׂיַּת בָּהּ חַבּוּרָה — it spoke of killing an animal, וְכָאן — and here — דִּבֵּר בְּהוֹרֵג בְּהֵמָה — it speaks of making a wound in it.

□ וּמַכֵּה אָדָם יוּמָת — AND ONE WHO STRIKES A PERSON SHALL BE PUT TO DEATH. — אֲפִלּוּ לֹא הֲרָגוֹ — Even **if he did not kill him,** אֶלָּא — but, rather, עָשָׂה בּוֹ חַבּוּרָה — he bruised him, שֶׁלֹּא נֶאֱמַר כָּאן ״נֶפֶשׁ״ — for נֶפֶשׁ, "mortally," is not stated here, as it is in verse 17 which speaks of killing. וּמַכֵּה אָבִיו וְאִמּוֹ — and it comes וּבָא לְהַקִּישׁ — The verse speaks of one who strikes his father or mother, דָּבָר הַכָּתוּב — and it comes to compare him לְמַכֵּה בְהֵמָה — to one who strikes an animal, as follows: מַה מַכֵּה בְהֵמָה — Just as

---

appeared. Hence Rashi followed *Targum Onkelos* in defining וַיִּקֹּב as other than cursing. But here, where no other word for cursing is used, Rashi chooses to follow the interpretation of the *Gemara* (see *Yosef Hallel*).

1. *Exodus* 21:12. See Rashi to that verse for a lengthy discussion of these two verses.

2. *Toras Kohanim*, perek 20:1.

3. *Bava Kamma* 84a. Had the Torah meant that the one who inflicted the injury should actually have injury inflicted upon him, it would have again used the same phrase here it used in the preceding verse, כֵּן יֵעָשֶׂה לוֹ, "so shall be done to him." The Torah substitutes the verb נתן, "to give," for עשה, "to do," to allude to payment of money (*Gur Aryeh*).

4. Verse 18 above.

315 / VAYIKRA/LEVITICUS — PARASHAS EMOR — 24/22-23

²² There shall be one law for you, it shall be for proselyte and native alike, for I, HASHEM, am your God.
²³ Moses spoke to the Children of Israel, and they took the blasphemer to the outside of the camp, and they pelted him with stones; and the Children of Israel did as HASHEM had commanded Moses.

כב מִשְׁפַּ֤ט אֶחָד֙ יִהְיֶ֣ה לָכֶ֔ם כַּגֵּ֥ר כָּאֶזְרָ֖ח יִהְיֶ֑ה כִּ֛י אֲנִ֥י יהו֖ה אֱלֹהֵיכֶֽם: כג וַיְדַבֵּ֣ר מֹשֶׁה֮ אֶל־בְּנֵ֣י יִשְׂרָאֵל֒ וַיּוֹצִ֣יאוּ אֶת־הַֽמְקַלֵּ֗ל אֶל־מִחוּץ֙ לַֽמַּחֲנֶ֔ה וַיִּרְגְּמ֥וּ אֹת֖וֹ אָ֑בֶן וּבְנֵֽי־יִשְׂרָאֵ֣ל עָשׂ֔וּ כַּאֲשֶׁ֛ר צִוָּ֥ה יהו֖ה אֶת־מֹשֶֽׁה: פ פ פ

THE HAFTARAH FOR EMOR APPEARS ON PAGE 400.

— אונקלוס —

כב דִּינָא חַד יְהֵי לְכוֹן בְּגִיּוֹרָא כְיַצִּיבָא יְהֵי אֲרֵי אֲנָא יְיָ אֱלָהֲכוֹן: כג וּמַלִּיל מֹשֶׁה עִם בְּנֵי יִשְׂרָאֵל וְאַפִּיקוּ יָת דְּאַרְגֵּז לְמִבְרָא לְמַשְׁרִיתָא וּרְגָמוּ יָתֵהּ אַבְנָא וּבְנֵי יִשְׂרָאֵל עֲבַדוּ כְּמָא דִי פַקִּיד יְיָ יָת מֹשֶׁה.

— רש״י —

מחיים אף מכה אביו [ואמו] מחיים, פרט למכה לאחר מיתה. [לפי שמליגו שהמקללו לאחר מיתה חייב הוצרך לומר במכה שפטור.] ומה בבהמה בחבלה, שאם אין חבלה אין תשלומין, אף מכה אביו [ואמו] אינו חייב עד שיעשה בו [שו״א בהם] חבורה (ת״כ פרק כ:ח): **(כב) אני ה׳ אלהיכם.** אלהי כולכם כשם שאני מיחד שמי עליכם כך אני מיחדו על הגרים: **(כג) ובני ישראל עשו.** כל המצוה האמורה בסקילה במקום אחר, דחייה, רגימה ותלייה (דברים כא:כב; ת״כ שם י):

— RASHI ELUCIDATED —

מֵחַיִּים — while it was **alive,**[1] **one who strikes an animal** is to be punished only if he struck it **אַף מַכֵּה** {וְאִמּוֹ} **אָבִיו — so, too,** when the Torah speaks of **one who strikes his father** {**or his mother**} being punished with death, **מֵחַיִּים —** it means that he strikes him **while** he is **alive, פְּרָט לְמַכֶּה לְאַחַר מִיתָה — to the exclusion of one who strikes** a parent **after death.** {**לְפִי שֶׁמָּצִינוּ — Since we have found** **שֶׁהַמְקַלְּלוֹ לְאַחַר מִיתָה חַיָּב — that one who curses [a parent] after** the parent's **death חַיָּב — is liable to** the death penalty,[2] **הֻצְרַךְ לוֹמַר — it had to say בְּמַכֶּה — about one who strikes** a parent after death **שֶׁפָּטוּר — that he is exempt** from the death penalty.[3]} **וּמָה בִּבְהֵמָה — And** we also learn from this comparison that **just as** regarding the animal **בְּחַבָּלָה — the** Torah speaks **about injury, שֶׁאִם אֵין חַבָּלָה — for if there is no injury אֵין תַּשְׁלוּמִין — there is no payment, אַף — so, too, מַכֶּה אָבִיו** {**וְאִמּוֹ**} — **one who strikes his father** {**or his mother**} **אֵינוֹ חַיָּב — is not liable** to the death penalty **עַד שֶׁיַּעֲשֶׂה בּוֹ** {**בָּהֶם**} **חַבּוּרָה — until he bruises him** {**them**}.[4]

22. אֲנִי ה׳ אֱלֹהֵיכֶם — I AM HASHEM, YOUR GOD. אֱלֹהֵי כֻּלְּכֶם — The God of all of you. כְּשֵׁם שֶׁאֲנִי מְיֻחָד — Just as I associate My Name uniquely upon you, שְׁמִי עֲלֵיכֶם — כָּךְ אֲנִי מְיַחֲדוֹ עַל הַגֵּרִים — so do I associate My Name uniquely upon the proselytes.

23. וּבְנֵי יִשְׂרָאֵל עָשׂוּ — AND THE CHILDREN OF ISRAEL DID כָּל הַמִּצְוָה — the entire commandment הָאֲמוּרָה בִסְקִילָה — that is stated regarding stoning בְּמָקוֹם אַחֵר — in another place, i.e., all the commandments stated with regard to stoning in other sources, namely: **דְּחִיָּה — pushing** the one being executed off a high place,[5] **רְגִימָה — stoning,** [6,7] **וּתְלִיָּה — and hanging** the corpse.[6,7]

---

1. For if the animal were dead, the Torah would not demand payment for striking it.
2. See 20:9 above and Rashi there.
3. Although one who strikes the corpse of a parent does not receive the death penalty, it is nonetheless a gross violation of the commandment to honor parents, for which one cannot escape punishment (*Mesiach Ilmim*).
4. *Toras Kohanim*, perek 20:8.
5. See *Exodus* 19:13 and Rashi there.
6. See *Deuteronomy* 21:22 and Rashi there, and *Sanhedrin* 45b. The verse has already said, "and they pelted him with stones." "And the Children of Israel did as HASHEM commanded Moses" appears redundant. Rashi explains that it refers to aspects of the procedure not mentioned by our verse (*Nachalas Yaakov*).
7. *Toras Kohanim*, perek 20:10.

פרשת בהר
Parashas Behar

25

¹ Hashem spoke to Moses on Mount Sinai, saying: **²** Speak to the Children of Israel and say to them: When you come into the land that I give you, the land shall observe a Sabbath rest for Hashem.

כה א וַיְדַבֵּר יהוה אֶל־מֹשֶׁה בְּהַר סִינַי לֵאמֹר: ב דַּבֵּר אֶל־בְּנֵי יִשְׂרָאֵל וְאָמַרְתָּ אֲלֵהֶם כִּי תָבֹאוּ אֶל־הָאָרֶץ אֲשֶׁר אֲנִי נֹתֵן לָכֶם וְשָׁבְתָה הָאָרֶץ שַׁבָּת לַיהוה:

אונקלוס

א וּמַלִּיל יְיָ עִם מֹשֶׁה בְּטוּרָא דְסִינַי לְמֵימָר: ב מַלֵּל עִם בְּנֵי יִשְׂרָאֵל וְתֵימַר לְהוֹן אֲרֵי תֵעֲלוּן לְאַרְעָא דִּי אֲנָא יָהֵב לְכוֹן וְתַשְׁמֵט אַרְעָא שְׁמִטְתָא קֳדָם יְיָ:

רש"י

(א) בהר סיני. מה ענין שמיטה אצל הר סיני והלא כל המצות נאמרו מסיני, אלא מה שמיטה נאמרו כללותיה [ופרטותיה] ודקדוקיה מסיני, אף כולן נאמרו כללותיהן ודקדוקיהן מסיני. כך שנויה בת"כ (פרשתא א:א). ונראה לי שכך פירושה, לפי שלא מצינו שמיטת קרקעות שנשנית בערבות מואב במשנה תורה, למדנו שכללותיה ופרטותיה [ס"א ופירושיה] כולן נאמרו מסיני, ובא הכתוב ולמד כאן על כל דבור שנדבר למשה שמסיני היו כולם, כללותיהן ודקדוקיהן, וחזרו ונשנו בערבות מואב: **(ב) שבת לה'.** כשם שנאמר בשבת בראשית (שמות כ"כ פרק א:כב):

RASHI ELUCIDATED

25.

1. בְּהַר סִינָי — ON MOUNT SINAI. מָה עִנְיַן שְׁמִטָּה אֵצֶל הַר סִינַי — **What is the matter of *shemittah*¹ doing next to Mount Sinai,** i.e., why does the Torah say "on Mount Sinai" specifically in the context of the laws of *shemittah* as opposed to other laws? וַהֲלֹא כָּל הַמִּצְוֹת נֶאֶמְרוּ מִסִּינַי — **Were not all of the commandments stated at Sinai?** אֶלָּא — **But,** it is written here to teach that מָה שְׁמִטָּה — **just as** with *shemittah* נֶאֶמְרוּ כְּלָלוֹתֶיהָ {וּפְרָטוֹתֶיהָ} וְדִקְדּוּקֶיהָ מִסִּינַי — **its general rules, {and its details,} and its fine points were stated at Sinai,** אַף כֻּלָּן — **so, too,** with all of [the commandments], נֶאֶמְרוּ כְּלָלוֹתֵיהֶן וְדִקְדּוּקֵיהֶן מִסִּינַי — **their general rules and their fine points were stated at Sinai.** כָּךְ שְׁנוּיָה בְּתוֹרַת כֹּהֲנִים² — **Thus is it taught in *Toras Kohanim*.²** וְנִרְאֶה לִי — **And it appears to me** שֶׁכָּךְ פֵּרוּשָׁהּ — **that this is its explanation:** לְפִי שֶׁלֹּא מָצִינוּ — **Since we do not find** שְׁמִטַּת קַרְקָעוֹת — a passage on *shemittah* of lands³ שֶׁנִּשְׁנֵית בְּעַרְבוֹת מוֹאָב — **which was repeated at the Plains of Moab⁴** בְּמִשְׁנֵה תוֹרָה,⁵ — **in *Mishneh Torah*,⁵** לָמַדְנוּ — **we have learned** שֶׁכְּלָלוֹתֶיהָ וּפְרָטוֹתֶיהָ⁶ כֻּלָּן נֶאֶמְרוּ מִסִּינַי — **that its general rules and its details⁶ were all stated at Sinai.** וּבָא הַכָּתוּב וְלִמֵּד כָּאן — **And Scripture comes and teaches us here** עַל כָּל דִּבּוּר שֶׁנִּדְבַּר לְמֹשֶׁה — about every statement that was communicated to Moses, i.e., all the commandments he was given, שֶׁמִּסִּינַי הָיוּ כֻלָּם — **that they were all from Sinai,** בִּכְלָלוֹתֵיהֶן וְדִקְדּוּקֵיהֶן — both **their general rules and their fine points,** וְחָזְרוּ וְנִשְׁנוּ בְּעַרְבוֹת מוֹאָב — **and they were repeated and reiterated at the Plains of Moab.⁷**

2. שַׁבָּת לַה' — A SABBATH REST FOR HASHEM. לְשֵׁם ה' — **For the sake of Hashem,⁸** כְּשֵׁם שֶׁנֶּאֱמַר בְּשַׁבָּת בְּרֵאשִׁית⁹,¹⁰ — **just as** it is said with regard to **the Sabbath of Creation,** i.e., the weekly Sabbath.⁹,¹⁰

---

1. Literally, "release." The seventh year of the seven-year cycle of laws pertaining to agriculture in the Land of Israel. The laws of that year include: "release" of fields, i.e., refraining from working them; allowing their produce to be taken by the public; and "release" of debts.

2. *Toras Kohanim, parshasa* 1·1

3. The law against working the fields during the seventh year. The law of release of debts during the seventh year, as opposed to the law of release of fields, is mentioned in *Deuteronomy* 15:1-2.

4. Rashi mentions the location at which Moses gave the Book of *Deuteronomy* to the Israelites by way of contrast to Mount Sinai.

5. Literally, "repetition of the Torah" (see *Metzudas David* to *Joshua* 8:32), an alternative name for the Book of *Deuteronomy*, which contains many repetitions of commandments found elsewhere in the Torah.

6. Some editions read וּפֵרוּשֶׁיהָ, "and its explanations" (see *Yosef Hallel*).

7. The law of "release" of fields on the seventh year was not repeated in the Book of *Deuteronomy*; we would assume, without being told so, that its laws must have all been given at Mount Sinai. The Torah nonetheless states the apparently superfluous בְּהַר סִינַי, "on Mount Sinai," to indicate to us that this law is to be viewed as a בִּנְיָן אָב, a paradigm from which to draw a general rule for all commandments — just as the law of release of fields on the seventh year was given at Sinai in full detail, so too all the other commandments, even those repeated in the Book of *Deuteronomy*, were given at Sinai (*Sefer Zikaron*).

8. The verse does not mean that it is a time when God rests (*Gur Aryeh*).

9. See *Exodus* 20:10. Just as we keep the weekly Sabbath to commemorate God's Creation of the world, so too we desist from agricultural work on the seventh year to commemorate God's act of Creation (*Mizrachi*).

10. *Toras Kohanim, perek* 1:2.

³ *For six years you may sow your field and for six years you may prune your vineyard; and you may gather in its crop.* ⁴ *But on the seventh year a complete rest there shall be for the land, a Sabbath for H*ASHEM; *your field you shall not sow and your vineyard you shall not prune.* ⁵ *The aftergrowth of your harvest you shall not reap and the grapes of your keeping away you shall not*

ג שֵׁשׁ שָׁנִים תִּזְרַע שָׂדֶךָ וְשֵׁשׁ שָׁנִים תִּזְמֹר כַּרְמֶךָ וְאָסַפְתָּ אֶת־תְּבוּאָתָהּ: ד וּבַשָּׁנָה הַשְּׁבִיעִת שַׁבַּת שַׁבָּתוֹן יִהְיֶה לָאָרֶץ שַׁבָּת לַיהוה שָׂדְךָ לֹא תִזְרָע וְכַרְמְךָ לֹא תִזְמֹר: ה אֵת סְפִיחַ קְצִירְךָ לֹא תִקְצוֹר וְאֶת־עִנְּבֵי נְזִירֶךָ לֹא

―――――――― אונקלוס ――――――――

ג שִׁית שְׁנִין תִּזְרַע חַקְלָךְ וְשִׁית שְׁנִין תִּכְסַח כַּרְמָךְ וְתִכְנוֹשׁ יָת עֲלַלְתַּהּ: ד וּבְשַׁתָּא שְׁבִיעֵתָא נְיָח שְׁמִטְּתָא יְהֵי לְאַרְעָא שְׁמִטְּתָא קֳדָם יְיָ חַקְלָךְ לָא תִזְרַע וְכַרְמָךְ לָא תִכְסַח: ה יָת כָּתָא דְחַצְדָךְ לָא תֶחֱצַד וְיָת עִנְּבֵי שִׁבְקָךְ לָא

―――――――― רש״י ――――――――

(ד) יִהְיֶה לָאָרֶץ. לַשָּׂדוֹת וְלַכְּרָמִים: **לֹא תִזְמֹר.** שֶׁקּוֹלְלִין זְמוֹרוֹתֶיהָ, וְתַרְגּוּמוֹ לָא תִכְסַח, וְדוֹמֶה לוֹ קוֹצִים כְּסוּחִים (ישעיה לג:יב), שְׂרוּפָה בָאֵשׁ כְּסוּחָה (תהלים פ:יז): **(ה) אֵת סְפִיחַ**

קְצִירְךָ. אֲפִילוּ לֹא זְרַעְתָּהּ וְהִיא צָמְחָה מִן הַזֶּרַע שֶׁנָּפַל בָּהּ בְּעֵת הַקָּצִיר, הוּא הַקָּרוּי סָפִיחַ: **לֹא תִקְצוֹר.** לִהְיוֹת מַחֲזִיק בּוֹ כִּשְׁאָר קָצִיר, אֶלָּא הֶפְקֵר יִהְיֶה לַכֹּל: **נְזִירֶךָ.** שֶׁהִנְזַרְתָּ וְהִפְרַשְׁתָּ

―――――――― RASHI ELUCIDATED ――――――――

4. יִהְיֶה לָאָרֶץ — THERE SHALL BE FOR THE LAND. לַשָּׂדוֹת — For the fields וְלַכְּרָמִים — and for the vineyards.[1]

☐ לֹא תִזְמֹר — YOU SHALL NOT PRUNE. The verb זמר is used here שֶׁקּוֹצְצִין זְמוֹרוֹתֶיהָ — because they cut off its vines,[2] וְתַרְגּוּמוֹ ,,לָא תִכְסָח'' — and it is rendered by *Targum Onkelos* as לָא תִכְסַח, "do not trim."[3] וְדוֹמֶה לוֹ — Similar to [the word used by *Targum Onkelos*] are the adjectives כְּסוּחִים in, ,,קוֹצִים כְּסוּחִים'',[4] "cut thorns,"[4] and כְּסוּחָה in, ,,שְׂרֻפָה בָאֵשׁ כְּסוּחָה'' — "burned by fire, cut off."[5]

5. אֶת סְפִיחַ קְצִירְךָ — THE AFTERGROWTH OF YOUR HARVEST. אֲפִילוּ לֹא זְרַעְתָּה — Even if you did not sow it מִן הַזֶּרַע שֶׁנָּפַל בָּהּ בְּעֵת הַקָּצִיר — from the seed that fell into [the ground] at the time of the previous year's harvest; וְהִיא צָמְחָה — and it sprouted וְהוּא קָרוּי ,,סָפִיחַ'' — that is what is called "aftergrowth."[6]

☐ לֹא תִקְצוֹר — YOU SHALL NOT REAP לִהְיוֹת מַחֲזִיק בּוֹ — to take possession of it כִּשְׁאָר קָצִיר — like other harvests. אֶלָּא — Rather, הֶפְקֵר יְהֵא — it shall be ownerless לַכֹּל — for all to take freely.[7]

☐ נְזִירֶךָ — OF YOUR KEEPING AWAY. שֶׁהִנְזַרְתָּ — That you kept away וְהִפְרַשְׁתָּ — and separated

---

1. "For the land" refers only to agricultural work, but non-agricultural work, e.g., excavation for construction, is permitted (*Mizrachi; Sifsei Chachamim*).

2. תִּזְמֹר is related to זְמוֹרָה, "vine," and means "pruning," for the purpose of pruning is to cut off excessive vines that impede a plant's growth. It is not related to "of the praiseworthy fruit of the land" (*Genesis* 43:11), which is derived from זֶמֶר, "song" (see Rashi there).

3. This is in contrast to זִמְרָה, which *Targum Onkelos* to *Genesis* 43:11 renders with the root שבח as noted by Rashi there.

4. *Isaiah* 33:12.

5. *Psalms* 80:17. The word תִזְמֹר appeared above in the preceding verse, וְשֵׁשׁ שָׁנִים תִּזְמֹר כַּרְמֶךָ, "and for six years you may prune your vineyard." Rashi did not define the word there, however, for in that context it might mean "you may add vines." [See next paragraph.] Here, however, לֹא תִזְמֹר must mean "you shall not prune" a vineyard, for it is parallel to "you shall not sow" a field. If it meant "you shall not add vines," it would not be parallel, for it would imply that you may

do work to enhance the yield of existing vines, whereas "your field you shall not sow" implies that you must let the field lie fallow, and not work it at all (*Levush HaOrah*).

That the root זמר can mean both "to plant vines" and "to prune vines" is an example of the phenomenon that Rashi describes as "the same Hebrew word alternating in meaning between בִּנְיָן וּסְתִירָה, building and tearing down." See Rashi to *Exodus* 27:3, s.v., לְדַשְּׁנוֹ, for other examples. This phenomenon occurs in other languages also. For example, "to root" can mean "to implant" or "to uproot."

6. Technically, the word "aftergrowth" refers to growth that continues after a harvest. For lack of a more precise English word, and to avoid the awkward "that which grows of its own accord," we have used "aftergrowth" to refer to the growth, during the next growing season, that comes from seeds dropped inadvertently while harvesting the previous year's crop.

7. Had the Torah meant that it is forbidden to take it under any circumstances, it would have said לֹא תִקַּח, "you shall not take" (*Gur Aryeh*).

תִּבְצֹר שְׁנַת שַׁבָּתוֹן יִהְיֶה לָאָרֶץ:
וְהָיְתָה שַׁבַּת הָאָרֶץ לָכֶם לְאָכְלָה לְךָ וּלְעַבְדְּךָ וְלַאֲמָתֶךָ וְלִשְׂכִירְךָ

pick; it shall be a year of rest for the land. **6** The resting of the land shall be yours to eat, for you, and for your slave, and for your maidservant; and for your hired worker

— אונקלוס —

תִּקְטוֹף שְׁנַת שְׁמִטְּתָא יְהֵי לְאַרְעָא: וּתְהֵי שְׁמִטַּת אַרְעָא יְהֵי לְמֵיכַל לָךְ וּלְעַבְדָּךְ וּלְאַמְתָךְ וְלַאֲגִירָךְ

— רש"י —

בני אדם מהם ולא הפקרתם: **לא תבצר**. אותם אינך בוצר אלא מן המופקר (ת"כ שם ג:): **(ו) והיתה שבת הארץ וגו׳**. אע"פ שאסרתים עליך, לא באכילה ולא בהנאה אסרתים, אלא שלא תנהוג בהם כבעל הבית אלא הכל יהיו שוים בה, אתה ושכירך ותושבך:

שבת הארץ לכם לאכלה. מן השבות אתה אוכל ואי אתה אוכל מן השמור (שם ה:): **לך ולעבדך ולאמתך**. לפי שנאמר ואכלו אביוני עמך (שמות כג:יא) יכול יהיו אסורים באכילה לעשירים, ת"ל לך ולעבדך ולאמתך, הרי בעלים ועבדים ושפחות אמורים כאן (ת"כ שם ו):

— RASHI ELUCIDATED —

בְּנֵי אָדָם מֵהֶם – **people from them,** וְלֹא הִפְקַרְתָּם – **and you did not relinquish ownership from them.** לֹא תִבְצֹר – **YOU SHALL NOT PICK.** אוֹתָם – **Those** that you wish to keep from others אֵינְךָ בּוֹצֵר – **you may not pick,**[1] אֶלָּא מִן הַמּוּפְקָר – **but** you may pick **from those whose ownership has been relinquished.**[1]

6. וְהָיְתָה שַׁבַּת הָאָרֶץ וְגוֹמֵר – **THE RESTING OF THE LAND SHALL BE, ETC.** אַף עַל פִּי שֶׁאֲסַרְתִּים עָלֶיךָ – **Even** though I forbade [the fruits of the seventh year] **to you,** לֹא בַּאֲכִילָה וְלֹא בַּהֲנָאָה אֲסַרְתִּים – **I did not forbid them for eating nor for** other benefit; אֶלָּא שֶׁלֹּא תִנְהוֹג בָּהֶם כְּבַעַל הַבַּיִת – **only that you should not treat them as an owner** does. אֶלָּא – **Rather,** הַכֹּל יִהְיוּ שָׁוִים בָּהּ – **all should be equal,** i.e., should have equal rights, **in [the produce of the seventh year],** אַתָּה וּשְׂכִירְךָ וְתוֹשָׁבְךָ – **you, and your hired worker, and one who resides with you.**

שַׁבַּת הָאָרֶץ לָכֶם לְאָכְלָה – **THE RESTING OF THE LAND [SHALL BE] YOURS TO EAT.** מִן הַשַּׁבּוּת אַתָּה אוֹכֵל – From that which has been rested from, i.e., from produce that grew from untilled land, **you may eat,**[2] וְאִי אַתָּה אוֹכֵל – **but you may not eat**[3] מִן הַשָּׁמוּר – **from that which has been kept.**[3]

לְךָ וּלְעַבְדְּךָ וְלַאֲמָתֶךָ – **FOR YOU, AND FOR YOUR SLAVE, AND FOR YOUR MAIDSERVANT.** לְפִי שֶׁנֶּאֱמַר – Since it says with reference to the seventh year, ״וְאָכְלוּ אֶבְיֹנֵי עַמֶּךָ״ – **"and the destitute of your people shall eat,"**[4] יָכוֹל יִהְיוּ אֲסוּרִים בַּאֲכִילָה לַעֲשִׁירִים – one might be able to think that [the fruits of the seventh year] should be forbidden to the rich with regard to eating. תַּלְמוּד לוֹמַר – To teach us otherwise, **the verse says,** ״לְךָ וּלְעַבְדְּךָ וְלַאֲמָתֶךָ״ – **"for you, and for your slave, and for your maidservant."** הֲרֵי בְּעָלִים – **See, now, that** owners וַעֲבָדִים – **and slaves** וּשְׁפָחוֹת – **and slavewomen** אֲמוּרִים כָּאן – **are stated here.**[5]

---

1. *Toras Kohanim, perek* 1:3. "The aftergrowth of your harvest you shall not reap" teaches that one may not reap the produce of the seventh year like the produce of other years, in that one must relinquish ownership of it. On the basis of that verse alone, however, we may have thought that if one does not relinquish ownership of crops that grew on their own, the produce becomes permanently forbidden. "The grapes of your keeping away you shall not pick" teaches us that it is forbidden only so long as there exists intent to keep it; if one relinquishes ownership before picking the produce, it is not forbidden (*Gur Aryeh*). Rashi's opinion stands in contrast to that of *Rabbeinu Tam* who holds that if the produce of the seventh year was kept, it is permanently forbidden. See *Pe'as HaShulchan* 22:1. See also note 3 below.

2. We would have expected the verse to use the more common expression, תְּבוּאַת הָאָרֶץ, "the produce of the land" (as in 23:39 above). It uses שַׁבַּת הָאָרֶץ to indicate that only that produced by "the resting of the land" may be eaten (*Mizrachi*; *Be'er Yitzchak*).

3. *Toras Kohanim, perek* 1:5. By "from that which has been kept," Rashi means that which has been grown from the start with intent to be kept, i.e., produce that grew as the result of forbidden agricultural work performed on the seventh year. Unlike produce that grew by itself but from which ownership was not relinquished (see note 1 above), produce that is the result of forbidden work may not be eaten even if it is subsequently made available to be taken for free by the public (*Mizrachi*; *Be'er Yitzchak*).

4. *Exodus* 23:11.

5. *Toras Kohanim, perek* 1:6. "You, your slave and your maidservant" are mentioned in the verse to indicate that although "you" are rich enough to own slaves, you may nonetheless eat of the fruits of the seventh year (*Mizrachi*; commentary of *Rabbeinu Hillel* to *Toras Kohanim*).

321 / VAYIKRA/LEVITICUS — PARASHAS BEHAR   25/7-8

and for one who resides with you. **⁷** *And for your animal and for the beast that is in your land shall all its crop be to eat.*

⁸ *You shall count for yourself seven sabbaths of years, seven years seven times; and the days of the seven sabbaths of years shall be for you forty-nine years.*

ז וּלְתוֹשָׁבְךָ הַגָּרִים עִמָּךְ: וְלִבְהֶמְתְּךָ
וְלַחַיָּה אֲשֶׁר בְּאַרְצֶךָ תִּהְיֶה כָל־
ח תְּבוּאָתָהּ לֶאֱכֹל: וְסָפַרְתָּ לְךָ
שֶׁבַע שַׁבְּתֹת שָׁנִים שֶׁבַע שָׁנִים
שֶׁבַע פְּעָמִים וְהָיוּ לְךָ יְמֵי שֶׁבַע
שַׁבְּתֹת הַשָּׁנִים תֵּשַׁע וְאַרְבָּעִים שָׁנָה:

—————— אונקלוס ——————

וּלְתוֹתָבָךְ דְּדָיְרִין עִמָּךְ: וְלִבְעִירָךְ וּלְחַיְתָא דִּי בְאַרְעָךְ תְּהֵא כָל עֲלַלְתַּהּ לְמֵיכָל: חוְתִמְנֵי לָךְ שְׁבַע
שְׁמִטִּין דִּשְׁנִין שְׁבַע שְׁנִין שְׁבַע זִמְנִין וִיהוֹן לָךְ יוֹמֵי שְׁבַע שְׁמִטִּין דִּשְׁנִין אַרְבְּעִין וּתְשַׁע שְׁנִין:

—————— רש"י ——————

(ז) **שַׁבְּתֹת שָׁנִים.** שְׁמִטּוֹת שָׁנִים. יָכוֹל יַעֲשֶׂה
שֶׁבַע שְׁמִטּוֹת רְצוּפוֹת שְׁמִטָּה וְיַעֲשֶׂה יוֹבֵל אַחֲרֵיהֶם, ת"ל שֶׁבַע שָׁנִים
שֶׁבַע פְּעָמִים, הֱוֵי אוֹמֵר כָּל שְׁמִטָּה וּשְׁמִטָּה בִּזְמַנָּהּ (ספרא פרשתא ב:א):
וְהָיוּ לְךָ יְמֵי שֶׁבַע וְגוֹ'. מַגִּיד לְךָ שֶׁאַע"פ שֶׁלֹּא עָשִׂיתָ שְׁמִטּוֹת
(ז) **וְלִשְׂכִירְךָ וּלְתוֹשָׁבְךָ.** אַף הַנָּכְרִים (שם ו):
וְלִבְהֶמְתְּךָ וְלַחַיָּה. אִם חַיָּה אוֹכֶלֶת בְּהֵמָה לֹא כָל שֶׁכֵּן, שֶׁמְּזוֹנוֹתֶיהָ
עָלֶיךָ, מַה ת"ל וְלִבְהֶמְתְּךָ, מַקִּישׁ בְּהֵמָה לְחַיָּה, כָּל זְמַן שֶׁחַיָּה אוֹכֶלֶת
מִן הַשָּׂדֶה הַאֲכֵל לִבְהֶמְתְּךָ מִן הַבַּיִת, כָּלָה לַחַיָּה מִן הַשָּׂדֶה כַּלֵּה לִבְהֶמְתְּךָ

—————— RASHI ELUCIDATED ——————

☐ וְלִשְׂכִירְךָ וּלְתוֹשָׁבְךָ — **AND FOR YOUR HIRED WORKER, AND FOR ONE WHO RESIDES WITH YOU,** אַף הַנָּכְרִים[1] — **even the non-Jews.**[1]

7. וְלִבְהֶמְתְּךָ וְלַחַיָּה — **AND FOR YOUR ANIMAL AND FOR THE BEAST.** אִם חַיָּה — **If a beast,** i.e., an undomesticated, ownerless animal, אוֹכֶלֶת — **may eat** the fruit of the seventh year, בְּהֵמָה לֹא כָל שֶׁכֵּן — **is it not true all the more so** that **a** domesticated **animal** may eat שֶׁמְּזוֹנוֹתֶיהָ עָלֶיךָ — **for its food is upon you,** i.e., feeding it is your responsibility? מַה תַּלְמוּד לוֹמַר ״וְלִבְהֶמְתְּךָ״ — **Why, then, does the verse mention "and for your** domesticated **animal"?** מַקִּישׁ בְּהֵמָה לְחַיָּה — **It compares a** domesticated **animal to a** wild **beast** as follows: כָּל זְמַן שֶׁחַיָּה אוֹכֶלֶת מִן הַשָּׂדֶה — **All the while that the** wild **beast eats from the field,** i.e., all the while that a particular type of produce is freely available for the wild beast, הַאֲכֵל לִבְהֶמְתְּךָ — **feed your animal** מִן הַבַּיִת — **from the house,** i.e., you may store a supply of that type of produce for your domestic animals. כָּלָה לַחַיָּה מִן הַשָּׂדֶה — **If it has been finished for the** wild **beast from the field,** i.e, if it is no longer found in the field, [2] כַּלֵּה לִבְהֶמְתְּךָ מִן הַבַּיִת — **get rid of it for your animal from the house,** i.e., take out what you have stored for your animal and make it available to all.[2]

8. שַׁבְּתֹת שָׁנִים — **SABBATHS OF YEARS.** שְׁמִטּוֹת שָׁנִים — **"Releases" of years,** i.e., periods of "release," a year in duration.[3] יָכוֹל יַעֲשֶׂה שֶׁבַע שָׁנִים רְצוּפוֹת שְׁמִטָּה — **One might be able** to think that **he should keep seven consecutive years of** *shemittah* at the end of the forty-nine-year cycle וְיַעֲשֶׂה יוֹבֵל — **and he should keep the** *yovel* **year**[4] אַחֲרֵיהֶם — **after them.** תַּלְמוּד לוֹמַר — To teach us otherwise, **the verse says,** ״שֶׁבַע שָׁנִים שֶׁבַע פְּעָמִים״ — **"seven years seven times."** הֱוֵי אוֹמֵר — **You should say** on the basis of that phrase,[5] כָּל שְׁמִטָּה וּשְׁמִטָּה בִּזְמַנָּהּ — **each and every** *shemittah* should be kept **at its distinct time.**[5]

☐ וְהָיוּ לְךָ יְמֵי שֶׁבַע וְגוֹמֵר — **AND THE DAYS OF THE SEVEN [SABBATHS OF YEARS] SHALL BE FOR YOU, ETC.** מַגִּיד לְךָ — **This tells you** שֶׁאַע״פ עַל פִּי שֶׁלֹּא עָשִׂיתָ שְׁמִטּוֹת — **that even if you did not keep the** *shemittah*

---

1. *Toras Kohanim,* perek 1:7. One may give the fruits of the seventh year only to "your hired worker, and one who resides with you," i.e., non-Jews whom you have an obligation to feed; otherwise non-Jews may not be given fruit that has the sanctity of the seventh year (*Maskil LeDavid;* see Rambam, Hil. Shemittah VeYovel 5:13; *Aruch HaShulchan HeAsid,* Hil. Shemittah VeYovel 24:14).

2. *Toras Kohanim,* perek 1:8.

3. The word שַׁבָּת when used with reference to days can mean "a week" (e.g., שַׁבָּתוֹת in 23:15 above) or "the Sabbath day." We may have thought that by the same token, when used with reference to years, it can mean a cycle of seven years or the seventh year. Rashi explains that here שָׁנִים שַׁבְּתֹת must mean *shemittah* years, for if the verse were saying, "you shall count for yourself seven series of seven years," the following words, שֶׁבַע שָׁנִים שֶׁבַע פְּעָמִים, "seven years seven times," would be redundant (*Mizrachi; Maskil LeDavid*).

4. See vv. 10-13 below.

5. *Toras Kohanim, parshasa* 2:1. "Seven years seven times" implies that each of the seven *shemittah*s is at

⁹ You shall sound a broken blast on the shofar, in the seventh month, on the tenth of the month; on Yom Kippur you shall sound the shofar throughout your land. ¹⁰ You shall sanctify the fiftieth year

ט וְהַעֲבַרְתָּ שׁוֹפַר תְּרוּעָה בַּחֹדֶשׁ הַשְּׁבִעִי בֶּעָשׂוֹר לַחֹדֶשׁ בְּיוֹם הַכִּפֻּרִים תַּעֲבִירוּ שׁוֹפָר בְּכָל־אַרְצְכֶם: י וְקִדַּשְׁתֶּם אֵת שְׁנַת הַחֲמִשִּׁים שָׁנָה

— אונקלוס —

ט וְתַעֲבַר שׁוֹפָר יַבָּבָא בְּיַרְחָא שְׁבִיעָאָה בְּעַשְׂרָא לְיַרְחָא בְּיוֹמָא דְכִפּוּרַיָּא תַּעְבְּרוּן שׁוֹפָרָא בְּכָל אַרְעֲכוֹן: י וּתְקַדְּשׁוּן יָת שְׁנַת חַמְשִׁין שְׁנִין

— רש"י —

עָשֵׂה יוֹבֵל לָסוֹף אַרְבָּעִים וָתֵשַׁע שָׁנָה וּפְשׁוּטוֹ שֶׁל מִקְרָא. יַעֲלֶה לְךָ חֶשְׁבּוֹן שְׁנוֹת הַשְּׁמִטּוֹת לְמִסְפַּר אַרְבָּעִים וָתֵשַׁע: (ט) וְהַעֲבַרְתָּ. לְשׁוֹן וַיַּעֲבִירוּ קוֹל בַּמַּחֲנֶה (שמות לו:ו) לְשׁוֹן הַכְרָזָה (ר"ה ל"ד.): בְּיוֹם הַכִּפֻּרִים. מִמַּשְׁמַע שֶׁנֶּאֱמַר בְּיוֹם הַכִּפּוּרִים אֵינִי יוֹדֵעַ שֶׁהוּא בֶּעָשׂוֹר לַחֹדֶשׁ אִם כֵּן לָמָּה נֶאֱמַר בֶּעָשׂוֹר לַחֹדֶשׁ אֶלָּא לוֹמַר לְךָ תְּקִיעַת עָשׂוֹר לַחֹדֶשׁ דּוֹחָה שַׁבָּת בְּכָל אַרְצְכֶם וְאֵין תְּקִיעַת רֹאשׁ הַשָּׁנָה דּוֹחָה שַׁבָּת בְּכָל אַרְצְכֶם אֶלָּא בְּבֵית דִּין (ת"כ שם ה): (י) וְקִדַּשְׁתֶּם. בִּכְנִיסָתָהּ מְקַדְּשִׁין אוֹתָהּ בְּב"ד

— RASHI ELUCIDATED —

— לְסוֹף אַרְבָּעִים וָתֵשַׁע שָׁנָה¹ — at the end of forty-nine years.¹ — עֲשֵׂה יוֹבֵל — keep a *yovel* year years, — וּפְשׁוּטוֹ שֶׁל מִקְרָא — And the simple meaning of the verse is: יַעֲלֶה לְךָ חֶשְׁבּוֹן שְׁנוֹת הַשְּׁמִטּוֹת — The total of the years of the *shemittos* shall add up — לְמִסְפַּר אַרְבָּעִים וָתֵשַׁע — to the number forty-nine.²

9. וְהַעֲבַרְתָּ — YOU SHALL SOUND. לְשׁוֹן — This word is **related to** וַיַּעֲבִירוּ in, ³,,וַיַּעֲבִירוּ קוֹל בַּמַּחֲנֶה — "**and they proclaimed in the camp.**"³ ⁴לְשׁוֹן הַכְרָזָה — **It means "announcing."**⁴

□ בְּיוֹם הַכִּפֻּרִים — ON YOM KIPPUR. מִמַּשְׁמַע שֶׁנֶּאֱמַר ,,בְּיוֹם הַכִּפּוּרִים'' — By implication of it being said, "on Yom Kippur," אֵינִי יוֹדֵעַ שֶׁהוּא בֶּעָשׂוֹר לַחֹדֶשׁ — don't I know that it is on the tenth of the month? אֶלָּא — But it is stated אִם כֵּן — If so, לָמָּה נֶאֱמַר ,,בֶּעָשׂוֹר לַחֹדֶשׁ'' — why did it say, "on the tenth of the month"?⁵ לוֹמַר לְךָ — to say to you, תְּקִיעַת עָשׂוֹר לַחֹדֶשׁ — the blowing the shofar on the tenth of the month דּוֹחָה שַׁבָּת — overrides the Sabbath ,,בְּכָל אַרְצְכֶם'', — "throughout your land," וְאֵין תְּקִיעַת רֹאשׁ הַשָּׁנָה דּוֹחָה שַׁבָּת — but the blowing of the shofar of Rosh Hashanah does not override the Sabbath בְּכָל אַרְצְכֶם — throughout your land; אֶלָּא — rather, it overrides the Sabbath בְּבֵית דִּין בִּלְבָד⁶ — in Court only.⁶

10. וְקִדַּשְׁתֶּם — YOU SHALL SANCTIFY. בִּכְנִיסָתָהּ⁷ — At its onset⁷ מְקַדְּשִׁין אוֹתָהּ בְּבֵית דִּין — they

the end of a seven-year cycle (*Korban Aharon*).
1. *Toras Kohanim, parshasa* 2:2. The end of our verse appears to be stating the obvious. It is meant to be read in conjunction with the beginning of the next verse, "The days of the seven sabbaths of years shall be for you forty-nine years" and when these forty-nine years elapse, whether you have kept the *shemittah* years or not, "you shall sound a broken blast on the shofar" (*Mizrachi*; *Sifsei Chachamim*).
2. In his first interpretation, Rashi dealt with the apparent obviousness of the concluding clause of our verse. In his explanation of the simple meaning of the verse, however, he deals with a different issue. Rashi in his comment at the beginning of this verse has stated that שַׁבְּתֹת שָׁנִים refers to the *shemittah* years themselves, not the seven-year cycles (see note 3 to v. 8 above). How then does our verse say that seven שָׁנִים amount to forty-nine years? Seven שַׁבְּתֹת are only seven years! He explains that here the verse means that the *period* during which you will count the seven years of *shemittah* will be a period of forty-nine years (*Mesiach Ilmim*).
3. Exodus 36:6.
4. *Rosh Hashanah* 34a. In other contexts, e.g., 18:21 below, לְהַעֲבִיר means "to make something pass from one place to another." Of our verse does not

mean that we should move the shofar from one place to another (*Mizrachi; Sifsei Chachamim*).
5. Although "on the tenth of the month" precedes "on Yom Kippur" in the verse, Rashi, based on *Toras Kohanim*, treats "on the tenth of the month" as the apparently unnecessary phrase. For it is the sanctity of Yom Kippur that leads to the shofar being blown on that day. The fact that the calendar date is the tenth of the month appears secondary (*Korban Aharon*).
6. *Toras Kohanim, parshasa* 2:5. Blowing the shofar does not fall under any of the categories of work forbidden on Shabbos and festivals. After the destruction of the *Beis HaMikdash*, R' Yochanan ben Zakkai, the head of the highest court, the Great Sanhedrin, decreed that the shofar may not be blown on Shabbos other than in the places where courts are located, lest people carry the shofar four *amos* in a public domain. This prohibition is of rabbinic origin. The prohibition suggested by our verse is an *asmachta*, an allusion by the Torah to a law of rabbinic origin (*Ramban*).
7. There is a dispute in *Rosh Hashanah* 8b as to when the *yovel* year is sanctified. According to one opinion, it is on Rosh Hashanah, while according to another opinion it is on Yom Kippur. Rashi uses the word בִּכְנִיסָתָהּ, "at its onset," rather than בִּתְחִלָּתָהּ, "at its beginning."

and you shall proclaim freedom throughout the land for all its inhabitants; it is a yovel year for you, and you shall return, each man to his ancestral heritage, and you shall return, each man to his family. [11] *It is a yovel —*

וּקְרָאתֶ֥ם דְּר֛וֹר בָּאָ֖רֶץ לְכָל־יֹשְׁבֶ֑יהָ יוֹבֵ֥ל הִוא֙ תִּהְיֶ֣ה לָכֶ֔ם וְשַׁבְתֶּ֗ם אִ֚ישׁ אֶל־אֲחֻזָּת֔וֹ וְאִ֥ישׁ אֶל־מִשְׁפַּחְתּ֖וֹ תָּשֻֽׁבוּ׃ יא יוֹבֵ֣ל הִ֔וא

— אונקלוס —

וְתִקְרוֹן חֵרוּתָא בְּאַרְעָא לְכָל יָתְבָהָא יוֹבֵלָא הִיא תְּהֵי לְכוֹן וּתְתוּבוּן גְּבַר לְאַחֲסַנְתֵּיהּ וּגְבַר לְזַרְעִיתֵיהּ תְּתוּבוּן: יא יוֹבֵלָא הִיא

— רש״י —

וּקְרָאתֶם דְּרוֹר: ר״ה (ח:); **דְּרוֹר.** לְשׁוֹן חֵרוּת. אָמַר ר׳ יְהוּדָה מַהוּ לְשׁוֹן דְּרוֹר כִּמְדַיֵּר בֵּי דַיְירָא וְכוּ׳ (ת״כ שם ב; ר״ה ע:) שֶׁדָּר בְּכָל מָקוֹם שֶׁהוּא רוֹצֶה וְאֵינוֹ בִּרְשׁוּת אֲחֵרִים: **יוֹבֵל הוּא.** שָׁנָה זֹאת מוּבְדֶּלֶת מִשְּׁאָר שָׁנִים בִּנְקִיבַת שֵׁם לָהּ לְבַדָּהּ, וּמַה שְּׁמָהּ, יוֹבֵל שְׁמָהּ, עַל שֵׁם תְּקִיעַת שׁוֹפָר: **וְשַׁבְתֶּם אִישׁ אֶל אֲחֻזָּתוֹ.** שֶׁהַשָּׂדוֹת חוֹזְרוֹת לְבַעֲלֵיהֶן: **וְאִישׁ אֶל מִשְׁפַּחְתּוֹ תָּשֻׁבוּ.** לְרַבּוֹת אֶת הַנִּרְצָע (ת״כ שם ה:)

— RASHI ELUCIDATED —

sanctify it in Court, וְאוֹמְרִים — and say, מְקֻדֶּשֶׁת הַשָּׁנָה[1] — "The year is sanctified."[1]

□ וּקְרָאתֶם דְּרוֹר — AND YOU SHALL PROCLAIM FREEDOM לָעֲבָדִים — for Hebrew servants, בֵּין נִרְצָע — whether he is one who has had his ear bored, בֵּין שֶׁלֹּא כָּלוּ לוֹ שֵׁשׁ שָׁנִים — or whether his six years have not expired מִשֶּׁנִּמְכַּר — from the time he was sold into service.[2]

אָמַר רַבִּי יְהוּדָה — The Tanna R' Yehudah says: מַהוּ לְשׁוֹן דְּרוֹר — What is meant by the term דְּרוֹר? How does it imply "freedom"? ³{וְכֻלְּהוּ} — "As one who dwells in a dwelling place, {etc.,}"[3] which means כִּמְדַיֵּר בֵּי דַיְירָא — שֶׁדָּר בְּכָל מָקוֹם שֶׁהוּא רוֹצֶה — that he lives wherever he pleases, וְאֵינוֹ בִּרְשׁוּת אֲחֵרִים — and is not under the authority of others.

□ יוֹבֵל הוּא — IT IS A YOVEL. שָׁנָה זֹאת מֻבְדֶּלֶת מִשְּׁאָר שָׁנִים — This year is distinct from other years בִּנְקִיבַת שֵׁם לָהּ לְבַדָּהּ — through the giving of a name to it alone. וּמַה שְּׁמָהּ — And what is its name? יוֹבֵל שְׁמָהּ — Yovel is its name, עַל שֵׁם תְּקִיעַת שׁוֹפָר — on account of the blowing of the shofar.[4]

□ וְשַׁבְתֶּם אִישׁ אֶל אֲחֻזָּתוֹ — AND YOU SHALL RETURN, EACH MAN TO HIS ANCESTRAL HERITAGE. שֶׁהַשָּׂדוֹת — For the fields which have been sold חוֹזְרוֹת לְבַעֲלֵיהֶן — return to their owners.[5]

□ וְאִישׁ אֶל מִשְׁפַּחְתּוֹ תָּשֻׁבוּ — AND YOU SHALL RETURN, EACH MAN TO HIS FAMILY. ⁶לְרַבּוֹת אֶת הַנִּרְצָע — To include the Hebrew servant who has had his ear bored.[6]

This seems to indicate that he is not decisively presenting the opinion that the sanctification is done on Rosh Hashanah, as some commentators assert; for בְּנִיסָה when used with reference to time can denote the early part of a longer period rather than its very beginning. See, for example, Rashi to *Pesachim* 106a, s.v., אין לי אלא ביום, where he uses כְּנִיסָה for the part of the Sabbath during which the essential Kiddush must be recited, although this need not be done at the very beginning of the Sabbath. On the other hand, Rashi uses תְּחִלָּה for the very beginning of a period, e.g., v. 28 below, s.v., עַד שְׁנַת הַיּוֹבֵל. The opinion cited in *Rosh Hashanah* that the *yovel* year is sanctified on Rosh Hashanah also uses מִתְחַלָּה rather than מִבְּנִיסָתָהּ (see *Nachalas Yaakov*).

1. *Toras Kohanim, perek* 2:1; *Rosh Hashanah* 8b. "You shall sanctify the fiftieth year" implies that there is a sanctification procedure other than the specific laws enumerated in this passage. Rashi explains that it refers to a proclamation by the Court (*Devek Tov*).

2. The standard term of a Hebrew servant is six years. See *Exodus* 21:2. A Hebrew servant who serves beyond the standard term is called a נִרְצָע, literally, "bored one," because his ear is bored. See *Exodus* 21:5-6 and Rashi there.

3. *Toras Kohanim, perek* 2:2; *Rosh Hashanah* 9b. The phrase in full reads, "as one who dwells in a dwelling place and carries on trade throughout the province."

4. יוֹבֵל means "ram's horn." It is related to the Arabic word for ram, *"yuvla"* (Rashi to *Exodus* 19:13, s.v., הַיֹּבֵל; see also *Targum Onkelos* there).

In this Rashi disagrees with both *Ibn Ezra*, who understands יוֹבֵל to mean "sent out," and *Ramban* who understands the term to mean "freedom of movement." According to them the word refers to the setting free of the servants.

5. See vv. 15-16 below.

6. *Toras Kohanim, perek* 2:5; see also note 2 above. "Until the *yovel* year shall he work with you" (v. 40 below) applies to one who, due to his poverty, sells himself as a servant for a six-year term, as indicated by the context. "He shall return to his family" (v. 41) is applied to a thief unable to make restitution, who is sold into servitude by the court for a six-year term. Hence, our verse is applied to one who has had his ear bored — the sign that he has accepted an unlimited term of servitude upon himself. He, too, goes free at the *yovel* year whether he has served briefly or for

ויקרא / פרשת בהר

שְׁנַת הַחֲמִשִּׁים שָׁנָה תִּהְיֶה לָכֶם לֹא תִזְרָעוּ וְלֹא תִקְצְרוּ אֶת־סְפִיחֶיהָ וְלֹא תִבְצְרוּ אֶת־נְזִרֶיהָ: יב כִּי יוֹבֵל הִוא קֹדֶשׁ תִּהְיֶה לָכֶם מִן־הַשָּׂדֶה תֹּאכְלוּ אֶת־תְּבוּאָתָהּ:

the fiftieth year — for you it shall be, you shall not sow, you shall not harvest its aftergrowth and you shall not pick what was set aside of it for yourself. [12] For it is a yovel, it shall be holy to you; from the field you may eat its crop.

—————— אונקלוס ——————

שְׁנַת חַמְשִׁין שְׁנִין תְּהֵי לְכוֹן לָא תִזְרְעוּן וְלָא תַחְצְדוּן יָת כַּתְּהָא וְלָא תִקְטְפוּן יָת שִׁבְקְתָהּ: יב אֲרֵי יוֹבְלָא הִיא קוּדְשָׁא תְּהֵי לְכוֹן מִן חַקְלָא תֵּיכְלוּן יָת עֲלַלְתַּהּ:

—————— רש"י ——————

(יא) יובל הוא שנת החמשים שנה. מה ת"ל, לפי שנאמר וקדשתם וגו', כדאיתא בר"ה (ח:) ובת"כ (פרק ג:ה): את נזריה. את הענבים המשומרים, אבל בוצר אתה מן המופקרים. כמו שנאמר בשביעית כך נאמר ביובל (שם ב):

(יב) קדש תהיה לכם. תופסת דמיה כהקדש. יכול תצא היא לחולין, ת"ל תהיה, בהויתה תהא (שם ג; קידושין נח.): מן השדה תאכלו. על ידי השדה אתה נמצא אוכל שתי שנים קדושות סמוכות זו לזו, שנת הארבעים ותשע שמטה ושנת החמשים יובל:

—————— RASHI ELUCIDATED ——————

11. יוֹבֵל הוּא שְׁנַת הַחֲמִשִּׁים שָׁנָה — IT IS A YOVEL — THE FIFTIETH YEAR. — מַה תַּלְמוּד לוֹמַר — Why is this verse stated? — לְפִי שֶׁנֶּאֱמַר — Since it says, וְקִדַּשְׁתֶּם וְגוֹמֵר — "you shall sanctify, etc.," — כִּדְאִיתָא — as it says in *Rosh Hashanah*[1] and *Toras Kohanim*.[2] — בְּרֹאשׁ הַשָּׁנָה וּבְתוֹרַת כֹּהֲנִים.

אֶת נְזִרֶיהָ — WHAT WAS SET ASIDE OF IT. This means אֶת הָעֲנָבִים הַמְשׁוּמָּרִים — the grapes that have been kept. — אֲבָל בּוֹצֵר אַתָּה — But you may pick מִן הַמֻּפְקָרִים — from those that have been rendered ownerless. — כְּשֵׁם שֶׁנֶּאֱמַר בַּשְּׁבִיעִית — As it has been said about the seventh year, כָּךְ נֶאֱמַר בַּיּוֹבֵל — so has it been said about the *yovel* year,[3] i.e., the agricultural laws stated with regard to the *yovel* year are identical to the agricultural laws stated with regard to the *shemittah* year. נִמְצְאוּ — It is thus found שְׁתֵּי שָׁנִים קְדוֹשׁוֹת — that there are **two holy years,** סְמוּכוֹת זוּ לָזוּ — **one immediately following the other;** שְׁנַת הָאַרְבָּעִים וָתֵשַׁע שְׁמִטָּה — **the forty-ninth year** is ***shemittah*,** וּשְׁנַת הַחֲמִשִּׁים יוֹבֵל — **and the fiftieth year** is ***yovel*.**

12. קֹדֶשׁ תִּהְיֶה לָכֶם — IT SHALL BE HOLY TO YOU. תּוֹפֶסֶת דָּמֶיהָ — It seizes its money כְּהֶקְדֵּשׁ — like that which is holy.[4] יָכוֹל תֵּצֵא הִיא לְחֻלִּין — One might be able to think that **it should go out to** be ***chullin*.**[5] תַּלְמוּד לוֹמַר — To teach us otherwise, **the verse says,** "תִּהְיֶה„ — "**it shall be**," which implies, בַּהֲוָיָתָהּ תְּהֵא — **it shall maintain its state** of holiness upon the fruit.[6]

מִן הַשָּׂדֶה תֹּאכְלוּ — FROM THE FIELD YOU MAY EAT. עַל יְדֵי הַשָּׂדֶה אַתָּה — By means of the field

---

a long time (*Kiddushin* 15a).

Although Rashi in his comment on the phrase וּקְרָאתֶם דְּרוֹר, "and you shall proclaim freedom," has said that that phrase refers to the freeing of Hebrew servants who have had their ear bored, he does not mean that that phrase is the source for the law that they go free in the *yovel* year. Rather, he means that once we have seen from the phrase "and you shall return, each man to his family" that even such servants go free at the *yovel* year, we can infer that "you shall proclaim" includes them, as well (*Minchas Yehudah*; *Sifsei Chachamim*).

1. *Rosh Hashanah* 8b. "Since it says, 'you shall sanctify the fiftieth year,' one might think that just as it becomes holy at its beginning, so it continues to be holy at its end [i.e., until Yom Kippur of the following year (Rashi)], for we add from the profane to the sacred [at the end of the Sabbath and of the festivals]. To teach us otherwise, the verse says, 'it is a *yovel* — the fiftieth year,' [which implies,] you must sanctify the fiftieth year, but you do not sanctify the fifty-first year."

2. *Toras Kohanim*, perek 3:1. The wording there is slightly different from that of *Rosh Hashanah*, but the meaning is the same.

3. *Toras Kohanim*, perek 3:2.

4. When property of the *Beis HaMikdash* is sold, its sanctity is transferred to the money with which it is purchased. The same holds true for the sanctity of fruits of the *yovel*, and of the *shemittah* years. See *Aruch HaShulchan HeAsid*, *Hilchos Shemittah VeYovel*, sections 25 and 26, for a discussion of the laws of the sanctity of the money which was used to buy fruits of *shemittah* and *yovel*.

5. *Chullin* refers to that which is not holy. One might think that once the sanctity of *yovel* leaves the fruit of *yovel* and falls upon the money with which it has been bought, the fruit should no longer have the sanctity of *yovel*, just as property of the *Beis HaMikdash* loses its sanctity once it has been bought.

6. *Toras Kohanim*, perek 3:3; *Kiddushin* 58a. Verbs of being such as תִּהְיֶה connote continuous states (see Rashi to 15:19 above and note 3 on p. 186). In our verse, it is understood to imply that the fruit remains in its state of holiness even after it has been sold.

13 In this yovel year you shall return, each man to his ancestral heritage. **14** When you make a sale to your fellow or when you buy from the hand of your

יג בִּשְׁנַת הַיּוֹבֵל הַזֹּאת תָּשֻׁבוּ אִישׁ אֶל־אֲחֻזָּתוֹ: יד וְכִי־תִמְכְּרוּ מִמְכָּר לַעֲמִיתֶךָ אוֹ קָנֹה מִיַּד עֲמִיתֶךָ

— אונקלוס —

יג בְּשַׁתָּא דְיוֹבֵלָא הָדָא תְּתוּבוּן גְּבַר לְאַחֲסַנְתֵּהּ: יד וַאֲרֵי תְזַבְּנוּן זְבוּן לְחַבְרָךְ אוֹ תִזְבּוּן מִידָא דְחַבְרָךְ

— רש״י —

אוֹכֵל מִן הַבַּיִת, שֶׁאִם כָּלָה לַחַיָּה מִן הַשָּׂדֶה צָרִיךְ אַתָּה לְבַעֵר מִן הַבַּיִת (ת"כ שם ו): כְּשֵׁם שֶׁנֶּאֱמַר בַּשְּׁבִיעִית כָּךְ נֶאֱמַר בַּיּוֹבֵל: (יג) תָּשׁוּבוּ אִישׁ אֶל אֲחֻזָּתוֹ. וַהֲרֵי כְבָר נֶאֱמַר וְשַׁבְתֶּם אִישׁ אֶל אֲחֻזָּתוֹ (לְעֵיל פָּסוּק י) אֶלָּא לְרַבּוֹת הַמּוֹכֵר שָׂדֵהוּ וְעָמַד בְּנוֹ וּגְאָלָהּ שֶׁחוֹזֶרֶת לְאָבִיו בַּיּוֹבֵל (ת"כ שם ו): (יד) וְכִי תִמְכְּרוּ וְגוֹ'. לְפִי פְשׁוּטוֹ כְּמַשְׁמָעוֹ. וְעוֹד יֵשׁ דְּרָשָׁה, מִנַּיִן כְּשֶׁאַתָּה מוֹכֵר מְכוֹר לְיִשְׂרָאֵל חֲבֵרְךָ, ת"ל וְכִי תִמְכְּרוּ מִמְכָּר לַעֲמִיתֶךָ, לַעֲמִיתֶךָ מְכֹר. וּמִנַּיִן שֶׁאִם בָּאתָ לִקְנוֹת קְנֵה מִיִּשְׂרָאֵל חֲבֵרְךָ, ת"ל אוֹ קָנֹה, מִיַּד עֲמִיתֶךָ (ת"כ פרשתא ג:א):

— RASHI ELUCIDATED —

that if [a שֶׁאִם כָּלָה חַיָּה מִן הַשָּׂדֶה — **you may eat from** the produce **in the house,** אוֹכֵל מִן הַבַּיִת — particular variety of produce] has been finished for the **wild beast from the field,** i.e., if it is no longer freely available to the wild beast, צָרִיךְ אַתָּה — **you are required**[1] **to** לְבַעֵר מִן הַבַּיִת — eliminate it from the house.[1] This is another example of the rule stated above:[2] כְּשֵׁם שֶׁנֶּאֱמַר בַּשְּׁבִיעִית — As it has been said about the seventh year, כָּךְ נֶאֱמַר בַּיּוֹבֵל — so has it been said about the *yovel* year.

13. וַהֲרֵי כְבָר נֶאֱמַר — תָּשֻׁבוּ אִישׁ אֶל אֲחֻזָּתוֹ — YOU SHALL RETURN, EACH MAN TO HIS ANCESTRAL HERITAGE. — Now, hasn't it already been said, וְשַׁבְתֶּם אִישׁ אֶל אֲחֻזָּתוֹ[3] — "you shall return, each man to his ancestral heritage"?[3] אֶלָּא — But it is repeated לְרַבּוֹת — to include הַמּוֹכֵר שָׂדֵהוּ — one who sells his field, וְעָמַד בְּנוֹ — and his son arose, i.e., took the initiative, וּגְאָלָהּ — and redeemed it, שֶׁחוֹזֶרֶת לְאָבִיו בַּיּוֹבֵל[4] — that it returns to his father at the *yovel* year.[4]

14. וְכִי תִמְכְּרוּ וְגוֹמֵר — WHEN YOU MAKE A SALE, ETC. לְפִי פְשׁוּטוֹ — The verse is to be understood according to its simple meaning, כְּמַשְׁמָעוֹ — as it sounds.[5] וְעוֹד — Furthermore, יֵשׁ דְּרָשָׁה — there is an exegetical interpretation of the verse: מִנַּיִן — What is the source that teaches כְּשֶׁאַתָּה מוֹכֵר — that when you sell, מְכוֹר לְיִשְׂרָאֵל חֲבֵרְךָ — you should sell to your fellow Jew? תַּלְמוּד לוֹמַר — The verse says, ״וְכִי תִמְכְּרוּ מִמְכָּר — "when you make a sale," לַעֲמִיתֶךָ״ — sell "to your fellow." וּמִנַּיִן — And what is the source that teaches שֶׁאִם בָּאתָ לִקְנוֹת — that if you have come to buy, קְנֵה מִיִּשְׂרָאֵל חֲבֵרְךָ — you should buy from your fellow Jew? תַּלְמוּד לוֹמַר — The verse says, ״אוֹ קָנֹה — "or when you buy," מִיַּד עֲמִיתֶךָ״[6] — "buy from the hand of your fellow."[6]

---

1. *Toras Kohanim, perek* 3:4. מִן is not to be taken as "from," for we may eat from the field every year; the verse is teaching us a law particular to the *yovel* (*Mesiach Ilmim*).

2. Rashi to v. 11, s.v., אֶת נְזִירֶיהָ.

3. Above v. 10.

4. *Toras Kohanim, perek* 3:6. With regard to certain laws, a son is viewed as his father's proxy by virtue of the fact that he is his father's potential heir. We might therefore have thought that if someone buys a field from the father, and the son buys the field from the buyer, the field would revert to the father at the *yovel* year, for his son stands in his place. Our apparently redundant verse teaches us that even in this situation, the father "shall return to his ancestral heritage" (*Mizrachi; Sifsei Chachamim*).

5. Our verse could apparently have made its point by saying, "When you make a sale to your fellow, one man should not victimize his brother." It would have been clear from the plural verb תונו that the verse uses for "victimize," that it is referring to both "one man" and "his brother," so that the prohibition applies equally to both buyer and seller. Had the prohibition applied to the seller alone, the verse would have used a singular verb. Rashi says that, nonetheless, the apparently superfluous אוֹ קָנֹה מִיַּד עֲמִיתֶךָ, "or buy from the hand of your fellow," can be understood as an explicit statement of something that could have been inferred, and does not change the simple meaning of the verse (see *Nachalas Yaakov*). The exegetical interpretation that Rashi goes on to give is a different justification for the necessity of the phrase אוֹ קָנֹה מִיַּד עֲמִיתֶךָ: to teach us that we should buy from fellow Jews.

6. *Toras Kohanim, parshasa* 3:1. Our verse could apparently have made its point by saying וְכִי תִמְכְּרוּ מִמְכָּר, אוֹ קָנֹה אַל תּוֹנוּ אִישׁ אֶת אָחִיו, "When you make a sale or buy, one man should not victimize his brother." It would have been clear from "one man should not victimize his brother" that the verse refers to transactions between Jews. לַעֲמִיתֶךָ is stated to teach us that we should sell to fellow Jews, and מִיַּד עֲמִיתֶךָ is stated to teach us that we should buy from fellow Jews (*Mishmeres HaKodesh*).

אַל־תּוֹנוּ אִישׁ אֶת־אָחִיו: בְּמִסְפַּר שָׁנִים אַחַר הַיּוֹבֵל תִּקְנֶה מֵאֵת עֲמִיתֶךָ בְּמִסְפַּר שְׁנֵי־תְבוּאֹת

fellow, do not victimize one another. ¹⁵ According to the number of years after the yovel shall you buy from your fellow; according to the number of crop-years

———————— אונקלוס ————————

לָא תוֹנוּן גְּבַר יָת אֲחוּהִי: טו בְּמִנְיַן שְׁנַיָּא בָּתַר יוֹבְלָא תִזְבּוֹן מִן חַבְרָךְ בְּמִנְיַן שְׁנֵי עֲלַלְתָּא

———————— רש"י ————————

אל תונו. זו אונאת ממון (שם ד; ב"מ נח:א): **(טו) במספר שנים אחר היובל תקנה.** זהו פשוטו לישב המקרא על אפניו. על האונאה בא להזהיר. כשתמכור או תקנה קרקע דעו כמה שנים יש עד היובל, ולפי השנים ותבואות השדה שהיא ראויה לעשות ימכור המוכר ויקנה הקונה. שהרי סופו להחזירה לו בשנת היובל, ואם יש שנים מועטות וזה מוכרה בדמים יקרים הרי נתאנה לוקח,

ואם יש שנים מרובות ואכל ממנה תבואות הרבה הרי נתאנה מוכר, לפיכך צריך לקנותה לפי הזמן. וזהו שנאמר במספר שני תבואות ימכר לך, לפי מנין שני התבואות שתהא עומדת ביד הלוקח תמכור לו. ורבותינו דרשו מכאן שהמוכר שדהו אינו רשאי לגאול פחות משתי שנים, שתעמוד שתי שנים ביד הלוקח מיום ליום, ואפילו יש שלש תבואות באותן שתי שנים כגון שמכרה לו בקמותיה.

———————— RASHI ELUCIDATED ————————

☐ **אַל תּוֹנוּ** — DO NOT VICTIMIZE. ¹ **זוֹ אוֹנָאַת מָמוֹן** — This is victimization in financial matters.¹

15. בְּמִסְפַּר שָׁנִים אַחַר הַיּוֹבֵל תִּקְנֶה — ACCORDING TO THE NUMBER OF YEARS AFTER THE *YOVEL* YEAR SHALL YOU BUY. **זֶהוּ פְּשׁוּטוֹ** — This which follows is the simple meaning **לְיַשֵּׁב הַמִּקְרָא עַל אָפְנָיו** — to put the verse in its proper setting: **עַל הָאוֹנָאָה בָּא לְהַזְהִיר** — [The verse] comes to enjoin us with regard to victimization. It tells us: **כְּשֶׁתִּמְכּוֹר אוֹ תִּקְנֶה קַרְקַע** — When you will sell or buy land, **דְּעוּ כַּמָּה שָׁנִים יֵשׁ עַד הַיּוֹבֵל** — know how many years there are until the *yovel*, **וּלְפִי הַשָּׁנִים** — and according to the number of years **וּתְבוּאוֹת הַשָּׂדֶה** — and the number of yields of crops of the field **שֶׁהִיא רְאוּיָה לַעֲשׂוֹת** — that it is fit to produce, **יִמְכּוֹר הַמּוֹכֵר** — shall the seller sell **וְיִקְנֶה הַקּוֹנֶה** — and the buyer buy. **שֶׁהֲרֵי סוֹפוֹ** — For, see now, the fate of [the buyer] is **לְהַחֲזִירָהּ לוֹ** — to return it to [the seller] **בִּשְׁנַת הַיּוֹבֵל** — at the *yovel* year. **וְאִם יֵשׁ שָׁנִים מוּעָטוֹת** — And if there are few years until the *yovel*, **וְזֶה מוֹכְרָהּ** — and this one sells it **בְּדָמִים יְקָרִים** — at a high price, **הֲרֵי נִתְאַנָּה לוֹקֵחַ** — see, now, that the buyer has been victimized. **וְאִם יֵשׁ שָׁנִים מְרֻבּוֹת** — And if there are many years until the *yovel*, **וְאָכַל מִמֶּנָּה תְּבוּאוֹת הַרְבֵּה** — and [the buyer] consumed many crops from it, **הֲרֵי נִתְאַנָּה מוֹכֵר** — see, now, that the seller has been victimized. **לְפִיכָךְ** — Therefore, **צָרִיךְ לִקְנוֹתָהּ לְפִי הַזְּמַן** — he must buy it at a price fixed according to the time remaining until the *yovel*. **וְזֶהוּ שֶׁנֶּאֱמַר** — This is what is meant by that which is stated, **״בְּמִסְפַּר שְׁנֵי תְבוּאוֹת יִמְכָּר לָךְ״** — "according to the number of crop-years shall he sell to you," that is, **לְפִי מִנְיַן שְׁנֵי הַתְּבוּאוֹת** — according to the amount of crop-years **שֶׁתְּהֵא עוֹמֶדֶת** — that it will remain **בְּיַד הַלּוֹקֵחַ** — in the hand of the buyer **תִּמְכּוֹר לוֹ** — you shall sell to him.

וְרַבּוֹתֵינוּ דָּרְשׁוּ מִכָּאן — Our Rabbis derived from here through exegesis **שֶׁהַמּוֹכֵר שָׂדֵהוּ** — that one who sells his field **אֵינוֹ רַשַּׁאי לִגְאוֹל** — is not permitted to redeem it **פָּחוֹת מִשְּׁתֵּי שָׁנִים** — within less than two years;² **שֶׁתַּעֲמוֹד שְׁתֵּי שָׁנִים** — that it should stay at least **two years** **בְּיַד הַלּוֹקֵחַ** — in the hand of the buyer **מִיּוֹם לְיוֹם** — from day to day, i.e., from the date of the purchase to the same date two years later, **וַאֲפִילוּ יֵשׁ שָׁלֹשׁ תְּבוּאוֹת** — even if there are three crops **בְּאוֹתָן שְׁתֵּי שָׁנִים** — in two years; **כְּגוֹן** — for example, **שֶׁמְּכָרָהּ לוֹ** — if he sold it to him **בְּקָמוֹתֶיהָ** — when the crop was standing in it.³

---

1. *Toras Kohanim, perek* 3:4; *Bava Metzia* 58b. This is in contrast to verse 17 below where the same word is used for verbal harassment.

2. According to this interpretation, שְׁנֵי is interpreted as "two," to imply that the sale must last for at least two years (*Gur Aryeh*; see *Gur Aryeh HaShalem*, note 104). This is an exegetical interpretation, for the plural feminine noun תְּבוּאוֹת should take the feminine number שְׁתֵּי rather than the masculine number שְׁנֵי (see *Maskil LeDavid*).

Alternatively, the Rabbis derive this law from the plural שְׁנֵי, "years of," which implies a minimum of two. This is considered an exegetical interpretation because

the flow of the language indicates that our verse is a continuation of the topic of financial victimization which was introduced in the preceding verse and which is continued in the following verse. The interpretation of the Rabbis has nothing to do with financial victimization. This is because the type of financial victimization referred to by the preceding verse, charging an exorbitant price, does not apply to real estate (*Sefer Zikaron*; see also *Be'er Yitzchak*; Rashi to *Arachin* 18b, s.v., שתי שנים שבשדה אחוזה appears to support *Sefer Zikaron's* position).

3. If one buys a field with the crop standing in it, he can harvest that crop, harvest another crop a year later,

shall he sell to you. *16 According to the greater number of years you shall increase its purchase, and according to the lesser number of years you shall reduce its purchase; for he is selling you the number of crops.*
17 Do not harass one another, and you

טז יִמְכָּר־לָךְ: לְפִי ׀ רֹב הַשָּׁנִים תַּרְבֶּה מִקְנָתוֹ וּלְפִי מְעֹט הַשָּׁנִים תַּמְעִיט מִקְנָתוֹ כִּי מִסְפַּר תְּבוּאֹת הוּא מֹכֵר לָךְ: יז וְלֹא תוֹנוּ אִישׁ אֶת־עֲמִיתוֹ

───── אונקלוס ─────

יְזַבֶּן לָךְ: טז לְפוּם סְגִיאוּת שְׁנַיָּא תַסְגֵּי זְבִינוֹהִי וּלְפוּם זְעֵירוּת שְׁנַיָּא תַזְעֵר זְבִינוֹהִי אֲרֵי מִנְיַן עֲלַלְתָּא הוּא מְזַבֵּן לָךְ: יז וְלָא תוֹנוּן גְּבַר יָת חַבְרֵהּ

───── רש"י ─────

ושני אינו יוצא מפשוטו, כלומר, מספר שנים של תבואות ולא של שדפון ומיעוט שנים (ת"כ שם י; ערכין כט:): (טז) **תרבה מקנתו.** תמכרנה ביוקר: **תמעיט מקנתו.** תמעיט בדמיה: (יז) **ולא תונו איש את עמיתו.** כאן הזהיר על אונאת דברים, שלא יקניט את חבירו ולא ישיאנו עצה שאינה הוגנת לו לפי דרכו. ואם תאמר מי יודע אם נתכוונתי לרעה, לכך נאמר "ויראת מאלהיך", היודע מחשבות הוא יודע. כל דבר המסור ללב, שאין מכיר אלא מי שהמחשבה בלבו, (ת"כ פרק ד:ח) שלא יקנים איש את חבירו ולא ישיאנו עצה שאינה הוגנת לו לפי דרכו והנאתו של יועץ. ואם תאמר מי יודע נתכוונתי לרעה, לכך נאמר ויראת מאלהיך, היודע מחשבות הוא יודע.

───── RASHI ELUCIDATED ─────

וּשְׁנֵי אֵינוֹ יוֹצֵא מִפְּשׁוּטוֹ — And the word שְׁנֵי does not leave its simple meaning,[1] כְּלוֹמַר — as if to say, וּמִעוּט שָׁנִים — but not of blight,[2] וְלֹא שֶׁל שִׁדָּפוֹן — a number of years of crops, מִסְפַּר שָׁנִים שֶׁל תְּבוּאוֹת — and the minimum of "years" is two.[3,4] שָׁנִים[4] —

16. תַּרְבֶּה מִקְנָתוֹ — YOU SHALL INCREASE ITS PURCHASE. תִּמְכְּרֶנָּה בְּיוֹקֶר — You shall sell it for a high price.

☐ **תַּמְעִיט מִקְנָתוֹ — YOU SHALL REDUCE ITS PURCHASE.** תַּמְעִיט בְּדָמֶיהָ — You shall reduce its price.[5]

17. וְלֹא תוֹנוּ אִישׁ אֶת עֲמִיתוֹ — DO NOT HARASS ONE ANOTHER. כָּאן הִזְהִיר — Here [the Torah] enjoins us עַל אוֹנָאַת דְּבָרִים — regarding verbal harassment;[6] שֶׁלֹּא יַקְנִיט אֶת חֲבֵרוֹ — that one should not annoy his fellow וְלֹא יַשִּׂיאֶנּוּ עֵצָה — nor give him advice שֶׁאֵינָהּ הוֹגֶנֶת לוֹ — that is not appropriate for him, לְפִי דַרְכּוֹ — but is in accord with the mode of life וַהֲנָאָתוֹ — and the benefit שֶׁל יוֹעֵץ — of the advisor.[7] וְאִם תֹּאמַר — And if you will say: מִי יוֹדֵעַ — "Who knows אִם נִתְכַּוַּנְתִּי לְרָעָה — if I had bad intentions when I gave the advice?" לְכָךְ נֶאֱמַר — This is why it says, "וְיָרֵאתָ מֵאֱלֹהֶיךָ" — "You shall have fear of your God", הוּא יוֹדֵעַ — the One Who knows thoughts, הַיּוֹדֵעַ מַחְשָׁבוֹת — He knows your intentions. כָּל דָּבָר הַמָּסוּר לַלֵּב — Anything given over to the heart, שֶׁאֵין מַכִּיר אֶלָּא מִי שֶׁהַמַּחֲשָׁבָה בְּלִבּוֹ — which no one can recognize except the one in whose heart the thought is,

---

and harvest a third crop the following year, before the second year expires.

1. According to *Gur Aryeh* (cited in note 2 on p. 326), Rashi here says that even the Rabbis who interpret שְׁנֵי as "two" to arrive at the minimum amount of time that the land must remain in the hands of the buyer do not ignore the simple meaning of the word in context, "years," in their interpretation. According to *Sefer Zikaron*, Rashi here tells us not to make the mistake of understanding that the interpretation of the Rabbis is based on an understanding of שְׁנֵי as "two."

2. The minimum two years must be two years of potential crops. Years of blight are not counted. This is a condition of the law that the field must stay in the hands of the purchaser for a minimum of two years. According to *Gur Aryeh*, Rashi cites it to show that even the Rabbis who interpreted שְׁנֵי as "two" did not reject the word's other meaning, "years," in their interpretation. According to *Sefer Zikaron*, Rashi cites this apparently parenthetic point in answer to a possible objection to his understanding of the Rabbis' interpretation. If we understand the Rabbis as *Gur Aryeh* does, with בְּמִסְפַּר שְׁנֵי תְבוּאוֹת meaning "by the number of two crops," the

word תְּבוּאֹת, "crops," is necessary. For the verse cannot just say, "by the number of two" — two of what? But according to his own interpretation which views the plural שְׁנֵי as the source for the basic law, why does the verse have to say תְּבוּאֹת? It could have said בְּמִסְפַּר שָׁנִים, "by the number of years." Rashi explains that the apparently superfluous תְּבוּאֹת was stated to teach us that the two years must be years of potential crops. See also Rashi to *Arachin* 30a, s.v., במספר שני תבואות.

3. According to *Sefer Zikaron*, here is where Rashi states that the Rabbis' interpretation is based on the plural of שְׁנֵי, without resorting to interpreting it as "two." According to *Gur Aryeh*, it is only the secondary law, that both of the minimum two years must not be years of blight, which is derived from the plural of שְׁנֵי.

4. *Toras Kohanim, parshasa* 3:10; *Arachin* 29b.

5. The verse does not mean "you shall increase or reduce the number of purchases he makes" (*Mizrachi; Sifsei Chachamim*).

6. *Toras Kohanim, perek* 4:1.

7. He should not give advice that benefits himself rather than the one to whom he offers the advice.

shall have fear of your God; for I am HASHEM, your God. *18* You shall perform My decrees, and observe My ordinances and perform them; and you shall dwell securely on the land.

19 The land will give its fruit and you will eat to satisfaction; and you will dwell securely upon it. *20* If you will say: What will we eat in the seventh year? — behold! we will not sow and we will not gather our crop! *21* I will ordain

וְיָרֵאתָ מֵאֱלֹהֶיךָ כִּי אֲנִי יהוה אֱלֹהֵיכֶם: וַעֲשִׂיתֶם אֶת־חֻקֹּתַי וְאֶת־מִשְׁפָּטַי תִּשְׁמְרוּ וַעֲשִׂיתֶם אֹתָם וִישַׁבְתֶּם עַל־הָאָרֶץ לָבֶטַח: וְנָתְנָה הָאָרֶץ פִּרְיָהּ וַאֲכַלְתֶּם לָשֹׂבַע וִישַׁבְתֶּם לָבֶטַח עָלֶיהָ: וְכִי תֹאמְרוּ מַה־נֹּאכַל בַּשָּׁנָה הַשְּׁבִיעִת הֵן לֹא נִזְרָע וְלֹא נֶאֱסֹף אֶת־תְּבוּאָתֵנוּ: וְצִוִּיתִי אֶת־

אונקלוס

וְתִדְחַל מֵאֱלָהָךְ אֲרֵי אֲנָא יְיָ אֱלָהֲכוֹן: יח וְתַעְבְּדוּן יָת קְיָמַי וְיָת דִּינַי תִּטְּרוּן וְתַעְבְּדוּן וְתֵיתְבוּן עַל אַרְעָא לְרָחֲצָן: יט וְתִתֵּן אַרְעָא אִבַּהּ וְתֵיכְלוּן לְמִשְׂבַּע וְתֵיתְבוּן לְרָחֲצָן עֲלַהּ: כ וַאֲרֵי תֵימְרוּן מָא נֵיכוֹל בְּשַׁתָּא שְׁבִיעֵתָא הָא לָא נִזְרַע וְלָא נִכְנוֹשׁ יָת עֲלַלְתָּנָא: כא וַאֲפַקֵּד יָת

רש"י

נֶאֱמַר בּוֹ וִירֵאתָ מֵאֱלֹהֶיךָ (שם כ, יד) מ"נח: (יח) וישבתם על הארץ לבטח. שֶׁבַּעֲוֹן שְׁמִטָּה יִשְׂרָאֵל גּוֹלִים, שֶׁנֶּאֱמַר אָז תִּרְצֶה הָאָרֶץ אֶת שַׁבְּתֹתֶיהָ, וְהִרְצָת אֶת שַׁבְּתֹתֶיהָ (לְהַלָּן כו, לד) וְשִׁבְעִים שָׁנָה שֶׁל גָּלוּת בָּבֶל כְּנֶגֶד שֶׁבַע שְׁמִטּוֹת שֶׁבִּטְּלוּ הָיוּ (דברי הימים ב לוכא):

(יט) ונתנה הארץ וגו' וישבתם לבטח עליה. שלא תדאגו משנת בצורת. ואבלתם לשבע. אף בתוך המעים תהא בו ברכה (ת"כ שם ד; שם מחוקותי פרק א/ח): (כ) ולא נאסף. אל הבית: את תבואתנו. כגון יין ופירות האילן וספיחין הבאים מאליהם:

RASHI ELUCIDATED

וְיָרֵאתָ מֵאֱלֹהֶיךָ — "you shall have fear of your God."[1] נֶאֱמַר בּוֹ – of it is it said,

18. וִישַׁבְתֶּם עַל הָאָרֶץ לָבֶטַח – AND YOU SHALL DWELL SECURELY ON THE LAND. שֶׁבַּעֲוֹן שְׁמִטָּה – For through the sin of not observing *shemittah* יִשְׂרָאֵל גּוֹלִים – Israel goes into exile,[2] שֶׁנֶּאֱמַר – for it says, אָז תִּרְצֶה הָאָרֶץ אֶת שַׁבְּתֹתֶיהָ, – "Then the land will appease its *shemittah* years ... וְהִרְצָת אֶת שַׁבְּתֹתֶיהָ[3] – and it will make its *shemittahs* appeasing."[3] וְשִׁבְעִים שָׁנָה – The seventy years שֶׁל גָּלוּת בָּבֶל – of the Babylonian Exile[4] כְּנֶגֶד שֶׁבַע שְׁמִטּוֹת שֶׁבִּטְּלוּ הָיוּ – corresponded to the seventy *shemittah* years that they neglected.[4]

19. וְנָתְנָה הָאָרֶץ וְגוֹמֵר וִישַׁבְתֶּם לָבֶטַח עָלֶיהָ – THE LAND WILL GIVE, ETC., AND YOU WILL DWELL SECURELY UPON IT. This means שֶׁלֹּא תִדְאֲגוּ – that you will have no worry מִשְּׁנַת בַּצֹּרֶת – of a year of drought.[5]

וַאֲכַלְתֶּם לָשֹׂבַע – AND YOU WILL EAT TO SATISFACTION. אַף בְּתוֹךְ הַמֵּעַיִם – Even within the innards תְּהֵא בּוֹ בְרָכָה[6] – there will be in it a blessing, i.e., one will feel satisfied after having eaten a small quantity.[6]

20. וְלֹא נֶאֱסֹף – AND WE WILL NOT GATHER אֶל הַבַּיִת – into the house.[7]

אֶת תְּבוּאָתֵנוּ – OUR CROP. כְּגוֹן – For instance, יַיִן – wine, וּפֵרוֹת הָאִילָן – and fruits of the tree, וּסְפִיחִין – and aftergrowths of fruits of the field, הַבָּאִים מֵאֲלֵיהֶם – which come, i.e., grow, on their own, without man having sown them.[8]

---

1. *Toras Kohanim, perek* 4:2; *Bava Metzia* 58b. See also Rashi to 19:14 and 19:32 above.
2. Rashi explains why this promise was given specifically in the context of the commandment to keep *shemittah* (*Devek Tov*).
3. Below 26:34.
4. See *II Chronicles* 36:21 which reads: "... until the land has appeased its sabbaticals ... to complete seventy years." See Rashi to that verse and to 26:35 below.
5. The security spoken of in this verse, as opposed to that in the preceding verse, has to do with the yield of crops mentioned at the beginning of the verse (*Be'er BaSadeh*).
6. *Toras Kohanim, perek* 4:4, and *Bechukosai, perek* 1:7. The verse has already said, "the land will give its fruit," which implies that there will be enough food. "You will eat to satisfaction" therefore does not refer to the quantity of food that will grow. Rather, it refers to the effect the food has after it is eaten; it is food that brings satisfaction (*Mizrachi; Sifsei Chachamim*).
7. See following note.
8. "Behold! we will not sow" in and of itself seems to imply "we will not gather our crop," for if there is no crop

329 / VAYIKRA/LEVITICUS — PARASHAS BEHAR   25/22-23

My blessing for you in the sixth year and it will yield a crop sufficient for the three years. ²² You will sow in the eighth year, but you will eat from the old crop; until the ninth year, until the arrival of its crop, you will eat the old.

²³ The land shall not be sold in per-

בְּרַכְתִּי לָכֶם בַּשָּׁנָה הַשִּׁשִּׁית וְעָשָׂת אֶת־הַתְּבוּאָה לִשְׁלֹשׁ הַשָּׁנִים: כּב וּזְרַעְתֶּם אֵת הַשָּׁנָה הַשְּׁמִינִת וַאֲכַלְתֶּם מִן־הַתְּבוּאָה יָשָׁן עַד ׀ הַשָּׁנָה הַתְּשִׁיעִת עַד־בּוֹא תְּבוּאָתָהּ תֹּאכְלוּ יָשָׁן: כּג וְהָאָרֶץ לֹא תִמָּכֵר

— אונקלוס —

בְּרַכְתִּי לְכוֹן בְּשַׁתָּא שְׁתִיתֵתָא וְתַעֲבֵד יָת עֲלַלְתָּא לִתְלָת שְׁנִין: כּב וְתִזְרְעוּן יָת שַׁתָּא תְמִינָאָה וְתֵיכְלוּן מִן עֲלַלְתָּא עַתִּיקָא עַד שַׁתָּא תְשִׁיעָאָה עַד מֵעַל עֲלַלְתַּהּ תֵּיכְלוּן עַתִּיקָא: כּג וְאַרְעָא לָא תִזְדַּבַּן

— רש״י —

(כא) **לשלש השנים.** לקצת השישית, מניסן ועד ר״ה, ולשביעית ולשמינית, שיזרעו בשמינית במרחשון ויקצרו בניסן: (כב) **עד השנה התשיעית.** עד חג הסכות של תשיעית שהוא עת בוא תבואתה של שמינית לתוך הבית, שכל ימות הקיץ היו בשדה בגרנות ובתשרי הוא עת האסיף לבית. ופעמים שהיתה צריכה לעשות לארבע שנים, בששית שלפני השמטה השביעית, שהן בטלין מעבודת קרקע שתי שנים רצופות, השביעית והיובל. ומקרא זה נאמר בשאר השמטות כולן: (כג) **והארץ לא תמכר וגו׳.** ליתן לאו על חזרת שדות לבעלים ביובל שלא יהא הלוקח כובשה (ת״כ פרק ד:ח)

— RASHI ELUCIDATED —

21. לִשְׁלֹשׁ הַשָּׁנִים – FOR THE THREE YEARS. לִקְצָת הַשִּׁשִּׁית – For part of the sixth, מִנִּיסָן וְעַד רֹאשׁ הַשָּׁנָה – from Nissan until Rosh Hashanah, וְלַשְּׁבִיעִית – and for the seventh, וְלַשְּׁמִינִית – and for the eighth, שֶׁיִּזְרְעוּ בַּשְּׁמִינִית – for they will sow in the eighth year בְּמַרְחֶשְׁוָן – in the autumn month of Marcheshvan, וְיִקְצְרוּ בְּנִיסָן – and they will reap in the spring month of Nissan.[1]

22. עַד הַשָּׁנָה הַתְּשִׁיעִית – UNTIL THE NINTH YEAR. עַד חַג הַסֻּכּוֹת – Until the Festival of *Succos* שֶׁל תְּשִׁיעִית – of the ninth year, שֶׁהוּא עֵת בּוֹא – which is the time of the coming תְּבוּאָתָהּ שֶׁל שְׁמִינִית – of the crop of the eighth year לְתוֹךְ הַבַּיִת – into the house. שֶׁכָּל יְמוֹת הַקַּיִץ – For all the days of the summer, הָיוּ בַשָּׂדֶה – [the crops] were in the field, בַּגֳּרָנוֹת – on the threshing floors. וּבְתִשְׁרֵי – And in the month of Tishrei, הוּא עֵת הָאָסִיף לַבַּיִת – it is the time of the gathering of the crops into the house.[2] וּפְעָמִים – There were times שֶׁהָיְתָה צְרִיכָה לַעֲשׂוֹת – that [the sixth year] had to produce crops לְאַרְבַּע שָׁנִים – for parts of four calendar years, בַּשִּׁשִּׁית – on the sixth year שֶׁהֵן בְּטֵלִין מֵעֲבוֹדַת – which precedes the seventh *shemittah* of the *yovel* cycle, קַרְקַע – when they are idle from the work of the land שְׁתֵּי שָׁנִים רְצוּפוֹת – two consecutive years, הַשְּׁבִיעִית וְהַיּוֹבֵל – the seventh year, and the *yovel* year. וּמִקְרָא זֶה נֶאֱמַר – This verse, which mentions only three years, is stated בִּשְׁאָר הַשְּׁמִטּוֹת כֻּלָּן – with regard to all of the other *shemittah* years.

23. וְהָאָרֶץ לֹא תִמָּכֵר וְגוֹמֵר – THE LAND SHALL NOT BE SOLD, ETC. This verse is stated לִתֵּן לָאו – to ordain a negative commandment עַל חֲזָרַת שָׂדוֹת לַבְּעָלִים – regarding returning fields to their original owners בַּיּוֹבֵל – on the *yovel* year,[3] שֶׁלֹּא יְהֵא הַלּוֹקֵחַ כּוֹבְשָׁהּ – that the buyer should not hold onto it.[3]

---

sown, no crop can be gathered. The verse states "we will not gather our crop" to include crops that grow without having been sown that year (*Minchas Yehudah; Sifsei Chachamim*). Rashi explains that the argument regarding such crops would be, "We will not gather them *into the house*"; that is, we cannot pick them and store them as an owner normally would, but must treat them as produce that has no owner (*Even Yaakov*).

1. The sixth-year crop will be used not for three full years, but for parts of three calendar years: the sixth year, from Nissan until the end of the year; the entire seventh year; and at least until Nissan of the eighth year, when the winter crop will be fully grown.

2. Rashi in his preceding comment stated that the crop of the eighth year will be ready for reaping by Nissan of the eighth year. But this does not contradict his statement here that crops of the sixth year will still be eaten into the ninth year. Although the crops of the eighth year will have been reaped by then, there will be such a surplus of crops from the sixth year, that the crops of the eighth year will remain in storage until the supply from the sixth is exhausted at the beginning of the ninth year (*Mizrachi; Sifsei Chachamim*).

3. *Toras Kohanim, perek* 4:8. Verses 10 and 13 have already ordained a positive commandment to this effect.

לִצְמִתֻת כִּי־לִי הָאָרֶץ כִּי־גֵרִים וְתוֹשָׁבִים אַתֶּם עִמָּדִי: וּבְכֹל אֶרֶץ אֲחֻזַּתְכֶם גְּאֻלָּה תִּתְּנוּ לָאָרֶץ: רביעי כִּי־יָמוּךְ אָחִיךָ וּמָכַר מֵאֲחֻזָּתוֹ וּבָא גֹאֲלוֹ הַקָּרֹב אֵלָיו וְגָאַל אֵת מִמְכַּר אָחִיו: וְאִישׁ

petuity, for the land is Mine; for you are sojourners and residents with Me. **24** In the entire land of your ancestral heritage you shall provide redemption for the land. **25** If your brother becomes impoverished and sells of his ancestral heritage, his redeemer who is closest to him shall come and redeem his brother's sale. **26** If a man

―――― אונקלוס ――――

לַחֲלוּטִין אֲרֵי דִילִי אַרְעָא אֲרֵי דַיָּרִין וְתוֹתָבִין אַתּוּן קֳדָמָי: כד וּבְכֹל אֲרַע אַחֲסַנְתְּכוֹן פֻּרְקָנָא תִתְּנוּן לְאַרְעָא: כה אֲרֵי יִתְמַסְכַּן אֲחוּךְ וִיזַבֵּן מֵאַחֲסַנְתֵּהּ וְיֵיתֵי פָרִיקֵהּ דְּקָרִיב לֵהּ וְיִפְרוֹק יָת זְבִינֵי אֲחוּהִי: כו וּגְבַר

―――― רש"י ――――

לצמתת. לפסיקה, למכירה פסוקה עולמית: **כי לי הארץ.** אל תרע עינך בה (שם) שאינה שלך: (כד) **ובכל ארץ אחזתכם.** לרבות בתים ועבד עברי, ודבר זה מפורש בקדושין בפרק א' (כא.). ולפי פשוטו סמוך לפרשה שלאחריו, שהמוכר אחוזתו רשאי לגאלה לאחר

שתי שנים או הוא או קרובו ואין הלוקח יכול לעכב: (כה) **כי ימוך אחיך ומכר.** מלמד שאין אדם רשאי למכור שדהו אלא מחמת דוחק עוני (ת"כ פרק ה:א): **מאחזתו.** ולא כולה, למדה תורה דרך ארץ שישייר שדה לעצמו (שם): **וגאל את ממכר אחיו.** ואין הלוקח יכול לעכב:

―――― RASHI ELUCIDATED ――――

☐ לִצְמִתֻת — IN PERPETUITY. This word is synonymous with לִפְסִיקָה — "for severing"; לַמְכִירָה פְּסוּקָה עוֹלָמִית — for a categorical, everlasting sale, i.e., a sale that "severs" the owner from his field.

☐ כִּי לִי הָאָרֶץ — FOR THE LAND IS MINE. אַל תֵּרַע עֵינְךָ בָּהּ — Let your eye not be evil upon it, i.e., do not return it begrudgingly,[1] שֶׁאֵינָהּ שֶׁלָּךְ — for it is not yours.

24. וּבְכֹל אֶרֶץ אֲחֻזַּתְכֶם — IN THE ENTIRE LAND OF YOUR ANCESTRAL HERITAGE. This verse is written לְרַבּוֹת בָּתִּים — to include houses וְעֶבֶד עִבְרִי — and a Hebrew servant.[2] וְדָבָר זֶה — This matter בְּפֶרֶק רִאשׁוֹן — in the first chapter.[3] in *Kiddushin*[3] בְּקִדּוּשִׁין — is explained מְפֹרָשׁ — And according to its simple meaning, סָמוּךְ לְפָרָשָׁה שֶׁלְּאַחֲרָיו — [our verse] is linked to the passage that follows it, שֶׁהַמּוֹכֵר אֲחֻזָּתוֹ — that one who sells his ancestral heritage רַשַּׁאי לְגָאֳלָהּ — is permitted to redeem it לְאַחַר שְׁתֵּי שָׁנִים — after two years have elapsed since the sale, אוֹ הוּא — either he אוֹ קְרוֹבוֹ — or his relative, וְאֵין הַלּוֹקֵחַ יָכוֹל לְעַכֵּב — and the buyer cannot prevent him.[4]

25. כִּי יָמוּךְ אָחִיךָ וּמָכַר — IF YOUR BROTHER BECOMES IMPOVERISHED. מְלַמֵּד — This teaches us שֶׁאֵין — אֶלָּא מֵחֲמַת דּוֹחַק עוֹנִי — to sell his field[5] לִמְכּוֹר שָׂדֵהוּ — that a person is not permitted אָדָם רַשַּׁאי — except when under the pressure of poverty.[5]

☐ מֵאֲחֻזָּתוֹ — OF HIS ANCESTRAL HERITAGE. וְלֹא כֻלָּהּ — But not all of it.[6] לִמְּדָה תוֹרָה דֶּרֶךְ אֶרֶץ — The Torah teaches us proper conduct, שֶׁיְּשַׁיֵּיר שָׂדֶה לְעַצְמוֹ[7] — that he should leave a field for himself.[7]

☐ וְגָאַל אֵת מִמְכַּר אָחִיו — AND REDEEM HIS BROTHER'S SALE. וְאֵין הַלּוֹקֵחַ יָכוֹל לְעַכֵּב — The buyer is not able to prevent him.

---

1. *Toras Kohanim, perek* 4:8.

2. The following verse states that fields which have been sold can be redeemed not only by the seller himself, but even by his relatives. This law does not explicitly refer to houses, or to Jews sold into servitude. The apparently superfluous וּבְכֹל of our verse teaches us that relatives can redeem in those cases, too. There are varying opinions among the commentators as to whether this interpretation refers to houses of a walled city (see vv. 29-30 below) or to unwalled towns (v. 31), and to whether it refers to a Jew sold to another Jew or to a Jew who has sold himself to a non-Jew. See *Mizrachi, Sefer Zikaron, Nachalas Yaakov,* and *Sifsei Chachamim*.

3. *Kiddushin* 21a.

4. Although redemption has been alluded to earlier (see v. 15 and Rashi there), Rashi says that according to the simple meaning our verse is linked to the following verse, for only in the following verse does the Torah begin explicit discussion of the laws of redemption (*Gur Aryeh*).

5. *Toras Kohanim, perek* 5:1.

6. "*Of* his ancestral heritage" implies less than the entire ancestral heritage. See Rashi to 1:2 above. See also Rashi to 4:2 and 22:7.

7. *Toras Kohanim, perek* 5:1.

331 / VAYIKRA/LEVITICUS — PARASHAS BEHAR — 25/27-28 — כה/כז-כח

will have no redeemer, but his means suffice and he acquires enough for its redemption, ²⁷ and he shall calculate the years of his sale and he shall return the excess to the man to whom he had sold it; and he shall return to his ancestral heritage. ²⁸ But if he does not acquire sufficient means to repay him,

כִּי לֹא יִהְיֶה־לּוֹ גֹּאֵל וְהִשִּׂיגָה יָדוֹ וּמָצָא כְּדֵי גְאֻלָּתוֹ: כז וְחִשַּׁב אֶת־שְׁנֵי מִמְכָּרוֹ וְהֵשִׁיב אֶת־הָעֹדֵף לָאִישׁ אֲשֶׁר מָכַר־לוֹ וְשָׁב לַאֲחֻזָּתוֹ: כח וְאִם לֹא־מָצְאָה יָדוֹ דֵּי הָשִׁיב לוֹ

― אונקלוס ―

אֲרֵי לָא יְהֵי לֵהּ פָּרִיק וְתַדְבֵּק יְדֵהּ וְיִשְׁכַּח כְּמִסַּת פֻּרְקָנֵהּ: כז וִיחַשַּׁב יָת שְׁנֵי זְבִינוֹהִי וְיָתֵב יָת מוֹתָרָא לִגְבַר דִּי זַבִּין לֵהּ וִיתוּב לְאַחֲסַנְתֵּהּ: כח וְאִם לָא תַשְׁכַּח יְדֵהּ כְּמִסַּת דְּאָתֵיב לֵהּ

― רש״י ―

(כו) ואיש כי לא יהיה לו גואל. וְכִי יֵשׁ לְךָ אָדָם בְּיִשְׂרָאֵל שֶׁאֵין לוֹ גוֹאֲלִים, אֶלָּא גוֹאֵל שֶׁיּוּכַל לִגְאוֹל מִמְכָּרוֹ (שם ב; קידושין כא.): **(כז) וחשב את שני ממכרו.** כַּמָּה שָׁנִים הָיוּ עַד הַיּוֹבֵל כָּךְ וְכָךְ, וּבְכַמָּה מְכַרְתִּיהָ לְךָ בְּכָךְ וְכָךְ, עָתִיד הָיִיתָ לְהַחֲזִירָהּ בַּיּוֹבֵל, נִמְצֵאתָ קוֹנֶה מִסְפַּר הַתְּבוּאוֹת כְּפִי חֶשְׁבּוֹן שֶׁל כָּל שָׁנָה,

אֲכַלְתָּ אוֹתָהּ שָׁלֹשׁ שָׁנִים אוֹ אַרְבַּע, הוֹצֵא אֶת דְּמֵיהֶן מִן הַחֶשְׁבּוֹן וְטוֹל אֶת הַשְּׁאָר. וְזֶהוּ: **והשיב את העדף.** בִּדְמֵי הַמֶּקַח עַל הָאֲכִילָה שֶׁאֲכָלָהּ, וְיִתְּנֵם לַלּוֹקֵחַ: **לאיש אשר מכר לו.** הַמּוֹכֵר הַזֶּה שֶׁבָּא לְגָאֳלָהּ (ת״כ שם כג; ערכין ל.): **(כח) [די השיב לו.** מִכָּאן שֶׁאֵינוֹ גּוֹאֵל לַחֲצָאִין (ת״כ שם ה; ערכין ל.-ל:):]

― RASHI ELUCIDATED ―

26. וְכִי יֵשׁ לְךָ אָדָם בְּיִשְׂרָאֵל — **Do you have,** i.e., is there, **a person in Israel** שֶׁאֵין לוֹ גוֹאֲלִים — **who has no redeemers?**[1] אֶלָּא — **But** the verse speaks of גּוֹאֵל שֶׁיּוּכַל — **a redeemer who is able,** i.e., who has the financial means, ²לִגְאוֹל מִמְכָּרוֹ — **to redeem that which [the seller] has sold.**[2]

27. וְחִשַּׁב אֶת שְׁנֵי מִמְכָּרוֹ — **AND HE SHALL CALCULATE THE YEARS OF HIS SALE.** The seller asks the buyer, כַּמָּה שָׁנִים הָיוּ עַד הַיּוֹבֵל — **"How many years were there** from the time you bought the field **until the** *yovel* **year?"** The buyer replies, כָּךְ וְכָךְ — **"Such and such** a number of years." וּבְכַמָּה מְכַרְתִּיהָ לְךָ — **"And for how much did I sell it to you?"** בְּכָךְ וְכָךְ — **"For such and such** an amount." The seller then calculates, עָתִיד הָיִיתָ לְהַחֲזִירָהּ בַּיּוֹבֵל — **"You were destined to return [the field]** to me **at the** *yovel* year. נִמְצֵאתָ קוֹנֶה — **It thus turns out that you have bought** מִסְפַּר הַתְּבוּאוֹת — **a number of crops** כְּפִי חֶשְׁבּוֹן שֶׁל כָּל שָׁנָה — **according to the total of each year.**[3] אֲכַלְתָּ אוֹתָהּ — **You have** consumed crops from it, שָׁלֹשׁ שָׁנִים אוֹ אַרְבַּע — **for three years or four.** הוֹצֵא אֶת דְּמֵיהֶן מִן הַחֶשְׁבּוֹן — **Deduct their value from the total** that you paid me, וְטוֹל אֶת הַשְּׁאָר — **and take** back **the rest."** וְזֶהוּ — **This is** what is meant by the next words of the verse,

□ וְהֵשִׁיב אֶת הָעֹדֵף — **AND HE SHALL RETURN THE EXCESS** בִּדְמֵי הַמֶּקַח — **of the purchase price** עַל הָאֲכִילָה שֶׁאֲכָלָהּ — **over the consuming which [the buyer] consumed** during the years he had the field, וְיִתְּנֵם לַלּוֹקֵחַ — **and he shall give it** back **to the buyer,** i.e., he returns to the buyer the difference between the purchase price and the value of the crops which the buyer harvested, that is,

□ לָאִישׁ אֲשֶׁר מָכַר לוֹ — **TO THE MAN TO WHOM HE HAD SOLD IT.** "He" refers to ⁴הַמּוֹכֵר הַזֶּה שֶׁבָּא לְגָאֳלָהּ — this seller who comes to redeem it.[4]

28. {דֵּי הָשִׁיב לוֹ — **SUFFICIENT MEANS TO REPAY HIM.** מִכָּאן — **From here** we learn ⁵שֶׁאֵינוֹ גּוֹאֵל לַחֲצָאִין — **that he does not redeem by fraction.**[5]}

---

1. The only Jews who have no blood relatives are childless converts. Our verse cannot refer to them because it speaks of those whose ancestors were allotted heritages in the Land of Israel, to the exclusion of converts (*Mizrachi; Sifsei Chachamim*).

2. *Toras Kohanim, perek* 5:2; *Kiddushin* 21a.

3. You have not bought the land per se, but rather one crop a year from the time of the purchase until the *yovel*.

4. *Toras Kohanim, perek* 5:3; *Arachin* 30a. Our verse teaches us that if the first buyer sells the field to another buyer at a higher rate than it was sold to him, the original seller does not redeem it from the second buyer at the higher rate, but rather from the first buyer at the lower rate (*Mizrachi; Sifsei Chachamim*). Furthermore, Rashi makes it clear that לָאִישׁ אֲשֶׁר מָכַר לוֹ means "to the man to whom he had sold it," i.e., the buyer; it does not mean "the man who sold it to him," i.e., the seller (*Mesiach Ilmim*).

5. *Toras Kohanim, perek* 5:5; see also *Arachin* 30a-b where this law is derived from a different source. The verse would have been clear without the word דֵּי, "sufficient." This word was written to teach us that if he does not have sufficient funds to redeem the entire

then his sale shall remain in possession of its purchaser until the yovel year; in the yovel, it shall leave and return to his ancestral heritage. ²⁹ If a man shall sell a residence house in a walled city, its redemption shall be until the end of the year of its sale; its period of redemption shall be days. ³⁰ But if it is not redeemed until its full year has elapsed,

וְהָיָה מִמְכָּרוֹ בְּיַד הַקֹּנֶה אֹתוֹ עַד
שְׁנַת הַיּוֹבֵל וְיָצָא בַיֹּבֵל וְשָׁב
לַאֲחֻזָּתוֹ: [חמישי [שלישי]] כט וְאִישׁ כִּי־
יִמְכֹּר בֵּית־מוֹשַׁב עִיר חוֹמָה וְהָיְתָה
גְאֻלָּתוֹ עַד־תֹּם שְׁנַת מִמְכָּרוֹ
יָמִים תִּהְיֶה גְאֻלָּתוֹ: ל וְאִם לֹא־
יִגָּאֵל עַד־מְלֹאת לוֹ שָׁנָה תְמִימָה

──────── אונקלוס ────────

וִיהֵי זְבִינוֹהִי בִּידָא דְזָבֵן יָתֵהּ עַד שַׁתָּא דְיוֹבֵלָא וְיִפּוֹק בְּיוֹבֵלָא וִיתוּב לְאַחֲסַנְתֵּהּ: כט וּגְבַר אֲרֵי יְזַבֵּן בֵּית מוֹתַב קַרְתָּא מַקְפָא שׁוּר וּתְהֵי פֻרְקָנֵהּ עַד מִשְׁלַם שַׁתָּא דִזְבִינוֹהִי עִדָּן בְּעִדָּן תְּהֵא פֻרְקָנֵהּ: ל וְאִם לָא יִתְפְּרֵק עַד מִשְׁלַם לֵהּ שַׁתָּא שְׁלֶמְתָּא

──────── רש״י ────────

עַד שְׁנַת הַיּוֹבֵל. שֶׁלֹּא יִכָּנֵס לְתוֹךְ אוֹתָהּ שָׁנָה כְּלוּם שֶׁהַיּוֹבֵל מְשַׁמֵּט בִּתְחִלָּתוֹ (ת״כ שם ז): (כט) בֵּית מוֹשַׁב עִיר חוֹמָה. בַּיִת בְּתוֹךְ עִיר הַמּוּקֶּפֶת חוֹמָה מִימוֹת יְהוֹשֻׁעַ בִּן נוּן (שם פרשתא ד:ה; ערכין לב.): וְהָיְתָה גְאֻלָּתוֹ. לְפִי שֶׁנֶּאֱ׳ בְּשָׂדֶה שִׁכֵּל לִגְאוֹל מִשְׁתֵּי שָׁנִים וְאֵילָךְ כָּל זְמַן שֶׁיִּרְצֶה, וּבְתוֹךְ שְׁתֵּי שָׁנִים הָרִאשׁוֹנִים אֵינוֹ יָכוֹל לִגְאוֹל, הוֹלֵךְ לְפָרֵשׁ בָּזֶה שֶׁהוּא חִלּוּף, שֶׁאִם רָצָה לִגְאוֹל בַּשָּׁנָה הָרִאשׁוֹנָה גּוֹאֲלָהּ, וּלְאַחַר מִכַּאן אֵינוֹ גּוֹאֲלָהּ: שֶׁל בַּיִת: יָמִים. יְמֵי שָׁנָה שְׁלֵמָה קְרוּיִים יָמִים וְכֵן תֵּשֵׁב הַנַּעֲרָ אִתָּנוּ יָמִים וגו׳ (בראשית כד:נה):

──────── RASHI ELUCIDATED ────────

□ עַד שְׁנַת הַיּוֹבֵל — UNTIL THE *YOVEL* YEAR. שֶׁלֹּא יִכָּנֵס — That he should not enter לְתוֹךְ אוֹתָהּ שָׁנָה into that year while in possession of the field כְּלוּם — at all, שֶׁהַיּוֹבֵל מְשַׁמֵּט — for the *yovel* year releases fields to their original owners בִּתְחִלָּתוֹ — at its beginning.[1]

□ **29.** בֵּית מוֹשַׁב עִיר חוֹמָה — A RESIDENCE HOUSE IN A WALLED CITY. בַּיִת בְּתוֹךְ עִיר — A house inside a city הַמּוּקֶּפֶת חוֹמָה — that is surrounded by a wall[3] מִימוֹת יְהוֹשֻׁעַ בִּן נוּן — from the days of Joshua the son of Nun.[2,3]

□ וְהָיְתָה גְאֻלָּתוֹ — ITS REDEMPTION SHALL BE. לְפִי שֶׁנֶּאֱמַר — Since it says בְּשָׂדֶה — about a field שֶׁיָּכוֹל לִגְאֹל — that he is able to redeem it מִשְּׁתֵּי שָׁנִים וְאֵילָךְ — from two years after the sale and onward, כָּל זְמַן שֶׁיִּרְצֶה — whenever he wishes, וּבְתוֹךְ שְׁתֵּי שָׁנִים הָרִאשׁוֹנִים — and that within the first two years after the sale אֵינוֹ יָכוֹל לִגְאֹל — he is not able to redeem it, הֻצְרַךְ לִפְרֹט בָּזֶה — [the Torah] needed to specify about this, the house in a walled city, שֶׁהוּא חִלּוּף — that it is the opposite; שֶׁאִם — רָצָה לִגְאֹל — that if he wants to redeem בַּשָּׁנָה הָרִאשׁוֹנָה — in the first year after the sale גּוֹאֲלָהּ — he may redeem it, וּלְאַחַר מִכָּאן — but after that point, אֵינוֹ גּוֹאֲלָהּ — he may not redeem it.

□ וְהָיְתָה גְאֻלָּתוֹ — ITS REDEMPTION SHALL BE, i.e., שֶׁל בַּיִת — the redemption of the house.[4]

□ יָמִים — DAYS. יְמֵי שָׁנָה שְׁלֵמָה — The days of a full year קְרוּיִים יָמִים — are called "days." וְכֵן — Similarly, in יָמִים [5] ,, תֵּשֵׁב הַנַּעֲרָ אִתָּנוּ יָמִים [וְגוֹמֵר] — "let the maiden live with us for days, [etc.]"[5]

---

field, he cannot redeem part of it (*Mizrachi; Sifsei Chachamim*).

1. *Toras Kohanim*, *perek* 5:7. This is in contrast to *shemittah* which releases debts at the end of the year. See *Arachin* 28b.

2. That is, from the time the nation entered the Land under Joshua.

3. *Toras Kohanim*, *parshasa* 4:1; *Arachin* 32a. בֵּית מוֹשַׁב עִיר חוֹמָה could have been understood as, "a residence house, a walled city," i.e., a residence house *or* a walled city, comparable to the phrase בֵּית וָעִיר אֲחֻזָּתוֹ in verse 33 (so Rashi there). Rashi explains that our verse means "a residence house *in* a walled city," as we see from the following verse which refers to "the house that is in the city" (*Gur Aryeh*; *Mesiach Ilmim*).

4. וְהָיְתָה גְאֻלָתוֹ could have been understood as, "*his* re-

demption can take place," referring to the seller. But the following verse says, וְאִם לֹא יִגָּאֵל, "but if it is not redeemed," with the passive *nifal* form יִגָּאֵל indicating that the passage has been talking about the house. If it were speaking of the seller, it would have used the active *kal* form, וְאִם לֹא יִגְאַל, "but if he will not redeem" (*Sefer Zikaron; Gur Aryeh*).

5. *Genesis* 24:55. When Abraham's slave Eliezer, whom Abraham had sent as his emissary, had come to terms with Rebecca's family regarding her betrothal to Abraham's son Isaac, Rebecca's brother and mother asked that Rebecca not go to Abraham's home immediately, but remain with them for a while. They said, "Let the maiden live with us for days or ten." Rashi there, based on *Kesubos* 57b, takes "days" to be a year, and "ten" to be ten months — rather than "(two) days" and "ten

then the house that is in the city that has a wall shall be established in perpetuity to the one who purchased it, for his generations; it shall not go out in the yovel. ³¹ *And the houses of the yards, which have no*

וְקָ֣ם הַבַּ֠יִת אֲשֶׁר־בָּעִיר֩ אֲשֶׁר־
°לֹ֨א חֹמָ֜ה לַצְּמִיתֻ֗ת לַקֹּנֶ֥ה
אֹת֛וֹ לְדֹרֹתָ֖יו לֹ֥א יֵצֵ֖א בַּיֹּבֵֽל: לוֹ ק׳
לא וּבָתֵּ֣י הַחֲצֵרִ֗ים אֲשֶׁ֤ר אֵין־לָהֶם֙

──────── אונקלוס ────────

וִיקוּם בֵּיתָא דִי בְקַרְתָּא דִי לֵהּ שׁוּרָא לַחֲלוּטִין לְדִזְבַן יָתֵהּ לְדָרוֹהִי לָא יִפּוֹק בְּיוֹבֵלָא: לא וּבָתֵּי פַצְחַיָּא דִּי לֵית לְהוֹן

──────── רש״י ────────

כה/נה: (**ל**) **וקם הבית וגו׳ לצמיתות.** יצא מכחו של מוכר ועומד בכחו של קונה: [**אשר לא חמה.** לו קרינן. אמרו רבותינו ז״ל אע״פ שאין לו עכשיו הואיל והיתה לו קודם לכן (ע״כ שם ז; ערכין שם) ועיר נקבה היא והוצרך לכתוב לה, אלא מתוך שצריך לכתוב לא, זה נופל על זה]: **לא יצא ביובל.** אמר רב ספרא אם פגע בו יובל בתוך שנתו לא יצא (ערכין לא:): (**לא**) **ובתי החצרים.** כתרגומו פצחיא עיירות פתוחות מאין חומה,

──────── RASHI ELUCIDATED ────────

30. וְקָם הַבַּיִת וְגוֹמֵר לַצְּמִיתֻת — THE HOUSE, ETC., SHALL BE ESTABLISHED IN PERPETUITY. יָצָא מִכֹּחוֹ שֶׁל מוֹכֵר — It has gone out from the authority of the seller וְעוֹמֵד בְּכֹחוֹ שֶׁל קוֹנֶה — and stands under the authority of the buyer.[1]

□ {אֲשֶׁר לֹא חֹמָה} — THAT HAS A WALL. Although the spelling is לֹא, "no" or "not," לוֹ קָרֵינָן — we read it as לוֹ, "to it."[2] אָמְרוּ רַבּוֹתֵינוּ זִכְרוֹנָם לִבְרָכָה — Our Rabbis of blessed memory said that the spelling of the word teaches us the following: אַף עַל פִּי שֶׁאֵין לוֹ עַכְשָׁיו — Even though it does not have a wall at present,[3] הוֹאִיל וְהָיְתָה לוֹ קוֹדֶם לָכֵן — since it had a wall previously, the law of a walled city applies to it.[3] וְעִיר נְקֵבָה הִיא — The word עִיר is feminine, וְהֻצְרַךְ לִכְתּוֹב לָהּ — and it should have written לָהּ,[4] אֶלָּא מִתּוֹךְ שֶׁצָּרִיךְ לִכְתּוֹב לֹא — but since it had to write לֹא, "not," בִּפְנִים — inside, i.e., in the written version of the text, תִּקְּנוּ לוֹ בַּמָּסֹרֶת — they fixed it as the masculine לוֹ in the reading of the text passed on through tradition. זֶה נוֹפֵל עַל זֶה — This one falls on that one, i.e., because לוֹ and לֹא have the identical pronunciation.}[5]

□ לֹא יֵצֵא בַּיּוֹבֵל — IT SHALL NOT GO OUT IN THE YOVEL. אָמַר רַב סַפְרָא — The Amora Rav Safra said, אִם פָּגַע בּוֹ יוֹבֵל — "If the yovel year encountered it בְּתוֹךְ שְׁנָתוֹ — within its year, i.e., if the yovel year began within the year after the sale of a house in a walled city, [6]לֹא יֵצֵא — it shall not go out of the possession of the buyer."[6]

31. וּבָתֵּי הַחֲצֵרִים — AND THE HOUSES OF THE YARDS. This is to be understood כְּתַרְגּוּמוֹ — as Targum Onkelos renders it, ",פַּצְחַיָּא" — which means, עֲיָרוֹת פְּתוּחוֹת — open towns מֵאֵין חוֹמָה — without

---

days," — because one does not ask for a small amount and then add, "If you don't agree to that, give me more than that."

1. In *Genesis* 23:17, the verb קם as applied to real estate denoted transfer of ownership from one party to another. In our verse it cannot have the identical meaning, for וְקָם refers to a stage that takes place a year after the sale, whereas the house becomes the property of the buyer at the time of the sale. Rashi therefore explains that וְקָם of our verse is linked to לַצְּמִיתֻת, as indicated by the heading. Although the purchase took place a year before, there is still an aspect of ownership that is not transferred to the buyer until a year has elapsed, namely, ownership in perpetuity, without the possibility of redemption (see *Mizrachi; Nachalas Yaakov; Sifsei Chachamim*).

2. According to the *mesorah*, the word לא, "not," is to be read (and understood) as if it were spelled לו, "to him." Rashi here explains both spellings and their respective interpretations. Although the phenomenon of

לֹא is written, לוֹ is read," appears at least fifteen times in Scripture, Rashi interprets both spellings in only five verses: *Exodus* 21:8; *Isaiah* 9:2; *Psalms* 139:16; *Proverbs* 19:7; and here. The other times it appears, Rashi interprets either according to only one of the two spellings, or not at all.

3. *Toras Kohanim, parshasa* 4:7; *Arachin* 32a.

4. "To it" should have been expressed by the feminine לָהּ rather than by the masculine לוֹ.

5. This comment does not appear in many of the early printed editions of Rashi. For that reason, and because this comment seems to contradict Rashi's commentary to *Arachin* 32a (s.v., חומה אשר לוא), *Yosef Hallel* suggests that this comment was not written by Rashi, but was added later.

6. *Arachin* 31b. In the preceding phrase, "the house . . . shall be established in perpetuity to the one who purchased it," the Torah has already told us that houses in walled cities do not return to their original owners at the yovel year, unlike fields. "It shall not go out in the

חֹמָה סָבִיב עַל־שְׂדֵה הָאָרֶץ
יֵחָשֵׁב גְּאֻלָּה תִּהְיֶה־לּוֹ וּבַיֹּבֵל
לב יֵצֵא: וְעָרֵי הַלְוִיִּם בָּתֵּי עָרֵי אֲחֻזָּתָם
לג גְּאֻלַּת עוֹלָם תִּהְיֶה לַלְוִיִּם: וַאֲשֶׁר

surrounding wall, shall be considered like the field of the land; it shall have redemption, and it shall go out in the yovel. **32** And the cities of the Levites, the houses in the cities of their ancestral heritage, the Levites shall have an eternal redemption. **33** And if

— אונקלוס —

מַקָּף שׁוּרִין סְחוֹר סְחוֹר עַל חֲקַל אַרְעָא יִתְחַשָּׁב פֻּרְקָנָא תְּהֵי לֵהּ וּבְיוֹבֵלָא יִפּוֹק: לב וְקִרְוֵי לֵיוָאֵי בָּתֵּי קִרְוֵי אֲחֲסַנְתְּהוֹן פֻּרְקַן עָלַם תְּהֵי לְלֵיוָאֵי: לג וְדִי

— רש״י —

וְהַרְבֵּה יֵשׁ בְּסֵפֶר יְהוֹשֻׁעַ (פרקים יג-יט) הֶעָרִים וְחַצְרֵיהֶם. בְּחַצְרֵיהֶם וּבְטִירֹתָם (בראשית כה:טז): **עַל שְׂדֵה הָאָרֶץ יֵחָשֵׁב.** הֲרֵי הֵן כַּשָּׂדוֹת, שֶׁנִּגְאָלִין עַד הַיּוֹבֵל, וְיוֹצְאִין בַּיּוֹבֵל לַבְּעָלִים אִם לֹא נִגְאָלוּ (ת"כ פרק ו:ב-ג; ערכין לג.): **גְּאֻלָּה תִּהְיֶה לוֹ.** מִיָּד אִם יִרְצֶה. וּבָזֶה **יָפֶה כֹּחוֹ** מִכֹּחַ שָׂדוֹת, שֶׁהַשָּׂדוֹת אֵין נִגְאָלוֹת עַד שְׁתֵּי שָׁנִים (שם): **וּבַיֹּבֵל יָצֵא.** בְּחִנָּם: **(לב) וְעָרֵי הַלְוִיִּם.** אַרְבָּעִים וּשְׁמֹנֶה עִיר שֶׁנִּתְּנוּ לָהֶם: **גְּאֻלַּת עוֹלָם.** גּוֹאֵל מִיָּד וַאֲפִלּוּ לִפְנֵי שְׁתֵּי שָׁנִים אִם מְכָרוּ שָׂדֶה מִשְּׂדוֹתֵיהֶם הַנְּתוּנוֹת לָהֶם בְּאַלְפַּיִם אַמָּה

— RASHI ELUCIDATED —

□ **וְהַרְבֵּה יֵשׁ** — a wall. — There are many examples of the word used in this sense — **בְּסֵפֶר יְהוֹשֻׁעַ** — in the Book of Joshua,[1] **הֶעָרִים וְחַצְרֵיהֶם** — "the walled cities and their open towns."[2] And elsewhere, **בְּחַצְרֵיהֶם וּבְטִירֹתָם**[3] — "in their open towns and in their cities."[3]

□ **עַל שְׂדֵה הָאָרֶץ יֵחָשֵׁב** — SHALL BE CONSIDERED LIKE THE FIELD OF THE LAND. — See, **הֲרֵי הֵן כַּשָּׂדוֹת** — now, they are like fields **שֶׁנִּגְאָלִין** — which can be redeemed **עַד הַיּוֹבֵל** — until the *yovel* year, **וְיוֹצְאִין בַּיּוֹבֵל לַבְּעָלִים** — and go out of the buyer's possession **to the** original **owner at the** *yovel* year **אִם לֹא נִגְאָלוּ**[4] — if they are not redeemed.[4]

□ **גְּאֻלָּה תִּהְיֶה לוֹ** — IT SHALL HAVE REDEMPTION **מִיָּד** — immediately, **אִם יִרְצֶה** — if [the original owner] wishes.[5] **וּבָזֶה** — And in this respect **יָפֶה כֹּחוֹ** — its power, i.e., the rights the original owner has to it, is greater **מִכֹּחַ שָׂדוֹת** — than the power of fields, i.e., than the rights of the original owners of sold fields, **שֶׁהַשָּׂדוֹת אֵין נִגְאָלוֹת** — for fields cannot be redeemed **עַד שְׁתֵּי שָׁנִים**[6] — until two years have passed since the time of the sale.[6]

□ **וּבַיֹּבֵל יָצֵא** — AND IT SHALL GO OUT IN THE YOVEL **בְּחִנָּם** — without payment.[5]

32. וְעָרֵי הַלְוִיִּם — AND THE CITIES OF THE LEVITES. **אַרְבָּעִים וּשְׁמֹנֶה עִיר** — Forty-eight cities **שֶׁנִּתְּנוּ לָהֶם** — which were given to the Levites.[7]

□ **גְּאֻלַּת עוֹלָם** — ETERNAL REDEMPTION. **גּוֹאֵל מִיָּד** — He may redeem immediately, **וַאֲפִלּוּ לִפְנֵי שְׁתֵּי שָׁנִים** — even before two years have passed since the sale. **אִם מָכְרוּ שָׂדֶה** — If they sold a field **מִשְּׂדוֹתֵיהֶם** — from among their fields **הַנְּתוּנוֹת לָהֶם** — which are given to them **בְּאַלְפַּיִם אַמָּה** — in

yovel year" teaches us that even if the *yovel* year begins before the year has elapsed, before the house has become the permanent property of the buyer, it does not revert automatically to the seller. He must redeem the house within the year if he wishes to regain possession of it (*Mizrachi*).

1. Chapters 13-19.
2. The exact phrase adduced by Rashi appears only one time (*Joshua* 13:28), and Rashi there translates עָרֵי הַפְּרָזִי בְּלֹא חוֹמָה, "unprotected towns, without a wall." Variations of this phrase appear more than two dozen times in the cited chapters. It is interesting to note that the verse cited by Rashi is the only one that uses the masculine pronominal suffix הֶם- with the feminine antecedent עָרִים. All the others use the feminine suffix הֶן-.
3. *Genesis* 25:16. See Rashi to that verse.
4. *Toras Kohanim*, *perek* 6:2-3; *Arachin* 33a.

5. The two phrases, "it shall have redemption," and, "and [it shall] go out in the *yovel*," could have been understood as a single law — the house can be redeemed, and if it is redeemed, it reverts to the original owner at the *yovel* year. In his comments to these two phrases, Rashi indicates that they delineate two separate laws: These houses can be redeemed and taken back immediately, or they can return to their original owners at the *yovel* year without redemption (*Mesiach Ilmim*; *Gur Aryeh*).

6. *Toras Kohanim*, *perek* 6:2-3; *Arachin* 33a.

7. The Levites were apportioned forty-eight cities throughout the land at the time that Joshua divided up the Land of Israel (see *Numbers* 35:7; the names of these cities and their locations are given in *Joshua* Ch. 21). If they come into possession of a city through other means, the laws of this passage do not apply (*Mizrachi*).

one will buy from the Levites — the selling of a house and the city of his ancestral heritage — shall go out in the yovel; for the houses of

יִגְאַל֙ מִן־הַלְוִיִּ֔ם וְיָצָ֧א מִמְכַּר־ בַּ֛יִת וְעִ֥יר אֲחֻזָּת֖וֹ בַּיֹּבֵ֑ל כִּ֣י בָתֵּ֞י

— אונקלוס —

יִפְרוֹק מִן לֵינָאֵי וְיִפּוֹק זְבִין בֵּיתָא וְקַרְתָּא דְאַחֲסַנְתֵּהּ בְּיוֹבֵלָא אֲרֵי בָתֵּי

— רש"י —

סְבִיבוּת הֶעָרִים, אוֹ אִם מָכְרוּ בֵּית בְּעִיר חוֹמָה, גּוֹאֲלִין לְעוֹלָם וְאֵינוֹ חָלוּט לְסוֹף שָׁנָה (ת"כ שָׁם ד"ה; עֲרָכִין שָׁם): (לג) וַאֲשֶׁר יִגְאַל מִן הַלְוִיִּם. וְאִם יִקְנֶה בַּיִת אוֹ עִיר מֵהֶם, וְיָצָא בַּיֹּבֵל, אוֹתוֹ מִמְכָּר שֶׁל בַּיִת אוֹ שֶׁל עִיר וְיָשׁוּב לַלֵּוִי שֶׁמְּכָרוֹ, וְלֹא יִהְיֶה חָלוּט כִּשְׁאָר בָּתֵּי עָרֵי חוֹמָה שֶׁל יִשְׂרָאֵל, וּגְאֻלָּה זוֹ לְשׁוֹן מְכִירָה. דָּבָר אַחֵר לְפִי שֶׁנֶּאֱמַר גְּאֻלַּת עוֹלָם תִּהְיֶה לַלְוִיִּם, יָכוֹל לֹא דִּבֶּר הַכָּתוּב אֶלָּא בְּלוֹקֵחַ יִשְׂרָאֵל שֶׁקָּנָה בַיִת בְּעָרֵי הַלְוִיִּם, אֲבָל לֵוִי שֶׁקָּנָה מְלֹא יִהְיֶה חָלוּט מִלּוֹ וַאֲשֶׁר יִגְאַל מִן הַלְוִיִּם, אַף הַגּוֹאֵל מִיַּד לֵוִי גּוֹאֵל גְּאֻלַּת עוֹלָם (ת"כ שָׁם ו; עֲרָכִין שָׁם): וְיָצָא מִמְכַּר בַּיִת. הֲרֵי זוֹ מִצְוָה אַחֶרֶת, וְאִם לֹא גְאָלָה

— RASHI ELUCIDATED —

the two thousand *amos* סְבִיבוּת הֶעָרִים — around the cities,[1] אוֹ אִם מָכְרוּ בַיִת — or if they sold a house בְּעִיר חוֹמָה — in a walled city, גּוֹאֲלִין לְעוֹלָם — they may redeem it forever, וְאֵינוֹ חָלוּט — and it does not become the absolute property of the buyer, with no further possibility of redemption, לְסוֹף שָׁנָה[2] — at the end of a year, as is the case when a non-Levite sells his house in a walled city.[2]

33. וַאֲשֶׁר יִגְאַל מִן הַלְוִיִּם — AND IF ONE WILL BUY FROM THE LEVITES. וְאִם יִקְנֶה — And if he will acquire בַּיִת — a house אוֹ עִיר — or a city[3] מֵהֶם — from them, וְיָצָא... בַּיֹּבֵל —[4] "it shall go out in the *yovel*";[4] "it" refers to אוֹתוֹ מִמְכָּר שֶׁל בַּיִת אוֹ שֶׁל עִיר — that sale of a house or of a city, וְיָשׁוּב לַלֵּוִי שֶׁמְּכָרוֹ — and it shall return to the Levite who sold it, וְלֹא יִהְיֶה חָלוּט — and it shall not become the absolute property of the buyer a year after the sale כִּשְׁאָר בָּתֵּי עָרֵי חוֹמָה שֶׁל יִשְׂרָאֵל — like other houses of walled cities of an Israelite, i.e., of non-Levites. וּגְאֻלָּה זוֹ לְשׁוֹן מְכִירָה — According to this interpretation, this גְּאֻלָּה, i.e., the word יִגְאַל used here, means selling, rather than redemption.[5] דָּבָר אַחֵר — Alternatively, לְפִי שֶׁנֶּאֱמַר — since it says in the preceding verse, גְּאֻלַּת עוֹלָם תִּהְיֶה לַלְוִיִּם — "the Levites shall have an eternal redemption," יָכוֹל — one might be able to think that לֹא דִּבֶּר הַכָּתוּב אֶלָּא בְּלוֹקֵחַ יִשְׂרָאֵל — the verse spoke only of an Israelite, i.e., non-Levite, buyer שֶׁקָּנָה בַיִת בְּעָרֵי הַלְוִיִּם — who bought a house in the cities of the Levites, אֲבָל לֵוִי שֶׁקָּנָה מִלּוֹ — but in the case of a Levite who bought from another Levite, יִהְיֶה חָלוּט — [the house] should become the buyer's absolute property if it was not redeemed within a year of the sale. תַּלְמוּד לוֹמַר — To teach us otherwise, the verse says, וַאֲשֶׁר יִגְאַל מִן הַלְוִיִּם — "and if one will redeem from the Levites," which implies, אַף הַגּוֹאֵל — even [a Levite] who redeems מִיַּד לֵוִי — from the hand of a fellow Levite גּוֹאֵל גְּאֻלַּת עוֹלָם — may redeem with the right of eternal redemption.[6]

☐ וְיָצָא מִמְכַּר בַּיִת — THE SELLING OF A HOUSE [AND THE CITY OF HIS ANCESTRAL HERITAGE] SHALL GO OUT. הֲרֵי זוֹ מִצְוָה אַחֶרֶת — This is a different commandment[7] as follows: וְאִם לֹא גְאָלָה — And if [the

---

1. The Levites were given two thousand *amos* of land around the walls of their forty-eight cities. The outer thousand *amos* of this land was allotted for cultivation (see Rashi to *Numbers* 35:4). Although the verse makes no explicit mention of the fields of the Levites, "eternal redemption" applies to the fields, as well, for the verse does refer to the cities of the Levites, and the cities include the thousand-*amah* belt designated for cultivation, which has the status of a field (*Malbim*).

2. *Toras Kohanim, perek* 6:4-5; *Arachin* 33a. "Eternal redemption" does not refer to the effect of the redemption, i.e., that the field stays redeemed eternally, for this is true of all redeemed real estate, not just that of the Levites. It refers to the period during which redemption may take place — Levites may redeem at any time, even at times denied to non-Levites.

3. Rashi follows the wording of the verse in mentioning the acquisition of a city. See *HaKesav VeHaKabbalah*

on our verse for a discussion of the sale of an entire Levite city.

4. In many editions, this phrase is the heading of a new comment.

5. If יִגְאַל is understood as redemption, the verse appears to say that if a non-Levite redeems property he has sold to a Levite, the property returns to the Levite at the *yovel* year. Rashi explains that this is not so. The verse speaks of one who *buys* property from a Levite, not one who redeems from him (*Mesiach Ilmim*).

6. *Toras Kohanim, perek* 6:6; *Arachin* 33a. This interpretation allows יִגְאַל to be taken in its normal sense of redemption.

7. This comment does not apply to the first interpretation given by Rashi that וַאֲשֶׁר יִגְאַל מִן הַלְוִיִּם refers to the non-Levite who *buys* from the Levites. By that view, "the selling of a house..." is a continuation of the first part of the verse, as Rashi has pointed out. However,

the Levite cities, that is their ancestral heritage among the Children of Israel! **³⁴** But the field of the open land of their cities may not be sold; for it is an eternal heritage for them.

³⁵ If your brother becomes impoverished and his hand falters in your proximity, you shall hold on to him — proselyte

עָרֵי הַלְוִיִּם הִוא אֲחֻזָּתָם בְּתוֹךְ בְּנֵי יִשְׂרָאֵל: לד וּשְׂדֵה מִגְרַשׁ עָרֵיהֶם לֹא יִמָּכֵר כִּי־אֲחֻזַּת עוֹלָם הוּא לָהֶם: לה וְכִי־יָמוּךְ אָחִיךָ וּמָטָה יָדוֹ עִמָּךְ וְהֶחֱזַקְתָּ בּוֹ גֵּר

──── אונקלוס ────

קִרְוֵי לֵיוָאֵי הִיא אַחֲסַנְתְּהוֹן בְּגוֹ בְּנֵי יִשְׂרָאֵל: לד וַחֲקַל רְוַח קִרְוֵיהוֹן לָא יִזְדַּבֵּן אֲרֵי אַחֲסָנַת עָלַם הוּא לְהוֹן: לה וַאֲרֵי יִתְמַסְכַּן אֲחוּךְ וּתְמוּט יְדֵהּ עִמָּךְ וְתִתְקֵף בֵּהּ דַּיָּר

──── רש"י ────

יוֹבְלוֹ בַּיּוֹבֵל, וְאֵינוֹ נֶחְלַט לְסוֹף [שָׁנָה] (ת"כ שָׁם): **כִּי בָתֵּי עָרֵי הַלְוִיִּם הִיא אֲחֻזָּתָם.** לֹא הָיָה לָהֶם נַחֲלַת שָׂדוֹת וּכְרָמִים אֶלָּא עָרִים לָשֶׁבֶת וּמִגְרְשֵׁיהֶם, לְפִיכָךְ הֵם לָהֶם בִּמְקוֹם שָׂדוֹת וְיֵשׁ לָהֶם גְּאֻלָּה כַּשָּׂדוֹת, כְּדֵי שֶׁלֹּא תוּפְקַע נַחֲלָתָם מֵהֶם (ת"כ שָׁם ח): (לד)

וּשְׂדֵה מִגְרַשׁ עָרֵיהֶם לֹא יִמָּכֵר. מֶכֶר גִּזְבָּר, שֶׁאִם הִקְדִּישׁ בֶּן לֵוִי אֶת שָׂדֵהוּ וְלֹא גְאָלָהּ וּמְכָרָהּ גִּזְבָּר, אֵינָהּ יוֹצְאָה לַכֹּהֲנִים בַּיּוֹבֵל כְּמוֹ שֶׁנֶּאֱמַר בְּיִשְׂרָאֵל וְאִם מָכַר אֶת הַשָּׂדֶה לְאִישׁ אַחֵר לֹא יִגָּאֵל עוֹד (לְהַלָּן כז,כ) אֲבָל בֶּן לֵוִי גּוֹאֵל לְעוֹלָם (ת"כ שָׁם ה,ט): (לה) **וְהֶחֱזַקְתָּ בּוֹ.** אַל תַּנִּיחֵהוּ שֶׁיֵּרֵד וְיִפּוֹל

──── RASHI ELUCIDATED ────

Levite] did not redeem it, יוֹצְאָה בַּיּוֹבֵל – **it goes out** of the possession of the buyer **at the** *yovel* **year,** וְאֵינוֹ נֶחְלָט – **and does not become** the **absolute** property of the buyer ¹{לְסוֹף שָׁנָה} – **at the end {of a year}**¹ ²כְּבֵית שֶׁל יִשְׂרָאֵל – **as** does the house **of an Israelite,** i.e., a non-Levite.²

☐ **כִּי בָתֵּי עָרֵי הַלְוִיִּם הִוא אֲחֻזָּתָם** – FOR THE HOUSES OF THE LEVITE CITIES, THAT IS THEIR ANCESTRAL HERITAGE. לֹא הָיָה לָהֶם נַחֲלַת שָׂדוֹת וּכְרָמִים – **They did not have an estate of fields and vineyards;** אֶלָּא עָרִים לָשֶׁבֶת – **only cities to live in,** וּמִגְרְשֵׁיהֶם – **and their open grounds.** לְפִיכָךְ – **Therefore,** הֵם לָהֶם בִּמְקוֹם שָׂדוֹת – [the cities] are to [the Levites] in place of fields, וְיֵשׁ לָהֶם גְּאֻלָּה כַּשָּׂדוֹת – **and they have redemption like fields,** ³כְּדֵי שֶׁלֹּא תוּפְקַע נַחֲלָתָם מֵהֶם – **so that their estate should not be revoked from them.**³

34. וּשְׂדֵה מִגְרַשׁ עָרֵיהֶם לֹא יִמָּכֵר – BUT THE FIELD OF THE OPEN LAND OF THEIR CITIES MAY NOT BE SOLD. This refers to מֶכֶר גִּזְבָּר – **a sale by a treasurer** of the *Beis HaMikdash*; שֶׁאִם הִקְדִּישׁ בֶּן לֵוִי אֶת שָׂדֵהוּ – **that if a Levite consecrated his field** וְלֹא גְאָלָהּ – **and did not redeem it,** וּמְכָרָהּ גִּזְבָּר – **and a treasurer** of the *Beis HaMikdash* **sold it,** אֵינָהּ יוֹצְאָה לַכֹּהֲנִים – **it does not go out** of the possession of the one who bought it **to the Kohanim** בַּיּוֹבֵל – **in the** *yovel* **year** כְּמוֹ שֶׁנֶּאֱמַר בְּיִשְׂרָאֵל – **as is stated with regard to an Israelite,** i.e., a non-Levite, וְאִם מָכַר אֶת הַשָּׂדֶה – **"And if he** [the treasurer] **had sold the field** consecrated by an Israelite לְאִישׁ אַחֵר – **to another man,** i.e., other than the original owner, ⁴לֹא יִגָּאֵל עוֹד – **it cannot be redeemed anymore."**⁴ ⁵אֲבָל בֶּן לֵוִי גּוֹאֵל לְעוֹלָם – **But a Levite may redeem forever.**⁵

35. וְהֶחֱזַקְתָּ בּוֹ – YOU SHALL HOLD ON TO HIM. אַל תַּנִּיחֵהוּ שֶׁיֵּרֵד – **Do not allow him to decline** וְיִפּוֹל

according to the alternative interpretation which takes וַאֲשֶׁר יִגְאַל as redemption, יִגְאַל מִן הַלְוִיִּם is linked to "the Levites shall have an eternal redemption" of the previous verse, as if to say, "The Levites shall have eternal rights of redemption, even as far as redeeming from other Levites." The rest of the verse stands apart from this and states "a different commandment" not related to the Levites' rights of redemption: that if they do not redeem, the property returns to them at the *yovel* year (*Chizkuni; Mizrachi; Sifsei Chachamim*).

1. The first printed edition of Rashi does not have the word שָׁנָה, "year." Accordingly, לְסוֹף, "at the end," refers to the end of the *yovel* cycle, i.e., the *yovel* year (*Yosef Hallel*).

2. *Toras Kohanim, perek* 6:7; *Arachin* 33a.

3. *Toras Kohanim, perek* 6:8.

4. Below 27:20. The following verse says that the field that was "sold to another man" goes to the Kohanim at the *yovel* year.

5. *Toras Kohanim, perek* 6:5,9. "May not be sold" does not mean that the Levites may not sell their property at all, for verse 32 above has said that they have eternal rights of redemption, which implies that they have the right to sell (see Rashi to that verse). Nor does it mean that they may not make an everlasting sale, for that is implied by the end of our verse, "it is an eternal heritage for them." Rather, the verse means that the field of a Levite, if it is consecrated, does not leave the possession of the Levite permanently if it is redeemed by another, as would a field consecrated by a non-Levite (*Sefer Zikaron*).

and resident — so that he can live with you. ³⁶ Do not take from him interest and increase; and you shall have fear of your God —

לּוֹ וְתוֹשָׁב וָחַי עִמָּךְ: אַל־תִּקַּח מֵאִתּוֹ נֶשֶׁךְ וְתַרְבִּית וְיָרֵאתָ מֵאֱלֹהֶיךָ

───── אונקלוס ─────

וְתוֹתָב (נ"א יְדוּר וְיֵיתַב) וְיֵיחֵי עִמָּךְ: לוֹ לָא תִסַּב מִנֵּהּ חִבּוּלְיָא וְרִבִּיתָא וְתִדְחַל מֵאֱלָהָךְ

───── רש"י ─────

(לוֹ) [נֶשֶׁךְ וְתַרְבִּית]. חַד שַׁוִּינְהוּ רַבָּנַן וְלַעֲבוֹר עָלָיו בִּשְׁנֵי לָאוִין (ב"מ ס:): וְיָרֵאתָ מֵאֱלֹהֶיךָ. לְפִי שֶׁדַּעְתּוֹ שֶׁל אָדָם נִמְשֶׁכֶת אַחַר הָרִבִּית וְקָשֶׁה לִפְרוֹשׁ הֵימֶנּוּ, וּמוֹרֶה לְעַצְמוֹ הֶתֵּר בִּשְׁבִיל מְעוֹתָיו שֶׁהָיוּ בְּטֵלוֹת אֶצְלוֹ, הֻצְרַךְ לוֹמַר וְיָרֵאתָ מֵאֱלֹהֶיךָ. אוֹ הַתּוֹלֶה מְעוֹתָיו בְּנָכְרִי כְּדֵי לְהַלְווֹתָם לְיִשְׂרָאֵל בְּרִבִּית הֲרֵי זֶה דָבָר הַמָּסוּר וְיִהְיֶה קָשֶׁה לַהֲקִימוֹ. לְמָה זֶה דוֹמֶה, לְמַשְּׂאוֹי שֶׁעַל הַחֲמוֹר. עוֹדֵהוּ בִּמְקוֹמוֹ [ס"א עַל הַחֲמוֹר], אֶחָד תּוֹפֵס בּוֹ וּמַעֲמִידוֹ. נָפַל לָאָרֶץ, חֲמִשָּׁה אֵין מַעֲמִידִין אוֹתוֹ (שם פָּרָשְׁתָא הא:ח): גֵּר וְתוֹשָׁב. אַף אִם הוּא גֵּר אוֹ תוֹשָׁב. וְאֵיזֶהוּ תּוֹשָׁב, כֹּל שֶׁקִּבֵּל עָלָיו שֶׁלֹּא לַעֲבוֹד ע"ז וְאוֹכֵל נְבֵלוֹת (שם):

───── RASHI ELUCIDATED ─────

וְיִהְיֶה קָשֶׁה לַהֲקִימוֹ – and then it will be difficult to raise him up. **אֶלָּא** – Rather, **הַחֲזִיקוֹ** – strengthen him **מִשְּׁעַת מוֹטַת הַיָּד** – from the time of the faltering of the hand, i.e., from the time his fortune begins to take a turn for the worse. **לְמָה זֶה דוֹמֶה** – What is this comparable to? **לְמַשְּׂאוֹי שֶׁעַל הַחֲמוֹר** – To a burden that is on a donkey.[1] **עוֹדֵהוּ בִּמְקוֹמוֹ** – While the donkey is still standing in its place[1] and it begins to slip off, **אֶחָד תּוֹפֵס בּוֹ** – one person can grab hold of it[2] **וּמַעֲמִידוֹ** – and set it in place. **נָפַל לָאָרֶץ** – Once it has fallen to the ground,[3] **חֲמִשָּׁה אֵין מַעֲמִידִין אוֹתוֹ** – five people cannot set it in place.[3]

□ **גֵּר וְתוֹשָׁב** – PROSELYTE AND RESIDENT. **אַף אִם הוּא גֵּר** – Even if he is a proselyte **אוֹ תוֹשָׁב** – or a resident.[4] **וְאֵיזֶהוּ תוֹשָׁב** – Who is "a resident"? **כֹּל שֶׁקִּבֵּל עָלָיו** – Any [non-Jew] who accepted upon himself **שֶׁלֹּא לַעֲבוֹד עֲבוֹדָה זָרָה** – not to worship idols,[5] **וְאוֹכֵל נְבֵלוֹת** – but eats unslaughtered carcasses.[5]

36. {**נֶשֶׁךְ וְתַרְבִּית** – INTEREST AND INCREASE. **חַד שַׁוִּינְהוּ רַבָּנָן** – The Rabbis considered these identical, **וְלַעֲבוֹר עָלָיו בִּשְׁנֵי לָאוִין** – and the Torah states them both to make one liable for transgressing two negative commandments if he charges interest.[6]}

□ **וְיָרֵאתָ מֵאֱלֹהֶיךָ** – AND YOU SHALL HAVE FEAR OF YOUR GOD. **לְפִי שֶׁדַּעְתּוֹ שֶׁל אָדָם** – Since a person's mind **נִמְשֶׁכֶת אַחַר הָרִבִּית** – is attracted to interest, **וְקָשֶׁה לִפְרוֹשׁ הֵימֶנּוּ** – and it is difficult to separate oneself from it, **וּמוֹרֶה לְעַצְמוֹ הֶתֵּר** – and he decides permission for himself, i.e., he gives himself license, **בִּשְׁבִיל מְעוֹתָיו** – because of his funds **שֶׁהָיוּ בְּטֵלוֹת אֶצְלוֹ** – which were unproductive for him while in [the borrower's] possession, **הֻצְרַךְ לוֹמַר** – [the Torah] had to say, **"וְיָרֵאתָ מֵאֱלֹהֶיךָ"** – "and you shall have fear of your God." **אוֹ** – Or, the verse also speaks of **הַתּוֹלֶה מְעוֹתָיו בְּנָכְרִי** – one who hangs his funds on a non-Jew, i.e., one who falsely claims that his money belongs to a non-Jew, **כְּדֵי לְהַלְווֹתָם לְיִשְׂרָאֵל** – in order to lend them to a Jew **בְּרִבִּית** – with interest.[7] **הֲרֵי זֶה דָבָר** – See, now, that this is a matter הַמָּסוּר

---

1. Some editions read עוֹדֵהוּ עַל הַחֲמוֹר, "while it is still on the donkey" (see Yosef Hallel).

2. Rashi's analogy to a situation in which one "grabs hold" of something is especially precise in light of his comments to Exodus 4:4, where he says that the meaning of לְהַחֲזִיק when followed by a ב prefix is always "to hold."

3. Toras Kohanim, parshasa 5:1.

4. The verse could be read as saying that "you shall hold on to him" refers only to a proselyte and resident. Rashi points out that it applies even to them, but that it applies to Jews by birth as well, as implied by the beginning of the verse, "If your brother becomes impoverished," which includes all Jews (Mesiach Ilmim; see also Mizrachi; Sifsei Chachamim). Furthermore, Rashi interprets the ו of וְתוֹשָׁב as "or."

5. Toras Kohanim, parshasa 5:1. A proselyte is fully Jewish and must keep all of the commandments of the Torah. A "resident" (elsewhere referred to as גֵּר תּוֹשָׁב, "resident stranger") according to Rashi, has accepted upon himself the prohibition against idolatry, but has not converted to the Jewish religion. He may be given unslaughtered carcasses to eat (see Deuteronomy 14:21). He is referred to as "a resident" because, unlike other non-Jews, he may establish permanent residence in the Land of Israel (see Rambam, Hilchos Avodah Zarah 10:6).

6. Bava Metzia 60b.

7. It is forbidden to borrow money from a Jew at interest, but it is permitted to do so from a non-Jew (see Deuteronomy 23:21). A Jew might be tempted to falsely claim that his money belongs to a non-Jew, so that he could lend it to another Jew at interest.

וְחֵי אָחִיךָ עִמָּךְ: אֶת־כַּסְפְּךָ לֹא־ ל
תִתֵּן לוֹ בְּנֶשֶׁךְ וּבְמַרְבִּית לֹא־תִתֵּן
אָכְלֶךָ: אֲנִי יהוה אֱלֹהֵיכֶם אֲשֶׁר־ לח
הוֹצֵאתִי אֶתְכֶם מֵאֶרֶץ מִצְרָיִם
לָתֵת לָכֶם אֶת־אֶרֶץ כְּנַעַן לִהְיוֹת
לָכֶם לֵאלֹהִים: [ששי רביעי] וְכִי־ לט
יָמוּךְ אָחִיךָ עִמָּךְ וְנִמְכַּר־
לָךְ לֹא־תַעֲבֹד בּוֹ עֲבֹדַת עָבֶד:

and let your brother live with you. **37** Do not give him your money for interest, and do not give your food for increase. **38** I am HASHEM, your God, Who took you out of the land of Egypt, to give you the land of Canaan, to be a God to you.

39 If your brother becomes impoverished with you and is sold to you; you shall not work him with slave labor.

— אונקלוס —

וְיֵחֵי אֲחוּךְ עִמָּךְ: לוֹ יָת כַּסְפָּךְ לָא תִתֵּן לֵהּ בְּחִבּוּלְיָא וּבְרִבִּיתָא לָא תִתֵּן מֵיכְלָךְ: לח אֲנָא יְיָ אֱלָהֲכוֹן דִּי אַפֵּיקִית יָתְכוֹן מֵאַרְעָא דְמִצְרָיִם לְמִתַּן לְכוֹן יָת אַרְעָא דִכְנַעַן לְמֶהֱוֵי לְכוֹן לֶאֱלָהּ: לט וַאֲרֵי יִתְמַסְכַּן אֲחוּךְ עִמָּךְ וְיִזְדַּבַּן לָךְ לָא תִפְלַח בֵּהּ פָּלְחַן עַבְדִין:

— רש"י —

כדעתו עליכם: **לתת לכם את ארץ בנען**. בשכר שתקבלו מלכות שמים: **להיות לכם לאלהים**. שכל הדר בארץ ישראל אני לו לאלהים, וכל היוצא ממנה כעובד ע"ז (ת"כ שם ד; כתובות קי"ב ע"ב): (**לט**) **עבודת עבד**. עבודה של גנאי שיהא ניכר בה כעבד, שלא יוליך כליו אחריו לבית המרחץ ולא ינעלו לו מנעליו (ת"כ פרק ז:ב):

ללבו של אדם ומחשבתו, לכך הולך לומר ויראת מאלהיך (שם נח:): סא"ו: (**לח**) **אשר הוצאתי וגו'**. והבחנתי בין בכור לשאינו בכור, אף אני יודע ונפרע מן המלוה מעות לישראל ברבית ואומר של נכרי הם (שם סא.). דבר אחר, אשר הוצאתי אתכם מארץ מצרים, על מנת שתקבלו עליכם מצותי (ת"כ שם ג) ואפילו הן

— RASHI ELUCIDATED —

לְכָךְ הֻצְרַךְ לוֹמַר – This is why it had to say, ",וְיָרֵאתָ מֵאֱלֹהֶיךָ" – "and you shall have fear of your God."[1]

38. אֲשֶׁר הוֹצֵאתִי וְגוֹמֵר – WHO TOOK [YOU] OUT, ETC. – וְהִבְחַנְתִּי – and I distinguished – בֵּין בְּכוֹר – between a firstborn – לְשֶׁאֵינוֹ בְכוֹר – and one who was not a firstborn. אַף אֲנִי יוֹדֵעַ – I also know וְנִפְרָע – and exact punishment – מִן הַמַּלְוָה מָעוֹת – from one who lends money – לְיִשְׂרָאֵל – to a Jew – בְּרִבִּית – with interest, וְאוֹמֵר שֶׁל נָכְרִי הֵם – [2] and says that it belongs to a non-Jew.[2] דָּבָר אַחֵר – Alternatively, אֲשֶׁר הוֹצֵאתִי אֶתְכֶם מֵאֶרֶץ מִצְרַיִם – "Who took you out of the land of Egypt" – עַל מְנָת – on condition – שֶׁתְּקַבְּלוּ עֲלֵיכֶם – that you would accept upon yourselves – מִצְוֹתַי – My commandments[3] – וַאֲפִילוּ הֵן כְּבֵדוֹת עֲלֵיכֶם – even if they are heavy upon you, i.e., even if keeping them is difficult.

□ שֶׁתְּקַבְּלוּ מִצְוֹתַי – as reward for accepting My commandments upon yourselves.

□ לִהְיוֹת לָכֶם לֵאלֹהִים – TO BE A GOD TO YOU. – שֶׁכָּל הַדָּר בְּאֶרֶץ יִשְׂרָאֵל – For whoever resides in the Land of Israel – אֲנִי לוֹ לֵאלֹהִים – I am a God to him; וְכָל הַיּוֹצֵא מִמֶּנָּה – and whoever leaves it – כְּעוֹבֵד עֲבוֹדָה זָרָה[4] – is like one who worships idols.[4]

39. עֲבֹדַת עָבֶד – SLAVE LABOR. This refers to עֲבוֹדָה שֶׁל גְּנַאי – demeaning labor, שֶׁיְּהֵא נִכָּר בָּהּ כְּעֶבֶד – by which he can be identified as a slave.[5] For example, שֶׁלֹּא יוֹלִיךְ כֵּלָיו אַחֲרָיו – that he should not carry [the master's] clothes behind [the master] – לְבֵית הַמֶּרְחָץ – to the bathhouse, וְלֹא יִנְעוֹל לוֹ מִנְעָלָיו[6] – and he should not put [the master's] shoes on [the master].[6]

---

1. *Bava Metzia* 58b, 61b.
2. *Bava Metzia* 61b. This explanation of "Who took you out of the land of Egypt" fits in with Rashi's second interpretation of "you shall have fear of your God" two verses earlier; according to that interpretation, that verse alludes to a situation in which a Jew claims that his money belongs to a non-Jew so that he can lend it at interest (*Be'er Yitzchak*).
3. *Toras Kohanim, parshasa* 5:3. This explanation fits in with Rashi's first interpretation of "you shall have

fear of your God" two verses earlier; according to that interpretation, that part of the verse was stated because refraining from taking interest is especially difficult (*Be'er Yitzchak*).

4. *Toras Kohanim, parshasa* 5:4; *Kesubos* 110b.

5. The verse does not mean to prohibit using a Hebrew servant for difficult labor (*Lifshuto shel Rashi*; see also *Rashbam* to our verse).

6. *Toras Kohanim, perek* 7:2.

40 *Like a hired laborer or a resident shall he be with you; until the yovel shall he work with you.* **41** *Then he shall leave you, he and his children with him; he shall return to his family, and he will return to the heritage of his ancestors.* **42** *For they are My slaves, whom I have taken out of the land of Egypt; they shall not be sold by a selling of a slave.* **43** *Do not subjugate him through hard labor*

מ כְּשָׂכִיר כְּתוֹשָׁב יִהְיֶה עִמָּךְ עַד־
מא שְׁנַת הַיֹּבֵל יַעֲבֹד עִמָּךְ: וְיָצָא
מֵעִמָּךְ הוּא וּבָנָיו עִמּוֹ וְשָׁב אֶל־
מִשְׁפַּחְתּוֹ וְאֶל־אֲחֻזַּת אֲבֹתָיו
מב יָשׁוּב: כִּי־עֲבָדַי הֵם אֲשֶׁר־הוֹצֵאתִי
אֹתָם מֵאֶרֶץ מִצְרָיִם לֹא יִמָּכְרוּ
מג מִמְכֶּרֶת עָבֶד: לֹא־תִרְדֶּה בוֹ בְּפָרֶךְ

──────── אונקלוס ────────

מ כַּאֲגִירָא כְּתוֹתָבָא יְהֵי עִמָּךְ עַד שַׁתָּא דְיוֹבֵלָא יִפְלַח עִמָּךְ: מא וְיִפּוֹק מֵעִמָּךְ הוּא וּבְנוֹהִי עִמֵּהּ וִיתוּב לְזַרְעִיתֵהּ וְלַאֲחֲסָנַת אֲבָהָתוֹהִי יְתוּב: מב אֲרֵי עַבְדַי אִנּוּן דִּי אַפֵּקִית יָתְהוֹן מֵאַרְעָא דְמִצְרָיִם לָא יִזְדַּבְּנוּן זְבִינֵי עַבְדִין: מג לָא תִפְלַח בֵּהּ בְּקַשְׁיוּ

──────── רש״י ────────

(מ) כשכיר כתושב. עֲבוֹדַת קַרְקַע וּמְלֶאכֶת אוּמָּנוּת כִּשְׁאָר שְׂכִירִים הִתְנַהֵג בּוֹ: **עד שנת היובל.** אִם פָּגַע בּוֹ יוֹבֵל לִפְנֵי שֵׁשׁ שָׁנִים הַיּוֹבֵל מוֹצִיאוֹ (שם ד): **(מא) הוא ובניו עמו.** אָמַר רַבִּי שִׁמְעוֹן אִם הוּא נִמְכַּר בָּנָיו מִי מְכָרָן אֶלָּא מִכָּאן שֶׁרַבּוֹ חַיָּב בִּמְזוֹנוֹת בָּנָיו (שם ג; קידושין כב.): **ואל אחזת**

אבותיו. אֶל כְּבוֹד אֲבוֹתָיו וְאֵין לְזַלְזְלוֹ בְּכָךְ (ת״כ שם ד; מכות יג.): **אחזת.** חֲזָקַת (שם): **(מב) כי עבדי הם.** שְׁטָרִי קוֹדֵם (ת״כ פרשתא ו:א): **לא ימכרו ממכרת עבד.** בְּהַכְרָזָה, כָּאן יֵשׁ עֶבֶד לִמְכּוֹר, וְלֹא יַעֲמִידֶנּוּ עַל אֶבֶן הַלֶּקַח (שם): **(מג) לא תרדה בו בפרך.** מְלָאכָה שֶׁלֹּא לְצוֹרֶךְ

──────── RASHI ELUCIDATED ────────

40. כְּשָׂכִיר כְּתוֹשָׁב — **LIKE A HIRED LABORER OR A RESIDENT.** עֲבוֹדַת קַרְקַע — **Labor of land,** i.e., agricultural labor, וּמְלֶאכֶת אוּמָּנוּת — **and work of a craft.** כִּשְׁאָר שְׂכִירִים הִתְנַהֵג בּוֹ — **Treat him like other hired workers.** ☐ עַד שְׁנַת הַיֹּבֵל — **UNTIL THE** *YOVEL* **YEAR.** אִם פָּגַע בּוֹ יוֹבֵל — **If the** *yovel* **encounters him,** i.e., if the *yovel* year begins, לִפְנֵי שֵׁשׁ שָׁנִים — **before** the end of his term of servitude of **six years,**[1] הַיּוֹבֵל מוֹצִיאוֹ — **the** *yovel* **takes him out** of slavery.[1]

41. הוּא וּבָנָיו עִמּוֹ — **HE AND HIS CHILDREN WITH HIM.** אָמַר רַבִּי שִׁמְעוֹן — The *Tanna* **R' Shimon said:** אִם הוּא נִמְכַּר — **If he was sold,** בָּנָיו מִי מְכָרָן — **who sold his children?** Why does the verse say that his children shall "leave you" if they were not sold into slavery? אֶלָּא — **But,** מִכָּאן — **from here** we see שֶׁרַבּוֹ מְחַיָּב — **that his master is obligated**[2] בִּמְזוֹנוֹת בָּנָיו — to supply the **food of his children.**[2] ☐ וְאֶל אֲחֻזַּת אֲבֹתָיו — **AND TO THE HERITAGE OF HIS ANCESTORS.** אֶל כְּבוֹד אֲבוֹתָיו — **To the dignity of his ancestors,**[3] וְאֵין לְזַלְזְלוֹ בְּכָךְ — **and he is not to be demeaned by this,** i.e., by the fact that he has been a servant.[4] ☐ אֲחֻזַּת — **HERITAGE OF,** that is, [4] חֲזָקַת — **the established position of.**[4]

42. כִּי עֲבָדַי הֵם — **FOR THEY ARE MY SLAVES.**[5] שְׁטָרִי קוֹדֵם — **My contract** which states that he is My slave **comes first,** before the contract of his present master.[5] ☐ לֹא יִמָּכְרוּ מִמְכֶּרֶת עָבֶד — **THEY SHALL NOT BE SOLD BY A SELLING OF A SLAVE.** בְּהַכְרָזָה — **through announcement:** כָּאן יֵשׁ עֶבֶד לִמְכּוֹר — **"Here is a slave for sale!"**[6] וְלֹא יַעֲמִידֶנּוּ עַל אֶבֶן הַלֶּקַח — **And** [the seller] should not stand [the slave] up on the selling block.[6]

43. לֹא תִרְדֶּה בוֹ בְּפָרֶךְ — **DO NOT SUBJUGATE HIM THROUGH HARD LABOR,** מְלָאכָה שֶׁלֹּא לְצוֹרֶךְ — **work**

---

1. *Toras Kohanim, perek* 7:4.

2. *Toras Kohanim, perek* 7:3; *Kiddushin* 22a. See also Rashi to *Exodus* 21:3, s.v., וְיָצְאָה אִשְׁתּוֹ עִמּוֹ.

3. In earlier verses, אֲחֻזָּה was used with reference to the portion of land passed down through inheritance, e.g., vv. 10, 36 (see Rashi there). Here "he will return to the heritage of his ancestors" cannot refer to his portion of land, for our verse does not deal with a person who has sold his portion of land (*Mizrachi; Sifsei Chachamim*).

4. *Toras Kohanim, perek* 7:4; *Makkos* 13a.

5. *Toras Kohanim, parshasa* 6:1. "For they are My slaves" of this verse is given as the reason for the servant's return to his family and heritage of his ancestors at the *yovel* year, mentioned in the preceding verse; you cannot buy another Jew permanently, for ultimately, he is the "property" of God (*Sefer Zikaron*).

6. *Toras Kohanim, parshasa* 6:1.

מד וְיָרֵאתָ מֵאֱלֹהֶיךָ: וְעַבְדְּךָ וַאֲמָתְךָ
אֲשֶׁר יִהְיוּ־לָךְ מֵאֵת הַגּוֹיִם
אֲשֶׁר סְבִיבֹתֵיכֶם מֵהֶם תִּקְנוּ

— *you shall have fear of your God.*
44 And your slave or your maidservant whom you may own, from the nations who surround you, from them you may purchase

———— אונקלוס ————

וְתִדְחַל מֵאֱלָהָךְ: מד וְעַבְדָּךְ וְאַמְתָךְ דִּי יְהוֹן לָךְ מִן עַמְמַיָּא דִּי בְסַחֲרָנֵיכוֹן מִנְּהוֹן תִּקְנוּן

———— רש"י ————

(מד) **ועבדך ואמתך אשר יהיו לך.** אם תאמר אם
כן, הרי הדבר הזה מסור ללב, לכך נאמר ויראת (שם ב):
לצורך, ואומר אני לו שהוא לצורך. שמא תאמר
אין מכיר בדבר אם לצורך אם לאו, הרי זה
אינו צריך, עבדור תחת הגפן עד שאבוא. שמא תאמר
כדי לענותו. אל תאמר לו החם לי את הכוס הזה והוא
לעבדים: **אשר סביבותיכם.** ולא שבתוך גבול ארצכם,
(ת"כ שם) שהרי בהם אמרתי לא תחיה כל נשמה
(דברים
כ:טז): אלא מי ישמשני: **מאת הגוים.** הם יהיו לך
אינו נוהל, שהרי הזהרתני לא תחיה כל נשמה (דברים
כן במה אשתמש (שם ג) [ובעבדי איני מושל, בז' אומות

———— RASHI ELUCIDATED ————

אַל תֹּאמַר לוֹ — Do not say to him, הַחֵם לִי אֶת הַכּוֹס הַזֶּה — "Warm up this cup for me," וְהוּא אֵינוֹ צָרִיךְ — and [the master] does not need it, or עֲדֹר תַּחַת הַגֶּפֶן — "Hoe under the vine עַד שֶׁאָבוֹא — until I come."[1] שֶׁמָּא תֹאמַר — Perhaps you will say, אֵין מַכִּיר בַּדָּבָר — "No one can tell about the matter אִם לְצֹרֶךְ — if it is for a need שֶׁהוּא לְצֹרֶךְ — that וְאוֹמֵר אֲנִי לוֹ — and I will tell [the slave] אִם לָאו — or not, הֲרֵי הַדָּבָר הַזֶּה מָסוּר לַלֵּב — See now that the matter is given over to the heart, i.e., no one but he knows his true intentions. לְכָךְ נֶאֱמַר — This is why it says, ,,וְיָרֵאתָ׳׳[2] — "and you shall have fear [of your God."[2]

44. אִם — וְעַבְדְּךָ וַאֲמָתְךָ אֲשֶׁר יִהְיוּ לָךְ — AND YOUR SLAVE OR YOUR MAIDSERVANT WHOM YOU MAY OWN. תֹּאמַר — If you will say, אִם כֵּן — "If so, that I may not use a Hebrew servant for personal services,[3] בַּמֶּה אֶשְׁתַּמֵּשׁ[4] — what (whom) will I use for such services?[4] {בַּעֲבָדַי אֵינִי מוֹשֵׁל — I do not hold full authority over my Hebrew servants, בְּשֶׁבַע אֻמּוֹת אֵינִי נוֹחֵל — nor may I take possession of members of the seven nations who occupy the Land of Canaan, שֶׁהֲרֵי הִזְהַרְתַּנִי — for, see, now, You have enjoined me, [5],,לֹא תְחַיֶּה כָּל נְשָׁמָה׳׳ — 'You shall not allow any soul to remain alive!'[5] אֶלָּא מִי יְשַׁמְּשֵׁנִי — Who, then, will serve me?" The Torah answers,}[6]

☐ מֵאֵת הַגּוֹיִם — FROM THE NATIONS, הֵם יִהְיוּ לָךְ לַעֲבָדִים — they shall be to you for slaves.[7]

☐ אֲשֶׁר סְבִיבֹתֵיכֶם — WHO SURROUND YOU. [8] וְלֹא שֶׁבְּתוֹךְ גְּבוּל אַרְצְכֶם — But not those who are within the boundary of your land,[8] שֶׁהֲרֵי בָּהֶם אָמַרְתִּי — for, see that of them I have said, ,,לֹא תְחַיֶּה כָּל נְשָׁמָה׳׳[9] — "You shall not allow any soul to remain alive."[9]

1. This is work with no need. Neither master nor slave knows in advance how long it will take until the master comes, so the master is giving him an unlimited task (see *Meshivas Nefesh; Lechem Mishneh, Hilchos Avadim* 1:6).

2. *Toras Kohanim, parshasa* 6:2. See Rashi to verse 36 and to 19:32 above.

3. See Rashi to verse 39.

4. *Toras Kohanim, parshasa* 6:3.

5. *Deuteronomy* 20:16.

6. The bracketed passage does not appear either in *Toras Kohanim* or in the first printed edition of Rashi.

7. Had the Torah merely wished to state that it is permissible to own non-Jewish slaves, it could have said it by using the conclusion of our verse alone — "from the nations who surround you, from them you may purchase a slave or a maidservant." The opening words, "your slave or your maidservant whom you may own," appear superfluous. Rashi explains that they serve to answer an implicit question to which the preceding verse gives rise. If Hebrew servants may not be employed for personal services, whom may we use for such work? The verse answers, "your slave or your maidservant whom you may own, from the nations" — the Torah teaches us that it is permitted to use non-Jewish slaves for personal services. Furthermore, Rashi clarifies that "from the nations" and "from them" of the verse do not mean that we are allowed to purchase a slave who is sold by a non-Jew. Rather, they are to be understood as "from *among* the nations . . . from *among* them," i.e, we are allowed to purchase slaves who *are* non-Jews (*Be'er BaSadeh*; *Mesiach Ilmim* notes that the apparently superfluous ו of וְעַבְדְּךָ, "*and* your slave," also indicates that our verse is linked to the subject matter of the preceding passage).

8. *Toras Kohanim, parshasa* 6:3.

9. *Deuteronomy* 20:16.

341 / VAYIKRA/LEVITICUS — PARASHAS BEHAR   25/45-46

מה עֶ֣בֶד וְאָמָ֑ה: ⁴⁵ וְ֠גַם מִבְּנֵ֨י הַתּוֹשָׁבִ֜ים הַגָּרִ֤ים עִמָּכֶם֙ מֵהֶ֣ם תִּקְנ֔וּ וּמִמִּשְׁפַּחְתָּם֙ אֲשֶׁ֣ר עִמָּכֶ֔ם אֲשֶׁ֥ר הוֹלִ֖ידוּ בְּאַרְצְכֶ֑ם וְהָי֥וּ לָכֶ֖ם לַֽאֲחֻזָּֽה: ⁴⁶ וְהִתְנַֽחַלְתֶּ֨ם אֹתָ֜ם לִבְנֵיכֶ֤ם אַֽחֲרֵיכֶם֙ לָרֶ֣שֶׁת אֲחֻזָּ֔ה

a slave or a maidservant. ⁴⁵ *Also from among the children of the residents who live with you, from them you may purchase, from their family that is with you, whom they begot in your land; and they shall remain yours as an ancestral heritage.* ⁴⁶ *You shall keep them in your possession for your sons after you to inherit as a possession,*

─────────────── אונקלוס ───────────────

עַבְדִּין וְאַמְהָן: מה וְאַף מִבְּנֵי תוֹתָבַיָּא עָרְלַיָּא דְּדָיְרִין עִמְּכוֹן מִנְּהוֹן תִּקְנוּן וּמִזַּרְעִיתְהוֹן דִּי עִמְּכוֹן דִּי אִתְיְלִידוּ בְּאַרְעֲכוֹן וִיהוֹן לְכוֹן לְאַחֲסָנָא: מו וְתַחְסְנוּן יָתְהוֹן לִבְנֵיכוֹן בַּתְרֵיכוֹן לְמֵירַת אַחֲסָנָא

─────────────── רש״י ───────────────

(מה) וגם מבני התושבים. שֶׁבָּאוּ מִסְּבִיבוֹתֵיכֶם לִשָּׂא נָשִׁים בְּאַרְצְכֶם וְיָלְדוּ לָהֶם, הַבֵּן הוֹלֵךְ אַחַר הָאָב וְאֵינוֹ בִכְלַל לֹא תְחַיֶּה אֶלָּא אַתָּה מוּתָּר לִקְנוֹתוֹ בְּעֶבֶד (ספ״ד; קידושין סז:): **מהם תקנו.** אוֹתָם: **תקנו: (מו) והתנחלתם אתם לבניכם.** הַחֲזִיקוּ בָהֶם לְנַחֲלָה לְצוֹרֶךְ בְּנֵיכֶם אַחֲרֵיכֶם. וְלֹא יִתָּכֵן לְפָרֵשׁ הַנְחִילוּם לִבְנֵיכֶם, שֶׁאִם כֵּן הָיָה לוֹ לִכְתּוֹב וְהִנְחַלְתֶּם אוֹתָם לִבְנֵיכֶם: **והתנחלתם:** כְּמוֹ וְהִתְחַזַּקְתֶּם.

─────────────── RASHI ELUCIDATED ───────────────

45. וְגַם מִבְּנֵי הַתּוֹשָׁבִים — ALSO FROM AMONG THE CHILDREN OF THE RESIDENTS שֶׁבָּאוּ מִסְּבִיבוֹתֵיכֶם — who came from the lands **around you**, i.e., who are not natives of the Land of Canaan, לִשָּׂא נָשִׁים — to marry Canaanite women בְּאַרְצְכֶם — **in your land**, וְיָלְדוּ לָהֶם — **and [those women] gave birth for them**, i.e., gave birth to children fathered by the "residents." הַבֵּן — The nationality of **the son** הוֹלֵךְ אַחַר הָאָב — **goes after the father**,[1] לֹא תְחַיֶּה — **and therefore [the child] is not included in** "You shall not allow [any soul] **to remain alive.**"[1] אֶלָּא — **Rather,** אַתָּה מוּתָּר לִקְנוֹתוֹ — **you are allowed to buy him** בְּעֶבֶד[2] — **as a slave.**[2]

□ מֵהֶם תִּקְנוּ — FROM THEM YOU MAY PURCHASE. אוֹתָם תִּקְנוּ — **You may purchase them.**[3]

46. וְהִתְנַחַלְתֶּם אֹתָם לִבְנֵיכֶם — YOU SHALL KEEP THEM IN YOUR POSSESSION FOR YOUR SONS. הַחֲזִיקוּ בָהֶם — **Hold on to them** לְנַחֲלָה — **as a possession** לְצוֹרֶךְ בְּנֵיכֶם אַחֲרֵיכֶם — **for the sake of your sons after you.** וְלֹא יִתָּכֵן — **It is not possible** לְפָרֵשׁ — **to explain** וְהִתְנַחַלְתֶּם אֹתָם לִבְנֵיכֶם as meaning, הַנְחִילוּם לִבְנֵיכֶם — **"bequeath them to your sons,"** שֶׁאִם כֵּן — **for if so,** הָיָה לוֹ לִכְתּוֹב — **it should have written,** וְהִנְחַלְתֶּם אֹתָם לִבְנֵיכֶם,, — **"you shall bequeath them to your sons,"** in the *hifil*.[4]

□ וְהִתְנַחַלְתֶּם — YOU SHALL KEEP THEM IN YOUR POSSESSION. כְּמוֹ ,,וְהִתְחַזַּקְתֶּם״ — This is **like, "you shall strengthen yourselves."**[5]

---

1. *Deuteronomy* 20:16.

2. *Toras Kohanim, parshasa* 6:4; *Kiddushin* 67b. If the father is a non-Canaanite and the mother is a Canaanite, the child has the nationality of the father (see *Kiddushin* 67b). Note that although Jewishness is determined matrilineally, tribal affiliations (whether among Jews or non-Jews) are patrilineal. However, see Rashi to 24.10 above (וַיֵּצֵא בֶּן אִשָּׁה יִשְׂרְאֵלִית), regarding the status of one born to a Jewish mother and non-Jewish father.

3. In *Deuteronomy* 14:21, the Torah commands us to grant a resident (see note 5 on page 337) privileges we would not grant other non-Jews. We might therefore have understood מֵהֶם תִּקְנוּ of our verse as "from them you *shall* purchase," i.e., the Torah grants them a franchise in the slave trade. Rashi explains that in our verse, as in the one which precedes it, מֵהֶם תִּקְנוּ means "from [among] them you may purchase."

4. Had the Torah meant a simple transitive verb, "you shall bequeath," it would have used the *hifil*, וְהִנְחַלְתֶּם. The *hispael*, וְהִתְנַחַלְתֶּם, is used here to indicate that the verb also has a reflexive quality, "you shall keep them for yourselves for your sons."

In many early editions, the following comment is not a new comment but a continuation of this one (see *Yosef Hallel*).

5. According to *Sefer Zikaron* (supported by Rashi's commentary to *Isaiah* 14:2), Rashi here refers to the word וְהִתְחַזַּקְתֶּם in *Numbers* 13:20 as an example of the reflexive quality of the *hispael*, for there וְהִתְחַזַּקְתֶּם clearly has no direct object. He apparently chose this particular word as his example out of all second-person plural, past, *hispael* verbs in the Torah because its vowelization resembles that of וְהִתְנַחַלְתֶּם [the *dagesh* of the second root letter of *hispael* verbs (ז in the case of וְהִתְחַזַּקְתֶּם) is omitted in the case of וְהִתְנַחַלְתֶּם because the letter ח never takes a *dagesh*, otherwise the vowelizations are identical].

According to *Mesiach Ilmim*, Rashi is not referring to the verse in *Numbers* at all, but rather cites וְהִתְחַזַּקְתֶּם as a synonym for וְהִתְנַחַלְתֶּם. וְהִתְנַחַלְתֶּם here, according to *Mesiach Ilmim*'s understanding of Rashi, does not you shall work with them forever; but with your brethren, the Children of Israel — a man with his brother — you shall not subjugate him through hard labor.

⁴⁷ If the hand of an alien and a resident with you will achieve, and your brother becomes impoverished with him, and he is sold to an alien, resident with you, or to an idol of an alien's family; ⁴⁸ after

לְעֹלָ֖ם בָּהֶ֣ם תַּעֲבֹ֑דוּ וּבְאַחֵיכֶ֣ם בְּנֵֽי־יִשְׂרָאֵ֗ל אִ֤ישׁ בְּאָחִיו֙ לֹא־תִרְדֶּ֥ה ב֖וֹ בְּפָֽרֶךְ: שביעי מז וְכִ֣י תַשִּׂ֗יג יַ֣ד גֵּ֤ר וְתוֹשָׁב֙ עִמָּ֔ךְ וּמָ֥ךְ אָחִ֖יךָ עִמּ֑וֹ וְנִמְכַּ֗ר לְגֵ֤ר תּוֹשָׁב֙ עִמָּ֔ךְ א֥וֹ לְעֵ֖קֶר מִשְׁפַּ֥חַת גֵּֽר: מח אַחֲרֵ֣י

───────── אונקלוס ─────────

לְעָלַם בְּהוֹן תִּפְלְחוּן וּבְאַחֵיכוֹן בְּנֵי יִשְׂרָאֵל גְּבַר בַּאֲחוּהִי לָא תִפְלַח בֵּהּ בְּקַשְׁיוּ: מז וַאֲרֵי תַדְבֵּק יַד עָרֵל (נ״א עֲרֵל) וְתוֹתָב עִמָּךְ וְיִתְמַסְכַּן אֲחוּךְ עִמֵּהּ וְיִזְדַּבַּן לְדַיָּר וְתוֹתָב עִמָּךְ אוֹ לְאַרְמַי זַרְעִית גִּיּוּרָא: מח בָּתַר

───────── רש"י ─────────

איש באחיו. להביא נשיא למלך וּמלך למשרתיו שלא לרדות בפרך: (מז) **יד גר ותושב.** גר והוא תושב. גר ותושב, כתרגומו ערל ותותב, וסופו מוכיח, ונמכר לגר תושב. וכי תשיג יד גר **ותושב עמך.** מי גרם לו שיעשיר דבוקו עמך (ת"כ פרק ח:א): **ומך אחיך עמו.** מי גרם לו שימוך דבוקו עמו ט"י שלמד ממעשיו (שם): **משפחת גר.** זה עובד כוכבים ומזלות, כשהוא

───────── RASHI ELUCIDATED ─────────

□ אִישׁ בְּאָחִיו — A MAN WITH HIS BROTHER. — לְהָבִיא נָשִׂיא בְּעַמָּיו — To include a leader with his people, וּמֶלֶךְ בִּמְשָׁרְתָיו — and a king with his servants, שֶׁלֹּא לִרְדּוֹת בְּפָרֶךְ — not to subjugate them through hard labor.[1]

47. יַד גֵּר וְתוֹשָׁב — THE HAND OF AN ALIEN AND A RESIDENT. — גֵּר וְהוּא תוֹשָׁב — An alien who is a resident;[2] כְּתַרְגּוּמוֹ — as Targum Onkelos renders it, "עָרֵל וְתוֹתָב" — "a resident non-Jew."[3] וְסוֹפוֹ מוֹכִיחַ — [The verse's] end proves that the "alien" and the "resident" are one and the same, for it says, "וְנִמְכַּר לְגֵר תּוֹשָׁב" — "and he is sold to an alien, resident with you."

□ וְכִי תַשִּׂיג יַד גֵּר וְתוֹשָׁב — IF THE HAND OF AN ALIEN AND A RESIDENT [WITH YOU] WILL ACHIEVE. — מִי גָרַם לוֹ שֶׁיַּעֲשִׁיר — Who caused him to become rich? דְּבוּקוֹ עִמָּךְ — His attachment "with you."[4]

□ וּמָךְ אָחִיךָ עִמּוֹ — AND YOUR BROTHER BECOMES IMPOVERISHED WITH HIM. — מִי גָרַם לוֹ שֶׁיִּמּוֹךְ — Who caused him to become impoverished? דְּבוּקוֹ עִמּוֹ — His attachment "with him," i.e., with the non-Jew, עַל יְדֵי שֶׁלָּמַד — through his having learned [5]מִמַּעֲשָׂיו — from [the non-Jew's] actions.[5]

□ מִשְׁפַּחַת גֵּר — AN ALIEN'S FAMILY.[6] — זֶה עוֹבֵד כּוֹכָבִים וּמַזָּלוֹת — This is an idolater.[7] כְּשֶׁהוּא

mean "you shall keep them in your possession," for the verb נחל in the sense of possessing applies only to property acquired by inheritance, and the slaves of our verse are not inherited but purchased. Rather, וְהִתְנַחַלְתֶּם here means הֶחֱזַקְתֶּם, "you shall hold."

1. The prohibition against using another Jew for pointless labor has already been stated in verse 43. It is repeated here to teach us that it applies not only to a slaveowner, but to a leader and a king, as well (Mizruchi).

2. This is in contradistinction to the way גֵּר וְתוֹשָׁב was used in verse 35 above. See Rashi there.

3. The fact that Targum Onkelos translates גֵּר with the word עָרֵל, literally, "one who is uncircumcised," indicates that גֵּר here is not to be taken as a גֵּר צֶדֶק, a proselyte who has converted to become part of the Jewish people, and who is subject to all of the laws of the Torah (Yosef Hallel). When Targum Onkelos understands גֵּר as גֵּר צֶדֶק, he renders it גִּיּוֹרָא, e.g., Exodus 12:48.

4. Toras Kohanim, perek 8:1. "With you" seems inappropriate with reference to a resident-alien, for he

is not part of the Jewish people (Zichron Moshe). It teaches us that that which "his hand will achieve," i.e., his wealth, mentioned in the beginning of the verse came about because it is "with you," through the Divine Providence manifest in the Land of Israel when it is inhabited by the Jewish people (Korban Aharon).

5. Toras Kohanim, perek 8:1. The apparently superfluous עִמּוֹ, "with him," teaches us that your brother's poverty is a punishment for aping the behavior of non-Jews — even resident-aliens who wish to reside among Jews in the Land of Israel — with whom he keeps company. For even actions permitted to non-Jews can be sinful for Jews (see Be'er Yitzchak).

6. The translation of לְעֵקֶר מִשְׁפַּחַת גֵּר as "to an idol of an alien's family" follows Targum Yonasan ben Uziel. According to Tosafos (Bava Metzia 71a) cited in Maskil LeDavid, the translation should be "to an idol, an alien's family."

7. The resident-alien is a non-Jew who has accepted upon himself not to worship idols as Rashi has mentioned in his comments to verse 35. His family are non-Jews who are idolaters (Korban Aharon).

343 / VAYIKRA/LEVITICUS — PARASHAS BEHAR — 25/49-50 — כה/מט-נ

he has been sold, he shall have redemption; one of his brothers shall redeem him; ⁴⁹ or his uncle, or his cousin shall redeem him, or a relative from his family shall redeem him; or if his own means become sufficient, he shall be redeemed. ⁵⁰ He shall make a calculation with his purchaser from the year he was sold to him until the yovel year; the money of his purchase shall be in the number of years, like the days of a hired worker he shall be

נִמְכַּ֔ר גְּאֻלָּ֖ה תִּֽהְיֶה־לּ֑וֹ אֶחָ֥ד מֵאֶחָ֖יו
מט יִגְאָלֶֽנּוּ׃ אוֹ־דֹד֞וֹ א֤וֹ בֶן־דֹּדוֹ֙ יִגְאָלֶ֔נּוּ
אֽוֹ־מִשְּׁאֵ֧ר בְּשָׂר֛וֹ מִמִּשְׁפַּחְתּ֖וֹ
יִגְאָלֶ֑נּוּ אוֹ־הִשִּׂ֥יגָה יָד֖וֹ וְנִגְאָֽל׃
נ וְחִשַּׁב֙ עִם־קֹנֵ֔הוּ מִשְּׁנַת֙ הִמָּ֣כְרוֹ ל֔וֹ
עַ֖ד שְׁנַ֣ת הַיֹּבֵ֑ל וְהָיָ֞ה כֶּ֤סֶף מִמְכָּרוֹ֙
בְּמִסְפַּ֣ר שָׁנִ֔ים כִּימֵ֥י שָׂכִ֖יר יִהְיֶ֥ה

────── אונקלוס ──────

דְּיִזְדַּבַּן פָּרְקָנָא תְּהֵי לֵהּ חַד מֵאֲחוֹהִי יִפְרְקִנֵּהּ: מט אוֹ אַח אֲבוּהִי אוֹ בַר אַח אֲבוּהִי יִפְרְקִנֵּהּ אוֹ מִקָרִיב בִּשְׂרֵהּ מִזַּרְעִיתֵהּ יִפְרְקִנֵּהּ אוֹ דְתַדְבֵּק יְדֵהּ וְיִתְפָּרֵק: נ וִיחַשֵּׁב עִם זָבְנֵהּ מִשַּׁתָּא דְאִזְדַּבַּן לֵהּ עַד שַׁתָּא דְיוֹבֵלָא וִיהֵי כְסַף זְבִינוֹהִי בְּמִנְיַן שְׁנַיָּא כְּיוֹמֵי אֲגִירָא יְהֵי

────── רש״י ──────

אוֹמֵר לְעֶקֶר זֶה הַנִּמְכָּר לַעֲבוֹדָה זָרָה עַצְמָהּ (שם; ב״ק קיג:) לִהְיוֹת לָהּ שַׁמָּשׁ, וְלֹא לֶאֱלֹהוּת אֶלָּא לַחֲטוֹב עֵצִים וְלִשְׁאוֹב מַיִם: (מח) גְּאֻלָּה תִּהְיֶה לּוֹ. מִיָּד, אַל תַּנִּיחֵהוּ שֶׁיִּטָּמַע (ת״כ שם): (נ) עַד שְׁנַת הַיֹּבֵל. שֶׁהֲרֵי כָל עַצְמוֹ לֹא קְנָאוֹ אֶלָּא לְעָבְדוֹ עַד הַיּוֹבֵל, שֶׁהֲרֵי בַיּוֹבֵל יֵצֵא כְּמוֹ שֶׁנֶּאֱ' לְמַטָּה וְיָצָא בִּשְׁנַת הַיּוֹבֵל (פסוק נד) וּבְנָכְרִי שֶׁתַּחַת יָדְךָ הַכָּתוּב מְדַבֵּר, וְאַעַפ״כ לֹא תָבֹא עָלָיו בַּעֲקִיפִין, מִפְּנֵי חִלּוּל הַשֵּׁם, אֶלָּא כְּשֶׁבָּא לִגָּאֵל יְדַקְדֵּק בַּחֶשְׁבּוֹן (ת״כ פרק ט:ב-ג; ב״ק קיג :) לְפִי הַמַּגִּיעַ בְּכָל שָׁנָה וְשָׁנָה יְנַכֶּה לוֹ הַגּוֹיִ מִן דָּמָיו. אִם הָיוּ עֶשְׂרִים שָׁנָה מִשֶּׁנִּמְכַּר עַד הַיּוֹבֵל וּקְנָאוֹ בְּעֶשְׂרִים מָנֶה, נִמְצָא

────── RASHI ELUCIDATED ──────

לַעֲבוֹדָה זָרָה עַצְמָהּ — this is one who is sold לָעֶקֶר — "to an idol," זֶה הַנִּמְכָּר — When it says, אוֹמֵר — to the idol itself,[1] לִהְיוֹת לָהּ שַׁמָּשׁ — to be a servant for it, וְלֹא לֶאֱלֹהוּת — but not for deification, i.e., he does not engage in the actual worship of the idol; אֶלָּא — rather, he is its servant לַחֲטוֹב עֵצִים — to chop wood וְלִשְׁאוֹב מַיִם — and to draw water.[2]

48. גְּאֻלָּה תִּהְיֶה לּוֹ — HE SHALL HAVE REDEMPTION, מִיָּד — immediately.[3] אַל תַּנִּיחֵהוּ שֶׁיִּטָּמַע — Do not let him become assimilated.[4]

50. עַד שְׁנַת הַיֹּבֵל — UNTIL THE *YOVEL* YEAR. שֶׁהֲרֵי — For, see now, כָּל עַצְמוֹ לֹא קְנָאוֹ — [the non-Jew] did not acquire [the Jewish slave's] person at all אֶלָּא לְעָבְדוֹ — other than to work for him עַד הַיּוֹבֵל — until the *yovel* year. שֶׁהֲרֵי בַיּוֹבֵל יֵצֵא — For, see now, that at the *yovel* year he goes out of slavery, כְּמוֹ שֶׁנֶּאֱמַר לְמַטָּה — as it says below, [5]וְיָצָא בִּשְׁנַת הַיּוֹבֵל — "he shall go out in the *yovel* year."[5] וּבְנָכְרִי שֶׁתַּחַת יָדְךָ הַכָּתוּב מְדַבֵּר — The verse speaks of a non-Jew who is under your hand, i.e., subject to your rule,[6] וְאַף עַל פִּי כֵן — and even so, לֹא תָבֹא עָלָיו בַּעֲקִיפִין — do not come upon him in a roundabout way, i.e., do not deal with him dishonestly, מִפְּנֵי חִלּוּל הַשֵּׁם — because of desecration of the Name of God. אֶלָּא — Rather, כְּשֶׁבָּא לִגָּאֵל — when [a Jewish slave] comes to be redeemed from a non-Jew [7]יְדַקְדֵּק בַּחֶשְׁבּוֹן — he should be meticulous in calculating the price of redemption.[7] לְפִי הַמַּגִּיעַ בְּכָל שָׁנָה וְשָׁנָה — According to that which was appropriated for each and every year,[8] יְנַכֶּה לוֹ הַגּוֹי — the non-Jew shall deduct for [the slave] מִן דָּמָיו — from his original price. אִם הָיוּ עֶשְׂרִים שָׁנָה — For example, if there were twenty years מִשֶּׁנִּמְכַּר — from the time he was sold עַד הַיּוֹבֵל — until the *yovel* year, וּקְנָאוֹ בְּעֶשְׂרִים מָנֶה — and he bought him for twenty *maneh*,[9] נִמְצָא —

1. *Toras Kohanim, perek* 8:1; *Bava Kamma* 113b; *Kiddushin* 20a; *Bava Metzia* 71a. לָעֶקֶר is from the root עקר, "to uproot." It denotes an idol, for idols are destined to be destroyed, uprooted (*Tosafos* to *Arachin* 30b, s.v., או לעקר).
2. Were he to practice idolatry, we would not be obligated to redeem him (*Maskil LeDavid*).
3. "He shall have redemption" of our verse appears superfluous, for the conclusion of our verse and the following verse go on to specify who shall redeem him. It is stated to teach us that he is to be redeemed immediately (*Malbim*).
4. *Toras Kohanim, perek* 8:1.
5. Below v. 54.
6. For it speaks of a non-Jew whom we can compel to release his Jewish slave at the *yovel* year (*Gur Aryeh*; *Sifsei Chachamim*).
7. *Toras Kohanim, perek* 9:2-3; *Bava Kamma* 113a-b.
8. That is, according to the amount paid for each year, determined by dividing the purchase price by the number of years from the time of purchase to the following *yovel* year.
9. A *maneh* is one hundred *dinars*, which equal twenty-five *shekels*.

with him. ⁵¹ *If there are yet many years, according to them he shall repay his redemption from the money of his purchase.* ⁵² *And if there are few years left until the yovel year, he shall calculate that with him; according to his years shall he repay his redemption.* ⁵³ *He shall be with him like a laborer hired by the year; he shall not subjugate him through hard labor in your sight.*

⁵⁴ *If he has not been redeemed by these [means], then he shall go out in the yovel year, he and his children with him.*

⁵⁵ *For the Children of Israel are slaves to Me,*

נא עִמּוֹ: אִם־ע֣וֹד רַבּ֣וֹת בַּשָּׁנִ֑ים לְפִיהֶן֙
נב יָשִׁ֣יב גְּאֻלָּת֔וֹ מִכֶּ֖סֶף מִקְנָת֑וֹ: וְאִם־
מְעַ֞ט נִשְׁאַ֧ר בַּשָּׁנִ֛ים עַד־שְׁנַ֥ת
הַיֹּבֵ֖ל וְחִשַּׁב־ל֑וֹ כְּפִ֣י שָׁנָ֔יו יָשִׁ֖יב
נג אֶת־גְּאֻלָּת֑וֹ: כִּשְׂכִ֥יר שָׁנָ֛ה בְּשָׁנָ֖ה
יִהְיֶ֣ה עִמּ֑וֹ לֹא־יִרְדֶּ֥נּוּ בְּפֶ֖רֶךְ
נד לְעֵינֶֽיךָ: וְאִם־לֹ֥א יִגָּאֵ֖ל בְּאֵ֑לֶּה
וְיָצָא֙ בִּשְׁנַ֣ת הַיֹּבֵ֔ל ה֖וּא וּבָנָ֥יו עִמּֽוֹ:
נה מפטיר כִּי־לִ֤י בְנֵֽי־יִשְׂרָאֵל֙ עֲבָדִ֔ים

― אונקלוס ―

עִמֵּהּ: נא אִם עוֹד סַגִיאִין בִּשְׁנַיָּא לְפוּמְהֶן יָתִיב פֻּרְקָנֵהּ מִכְּסַף זְבִינוֹהִי: נב וְאִם זְעֵר יִשְׁתְּאַר בִּשְׁנַיָּא עַד שַׁתָּא דְיוֹבֵלָא וִיחַשֵׁב לֵהּ כְּפוּם שְׁנוֹהִי יָתֵיב יָת פֻּרְקָנֵהּ: נג כַּאֲגִיר שְׁנָא בִּשְׁנָא יְהֵי עִמֵּהּ לָא יִפְלַח בֵּהּ בְּקַשְׁיוּ לְעֵינָיךְ: נד וְאִם לָא יִתְפְּרַק בְּאִלֵּין וְיִפּוֹק בְּשַׁתָּא דְיוֹבֵלָא הוּא וּבְנוֹהִי עִמֵּהּ: נה אֲרֵי דִילִי בְּנֵי יִשְׂרָאֵל עַבְדִּין

― רש"י ―

שקנה הנכרי עבודת שנה במנה, ואם שהה זה אללו חמש שנים ובא ליגאל ינכה לו חמשה מנים ויתן לו העבד חמשה עשר מנים, וזהו והיה כסף ממכרו במספר שנים כימי שכיר יהיה עמו, חשבון המגיע לכל שנה ושנה יתחשב כאלו נשכר עמו כל שנה במנה וינכה לו: (נא) **אִם עוֹד רַבּוֹת** **בַּשָּׁנִים**. עַד הַיּוֹבֵל: **לְפִיהֶן וְגוֹ׳**. הַכֹּל כְּמוֹ שֶׁפֵּרַשְׁתִּי: (נג) **לֹא יִרְדֶּנּוּ בְּפֶרֶךְ לְעֵינֶיךָ**. כְּלוֹמַר וְאַתָּה רוֹאֶה: (נד) **וְאִם לֹא יִגָּאֵל בְּאֵלֶּה**. בְּאֵלֶּה הוּא נִגְאָל וְאֵינוֹ נִגְאָל בְּשֵׁשׁ (קידושין ט״ו): [**הוּא וּבָנָיו עִמּוֹ**. הַגּוֹי חַיָּב בִּמְזוֹנוֹת בָּנָיו]: (נה) **כִּי לִי בְנֵי יִשְׂרָאֵל עֲבָדִים**. שְׁטָרִי קוֹדֵם:

― RASHI ELUCIDATED ―

בְּמָנֶה – it turns out שֶׁקָּנָה הַנָּכְרִי עֲבוֹדַת שָׁנָה – that the non-Jew purchased the labor of one year for a *maneh*, וְאִם שָׁהָה זֶה אֶצְלוֹ חָמֵשׁ שָׁנִים – and if this [slave] spent five years with him וּבָא לִגָּאֵל – and he comes to be redeemed, יְנַכֶּה לוֹ – [the non-Jew] shall deduct for him חֲמִשָּׁה מָנִים – five *maneh*, וְיִתֵּן לוֹ הָעֶבֶד – and the slave will give him חֲמִשָּׁה עָשָׂר מָנִים – fifteen *maneh*. וְזֶהוּ – And this is what is meant by, ,,וְהָיָה כֶּסֶף מִמְכָּרוֹ בְּמִסְפַּר שָׁנִים – "The money of his purchase shall be in the number of years, כִּימֵי שָׂכִיר יִהְיֶה עִמּוֹ'' – like the days of a hired worker he shall be with him''; חֶשְׁבּוֹן הַמַּגִּיעַ לְכָל שָׁנָה וְשָׁנָה יְחַשֵּׁב – he shall calculate the amount that was appropriated for each and every year, כְּאִלּוּ נִשְׂכַּר עִמּוֹ – as if he were hired with him, i.e., to work for him, כָּל שָׁנָה בְּמָנֶה – each year for a *maneh*, וִינַכֶּה לוֹ – and [the non-Jew] shall deduct it for [the slave] from the purchase price to arrive at the price of redemption.

51. אִם עוֹד רַבּוֹת בַּשָּׁנִים – IF THERE ARE YET MANY YEARS עַד הַיּוֹבֵל – until the *yovel* year.

☐ לְפִיהֶן וְגוֹמֵר – ACCORDING TO THEM, ETC. הַכֹּל כְּמוֹ שֶׁפֵּרַשְׁתִּי – It is all as I have explained.

53. לֹא יִרְדֶּנּוּ בְּפֶרֶךְ לְעֵינֶיךָ – HE SHALL NOT SUBJUGATE HIM THROUGH HARD LABOR IN YOUR SIGHT. כְּלוֹמַר – That is to say, וְאַתָּה רוֹאֶה – and you view it.[1]

54. וְאִם לֹא יִגָּאֵל בְּאֵלֶּה – IF HE HAS NOT BEEN REDEEMED BY THESE [MEANS]. ,,בְּאֵלֶּה'' – "By these means" הוּא נִגְאָל – he can be redeemed, וְאֵינוֹ נִגְאָל – but he is not redeemed ²בְּשֵׁשׁ – through completion of a term of **six** years, as is a Hebrew servant sold to another Jew.[2]

☐ הוּא וּבָנָיו עִמּוֹ – HE AND HIS CHILDREN WITH HIM. הַגּוֹי חַיָּב בִּמְזוֹנוֹת בָּנָיו – The non-Jew is responsible for the food of his children.[3]}

55. כִּי לִי בְנֵי יִשְׂרָאֵל עֲבָדִים – FOR THE CHILDREN OF ISRAEL ARE SLAVES TO ME. שְׁטָרִי – My contract קוֹדֵם – comes first.

---

1. The verse could have been understood as prohibiting the non-Jew from subjugating the Jewish slave through hard labor only in the presence of another Jew. But this is not so. For if the Torah forbids a non-Jew to subjugate a Jewish slave through hard labor, it stands to reason that the prohibition applies whether another Jew is present or not. Rather, the verse forbids another Jew from viewing such subjugation passively without taking action to stop it (*Gur Aryeh*).

2. *Kiddushin* 15b. See *Exodus* 21:2.

3. See Rashi to v. 41.

345 / VAYIKRA/LEVITICUS — PARASHAS BEHAR — 26/1

עֲבָדַי הֵם אֲשֶׁר־הוֹצֵאתִי אֹתָם
מֵאֶרֶץ מִצְרָיִם אֲנִי יהוה
אֱלֹהֵיכֶם: לֹא־תַעֲשׂוּ לָכֶם אֱלִילִם
וּפֶסֶל וּמַצֵּבָה לֹא־תָקִימוּ לָכֶם

they are My slaves, whom I have taken out of the land of Egypt — I am HASHEM, your God.

26 ¹ **Y**ou shall not make idols for yourselves, and you shall not erect for yourselves a statue or a pillar,

———— אונקלוס ————

עַבְדַי אִנּוּן דִּי אַפֵּקִית יָתְהוֹן מֵאַרְעָא דְמִצְרָיִם אֲנָא יְיָ אֱלָהֲכוֹן:
א לָא תַעְבְּדוּן לְכוֹן טַעֲוָן וְצֶלֶם וְקָמָא לָא תְקִימוּן לְכוֹן

———— רש"י ————

אני ה' אלהיכם. כל המשתעבד בהן כאילו משתעבד [בהן] מלמעלן (ת"כ שם ד): **(א) לא תעשו לכם אלילם.** כנגד זה הנמכר לגוי, שלא יאמר הואיל ורבי מגלה עריות אף אני כמותו, הואיל ורבי עובד עבודה זרה אף אני כמותו, הואיל ורבי מחלל שבת אף אני כמותו, לכך נאמרו מקראות הללו (שם ו). ואף הפרשיות הללו נאמרו על הסדר. בתחלה הזהיר על השביעית, ואם חמד ממון ונחשד על השביעית סופו למכור מטלטליו, לכך סמך לה (לעיל כה:יד) [ומה כתיב ביה או קנה מיד עמיתך] דבר הנקנה מיד ליד. לא חזר בו, סוף מוכר אחוזתו. לא חזר בו, סוף מוכר את ביתו. לא חזר בו, סוף לוה ברבית.

———— RASHI ELUCIDATED ————

□ אֲנִי ה' אֱלֹהֵיכֶם — I AM HASHEM, YOUR GOD. — כָּל הַמִּשְׁתַּעְבֵּד בָּהֶן מִלְּמַטָּן — Whoever subjugates them below, i.e., on earth, {בָּהֶן} כְּאִלּוּ מִשְׁתַּעְבֵּד — is as if he is subjugating {them} מִלְמַעְלָן — above.[1]

26.

1. לֹא תַעֲשׂוּ לָכֶם אֱלִילִם — YOU SHALL NOT MAKE IDOLS FOR YOURSELVES. — כְּנֶגֶד זֶה — The verse is directed toward this one הַנִּמְכָּר לְנָכְרִי — who has been sold as a slave to a non-Jew, שֶׁלֹא יֹאמַר — that he should not say, הוֹאִיל וְרַבִּי מְגַלֶּה עֲרָיוֹת — "Since my master practices sexual immorality, אַף אֲנִי כְּמוֹתוֹ — I will too, like him; הוֹאִיל וְרַבִּי עוֹבֵד עֲבוֹדָה זָרָה — since my master worships idols, אַף אֲנִי כְּמוֹתוֹ — I will too, like him; הוֹאִיל וְרַבִּי מְחַלֵּל שַׁבָּת — since my master desecrates Shabbos, אַף אֲנִי כְּמוֹתוֹ — I will too, like him." לְכָךְ נֶאֶמְרוּ מִקְרָאוֹת הַלָּלוּ — That is why these verses have been stated.[2] וְאַף הַפָּרָשִׁיּוֹת הַלָּלוּ נֶאֶמְרוּ עַל הַסֵּדֶר — These passages of the Torah, from the beginning of Chapter 25 up to this point, were also stated in sequential order: בַּתְּחִלָּה הִזְהִיר עַל הַשְּׁבִיעִית — At first [the Torah] enjoined us with regard to the seventh year. וְאִם חָמַד מָמוֹן — If he desired money וְנֶחְשַׁד עַל הַשְּׁבִיעִית — and became suspect with regard to the seventh year,[3] סוֹפוֹ לִמְכּוֹר מִטַּלְטְלָיו — his fate is to sell his chattels. לְכָךְ סָמַךְ לָהּ — This is why [the Torah] put next to [the passage dealing with the seventh year], "וְכִי תִמְכְּרוּ מִמְכָּר וְגוֹמֵר״, — "when you make a sale, etc."[4] מַה כְּתִיב בֵּיהּ — What is written in [that verse]? "אוֹ קָנֹה מִיַּד עֲמִיתֶךָ״, — "Or buy from the hand of your fellow." דָּבָר הַנִּקְנֶה מִיַּד לְיָד — The verse refers to something which is bought from hand to hand, i.e., chattels which are passed from hand to hand.[5]} לֹא חָזַר בּוֹ — If he did not repent, סוֹף מוֹכֵר אֲחוּזָתוֹ — in the end he sells his ancestral heritage. לֹא חָזַר בּוֹ — If he still did not repent, סוֹף מוֹכֵר אֶת בֵּיתוֹ — in the end he sells his house. לֹא חָזַר בּוֹ — If he still did not repent, סוֹף לֹוֶה בְּרִבִּית — in the end he borrows

---

1. *Toras Kohanim, perek* 9:4. Whoever subjugates them on earth also bears the responsibility of subjugating the Divine source of their soul (*Maskil LeDavid*).

2. *Toras Kohanim, perek* 9:6. The commandments not to worship idols, to keep Shabbos, and to have reverence for the Sanctuary have been stated above in 19:4,30. They are repeated in our verse and the following one because they have special relevance for a Jew who has been sold as a slave to a non-Jew. He might be prone to emulate the conduct of his master and violate these three commandments. "Reverence for the Sanctuary" is taken by Rashi as an allusion to sexual morality, as Rashi stated above in his comments to 19:2 above; קְדֻשָּׁה, "sanctity," which shares the root קדש with וּמִקְדָּשִׁי, "and My Sanctuary," is present only where there is restriction against sexual immorality (*Be'er BaSadeh*; *Lifshuto shel Rashi*).

3. Rashi uses וְנֶחְשַׁד, "became suspect [with regard to the seventh year]," rather than the stronger עָבַר, "violated [the law of the seventh year]," because he refers to one who violates the lesser prohibition against doing business with produce of the seventh year, rather than the more severe prohibition against doing agricultural work. This is implied by Rashi's statement that "he desired money," i.e., he wished to profit by doing business with the produce of the seventh year (*Nachalas Yaakov*).

4. Above 25:14.

5. The verse appears to deal with a field. But the apparently superfluous מִיַּד, "from the hand," teaches that it applies to chattels, movable goods, also.

and in your land you shall not emplace a flooring stone upon which to prostrate oneself — for I am HASHEM, your God. ² *My Sabbaths shall you observe and My Sanctuary shall you revere — I am HASHEM.*

וְאֶבֶן מַשְׂכִּית לֹא תִתְּנוּ בְּאַרְצְכֶם לְהִשְׁתַּחֲוֹת עָלֶיהָ כִּי אֲנִי יהוה אֱלֹהֵיכֶם: אֶת־שַׁבְּתֹתַי תִּשְׁמֹרוּ וּמִקְדָּשִׁי תִּירָאוּ אֲנִי יהוה: פ פ פ

THE HAFTARAH FOR BEHAR APPEARS ON PAGE 401.
During non-leap years Behar is always read together with Bechukosai.
The Haftarah of Bechukosai is then read.

— אונקלוס —

וְאֶבֶן סָגְדָּא לָא תִתְּנוּן בְּאַרְעֲכוֹן לְמִסְגַּד עֲלַהּ אֲרֵי אֲנָא יְיָ אֱלָהֲכוֹן: יָת יוֹמֵי שַׁבַּיָּא דִּילִי תִּטְרוּן וּלְבֵית מַקְדְּשִׁי תְּהוֹן דָּחֲלִין אֲנָא יְיָ:

— רש״י —

כל אלו האחרונות קשות מן הראשונות. לא חזר בו, סוף מוכר את עצמו. לא חזר בו, לא דיו לישראל אלא אפילו לנכרי (קידושין כ.): **וְאֶבֶן מַשְׂכִּית.** ל׳ כסוי כמו ושכותי כפי (שמות לג:כב). שמכסין הקרקע ברצפת אבנים: **לְהִשְׁתַּחֲוֹת עָלֶיהָ.** אפילו לשמים. לפי שהשתחואה בפשוט ידים ורגלים היא ואסרה תורה לעשות כן חוץ מן המקדש (ת״כ שם ה; מגילה כב:): **(ב) אֲנִי ה׳.** נאמן לשלם שכר (ת״כ שם ו):

— RASHI ELUCIDATED —

on interest. — **כָּל אֵלּוּ הָאַחֲרוֹנוֹת** — **All of these later ones** **קָשׁוֹת מִן הָרִאשׁוֹנוֹת** — **are harsher than the earlier ones,** i.e., each of these stages is harsher than the one that preceded it.¹ — **לֹא חָזַר בּוֹ** — **If he still did not repent,** **סוֹף מוֹכֵר אֶת עַצְמוֹ** — **in the end he sells himself** as a slave. — **לֹא חָזַר בּוֹ** — **If he still did not repent,** **לֹא דַּיּוֹ לְיִשְׂרָאֵל** — **it is not enough for him** that he will have to sell himself **to an Israelite,** **אֶלָּא** — **but** he will have to sell himself ²**אֲפִילּוּ לְנָכְרִי** — **even to a non-Jew.**²

☐ **וְאֶבֶן מַשְׂכִּית** — **A FLOORING STONE.** **מַשְׂכִּית** — **לְשׁוֹן כִּסּוּי** means **"covering"**³ **כְּמוֹ** — **like** **וְשַׂכֹּתִי** in, **"וְשַׂכֹּתִי כַפִּי,,**⁴ — **"and I shall cover** [you] **with My palm."**⁴ **שֶׁמְּכַסִּין הַקַּרְקַע** — The word for **"flooring stone"** is related to **"covering," for they cover the ground** **בְּרִצְפַת אֲבָנִים** — **with a floor of stones.**

☐ **לְהִשְׁתַּחֲוֹת עָלֶיהָ** — **UPON WHICH TO PROSTRATE ONESELF.** **אֲפִילּוּ לַשָּׁמַיִם** — **Even for** the sake of **Heaven.** **לְפִי שֶׁהִשְׁתַּחֲוָאָה** — **For prostration** **בְּפִשּׁוּט יָדַיִם וְרַגְלַיִם הִיא** — **is** performed **through stretching out the hands and feet,** **וְאָסְרָה תוֹרָה לַעֲשׂוֹת כֵּן** — **and the Torah forbade doing so** even for the sake of Heaven,⁵ ⁶**חוּץ מִן הַמִּקְדָּשׁ** — **outside the** *Beis HaMikdash*.⁶

2. אֲנִי ה׳ — **I AM HASHEM.** ⁷**נֶאֱמָן לְשַׁלֵּם שָׂכָר** — **Faithful to pay reward.**⁷

---

1. Rashi mentions this at this particular point, for we may have thought that borrowing on interest is not as harsh as selling one's ancestral lands. But this is not so, for ancestral lands may be redeemed, whereas interest creates a permanent and constantly increasing loss (*Nachalas Yaakov*).

2. *Kiddushin* 20a.

3. This is an example of two roots with identical meanings and formed of the same letters, but in different order. כסוי is from the root כסה, while משכית is from the root סכה (ס and שׂ are interchangeable; see *Yosef Hallel*).

4. *Exodus* 33:22.

5. Rashi speaks here only of the law which is *de'oraisa* (of Scriptural origin). See *Shulchan Aruch, Orach Chaim* 131:8 and *Mishneh Brurah* there for a discussion of the related rabbinic prohibition.

6. *Toras Kohanim, perek* 9:5; *Megillah* 22b. "In your land" implies the Land of Israel outside the grounds of the *Beis HaMikdash*, for that is not "your land"; it is the property of God in a more immediate sense than the rest of the world (*Sefer Zikaron*).

Rashi is of the opinion that prostration upon flooring stones is forbidden because the Torah did not want places of worship other than the *Beis HaMikdash* to have floors of stone (see Rashi to *Megillah* 22b, s.v., לא אסרה תורה). This stands in contrast to the opinion of the *Rambam*, who understands אֶבֶן מַשְׂכִּית as a stone with decorative engravings of a sort that was worshiped by pagans. The Torah forbids making this sort of stone even if it is meant as a vehicle for worshiping God, for it is similar to the practice of the pagans (see *Sefer HaMitzvos, lavin* 12; *Yad HaChazakah, Hilchos Avodas Kochavim*, 6:6-7). According to this opinion, מַשְׂכִּית is from the root שכה, "to gaze" or "view," for people would look at the engravings on the אֶבֶן מַשְׂכִּית (*Radak*). See *Minchas Chinuch*, 349, for further discussion of the dispute between Rashi and the *Rambam*.

7. *Toras Kohanim, perek* 9:6.

פרשת בחקתי

Parashas Bechukosai

³ *If you will go in My statutes and observe My commandments and perform them;* **⁴** *then I will provide your rains in their time, and the land will give its produce and the tree of the field will give its fruit.*

ג אִם־בְּחֻקֹּתַ֖י תֵּלֵ֑כוּ וְאֶת־מִצְוֺתַ֣י תִּשְׁמְר֔וּ וַעֲשִׂיתֶ֖ם אֹתָֽם: ד וְנָתַתִּ֥י גִשְׁמֵיכֶ֖ם בְּעִתָּ֑ם וְנָתְנָ֤ה הָאָ֙רֶץ֙ יְבוּלָ֔הּ וְעֵ֥ץ הַשָּׂדֶ֖ה יִתֵּ֥ן פִּרְיֽוֹ:

── אונקלוס ──

ג אִם בִּקְיָמַי תְּהָכוּן וְיָת פִּקּוּדַי תִּטְּרוּן וְתַעְבְּדוּן יָתְהוֹן: ד וְאֶתֵּן מַטְרֵיכוֹן בְּעִדָּנְהוֹן וְתִתֵּן אַרְעָא עֲלַלְתַּהּ וְאִילָן חַקְלָא יִתֵּן אִבֵּהּ:

── רש"י ──

(ג) אם בחקתי תלכו. יכול זה קיום המצות כשהוא אומר ואת מצותי תשמרו ועשיתם אתם הרי קיום המצות אמור הא מה אני מקיים אם בחקתי תלכו שתהיו עמלים בתורה (ת"כ בחקותי פרשתא א:ב): **ואת מצותי תשמרו.** הוו עמלים בתורה על מנת לשמור ולקיים כמו שנאמר ולמדתם אתם ושמרתם לעשותם (דברים ה:א): **(ד) בעתם.** בשעה שאין דרך בני אדם לצאת כגון (בלילי רביעיות) בלילי שבתות (ת"כ פרק א:ח; תענית כג.): **ועץ השדה.** הן אילני סרק

──── RASHI ELUCIDATED ────

3. אִם בְּחֻקֹּתַי תֵּלֵכוּ — IF YOU WILL GO IN MY STATUTES. יָכוֹל זֶה קִיּוּם הַמִּצְוֹת — One might be able to think that this refers to fulfillment of the commandments. כְּשֶׁהוּא אוֹמֵר — When it says, {וְאֶת מִצְוֺתַי תִּשְׁמְרוּ — "and observe My commandments"} וַעֲשִׂיתֶם אֹתָם — "and perform them,"[1] הֲרֵי קִיּוּם הַמִּצְוֹת אָמוּר — see that fulfillment of the commandments has been stated. הָא מָה אֲנִי מְקַיֵּם — What, then, do I maintain is meant by אִם בְּחֻקֹּתַי תֵּלֵכוּ — "if you will go in My statutes"? שֶׁתִּהְיוּ עֲמֵלִים בַּתּוֹרָה[2] — That you should be laboring in the Torah.[2]

□ וְאֶת מִצְוֹתַי תִּשְׁמְרוּ — AND OBSERVE MY COMMANDMENTS. הֱווּ עֲמֵלִים בַּתּוֹרָה — Be laboring in the Torah[3] עַל מְנָת לִשְׁמֹר וּלְקַיֵּם — in order to observe and to fulfill that which you learn,[4] כְּמוֹ שֶׁנֶּאֱמַר — as it says, וּלְמַדְתֶּם אֹתָם וּשְׁמַרְתֶּם לַעֲשׂוֹתָם[5] — "and you shall study them, and you shall observe them to perform them."[5]

4. בְּעִתָּם — IN THEIR TIME. בְּשָׁעָה — At a time שֶׁאֵין דֶּרֶךְ בְּנֵי אָדָם — when it is not the manner of people לָצֵאת — to go outside;[6] כְּגוֹן — for instance,[7] בְּלֵילֵי שַׁבָּתוֹת — on the nights of Shabbos, i.e., on Friday nights.[7]

□ וְעֵץ הַשָּׂדֶה — AND THE TREE OF THE FIELD. הֵן אִילָנֵי סְרָק — These trees which do not bear fruit,

---

1. The version of Rashi cited by *Mizrachi, Sifsei Chachamim,* et al., omits the phrase וְאֶת מִצְוֹתַי תִּשְׁמְרוּ "and observe My commandments." In most printed editions, however, that phrase is adduced here, either with or without the additional וְגוֹמֵר, "etc.," which refers to the phrase וַעֲשִׂיתֶם אֹתָם "and perform them." *Toras Kohanim,* Rashi's source for this comment, adduces both phrases.

2. *Toras Kohanim, parshasa* 1:2. תֵּלְכוּ, "you will go," connotes movement from place to place, and alludes to the process of Torah study, in which one regularly progresses to increasingly more sophisticated levels of understanding. תֵּלְכוּ also means "you will walk," which can be a laborious activity; thus, "you should be laboring in Torah" (*Gur Aryeh*).

3. According to the version cited by *Mizrachi* (see note 1 above), the first phrase, אִם בְּחֻקֹּתַי תֵּלֵכוּ, "if you will go in My decrees," refers to laboring in Torah study; the second phrase, וְאֶת מִצְוֺתַי תִּשְׁמְרוּ, "and observe My commandments," refers to laboring in Torah study for the sake of fulfillment, a much higher purpose than that implied by the first phrase; and the third phrase וַעֲשִׂיתֶם אֹתָם, "and perform them," refers to the actual fulfillment of the commandments.

According to the other versions, the first phrase refers to laboring in Torah study; the second explains that the purpose of that labor should be for the sake of fulfillment; and the third phrase speaks of the actual fulfillment.

4. *Toras Kohanim, parshasa* 1:5.

5. *Deuteronomy* 5:1. It is clear from this verse that "observing" is not the performance itself, but rather a stage that precedes performance (see *Mizrachi*).

6. בְּעִתָּם, "in their time," is not to be understood as "in their season," for that would be superfluous; if God gives rain and the land brings forth its produce and the tree its fruit, it is obvious that the rain falls in its proper season. Rather, בְּעִתָּם should be understood as at the time of the week when it causes the least bother (*Sefer Zikaron*; cf. Rashi to *Deuteronomy* 11:14).

7. *Toras Kohanim, perek* 1:1; *Taanis* 23a. People go out less on Friday nights than on other nights because their activities are limited (*Mizrachi*).

Alternative texts of Rashi read בְּלֵילֵי רְבִיעִיּוֹת, "on the nights of the fourth day," i.e., Tuesday nights. The Gemara in *Taanis* mentions both nights. Rashi there explains that a harmful spirit roams about on Tuesday nights, and because of this, people tend to stay home. According to the Gemara in *Pesachim* 112b, that spirit roams about on both Tuesday and Friday nights.

26/5-7 — בו/ה-ז

⁵ *Threshing will overtake vintage for you, and the vintage will last until the sowing; you will eat your bread to satiety and you will dwell securely in your land.* ⁶ *I will provide peace in the land, and you will lie down with none to frighten you; I will cause wild beasts to withdraw from the land, and a sword will not cross your land.* ⁷ *You will pursue your enemies;*

ה וְהִשִּׂיג לָכֶם דַּיִשׁ אֶת־בָּצִיר וּבָצִיר
יַשִּׂיג אֶת־זָרַע וַאֲכַלְתֶּם לַחְמְכֶם
לָשֹׂבַע וִישַׁבְתֶּם לָבֶטַח בְּאַרְצְכֶם:
ו וְנָתַתִּי שָׁלוֹם בָּאָרֶץ וּשְׁכַבְתֶּם
וְאֵין מַחֲרִיד וְהִשְׁבַּתִּי חַיָּה רָעָה
מִן־הָאָרֶץ וְחֶרֶב לֹא־תַעֲבֹר
בְּאַרְצְכֶם: ז וּרְדַפְתֶּם אֶת־אֹיְבֵיכֶם

--- אונקלוס ---

ה וִיעָרַע לְכוֹן דְּיָשָׁא לִקְטָפָא וּקְטָפָא יְעָרַע לְאַפּוּקֵי בַר זַרְעָא וְתֵיכְלוּן לַחְמְכוֹן לְמִשְׂבַּע וְתֵיתְבוּן לְרָחְצָן בְּאַרְעֲכוֹן: ו וְאֶתֵּן שְׁלָמָא בְּאַרְעָא וְתִשְׁרוֹן וְלֵית דְּמָנִיד וַאֲבַטֵּל חַיְתָא בִישְׁתָּא מִן אַרְעָא וּדְקָטְלִין בְּחַרְבָּא לָא יַעְדּוּן בְּאַרְעֲכוֹן: ז וְתִרְדְּפוּן יָת בַּעֲלֵי דְבָבֵיכוֹן

--- רש"י ---

(ה) והשיג לכם דיש את בציר. שיהא הדיש מרובה ואתם עסוקים בו עד הבציר ובבציר עד שעת הזרע (שם ז): **ואכלתם לחמכם לשבע.** אוכל קִמְעָא וְהוּא מִתְבָּרֵךְ בְּמֵעָיו (שם): (ו) **ונתתי שלום.** שֶׁמָּא תֹאמְרוּ הֲרֵי מַאֲכָל הֲרֵי מִשְׁתֶּה אִם אֵין שָׁלוֹם אֵין כְּלוּם, תַּ"ל אַחַר כָּל זֹאת וְנָתַתִּי שָׁלוֹם בָּאָרֶץ, מִכָּאן שֶׁהַשָּׁלוֹם שָׁקוּל כְּנֶגֶד הַכֹּל, וְכֵן הוּא אוֹמֵר עוֹשֶׂה שָׁלוֹם וּבוֹרֵא אֶת הַכֹּל (ברכות יא:): **וחרב לא תעבר בארצכם.** אֵין צָרִיךְ לוֹמַר שֶׁלֹּא יָבֹאוּ לְמִלְחָמָה, אֶלָּא אֲפִלּוּ לַעֲבֹר דֶּרֶךְ אַרְצְכֶם מִמְּדִינָה

--- RASHI ELUCIDATED ---

וַעֲתִידִין לַעֲשׂוֹת פֵּרוֹת¹ — *and they are destined to produce fruit.*¹

שֶׁיְּהֵא הַדַּיִשׁ מְרֻבֶּה — **For the threshing will be plentiful,** וְאַתֶּם עֲסוּקִים בּוֹ — *and you will be busy with it* עַד הַבָּצִיר — **until the vintage,** וּבַבָּצִיר — *and you will be busy with the vintage* עַד שְׁעַת הַזָּרַע² — **until the time of sowing.**²

5. וְהִשִּׂיג לָכֶם דַּיִשׁ אֶת בָּצִיר — **THRESHING WILL OVERTAKE VINTAGE FOR YOU.**

וַאֲכַלְתֶּם לַחְמְכֶם לָשֹׂבַע — **YOU WILL EAT YOUR BREAD TO SATIETY.** אוֹכֵל קִמְעָא — *He will eat a bit,* וְהוּא מִתְבָּרֵךְ בְּמֵעָיו³ — *and it will become blessed in his innards.*³

6. וְנָתַתִּי שָׁלוֹם — **I WILL PROVIDE PEACE.** שֶׁמָּא תֹאמְרוּ — *Perhaps you will say,* הֲרֵי מַאֲכָל — *"Here is food,* וַהֲרֵי מִשְׁתֶּה — *and here is drink;* אִם אֵין שָׁלוֹם — *but if there is no peace,* אֵין כְּלוּם — *there is nothing!"* תַּלְמוּד לוֹמַר — *In answer the verse says* אַחַר כָּל זֹאת — *after all this,* וְנָתַתִּי שָׁלוֹם בָּאָרֶץ — *"I will provide peace in the land."* מִכָּאן — *From here we see* שֶׁהַשָּׁלוֹם שָׁקוּל כְּנֶגֶד הַכֹּל — *that peace is as weighty as everything* else combined.⁴ וְכֵן הוּא אוֹמֵר — *And so it says,* עוֹשֶׂה שָׁלוֹם — *"He makes peace* וּבוֹרֵא אֶת הַכֹּל⁵ — *and creates everything."*⁵

וְחֶרֶב לֹא תַעֲבֹר בְּאַרְצְכֶם — **AND A SWORD WILL NOT CROSS YOUR LAND.** אֵין צָרִיךְ לוֹמַר — *It does not have to say* שֶׁלֹּא יָבֹאוּ לְמִלְחָמָה — *that [foreign swords] will not come for war,* אֶלָּא — *but* אֲפִילוּ לַעֲבוֹר — *even to cross* דֶּרֶךְ אַרְצְכֶם — *by way of your land* מִמְּדִינָה — *they will not come*

---

1. *Toras Kohanim, perek* 1:6. הַשָּׂדֶה, "of the field," appears superfluous. It teaches us that even trees of the field, as opposed to fruit-bearing trees of the orchard, will yield fruit (*Mizrachi; Sifsei Chachamim*).

2. *Toras Kohanim, perek* 1:7.

3. *Toras Kohanim, perek* 1:7. The beginning of the verse has already stated that the earth will yield plentiful produce. "You will eat your bread to satiety" therefore refers to the quality of the bread rather than its quantity; it will be unusually satisfying (*Mizrachi; Sifsei Chachamim*).

4. The passage has been speaking of the blessing of plentiful produce. It now shifts to the subject of peace. It goes back to the subject of plenty in verse 10. This indicates that peace is not only a blessing in itself; it is a feature of the blessing of plenty. Without peace, we cannot enjoy plenty (*Mizrachi; Sifsei Chachamim*).

5. *Berachos* 11b (according to *Hagahos HaBach*). This quotation is from the daily prayers and is based on *Isaiah* 45:7. In it, "peace" is compared to "everything," i.e., all that is good.

Alternative texts (based on *Toras Kohanim, perek* 1:8, and the standard version of *Berachos* 11b) adduce the original phrase from *Isaiah* 45:7, עוֹשֶׂה שָׁלוֹם וּבוֹרֵא רָע, "He makes peace and creates evil." That verse begins, "He forms light and creates darkness." Just as the verse's contrast between light and darkness is absolute, so, too, its contrast between peace and evil; just as "evil" includes all evil, so "peace" must include all that is good (*Sefer Zikaron*).

וְנָפְל֥וּ לִפְנֵיכֶ֖ם לֶחָֽרֶב: וְרָדְפ֨וּ ח
מִכֶּ֤ם חֲמִשָּׁה֙ מֵאָ֔ה וּמֵאָ֥ה מִכֶּ֖ם
רְבָבָ֣ה יִרְדֹּ֑פוּ וְנָפְל֧וּ אֹיְבֵיכֶ֛ם
לִפְנֵיכֶ֖ם לֶחָֽרֶב: וּפָנִ֣יתִי אֲלֵיכֶ֗ם ט

and they will fall before you by the sword. **8** Five from among you will pursue a hundred, and a hundred from among you will pursue ten thousand; and your enemies will fall before you by the sword. **9** I will turn to you, I will

— אונקלוס —

וְיִפְּלוּן קֳדָמֵיכוֹן לְחַרְבָּא: חוְיִרְדְּפוּן מִנְּכוֹן חַמְשָׁא לִמְאָה וּמְאָה מִנְּכוֹן מִנְבוֹן לְרִבְּוָתָא יִרְדְפוּן וְיִפְּלוּן בַּעֲלֵי דְבָבֵיכוֹן קֳדָמֵיכוֹן לְחַרְבָּא: טוְאֶתְפְּנִי בְמֵימְרִי לְאוֹטָבָא לְכוֹן

— רש״י —

(ז) **לפניכם לחרב.** אִישׁ בְּחֶרֶב רֵעֵהוּ. למדינה (ת״כ פרק ב:ג):
(ח) **ורדפו מכם.** מִן הַחֲלָשִׁים שֶׁבָּכֶם וְלֹא מִן הַגִּבּוֹרִים שֶׁבָּכֶם (שם): **חמשה מאה ומאה מכם רבבה.** וְכִי כָּךְ הוּא הַחֶשְׁבּוֹן? וַהֲלֹא לֹא הָיָה צָרִיךְ לוֹמַר אֶלָּא וּמֵאָה מִכֶּם שְׁנֵי אֲלָפִים יִרְדֹּפוּ, אֶלָּא אֵינוֹ דוֹמֶה מוּעָטִין הָעוֹשִׂין אֶת הַתּוֹרָה לִמְרֻבִּין הָעוֹשִׂין אֶת הַתּוֹרָה (שם): **ונפלו איביכם וגו׳.** שֶׁיִּהְיוּ נוֹפְלִים לִפְנֵיכֶם שֶׁלֹּא כְדֶרֶךְ הָאָרֶץ (שם):
(ט) **ופניתי אליכם.** אֶפְנֶה מִכָּל עֲסָקַי לְשַׁלֵּם שְׂכַרְכֶם. מָשָׁל לְמָה הַדָּבָר דּוֹמֶה, לְמֶלֶךְ שֶׁשָּׂכַר פּוֹעֲלִים וְכוּ׳ כִּדְאִיתָא בת״כ (שם ה):

— RASHI ELUCIDATED —

לִמְדִינָה¹ — **from** one **country to** another **country**.¹

7. לִפְנֵיכֶם לֶחָרֶב — BEFORE YOU BY THE SWORD. ²אִישׁ בְּחֶרֶב רֵעֵהוּ — **A man by the sword of his fellow,** i.e., by the sword of his comrade-in-arms.²

8. וְרָדְפוּ מִכֶּם — [FIVE] FROM AMONG YOU WILL PURSUE. מִן הַחַלָּשִׁים שֶׁבָּכֶם — **From the weak who are among you,** ³וְלֹא מִן הַגִּבּוֹרִים שֶׁבָּכֶם — **and not from the mighty who are among you.**³ □ חֲמִשָּׁה מֵאָה וּמֵאָה מִכֶּם רְבָבָה — FIVE [FROM AMONG YOU WILL PURSUE] A HUNDRED, AND A HUNDRED FROM AMONG YOU [WILL PURSUE] TEN THOUSAND. וְכִי כָּךְ הוּא הַחֶשְׁבּוֹן — **Is this the** correct **calculation?** וַהֲלֹא לֹא הָיָה צָרִיךְ לוֹמַר אֶלָּא וּמֵאָה מִכֶּם — **Should it not rather be said, "and a hundred from among you** שְׁנֵי אֲלָפִים יִרְדֹּפוּ — **will pursue two thousand?"** אֶלָּא — **But,** אֵינוֹ דוֹמֶה — **you cannot compare,** מוּעָטִין הָעוֹשִׂין אֶת הַתּוֹרָה — **a few who perform** the commandments **of the Torah** לִמְרֻבִּין הָעוֹשִׂין אֶת הַתּוֹרָה⁴ — **to many who perform** the commandments **of the Torah.**⁴ □ וְנָפְלוּ אֹיְבֵיכֶם וְגוֹמֵר — AND YOUR ENEMIES WILL FALL, ETC. This means שֶׁיִּהְיוּ נוֹפְלִים לִפְנֵיכֶם — **that they will fall before you** ⁵שֶׁלֹּא כְדֶרֶךְ הָאָרֶץ — **unlike the way of the land,** i.e., in an unnatural manner.⁵

9. וּפָנִיתִי אֲלֵיכֶם — I WILL TURN TO YOU. אֶפְנֶה מִכָּל עֲסָקַי — **I will turn away from all of My concerns** לְשַׁלֵּם שְׂכַרְכֶם — in order **to pay your reward.** מָשָׁל לְמָה הַדָּבָר דּוֹמֶה — **What can this matter be compared to?** לְמֶלֶךְ — **To a king** שֶׁשָּׂכַר פּוֹעֲלִים וְכוּלְהוּ — **who hired workers, etc.,** כִּדְאִיתָא בְּתוֹרַת כֹּהֲנִים⁶ — **as stated in** *Toras Kohanim*.⁶

1. *Toras Kohanim, perek* 2:3. The verse has said, "I will provide peace in the land." This already implies that "a sword" will not come to your land to wage war against you. The seemingly superfluous "and a sword will not cross your land" implies that foreign armies will not even cross your land to get to some other destination (*Minchas Yehudah; Sifsei Chachamim*; see also *Taanis* 22b, and Rashi there, s.v., הא כתיב ונתתי שלום בארץ).

2. *Toras Kohanim, perek* 2:3. The verse could have said, "You will pursue your enemies; and they will fall by the sword." It would have been understood that they will fall by *your* sword. The apparently superfluous לִפְנֵיכֶם, "before you" or "in front of you," indicates that they will not fall by your sword but by their own, while they are in flight ahead of you (*Be'er Mayim Chaim* by R' Yaakov ben Yitzchak HaKohen Shapira).

3. *Toras Kohanim, perek* 2:4. We would have expected the verse to use וּרְדַפְתֶּם, "you will pursue," as it did in verse 7. וְרָדְפוּ מִכֶּם, "*from among you* will pursue," implies that the verse refers to some, but not to all. Since the verse speaks of a blessing, it stands to reason that it describes how great will be the fear that the enemy has for the weakest of the Israelites, but that their fear of the strongest will be even greater (*Mesiach Ilmim*).

4. *Toras Kohanim, perek* 2:4.

5. *Toras Kohanim, perek* 2:4. Verse 12 has already stated that our enemies will fall before us by the sword. It is repeated here to teach us that they will fall in an unnatural manner (*Mizrachi; Sifsei Chachamim*).

6. *Toras Kohanim, perek* 2:5. What can this matter be compared to? To a king who hired many workers. There was one worker there who had worked for a long time. The workers went to collect their wages, and this worker went with them. The king said to that worker, "My son, I turn to [deal with] you. These [other] young men worked little for me, and I pay them little. But I have a substantial account to settle with you." So, too, Israel in this world requests their reward from God, and the [other] nations of the world request their reward from God. God says to Israel, "My son, I will turn to [deal with] you. These [other] nations of the world worked little for Me, and I pay them little. But I have a substantial account to settle with you." This is

וְהִפְרֵיתִי אֶתְכֶם וְהִרְבֵּיתִי אֶתְכֶם וַהֲקִימֹתִי אֶת־בְּרִיתִי אִתְּכֶם: [חמישי] וַאֲכַלְתֶּם יָשָׁן נוֹשָׁן וְיָשָׁן מִפְּנֵי חָדָשׁ תּוֹצִיאוּ: וְנָתַתִּי

make you fruitful and increase you; and I will establish My covenant with you. [10] And you will eat that which is very old and remove the old to make way for the new. [11] I will place My

— אונקלוס —

וְאַפֵּשׁ יָתְכוֹן וְאַסְגֵּי יָתְכוֹן וַאֲקֵם יָת קְיָמִי עִמְּכוֹן: וְתֵיכְלוּן עַתִּיקָא דְעַתִּיק וְעַתִּיק מִן קֳדָם חֲדַתָּא תְּפַנּוּן: יא וְאֶתֵּן

— רש"י —

והפריתי אתכם. בפריה ורביה: **והרביתי אתכם.** בקומה זקופה (שם): **והקימתי את בריתי אתכם.** ברית חדשה, לא כברית הראשונה שהפרתם אותה אלא ברית חדשה שלא תופר, שנאמר וכרתי את בית ישראל ואת בית יהודה ברית חדשה (ירמיה ל"א:ל"ב; ת"ל שם ו'): (י) **ואכלתם ישן נושן.** הפירות יהיו משתמרין וטובים להתיישן, שיהא יין הנושן של שלש שנים יפה לאכול משל אשתקד (ת"כ פרק ג:א): **וישן מפני חדש תוציאו.** שיהיו הגרנות מלאות חדש והאוצרות מלאות ישן,

— RASHI ELUCIDATED —

☐ וְהִפְרֵיתִי אֶתְכֶם — I WILL MAKE YOU FRUITFUL, בִּפְרִיָה — with fruitfulness וּרְבִיָה — and proliferation, i.e., with increase of population.[1]

☐ וְהִרְבֵּיתִי אֶתְכֶם — AND INCREASE YOU, בְּקוֹמָה זְקוּפָה — with erect bearing.[1]

☐ וַהֲקִימֹתִי אֶת בְּרִיתִי אִתְּכֶם — AND I WILL ESTABLISH MY COVENANT WITH YOU. בְּרִית חֲדָשָׁה — A new covenant,[2] לֹא כַּבְּרִית הָרִאשׁוֹנָה — unlike the first covenant שֶׁהֲפַרְתֶּם אוֹתָהּ — which you annulled at the sin of the Golden Calf, אֶלָּא בְּרִית חֲדָשָׁה — but a new covenant, שֶׁלֹּא תוּפַר — which will not be annulled, שֶׁנֶּאֱמַר — as it says, ״וְכָרַתִּי אֶת בֵּית יִשְׂרָאֵל — "And I will enter into[3] with the House of Israel וְאֶת בֵּית יְהוּדָה — and the House of Judah[4] בְּרִית חֲדָשָׁה — a new covenant; לֹא כַבְּרִית — unlike the covenant, etc."[4,5] וְגוֹמֵר —

10. וַאֲכַלְתֶּם יָשָׁן נוֹשָׁן — AND YOU WILL EAT THAT WHICH IS VERY OLD. הַפֵּרוֹת יִהְיוּ מִשְׁתַּמְּרִין — The fruits will be preserved וְטוֹבִים לְהִתְיַישֵׁן — and good for being aged,[6] שֶׁיְּהֵא יָשָׁן הַנּוֹשָׁן — for the old which has been aged, שֶׁל שָׁלֹשׁ שָׁנִים — of three years, i.e., three years old,[7] יָפֶה לֶאֱכוֹל — will be better to eat מִשֶּׁל אֶשְׁתָּקַד — than that of last year.[8]

☐ וְיָשָׁן מִפְּנֵי חָדָשׁ תּוֹצִיאוּ — AND [YOU WILL] REMOVE THE OLD TO MAKE WAY FOR THE NEW. שֶׁיִּהְיוּ הַגְּרָנוֹת — For the threshing floors will be full of the new crop, וְהָאוֹצָרוֹת מְלֵאוֹת יָשָׁן — and the

why it says, "I will turn to you" (*Toras Kohanim*).

God has no limitations and need not "turn" from one thing to another. The Torah nonetheless uses this language to indicate how great is the reward in store for Israel, as if God would have to free Himself from other concerns in order to deal with Israel (*Be'er Yitzchak*).

1. *Toras Kohanim, perek* 2:5. "I will make you fruitful and increase you" could have been taken as referring only to increase in population. "I will make you fruitful" would have implied that they would not be childless, and "and increase you" would have implied that not only would they not have been childless, but they would have many children. But if this were the intent of the verse, it would have said וְהִפְרֵיתִי וְהִרְבֵּיתִי אֶתְכֶם, without repeating אֶתְכֶם. The apparently superfluous אֶתְכֶם teaches us that וְהִפְרֵיתִי and וְהִרְבֵּיתִי are two distinct blessings. וְהִפְרֵיתִי refers to population. Since it appears in the context of a blessing, Rashi presumes it means not only that they will not be childless, but that they will proliferate. וְהִרְבֵּיתִי refers to dignified bearing (*Nachalas Yaakov*).

2. Our passage lists blessings that will befall Israel for observing the Torah. Maintaining the old covenant is not a blessing; it is merely the absence of a curse. Thus, our verse refers to the establishment of a new covenant (*Be'er Yitzchak*).

3. וְכָרַתִּי means literally, "and I will cut." "To cut" is used because it was customary to cut an animal, and pass between the pieces when entering a treaty or covenant. See Rashi to *Genesis* 15:10, s.v., וַיְבַתֵּר אֹתָם; *Deuteronomy* 29:11, s.v., לְעָבְרְךָ בִּבְרִית; and *Jeremiah* 34:18.

4. *Jeremiah* 31:30-31. The passage then continues: "I entered into with their ancestors on the day I held their hand to take them out of the land of Egypt, for they have annulled My covenant; yet I have been a faithful Master to them — the word of Hashem. For this covenant that I shall enter into with the House of Israel . . . and I shall be a God to them and they shall be a nation to Me."

5. *Toras Kohanim, perek* 2:6.

6. The verse does not mean that you will eat old, stale food; that would not be a blessing (*Minchas Yehudah; Sifsei Chachamim*).

7. The crop of the present year is called חָדָשׁ, "new." By itself, יָשָׁן, "old," would imply last year's crop. יָשָׁן נוֹשָׁן, literally, "old which has become old," implies the crop of the year before last (*Nachalas Yaakov; Be'er Mayim Chaim*). The "three years" are then: this year, last year, and the year before last.

8. *Toras Kohanim, perek* 3:1.

Tabernacle among you; and My Soul will not purge itself of you. ¹² *I will walk among you, I will be a God to you and you will be a people unto Me.* ¹³ *I am* HASHEM, *your God, Who took you out of the land of Egypt from being their*

מִשְׁכָּנִ֖י בְּתוֹכְכֶ֑ם וְלֹֽא־תִגְעַ֥ל נַפְשִׁ֖י
אֶתְכֶֽם: וְהִתְהַלַּכְתִּי֙ בְּתוֹכְכֶ֔ם וְהָיִ֥יתִי
לָכֶ֖ם לֵֽאלֹהִ֑ים וְאַתֶּ֖ם תִּֽהְיוּ־לִ֥י לְעָֽם:
אֲנִ֞י יְהֹוָ֣ה אֱלֹֽהֵיכֶ֗ם אֲשֶׁ֨ר הוֹצֵ֤אתִי
אֶתְכֶם֙ מֵאֶ֣רֶץ מִצְרַ֔יִם מִֽהְיֹ֥ת לָהֶ֖ם

יב

יג

— אונקלוס —

מַקְדְּשִׁי בֵּינֵיכוֹן וְלָא יְרָחֵק מֵימְרִי יָתְכוֹן: יב וַאֲשָׁרֵי שְׁכִינְתִּי בֵּינֵיכוֹן וְאֶהֱוֵי לְכוֹן לֶאֱלָהּ וְאַתּוּן
תְּהוֹן קֳדָמַי לְעָם: יג אֲנָא יְיָ אֱלָהֲכוֹן דִּי אַפֵּקִית יָתְכוֹן מֵאַרְעָא דְמִצְרַיִם מִלְּמֶהֱוֵי לְהוֹן

— רש"י —

יקוב העור: (יב) והתהלכתי בתוככם. אטייל עמכם בגן עדן
כאחד מכם ולא תהיו מזדעזעים ממני. יכול לא תיראו ממני,
ת"ל אני ה' אלהיכם: (יג) אני ה' אלהיכם וגו'.
כדאי אני שתאמינו בי שאני יכול לעשות כל אלה שהרי
הוצאתי אתכם מארץ מצרים ועשיתי לכם נסים גדולים (שם ד):

וּלְרֵיקִים אַתֶּם לְפַנּוֹת הָאוֹצָרוֹת לְמָקוֹם אַחֵר לָתֵת הֶחָדָשׁ לְתוֹכוֹ (שם).
(יא) וְנָתַתִּי מִשְׁכָּנִי. זֶה בֵּית הַמִּקְדָּשׁ (שם ב): וְלֹא תִגְעַל נַפְשִׁי.
אֵין רוּחִי קָצָה בָּכֶם. כָּל גְּעִילָה ל' פְּלִיטַת דָּבָר הַבָּלוּעַ בְּדָבָר, כְּמוֹ כִּי
שָׁם נִגְעַל מָגֵן גִּבּוֹרִים (שמואל ב' א:כא) לֹא קִבֵּל הַמְּשִׁיחָה, שֶׁמּוֹשְׁחִין
מָגֵן שֶׁל עוֹר בְּחֵלֶב מְבֻשָּׁל כְּדֵי לְהַחֲלִיק מֵעָלָיו מַכַּת חֵץ אוֹ חֲנִית שֶׁלֹּא

— RASHI ELUCIDATED —

וּצְרִיכִים אַתֶּם לְפַנּוֹת הָאוֹצָרוֹת — and you will need to empty the storehouses will be full of the old, לְמָקוֹם אַחֵר — to some other place [1] לָתֵת הֶחָדָשׁ לְתוֹכְךָ — so as to put the new crop into them.[1] storehouses and take their contents

11. וְנָתַתִּי מִשְׁכָּנִי — I WILL PLACE MY TABERNACLE. [2] זֶה בֵּית הַמִּקְדָּשׁ — This is the *Beis HaMikdash*.[2]

☐ וְלֹא תִגְעַל נַפְשִׁי — AND MY SOUL WILL NOT PURGE ITSELF OF YOU. אֵין רוּחִי קָצָה בָּכֶם — My Spirit is not disgusted by you. כָּל גְּעִילָה — Any form of the word גְּעִילָה, i.e., the root געל, found in Scripture לְשׁוֹן פְּלִיטַת דָּבָר הַבָּלוּעַ בְּדָבָר — means expelling something that had been absorbed by something else,[3] כְּמוֹ — like נִגְעַל in, "כִּי שָׁם נִגְעַל מָגֵן גִּבּוֹרִים" — "for there the shield of the mighty was purged,"[4] which means, לֹא קִבֵּל הַמְּשִׁיחָה — it did not take, i.e., absorb, the smearing, בְּחֵלֶב מְבֻשָּׁל — with cooked fat שֶׁמּוֹשְׁחִין מָגֵן שֶׁל עוֹר — for they smear a shield of leather כְּדֵי לְהַחֲלִיק מֵעָלָיו — in order to make slide off it מַכַּת חֵץ — the blow of an arrow אוֹ חֲנִית — or a spear שֶׁלֹּא יָקוֹב הָעוֹר — so that it should not puncture the leather.

12. וְהִתְהַלַּכְתִּי בְּתוֹכְכֶם — I WILL WALK AMONG YOU. אֲטַיֵּל עִמָּכֶם — I will stroll with you בְּגַן עֵדֶן — in the Garden of Eden כְּאֶחָד מִכֶּם — like one of you,[5] וְלֹא תִהְיוּ מִזְדַּעְזְעִים מִמֶּנִּי — and you will not tremble because of Me. יָכוֹל — One might be able to think לֹא תִירְאוּ מִמֶּנִּי — that you will not fear Me. תַּלְמוּד לוֹמַר — To teach us otherwise, the verse says, "וְהָיִיתִי לָכֶם לֵאלֹהִים" — "I will be a God to you."[6]

13. אֲנִי ה' אֱלֹהֵיכֶם וְגוֹמֵר — I AM HASHEM, YOUR GOD, ETC. כְּדַאי אֲנִי — I deserve שֶׁתַּאֲמִינוּ בִּי — that you should believe in Me, שֶׁאֲנִי יָכוֹל לַעֲשׂוֹת כָּל אֵלֶּה — that I can do all of these things, שֶׁהֲרֵי — for, see now, הוֹצֵאתִי אֶתְכֶם מֵאֶרֶץ מִצְרַיִם — I have taken you out of the land of Egypt וְעָשִׂיתִי לָכֶם — and I have performed for you [7] נִסִּים גְּדוֹלִים — great miracles.[7]

1. *Toras Kohanim, perek* 3:1.
2. *Toras Kohanim, perek* 3:2. "Tabernacle" here does not refer to the *Mishkan*. For the *Mishkan* already accompanied the Israelites during their sojourn in the desert, while our verse refers to a future blessing (*Nachalas Yaakov* based on Rashi to *Eruvin* 2a, s.v., ונתתי משכני בתוככם).
3. In our verse, if the Soul of God is disgusted by Israel, they are expelled and banished from His thoughts and presence (*Be'er Yitzchak*).
4. *II Samuel* 1:21. That verse continues, ". . . as though it were not smeared with oil" (see Rashi there).
5. Had the verse said, וְהָלַכְתִּי בְּתוֹכְכֶם, "I will go (or, "walk") among you," it would have implied manifestation of the Divine Presence in this world. וְהִתְהַלַּכְתִּי literally, "I will make Myself walk," implies an expression of the Divine Presence in a manner in which it is seen as "walking." This can only happen in the spiritual dimension of the Garden of Eden. "Strolling" or "walking" with God are used as metaphors for intense apprehension of the Presence of God (*Korban Aharon*; *Tzeidah LaDerech*).
6. *Toras Kohanim, perek* 3:3-4.
7. *Toras Kohanim, perek* 3:4.

עֲבָדִ֑ים וָאֶשְׁבֹּר֙ מֹטֹ֣ת עֻלְּכֶ֔ם וָאוֹלֵ֥ךְ
אֶתְכֶ֖ם קֽוֹמְמִיּֽוּת׃
יד וְאִם־לֹ֥א תִשְׁמְע֖וּ לִ֑י וְלֹ֣א תַעֲשׂ֔וּ

slaves; I broke the pegs of your yoke and I led you erect.
14 But if you will not listen to Me and will not perform all of these

---
אונקלוס

עַבְדִּין וְתַבָּרִית נִיר עַמְמַיָּא מִנְּכוֹן וְדַבָּרִית יָתְכוֹן לְחֵרוּתָא (נ״א בְּחֵרוּתָא): יד וְאִם לָא תְקַבְּלוּן לְמֵימְרִי וְלָא תַעְבְּדוּן

רש״י

מטת. כְּמִין יָתֵד בִּשְׁנֵי רָאשֵׁי הָעוֹל הַמְעַכְּבִים הַמּוֹסֵרָה שֶׁלֹּא תֵּצֵא מֵרֹאשׁ הַשּׁוֹר וִיתִיר הַקֶּשֶׁר, כְּמוֹ "עֲשֵׂה לְךָ מוֹסֵרוֹת וּמֹטוֹת" (ירמיה כז:ב), קביל״א בלע״ז: **קוממיות.** בְּקוֹמָה זְקוּפָה. **(יד) ואם לא תשמעו לי.** לִהְיוֹת עֲמֵלִים בַּתּוֹרָה [וְלָדַעַת] מִדְרַשׁ חֲכָמִים. יָכוֹל לְקִיּוּם הַמִּצְוֹת, כְּשֶׁהוּא אוֹמֵר וְלֹא תַעֲשׂוּ וְגוֹ׳ הֲרֵי קִיּוּם מִצְוֹת אָמוּר, הָא מָה אֲנִי מְקַיֵּם וְאִם לֹא

תִּשְׁמְעוּ לִי, לִהְיוֹת עֲמֵלִים בַּתּוֹרָה. וּמַה תַּלְמוּד לוֹמַר לִי, אֵין לִי אֶלָּא, זֶה הַמַּכִּיר אֶת רִבּוֹנוֹ וּמִתְכַּוֵּן לִמְרֹד בּוֹ, וְכֵן בְּנִמְרוֹד "גִּבּוֹר צַיִד לִפְנֵי ה׳", שֶׁמַּכִּירוֹ וּמִתְכַּוֵּן לִמְרֹד בּוֹ, וְכֵן בְּאַנְשֵׁי סְדוֹם "רָעִים וְחַטָּאִים לַה׳ מְאֹד" (ת״כ פרשתא ב:ג), מַכִּירִים אֶת רִבּוֹנָם וּמִתְכַּוְּנִים לִמְרֹד בּוֹ (ת״כ פרשתא ב:ב): **ולא תעשו.** מִשֶּׁלֹּא תִּלְמְדוּ לֹא תַּעֲשׂוּ,

---
RASHI ELUCIDATED

□ מֹטֹת — PEGS. — כְּמִין יָתֵד — A type of peg — בִּשְׁנֵי רָאשֵׁי הָעוֹל — at the two ends of the yoke הַמְעַכְּבִים — הַמּוֹסֵרָה — which stop the reins — שֶׁלֹּא תֵּצֵא מֵרֹאשׁ הַשּׁוֹר — so that it not come off the head of the ox, וִיתִיר הַקֶּשֶׁר — and undo the tie.[1] — כְּמוֹ — Like וּמֹטוֹת in the phrase, "עֲשֵׂה לְךָ מוֹסֵרוֹת וּמֹטוֹת"[2] — "make yourself reins and pegs."[2] — קביל״א בְּלַעַז — Cheville in Old French.[3]

□ קוממיות — ERECT. — בְּקוֹמָה זְקוּפָה — With erect bearing.

14. וְאִם לֹא תִשְׁמְעוּ לִי — BUT IF YOU WILL NOT LISTEN TO ME, — לִהְיוֹת עֲמֵלִים בַּתּוֹרָה — to be laboring in Torah, — לָדַעַת — to know[4] the exposition — מִדְרַשׁ חֲכָמִים — of the Written Torah by the Sages. — יָכוֹל — One might be able to think that the verse refers — לְקִיּוּם הַמִּצְוֹת — to fulfillment of the commandments. — כְּשֶׁהוּא אוֹמֵר — When it says, "וְלֹא תַעֲשׂוּ וְגוֹמֵר" — "and will not perform, etc.," — הֲרֵי קִיּוּם מִצְוֹת אָמוּר — see now, that fulfillment of the commandments is stated in that phrase. הָא — מָה אֲנִי מְקַיֵּם — What, then, do I maintain "וְאִם לֹא תִשְׁמְעוּ לִי" — "but if you will not listen to Me" refers to?[5] — לִהְיוֹת עֲמֵלִים בַּתּוֹרָה — To be laboring in Torah.[5] — וּמַה תַּלְמוּד לוֹמַר "לִי" — And why does the verse say "to Me"? — אֵין לִי אֶלָּא — I have, i.e., the verse refers to, none but — זֶה הַמַּכִּיר אֶת רִבּוֹנוֹ — this one who is aware of his Master, — וּמִתְכַּוֵּן לִמְרֹד בּוֹ — yet intends to rebel against Him. — וְכֵן בְּנִמְרֹד — Similarly, regarding Nimrod it says, "גִּבּוֹר צַיִד לִפְנֵי ה׳"[6] — "a mighty hunter before Hashem."[6] — שֶׁמַּכִּירוֹ — "Before Hashem" implies that he is aware of Him — וּמִתְכַּוֵּן לִמְרֹד בּוֹ — yet intends to rebel against Him. — וְכֵן בְּאַנְשֵׁי סְדוֹם — Similarly, regarding the people of Sodom it says, "רָעִים וְחַטָּאִים לַה׳ מְאֹד"[7] — "evil and sinful unto Hashem, very greatly."[7] — מַכִּירִים אֶת רִבּוֹנָם — "Unto Hashem" implies that they are aware of their Master — וּמִתְכַּוְּנִים לִמְרֹד בּוֹ[8] — and intend to rebel against Him.[8]

□ וְלֹא תַעֲשׂוּ — AND WILL NOT PERFORM. — מִשֶּׁלֹּא תִּלְמְדוּ — Once you will not study, — לֹא תַעֲשׂוּ — you

---

YOKE — מֹט — PEG

1. The yoke described by Rashi consists of a wooden bar with a hole at each end that rests on the back of the animal's neck. A rope goes through the hole at one end, under the animal's neck, and then through the hole at the other end. The wooden bar and rope thus encircle the neck of the animal. To prevent the rope from slipping, pegs are jammed into the holes. These pegs are the מֹטֹת of our verse.

2. Jeremiah 27:2.

3. This Old French word and its Modern French derivative *cheville* mean a "peg or a plug used to fill a gap." The Modern English word "cheville" describes a word

or phrase whose only purpose is to plug a metrical gap in a line of poetry or to fill out an unbalanced sentence in prose. Thus, מֹטֹת are pegs inserted into the holes of the yoke to fill the part of the hole not filled by the reins, thereby fixing the reins in place.

4. Some editions read וְלָדַעַת, "*and* to know," in which case "to be laboring in Torah" and "to know the exposition by the Sages" are independent phrases. According to our text, however, the conjunctive ו, "and," does not appear and the passage means "to be laboring in Torah [in order] to hear the exposition by the Sages" (see *Yosef Hallel*).

5. *Toras Kohanim, parshasa* 1:2; cf. *parshasa* 2:1.

6. *Genesis* 10:9. See Rashi there, s.v., לִפְנֵי ה׳.

7. *Genesis* 13:13. See Rashi there, s.v., לַה׳ מְאֹד.

8. *Toras Kohanim, parshasa* 2:2.

טו אֶת כָּל־הַמִּצְוֺת הָאֵלֶּה: וְאִם־בְּחֻקֹּתַי תִּמְאָסוּ וְאִם אֶת־מִשְׁפָּטַי תִּגְעַל נַפְשְׁכֶם לְבִלְתִּי עֲשׂוֹת אֶת־כָּל־מִצְוֺתַי לְהַפְרְכֶם אֶת־בְּרִיתִי: טז אַף־אֲנִי אֶעֱשֶׂה־זֹּאת לָכֶם וְהִפְקַדְתִּי עֲלֵיכֶם בֶּהָלָה אֶת־הַשַּׁחֶפֶת וְאֶת

commandments; [15] *and if you will consider My statutes revolting, and if your being rejects My ordinances, so as not to perform all My commandments, to annul My covenant —* [16] *then I, too, will do this to you; I will assign over you panic, and the wasting away, and will not perform.*

— אונקלוס —

יָת כָּל פִּקּוּדַיָּא הָאִלֵּין: טז וְאִם בִּקְיָמַי תְּקוּצוּן וְאִם יָת דִּינַי תְּרַחֵק נַפְשְׁכוֹן בְּדִיל דְּלָא לְמֶעְבַּד יָת כָּל פִּקּוּדַי לְאַשְׁנָיוּתְכוֹן יָת קְיָמִי: טז אַף אֲנָא אֶעְבֵּד דָּא לְכוֹן וְאַסְעַרִית עֲלֵיכוֹן בַּהֲלָתָא יָת שַׁחֶפְתָּא וְיָת

— רש"י —

הֲרֵי שְׁתֵּי עֲבֵירוֹת (שם ג): (טו) וְאִם בְּחֻקֹּתַי תִּמְאָסוּ. מוֹאֵס בַּאֲחֵרִים הָעוֹשִׂים (שם): מִשְׁפָּטַי תִּגְעַל נַפְשְׁכֶם. שׂוֹנֵא הַחֲכָמִים (שם): לְבִלְתִּי עֲשׂוֹת. מוֹנֵעַ אֶת אֲחֵרִים מֵעֲשׂוֹת (שם): אֶת כָּל מִצְוֺתָי. כּוֹפֵר שֶׁלֹּא נִצְטַוּוּ, לְכָךְ נֶאֱמַר אֶת כָּל מִצְוֺתַי וְלֹא נֶאֱמַר אֶת כָּל הַמִּצְוֺת (שם): לְהַפְרְכֶם אֶת בְּרִיתִי. כּוֹפֵר בָּעִיקָר. הֲרֵי שֶׁבַע עֲבֵירוֹת, הָרִאשׁוֹנָה גּוֹרֶרֶת הַשְּׁנִיָּה וְכֵן עַד הַשְּׁבִיעִית, וְאֵלּוּ הֵן. לֹא לָמַד. וְלֹא עָשָׂה. מוֹאֵס בַּאֲחֵרִים הָעוֹשִׂים. שׂוֹנֵא אֶת הַחֲכָמִים. מוֹנֵעַ אֶת הָאֲחֵרִים. כּוֹפֵר בְּמִצְוֺת. כּוֹפֵר בָּעִיקָר: (טז) וְהִפְקַדְתִּי עֲלֵיכֶם. וְצִוִּיתִי עֲלֵיכֶם: שַׁחֶפֶת. חֹלִי שֶׁמְּשַׁחֵף אֶת הַבָּשָׂר (שם פרק ד:ג) אנפולי"ש בלע"ז דּוֹמֶה לִנְפוּחַ

RASHI ELUCIDATED

will not perform.[1] — הֲרֵי שְׁתֵּי עֲבֵרוֹת — **See now,** that there are **two sins.**[1]

15. וְאִם בְּחֻקֹּתַי תִּמְאָסוּ — **AND IF YOU WILL CONSIDER MY STATUTES REVOLTING,** — מוֹאֵס בַּאֲחֵרִים הָעוֹשִׂים — **He abhors others who perform** the statutes.[2]

□ מִשְׁפָּטַי תִּגְעַל נַפְשְׁכֶם — **YOUR BEING REJECTS MY ORDINANCES,** i.e.,[3] שׂוֹנֵא הַחֲכָמִים — **he hates the** Torah **scholars.**[3]

□ לְבִלְתִּי עֲשׂוֹת — **NOT TO PERFORM.** מוֹנֵעַ אֶת אֲחֵרִים — **He prevents others** מֵעֲשׂוֹת — **from performing.**[3]

□ אֶת כָּל מִצְוֺתָי — **ALL MY COMMANDMENTS.** כּוֹפֵר — **He renounces** the commandments — שֶׁלֹּא צִוִּיתִים — by saying **that I did not command them.** לְכָךְ נֶאֱמַר אֶת כָּל מִצְוֺתַי — **This is why it says,** "**all** *My* **commandments,**" וְלֹא נֶאֱמַר — **and it does not say,**[3] אֶת כָּל הַמִּצְוֺת — "**all** *the* **commandments.**"[3]

□ לְהַפְרְכֶם אֶת בְּרִיתִי — **TO ANNUL MY COVENANT.** כּוֹפֵר בָּעִיקָר — **He renounces that which is essential,** i.e., he denies belief in God. הֲרֵי שֶׁבַע עֲבֵרוֹת — **See now,** that there are **seven sins.** הָרִאשׁוֹנָה גּוֹרֶרֶת הַשְּׁנִיָּה — **The first brings on the second,** וְכֵן עַד הַשְּׁבִיעִית — **and so forth, until the seventh.** וְאֵלּוּ הֵן — **They are the following:** לֹא לָמַד — **He did not study,** וְלֹא עָשָׂה — **and he did not perform;** מוֹאֵס בַּאֲחֵרִים הָעוֹשִׂים — **he abhors others who perform;** שׂוֹנֵא אֶת הַחֲכָמִים — **he hates the** Torah **scholars;** מוֹנֵעַ אֶת הָאֲחֵרִים — **he prevents others** from performing the commandments; כּוֹפֵר בְּמִצְוֺת — **he renounces the commandments;**[3] כּוֹפֵר בָּעִיקָר — **he renounces that which is essential.**[3]

16. וְהִפְקַדְתִּי עֲלֵיכֶם — **I WILL ASSIGN OVER YOU.** This means, וְצִוִּיתִי עֲלֵיכֶם — **I will command upon you.**

□ שַׁחֶפֶת — **WASTING AWAY.** חֹלִי — An illness[4] שֶׁמְּשַׁחֵף אֶת הַבָּשָׂר — that wears away the flesh.[4]

□ אנפולי"ש בלע"ז — *Anpoles* in Old French.[5] דּוֹמֶה לִנְפוּחַ — **He is like one who has been swollen**

---

1. *Toras Kohanim, parshasa* 2:3. The clause that precedes "and will not perform" begins with וְאִם, "but if," as do the clauses that follow it. The fact that וְלֹא תַעֲשׂוּ is not set off from וְאִם לֹא תִשְׁמְעוּ לִי by וְאִם could be taken to indicate that it is part of the same sin as וְאִם לֹא תִשְׁמְעוּ לִי. But this is not so, for, according to Rashi, verse 18 implies that there are seven sins mentioned in this passage (see Rashi there). If וְלֹא תַעֲשׂוּ were not an independent sin, there would only be six. Hence, Rashi concludes that "these are two sins." The second וְאִם does not appear because the Torah wants to show the relationship between the two sins — if you do not study, it is inevitable

that you will not perform (see *Devek Tov*).

2. *Toras Kohanim, parshasa* 2:3. The preceding verse has already mentioned failure to perform the commandments. Here the verse refers to the next stage, disgust at others who perform the commandments (*Mizrachi; Sifsei Chachamim*).

3. *Toras Kohanim, parshasa* 2:3.

4. *Toras Kohanim, perek* 4:3.

5. This and its Modern French equivalent *ampoule* mean "puffed out" or "swollen." In both Modern English (usually *ampule*) and Modern French this word

355 / VAYIKRA/LEVITICUS — PARASHAS BECHUKOSAI — 26/17 — בו/יז

הַקַּדַּ֣חַת מְכַלּ֥וֹת עֵינַ֖יִם וּמְדִיבֹ֣ת
נָ֑פֶשׁ וּזְרַעְתֶּ֤ם לָרִיק֙ זַרְעֲכֶ֔ם
יו וַאֲכָלֻ֖הוּ אֹיְבֵיכֶֽם: וְנָתַתִּ֤י פָנַי֙ בָּכֶ֔ם
וְנִגַּפְתֶּ֖ם לִפְנֵ֣י אֹיְבֵיכֶ֑ם וְרָד֤וּ בָכֶם֙
שֽׂנְאֵיכֶ֔ם וְנַסְתֶּ֖ם וְאֵין־רֹדֵ֥ף אֶתְכֶֽם:

the fever, causing eyes to pine and souls to feel anguish; you will sow your seed in vain, and your enemies will eat it. [17] *And I will direct My face against you, you will be struck down before your enemies; those who hate you will subjugate you — you will flee but there will be no one pursuing you.*

— אונקלוס —

קַדַּחְתָּא מְחַשְׁכָן עַיְנִין וּמַפְּחָן נְפָשׁ וְתִזְרְעוּן לְרֵקָנוּ זַרְעֲכוֹן וְיֵיכְלֻנֵּהּ בַּעֲלֵי דְבָבֵיכוֹן: יו וְאֶתֵּן רוּגְזִי בְכוֹן וְתִתַּבְרוּן קֳדָם בַּעֲלֵי דְבָבֵיכוֹן וְיִרְדּוּן בְּכוֹן סָנְאֵיכוֹן וְתֵעִרְקוּן וְלֵית דְּרָדִיף יָתְכוֹן:

— רש״י —

קדחת. חוֹלִי שֶׁמַּקְדִּיחַ אֶת הַגּוּף וּמְחַמְּמוֹ וּמַבְעִירוֹ כְּמוֹ כִּי אֵשׁ קָדְחָה בְאַפִּי (דברים לב:כב). **מכלות עינים ומדיבת נפש.** הָעֵינַיִם צוֹפוֹת וְכָלוֹת לִרְאוֹת שֶׁיָּקֵל וְיִרְפָּא וְסוֹף שֶׁלֹּא יִרְפֵּא וְיִדְאֲבוּ הַנְּפָשׁוֹת שֶׁל מִשְׁפַּחְתּוֹ בְּמוֹתוֹ. כָּל תְּאָוָה שֶׁאֵינָהּ בָּאָה וְתוֹחֶלֶת מְמֻשָּׁכָה קְרוּיָה כִּלְיוֹן עֵינַיִם. **וזרעתם לריק.** תִּזְרְעוּ וְלֹא תִצְמַח שֶׁאִם כֵּן מַה יֹּאכְלוּ אוֹיְבֵיכֶם (שם), אֶלָּא מָה תַּלְמוּד לוֹמַר **ואכלהו אויביכם** (שם ז): **ונתתי פני.** פְּנַאי שֶׁלִּי, פּוֹנֶה אֲנִי מִכָּל עֲסָקַי לְהָרַע לָכֶם (שם ד): **ורדו בכם שנאיכם.** כְּמַשְׁמָעוֹ יִשְׁלְטוּ בָכֶם: **זו אף אני אעשה זאת.** אֵינִי מְדַבֵּר אֶלָּא בְאַף (אגדת תורת כוהנים מפרשה זו פרק ד:א)

ממוסכה קרויה כליון עיניים. תזרעו ולא תלמח ואם תלמח ואכלוהו אויביכם

— RASHI ELUCIDATED —

וּמַרְאִית פָּנָיו זְעוּפָה — **and the countenance of whose face** שֶׁהוּקְלָה נְפִיחָתוֹ — **whose swelling has eased, appears sullen** due to the sagging of his flesh.

□ קַדַּחַת — **FEVER.** ¹חוֹלִי שֶׁמַּקְדִּיחַ אֶת הַגּוּף — **An illness that inflames the body** וּמְחַמְּמוֹ — **and heats** וּמַבְעִירוֹ — **and makes it burn.** ²קַדַּחַת — קַדַּחַת **is similar to** קָדְחָה **in the phrase,** "for a fire burns in My nostrils."²

□ מְכַלּוֹת עֵינַיִם וּמְדִיבֹת נָפֶשׁ — **CAUSING EYES TO PINE AND SOULS TO FEEL ANGUISH.** הָעֵינַיִם צוֹפוֹת — **The eyes look forward** וְכָלוֹת — **and pine** לִרְאוֹת — **to see** שֶׁיָּקֵל — **that he will be relieved** וְיִרְפָּא — **and be cured.** וְסוֹף — **But the end** will be שֶׁלֹּא יֵרָפֵא — **that he will not be cured** וְיִדְאֲבוּ הַנְּפָשׁוֹת — **and the souls** שֶׁל מִשְׁפַּחְתּוֹ — **of his family will feel anguish** בְּמוֹתוֹ — **by his death.** כָּל תַּאֲוָה — **Any desire** שֶׁאֵינָהּ בָּאָה — **that does not come,** i.e., that is not fulfilled, וְתוֹחֶלֶת מְמֻשָּׁכָה — **and extended yearning** קְרוּיָה — **is called** "pining of the eyes." "כִּלְיוֹן עֵינַיִם"

□ וּזְרַעְתֶּם לָרִיק — **YOU WILL SOW [YOUR SEED] IN VAIN.** תִּזְרְעוּ — **You will sow** וְלֹא תִצְמַח — **but it will not sprout,** וְאִם תִּצְמַח — **and if it will sprout,** ³"וַאֲכָלֻהוּ אֹיְבֵיכֶם" — **"and your enemies will eat it."**³

□ **17.** וְנָתַתִּי פָנַי — **AND I WILL DIRECT MY FACE.** פְּנַאי שֶׁלִּי — **My attention.**⁴ פּוֹנֶה אֲנִי — **I turn away** מִכָּל עֲסָקַי — **from all My concerns** ⁵לְהָרַע לָכֶם — **to harm you.**⁵

□ וְרָדוּ בָכֶם שֹׂנְאֵיכֶם — **THOSE WHO HATE YOU WILL SUBJUGATE YOU.** This is to be understood כְּמַשְׁמָעוֹ — **as it sounds,** יִשְׁלְטוּ בָכֶם — **they will rule over you.**⁶

□ אַגָּדַת תּוֹרַת כֹּהֲנִים מִפָּרָשָׁה זוֹ — **The** *Toras Kohanim*'s **aggadic interpretation of this passage** beginning with verse 16 is as follows:⁷

□ אַף אֲנִי אֶעֱשֶׂה זֹּאת — **I, TOO, WILL DO THIS.** ⁸אֵינִי מְדַבֵּר אֶלָּא בְאַף — **I shall not speak except with rage,**⁸

also describes a bulb-like (i.e., puffed out) container or tube.

1. *Toras Kohanim, perek* 4:3.
2. *Deuteronomy* 32:22.
3. *Toras Kohanim, perek* 4:3. "You will sow your seed in vain, and your enemies will eat it" could have been understood as a single curse, that your crop will be eaten by your enemies. But if this were the verse's sole intent, it could have said, "You will sow in vain, and your enemies will eat it." זַרְעֲכֶם, "your seed," would have been superfluous. It is written to teach us that the futility of sowing begins from the seed itself; it will not sprout (*Be'er BaSadeh*). Our verse means, "You will

sow your seed in vain, *or your enemies will eat it*" (*Be'er Yitzchak*).

4. See Rashi to 17:10 and note 3 there.
5. *Toras Kohanim, perek* 4:4.
6. This is in contrast to the aggadic interpretation Rashi gives below, which interprets וְרָדוּ and בָכֶם differently (*Be'er BaSadeh;* see note 7 on page 357 below).
7. Up to this point, Rashi has given the straightforward meaning of the text. He goes on to give an exegetical interpretation alluded to by the text.
8. *Toras Kohanim, perek* 4:1. In the context of the verse, אַף means "too." The aggadic interpretation views it in its sense of "rage." This is because more generally, "I,

רש"י

וכן והלכתי אף אני עמכם בקרי (להגן פסוק כד) ׀וס"א אף אני אלך עמם בקרי (להגן פסוק מא)׀: **והפקדתי עליכם.** שיהיו המכות פוקדות אתכם מזו לזו, עד שהראשונה פקודה אצלכם אביא אחרת ואסמכנה לה (שם ב): **בהלה.** מכה המבהלת את הבריות, ואיזו זו מכת מותן (שם): **את השחפת.** יש לך אדם שהוא חולה ומוטל במטה אבל בשרו שמור עליו, ת"ל שחפת, שהוא נשחף. או עתים שהוא נשחף, אבל נוח ואינו מקדיח, ת"ל ואת הקדחת, מלמד שהוא מקדיח. או עתים שהוא מקדיח וסבור הוא בעצמו שיחיה, ת"ל מכלות עינים, או הוא אינו סבור בעצמו אבל אחרים סבורים שיחיה, ת"ל ומדיבות נפש. **וזרעתם לריק זרעכם.** זורעה ואינה מצמחת. ומעתה מה אויביכם באים ואוכלים ומה ת"ל ואכלוהו אויביכם, הא כיצד, זורעה שנה ראשונה ואינה מצמחת, שנה שניה מצמחת, ואויבים באים ומולאים תבואה לימי המצור, ושבפנים מתים ברעב, שלא לקטו תבואה אשתקד. ד"א וזרעתם לריק זרעכם כנגד

RASHI ELUCIDATED

וְכֵן — **and similarly,** אַף **is expounded as** "**rage" in the verse,** ¹וְהָלַכְתִּי אַף אֲנִי עִמָּכֶם בְּקֶרִי — "**then I, too, will behave toward you with casualness."**[1]

□ וְהִפְקַדְתִּי עֲלֵיכֶם — **I WILL ASSIGN OVER YOU.** שֶׁיִּהְיוּ הַמַּכּוֹת פּוֹקְדוֹת אֶתְכֶם — **That the plagues will visit you** מִזּוֹ לָזוֹ — **from this one to that one;** עַד שֶׁהָרִאשׁוֹנָה פְּקוּדָה אֶצְלְכֶם — **while the first one is still visiting you,** אָבִיא אַחֶרֶת — **I will bring another** וְאַסְמִּכֶנָּה לָהּ — **and put it next to it.**[2]

□ בֶּהָלָה — **PANIC.** מַכָּה הַמַּבְהֶלֶת אֶת הַבְּרִיּוֹת — **A plague that panics the people.** וְאֵיזוֹ — **And which plague is this?** ³זוֹ מַכַּת מוֹתָן — **This is the plague** that is a herald **of their death.**[3]

□ אֶת הַשַּׁחֶפֶת — **THE WASTING AWAY.** יֵשׁ לְךָ אָדָם — **You have a person,** i.e., there can be a person, שֶׁהוּא חוֹלֶה — **who is sick** וּמוּטָל בְּמִטָּה — **and bedridden,** אֲבָל בְּשָׂרוֹ שָׁמוּר עָלָיו — **but his flesh is** still **preserved upon him.** To teach us that this is not so here, תַּלְמוּד לוֹמַר — **the verse says,** "שַׁחֶפֶת„ — "**and the wasting away,"** which implies, שֶׁהוּא נִשְׁחָף — **that he is worn away.** אוֹ עִתִּים שֶׁהוּא — Or there can be times when he is worn away, וְאֵינוֹ מַקְדִּיחַ — נִשְׁחָף **Or** there can be times when he is worn away, אֲבָל נוֹחַ — **but he is at ease** and he is not feverish. To teach us that this is not so here תַּלְמוּד לוֹמַר — **the verse says,** "וְאֶת, „הַקַּדַּחַת — "**and the fever,"** מְלַמֵּד — **this teaches** us שֶׁהוּא מַקְדִּיחַ — **that he is feverish.** אוֹ עִתִּים שֶׁהוּא מַקְדִּיחַ — **Or** there can be times when he is feverish וְסָבוּר הוּא בְּעַצְמוֹ — **but he is under the impression about himself** שֶׁיִּחְיֶה — **that he will survive.** To teach us that this is not so here תַּלְמוּד לוֹמַר — **the verse says,** "מְכַלּוֹת עֵינַיִם„ — "**causing eyes to pine."** אוֹ הוּא אֵינוֹ סָבוּר בְּעַצְמוֹ — **Or** he **might not be under the impression about himself** שֶׁיִּחְיֶה — **that he will survive,** אֲבָל אֲחֵרִים — **but others** סְבוּרִים — are nonetheless **under the impression** שֶׁיִּחְיֶה — **that he will survive.** To teach us that this is not so here, תַּלְמוּד לוֹמַר — **the verse says,** ⁴"וּמְדִיבוֹת נָפֶשׁ„ — "**and** [causing] **souls to feel anguish."**[4]

□ וּזְרַעְתֶּם לָרִיק זַרְעֲכֶם — **YOU WILL SOW YOUR SEED IN VAIN.** זוֹרְעָהּ — **He sows it** וְאֵינָהּ מְצַמַּחַת — **but it does not sprout.** וּמֵעַתָּה מַה אוֹיְבֵיכֶם בָּאִים וְאוֹכְלִים — **Now, what do enemies come and eat?** וּמַה — "וַאֲכָלֻהוּ אֹיְבֵיכֶם„ — "**and your enemies will eat it"?** הָא — תַּלְמוּד לוֹמַר — **Why does the verse say,** כֵּיצַד — **How can this be?** It must mean that זוֹרְעָהּ שָׁנָה רִאשׁוֹנָה — **he sows it the first year** וְאֵינָהּ — מְצַמַּחַת — **and it does not sprout.** שָׁנָה שְׁנִיָּה — **In the second year** מְצַמַּחַת — **it sprouts** וְאוֹיְבִים בָּאִים — **and enemies** come וּמוֹצְאִים תְּבוּאָה — **and find crops** to supply them לִימֵי הַמָּצוֹר — **for the days of the siege.** וְשֶׁבִּפְנִים — **Those within** the city walls מֵתִים בָּרָעָב — **die of starvation** שֶׁלֹּא — לָקְטוּ תְּבוּאָה — **for they did not gather crops** אֶשְׁתָּקַד — **the year before.** דָּבָר אַחֵר — **Alternatively:** "וּזְרַעְתֶּם לָרִיק זַרְעֲכֶם„ — "**And you will sow your seed in vain,"** כְּנֶגֶד

---

too" in Scripture is גַּם אֲנִי. That appears over twenty times. אַף אֲנִי, on the other hand, appears only four times outside of our chapter, in Genesis 40:16, Isaiah 48:12, and Job 32:10,17. The fact that the Torah uses אַף here, in contrast to גַּם which appears in verse 24, indicates that it may also be interpreted as "rage" (see Nachalas Yaakov).

1. Below v. 24. According to this aggadic interpretation, that verse reads, "in rage, I will behave toward you with casualness."

Some editions adduce verse 41 instead of verse 24. According to this aggadic interpretation, the verse reads אַף אֲנִי אֵלֵךְ עִמָּם בְּקֶרִי, "in rage, I will behave towards them with casualness."

2. Toras Kohanim, perek 4:2. According to this interpretation, פקד is used here in the sense of "to visit," rather than "to assign or command," as Rashi explained it in his comments to verse 16.

3. Toras Kohanim, perek 4:2. The vowelization and translation of מַכַּת מוֹתָן follow Korban Aharon (see also Targum Yonasan ben Uziel). Sefer Zikaron suggests מַכַּת מוֹתֶן, "a blow to the loins" (see Rashi to Deuteronomy 33:11, s.v., מְחַץ מָתְנַיִם קָמָיו).

4. Toras Kohanim, perek 4:3.

— רש"י —

הבנים והבנות הכתוב מדבר, שאתה עמל בהן ומגדלן והחטא בא
ומכלה אותם, שנאמר אשר טפחתי ורביתי אויבי כלם (איכה ב:כב):
ת"כ שם: **ונתתי פני בכם.** כמו שנאמר בטובה ופניתי אליכם כך
נאמר ברעה ונתתי פני. משלו משל, למלך שאמר לעבדיו פונה אני
מכל עסקי ועוסק אני עמכם לרעה (שם ד): **ונגפתם לפני
איביכם.** שיהא המות הורג אתכם מבפנים ובעלי דבביכון מקיפין

אתכם מבחוץ (שם ה): **ורדו בכם שנאיכם.** שאיני מעמיד שונאים
אלא מכם ובכם, שבשעה שאומות העולם עומדים על ישראל אינם
מבקשים אלא מה שבגלוי, שנאמר והיה אם זרע ישראל ועלה מדין
ועמלק ובני קדם וגו' ויחנו עליהם וישחיתו את יבול הארץ (שופטים
ו:ג-ד) אבל בשעה שאעמיד עליכם מכם ובכם הם מחפשים
אחר המטמוניות שלכם, וכן הוא אומר ואשר אכלו שאר עמי

——————— RASHI ELUCIDATED ———————

הַבָּנִים וְהַבָּנוֹת הַכָּתוּב מְדַבֵּר – the verse speaks these words with reference to the sons and the daughters. שָׁאַתָּה עָמֵל בָּהֶן – For you toil with them, וּמְגַדְּלָן – and raise them, וְהַחֵטְא בָּא – and the punishment for the sin comes וּמְכַלֶּה אוֹתָם – and annihilates them, שֶׁנֶּאֱמַר – as it says, "אֲשֶׁר טִפַּחְתִּי – "Those whom I cared for וְרִבִּיתִי – and nurtured, אֹיְבַי כִלָּם"[1,2] – my enemy has annihilated."[1,2]

□ וְנָתַתִּי פָנַי בָּכֶם – AND I WILL DIRECT MY FACE. כְּמוֹ שֶׁנֶּאֱמַר – Just as it says בְּטוֹבָה – about the good that God will do to Israel if they keep His commandments, "וּפָנִיתִי אֲלֵיכֶם",[3] – "I will turn to you,"[3] כָּךְ נֶאֱמַר בְּרָעָה – so it says about the evil, "וְנָתַתִּי פָנַי" – "and I will direct My face." מָשְׁלוּ מָשָׁל – They, i.e., the Sages, made a parable of this idea, in which God is compared to a king שֶׁאָמַר לַעֲבָדָיו – who told his slaves, "פּוֹנֶה אֲנִי – "I turn away מִכָּל עֲסָקַי – from all of my concerns, וְעוֹסֵק אֲנִי עִמָּכֶם – and concern myself with you לְרָעָה"[4] – for bad, i.e., to punish you."[4]

□ וְנִגַּפְתֶּם לִפְנֵי אֹיְבֵיכֶם – YOU WILL BE STRUCK DOWN BEFORE YOUR ENEMIES. שֶׁיְּהֵא הַמָּוֶת הוֹרֵג אֶתְכֶם – That the death, i.e., epidemic, will kill you מִבִּפְנִים – on the inside, i.e., inside the walls of your besieged city, וּבַעֲלֵי דְבָבֵיכוֹן מַקִּיפִין אֶתְכֶם – while your enemies surround you מִבַּחוּץ[5] – on the outside.[5]

□ וְרָדוּ בָכֶם שֹׂנְאֵיכֶם – THOSE WHO HATE YOU WILL SUBJUGATE YOU. שֶׁאֵינִי מַעֲמִיד שׂוֹנְאִים אֶלָּא מִכֶּם וּבָכֶם – For I do not give rise to those who hate you except from among your very selves, שֶׁבְּשָׁעָה שֶׁאֻמּוֹת הָעוֹלָם – for at the time that the nations of the world עוֹמְדִים עַל יִשְׂרָאֵל – stand against Israel, אֵינָם מְבַקְּשִׁים אֶלָּא מַה שֶּׁבַּגָּלוּי – they seek nothing but that which is in the open, שֶׁנֶּאֱמַר – as it says, "וְהָיָה אִם זָרַע יִשְׂרָאֵל – "It would be, that when Israel would sow, וְעָלָה מִדְיָן וַעֲמָלֵק וּבְנֵי קֶדֶם וְגוֹמֵר – and Midian, and Amalek, and the people of the East would ascend, etc., וַיַּחֲנוּ עֲלֵיהֶם – and encamp against them, וַיַּשְׁחִיתוּ אֶת יְבוּל הָאָרֶץ"[6] – and they would destroy the crop of the land."[6] אֲבָל בְּשָׁעָה שֶׁאַעֲמִיד עֲלֵיכֶם – But at the time that I give rise against you to those who hate you מִכֶּם וּבָכֶם – from among your very selves, הֵם מְחַפְּשִׂים אַחַר הַמַּטְמוֹנִיּוֹת שֶׁלָּכֶם – they search for your hidden treasures.[7] וְכֵן הוּא אוֹמֵר – Similarly, it says, "וַאֲשֶׁר אָכְלוּ שְׁאֵר עַמִּי – "And who ate the flesh of

---

1. *Lamentations* 2:22.
2. *Toras Kohanim, perek* 4:3.
3. Above v. 9.
4. *Toras Kohanim, perek* 4:4.
5. *Toras Kohanim, perek* 4:5. The verse does not refer here to being struck down by the enemy in battle, for it concludes, "You will flee but there will be no one pursuing you." Being struck down in the battle by the enemy follows flight. This part of the verse refers to a stage that precedes flight, namely, epidemic during siege (*Be'er BaSadeh*). Alternatively: Being struck down in battle would normally be expressed by וְנָפַלְתֶּם, "you will fall," rather than וְנִגַּפְתֶּם. See for example verse 8 above which uses וְנָפְלוּ. This verse uses וְנִגַּפְתֶּם because it is related to מַגֵּפָה, "epidemic" (*Gur Aryeh*).
6. *Judges* 6:3-4. Rashi to *Deuteronomy* 11:14 interprets that verse as referring not only to destruction of crops, but to the enemies gathering the crops of the Israelites. The preceding verse (6:2) states that the Israelites would employ tunnels and caves against the foreign menace, implying that their enemies would take only that which was out in the open.

7. According to this interpretation, וְרָדוּ is understood as "and they will take out," and בָכֶם is understood as "from among you"; the verse means, "those who hate you, from among you, will take out" (*Be'er BaSadeh*). According to both this interpretation and the simple meaning of the verse which Rashi refers to at the beginning of his comments to this verse (see note 6 on page 355 above), the root of וְרָדוּ is רדה. We find this root used in the sense of "to subjugate," as it is understood according to the simple meaning, in *Genesis* 1:28, וּרְדוּ בִּדְגַת הַיָּם, "and rule over the fish of the sea." We find it in the sense of "to take out," as it is understood in this interpretation, in *Judges* 14:9, כִּי מִגְוִיַּת הָאַרְיֵה רָדָה הַדְּבָשׁ, "for he took the honey out of the carcass of the lion."

וְאִם־עַד־אֵלֶּה לֹא תִשְׁמְעוּ לִי וְיָסַפְתִּי לְיַסְּרָה אֶתְכֶם שֶׁבַע עַל־חַטֹּאתֵיכֶם: וְשָׁבַרְתִּי אֶת־גְּאוֹן עֻזְּכֶם וְנָתַתִּי אֶת־שְׁמֵיכֶם כַּבַּרְזֶל וְאֶת־אַרְצְכֶם כַּנְּחֻשָׁה: וְתַם לָרִיק כֹּחֲכֶם

[18] And if during these you will not heed Me, I will increase tormenting you, seven for your sins. [19] I will break the pride of your might; I will make your heavens like iron and your land like copper. [20] Your strength will be spent in vain;

───────── אונקלוס ─────────

יח וְאִם עַד אִלֵּין לָא תְקַבְּלוּן לְמֵימְרִי וְאוֹסֵף לְמִרְדֵּי יָתְכוֹן שְׁבַע עַל חוֹבֵיכוֹן: יט וְאֶתְבַּר יָת יְקָר תָּקְפְּכוֹן וְאֶתֵּן יָת שְׁמַיָּא דִי עֲלָוֵיכוֹן תַּקִּיפִין כְּפַרְזְלָא מִלְּאַחָתָא מִטְרָא וְאַרְעָא דִתְחוֹתֵיכוֹן חֲסִינָא כִנְחָשָׁא מִלְּמֶעְבַּד פֵּרִין: כ וִיסוּפוּן לְרֵיקָנוּ חֵילֵיכוֹן

───────── רש"י ─────────

ושברתי את גאון עזכם. זה בית המקדש. וכן הוא אומר הנני מחלל את מקדשי גאון עזכם (יחזקאל כד:כא): ונתתי את שמיכם כברזל ואת ארצכם כנחשה. זו קשה משל משה, שהוא אומר והיו שמיך אשר על ראשך נחשת וגו' (דברים כח:כג), שיהיו השמים מזיעין כדרך שהנחשת מזיעה, והארץ אינה

ועורס מעליהם הפשיטו וגו' (מיכה ג:ג), ת"כ שם ה): ונסתם. מפני אימה (שם): ואין רודף אתכם. מבלי כח (שם): (יח) ואם עד אלה. ואם בעוד אלה (עליכם) לא תשמעו (לי), ויספתי עוד יסורין אחרים (שם פרק ה:א): שבע על חטאתיכם. שבע פורענויות על שבע עבירות האמורות למעלה (שם): (יט)

───────── RASHI ELUCIDATED ─────────

וְעֹרָם מֵעֲלֵיהֶם הִפְשִׁיטוּ וְגוֹמֵר' — and stripped their flesh from upon them, etc."[1,2] My people,

□ וְנַסְתֶּם — YOU WILL FLEE — מִפְּנֵי אֵימָה — as a result of terror,[2]

□ וְאֵין רֹדֵף אֶתְכֶם — BUT THERE WILL BE NO ONE PURSUING YOU, — מִבְּלִי כֹחַ — for lack of strength.[3]

18. וְאִם עַד אֵלֶּה — AND IF DURING THESE. {עֲלֵיכֶם — וְאִם בְּעוֹד אֵלֶּה — And if while these tribulations {are upon you}[4] וְיָסַפְתִּי — "I will increase" עוֹד יִסּוּרִין אֲחֵרִים — yet other torments.[5]

□ שֶׁבַע עַל חַטֹּאתֵיכֶם — SEVEN FOR YOUR SINS. — שֶׁבַע פּוּרְעָנִיּוֹת — Seven punishments — עַל שֶׁבַע עֲבֵרוֹת הָאֲמוּרוֹת לְמַעְלָה — for the seven sins that are stated above.[6]

19. וְשָׁבַרְתִּי אֶת גְּאוֹן עֻזְּכֶם — I WILL BREAK THE PRIDE OF YOUR MIGHT. — זֶה בֵּית הַמִּקְדָּשׁ — This is the Beis HaMikdash. וְכֵן הוּא אוֹמֵר — And similarly it says, "הִנְנִי מְחַלֵּל אֶת מִקְדָּשִׁי — "Behold, I defile My Sanctuary, גְּאוֹן עֻזְּכֶם"[7,8] — the pride of your might."[7,8]

□ וְנָתַתִּי אֶת שְׁמֵיכֶם כַּבַּרְזֶל וְאֶת אַרְצְכֶם כַּנְּחֻשָׁה — I WILL MAKE YOUR HEAVENS LIKE IRON AND YOUR LAND LIKE COPPER. — זוֹ קָשָׁה מִשֶּׁל מֹשֶׁה — This punishment is harsher than that mentioned in the curses enumerated by Moses, — שֶׁשָּׁם הוּא אוֹמֵר — for there it says, "וְהָיוּ שָׁמֶיךָ אֲשֶׁר עַל רֹאשְׁךָ נְחֹשֶׁת וְגוֹמֵר"[9] — "and the heavens over your head will be copper, etc."[9] mentioned by Moses, the heavens would sweat, i.e., bring forth some moisture, כַּדֶּרֶךְ שֶׁהַנְּחֹשֶׁת מַזִּיעָה — in the manner that copper sweats, i.e., has condensation of moisture on its surface; וְהָאָרֶץ אֵינָהּ — שֶׁיִּהְיוּ הַשָּׁמַיִם מַזִּיעִין — For in the curse

─────────────────────

1. *Micah* 3:3. That verse continues, "and cracked open their bones." According to Rashi, cracking open the bones to extract the marrow is a metaphor for taking hidden stores (see *Yosef Hallel*).

2. *Toras Kohanim, perek* 4:5.

3. *Toras Kohanim, perek* 4:5. The enemies will not bother pursuing you because they know that you no longer pose a threat to them for lack of strength (*Mizrachi; Sifsei Chachamim*).

4. Rashi interprets עַד as if it read עוֹד, "while." The word has this meaning in *Job* 1:18. Verses 14-17 there describe a series of messages received by Job from successive messengers. After verses 14 and 15 relate the first messenger's words, verses 16 and 17 each begin, עוֹד זֶה מְדַבֵּר וְזֶה בָּא, "while this one was speaking,

another one came." In verse 18, the parallel phrase reads עַד זֶה מְדַבֵּר וְזֶה בָּא (see *Metzudos David* there).

5. *Toras Kohanim, perek* 5:1. "I will increase tormenting you" does not mean "I will intensify the torments I have already inflicted," for the passage goes on to mention new torments (*Mizrachi; Sifsei Chachamim*).

6. *Toras Kohanim, perek* 5:1. See Rashi to verse 15 above. The verse does not mean that they will be punished seven times as much as they deserve, for God is just and does not punish unfairly (*Mizrachi; Sifsei Chachamim*).

7. *Ezekiel* 24:21.

8. *Toras Kohanim, perek* 5:2.

9. *Deuteronomy* 28:23. That verse continues, "and the land beneath you iron."

359 / VAYIKRA/LEVITICUS — PARASHAS BECHUKOSAI — 26/20 — כו/כ

וְלֹא־תִתֵּן אַרְצְכֶם אֶת־יְבוּלָהּ
וְעֵץ הָאָרֶץ לֹא יִתֵּן פִּרְיוֹ:

your land will not give its produce and the tree of the land will not give its fruit.

— אונקלוס —

וְלָא תִתֵּן אַרְעֲכוֹן יָת עֲלַלְתַּהּ וְאִילָן אַרְעָא לָא יִתֵּן אִבֵּהּ:

— רש"י —

מֵזִיעָה כְּדַרְכָּהּ שֶׁאֵין הַבַּרְזֶל מֵזִיעַ וְהִיא מְשַׁמֶּרֶת פֵּירוֹתֶיהָ, אֲבָל כָּאן הַשָּׁמַיִם לֹא יִהְיוּ מַזִּיעִין כְּדַרְכָּן שֶׁאֵין הַבַּרְזֶל מֵזִיעַ וִיהֵא חֹרֶב בָּעוֹלָם, וְהָאָרֶץ תְּהֵא מַזִּיעָה כְּדֶרֶךְ שֶׁהַנְּחֹשֶׁת מַזִּיעָה וְהִיא מְאַבֶּדֶת פֵּירוֹתֶיהָ (ת"כ שם ג): (כ) וְתַם לָרִיק כֹּחֲכֶם. הֲרֵי אָדָם שֶׁלֹּא עָמַל שֶׁלֹּא חָרַשׁ שֶׁלֹּא זָרַע שֶׁלֹּא נִכֵּשׁ שֶׁלֹּא כִסַּח שֶׁלֹּא עָדַר, וּבִשְׁעַת הַקָּצִיר בָּא שִׁדָּפוֹן וּמַלְקֶה אוֹתוֹ, אֵין בְּכָךְ כְּלוּם,

אֲבָל אָדָם שֶׁעָמַל וְחָרַשׁ וְזָרַע וְנִכֵּשׁ וְכִסַּח וְעָדַר, וּבָא שִׁדָּפוֹן וּמַלְקֶה אוֹתוֹ, הֲרֵי שִׁנָּיו שֶׁל זֶה קֵהוֹת (ת"כ שם ד): וְלֹא תִתֵּן אַרְצְכֶם אֶת יְבוּלָהּ. אַף מַה שֶׁאַתָּה מוֹבִיל לָהּ בִּשְׁעַת הַזֶּרַע: וְעֵץ הָאָרֶץ. אֲפִילוּ מִן הָאָרֶץ, לְפִי מַה שֶׁאָרֶץ תְּהֵא לָקוּי, שֶׁלֹּא יַחֲנִיטוּ פֵּירוֹתָיו בִּשְׁעַת הַחֲנָטָה (שם): לֹא יִתֵּן. מִשֶּׁמַּח לְמַעְלָה וּלְמַטָּה, אֵץ וָפֶרִי: לֹא יִתֵּן פִּרְיוֹ. כְּשֶׁהוּא מַפְרֶה מַשִּׁיר

— RASHI ELUCIDATED —

מַזִּיעָה – **but the land would not sweat,** i.e., become moist, כְּדֶרֶךְ שֶׁאֵין הַבַּרְזֶל מַזִּיעַ – **in the manner that iron does not sweat,** וְהִיא מְשַׁמֶּרֶת פֵּירוֹתֶיהָ – **and [the land] thus preserves its fruit.**[1] אֲבָל כָּאן – But here, כְּדֶרֶךְ שֶׁאֵין הַבַּרְזֶל מֵזִיעַ – in the manner that iron does not sweat, הַשָּׁמַיִם לֹא יִהְיוּ מַזִּיעִין – **the heavens will not sweat,** וִיהֵא חֹרֶב בָּעוֹלָם – **and there will be a drought in the world.** וְהָאָרֶץ תְּהֵא מַזִּיעָה – **But the land will sweat,** כְּדֶרֶךְ שֶׁהַנְּחֹשֶׁת מַזִּיעָה – **in the manner that copper sweats,** וְהִיא מְאַבֶּדֶת פֵּירוֹתֶיהָ – **and it will destroy its fruits.**[2]

20. וְתַם לָרִיק כֹּחֲכֶם – **YOUR STRENGTH WILL BE SPENT IN VAIN.** הֲרֵי אָדָם שֶׁלֹּא עָמַל – **Now, a person who has not toiled,** שֶׁלֹּא חָרַשׁ – **who has not plowed,** שֶׁלֹּא זָרַע – **who has not sown,** שֶׁלֹּא נִכֵּשׁ – **who has not weeded,** שֶׁלֹּא כִסַּח – **who has not cleared land,** שֶׁלֹּא עָדַר – **who has not hoed,** וּבִשְׁעַת הַקָּצִיר – **and at the time of the harvest,** בָּא שִׁדָּפוֹן – **blight comes** וּמַלְקֶה אוֹתוֹ – **and strikes him,** אֵין בְּכָךְ כְּלוּם – **there is nothing to that,** i.e., it is not considered a punishment. אֲבָל אָדָם שֶׁעָמַל – **But a person who has toiled** וְחָרַשׁ – **and plowed,** וְזָרַע – **and sown,** וְנִכֵּשׁ – **and weeded,** וְכִסַּח – and, וְעָדַר – **and hoed,** וּבָא שִׁדָּפוֹן – **and blight comes** וּמַלְקֶה אוֹתוֹ – **and strikes him,**[3] הֲרֵי שִׁנָּיו שֶׁל זֶה קֵהוֹת – **now, this person's teeth are set on edge,** i.e., he suffers greatly.[3]

☐ וְלֹא תִתֵּן אַרְצְכֶם אֶת יְבוּלָהּ – **YOUR LAND WILL NOT GIVE ITS PRODUCE.** אַף מַה שֶׁאַתָּה מוֹבִיל לָהּ – **It will not give forth even that** quantity **which you convey to it** בִּשְׁעַת הַזֶּרַע – **at the time of sowing.**[4]

☐ וְעֵץ הָאָרֶץ – **AND THE TREE OF THE LAND.** אֲפִילוּ מִן הָאָרֶץ – **Even from the land** יְהֵא לָקוּי – it will be stricken, שֶׁלֹּא יַחֲנִיטוּ פֵּירוֹתָיו – in that it will not ripen[5] its fruits בִּשְׁעַת הַחֲנָטָה – **at the time of ripening.**[6]

☐ לֹא יִתֵּן – **WILL NOT GIVE.** This phrase מְשַׁמֵּשׁ – serves as a predicate לְמַעְלָה – **for** the word **above,** וּלְמַטָּה – **and for** the word **below,** that is, אַעֵץ – **for** עֵץ, "**tree,**" which precedes it, וְאַפְּרִי – **and for** פְּרִי, "**fruit,**" which follows it.[7]

☐ לֹא יִתֵּן פִּרְיוֹ – **WILL NOT GIVE ITS FRUIT.** כְּשֶׁהוּא מַפְרֶה – **When it does produce fruit,** מַשִּׁיר

---

1. If the land were damp, it would cause the fruit to rot.
2. *Toras Kohanim, perek* 5:3. By his prayers, Moses was able to mitigate the curses mentioned here (*Be'er BaSadeh*).
3. *Toras Kohanim, perek* 5:4.
4. *Toras Kohanim, perek* 5:4. The preceding verse and the beginning of this verse have already said that there will be a shortage of crops. The apparently superfluous "your land will not give its produce" is stated so that we should expound the word יְבוּלָהּ, "its produce," comes from the root יבל, "to convey" (see e.g., *Psalms* 68:30). It is used by our verse to imply that the earth will not even give forth the quantity of seed that was conveyed to it when it was sown (see *Maskil LeDavid*; *Mizrachi*; *Sifsei Chachamim*).
5. חֲנָטָה, which is here translated as "ripening," specif-

ically denotes the first appearance of budding fruits.
6. *Toras Kohanim, perek* 5:4. "Of the land" appears superfluous (*Mizrachi*; *Sifsei Chachamim*). It is written to teach us that the land itself will be a source of punishment; it will not provide sufficient nourishment for the fruit of the tree to ripen (*Sefer Zikaron*).
7. In line with his comment above (v. 18) that this passage lists a series of seven punishments, Rashi sees לֹא יִתֵּן serving as the predicate of two clauses. In his preceding comment, Rashi has said that the fruit will not even ripen. According to this, וְעֵץ הָאָרֶץ לֹא יִתֵּן, "and the tree of the land will not give," is viewed as an independent clause – it will not give fruit at all. In his next comment Rashi shows how לֹא יִתֵּן can also be viewed as the predicate of a clause – "it will not give its fruit" (see following note) – which includes the word פְּרִי (*Sefer Zikaron*).

כא וְאִם־תֵּלְכוּ עִמִּי קֶרִי וְלֹא תֹאבוּ לִשְׁמֹעַ לִי וְיָסַפְתִּי עֲלֵיכֶם מַכָּה שֶׁבַע כְּחַטֹּאתֵיכֶם: כב וְהִשְׁלַחְתִּי בָכֶם אֶת־חַיַּת הַשָּׂדֶה וְשִׁכְּלָה אֶתְכֶם

21 *If you behave casually with Me and refuse to heed Me, then I shall lay a further blow upon you — seven, like your sins.* **22** *I will send the wildlife of the field against you and it will bereave you,*

אונקלוס

כא וְאִם תְּהָכוּן קֳדָמַי בְּקַשְׁיוּ וְלָא תֵּיבוּן לְקַבָּלָא בְּמֵימְרִי וְאוֹסֵף לְאֵתָאָה (נ"א לְאַיְתָאָה) עֲלֵיכוֹן מָחָא שְׁבַע כְּחוֹבֵיכוֹן: כב וַאֲגָרֵי בְכוֹן יָת חֵיוַת בָּרָא וּתְתַכֵּל יָתְכוֹן

רש"י

פירותיו (שם) [שתי קללות ויש] כאן שבע פורעניות: (כא) **ואם תלכו עמי קרי.** רבותינו אמרו עראי. במקרה (שם ה) שאינו אלא לפרקים כן תלכו עראי במצות. ומנחם פירש לשון מניעה, וכן הוקר רגלך (משלי כה:יז) וכן יקר רוח (שם ז:כו)

וקרוב לשון זה לתרגומו של אונקלוס, לשון קושי, שמקשים לבם להמנע מהתקרב אלי: שבע **בחטאתיכם.** שבע פורעניות אחרות במספר שבע כחטאתיכם (ת"כ שם ה): (כב) **והשלחתי. ושכלה אתכם.** אין לי אלא חיה משכלת לשון גירוי,

---

RASHI ELUCIDATED

פֵּירוֹתָיו[1] — *it drops its fruit* on the ground, and makes it unfit for consumption.[1] {הֲרֵי} {שְׁתֵּי קְלָלוֹת} Now, there are {two curses,} {וְיֵשׁ} כָּאן שֶׁבַע פּוּרְעָנִיוֹת – {and there are} seven punishments here.[2]

21. וְאִם תֵּלְכוּ עִמִּי קֶרִי — IF YOU BEHAVE CASUALLY WITH ME. רַבּוֹתֵינוּ אָמְרוּ — Our Rabbis said[3] עֲרַאי — that קֶרִי means **casually**,[3] בְּמִקְרֶה — by chance, שֶׁאֵינוֹ אֶלָּא לְפְרָקִים — a thing that occurs only sometimes. כֵּן תֵּלְכוּ עֲרַאי — So will you behave casually בַּמִּצְוֹת — about the commandments.[4] וְכֵן — {וּמְנַחֵם פֵּרֵשׁ — Menachem[5] explains קֶרִי לְשׁוֹן מְנִיעָה — as an expression of "holding back." וְכֵן — And so he explains הֹקַר in the phrase, הֹקַר רַגְלְךָ,[6] — "**hold back your foot.**"[6] וְכֵן — And so he explains יְקַר in, יְקַר רוּחַ,[7] — "**withheld of spirit**,"[7] i.e., one who does not give vent to his emotions. וְקָרוֹב לָשׁוֹן זֶה — This meaning ascribed to the word by Menachem **is close** לְתַרְגּוּמוֹ שֶׁל אוּנְקְלוּס — **to** Onkelos' translation,[8] לְשׁוֹן קוֹשִׁי — in which he uses **the meaning "hardness,"** שֶׁמַּקְשִׁים לִבָּם — for **they harden their hearts** לְהִמָּנַע — **to hold** themselves **back** מֵהִתְקָרֵב אֵלָי — **from bringing themselves close to Me**.

☐ שֶׁבַע כְּחַטֹּאתֵיכֶם — SEVEN, LIKE YOUR SINS. שֶׁבַע פּוּרְעָנִיוֹת אֲחֵרוֹת — Seven other punishments, בְּמִסְפַּר שֶׁבַע — **seven in number**,[9] כְּחַטֹּאתֵיכֶם — like your sins.[9]

22. וְהִשְׁלַחְתִּי — I WILL SEND. לְשׁוֹן גֵּרוּי — This is an expression of **inciting**.[10]

☐ וְשִׁכְּלָה אֶתְכֶם — AND IT WILL BEREAVE YOU. אֵין לִי אֶלָּא חַיָּה מְשַׁכֶּלֶת — On the basis of this verse, **I know**

---

1. *Toras Kohanim, perek* 5:4. Here, לֹא יִתֵּן פִּרְיוֹ is seen as an independent clause — even if the fruit of a tree should ripen, "it will not give its fruit" — the fruit will be made unavailable to you.

2. The seven punishments are: (a) I will break the pride of your might; (b) your heavens will be like iron; (c) your land will be like copper; (d) you will spend your strength in vain; (e) your land will not give its produce; (f) the tree of the land will not give; (g) it will not give its fruit.

3. *Toras Kohanim, perek* 5:5.

4. The word כֵּן ("so") appears unnecessary in this comment. If Rashi is interested in paraphrasing וְאִם תֵּלְכוּ עִמִּי קֶרִי, he should have said only, תֵּלְכוּ עֲרַאי בַּמִּצְוֹת, "You will behave casually about the commandments." *Yosef Hallel* notes that the first printed edition of Rashi has בְּמִקְרֶה, "like an event," instead of בְּמִקְרֶה, "by chance," which appears in most printed editions. According to this version, the word כֵּן fits nicely into the text. Rashi says, "Like an event that occurs only sometimes, so will you behave casually about the commandments."

5. Menachem ben Saruk (Spain, c. 920-980) compiled *Machberes,* a dictionary of the Hebrew language frequently quoted by Rashi.

6. *Proverbs* 25:17; see Rashi there.

7. *Proverbs* 17:27; see Rashi there.

8. Onkelos translates קֶרִי as בְּקַשְׁיוּ.

9. *Toras Kohanim, perek* 5:5. וְיָסַפְתִּי עֲלֵיכֶם מַכָּה, "I shall lay a further blow upon you," using the singular מַכָּה, could be understood as referring to a single punishment. If this were so, שֶׁבַע כְּחַטֹּאתֵיכֶם would mean "seven times as much as your sins." But this cannot be so, for God does not punish unfairly. Thus, שֶׁבַע כְּחַטֹּאתֵיכֶם is understood as seven punishments for seven sins (see *Mizrachi*).

10. The root שלח, "to send," in the simple *kal* implies an act done through an agent acting consciously on behalf of the one who sent him. But in the *hifil*, as it appears here, it implies that the sender consciously dispatches his agent, but the agent does not know he is being sent; e.g., when one sics an animal on another person, the animal is unaware that he has become an agent for the one who incited him (see *Minchas Yehudah; Sifsei Chachamim*).

VAYIKRA/LEVITICUS — PARASHAS BECHUKOSAI

וְהִכְרַ֤יתִי אֶת־בְּהֶמְתְּכֶם֙ וְהִמְעִ֣יטָה
אֶתְכֶ֔ם וְנָשַׁ֖מּוּ דַּרְכֵיכֶֽם: כג וְאִם־בְּאֵ֕לֶּה
לֹ֥א תִוָּסְר֖וּ לִ֑י וַהֲלַכְתֶּ֥ם עִמִּ֖י קֶֽרִי:

exterminate your cattle, and diminish your number; and your roads will become desolate. ²³ *If despite these you will not be chastised to Me, and you behave casually with Me,*

---------- אונקלוס ----------

וּתְשֵׁיצֵי יָת בְּעִירְכוֹן וְתַזְעֵר יָתְכוֹן וִיצַדְיָן אוֹרְחָכוֹן: כג וְאִם בְּאִלֵּין לָא תִתְרַדְרוּן קֳדָמַי וּתְהָכוּן קֳדָמַי בְּקַשְׁיוּ:

---------- רש"י ----------

אתכם. אֵלּוּ הַקְּטַנִּים (שם ז): **וְהִכְרִיתִי אֶת בְּהֶמְתְּכֶם.** מִבַּחוּץ (שם): **וְהִמְעִיטָה אֶתְכֶם.** מִבִּפְנִים (שם): **וְנָשַׁמּוּ דַּרְכֵיכֶם.** שְׁבִילִים גְּדוֹלִים וּשְׁבִילִים קְטַנִּים הֲרֵי שֶׁבַע פֻּרְעָנִיּוֹת. שֵׁן בְּהֵמָה, וְשֵׁן חַיָּה, חֲמַת זוֹחֲלֵי עָפָר, וְשַׁכְּלָה, וְהִכְרִיתָהּ, וְהִמְעִיטָה, וְנַשַּׁמּוּ: (כג) **לֹא תִוָּסְרוּ לִי.** לָשׁוּב אֵלָי:

שֶׁדַּרְכָּהּ בְּכָךְ, בְּהֵמָה שֶׁאֵין דַּרְכָּהּ בְּכָךְ מִנַּיִן, ת"ל וְשֵׁן בְּהֵמוֹת אֲשַׁלַּח בָּם (דברים לב:כד) הֲרֵי שְׁתַּיִם. וּמִנַּיִן שֶׁתְּהֵא מְמִיתָה בִּנְשִׁיכָתָהּ, ת"ל עִם חֲמַת זוֹחֲלֵי עָפָר (שם) מַה אֵלּוּ נוֹשְׁכִין וּמְמִיתִין אַף אֵלּוּ נוֹשְׁכִין וּמְמִיתִין. כְּבָר הָיוּ שָׁנִים בְּאֶרֶץ יִשְׂרָאֵל חֲמוֹר נוֹשֵׁךְ וּמֵמִית עָרוֹד נוֹשֵׁךְ וּמֵמִית (ת"כ שם ו): **וְשִׁכְּלָה**

---------- RASHI ELUCIDATED ----------

only that a beast bereaves, שֶׁדַּרְכָּהּ בְּכָךְ — **for its way,** i.e., nature, **is so.** בְּהֵמָה — **A domestic animal,** שֶׁאֵין דַּרְכָּהּ בְּכָךְ — **whose way is not so,** מִנַּיִן — **from where do we know** that it, too, will attack you? תַּלְמוּד לוֹמַר — To provide this source, **the verse says,** [1]״וְשֵׁן בְּהֵמוֹת אֲשַׁלַּח בָּם״ — **"and I will send the tooth of domestic animals against them."**[1] הֲרֵי שְׁתַּיִם — See, now, that there are **two** punishments implicit in ״וְהִשְׁלַחְתִּי בָכֶם אֶת חַיַּת הַשָּׂדֶה״.[2] וּמִנַּיִן — **And from where do we know** שֶׁתְּהֵא מְמִיתָה בִּנְשִׁיכָתָהּ — **that it will kill with its bite?** תַּלְמוּד לוֹמַר — To provide this source, **the verse says,** ״עִם חֲמַת זוֹחֲלֵי עָפָר״[1] — **"with the venom of those that slither on the ground."**[1] מַה אֵלּוּ נוֹשְׁכִין — **Just as these** snakes **bite** וּמְמִיתִין — **and kill,** אַף אֵלּוּ — **so, too, these** animals נוֹשְׁכִין וּמְמִיתִין — **bite and kill.** כְּבָר הָיוּ שָׁנִים — **There have already been years** בְּאֶרֶץ יִשְׂרָאֵל — **in the Land of Israel** חֲמוֹר נוֹשֵׁךְ וּמֵמִית — in which **a donkey bites and kills,** [3]עָרוֹד נוֹשֵׁךְ וּמֵמִית — and **a wild donkey bites and kills,** i.e., there were years in which the tame donkey was just as deadly as the wild one.[3]

□ וְשִׁכְּלָה אֶתְכֶם — AND IT WILL BEREAVE YOU.[4] אֵלּוּ הַקְּטַנִּים — These are the minors.[4]

□ וְהִכְרִיתָה אֶת בְּהֶמְתְּכֶם — EXTERMINATE YOUR CATTLE — [5]מִבַּחוּץ — **on the outside.**[5]

□ וְהִמְעִיטָה אֶתְכֶם — AND DIMINISH YOUR NUMBER — [5]מִבִּפְנִים — **on the inside.**[5]

□ וְנָשַׁמּוּ דַּרְכֵיכֶם — AND YOUR ROADS WILL BECOME DESOLATE. שְׁבִילִים גְּדוֹלִים — Major trails קְטַנִּים — and minor trails.[6] הֲרֵי שֶׁבַע פֻּרְעָנִיּוֹת — See, now, that there are **seven punishments:** שֵׁן בְּהֵמָה — **Tooth of cattle;** וְשֵׁן חַיָּה — **and tooth of beast;** חֲמַת זוֹחֲלֵי עָפָר — **the venom of those that slither on the ground;** ״וְשִׁכְּלָה״ — **"and it will bereave";** ״וְהִכְרִיתָה״ — **"and [it will] exterminate";** ״וְהִמְעִיטָה״ — **"and [it will] diminish";** ״וְנַשַּׁמּוּ״ — **"and [your roads] will become desolate."**

23. לֹא תִוָּסְרוּ לִי — YOU WILL NOT BE CHASTISED TO ME, i.e., לָשׁוּב אֵלָי — to repent unto Me.[7]

---

1. *Deuteronomy* 32:24.

2. The use of the verb שלח by both our verse and the one in *Deuteronomy* indicates that our verse speaks of domestic animals, just as the other verse (see Rashi there; *Minchas Yehudah; Sifsei Chachamim* ; see also commentary of *Rash MiShantz* to *Toras Kohanim*). Alternatively, the word חַיָּה, "beast," can also include domesticated animals (see Rashi to 11:2 above). The verse from *Deuteronomy* indicates that it is to be understood this way in our verse (*Be'er BaSadeh*). Thus, וְהִשְׁלַחְתִּי בָכֶם אֶת חַיַּת הַשָּׂדֶה implies two punishments, that wild beasts will attack them, and that animals which are normally tame will attack them.

3. *Toras Kohanim, perek* 5:6. The text of *Toras Kohanim* , which is apparently Rashi's source, reads שׁוֹר, "an ox," in place of עָרוֹד, "a wild donkey."

4. *Toras Kohanim, perek* 5:7. The verse refers to bereavement of the parents through the death of their children.

5. *Toras Kohanim, perek* 5:7. Your cattle, which are on the outside without any protection, will be exterminated, but you, who are protected inside your fortifications, will be diminished in number, but not exterminated entirely. Rashi stresses this difference between וְהִכְרִיתָה and וְהִמְעִיטָה to show that they are two different punishments, so that he can arrive at the total of seven punishments in this series (see *Sefer Zikaron* ; *Minchas Yehudah; Sifsei Chachamim*).

6. *Toras Kohanim, perek* 5:7. The verse could have said וְנָשַׁמּוּ דְרָכִים, "roads will become desolate." The lengthier דַּרְכֵיכֶם, "your roads," implies that all roads will become desolate, even minor ones. Rashi uses שְׁבִילִים, "trails," as a synonym for דְּרָכִים, "roads," because all other instances of דַּרְכֵיכֶם in Scripture mean "your ways," i.e., patterns of behavior. Rashi points out that here it means "your roads," both major and minor.

7. תִוָּסְרוּ is a *nifal* form of the root יסר. This root in the *nifal*

²⁴ then I, too, will behave toward you with casualness; and I will strike you, even I, seven ways for your sins. ²⁵ I will bring upon you a sword, avenging the vengeance of a covenant, you will be gathered into your cities; and I will send pestilence among you and you will be delivered into the hand of the enemy. ²⁶ When I break for you the staff of bread,

כד וְהָלַכְתִּי אַף־אֲנִי עִמָּכֶם בְּקֶרִי וְהִכֵּיתִי אֶתְכֶם גַּם־אָנִי שֶׁבַע עַל־חַטֹּאתֵיכֶם: כה וְהֵבֵאתִי עֲלֵיכֶם חֶרֶב נֹקֶמֶת נְקַם־בְּרִית וְנֶאֱסַפְתֶּם אֶל־עָרֵיכֶם וְשִׁלַּחְתִּי דֶבֶר בְּתוֹכְכֶם וְנִתַּתֶּם בְּיַד־אוֹיֵב: כו בְּשִׁבְרִי לָכֶם מַטֵּה־לֶחֶם

— אונקלוס —

כד וְאֵהַךְ אַף אֲנָא עִמְּכוֹן בְּקַשְׁיוּ וְאַלְקֵי יַתְכוֹן אַף אֲנָא שְׁבַע עַל חוֹבֵיכוֹן: כה וְאַיְתִי עֲלֵיכוֹן דְּקָטְלִין בְּחַרְבָּא וְיִתְפָּרַע מִנְּכוֹן פֻּרְעֲנוּתָא עַל דַּעֲבַרְתּוּן עַל פִּתְגָמֵי אוֹרָיְתָא וְתִתְכַּנְּשׁוּן לְקִרְוֵיכוֹן וַאֲגָרֵי מוֹתָנָא בֵּכוֹן וְתִתְמַסְּרוּן בִּידָא דְסַנְאָה: כו בִּדְאֶתְבַּר לְכוֹן סְעִיד מֵיכְלָא

— רש"י —

(כה) נֶקֶם בְּרִית. וְיֵשׁ נָקָם שֶׁאֵינוֹ בַּבְּרִית כְּדֶרֶךְ שְׁאָר נְקָמוֹת, וְזֶהוּ סִמּוּי עֵינָיו שֶׁל צִדְקִיָּהוּ (מלכים ב כה:ז; ת"כ פרק ו:ח). ד"א, נֶקֶם בְּרִית נִקְמַת בְּרִיתִי אֲשֶׁר עֲבַרְתֶּם. כָּל הֲבָאַת חֶרֶב שֶׁבַּמִּקְרָא הִיא מִלְחֶמֶת חֲיָלוֹת אוֹיְבִים. וְנֶאֱסַפְתֶּם. מִן הַחוּץ אֶל תּוֹךְ הֶעָרִים מִפְּנֵי הַמָּצוֹר: וְשִׁלַּחְתִּי דֶבֶר בְּתוֹכְכֶם. וְעַל יְדֵי הַדֶּבֶר וְנִתַּתֶּם בְּיַד הָאוֹיְבִים הַצָּרִים עֲלֵיכֶם, לְפִי שֶׁאֵין מְלִינִים אֶת הַמֵּת בִּירוּשָׁלַיִם (ב"ק פב:), וּכְשֶׁהֵם מוֹצִיאִים אֶת הַמֵּת לְקָבְרוֹ נִתָּנִים בְּיַד אוֹיֵב (ת"כ שם): (כו) מַטֵּה לֶחֶם. לְשׁוֹן מִשְׁעָן, כְּמוֹ מַטֵּה עֹז (ירמיה מח:יז):

— RASHI ELUCIDATED —

25. נְקַם בְּרִית — **THE VENGEANCE OF A COVENANT.** וְיֵשׁ נָקָם — **There is vengeance** שֶׁאֵינוֹ בַּבְּרִית — **which is not in the Covenant,** כְּדֶרֶךְ שְׁאָר נְקָמוֹת — **in the manner of other vengeances,** וְזֶהוּ סִמּוּי עֵינָיו שֶׁל צִדְקִיָּהוּ — **and this is the blinding of the eyes of Zedekiah.**[1]

נִקְמַת בְּרִיתִי — **Alternatively,** נֶקֶם בְּרִית — **"vengeance of a covenant"** means, נִקְמַת בְּרִיתִי — **vengeance of My covenant** אֲשֶׁר עֲבַרְתֶּם — **which you violated.**[2]

כָּל הֲבָאַת חֶרֶב שֶׁבַּמִּקְרָא — **Any "bringing of a sword" in Scripture** הִיא מִלְחֶמֶת חֲיָלוֹת אוֹיְבִים — **is war with enemy armies.**

□ וְנֶאֱסַפְתֶּם — **YOU WILL BE GATHERED.** מִן הַחוּץ — **From the outside** אֶל תּוֹךְ הֶעָרִים — **to the inside of the cities** מִפְּנֵי הַמָּצוֹר — **because of the siege.**[3]

□ וְשִׁלַּחְתִּי דֶבֶר בְּתוֹכְכֶם — **AND I WILL SEND PESTILENCE AMONG YOU.** וְעַל יְדֵי הַדֶּבֶר — **And by means of the pestilence,** וְנִתַּתֶּם בְּיַד הָאוֹיְבִים — **you will be delivered into the hand of the enemies** הַצָּרִים עֲלֵיכֶם — **who besiege you;** לְפִי שֶׁאֵין מְלִינִים אֶת הַמֵּת — **because they do not leave a corpse overnight** בִּירוּשָׁלַיִם — **in Jerusalem,**[4] וּכְשֶׁהֵם מוֹצִיאִים אֶת הַמֵּת — **and when they take out the corpse** לְקָבְרוֹ — **to bury it,**[5] נִתָּנִים בְּיַד אוֹיֵב — **they are delivered into the hand of the enemy.**[5]

26. מַטֵּה לֶחֶם — **STAFF OF BREAD.** מַטֵּה — מַטֵּה in our verse **means a source of support,** כְּמוֹ לְשׁוֹן מִשְׁעָן — **as** it does in the phrase, מַטֵּה עֹז — **"a staff of strength."**[6]

---

means "to accept chastisement," as stated by Rashi to *Jeremiah* 6:8. Consequently, our verse should have said, לֹא תֻנַּסְרוּ מִמֶּנִּי, "you will not be chastised *by* Me" or "*from* Me," rather than "*to* Me"; or the clause should have ended with the words לֹא תֻנַּסְרוּ. The verse uses "*to* Me," because implicit in it is "to repent" (see *Be'er BaSadeh*).

1. *Toras Kohanim, perek* 6:1. See *II Kings* 25:7, which states that Zedekiah, the last king of Judea, was blinded by Nebuchadnezzar, king of Babylonia.
The "Covenant" mentioned here is the Torah. "Vengeance of a Covenant" means "vengeance which is mentioned in the Covenant, i.e., the Torah." This excludes punishments such as putting out one's eyes, which Zedekiah suffered, which the Torah never mentions (*Chizkuni*; see also Rashi to *Ezekiel* 23:37).

2. According to the first explanation, "vengeance of a covenant" means vengeance which is mentioned in "a covenant." According to the second explanation,

"vengeance of a covenant" means vengeance for violation of "a covenant."

3. אסף can mean "gathering that which is scattered" or "gathering in from the outside." Rashi notes that here it is used in the second sense. See also Rashi to *Genesis* 30:23, 49:29, 49:33; *Exodus* 9:19, 23:10, 23:16, 34:22; *Numbers* 11:30, 12:14; *Isaiah* 60:20; *Jeremiah* 16:5; *Joel* 2:10, 4:15.

4. *Bava Kamma* 82b.

5. *Toras Kohanim, perek* 6:1. Pestilence causes death, yet our verse makes it sound as if it brings about delivery into the hand of the enemy. Rashi explains that through the death of those who are stricken with pestilence, the survivors will be delivered into the hand of the enemy (*Mizrachi; Sifsei Chachamim*).

6. *Jeremiah* 48:17. Bread, i.e., food (see next note), is referred to as a "staff" because the body is supported, i.e., sustained, by it just as a man is supported by his staff (*Mizrachi*).

| ten women will bake your bread in the same oven, and they will bring back your bread by weight; you will eat and not be sated. ²⁷ If despite this you will not heed Me, and you behave toward Me with casualness, ²⁸ I will behave toward you with a fury of casualness; I will chastise you, even I, seven ways for your sins. ²⁹ You will eat the flesh of your sons; and the flesh of your daughters will you eat. | וְאָפוּ עֶשֶׂר נָשִׁים לַחְמְכֶם בְּתַנּוּר אֶחָד וְהֵשִׁיבוּ לַחְמְכֶם בַּמִּשְׁקָל וַאֲכַלְתֶּם וְלֹא תִשְׂבָּעוּ: כז וְאִם־ בְּזֹאת לֹא תִשְׁמְעוּ לִי וַהֲלַכְתֶּם עִמִּי בְּקֶרִי: כח וְהָלַכְתִּי עִמָּכֶם בַּחֲמַת־ קֶרִי וְיִסַּרְתִּי אֶתְכֶם אַף־אָנִי שֶׁבַע עַל־חַטֹּאתֵיכֶם: כט וַאֲכַלְתֶּם בְּשַׂר בְּנֵיכֶם וּבְשַׂר בְּנֹתֵיכֶם תֹּאכֵלוּ: |

———————— אונקלוס ————————

וְיָפְיָן עֲסַר נְשִׁין לַחְמְכוֹן בְּתַנּוּרָא חַד וִיתִיבוּן לַחְמְכוֹן בְּמַתְקְלָא וְתֵיכְלוּן וְלָא תִשְׂבְּעוּן: כז וְאִם בְּדָא לָא תְקַבְּלוּן בְּמֵימְרִי וּתְהָכוּן קֳדָמַי בְּקַשְׁיוּ: כח וְאֶהָךְ עִמְּכוֹן בִּתְקוֹף רְגַז וְאַלְקֵי (נ"א וְאַרְדֵּי) יָתְכוֹן אַף אֲנָא שְׁבַע עַל חוֹבֵיכוֹן: כט וְתֵיכְלוּן בְּשַׂר בְּנֵיכוֹן וּבְשַׂר בְּנָתֵיכוֹן תֵּיכְלוּן:

———————— רש"י ————————

בשברי לכם מטה לחם. אֶשְׁבּוֹר לָכֶם כָּל מִסְעַד אוֹכֶל (ת"כ שם ג) וְהֵם חֲלֵי רָעָב: **ואפו עשר נשים לחמכם בתנור אחד.** מֵחוֹסֶר עֵצִים (שם): **והשיבו לחמכם במשקל.** שֶׁתְּהֵא הַתְּבוּאָה נִרְקֶבֶת וְנַעֲשֵׂית פַּת נְפוּלָה וּמִשְׁתַּבֶּרֶת בַּתַּנּוּר וְהֵן יוֹשְׁבוֹת וְשׁוֹקְלוֹת אֶת הַשְּׁבָרִים לְחַלֵּק בֵּינֵיהֶם (שם): **ואכלתם ולא תשבעו.** זוֹהִי מְאֵרָה בְּתוֹךְ הַמֵּעַיִם בַּלֶּחֶם. הֲרֵי שֶׁבַע פּוּרְעָנִיּוֹת. חֶרֶב, מָצוֹר, דֶּבֶר, שֶׁבֶר מַטֵּה לֶחֶם, חוֹסֶר עֵצִים, פַּת נְפוּלָה, מְאֵרָה בַּמֵּעַיִם. וְנִתַּתֶּם אֵינָהּ מִן הַמִּנְיָן, הִיא הַחֶרֶב:

———————— RASHI ELUCIDATED ————————

□ **אֶשְׁבּוֹר לָכֶם** — I will break for you **בְּשִׁבְרִי לָכֶם מַטֵּה לֶחֶם** — WHEN I BREAK FOR YOU THE STAFF OF BREAD. **כָּל מִסְעַד אוֹכֵל** — all sustenance of food.[1] **וְהֵם חִצֵּי רָעָב** — These are "the arrows of hunger."[2]

□ **וְאָפוּ עֶשֶׂר נָשִׁים לַחְמְכֶם בְּתַנּוּר אֶחָד** — TEN WOMEN WILL BAKE YOUR BREAD IN THE SAME OVEN, **מֵחוֹסֶר עֵצִים** — for lack of wood.[3]

□ **וְהֵשִׁיבוּ לַחְמְכֶם בַּמִּשְׁקָל** — AND THEY WILL BRING BACK YOUR BREAD BY WEIGHT. **שֶׁתְּהֵא הַתְּבוּאָה נִרְקֶבֶת** — For the grain will rot, **וְנַעֲשֵׂית פַּת נְפוּלָה** — and it becomes crumbly bread, **וּמִשְׁתַּבֶּרֶת בַּתַּנּוּר** — and breaks apart in the oven. **וְהֵן יוֹשְׁבוֹת** — [The ten women] sit **וְשׁוֹקְלוֹת** — and weigh the broken pieces **אֶת הַשְּׁבָרִים** **לְחַלְּקָם בֵּינֵיהֶם** — to divide them among themselves.[4]

□ **בְּתוֹךְ הַמֵּעַיִם** – **וַאֲכַלְתֶּם וְלֹא תִשְׂבָּעוּ** — YOU WILL EAT AND NOT BE SATED. **זוֹהִי מְאֵרָה** — This is a curse inside the innards, i.e., a curse which prevents the body from deriving satisfaction from food {**בַּלֶּחֶם** — regarding bread.}[5]

הֲרֵי שֶׁבַע פּוּרְעָנִיּוֹת — See, now, that there are **seven punishments:** **חֶרֶב** — sword, **מָצוֹר** — siege, **דֶּבֶר** — pestilence, **שֶׁבֶר מַטֵּה לֶחֶם** — breaking the staff of bread, **חוֹסֶר עֵצִים** — lack of wood, **פַּת נְפוּלָה** — crumbly bread, **מְאֵרָה בַּמֵּעַיִם** — and curse in the innards. "**וְנִתַּתֶּם,**" — However, the curse, "**you will be delivered** [into the hand of the enemy]," **אֵינָהּ מִן הַמִּנְיָן** — is not among the number, **הִיא הַחֶרֶב** — because **it is the sword** already mentioned.

---

1. *Toras Kohanim, perek* 6:2. Rashi here takes לֶחֶם as referring to all food, as he does above 3:11, 21:17, 21:21, and in many other places in his commentaries. This is in contrast to the way it is used in the next clause of the verse, וְאָפוּ עֶשֶׂר נָשִׁים לַחְמְכֶם בְּתַנּוּר אֶחָד, where it means "bread" in the narrower sense of the word.

2. *Ezekiel* 5:16 says that when God sends חִצֵּי הָרָעָב, "the arrows of the hunger," He "breaks the staff of bread." Rashi refers to this verse to show that

"breaking the staff of bread" is to be taken as a metaphor for hunger, and does not mean the breaking of some actual staff.

3. *Toras Kohanim, perek* 6:2. But not for lack of bread; this is a punishment distinct from hunger referred to at the beginning of the verse (*Gur Aryeh*; *Sifsei Chachamim*).

4. *Toras Kohanim, perek* 6:2.

5. The word בַּלֶּחֶם does not appear in the first printed edition of Rashi.

ל וְהִשְׁמַדְתִּ֞י אֶת־בָּמֹֽתֵיכֶ֗ם וְהִכְרַתִּי֙
אֶת־חַמָּ֣נֵיכֶ֔ם וְנָֽתַתִּי֙ אֶת־פִּגְרֵיכֶ֔ם
עַל־פִּגְרֵ֖י גִּלּוּלֵיכֶ֑ם וְגָעֲלָ֥ה נַפְשִׁ֖י
אֶתְכֶֽם: לא וְנָתַתִּ֤י אֶת־עָרֵיכֶם֙ חָרְבָּ֔ה
וַהֲשִׁמּוֹתִ֖י אֶת־מִקְדְּשֵׁיכֶ֑ם וְלֹ֣א

30 I will destroy your high places and decimate your sun-images, I will put your carcasses upon the carcasses of your idols, and My Spirit will reject you. 31 I will put your cities to ruin and I will make your sanctuaries desolate; I will not

---- אונקלוס ----

לוֶאֱשֵׁיצֵי יָת בָּמָתְכוֹן וַאֲקַצֵּץ יָת חֲנִיסְנֵסַיְכוֹן וְאֶתֵּן יָת פִּגְרֵיכוֹן עַל פְּגַר טַעֲוָתְכוֹן וִירַחֵק מֵימְרִי יָתְכוֹן: לאוְאֶתֵּן יָת קִרְוֵיכוֹן צָדְיָא וְאֶצְדֵּי יָת מַקְדְּשֵׁיכוֹן וְלָא

---- רש"י ----

(ל) במתיכם. מגדלים ובירניות: חמניכם. מין עבודה זרה שמעמידין על הגגות, ועל שם שמעמידין בחמה קרויין חמנים: ונתתי את פגריכם. תפוחי רעב היו, ומוליאים יראתם מחיקם ומנשקים אותם, וכרסן נבקעת ונופל עליה (שם ד): וגעלה נפשי אתכם. זה סילוק שכינה (שם): (לא) ונתתי את עריכם חרבה. יכול מאדם, כשהוא אומר והשמותי אני את הארץ (פסוק לב) הרי אדם אמור. הא מה אני מקיים חרבה, מעובר ושב (ת"כ פרשתא ו:ד): והשמותי את מקדשיכם. יכול מן הקרבנות, כשהוא אומר ולא אריח הרי קרבנות אמורים, הא מה אני מקיים והשמותי את מקדשיכם, מן הגדודיות (שם) שיירות של ישראל שהיו מתקדשות ונועדות לבא שם. הרי שבע פורעניות. אכילת בשר בנים ובנות. והשמדת במות הרי שתים.

---- RASHI ELUCIDATED ----

30. בָּמֹתֵיכֶם — YOUR HIGH PLACES. מִגְדָּלִים — Towers וּבִירָנִיּוֹת — and castles.[1]

□ חַמָּנֵיכֶם — YOUR SUN-IMAGES. מִין עֲבוֹדָה זָרָה — A type of idol שֶׁמַּעֲמִידִין עַל הַגַּגוֹת — which they set up on the rooftops. וְעַל שֵׁם שֶׁמַּעֲמִידִין בַּחַמָּה — Because they stand them in the sun, קְרוּיִין חַמָּנִים — they are called "sun-images."

□ וְנָתַתִּי אֶת פִּגְרֵיכֶם — I WILL PUT YOUR CARCASSES. תְּפוּחֵי רָעָב הָיוּ — They were swollen from hunger, וּמְנַשְּׁקִים אוֹתָם — and kiss it; וּכְרֵיסָן נִבְקַעַת — and their belly would burst, [2] וְנוֹפֵל עָלֶיהָ — and [the idolater] would fall on [the idol].[2]

□ וְגָעֲלָה נַפְשִׁי אֶתְכֶם — AND MY SPIRIT WILL REJECT YOU. [3] זֶה סִלּוּק שְׁכִינָה — This is departure of the Divine Presence.[3]

31. וְנָתַתִּי אֶת עָרֵיכֶם חָרְבָּה — I WILL PUT YOUR CITIES TO RUIN. יָכוֹל מֵאָדָם — One might be able to think that this means barren of man, i.e., of inhabitants, כְּשֶׁהוּא אוֹמֵר — when it says, "וַהֲשִׁמֹּתִי אֲנִי אֶת הָאָרֶץ" — "I will make the land desolate,"[4] הֲרֵי אָדָם אָמוּר — see, now, that being barren of man has been stated in that verse. הָא מַה אֲנִי מְקַיֵּם "חָרְבָּה" — What, then do I maintain that "to ruin" means? מֵעוֹבֵר וָשָׁב — That it will be empty even of those who pass through.[5]

□ וַהֲשִׁמֹּתִי אֶת מִקְדְּשֵׁיכֶם — AND I WILL MAKE YOUR SANCTUARIES DESOLATE. יָכוֹל מִן הַקָּרְבָּנוֹת — One might be able to think that the verse means that the sanctuaries will be desolate of offerings. כְּשֶׁהוּא אוֹמֵר — When it says, "וְלֹא אָרִיחַ" — "I will not smell [your satisfying aromas]," הֲרֵי קָרְבָּנוֹת אֲמוּרִים — see, now, that the suspension of offerings is stated in this verse. הָא מַה אֲנִי מְקַיֵּם — What, then, do I maintain that וַהֲשִׁמֹּתִי אֶת מִקְדְּשֵׁיכֶם — "and I will make your sanctuaries desolate" means? [5] מִן הַגְּדוּדִיוֹת — It means desolate from the throngs,[5] שַׁיָּרוֹת שֶׁל יִשְׂרָאֵל — caravans of Israelites שֶׁהָיוּ מִתְקַדְּשׁוֹת — who would ready themselves, וְנוֹעָדוֹת — and meet לָבֹא שָׁם — to come there, i.e., to the Beis HaMikdash. הֲרֵי שֶׁבַע פּוּרְעָנִיּוֹת — See, now, that there are seven punishments: אֲכִילַת בְּשַׂר בָּנִים וּבָנוֹת — Eating the flesh of sons and daughters; וְהַשְׁמָדַת בָּמוֹת — and destruction of high places; הֲרֵי שְׁתַּיִם — see

---

1. בָּמָה often means "an altar." Here, however, Rashi defines it as a high building, for it allows him to combine the destruction of high places and the destruction of sun-images into one punishment, and thus arrive at the total of seven for this series, as he explains in his comments to the next verse. If בָּמֹתֵיכֶם of our verse meant altars, there would be a total of eight.

2. *Toras Kohanim, perek* 6:4. This explains how "I will put your carcasses upon the carcasses of your idols" was fulfilled (*Minchas Yehudah; Sifsei Chachamim*).

3. *Toras Kohanim, perek* 6:4.

4. Below v. 32.

5. *Toras Kohanim, parshasa* 1:7.

לב אָרִיחַ בְּרֵיחַ נִיחֹחֲכֶם: וַהֲשִׁמֹּתִי אֲנִי אֶת־הָאָרֶץ וְשָׁמְמוּ עָלֶיהָ אֹיְבֵיכֶם לג הַיֹּשְׁבִים בָּהּ: וְאֶתְכֶם אֱזָרֶה בַגּוֹיִם וַהֲרִיקֹתִי אַחֲרֵיכֶם חָרֶב

smell your satisfying aromas. ³² *I will make the land desolate; and your foes who dwell upon it will be desolate.* ³³ *And you, I will separate among the nations, I will empty the sword after you;*

— אונקלוס —

אֲקַבֵּל בְּרַעֲוָא קֻרְבָּן כְּנִשְׁתְּכוֹן: לב וְאֵצְדֵּי אֲנָא יָת אַרְעָא וִיצָדוּן עֲלַהּ בַּעֲלֵי דְבָבֵיכוֹן דְּיָתְבִין בַּהּ: לג וְיָתְכוֹן אֲבַדַּר בֵּינֵי עַמְמַיָּא וַאֲגָרֵי בַתְרֵיכוֹן דְּקַטְלִין בְּחַרְבָּא

— רש"י —

(לג) וְאֶתְכֶם אֱזָרֶה בַגּוֹיִם. זוֹ מִדָּה קָשָׁה, שֶׁבְּשָׁעָה שֶׁבְּנֵי מְדִינָה גּוֹלִים לְמָקוֹם אֶחָד רוֹאִים זֶה אֶת זֶה וּמִתְנַחֲמִין, וְיִשְׂרָאֵל נִזְרוּ כִּבְמַזְרֶה, כְּאָדָם הַזּוֹרֶה שְׂעוֹרִים בְּנָפָה וְאֵין אַחַת מֵהֶן דְּבוּקָה בַחֲבֶרְתָּהּ (שם ו): וַהֲרִיקֹתִי. כְּשֶׁשּׁוֹלֵף הַחֶרֶב מִתְרוֹקֵן הַנָּדָן. וּמִדְרָשׁוֹ, חֶרֶב הַנִּשְׁמֶטֶת אַחֲרֵיכֶם אֵינָהּ חוֹזֶרֶת מַהֵר, כְּאָדָם שֶׁמֵּרִיק אֶת הַמַּיִם וְאֵין סוֹפָן לַחֲזוֹר (שם ז):

כְּרִיתַת חַמָּנִים אֵין כָּאן פֻּרְעָנוּת אֶלָּא ע"י הַשְׁמָדַת הַבִּירָנִיּוֹת יִפְּלוּ הַחַמָּנִים שֶׁבְּרָאשֵׁי הַגַּגוֹת. וְנָתַתִּי אֶת פִּגְרֵיכֶם וְגוֹ' הֲרֵי שָׁלֹשׁ. סִלּוּק שְׁכִינָה אַרְבַּע. חֻרְבַּן עָרִים. שִׁמְמוֹן מִקְדָּשׁ מִן הַגְּדוּדִיּוֹת. וְלֹא אָרִיחַ קָרְבָּנוֹת. הֲרֵי שֶׁבַע: (לב) וַהֲשִׁמֹּתִי אֲנִי אֶת הָאָרֶץ. זוֹ מִדָּה טוֹבָה לְיִשְׂרָאֵל, שֶׁלֹּא יִמְצְאוּ הָאוֹיְבִים נַחַת רוּחַ בְּאַרְצָם שֶׁתְּהֵא שׁוֹמֵמָה מִיּוֹשְׁבֶיהָ (שם פרק ו:ה):

— RASHI ELUCIDATED —

now, that there are two. בְּרִיתַת חַמָּנִים — **Cutting down sun-images,** אֵין כָּאן פֻּרְעָנוּת — **there is not a punishment here,** i.e., it is not counted among the seven punishments, אֶלָּא — **rather,** עַל יְדֵי — **the** הַשְׁמָדַת הַבִּירָנִיּוֹת — **through destruction of the castles,** יִפְּלוּ הַחַמָּנִים שֶׁבְּרָאשֵׁי הַגַּגוֹת — **sun-images on the rooftops will fall** וְיִכָּרְתוּ — **and be cut down.** ,,וְנָתַתִּי אֶת פִּגְרֵיכֶם וְגוֹ'" — **"I will put your carcasses, etc.,"** הֲרֵי שָׁלֹשׁ — **see now, that there are three;** סִלּוּק שְׁכִינָה — **departure of the Divine Presence,** אַרְבַּע — **four;** חֻרְבַּן עָרִים — **destruction of cities;** שִׁמְמוֹן מִקְדָּשׁ מִן הַגְּדוּדִיּוֹת — **desolation of the *Beis HaMikdash* from throngs;** ,,וְלֹא אָרִיחַ" קָרְבָּנוֹת — **"and I will not smell" offerings.** הֲרֵי שֶׁבַע — **See, now, that there are seven.**

32. וַהֲשִׁמֹּתִי אֲנִי אֶת הָאָרֶץ — **I WILL MAKE THE LAND DESOLATE.** זוֹ מִדָּה טוֹבָה לְיִשְׂרָאֵל — **This is a good measure,** i.e., a matter of benefit, **for Israel,** שֶׁלֹּא יִמְצְאוּ הָאוֹיְבִים — **that the enemies will not find** נַחַת רוּחַ — **contentment** בְּאַרְצָם — **in [Israel's] land;**[1] שֶׁתְּהֵא שׁוֹמֵמָה מִיּוֹשְׁבֶיהָ — **for it will be desolate of its inhabitants.**[1]

33. וְאֶתְכֶם אֱזָרֶה בַגּוֹיִם — **AND YOU, I WILL SEPARATE AMONG THE NATIONS.** זוֹ מִדָּה קָשָׁה — **This is a harsh measure,** שֶׁבְּשָׁעָה שֶׁבְּנֵי מְדִינָה — **because at a time when the inhabitants of a country** גּוֹלִים לְמָקוֹם אֶחָד — **are exiled to one place,** רוֹאִים זֶה אֶת זֶה — **they see one another** וּמִתְנַחֲמִין — **and are consoled.** וְיִשְׂרָאֵל נִזְרוּ — **But Israel was separated** from each other כִּבְמַזְרֶה — **as if with a winnowing basket,** בְּנָפָה — **with a** כְּאָדָם הַזּוֹרֶה שְׂעוֹרִים — **like a person who winnows barley** sifter, וְאֵין אַחַת מֵהֶן — **and not one of them** דְּבוּקָה בַחֲבֶרְתָּהּ[2] — **is stuck to another.**[2] וַהֲרִיקֹתִי □ — **I WILL EMPTY.** כְּשֶׁשּׁוֹלֵף הַחֶרֶב — **When he draws the sword** מִתְרוֹקֵן הַנָּדָן — **the sheath is emptied.**[3] וּמִדְרָשׁוֹ — **And it is expounded** midrashically as follows: חֶרֶב הַנִּשְׁמֶטֶת אַחֲרֵיכֶם — **The sword which is released after you,** i.e., to pursue you, אֵינָהּ חוֹזֶרֶת מַהֵר — **does not return quickly;** כְּאָדָם שֶׁמֵּרִיק אֶת הַמַּיִם — **like a person who spills out the water,**[4] וְאֵין סוֹפָן לַחֲזוֹר — **and it is not destined to come back,** i.e., and the water will not come back to its container.[4]

---

1. *Toras Kohanim, perek* 6:5.

2. *Toras Kohanim, perek* 6:6. Rashi to *Jeremiah* 15:7 uses נָפָה as a synonym to define מִזְרֶה. He translates both words with the Old French word *van*, a willow basket used to separate kernels of grain from the chaff.

3. According to Rashi, the object of the transitive לְהָרִיק, "to empty," can be either the container which is emptied, or that which comes out of it and leaves it empty, such as the sword of our verse. See also Rashi to *Exodus* 15:9, s.v., אָרִיק חַרְבִּי.

4. *Toras Kohanim, perek* 6:7. This midrashic interpretation apparently accepts the opinion held by some commentators (e.g., *Rabbeinu Meyuchas* and *Bechor Shor* to *Exodus* 15:9) that the object of the transitive verb לְהָרִיק is the container which is emptied, not that which comes out of it. Even according to this opinion, however, when לְהָרִיק refers to liquids, it means "to spill," and can take the liquid which is spilled out of the container as its direct object. By using חֶרֶב as the direct object of וַהֲרִיקֹתִי, the verse compares the sword to water, which does not return to its container once it has been spilled (see commentary of *Ra'avad* to *Toras Kohanim; Nachalas Yaakov*).

your land will be desolate and your cities will be put to ruin. **34** Then the land will appease its *shemittah* years during all the years of its desolation, while you are in the land of your foes; then the land will rest and it will make its *shemittah* years appeasing. **35** All the days of its being desolate it will rest, whatever it did not rest during your *shemittah* years when you dwelled upon her.

וְהָיְתָה אַרְצְכֶם שְׁמָמָה וְעָרֵיכֶם יִהְיוּ חָרְבָּה: לד אָז תִּרְצֶה הָאָרֶץ אֶת־שַׁבְּתֹתֶיהָ כֹּל יְמֵי הָשַּׁמָּה וְאַתֶּם בְּאֶרֶץ אֹיְבֵיכֶם אָז תִּשְׁבַּת הָאָרֶץ וְהִרְצָת אֶת־שַׁבְּתֹתֶיהָ: לה כָּל־יְמֵי הָשַּׁמָּה תִּשְׁבֹּת אֵת אֲשֶׁר לֹא־שָׁבְתָה בְּשַׁבְּתֹתֵיכֶם בְּשִׁבְתְּכֶם עָלֶיהָ:

---- אונקלוס ----

וּתְהֵי אַרְעֲכוֹן צָדְיָא וְקִרְוֵיכוֹן יְהוֹן חָרְבָּן: לד בְּכֵן תַּרְעֵי אַרְעָא יָת שְׁמִטָּהָא כֹּל יוֹמִין דִּי צָדְיָאת וְאַתּוּן בַּאֲרַע בַּעֲלֵי דְבָבֵיכוֹן בְּכֵן תַּשְׁמֵט אַרְעָא וְתַרְעֵי יָת שְׁמִטָּהָא: לה כָּל יוֹמִין דִּי צָדְיָא תַּשְׁמֵט יָת דִּי לָא שְׁמַטַת בִּשְׁמִטֵּיכוֹן כַּד הֲוֵיתוּן יָתְבִין עֲלָהּ:

---- רש"י ----

והיתה ארצכם שממה. שלא תמהרו לשוב לתוכה, ומתוך כך עריכם יהיו חרבות נראות לכם חרבות, שבשעה שאדם גולה מביתו ומכרמו ומעירו וסופו לחזור כאלו אין כרמו וביתו חרבים. כך שנויה בתורת כהנים: **(לד) אז תרצה.** תפיים

אֶת כַּעַס הַמָּקוֹם שֶׁכָּעַס עַל שְׁמִטּוֹתֶיהָ: **והרצת.** לַמֶּלֶךְ [נס"א למלאת] אֶת שַׁבְּתוֹתֶיהָ: **(לה) כל ימי השמה.** לְשׁוֹן הָעָשׂוֹת. ומ"ס דָּגֵשׁ בְּמָקוֹם כְּפַל שְׁמָמָה. **את אשר לא שבתה.** שִׁבְעִים שָׁנָה שֶׁל גָּלוּת בָּבֶל הֵן הָיוּ כְּנֶגֶד שְׁבִיעִיּוֹת שְׁנוֹת הַשְּׁמִטָּה

---- RASHI ELUCIDATED ----

□ וְהָיְתָה אַרְצְכֶם שְׁמָמָה — YOUR LAND WILL BE DESOLATE. שֶׁלֹּא תְמַהֲרוּ לָשׁוּב לְתוֹכָהּ — For you will not come back into it quickly, וּמִתּוֹךְ כָּךְ — and as a result עָרֵיכֶם יִהְיוּ חָרְבָּה — "your cities will be put to ruin"; i.e., חֲרֵבוֹת נִרְאוֹת לָכֶם — they will seem ruined to you. שֶׁבְּשָׁעָה שֶׁאָדָם גּוֹלֶה — For at a time that a person goes into exile מִבֵּיתוֹ — from his house וּמִכַּרְמוֹ — and from his vineyard, וּמֵעִירוֹ — and from his city, וְסוֹפוֹ לַחֲזוֹר — and he is destined to return, כְּאִלּוּ אֵין כַּרְמוֹ וּבֵיתוֹ חֲרֵבִים — it is as if his vineyard and his house are not ruined.[1] כָּךְ שְׁנוּיָה בְּתוֹרַת כֹּהֲנִים — Thus it has been taught in *Toras Kohanim*.[1]

34. אָז תִּרְצֶה — THEN [THE LAND] WILL APPEASE. תְּפַיֵּס אֶת כַּעַס הַמָּקוֹם — It will appease the anger of the Omnipresent, שֶׁכָּעַס עַל שְׁמִטּוֹתֶיהָ — Who was angered over its *shemittah* years.[2]

□ וְהִרְצָת — AND IT WILL MAKE . . . APPEASING [3] לַמֶּלֶךְ — to the King[3] אֶת שַׁבְּתֹתֶיהָ — its *shemittah* years.[4]

35. כָּל יְמֵי הָשַּׁמָּה — ALL THE DAYS OF ITS BEING DESOLATE. לְשׁוֹן הֵעָשׂוֹת — This is an expression of a passive infinitive.[5] וּמֵ"ם דָּגֵשׁ — The letter מ is marked with a *dagesh* בְּמָקוֹם כְּפֶל שְׁמָמָה — because it stands **in place of the double** מ of שְׁמָמָה.[6]

□ אֵת אֲשֶׁר לֹא שָׁבְתָה — WHATEVER IT DID NOT REST. שִׁבְעִים שָׁנָה — The seventy years שֶׁל גָּלוּת בָּבֶל — of the Babylonian exile[7] הֵן הָיוּ כְּנֶגֶד שִׁבְעִים שְׁנוֹת הַשְּׁמִטָּה — corresponded to the seventy years of

---

1. *Toras Kohanim, perek* 7:1.

2. The verse reads, "then the land will appease its *shemittah* years." But the *shemittah* years do not need appeasing. The object "the Omnipresent" is implicit in the verse. It means to say, "then the land will appease the Omnipresent for its *shemittah* years" (*Gur Aryeh*).

3. *Yosef Hallel* notes that the text of early printed editions of Rashi reads, לְמַלֹּאות אֶת שַׁבְּתֹתֶיהָ, "to compensate for its *shemittah* years," instead of לַמֶּלֶךְ אֶת שַׁבְּתֹתֶיהָ. Note, too, that the word לְמַלֹּאות is used in *II Chronicles* 36:21 with reference to compensating for *shemittah* years which were not kept.

4. וְהִרְצָת means "to give something an appeasing quality." Here, an implicit object need not be supplied, as was needed at the beginning of the verse; the object

of וְהִרְצָת is שַׁבְּתֹתֶיהָ, "its *shemittah* years." It will make the *shemittah* years appeasing to the King (*Gur Aryeh*).

5. Although הֵעָשׂוֹת is an infinitive in the *nifal*, while הָשַּׁמָּה is an infinitive in the *hofal*, they share in common the characteristic of being passive infinitives.

6. Both הָשַּׁמָּה ("being desolate") and שְׁמָמָה ("desolation") share the root שׁממ. The *dagesh* in the מ of הָשַּׁמָּה stands in place of the missing מ of the root.

7. That is, the seventy years between the First and Second *Beis HaMikdash*. Although the Babylonian domination ended and the Persian-Medean domination began at some time during this period, Rashi calls the entire period "the Babylonian exile" because it was the Babylonians who destroyed the *Beis HaMikdash* and ushered in this period of exile.

367 / VAYIKRA/LEVITICUS — PARASHAS BECHUKOSAI

ויובל שהיו בשנים שהכעיסו ישראל בארצם לפני המקום, ארבע מאות ושלשים שנה. שלש מאות ותשעים היו שני עוגם משנכנסו לארץ עד שגלו עשרת השבטים, ובני יהודה הכעיסו לפניו ארבעים שנה משגלו עשרת השבטים עד חרבות ירושלים. הוא שנאמר ביחזקאל ואתה שכב על צדך השמאלי וגו' וכלית את אלה וגו' ושכבת על צדך הימני וגו' ונשאת את עון בית יהודה ארבעים יום (יחזקאל ד:ד־ו) ונבואה זו נאמרה ליחזקאל בשנה החמישית

לגלות המלך יהויכין (שם א:ב) ועוד עשו שם שנים עד גלות צדקיהו הרי ארבעים ושש. ואם תאמר שנות מנשה חמשים וחמש היו (מלכים ב כא:א) מנשה עשה תשובה שלשים ושלש שנה, וכל שנות רשעו עשרים ושתים, כמו שאמרו באגדת חלק (סנהדרין קג.) ושל אמון שתים (מלכים ב כא:יט) ואחת עשרה ליהויקים (שם כג:לו) וכנגדן לצדקיהו (שם כד:יח). צא וחשוב לארבע מאות ושלשים ושש שנה שמיטין ויובלות שבהס, והס שש עשרה למאה,

--- RASHI ELUCIDATED ---

שֶׁהִבְעִיסוּ יִשְׂרָאֵל – that **וַיּוֹבֵל** – and *yovel* **שֶׁהָיוּ בַשָּׁנִים** – which took place in the years **יִשְׂרָאֵל** Israel brought about anger **בְּאַרְצָם** – in their land **לִפְנֵי הַמָּקוֹם** – before the Omnipresent, a total of **אַרְבַּע מֵאוֹת וּשְׁלֹשִׁים שָׁנָה** – four hundred and thirty years. **שְׁלֹשׁ מֵאוֹת וְתִשְׁעִים** – Three hundred and ninety **הָיוּ שְׁנֵי עֲוֹנָם** – were the years of their sinfulness **מִשֶּׁנִּכְנְסוּ לָאָרֶץ** – from when they entered the Land of Israel **עַד שֶׁגָּלוּ עֲשֶׂרֶת הַשְּׁבָטִים** – until the Ten Tribes went into exile;[1] **וּבְנֵי יְהוּדָה** – and the Children of the Tribe of Judah **הִכְעִיסוּ לְפָנָיו** – brought about anger before Him **אַרְבָּעִים שָׁנָה** – for forty years **מִשֶּׁגָּלוּ עֲשֶׂרֶת הַשְּׁבָטִים** – from the time that the Ten Tribes went into exile **עַד חָרְבוֹת יְרוּשָׁלַיִם** – until the destruction of Jerusalem.[2] **הוּא שֶׁנֶּאֱמַר בִּיחֶזְקֵאל** – This is what is referred to in *Ezekiel* in the verses, **"וְאַתָּה שְׁכַב עַל צִדְּךָ הַשְּׂמָאלִי וְגוֹמֵר** – "And you, lie on your left side, etc. **וְכִלִּיתָ אֶת אֵלֶּה** – You shall complete these **וְשָׁכַבְתָּ עַל צִדְּךָ הַיְמָנִי וְגוֹמֵר** – and you shall lie on your right side, etc., **וְנָשָׂאתָ אֶת עֲוֹן בֵּית יְהוּדָה** – and you shall bear the sin of the House of Judah **אַרְבָּעִים יוֹם"** – for forty days..."[3] **וּנְבוּאָה זוֹ** – This prophecy **נֶאֶמְרָה לִיחֶזְקֵאל** – was said to Ezekiel[4] **בַּשָּׁנָה הַחֲמִישִׁית לְגָלוּת הַמֶּלֶךְ יְהוֹיָכִין** – in the fifth year of the exile of King Jehoiachin.[4] **וְעוֹד עָשׂוּ שֵׁשׁ שָׁנִים** – And they spent another six years in the Land of Israel **עַד גָּלוּת צִדְקִיָּהוּ** – until the exile of Zedekiah, the last king of Judah; **הֲרֵי אַרְבָּעִים וָשֵׁשׁ** – see, now, that there were forty-six years of sinfulness during the period extending from the time of the exile of the Ten Tribes until the exile of the Tribe of Judah.

וְאִם תֹּאמַר – And if you will say, **שְׁנוֹת מְנַשֶּׁה** – the years of the reign of Manasseh, a wicked king who ruled over Judah after the exile of the Ten Tribes, **חֲמִשִּׁים וְחָמֵשׁ הָיוּ** – were fifty-five,[5] so how could there have been only forty years that Judah angered God after the exile of the Ten Tribes? **מְנַשֶּׁה עָשָׂה תְשׁוּבָה** – Manasseh was repentant **שְׁלֹשִׁים וְשָׁלֹשׁ שָׁנָה** – for thirty-three years, **וְכָל שְׁנוֹת רִשְׁעוֹ** – and all the years of his wickedness add up to only **עֶשְׂרִים וּשְׁתַּיִם** – twenty-two, **כְּמוֹ שֶׁאָמְרוּ** – as they said **בְּאַגָּדַת חֵלֶק** – in the aggadic section of *Cheilek*.[6] **וְשֶׁל אָמוֹן שְׁתַּיִם** – The years of the reign of Amon,[7] who followed Manasseh, were two; **וְאַחַת עֶשְׂרֵה לִיהוֹיָקִים** – there were eleven years of the reign of Jehoiakim,[8] who followed Amon; **וּכְנֶגְדָּן לְצִדְקִיָּהוּ** – and a corresponding number (eleven) for the reign of Zedekiah,[9] who followed Jehoiakim.[10] **צֵא וַחֲשׁוֹב** – Go and calculate **לְאַרְבַּע מֵאוֹת וּשְׁלֹשִׁים וָשֵׁשׁ שָׁנָה** – for four hundred and thirty-six years **שְׁמִטִּין וְיוֹבְלוֹת שֶׁבָּהֶם** – the *shemittah* and *yovel* years that are among them, **וְהֵם שֵׁשׁ עֶשְׂרֵה לְמֵאָה** – and they are sixteen per

---

1. There were 440 years from the time that the Israelites entered the Land of Israel until the completion of the *Beis HaMikdash*. The *Beis HaMikdash* stood for 410 years. The exile of the Ten Tribes took place more than forty years before the destruction of the *Beis HaMikdash*. Of the nearly eight hundred years before the exile of the Ten Tribes, Israel was sinful for three hundred and ninety (*Sefer Zikaron*).

2. The phrase חָרְבוֹת יְרוּשָׁלַיִם is taken from *Isaiah* 52:9 and *Daniel* 9:2.

3. *Ezekiel* 4:4-6. The verses read in full: "And you, lie on your left side, and put the sin of the House of Israel upon it; the number of days you will lie upon it, you will bear their sin. I have given you the years of their sin corresponding to the number of days — three hundred and ninety days; and you shall bear the sin of the House of Israel. You shall complete these and you

shall lie on your right side, a second time, and you shall bear the sin of the House of Judah for forty days, a day for a year, a day for a year, have I given you."

4. See *Ezekiel* 1:2.

5. See *II Kings* 21:1.

6. *Sanhedrin* 103a. The eleventh chapter of *Sanhedrin* is called חֵלֶק, *Cheilek*.

7. See *II Kings* 21:19.

8. See *II Kings* 23:36.

9. See *II Kings* 24:18.

10. There were three kings of Judah who ruled after the exile of the Ten Tribes whom Rashi does not mention: Josiah, because he was righteous (*II Kings* 22:1-2), and Jehoachaz (23:31) and Jehoiachin (24:8), because they ruled for only three months each (*Sefer Zikaron*).

36 The survivors among you — I will bring intimidation into their hearts in the lands of their foes; the sound of a rustling leaf will pursue them, and they will flee the flight of a sword, and they will fall, but without a pursuer.

לו וְהַנִּשְׁאָרִים בָּכֶם וְהֵבֵאתִי מֹרֶךְ בִּלְבָבָם בְּאַרְצֹת אֹיְבֵיהֶם וְרָדַף אֹתָם קוֹל עָלֶה נִדָּף וְנָסוּ מְנֻסַת־חֶרֶב וְנָפְלוּ וְאֵין רֹדֵף:

―――――― אונקלוס ――――――

לו וְדִישְׁתָּאֲרוּן בְּכוֹן וְאָעֵל תַּבְרָא בְּלִבְּהוֹן בְּאַרְעָתָא דְסָנְאֵיהוֹן וְיִרְדּוֹף יָתְהוֹן קָל טַרְפָּא דְשָׁקִיף וְיֵעַרְקוּן כַּד מֵעִירוּקִין מִן קֳדָם דְקָטְלִין בְּחַרְבָּא וְיִפְּלוּן וְלֵית דְרָדִיף:

―――――― רש"י ――――――

אַרְבַּע עֶשְׂרָה שְׁמִטִּין וּשְׁנֵי יוֹבְלוֹת, הֲרֵי לְאַרְבַּע מֵאוֹת שָׁנָה שִׁשִּׁים וְאַרְבַּע, לִשְׁלֹשִׁים וְשֵׁשׁ שָׁנָה חֲמֵשׁ שְׁמִטּוֹת, הֲרֵי שִׁבְעִים חָסֵר אֶחָת, וְעוֹד שָׁנָה יְתֵירָה שֶׁנִּכְנְסָה בַּשְּׁמִטָּה הַמַּשְׁלֶמֶת לְשִׁבְעִים [ס"א וְאוֹתוֹ יוֹבֵל שֶׁגָּלוּ שֶׁלֹא נִגְמַר בְּעֶוְנָם נֶחְשַׁב לָהֶם], וַעֲלֵיהֶם נִגְזַר שִׁבְעִים שָׁנָה שְׁלֵמִים. וְכֵן הוּא אוֹמֵר בְּדִבְרֵי הַיָּמִים הֵימִים עַד רָצְתָה הָאָרֶץ אֶת שַׁבְּתוֹתֶיהָ וגו' לְמַלֹּאות שִׁבְעִים שָׁנָה [דה"ב לו:כא]: **(לו) וְהֵבֵאתִי מֹרֶךְ.** פַּחַד וְרֹךְ לֵבָב [ת"א פְּרַק זָג.]. מ"ם שֶׁל מֹרֶךְ יְסוֹד נוֹפֵל הוּא, כְּמוֹ מ"ם שֶׁל מוֹעֵד וְשֶׁל מוֹקֵשׁ: **וְנָסוּ מְנֻסַת חָרֶב.** כְּאִלּוּ רוֹדְפִים הוֹרְגִים אוֹתָם: **עָלֶה נִדָּף.** שֶׁהָרוּחַ דּוֹחֲפוֹ [ס"א הוֹדְפוֹ] וּמַכֵּהוּ עַל עָלֶה אַחֵר

―――――― RASHI ELUCIDATED ――――――

וּשְׁנֵי יוֹבְלוֹת – **and two** *yovel* **years.**[1] אַרְבַּע עֶשְׂרָה שְׁמִטִּין – **fourteen** *shemittah* **years,** שִׁשִּׁים וְאַרְבַּע – **there are sixty-four** הֲרֵי לְאַרְבַּע מֵאוֹת שָׁנָה – **See, now, that for four hundred years** *shemittah* and *yovel* years. לִשְׁלֹשִׁים וָשֵׁשׁ שָׁנָה – **For the thirty-six years beyond the four hundred,** חָמֵשׁ שְׁמִטּוֹת – **there are five** *shemittah* **years.** הֲרֵי שִׁבְעִים חָסֵר אֶחָת – **See, now, that there is a total of seventy minus one.** וְעוֹד שָׁנָה יְתֵירָה – **And there is yet an additional year,** i.e., the four hundred and thirty-sixth year, which followed a *shemittah* year, שֶׁנִּכְנְסָה בַּשְּׁמִטָּה – **that enters the** *shemittah*, i.e., that began a new *shemittah* cycle, הַמַּשְׁלֶמֶת לְשִׁבְעִים – **which completes the total of seventy** *shemittah* and *yovel* years not kept.[2] וַעֲלֵיהֶם – **On their account** נִגְזַר – **there was decreed** שִׁבְעִים שָׁנָה שְׁלֵמִים – **seventy complete years** of exile. וְכֵן הוּא אוֹמֵר – **And so it says** בְּדִבְרֵי הַיָּמִים – **in** *Chronicles*, "עַד רָצְתָה הָאָרֶץ אֶת שַׁבְּתוֹתֶיהָ וגומר, – "**until the land has appeased its rest years, etc.** לְמַלֹּאות שִׁבְעִים שָׁנָה"[3] – **to compensate seventy years.**"[3]

36. וְהֵבֵאתִי מֹרֶךְ – **I WILL BRING INTIMIDATION.** מֹרֶךְ means פַּחַד – **fright** [4] וְרֹךְ לֵבָב – **and softness of the heart.**[4] מ"ם שֶׁל מֹרֶךְ – **The מ of** מֹרֶךְ יְסוֹד נוֹפֵל הוּא – **is an essential element which falls,** i.e., which does not appear in all forms of the word,[5] כְּמוֹ מ"ם שֶׁל מוֹעֵד – **like the מ of** מוֹעֵד, "**fixed time, festival,**" וְשֶׁל מוֹקֵשׁ – **and of** מוֹקֵשׁ, "**snare.**" ☐ וְנָסוּ מְנֻסַת חֶרֶב – **AND THEY WILL FLEE THE FLIGHT OF A SWORD.** כְּאִלּוּ רוֹדְפִים – **As if pursuers** הוֹרְגִים אוֹתָם – **are killing them.**[6] ☐ עָלֶה נִדָּף – **A RUSTLING LEAF.** שֶׁהָרוּחַ דּוֹחֲפוֹ [7] – **That the wind pushes it** וּמַכֵּהוּ עַל עָלֶה אַחֵר – **and**

---

1. Seven *shemittah* cycles cover a forty-nine-year period. The *yovel* year is not included in that count. Thus each fifty-year period contains seven *shemittah* years and one *yovel* year, a total of eight years (see *Rosh Hashanah* 9a with *Tosafos*, s.v., לאפוקי מדר״י; *Kesef Mishneh*, Hil. *Shemittah VeYovel* 10:3).

2. The 436th year was the first year of a *shemittah* cycle. The intent not to keep the *shemittah* year of the cycle which had begun counts as the seventieth *shemittah* not observed. Although God normally does not punish for an evil intention which is not carried out, this does not hold true for one who has repeatedly transgressed a particular sin (see statement of Ulla in *Kiddushin* 40a, and Rashi there, s.v. עולא אמר).

Some editions of Rashi read: וְאוֹתוֹ יוֹבֵל שֶׁגָּלוּ, "and that *yovel* [read, *shemittah*] in which they were exiled," שֶׁלֹא נִגְמַר בַּעֲוֹנָם, "which was not completed in their sin," נֶחְשַׁב לָהֶם, "is [nevertheless] counted for them."

3. II *Chronicles* 36:21.

4. *Toras Kohanim*, *perek* 7:3.

5. According to *Mesiach Ilmim* and *Be'er Rechovos*, Rashi is of the opinion that מֹרֶךְ is from the root רכך. When Rashi says that the מ is "an essential element," he does not mean that it is part of the root. Rather, he means that it is an essential part of the noun form, not a prefix. According to *Sefer Zikaron*, however, Rashi holds that the root of מֹרֶךְ is מרך. The term נִיטוּ נְעִמוּ (לִפְרָקִים), "an essential element which falls out (at times)," is a term coined by Rashi. It also appears in Rashi to *Genesis* 17:11, 49:10, *Exodus* 18:8, *Ezekiel* 21:20, *Psalms* 119:5.

6. Some editions read, כְּאִלּוּ הוֹרְגִים רוֹדְפִים אוֹתָם, "as if killers are pursuing them."

"The flight of a sword" cannot mean flight from an actual sword, for the verse concludes, "but without a pursuer." It means flight *as if* there were deadly pursuit (*Mizrachi*; *Sifsei Chachamim*). Had the verse meant that they would flee from an actual sword, it would have said, וְנָסוּ מֵחֶרֶב, "and they will flee from a sword" (*Be'er Yitzchak*).

7. Some editions read הוֹדְפוֹ, but the meaning is the same.

37 *They will stumble, each man over his brother as if from before a sword, but there is no pursuer; you will not have the power to withstand your foes.* **38** *You will become lost among the nations; the land of your enemies will consume you.*

לז וְכָשְׁלוּ אִישׁ־בְּאָחִיו כְּמִפְּנֵי־חֶרֶב וְרֹדֵף אָיִן וְלֹא־תִהְיֶה לָכֶם תְּקוּמָה לִפְנֵי אֹיְבֵיכֶם: לח וַאֲבַדְתֶּם בַּגּוֹיִם וְאָכְלָה אֶתְכֶם אֶרֶץ אֹיְבֵיכֶם:

— אונקלוס —

לז וְיִתַּקְלוּן גְּבַר בַּאֲחוּהִי כְּמִקֳדָם דְּקָטְלִין בְּחַרְבָּא וְרָדִיף לַיִת וְלָא תְּהֵי לְכוֹן תְּקוּמָה קֳדָם בַּעֲלֵי דְבָבֵיכוֹן: לח וְתִתְבַּדְרוּן בֵּינֵי עַמְמַיָּא וּתְגַמַּר יָתְכוֹן אֲרַע בַּעֲלֵי דְבָבֵיכוֹן:

— רש"י —

וּמַקְשְׁקֵשׁ וּמוֹצִיא קוֹל, וְכֵן תַּרְגּוּמוֹ קָל טַרְפָּא דְשָׁקִיף, לְשׁוֹן חֲבָטָה, כְּמוֹ שְׁדוּפוֹת קָדִים (בראשית מא:ו) שְׁקִיפָן קִדּוּם, וְהוּא לְשׁוֹן מַשְׁקוֹף (שמות יב:כב) מְקוֹם חֲבָטַת הַדֶּלֶת, וְכֵן תַּרְגּוּמוֹ שֶׁל חַבּוּרָה (שם כא:כה) מַשְׁקוֹפֵי: **(לז) וּבָשְׁלוּ אִישׁ בְּאָחִיו.** כְּשֶׁיִּרְצוּ לָנוּס יִכָּשְׁלוּ זֶה בָּזֶה כִּי יִבָּהֲלוּ לָרוּץ: **כְּמִפְּנֵי חָרֶב.** כְּאִלּוּ בּוֹרְחִים מִלִּפְנֵי הוֹרְגִים שֶׁיְּהֵא בִּלְבָבָם פַּחַד וְכָל שָׁעָה סְבוּרִים שֶׁאָדָם רוֹדְפָם. וּמִדְרָשׁוֹ (ת"כ שם ה. סנהדרין כז:) וְכָשְׁלוּ אִישׁ בְּאָחִיו [וס"א בִּשְׁבִיל אָחִיו] זֶה נִכְשָׁל בַּעֲוֹנוֹ שֶׁל זֶה שֶׁכָּל יִשְׂרָאֵל עֲרֵבִים זֶה לָזֶה [וס"א בָּזֶה]: **(לח) וַאֲבַדְתֶּם בַּגּוֹיִם.** כְּשֶׁתִּהְיוּ פְזוּרִים תִּהְיוּ אֲבוּדִים זֶה מִזֶּה: **וְאָכְלָה אֶתְכֶם.** אֵלּוּ הַמֵּתִים בַּגּוֹלָה:

— RASHI ELUCIDATED —

strikes it against another leaf, וּמְקַשְׁקֵשׁ – and it rattles, וּמוֹצִיא קוֹל – and produces a sound.[1] וְכֵן תַּרְגּוּמוֹ – And thus does *Targum Onkelos* render it, ״קָל טַרְפָּא דְשָׁקִיף״ – "the sound of a rustling leaf." דְּשָׁקִיף – לְשׁוֹן חֲבָטָה means "knocking," כְּמוֹ – like the phrase ״שְׁדוּפוֹת קָדִים״[2] – "beaten by the east wind." שְׁדוּפוֹת קָדִים which is rendered by *Targum Onkelos* as, ״שְׁקִיפָן קִדּוּם״ – וְהוּא לְשׁוֹן ״מַשְׁקוֹף״ And שְׁקִיפָן and דְּשָׁקִיף are related to מַשְׁקוֹף, "lintel,"[3] – מְקוֹם חֲבָטַת הַדֶּלֶת – the place where the door bangs. וְכֵן – Similarly,[4] תַּרְגּוּמוֹ שֶׁל חַבּוּרָה – *Targum Onkelos'* translation of "bruise"[4] ״מַשְׁקוֹפֵי״, – is, literally, "a knocking."[5]

37. וְכָשְׁלוּ אִישׁ בְּאָחִיו – THEY WILL STUMBLE, EACH MAN OVER HIS BROTHER. כְּשֶׁיִּרְצוּ לָנוּס – When they will run to escape,[6] יִכָּשְׁלוּ זֶה בָּזֶה – they will stumble over one another, כִּי יִבָּהֲלוּ לָרוּץ – because they will run confusedly.[7]

❑ כְּמִפְּנֵי חֶרֶב – AS IF FROM BEFORE A SWORD. כְּאִלּוּ בּוֹרְחִים – As if they are fleeing מִלִּפְנֵי הוֹרְגִים – from before killers, שֶׁיְּהֵא בִּלְבָבָם פַּחַד – for there will be fright in their heart, וְכָל שָׁעָה סְבוּרִים – and they are always under the impression שֶׁאָדָם רוֹדְפָם – that someone is pursuing them. וּמִדְרָשׁוֹ – And it is expounded as follows: ״וְכָשְׁלוּ אִישׁ בְּאָחִיו״,[8] – "They will stumble, each man over his brother,"[8] means זֶה נִכְשָׁל – one stumbles בַּעֲוֹנוֹ שֶׁל זֶה – through the sin of another, שֶׁכָּל יִשְׂרָאֵל – for all of Israel עֲרֵבִים זֶה לָזֶה – are guarantors for one another.[9]

38. וַאֲבַדְתֶּם בַּגּוֹיִם – YOU WILL BECOME LOST AMONG THE NATIONS. כְּשֶׁתִּהְיוּ פְזוּרִים – When you will be scattered, תִּהְיוּ אֲבוּדִים זֶה מִזֶּה – you will be lost from one another.[10]

❑ וְאָכְלָה אֶתְכֶם – [THE LAND OF YOUR ENEMIES] WILL CONSUME YOU. אֵלּוּ הַמֵּתִים בַּגּוֹלָה – These are the ones who die in the Diaspora.

---

1. נִדָּף means literally "pushed." But a leaf does not make a noise when it is pushed. Rashi explains that the verse refers to a leaf that is pushed against another, causing a rustling sound (*Mizrachi; Sifsei Chachamim*). He goes on to cite *Targum Onkelos* in support of this interpretation.
2. *Genesis* 41:6.
3. *Exodus* 12:22.
4. *Exodus* 21:25. See Rashi there.
5. That is, a place where the body has been bruised or "knocked."
6. Some editions read כְּשֶׁיִּרְצוּ לָנוּס, "when they desire to escape" (see *Yosef Hallel*).
7. אִישׁ בְּאָחִיו does not have the same meaning in our verse as it does in 25:46, וּבְאַחֵיכֶם בְּנֵי יִשְׂרָאֵל אִישׁ בְּאָחִיו לֹא תִרְדֶּה בּוֹ בְּפֶרֶךְ, "But with your brethren, the Children of Israel — a man with his brother — you shall not subjugate him

through hard labor." There, there was not a mutual relationship between "a man" and "his brother." A man was subjugating, and "his brother" was being subjugated. Here, however, אִישׁ בְּאָחִיו implies mutuality. The verse does not mean that one man will stumble over another who remains firm upright. It means that both will stumble over one another.
8. Some early texts read וְכָשְׁלוּ אִישׁ בִּשְׁבִיל אָחִיו, "they will stumble, each man because of his brother." If so, Rashi is not citing the words of the verse, rather he is interpreting the ב prefix of בְּאָחִיו as a contraction of בִּשְׁבִיל, "because of." Other places where Rashi interprets the ב prefix in this way include: *Genesis* 1:1, 6:3, 39:22, 49:44; *Exodus* 10:12; and *Numbers* 14:11.
9. *Toras Kohanim, perek* 7:5; *Sanhedrin* 27b. Some texts read בָּזֶה. The meaning, however, is unchanged.
10. It does not mean that they will perish, for in verse 44

39 Because of their iniquity, your remnant will disintegrate in the lands of your foes; and because the sins of their forefathers are with them as well, they will disintegrate. **40** Then they will confess their sin and the sin of their forefathers, for the treachery with which they betrayed Me, and also for having behaved toward Me with casualness. **41** I, too, will behave toward them with casualness and I will bring them in the land of

לט וְהַנִּשְׁאָרִים בָּכֶם יִמַּקּוּ בַּעֲוֹנָם בְּאַרְצֹת אֹיְבֵיכֶם וְאַף בַּעֲוֹנֹת אֲבֹתָם אִתָּם יִמָּקּוּ: מ וְהִתְוַדּוּ אֶת־עֲוֹנָם וְאֶת־עֲוֹן אֲבֹתָם בְּמַעֲלָם אֲשֶׁר מָעֲלוּ־בִי וְאַף אֲשֶׁר־הָלְכוּ עִמִּי בְּקֶרִי: מא אַף־אֲנִי אֵלֵךְ עִמָּם בְּקֶרִי וְהֵבֵאתִי אֹתָם בְּאֶרֶץ

──────── אונקלוס ────────

לט וּדְיִשְׁתָּאֲרוּן בְּכוֹן יִתְּמְסוּן בְּחוֹבֵיהוֹן בְּאַרְעֲתָא דְּבַעֲלֵי דְבָבֵיכוֹן וְאַף בְּחוֹבֵי אֲבָהָתְהוֹן בִּישַׁיָּא דַּאֲחִידִין בִּידֵיהוֹן יִתְּמְסוּן: מ וִיוַדּוּן יָת חוֹבֵיהוֹן וְיָת חוֹבֵי אֲבָהָתְהוֹן בְּשִׁקְרוּתְהוֹן דְּשַׁקַּרוּ בְמֵימְרִי וְאַף דְּהַלִּיכוּ קֳדָמַי בְּקַשְׁיוּ: מא אַף אֲנָא אֲהַךְ עִמְּהוֹן בְּקַשְׁיוּ וְאָעֵל יָתְהוֹן בַּאֲרַע

──────── רש"י ────────

(לט) בעונת אבותם אתם. [כשעונות אבותם אתם] כשאוחזים מעשה אבותיהם בידיהם (ת"כ פרק ח:ב): **ימקו.** לשון המסה כמו ימסו וכמוהו תמקנה בחוריהן (זכריה יד:יב), נמקו חבורותי (תהלים לח:ו): **(מא) והבאתי אתם.** אני בעצמי אביאם. זו מדה טובה לישראל, שלא יהיו אומרים הואיל וגלינו בין האומות נעשה כמעשיהם, אני איני מניחם אלא מעמיד אני את נביאי ומחזירן לתחת כנפי, שנאמר והעולה על רוחכם היו לא תהיה וגו' חי אני וגו' אם לא ביד חזקה וגו' (יחזקאל כ:לב-לג; ת"כ שם ה):

──────── RASHI ELUCIDATED ────────

39. בַּעֲוֹנֹת אֲבֹתָם — **BECAUSE THE SINS OF THEIR FOREFATHERS ARE WITH THEM.** {כְּשֶׁעֲוֹנוֹת אֲבוֹתָם אִתָּם — **When the sins of their forefathers are with them,**}[1] כְּשֶׁאוֹחֲזִים מַעֲשֵׂה אֲבוֹתֵיהֶם בִּידֵיהֶם — **when they hold the action of their forefathers in their hand,** i.e., when they continue the sinful conduct of their forefathers.[1]

□ יִמַּקּוּ — **WILL DISINTEGRATE.** לְשׁוֹן הַמַּסָּה — **This means "dissolving."** כְּמוֹ יִמַּסּוּ — **It has the same meaning as, "will dissolve."** וְכָמוֹהוּ — **Like it is** תִּמַּקְנָה בְחֹרֵיהֶן,[2] — ,,**תִּמַּקְנָה בְחֹרֵיהֶן** — "will dissolve in their sockets,"**[2]** נָמַקּוּ חַבּוּרֹתָי,, — and נָמַקּוּ in, "my wounds moldered."[3]

41. וְהֵבֵאתִי אֹתָם — **AND I WILL BRING THEM.** אֲנִי בְעַצְמִי — **I, Myself,** אֲבִיאָם — **will bring them.** זוֹ מִדָּה טוֹבָה — **This is a good measure,** i.e., a matter of benefit, לְיִשְׂרָאֵל — **for Israel;**[4] שֶׁלֹּא יִהְיוּ אוֹמְרִים — **that they will not say,** הוֹאִיל וְגָלִינוּ — "**Since we have gone into exile** בֵּין הָאֻמּוֹת — **among the nations,** נַעֲשֶׂה כְּמַעֲשֵׂיהֶם — **let us do like their acts,** i.e., mimic their behavior." אֲנִי אֵינִי מַנִּיחָם — **I shall not let them** do this. אֶלָּא — **Rather,** מַעֲמִיד אֲנִי אֶת נְבִיאַי — **I shall raise up My prophets** וּמַחֲזִירָן — **and bring them back** לְתַחַת כְּנָפַי — **under My wings,**[5] שֶׁנֶּאֱמַר — **as it says,** ,,וְהָעֹלָה עַל רוּחֲכֶם — "**That which enters your mind** הָיוֹ לֹא תִהְיֶה וְגוֹמֵר — **will not be, etc.,** חַי אֲנִי וְגוֹמֵר — **as I live, etc.,** אִם לֹא בְּיָד חֲזָקָה וְגוֹמֵר,, — **if not by a strong hand, etc."**[6,7]

below, God promises that He will not reject Israel forever (*Mizrachi; Sifsei Chachamim*).

1. *Toras Kohanim, perek* 8:2. God does not punish children for the sins of the fathers. As it says, "Fathers shall not be put to death because of children, and children shall not be put to death because of fathers etc." (*Deuteronomy* 24:16). The apparently superfluous אִתָּם, "with them," of our verse teaches us that the sin of the fathers is taken into consideration against the children only when the children maintain the fathers' sinful behavior (*Mizrachi; Sifsei Chachamim; Korban Aharon*).

2. *Zechariah* 14:12.

3. *Psalms* 38:6.

4. The verse seems to prophesy a punishment of exile for Israel. But the preceding verse has said that Israel will confess their sin. It thus stands to reason that our verse refers to a turn for the better for them. "I will bring them" is therefore interpreted as "I will bring them to Me." This is supported by the verse's use of בְּאֶרֶץ אֹיְבֵיהֶם, "*in* the land of their enemies," rather than אֶל אֶרֶץ אֹיְבֵיהֶם, "*to* the land of their enemies." "*To* the land of their enemies" would express being brought in exile to the land of the enemies. "*In* the land of their enemies" expresses a "bringing" which takes place after they are already exiled in the land of the enemies (*Korban Aharon*).

5. Alternatively, כְּנָפַי means "the corners of My coat." See Rashi to *Sotah* 13b, s.v., בכנפי השכינה, and to *Isaiah* 30:20, s.v., וְלֹא יִכָּנֵף.

6. *Ezekiel* 20:32-33. The verses read in full, "That which enters your mind will not be, that which you say, 'We will be like the nations, like the families of the earth, to serve wood and stone.' As I live, says my Lord HASHEM/ELOHIM, if not by a strong hand, and an outstretched arm, and with wrath outpoured shall I rule over you!"

7. *Toras Kohanim, perek* 8:5.

their enemies — perhaps then their unfeeling heart will be humbled and then they will gain appeasement for their sin. **⁴²** *I will remember My covenant with Jacob and also My covenant*

אֹיְבֵיהֶם אוֹ־אָז יִכָּנַע לְבָבָם הֶעָרֵל וְאָז יִרְצוּ אֶת־עֲוֹנָם: מב וְזָכַרְתִּי אֶת־ בְּרִיתִי יַעֲקוֹב וְאַף אֶת־בְּרִיתִי

―――――― אונקלוס ――――――

בַּעֲלֵי דְבָבֵיהוֹן אוֹ בְכֵן יִתְּבַר לִבְּהוֹן טַפְּשָׁא וּבְכֵן יִרְעוּן יָת חוֹבֵיהוֹן: מב וְדָכִירְנָא יָת קְיָמִי דְעִם יַעֲקֹב וְאַף יָת קְיָמִי דְעִם

―――――― רש"י ――――――

או אז יכנע. כְּמוֹ אוֹ נוֹדַע כִּי שׁוֹר נַגָּח הוּא (שמות כא:לו) אִם אָז יִכָּנַע. [לָשׁוֹן אַחֵר,] אוּלַי, שֶׁמָּא אָז יִכָּנַע לְבָבָם וְגוֹ'. **ואז ירצו את עונם.** יְכַפְּרוּ עַל עֲווֹנָם בְּיִסּוּרֵיהֶם: **(מב) וזכרתי את בריתי יעקוב.** בַּחֲמִשָּׁה מְקוֹמוֹת נִכְתַּב מָלֵא, וְאֵלִיָּהוּ חָסֵר בַּחֲמִשָּׁה מְקוֹמוֹת. יַעֲקֹב נָטַל אוֹת

מִשְּׁמוֹ שֶׁל אֵלִיָּהוּ עֵרָבוֹן שֶׁיָּבוֹא וִיבַשֵּׂר גְּאֻלַּת בָּנָיו: **וזברתי את בריתי יעקוב.** לָמָּה נִמְנוּ אֲחוֹרַנִּית, כְּלוֹמַר כְּדַאי הוּא יַעֲקֹב הַקָּטֹן לְכָךְ, וְאִם אֵינוֹ כְדַאי הֲרֵי יִצְחָק עִמּוֹ, וְאִם אֵינוֹ כְדַאי הֲרֵי אַבְרָהָם עִמּוֹ שֶׁהוּא כְדַאי (ת"כ שָׁם ז). וְלָמָּה לֹא נֶאֶמְרָה זְכִירָה בְּיִצְחָק, אֶלָּא אֶפְרוֹ שֶׁל יִצְחָק

―――――― RASHI ELUCIDATED ――――――

☐ אוֹ אָז יִכָּנַע — PERHAPS THEN [THEIR UNFEELING HEART] WILL BE HUMBLED. כְּמוֹ — אוֹ is used here as it is in, אוֹ נוֹדַע כִּי שׁוֹר נַגָּח הוּא[1] — "if it was known that it was a goring ox."[1] אוֹ אָז יִכָּנַע — אִם אָז יִכָּנַע is the equivalent of אִם אָז יִכָּנַע.[2] אוּלַי — אִם is used in the sense of **maybe.** שֶׁמָּא אָז יִכָּנַע לְבָבָם, וְגוֹמֵר — The phrase means, **"perhaps their** [unfeeling] **heart will be humbled, etc."**

☐ וְאָז יִרְצוּ אֶת עֲוֹנָם — AND THEN THEY WILL GAIN APPEASEMENT FOR THEIR SIN. יְכַפְּרוּ עַל עֲווֹנָם — **They will atone for their sin** בְּיִסּוּרֵיהֶם — **through their sufferings.**

42. וְזָכַרְתִּי אֶת בְּרִיתִי יַעֲקוֹב — I WILL REMEMBER MY COVENANT WITH JACOB. בַּחֲמִשָּׁה מְקוֹמוֹת — **In five places** נִכְתָּב מָלֵא — [the name יַעֲקוֹב] is written in **full,** i.e., spelled with the letter ו,[3] וְאֵלִיָּהוּ חָסֵר — and אֵלִיָּהוּ is written with its ו missing בַּחֲמִשָּׁה מְקוֹמוֹת — **in five places.**[4] יַעֲקֹב נָטַל אוֹת — **Jacob took a letter** מִשְּׁמוֹ שֶׁל אֵלִיָּהוּ — **from the name of Elijah** עֵרָבוֹן — **as security,**[5] שֶׁיָּבוֹא — **so that [Elijah] will come** וִיבַשֵּׂר — **and herald** גְּאֻלַּת בָּנָיו — **the redemption of [Jacob's] children.**

☐ וְזָכַרְתִּי אֶת בְּרִיתִי יַעֲקוֹב — I WILL REMEMBER MY COVENANT WITH JACOB. לָמָּה נִמְנוּ אֲחוֹרַנִּית — **Why were [the Patriarchs] listed in reverse order** in our verse?[6] כְּלוֹמַר — **As if to say,** כְּדַאי הוּא יַעֲקֹב הַקָּטֹן לְכָךְ — **Jacob, the youngest** of the Patriarchs, **is** alone **sufficient for this,** i.e., that Israel should be redeemed through his merit, וְאִם אֵינוֹ כְדַאי — **and if he is not sufficient,** הֲרֵי יִצְחָק עִמּוֹ — **see now, that Isaac is with him,** וְאִם אֵינוֹ כְדַאי — **and if he is not sufficient,** הֲרֵי אַבְרָהָם עִמּוֹ — **see now, that Abraham is with him,** שֶׁהוּא כְדַאי[7] — **for he is sufficient.**[7]

וְלָמָּה לֹא נֶאֶמְרָה זְכִירָה בְּיִצְחָק — Why was "remembering" not stated by the verse **with reference to Isaac?**[8] אֶלָּא — But "remembering" is not necessary in the case of Isaac, אֶפְרוֹ שֶׁל יִצְחָק — because the

―――――――――――――――――

1. *Exodus* 21:36.

2. In many editions of Rashi, the words לָשׁוֹן אַחֵר, "alternatively," appear at this point. This implies that Rashi presents אוּלַי, "maybe," as a definition of אוֹ in contrast to אִם, "if," which he gave as a definition at the beginning of his comment. If Rashi brings אוּלַי in contrast to אִם, he understands אִם as the conditional "if." *Mizrachi* notes that this text is problematic, for then, according to his first explanation, Rashi understands the verse as saying, "and I will bring them [under My wings] in the land of their enemies if their unfeeling heart will be humbled." This implies that God's bringing them under His wings is contingent upon their humbling themselves. But the verse Rashi cited in support of his interpretation of "I will bring them" as referring to bringing them under His wings says that He will do so "with a strong hand," whether they humble themselves or not. Our text which omits לָשׁוֹן אַחֵר follows the first printed edition of Rashi. According to this version Rashi brings אוּלַי not as a contrast to אִם, but as its explanation, to say that אוֹ here is used as the equivalent

of אִם but in the sense of "perhaps" rather than the sense of "on the condition that." See *Yosef Hallel*.

3. In addition to our verse, *Jeremiah* 30:18, 33:26, 46:27, and 51:19.

4. *II Kings* 1:3, 1:4, 1:8, 1:12, and *Malachi* 3:23.

5. The giving of a security was sealed by a handshake, as seen from *Proverbs* 6:1,3. The letter ו resembles a finger. Five of them represent the hand which finalizes the giving of security. By taking the ו from Elijah five times, Jacob took his "hand" as a security to ensure that he would redeem his children. This is also alluded to through the fact that the numerical value of ו is six. Five times six equals thirty. The Mishnah in *Oholos* 1:8 says that the hand is composed of thirty segments (*Gur Aryeh*).

6. This is the only place in Scripture that the Patriarchs are listed in reverse order.

7. *Toras Kohanim, perek* 8:6 (7).

8. As it says וְזָכַרְתִּי in conjunction with Jacob, and אֶזְכֹּר in conjunction with Abraham.

with Isaac, and also My covenant with Abraham will I remember, and I will remember the Land. ⁴³ The Land will be bereft of them; and it will be appeased for its shemittah years having become desolate of them; and they must gain appeasement for their iniquity; as retribution, indeed, as retribution for having rejected My ordinances and because their spirit rejected My decrees.

⁴⁴ But also, even though there is this, while they are in the land of their enemies, I will not have been abhorred by them nor will I have rejected them to obliterate them, to annul My covenant with them — for I am Hashem, their God. ⁴⁵ I will remember for them the covenant of the forebears, those whom I have taken out of the land of Egypt before the eyes of the nations, to be God unto them — I am Hashem.

⁴⁶ These are the decrees, the ordinances,

יִצְחָק וְאַף אֶת־בְּרִיתִי אַבְרָהָם מג אֶזְכֹּר וְהָאָרֶץ אֶזְכֹּר: וְהָאָרֶץ תֵּעָזֵב מֵהֶם וְתִרֶץ אֶת־שַׁבְּתֹתֶיהָ בָּהְשַׁמָּה מֵהֶם וְהֵם יִרְצוּ אֶת־עֲוֹנָם יַעַן וּבְיַעַן בְּמִשְׁפָּטַי מָאָסוּ מד וְאֶת־חֻקֹּתַי גָּעֲלָה נַפְשָׁם: וְאַף גַּם־זֹאת בִּהְיוֹתָם בְּאֶרֶץ אֹיְבֵיהֶם לֹא־מְאַסְתִּים וְלֹא־גְעַלְתִּים לְכַלֹּתָם לְהָפֵר בְּרִיתִי אִתָּם כִּי מה אֲנִי יהוה אֱלֹהֵיהֶם: וְזָכַרְתִּי לָהֶם בְּרִית רִאשֹׁנִים אֲשֶׁר הוֹצֵאתִי־אֹתָם מֵאֶרֶץ מִצְרַיִם לְעֵינֵי הַגּוֹיִם לִהְיוֹת לָהֶם לֵאלֹהִים אֲנִי מו יהוה: אֵלֶּה הַחֻקִּים וְהַמִּשְׁפָּטִים

───────── אונקלוס ─────────

יִצְחָק וְאַף יָת קְיָמִי דְּעִם אַבְרָהָם אֲנָא דְכִיר: מג וְאַרְעָא תִתְרְטֵשׁ מִנְּהוֹן וְתִרְעֵי יָת שְׁמִטָּהָא בִּדְצַדִּיאַת מִנְּהוֹן וְאִנּוּן יְרַעוּן יָת חוֹבֵיהוֹן לְנָטִיל חֲלַף בְּרַכַן אִיתַי עֲלֵיהוֹן לִדְדִינֵי קָצוּ וְיָת קְיָמֵי רַחֲקַת נַפְשְׁהוֹן: מד וְאַף בְּרַם (בְּ)דָא בְמֶהֱוֵיהוֹן בַּאֲרַע בַּעֲלֵי דְבָבֵיהוֹן לָא אַרְטַשְׁנּוּן וְלָא אַרְחֵקְנּוּן לְשֵׁיצָיוּתְהוֹן לְאַשְׁנָאָה קְיָמִי עִמְּהוֹן אֲרֵי אֲנָא יְיָ אֱלָהֲהוֹן: מה וּדְכִירְנָא לְהוֹן קְיָם קַדְמָאֵי דִּי אַפֵּיקִת יָתְהוֹן מֵאַרְעָא דְמִצְרַיִם לְעֵינֵי עַמְמַיָּא לְמֶהֱוֵי לְהוֹן לֶאֱלָהּ אֲנָא יְיָ: מו אִלֵּין קְיָמַיָּא וְדִינַיָּא

───────── רש״י ─────────

נִרְאֶה לְפָנַי לִבּוֹר וּמוּנָח עַל הַמִּזְבֵּחַ (שם ח): (מג) יַעַן וּבְיַעַן. גְּמוּל וּבִגְמוּל אֲשֶׁר בְּמִשְׁפָּטַי מָאָסוּ: (מד) וְאַף גַּם זֹאת. וְאַף אֲפִי אֲנִי עוֹשֶׂה עִמָּהֶם זֹאת הַפּוּרְעָנוּת אֲשֶׁר אָמַרְתִּי, בִּהְיוֹתָם בְּאֶרֶץ אוֹיְבֵיהֶם לֹא אֶמְאָסֵם לְכַלּוֹתָם וּלְהָפֵר בְּרִיתִי אֲשֶׁר אִתָּם: (מה) בְּרִית רִאשֹׁנִים. שֶׁל שְׁבָטִים (ת״כ שם יב):

───────── RASHI ELUCIDATED ─────────

ashes of Isaac[1] – נִרְאֶה לְפָנַי – appear before Me, צָבוּר – gathered up,[2] וּמֻנָּח עַל הַמִּזְבֵּחַ – and placed on the *Mizbe'ach*.[2]

43. יַעַן וּבְיַעַן – AS RETRIBUTION, INDEED, AS RETRIBUTION. גְּמוּל וּבִגְמוּל – In compensation, indeed, in compensation אֲשֶׁר בְּמִשְׁפָּטַי מָאָסוּ – for having rejected My ordinances.

44. וְאַף גַּם זֹאת – BUT ALSO, EVEN THOUGH [THERE IS] THIS. וְאַף – But also, אֲפִילוּ אֲנִי עוֹשֶׂה עִמָּהֶם – even though I do to them[3] זֹאת הַפּוּרְעָנוּת – this punishment אֲשֶׁר אָמַרְתִּי – that I have said, "בִּהְיוֹתָם בְּאֶרֶץ אֹיְבֵיהֶם" – "while they are in the land of their enemies," לֹא אֶמְאָסֵם – I will not abhor them, לְכַלּוֹתָם – to the point of obliterating them וּלְהָפֵר בְּרִיתִי אֲשֶׁר אִתָּם – and annulling My covenant that is with them.

45. בְּרִית רִאשֹׁנִים – THE COVENANT OF THE FOREBEARS, שֶׁל שְׁבָטִים[4] – of the Tribes.[4]

---

1. This refers either to the ashes of the ram which was offered in place of Isaac (see *Genesis* 22:13), or the ashes which Abraham envisioned as the result of the burning of Isaac's slaughtered corpse as a burnt-offering (*Maharsha* to *Berachos* 62b).

2. *Toras Kohanim, perek* 8:7 (8).

3. וְאַף גַּם seems redundant, because both אַף and גַּם usually mean "also." Rashi explains that our verse uses it as "but also, even though" (*Lifshuto shel Rashi*). He goes on to explain what "this" of the verse refers to.

4. *Toras Kohanim, perek* 8:10 (11,12). The "forebears" cannot refer to the Patriarchs, for the covenants with them have already been mentioned in verse 42. Furthermore, the verse says that the "forebears" were taken out of the land of Egypt. This cannot apply to the Patriarchs, for Isaac was never in Egypt or anywhere else outside of Canaan. Accordingly, the "forebears" are the Israelite tribes that went out of Egypt (*Sefer Zikaron*).

וְהַתּוֹרֹת֙ אֲשֶׁ֣ר נָתַ֣ן יהו֔ה בֵּינ֕וֹ וּבֵ֖ין בְּנֵ֣י יִשְׂרָאֵ֑ל בְּהַ֥ר סִינַ֖י בְּיַד־מֹשֶֽׁה׃
כז א וַיְדַבֵּ֥ר יהו֖ה אֶל־מֹשֶׁ֥ה לֵּאמֹֽר׃ ב דַּבֵּ֞ר אֶל־בְּנֵ֤י יִשְׂרָאֵל֙ וְאָמַרְתָּ֣ אֲלֵהֶ֔ם אִ֕ישׁ כִּ֥י יַפְלִ֖א נֶ֑דֶר בְּעֶרְכְּךָ֥ נְפָשֹׁ֖ת לַיהוָֽה׃ ג וְהָיָ֤ה עֶרְכְּךָ֙ הַזָּכָ֔ר מִבֶּן֙ עֶשְׂרִ֣ים שָׁנָ֔ה וְעַ֖ד בֶּן־שִׁשִּׁ֣ים שָׁנָ֑ה וְהָיָ֣ה עֶרְכְּךָ֗ חֲמִשִּׁ֛ים שֶׁ֥קֶל כֶּ֖סֶף בְּשֶׁ֥קֶל הַקֹּֽדֶשׁ׃ ד וְאִ֣ם

and the Torahs that HASHEM gave, between Himself and the Children of Israel, at Mount Sinai, through Moses.

27 [1] HASHEM spoke to Moses, saying: [2] Speak to the Children of Israel and say to them: When a man will express a vow to HASHEM regarding a valuation of souls, [3] the valuation of a male shall be: for someone twenty years of age to sixty years of age, the valuation shall be fifty silver shekels, of the sacred shekel. [4] If

---
אונקלוס

וְאוֹרַיְתָא דִּי יְהַב יְיָ בֵּין מֵימְרֵהּ וּבֵין בְּנֵי יִשְׂרָאֵל בְּטוּרָא דְסִינַי בִּידָא דְמֹשֶׁה: א וּמַלִּיל יְיָ עִם מֹשֶׁה לְמֵימָר: ב מַלֵּל עִם בְּנֵי יִשְׂרָאֵל וְתֵימַר לְהוֹן גְּבַר אֲרֵי יְפָרֵשׁ נְדַר בְּפֻרְסָנֵהּ נַפְשָׁתָא קֳדָם יְיָ: ג וִיהֵי פֻרְסָנָהּ דְכוּרָא מִבַּר עַסְרִין שְׁנִין וְעַד בַּר שִׁתִּין שְׁנִין וִיהֵי פֻרְסָנֵהּ חַמְשִׁין סִלְעִין דִּכְסַף בְּסִלְעֵי קוּדְשָׁא: ד וְאִם

רש"י

(מו) **וְהַתּוֹרֹת.** אַחַת בִּכְתָב וְאַחַת בְּעַל פֶּה מַגִּיד שֶׁכֻּלָּם נִתְּנוּ לְמֹשֶׁה בְּסִינַי (שם יג): (ב) **כִּי יַפְלִא.** יְפָרֵשׁ בְּפִיו: **בְּעֶרְכְּךָ נְפָשֹׁת.** לִתֵּן עֵרֶךְ נַפְשׁוֹ, לוֹמַר עֵרֶךְ דָּבָר שֶׁנַּפְשׁוֹ תְּלוּיָה בּוֹ עָלַי (שם פרשתא ג:ו; ערכין ד.): (ג) **וְהָיָה עֶרְכְּךָ וְגוּ׳.** אֵין עֵרֶךְ זֶה לְשׁוֹן דָּמִים, אֶלָּא בֵּין שֶׁהוּא יָקָר בֵּין שֶׁהוּא זוֹל אֵין עֶרְכּוֹ אֶלָּא כְּפִי שָׁנָיו הוּא הָעֵרֶךְ הַקָּצוּב עָלָיו בְּפָרָשָׁה זוֹ: **עֶרְכְּךָ.** כְּמוֹ עֵרֶךְ, וְכֶפֶל הַכַּפִּי״ן

RASHI ELUCIDATED

46. וְהַתּוֹרֹת — AND THE TORAHS. The plural word "Torahs" refers to the two parts of the Torah, אַחַת בִּכְתָב — one written,[1] וְאַחַת בְּעַל פֶּה — and one oral.[2] מַגִּיד — [The verse] tells us שֶׁכֻּלָּם נִתְּנוּ לְמֹשֶׁה — that both of them were given to Moses בְּסִינַי[3] — on Sinai.[3]

27.

2. כִּי יַפְלִא — WHEN [A MAN] WILL EXPRESS. יְפָרֵשׁ בְּפִיו — יַפְלִא means express orally.[4]

□ בְּעֶרְכְּךָ נְפָשֹׁת — REGARDING A VALUATION OF SOULS. לִתֵּן — To give to the *Beis HaMikdash* עֵרֶךְ — נְפָשׁוֹת — the value of souls,[5] לוֹמַר — by saying, עֵרֶךְ דָּבָר שֶׁנַּפְשׁוֹ תְּלוּיָה בּוֹ עָלַי — "The valuation of something" — i.e., a part of the body, upon which life depends "is incumbent upon me to donate to the *Beis HaMikdash*."[6]

3. וְהָיָה עֶרְכְּךָ וְגוּמֵר — THE VALUATION [OF A MALE] SHALL BE, ETC. אֵין עֵרֶךְ זֶה לְשׁוֹן דָּמִים — This "valuation" does not mean market value as a slave, אֶלָּא — Rather, בֵּין שֶׁהוּא יָקָר — whether [the one whose valuation is being pledged] is expensive, i.e., would fetch a high price if sold as a slave, בֵּין שֶׁהוּא זוֹל — or whether he is cheap, i.e., he would fetch a low price, כְּפִי שָׁנָיו — based on his age הוּא הָעֵרֶךְ הַקָּצוּב עָלָיו — is the valuation that is fixed for him בְּפָרָשָׁה זוֹ — in this section of the Torah.

□ עֶרְכְּךָ — VALUATION. כְּמוֹ עֵרֶךְ — This has the same meaning as עֵרֶךְ, without the ךְ suffix. וְכֶפֶל הַכַּפִּי״ן

---

1. That is, the Written Torah, or Scriptures.
2. That is, the Oral Torah, or Talmud, which explains the Scriptures.
3. *Toras Kohanim*, *perek* 8:11 (12,13).
4. See Rashi to *Chagigah* 10a, s.v., אחת הפלאה לאיסר. The vowelization יַפְלִא follows most early printed editions. *Sefer Zikaron* however, follows the Zamora edition which reads, יַפְרִישׁ בְּפִיו, "set aside orally," or "designate." Although our verse does not speak of setting aside a particular object, "designate," is nonetheless applicable for it does not necessarily connote the designation of a specific object; it can apply to vows in general (*Sefer Zikaron*).

5. The verse speaks of "a vow regarding a valuation of souls," but does not tell us what obligation is undertaken through the vow. Rashi explains that "to give" is implicit in the verse (*Mizrachi*).
6. *Toras Kohanim*, *parshasa* 3:6; *Arachin* 4a. It is clear from our passage that we are dealing with the valuation of people. Our verse uses "souls" to teach us that not only is one obligated to pay when he pledges the valuation of an individual, he is obligated to pay even when he pledges the valuation of a vital organ of an individual. If, however, he pledges the valuation of a non-vital organ or limb, such as an arm or a leg, he is exempt from any payment (*Maskil LeDavid*).

נְקֵבָה הִוא וְהָיָה עֶרְכְּךָ שְׁלֹשִׁים שָׁקֶל: הוְאִם מִבֶּן־חָמֵשׁ שָׁנִים וְעַד בֶּן־עֶשְׂרִים שָׁנָה וְהָיָה עֶרְכְּךָ הַזָּכָר עֶשְׂרִים שְׁקָלִים וְלַנְּקֵבָה עֲשֶׂרֶת שְׁקָלִים: וּוְאִם מִבֶּן־חֹדֶשׁ וְעַד בֶּן־חָמֵשׁ שָׁנִים וְהָיָה עֶרְכְּךָ הַזָּכָר חֲמִשָּׁה שְׁקָלִים כָּסֶף וְלַנְּקֵבָה עֶרְכְּךָ שְׁלֹשֶׁת שְׁקָלִים כָּסֶף: זוְאִם מִבֶּן־שִׁשִּׁים שָׁנָה וָמַעְלָה אִם־זָכָר וְהָיָה עֶרְכְּךָ חֲמִשָּׁה עָשָׂר שָׁקֶל וְלַנְּקֵבָה עֲשָׂרָה שְׁקָלִים: חוְאִם־מָךְ הוּא

she is female, the valuation shall be thirty shekels. ⁵ *And if from five years of age to twenty years of age, the valuation of a male shall be twenty shekels and of a female ten shekels.* ⁶ *And if from one month of age to five years of age, the valuation of a male shall be five silver shekels; and for a female, the valuation shall be three silver shekels.* ⁷ *And if from sixty years of age and up, if for a male, the valuation shall be fifteen shekels; and for a female, ten shekels.* ⁸ *But if he is destitute for the*

──────── אונקלוס ────────

נְקוּבְתָא הִיא וִיהֵי פֻּרְסָנָהּ תְּלָתִין סִלְעִין: הוְאִם מִבַּר חֲמֵשׁ שְׁנִין וְעַד בַּר עַסְרִין שְׁנִין וִיהֵי פֻּרְסָנֵהּ דְּכוּרָא עַסְרִין סִלְעִין וְלִנְקוּבְתָא עֲסַר סִלְעִין: ווְאִם מִבַּר יַרְחָא וְעַד בַּר חֲמֵשׁ שְׁנִין וִיהֵי פֻּרְסָנֵהּ דְּכוּרָא חַמְשָׁא סִלְעִין דִּכְסַף וְלִנְקוּבְתָא פֻּרְסָנָהּ תְּלָתָא סִלְעִין דִּכְסַף: זוְאִם מִבַּר שִׁתִּין שְׁנִין וּלְעֵלָּא אִם דְּכוּרָא וִיהֵי פֻּרְסָנֵהּ חַמְשָׁא עֲסַר סִלְעִין וְלִנְקוּבְתָא עֲסַר סִלְעִין: חוְאִם מִסְכֵּן הוּא

──────── רש"י ────────

לֹא יָדַעְתִּי מָאִיזֶה לָשׁוֹן הוּא: (ה) **וְאִם מִבֶּן חָמֵשׁ שָׁנִים.** לֹא שֶׁיְּהֵא הַנּוֹדֵר קָטָן, שֶׁאֵין בְּדִבְרֵי קָטָן כְּלוּם, אֶלָּא גָּדוֹל שֶׁאָמַר עֶרֶךְ קָטָן זֶה שֶׁהוּא בֶן חָמֵשׁ שָׁנִים עָלַי: (ז) **וְאִם מִבֶּן שִׁשִּׁים שָׁנָה וְגוֹ׳.** מַשְׁמַגִּיט [ס"א כְּשֶׁמַּגִּיט] לִימֵי הַזִּקְנָה הָאִשָּׁה קְרוֹבָה לְהַחָשֵׁב כְּאִישׁ, שֶׁהֲרֵי הָאִישׁ פּוֹחֵת בְּהִזְדַּקְּנוֹ יוֹתֵר מִשְּׁלִישׁ בְּעֶרְכּוֹ, וְהָאִשָּׁה אֵינָהּ פּוֹחֶתֶת אֶלָּא שְׁלִישׁ מֶעֶרְכָּהּ, דְּאָמְרֵי אִינָשֵׁי סָבָא בְּבֵיתָא, פָּחָא בְּבֵיתָא, סָבְתָא בְּבֵיתָא, סִימָא טָבָא בְּבֵיתָא: (ח) **וְאִם מָךְ הוּא.** שֶׁאֵין יְדוֹ מַשֶּׂגֶת

──────── RASHI ELUCIDATED ────────

— And as for **the repetition of the letter ב**, לֹא יָדַעְתִּי מֵאֵיזֶה לָשׁוֹן הוּא — **I do not know its linguistic significance.**[1]

5. וְאִם מִבֶּן חָמֵשׁ שָׁנִים — AND IF FROM FIVE YEARS OF AGE. לֹא שֶׁיְּהֵא הַנּוֹדֵר קָטָן — **Not that the one who makes the vow would be a minor,** שֶׁאֵין בְּדִבְרֵי קָטָן כְּלוּם — **for there is nothing to a minor's words,** i.e., he can incur no obligations through his speech. אֶלָּא — **Rather,** the verse speaks of גָּדוֹל שֶׁאָמַר — **an adult who said,** עֶרֶךְ קָטָן זֶה — **"The valuation of this minor"** שֶׁהוּא בֶן חָמֵשׁ שָׁנִים — **who is** at least **five years of age** עָלַי — **"is incumbent upon me** to pay to the *Beis HaMikdash*."

7. וְאִם מִבֶּן שִׁשִּׁים שָׁנָה וְגוֹמֵר — AND IF FROM SIXTY YEARS OF AGE, ETC. מַשְׁמַגִּיט[2] לִימֵי הַזִּקְנָה — **Once they reach**[2] **the days of old age,** הָאִשָּׁה קְרוֹבָה לְהֵחָשֵׁב כְּאִישׁ — **a woman comes close to being reckoned in** terms of the sum of the valuation **as a man,** {שֶׁהֲרֵי הָאִישׁ פּוֹחֵת בְּהִזְדַּקְּנוֹ — **for, see now,**[3] **that a man decreases** in the sum of his valuation **as he reaches old age** יוֹתֵר מִשְּׁלִישׁ בְּעֶרְכּוֹ — **by more than a third of his valuation,** וְהָאִשָּׁה אֵינָהּ פּוֹחֶתֶת אֶלָּא שְׁלִישׁ מֵעֶרְכָּהּ — **while a woman decreases by only a third of her valuation,**} דְּאָמְרֵי אִינָשֵׁי — **for people say,** סָבָא בְּבֵיתָא — "If there is **an old man in the house,** פָּחָא בְּבֵיתָא[4] — **there is something broken**[4] **in the house.** סָבְתָא בְּבֵיתָא — If there is **an old woman in the house,** [5] סִימָא טָבָא בְּבֵיתָא[5] — **there is a treasure in the house**[5] **and a good sign in the house."**

8. וְאִם מָךְ הוּא — BUT IF HE IS DESTITUTE. שֶׁאֵין יָדוֹ מַשֶּׂגֶת — **That his hand does not attain,** i.e., that he

---

1. The ךָ suffix does not mean "your" as it usually does, for verses 2 and 8 speak of one who makes the vow in the third person, not the second person. Furthermore, it is clear from context that עֶרְכְּךָ cannot mean "*your* valuation" in verses 12 and 23 (see *Maskil LeDavid*).

2. Our text follows the early editions. Most modern editions read כְּשֶׁמַּגִּיעַ, "as they reach." The meaning is basically the same.

3. Our text, which reads שֶׁהֲרֵי, follows *Mizrachi* and *Ho'il Moshe*. Many texts read לְפִיכָךְ, "therefore," instead of שֶׁהֲרֵי. The bracketed words do not appear in the first printed edition of Rashi.

4. Rashi (to *Arachin* 19a) cites the variant reading פֶּחָא, "one dressed in tatters."

5. *Arachin* 19a.

VAYIKRA/LEVITICUS — PARASHAS BECHUKOSAI — 27/9-10

מַעֲרִיכְךָ וְהֶעֱמִידוֹ לִפְנֵי הַכֹּהֵן וְהֶעֱרִיךְ אֹתוֹ הַכֹּהֵן עַל־פִּי אֲשֶׁר תַּשִּׂיג יַד הַנֹּדֵר יַעֲרִיכֶנּוּ הַכֹּהֵן: ט וְאִם־בְּהֵמָה אֲשֶׁר יַקְרִיבוּ מִמֶּנָּה קָרְבָּן לַיהוה כֹּל אֲשֶׁר יִתֵּן מִמֶּנּוּ לַיהוה יִהְיֶה־קֹּדֶשׁ: י לֹא יַחֲלִיפֶנּוּ וְלֹא־יָמִיר אֹתוֹ טוֹב בְּרָע אוֹ־רַע בְּטוֹב

valuation, then he should have him stand before the Kohen, and the Kohen should set his valuation; according to what the hand of the person who makes the vow can attain should the Kohen set his evaluation.

⁹ If it is the kind of animal that one can bring as an offering to HASHEM, *whatever he may give of it to* HASHEM *shall be holy.* *¹⁰ He shall not exchange it nor substitute it, whether good for bad or bad for good;*

---- אונקלוס ----

מפרסנה ויקימנה קדם כהנא ויפרוס על מימר די תדבק ידא דנודרא יפרסנה כהנא: ט ואם בעירא די יקרבון מנה קרבנא קדם יי כל די יתן מנה קדם יי יהי קודשא: י לא יחלפנה ולא יעבר יתה טב בביש או ביש בטב

---- רש"י ----

ליתן הערך הזה: **והעמידו.** לנערך [ס"א ליערך] לפני הכהן, ויעריכנו לפי השגת ידו של מעריך: **על פי אשר תשיג.** לפי מה שיש לו יסדרנו וישאיר לו כדי חייו, מטה כר וכסת וכלי אומנות, אם היה חמר משאיר לו חמורו (ערכין

כג.): (ט) **כל אשר יתן ממנו.** אמר רגלה של זו עולה דבריו קיימין ותמכר ולדמי עולה ולדמי חולין חוץ מדמי אותו האבר (ת"כ פרק ט:א; ערכין ה.; תמורה יא:): (י) **טוב ברע.** תם בבעל מום: **או רע בטוב:** וכל שכן טוב בטוב

---- RASHI ELUCIDATED ----

cannot afford, לָתֵת הָעֵרֶךְ הַזֶּה — **to give this valuation.**

□ וְהֶעֱמִידוֹ — THEN HE SHOULD HAVE HIM STAND, i.e., the Kohen shall cause לַנֶּעֱרָךְ — **the one whose value is being pledged** to stand¹ לִפְנֵי הַכֹּהֵן — **before the Kohen,** וְיַעֲרִיכֶנּוּ — **and the [Kohen] should set the valuation of [the one whose valuation is being pledged]** לְפִי הַשָּׂגַת יָדוֹ שֶׁל מַעֲרִיךְ — **according to the attainment of the hand of the one pledging the valuation,** i.e., according to what the one pledging the valuation can afford.

□ עַל פִּי אֲשֶׁר תַּשִּׂיג — ACCORDING TO WHAT [THE HAND OF THE PERSON WHO MAKES THE VOW] CAN ATTAIN. לְפִי מַה שֶּׁיֵּשׁ לוֹ — **According to what he has,**² יְסַדְּרֶנּוּ — **[the Kohen] will arrange for him** וְיַשְׁאִיר לוֹ — **and leave for him** כְּדֵי חַיָּיו — means **sufficient for his life's needs:** מִטָּה — **a bed;** כַּר — **a pillow,** וָכֶסֶת — **and a cover;** וּכְלֵי אֻמָּנוּת — **and tools of** his trade, for example, אִם הָיָה חַמָּר — **if he was a donkey driver,** ³ מַשְׁאִיר לוֹ חֲמוֹרוֹ — **[the Kohen] leaves his donkey for him.**³

9. כֹּל אֲשֶׁר יִתֵּן מִמֶּנּוּ — WHATEVER HE MAY GIVE OF IT. אָמַר — If he said, רַגְלָהּ שֶׁל זוֹ עוֹלָה — "The foot of this animal is an *olah*-offering," דְּבָרָיו קַיָּמִין — his words are upheld, i.e., his pledge takes effect,⁴ וְתִמָּכֵר — and [the animal] should be sold לְצָרְכֵי עוֹלָה — for the needs of an *olah*-offering, i.e., it is sold to somebody who will use it for an *olah*-offering, וְדָמֶיהָ חֻלִּין — and its money, i.e., the money paid for it, is not holy, ⁵ חוּץ מִדְּמֵי אוֹתוֹ הָאֵבֶר — except for the value of that limb which had been consecrated, for the buyer does not pay at all for that limb.⁵

10. טוֹב בְּרָע — GOOD FOR BAD. This means תָּם בְּבַעַל מוּם — an **unblemished one for a blemished one.**⁶

□ אוֹ רַע בְּטוֹב — OR BAD FOR GOOD — וְכָל שֶׁכֵּן — **And all the more so** טוֹב בְּטוֹב — **good for good**

---

1. The Torah does not specify who is to stand before the Kohen. Rashi and *Rambam* (*Hil. Arachin VeCharamin* 1:21, see *Lechem Mishneh*) hold that it is the one whose valuation has been pledged. *Tosafos* (*Arachin* 4a, s.v., ולא הגוסס אוציא את) holds that it is the one who makes the pledge. (See *HaKesav VeHaKabbalah* to our verse.)

2. Although תַּשִּׂיג is in the future tense, it refers to what the one who made the pledge has in the present, not to what he might acquire at some time after the Kohen fixes the sum of the valuation.

3. *Arachin* 23b.

4. This is in contrast to the valuation of people, where the pledge of a non-vital organ does not take effect (see Rashi to v. 2 above; *Mizrachi*; *Sifsei Chachamim*).

5. *Toras Kohanim, perek* 9:1; *Arachin* 5a; *Temurah* 11b. The one who buys the animal does not pay for the limb that has been consecrated. It may not be sold, because it is already the property of the *Beis HaMikdash* by virtue of its having the sanctity of an *olah*-offering. Nevertheless, the entire animal is considered offered by the one who bought it.

6. Rashi knows that בְּרָע of our verse refers to that which is blemished because *Deuteronomy* 17:1 uses "bad" to describe a blemished animal (*Mizrachi*; see next note).

but if he does substitute one animal for another animal, then it and its substitute shall be holy. ¹¹ And if it is any impure animal from which they may not bring an offering to HASHEM, then he shall stand the animal before the Kohen. ¹² The Kohen shall evaluate it, whether good or bad; like the Kohen's evaluation so shall it be. ¹³ But if he redeems it,

וְאִם־הָמֵר יָמִיר בְּהֵמָה בִּבְהֵמָה וְהָיָה־הוּא וּתְמוּרָתוֹ יִהְיֶה־קֹּדֶשׁ:
יא וְאִם כָּל־בְּהֵמָה טְמֵאָה אֲשֶׁר לֹא־יַקְרִיבוּ מִמֶּנָּה קָרְבָּן לַיהוָה וְהֶעֱמִיד
יב אֶת־הַבְּהֵמָה לִפְנֵי הַכֹּהֵן: וְהֶעֱרִיךְ הַכֹּהֵן אֹתָהּ בֵּין טוֹב וּבֵין רָע כְּעֶרְכְּךָ
יג הַכֹּהֵן כֵּן יִהְיֶה: וְאִם־גָּאֹל יִגְאָלֶנָּה

― אונקלוס ―

וְאִם חַלָּפָא יְחַלַּף בְּעִירָא בִּבְעִירָא וִיהֵי הוּא וְחִלּוּפֵהּ יְהֵי קַדִּישׁ: יא וְאִם כָּל בְּעִירָא מְסָאָבָא דִּי לָא יְקָרְבוּן מִנַּהּ קֻרְבָּנָא קֳדָם יְיָ וִיקִים יָת בְּעִירָא קֳדָם כַּהֲנָא: יב וְיִפְרוֹס כַּהֲנָא יָתַהּ בֵּין טַב וּבֵין בִּישׁ כְּפָרְסָנָא דְכַהֲנָא כֵּן יְהֵי: יג וְאִם מִפְרַק יִפְרְקִנַּהּ

― רש"י ―

ורע ברע (תמורה ט.): (יא) ואם בל בהמה טמאה. הבהן בן יהיה. לשאר כל אדם הבא לקנותה מיד הקדש: (יג) ואם גאל יגאלנה. בבעלים החמיר הכתוב בבעלת מום הכתוב מדבר שהיא טמאה להקרבה ולמדך הכתוב שאין קדשים תמימים יוצאין לחולין בפדיון אלא א"כ להוסיף חומש, וכן במקדיש בית וכן במקדיש את השדה הוממו (ת"כ פרשתא ד:ח; תמורה לב:): (יב) בערבך וכן בפדיון מעשר שני הבעלים מוסיפין חומש ולא שאר כל

― RASHI ELUCIDATED ―

וְרַע בְּרָע¹ – and bad for bad.¹

11. וְאִם כָּל בְּהֵמָה טְמֵאָה – AND IF IT IS ANY IMPURE ANIMAL. – בְּבַעֲלַת מוּם הַכָּתוּב מְדַבֵּר – The verse speaks of one that is blemished, שֶׁהִיא טְמֵאָה לְהַקְרָבָה – for it is "impure" for offering. וְלִמֶּדְךָ הַכָּתוּב – Thus, the verse teaches you שֶׁאֵין קָדָשִׁים תְּמִימִים יוֹצְאִין לְחוּלִין – that unblemished holy objects, i.e., unblemished animals which have been consecrated as offerings, do not go out of their sanctity to become that which is not holy בְּפִדְיוֹן – through redemption² אֶלָּא אִם כֵּן הוּמְמוּ – unless they become blemished.²

12. כְּעֶרְכְּךָ הַכֹּהֵן כֵּן יִהְיֶה – LIKE THE KOHEN'S EVALUATION SO SHALL IT BE – לִשְׁאָר כָּל אָדָם – for any other person הַבָּא לִקְנוֹתָהּ – who comes to buy it מִיַּד הֶקְדֵּשׁ – from the possession of the *Beis HaMikdash*.³

13. וְאִם גָּאֹל יִגְאָלֶנָּה – BUT, IF HE REDEEMS IT. בַּבְּעָלִים – With regard to the original owner of the consecrated animal, הֶחֱמִיר הַכָּתוּב – Scripture was more stringent, לְהוֹסִיף חוֹמֶשׁ – by adding a fifth⁴ of the evaluation to the price of redemption. וְכֵן בְּמַקְדִּישׁ בַּיִת – Similarly with regard to one who consecrates a house,⁵ וְכֵן בְּמַקְדִּישׁ אֶת הַשָּׂדֶה – and similarly with regard to one who consecrates a field,⁶ וְכֵן בְּפִדְיוֹן מַעֲשֵׂר שֵׁנִי – and similarly with regard to the redemption of the second tithe,⁷ הַבְּעָלִים – the original owner מוֹסִיפִין חוֹמֶשׁ – adds a fifth, וְלֹא שְׁאָר כָּל

1. *Temurah* 9a. Rashi's reasoning is as follows: If when one substitutes a bad animal for a good animal, the inferior animal becomes holy, all the more should the substituted animal become holy when he substitutes an animal of equal quality. But according to Rashi's reasoning, "good for bad" is even more certain to become holy. If so, why must the Torah state, "good for bad"? This is stated to teach us that making a substitution for an offering is forbidden even when one attempts to improve the quality of the offering (*Mizrachi*; *Sifsei Chachamim*).

2. *Toras Kohanim, parshasa* 4:1; *Temurah* 32b. "Impure," i.e., non-kosher animals, are also discussed in verse 27. Our verse is seen as referring to animals of kosher species that have become blemished because it says, "from which they may not bring an offering to HASHEM," implying that the impurity is one that prevents offering alone, but the animal may be eaten if properly slaughtered. Thus, verse 27, which includes no such qualification, refers to animals of non-kosher species, which may not even be eaten (*Nachalas Yaakov*).

3. Our verse, which fixes the cost equal to the evaluation of the Kohen, applies when any person other than the one who consecrated it wishes to buy it. The following verse, which says that a fifth must be added to the evaluation, applies when the one who consecrated it redeems it (*Mizrachi*; *Sifsei Chachamim*).

4. See note 7 on page 51 for the formula by which one-fifth is figured.

5. Below v. 15.

6. Below v. 19.

7. Below v. 31.

he must add a fifth to the valuation. **14** *If a man consecrates his house to be holy to* Hashem, *the Kohen shall evaluate it, whether good or bad; as the Kohen shall evaluate it, so shall it remain.* **15** *If the one who sanctified it will redeem his house, he shall add a fifth of the money-valuation onto the money of valuation, and it shall be his.* **16** *If a man consecrates a field from his ancestral heritage to* Hashem, *the valuation shall be according to its seeding: an area seeded by a chomer of barley*

יד וְיָסַף חֲמִישִׁתוֹ עַל־עֶרְכֶּךָ: וְאִישׁ
כִּי־יַקְדִּשׁ אֶת־בֵּיתוֹ קֹדֶשׁ לַיהוה
וְהֶעֱרִיכוֹ הַכֹּהֵן בֵּין טוֹב וּבֵין רָע
כַּאֲשֶׁר יַעֲרִיךְ אֹתוֹ הַכֹּהֵן כֵּן יָקוּם:
טו וְאִם־הַמַּקְדִּישׁ יִגְאַל אֶת־בֵּיתוֹ
וְיָסַף חֲמִישִׁית כֶּסֶף־עֶרְכְּךָ עָלָיו
וְהָיָה לּוֹ: טז [חמישי] [שביעי] וְאִם | מִשְּׂדֵה
אֲחֻזָּתוֹ יַקְדִּישׁ אִישׁ לַיהוה וְהָיָה
עֶרְכְּךָ לְפִי זַרְעוֹ זֶרַע חֹמֶר שְׂעֹרִים

— אונקלוס —

וְיוֹסֵף חֻמְשֵׁהּ עַל פֻּרְסָנֵהּ: יד וּגְבַר אֲרֵי יַקְדֵּשׁ יָת בֵּיתֵהּ קוּדְשָׁא קֳדָם יְיָ וְיִפְרְסִנֵּהּ כַּהֲנָא בֵּין טַב וּבֵין בִּישׁ כְּמָא דִי יִפְרוֹס יָתֵהּ כַּהֲנָא כֵּן יְקוּם: טו וְאִם דְּאַקְדֵּשׁ יִפְרוֹק יָת בֵּיתֵהּ וְיוֹסֵף חֲמֵשׁ כְּסַף פֻּרְסָנֵהּ עֲלוֹהִי וִיהֵי לֵהּ: טז וְאִם מֵחֲקַל אַחֲסַנְתֵּהּ יַקְדֵּשׁ גְּבַר קֳדָם יְיָ וִיהֵי פֻּרְסָנֵהּ לְפוּם זַרְעֵהּ בַּר זְרַע כּוֹר שְׂעוֹרִין

— רש"י —

אדם (ת"כ שם ז; ערכין כה.): (טז) **והיה ערכך לפי זרעו.** ולא כפי שוויה, אחת שדה טובה ואחת שדה רעה פדיון הקדש שוה, בית כור שעורים בחמשים שקלים, כך גזירת הכתוב (ת"כ פרק יב; ערכין יד.) והוא שבא לגאלה בתחלת היובל, ואם בא לגאלה

באמצעו נותן לפי החשבון סלע ופונדיון לשנה, לפי שאינה הקדש אלא למנין שני היובל, שאם נגאלה הרי טוב, ואם לאו הגזבר מוכרה בדמים הללו לאחר ועומדת ביד הלוקח עד היובל כשאר כל השדות המכורות, וכשהיא יוצאה מידו חוזרת לכהנים של אותו משמר

— RASHI ELUCIDATED —

אָדָם – **but not any other person.**[1]

16. וְלֹא כְּפִי שְׁוְיָהּ – **And** וְהָיָה עֶרְכְּךָ לְפִי זַרְעוֹ – THE VALUATION SHALL BE ACCORDING TO ITS SEEDING. **not according to its worth** on the market. אַחַת שָׂדֶה טוֹבָה וְאַחַת שָׂדֶה רָעָה – **Regarding both a good field and a bad field,** פִּדְיוֹן הֶקְדֵּשָׁן שָׁוֶה – **the redemption of their sanctity is equal;** בֵּית כּוֹר שְׂעוֹרִים – **the area which is sown with a** *kor*[2] **of barley seed** בַּחֲמִשִּׁים שְׁקָלִים – **is redeemed for fifty shekels.**[3] כָּךְ גְּזֵרַת הַכָּתוּב – **Thus is the decree of Scripture.**[3] וְהוּא שֶׁבָּא לְגָאֲלָהּ – **This is,** i.e., this price is paid, **if he comes to redeem it** בִּתְחִלַּת הַיּוֹבֵל – **at the beginning of the** *yovel* cycle.[4] וְאִם בָּא לְגָאֲלָהּ – **But if he comes to redeem it** בְּאֶמְצָעוֹ – **in its middle,** i.e., after the first year of the *yovel* cycle has elapsed, נוֹתֵן – **he gives** the price of redemption לְפִי הַחֶשְׁבּוֹן – **according to the calculation** סֶלַע – **of a** *shekel*[5] וּפֻנְדְיוֹן – **and a** *pundyon* (a forty-eighth of a *shekel*) לְשָׁנָה – **per year.** לְפִי שֶׁאֵינָהּ הֶקְדֵּשׁ אֶלָּא לְמִנְיַן שְׁנֵי הַיּוֹבֵל – **For it is holy only for the number of years of the** *yovel,* i.e., the number of years until the *yovel* year, שֶׁאִם נִגְאֲלָה – **for if it is redeemed,** הֲרֵי טוֹב – **then fine,** it is clear that it is not holy beyond the *yovel* year, וְאִם לָאו – **and if not,** הַגִּזְבָּר מוֹכְרָהּ – **the treasurer** of the *Beis HaMikdash* **sells it** בְּדָמִים הַלָּלוּ – **for this price,** i.e., a *shekel* and a *pundyon* per year until the *yovel,* לְאַחֵר – **to someone else,** וְעוֹמֶדֶת בְּיַד הַלּוֹקֵחַ – **and it remains in the possession of the buyer** עַד הַיּוֹבֵל – **until the** *yovel* **year** כִּשְׁאָר כָּל הַשָּׂדוֹת – **like all other fields** הַמְּכוּרוֹת – **which have been sold.**[6] וּכְשֶׁהִיא יוֹצְאָה מִיָּדוֹ – **When it leaves his possession** at the *yovel* year, חוֹזֶרֶת לַכֹּהֲנִים – **it reverts to the Kohanim** שֶׁל אוֹתוֹ מִשְׁמָר – **of that watch**[7]

---

1. *Toras Kohanim, parshasa* 4:7; *Arachin* 25a.
2. A *chomer,* referred to in Mishnaic terminology as a *kor,* is equal to thirty *se'ah,* and has a volume of 4,320 eggs. The area requiring this amount of seed is 75,000 square cubits. Opinions regarding modern equivalents range from 67 to 120 gallons for the *kor,* and from 170,000 to 300,000 square feet for the *beis kor.*
3. *Toras Kohanim, perek* 10:3; *Arachin* 14a. A "decree of Scripture" is a law of the Torah whose rationale man does not understand.
4. See 25:8-13 above.
5. For purposes of this passage, *sela* and *shekel* are the same coin.
6. See 25:28 above.
7. The Kohanim are divided into twenty-four "watches," i.e., family groupings. Each watch officiated in the *Beis HaMikdash* according to a regular rotation, for two (or three) one-week periods during the year. Fields which were bought from the *Beis HaMikdash* by someone other than the original owner go to the watch that officiates on Yom Kippur of the *yovel* year.

378 / ויקרא – פרשת בחקתי

יז בַּחֲמִשִּׁים שֶׁקֶל כָּסֶף: אִם־מִשְּׁנַת הַיֹּבֵל יַקְדִּישׁ שָׂדֵהוּ כְּעֶרְכְּךָ יָקוּם: יח וְאִם־אַחַר הַיֹּבֵל יַקְדִּישׁ שָׂדֵהוּ וְחִשַּׁב־לוֹ הַכֹּהֵן אֶת־הַכֶּסֶף עַל־פִּי הַשָּׁנִים הַנּוֹתָרֹת עַד שְׁנַת הַיֹּבֵל

for fifty silver shekels. [17] *If he consecrates his field from the yovel year, it shall remain at its valuation.* [18] *And if he consecrates his field after the yovel, the Kohen shall calculate the money for him according to the remaining years until the yovel year,*

—— אונקלוס ——

בְּחַמְשִׁין סִלְעִין דִּכְסַף: יז אִם מִשַּׁתָּא דְיוֹבֵלָא יַקְדֵּישׁ חַקְלֵהּ כְּפָרְסָנֵהּ יְקוּם: יח וְאִם בָּתַר יוֹבֵלָא יַקְדֵּישׁ חַקְלֵהּ וִיחַשֵּׁב לֵהּ כַּהֲנָא יָת כַּסְפָּא עַל פּוּם שְׁנַיָּא דְּיִשְׁתָּאֲרָן עַד שַׁתָּא דְיוֹבֵלָא

—— רש"י ——

שֶׁהַיּוֹבֵל פּוֹגֵעַ בּוֹ וּמִתְחַלֶּקֶת בֵּינֵיהֶם. זֶהוּ הַמִּשְׁפָּט הָאָמוּר בְּמַקְדִּישׁ שָׂדֶה. וְעַכְשָׁיו אֲפָרְשֶׁנּוּ עַל סֵדֶר הַמִּקְרָאוֹת: (יז) **אִם מִשְּׁנַת הַיֹּבֵל יַקְדִּישׁ וְגוֹ'.** אִם מִשֶּׁעָבְרָה שְׁנַת הַיּוֹבֵל מִיָּד הִקְדִּישָׁהּ וּבָא זֶה לְגָאֳלָהּ מִיָּד, כְּעֶרְכְּךָ יָקוּם, כָּעֵרֶךְ הַזֶּה הָאָמוּר יִהְיֶה, חֲמִשִּׁים כֶּסֶף יִתֵּן: (יח) **וְאִם אַחַר הַיֹּבֵל יַקְדִּישׁ.** וְכֵן אִם הִקְדִּישָׁהּ מִשְּׁנַת הַיּוֹבֵל וְנִשְׁתַּהָה בְּיַד גִּזְבָּר וּבָא זֶה לְגָאֳלָהּ אַחַר הַיּוֹבֵל: **וְחִשַּׁב לוֹ הַכֹּהֵן אֶת הַכֶּסֶף עַל פִּי הַשָּׁנִים הַנּוֹתָרוֹת.** כְּפִי חֶשְׁבּוֹן, כֵּיצַד, הֲרֵי קָצַב דָּמֶיהָ שֶׁל אַרְבָּעִים וָתֵשַׁע שָׁנִים חֲמִשִּׁים שֶׁקֶל, הֲרֵי שֶׁקֶל לְכָל שָׁנָה וְשֶׁקֶל יָתֵר עַל כֻּלָּן. וְהַשֶּׁקֶל אַרְבָּעִים וּשְׁמוֹנֶה פּוּנְדְּיוֹנִין, הֲרֵי סֶלַע וּפוּנְדְּיוֹן לְשָׁנָה, אֶלָּא שֶׁחָסֵר פּוּנְדְּיוֹן אֶחָד לְכֻלָּן, וְאָמְרוּ רַבּוֹתֵינוּ

—— RASHI ELUCIDATED ——

שֶׁהַיּוֹבֵל פּוֹגֵעַ בּוֹ — **which the** *yovel* **encounters,** i.e., the watch which is officiating on Yom Kippur of the *yovel* year וּמִתְחַלֶּקֶת בֵּינֵיהֶם — **and is divided among them.** זֶהוּ הַמִּשְׁפָּט — **This is the law** הָאָמוּר — **that is stated** בְּמַקְדִּישׁ שָׂדֶה — **regarding one who consecrates a field.** וְעַכְשָׁיו אֲפָרְשֶׁנּוּ — **Now I will explain [that law]** עַל סֵדֶר הַמִּקְרָאוֹת — **in the order of the verses,** i.e., I will show how the verses provide the details of the law stated above.

17. אִם מִשֶּׁעָבְרָה שְׁנַת — אִם מִשְּׁנַת הַיֹּבֵל יַקְדִּישׁ וְגוֹמֵר — **IF HE CONSECRATES . . . FROM THE** *YOVEL* **YEAR, ETC.** הַיּוֹבֵל — **If once the** *yovel* **year has passed,** מִיָּד הִקְדִּישָׁהּ — **he consecrates it immediately,** i.e., before another year has passed, וּבָא זֶה לְגָאֳלָהּ מִיָּד — **and this one comes to redeem it immediately,** i.e., during that first year after *yovel*,[1] כְּעֶרְכְּךָ יָקוּם — **"it shall remain at its valuation,"** that is, כָּעֵרֶךְ הַזֶּה הָאָמוּר — **like this valuation which has been stated** in the preceding verse יִהְיֶה — **it shall be;** חֲמִשִּׁים כֶּסֶף יִתֵּן — **he shall give fifty silver** *shekels.*

18. וְאִם אַחַר הַיֹּבֵל יַקְדִּישׁ — **AND IF HE CONSECRATES [HIS FIELD] AFTER THE** *YOVEL.* וְכֵן — **Similarly, the** law of our verse holds true אִם הִקְדִּישָׁהּ — **if he consecrated it** מִשְּׁנַת הַיּוֹבֵל — **from the** *yovel* **year,** i.e., during the year immediately following the *yovel* year, וְנִשְׁתַּהָה בְּיַד גִּזְבָּר — **and it remained in the possession** of the *Beis HaMikdash* beyond that year, וּבָא זֶה לְגָאֳלָהּ — **and this one comes to redeem it** אַחַר הַיּוֹבֵל — **after the** *yovel* year, i.e., during a year other than the one immediately following the *yovel* year.

וְחִשַּׁב לוֹ הַכֹּהֵן אֶת הַכֶּסֶף עַל פִּי הַשָּׁנִים הַנּוֹתָרוֹת — **THE KOHEN SHALL CALCULATE THE MONEY FOR HIM ACCORDING TO THE REMAINING YEARS.** כְּפִי חֶשְׁבּוֹן — **According to calculation.**[2] כֵּיצַד — **How?** הֲרֵי — **See now, [the Torah] has fixed** דָּמֶיהָ — **the price** of redemption קָצַב — **of** שֶׁל אַרְבָּעִים וָתֵשַׁע שָׁנָה — **of forty-nine years** חֲמִשִּׁים שֶׁקֶל — **at fifty** *shekels.* הֲרֵי שֶׁקֶל לְכָל שָׁנָה — **There you have a** *shekel* **for each year,** וְשֶׁקֶל יָתֵר עַל כֻּלָּן — **plus one** *shekel* **more than all of [the forty-nine years].** וְהַשֶּׁקֶל — **The** *shekel* אַרְבָּעִים וּשְׁמוֹנֶה פּוּנְדְּיוֹנִין — **is forty-eight** *pundyons.* הֲרֵי סֶלַע וּפוּנְדְּיוֹן לְשָׁנָה — **See now, that there are a** *shekel* **and** *pundyon* **per year,** אֶלָּא שֶׁחָסֵר פּוּנְדְּיוֹן אֶחָד — **except that there is one** *pundyon* **lacking** לְכֻלָּן — **for all of [the forty-nine years].**[3] וְאָמְרוּ רַבּוֹתֵינוּ — **Our Rabbis said**

---

1. Only whole years are counted as having passed (*Maskil LeDavid*).

2. Our verse uses וְחִשַּׁב לוֹ הַכֹּהֵן, "the Kohen shall calculate for him," in contrast to וְהֶעֱרִיךְ הַכֹּהֵן, "the Kohen shall evaluate," of verse 12, because that verse refers to a value determined by the Kohen's judgment, whereas ours refers to a value arrived at by a fixed system of calculation.

3. If one redeems a field in the middle of the *yovel* cycle, the rate of payment is one *sela* and one *pundyon* per year. Projected over forty-nine years, this comes to forty-nine *selas* and forty-nine *pundyons*, which is fifty *selas* and one *pundyon*. Yet the Torah requires payment of only fifty *selas* for forty-nine years — a figure which leaves "one *pundyon* lacking" when compared to the rate of one *sela* and one *pundyon* per year.

and it shall be subtracted from the valuation. ¹⁹ *And if the one who consecrated it shall redeem the field, he shall add a fifth of the money-valuation onto the money of valuation, and it shall be his.* ²⁰ *But if he does not redeem the field, and if he had sold the field to another man, it cannot be redeemed anymore.* ²¹ *Then, when the field goes out in the yovel,*

יט וְנִגְרַע מֵעֶרְכֶּךָ: וְאִם־גָּאֹל יִגְאַל אֶת־הַשָּׂדֶה הַמַּקְדִּישׁ אֹתוֹ וְיָסַף חֲמִשִׁית כֶּסֶף־עֶרְכְּךָ עָלָיו וְקָם לוֹ: כ וְאִם־לֹא יִגְאַל אֶת־הַשָּׂדֶה וְאִם־מָכַר אֶת־הַשָּׂדֶה לְאִישׁ אַחֵר לֹא־יִגָּאֵל עוֹד: כא וְהָיָה הַשָּׂדֶה בְּצֵאתוֹ בַיֹּבֵל

—————— אונקלוס ——————

וְיִתְמְנַע מִפֻּרְסָנָהּ: יט וְאִם מִפְרַק יִפְרוֹק יָת חַקְלָא דְּאַקְדְּשֵׁהּ הַמַּקְדִּישׁ יָתֵהּ וְיוֹסֵף חֻמְשׁ כְּסַף פֻּרְסָנֵהּ עֲלוֹהִי וִיקוּם לֵהּ: כ וְאִם לָא יִפְרוֹק יָת חַקְלָא וְאִם זַבִּין יָת חַקְלָא לִגְבַר אָחֳרָן לָא יִתְפְּרֵק עוֹד: כא וִיהֵי חַקְלָא בְּמִפְּקֵהּ בְּיוֹבֵלָא

—————— רש"י ——————

אוֹתוֹ. יוֹסִיף חוּמֶשׁ עַל הַקְּצָבָה הַזֹּאת: **(כ) וְאִם לֹא יִגְאַל אֶת הַשָּׂדֶה.** הַמַּקְדִּישׁ: **וְאִם מָכַר.** הַגִּזְבָּר: **אֶת הַשָּׂדֶה לְאִישׁ אַחֵר לֹא יִגְאֵל עוֹד.** לָשׁוּב לְיַד הַמַּקְדִּישׁ: **(כא) וְהָיָה הַשָּׂדֶה בְּצֵאתוֹ בַיֹּבֵל.** מִיַּד הַלּוֹקְחוֹ מִן הַגִּזְבָּר

שֶׁאוֹתוֹ לְפֻרְטָרוֹט וְהָבָא לִגְאוֹל יִתֵּן סֶלַע וּפֻנְדְיוֹן לְכָל שָׁנָה לַשָּׁנִים הַנּוֹתָרוֹת עַד שְׁנַת הַיּוֹבֵל (ת"כ פרק יה; בכורות נ.): **וְנִגְרַע מֵעֶרְכְּךָ.** מִנְיַן הַשָּׁנִים מִשְּׁנַת הַיּוֹבֵל עַד שְׁנַת הַפִּדְיוֹן: **(יט) וְאִם גָּאֹל יִגְאַל הַמַּקְדִּישׁ**

—————— RASHI ELUCIDATED ——————

קַלְבּוֹן לִפְרוֹטְרוֹט — is a premium for exchange of money.[1] שֶׁאוֹתוֹ פֻּנְדְיוֹן — that that extra *pundyon* וְהַבָּא לִגְאוֹל — One who comes to redeem יִתֵּן סֶלַע וּפֻנְדְיוֹן — shall give a *shekel* and a *pundyon* לְכָל שָׁנָה — for each year לַשָּׁנִים הַנּוֹתָרוֹת — for the years that remain עַד שְׁנַת הַיּוֹבֵל — until the *yovel* year.[2]

☐ וְנִגְרַע מֵעֶרְכְּךָ — AND IT SHALL BE SUBTRACTED FROM THE VALUATION. מִנְיַן הַשָּׁנִים — The number of years מִשְּׁנַת הַיּוֹבֵל — from the preceding *yovel* year עַד שְׁנַת הַפִּדְיוֹן — until the year of the redemption.[3]

19. וְאִם גָּאֹל יִגְאַל . . . הַמַּקְדִּישׁ אוֹתוֹ — AND IF THE ONE WHO CONSECRATED IT SHALL REDEEM, יוֹסִיף חוּמֶשׁ — he shall add[4] a fifth עַל הַקְּצָבָה הַזֹּאת — onto this rate.[5]

20. וְאִם לֹא יִגְאַל אֶת הַשָּׂדֶה — BUT IF HE DOES NOT REDEEM THE FIELD, i.e., הַמַּקְדִּישׁ — the one who consecrated the field.

☐ וְאִם מָכַר — AND IF HE HAD SOLD, i.e., הַגִּזְבָּר — the treasurer of the *Beis HaMikdash*.

☐ אֶת הַשָּׂדֶה לְאִישׁ אַחֵר לֹא יִגָּאֵל עוֹד — THE FIELD TO ANOTHER MAN, IT CANNOT BE REDEEMED ANYMORE לָשׁוּב לְיַד הַמַּקְדִּישׁ — to go back to the possession of the one who consecrated it, when the *yovel* year comes.[6]

21. וְהָיָה הַשָּׂדֶה בְּצֵאתוֹ בַיֹּבֵל — THEN, WHEN THE FIELD GOES OUT IN THE *YOVEL* מִיַּד הַלּוֹקְחוֹ מִן הַגִּזְבָּר —

---

1. The first printed edition of Rashi, as well as the Alkabetz edition (1476 C.E.), include additional words in which Rashi explains the nature of the premium. A whole *shekel* is preferable to a *shekel* composed of forty-eight *pundyons* because it is more dignified to pay with a large coin than with small change, and because it is easier to watch a large coin. The additional fraction of a *pundyon* which is paid per year when one redeems for less than forty-nine years is a "premium for exchange of money" — it is compensation for paying the fiftieth *shekel*, or fraction thereof, in small coin.

2. *Toras Kohanim, perek* 10:5; *Bechoros* 50a.

3. The verse could be understood as saying that the years remaining until the next *yovel* should be subtracted. But this would not be reasonable, for these are the years that the redeemer has use of the field. These are the years that he should pay for. Rather, it is the years which have elapsed since the preceding *yovel* which are subtracted (*Mizrachi; Sifsei Chachamim*).

4. Rashi points out that the ו of וְיָסַף is not to be understood as "and" or "if" in this context. It serves only as the conversive prefix to change the tense of the verb from the past form to the future (*Mizrachi*). See also Rashi to *Exodus* 15:2, s.v., עָזִּי וְזִמְרָת, which points out other examples of the conversive ו used in this manner.

5. The verse says that he shall add a fifth onto "the money of valuation." This could have been understood as referring to the valuation of fifty *shekels* per unit of land, for "valuation" was used in this sense in verse 16. Rashi explains that here it is used for "this rate"; that is, the partial valuation of the preceding verse by which he redeems after more than a year has elapsed since the *yovel* (*Mizrachi*).

6. The verse does not mean that it cannot be redeemed under any circumstances. If, for example, the one who redeemed it subsequently consecrates it, he or another may redeem it again.

it will be holy to HASHEM, like a segregated field; his ancestral heritage shall become the Kohen's. *²² But if he will sanctify to HASHEM a field of his acquisition, that is not of the field of his ancestral heritage, ²³ then the Kohen shall calculate for him the sum of the valuation until the yovel year; and he shall pay the valuation of that day, it is holy*

כב קֹ֣דֶשׁ לַיהֹוָ֑ה כִּשְׂדֵ֥ה הַחֵ֖רֶם לַכֹּהֵ֥ן תִּֽהְיֶ֥ה אֲחֻזָּתֽוֹ: שּׁשׁי וְאִם֙ אֶת־שְׂדֵ֣ה מִקְנָת֔וֹ אֲשֶׁ֕ר לֹ֖א מִשְּׂדֵ֣ה אֲחֻזָּת֑וֹ כג יַקְדִּ֖ישׁ לַֽיהוָֹֽה: וְחִשַּׁב־ל֣וֹ הַכֹּהֵ֗ן אֵ֚ת מִכְסַ֣ת הָֽעֶרְכְּךָ֔ עַ֖ד שְׁנַ֣ת הַיֹּבֵ֑ל וְנָתַ֤ן אֶת־הָֽעֶרְכְּךָ֙ בַּיּ֣וֹם הַה֔וּא קֹ֖דֶשׁ

— אונקלוס —

קוּדְשָׁא קֳדָם יְיָ כַּחֲקַל חֶרְמָא לְכַהֲנָא תְּהֵי אַחֲסַנְתֵּהּ: כבוְאִם יָת חֲקַל זְבִינוֹהִי דִּי לָא מֵחֲקַל אַחֲסַנְתֵּהּ יַקְדֵּשׁ קֳדָם יְיָ: כג וִיחַשֵּׁב לֵהּ כַּהֲנָא יָת מִנְיַן פֻּרְסָנָא עַד שַׁתָּא דְיוֹבְלָא וְיִתֵּן יָת פֻּרְסָנָא בְּיוֹמָא הַהוּא קוּדְשָׁא

— רש״י —

כְּדֶרֶךְ שְׁאָר שָׂדוֹת הַיּוֹצְאוֹת מִיַּד לוֹקְחֵיהֶם בַּיּוֹבֵל: קֹדֶשׁ לַה'. לֹא שֶׁיָּשׁוּב לְהֶקְדֵּשׁ בֶּדֶק הַבַּיִת לְיַד הַגִּזְבָּר, אֶלָּא כְּשָׂדֶה הַחֵרֶם הַנִּתּוּן לַכֹּהֲנִים, שֶׁנֶּאֱמַר: כָּל חֵרֶם בְּיִשְׂרָאֵל לְךָ יִהְיֶה (במדבר יח:יד) אַף זוֹ תִּתְחַלֵּק לַכֹּהֲנִים שֶׁל אוֹתוֹ מִשְׁמַר שִׁיּוּם הַכִּפּוּרִים שֶׁל יוֹבֵל פּוֹגֵעַ בּוֹ (ערכין כח:): (כב) וְאִם אֶת שְׂדֵה מִקְנָתוֹ וְגוֹ'. חִלּוּק יֵשׁ בֵּין שְׂדֵה מִקְנָה לִשְׂדֵה אֲחֻזָּה, שֶׁשְּׂדֵה מִקְנָה לֹא תִּתְחַלֵּק לַכֹּהֲנִים בַּיּוֹבֵל לְפִי שֶׁאֵינוֹ יָכוֹל לְהַקְדִּישָׁהּ אֶלָּא עַד הַיּוֹבֵל, שֶׁהֲרֵי בַּיּוֹבֵל הָיְתָה עֲתִידָה לָצֵאת מִיָּדוֹ וְלָשׁוּב לַבְּעָלִים. לְפִיכָךְ אִם בָּא לְגָאֳלָהּ, יִגְאַל בַּדָּמִים הַלָּלוּ הַקְּצוּבִים לִשְׂדֵה אֲחֻזָּה, וְאִם לֹא יִגְאַל

— RASHI ELUCIDATED —

כְּדֶרֶךְ שְׁאָר שָׂדוֹת — in the way of other fields **הַיּוֹצְאוֹת מִיַּד לוֹקְחֵיהֶם** — which go out of the possession of those who bought them **בַּיּוֹבֵל** — in the *yovel* year.[1]

קֹדֶשׁ לַה' — HOLY TO HASHEM. **לֹא שֶׁיָּשׁוּב** — Not that it should return **לְהֶקְדֵּשׁ בֶּדֶק הַבַּיִת** — to the fund for the upkeep of the *Beis HaMikdash* **לְיַד הַגִּזְבָּר** — to the hand of the treasurer. **אֶלָּא** — Rather, **כְּשָׂדֵה הַחֵרֶם** — it should be like a banned field, **הַנִּתּוּן לַכֹּהֲנִים** — which is given to the Kohanim, **שֶׁנֶּאֱמַר** — as it says, **"כָּל חֵרֶם בְּיִשְׂרָאֵל לְךָ יִהְיֶה"** — "any segregated property among Israel shall be yours."[2] **אַף זוֹ** — This, too, **תִּתְחַלֵּק לַכֹּהֲנִים** — shall be apportioned to the Kohanim **שֶׁל אוֹתוֹ מִשְׁמָר** — of that watch[3] **שִׁיּוּם הַכִּפּוּרִים שֶׁל יוֹבֵל פּוֹגֵעַ בּוֹ** — which the Yom Kippur of the *yovel* year encounters, i.e., the watch officiating on Yom Kippur of the *yovel* year.[4]

22. וְאִם אֶת שְׂדֵה מִקְנָתוֹ וְגוֹמֵר — BUT IF [HE WILL SANCTIFY TO HASHEM] A FIELD OF HIS ACQUISITION, ETC. **חִלּוּק יֵשׁ** — There is a difference **בֵּין שְׂדֵה מִקְנָה** — between a field of acquisition, i.e., a field bought or received as a gift, **לִשְׂדֵה אֲחֻזָּה** — and a field of ancestral heritage, **שֶׁשְּׂדֵה מִקְנָה** — in that a field of acquisition **לֹא תִּתְחַלֵּק** — will not be apportioned **לַכֹּהֲנִים** — to the Kohanim **בַּיּוֹבֵל** — in the *yovel* year, **לְפִי שֶׁאֵינוֹ יָכוֹל לְהַקְדִּישָׁהּ** — because [the one who acquired it] is unable to consecrate it **אֶלָּא עַד הַיּוֹבֵל** — except until the time of the *yovel;* **שֶׁהֲרֵי** — for, see now, **בַּיּוֹבֵל** — at the *yovel* **הָיְתָה עֲתִידָה** — [the field] was destined **לָצֵאת מִיָּדוֹ** — to leave his possession **וְלָשׁוּב לַבְּעָלִים** — and to return to the original owner. **לְפִיכָךְ** — Therefore, **אִם בָּא לְגָאֳלָהּ** — if he comes to redeem it, **יִגְאַל בַּדָּמִים הַלָּלוּ** — he shall redeem for this price **הַקְּצוּבִים לִשְׂדֵה אֲחֻזָּה** — which has been fixed for a field of ancestral heritage.[5] **וְאִם לֹא יִגְאַל** — And if [the one who acquired and consecrated it]

---

1. But the verse does not refer to fields that have not been redeemed and are in the possession of the *Beis HaMikdash* at the *yovel*. Such fields do not "go out" at the *yovel* (*Mizrachi; Sifsei Chachamim*).

2. *Numbers* 18:14. The verse is addressed to Aaron the Kohen.

3. See note 7 to v. 16 above.

4. *Arachin* 28b.

5. There is a dispute in the Mishnah in *Arachin* 14a as to the price of redemption of a field one has acquired through purchase or a gift, and then consecrated. The Rabbis are of the opinion that it is redeemed at market value, while the Tanna R' Eliezer holds that it is redeemed at the rate fixed in verses 16-19 for a field of ancestral heritage. Rashi here appears to explain our verse according to the view of R' Eliezer which is the minority opinion, although the halachah generally follows the majority. To avoid having to put Rashi in this difficult position, *Panim Yafos* and *Malbim* explain that when Rashi says, "If he comes to redeem it, he shall redeem it for the price which has been fixed for a field of ancestral heritage," he refers to a situation in which the original owner redeems it after the one who acquired it from him has consecrated it. Then, although

to Hashem. **24** In the yovel year the field shall return to the original owner from whom he acquired it; to him who has it as ancestral heritage of the land. **25** Every valuation shall be in the shekel of the sanctuary; that shekel shall be twenty geirah.

26 However, a firstborn that will become a firstling for Hashem among livestock,

כד לַיהוָה: בִּשְׁנַת הַיּוֹבֵל יָשׁוּב הַשָּׂדֶה לַאֲשֶׁר קָנָהוּ מֵאִתּוֹ לַאֲשֶׁר־לוֹ אֲחֻזַּת הָאָרֶץ: כה וְכָל־עֶרְכְּךָ יִהְיֶה בְּשֶׁקֶל הַקֹּדֶשׁ עֶשְׂרִים גֵּרָה יִהְיֶה הַשָּׁקֶל: כו אַךְ־בְּכוֹר אֲשֶׁר־יְבֻכַּר לַיהוָה בִּבְהֵמָה

— אונקלוס —

קֳדָם יְיָ: כד בְּשַׁתָּא דְיוֹבֵלָא יְתוּב חַקְלָא לִדְנַבְנֵהּ מִנֵּהּ לִדְלֵהּ אַחֲסָנַת אַרְעָא: כה וְכָל פֻּרְסָנֵהּ יְהֵי בְסִלְעֵי קוּדְשָׁא עֶשְׂרִין מָעִין יְהֵי סִלְעָא: כו בְּרַם בּוּכְרָא דִּי בַכַּר קֳדָם יְיָ בִּבְעִירָא

— רש"י —

(ת"כ פרק יח:ז; ערכין כו:א'-ב'): (כה) וכל ערכך יהיה בשקל הקדש. כל ערך שכתוב בו שקלים יהיה בשקל הקדש: **עשרים גרה.** עשרים מעות. כך היו מתחלה, ולאחר מכאן הוסיפו שתות ואמרו רבותינו שש מעה כסף דינר, עשרים וארבע מעות

וימכרנה גזבר לאחר, או אם יגאל הוא, בשנת היובל ישוב השדה לאשר קנהו מאתו לאשר שהקדישה. ופן תאמר לאשר קנהו הלוקח הזה האחרון מאתו, וזהו הגזבר, לכך הוצרך לומר לאשר לו אחוזת הארץ מירושת אבות, וזהו בעליו הראשונים שמכרוה למקדיש.

— RASHI ELUCIDATED —

או – **does not redeem** it וּמְכָרָהּ גִּזְבָּר לְאַחֵר – **and the treasurer will sell it to someone else,** אִם יִגְאַל הוּא – **or if [the one who acquired and consecrated it] will redeem** it, בִּשְׁנַת הַיּוֹבֵל יָשׁוּב – "**in the** *yovel* **year the field shall return to the** [original owner] **from whom he acquired it,**" הַשָּׂדֶה לַאֲשֶׁר קָנָהוּ מֵאִתּוֹ – i.e., to the one from whom שֶׁהִקְדִּישָׁהּ – **the one that consecrated it** had bought it. וּפֶן תֹּאמַר – **But perhaps you will say** that the verse means לַאֲשֶׁר קְנָהוּ – **the one from whom** הַלּוֹקֵחַ הַזֶּה הָאַחֲרוֹן מֵאִתּוֹ – **the one from whom this last buyer** who redeemed it from the *Beis HaMikdash* **acquired it,** וְזֶהוּ הַגִּזְבָּר – **and that is the treasurer** of the *Beis HaMikdash*. לְכָךְ הֻצְרַךְ לוֹמַר – **This is why** [the verse] **had to say,** ״לַאֲשֶׁר לוֹ אֲחֻזַּת הָאָרֶץ״ – "**to him who has it as ancestral heritage of the land**" מִירוּשַׁת אָבוֹת – **through inheritance from ancestors,** וְזֶהוּ בְּעָלִים הָרִאשׁוֹנִים – **and this is the original owner,** שֶׁמְּכָרוּהוּ לַמַּקְדִּישׁ[1] – **who sold it to the one who consecrated** it.[1]

25. וְכָל עֶרְכְּךָ יִהְיֶה בְּשֶׁקֶל הַקֹּדֶשׁ – EVERY VALUATION SHALL BE IN THE *SHEKEL* OF THE SANCTUARY. כָּל עֶרֶךְ – Any valuation שֶׁכָּתוּב בּוֹ שְׁקָלִים – about which *shekels* are written[2] יִהְיֶה בְּשֶׁקֶל הַקֹּדֶשׁ – shall be in the *shekel* of the Sanctuary.[3]

□ עֶשְׂרִים גֵּרָה – TWENTY *GEIRAH*. עֶשְׂרִים מָעוֹת – Twenty *ma'ah*.[4] כָּךְ הָיוּ מִתְּחִלָּה – So they were at first, i.e., such was the original relationship between the *shekel* and the *geirah*. וּלְאַחַר מִכָּאן – Later on הוֹסִיפוּ שְׁתוּת – they added a sixth,[5] וְאָמְרוּ רַבּוֹתֵינוּ – and our Rabbis said, שֵׁשׁ מָעָה כֶסֶף – six *ma'ah*, i.e., *geirah*, of silver דִּינָר – are a *dinar*; עֶשְׂרִים וְאַרְבַּע מָעוֹת – twenty-four *ma'ah*

the one who acquired it would redeem it at market value, in accordance with the opinion of the Rabbis, it still retains the status of a field of ancestral heritage insofar as the original owner is concerned, and he redeems it at the fixed rate.

1. *Toras Kohanim, perek* 11:7; *Arachin* 26a-b.

2. That is, any payment which the Torah states explicitly must be in *shekalim*, such as the redemption of a firstborn son (see *Numbers* 18:16), or compensation for a slave killed by one's ox (see *Exodus* 21:32).

3. But valuations regarding which the Torah makes no reference to *shekels*, such as the valuations of animals or houses mentioned in our chapter, need not be a minimum of a *shekel*. They may even be as little as a *perutah* (*Gur Aryeh*; *Sefer Zikaron*; there are 768 *perutahs* in a *shekel*).

4. Our verse states that there are twenty *geirah* per *shekel*. It is commonly known that there are twenty-four *ma'ah* per *shekel*. We might have thought that a *ma'ah* is a coin of slightly less value than a *geirah*. Rashi begins his comment by dispelling this notion and saying that a *geirah* is identical to a *ma'ah*. He goes on to explain the discrepancy in figures.

5. The full *shekel* was four *zuz* times five *ma'ah* per *zuz*, or twenty *ma'ah* (in the language of our verse, "twenty *geirah*"). Yet the Talmud often speaks of the *shekel* as containing twenty-four *ma'ah*. Rashi explains that the *shekel* of the Torah indeed weighted twenty *ma'ah*, but later generations increased the weight of the *zuz* to six *ma'ah*, thus increasing the *shekel* to

לֹא־יַקְדִּישׁ אִישׁ אֹתוֹ אִם־שׁוֹר אִם־שֶׂה לַיהוה הוּא: וְאִם בַּבְּהֵמָה הַטְּמֵאָה וּפָדָה בְעֶרְכֶּךָ וְיָסַף חֲמִשִׁתוֹ עָלָיו וְאִם־לֹא יִגָּאֵל וְנִמְכַּר בְּעֶרְכֶּךָ:

a man shall not consecrate it; whether it is of oxen or of the flock, it is HASHEM'*s.* [27] *If among the impure livestock he shall redeem [it] according to the valuation and add a fifth to it; and if it is not redeemed it shall be sold for the valuation.*

—————————— אונקלוס ——————————

לָא יַקְדֵּשׁ גְּבַר יָתֵהּ אִם תּוֹר אִם אִמַּר קֳדָם יְיָ הוּא: [כז] וְאִם בִּבְעִירָא מְסָאֲבָא וְיִפְרוֹק בְּפֻרְסָנֵהּ וְיוֹסֵף חֻמְשֵׁהּ עֲלוֹהִי וְאִם לָא יִתְפְּרֵק וְיִזְדַּבַּן בְּפֻרְסָנֵהּ:

—————————— רש"י ——————————

לְסֶלַע (בכורות נ.): (כו) לֹא יַקְדִּישׁ אִישׁ אֹתוֹ. לְשֵׁם קָרְבָּן אַחֵר (ת"כ פרשתא ח:ב,ז; ערכין כט.), לְפִי שֶׁאֵינוֹ שֶׁלּוֹ: (כז) וְאִם בַּבְּהֵמָה הַטְּמֵאָה וְגוֹ'. אֵין הַמִּקְרָא הַזֶּה מוּסָב עַל הַבְּכוֹר, שֶׁאֵין לוֹמַר בִּבְכוֹר בְּהֵמָה טְמֵאָה וּפָדָה בְעֶרְכֶּךָ [וחומש], וַחֲמוֹר אֵין זֶה, שֶׁהֲרֵי אֵין פִּדְיוֹן פֶּטֶר חֲמוֹר אֶלָּא טָלֶה, וְהוּא מַתָּנָה לַכֹּהֵן וְאֵינוֹ לְהֶקְדֵּשׁ. אֶלָּא הַכָּתוּב מוּסָב עַל הַהֶקְדֵּשׁ, שֶׁהַכָּתוּב שֶׁלְּמַעְלָה דִּבֵּר בְּפִדְיוֹן בְּהֵמָה טְהוֹרָה שֶׁהוּמְּמָה, וְכָאן דִּבֶּר בְּמַקְדִּישׁ בְּהֵמָה טְמֵאָה לְבֶדֶק הַבַּיִת: וּפָדָה בְעֶרְכֶּךָ. כְּפִי מַה שֶּׁיַּעֲרִיכֶנָּה הַכֹּהֵן: וְאִם לֹא יִגָּאֵל. בְּעָלִים (ת"כ פרק יב:ב:ג): וְנִמְכַּר בְעֶרְכֶּךָ. לַאֲחֵרִים (שם):

—————————— RASHI ELUCIDATED ——————————

לְסֶלַע — per *shekel.*[1]

26. לֹא יַקְדִּישׁ אִישׁ אֹתוֹ — A MAN SHALL NOT CONSECRATE IT לְשֵׁם קָרְבָּן אַחֵר — for the sake of a different offering,[2] לְפִי שֶׁאֵינוֹ שֶׁלּוֹ — because it does not belong to him.

27. וְאִם בַּבְּהֵמָה הַטְּמֵאָה וְגוֹמֵר — IF AMONG THE IMPURE LIVESTOCK, ETC. אֵין הַמִּקְרָא הַזֶּה מוּסָב — This verse does not refer עַל הַבְּכוֹר — to the firstborn, which is the subject of the preceding verse, שֶׁאֵין לוֹמַר — for it cannot be said בִּבְכוֹר בְּהֵמָה טְמֵאָה — of the firstborn of impure, i.e., non-kosher, livestock, וּפָדָה בְעֶרְכֶּךָ — "he shall redeem [it] according to the valuation." וַחֲמוֹר אֵין זֶה — And this "impure livestock" is also not a donkey, to which the law of the firstborn *does* apply,[4] שֶׁהֲרֵי אֵין — for, see now, that there is no redemption of a firstborn donkey אֶלָּא טָלֶה — other than through a lamb,[5] not through the valuation of our verse, וְהוּא מַתָּנָה לַכֹּהֵן — and [the lamb] is a gift to the Kohen, וְאֵינוֹ לְהֶקְדֵּשׁ — and it does not go to the Beis HaMikdash, as does the valuation of redemption of our verse. אֶלָּא — Rather, הַכָּתוּב מוּסָב עַל הַהֶקְדֵּשׁ — the verse refers to that which is consecrated to the Beis HaMikdash, שֶׁהַכָּתוּב שֶׁלְּמַעְלָה — for the verse above[6] דִּבֵּר בְּפִדְיוֹן בְּהֵמָה — spoke of the redemption of a kosher animal שֶׁהוּמְּמָה — that became blemished after it had been consecrated as an offering, וְכָאן דִּבֶּר — and here it speaks בְּמַקְדִּישׁ בְּהֵמָה טְמֵאָה — of one who consecrates a non-kosher animal לְבֶדֶק הַבַּיִת — for the upkeep of the Beis HaMikdash.[7]

□ וּפָדָה בְעֶרְכֶּךָ — HE SHALL REDEEM [IT] ACCORDING TO THE VALUATION, i.e., כְּפִי מַה שֶּׁיַּעֲרִיכֶנָּה הַכֹּהֵן — according to what the Kohen will assess it for.[8]

□ וְאִם לֹא יִגָּאֵל — AND IF IT IS NOT REDEEMED [9] עַל יְדֵי בְעָלִים — by the original owner,[9]

□ וְנִמְכַּר בְעֶרְכֶּךָ — IT SHALL BE SOLD FOR THE VALUATION [9] לַאֲחֵרִים — to others.[9]

twenty-four (see *Mizrachi; Sifsei Chachamim*).
   See note 7 on page 51 for the formula by which one-sixth is figured.
1. *Bechoros* 50a.
2. *Toras Kohanim, parshasa* 8:2,7; *Arachin* 29a. He may not consecrate it for the sake of a different offering, but other types of consecration apply. According to one opinion, he may consecrate the value of his right to give the firstborn to whichever Kohen he pleases. According to another opinion, he must consecrate it verbally with the sanctity of the firstborn (see Rashi to *Deuteronomy* 15:19).
3. Because the law of the firstborn applies to no non-kosher species other than the donkey (see Rashi to *Exodus* 13:12, s.v., שגר בהמה, and to *Exodus* 13:13,

s.v., פטר חמור).
4. The first printed edition of Rashi omits the phrase וַחֲמוֹר אֵין זֶה, "and this is not a donkey." Instead the word וְחֹמֶשׁ, "and a fifth," appears in its place. Accordingly, Rashi is saying: "... for it cannot be said that the firstborn of a non-kosher species, i.e., the firstborn of a donkey, 'he shall redeem [it] according to the valuation and a fifth,' for, see now, . . ."
5. See *Exodus* 13:13.
6. Verses 11-13.
7. *Menachos* 101a.
8. Here the valuation is not based on a fixed rate, as are the valuations of souls and of fields of ancestral heritage.
9. *Toras Kohanim, perek* 12:2.

28 However, any segregated property that a man will segregate for the sake of HASHEM, of all that he has — of a man, and an animal, and of a field of his ancestral heritage — may not be sold and may not be redeemed, any segregated property is most holy

כח אַךְ כָּל־חֵרֶם אֲשֶׁר יַחֲרִם אִישׁ לַיהוה מִכָּל־אֲשֶׁר־לוֹ מֵאָדָם וּבְהֵמָה וּמִשְּׂדֵה אֲחֻזָּתוֹ לֹא יִמָּכֵר וְלֹא יִגָּאֵל כָּל־חֵרֶם קֹדֶשׁ־קָדָשִׁים

— אונקלוס —

כח בְּרַם כָּל חֶרְמָא דִּי יַחֲרֵם גְּבַר קֳדָם יְיָ מִכֹּל דִּי לֵהּ מֵאֱנָשָׁא וּבְעִירָא וּמֵחֲקַל אַחֲסַנְתֵּהּ לָא יִזְדַּבַּן וְלָא יִתְפְּרֵק כָּל חֶרְמָא קֹדֶשׁ קוּדְשִׁין

— רש"י —

(כח) **אך כל חרם וגו'.** נֶחְלְקוּ רַבּוֹתֵינוּ בַּדָּבָר. יֵשׁ אוֹמְרִים סְתָם חֲרָמִים לְהֶקְדֵּשׁ, וּמָה אֲנִי מְקַיֵּם כָּל חֵרֶם בְּיִשְׂרָאֵל לְךָ יִהְיֶה (במדבר יח:יד) בְּחֶרְמֵי כֹהֲנִים, שֶׁפֵּרֵשׁ וְאָמַר הֲרֵי זֶה חֵרֶם לַכֹּהֵן. וְיֵשׁ אוֹמְרִים סְתָם חֲרָמִים לַכֹּהֲנִים (ת"כ פרק יב:ד-ה; ערכין כח:-כט.): **לא ימכר ולא יגאל.** אֶלָּא יִנָּתֵן לַכֹּהֵן. לְדִבְרֵי הָאוֹמֵר סְתָם חֲרָמִים לַבֶּדֶק הַבַּיִת מְפָרֵשׁ מִקְרָא זֶה בְּסֶתֶם חֲרָמִים, שֶׁהַכֹּל מוֹדִים חֶרְמֵי כֹהֲנִים אֵין לָהֶם פִּדְיוֹן עַד שֶׁיָּבוֹאוּ לְיַד כֹּהֵן, וְחֶרְמֵי גָבוֹהַּ נִפְדִּים (ערכין שם): **כל חרם קדש קדשים הוא.** הָאוֹמֵר סְתָם חֲרָמִים לַבֶּדֶק הַבַּיִת מֵבִיא רְאָיָה מִכָּאן (ת"כ שם ה; ערכין שם).

— RASHI ELUCIDATED —

28. אַךְ כָּל חֵרֶם וְגוֹמֵר — HOWEVER, ANY SEGREGATED PROPERTY, ETC. נֶחְלְקוּ רַבּוֹתֵינוּ — Our Rabbis are in dispute בַּדָּבָר — about the matter. יֵשׁ אוֹמְרִים — There are those who say סְתָם חֲרָמִים — that unspecified vows of segregated property, i.e., vows that do not specify to whom the property should go, לְהֶקְדֵּשׁ — go for the upkeep of the *Beis HaMikdash*. וּמָה אֲנִי מְקַיֵּם — What, then, do I maintain כָּל חֵרֶם בְּיִשְׂרָאֵל לְךָ יִהְיֶה — that "any segregated property among Israel shall be yours"[1] means? בְּחֶרְמֵי כֹהֲנִים — It speaks of vows of segregated property of the Kohanim, שֶׁפֵּרֵשׁ — where he spoke explicitly וְאָמַר — and said, הֲרֵי זֶה חֵרֶם לַכֹּהֵן — "Behold, this is segregated property for the Kohen." וְיֵשׁ שֶׁאָמְרוּ — And there are those Rabbis who said סְתָם חֲרָמִים — that unspecified vows of segregated property לַכֹּהֲנִים — go to the Kohanim.[2]

□ לֹא יִמָּכֵר וְלֹא יִגָּאֵל — MAY NOT BE SOLD AND MAY NOT BE REDEEMED. אֶלָּא — Rather, יִנָּתֵן לַכֹּהֵן — it shall be given to the Kohen. לְדִבְרֵי הָאוֹמֵר — According to the words of the one who says סְתָם חֲרָמִים — unspecified vows of segregated property לַכֹּהֲנִים — go to the Kohanim, מְפָרֵשׁ מִקְרָא זֶה — he explains this part of the verse בְּסֶתֶם חֲרָמִים — as speaking of unspecified vows of segregated property; the property may be neither sold nor redeemed, but goes directly to the Kohen.[3] וְהָאוֹמֵר — And the one who says סְתָם חֲרָמִים — unspecified vows of segregated property לְבֶדֶק הַבַּיִת — go for the upkeep of the *Beis HaMikdash* בְּחֶרְמֵי כֹהֲנִים — explains this part of the verse מְפָרֵשׁ מִקְרָא זֶה — as speaking of vows of segregated property of the Kohanim. שֶׁהַכֹּל מוֹדִים — For all, i.e., both of the above opinions, agree שֶׁחֶרְמֵי כֹהֲנִים — that segregated properties of the Kohanim אֵין לָהֶם פִּדְיוֹן — have no redemption עַד שֶׁיָּבוֹאוּ — until they come לְיַד כֹּהֵן — into the possession of a Kohen,[4] וְחֶרְמֵי גָבוֹהַּ — but segregated properties of Him Who is on High נִפְדִּים — may be redeemed.[5]

□ כָּל חֵרֶם קֹדֶשׁ קָדָשִׁים הוּא — ANY SEGREGATED PROPERTY IS MOST HOLY TO HASHEM. הָאוֹמֵר — The one who says סְתָם חֲרָמִים — unspecified vows of segregated property לְבֶדֶק הַבַּיִת — are for the upkeep of the *Beis HaMikdash* מֵבִיא רְאָיָה מִכָּאן — brings proof for his position from here.[6]

---

1. *Numbers* 18:14. The verse is addressed to Aaron the Kohen.

2. *Toras Kohanim*, perek 12:4-5; *Arachin* 28b-29a.

3. Although the verse speaks of property segregated "for the sake of HASHEM," it can still be maintained that the verse speaks of property which ultimately goes to the Kohanim, for the Gemara (*Arachin* 29a) derives from the beginning of the verse that property segregated for the Kohanim has the status of "for the sake of HASHEM," i.e., property of the *Beis HaMikdash*, insofar as it is forbidden to derive personal benefit from it, until it comes into the possession of the Kohanim (see, too, *Arachin* 28b, *Rashi*, s.v., הרי הן כהקדש).

4. The segregated item itself must be given to a Kohen: One may not redeem it and give the value to a Kohen (*Be'er Yitzchak*). Rashi does not mean to imply that redemption of any sort is required once the segregated properties come into the possession of the Kohen. Rather, it means that coming into the possession of the Kohen is the equivalent of redemption, in that it removes all sanctity from the property (*Gur Aryeh*).

5. *Arachin* 28b-29a.

6. *Toras Kohanim*, perek 12:5; *Arachin* 28b-29a.

to Hashem. *²⁹ Any banishment which shall be banned from among man, he shall not be redeemed; he shall be put to death.*

כט הוּא לַיהוה: שביעי כָּל־חֵרֶם אֲשֶׁר יָחֳרַם מִן־הָאָדָם לֹא יִפָּדֶה מוֹת יוּמָת:

―――――― אונקלוס ――――――

כט הוּא קֳדָם יְיָ: כָּל חֶרְמָא דִּי יִתַּחֲרַם מִן אֲנָשָׁא לָא יִתְפְּרַק אִתְקְטָלָא יִתְקְטֵל:

―――――― רש״י ――――――

(כט) בָּל חֵרֶם אֲשֶׁר יָחֳרַם וגו'. הַיּוֹצֵא לֵיהָרֵג וְאָמַר אֶחָד עֶרְכּוֹ עָלַי לֹא אָמַר כְּלוּם (ערכין ו:): מוֹת יוּמָת. הֲרֵי הוֹלֵךְ לָמוּת לְפִיכָךְ לֹא יִפָּדֶה אֵין לוֹ דָמִים וְלֹא עֵרֶךְ (ערכין שם):

והאומר סתם חרמים להכנים מפרש כל חרם קדש קדשים הוא לה׳ ללמד שחרמי כהנים חלים על קדשי קדשים ועל קדשים קלים ונותן לכהן, כמו ששנינו במסכת ערכין (שם כת:) אם נדר נותן דמיהם ואם נדבה נותן את טובתה: מֵאָדָם. כגון שהחרים עבדיו ושפחותיו הכנענים (ת״כ שם ג; ערכין כת.): בָּל חֵרֶם אֲשֶׁר יָחֳרַם וגו'. הַיּוֹצֵא לֵיהָרֵג וְאָמַר אֶחָד עֶרְכּוֹ עָלַי לֹא אָמַר כְּלוּם (ערכין ו:): מוֹת יוּמָת. הֲרֵי הוֹלֵךְ לָמוּת לְפִיכָךְ לֹא יִפָּדֶה אֵין לוֹ דָמִים וְלֹא עֵרֶךְ (ערכין שם):

―――――― RASHI ELUCIDATED ――――――

□ וְהָאוֹמֵר — **And the one who says** סְתָם חֲרָמִים — **unspecified vows of segregated property** לַכֹּהֲנִים — **are for the Kohanim** מְפָרֵשׁ — **explains** ״כָּל קֹדֶשׁ קָדָשִׁים הוּא לַה׳״: — **"any segregated property is most holy to Hashem"** is meant לְלַמֵּד — **to teach us** שֶׁחֶרְמֵי כֹהֲנִים — **that vows of segregated property of the Kohanim** חָלִים — **take effect** עַל קָדְשֵׁי קָדָשִׁים — **upon that which is holy of the highest degree** וְעַל קָדָשִׁים קַלִּים — **and that which is holy of the lesser degree.**[1] וְנוֹתֵן לַכֹּהֵן — **In this situation he gives the Kohen**[2] כְּמוֹ שֶׁשָּׁנִינוּ בְּמַסֶּכֶת עֲרָכִין — **as we have learned in Tractate *Arachin*:**[2] אִם נֶדֶר — **If it is a vow**[3] נוֹתֵן דְּמֵיהֶם — **he gives their value,** וְאִם נְדָבָה — **and if it is a voluntary-offering**[3] נוֹתֵן אֶת טוֹבָתָהּ — **he gives its benefit.**[4]

□ מֵאָדָם — OF A MAN. כְּגוֹן — **For instance,** שֶׁהֶחֱרִים — **if he pledged as segregated property** עֲבָדָיו וְשִׁפְחוֹתָיו הַכְּנַעֲנִים — **his Canaanite,** i.e., non-Jewish, **slaves and slavewomen.**[5]

29. כָּל חֵרֶם אֲשֶׁר יָחֳרַם וגו׳ — ANY BANISHMENT WHICH SHALL BE BANNED, ETC. הַיּוֹצֵא לֵיהָרֵג — **If one goes forth to be executed** by the decision of the court, וְאָמַר אֶחָד — **and someone says,** עֶרְכּוֹ עָלַי — **"It is** incumbent **upon me** to pay **his valuation,"** לֹא אָמַר כְּלוּם — **he has not said anything,** i.e., the pledge does not take effect.[6]

□ מוֹת יוּמָת — HE SHALL BE PUT TO DEATH. הֲרֵי הוֹלֵךְ לָמוּת — **See now, that he is going to die,** i.e., the process of his death has begun. לְפִיכָךְ — **Therefore,** לֹא יִפָּדֶה — **"he shall not be redeemed";** אֵין לוֹ דָמִים — **he has neither worth**[7] וְלֹא עֵרֶךְ — **nor valuation.**[8]

---

1. קֹדֶשׁ of our verse implies that the law of segregated property takes effect on that which is holy of the lesser degree. קָדָשִׁים implies that it takes effect on that which is holy of the highest degree (*Toras Kohanim, perek* 12:6).

2. *Arachin* 28b.

3. See Rashi to 22:18 above.

4. In the case of a vow, the one who made the pledge has an obligation to bring an offering even if the animal he originally set aside becomes lost, becomes disqualified, or dies. Thus, when that animal is before us in a state suitable for offering, the owner's stake in it is equivalent to its entire value, for if something should happen to disqualify it, the owner would have to bring an equivalent animal as an offering. Therefore, when he pledges it as segregated property, he must give its entire value to the Kohen.

In the case of a voluntary-offering, however, the one who made the pledge need not make a substitution should the animal designated as the offering become disqualified, or lost, or die. His stake in the animal is therefore less than its full value. It is assessed as the equivalent of what somebody who is not obligated to bring would pay to have this animal for an offering. It is this value that the owner of the offering gives to the Kohen if he pledges a voluntary-offering as segregated property (Rashi to *Arachin* 28b).

5. *Toras Kohanin, perek* 12:3; *Arachin* 28a. To the exclusion of Hebrew servants, who are not the property of their masters (*Mizrachi*).

6. *Toras Kohanin, perek* 12:7; *Arachin* 6b. Although our verse uses חֵרֶם, the word used by the preceding verse for "segregated property," it cannot be understood in that sense in our verse. For then the verse would be saying that any person pledged by another as segregated property should be put to death — an impossible situation. Rather, חֵרֶם is used here in the sense of destruction, being sentenced to death (*Mesiach Ilmim*; *Sefer Zikaron*).

7. If someone pledges a person's דָּמִים, "worth," he pays the price that the person would fetch were he sold as a servant.

8. *Arachin* 6b.

385 / VAYIKRA/LEVITICUS — PARASHAS BECHUKOSAI — 27/30-32

ל וְכָל־מַעְשַׂר הָאָרֶץ מִזֶּרַע הָאָרֶץ מִפְּרִי
הָעֵץ לַיהוה הוּא קֹדֶשׁ לַיהוה: לא וְאִם־
גָּאֹל יִגְאַל אִישׁ מִמַּעַשְׂרוֹ חֲמִשִׁיתוֹ
יֹסֵף עָלָיו: מפטיר לב וְכָל־מַעְשַׂר בָּקָר וָצֹאן
כֹּל אֲשֶׁר־יַעֲבֹר תַּחַת הַשָּׁבֶט הָעֲשִׂירִי

³⁰ Any tithe of the land, of the seed of the land, of the fruit of the tree, belongs to HASHEM; it is holy to HASHEM. ³¹ If a person shall redeem of his tithe, he shall add his fifth to it.
³² Any tithe of cattle or of the flock, any that passes under the staff, the tenth one

— אונקלוס —

וּלְכָל מַעְשְׂרָא דְאַרְעָא מִזַּרְעָא דְאַרְעָא מִפֵּרֵי אִילָנָא דַּיָּי הוּא קוּדְשָׁא קֳדָם יְיָ: לא וְאִם מִפְרַק יִפְרוֹק גְּבַר מִמַּעַשְׂרֵהּ חֻמְשֵׁהּ יוֹסֵף עֲלוֹהִי: לב וְכָל מַעְשַׂר תּוֹרִין וְעָן כֹּל דְּיֵעִיבַּר תְּחוֹת חֻטְרָא עֲשִׂירָאָה

— רש"י —

(ל) **וכל מעשר הארץ.** במקרא שני הכתוב מדבר: **מזרע הארץ.** דגן: **מפרי העץ.** תירוש ויצהר: **לה' הוא.** קנאו השם ומשולחנו לוה לך לעלות ולאכול וס"א לעלותו לאכלו בירושלים (קידושין כד.) כמו שנאמר ואכלת לפני ה' אלהיך מעשר דגנך תירושך וגו' (דברים יד:כג). ולא **(לא) ממעשרו.** ממעשר חבירו, הפודה מעשר של חבירו אין מוסיף חומש (מעשר שני ד:ג; קידושין כד.) ומה היא גאולתו, (יפדנו) כדי להתירו באכילה בכל מקום והמעות יעלה ויאכל בירושלים כמו שכתוב ונתתה בכסף וגו' (דברים יד:כה): **(לב) תחת השבט.** כשבא לעשרן מוציאן מולין בפתח זה אחר זה והעשירי

— RASHI ELUCIDATED —

30. וְכָל מַעְשַׂר הָאָרֶץ — ANY TITHE OF THE LAND. בְּמַעֲשֵׂר שֵׁנִי הַכָּתוּב מְדַבֵּר — The verse speaks of the second tithe.[1]

☐ מִזֶּרַע הָאָרֶץ — OF THE SEED OF THE LAND, i.e., דָּגָן — grain.

☐ מִפְּרִי הָעֵץ — OF THE FRUIT OF THE TREE, i.e., תִּירוֹשׁ וְיִצְהָר — wine and oil.[2]

☐ לַה' הוּא — BELONGS TO HASHEM. קְנָאוֹ הַשֵּׁם — HASHEM has taken possession of it, וּמִשֻּׁלְחָנוֹ צִוָּה לְךָ לַעֲלוֹת וְלֶאֱכוֹל[3] בִּירוּשָׁלַיִם[4] — and He has commanded you to go up and to eat,[3] in Jerusalem, from His table,[4] כְּמוֹ שֶׁנֶּאֱמַר — as it says, "וְאָכַלְתָּ, — "And you shall eat לִפְנֵי ה' אֱלֹהֶיךָ — before HASHEM, your God, [in the place where He will choose to rest His Name] מַעְשַׂר דְּגָנְךָ תִּירשְׁךָ וְגוֹמֵר" — the tithe of your grain, wine, etc."[5]

31. מִמַּעַשְׂרוֹ — OF HIS TITHE, וְלֹא מִמַּעְשַׂר חֲבֵרוֹ — but not of the tithe of his fellow. הַפּוֹדֶה מַעְשַׂר שֶׁל חֲבֵרוֹ — One who redeems the tithe of his fellow אֵין מוֹסִיף חוֹמֶשׁ[6] — does not add a fifth.[6] וּמָה הִיא גְּאֻלָּתוֹ — What is its redemption?[7] {יִפְדֶּנּוּ} — He will redeem it כְּדֵי לְהַתִּירוֹ בַּאֲכִילָה — in order to permit it to be eaten בְּכָל מָקוֹם — in any place.[8] וְהַמָּעוֹת — And the money with which the tithe was redeemed יַעֲלֶה — he should take up וְיֹאכַל — and consume, i.e., and use to buy food, to be eaten בִּירוּשָׁלַיִם — in Jerusalem, כְּמוֹ שֶׁכָּתוּב — as it is written, "וְנָתַתָּה בַּכֶּסֶף וְגוֹמֵר"[9] — "and you shall give [it] for money, etc."[9]

32. תַּחַת הַשָּׁבֶט — UNDER THE STAFF. כְּשֶׁבָּא לְעַשְּׂרָן — When he comes to tithe them מוֹצִיאָן בַּפֶּתַח — he brings them out through the entrance זֶה אַחַר זֶה — one after the other, וְהָעֲשִׂירִי — and the

---

1. See *Deuteronomy* 14:22-26. The tithe of our verse is described as holy. This is characteristic only of the second tithe, which must be eaten in Jerusalem, in a state of ritual purity. Indeed, *Deuteronomy* 26:10 refers to this tithe as "holy" (see Rashi there). The first tithe and the tithe of the poor have no particular sanctity (*Mizrachi*; see, too, Rashi to *Numbers* 18:31 which states that the first tithe may be eaten even in a cemetery).

2. *Mizrachi* here states that Rashi agrees with the opinion of the *Rambam* that grain, wine, and oil are representative of the entire category of תְּבוּאָה "produce," i.e., foods, other than vegetables, that grow from the ground, to which the law of the second tithe applies. *Maskil LeDavid* notes, however, that Rashi to *Berachos* 36a, s.v. גבי מעשר, states explicitly that by Torah law, the second tithe applies only to grain, wine, and oil. The Rabbis extended the law to apply to other produce.

3. Some editions read . . . לַעֲלוֹתוֹ לְאָכְלוֹ, "to bring it up to eat it in Jerusalem."

4. *Kiddushin* 54b. "Belongs to HASHEM" does not mean that it is forbidden to man. It means that man eats it "from God's table," so to speak (*Mizrachi*; *Sifsei Chachamim*).

5. *Deuteronomy* 14:23.

6. *Maaser Sheni* 4:3; *Kiddushin* 24a.

7. That is, what is the point of redeeming it? It may be eaten even if it has not been redeemed (*Leket Bahir*).

8. Before redemption, it could be eaten only within the walls of Jerusalem.

9. *Deuteronomy* 14:25-26, which continues: "and bind the money in your hand, and go to the place which HASHEM, your God, shall choose. And you will give the money for anything your soul desires, for cattle and flocks and wine

shall be holy to Hashem. ³³ He shall not distinguish between good and bad and he should not substitute for it; and if he does substitute for it, then it and its substitute shall be holy, it may not be redeemed.

³⁴ These are the commandments that Hashem commanded Moses to the Children of Israel on Mount Sinai.

לג יִהְיֶה־קֹּדֶשׁ לַיהוָה: לֹא יְבַקֵּר בֵּין־טוֹב לָרַע וְלֹא יְמִירֶנּוּ וְאִם־הָמֵר יְמִירֶנּוּ וְהָיָה־הוּא וּתְמוּרָתוֹ יִהְיֶה־קֹדֶשׁ לֹא יִגָּאֵל: לד אֵלֶּה הַמִּצְוֹת אֲשֶׁר צִוָּה יְהוָה אֶת־מֹשֶׁה אֶל־בְּנֵי יִשְׂרָאֵל בְּהַר סִינָי:

At the conclusion of each of the five books of of the Torah, it is customary for the congregation followed by the reader to proclaim:

חֲזַק! חֲזַק! וְנִתְחַזֵּק!

"Chazak! Chazak! Venischazeik! (Be strong! Be strong! And may we be strengthened!)"

THE HAFTARAH FOR BECHUKOSAI APPEARS ON PAGE 402.

— אונקלוס —

יְהֵי קַדִּישׁ קֳדָם יְיָ: לג לָא יְבַקַּר בֵּין טָב לְבִישׁ וְלָא יַחְלְפִנֵּהּ וְאִם חַלָּפָא יַחְלְפִנֵּהּ וִיהֵי הוּא וְחִלּוּפֵהּ יְהֵי קֻדְשָׁא לָא יִתְפָּרֵק: לד אִלֵּין פִּקּוֹדַיָּא דִּי פַקִּיד יְיָ יָת מֹשֶׁה לִבְנֵי יִשְׂרָאֵל בְּטוּרָא דְסִינָי:

— רש"י —

(לג) לא יבקר וגו׳. לְפִי שֶׁנֶּאֱמַר בְּמִקְרָא לִהְיוֹת שָׂהוּא מַעֲשֵׂר נִכָּר שְׁהוּא לְטָעֲגִים וְלִטְלָאִים שֶׁל כָּל שָׁנָה וְשָׁנָה: יהיה קדש. לִיקְרַב יִבְחַר) יָכוֹל יְהֵא בּוֹרֵר וּמוֹצִיא אֶת הַיָּפָה, ת"ל לֹא יְבַקֵּר בֵּין טוֹב לָרַע, בֵּין תָּם בֵּין בַּעַל מוּם חָלָה עָלָיו קְדֻשָּׁה, וְלֹא שֶׁיִּקְרַב בַּעַל מוּם אֶלָּא יֵאָכֵל בְּתוֹרַת מַעֲשֵׂר וְאָסוּר לִגָּזֵז וּלְעָבֵד (בכורות יד:): לַמִּזְבֵּחַ דָּמוֹ וְאֵמוּרָיו, וְהַבָּשָׂר נֶאֱכָל לַבְּעָלִים שֶׁהֲרֵי לֹא נִמְנָה עִם שְׁאָר מַתְּנוֹת כְּהֻנָּה וְלֹא מָצִינוּ שֶׁיְּהֵא נִתָּן בְּשָׂרוֹ לַכֹּהֲנִים (זבחים נו:):

— RASHI ELUCIDATED —

לִהְיוֹת נִכָּר — **he strikes with a staff colored with red pigment** מַכֶּה בַּשֵּׁבֶט שֶׁבוּעַ צָבוּעַ בְּסִיקְרָא — **tenth one so that it will be discernible.**¹ שֶׁהוּא מַעֲשֵׂר — **that it is** of the tithe.¹ כֵּן עוֹשֶׂה — **So he does** לָעֲגָלִים — **to the calves** וְלַטְּלָאִים — **and to the lambs** שֶׁל כָּל שָׁנָה וְשָׁנָה — **of each and every year**'s yield.

□ יִהְיֶה קֹּדֶשׁ — SHALL BE HOLY לִקְרַב לַמִּזְבֵּחַ דָּמוֹ וְאֵמוּרָיו — **for its blood and specified parts to be offered on the** Mizbe'ach, וְהַבָּשָׂר נֶאֱכָל לַבְּעָלִים — **and the meat is eaten by the owner,**² שֶׁהֲרֵי לֹא נִמְנָה — **for, see now, it has not been listed** עִם שְׁאָר מַתְּנוֹת כְּהֻנָּה — **among the rest of the gifts of priesthood,** i.e., gifts that are the portion of the Kohanim, וְלֹא מָצִינוּ — **nor have we found** שֶׁיְּהֵא נָתוּן בְּשָׂרוֹ — **that its meat should be given** ³לַכֹּהֲנִים — **to the Kohanim.**³

33. ״וְכָל מִבְחַר נִדְרֵיכֶם״ — HE SHALL NOT DISTINGUISH, ETC. לְפִי שֶׁנֶּאֱמַר — **Since it says,** ⁴"**all the choicest of your vows,**"⁴ יָכוֹל — **one might be able** to think יְהֵא בּוֹרֵר — **that he should select** וּמוֹצִיא — **and take out** אֶת הַיָּפָה — **the nicest** of his cattle for the tithe. תַּלְמוּד לוֹמַר — To teach us otherwise, the verse says, ״לֹא יְבַקֵּר בֵּין טוֹב לָרַע״ — "**he shall not distinguish between good and bad**"; בֵּין תָּם — **whether it is one that is free of blemish** בֵּין בַּעַל מוּם — **or whether it is one that is blemished,** חָלָה עָלָיו קְדֻשָּׁה — **sanctity** of the tithe **takes effect upon it** if it is the tenth to emerge through the entrance. וְלֹא שֶׁיִּקְרַב בַּעַל מוּם — **Not that it should be offered** on the Mizbe'ach **in a blemished state,** אֶלָּא יֵאָכֵל בְּתוֹרַת מַעֲשֵׂר — **but that it should be eaten with the law of the tithe,**⁵ וְאָסוּר לִגָּזֵז — **and it may not be shorn** of its fleece ⁶וְלַעֲבֹד — **nor be used for work.**⁶

---

and hard drink, and for anything your soul will ask of you. And you will eat there, before Hashem, your God."

1. *Bechoros* 58b.
2. Or by any Jew to whom the owner chooses to give it, providing he is ritually pure, and not in mourning.
3. *Zevachim* 56b.
4. *Deuteronomy* 12:11. Rashi there notes that the verse implies that animals selected as an offering should be selected from those of the highest quality.
5. It may not be sold unless it is both blemished and the property of orphans. Even then, it may not be sold in a butcher shop, or by weight (*Bechoros* 31b).
6. *Bechoros* 14b.

ההפטרות
The Haftaros

BLESSINGS OF THE HAFTARAH / ברכות ההפטרה

After the Torah Scroll has been tied and covered, the Maftir recites the Haftarah blessings.

Blessed are You, HASHEM, our God, King of the universe, Who has chosen good prophets and was pleased with their words that were uttered with truth. Blessed are You, HASHEM, Who chooses the Torah; Moses, His servant; Israel, His nation; and the prophets of truth and righteousness. (Cong. — Amen.)

בָּרוּךְ אַתָּה יהוה אֱלֹהֵינוּ מֶלֶךְ הָעוֹלָם, אֲשֶׁר בָּחַר בִּנְבִיאִים טוֹבִים, וְרָצָה בְדִבְרֵיהֶם הַנֶּאֱמָרִים בֶּאֱמֶת, בָּרוּךְ אַתָּה יהוה, הַבּוֹחֵר בַּתּוֹרָה וּבְמֹשֶׁה עַבְדּוֹ, וּבְיִשְׂרָאֵל עַמּוֹ, וּבִנְבִיאֵי הָאֱמֶת וָצֶדֶק. (קהל – אָמֵן)

The Haftarah is read, after which the Maftir recites the following blessings.

Blessed are You, HASHEM, our God, King of the universe, Rock of all eternities, Righteous in all generations, the trustworthy God, Who says and does, Who speaks and fulfills, all of Whose words are true and righteous. Trustworthy are You HASHEM, our God, and trustworthy are Your words, not one of Your words is turned back to its origin unfulfilled, for You are God, trustworthy (and compassionate) King. Blessed are You, HASHEM, the God Who is trustworthy in all His words. (Cong. — Amen.)

בָּרוּךְ אַתָּה יהוה אֱלֹהֵינוּ מֶלֶךְ הָעוֹלָם, צוּר כָּל הָעוֹלָמִים, צַדִּיק בְּכָל הַדּוֹרוֹת, הָאֵל הַנֶּאֱמָן הָאוֹמֵר וְעֹשֶׂה, הַמְדַבֵּר וּמְקַיֵּם, שֶׁכָּל דְּבָרָיו אֱמֶת וָצֶדֶק. נֶאֱמָן אַתָּה הוּא יהוה אֱלֹהֵינוּ, וְנֶאֱמָנִים דְּבָרֶיךָ, וְדָבָר אֶחָד מִדְּבָרֶיךָ אָחוֹר לֹא יָשׁוּב רֵיקָם, כִּי אֵל מֶלֶךְ נֶאֱמָן (וְרַחֲמָן) אָתָּה. בָּרוּךְ אַתָּה יהוה, הָאֵל הַנֶּאֱמָן בְּכָל דְּבָרָיו. (קהל – אָמֵן)

Have mercy on Zion for it is the source of our life; to the one who is deeply humiliated bring salvation speedily, in our days. Blessed are You, HASHEM, Who gladdens Zion through her children. (Cong. — Amen.)

רַחֵם עַל צִיּוֹן כִּי הִיא בֵּית חַיֵּינוּ, וְלַעֲלוּבַת נֶפֶשׁ תּוֹשִׁיעַ בִּמְהֵרָה בְיָמֵינוּ. בָּרוּךְ אַתָּה יהוה, מְשַׂמֵּחַ צִיּוֹן בְּבָנֶיהָ. (קהל – אָמֵן)

Gladden us, HASHEM, our God, with Elijah the prophet Your servant, and with the kingdom of the House of David, Your anointed, may he come speedily and cause our heart to exult. On his throne let no stranger sit nor let others continue to inherit his honor, for by Your holy Name You swore to him that his lamp will not be extinguished forever and ever. Blessed are You, HASHEM, Shield of David. (Cong. — Amen.)

שַׂמְּחֵנוּ יהוה אֱלֹהֵינוּ בְּאֵלִיָּהוּ הַנָּבִיא עַבְדֶּךָ, וּבְמַלְכוּת בֵּית דָּוִד מְשִׁיחֶךָ, בִּמְהֵרָה יָבֹא וְיָגֵל לִבֵּנוּ, עַל כִּסְאוֹ לֹא יֵשֶׁב זָר וְלֹא יִנְחֲלוּ עוֹד אֲחֵרִים אֶת כְּבוֹדוֹ, כִּי בְשֵׁם קָדְשְׁךָ נִשְׁבַּעְתָּ לּוֹ, שֶׁלֹּא יִכְבֶּה נֵרוֹ לְעוֹלָם וָעֶד. בָּרוּךְ אַתָּה יהוה, מָגֵן דָּוִד. (קהל – אָמֵן)

For the Torah reading, for the prayer service, for the reading from the Prophets and for this Sabbath day that You, HASHEM, our God, have given us for holiness and contentment, for glory and splendor — for all this, HASHEM, our God, we gratefully thank You and bless You. May Your Name be blessed by the mouth of all the living always, for all eternity. Blessed are You, HASHEM, Who sanctifies the Sabbath. (Cong. — Amen.)

עַל הַתּוֹרָה, וְעַל הָעֲבוֹדָה, וְעַל הַנְּבִיאִים, וְעַל יוֹם הַשַּׁבָּת הַזֶּה, שֶׁנָּתַתָּ לָּנוּ יהוה אֱלֹהֵינוּ לִקְדֻשָּׁה וְלִמְנוּחָה, לְכָבוֹד וּלְתִפְאָרֶת. עַל הַכֹּל יהוה אֱלֹהֵינוּ, אֲנַחְנוּ מוֹדִים לָךְ, וּמְבָרְכִים אוֹתָךְ, יִתְבָּרַךְ שִׁמְךָ בְּפִי כָּל חַי תָּמִיד לְעוֹלָם וָעֶד. בָּרוּךְ אַתָּה יהוה, מְקַדֵּשׁ הַשַּׁבָּת. (קהל – אָמֵן)

HAFTARAS VAYIKRA / הפטרת ויקרא

Isaiah 43:21-44:23 / ישעיה מג:כא-מד:כג

43 [21] I fashioned this people for Myself that it might declare My praise. [22] But you did not call to Me, O Jacob, for you grew weary of Me, O Israel. [23] You did not bring Me sheep for your olah-offerings, nor did you honor Me with your peace-offerings; I did not burden you with a meal-offering, nor did I weary you with frankincense. [24] You bought Me no cinnamon with silver, nor did you satisfy Me with the fat of your offerings — but you burdened Me with your sins, you wearied Me with your iniquities. [25] I, only I, am the One Who wipes away your willful sins for My sake, and I shall not recall your sins. [26] Remind Me! — let us contest one another; tell your side first that you may be vindicated. [27] Your first patriarch erred, and your advocates betrayed Me. [28] So I have profaned the holy princes; I handed Jacob to devastation and Israel to rebukes.

44 [1] And now, listen, Jacob My servant; and Israel whom I have chosen. [2] So says Hashem Who made you and fashioned you from the womb — He will help you; fear not, My servant Jacob, and Jeshurun whom I have chosen. [3] Just as I pour water upon the thirsty land and streams upon the dry ground, so shall I pour My spirit upon your offspring and My blessing upon your children. [4] They will flourish among the grass like willows by streams of water. [5] This one will say: "I am Hashem's," and the other one will call in the name of Jacob; one will sign his allegiance to Hashem, and another will adopt the name Israel.

[6] So said Hashem, King of Israel and its Redeemer, Hashem, Master of Legions: I am the first and I am the last, and aside from Me there is no God. [7] Who can declare that he, like Me, can proclaim and order events since I emplaced the people of antiquity? And let them tell us miracles that will yet come. [8] Be not afraid and be not terrified! Did I not let you hear and tell you of yore? And you are My witnesses — is there a god beside Me? There is no rock I do not know! [9] All who fashion statues are empty, and their treasures will not avail; they bear witness on themselves for they see not and know not, let their worshipers be shamed. [10] Who would fashion a god or a molten statue that has no purpose? [11] Behold! all who join it will be shamed, and the artisans — they are but human! Let them all gather and stand, they shall be frightened and shamed together.

[12] The ironsmith makes his tool and works with charcoal, and fashions [an idol] with hammers; he crafts it with all his strength, though he may be hungry and without strength, he drinks no water and grows faint. [13] The woodworker stretches a line

מג כא עַם־זוּ֙ יָצַ֣רְתִּי לִ֔י תְּהִלָּתִ֖י יְסַפֵּֽרוּ׃ כב וְלֹא־אֹתִ֥י קָרָ֖אתָ יַעֲקֹ֑ב כִּֽי־יָגַ֥עְתָּ בִּ֖י יִשְׂרָאֵֽל׃ כג לֹֽא־הֵבֵ֤יאתָ לִּי֙ שֵׂ֣ה עֹלֹתֶ֔יךָ וּזְבָחֶ֖יךָ לֹ֣א כִבַּדְתָּ֑נִי לֹ֤א הֶעֱבַדְתִּ֨יךָ֙ בְּמִנְחָ֔ה וְלֹ֥א הוֹגַעְתִּ֖יךָ בִּלְבוֹנָֽה׃ כד לֹֽא־קָנִ֨יתָ לִּ֤י בַכֶּ֨סֶף֙ קָנֶ֔ה וְחֵ֥לֶב זְבָחֶ֖יךָ לֹ֣א הִרְוִיתָ֑נִי אַ֗ךְ הֶעֱבַדְתַּ֨נִי֙ בְּחַטֹּאותֶ֔יךָ הוֹגַעְתַּ֖נִי בַּעֲוֺנֹתֶֽיךָ׃ כה אָנֹכִ֨י אָנֹכִ֥י ה֛וּא מֹחֶ֥ה פְשָׁעֶ֖יךָ לְמַעֲנִ֑י וְחַטֹּאתֶ֖יךָ לֹ֥א אֶזְכֹּֽר׃ כו הַזְכִּירֵ֕נִי נִשָּׁפְטָ֖ה יָ֑חַד סַפֵּ֥ר אַתָּ֖ה לְמַ֥עַן תִּצְדָּֽק׃ כז אָבִ֥יךָ הָרִאשׁ֖וֹן חָטָ֑א וּמְלִיצֶ֖יךָ פָּ֥שְׁעוּ בִֽי׃ כח וַאֲחַלֵּ֖ל שָׂ֣רֵי קֹ֑דֶשׁ וְאֶתְּנָ֤ה לַחֵ֨רֶם֙ יַעֲקֹ֔ב וְיִשְׂרָאֵ֖ל לְגִדּוּפִֽים׃

מד א וְעַתָּ֥ה שְׁמַ֖ע יַעֲקֹ֣ב עַבְדִּ֑י וְיִשְׂרָאֵ֖ל בָּחַ֥רְתִּי בֽוֹ׃ ב כֹּה־אָמַ֨ר יְהֹוָ֥ה עֹשֶׂ֛ךָ וְיֹצֶרְךָ֥ מִבֶּ֖טֶן יַעְזְרֶ֑ךָּ אַל־תִּירָא֙ עַבְדִּ֣י יַעֲקֹ֔ב וִישֻׁר֖וּן בָּחַ֥רְתִּי בֽוֹ׃ ג כִּ֤י אֶצָּק־מַ֨יִם֙ עַל־צָמֵ֔א וְנֹזְלִ֖ים עַל־יַבָּשָׁ֑ה אֶצֹּ֤ק רוּחִי֙ עַל־זַרְעֶ֔ךָ וּבִרְכָתִ֖י עַל־צֶאֱצָאֶֽיךָ׃ ד וְצָמְח֖וּ בְּבֵ֣ין חָצִ֑יר כַּעֲרָבִ֖ים עַל־יִבְלֵי־מָֽיִם׃ ה זֶ֤ה יֹאמַר֙ לַיהֹוָ֣ה אָ֔נִי וְזֶ֖ה יִקְרָ֣א בְשֵֽׁם־יַעֲקֹ֑ב וְזֶ֗ה יִכְתֹּ֤ב יָדוֹ֙ לַֽיהֹוָ֔ה וּבְשֵׁ֥ם יִשְׂרָאֵ֖ל יְכַנֶּֽה׃ ו כֹּֽה־אָמַ֨ר יְהֹוָ֧ה מֶֽלֶךְ־יִשְׂרָאֵ֛ל וְגֹאֲל֖וֹ יְהֹוָ֣ה צְבָא֑וֹת אֲנִ֤י רִאשׁוֹן֙ וַאֲנִ֣י אַחֲר֔וֹן וּמִבַּלְעָדַ֖י אֵ֥ין אֱלֹהִֽים׃ ז וּמִֽי־כָמ֣וֹנִי יִקְרָ֗א וְיַגִּידֶ֤הָ וְיַעְרְכֶ֨הָ֙ לִ֔י מִשּׂוּמִ֖י עַם־עוֹלָ֑ם וְאֹתִיּ֛וֹת וַאֲשֶׁ֥ר תָּבֹ֖אנָה יַגִּ֥ידוּ לָֽמוֹ׃ ח אַֽל־תִּפְחֲדוּ֙ וְאַל־תִּרְה֔וּ הֲלֹ֥א מֵאָ֛ז הִשְׁמַעְתִּ֥יךָ וְהִגַּ֖דְתִּי וְאַתֶּ֣ם עֵדָ֑י הֲיֵ֤שׁ אֱל֨וֹהַּ֙ מִבַּלְעָדַ֔י וְאֵ֥ין צ֖וּר בַּל־יָדָֽעְתִּי׃ ט יֹֽצְרֵי־פֶ֤סֶל כֻּלָּם֙ תֹּ֔הוּ וַחֲמוּדֵיהֶ֖ם בַּל־יוֹעִ֑ילוּ וְעֵדֵיהֶ֣ם הֵ֗מָּה [נקוד על המה] בַּל־יִרְאוּ֙ וּבַל־יֵ֣דְע֔וּ לְמַ֖עַן יֵבֹֽשׁוּ׃ י מִֽי־יָצַ֥ר אֵ֖ל וּפֶ֣סֶל נָסָ֑ךְ לְבִלְתִּ֖י הוֹעִֽיל׃ יא הֵ֤ן כָּל־חֲבֵרָיו֙ יֵבֹ֔שׁוּ וְחָרָשִׁ֥ים הֵ֖מָּה מֵֽאָדָ֑ם יִֽתְקַבְּצ֤וּ כֻלָּם֙ יַֽעֲמֹ֔דוּ יִפְחֲד֖וּ יֵבֹ֥שׁוּ יָֽחַד׃ יב חָרַ֣שׁ בַּרְזֶ֗ל מַֽעֲצָד֙ וּפָעַ֣ל בַּפֶּחָ֔ם וּבַמַּקָּב֖וֹת יִצְּרֵ֑הוּ וַיִּפְעָלֵ֨הוּ֙ בִּזְר֣וֹעַ כֹּח֔וֹ גַּם־רָעֵב֙ וְאֵ֣ין כֹּ֔חַ לֹא־שָׁ֥תָה מַ֖יִם וַיִּיעָֽף׃ יג חָרַ֣שׁ עֵצִ֔ים נָ֖טָה קָ֑ו

and marks his shape with a chalk, he works on [an idol] with planes and marks it with a compass; he makes it like a human form, like human splendor, only to be deposited in a house. [14] He cuts himself cedar trees; he takes shade trees and oak trees and strengthens them with trees of the forest; he plants a fir tree and the rain makes it grow. [15] It will be fuel for man, he will take some of them and warm himself and even make a fire and bake bread — and he will even make of it a god and prostrate himself, he will make a graven image and worship it!

[16] He burns half of it in the fire, with half he prepares meat to eat, roasting it and sating himself; he will even warm himself and say, "Ah, I have warmed myself, I enjoy the fire." [17] And with the rest he makes a god as his graven image; he will bow to it, prostrate himself and pray to it; he will say, "Save me, for you are my god!" [18] They do not know, they do not understand; a coating prevents their eyes from seeing and their hearts from comprehending. [19] He does not rebuke his heart; there is no wisdom or insight to say: "I burned half of it in the fire and I baked bread on its coals, I roasted meat and ate it — could I make an abomination of the rest, could I bow to the branch of a tree?"

[20] His "shepherd" is but ashes, his mocking heart deceived him; he cannot even save himself, yet he does not say: "There is falsehood in my right hand."

[21] Remember this, O Jacob and Israel, for you are My servant — I fashioned you to be My servant — O Israel, do not forget Me! [22] I will have wiped away your willful sins like a cloud and your errors like a wisp — return to Me, for I will have redeemed you. [23] Sing glad song, O heaven, for what HASHEM has done; call out, O core of the earth; break out, O mountains, in glad song, O forest and every tree within it; for HASHEM will have redeemed Jacob, and He will glorify Himself in Israel.

HAFTARAS TZAV / הפטרת צו
Jeremiah 7:21 — 8:3, 9:22-23

7 [21] So said HASHEM, Master of Legions, God of Israel: Pile your olah-offerings upon your peace-offerings and eat flesh. [22] For I did not speak with your forefathers nor did I command them — on the day I took them out of the land of Egypt — concerning olah-offering or peace-offering. [23] Rather, I commanded them regarding only this matter, saying: "Hear My voice that I may be a God unto you and you will be a people unto Me; and you shall follow along the entire path in which I command you, so that it will go well for you."

[24] But they did not hear, they did not incline their ear, and they followed their own counsels and the fancies of their evil heart; they went backwards and not forward. [25] From the day your forefathers left the land of Egypt until this day,

I sent them all My servants the prophets, every day I would send them early in the morning. ²⁶ *But they would not listen to Me, and they would not incline their ear; they stiffened their neck and became more evil than their forefathers.*

²⁷ *You will tell them all these things but they will not listen to you; you will call to them but they will not answer you.*

²⁸ *You shall tell them, "This is the nation that will not listen to the voice of* HASHEM, *its God, and will not accept rebuke; its faith is lost and cut off from their mouth."*

²⁹ *Tear out your hair and throw it away, proclaim lament from the heights; for* HASHEM *has despised and forsaken the generation of His wrath.* ³⁰ *For the children of Judah have done what is evil in My eyes — the word of* HASHEM — *they have placed their abominations in the House upon which My Name was proclaimed, to contaminate it.* ³¹ *They have built the high altars of Topheth that are in the Valley of the Son of Hinnom, to burn their sons and daughters in the fire — which I have not commanded and have not contemplated!*

³² *Therefore, behold! days are coming — the word of* HASHEM — *when it will no longer be called the Topheth and the Valley of the Son of Hinnom, but the Valley of Murder; and they will bury in Topheth until there is no more room.* ³³ *The carcass of this people will be food for the bird of the heaven and the animal of the earth, and none will frighten them away.* ³⁴ *I will suspend from the cities of Judah and the streets of Jerusalem the sound of joy and the sound of gladness, the voice of the groom and the voice of the bride; for the land will become ruin.*

8 ¹ At that time — the word of HASHEM — they will remove the bones of the kings of Judah, the bones of its ministers, the bones of the priests, the bones of the prophets, and the bones of Jerusalem's inhabitants from their graves. ² *They will spread them out in the sun and the moon and all the heavenly legions, which the people loved and which they worshiped and followed, and which they sought out and to which they prostrated themselves; [the bones] will not be gathered together nor buried — they will be dung upon the face of the earth.* ³ *Death will be preferable to life for the remnant of those who survive from this evil family, who survive in all the places where I have driven them — the word of* HASHEM, *Master of Legions.*

9 ²² So says HASHEM; *Let a wise man not glory in his wisdom, nor let the strong one glory in his strength, nor let a wealthy one glory in his wealth.* ²³ *Only in this may one who glories glorify himself: in discerning and knowing Me, for I am* HASHEM, *Who performs kindness, judgment, and righteousness in the world; for these are what I desire — the word of* HASHEM.

וָאֶשְׁלַ֤ח אֲלֵיכֶם֙ אֶת־כָּל־עֲבָדַ֣י הַנְּבִיאִ֔ים י֖וֹם הַשְׁכֵּ֣ם וְשָׁלֹ֑חַ: כו וְל֤וֹא שָׁמְעוּ֙ אֵלַ֔י וְלֹ֥א הִטּ֖וּ אֶת־אָזְנָ֑ם וַיַּקְשׁוּ֙ אֶת־עָרְפָּ֔ם הֵרֵ֖עוּ מֵאֲבוֹתָֽם: כז וְדִבַּרְתָּ֤ אֲלֵיהֶם֙ אֶת־כָּל־הַדְּבָרִ֣ים הָאֵ֔לֶּה וְלֹ֥א יִשְׁמְע֖וּ אֵלֶ֑יךָ וְקָרָ֥אתָ אֲלֵיהֶ֖ם וְלֹ֥א יַעֲנֽוּכָה: כח וְאָמַרְתָּ֣ אֲלֵיהֶ֔ם זֶ֣ה הַגּ֗וֹי אֲשֶׁ֤ר לֽוֹא־שָֽׁמְעוּ֙ בְּקוֹל֙ יְהֹוָ֣ה אֱלֹהָ֔יו וְלֹ֥א לָקְח֖וּ מוּסָ֑ר אָבְדָה֙ הָאֱמוּנָ֔ה וְנִכְרְתָ֖ה מִפִּיהֶֽם: כט גָּזִּ֤י נִזְרֵךְ֙ וְֽהַשְׁלִ֔יכִי וּשְׂאִ֥י עַל־שְׁפָיִ֖ם קִינָ֑ה כִּ֚י מָאַ֣ס יְהֹוָ֔ה וַיִּטֹּ֖שׁ אֶת־דּ֥וֹר עֶבְרָתֽוֹ: ל כִּֽי־עָשׂ֨וּ בְנֵֽי־יְהוּדָ֥ה הָרַ֛ע בְּעֵינַ֖י נְאֻם־יְהוָֹ֑ה שָׂ֣מוּ שִׁקּֽוּצֵיהֶ֗ם בַּבַּ֛יִת אֲשֶׁר־נִקְרָא־שְׁמִ֥י עָלָ֖יו לְטַמְּאֽוֹ: לא וּבָנ֞וּ בָּמ֣וֹת הַתֹּ֗פֶת אֲשֶׁר֙ בְּגֵ֣יא בֶן־הִנֹּ֔ם לִשְׂרֹ֛ף אֶת־בְּנֵיהֶ֥ם וְאֶת־בְּנֹתֵיהֶ֖ם בָּאֵ֑שׁ אֲשֶׁר֙ לֹ֣א צִוִּ֔יתִי וְלֹ֥א עָלְתָ֖ה עַל־לִבִּֽי: לב לָכֵ֞ן הִנֵּ֤ה יָמִים֙ בָּאִ֣ים נְאֻם־יְהֹוָ֔ה וְלֹא־יֵאָמֵ֨ר ע֤וֹד הַתֹּ֙פֶת֙ וְגֵ֣יא בֶן־הִנֹּ֔ם כִּ֖י אִם־גֵּ֣יא הַהֲרֵגָ֑ה וְקָבְר֥וּ בְתֹ֖פֶת מֵאֵ֥ין מָקֽוֹם: לג וְֽהָיְתָ֞ה נִבְלַת֙ הָעָ֣ם הַזֶּ֔ה לְמַֽאֲכָ֛ל לְע֥וֹף הַשָּׁמַ֖יִם וּלְבֶֽהֱמַ֣ת הָאָ֑רֶץ וְאֵ֖ין מַֽחֲרִֽיד: לד וְהִשְׁבַּתִּ֣י ׀ מֵעָרֵ֣י יְהוּדָ֗ה וּמֵֽחֻצוֹת֙ יְר֣וּשָׁלִַ֔ם ק֤וֹל שָׂשׂוֹן֙ וְק֣וֹל שִׂמְחָ֔ה ק֥וֹל חָתָ֖ן וְק֣וֹל כַּלָּ֑ה כִּ֥י לְחָרְבָּ֖ה תִּֽהְיֶ֥ה הָאָֽרֶץ: ח א בָּעֵ֨ת הַהִ֜יא נְאֻם־יְהֹוָ֗ה יוֹצִ֜יאוּ [יוֹצִ֜יאוּ כ׳] אֶת־עַצְמ֣וֹת מַלְכֵֽי־יְהוּדָ֠ה וְאֶת־עַצְמ֨וֹת שָׂרָ֜יו וְאֶת־עַצְמ֣וֹת הַכֹּֽהֲנִ֗ים וְאֵ֚ת ׀ עַצְמ֣וֹת הַנְּבִיאִ֔ים וְאֵ֖ת עַצְמ֣וֹת יֽוֹשְׁבֵֽי־יְרֽוּשָׁלִָ֑ם מִקִּבְרֵיהֶֽם: ב וּשְׁטָחוּם֩ לַשֶּׁ֨מֶשׁ וְלַיָּרֵ֜חַ וּלְכֹ֣ל ׀ צְבָ֣א הַשָּׁמַ֗יִם אֲשֶׁ֨ר אֲהֵב֜וּם וַֽאֲשֶׁ֤ר עֲבָדוּם֙ וַֽאֲשֶׁר֙ הָֽלְכ֣וּ אַֽחֲרֵיהֶ֔ם וַֽאֲשֶׁ֣ר דְּרָשׁ֔וּם וַֽאֲשֶׁ֥ר הִשְׁתַּֽחֲו֖וּ לָהֶ֑ם לֹ֤א יֵאָֽסְפוּ֙ וְלֹ֣א יִקָּבֵ֔רוּ לְדֹ֛מֶן עַל־פְּנֵ֥י הָאֲדָמָ֖ה יִֽהְיֽוּ: ג וְנִבְחַ֣ר מָ֗וֶת מֵֽחַיִּ֔ים לְכֹ֗ל הַשְּׁאֵרִית֙ הַנִּשְׁאָרִ֔ים מִן־הַמִּשְׁפָּחָ֥ה הָֽרָעָ֖ה הַזֹּ֑את בְּכָל־הַמְּקֹמ֤וֹת הַנִּשְׁאָרִים֙ אֲשֶׁ֣ר הִדַּחְתִּ֣ים שָׁ֔ם נְאֻ֖ם יְהֹוָ֥ה צְבָאֽוֹת: ט כב כֹּ֣ה ׀ אָמַ֣ר יְהֹוָ֗ה אַל־יִתְהַלֵּ֤ל חָכָם֙ בְּחָכְמָת֔וֹ וְאַל־יִתְהַלֵּ֥ל הַגִּבּ֖וֹר בִּגְבֽוּרָת֑וֹ אַל־יִתְהַלֵּ֥ל עָשִׁ֖יר בְּעָשְׁרֽוֹ: כג כִּ֣י אִם־בְּזֹ֞את יִתְהַלֵּ֣ל הַמִּתְהַלֵּ֗ל הַשְׂכֵּל֘ וְיָדֹ֣עַ אוֹתִי֒ כִּ֚י אֲנִ֣י יְהֹוָ֔ה עֹ֥שֶׂה חֶ֛סֶד מִשְׁפָּ֥ט וּצְדָקָ֖ה בָּאָ֑רֶץ כִּֽי־בְאֵ֥לֶּה חָפַ֖צְתִּי נְאֻם־יְהוָֹֽה:

HAFTARAS SHEMINI / הפטרת שמיני

II Samuel 6:1 — 7:17 / שמואל ב ו:א — ז:יז

ו ¹ **D**avid once again gathered every chosen one in Israel, thirty thousand. ² David rose up and went, with the entire people that was with him, from Baale-judah to bring up from there the Ark of God upon which is called the Name: the Name of Hashem — Master of Legions, Who is enthroned upon the Cherubim — is upon it. ³ They placed the Ark of God upon a new wagon and bore it from the house of Abinadab that was in Gibeah, and Uzzah and Ahio the sons of Abinadab guided the new wagon. ⁴ They bore it from the house of Abinadab that was in Gibeah, with the Ark of God, and Ahio walked in front of the Ark. ⁵ David and the entire House of Israel were rejoicing before Hashem with all the cypress-wood instruments, with harps, lyres, and drums, with timbrels and cymbals. ⁶ They came to the threshing-floor of Nahon — and Uzzah reached out to the Ark of God and grasped it, for the oxen had shifted it. ⁷ The anger of Hashem flared up against Uzzah and God struck him there for the error; Uzzah died there by the Ark of God.

⁸ David was upset because of the breach with which Hashem had broken forth against Uzzah; he called that place Breach of Uzzah to this very day. ⁹ David feared Hashem on that day, and he said: "How can the Ark of Hashem come to me?" ¹⁰ David refused to remove the Ark of Hashem to himself to the City of David; and David diverted it to the house of Obed-edom the Gittite.

¹¹ The Ark remained in the house of Obed-edom the Gittite for three months, and Hashem blessed Obed-edom and his entire household. ¹² It was related to King David, saying: "Hashem has blessed the house of Obed-edom and all that is his because of the Ark of God." So David went and he brought up the Ark of God from the house of Obed-edom to the City of David, with gladness. ¹³ Whenever the bearers of the Ark of Hashem walked six paces, he slaughtered an ox and a fatted ox. ¹⁴ David danced with all his strength before Hashem, and David was girdled in a linen tunic. ¹⁵ David and the entire House of Israel brought up the Ark of Hashem with loud joyous sound and the sound of the shofar.

¹⁶ When the Ark of Hashem arrived at the City of David, Michal daughter of Saul looked out the window and saw King David leaping and dancing before Hashem, and she was contemptuous of him in her heart.

¹⁷ They brought the Ark of Hashem and set it up in its place, in the tent that David had pitched for it;

ו א וַיֹּסֶף עוֹד דָּוִד אֶת־כָּל־בָּחוּר בְּיִשְׂרָאֵל שְׁלֹשִׁים אָלֶף: ב וַיָּקָם ׀ וַיֵּלֶךְ דָּוִד וְכָל־הָעָם אֲשֶׁר אִתּוֹ מִבַּעֲלֵי יְהוּדָה לְהַעֲלוֹת מִשָּׁם אֵת אֲרוֹן הָאֱלֹהִים אֲשֶׁר־נִקְרָא שֵׁם שֵׁם יְהוָה צְבָאוֹת יֹשֵׁב הַכְּרֻבִים עָלָיו: ג וַיַּרְכִּבוּ אֶת־אֲרוֹן הָאֱלֹהִים אֶל־עֲגָלָה חֲדָשָׁה וַיִּשָּׂאֻהוּ מִבֵּית אֲבִינָדָב אֲשֶׁר בַּגִּבְעָה וְעֻזָּא וְאַחְיוֹ בְּנֵי אֲבִינָדָב נֹהֲגִים אֶת־הָעֲגָלָה חֲדָשָׁה: ד וַיִּשָּׂאֻהוּ מִבֵּית אֲבִינָדָב אֲשֶׁר בַּגִּבְעָה עִם אֲרוֹן הָאֱלֹהִים וְאַחְיוֹ הֹלֵךְ לִפְנֵי הָאָרוֹן: ה וְדָוִד ׀ וְכָל־בֵּית יִשְׂרָאֵל מְשַׂחֲקִים לִפְנֵי יְהוָה בְּכֹל עֲצֵי בְרוֹשִׁים וּבְכִנֹּרוֹת וּבִנְבָלִים וּבְתֻפִּים וּבִמְנַעַנְעִים וּבְצֶלְצֶלִים: ו וַיָּבֹאוּ עַד־גֹּרֶן נָכוֹן וַיִּשְׁלַח עֻזָּה אֶל־אֲרוֹן הָאֱלֹהִים וַיֹּאחֶז בּוֹ כִּי שָׁמְטוּ הַבָּקָר: ז וַיִּחַר־אַף יְהוָה בְּעֻזָּה וַיַּכֵּהוּ שָׁם הָאֱלֹהִים עַל־הַשַּׁל וַיָּמָת שָׁם עִם אֲרוֹן הָאֱלֹהִים: ח וַיִּחַר לְדָוִד עַל אֲשֶׁר פָּרַץ יְהוָה פֶּרֶץ בְּעֻזָּה וַיִּקְרָא לַמָּקוֹם הַהוּא פֶּרֶץ עֻזָּה עַד הַיּוֹם הַזֶּה: ט וַיִּרָא דָוִד אֶת־יְהוָה בַּיּוֹם הַהוּא וַיֹּאמֶר אֵיךְ יָבוֹא אֵלַי אֲרוֹן יְהוָה: י וְלֹא־אָבָה דָוִד לְהָסִיר אֵלָיו אֶת־אֲרוֹן יְהוָה עַל־עִיר דָּוִד וַיַּטֵּהוּ דָוִד בֵּית עֹבֵד־אֱדֹם הַגִּתִּי: יא וַיֵּשֶׁב אֲרוֹן יְהוָה בֵּית עֹבֵד אֱדֹם הַגִּתִּי שְׁלֹשָׁה חֳדָשִׁים וַיְבָרֶךְ יְהוָה אֶת־עֹבֵד אֱדֹם וְאֶת־כָּל־בֵּיתוֹ: יב וַיֻּגַּד לַמֶּלֶךְ דָּוִד לֵאמֹר בֵּרַךְ יְהוָה אֶת־בֵּית עֹבֵד אֱדֹם וְאֶת־כָּל־אֲשֶׁר־לוֹ בַּעֲבוּר אֲרוֹן הָאֱלֹהִים וַיֵּלֶךְ דָּוִד וַיַּעַל אֶת־אֲרוֹן הָאֱלֹהִים מִבֵּית עֹבֵד אֱדֹם עִיר דָּוִד בְּשִׂמְחָה: יג וַיְהִי כִּי צָעֲדוּ נֹשְׂאֵי אֲרוֹן־יְהוָה שִׁשָּׁה צְעָדִים וַיִּזְבַּח שׁוֹר וּמְרִיא: יד וְדָוִד מְכַרְכֵּר בְּכָל־עֹז לִפְנֵי יְהוָה וְדָוִד חָגוּר אֵפוֹד בָּד: טו וְדָוִד וְכָל־בֵּית יִשְׂרָאֵל מַעֲלִים אֶת־אֲרוֹן יְהוָה בִּתְרוּעָה וּבְקוֹל שׁוֹפָר: טז וְהָיָה אֲרוֹן יְהוָה בָּא עִיר דָּוִד וּמִיכַל בַּת־שָׁאוּל נִשְׁקְפָה ׀ בְּעַד הַחַלּוֹן וַתֵּרֶא אֶת־הַמֶּלֶךְ דָּוִד מְפַזֵּז וּמְכַרְכֵּר לִפְנֵי יְהוָה וַתִּבֶז לוֹ בְּלִבָּהּ: יז וַיָּבִאוּ אֶת־אֲרוֹן יְהוָה וַיַּצִּגוּ אֹתוֹ בִּמְקוֹמוֹ בְּתוֹךְ הָאֹהֶל אֲשֶׁר נָטָה־לוֹ דָּוִד

and David brought up olah-offerings before HASHEM, and peace-offerings. ¹⁸ When David had finished bringing up the olah-offering and the peace-offering, he blessed the people with the Name of HASHEM, Master of Legions. ¹⁹ He distributed to all the people, to all the multitude of Israel, to man and woman alike, a loaf of bread, a portion of beef, and a container of wine;

Sephardim conclude the Haftarah here:

then the entire people, everyone, went to his home. ²⁰ David returned to bless his household. Michal daughter of Saul went out to meet David and she said, "How honored was the king of Israel today, who exposed himself today in the eyes of his servants' maidservants, as one of the boors might expose himself!" ²¹ David answered Michal, "Before HASHEM Who chose me over your father and over his entire household to appoint me as ruler over the people of HASHEM, of Israel — before HASHEM did I rejoice. ²² Had I held myself even more lightly than this and had I been lowly in my own eyes — and with the maidservants of whom you spoke, among them will I be honored!" ²³ Michal daughter of Saul had no child, until the day of her death.

7 ¹ When the king dwelled in his home and HASHEM had given him rest from his enemies all around, ² the king said to Nathan the prophet, "See now, I dwell in a house of cedarwood while the Ark of God dwells within the curtain!" ³ Nathan said to the king, "Whatever is in your heart, go and do, for HASHEM is with you."

⁴ That night the word of HASHEM came to Nathan, saying: ⁵ "Go and say to My servant, to David, 'So says HASHEM, will you build a house for My dwelling? ⁶ For I have not dwelt in a house from the day I brought the Children of Israel up from Egypt to this day, and I have moved about in a tent and a tabernacle. ⁷ Wherever I moved about among all the Children of Israel, did I say a word to one of the leaders of Israel, whom I have appointed to shepherd My people Israel, saying: "Why have you not built Me a house of cedarwood?" ' ⁸ And now, so shall you say to My servant David, 'So says HASHEM, Master of Legions, I have taken you from the sheepfold, from following the flock, to become ruler over My people, over Israel. ⁹ And I was with you wherever you went, I cut down all your enemies before you, and I gave you great renown, like the renown of the great men who are in the world. ¹⁰ I dedicated a place for My people, for Israel; I planted him there and he dwelt in his place so that he shall tremble no more;

iniquitous people will no more afflict him as before. **11** From the day that I appointed judges over My people Israel and gave you rest from all your enemies, and HASHEM told you that HASHEM will make a dynasty for you. **12** When your days are completed and you lay with your forefathers, I shall establish after you your offspring who will issue from your loins, and I shall establish his kingdom. **13** He shall build a house for My sake, and I shall establish the throne of his kingdom forever. **14** I shall be a Father unto him and he shall be a son unto Me; therefore, when he sins, I shall chastise him with the rod of men and with afflictions of human beings. **15** But My kindness will not be removed from him as I removed it from Saul, whom I removed from before you. **16** The security of your house and your kingdom will be forever before you; your throne will be established forever.' "

17 In accordance with all these words and this entire vision, so Nathan spoke to David.

HAFTARAS TAZRIA / הפטרת תזריע
II Kings 4:42 — 5:19 / מלכים ב ד:מב – ה:יט

4 **42** And a man came from Baal-shalishah and he brought to the man of God food from the first reaping: twenty loaves of barley bread, and young ears of grain in their chaff: [Elisha] said, "Give it to the people and let them eat."

43 His servant said, "How can I place this in front of a hundred men?"

So he said, "Give the people and let them eat, for so said HASHEM, 'They will eat and leave over.' " **44** So he placed it before them; they ate and left over, as HASHEM had said.

5 **1** Naaman, general of the army of the king of Aram, was an eminent person in his master's presence and highly honored, for through him had HASHEM given victory to Aram; the man was a great warrior — a metzora. **2** Aram had gone out in raiding parties and had captured a young girl from the Land of Israel; and she served Naaman's wife. **3** She said to her mistress, "My master's prayers should be directed to the prophet who is in Samaria; then he will heal him from his tzara'as."

4 So [Naaman] went and told his master, saying, "Such-and-such spoke the girl from the Land of Israel." **5** The king of Aram said, "Go to him, and I will send a letter to the king of Israel." He went and took with him ten talents of silver, six thousand gold coins, and ten changes of clothes.

6 He brought to the king of Israel the letter which said, "And now, when this letter comes to you, behold I have sent my servant Naaman to you, that you shall heal him from his tzara'as."

7 When [Jehoram] the king of Israel read the letter, he tore his clothes and said, "Am I God that I can kill and give life, that this person sends to me to heal a man of his tzara'as? Know now and see that he seeks a pretext against me!"

⁸ When Elisha, the man of God, heard that the king of Israel had torn his clothes, he sent to the king, saying, "Why did you tear your clothes? Let him come to me now and he will know that there is a prophet in Israel!"

⁹ Naaman came with his horses and chariot and stood at the entrance of Elisha's house. ¹⁰ Elisha sent him a messenger, saying, "Go and bathe seven times in the Jordan, and your normal flesh will come back and you will become cleansed."

¹¹ Naaman was enraged and he left; he said, "Behold, I thought that he would come out to me, stand up and call out in the Name of HASHEM, his God, and lift his hands to the Omnipresent One — and the metzora would be healed! ¹² Are not Amanah and Pharpar, the rivers of Damascus, better than all the waters of Israel? I will bathe in them and become cleansed!" Then he turned and left in a fury.

¹³ But his servants approached and spoke to him, saying, "My father, had the prophet told you to do a difficult thing, would you not have done it? — surely since he has told you only 'bathe and become cleansed.' "

¹⁴ So he descended and immersed himself seven times in the Jordan, as the word of the man of God; and his flesh was transformed to the flesh of a young boy, and he became cleansed. ¹⁵ He returned to the man of God, he and his entire retinue; he came and stood before him and said, "Behold, now I know that there is no God in the whole world, except in Israel; and now please accept a tribute from your servant."

¹⁶ But he answered, "By the life of HASHEM before Whom I have stood, I will not accept." He imposed upon him to accept, but he refused.

¹⁷ Naaman said, "May there at least be given to your servant two mule-loads of earth — for your servant will never again offer a burnt-offering or a peace-offering to other gods, only to HASHEM. ¹⁸ And may HASHEM forgive your servant for this matter: When my master comes to the temple of Rimmon to prostrate himself there, he leans on my arm, so I must bow in the temple of Rimmon — may HASHEM forgive your servant for this thing."

¹⁹ He said to him, "Go to peace." He traveled a stretch of land from him.

HAFTARAS METZORA / הפטרת מצורע
II Kings 7:3-20 / מלכים ב ז:ג-כ

7 ³ **F**our men, metzoraim, were outside the gate; each one said to his friend, "Why are we sitting here until we die? ⁴ If we propose to come to the city, there is a famine in the city and we will die there, and if we remain here we will die; let us now go and throw ourselves upon the camp of Aram; if they let us live, we will live; and if they put us to death, we will die."

⁵ They stood up at evening to come to the Aramean camp and they arrived at the edge of the Aramean camp, and behold! — not a man was there. ⁶ HASHEM had caused the Aramean camp to hear the sound of chariot and the sound of horse, the sound of a great army; and they said one to another, 'Behold! — the King of Israel has hired the Hittite kings and the Egyptian kings to come upon us!' ⁷ So they stood up and fled into the evening; they abandoned their tents, their horses, and their donkeys — the camp just as it was — and they fled for their lives. ⁸ These metzoraim arrived at the edge of the camp; they came to a tent and ate and drank. From it they carried away silver, gold, and garments, and went and hid them; then they returned and went to another tent, carried away from there, and went and hid it. ⁹ One said to his fellow, "We are not acting properly — today is a day of good news, yet we remain silent! If we wait until the light of dawn we will be adjudged as sinners. Now come, let us go and report to the king's palace!" ¹⁰ They arrived and called out to the gatekeepers of the city and declared to them, saying, "We came to the Aramean camp and behold! — not a man or a human sound is there, only the horses are tethered and the donkeys are tethered, and the tents are as they were." ¹¹ The gatekeepers announced it; and it was related inside the king's palace.

¹² The king arose in the night and said to his servants, "I will tell you now what Aram has done to us; they knew that we are famished, so they left the camp to conceal themselves in the field, thinking, 'When they leave the city we will capture them alive, and then enter the city.'" ¹³ One of his servants spoke up and said, "Let them take five of the remaining horses that are still here — they are like the entire multitude of Israel that still survives within, which are like the entire multitude of Israel that has perished — let us send them and we will see."

¹⁴ They took two horsemen and the king sent them after the Aramean camp, saying, "Go and see." ¹⁵ They followed them until the Jordan and behold! — the whole way was filled with garments and gear that Aram had thrown away in their haste; the messengers returned and told the king.

¹⁶ The people went out and plundered the Aramean camp; a se'ah of fine flour cost a shekel and two se'ah of barley cost a shekel — like the word of HASHEM.

¹⁷ In charge of the gate, the king appointed the official on whose arm he leaned; the people trampled him in the gateway and he died, as the

לְכוּ וְנִפְּלָה אֶל־מַחֲנֵה אֲרָם אִם־יְחַיֻּנוּ נִחְיֶה וְאִם־יְמִיתֻנוּ וָמָתְנוּ: ה וַיָּקֻמוּ בַנֶּשֶׁף לָבוֹא אֶל־מַחֲנֵה אֲרָם וַיָּבֹאוּ עַד־קְצֵה מַחֲנֵה אֲרָם וְהִנֵּה אֵין־שָׁם אִישׁ: ו וַאדֹנָי הִשְׁמִיעַ ׀ אֶת־מַחֲנֵה אֲרָם קוֹל רֶכֶב קוֹל סוּס קוֹל חַיִל גָּדוֹל וַיֹּאמְרוּ אִישׁ אֶל־אָחִיו הִנֵּה שָׂכַר־עָלֵינוּ מֶלֶךְ יִשְׂרָאֵל אֶת־מַלְכֵי הַחִתִּים וְאֶת־מַלְכֵי מִצְרַיִם לָבוֹא עָלֵינוּ: ז וַיָּקוּמוּ וַיָּנוּסוּ בַנֶּשֶׁף וַיַּעַזְבוּ אֶת־אָהֳלֵיהֶם וְאֶת־סוּסֵיהֶם וְאֶת־חֲמוֹרֵיהֶם הַמַּחֲנֶה כַּאֲשֶׁר־הִיא וַיָּנֻסוּ אֶל־נַפְשָׁם: ח וַיָּבֹאוּ הַמְצֹרָעִים הָאֵלֶּה עַד־קְצֵה הַמַּחֲנֶה וַיָּבֹאוּ אֶל־אֹהֶל אֶחָד וַיֹּאכְלוּ וַיִּשְׁתּוּ וַיִּשְׂאוּ מִשָּׁם כֶּסֶף וְזָהָב וּבְגָדִים וַיֵּלְכוּ וַיַּטְמִנוּ וַיָּשֻׁבוּ וַיָּבֹאוּ אֶל־אֹהֶל אַחֵר וַיִּשְׂאוּ מִשָּׁם וַיֵּלְכוּ וַיַּטְמִנוּ: ט וַיֹּאמְרוּ אִישׁ אֶל־רֵעֵהוּ לֹא־כֵן ׀ אֲנַחְנוּ עֹשִׂים הַיּוֹם הַזֶּה יוֹם־בְּשֹׂרָה הוּא וַאֲנַחְנוּ מַחְשִׁים וְחִכִּינוּ עַד־אוֹר הַבֹּקֶר וּמְצָאָנוּ עָווֹן וְעַתָּה לְכוּ וְנָבֹאָה וְנַגִּידָה בֵּית הַמֶּלֶךְ: י וַיָּבֹאוּ וַיִּקְרְאוּ אֶל־שֹׁעֵר הָעִיר וַיַּגִּידוּ לָהֶם לֵאמֹר בָּאנוּ אֶל־מַחֲנֵה אֲרָם וְהִנֵּה אֵין־שָׁם אִישׁ וְקוֹל אָדָם כִּי אִם־הַסּוּס אָסוּר וְהַחֲמוֹר אָסוּר וְאֹהָלִים כַּאֲשֶׁר הֵמָּה: יא וַיִּקְרָא הַשֹּׁעֲרִים וַיַּגִּידוּ בֵּית הַמֶּלֶךְ פְּנִימָה: יב וַיָּקָם הַמֶּלֶךְ לַיְלָה וַיֹּאמֶר אֶל־עֲבָדָיו אַגִּידָה־נָּא לָכֶם אֵת אֲשֶׁר־עָשׂוּ לָנוּ אֲרָם יָדְעוּ כִּי־רְעֵבִים אֲנַחְנוּ וַיֵּצְאוּ מִן־הַמַּחֲנֶה לְהֵחָבֵה בַשָּׂדֶה [בהשדה כ׳] לֵאמֹר כִּי־יֵצְאוּ מִן־הָעִיר וְנִתְפְּשֵׂם חַיִּים וְאֶל־הָעִיר נָבֹא: יג וַיַּעַן אֶחָד מֵעֲבָדָיו וַיֹּאמֶר וְיִקְחוּ־נָא חֲמִשָּׁה מִן־הַסּוּסִים הַנִּשְׁאָרִים אֲשֶׁר נִשְׁאֲרוּ־בָהּ הִנָּם כְּכָל־הֶהָמוֹן [ההמון כ׳] יִשְׂרָאֵל אֲשֶׁר נִשְׁאֲרוּ־בָהּ הִנָּם כְּכָל־הֲמוֹן יִשְׂרָאֵל אֲשֶׁר־תָּמּוּ וְנִשְׁלְחָה וְנִרְאֶה: יד וַיִּקְחוּ שְׁנֵי רֶכֶב סוּסִים וַיִּשְׁלַח הַמֶּלֶךְ אַחֲרֵי מַחֲנֵה־אֲרָם לֵאמֹר לְכוּ וּרְאוּ: טו וַיֵּלְכוּ אַחֲרֵיהֶם עַד־הַיַּרְדֵּן וְהִנֵּה כָל־הַדֶּרֶךְ מְלֵאָה בְגָדִים וְכֵלִים אֲשֶׁר־הִשְׁלִיכוּ אֲרָם בְּחָפְזָם [בהחפזם כ׳] וַיָּשֻׁבוּ הַמַּלְאָכִים וַיַּגִּדוּ לַמֶּלֶךְ: טז וַיֵּצֵא הָעָם וַיָּבֹזּוּ אֵת מַחֲנֵה אֲרָם וַיְהִי סְאָה־סֹלֶת בְּשֶׁקֶל וְסָאתַיִם שְׂעֹרִים בְּשֶׁקֶל כִּדְבַר יְהוָה: יז וְהַמֶּלֶךְ הִפְקִיד אֶת־הַשָּׁלִישׁ אֲשֶׁר־נִשְׁעָן עַל־יָדוֹ עַל־הַשַּׁעַר וַיִּרְמְסֻהוּ הָעָם בַּשַּׁעַר וַיָּמֹת כַּאֲשֶׁר

man of God had spoken, as he had spoken when the king descended to him. *18* And it happened just as the man of God had spoken to the king, saying, "Two se'ah of barley will cost a shekel and a se'ah of fine flour will cost a shekel at this time tomorrow in the gate of Samaria."

19 And that official had answered the man of God and said, "Behold! — if HASHEM were to make windows in the sky, could such a thing happen?"

And he said, "You will see it with your own eyes, but you will not eat from it!"

20 And so it happened to him: the people trampled him in the gate and he died.

HAFTARAS ACHAREI / הפטרת אחרי

We give this reading as the *Haftarah* of *Acharei* based on the ruling of *Rama* (*Orach Chaim* 428:8), with which most authorities concur. The version found in most *Chumashim*, that this is the *Haftarah* of *Kedoshim*, is in error. Although the general rule is that when two *Sidros* are read together, the *Haftarah* is that of the second one, the *Sidros* of *Acharei* and *Kedoshim* are exceptions. When *Acharei* and *Kedoshim* are combined, the *Haftarah* of *Acharei* is read. Similarly, when *Acharei* falls on the day before Rosh Chodesh or on *Shabbos Hagadol*, which have special *Haftaros*, the *Haftarah* of *Acharei* is read on the Sabbath of *Kedoshim*. See *Mishnah Berurah*, 428:26.

According to the *Sephardic* custom, the *Haftarah* of *Acharei* can be found below as the *Ashkenazic Haftarah* of *Kedoshim* (Ezekiel 22:1-16). According to the *Ashkenazic* custom, the following *Haftarah* is read.

Amos 9:7-15 / עמוס ט:ז-טו

9 *7* **A**re you not to Me like the children of Ethiopians, O Children of Israel? — the words of HASHEM — have I not brought up Israel from the land of Egypt, the Philistines from Caphtor, and Aram from Kir? *8* Behold! — the eyes of my Lord HASHEM/ELOHIM are upon the sinful monarchy, and I will waste it from upon the face of the earth; but I will not utterly destroy the House of Jacob — the words of HASHEM. *9* For behold I command! I shall shake the House of Israel among all the nations as one shakes [grain] in a sieve, and no pebble shall fall to the ground. *10* By the sword will all the sinners of My people die, those who say, "The evil will not approach and overtake us!"

11 On that day I will erect David's fallen booth; I will repair their breaches and erect his ruins, and I will rebuild it as in days of old. *12* So that they will conquer the remnant of Edom and all the nations, for My Name is upon them — the words of HASHEM Who brings this about.

13 Behold — days are coming — the words of HASHEM — when the plower will encounter the reaper, and he who treads upon the grapes will meet the one who brings the seeds; the mountains will drip with wine and the hills will melt [with fat]. *14* I shall bring back the captivity of My people Israel, and they will rebuild desolate cities; they will return and plant vineyards and drink their wine; they will make gardens and eat their fruit. *15* I shall implant them upon their Land; they will not be uprooted again from upon their Land that I have given them, says HASHEM, your God.

HAFTARAS KEDOSHIM / הפטרת קדושים

According to the *Sephardic* custom, the following *Haftarah* is read for *Acharei*.
According to the *Ashkenazic* custom, it is read for *Kedoshim*.

Ezekiel 22:1-16 / יחזקאל כב:א-טז

22 ¹ The word of HASHEM came to me saying: ² Now you Ben Adam, will you rebuke, will you rebuke the city of bloodshed and let her know all her abominations? ³ And say: "Thus says my Lord HASHEM/ELOHIM: O city, shedding blood in her midst to hasten her time, and which fashioned idols within herself for contamination. ⁴ Through your blood that you shed you became guilty and through your idols that you fashioned you became contaminated; thus you brought your days near and reached the limit of your years; therefore have I made you a shame to the nations, and a mockery for all the lands. ⁵ Those who are near and those who are far will mock you: 'Contaminated of name! Great of confusion!' ⁶ Behold! the princes of Israel, every man was in you for his own power, for the sake of bloodshed. ⁷ Father and mother have they slighted within you; toward the stranger they have acted oppressively in your midst; orphan and widow have they wronged within you. ⁸ My sanctities have you spurned; My Sabbaths have you desecrated. ⁹ Talebearers were among you, in order to shed blood; upon the mountains they ate among you; evil plans did they lay in your midst. ¹⁰ A father's nakedness he uncovered within you; they afflicted menstruant women within you. ¹¹ A man would commit abomination against his neighbor's wife; a man would defile his daughter-in-law with lewdness; a man would afflict his sister, his father's daughter, within you. ¹² They took bribery within you, in order to shed blood; interest and increase have you taken, and enriched your friends with loot; but Me you have forgotten — the words of my Lord HASHEM/ELOHIM.

¹³ "Now behold! I have pounded My hand because of your robbery that you have committed, and because of your bloodshed that was in your midst. ¹⁴ Can your heart endure, can your hands be strong in the days when I shall deal with you? I, HASHEM, have spoken and done.

¹⁵ "Then I shall scatter you among the nations and disperse you among the lands and remove all your contamination from you. ¹⁶ Then you shall be caused to re-inherit yourself in the sight of the nations, and you shall know that I am HASHEM."

Haftarah of Kedoshim according to the *Sephardic* and Italian custom.
According to this custom, it is also read when the two *Sidros Acharei* and *Kedoshim* are combined.

Ezekiel 20:2-20 / יחזקאל כ:ב-כ

20 ² Then the word of HASHEM came to me saying: ³ Ben Adam, speak to the Elders of Israel and say to them: "Thus spoke my Lord HASHEM/ELOHIM: Is it to seek of Me that you come? As I live, I will not make Myself accessible to you — the words of my Lord HASHEM/ELOHIM."

THE HAFTAROS — KEDOSHIM

⁴ Would you rebuke them, would you rebuke, Ben Adam? Inform them of the abominations of their fathers, ⁵ and say to them: "So said my Lord HASHEM/ELOHIM: On the day I chose Israel, when I swore to the seed of Jacob's family and made Myself known to them in Egypt, then I swore to them saying, 'I am HASHEM your God.' ⁶ On that day I swore to them to take them out from the land of Egypt, to a land that I had sought out for them, flowing with milk and honey, a splendor for all the lands. ⁷ And I said to them: 'Every man, cast away the detestable idols of his eyes and do not defile yourselves with the idols of Egypt, I am HASHEM, your God.'

⁸ "But they rebelled against Me and did not want to listen to Me; not a man cast out the detestable idols of their eyes, and they did not forsake the idols of Egypt; so I intended to pour My fury upon them, to spend My anger upon them, in the midst of the land of Egypt. ⁹ But I acted for the sake of My Name, that it not be desecrated in the eyes of the nations amid which they are; and in whose sight I had made Myself known to them to remove them from the land of Egypt. ¹⁰ And I took them out of the land of Egypt and brought them to the Wilderness; ¹¹ and I gave them My decrees and made known to them My ordinances through which a man will live if he performs them. ¹² And also My Sabbaths have I given them to be a sign between Me and them; to know that I am HASHEM Who sanctifies them.

¹³ "But the House of Israel rebelled against Me in the Wilderness; they did not walk in My decrees and they spurned My ordinances through which a man will live if he performs them, and they desecrated My Sabbaths exceedingly; so I intended to pour My fury upon them in the Wilderness — to make an end of them.

¹⁴ "But I acted for the sake of My Name, that it should not be desecrated in the eyes of the nations, in whose sight I had taken them out. ¹⁵ And also I swore to them in the Wilderness not to bring them to the Land that I had given, flowing with milk and honey; it is a splendor for all the lands. ¹⁶ For they spurned My ordinances and did not walk in My decrees; they desecrated My Sabbaths because their heart goes after their idols. ¹⁷ Yet My eye pitied them rather than destroy them, and I did not put an end to them in the Wilderness. ¹⁸ But I said to their children in the Wilderness: Do not walk in the decrees of your fathers, do not observe their ordinances, and do not defile yourselves with their idols. ¹⁹ I am HASHEM your God: Walk in My decrees, observe My ordinances and perform them. ²⁰ Sanctify My Sabbaths and they will be a sign between Me and you, to know that I am HASHEM, your God."

ד הֲתִשְׁפֹּט אֹתָם הֲתִשְׁפּוֹט בֶּן־אָדָם אֶת־תּוֹעֲבֹת אֲבוֹתָם הוֹדִיעֵם: ה וְאָמַרְתָּ אֲלֵיהֶם כֹּה־אָמַר אֲדֹנָי יֱהֹוִה בְּיוֹם בָּחֳרִי בְיִשְׂרָאֵל וָאֶשָּׂא יָדִי לְזֶרַע בֵּית יַעֲקֹב וָאִוָּדַע לָהֶם בְּאֶרֶץ מִצְרָיִם וָאֶשָּׂא יָדִי לָהֶם לֵאמֹר אֲנִי יְהֹוָה אֱלֹהֵיכֶם: ו בַּיּוֹם הַהוּא נָשָׂאתִי יָדִי לָהֶם לְהוֹצִיאָם מֵאֶרֶץ מִצְרָיִם אֶל־אֶרֶץ אֲשֶׁר־תַּרְתִּי לָהֶם זָבַת חָלָב וּדְבַשׁ צְבִי הִיא לְכָל־הָאֲרָצוֹת: ז וָאֹמַר אֲלֵהֶם אִישׁ שִׁקּוּצֵי עֵינָיו הַשְׁלִיכוּ וּבְגִלּוּלֵי מִצְרַיִם אַל־תִּטַּמָּאוּ אֲנִי יְהֹוָה אֱלֹהֵיכֶם: ח וַיַּמְרוּ־בִי וְלֹא אָבוּ לִשְׁמֹעַ אֵלַי אִישׁ אֶת־שִׁקּוּצֵי עֵינֵיהֶם לֹא הִשְׁלִיכוּ וְאֶת־גִּלּוּלֵי מִצְרַיִם לֹא עָזָבוּ וָאֹמַר לִשְׁפֹּךְ חֲמָתִי עֲלֵיהֶם לְכַלּוֹת אַפִּי בָּהֶם בְּתוֹךְ אֶרֶץ מִצְרָיִם: ט וָאַעַשׂ לְמַעַן שְׁמִי לְבִלְתִּי הֵחֵל לְעֵינֵי הַגּוֹיִם אֲשֶׁר־הֵמָּה בְתוֹכָם אֲשֶׁר נוֹדַעְתִּי אֲלֵיהֶם לְעֵינֵיהֶם לְהוֹצִיאָם מֵאֶרֶץ מִצְרָיִם: י וָאוֹצִיאֵם מֵאֶרֶץ מִצְרַיִם וָאֲבִאֵם אֶל־הַמִּדְבָּר: יא וָאֶתֵּן לָהֶם אֶת־חֻקּוֹתַי וְאֶת־מִשְׁפָּטַי הוֹדַעְתִּי אוֹתָם אֲשֶׁר יַעֲשֶׂה אוֹתָם הָאָדָם וָחַי בָּהֶם: יב וְגַם אֶת־שַׁבְּתוֹתַי נָתַתִּי לָהֶם לִהְיוֹת לְאוֹת בֵּינִי וּבֵינֵיהֶם לָדַעַת כִּי אֲנִי יְהֹוָה מְקַדְּשָׁם: יג וַיַּמְרוּ־בִי בֵית־יִשְׂרָאֵל בַּמִּדְבָּר בְּחֻקּוֹתַי לֹא־הָלָכוּ וְאֶת־מִשְׁפָּטַי מָאָסוּ אֲשֶׁר יַעֲשֶׂה אֹתָם הָאָדָם וָחַי בָּהֶם וְאֶת־שַׁבְּתֹתַי חִלְּלוּ מְאֹד וָאֹמַר לִשְׁפֹּךְ חֲמָתִי עֲלֵיהֶם בַּמִּדְבָּר לְכַלּוֹתָם: יד וָאֶעֱשֶׂה לְמַעַן שְׁמִי לְבִלְתִּי הֵחֵל לְעֵינֵי הַגּוֹיִם אֲשֶׁר הוֹצֵאתִים לְעֵינֵיהֶם: טו וְגַם־אֲנִי נָשָׂאתִי יָדִי לָהֶם בַּמִּדְבָּר לְבִלְתִּי הָבִיא אוֹתָם אֶל־הָאָרֶץ אֲשֶׁר־נָתַתִּי זָבַת חָלָב וּדְבַשׁ צְבִי הִיא לְכָל־הָאֲרָצוֹת: טז יַעַן בְּמִשְׁפָּטַי מָאָסוּ וְאֶת־חֻקּוֹתַי לֹא־הָלְכוּ בָהֶם וְאֶת־שַׁבְּתוֹתַי חִלֵּלוּ כִּי אַחֲרֵי גִלּוּלֵיהֶם לִבָּם הֹלֵךְ: יז וַתָּחָס עֵינִי עֲלֵיהֶם מִשַּׁחֲתָם וְלֹא־עָשִׂיתִי אוֹתָם כָּלָה בַּמִּדְבָּר: יח וָאֹמַר אֶל־בְּנֵיהֶם בַּמִּדְבָּר בְּחוּקֵּי אֲבוֹתֵיכֶם אַל־תֵּלֵכוּ וְאֶת־מִשְׁפְּטֵיהֶם אַל־תִּשְׁמֹרוּ וּבְגִלּוּלֵיהֶם אַל־תִּטַּמָּאוּ: יט אֲנִי יְהֹוָה אֱלֹהֵיכֶם בְּחֻקּוֹתַי לֵכוּ וְאֶת־מִשְׁפָּטַי שִׁמְרוּ וַעֲשׂוּ אוֹתָם: כ וְאֶת־שַׁבְּתוֹתַי קַדֵּשׁוּ וְהָיוּ לְאוֹת בֵּינִי וּבֵינֵיכֶם לָדַעַת כִּי אֲנִי יְהֹוָה אֱלֹהֵיכֶם:

HAFTARAS EMOR / הפטרת אמור

Ezekiel 44:15-31 / יחזקאל מד:טו-לא

44 ¹⁵ But the Levite-Kohanim — descendants of Zadok who safeguarded the charge of My Sanctuary when the Children of Israel strayed from Me — let them draw near to Me to serve Me, let them stand before Me to offer Me fat and blood — the words of my Lord HASHEM/ELOHIM. ¹⁶ They shall come to My Sanctuary, and they shall approach My table to serve Me, and they shall safeguard My charge.

¹⁷ Now when they come to the gates of the Inner Courtyard they are to wear linen clothes; let no wool be upon them when they serve in the gates of the Inner Courtyard and within. ¹⁸ Linen turbans shall be on their heads and linen breeches shall be on their loins; let them not gird themselves where one perspires. ¹⁹ Now when they leave for the Outer Courtyard, to the Outer Courtyard to the people, let them remove the clothes in which they minister and leave them in the holy chambers; let them don other garments and let them not mingle with people in their clothes. ²⁰ Their heads they may not shear nor a wild growth may they permit; they shall keep their heads trimmed. ²¹ They shall not drink wine — any Kohen — when they enter the Inner Courtyard. ²² Widow or divorcee they may not take themselves for wives, only virgins from the offspring of the House of Israel; but a widow who shall only be widowed, some Kohanim may take. ²³ They shall instruct My people concerning the differences between holy and ordinary; let them inform them of the difference between contaminated and clean. ²⁴ Concerning a grievance let them stand in judgment, and according to My laws are they to adjudicate it; my teachings and decrees regarding My appointed times are they to protect; and My Sabbaths are they to sanctify. ²⁵ To a human corpse they are not to come to become contaminated, except for a father and mother, son and daughter, brother, and sister who had never been married to a man, they may become contaminated. ²⁶ After his cleansing, let them count seven days for him. ²⁷ Now on the day of his entry into the Sanctuary, to the Inner Courtyard, to minister in the Sanctuary, let him bring his sin-offering — the words of my Lord HASHEM/ELOHIM.

²⁸ And it shall be a heritage for them; I am their heritage; give them no ancestral possession in Israel; I am their ancestral possession. ²⁹ They shall eat the meal-offering, the sin-offering, and the guilt-offering; any cherem-vow in Israel shall be for them. ³⁰ All the choice first fruits of every kind and all terumah

of any kind — of all your terumah gifts — shall go to the Kohanim; the first yield of your dough shall you give to the Kohen, to make a blessing rest upon your home. ³¹ Any carcass or torn animal of fowl or livestock, the Kohanim may not eat.

HAFTARAS BEHAR / הפטרת בהר
Jeremiah 32:6-27 / ירמיה לב:ו-כז

32 ⁶ Jeremiah said: The word of HASHEM came to me, saying: ⁷ "Behold! — Hanamel, son of Shallum your uncle, is coming to you to say: 'Buy for yourself my field that is in Anasoth, for the right of redemption is yours.' "

⁸ Hanamel, my cousin, came to me as HASHEM had spoken, to the courtyard of the prison, and he said to me, "Buy for yourself my field in Anasoth, that is in the territory of Benjamin, for yours is the right of inheritance and yours is the redemption; buy it for yourself." And I knew that it was the word of HASHEM.

⁹ So I bought the field that was in Anasoth from Hanamel, my cousin; and I weighed out the silver for him: seven shekalim and ten selaim. ¹⁰ I wrote out the deed, sealed it, and appointed witnesses; and I weighed out the silver on the scales. ¹¹ I took the bill of sale, the sealed one made according to the ordinances and the decrees, and the unsealed one. ¹² I gave the bill of sale to Baruch son of Neriah son of Mahseiah before the eyes of Hanamel my uncle['s son] and before the eyes of the witnesses who signed the bill of sale, before the eyes of all the Jews who were sitting in the courtyard of the prison.

¹³ I instructed Baruch before their eyes, saying: ¹⁴ "So said HASHEM, Master of Legions, God of Israel: 'Take these documents, this bill of sale, the sealed one and this unsealed document, and place them in an earthenware vessel so that they will last for many days.' ¹⁵ For so said HASHEM, Master of Legions, God of Israel: 'Houses, fields, and vineyards will yet be bought in this land.' "

¹⁶ I prayed to HASHEM, after giving the bill of sale to Baruch, son of Neriah, saying: ¹⁷ "Alas, my Lord, HASHEM/ELOHIM, behold! — You made the heaven and the earth with Your great strength and Your outstretched arm; nothing is hidden from You; ¹⁸ Who does kindness to thousands [of generations], and repays the sin of parents in the bosom of the children after them; the great and strong God, His Name is HASHEM, Master of Legions; ¹⁹ great of counsel and mighty of deed, Whose eyes are cognizant of all

כֹּל מִכָּל תְּרוּמֹתֵיכֶם לַכֹּהֲנִים יִהְיֶה: וְרֵאשִׁית עֲרִיסוֹתֵיכֶם תִּתְּנוּ לַכֹּהֵן לְהָנִיחַ בְּרָכָה אֶל־בֵּיתֶךָ: לֹא כָל־נְבֵלָה וּטְרֵפָה מִן־הָעוֹף וּמִן־הַבְּהֵמָה לֹא יֹאכְלוּ הַכֹּהֲנִים:

לב ו וַיֹּאמֶר יִרְמְיָהוּ הָיָה דְבַר־יהוה אֵלַי לֵאמֹר: ז הִנֵּה חֲנַמְאֵל בֶּן־שַׁלֻּם דֹּדְךָ בָּא אֵלֶיךָ לֵאמֹר קְנֵה לְךָ אֶת־שָׂדִי אֲשֶׁר בַּעֲנָתוֹת כִּי לְךָ מִשְׁפַּט הַגְּאֻלָּה לִקְנוֹת: ח וַיָּבֹא אֵלַי חֲנַמְאֵל בֶּן־דֹּדִי כִּדְבַר יהוה אֶל־חֲצַר הַמַּטָּרָה וַיֹּאמֶר אֵלַי קְנֵה נָא אֶת־שָׂדִי אֲשֶׁר־בַּעֲנָתוֹת אֲשֶׁר ׀ בְּאֶרֶץ בִּנְיָמִין כִּי־לְךָ מִשְׁפַּט הַיְרֻשָּׁה וּלְךָ הַגְּאֻלָּה קְנֵה־לָךְ וָאֵדַע כִּי דְבַר־יהוה הוּא: ט וָאֶקְנֶה אֶת־הַשָּׂדֶה מֵאֵת חֲנַמְאֵל בֶּן־דֹּדִי אֲשֶׁר בַּעֲנָתוֹת וָאֶשְׁקֲלָה־לּוֹ אֶת־הַכֶּסֶף שִׁבְעָה שְׁקָלִים וַעֲשָׂרָה הַכָּסֶף: י וָאֶכְתֹּב בַּסֵּפֶר וָאֶחְתֹּם וָאָעֵד עֵדִים וָאֶשְׁקֹל הַכֶּסֶף בְּמֹאזְנָיִם: יא וָאֶקַּח אֶת־סֵפֶר הַמִּקְנָה אֶת־הֶחָתוּם הַמִּצְוָה וְהַחֻקִּים וְאֶת־הַגָּלוּי: יב וָאֶתֵּן אֶת־הַסֵּפֶר הַמִּקְנָה אֶל־בָּרוּךְ בֶּן־נֵרִיָּה בֶּן־מַחְסֵיָה לְעֵינֵי חֲנַמְאֵל דֹּדִי וּלְעֵינֵי הָעֵדִים הַכֹּתְבִים בְּסֵפֶר הַמִּקְנָה לְעֵינֵי כָּל־הַיְּהוּדִים הַיֹּשְׁבִים בַּחֲצַר הַמַּטָּרָה: יג וָאֲצַוֶּה אֶת־בָּרוּךְ לְעֵינֵיהֶם לֵאמֹר: יד כֹּה־אָמַר יהוה צְבָאוֹת אֱלֹהֵי יִשְׂרָאֵל לָקוֹחַ אֶת־הַסְּפָרִים הָאֵלֶּה אֵת סֵפֶר הַמִּקְנָה הַזֶּה וְאֵת הֶחָתוּם וְאֵת סֵפֶר הַגָּלוּי הַזֶּה וּנְתַתָּם בִּכְלִי־חָרֶשׂ לְמַעַן יַעַמְדוּ יָמִים רַבִּים: טו כִּי כֹה אָמַר יהוה צְבָאוֹת אֱלֹהֵי יִשְׂרָאֵל עוֹד יִקָּנוּ בָתִּים וְשָׂדוֹת וּכְרָמִים בָּאָרֶץ הַזֹּאת: טז וָאֶתְפַּלֵּל אֶל־יהוה אַחֲרֵי תִתִּי אֶת־סֵפֶר הַמִּקְנָה אֶל־בָּרוּךְ בֶּן־נֵרִיָּה לֵאמֹר: יז אֲהָהּ אֲדֹנָי יֱהוִֹה הִנֵּה ׀ אַתָּה עָשִׂיתָ אֶת־הַשָּׁמַיִם וְאֶת־הָאָרֶץ בְּכֹחֲךָ הַגָּדוֹל וּבִזְרֹעֲךָ הַנְּטוּיָה לֹא־יִפָּלֵא מִמְּךָ כָּל־דָּבָר: יח עֹשֶׂה חֶסֶד לַאֲלָפִים וּמְשַׁלֵּם עֲוֹן אָבוֹת אֶל־חֵיק בְּנֵיהֶם אַחֲרֵיהֶם הָאֵל הַגָּדוֹל הַגִּבּוֹר יהוה צְבָאוֹת שְׁמוֹ: יט גְּדֹל הָעֵצָה וְרַב הָעֲלִילִיָּה אֲשֶׁר־עֵינֶיךָ פְקֻחוֹת עַל־כָּל־

the ways of humankind, to give each man according to his ways and the fruit of his deeds; [20] Who placed signs and wonders in the land of Egypt that are known until this day, and upon Israel as upon man, and You made Yourself a reputation like this very day. [21] And You took Your people Israel out of the land of Egypt, with signs and wonders, with a strong hand, an outstretched arm, and with great awe. [22] And You gave them this land that You swore to their forefathers to give them, a land flowing with milk and honey. [23] They came and conquered it, but they did not listen to Your voice and did not follow Your teaching; everything that You commanded them to do they did not do, so You caused all this evil to befall them. [24] Behold! — upon mounds of earth they came to the city to capture it, and the city was handed over to the Chaldeans who are attacking it, in the face of the sword, the famine, and the pestilence; what You declared has happened — and You see it! [25] Yet You said to me, my Lord HASHEM/ELOHIM, 'Buy for yourself a field with silver, and appoint witnesses — but the city has been handed over to the Chaldeans!' "

[26] Then the word of HASHEM came to Jeremiah, saying: [27] "Behold! — I am HASHEM, the God of all flesh; is anything hidden from Me?"

HAFTARAS BECHUKOSAI / הפטרת בחקתי

Jeremiah 16:19 — 17:14 / ירמיהו טז:יט — יז:יד

16 [19] **H**ASHEM — my Strength, my Stronghold and my Refuge in the day of travail — to You nations will come from the ends of the earth, and say: "Our ancestors inherited only falsehood, futility that has no purpose. [20] Can a man make a god for himself? — they are not gods!" [21] Therefore, behold I inform them upon this occasion, I shall let them know of My hand and My strength; and they shall know that My Name is HASHEM.

17 [1] The sin of Judah is inscribed with an iron quill, with a diamond-like fingernail, engraved into the slate of their heart and the corners of your altars. [2] As they remember their children, so [they remember] their altars and their idol-trees beside luxuriant trees upon lofty hills. [3] O worshipers on mountains, in the field: your wealth, all your treasures, shall I make into booty, because of your high altars made in sin throughout your boundaries. [4] You will be forced to withdraw from the heritage that I have given you, and I will put you to work for your enemies in a land that you know not; for you have ignited a fire in My nostrils, it will burn forever.

⁵ *So says* HASHEM: *"Accursed is the man who trusts in people and makes mortals his strength, and turns his heart away from* HASHEM. ⁶ *He will be like a lone tree in the wilderness and will not see when goodness comes; he will dwell in the arid desert, in a sulfurous, uninhabited land.* ⁷ *Blessed is the man who trusts in* HASHEM, *then* HASHEM *will be his security.* ⁸ *He will be like a tree that is planted near water, which will spread its roots alongside brooks and will not see when heat comes, whose foliage will be ever fresh, who will not worry in years of drought and will never stop producing fruit.*

⁹ *"The heart is most deceitful of all and it is fragile; who can know it?* ¹⁰ *I,* HASHEM, *plumb the heart and test the mind; to give to man according to his ways, like the fruit of his deeds.* ¹¹ *Like a bird chirpingly attracting those it did not beget is one who amasses wealth without justice; in half his days it will desert him, and at his end he will be a degenerate."*

¹² *Like the Throne of Glory, exalted from the beginning, is the place of our Sanctuary.* ¹³ *The hope of Israel is* HASHEM, *all who forsake You will be shamed — "Those who forsake Me will be inscribed for earthly depths" — for they have forsaken* HASHEM, *the Source of living waters.* ¹⁴ *Heal me,* HASHEM, *and I will be healed; save me, and I will be saved — for You are my praise.*

HAFTARAS SHABBAS EREV ROSH CHODESH / הפטרת שבת ערב ראש חודש
I Samuel 20:18-42 / שמואל א כ:יח-מב

20 ¹⁸ *Jonathan said to [David], "Tomorrow is the New Moon, and you will be missed because your seat will be empty.* ¹⁹ *For three days you are to go far down and come to the place where you hid on the day of the deed, and remain near the marker stone.* ²⁰ *I will shoot three arrows in that direction as if I were shooting at a target.* ²¹ *Behold! — I will then send the lad, 'Go, find the arrows.' If I call out to the lad, 'Behold! — the arrows are on this side of you!' then you should take them and return, for it is well with you and there is no concern, as* HASHEM *lives.* ²² *But if I say this to the boy, 'Behold! — the arrows are beyond you!' then go, for* HASHEM *will have sent you away.* ²³ *This matter of which we have spoken, I and you, behold! —* HASHEM *remains [witness] between me and you forever."*

²⁴ *David concealed himself in the field. It was the New Moon and the king sat at the feast to eat.* ²⁵ *The king sat on his seat as usual, on the seat by the wall; and Jonathan stood up so that Abner could sit at Saul's side, and David's seat was empty.* ²⁶ *Saul said nothing on that day, for he thought, "It is a coincidence, he must be impure, for he has not been cleansed."*

ה כֹּה ׀ אָמַ֣ר יְהֹוָ֗ה אָר֤וּר הַגֶּ֙בֶר֙ אֲשֶׁ֣ר יִבְטַ֣ח בָּאָדָ֔ם וְשָׂ֥ם בָּשָׂ֖ר זְרֹע֑וֹ וּמִן־יְהֹוָ֖ה יָס֥וּר לִבּֽוֹ: ו וְהָיָה֙ כְּעַרְעָ֣ר בָּֽעֲרָבָ֔ה וְלֹ֥א יִרְאֶ֖ה כִּי־יָב֣וֹא ט֑וֹב וְשָׁכַ֤ן חֲרֵרִים֙ בַּמִּדְבָּ֔ר אֶ֥רֶץ מְלֵחָ֖ה וְלֹ֥א תֵשֵֽׁב: ז בָּר֣וּךְ הַגֶּ֔בֶר אֲשֶׁ֥ר יִבְטַ֖ח בַּיהֹוָ֑ה וְהָיָ֥ה יְהֹוָ֖ה מִבְטַחֽוֹ: ח וְהָיָ֞ה כְּעֵ֣ץ ׀ שָׁת֣וּל עַל־מַ֗יִם וְעַל־יוּבַל֙ יְשַׁלַּ֣ח שָֽׁרָשָׁ֔יו וְלֹ֤א יִרְאֶה [ירא כ׳] כִּֽי־יָבֹ֣א חֹ֔ם וְהָיָ֥ה עָלֵ֖הוּ רַעֲנָ֑ן וּבִשְׁנַ֤ת בַּצֹּ֙רֶת֙ לֹ֣א יִדְאָ֔ג וְלֹ֥א יָמִ֖ישׁ מֵעֲשׂ֥וֹת פֶּֽרִי: ט עָקֹ֥ב הַלֵּ֛ב מִכֹּ֖ל וְאָנֻ֣שׁ ה֑וּא מִ֖י יֵדָעֶֽנּוּ: י אֲנִ֧י יְהֹוָ֛ה חֹקֵ֥ר לֵ֖ב בֹּחֵ֣ן כְּלָי֑וֹת וְלָתֵ֤ת לְאִישׁ֙ כִּדְרָכָ֔יו [כדרכו כ׳] כִּפְרִ֖י מַעֲלָלָֽיו: יא קֹרֵ֤א דָגַר֙ וְלֹ֣א יָלָ֔ד עֹ֥שֶׂה עֹ֖שֶׁר וְלֹ֣א בְמִשְׁפָּ֑ט בַּחֲצִ֤י יָמָו [ימו כ׳] יַעַזְבֶ֔נּוּ וּבְאַחֲרִית֖וֹ יִֽהְיֶ֥ה נָבָֽל: יב כִּסֵּ֣א כָב֔וֹד מָר֖וֹם מֵרִאשׁ֑וֹן מְק֖וֹם מִקְדָּשֵֽׁנוּ: יג מִקְוֵ֨ה יִשְׂרָאֵ֜ל יְהֹוָ֗ה כָּל־עֹזְבֶ֙יךָ֙ יֵבֹ֔שׁוּ וְסוּרַי֙ [יסורי כ׳] בָּאָ֣רֶץ יִכָּתֵ֔בוּ כִּ֤י עָזְבוּ֙ מְק֣וֹר מַֽיִם־חַיִּ֔ים אֶת־יְהֹוָֽה: יד רְפָאֵ֤נִי יְהֹוָה֙ וְאֵ֣רָפֵ֔א הוֹשִׁיעֵ֖נִי וְאִוָּשֵׁ֑עָה כִּ֥י תְהִלָּתִ֖י אָֽתָּה:

כ יח וַיֹּֽאמֶר־ל֥וֹ יְהוֹנָתָ֖ן מָחָ֣ר חֹ֑דֶשׁ וְנִפְקַ֕דְתָּ כִּ֥י יִפָּקֵ֖ד מוֹשָׁבֶֽךָ: יט וְשִׁלַּשְׁתָּ֙ תֵּרֵ֣ד מְאֹ֔ד וּבָאתָ֙ אֶל־הַמָּק֔וֹם אֲשֶׁר־נִסְתַּ֥רְתָּ שָּׁ֖ם בְּי֣וֹם הַֽמַּעֲשֶׂ֑ה וְיָ֣שַׁבְתָּ֔ אֵ֖צֶל הָאֶ֥בֶן הָאָֽזֶל: כ וַאֲנִ֕י שְׁלֹ֥שֶׁת הַחִצִּ֖ים צִדָּ֣ה אוֹרֶ֑ה לְשַׁלַּֽח־לִ֖י לְמַטָּרָֽה: כא וְהִנֵּה֙ אֶשְׁלַ֣ח אֶת־הַנַּ֔עַר לֵ֖ךְ מְצָ֣א אֶת־הַחִצִּ֑ים אִם־אָמֹר֩ אֹמַ֨ר לַנַּ֜עַר הִנֵּ֥ה הַחִצִּ֣ים ׀ מִמְּךָ֣ וָהֵ֗נָּה קָחֶ֧נּוּ ׀ וָבֹ֛אָה כִּֽי־שָׁל֥וֹם לְךָ֖ וְאֵ֣ין דָּבָ֑ר חַי־יְהֹוָֽה: כב וְאִם־כֹּ֤ה אֹמַר֙ לָעֶ֔לֶם הִנֵּ֥ה הַחִצִּ֖ים מִמְּךָ֣ וָהָ֑לְאָה לֵ֕ךְ כִּ֥י שִֽׁלַּחֲךָ֖ יְהֹוָֽה: כג וְהַ֨דָּבָ֔ר אֲשֶׁ֥ר דִּבַּ֖רְנוּ אֲנִ֣י וָאָ֑תָּה הִנֵּ֧ה יְהֹוָ֛ה בֵּינִ֥י וּבֵינְךָ֖ עַד־עוֹלָֽם: כד וַיִּסָּתֵ֥ר דָּוִ֖ד בַּשָּׂדֶ֑ה וַיְהִ֣י הַחֹ֔דֶשׁ וַיֵּ֧שֶׁב הַמֶּ֛לֶךְ אֶל־[על כ׳] הַלֶּ֖חֶם לֶאֱכֽוֹל: כה וַיֵּ֣שֶׁב הַ֠מֶּ֠לֶךְ עַל־מ֨וֹשָׁב֜וֹ כְּפַ֣עַם ׀ בְּפַ֗עַם אֶל־מוֹשַׁב֙ הַקִּ֔יר וַיָּ֙קָם֙ יְה֣וֹנָתָ֔ן וַיֵּ֥שֶׁב אַבְנֵ֖ר מִצַּ֣ד שָׁא֑וּל וַיִּפָּקֵ֖ד מְק֥וֹם דָּוִֽד: כו וְלֹא־דִבֶּ֥ר שָׁא֛וּל מְא֖וּמָה בַּיּ֣וֹם הַה֑וּא כִּ֣י אָמַ֗ר מִקְרֶ֥ה ה֛וּא בִּלְתִּ֥י טָה֖וֹר ה֑וּא כִּי־לֹ֥א טָהֽוֹר:

English	Hebrew

²⁷ It was the day after the New Moon, the second day, and David's place was empty; Saul said to Jonathan, his son, "Why did the son of Jesse not come to the feast yesterday or today?"

²⁸ Jonathan answered Saul, "David asked me for permission to go Bethlehem. ²⁹ He said, 'Please send me away, for we have a family feast in the city, and he, my brother, ordered me [to come]; so now, if I have found favor in your eyes, excuse me, please, and let me see my brothers.' Therefore, he has not come to the king's table."

³⁰ Saul's anger flared up at Jonathan, and he said to him, "Son of a pervertedly rebellious woman, do I not know that you prefer the son of Jesse, for your own shame and the shame of your mother's nakedness! ³¹ For all the days that the son of Jesse is alive on the earth, you and your kingdom will not be secure! And now send and bring him to me, for he is deserving of death."

³² Jonathan answered his father Saul and he said to him, "Why should he die; what has he done?"

³³ Saul hurled his spear at him to strike him; so Jonathan realized that it was decided by his father to kill David. ³⁴ Jonathan arose from the table in a burning anger; he did not partake of food on that second day of the month, for he was saddened over David because his father had humiliated him.

³⁵ It happened in the morning that Jonathan went out to the field for the meeting with David, and a young lad was with him. ³⁶ He said to his lad, "Run — please find the arrows that I shoot." The lad ran, and he shot the arrow to make it go further. ³⁷ The lad arrived at the place of the arrow that Jonathan had shot, and Jonathan called out after the lad, and he said, "Is not the arrow beyond you?"

³⁸ And Jonathan called out after the lad, "Quickly, hurry, do not stand still!" The lad gathered the arrows and came to his master. ³⁹ The lad knew nothing, only Jonathan and David understood the matter. ⁴⁰ Jonathan gave his equipment to his lad and said to him, "Go bring it to the city."

⁴¹ The lad went and David stood up from near the south [side of the stone], and he fell on his face to the ground and prostrated himself three times. They kissed one another and they wept with one another, until David [wept] greatly.

⁴² Jonathan said to David, "Go to peace. What the two of us have sworn in the Name of HASHEM — saying, 'HASHEM shall be between me and you, and between my children and your children' — shall be forever!"

MAFTIR SHABBAS ROSH CHODESH / מפטיר לשבת ראש חודש
Numbers 28:9-15 / במדבר כח:ט-טו

28 ⁹ And on the Sabbath day: two male lambs in their first year, unblemished, two tenth-ephah of fine flour for a meal-offering, mixed with oil, and its libation. ¹⁰ The olah-offering of each Sabbath on its own Sabbath, in addition to the continual olah-offering and its libation.

¹¹ On your New Moons, you shall bring an olah-offering to HASHEM: two young bulls, one ram, seven male lambs in their first year, unblemished. ¹² And three tenth-ephah of fine flour for a meal-offering mixed with oil, for each bull; and two tenth-ephah of fine flour mixed with oil, for each ram; ¹³ and a tenth-ephah of fine flour for a meal-offering, mixed with oil, for each lamb — an olah-offering, a satisfying aroma, a fire-offering to HASHEM. ¹⁴ And their libations: a half-hin for a bull, a third-hin for a ram, a quarter-hin for a lamb — of wine. This is the olah-offering of each month in its own month for the months of the year. ¹⁵ And one male of the goats for a sin-offering to HASHEM. In addition to the continual olah-offering, shall it be made, and its libation.

HAFTARAS SHABBAS ROSH CHODESH / הפטרת שבת ראש חודש
Isaiah 66:1-24 / ישעיה סו:א-כד

66 ¹ So said HASHEM, the heaven is My throne and the earth is My footstool; what House could you build for Me, and what could be My resting place? ² My hand made all these and thus they came into being, the words of HASHEM — but it is to this that I look: to the poor and broken-spirited person who is zealous regarding My Word.

³ He who slaughters an ox is as if he slays a man; he who offers a sheep is as if he breaks a dog's neck; he who brings up a meal-offering is as if he offers a swine's blood; one who brings a frankincense remembrance is as if he brings a gift of extortion; they have even chosen their ways, and their souls have desired their abominations.

⁴ I, too, will choose to mock them and what they dread I will bring upon them — because I have called, but no one responded; I have spoken, but they did not hear; they did what is evil in My eyes and what I did not desire they chose.

⁵ Listen to the Word of HASHEM, those who are zealous regarding His Word; your brethren who hate you and distance themselves from you say, "HASHEM is glorified because of my reputation" — but we shall see your gladness and they will be shamed. ⁶ A tumultuous sound comes from the city, a sound from the Sanctuary, the sound of HASHEM dealing retribution to His enemies. ⁷ When she has not yet felt her labor, she will have given birth! When the pain has not yet come to her, she will have delivered a son! ⁸ Who has heard such a thing? Who has seen its like? Has a land gone through its labor in one day? Has a nation been born

פַּעַם אֶחָת כִּי־חָלָה גַּם־יָלְדָה צִיּוֹן אֶת־בָּנֶיהָ: ט הַאֲנִי אַשְׁבִּיר וְלֹא אוֹלִיד יֹאמַר יְהוָה אִם־אֲנִי הַמּוֹלִיד וְעָצַרְתִּי אָמַר אֱלֹהָיִךְ: י שִׂמְחוּ אֶת־יְרוּשָׁלַם וְגִילוּ בָהּ כָּל־אֹהֲבֶיהָ שִׂישׂוּ אִתָּהּ מָשׂוֹשׂ כָּל־הַמִּתְאַבְּלִים עָלֶיהָ: יא לְמַעַן תִּינְקוּ וּשְׂבַעְתֶּם מִשֹּׁד תַּנְחֻמֶיהָ לְמַעַן תָּמֹצּוּ וְהִתְעַנַּגְתֶּם מִזִּיז כְּבוֹדָהּ: יב כִּי־כֹה ׀ אָמַר יְהוָה הִנְנִי נֹטֶה־אֵלֶיהָ כְּנָהָר שָׁלוֹם וּכְנַחַל שׁוֹטֵף כְּבוֹד גּוֹיִם וִינַקְתֶּם עַל־צַד תִּנָּשֵׂאוּ וְעַל־בִּרְכַּיִם תְּשָׁעֳשָׁעוּ: יג כְּאִישׁ אֲשֶׁר אִמּוֹ תְּנַחֲמֶנּוּ כֵּן אָנֹכִי אֲנַחֶמְכֶם וּבִירוּשָׁלַם תְּנֻחָמוּ: יד וּרְאִיתֶם וְשָׂשׂ לִבְּכֶם וְעַצְמוֹתֵיכֶם כַּדֶּשֶׁא תִפְרַחְנָה וְנוֹדְעָה יַד־יְהוָה אֶת־עֲבָדָיו וְזָעַם אֶת־אֹיְבָיו: טו כִּי־הִנֵּה יְהוָה בָּאֵשׁ יָבוֹא וְכַסּוּפָה מַרְכְּבֹתָיו לְהָשִׁיב בְּחֵמָה אַפּוֹ וְגַעֲרָתוֹ בְּלַהֲבֵי־אֵשׁ: טז כִּי בָאֵשׁ יְהוָה נִשְׁפָּט וּבְחַרְבּוֹ אֶת־כָּל־בָּשָׂר וְרַבּוּ חַלְלֵי יְהוָה: יז הַמִּתְקַדְּשִׁים וְהַמִּטַּהֲרִים אֶל־הַגַּנּוֹת אַחַר אַחַת [אחד כ'] בַּתָּוֶךְ אֹכְלֵי בְּשַׂר הַחֲזִיר וְהַשֶּׁקֶץ וְהָעַכְבָּר יַחְדָּו יָסֻפוּ נְאֻם־יְהוָה: יח וְאָנֹכִי מַעֲשֵׂיהֶם וּמַחְשְׁבֹתֵיהֶם בָּאָה לְקַבֵּץ אֶת־כָּל־הַגּוֹיִם וְהַלְּשֹׁנוֹת וּבָאוּ וְרָאוּ אֶת־כְּבוֹדִי: יט וְשַׂמְתִּי בָהֶם אוֹת וְשִׁלַּחְתִּי מֵהֶם ׀ פְּלֵיטִים אֶל־הַגּוֹיִם תַּרְשִׁישׁ פּוּל וְלוּד מֹשְׁכֵי קֶשֶׁת תֻּבַל וְיָוָן הָאִיִּים הָרְחֹקִים אֲשֶׁר לֹא־שָׁמְעוּ אֶת־שִׁמְעִי וְלֹא־רָאוּ אֶת־כְּבוֹדִי וְהִגִּידוּ אֶת־כְּבוֹדִי בַּגּוֹיִם: כ וְהֵבִיאוּ אֶת־כָּל־אֲחֵיכֶם מִכָּל־הַגּוֹיִם ׀ מִנְחָה ׀ לַיהוָה בַּסּוּסִים וּבָרֶכֶב וּבַצַּבִּים וּבַפְּרָדִים וּבַכִּרְכָּרוֹת עַל הַר קָדְשִׁי יְרוּשָׁלַם אָמַר יְהוָה כַּאֲשֶׁר יָבִיאוּ בְנֵי יִשְׂרָאֵל אֶת־הַמִּנְחָה בִּכְלִי טָהוֹר בֵּית יְהוָה: כא וְגַם־מֵהֶם אֶקַּח לַכֹּהֲנִים לַלְוִיִּם אָמַר יְהוָה: כב כִּי כַאֲשֶׁר הַשָּׁמַיִם הַחֳדָשִׁים וְהָאָרֶץ הַחֲדָשָׁה אֲשֶׁר אֲנִי עֹשֶׂה עֹמְדִים לְפָנַי נְאֻם־יְהוָה כֵּן יַעֲמֹד זַרְעֲכֶם וְשִׁמְכֶם: כג וְהָיָה מִדֵּי־חֹדֶשׁ בְּחָדְשׁוֹ וּמִדֵּי שַׁבָּת בְּשַׁבַּתּוֹ יָבוֹא כָל־בָּשָׂר לְהִשְׁתַּחֲוֺת לְפָנַי אָמַר יְהוָה: כד וְיָצְאוּ וְרָאוּ בְּפִגְרֵי הָאֲנָשִׁים הַפֹּשְׁעִים בִּי כִּי תוֹלַעְתָּם לֹא תָמוּת וְאִשָּׁם לֹא תִכְבֶּה וְהָיוּ דֵרָאוֹן לְכָל־בָּשָׂר:
וְהָיָה מִדֵּי־חֹדֶשׁ בְּחָדְשׁוֹ וּמִדֵּי שַׁבָּת בְּשַׁבַּתּוֹ יָבוֹא כָל־בָּשָׂר לְהִשְׁתַּחֲוֺת לְפָנַי אָמַר יְהוָה:

---

at one time, as Zion went through labor and gave birth to her children? ⁹ Shall I bring [a woman] to the birthstool and not have her give birth? says HASHEM. Shall I, Who causes birth, hold it back? says your God.

¹⁰ Be glad with Jerusalem and rejoice in her, all who love her; exult with her exultation, all who mourned for her; ¹¹ so that you may nurse and be sated from the breast of her consolations; so that you may suck and delight from the glow of her glory. ¹² For so said HASHEM, Behold! — I shall direct peace to her like a river, and the honor of nations like a surging stream and you shall suckle; you will be carried on a shoulder and dandled on knees. ¹³ Like a man whose mother consoled him, so will I console you, and in Jerusalem will you be consoled. ¹⁴ You shall see and your heart will exult, and your bones will flourish like grass; the hand of HASHEM will be known to His servants, and He will be angry with His enemies. ¹⁵ For behold! — HASHEM will arrive in fire and His chariots like the whirlwind, to requite His anger with wrath, and His rebuke with flaming fire. ¹⁶ For with fire HASHEM will judge, and with His sword against all flesh; many will be those slain by HASHEM.

¹⁷ Those who prepare and purify themselves [to storm] the gardens go one after another to the midst [of the fray]; together will be consumed those who eat the flesh of swine, of abominable creatures and rodents — the words of HASHEM. ¹⁸ [I am aware of] their deeds and their thoughts; [the time] has come to gather in all the nations and tongues; they shall come and see My glory.

¹⁹ I shall put a sign upon them and send some as survivors to the nations: Tarshish, Pul and Lud, the bow-drawers, Tubal, and Yavan; the distant islands, who have not heard of My fame and not seen My glory, and they will declare My glory among the nations. ²⁰ They will bring all your brethren from all the nations as an offering to HASHEM, on horses, on chariot, on covered wagons, on mules, and with joyful dances upon My holy mountain, Jerusalem, said HASHEM; just as the Children of Israel bring their offering in a pure vessel to the House of HASHEM. ²¹ From them, too, will I take to be Kohanim and Levites, said HASHEM.

²² For just as the new heavens and the new earth that I will make will endure before Me — the words of HASHEM — so will your offspring and your name endure. ²³ And it shall be that, from New Moon to New Moon, and from Sabbath to Sabbath, all flesh shall come to prostrate themselves before Me, said HASHEM.

²⁴ They shall go out and see the corpses of those who rebel against Me, for their worms will not die and their fire will not go out, and they shall be a disgrace for all flesh.

And it shall be that, from New Moon to New Moon, and from Sabbath to Sabbath, all flesh shall come to prostrate themselves before Me, said HASHEM.

When the second day Rosh Chodesh falls on Sunday, some congregations add the first and last verses of the Haftarah for Shabbas Erev Rosh Chodesh:

Jonathan said to [David], "Tomorrow is the New Moon, and you will be missed because your seat will be empty." Jonathan said to David, "Go to peace. What the two of us have sworn in the Name of HASHEM — saying, 'HASHEM shall be between me and you, and between my children and your children' — shall be forever!"

וַיֹּאמֶר־לוֹ יְהוֹנָתָן מָחָר חֹדֶשׁ וְנִפְקַדְתָּ כִּי יִפָּקֵד מוֹשָׁבֶךָ: וַיֹּאמֶר יְהוֹנָתָן לְדָוִד לֵךְ לְשָׁלוֹם אֲשֶׁר נִשְׁבַּעְנוּ שְׁנֵינוּ אֲנַחְנוּ בְּשֵׁם יהוה לֵאמֹר יהוה יִהְיֶה ׀ בֵּינִי וּבֵינֶךָ וּבֵין זַרְעִי וּבֵין זַרְעֲךָ עַד־עוֹלָם:

MAFTIR PARASHAS ZACHOR / מפטיר לפרשת זכור
Deuteronomy 25:17-19 / דברים כה:יז-יט

25 ¹⁷ Remember what Amalek did to you, on the way when you were leaving Egypt, ¹⁸ that he happened upon you on the way, and he struck those of you who were hindmost, all the weaklings at your rear, when you were faint and exhausted, and he did not fear God. ¹⁹ It shall be that when HASHEM, your God, gives you rest from all your enemies all around, in the Land that HASHEM, your God, gives you as an inheritance to possess it, you shall wipe out the memory of Amalek from under the heaven — you shall not forget!

כה יז זָכוֹר אֵת אֲשֶׁר־עָשָׂה לְךָ עֲמָלֵק בַּדֶּרֶךְ בְּצֵאתְכֶם מִמִּצְרָיִם: יח אֲשֶׁר קָרְךָ בַּדֶּרֶךְ וַיְזַנֵּב בְּךָ כָּל־הַנֶּחֱשָׁלִים אַחֲרֶיךָ וְאַתָּה עָיֵף וְיָגֵעַ וְלֹא יָרֵא אֱלֹהִים: יט וְהָיָה בְּהָנִיחַ יהוה אֱלֹהֶיךָ ׀ לְךָ מִכָּל־אֹיְבֶיךָ מִסָּבִיב בָּאָרֶץ אֲשֶׁר יהוה־אֱלֹהֶיךָ נֹתֵן לְךָ נַחֲלָה לְרִשְׁתָּהּ תִּמְחֶה אֶת־זֵכֶר עֲמָלֵק מִתַּחַת הַשָּׁמָיִם לֹא תִּשְׁכָּח:

HAFTARAS PARASHAS ZACHOR / הפטרת פרשת זכור
I Samuel 15:1-34 / שמואל א טו:א-לד
According to most authorities the first verse is omitted and the Haftarah begins with verse 2.

15 (¹ Samuel said to Saul: "HASHEM sent me to anoint you as king over His people, over Israel, so now hear the sound of HASHEM's words.)
² "So said HASHEM, Master of Legions: I remembered what Amalek did to Israel, [the ambush] he emplaced against him on the way, as he went up from Egypt. ³ Now go and strike down Amalek and destroy everything he has, have no pity on him; kill man and woman alike, infant and suckling alike, ox and sheep alike, camel and donkey alike."
⁴ Saul had all the people summoned and he counted them through lambs: two hundred thousand infantry, and the men of Judah were ten thousand. ⁵ Saul came up to the city of Amalek, and he made war in the valley. ⁶ Saul said to the Kenites, "Go, withdraw, descend from among the Amalekites lest I destroy you with them; for you performed kindness with all the Children of Israel when they went up from Egypt." The Kenites withdrew from among Amalek.
⁷ Saul struck down Amalek from Havilah to the approach to Shur, which faces Egypt. ⁸ He captured Agag, the king of Amalek, alive, and the entire people he destroyed by the sword. ⁹ Saul and the people took pity on Agag; on the best of the sheep and cattle, the fatted bulls and the fatted sheep; and on all that was good; and they did not destroy them; only what was despicable and deteriorated did they destroy.
¹⁰ The word of HASHEM came to Samuel, saying,

טו א וַיֹּאמֶר שְׁמוּאֵל אֶל־שָׁאוּל אֹתִי שָׁלַח יהוה לִמְשָׁחֲךָ לְמֶלֶךְ עַל־עַמּוֹ עַל־יִשְׂרָאֵל וְעַתָּה שְׁמַע לְקוֹל דִּבְרֵי יהוה: ב כֹּה אָמַר יהוה צְבָאוֹת פָּקַדְתִּי אֵת אֲשֶׁר־עָשָׂה עֲמָלֵק לְיִשְׂרָאֵל אֲשֶׁר־שָׂם לוֹ בַּדֶּרֶךְ בַּעֲלֹתוֹ מִמִּצְרָיִם: ג עַתָּה לֵךְ וְהִכִּיתָה אֶת־עֲמָלֵק וְהַחֲרַמְתֶּם אֶת־כָּל־אֲשֶׁר־לוֹ וְלֹא תַחְמֹל עָלָיו וְהֵמַתָּה מֵאִישׁ עַד־אִשָּׁה מֵעֹלֵל וְעַד־יוֹנֵק מִשּׁוֹר וְעַד־שֶׂה מִגָּמָל וְעַד־חֲמוֹר: ד וַיְשַׁמַּע שָׁאוּל אֶת־הָעָם וַיִּפְקְדֵם בַּטְּלָאִים מָאתַיִם אֶלֶף רַגְלִי וַעֲשֶׂרֶת אֲלָפִים אֶת־אִישׁ יְהוּדָה: ה וַיָּבֹא שָׁאוּל עַד־עִיר עֲמָלֵק וַיָּרֶב בַּנָּחַל: ו וַיֹּאמֶר שָׁאוּל אֶל־הַקֵּינִי לְכוּ סֻּרוּ רְדוּ מִתּוֹךְ עֲמָלֵקִי פֶּן־אֹסִפְךָ עִמּוֹ וְאַתָּה עָשִׂיתָה חֶסֶד עִם־כָּל־בְּנֵי יִשְׂרָאֵל בַּעֲלוֹתָם מִמִּצְרָיִם וַיָּסַר קֵינִי מִתּוֹךְ עֲמָלֵק: ז וַיַּךְ שָׁאוּל אֶת־עֲמָלֵק מֵחֲוִילָה בּוֹאֲךָ שׁוּר אֲשֶׁר עַל־פְּנֵי מִצְרָיִם: ח וַיִּתְפֹּשׂ אֶת־אֲגַג מֶלֶךְ־עֲמָלֵק חָי וְאֶת־כָּל־הָעָם הֶחֱרִים לְפִי־חָרֶב: ט וַיַּחְמֹל שָׁאוּל וְהָעָם עַל־אֲגָג וְעַל־מֵיטַב הַצֹּאן וְהַבָּקָר וְהַמִּשְׁנִים וְעַל־הַכָּרִים וְעַל־כָּל־הַטּוֹב וְלֹא אָבוּ הַחֲרִימָם וְכָל־הַמְּלָאכָה נְמִבְזָה וְנָמֵס אֹתָהּ הֶחֱרִימוּ: י וַיְהִי דְּבַר־יהוה אֶל־שְׁמוּאֵל לֵאמֹר:

¹¹ "I have regretted that I made Saul king, for he has turned away from Me and has not fulfilled My word!" It aggrieved Samuel and he cried out to Hashem the entire night. ¹² Samuel woke up early in the morning to meet Saul. It was told to Samuel, saying: "Saul came to the Carmel and behold! — he set up an altar and then he turned around and descended to the Gilgal." ¹³ Samuel came to Saul. Saul said to him, "Blessed are you to Hashem, I have fulfilled the word of Hashem." ¹⁴ Samuel said, "And what is this sound of the sheep in my ears and the sound of the cattle that I hear?" ¹⁵ Saul said, "I have brought them from the Amalekites, for the people took pity on the best of the sheep and cattle in order to slaughter them to Hashem, your God, but we have destroyed the remainder." ¹⁶ Samuel said to Saul, "Wait. I shall tell you what Hashem spoke to me last night." He said to him, "Speak." ¹⁷ Samuel said, "Is this not so? — Though you are small in your own eyes, you are the head of the tribes of Israel; and Hashem has anointed you to be king over Israel. ¹⁸ Hashem sent you on the way, and He said, 'Go and destroy the sinners, the Amalekites, and wage war with them until you have exterminated them.' ¹⁹ Why did you not obey the voice of Hashem? You rushed to the loot, and you did what was evil in the eyes of Hashem." ²⁰ Saul said to Samuel, "But I heeded the voice of Hashem and I walked the path on which Hashem sent me! I brought Agag, king of Amalek, and I destroyed Amalek! ²¹ The people took the sheep and the cattle from the loot, the best of what was to be destroyed, in order to bring offerings to Hashem, your God, in Gilgal." ²² Samuel said, "Does Hashem take delight in olah-offerings and feast-offerings as in obedience to the voice of Hashem? Behold! — obedience is better than a choice offering, attentiveness than the fat of rams. ²³ For rebelliousness is like the sin of sorcery, and verbosity is like the iniquity of idolatry; because you have rejected the word of God, He has rejected you as king!" ²⁴ Saul said to Samuel, "I have sinned since I have transgressed the word of Hashem and your word, for I have feared the people and I obeyed their voice. ²⁵ And now, please forgive my sin and return with me, and I will prostrate myself to Hashem." ²⁶ Samuel said to Saul, "I will not return with you for you have rejected the word of Hashem and Hashem has rejected you from being king over Israel!" ²⁷ Samuel turned away to leave, and [Saul] grabbed the hem of his tunic, and it tore. ²⁸ Samuel said to him, "Hashem has torn the kingship of Israel away from you today and has given it to your fellow who is better than you. ²⁹ Moreover, the Eternal One of Israel

יא נִחַ֕מְתִּי כִּֽי־הִמְלַ֥כְתִּי אֶת־שָׁא֖וּל לְמֶ֑לֶךְ כִּי־שָׁ֣ב מֵאַחֲרַ֗י וְאֶת־דְּבָרַ֖י לֹ֣א הֵקִ֑ים וַיִּ֙חַר֙ לִשְׁמוּאֵ֔ל וַיִּזְעַ֥ק אֶל־יְהוָ֖ה כָּל־הַלָּֽיְלָה׃ יב וַיַּשְׁכֵּ֧ם שְׁמוּאֵ֛ל לִקְרַ֥את שָׁא֖וּל בַּבֹּ֑קֶר וַיֻּגַּ֨ד לִשְׁמוּאֵ֜ל לֵאמֹ֗ר בָּֽא־שָׁא֤וּל הַכַּרְמֶ֙לָה֙ וְהִנֵּ֨ה מַצִּ֥יב לוֹ֙ יָ֔ד וַיִּסֹּב֙ וַֽיַּעֲבֹ֔ר וַיֵּ֖רֶד הַגִּלְגָּֽל׃ יג וַיָּבֹ֥א שְׁמוּאֵ֖ל אֶל־שָׁא֑וּל וַיֹּ֨אמֶר ל֤וֹ שָׁאוּל֙ בָּר֤וּךְ אַתָּה֙ לַֽיהוָ֔ה הֲקִימֹ֖תִי אֶת־דְּבַ֥ר יְהוָֽה׃ יד וַיֹּ֣אמֶר שְׁמוּאֵ֔ל וּמֶ֛ה קוֹל־הַצֹּ֥אן הַזֶּ֖ה בְּאָזְנָ֑י וְק֣וֹל הַבָּקָ֔ר אֲשֶׁ֥ר אָנֹכִ֖י שֹׁמֵֽעַ׃ טו וַיֹּ֨אמֶר שָׁא֜וּל מֵעֲמָלֵקִ֣י הֱבִיא֗וּם אֲשֶׁ֨ר חָמַ֤ל הָעָם֙ עַל־מֵיטַ֤ב הַצֹּאן֙ וְהַבָּקָ֔ר לְמַ֥עַן זְבֹ֖חַ לַיהוָ֣ה אֱלֹהֶ֑יךָ וְאֶת־הַיּוֹתֵ֖ר הֶחֱרַֽמְנוּ׃ טז וַיֹּ֤אמֶר שְׁמוּאֵל֙ אֶל־שָׁא֔וּל הֶ֗רֶף וְאַגִּ֤ידָה לְּךָ֙ אֵת֩ אֲשֶׁ֨ר דִּבֶּ֧ר יְהוָ֛ה אֵלַ֖י הַלָּ֑יְלָה וַיֹּ֥אמֶר [וַיֹּאמְרוּ כ׳] ל֖וֹ דַּבֵּֽר׃ יז וַיֹּ֣אמֶר שְׁמוּאֵ֗ל הֲל֗וֹא אִם־קָטֹ֤ן אַתָּה֙ בְּעֵינֶ֔יךָ רֹ֛אשׁ שִׁבְטֵ֥י יִשְׂרָאֵ֖ל אָ֑תָּה וַיִּמְשָׁחֲךָ֧ יְהוָ֛ה לְמֶ֖לֶךְ עַל־יִשְׂרָאֵֽל׃ יח וַיִּשְׁלָחֲךָ֥ יְהוָ֖ה בְּדָ֑רֶךְ וַיֹּ֗אמֶר לֵ֣ךְ וְהַחֲרַמְתָּ֞ה אֶת־הַֽחַטָּאִים֙ אֶת־עֲמָלֵ֔ק וְנִלְחַמְתָּ֣ ב֔וֹ עַ֥ד כַּלּוֹתָ֖ם אֹתָֽם׃ יט וְלָ֛מָּה לֹא־שָׁמַ֥עְתָּ בְּק֣וֹל יְהוָ֑ה וַתַּ֙עַט֙ אֶל־הַשָּׁלָ֔ל וַתַּ֥עַשׂ הָרַ֖ע בְּעֵינֵ֥י יְהוָֽה׃ כ וַיֹּ֨אמֶר שָׁא֜וּל אֶל־שְׁמוּאֵ֗ל אֲשֶׁ֤ר שָׁמַ֙עְתִּי֙ בְּק֣וֹל יְהוָ֔ה וָאֵלֵ֕ךְ בַּדֶּ֖רֶךְ אֲשֶׁר־שְׁלָחַ֣נִי יְהוָ֑ה וָאָבִ֗יא אֶת־אֲגַג֙ מֶ֣לֶךְ עֲמָלֵ֔ק וְאֶת־עֲמָלֵ֖ק הֶחֱרַֽמְתִּי׃ כא וַיִּקַּ֨ח הָעָ֧ם מֵהַשָּׁלָ֛ל צֹ֥אן וּבָקָ֖ר רֵאשִׁ֣ית הַחֵ֑רֶם לִזְבֹּ֛חַ לַיהוָ֥ה אֱלֹהֶ֖יךָ בַּגִּלְגָּֽל׃ כב וַיֹּ֣אמֶר שְׁמוּאֵ֗ל הַחֵ֤פֶץ לַֽיהוָה֙ בְּעֹל֣וֹת וּזְבָחִ֔ים כִּשְׁמֹ֖עַ בְּק֣וֹל יְהוָ֑ה הִנֵּ֤ה שְׁמֹ֙עַ֙ מִזֶּ֣בַח ט֔וֹב לְהַקְשִׁ֖יב מֵחֵ֥לֶב אֵילִֽים׃ כג כִּ֤י חַטַּאת־קֶ֙סֶם֙ מֶ֔רִי וְאָ֥וֶן וּתְרָפִ֖ים הַפְצַ֑ר יַ֗עַן מָאַ֙סְתָּ֙ אֶת־דְּבַ֣ר יְהוָ֔ה וַיִּמְאָסְךָ֖ מִמֶּֽלֶךְ׃ כד וַיֹּ֨אמֶר שָׁא֤וּל אֶל־שְׁמוּאֵל֙ חָטָ֔אתִי כִּֽי־עָבַ֥רְתִּי אֶת־פִּֽי־יְהוָ֖ה וְאֶת־דְּבָרֶ֑יךָ כִּ֤י יָרֵ֙אתִי֙ אֶת־הָעָ֔ם וָאֶשְׁמַ֖ע בְּקוֹלָֽם׃ כה וְעַתָּ֕ה שָׂ֥א נָ֖א אֶת־חַטָּאתִ֑י וְשׁ֣וּב עִמִּ֔י וְאֶֽשְׁתַּחֲוֶ֖ה לַֽיהוָֽה׃ כו וַיֹּ֤אמֶר שְׁמוּאֵל֙ אֶל־שָׁא֔וּל לֹ֥א אָשׁ֖וּב עִמָּ֑ךְ כִּ֤י מָאַ֙סְתָּה֙ אֶת־דְּבַ֣ר יְהוָ֔ה וַיִּמְאָסְךָ֣ יְהוָ֔ה מִהְי֥וֹת מֶ֖לֶךְ עַל־יִשְׂרָאֵֽל׃ כז וַיִּסֹּ֥ב שְׁמוּאֵ֖ל לָלֶ֑כֶת וַיַּחֲזֵ֥ק בִּכְנַף־מְעִיל֖וֹ וַיִּקָּרַֽע׃ כח וַיֹּ֤אמֶר אֵלָיו֙ שְׁמוּאֵ֔ל קָרַ֨ע יְהוָ֜ה אֶת־מַמְלְכ֧וּת יִשְׂרָאֵ֛ל מֵעָלֶ֖יךָ הַיּ֑וֹם וּנְתָנָ֕הּ לְרֵעֲךָ֖ הַטּ֥וֹב מִמֶּֽךָּ׃ כט וְגַם֙ נֵ֣צַח יִשְׂרָאֵ֔ל

does not lie and does not relent, for He is not a human that He should relent."

³⁰ He said, "I have sinned. Now, please honor me in the presence of the elders of my people and in the presence of Israel; return with me, and I shall prostrate myself to HASHEM, your God." ³¹ Samuel returned after Saul and Saul prostrated himself before HASHEM.

³² Samuel said, "Bring to me Agag, king of Amalek." Agag went to him in chains; Agag said, "Truly, the bitterness of death has passed."

³³ Samuel said, "Just as your sword made women childless so shall your mother be childless among the women!" And Samuel split Agag before HASHEM in Gilgal. ³⁴ Samuel went to Ramah; and Saul went up to his home at Gibeah of Saul.

MAFTIR PARASHAS PARAH / מפטיר לפרשת פרה

Numbers 19:1-22 / במדבר יט:א-כב

19 ¹ HASHEM spoke to Moses and to Aaron, saying: ² This is the decree of the Torah, which HASHEM has commanded, saying: Speak to the Children of Israel, and they shall take to you a completely red cow, which is without blemish, and upon which a yoke has not come. ³ You shall give it to Elazar the Kohen; he shall take it to the outside of the camp and someone shall slaughter it in his presence. ⁴ Elazar the Kohen shall take some of its blood with his forefinger, and sprinkle some of its blood toward the Tent of Meeting seven times. ⁵ Someone shall burn the cow before his eyes — its hide, and its flesh, and its blood, with its dung, shall he burn. ⁶ The Kohen shall take cedarwood, hyssop, and crimson thread, and he shall throw these into the burning of the cow.

⁷ The Kohen shall immerse his clothing and immerse himself in water, and afterwards he may enter the camp; and the Kohen shall remain contaminated until evening. ⁸ The one who burns it shall immerse his clothing and immerse himself in water; and he shall remain contaminated until evening. ⁹ A pure man shall gather the ash of the cow and place it outside the camp in a pure place. For the assembly of Israel it shall remain as a safekeeping, for water of sprinkling; it is for purification. ¹⁰ The one who gathered the ash of the cow shall immerse his clothing and remain contaminated until evening. It shall be for the Children of Israel and for the proselyte who dwells among them as an eternal decree.

¹¹ Whoever touches the corpse of any human being shall be contaminated for seven days. ¹² He shall purify himself with it on the third day and on the seventh day become pure; but if he will not purify himself on the third day, then on the seventh day he will not become pure. ¹³ Whoever touches the dead body of a human being who will have died and will not have purified himself — if he shall have contaminated the Tabernacle of HASHEM,

that person shall be cut off from Israel; because the water of sprinkling has not been thrown upon him, he shall remain contaminated; his contamination is still upon him.

¹⁴ This is the teaching regarding a man who would die in a tent: Anything that enters the tent and anything that is in the tent shall be contaminated for seven days. ¹⁵ Any open vessel that has no cover fastened to it is contaminated. ¹⁶ On the open field: Anyone who touches one slain by the sword, or one that died, or a human bone, or a grave, shall be contaminated for seven days. ¹⁷ They shall take for the contaminated person some of the ashes of the burning of the purification [animal], and put upon it spring water in a vessel. ¹⁸ A pure man shall take hyssop and dip it in the water, and sprinkle upon the tent, upon all the vessels, upon the people who were there, and upon the one who touched the bone, or the slain one, or the one that died, or the grave. ¹⁹ The pure person shall sprinkle upon the contaminated person on the third day and on the seventh day, and shall purify him on the seventh day; then he shall immerse his clothing and immerse himself in water and become purified in the evening. ²⁰ But a man who becomes contaminated and does not purify himself, that person shall be cut off from the midst of the congregation, if he shall have contaminated the Sanctuary of Hashem; because the water of sprinkling has not been thrown upon him, he is contaminated.

²¹ This shall be for them an eternal decree. And the one who sprinkles the water of sprinkling shall immerse his clothing, and one who touches water of sprinkling shall be contaminated until evening. ²² Anything that the contaminated one may touch shall become contaminated, and the person who touches him shall become contaminated until evening.

HAFTARAS PARASHAS PARAH / הפטרת פרשת פרה
Ezekiel 36:16-38 / יחזקאל לו:טז-לח

36 ¹⁶The word of Hashem came to me, saying: ¹⁷ Ben Adam, the House of Israel dwell on their land and contaminate it, by their way and by their actions. Like the contamination of a menstruous woman was their way before Me. ¹⁸ So I poured My anger upon them because of the blood that they poured upon the earth — and they defiled it with their idols — ¹⁹ so I scattered them among the nations and they were dispersed among the lands. According to their ways and their doings did I judge them; ²⁰ and they came to the nations to which they came, and they desecrated My holy Name when it was said of them, "These are Hashem's people, but they departed His land"; ²¹ but I pitied My holy Name that the House of Israel desecrated among the nations to which they came.

²² Therefore say to the House of Israel: "Thus says my Lord Hashem/Elohim: Not for your sake

וְנִכְרְתָה הַנֶּפֶשׁ הַהִוא מִיִּשְׂרָאֵל כִּי מֵי נִדָּה לֹא־זֹרַק עָלָיו טָמֵא יִהְיֶה עוֹד טֻמְאָתוֹ בוֹ: יד זֹאת הַתּוֹרָה אָדָם כִּי־יָמוּת בְּאֹהֶל כָּל־הַבָּא אֶל־הָאֹהֶל וְכָל־אֲשֶׁר בָּאֹהֶל יִטְמָא שִׁבְעַת יָמִים: טו וְכֹל כְּלִי פָתוּחַ אֲשֶׁר אֵין־צָמִיד פָּתִיל עָלָיו טָמֵא הוּא: טז וְכֹל אֲשֶׁר־יִגַּע עַל־פְּנֵי הַשָּׂדֶה בַּחֲלַל־חֶרֶב אוֹ בְמֵת אוֹ־בְעֶצֶם אָדָם אוֹ בְקָבֶר יִטְמָא שִׁבְעַת יָמִים: יז וְלָקְחוּ לַטָּמֵא מֵעֲפַר שְׂרֵפַת הַחַטָּאת וְנָתַן עָלָיו מַיִם חַיִּים אֶל־כֶּלִי: יח וְלָקַח אֵזוֹב וְטָבַל בַּמַּיִם אִישׁ טָהוֹר וְהִזָּה עַל־הָאֹהֶל וְעַל־כָּל־הַכֵּלִים וְעַל־הַנְּפָשׁוֹת אֲשֶׁר הָיוּ־שָׁם וְעַל־הַנֹּגֵעַ בַּעֶצֶם אוֹ בֶחָלָל אוֹ בַמֵּת אוֹ בַקָּבֶר: יט וְהִזָּה הַטָּהֹר עַל־הַטָּמֵא בַּיּוֹם הַשְּׁלִישִׁי וּבַיּוֹם הַשְּׁבִיעִי וְחִטְּאוֹ בַּיּוֹם הַשְּׁבִיעִי וְכִבֶּס בְּגָדָיו וְרָחַץ בַּמַּיִם וְטָהֵר בָּעָרֶב: כ וְאִישׁ אֲשֶׁר־יִטְמָא וְלֹא יִתְחַטָּא וְנִכְרְתָה הַנֶּפֶשׁ הַהִוא מִתּוֹךְ הַקָּהָל כִּי אֶת־מִקְדַּשׁ יְהוָה טִמֵּא מֵי נִדָּה לֹא־זֹרַק עָלָיו טָמֵא הוּא: כא וְהָיְתָה לָּהֶם לְחֻקַּת עוֹלָם וּמַזֵּה מֵי־הַנִּדָּה יְכַבֵּס בְּגָדָיו וְהַנֹּגֵעַ בְּמֵי הַנִּדָּה יִטְמָא עַד־הָעָרֶב: כב וְכֹל אֲשֶׁר־יִגַּע־בּוֹ הַטָּמֵא יִטְמָא וְהַנֶּפֶשׁ הַנֹּגַעַת תִּטְמָא עַד־הָעָרֶב:

לו טז וַיְהִי דְבַר־יְהוָה אֵלַי לֵאמֹר: יז בֶּן־אָדָם בֵּית יִשְׂרָאֵל יֹשְׁבִים עַל־אַדְמָתָם וַיְטַמְּאוּ אוֹתָהּ בְּדַרְכָּם וּבַעֲלִילוֹתָם כְּטֻמְאַת הַנִּדָּה הָיְתָה דַרְכָּם לְפָנָי: יח וָאֶשְׁפֹּךְ חֲמָתִי עֲלֵיהֶם עַל־הַדָּם אֲשֶׁר־שָׁפְכוּ עַל־הָאָרֶץ וּבְגִלּוּלֵיהֶם טִמְּאוּהָ: יט וָאָפִיץ אֹתָם בַּגּוֹיִם וַיִּזָּרוּ בָּאֲרָצוֹת כְּדַרְכָּם וְכַעֲלִילוֹתָם שְׁפַטְתִּים: כ וַיָּבוֹא אֶל־הַגּוֹיִם אֲשֶׁר־בָּאוּ שָׁם וַיְחַלְּלוּ אֶת־שֵׁם קָדְשִׁי בֶּאֱמֹר לָהֶם עַם־יְהוָה אֵלֶּה וּמֵאַרְצוֹ יָצָאוּ: כא וָאֶחְמֹל עַל־שֵׁם קָדְשִׁי אֲשֶׁר חִלְּלוּהוּ בֵּית יִשְׂרָאֵל בַּגּוֹיִם אֲשֶׁר־בָּאוּ שָׁמָּה: כב לָכֵן אֱמֹר לְבֵית־יִשְׂרָאֵל כֹּה אָמַר אֲדֹנָי יְהוִה לֹא לְמַעַנְכֶם

do I act, O House of Israel, but for My holy Name that you have desecrated among the nations to which you came. **23** And I will sanctify My great Name that was desecrated among the nations, that you desecrated among them. Then the nations shall know that I am Hashem — the words of my Lord Hashem/Elohim — when I become sanctified through you in their sight; **24** and I shall take you from the nations and gather you in from all the countries, and I shall bring you to your Land; **25** and I shall sprinkle pure water upon you, that you be cleansed. From all your contamination and from all your filth I will cleanse you; **26** and I shall give you a new heart, and a new spirit shall I put within you; I shall remove the heart of stone from your flesh and give you a heart of flesh; **27** and My spirit shall I put within you, and I shall cause you to go by My decrees and guard My laws and perform them; **28** and you shall dwell in the land that I gave your fathers; and you shall be to Me a people and I shall be your God; **29** and I shall save you from all your contaminations, and I shall summon the grain and increase it, and I shall not place famine upon you; **30** and I shall increase the fruit of the tree and the produce of the field so that you no longer accept the shame of hunger among the nations. **31** Then you will remember your evil ways and your doings that were not good, and you shall loathe yourselves in your own sight because of your sins and your abominations. **32** Not for your sake do I act — the words of my Lord Hashem/Elohim — let it be known to you. Be ashamed and humiliated because of your ways, O House of Israel.

33 Thus says my Lord Hashem/Elohim: On the day when I cleanse you from all your sins, and cause the cities to be inhabited and the ruins to be built, **34** and the desolated land to be tilled instead of being desolate in the eyes of every passerby; **35** then they shall say, "This very land that was desolate has become a Garden of Eden; and the cities that were destroyed and were desolate and ruined shall be fortified — inhabited!" **36** And the nations that will remain around you will know that I am Hashem. I will have rebuilt the ruins, replanted the wasteland. I, Hashem, have spoken and acted.

Sephardim conclude the Haftarah here. Ashkenazim continue.

37 Thus says my Lord Hashem/Elohim: Furthermore I will make Myself accessible to the House of Israel to act for them. I shall increase them — the men — like sheep. **38** Like the sheep for Divine service, like the sheep of Jerusalem on her festivals, so shall the destroyed cities be filled by sheep-men — and they shall know that I am Hashem.

אֲנִי עֹשֶׂה בֵּית יִשְׂרָאֵל כִּי אִם־לְשֵׁם־קָדְשִׁי אֲשֶׁר חִלַּלְתֶּם בַּגּוֹיִם אֲשֶׁר־בָּאתֶם שָׁם: כג וְקִדַּשְׁתִּי אֶת־שְׁמִי הַגָּדוֹל הַמְחֻלָּל בַּגּוֹיִם אֲשֶׁר חִלַּלְתֶּם בְּתוֹכָם וְיָדְעוּ הַגּוֹיִם כִּי־אֲנִי יְהוָה נְאֻם אֲדֹנָי יֱהוִֹה בְּהִקָּדְשִׁי בָכֶם לְעֵינֵיהֶם: כד וְלָקַחְתִּי אֶתְכֶם מִן־הַגּוֹיִם וְקִבַּצְתִּי אֶתְכֶם מִכָּל־הָאֲרָצוֹת וְהֵבֵאתִי אֶתְכֶם אֶל־אַדְמַתְכֶם: כה וְזָרַקְתִּי עֲלֵיכֶם מַיִם טְהוֹרִים וּטְהַרְתֶּם מִכֹּל טֻמְאוֹתֵיכֶם וּמִכָּל־גִּלּוּלֵיכֶם אֲטַהֵר אֶתְכֶם: כו וְנָתַתִּי לָכֶם לֵב חָדָשׁ וְרוּחַ חֲדָשָׁה אֶתֵּן בְּקִרְבְּכֶם וַהֲסִרֹתִי אֶת־לֵב הָאֶבֶן מִבְּשַׂרְכֶם וְנָתַתִּי לָכֶם לֵב בָּשָׂר: כז וְאֶת־רוּחִי אֶתֵּן בְּקִרְבְּכֶם וְעָשִׂיתִי אֵת אֲשֶׁר־בְּחֻקַּי תֵּלֵכוּ וּמִשְׁפָּטַי תִּשְׁמְרוּ וַעֲשִׂיתֶם: כח וִישַׁבְתֶּם בָּאָרֶץ אֲשֶׁר נָתַתִּי לַאֲבֹתֵיכֶם וִהְיִיתֶם לִי לְעָם וְאָנֹכִי אֶהְיֶה לָכֶם לֵאלֹהִים: כט וְהוֹשַׁעְתִּי אֶתְכֶם מִכֹּל טֻמְאוֹתֵיכֶם וְקָרָאתִי אֶל־הַדָּגָן וְהִרְבֵּיתִי אֹתוֹ וְלֹא־אֶתֵּן עֲלֵיכֶם רָעָב: ל וְהִרְבֵּיתִי אֶת־פְּרִי הָעֵץ וּתְנוּבַת הַשָּׂדֶה לְמַעַן אֲשֶׁר לֹא תִקְחוּ עוֹד חֶרְפַּת רָעָב בַּגּוֹיִם: לא וּזְכַרְתֶּם אֶת־דַּרְכֵיכֶם הָרָעִים וּמַעַלְלֵיכֶם אֲשֶׁר לֹא־טוֹבִים וּנְקֹטֹתֶם בִּפְנֵיכֶם עַל עֲוֹנֹתֵיכֶם וְעַל תּוֹעֲבוֹתֵיכֶם: לב לֹא לְמַעַנְכֶם אֲנִי־עֹשֶׂה נְאֻם אֲדֹנָי יֱהוִֹה יִוָּדַע לָכֶם בּוֹשׁוּ וְהִכָּלְמוּ מִדַּרְכֵיכֶם בֵּית יִשְׂרָאֵל: לג כֹּה אָמַר אֲדֹנָי יֱהוִֹה בְּיוֹם טַהֲרִי אֶתְכֶם מִכֹּל עֲוֹנוֹתֵיכֶם וְהוֹשַׁבְתִּי אֶת־הֶעָרִים וְנִבְנוּ הֶחֳרָבוֹת: לד וְהָאָרֶץ הַנְּשַׁמָּה תֵּעָבֵד תַּחַת אֲשֶׁר הָיְתָה שְׁמָמָה לְעֵינֵי כָּל־עוֹבֵר: לה וְאָמְרוּ הָאָרֶץ הַלֵּזוּ הַנְּשַׁמָּה הָיְתָה כְּגַן־עֵדֶן וְהֶעָרִים הֶחֳרֵבוֹת וְהַנְשַׁמּוֹת וְהַנֶּהֱרָסוֹת בְּצוּרוֹת יָשָׁבוּ: לו וְיָדְעוּ הַגּוֹיִם אֲשֶׁר יִשָּׁאֲרוּ סְבִיבוֹתֵיכֶם כִּי ׀ אֲנִי יְהוָה בָּנִיתִי הַנֶּהֱרָסוֹת נָטַעְתִּי הַנְּשַׁמָּה אֲנִי יְהוָה דִּבַּרְתִּי וְעָשִׂיתִי:

לז כֹּה אָמַר אֲדֹנָי יֱהוִֹה עוֹד זֹאת אִדָּרֵשׁ לְבֵית־יִשְׂרָאֵל לַעֲשׂוֹת לָהֶם אַרְבֶּה אֹתָם כַּצֹּאן אָדָם: לח כְּצֹאן קָדָשִׁים כְּצֹאן יְרוּשָׁלִַם בְּמוֹעֲדֶיהָ כֵּן תִּהְיֶינָה הֶעָרִים הֶחֳרֵבוֹת מְלֵאוֹת צֹאן אָדָם וְיָדְעוּ כִּי־אֲנִי יְהוָה:

MAFTIR PARASHAS HACHODESH / מפטיר לפרשת החודש

Exodus 12:1-20 / שמות יב:א-כ

HASHEM said to Moses and Aaron in the land of Egypt, saying, ² "This month shall be for you the beginning of the months, it shall be for you the first of the months of the year.

³ "Speak to the entire assembly of Israel, saying: On the tenth of this month they shall take for themselves — each man — a lamb or kid for each father's house, a lamb or kid for the household. ⁴ But if the household is too small for a lamb or kid, then he and his neighbor who is near his house shall take according to the number of people; everyone according to what he eats shall be counted for the lamb or kid. ⁵ An unblemished lamb or kid, a male, within its first year shall it be for you; from the sheep or goats shall you take it. ⁶ It shall be yours for examination until the fourteenth day of this month; the entire congregation of the assembly of Israel shall slaughter it in the afternoon. ⁷ They shall take some of its blood and place it on the two doorposts and on the lintel of the houses in which they will eat it. ⁸ They shall eat the flesh on that night — roasted over the fire — and matzos; with bitter herbs shall they eat it.

⁹ "You shall not eat it partially roasted or cooked in water; only roasted over fire — its head, its legs, with its innards. ¹⁰ You shall not leave any of it until morning; any of it that is left until morning you shall burn in the fire.

¹¹ "So shall you eat it: your loins girded, your shoes on your feet, and your staff in your hand; you shall eat it in haste — it is a pesach-offering to HASHEM.

¹² "I shall go through Egypt on this night, and I shall strike every firstborn in the land of Egypt, from man to beast; and against all the gods of Egypt I shall mete out punishment — I am HASHEM. ¹³ The blood shall be a sign for you upon the houses where you are; when I see the blood I shall pass over you; there shall not be a plague of destruction upon you when I strike in the land of Egypt.

¹⁴ "This day shall become a remembrance for you and you shall celebrate it as a festival for HASHEM; for your generations, as an eternal decree shall you celebrate it. ¹⁵ For a seven-day period shall you eat matzos, but on the previous day you shall nullify the leaven from your homes; for anyone who eats leavened food — that soul shall be cut off from Israel, from the first day to the seventh day.

¹⁶ "On the first day shall be a holy convocation and on the seventh day shall be a holy convocation for you, no work may be done on them, except for what must be eaten for any person — only that may be done for you.

¹⁷ "You shall safeguard the matzos, for on this very day I will have taken your legions out of the land of Egypt; you shall observe this day for

יב א וַיֹּ֣אמֶר יְהֹוָ֗ה אֶל־מֹשֶׁ֧ה וְאֶל־אַהֲרֹ֛ן בְּאֶ֥רֶץ מִצְרַ֖יִם לֵאמֹֽר: ב הַחֹ֧דֶשׁ הַזֶּ֛ה לָכֶ֖ם רֹ֣אשׁ חֳדָשִׁ֑ים רִאשׁ֥וֹן הוּא֙ לָכֶ֔ם לְחָדְשֵׁ֖י הַשָּׁנָֽה: ג דַּבְּר֗וּ אֶֽל־כָּל־עֲדַ֤ת יִשְׂרָאֵל֙ לֵאמֹ֔ר בֶּעָשֹׂ֖ר לַחֹ֣דֶשׁ הַזֶּ֑ה וְיִקְח֣וּ לָהֶ֗ם אִ֛ישׁ שֶׂ֥ה לְבֵית־אָבֹ֖ת שֶׂ֥ה לַבָּֽיִת: ד וְאִם־יִמְעַ֣ט הַבַּיִת֮ מִֽהְיֹ֣ת מִשֶּׂה֒ וְלָקַ֣ח ה֗וּא וּשְׁכֵנ֛וֹ הַקָּרֹ֥ב אֶל־בֵּית֖וֹ בְּמִכְסַ֣ת נְפָשֹׁ֑ת אִ֚ישׁ לְפִ֣י אָכְל֔וֹ תָּכֹ֖סּוּ עַל־הַשֶּֽׂה: ה שֶׂ֥ה תָמִ֛ים זָכָ֥ר בֶּן־שָׁנָ֖ה יִהְיֶ֣ה לָכֶ֑ם מִן־הַכְּבָשִׂ֥ים וּמִן־הָעִזִּ֖ים תִּקָּֽחוּ: ו וְהָיָ֤ה לָכֶם֙ לְמִשְׁמֶ֔רֶת עַ֣ד אַרְבָּעָ֥ה עָשָׂ֛ר י֖וֹם לַחֹ֣דֶשׁ הַזֶּ֑ה וְשָׁחֲט֣וּ אֹת֗וֹ כֹּ֛ל קְהַ֥ל עֲדַֽת־יִשְׂרָאֵ֖ל בֵּ֥ין הָעַרְבָּֽיִם: ז וְלָֽקְחוּ֙ מִן־הַדָּ֔ם וְנָֽתְנ֛וּ עַל־שְׁתֵּ֥י הַמְּזוּזֹ֖ת וְעַל־הַמַּשְׁק֑וֹף עַ֚ל הַבָּ֣תִּ֔ים אֲשֶׁר־יֹֽאכְל֥וּ אֹת֖וֹ בָּהֶֽם: ח וְאָֽכְל֥וּ אֶת־הַבָּשָׂ֖ר בַּלַּ֣יְלָה הַזֶּ֑ה צְלִי־אֵ֣שׁ וּמַצּ֔וֹת עַל־מְרֹרִ֖ים יֹֽאכְלֻֽהוּ: ט אַל־תֹּֽאכְל֤וּ מִמֶּ֨נּוּ֙ נָ֔א וּבָשֵׁ֥ל מְבֻשָּׁ֖ל בַּמָּ֑יִם כִּ֣י אִם־צְלִי־אֵ֔שׁ רֹאשׁ֥וֹ עַל־כְּרָעָ֖יו וְעַל־קִרְבּֽוֹ: י וְלֹֽא־תוֹתִ֥ירוּ מִמֶּ֖נּוּ עַד־בֹּ֑קֶר וְהַנֹּתָ֥ר מִמֶּ֛נּוּ עַד־בֹּ֖קֶר בָּאֵ֥שׁ תִּשְׂרֹֽפוּ: יא וְכָ֘כָה֘ תֹּֽאכְל֣וּ אֹתוֹ֒ מָתְנֵיכֶ֣ם חֲגֻרִ֔ים נַֽעֲלֵיכֶם֙ בְּרַגְלֵיכֶ֔ם וּמַקֶּלְכֶ֖ם בְּיֶדְכֶ֑ם וַֽאֲכַלְתֶּ֤ם אֹתוֹ֙ בְּחִפָּז֔וֹן פֶּ֥סַח ה֖וּא לַֽיהֹוָֽה: יב וְעָֽבַרְתִּ֣י בְאֶֽרֶץ־מִצְרַ֘יִם֘ בַּלַּ֣יְלָה הַזֶּה֒ וְהִכֵּיתִ֤י כָל־בְּכוֹר֙ בְּאֶ֣רֶץ מִצְרַ֔יִם מֵֽאָדָ֖ם וְעַד־בְּהֵמָ֑ה וּבְכָל־אֱלֹהֵ֥י מִצְרַ֛יִם אֶֽעֱשֶׂ֥ה שְׁפָטִ֖ים אֲנִ֥י יְהֹוָֽה: יג וְהָיָה֩ הַדָּ֨ם לָכֶ֜ם לְאֹ֗ת עַ֤ל הַבָּתִּים֙ אֲשֶׁ֣ר אַתֶּ֣ם שָׁ֔ם וְרָאִ֨יתִי֙ אֶת־הַדָּ֔ם וּפָֽסַחְתִּ֖י עֲלֵכֶ֑ם וְלֹֽא־יִֽהְיֶ֨ה בָכֶ֥ם נֶ֨גֶף֙ לְמַשְׁחִ֔ית בְּהַכֹּתִ֖י בְּאֶ֥רֶץ מִצְרָֽיִם: יד וְהָיָה֩ הַיּ֨וֹם הַזֶּ֤ה לָכֶם֙ לְזִכָּר֔וֹן וְחַגֹּתֶ֥ם אֹת֖וֹ חַ֣ג לַֽיהֹוָ֑ה לְדֹרֹ֣תֵיכֶ֔ם חֻקַּ֥ת עוֹלָ֖ם תְּחָגֻּֽהוּ: טו שִׁבְעַ֤ת יָמִים֙ מַצּ֣וֹת תֹּאכֵ֔לוּ אַ֚ךְ בַּיּ֣וֹם הָֽרִאשׁ֔וֹן תַּשְׁבִּ֥יתוּ שְּׂאֹ֖ר מִבָּֽתֵּיכֶ֑ם כִּ֣י | כָּל־אֹכֵ֣ל חָמֵ֗ץ וְנִכְרְתָ֞ה הַנֶּ֤פֶשׁ הַהִוא֙ מִיִּשְׂרָאֵ֔ל מִיּ֥וֹם הָֽרִאשֹׁ֖ן עַד־י֥וֹם הַשְּׁבִעִֽי: טז וּבַיּ֤וֹם הָֽרִאשׁוֹן֙ מִקְרָא־קֹ֔דֶשׁ וּבַיּוֹם֙ הַשְּׁבִיעִ֔י מִקְרָא־קֹ֖דֶשׁ יִֽהְיֶ֣ה לָכֶ֑ם כָּל־מְלָאכָה֙ לֹֽא־יֵֽעָשֶׂ֣ה בָהֶ֔ם אַ֚ךְ אֲשֶׁ֣ר יֵֽאָכֵ֣ל לְכָל־נֶ֔פֶשׁ ה֥וּא לְבַדּ֖וֹ יֵֽעָשֶׂ֥ה לָכֶֽם: יז וּשְׁמַרְתֶּם֘ אֶת־הַמַּצּוֹת֒ כִּ֗י בְּעֶ֨צֶם֙ הַיּ֣וֹם הַזֶּ֔ה הוֹצֵ֥אתִי אֶת־צִבְאֽוֹתֵיכֶ֖ם מֵאֶ֣רֶץ מִצְרָ֑יִם וּשְׁמַרְתֶּ֞ם אֶת־הַיּ֤וֹם הַזֶּה֙

your generations as an eternal decree. *¹⁸ On the first day, on the fourteenth day of the month in the evening shall you eat matzos, until the twenty-first day of the month in the evening.*

¹⁹ "For seven days, leaven may not be found in your houses, for anyone who eats leavening — that soul shall be cut off from the assembly of Israel, whether a convert or a native of the land. ²⁰ You shall not eat any leavening; in all your dwellings shall you eat matzos."

HAFTARAS PARASHAS HACHODESH / הפטרת פרשת החודש

Ezekiel 45:16 — 46:18 / יחזקאל מה:טז — מו:יח

Most communities begin the *Haftarah* here. However, some *Sephardic* communities begin with 45:18.

45 ¹⁶ The entire population of the land must join in this terumah with the prince of Israel.

¹⁷ The prince's responsibility shall be the olah-offerings, the meal-offerings and the libations on the festive days, the New Moons, and the Sabbaths — all festivals — of the House of Israel. He shall make the sin-offering, the meal-offering, the olah-offering and the peace-offering to atone for the House of Israel.

¹⁸ Thus says my Lord HASHEM/ELOHIM: In the first month on the first of the month you shall take a young bull without blemish, and you shall cleanse the Sanctuary. ¹⁹ And the Kohen shall take some of the blood of the sin-offering and apply it to the doorposts of the House and on the four corners of the Altar's Courtyard and on the doorposts of the gate of the Inner Courtyard. ²⁰ And so shall you do for a week in the month — from [contamination caused by] an unwitting or ignorant person shall you cleanse the House. ²¹ In the first month on the fourteenth day of the month, you shall have the Pesach, a festival of seven days; matzos shall be eaten. ²² The prince shall make on that day, for himself and for the entire population, a bull for a sin-offering. ²³ During the first seven days of the festival he shall bring an olah-offering for HASHEM: seven bulls and seven rams without a blemish daily for seven days, and, as a sin-offering, a goat daily; ²⁴ and, as a meal-offering, an ephah for the bull and an ephah for the ram is he to bring; and a hin of oil for each ephah. ²⁵ In the seventh month on the fifteenth day of the month, on the festival, let him bring the same for the seven days. Like the sin-offering, like the olah-offering, like the meal-offering and like the oil.

46 ¹ Thus says my Lord HASHEM/ELOHIM: The gate of the Inner Courtyard that faces eastward shall be closed during the six days of labor, but on the Sabbath day it shall be opened, and on the day of the New Moon it shall be opened. ² Then the prince shall enter by way of the hall of the gate from the outside and stand by the doorpost of the gate by which the Kohanim bring his olah-offerings and his peace-offerings. He shall then prostrate himself at the threshold of the gate and depart, and the gate shall not be closed until the evening.

יח בָּרִאשֹׁן בְּאַרְבָּעָה עָשָׂר יוֹם לַחֹדֶשׁ בָּעֶרֶב תֹּאכְלוּ מַצֹּת עַד יוֹם הָאֶחָד וְעֶשְׂרִים לַחֹדֶשׁ בָּעָרֶב: יט שִׁבְעַת יָמִים שְׂאֹר לֹא יִמָּצֵא בְּבָתֵּיכֶם כִּי ׀ כָּל־אֹכֵל מַחְמֶצֶת וְנִכְרְתָה הַנֶּפֶשׁ הַהִוא מֵעֲדַת יִשְׂרָאֵל בַּגֵּר וּבְאֶזְרַח הָאָרֶץ: כ כָּל־מַחְמֶצֶת לֹא תֹאכֵלוּ בְּכֹל מוֹשְׁבֹתֵיכֶם תֹּאכְלוּ מַצּוֹת:

מה טז כֹּל הָעָם הָאָרֶץ יִהְיוּ אֶל־הַתְּרוּמָה הַזֹּאת לַנָּשִׂיא בְּיִשְׂרָאֵל: יז וְעַל־הַנָּשִׂיא יִהְיֶה הָעוֹלוֹת וְהַמִּנְחָה וְהַנֵּסֶךְ בַּחַגִּים וּבֶחֳדָשִׁים וּבַשַּׁבָּתוֹת בְּכָל־מוֹעֲדֵי בֵּית יִשְׂרָאֵל הוּא־יַעֲשֶׂה אֶת־הַחַטָּאת וְאֶת־הַמִּנְחָה וְאֶת־הָעוֹלָה וְאֶת־הַשְּׁלָמִים לְכַפֵּר בְּעַד בֵּית־יִשְׂרָאֵל: יח כֹּה־אָמַר אֲדֹנָי יֱהֹוִה בָּרִאשׁוֹן בְּאֶחָד לַחֹדֶשׁ תִּקַּח פַּר־בֶּן־בָּקָר תָּמִים וְחִטֵּאתָ אֶת־הַמִּקְדָּשׁ: יט וְלָקַח הַכֹּהֵן מִדַּם הַחַטָּאת וְנָתַן אֶל־מְזוּזַת הַבַּיִת וְאֶל־אַרְבַּע פִּנּוֹת הָעֲזָרָה לַמִּזְבֵּחַ וְעַל־מְזוּזַת שַׁעַר הֶחָצֵר הַפְּנִימִית: כ וְכֵן תַּעֲשֶׂה בְּשִׁבְעָה בַחֹדֶשׁ מֵאִישׁ שֹׁגֶה וּמִפֶּתִי וְכִפַּרְתֶּם אֶת־הַבָּיִת: כא בָּרִאשׁוֹן בְּאַרְבָּעָה עָשָׂר יוֹם לַחֹדֶשׁ יִהְיֶה לָכֶם הַפָּסַח חָג שְׁבֻעוֹת יָמִים מַצּוֹת יֵאָכֵל: כב וְעָשָׂה הַנָּשִׂיא בַּיּוֹם הַהוּא בַּעֲדוֹ וּבְעַד כָּל־עַם הָאָרֶץ פַּר חַטָּאת: כג וְשִׁבְעַת יְמֵי־הֶחָג יַעֲשֶׂה עוֹלָה לַיהֹוָה שִׁבְעַת פָּרִים וְשִׁבְעַת אֵילִים תְּמִימִם לַיּוֹם שִׁבְעַת הַיָּמִים וְחַטָּאת שְׂעִיר עִזִּים לַיּוֹם: כד וּמִנְחָה אֵיפָה לַפָּר וְאֵיפָה לָאַיִל יַעֲשֶׂה וְשֶׁמֶן הִין לָאֵיפָה: כה בַּשְּׁבִיעִי בַּחֲמִשָּׁה עָשָׂר יוֹם לַחֹדֶשׁ בֶּחָג יַעֲשֶׂה כָאֵלֶּה שִׁבְעַת הַיָּמִים כַּחַטָּאת כָּעֹלָה וְכַמִּנְחָה וְכַשָּׁמֶן:

מו א כֹּה־אָמַר אֲדֹנָי יֱהֹוִה שַׁעַר הֶחָצֵר הַפְּנִימִית הַפֹּנֶה קָדִים יִהְיֶה סָגוּר שֵׁשֶׁת יְמֵי הַמַּעֲשֶׂה וּבְיוֹם הַשַּׁבָּת יִפָּתֵחַ וּבְיוֹם הַחֹדֶשׁ יִפָּתֵחַ: ב וּבָא הַנָּשִׂיא דֶּרֶךְ אוּלָם הַשַּׁעַר מִחוּץ וְעָמַד עַל־מְזוּזַת הַשַּׁעַר וְעָשׂוּ הַכֹּהֲנִים אֶת־עוֹלָתוֹ וְאֶת־שְׁלָמָיו וְהִשְׁתַּחֲוָה עַל־מִפְתַּן הַשַּׁעַר וְיָצָא וְהַשַּׁעַר לֹא־יִסָּגֵר עַד־הָעָרֶב:

³ And the people of the land shall prostrate themselves at the entrance of that gate — on Sabbaths and on New Moons — before HASHEM.
⁴ This is the olah-offering that the prince shall bring to HASHEM: on the Sabbath day, six sheep without blemish and a ram without blemish; ⁵ with a meal-offering of one ephah for the ram; and for the sheep, a meal-offering according to what his hand can give, and a hin of oil for each ephah. ⁶ And on the New Moon, a bull from the herd without blemish, and six sheep and a ram; they shall be without blemish. ⁷ An ephah for the bull and an ephah for the ram is he to make as the meal-offering; and for the sheep according to his means. And one hin of oil for an ephah.
⁸ Now when the prince enters, by way of the hall of the gate is he to enter, and by the same way is he to leave. ⁹ But when the people of the land come before HASHEM, on the appointed days, whoever enters by way of the northern gate to worship is to leave by way of the southern gate, and whoever enters by way of the southern gate is to leave by way of the northern gate. He should not withdraw by way of the gate through which he entered, rather he is to leave by way of the opposite one. ¹⁰ And as for the prince among them, as they shall enter is he to enter, and as they leave is he to leave. ¹¹ And on the festivals and the appointed times, the meal-offering shall be an ephah for the bull and an ephah for the ram. And for the sheep, according to what his hand can give, and a hin of oil for each ephah. ¹² Now when the prince offers a voluntary-offering — an olah-offering or a peace-offering as a voluntary-offering to HASHEM — then one should open for him the gate facing eastward. He shall make his olah-offering and his peace-offerings as he does on the Sabbath day; then he shall depart, and one is to close the gate after his departure.
¹³ A sheep in its first year without blemish are you to make as a daily olah-offering for HASHEM. Every morning are you to make it. ¹⁴ You shall bring a meal-offering with it every morning — one-sixth of an ephah and one-third of a hin of oil with which to mix the flour; a meal-offering to HASHEM — an eternal decree, continually. ¹⁵ And they shall make the sheep and the meal-offering and the oil every morning as a continual offering.

Sephardim conclude the Haftarah here. Ashkenazim continue.

¹⁶ So says my Lord HASHEM/ELOHIM: If the prince makes a gift to one of his sons — since it is his heritage that will belong to him — it is their holding by inheritance. ¹⁷ But if he makes a gift from his inheritance to one of his subjects, it shall remain his until the year of freedom, then it shall revert to the prince; his inheritance must by all means pass to his sons. ¹⁸ So that the prince shall not take from the inheritance of the people to rob them of their holdings. From his own property is he to endow his sons in order that My people be not scattered, each man from his holding.

וְהִשְׁתַּחֲווּ עַם־הָאָרֶץ פֶּתַח הַשַּׁעַר הַהוּא בַּשַּׁבָּתוֹת וּבֶחֳדָשִׁים לִפְנֵי יהוה: ד וְהָעֹלָה אֲשֶׁר־יַקְרִב הַנָּשִׂיא לַיהוה בְּיוֹם הַשַּׁבָּת שִׁשָּׁה כְבָשִׂים תְּמִימִם וְאַיִל תָּמִים: ה וּמִנְחָה אֵיפָה לָאַיִל וְלַכְּבָשִׂים מִנְחָה מַתַּת יָדוֹ וְשֶׁמֶן הִין לָאֵיפָה: ו וּבְיוֹם הַחֹדֶשׁ פַּר בֶּן־בָּקָר תְּמִימִם וְשֵׁשֶׁת כְּבָשִׂים וָאַיִל תְּמִימִם יִהְיוּ: ז וְאֵיפָה לַפָּר וְאֵיפָה לָאַיִל יַעֲשֶׂה מִנְחָה וְלַכְּבָשִׂים כַּאֲשֶׁר תַּשִּׂיג יָדוֹ וְשֶׁמֶן הִין לָאֵיפָה: ח וּבְבוֹא הַנָּשִׂיא דֶּרֶךְ אוּלָם הַשַּׁעַר יָבוֹא וּבְדַרְכּוֹ יֵצֵא: ט וּבְבוֹא עַם־הָאָרֶץ לִפְנֵי יהוה בַּמּוֹעֲדִים הַבָּא דֶּרֶךְ־שַׁעַר צָפוֹן לְהִשְׁתַּחֲוֺת יֵצֵא דֶּרֶךְ־שַׁעַר נֶגֶב וְהַבָּא דֶּרֶךְ־שַׁעַר נֶגֶב יֵצֵא דֶּרֶךְ־שַׁעַר צָפוֹנָה לֹא יָשׁוּב דֶּרֶךְ הַשַּׁעַר אֲשֶׁר־בָּא בוֹ כִּי נִכְחוֹ יֵצֵא [יצאו כ׳]: י וְהַנָּשִׂיא בְּתוֹכָם בְּבוֹאָם יָבוֹא וּבְצֵאתָם יֵצֵאוּ: יא וּבַחַגִּים וּבַמּוֹעֲדִים תִּהְיֶה הַמִּנְחָה אֵיפָה לַפָּר וְאֵיפָה לָאַיִל וְלַכְּבָשִׂים מַתַּת יָדוֹ וְשֶׁמֶן הִין לָאֵיפָה: יב וְכִי־יַעֲשֶׂה הַנָּשִׂיא נְדָבָה עוֹלָה אוֹ־שְׁלָמִים נְדָבָה לַיהוה וּפָתַח לוֹ אֶת־הַשַּׁעַר הַפֹּנֶה קָדִים וְעָשָׂה אֶת־עֹלָתוֹ וְאֶת־שְׁלָמָיו כַּאֲשֶׁר יַעֲשֶׂה בְּיוֹם הַשַּׁבָּת וְיָצָא וְסָגַר אֶת־הַשַּׁעַר אַחֲרֵי צֵאתוֹ: יג וְכֶבֶשׂ בֶּן־שְׁנָתוֹ תָּמִים תַּעֲשֶׂה עוֹלָה לַיּוֹם לַיהוה בַּבֹּקֶר בַּבֹּקֶר תַּעֲשֶׂה אֹתוֹ: יד וּמִנְחָה תַעֲשֶׂה עָלָיו בַּבֹּקֶר בַּבֹּקֶר שִׁשִּׁית הָאֵיפָה וְשֶׁמֶן שְׁלִישִׁית הַהִין לָרֹס אֶת־הַסֹּלֶת מִנְחָה לַיהוה חֻקּוֹת עוֹלָם תָּמִיד: טו יַעֲשׂוּ [ועשו כ׳] אֶת־הַכֶּבֶשׂ וְאֶת־הַמִּנְחָה וְאֶת־הַשֶּׁמֶן בַּבֹּקֶר בַּבֹּקֶר עוֹלַת תָּמִיד:

טז כֹּה־אָמַר אֲדֹנָי יֱהוִֹה כִּי־יִתֵּן הַנָּשִׂיא מַתָּנָה לְאִישׁ מִבָּנָיו נַחֲלָתוֹ הִיא לְבָנָיו תִּהְיֶה אֲחֻזָּתָם הִיא בְּנַחֲלָה: יז וְכִי־יִתֵּן מַתָּנָה מִנַּחֲלָתוֹ לְאַחַד מֵעֲבָדָיו וְהָיְתָה לּוֹ עַד־שְׁנַת הַדְּרוֹר וְשָׁבַת לַנָּשִׂיא אַךְ נַחֲלָתוֹ בָּנָיו לָהֶם תִּהְיֶה: יח וְלֹא־יִקַּח הַנָּשִׂיא מִנַּחֲלַת הָעָם לְהוֹנֹתָם מֵאֲחֻזָּתָם מֵאֲחֻזָּתוֹ יַנְחִל אֶת־בָּנָיו לְמַעַן אֲשֶׁר לֹא־יָפֻצוּ עַמִּי אִישׁ מֵאֲחֻזָּתוֹ:

When Rosh Chodesh Nissan falls on *Shabbos*, some congregations add the first and last verses of the *Haftarah* for *Shabbas* Rosh Chodesh:

So said HASHEM, the heaven is My throne and the earth is My footstool; what House could you build for Me, and what could be My resting place? And it shall be that, from New Moon to New Moon, and from Sabbath to Sabbath, all flesh shall come to prostrate themselves before Me, said HASHEM.

כֹּה אָמַר יהוה הַשָּׁמַיִם כִּסְאִי וְהָאָרֶץ הֲדֹם רַגְלָי אֵי־זֶה בַיִת אֲשֶׁר תִּבְנוּ־לִי וְאֵי־זֶה מָקוֹם מְנוּחָתִי: וְהָיָה מִדֵּי־חֹדֶשׁ בְּחָדְשׁוֹ וּמִדֵּי שַׁבָּת בְּשַׁבַּתּוֹ יָבוֹא כָל־בָּשָׂר לְהִשְׁתַּחֲוֺת לְפָנַי אָמַר יהוה:

When Rosh Chodesh Nissan falls on Sunday, some congregations add the first and last verses of the *Haftarah* for *Shabbas* Erev Rosh Chodesh:

Jonathan said to [David], "Tomorrow is the New Moon, and you will be missed because your seat will be empty." Jonathan said to David, "Go to peace. What the two of us have sworn in the Name of HASHEM — saying, 'HASHEM shall be between me and you, and between my children and your children' — shall be forever!"

וַיֹּאמֶר־לוֹ יְהוֹנָתָן מָחָר חֹדֶשׁ וְנִפְקַדְתָּ כִּי יִפָּקֵד מוֹשָׁבֶךָ: וַיֹּאמֶר יְהוֹנָתָן לְדָוִד לֵךְ לְשָׁלוֹם אֲשֶׁר נִשְׁבַּעְנוּ שְׁנֵינוּ אֲנַחְנוּ בְּשֵׁם יהוה לֵאמֹר יהוה יִהְיֶה ׀ בֵּינִי וּבֵינֶךָ וּבֵין זַרְעִי וּבֵין זַרְעֲךָ עַד־עוֹלָם:

HAFTARAS SHABBAS HAGADOL / הפטרת שבת הגדול

There are various customs regarding the *Haftarah* of *Shabbas HaGadol*. According to many authorities it is read only if Erev Pesach falls on the Sabbath (see *Ba'er Heitev* 430:1). The custom of the Vilna Gaon was to read it on all days except Erev Pesach. Most communities read it on the Sabbath before Pesach, regardless of the date.

Malachi 3:4-24 / מלאכי ג:ד-כד

3 **⁴** Then the offering of Judah and Jerusalem will be pleasing to HASHEM, as in days of old and in former years. ⁵ I shall approach you for judgment, and I will be an urgent witness against the sorcerers, the adulterers, those who swear falsely, those who withhold the wage of laborer, widow, and orphan, who pervert the judgment of the stranger, and do not fear Me — so says HASHEM, Master of Legions.

⁶ For I, HASHEM, have not changed; and you, O children of Jacob, have not ceased to be. ⁷ From the days of your forefathers you strayed from My decrees and did not observe them — return to Me and I will return to you, says HASHEM, Master of Legions. Yet you say: "For what should we repent?" ⁸ Should a man rob God, as you rob Me? Yet you say: "How have we robbed You?" — through the tithe and the priestly gift! ⁹ You are afflicted with a curse, yet Me you still rob, the entire nation.

¹⁰ Bring the entire tithe to the storehouse and let there be food in My House — and test Me now thereby, says HASHEM, Master of Legions, if I will not open for you the windows of heaven and pour down for you blessing beyond your capacity. ¹¹ I shall frighten away the devouring [locust] and it will not destroy the fruit of the land, and the vine of the field will not lose its fruit, says HASHEM, Master of Legions. ¹² All the nations will praise you, for you will be a desirable land, says HASHEM, Master of Legions.

¹³ You have spoken harshly against Me, says HASHEM, yet you say: "How have we spoken against You?" ¹⁴ You said: "To serve God is useless, and what did we gain for keeping His charge or for walking submissively before HASHEM, Master of Legions? ¹⁵ So now we praise wanton sinners, those who did

ג וְעָרְבָה לַיהוה מִנְחַת יְהוּדָה וִירוּשָׁלָםִ כִּימֵי עוֹלָם וּכְשָׁנִים קַדְמֹנִיּוֹת: ה וְקָרַבְתִּי אֲלֵיכֶם לַמִּשְׁפָּט וְהָיִיתִי ׀ עֵד מְמַהֵר בַּמְכַשְּׁפִים וּבַמְנָאֲפִים וּבַנִּשְׁבָּעִים לַשָּׁקֶר וּבְעֹשְׁקֵי שְׂכַר־שָׂכִיר אַלְמָנָה וְיָתוֹם וּמַטֵּי־גֵר וְלֹא יְרֵאוּנִי אָמַר יהוה צְבָאוֹת: ו כִּי אֲנִי יהוה לֹא שָׁנִיתִי וְאַתֶּם בְּנֵי־יַעֲקֹב לֹא כְלִיתֶם: ז לְמִימֵי אֲבֹתֵיכֶם סַרְתֶּם מֵחֻקַּי וְלֹא שְׁמַרְתֶּם שׁוּבוּ אֵלַי וְאָשׁוּבָה אֲלֵיכֶם אָמַר יהוה צְבָאוֹת וַאֲמַרְתֶּם בַּמֶּה נָשׁוּב: ח הֲיִקְבַּע אָדָם אֱלֹהִים כִּי אַתֶּם קֹבְעִים אֹתִי וַאֲמַרְתֶּם בַּמֶּה קְבַעֲנוּךָ הַמַּעֲשֵׂר וְהַתְּרוּמָה: ט בַּמְּאֵרָה אַתֶּם נֵאָרִים וְאֹתִי אַתֶּם קֹבְעִים הַגּוֹי כֻּלּוֹ: י הָבִיאוּ אֶת־כָּל־הַמַּעֲשֵׂר אֶל־בֵּית הָאוֹצָר וִיהִי טֶרֶף בְּבֵיתִי וּבְחָנוּנִי נָא בָּזֹאת אָמַר יהוה צְבָאוֹת אִם־לֹא אֶפְתַּח לָכֶם אֵת אֲרֻבּוֹת הַשָּׁמַיִם וַהֲרִיקֹתִי לָכֶם בְּרָכָה עַד־בְּלִי־דָי: יא וְגָעַרְתִּי לָכֶם בָּאֹכֵל וְלֹא־יַשְׁחִת לָכֶם אֶת־פְּרִי הָאֲדָמָה וְלֹא־תְשַׁכֵּל לָכֶם הַגֶּפֶן בַּשָּׂדֶה אָמַר יהוה צְבָאוֹת: יב וְאִשְּׁרוּ אֶתְכֶם כָּל־הַגּוֹיִם כִּי־תִהְיוּ אַתֶּם אֶרֶץ חֵפֶץ אָמַר יהוה צְבָאוֹת: יג חָזְקוּ עָלַי דִּבְרֵיכֶם אָמַר יהוה וַאֲמַרְתֶּם מַה־נִּדְבַּרְנוּ עָלֶיךָ: יד אֲמַרְתֶּם שָׁוְא עֲבֹד אֱלֹהִים וּמַה־בֶּצַע כִּי שָׁמַרְנוּ מִשְׁמַרְתּוֹ וְכִי הָלַכְנוּ קְדֹרַנִּית מִפְּנֵי יהוה צְבָאוֹת: טו וְעַתָּה אֲנַחְנוּ מְאַשְּׁרִים זֵדִים גַּם־נִבְנוּ עֹשֵׂי

evil were even built up, they have even tested God and been spared."

¹⁶ Then those who fear HASHEM spoke to one another, and HASHEM listened and heard; it was inscribed before Him in a book of remembrance of those who fear HASHEM and meditate upon His Name. ¹⁷ They shall remain Mine as a treasure — says HASHEM, Master of Legions — of the days when I make [judgment] — and I shall have compassion on them, as a man has compassion on his son who serves him. ¹⁸ Then you will return and see the difference between the righteous and the wicked, between one who serves God and one who does not serve Him.

¹⁹ For behold! the day is coming, burning like an oven; all the wanton ones and all the evildoers will be stubble and the coming day will set them ablaze, says HASHEM, Master of Legions, it will leave them no root or branch. ²⁰ But for you that revere My Name, a sun of righteousness will shine forth, with healing on its wings; and you shall go forth and prosper like fatted calves. ²¹ You will trample the wicked, for they will be like dust under the soles of your feet, on the day that I prepare, says HASHEM, Master of Legions.

²² Remember the teaching of Moses, My servant, which I commanded him at Horeb for all Israel, decrees and ordinances. ²³ Behold! I send you Elijah the prophet, before the great and awesome day of HASHEM. ²⁴ He shall restore the heart of fathers to children and the heart of children to their fathers, lest I come and strike the land with destruction.

Behold! I send you Elijah the prophet, before the great and awesome day of HASHEM.

רִשְׁעָה גַּם בָּחֲנוּ אֱלֹהִים וַיִּמָּלֵטוּ: טז אָז נִדְבְּרוּ יִרְאֵי יהוה אִישׁ אֶל־רֵעֵהוּ וַיַּקְשֵׁב יהוה וַיִּשְׁמָע וַיִּכָּתֵב סֵפֶר זִכָּרוֹן לְפָנָיו לְיִרְאֵי יהוה וּלְחֹשְׁבֵי שְׁמוֹ: יז וְהָיוּ לִי אָמַר יהוה צְבָאוֹת לַיּוֹם אֲשֶׁר אֲנִי עֹשֶׂה סְגֻלָּה וְחָמַלְתִּי עֲלֵיהֶם כַּאֲשֶׁר יַחְמֹל אִישׁ עַל־בְּנוֹ הָעֹבֵד אֹתוֹ: יח וְשַׁבְתֶּם וּרְאִיתֶם בֵּין צַדִּיק לְרָשָׁע בֵּין עֹבֵד אֱלֹהִים לַאֲשֶׁר לֹא עֲבָדוֹ: יט כִּי־הִנֵּה הַיּוֹם בָּא בֹּעֵר כַּתַּנּוּר וְהָיוּ כָל־זֵדִים וְכָל־עֹשֵׂה רִשְׁעָה קַשׁ וְלִהַט אֹתָם הַיּוֹם הַבָּא אָמַר יהוה צְבָאוֹת אֲשֶׁר לֹא־יַעֲזֹב לָהֶם שֹׁרֶשׁ וְעָנָף: כ וְזָרְחָה לָכֶם יִרְאֵי שְׁמִי שֶׁמֶשׁ צְדָקָה וּמַרְפֵּא בִּכְנָפֶיהָ וִיצָאתֶם וּפִשְׁתֶּם כְּעֶגְלֵי מַרְבֵּק: כא וְעַסּוֹתֶם רְשָׁעִים כִּי־יִהְיוּ אֵפֶר תַּחַת כַּפּוֹת רַגְלֵיכֶם בַּיּוֹם אֲשֶׁר אֲנִי עֹשֶׂה אָמַר יהוה צְבָאוֹת: כב זִכְרוּ תּוֹרַת מֹשֶׁה עַבְדִּי אֲשֶׁר צִוִּיתִי אוֹתוֹ בְחֹרֵב עַל־כָּל־יִשְׂרָאֵל חֻקִּים וּמִשְׁפָּטִים: כג הִנֵּה אָנֹכִי שֹׁלֵחַ לָכֶם אֵת אֵלִיָּה הַנָּבִיא לִפְנֵי בּוֹא יוֹם יהוה הַגָּדוֹל וְהַנּוֹרָא: כד וְהֵשִׁיב לֵב־אָבוֹת עַל־בָּנִים וְלֵב בָּנִים עַל־אֲבוֹתָם פֶּן־אָבוֹא וְהִכֵּיתִי אֶת־הָאָרֶץ חֵרֶם:

הִנֵּה אָנֹכִי שֹׁלֵחַ לָכֶם אֵת אֵלִיָּה הַנָּבִיא לִפְנֵי בּוֹא יוֹם יהוה הַגָּדוֹל וְהַנּוֹרָא: